The Blackwell Companion to Organizations

In loving memory of my grandparents, Harry and Ray Baum, and Henry and Beatrice Cieman,
and my godparents, Lou and Rhoda Marks.
And, for my parents, David and Rochelle.
All companions of mine.

The Blackwell

Companion to Organizations

EDITED BY JOEL A. C. BAUM

Blackwell
Publishing

© 2002, 2005 by Blackwell Publishing Ltd
Editorial matter and arrangement © 2002, 2005 by Joel A. C. Baum

BLACKWELL PUBLISHING
350 Main Street, Malden, MA 02148-5020, USA
9600 Garsington Road, Oxford OX4 2DQ, UK
550 Swanston Street, Carlton, Victoria 3053, Australia

The moral right of Joel A. C. Baum to be identified as author of the editorial material has been asserted
in accordance with the Copyright, Designs and Patents Act 1988.

First published 2002
First published in paperback 2005 by Blackwell Publishing Ltd

1   2005

Library of Congress Cataloging-in-Publication Data

The Blackwell companion to organizations / edited by Joel A. C. Baum.
  p. cm.
 Includes bibliographical references and index.
 ISBN 0-631-21694-4 (alk. paper) – ISBN-10: 0-631-21695-2 (pbk. : alk. paper)
 1. Organizational behavior. 2. Organization. 3. Management. I. Baum, Joel A. C.

 HD58.7 .C626 2002
 302.3′5–dc21

                                                                2001037530

   ISBN-13: 978-0-631-21694-0 (alk. paper) – ISBN-13: 978-0-631-21695-7 (pbk. : alk. paper)

A catalogue record for this title is available from the British Library.

Typeset in 10 on 12 pt Photina
by Ace Filmsetting Ltd, Frome, Somerset
Printed in the United Kingdom
by TJ International, Padstow, Cornwall

The publisher's policy is to use permanent paper from mills that operate a sustainable forestry policy, and
which has been manufactured from pulp processed using acid-free and elementary chlorine-free practices.
Furthermore, the publisher ensures that the text paper and cover board used have met acceptable
environmental accreditation standards.

For further information on
Blackwell Publishing, visit our website:
www.blackwellpublishing.com

Table of Contents

List of Figures   viii
List of Tables   ix
Contributors   xi
Preface   xxvii
    Howard E. Aldrich

Acknowledgments   xxx

Companion to Organizations: An Introduction   1
    Joel A. C. Baum and Tim J. Rowley

Part I: Intraorganizational Level   35

1   Intraorganizational Institutions   37
    Kimberly D. Elsbach

2   Intraorganizational Networks   58
    Holly Raider and David J. Krackhardt

3   Intraorganizational Ecology   75
    D. Charles Galunic and John R. Weeks

4   Intraorganizational Evolution   98
    Massimo Warglien

5   Intraorganizational Cognition and Interpretation   119
    C. Marlene Fiol

6   Intraorganizational Power and Dependence   138
    Daniel J. Brass

7   Intraorganizational Technology   158
    Melissa A. Schilling

8   Intraorganizational Learning   181
    Linda Argote and Ron Ophir

9   Intraorganizational Complexity and Computation   208
    Kathleen M. Carley

10 Intraorganizational Economics   233
    Edward J. Zajac and James D. Westphal

Part II: Organizational Level   257

11 Organizational Institutions   259
    Donald A. Palmer and Nicole Woolsey Biggart

12 Organizational Networks   281
    Ranjay Gulati, Dania A. Dialdin, and Lihua Wang

13 Organizational Ecology   304
    Joel A. C. Baum and Terry L. Amburgey

14 Organizational Evolution   327
    Terry L. Amburgey and Jitendra V. Singh

15 Organizational Cognition and Interpretation   344
    Theresa K. Lant

16 Organizational Power and Dependence   363
    William Ocasio

17 Organizational Technology   386
    Michael L. Tushman and Wendy Smith

18 Organizational Learning   415
    Martin Schulz

19 Organizational Complexity and Computation   442
    Kathleen M. Eisenhardt and Mahesh M. Bhatia

20 Organizational Economics   467
    Brian S. Silverman

Part III: Interorganizational Level   495

21 Interorganizational Institutions   497
    David Strang and Wesley D. Sine

22 Interorganizational Networks   520
    Wayne E. Baker and Robert R. Faulkner

23 Interorganizational Ecology 541
Hayagreeva Rao

24 Interorganizational Evolution 557
Henrich R. Greve

25 Interorganizational Cognition and Interpretation 579
Joseph F. Porac, Marc J. Ventresca, and Yuri Mishina

26 Interorganizational Power and Dependence 599
Mark S. Mizruchi and Mina Yoo

27 Interorganizational Technology 621
Toby E. Stuart

28 Interorganizational Learning 642
Paul Ingram

29 Interorganizational Complexity and Computation 664
Olav Sorenson

30 Interorganizational Economics 686
Arjen Van Witteloostuijn

Part IV: Organizational Epistemology and Research Methods 713

31 Updating Organizational Epistemology 715
Jane Azevedo

32 Contemporary Debates in Organizational Epistemology 733
Mihnea C. Moldoveanu and Joel A. C. Baum

33 Model-Centered Organization Science Epistemology 752
Bill McKelvey

34 Survey Research Methods 781
David Knoke, Peter V. Marsden and Arne L. Kalleberg

35 Archival Research Methods 805
Marc J. Ventresca and John W. Mohr

36 Simulation Research Methods 829
Kevin Dooley

37 Grounded Theory Research Methods 849
Deborah Dougherty

38 Field Research Methods 867
Andrew H. Van de Ven and Marshall Scott Poole

Appendix: Glossary of Epistemology Terms 889
Bill McKelvey

Index 899

Figures

0.1	Mapping contemporary perspectives on organizations: Rational, natural and open systems	11
0.2	Mapping contemporary perspectives on organizations: Overlapping fish-scales	22
0.3	Mapping contemporary perspectives on organizations: An evolutionary meta-framework	25
5.1	Possible relationships between symbolic and connectionist architectures	126
12.1	Example of an egocentric network	290
17.1	Technology cycles over time	389
17.2	Innovation streams	393
17.3	Ambidextrous organizations: Exploitation and exploration within business units	397
18.1	Four possible disconnects in the learning cycle	417
22.1	The ION box	522
25.1	The enactment of industry belief systems	585
29.1	2-dimensional cellular automata	669
29.2	Landscape without interdependence ($N = 3$, $K = 0$)	671
29.3	Landscape with maximal interdependence ($N = 3$, $K = 2$)	671
30.1	IO's model of market performance	688
30.2	The IO–OS cross-fertilization circle	698
30.3	Sales-motivated behavior	700
30.4	Information-defective investment	701
30.5	Status-driven rivalry	702
32.1	Epistemological misattribution in the "paradigm wars": Summary	735
33.1	Conceptions of the axiom–theory–model–phenomena relationship	764
33.2	Guttman scale	770
35.1	Articles employing archival methods published in the *Administrative Science Quarterly*, 1970–98	809
36.1	Cellular automata example	839
38.1	Process theories of organizational development and change	871
38.2	Barley's parallel, synchronic, and diachronic research design	876

Tables

0.1	Key topics and themes across perspectives and levels of organization	27
1.1	Selected research on intraorganizational institutions	39
2.1	Selected studies of intraorganizational networks	60
2.2	Framework of intraorganizational network studies	62
3.1	Summary of the seminal works in intraorganizational ecology	77
4.1	Synopsis of selected empirical studies on intraorganizational evolution	109
5.1	Exemplar intraorganizational cognition and interpretation collections	122
5.2	Exemplar intraorganizational cognition and interpretation studies	123
6.1	Selected research on intraorganizational power and dependence	142
7.1	Selected studies in intraorganizational technology	159
8.1	Key empirical studies on intraorganizational learning	184
9.1	Summary of intraorganizational complexity and computation studies	210
9.2	A meta-network approach to organizational representation	225
10.1	Research on intraorganizational economics	236
11.1	Selected research on organizational institutions	261
12.1	Selected studies of organizational networks	283
13.1	Selected studies in organizational ecology	306
13.2	Elaborations of the density dependence model	314
14.1	Summary of organizational evolution studies	330
15.1	Key empirical studies: Information processing perspective	348
15.2	Key empirical studies: Enactment perspective	353
16.1	Selected research on organizational power and dependence	365
17.1	Technology cycles and dominant designs	390
17.2	Innovation types and innovation streams	394
17.3	Ambidextrous organizations	398
17.4	Senior teams	403
18.1	Selected organizational learning studies	419
19.1	Selected empirical studies illustrating loose coupling and NK phenomena	446
19.2	Selected empirical studies illustrating the edge of chaos	449

19.3	Selected empirical studies illustrating simple schemata, complex behavior	452
19.4	Selected empirical studies illustrating emergence of complex adaptive systems	454
19.5	Selected empirical studies illustrating recombination and evolution	457
20.1	Transaction cost economics: Representative empirical studies	471
20.2	Resource-based view: Representative empirical studies	477
21.1	Selected research on interorganizational institutions and institutional change	500
22.1	Key studies of interorganizational networks	524
23.1	Select studies in interorganizational ecology	546
24.1	Summary of key interorganizational evolution studies	567
25.1	Summary of key interorganizational cognition and interpretation studies and findings	581
26.1	Summary of key interorganizational power and dependence studies	612
27.1	Summary of selected interorganizational technology studies	623
28.1	Selected interorganizational learning studies	644
29.1	Selected interorganizational complexity and computational studies	666
30.1	Eight illustrative IO studies	691
30.2	Three examples of humanized IO's theory	706
33.1	Suggested tenets for a Campbellian Realist organization science	757
33.2	Model substructures defined	767
34.1	Examples of organizational surveys	784
34.2	Implementation guide for organizational surveys	786
34.3	Private-sector employment by organization size, 1994	788
35.1	Major analytic distinctions and the three modes of archival analysis	814
35.2	Research goals, data sources, and methods for archival research on organizations	819
36.1	Characteristics of three different simulation approaches	834
36.2	Issues and challenges in organizational simulation	842
37.1	Principles that guide grounded theory-based research	851
38.1	Key steps, decisions, and suggestions for process research in field studies	870
38.2	Evolution of innovation concepts during MIRP	880

Contributors

Terry L. Amburgey [Organizational Ecology; Organizational Evolution] is Professor of Strategy and Organization at the Joseph L. Rotman School of Management, University of Toronto [E-mail: amburgey@rotman.utoronto.ca]. His current research focuses on the evolution of organizational networks, learning races among organizations, social issue framing and dynamic modeling. He has authored several articles on organizational ecology and organizational change, which have appeared in *Academy of Management Journal*, *Administrative Science Quarterly*, and *Strategic Management Journal*. He received his Ph.D. in sociology from Stanford University.

Linda Argote [Intraorganizational Learning] holds the David M. and Barbara A. Kirr Chair in Organizational Behavior in the Graduate School of Industrial Administration and (by courtesy) in the Department of Social and Decision Sciences, Carnegie Mellon University [E-mail: argote@cmu.edu]. Her research interests include group and organizational learning, memory, knowledge transfer, and performance. Recent publications include *Organizational Learning: Creating, Retaining, and Transferring Knowledge* (1999) and "Knowledge Transfer in Organizations: A Basis for Competitive Advantage in Firms," with P. Ingram (*Organizational Behavior and Human Decision Processes*, 2000). She received her Ph.D. in organizational psychology from the University of Michigan.

Jane Azevedo (1949–2000) [Updating Organizational Epistemology] was a sociologist and philosopher of science whose own work was greatly influenced by her dissertation supervisor, Cliff A. Hooker (University of Newcastle). At the time of her death, Jane was Senior Lecturer in Social and Community Studies at Sunshine Coast University College in Queensland, Australia. In her book, *MAPPING REALITY: An Evolutionary Realist Methodology for the Natural and Social Sciences* (1997), Jane used insights from evolutionary epistemology to develop a new naturalist realist methodology of science, and applied it to the conceptual, practical, and ethical problems of the social sciences. She was an active member of the Australasian Association for the History, Philosophy, and Social Studies of Science, organizing their July 1999 annual meeting at her home institution.

Wayne E. Baker [Interorganizational Networks] is Professor of Management and

and Human Resource Management, and Director of the Center for Society & Economy, at the University of Michigan Business School [E-mail: wayneb@umich.edu]. He is a Faculty Associate at the Institute for Social Research. His research interests include economic sociology, networks, organizations, and culture. Winner with Robert Faulkner of the American Sociological Association's Max Weber Award for Distinguished Scholarship, he is a recipient of the Emory Williams Award for Excellence in Teaching.

Joel A. C. Baum [Companion to Organizations: An Introduction; Organizational Ecology; Contemporary Debates in Organizational Epistemology] is Canadian National Professor of Strategy and Organization at the Rotman School of Management (with a cross-appointment to the Department of Sociology), University of Toronto [E-mail: baum@rotman.utoronto.ca]. Studying economic phenomena from the point of view of a sociologist, Joel is concerned with how institutions, interorganizational relations, and managers shape patterns of strategic interaction among firms. His recent publications have appeared in the *Academy of Management Journal*, *Administrative Science Quarterly*, *Management Science*, *Social Forces*, *Social Science Research*, and *Strategic Management Journal*. Joel has also recently co-edited three books: *Variations in Organization Science: In Honor of Donald T. Campbell* (1999), with Bill McKelvey, *Economics Meets Sociology in Strategic Management* (*Advances in Strategic Management*, vol. 17, 2000), with Frank Dobbin, and *Multiunit Organization and Multimarket Strategy* (*Advances in Strategic Management*, vol. 18, 2001), with Henrich R. Greve. Joel is a member of the editorial boards of *Administrative Science Quarterly* and *Academy of Management Journal*, editor-in-chief of *Advances in Strategic Management*, and Organization and Management Theory Division Program Chair for the Academy of Management meetings in Washington, DC, 2001. Joel received his Ph.D. in organizational behavior from the University of Toronto.

Mahesh M. Bhatia [Organizational Complexity and Computation] is a doctoral student in Strategy and Organization at the Department of Management Science and Engineering, Stanford University [E-mail: mbhatia@stanford.edu]. Bhatia's research interests center around organizational experimentation and probing strategies in high-velocity environments. Prior to joining Stanford, he earned Masters degrees in technology and policy from the Massachusetts Institute of Technology and in biomedical engineering from the Indian Institute of Technology, Madras. He has a Bachelors degree in electronics and telecommunications engineering from the Government College of Engineering, Pune, India. Mahesh has published several journal, conference papers, and book chapters in the areas of biomedical engineering and public policy. He has also worked for two years in hardware/software development and strategy consulting in the USA and India.

Nicole Woolsey Biggart [Organizational Institutions] is Professor of Management and Sociology at the Graduate School of Management, University of California, Davis [E-mail: nwbiggart@ucdavis.edu]. Her current research, funded by the California Institute for Energy Efficiency, concerns the institutional structure of the commercial buildings industry in the USA. She is trying to understand how the market structure and communities of practice of an industry shapes its potential for innovation, in this case, producing energy efficient products. She is editing an economic sociology volume (Blackwell Publishers, forthcoming) and continues to be interested in the social bases of economic activity. Nicole received her Ph.D. in sociology from the University of California at Berkeley.

Daniel J. Brass [Intraorganizational Power and Dependence] is the Henning Hilliard Professor of Innovative Management in the School of Management, Gatton College of

Business and Economics, University of Kentucky [E-mail: dbrass@pop.uky.edu]. His research focuses on the antecedents and consequences of social networks in organizations. Recent publications include "At the Margins: A Distinctiveness Approach to the Social Identity and Social Networks of Underrepresented Groups," with A. M. Mehra and M. Kilduff (*Academy of Management Journal*, 1998), "Social Capital, Social Liabilities, and Social Resources Management," with G. Labianca in *Corporate Social Capital and Liability* (eds., R. Th. A. J. Leenders and S. Gabby, 1999), and "The Right Person and the Right Place: The Effects of Self-Monitoring and Structural Position on Workplace Performance," with A. M. Mehra and M. Kilduff (*Administrative Science Quarterly*, 2001). He received his Ph.D. in business administration from the University of Illinois.

Kathleen M. Carley [Intraorganizational Complexity and Computation] is a Professor of Sociology and Organizations at Carnegie Mellon University [E-mail: katheen.carley@andrew.cmu.edu]. Her research is in the areas of computational organization theory, social and organizational adaptation and evolution, statistical models for network analysis and evolution, computational text analysis, and the impact of telecommunication technologies on communication, information diffusion, knowledge networks, information security, and e-commerce. Recent work focuses on the co-evolution of social and knowledge networks, transactive memory, information diffusion and the internet, and adaptive architectures for command and control. Her work blends social networks, cognitive science, and multi-agent modeling. She has written over 60 papers and is co-author of two books using computational models to explore the impact of group and organizational processes on individual and organizational learning, interaction, and response to changing social and technological conditions. Carley directs the center for computational analysis of social and organizational systems (CASOS) at Carnegie Mellon. She and Mike Prietula founded and run the annual workshop in computational and mathematical social and organization theory, and with Al Wallace she is founding editor of the journal *Computational and Mathematical Organization Theory*. She received her Ph.D. from Harvard University.

Dania A. Dialdin [Organizational Networks] is a doctoral candidate at the Department of Management and Organizations, Kellogg Graduate School of Management, Northwestern University [E-mail: ddialdin@kellogg.nwu.edu]. Her research interests include social networks, strategic alliances, and cross-cultural negotiations. Her current research focuses on the impact of social networks on the performance of firms. She received her M.A. from Stanford University and her B.A. from Wellesley College.

Kevin Dooley [Simulation Research Methods] has a joint appointment with the Department of Industrial Engineering and the Department of Management at Arizona State University [E-mail: Kevin.Dooley@asu.edu]. Kevin's research interests lie in the areas of complex systems theory, quality management, innovation and new product development, organizational change, knowledge management, text analysis, information technology, and health care management. He is currently President of the *Society for Chaos Theory in Psychology and the Life Sciences*, an international society devoted to applying complexity science to the study of living systems. He is on the editorial boards of *Journal of Operations Management, Quality Management Journal, Journal of Quality Management, Nonlinear Dynamics, Psychology, & the Life Sciences, Production and Operations Management*, and *Emergence*. He has consulted with over 100 companies in the areas of quality, organizational change, and innovation. Kevin received his Ph.D. in mechanical engineering from the University of Illinois, in 1987.

Deborah Dougherty [Grounded Theory Research Methods] is Associate Professor at Rutgers University where she teaches principles of management, managing technology, qualitative methods, and managing innovation [E-mail: doughert@business.rutgers.edu]. She has also taught at McGill University and the Wharton School. Her research concerns how to organize for sustained product/service innovation in complex organizations, rethinking the organization of work, knowledge and human relations to support innovation, and knowledge management. She has published over 20 articles and book chapters on these topics. All her empirical articles use a grounded theory building approach. Deborah was 2000–2001 Chair of the Technology and Innovation Management Division of the Academy of Management, serves on three journal editorial boards (*Academy of Management Review*, *Journal of Product Innovation Management*, and *Organization Science*), and is co-editor of essays for *The Journal of Management Inquiry*. After working in the trenches of large organizations for ten years, Deborah returned to school and received a Ph.D. in management from MIT in 1987.

Kathleen M. Eisenhardt [Organizational Complexity and Computation] is Professor of Strategy and Organization at the Department of Management Science and Engineering, Stanford University [E-mail: kme@leland.stanford.edu]. Kathy's research interests center on strategy and organization in high-velocity industries. She is currently studying the acquisition of entrepreneurial firms, creation of cross-business synergies, and the concept of boundaries for contemporary organizations. She is a co-author of *Competing on the Edge: Strategy as Structured Chaos* (1998), winner of the Academy of Management's George R. Terry Award for outstanding contribution to management thinking. She has published in journals including *Administrative Science Quarterly*, *Harvard Business Review*, *Academy of Management Review*, and *Organization Science*. Her recent publications include "Dynamic Capabilities: What are They?" with J. A. Martin (*Strategic Management Journal*, 2000), "Strategy as Simple Rules," with D. N. Sull (*Harvard Business Review*, 2001), and "Architectural Innovation and Modular Corporate Forms," with D. C. Galunic (*Academy of Management Journal*, 2001). Kathy serves on the editorial boards of *Administrative Science Quarterly* and *Strategic Management Journal*, and has been elected a Fellow of the Academy of Management. She is also a Fellow of the World Economic Forum. Her Ph.D. is from Stanford's Graduate School of Business.

Kimberly D. Elsbach [Intraorganizational Institutions] is an Associate Professor of Management and Chancellor's Fellow at the Graduate School of Management, University of California, Davis [E-mail: kdelsbach@ucdavis.edu]. Her research focuses on the perception and management of individual and organizational images, identities, and reputations. She has studied these symbolic processes in variety of contexts ranging from the California cattle industry, and the National Rifle Association, to radical environmentalist groups, and Hollywood screenwriters. Using a combination of qualitative field methods and experimental lab methods, her work aims to build theory about the cognitive and emotional processes organizational members use in perceiving their organization, their co-workers, and themselves. Her work has been published in a number of scholarly outlets, including *Administrative Science Quarterly*, *Academy of Management Journal*, *Organization Science*, and *Research in Organizational Behavior*. Kim has served on a number of editorial boards and is currently a senior editor for *Organization Science* and *Advances in Qualitative Organizational Research*. Her paper on managing organizational legitimacy in the California cattle industry won the 1993 Louis Pondy Award for best paper based on a dissertation, from the Organization and Management Theory Division of the Academy of Management. She currently serves as an OMT division representative-at-large, in the Academy of Management. She received her Ph.D. from Stanford University in 1993.

Robert R. Faulkner [Interorganizational Networks] is Professor of Sociology, University of Massachusetts, Amherst, and research associate in The Social and Demographic Research Institute [E-mail: faulkner@soc.umass.edu]. His research interests include organizations, careers, corporate crime, and the sociology of jazz. He has written on careers in the film industry, markets in the advertising business, and interorganizational collusion. He is currently at work on a project studying schism and the culture of opportunism in price-fixing conspiracies. Winner with Wayne Baker of the American Sociological Association's Max Weber Award for Distinguished Scholarship, he is a recipient of his university's College Outstanding Teaching Award, College of Social and Behavioral Science.

C. Marlene Fiol [Intraorganizational Cognition and Interpretation] is an Associate Professor of Strategic Management at the Graduate School of Business, University of Colorado at Denver [E-mail: marlena.fiol@cudenver.edu], where she teaches strategy and entrepreneurship. Her research interests include organizational cognition and interpretation, organizational learning, knowledge management, and entrepreneurship. Marlene is one of the founders of the Managerial and Organizational Cognition Division of the Academy of Management, and she remains deeply committed to cognition research that crosses organizational levels and disciplines to address the role of cognitive processes in strategic decision making. Recent publications include "All for One and One for All? The Development and Transfer of Power across Organizational Levels," with E. O'Connor and H. Aguinis, (*Academy of Management Review*, 2001), and *Entrepreneurship in Healthcare*, with E. O'Connor (*American College of Physician Executives*, 2001). She received her Ph.D. in strategic management from the University of Illinois at Urbana-Champaign.

D. Charles Galunic [Intraorganizational Ecology] is an Associate Professor of Organizational Behavior at INSEAD [E-mail: charles.galunic@insead.fr]. His work examines organizational innovation, change, and learning. His recent most work has explored how managerial networks and corporate systems contribute to the creation and transfer of knowledge resources within the firm. He has also examined how human resource investment strategies impact the development of human capital. His work on the continuous change processes of multidivisional firms has been recognized in several places, including awards from the Academy of Management. He serves on the editorial boards of *Organization Science* and *Strategic Management Journal*, and was 1998 convenor for the *European Group for Organization Studies*. His publications have appeared in the *Academy of Management Journal*, *Strategic Management Journal*, *Organization Science*, *Research in Organizational Behavior*, and *Harvard Business Review*. Charles holds a Ph.D. in organizational behavior from Stanford University; a B.A. in philosophy, politics and economics from Oxford University (Canadian Rhodes Scholar); and a B.Sc. in chemical engineering from Queen's University, Canada.

Henrich R. Greve [Interorganizational Evolution] is an Associate Professor at the University of Tsukuba (Institute of Policy and Planning Science, Japan [E-mail: greve@shako.sk.tsukuba.ac.jp]. In the spring of 2002 he will join the Norwegian School of Management, Norway [E-mail: henrich.greve@bi.no]. Henrich's work has been published in *Administrative Science Quarterly*, *Strategic Management Journal*, *Academy of Man-*

agement Journal, American Journal of Sociology and elsewhere. His current research includes work on performance and aspiration levels effects on organizational investment and innovation strategies, research on spatial competition in organizational fields, and research on heterogeneous influence among organizations (including methodological work jointly with Nancy Brandon Tuma). The research on heterogeneous influence extends his earlier methodological and empirical work on heterogeneous diffusion process into other kinds of influence such as competition. Recent publications include "Market Niche Entry Decisions: Competition, Learning, and Strategy in Tokyo Banking, 1894–1936" (*Academy of Management Journal*, 2000), "Estimation of diffusion processes from incomplete data: A simulation study" (*Sociological Methodology and Research*, 2001), with Nancy Brandon Tuma and David Strang, and *Multiunit Organization and Multiunit Strategy: Advances in Strategic Management*, vol. 18 (2001), co-edited with Joel A. C. Baum. He received his Ph.D. in organizational behavior from the Graduate School of Business, Stanford University.

Ranjay Gulati [Organizational Networks] is the Michael L. Nemmers Associate Professor of Technology and E-Commerce at the Kellogg Graduate School of Management, Northwestern University [E-mail: r-gulati@nwu.edu], where he is Research Director of the Center for Research on Technology, Innovation, and E-Commerce, and a member of the Management and Organizations Department. He recently edited a special issue of the *Strategic Management Journal* (2000) on Alliances and Strategic Networks. He is presently completing a book titled *Digital Strategy and Organizations* (2001). Ranjay holds a Ph.D. from the Harvard Business School, an M.B.A. from the MIT Sloan School of Management, a B.Sc. in computer science from Washington State University, and a B.A. in economics from St. Stephen's College, New Delhi.

Paul Ingram [Interorganizational Learning] is the David W. Zalaznick Associate Professor of Business at the Graduate School of Business, Columbia University [E-mail: pi17@columbia.edu]. He studies the interdependence between organizations and institutions. Past work has examined interorganizational learning in the hotel industry, and among Israeli kibbutzim. Current research examines the influence of informal and formal institutions on organizational outcomes, including the anti-competitive norms that emerge from managerial friendships in the Sydney hotel industry; the mechanisms for experience sharing in groups of organizations; and the competition to supply order in Palestine and Israel. Recent publications include "Friendships among Competitors in the Sydney Hotel Industry," with Peter Roberts (*American Journal of Sociology*, 2000); "The Choice-Within-Constraints New Institutionalism and Implications for Sociology," with Karen Clay (*Annual Review of Sociology*, 2000); "Knowledge Transfer: A Basis for the Competitive Advantage of Firms," with Linda Argote (*Organizational Behavior and Human Decision Processes*, 2000); and "The Kibbutz for Organizational Behavior," with Tal Simons (*Research in Organizational Behavior*, 2000). He received his M.Sc. and Ph.D. in organization theory from Cornell University.

Arne L. Kalleberg [Survey Research Methods] is Kenan Professor of Sociology at the University of North Carolina at Chapel Hill [E-mail: arne_kalleberg@unc.edu]. He is spending 2000–2001 as a Visiting Scholar at the Russell Sage Foundation in New York City. His current research focuses on: US organizations' use of flexible staffing arrangements (especially in the health care industry); the consequences of nonstandard employment for workers; cross-national differences in the work attitudes of nonstandard vs. regular full-time workers; what companies can do to promote work-life balance; high performance work organizations in the US medical, electronics, apparel, and steel industries; and changing employment relations in the USA and Norway. Recent publications include *Manufacturing Advantage: Why High-Performance Work Systems Pay Off* (with Eileen Appelbaum, Thomas Bailey and Peter Berg, 2000) and *Sourcebook on Labor Markets: Evolving Structures and Processes* (with Ivar Berg; 2001).

David Knoke [Survey Research Methods] is Professor of Sociology at the University of Minnesota [E-mail: knoke@atlas.socsci.umn.edu]. His research interests are in organizations and social networks, combined in a current project on the development of strategic alliances in the global information sector. He also teaches social statistics to graduate and undergraduate students. Recent publications include *Changing Organizations: Business Networks in the Changing Political Economy* (2000) and *Organizations in America* (with Arne Kalleberg, Peter Marsden, and Joe Spaeth, 1996).

David J. Krackhardt [Intraorganizational Networks] is a Professor of Organizations at the Heinz School of Public Policy and Management and at the Graduate School of Industrial Administration, Carnegie Mellon University [E-mail: krack+@andrew.cmu.edu]. His research focuses social networks, and emphasizes how the theoretical insights and methodological innovations of network analysis enhance our understanding of how organizations function. His methodological work includes the adaptation of the quadratic assignment procedure to multiple regression analysis, and tools for using graph theory to study the structure of organizations as a whole. Currently, David applies his theoretical and methodological interests to developing models of diffusion of controversial innovations, exploring and testing visual representations of networks, identifying effective leverage points for organizational change, and exploring the roles of Simmelian (super-strong) ties in organizations. David edits the new peer-reviewed and paperless e-journal, the *Journal of Social Structure* (http://www.heinz.cmu.edu/project/INSNA/joss/) and is area editor of *Computational and Mathematical Organizational Theory*.

Theresa K. Lant [Organizational Cognition and Interpretation] is an Associate Professor of Management at the Stern School of Business, New York University [E-mail: tlant@stern.nyu.edu]. She has served as a Senior Editor of *Organization Science* and as Chair of the Managerial and Organizational Cognition Division of the Academy of Management. Theresa's research focuses on the processes of managerial cognition, organizational learning and strategic adaptation. She and Zur Shapira have recently completed a book that investigates the role of cognition in organizations. Currently, she is studying the emergence of the new media sectors in New York City. Her publications have appeared in the *Strategic Management Journal, Advances in Strategic Management, Organization Science, Management Science*, and the *Journal of Management*. She received her Ph.D. from Stanford University in 1987, and her A.B. from the University of Michigan in 1981.

Bill McKelvey [Model-Centered Organization Science Epistemology] is currently Professor of Strategic Organizing at the Anderson Graduate School of Management, University of California – Los Angeles [E-mail: mckelvey@anderson.ucla.edu]. Bill's early articles focus on organization and socio-technical systems design. His book, *Organizational Systematics* (1982) remains the definitive treatment of organizational taxonomy and evolutionary theory. He chaired the building committee that produced the $110,000,000 Anderson Complex at UCLA, which opened in 1994. In 1997 he became Director of the Center for Rescuing Strategy and Organization Science (SOS). From this Center he initiated activities leading to the founding of UCLA's Center for Computational Social

Science. He now organizes various agent-modeling speaker programs and conferences at UCLA. Recently Bill co-edited *Variations in Organization Science* (with Joel A. C. Baum, 1999) and a special issue of the journal *Emergence* containing 55 reviews of 34 books applying complexity theory to management (with Steve Maguire, 1999). Current publications focus on philosophy of organization science, complexity science and emergence, self-organization vs. selectionist order-creation, coevolutionary theory; human and social capital aspects of competitive strategy, distributed intelligence, organizational microstate rate dynamics, knowledge-flow dynamics, and computational agent-based adaptive-learning models. Bill received his Ph.D. from the Sloan School of Management at MIT in 1967.

Peter V. Marsden [Survey Research Methods] is a Professor in the Department of Sociology at Harvard University [E-mail: pvm@wjh.harvard.edu]. He teaches and does research on social organization, social networks, and social science methodology. With James A. Davis and Tom W. Smith, he is a principal investigator of the General Social Survey, which has tracked trends in attitudes and behaviors of US adults since 1972. With Arne L. Kalleberg, David Knoke, and Joe L. Spaeth, he was a principal investigator of the 1991 National Organizations Study, which assembled data on organizational structures and human resource practices for a representative sample of US establishments. Among Marsden's recent projects are studies of recruitment and selection methods used by US organizations, of the interpretation of name generators used to elicit personal networks in social surveys, of interviewer effects on the number of names elicited by name generators, and of how involvement in and attitudes toward the arts differ by religiosity. He received his Ph.D. in sociology from the University of Chicago in 1979.

Yuri Mishina [Interorganizational Cognition and Interpretation] is a doctoral student at the University of Illinois at Urbana-Champaign [E-mail: Yuri_Mishina@bus.emory.edu]. His research interests focus on the influences of managerial cognition on strategy, growth, and technology. He is currently pursuing research on shareholder resolutions, high-growth firms, and minivans. His recent publications include "Entrepreneurial Narratives and the Dominant Logics of High Growth Firms," with Joseph Porac and Timothy Pollock in *Mapping Strategic Knowledge* (eds, A. S. Huff and M. Jenkins, 2001).

Mark S. Mizruchi [Interorganizational Power and Dependence] is a Professor of Sociology and Business Administration at the University of Michigan [E-mail: mizruchi@umich.edu]. Mark's research is focused on the economic and political behavior of large American corporations, using the methods of social network analysis. He has also published articles on circadian rhythms of blood minerals in humans, substance abuse among psychiatric inpatients, and two (scholarly) papers on professional basketball teams. His current work includes a study of the deal-making process among bankers in a major commercial bank, a longitudinal study of corporate financing, and a study of the uses and diffusion of knowledge in the sociology of organizations. His publications include three books, *The Structure of Corporate Political Action* (1992), *Intercorporate Relations* (co-edited with Michael Schwartz, 1987), and *The American Corporate Network, 1904–1974* (1982), and more than 70 articles and reviews. Among Mark's awards are an invited fellowship to the Center for Advanced Study in the Behavioral Sciences and a National Science Foundation Presidential Young Investigator Award. He has served as an associate editor of *Administrative Science Quarterly*, a consulting editor of the *American Journal of Sociology*, and a reviewer for numerous academic journals, publishers, and granting agencies. He received his Ph.D. in sociology from the State University of New York at Stony Brook.

John W. Mohr [Archival Research Methods] is an Associate Professor of Sociology (and Associate Dean of the Graduate Division) at the University of California, Santa Barbara [E-mail: mohr@sscf.ucsb.edu]. He has studied the history of social welfare organizations in New York City from the nineteenth century up through the New Deal period, focusing in particular on the way in which category systems operate and how new organizational forms are created. More generally, John has a longstanding interest in the formal analysis of culture. In this respect he has published articles (with Paul DiMaggio) applying Bourdieu's concept of cultural capital to the study of social stratification among American high school students. He has also published a number of papers that apply relational (network) methodologies to the interpretation of archival texts, and edited a special issue of the journal *Poetics* (March, 2000) highlighting developments in this style of work. He is currently working on a project concerning the politics of post-affirmative action at the University of California and he is editing a book with Roger Friedland based on the "Cultural Turn" conference series hosted biannually at UC-Santa Barbara. He received his Ph.D. from Yale University in 1991.

Mihnea C. Moldoveanu [Contemporary Debates in Organizational Epistemology] is Assistant Professor of Strategic Management at the Rotman School of Management at the University of Toronto [E-mail: micamo@rotman.utoronto.ca]. He studies organizational learning processes and outcomes, the relationship between interorganizational network structures and organizational information strategies and the processes by which researchers study and debate about organizational phenomena. He holds a D.B.A. from Harvard University.

William Ocasio [Organizational Power and Dependence] is a Professor at the Kellogg Graduate School of Management and, by courtesy, in the Department of Sociology, Northwestern University [E-mail: wocasio@nwu.edu], and was previously on the faculty at the MIT Sloan School of Management. His work focuses on the interplay between politics, organizational cognition, and institutions and their consequences for organizational decisions and outcomes, bringing these perspectives together through cross-level theory and research on organizational and industry attention. His paper with Patricia Thornton on institutional logics and executive succession (*American Journal of Sociology*, 1999), received the 2000 W. Richard Scott Award, from the American Sociological Association's Section on Organizations, Occupations, and Work for the best paper published during the previous three years. Recent publications include "How do organizations think?" in *Organizational Cognition: Computation and Interpretation* (eds., Theresa Lant and Zur Shapira, 2001). He received a B.A. in economics from the University of Puerto Rico, Mayaguez, an M.B.A. from the Harvard Business School, and his Ph.D. in organizational behavior from Stanford University.

Ron Ophir [Intraorganizational Learning] is a doctoral candidate in Organizational Behavior and Theory at the Graduate School of Industrial Administration, Carnegie Mellon University [E-mail: ophir@cmu.edu]. His research focuses on group and organizational learning, and transfer of knowledge within and between organizations and organizational units.

Donald A. Palmer [Organizational Institutions] is Professor of Management and Sociology at the Graduate School of Management, University of California, Davis [E-mail:

dapalmer@ucdavis.edu]. His current research focuses on the institutional and social class structures that shaped the behavior of large corporations in the 1960s, a period in which now common corporate tactics, strategies, and structures first emerged. He has published papers on the factors that lead large firms to adopt the multi-divisional form and to pursue diversifying acquisitions, as well as fall victim to hostile takeovers, in this period. Don is currently an Associate Editor of *Administrative Science Quarterly*. He received his Ph.D. in sociology from the State University of New York at Stony Brook.

Marshall Scott Poole [Field Research Methods] is Professor of Speech-Communication at Texas A&M University [E-mail: mspoole@acs.tamu.edu]. He has conducted research and published extensively on the topics of group and organizational communication, computer-mediated communication systems, conflict management, and organizational innovation. These research projects include research funded by the National Science Foundation, Hewlett Foundation, and Texaco, Inc. Scott has co-authored or edited eight books including *Communication and Group Decision-Making*, *Research on the Management of Innovation*, and *Organizational Change and Innovation Processes: Theory and Methods for Research*. He has published in a number of journals, including *Management Science*, *MIS Quarterly*, *Human Communication Research*, *Academy of Management Journal*, and *Communication Monographs*. He is currently a Senior Editor of *Information Systems Research* and *Organization Science*. He received his Ph.D. from the University of Wisconsin at Madison.

Joseph F. Porac [Interorganizational Cognition and Interpretation] is a Professor of Organization at the Goizueta Business School at Emory University [E-mail: Joe_Porac@bus.emory.edu]. His research interests center on the cognitive bases of markets and organizations, and he is currently pursuing research on minivans, motorcycles, the US paper industry, and the use of information technologies. His research has appeared in a variety of organizational journals, and his most recent papers include "Industry Categories and the Politics of the Comparable Firm in CEO Compensation," with James Wade and Timothy Pollock (*Administrative Science Quarterly*, 1999), "Sociocognitive Dynamics in a Product Market," with Jose Antonio Rosa, Jelena Runser-Spanjol, and Michael S. Saxon (*Journal of Marketing*, 1999), and *Cognition, Knowledge and Organizations* (1999) which he coedited with Raghu Garud. Joe is currently an Associate Editor of *Administrative Science Quarterly*. He received his Ph.D. from the University of Rochester.

Holly Raider [Intraorganizational Networks] is an Assistant Professor of Organization Behavior at INSEAD, where her teaching includes general management and organization change [E-mail: holly.raider@insead.fr]. Her primary research interest is contracts and transactional governance. Her current research focuses on relational governance in economic transactions, examining how relationship qualities between transacting dyads affect formal governance structures (contracts) and pricing of deals. Holly's other research interests include social network effects on careers, and technological innovation. Holly earned her B.A. at Barnard College, and studied for her Ph.D. at Columbia University and at the Interuniversity Center for Social Science Theory and Methodology, Groningen, the Netherlands.

Hayagreeva Rao [Interorganizational Ecology] is Professor of Organization and Management, Goizueta Business School, and an Adjunct Professor in the Department of Sociology, Emory University [E-mail: hayagreeva_rao@bus.emory.edu]. His research, which analyzes the social foundations of economic outcomes, has appeared in the *American Journal of Sociology*, *Administrative Science Quarterly*, *Academy of Management Journal*, *Organization Science*, *Strategic Management Journal*, and the *Journal of Marketing*. His recent publications include "Embeddedness, Social Identity and Mobility: Why Firms Leave NASDAQ and Join NYSE" (*Administrative Science Quarterly*, 2000), co-authored with Gerald Davis and Andrew Ward, and "Power Plays: How Social Movements and Collective Action Create New Organizational Forms" (*Research in Organizational Behavior*, 2000) co-authored with Mayer Zald and Cal Morrill. He is a Consulting Editor of the *American Journal of Sociology*, Senior Editor at *Organization Science* and serves on the editorial boards of *Administrative Science Quarterly* and *Academy of Management Review*. He has also served as a guest co-editor of the *Academy of Management Journal*'s Special Research Forum "Extending the Frontiers of Organizational Ecology." He completed his Ph.D. in organizational behavior at Case Western Reserve University.

Tim J. Rowley [Companion to Organizations: An Introduction] is the Deloitte & Touche Assistant Professor of Strategy at the University of Toronto's Rotman School of Management [E-mail: rowley@rotman.utoronto.ca]. His current research interests include alliance formation and interorganizational networks and their evolutionary processes. He received the Best Paper Award (with Stan X. Li) from the Business Policy and Strategy Division of the Academy of Management, 2000. His work has been published in the *Academy of Management Review* and *Business & Society* and most recently a paper titled "Redundant Governance Structures: An Analysis of Structural and Relational Embeddedness in the Steel and Semiconductor Industries" in the *Strategic Management Journal* (with Dean Behrens and David Krackhardt).

Melissa A. Schilling [Intraorganizational Technology] is an Assistant Professor at the Stern School of Business, New York University [E-mail: mschilli@stern.nyu.edu]. Previously she was an Assistant Professor of Strategy and Policy at Boston University's School of Management. Her primary research interests include the study of technology trajectories and standards, modularity at the product, organizational, and general system levels, and mechanisms underlying organizational learning and cognitive insight. Recent publications include "Technology Success and Failure in Winner-take-all Markets: Testing a Model of Technological Lock Out" (*Academy of Management Journal*, 2001), "Towards a General Modular Systems Theory and its Application to Inter-Firm Product Modularity" (*Academy of Management Review*, 2000), "Product and Process Technological Change and the Adoption of Modular Organizational Forms," in *Winning Strategies in a Deconstructing World* (eds, R. Bresser, M. Hitt, R. Nixon, and D. Heuskel, 2000), and "Technological Lock Out: An Integrative Model of the Economic and Strategic Factors Driving Technology Success and Failure" (*Academy of Management Review*, 1998). She received her Ph.D. in strategic management from the University of Washington in 1997.

Martin Schulz [Organizational Learning] is an Associate Professor of Organizational Behavior and Human Resources in the Faculty of Commerce and Business Administration at the University of British Columbia [E-mail: martinus@commerce.ubc.ca]. Previously he was an Assistant Professor of Management and Organization at the Business School, University of Washington. His primary research interests focus on organizational learning and organizational knowledge. His empirical work on these topics has included studies of organizational rule change and organizational knowledge flows. Recent publications include "Limits to Bureaucratic Growth: The Density Dependence of Organizational Rule Births," (*Administrative Science Quarterly*, 1998), "The Uncertain Relevance of Newness: Organizational Learning and Knowledge Flows," (*Academy of Management Journal*, 2001), "Codification and Tacitness as Knowledge Management Strategies: An Empirical Exploration," with Lloyd A. Jobe (*Journal of High Technology*

Management Research, 2001), and *The Dynamics of Rules: Change in Written Organizational Codes*, with James G. March and Xueguang Zhou (2000). He received his Ph.D. in sociology from Stanford University.

Brian S. Silverman [Organizational Economics] is an Associate Professor of Strategy at the Rotman School of Management, University of Toronto [E-mail: silverman@rotman.utoronto.ca]. Previously he was Assistant Professor of Competition and Strategy at Harvard Business School. His research interests include the efficient governance of innovation and the intersection of competitive strategy and organizational economics. Recent publications include "Technological Resources and the Direction of Corporate Diversification" (*Management Science*, 1999) and "Don't Go It Alone: Alliance Networks and Startups' Performance in Canadian Biotechnology," with J. A. C. Baum and T. Calabrese (*Strategic Management Journal*, 2000). Currently, with Paul Ingram, he is co-editing *The New Institutionalism in Strategic Management* (*Advances in Strategic Management*, vol. 19, 2002). He received his Ph.D. in business and public policy and strategy from the Haas School of Business at the University of California, Berkeley.

Wesley D. Sine [Interorganizational Institutions] is an Assistant Professor at the University of Maryland Business School [E-mail: wsine@rhsmith.umd.edu]. His current research examines the emergence, diffusion, and decline of institutions and the role institutional structures play in shaping organizational populations. Current projects include an analysis of the institutional barriers to entry that inhibit alternative energy entrepreneurs. A second study examines the diffusion of management innovations across national borders. He received his Ph.D. in industrial and labor relations from Cornell University.

Jitendra V. Singh [Organizational Evolution] is Saul P. Steinberg Professor of Management and Vice Dean for International Academic Affairs, the Wharton School, University of Pennsylvania [E-mail: singhj@wharton.upenn.edu]. He has been a faculty member at Wharton since 1987 and moved there from University of Toronto, Canada where he was an Associate Professor in the (now) Rotman School of Business. His current research interests focus on the intersection of strategy, technology and organization, with a specific focus on high technology organizations. He has published over 35 papers in leading management journals, and has also edited two books: *Organizational Evolution: New Directions* (1990), and *Evolutionary Dynamics of Organizations* (with Joel A. C. Baum, 1994). His current research project (with Terry Amburgey and Tina Dacin) examines dynamics of foundings, exits, initial public offerings and joint ventures by US new biotechnology firms, 1973–93. Jitendra currently serves on the editorial boards of *Asia Pacific Journal of Management, Strategic Management Journal* and *Organization Science*. Previously, he has also served on the editorial boards of *Academy of Management Journal* and *Administrative Science Quarterly*. He received his B.Sc. (physics, maths, statistics) from Lucknow University in India in 1972, his M.B.A. from the Indian Institute of Management, Ahmedabad, India, in 1975, and his Ph.D. from Stanford University in 1983.

Wendy Smith [Organizational Technology] is a doctoral student in Organizational Behavior at the Harvard Business School [E-mail: wesmith@hbs.edu]. Her research explores the role of senior teams in organizational change. She has a joint degree in psychology and political science from Yale, was a research assistant at Harvard Business School, and was a management consultant with Mercer Management Consulting prior to joining the Ph.D. program.

Olav Sorenson [Interorganizational Complexity and Computation] is an Assistant Professor of Policy at the Anderson Graduate School of Management, University of California – Los Angeles [E-mail: olav.sorenson@anderson.ucla.edu]. Prior to joining UCLA, he served on the faculty at the University of Chicago's Graduate School of Business. His current research examines how several factors – including organizational structure, competition and product strategy – influence an organization's ability to adapt. Other research investigates the role that social networks play in determining the geographic distribution of industry. Recent publications include "Technology as a Complex Adaptive System: Evidence from Patent Data" (with Lee Fleming, *Research Policy*, 2000), "Letting the Market work for you: An Evolutionary Perspective on Product Strategy" (*Strategic Management Journal*, 2000) and "Syndication Networks and the Spatial Distribution of Venture Capital Investment" (with Toby Stuart, *American Journal of Sociology*, 2001). Olav holds a Ph.D. from Stanford University.

David Strang [Interorganizational Institutions] is an Associate Professor in the Department of Sociology, Cornell University [E-mail: ds20@cornell.edu]. His research examines diffusion dynamics and organizational change, focusing particularly on the role of rhetorics, professional communities, organizational networks, and organizational learning. Recent papers include "In Search of Excellence: Fads, Success Stories, and Adaptive Emulation" with Michael Macy (*American Journal of Sociology*, 2001), "Theorizing Legitimacy or Legitimating Theory? Neo-Liberal Discourse and HMO Policy, 1970–89" with Ellen Bradburn (in *The Second Movement in Institutional Analysis*, edited by John Campbell and Ove Pedersen), and "Diffusion in Organizations and Social Movements: From Hybrid Corn to Poison Pills" with Sarah Soule (*Annual Review of Sociology*, 1998). A current project examines the rise and fall of "quality" programs both within a firm and across the business community as a whole. He received his Ph.D. in sociology from Stanford University.

Toby E. Stuart [Interorganizational Technology] is Fred G. Steingraber–A.T. Kearney Professor of Organizations and Strategy at the Graduate School of Business, University of Chicago [E-mail: toby.stuart@gsb.uchicago.edu]. His research examines how intercorporate social networks affect the evolution of high technology industries. His recent articles have appeared in *Administrative Science Quarterly*, *American Journal of Sociology*, *Strategic Management Journal*, *Industrial and Corporate Change*, and *Management Science*. Toby is an associate editor of the American Journal of Sociology and a member of the editorial board of *Industrial and Corporate Change*. He received his Ph.D. in 1995 from Stanford University, Graduate School of Business.

Michael L. Tushman [Organizational Technology] is the Paul R. Lawrence, Class of 1942 Professor of Business Administration at the Harvard Business School [E-mail: mtushman@hbs.edu]. His research explores the linkages between technological change, senior team characteristics, organization designs, and organizational change. Recent publications include "From the Technology Cycle to the Entrepreneurship Dynamic: Placing Dominant Designs in Social Context" (with J. Peter Murmann) in *The Entrepreneurship Dynamic: The Origins of Entrepreneurship and Its Role in Industry Evolution* (eds, K. Schoonhoven and E. Romanelli, 2001); "Dominant Designs, Innovation Types and Organizational Outcomes " (with J. Peter Murmann), *Research in Organization Behavior*, vol. 20 (eds, B. Staw and L. Cummings, 1998), and "The Coevolution of Community Networks and Technology: Lessons From the Flight Simulation Industry" (with Lori Rosenkopf), *Industrial and Corporate Change* (1998). He received his Ph.D. in organization studies at the Sloan School of Management at MIT.

Andrew H. Van de Ven [Field Research Methods] is Vernon H. Heath Professor of Organizational Innovation and Change in the Carlson School of Management of the University of Minnesota [E-mail: avandeven@csom.umn.edu]. Previously, he taught at Kent State University and the Wharton School of the University of Pennsylvania. Since 1994 he has been conducting a real-time field study of changes unfolding in healthcare organizations. He is co-author of *The Innovation Journey* (1999), and *Organizational Change and Innovation Processes: Theory and Methods for Research* (2000). Andy is 2000–2001 President of the Academy of Management, and was Program Chair of the Chicago '99 conference. He received his Ph.D. from the University of Wisconsin at Madison in 1972.

Arjen van Witteloostuijn [Interorganizational Economics] is Professor of International Economics and Business at the University of Groningen in the Netherlands [E-mail: a.van.witteloostuijn@eco.rug.nl]. Previously, he was affiliated with the University Maastricht (the Netherlands), New York University (USA) and Warwick Business School (UK). In 1996–98, he was Dean of the Maastricht Faculty of Economics and Business Administration. Arjen is founder of the Netherlands Institute of Business Organization and Strategy Research (NIBOR), and member of the editorial boards of *Academische boekengids, Academy Management Journal, Bedrijfskunde: tijdschrift voor modern management, Industrial and Corporate Change, Longe Range Planning, Maandblad voor accountancy en bedrijfseconomie, M&O, Organization Studies* and *Tijdschrift voor Bedrijfsadministratie.* He is a member of the Executive Committee of the European Association of Research in Industrial Economics (EARIE) and President of the Nederlands-Vlaamse Academie voor Management (NVAM). In addition to numerous book chapters and articles in Dutch dailies and journals, he has published in journals including the *Academy of Management Journal, Economica, European Journal of Political Economy, History of Political Economy, Journal of Economic Behavior and Organization, Journal of Economic Psychology, Journal of Management Studies, Management Science, Organization Studies, Personality and Individual Differences, Scandinavian Journal of Management* and *Strategic Management Journal.* He holds degrees in business, economics, and psychology.

Marc J. Ventresca [Interorganizational Cognition and Interpretation; Archival Research Methods] is an Assistant Professor of Management and Organizations, Kellogg Graduate School of Management (and, by courtesy, of Sociology, and Research Associate, Institute for Policy Research), Northwestern University [E-mail: m-ventresca@nwu.edu]. His current research interests investigate the interplay of regulation and activity as sources of new organizational forms, in three empirical contexts: governance innovations in the global stock exchanges industry, the emergence of online information services, and higher education policy. Recent publications are "Ideology and Field-Level Analysis," with Trex Proffitt (*Research in Social Movements, Conflict, and Change,* 2001), "The Embeddedness of Organizations," with Tina Dacin and Brent Beal (*Journal of Management,* 1999), and "The Institutional Framing of Policy Debates," with Andy Hoffman (*American Behavioral Scientist,* 1998). He is co-editor, with Joe Porac, of *Constructing Markets and Industries* (2001), and with Andy Hoffman, *Organizations, Policy, and the Natural Environment* (2001). He received his Ph.D. from Stanford University in 1995.

Lihua Wang [Organizational Networks] is a doctoral candidate at the Department of Management and Organizations, Kellogg Graduate School of Management, Northwestern University [E-mail: l-wang@nwu.edu]. Her research interests include mergers and acquisitions and strategic alliances. Her recent work studies stock market reactions to joint venture formation from a social network perspective.

Massimo Warglien [Intraorganizational Evolution] is Professor of Industrial Management and Decision Making at the Ca' Foscari University of Venezia, Italy [E-mail: warglien@unive.it]. His current research interests include evolutionary theories of the firm, mental models of strategic interaction, and conversational games. Recent publications include: "Talking about Routines in the Field: The Emergence of Organizational Capabilities in a New Cellular Phone Network Company," with A. Narduzzo and E. Rocco (eds, G. Dosi, R. Nelson, and S. Winter), *The Nature and Dynamics of Organizational Capabilities*, 2000), "Playing Conversation Games" (ed. B. Brogaard), *Rationality and Irrationality* (2000), and "Landscape Design. Designing for Local Action in Complex Worlds," with D. Levinthal (*Organization Science*, 1999). Massimo is also editor of the *Journal of Management and Governance*.

John R. Weeks [Intraorganizational Ecology] is an assistant Professor of Organizational Behavior at INSEAD [E-mail: john.weeks@insead.fr]. His work focuses on issues of organizational culture, innovation, and change. He is particularly interested in how national and organizational cultures evolve, and how "lay ethnography," or the views of people about their own culture, shapes culture change. John's forthcoming book is a study of the causes and consequences of the "unpopular culture" of a large British bank where everyone from the CEO to the most junior clerk agrees that a radical change of culture is necessary and desirable, and yet they also agree that such change is practically impossible. His most recent work is a study of the evolution of culture in an Internet startup company. His research has appeared in the *Academy of Management Review* and *Human Relations*. John holds a Ph.D. in management from the MIT Sloan School of management, an M.Phil. in management from Oxford University, and a B.A. in computer science from the University of California, Berkeley.

James D. Westphal [Intraorganizational Economics] is a Professor at the McCombs School of Business, University of Texas, Austin [E-mail: westphal@bus.utexas.edu]. His current research interests include corporate governance, institutional processes, and interorganizational networks. Recent publications include "The Strategic Context of Social Network Ties: Examining the Impact of Director Appointments on Board Involvement in Strategic Decision Making," with Mason A. Carpenter (*Academy of Management Journal*, 2001), "How Experience and Network Ties affect the Influence of Demographic Minorities on Corporate Boards," with Laurie P. Milton (*Administrative Science Quarterly*, 2000), "Collaboration in the Boardroom: The Consequences of Social Ties in the CEO/Board Relationship," (*Academy of Management Journal*, 1999), "Cooperative or Controlling? The Effects of CEO-Board Relations and the Content of Interlocks on the Formation of Joint Ventures," with Ranjay Gulati (*Administrative Science Quarterly*, 1999), and "The Symbolic Management of Stockholders: Corporate Governance Reforms and Shareholder Reactions", with Edward J. Zajac (*Administrative Science Quarterly*, 1998). He received his Ph.D. in organization behavior from Northwestern University.

Mina Yoo [Interorganizational Power and Dependence] is a doctoral candidate in Sociology at the University of Michigan [E-mail: minayoo@umich.edu] and in Organizational Behavior at the University of Michigan Business School. Her interests include entrepreneurship, social networks, globalization, and knowledge creation. She has conducted research examining the factors influencing organizational governance structures in educational settings. She has also examined the conditions under which an organization's culture is transferred successfully across national boundaries. Most recently (with Gerald Davis and Wayne Baker), she has investigated the network and demographic properties of *Fortune* 1000 board interlocks over time. She received her B.A. from Brown University.

Edward J. Zajac [Intraorganizational Economics] is the James F. Beré Distinguished Professor of Management and Organizations at the Kellogg Graduate School of Management, Northwestern University [E-mail: e-zajac@northwestern.edu]. His research focuses on the integration of economic and behavioral perspectives in the study of corporate governance, strategic adaptation, and strategic alliances. Recent publications include "Explaining Institutional Decoupling: The Case of Stock Repurchase Programs," with James D. Westphal (*Administrative Science Quarterly*, 2001), "How Resources Affect Strategic Change and Performance in Turbulent Environments: Theory and Evidence," with Matthew S. Kraatz (*Organization Science*, 2001), and "When Will Boards Influence Strategy? Inclination × Power = Strategic Change," with Brian R. Golden (*Strategic Management Journal*, 2001). He received his Ph.D. in organization and strategy at the Wharton School, University of Pennsylvania.

Preface

HOWARD E. ALDRICH

When I walked into Steve Berkowitz's office, in the winter of 1965, and saw the thick red book on his desk, I thought, "Why does he need a *Handbook of Organizations*? Is he thinking of becoming a Boy Scout leader or something?" I was in my first year of graduate school at the University of Michigan and Al Reiss had yet to implant in my mind the notion of organizations as units of analysis. Months passed before my curiosity got the better of me and I opened the book. The book's sections – foundations, methodologies, theoretical-substantive areas, and applications – struck me as arbitrary, and I ignored Stinchcombe's brilliantly prescient chapter for another year or so. So much for my abilities as a clairvoyant.

In his introduction, Jim March (1965: ix) made an astonishing claim: "we wish to summarize and report the present state of knowledge about human organizations." In 1247 pages! He noted the growing amount of multi-disciplinary work on organizations and the emerging boundaries of organizations as an area of study. Self-effacing as always, Jim (1965: xiv) admitted, "I do not know where the study of organizations is going. The vitality, represented by the contributors to this *Handbook*, and by contemporary organizations, suggests that it is going somewhere." And indeed, it has.

The first issue of *Administrative Science Quarterly*, founded by James Thompson, had appeared in June 1956. Thus, March was clearly right when he said that his *Handbook* "could not have been written 15 years ago." However, he was clearly wrong when he said, "certainly, it will not survive another 15." Nothing of comparable scope appeared again until Paul Nystrom and Bill Starbuck's 1981 *Handbook of Organizational Design*. By then, I was a lot more professionally savvy, and so when Bill asked me in 1973 if I were interested in contributing, I knew what a "Handbook" was. I didn't know how long they took to produce, however. Luckily, I already had tenure at that point. My coauthor, Dave Whetten, didn't, but that's another story. Paul and Bill followed March's lead and created a somewhat idiosyncratic set of sections for their *Handbook*: organizations' adaptive capabilities, implications of societal environments, interactions in interorganizational environments, organizations' operating characteristics, and consequences of organizations' activities.

Perhaps in keeping with March's implicit 15-year cycle of obsolescence, the next major Handbook appeared in 1996, edited by Stewart Clegg, Cynthia Hardy, and Walt Nord. I was recruited to their editorial board. In editing the *Handbook of Organization Studies*, Clegg et al. saw their task as quite different from previous editors. Whereas March offered us a synthesis of existing knowledge and Nystrom and Starbuck were concerned with improving organizational design, Clegg et al. wrote of offering a map of the terrain, stimulating a series of conversations, and opening up the field to diverse influences. The subdivisions of their *Handbook* reflected their embrace of multiple views: frameworks for analysis, current issues, and reflections on research, theory, and practice.

In keeping with their more eclectic definition of the field, only 65 percent of Clegg et al.'s contributors were based in North America, compared to 83 percent in Nystrom and Starbuck. The *Companion*'s share of North American contributors is the same as Paul and Bill's. In contrast, back in 1965, the study of organizations was hegemonically North American.

Had Joel stuck with March's 15-year cycle, this volume should have appeared in 2011! Luckily, we have no reason to wait that long. High-quality theory-driven research has been accumulating so quickly that I have no doubt that we'll need another Handbook before 15 years elapse again. I specifically mention "theory-driven" research because Jim March's prediction about an emerging structure has been realized, and Joel has taken advantage of it in organizing the *Companion*. Three levels of analysis – intraorganizational, organizational, and interorganizational – provide a coherent framework within which authors address common processes occurring at multiple levels, such as learning and networking.

What about the content of these Handbooks? What was there to write about? March's authors were limited by the scarcity of journals devoted specifically to studies of organizations as units of analysis. However, since 1965, dozens of new journals and thousands of articles and books have appeared. Too much information has been generated, in fact, for one scholar to comprehend. Handbooks serve the valuable function of collecting and organizing, from various perspectives, what we think we know about organizations.

In that respect, contributors to Joel's *Companion* are much better positioned than their predecessors. When Gerry Salancik and I were co-editing *Administrative Science Quarterly*, back in the 1970s and early 1980s under Karl Weick's editorship, we used to joke that for every empirical paper we published, we subsequently received at least two review papers, trying to interpret the empirical one! The emergence of the *Academy of Management Review*, in 1976, put added pressure on researchers to come up with enough new ideas to allow purely conceptual papers, but the field survived. Its survival, in part, reflects the difference between the study of organizations and the study of other entities.

Unlike economics, sociology, and some other social sciences, our field is not divided up between an elite cadre of theorists and another group who collect the data on which (mostly) the theorists depend. Instead, as the 50 plus contributors to the *Companion* superbly demonstrate, our most vigorous theorists are also our most vigorous researchers. Indeed, the authors who write about research methods in the *Companion* all have actually used those methods in their own research. In that respect, a strong thread of continuity runs between March's *Handbook* and the *Companion*.

Finally, I am delighted to see the powerful influence that Donald Campbell has had on the conception and development of the *Companion*. Reading his work on evolutionary theory, back in the 1960s, started me on what I now understand, under Bill McKelvey's tutelage, as the scientific realist approach to theory corroboration. The evolutionary approach that underlies the structure of the *Companion* is committed to a constant search for new arenas in which to test propositions, as well as to open debate among scholars. As Joel and co-author Tim Rowley note in their introduction, everything in the *Companion* is provisional in nature and subject to further criticism. I wish this book had been the one on Steve's desk, back in 1965, although the one I actually found there wasn't too shabby, either.

Acknowledgments

In the dozen years before and since my joining the field, the study of organization has experienced unprecedented vitality and produced a dramatic growth in knowledge. The field has also been increasingly influenced *less* by normal science post-positivisms and *more* by relativist and postmodernist post-positivisms calling for a different research approach, one somehow "more relevant to social sciences." The field is ripe for a critical accounting of what we now know about organizations, and how we know it.

I conceived the *Companion* as a comprehensive, interdisciplinary survey that consolidates and evaluates what we know (and don't) about organizations and to focus critical attention to the possibilities for epistemological and methodological elaboration. A "companion" is a person you spend a lot of time with either because you are friends, or because you are traveling together – a companion is an associate, a comrade, a consort, a partner, an ally, or an accomplice. A companion is also a type of book that gives you information on a particular subject, or tells you how to do something. This Companion is, of course, a book. But, as you travel the field of organizations, I hope that it becomes a friend too – an indispensable source of reference and fresh insight into the modern organizational world we inhabit.

For newcomers, the *Companion* is an introduction to and contemporary mapping of the field that provides a foundation for understanding and navigating the complex world of complex organizations. For those already studying and working in the field, it is an exhaustive resource and rich source of inspiration, ideas and insight. The *Companion* sets the stage for the field to construct a more comprehensive "multiscience," in Donald Campbell's (1969) terms, in which a continuous texture of overlapping specialized perspectives contribute to a fuller understanding of the organizational world.

The *Companion* is a compilation of the thoughtful insights of more than 50 researchers on four continents, who, in a leap of faith, agreed to join me in this venture. Among them brave young scholars who, despite tenure clocks ticking loudly, agreed to contribute their fresh and exciting views, as well as more experienced scholars who have carefully and thoughtfully compressed decades of scholarship into sharp and percipient statements. Each author is – or is becoming – a vital contributor to the area on which they have written. Together, in my view, they have created a masterwork. I hope that you, readers of this *Companion*, will arrive at a similar conclusion.

Some specific thanks are in order. The first is an unhappy one. Jane Azevedo was diagnosed with breast cancer early in the fall of 1999 and died May 9, 2000. Jane wrote much of her chapter, Updating Organizational Epistemology, as she endured treatment. On several occasions, she reported that the writing was a great source of distraction from her daily regime; the product of her "distraction" is wonderful resource for students and scholars of organization. Thank you Jane. I also owe a debt of gratitude to all the contributors to the *Companion* who, completed thoughtful revisions (sometimes several) and generally met (and put up with) the annoying deadlines I set – and, more than once, reset! Thanks are also due to Blackwell's Susan Rabinowitz for somehow persuading me to undertake this mammoth project – What was I thinking? – and Rosemary Nixon, who ultimately got me through it, largely in tact. Finally, and most importantly, Kathy, Sara Bea, Zachary, and yes, Peanut too, thanks for enduring my manuscript piles, hours reading in the jungle chair, and late night e-mailing sprees. I wouldn't want to be anywhere else but with you all.

JACB, Toronto, January 2001

Companion to Organizations: An Introduction

JOEL A. C. BAUM AND TIM J. ROWLEY

Organizations dominate our socioeconomic landscape. Their influence in our everyday lives has increased steadily over time, particularly in the most developed regions of the world during the twentieth century. Today, we are born, work, pray and die in organizations, and, along the way, many of us derive our identities from our associations with them. Organizations are the building blocks of our societies, and a basic vehicle for collective action. They produce the infrastructure of our societies and they will fundamentally shape our futures. Because they are such an integral part of modern societies, we readily turn to them, or construct them when a problem exceeds our own personal abilities or resources.

The ubiquity of organizations prompted Nobel Laureate Herbert Simon (1991) to question the use of the term "market economy" to describe the structure of economic interactions, suggesting that "organizational economy" would be the more appropriate term. As Richard Scott (1992, p. 3) points out, however, because organizations are so ubiquitous, they tend to "fade into the background, and we need to be reminded of their impact." Still, most of us are of two minds about the organizations in our lives. While we wonder in amazement at their innovative achievements and bask in the recognition and status they confer on us, we damn them when they don't (or won't) work for us and worry that we are powerless to take them on.

To understand organizations *is* to understand our world.

The perspectives and theories constituting our current understanding of organizations are different from those employed twenty years ago. Scott (1998) wonders whether these changes are due to an evolution in the nature of organizations themselves or in the theorists' interests and manner of creating knowledge. That is, changes in perspectives on organizations could represent development of a deeper level of understanding, replacement of old theories and ideas with new ones to match the changes in organizations while maintaining previous levels of understanding, or simply the adoption of new languages corresponding to different knowledge creation approaches with no significant increase – and perhaps even a decrease – in our understanding.

Does the diversity of perspectives on organizations enrich or fragment our understanding of them? Or worse still, does it undermine our understanding by encouraging a proliferation of uncorroborated ideas? The answers to these questions remain open, and are hotly debated by some theorists. This diversity has also generated disagreement over whether or not research on organizations has advanced sufficiently to be deemed "organization *science.*" Many believe "organization *studies*" is a more appropriate label (Clegg et al., 1996), the field's multiple perspectives providing evidence that it is *prescientific* in Thomas Kuhn's (1962) famous classification. As Kuhn also counsels, however, we should not be surprised to find in the early stages of development of a science that researchers studying the same phenomena describe and interpret them in the different ways. Here, we follow McKelvey (this volume, 2001) and refer to the field as organization "science" to signify our collective efforts in the field and within the *Companion* toward constructing a science of organizations.

The *Companion* presents a survey that consolidates and evaluates ten contemporary perspectives on organizations, providing you with the opportunity to explore what we know about organizations, and how we have come to know it. To set the stage for your exploration, in this introductory chapter, we perform three tasks. First, we review the fundamental definitions of organizations that underlie contemporary perspectives. Second, we provide an overview of the perspectives themselves. And third, we discuss approaches to knowledge creation in organization science.

Three Definitions of "Organization"

Although most of us "know an organization when we see one," the diversity and complexity of organizations and their activities is difficult to capture in a single formal definition. As a result, multiple, sometimes contrary, conceptions of organizations exist, each one highlighting particular features of organizations, but necessarily providing only partial and incomplete views. Also contributing to the definitional difficulties, most words ending in "-tion" are ambiguous between process and product – between the way one gets there, and the result. Our word, organization, shares this ambivalence, itself referring to the process of "organizing," or, to the result of organizing. Although the range of definitions can create confusion, together, they also provide a means of capturing the full breadth of organizational life.

Scott (1998, pp. 24–8) articulates three prominent definitions that capture well the spectrum of how organizations are conceived. Each definition calls attention to certain significant, enduring and essential features of organizations that distinguish them from related types of collectivities (e.g., families, small groups), and embodies different assumptions and beliefs about the nature of organizations. The definitions are given in order of their historical appearance, and each can be seen, at least in part, as a critical response to perceived inadequacies and limitations of the prior conceptions.

- *Rational system*: Organizations are collectivities oriented to the pursuit of relatively specific goals and exhibiting relatively highly formalized social structures.
- *Natural system*: Organizations are collectivities whose participants share a common interest in the survival of the system and who engage in collective activities, informally structured, to secure this end.
- *Open system*: Organizations are systems of interdependent activities linking shift-

ing coalitions of participants; the systems are embedded in – dependent on continuing exchanges with and constituted by – the environment in which they operate.

Although historically, rational, natural and open systems definitions have been associated with distinct research programs, each with its own conceptual frameworks, guiding assumptions, and empirical approaches, contemporary perspectives built on these foundations invariably take an open systems view, and combine it with either a rational or a natural systems orientation; see, for example, the typology of contemporary theorists (Scott, 1998, p. 107, Table 5-1). Thus, most recent definitions of organizations tend to combine elements of rational, natural, and open systems definitions. Aldrich (1979 – cf. Aldrich 1999, p. 2) – for example, defines organizations as "goal-directed, boundary-maintaining, and socially constructed systems of human activity." Notably, the rise of open systems approaches has, as we will see, increasingly focused researchers' attention away from behavior *within* organizations, which had been the primary focus of rational and natural systems approaches, and toward the behavior *of* organizations as entities in and of themselves.

Although some researchers continue to seek a parsimonious formal definition that captures the essential features of all organizations, others have concluded that no single definition will travel well across all organizations (Pfeffer, 1997). Further, some observers suggest that these definitions correspond to different types of organizations operating in environments demanding different features and structures (Lawrence and Lorsch, 1967). Others argue that these definitions capture different aspects of organization. For example, the rational, natural and open system views correspond to the technical, managerial and institutional dimensions of organizations, respectively (Thompson, 1967).

It is impossible for us to do justice to either the range of imaginative rational, natural and open system ideas from which contemporary perspectives on organizations emerged, or even, for that matter, to the subtleties of those approaches selected for mention; see Scott (1998) for a detailed examination. But we will note some of the main lines of thinking within each conception, and attempt to capture the basic spirit of the ideas. Afterward, we turn to ten perspectives that evolved from these definitions and form the corpus of the *Companion.*

Rational system origins

The Greek root of organization, "organon," meaning instrument or tool, captures the image projected in the rational system view. Organizations are designed (created) to achieve specific goals; and rational view theorists normatively and descriptively argue that organizational designs involve formal structures – rules, roles and relationships – that are created to emphasize efficiency in achieving well-defined objectives. In this view, organizations are portrayed as machine-like bureaucracies in which all actions and behaviors are controlled and coordinated to ensure goal achievement in the greatest economy. They are comprised of standard operating procedures and formal structures, which specify responsibilities and ensure that these all procedures are reliably performed.

Historically, the study of organizations has been dominated by the rational system definition, and its early focus on goal-directed activity-systems was critical to establishing "complex organizations" as a distinctive field of study. The rational systems approach emerged in Europe and North America alongside the rapid industrialization and increasing rationalization of business enterprises at the turn of the twentieth century. In Europe, Max Weber ([1922] 1978) and Robert Michels ([1911] 1949) documented the rise of the "bureaucracy," an organizational form based on a belief in normative rules and a hierarchy of officials elevated to authority under those rules who issue commands. In North America, Frederick Taylor and his followers (e.g., Frank and Lillian Gilbreth and Henry Gantt) championed "scientific management," which aimed to rationalize the activities of both managers and workers based on an analytical "regimen of science." On both continents, business practitioners – most notably French industrialist Henri Fayol and General Motors executives James Mooney and Allan Reiley – searched for a universal set of principles of administration to guide the specialization, grouping, and coordination of work activities. The enduring contribution of these early thinkers was the elaboration of the concept of the formal organization as an instrument purposefully designed to achieve explicit goals with the greatest economy of resources.

Perhaps the most influential rational system contribution, however, is the pioneering work of Herbert Simon and his colleagues James March and Richard Cyert, known collectively as "the Carnegie School" (Simon, 1945; March and Simon, 1958; Cyert and March, 1963). Many of the themes they introduced – among them, goals and constraints, formalized structure, bounded rationality, information processing, decision-making, political coalitions, and performance programs – remain central to contemporary organizational research. Simon and his colleagues were highly critical of earlier "prescriptive" efforts both for searching for a simple set of "dos and don'ts" and for focusing on *activities* rather than the *choices* that determined them. Underlying their model is a conception of human cognitive limits in which incomplete information about means and ends – bounded rationality – leads to "satisficing" choices that meet some minimum set of criteria, rather than best possible choices. Thus, while, like neoclassical "economic man" motivated by self-interests, Simon's (1945) "administrative man" does not always know what his interests are, is aware of only a few alternatives, and is willing to settle for an adequate solution.

In their "behavioral theory of the firm" Cyert and March (1963), formalized structure economizes on human cognitive limits and promotes rational decision making by providing a set of "givens" in which choice and action takes place. Rationality thus resides in the structure itself – in specialized roles, rules, training programs and operating procedures that assure members will behave in ways designed to achieve desired objectives, in control arrangements that evaluate performance and detect deviations, in reward systems that give members incentives to perform proscribed tasks, and in criteria for hiring, firing, and promotion. Their conceptualization reveals a tension between two images of adaptation, however. On the one hand, organizations' behavior is directed toward performance improvement, compatible with rationalistic assumptions of traditional economic theories of the firm. On the other hand, their behavior tends to be complex, slow and sensitive to organizational conditions, characteristic of bounded rationality. Thus, while *intendedly* adaptive, organizations' behavior might not necessarily result in performance improvement – structures developed to promote rationality may, under some conditions, have the opposite effect.

NATURAL SYSTEM ORIGINS

If goals, formal structure and efficiency best describe the rational system view, emergent purpose, informal structure and adaptation depict the natural system view. In addition, natural system theorists put little emphasis on formal structure, arguing that the informal structure of roles and relationships that emerge among individuals and groups shape organizational activities and goals. In this view, organizations are not purposively designed instruments performing tasks with machine-like efficiency, but rather organic entities that become infused value and meaning beyond the purpose intended in the formal structure. So, organizations may initially be created to pursue specific goals, but alternative (supplementing or supplanting) purposes and meanings emerge through human interaction and displace the initial objectives.

Although there is no single "unified" natural systems model of organizations, what sets natural systems models apart is their focus on the nonrational, informal and moral bases of social conduct and cooperation. Starting with Chester Barnard (1938), Elton Mayo (1945), and Fritz Roethlisberger and William Dickson (1939), the interplay between formal and informal structures is a recurring natural system theme. Whereas formal structure is viewed as a conscious expression of a cost-and-efficiency logic, informal structure represents the spontaneous logic of human sentiments and needs. Informal relationships facilitate communication and getting things done, maintain cohesion, and are at the center of political life in organizations. Some, including George Homans (1950), concluded from this view that small face-to-face groups, joined together by reciprocal bonds of activities, interactions and feelings were the basic building blocks of organizations. Others, including Robert Merton (1957), drew less "reductionist" conclusions, viewing organizations more holistically as finely balanced systems of mutual social constraint in which each individual's actions are shaped by the demands and expectations in his or her "role set."

Another natural system pioneer and Merton student, Philip Selznick (1949, 1957) stressed that, although organizations are "instruments designed to attain specific goals," they are also "adaptive organisms" that take on lives of their own, changing their unifying purposes and very reasons for existence in order to perpetuate themselves. Over time, he suggests, each organization develops a "distinctive character and competence" and becomes "infused with value beyond the technical requirements of the task at hand" (1957, p. 17). Selznick referred to the process by which an organization developed a distinctive character and became invested with meaning beyond its utilitarian value as *institutionalization.* Selznick's natural system approach is the foundation for contemporary research in the institutional perspective, or "neo-institutionalism," and has also influenced research on power and dependence. Selznick's institutionalism and its descendants follow the Weberian ([1922] 1978) tradition of focusing on *verstehen* – the subjective meaning of action – and on the effects of institutional structure. Subjective meaning underpins human behavior – we behave in ways that are meaningful to us, whether that meaning is associated with salvation or with material accumulation.

Also influential, and anticipating many themes pursued by open system models to follow, was Talcott Parsons's (1960) general analytic model identifying a set of functional needs that all social systems – from face-to-face groups, to organizations, to societies – must satisfy in order to survive. His model is identified by the acronym

"AGIL," which represents the four basic system-survival functions, **A**daptation (securing resources), **G**oal attainment (setting an implementing goals), **I**ntegration (maintaining solidarity and coordination), and **L**atency (creating, preserving and transmitting cultural values). In his examination of organizations, Parsons applied his model at three levels: "ecological," (i.e., the organization's social function); "structural" (i.e., horizontal functional differentiation and integration, and vertical differentiation among technical, managerial and institutional systems within organizations); and "social psychological" (i.e., finer micro-level subsystems such as face-to-face groups). Thus, although like many natural system models in his focus on functional needs, Parsons departed from most in his conception of organizations as a distinctive class of social system differentiated by their goal directedness.

OPEN SYSTEM ORIGINS

In the rational and natural system views, organizations and their environments are separate entities with clear boundaries. In the open system perspective, however, this distinction is not so obvious, and focus is placed on the relationship and interdependencies between organizations and environments. Inspired by general systems theory and cybernetics (Boulding, 1956; Buckley, 1967; Katz and Kahn [1966] 1978), open systems models conceive organizations as both systems of internal relationships and as inhabitants of a larger system encompassing the environments in which they operate and on which they depend for resources. Organizations are conceived of as a throughput model, obtaining resources from the environment, processing them and distributing the output back to the environment. If the rational view projects a machine image and the natural systems view an organic one, the open system view suggests an organism analogy – organizations are adaptive and interdependent systems, comprised of various interrelated – possibly conflicting subsystems – attempting to meet and influence the dynamic demands of the environment.

Early open systems work focused on development of a "contingency theory" in which the best way to organize depended on the demands placed on the organization by the environment in which it operated, in addition to internal characteristics including the complexity of inputs, processes, and knowledge (Burns and Stalker, 1961; Lawrence and Lorsch, 1967; Perrow, 1967; Thompson, 1967; Woodward, 1965). For example, environments characterized by uncertainty and rapid technological or market change place different demands on organizations than do stable environments. Because different organizational subunits (e.g., research and development vs. production) may confront different environments, they may require specialized subunits with differing features. The more differentiated the organizational structure, the more difficult it will be to coordinate various subunit activities, and so, the greater the need for coordinating mechanisms. Thus, combining open and rational system logics, contingency theory asked: "Given that an organization is open to the uncertainties of its environment, how can it function as a rational system?" (Scott, 1998, p. 111)

In contrast to contingency theorists' content-oriented, "rational-open" systems approach, Karl Weick (1969, 1979) advanced a process-oriented, "natural-open" systems model of "organizing," in which organizational activities are directed toward resolving equivocal informational inputs from the environment. Organizational activities are carried out in three stages – enactment, selection, and retention – a translation of Donald Campbell's (1965) influential variation-selection-retention model of sociocultural evolution. Weick replaces "variation" with "enactment" to emphasize the active role organizational members play in defining, giving meaning to, and influencing their environments. Over time, organizational activities become structured as loosely coupled systems of repeated, contingent, interlocked behaviors that establish a workable level of certainty for organizational members, but also allow variation in interpretation and action as organizational members selectively attend to their environments. Although, like Simon and colleagues, Weick gives great attention to the role of cognition in creating and sustaining organizations, his focus is on "interpretation" and "meaning creation" rather than on "computation" and "information processing."

Levels of Organization

The rise of open systems perspectives had several important side effects on organization science. Key among these was the increasing clarity and explicitness with which different levels of organization were recognized, conceptualized and studied – from individual members, to face-to-face groups, to departments, to organizations, to organizational populations and communities. These different levels can be seen as forming an *inclusive* hierarchy with the levels nested one within the other. Each "whole" is composed of parts at lower levels of organization, and are themselves parts of more extensive wholes. Organizational communities, for example, are composed of populations of organizations, themselves composed of organizations, and so on. A multilevel approach is thus useful because organizational systems are hierarchically arranged (Baum and Singh, 1994).

Although it is possible to identify a great number of organizational levels, in the *Companion* each perspective is approached from three commonly studied levels of organization. The levels are distinguished primarily by the phenomenon of interest to be explained (i.e., the dependent variable). At the *intraorganizational level*, the focus is on understanding the people, groups, knowledge, tools and tasks that make up organizations. At the *organizational level*, the focus is on understanding organizational processes, boundaries, activity-systems and strategies. At the *interorganizational level*, the focus is on understanding the relationships and interactions within and among aggregates of organizations.

Although accompanying the shift of focus over time from rational, to natural, to open systems conceptions of organizations was a tendency to shift attention from intraorganizational to organizational, and to interorganizational levels, perspectives originally conceived at one level are now commonly applied at multiple levels. This has helped to foster research that spans multiple levels, and opened a great opportunity to connect research across levels of organization and to better reflect the hierarchically nested nature of organizational phenomena. So, while this differentiation among levels serves to organize, simplify, and reflect the complexity of the field (and of organizational systems), the particular distinctions among organizational levels are a matter of analytic convenience, and researchers at each level cognizant of the other levels.

Researchers have attempted to better demarcate levels of organizations – and in particular organizations – through efforts to conceptualize and study organizational boundaries. As Scott (1992, p. 181) points out, however, "accepting the notion of organizations as open systems is to acknowledge that organizations are penetrated by their environments in ways that blur and confound any simple criterion for distinguishing one from the other." Two approaches to defining organizational boundaries, and social boundaries more generally, are the "realist" approach, which adopts a participants' perspective to identify boundaries salient to the participants themselves, and the "nominalist" approach, which adopts a conceptual perspective to locate theoretically salient boundaries (Scott 1998, p. 183). Regardless of the perspective taken, what features of the situation to attend to must be determined. One option is to focus on relationships among people, locating organizational boundaries where interpersonal relationships become sparse (Weick, 1979). A second is to focus on the nature of peoples' activities, identifying boundaries where the nature of activities and control over them change (Pfeffer and Salancik, 1978). A third possibility is to focus on normative criteria for membership and inclusion, and constitutive rules and norms that are applicable to participants, which locates boundaries where applicable criteria and rules change. Not surprisingly relational, activity-based and normative boundaries often do not coincide, and so organizational boundaries will typically be somewhat blurred. Thus, notwithstanding the efforts of groups and organizations to differentiate members from nonmembers, it will often be the case that formal group and organizational boundaries fail to delineate all key activities and relations.

Organizational Environments

A second, and perhaps the most fundamental development accompanying the rise of open systems thinking, was the systematic conceptualization of the nature of organizational environments. Most commonly, organizational environments are conceived as *task environments*. First proposed by William Dill as encompassing all aspects of the environment "potentially relevant to goal setting and goal attainment" (1958, p. 410), in practice, the task environment is more narrowly conceived as comprised of sources for inputs, markets for outputs, competitors, and regulators (Scott, 1998). A closely related conception, the *technical environment*, is one in which organizations produce a product or service and are rewarded in the market for outputs for high quality and efficient performance (Scott and Meyer, 1983).

Task and technical conceptions of environments emphasize the rational system idea that organizations are activity systems created to economically achieve goals. Since organizations are not self-sufficient, to survive, they must enter into exchanges with the environment to acquire needed resources and information. Organizations' need for information creates uncertainty (Thompson, 1967); their need for resources creates dependence (Pfeffer and Salancik, 1978). In general, the more complex, unstable, interconnected and uncoordinated the environment, the greater the uncertainty it creates. And, the scarcer the resources, and more concentrated and coordinated their sources, the greater the dependence. Although it is possible to characterize an organization's general task environment as "complex" or "munificent," it is not necessarily informative to do so because the specific location an organization occupies within its environment strongly influences the conditions it faces, and, in addition, because different subunits of a given organization may confront quite different task environmental conditions.

Organizational environments are more than simply sources for inputs, information, and markets for outputs, however. Symbolic and normative aspects of environments – institutionalized rules and beliefs about organizations also figure prominently (DiMaggio and Powell, 1983; Meyer and Rowan, 1977). Institutional theorists emphasize that organizations must conform to these rules and requirements if they are to receive support and be perceived as legitimate. In *institutional environments* organizations are rewarded for using acceptable structures and practices, not the quantity and quality of their outputs (Scott and Meyer, 1983). The state, professions, unions, and trade associations are among the most consequential sources of institutional structures in modern societies. The role of such normative and cognitive (as opposed to task and technical) constraints has figured with increasing prominence in organizational research as natural-open systems thinking has expanded.

Some view the relationship between technical and institutional environments as complementary, suggesting that they be treated as dimensions along which environments vary, with organizations inhabiting environments with varied intensities of technical and institutional pressures (Scott, 1998). Schools, for example, experience stronger institutional than technical demands, while commercial airlines experience the opposite. Some organizations also inhabit environments in which both technical and institutional demands are significant (e.g., banks), while others experience little of either (e.g., restaurants). Increasingly, however, institutional environments are conceived as contextual to technical environments – the relationship between them is not only complementary; it is also "hierarchical" (Tucker et al., 1992). From this point of view, the institutional environment constitutes the broader social context for defining technical processes – the institutional environment may prescribe the technical criteria for judging whether an organization is worthy of environmental support. The markets that reward organizations for efficient performance, for example, are institutionally constituted and structured by rules regarding property rights, norms governing exchange, and so on.

Although influential and common, the distinction between technical and institutional environments has not been without critics. Powell (1991; 1996, p. 295) argues vehemently that this separation is "wrongheaded" and "simple minded," perpetuated more by scholarly turf fighting than substantive debate over how to accurately conceptualize environments and their relationship to organizations. In Powell's view, these distinctions are purely analytical; all organizational environments include *both* technical and institutional elements. Recognizing and acknowledging this, according to Powell, provides a more accurate and useful conception of organization–environment interactions than those relying on two or more separate environments conceived as interacting independently with organizations. Even advocates of the technical/institutional distinction do not appear to dispute this claim, however. Scott (1992, p. 140), for example, thinks that all organizations operate in both technical and institutional environments. And, therefore, that we "must not overlook the institutional supports of even the most technically oriented organizations . . . the markets that reward organizations for effective and efficient performance are themselves institutionally constituted and structured."

Because organizations must respond effectively to the demands of the environment (or environments) if they are to acquire the information and resources they need to survive, how organizations relate to their environments is an important conceptual question. For the environmental demand to influence an organization's decisions and actions, the organization's members must have knowledge of it. Environments may not only be *observed* and *(mis)interpreted*, however, they may be *enacted* as organizational members actively constitute and give meaning to them (Weick, 1969). How the environment is enacted (and responded to) depends, among other factors, on how organizational members' attention is structured by organizational arrangements and information collection practices. Of course, not only perception and enactment matter. What organizational members do not know (or do not know all that well) can impact organizational outcomes – for better or worse. Organizations produce outputs (products and services) whose quality, quantity and form is largely under their members' control. But organizational performance reflects the interaction of organizational outputs and an environmental response that is much less under their members' control. And, the environment will respond regardless of whether or not it is known.

Contemporary Perspectives

The *Companion* presents ten contemporary perspectives on organizations. Figure 0.1 lists the perspectives, and maps them in relation to rational, natural and open system definitions. Although by no means exhaustive, together these ten perspectives encompass most areas of inquiry into organizations. As with their rational, natural and open systems predecessors, these current perspectives are based partly on different disciplines (e.g., economics, sociology, psychology, anthropology, and biology). They also reflect differences between "subjectivists," who hold that knowledge is constitutively a social product, and "objectivists," who see knowledge as being distinct from and independent of the social realm. A majority of the perspectives, however, draw on multiple disciplines and include both subjectivist and objectivist accounts. Selected perspectives include some that are well established (e.g., economics, ecology, institutions, power and dependence), some that are now expanding rapidly (e.g., cognition and interpretation, networks, learning, technology), and some that are still emerging (e.g., complexity and computation, evolution). As noted earlier, contemporary perspectives on organizations invariably take an open system view, and combine it with either a rational or a natural systems orientation. Nine perspectives combine open and natural systems thinking, although five of these have a rational-open system substream. Economics is the lone remaining perspective dominated by rational system thinking. As such, as we will see, it is often viewed with great skepticism, and even "fear and loathing" (Pfeffer, 1993).

These perspectives are not "theories" (i.e., descriptive or explanatory frameworks), but comprise multiple theories. The economics perspective, for example, includes agency, resource-based, transaction cost, industrial organization, and game theories. Nor are they "paradigms" (Kuhn, 1962). Although each perspective has its own core conceptual frameworks, distinctive processes, and guiding assumptions that help to establish the importance of various research problems and how to conduct research to solve them, they are not "incommensurable." Rather than adoption of concepts from one perspective rendering concepts from the others meaningless, as Kuhn's incommensurability implies, the perspectives *complement* one another either by focusing on different organizational phenomena and problems, or by emphasizing different aspects of similar phenomena and problems. The institutional perspective, for example, is concerned with how routine organizational practices become taken-for-granted and meaningful. The network perspective is concerned with how organizational practices are developed in a

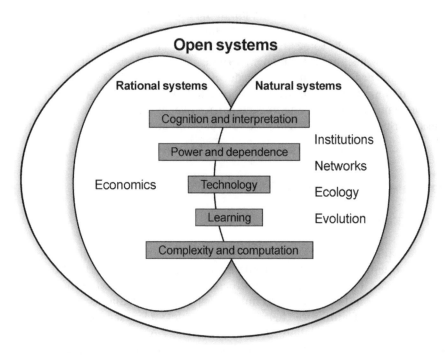

Figure 0.1   Mapping contemporary perspectives on organizations: Rational, natural and open systems

social milieu, and with how they are constrained by that milieu. The power and dependence perspective is concerned with how power influences economic patterns and the rise and fall of organizational practices. The economics perspective is concerned with how competitive pressures and the quest for efficiency shape firm behavior and organizational arrangements. Less frequently, perspectives *compete* with one another by offering alternative explanations for particular features of similar phenomena and problems.

In practice, research within each perspective thus tends to draw on, rather than challenge, the others. Rather than seeking to disprove (or ignore) the other perspectives, researchers based in one perspective typically borrow from others liberally. Indeed, in contemporary research, the perspectives are less frequently used alone than they are in combination. McGuire and Granovetter (2001), for example, use a structural theory of power in their network-based study of electricity generation to explain technological choices. Some institutionalists, including Strang and Meyer (1993), use network theory to explain how organizational practices diffuse. Others, notably Davis et al. (1994), incorporate an economic perspective into their account. Power and dependence theorists, particularly Fligstein (1990, 1996), have incorporated both institutional and network elements to explain how new norms and practices diffuse across corporations. Ecological researchers, including Baum and his colleagues (Baum and Haveman, 1997; Baum and Mezias, 1992; Baum and Oliver, 1991, 1992), have increasingly used institutional, network and economic concepts and measures in their models of organizational population dynamics.

Although this wealth of perspectives might appear as an embarrassment of riches, as we noted at the outset of this chapter, the value of this diversity is currently a point of heated contention. While some organization theorists celebrate the multiple perspectives as sources of new insight (Van Maanen, 1995a, 1995b), others criticize the fragmentation and diminished consensus they produce (Pfeffer, 1993, 1995). Later, we address the question of multiple perspectives in more detail; before doing so, however, we introduce some main lines of thinking in each perspective, again attempting only to capture the basic spirit of the work, leaving the task of detail and subtlety to the chapters that follow.

Natural-Open Systems

INSTITUTIONS

Dissatisfied with the rational system view of organizations as dominated by environmental constraints and efficiency considerations, John Meyer and Brian Rowan (1977) and Lynne Zucker (1977) proposed that the increasing rationalization of cultural rules provided a basis – independent of technical and economic demands – for constructing organizations. Two features set their "neoinstitutional" approach apart from Selznick's (1949, 1957) earlier formulation. One is the centrality of *cognitive* (vs. normative) elements of institutions – the rules and symbols that constitute the nature of reality, the frames through which meaning is made, and social action constructed – and associated *social constructionist* or *phenomenological* orientation (Berger and Luckmann, 1966). The other is a focus on institutional effects – how organizations are influenced by institutionalized rules and institutional environments, rather than on how organizations become institutions in the first place. Meyer, Rowan and Zucker portray organizations as complexes of cultural rules rationalized through the actions of professions, the state, and mass media. Institutional processes create both *structural* and *cognitive* constraints – an "iron cage" in Max Weber's terms – limiting not only organizational structures by rendering some options *unfeasible*, but organizational members' imaginations by rendering some options *unimaginable*. Formal structures signal organizations' commitment and conformity to acceptable standards of organizing. Formal structures may be adopted in the absence of specific, immediate coordination and control problems, and so are only loosely coupled with actual behavior. Organizational performance is inherently *social*, depending not on technical and economic competence, but on conformity to rationalized rules and requirements necessary to acquire needed social support and resources and to be perceived as legitimate. Emphasizing *isomorphism* (i.e., similarity) among organizations as basic product of institutional processes Paul DiMaggio and Walter Powell (1983) elaborated a set of mechanisms – *coercive*, *normative*, and *mimetic* – through which institutionalized rules and practices are diffused among organizations as they follow the actions of other organizations to reduce uncertainty and acquire legitimacy.

NETWORKS

The study of networks has a long history in organization science. Like the institutional perspective, the network perspective is *phenomenological*, in the sense that it focuses on the *content* of networks of interpersonal and interorganizational relations and the meaning of action as defined by the network. Sociological network theory builds closely on Émile Durkheim's ([1893] 1933) concern with how social milieu produces social identity and, in so doing, shapes the actions of individuals – not merely in the negative sense of undermining antisocial behavior, but in the positive sense of establishing accepted, rational forms of action. Over time, the network concept has evolved from a metaphor for "informal structure" to a formal research tool (White et al., 1976), and also shifted levels of analysis from a focus on patterns of relations among people *within* organizations, to focus on how organizational environments are constituted. The shift to formal tool lends itself to quantitative analysis and is a valuable and flexible device for characterizing and analyzing the actual interconnectedness among individuals and organizations. The shift in level was sparked in part by Harrison White's (1981) pioneering "sociology of markets," which became a call to action to network theorists in sociology. White's work was reinforced by Mark Granovetter's (1985) revival of Karl Polanyi's (1944) concept of "embeddedness" – the notion that organizations and the economy are part of a larger institutional and interorganizational structure, and that the context of human and organizational action shapes rational choice in market situations. Building on the basic insight that much of organizational behavior takes place within dense networks of ties among organizations and their members, research has made great headway, particularly over the last decade, in explaining how the structural and informational properties of networks and network positions can predict organizational behavior.

ECOLOGY

Until the mid-1970s, the prominent approach in organization science emphasized adaptive change in organizations. In this view, as the environment changes, leaders or dominant coalitions in organizations alter appropriate features to realign their fit to environmental demands. Since then, an ecological approach to studying organizational change that places more emphasis on selection processes has become increasingly influential. Inspired by Michael Hannan and John Freeman's question, *Why are there so many kinds of organizations?* (1977, p. 936), organizational ecologists seek to explain how social, economic, and political conditions affect the relative abundance and diversity of organizations and attempt to account for their changing composition over time. Ecological theory stresses the difficulty organizational members have changing their organizations' strategies and structures to keep pace with the demands of uncertain, changing environments. Longitudinal studies of founding and failure in organizational populations – sets of organizations engaged in similar activities and with similar patterns of resource utilization – thus figure prominently in ecological research because they affect the relative abundance and diversity of organizations. The focus of organizational ecology research has transformed dramatically since Hannan and Freeman's (1977) original theoretical statement. Some researchers have turned their attention inside organizations to focus on processes of organizational change and selection of routines and strategies. Others have begun to investigate how the links binding a set of organizational populations into a "community" affect the likelihood of persistence and stability of the community as a whole and the creation and disappearance of entire populations of organizations. As ecological models have spanned multiple levels of organization, the kinds of organizations surviving are increasingly conceived as the result of a multilevel interplay: the order that is favorably selected ecologically is the result of ecological processes boiling up from within (Aldrich, 1999; Baum and Singh, 1994). The implication of this view is that organizational change is best studied by examining how social and environmental conditions and interactions within and between organizations and organizational populations jointly influence the rates at which new organizations and new populations are created, existing organizations and organizational forms die out, and individual organizations change.

EVOLUTION

Organizational evolution reflects the operation of three basic processes: *Variation, Selection,* and *Retention,* or *VSR* (Aldrich, 1979, 1999; Baum and McKelvey, 1999; McKelvey, 1982). This view of change, which is derived from Donald Campbell's (1965) seminal article "Variation and selective retention in socio-cultural evolution," is based on an analogy between "natural selection in biological evolution and the selective propagation of cultural forms" (1965, p. 26). The three elements of the model are V) occurrence of variations – "blind," "chance," or "random" but in any event variable, S) consistent selection criteria – selective elimination of certain types of variations, and R) a mechanism for the preservation, duplication or propagation of the positively selected variants. Combined, *blind* variation and selective retention generate "evolution in the direction of better fit to the selective system" (Campbell, 1965, p. 27). Variation generates the raw material from which selection is made. Retention processes preserve and transmit the selected variation. If any of the three components is missing, however, no fit or order will occur. Campbell emphasized the "blindness" of variation to highlight the danger of basing variations on restrictive *a priori* understanding or knowledge of their outcomes and the possibility that elaborate adaptive social systems could emerge *without* conscious planning or foresight. From an evolutionary perspective, adaptation requires exploring the unknown, going beyond existing knowledge and recipes, and "fumbling in the dark" (Campbell, 1974a, p. 147). Although ecological research has informed us about the selection component of Campbell's model, the variation component has seen far less attention, perhaps because as the work of technological, organizational and institutional innovators it is seen as less amenable to systematic study (Aldrich and Kenworthy, 1999; Romanelli, 1999). We also know very little about the "genealogical" side of organizational evolution – the structures of organizational inheritance and transmission. Whereas biological inheritance is based primarily on propagation of genes, inheritance processes for social organizations appear very different, suggesting more equivocal patterns of organizational descent and evolutionary dynamics perhaps strikingly different from those expected with purely genetic transmission.

Natural/Rational-Open Systems

COGNITION AND INTERPRETATION

The application of cognitive concepts to organization originated with the open-rational systems view pioneered by Simon and his colleagues (Simon, 1945; March and Simon, 1958; Cyert and March, 1963). The role of cognition in organizations has been seen differently, depending on whether organizations are seen as systems of *information* or systems of *meaning* (Lant and Shapira, 2000). March, Simon, and Cyert view organizations as information processing systems that code and enact information in a computational manner. That is, the problem that organizations face is one of searching and processing relevant information when such search is costly and decision makers are boundedly rational. Other cognition researchers adopt a natural systems view. Following Karl Weick (1969, 1995), they conceive organizations as social entities whose members enact their world, and emphasize the cognitive processes entailed in creating and sustaining organizations. While the information processing approach emphasizes prospective, intended (though bounded) rationality, the enactment approach emphasizes the retrospectively rational nature of human behavior, that is, that individuals and organizations will take actions to make sense of or to appear to be consistent with their prior actions. These two views represent distinct branches of cognition research in organizations. The "computational" stream of research examines the processes by which organizations and their members *process information* and make decisions. The "interpretive" approach investigates how *meaning* is created around information in a social context.

POWER AND DEPENDENCE

Dissatisfied with the rational system view of organizations as ruled by environmental constraints and efficiency considerations, the power and dependence perspective, a descendant of Karl Marx ([1894] 1954), stresses the importance of varying interests and goals and particularly the role of power in determining whose interests are most likely to prevail. The focus is on how powerful groups manage to get their way using force and persuasion to promote the practices and policies they favor. One stream, the legacy of C. Wright Mills (1956), explores the structure and influence of the "corporate elite." The main idea is that elite networks whose interests transcend those of particular organizations develop strategies collectively, shaping organizations and public policy (Useem, 1984). A second stream concerns the exercise of power within and between organizations. Contemporary research in this stream has its origins in political economy (Zald, 1970), exchange (Emerson, 1962; Thompson, 1967), strategic contingency (Hickson et al., 1971) resource dependence (Pfeffer and Salancik, 1978), and network (Burt, 1980) theories of power and dependence. A power struggle among competing management groups – marketing versus finance managers, for example – may determine corporate response, and the group that wins control of the organization may direct future decisions for some time to come (Fligstein, 1990). Of course, power struggles for control also go on between organizations. Financial corporations, for example, use their economic leverage to coerce desired behavior from nonfinancial firms (Mintz and Schwartz, 1985). Contrasting, but complementing these *structural* theories focused on resource acquisition and control, are *behavioral* theories focused on an individual's ability to use resources, and *personal* theories focused on individual characteristics such as expertise or personality that have been researched extensively at the intraorganizational level.

TECHNOLOGY

In contingency theories advanced by Charles Perrow, James Thompson, Joanne Woodward and others during the 1960s, technology played a vital role in shaping organizational structure (Perrow, 1967; Thompson, 1967; Woodward, 1965). The greater the technical complexity, the greater the structural complexity; the greater the technical uncertainty, the greater the decentralization and lower the formalization; the greater the technical interdependence, the greater the need for coordination. Technology lost its prominent position, however, as empirical research failed to support theoretical predictions, and evidence mounted that technology and technology-structure relations were both influenced by informal structures within organizations and the broader social context. Technology increasingly became seen not as a product of technological determinism or economic efficiency, but as socially shaped – a combination of what is technically feasible and what is socially acceptable (Bijker et al., 1987; Piore and Sable, 1984). In contrast to the contingency view, organizational politics and arrangements were seen as shaping and selecting successful technologies, which focused attention on the role of organizations in fostering technological change and supporting and diffusing new technologies. Attention also shifted to broader patterns of technological change in organizational environments (Abernathy, 1978; Dosi, 1982; Tushman and Anderson, 1986) and competition among rival technologies (e.g., Arthur, 1989; David, 1985). Drawing inspiration from Joseph Schumpeter ([1942] 1976), this work characterized technological change as a process of "creative destruction" in which technologies evolve over time through cycles of long periods of incremental change punctuated by the arrival of new, radically superior technologies, which displace old, inferior ones. Organizations are "carriers" of technology whose fates are influenced profoundly by these technological dynamics. Recently, as the idea that "knowledge" is key to superior organizational performance has become more influential, attention to technology has increased dramatically in organization science.

LEARNING

Interest in knowledge has also sparked an interest in organizational learning. Organizational learning involves processes through which organizations and their subunits change as a result of experience. Organizational learning occurs when new knowledge is embedded in various repositories – organizational routines, technologies, and individuals, for example – so that it is retained over time (Argote and Ingram, 2000). Learning need not always, or even often, lead to improved outcomes. Organizations can, for example, learn to do things that are not valued by their environments. Further complicating matters, learning from experience is not an unbiased activity; rather it is myopic – when organizational members mistakenly credit a practice or skill for good performance, they rarely receive any information that might reveal their error, making it more likely that any false or superstitious beliefs they hold will be reinforced. That said, organizations can try to learn from both their own direct experience and from the experience of other subunits and organizations. Knowledge transfer is the process through which an organization or subunit is affected by the experience of another. Historically, research on organizational learning has emphasized organizations' learning from their own experience (Yelle, 1979; Argote, 1999). This research has documented a robust phenomenon known as the *learning curve*: as organizations gain experience producing a given output, their cost and/or time to produce decreases, although at a decreasing rate. Notably, even though accumulating experience may lead to internal efficiencies, such experiential learning can become harmful, however, if the criteria for organizational success change after the organization has learned. Then the organization may perform poorly and even fail by doing well what it learned in the past; it may suffer the so-called "competency trap" (Levitt and March, 1988). There is no contradiction in this: experience simultaneously enhances performance in the short run and lowers it in long run. More recently, attention has shifted to "transfer learning" among organizations and their subunits (Argote and Ingram, 2000). Transfer learning occurs when one organization or subunit causes a change in the capacities of another, either through direct experience sharing, or by somehow stimulating innovation – inferential learning from observation that sparks imitation, for example.

COMPLEXITY AND COMPUTATION

Many dynamic systems fail to reach equilibrium and so appear to behave randomly. Processes that appear random may, however, be chaotic. Chaotic processes follow rules, but even simple rules can produce great complexity. Interest in applying complexity theory to organizations has been great in recent years, driven by the promise of this new branch of mathematics to untangle and elicit order from seeming disorder. Complexity theory suggests that adaptive systems tend to steer themselves toward "the edge of chaos" by regulating levels of autonomy and dependence, both among components of the system and between the system and other systems in its environment (Kauffman, 1993). Consider an organizational example. If an organization's subunits are too tightly coupled, there may be excessive interdependence and rigidity – if every act of one subunit influences every other, then the repercussions of any given action can destabilize the entire organization. Coupling that is too tight thus leaves no room for desirable subunit autonomy, making change difficult to mount. If, in contrast, subunits are too loosely coupled, there is no coherence. Coordination is problematic, knowledge fails to diffuse or accumulate, confusion sets in, and the organization begins to disintegrate. In short, "too much structure creates gridlock . . . too little structure creates chaos" (Brown and Eisenhardt, 1998, p. 14). The edge of chaos lies between these extremes, where partially connected subunits never quite reach equilibrium, but never quite fly apart either. It is a transitional realm in which organizations, characterized by a relatively few simple structures, enjoy a balance between interdependence and autonomy that generates unpredictable, adaptive behavior. In the emerging organizational literature, complexity theory tends to be invoked mainly metaphorically, with increased turbulence and accelerating environmental change sufficient to motivate the label "chaotic," and so fails to take advantage of complexity theory's rich conceptual models and empirical techniques for detecting and analyzing complex behavior. Despite the limited serious theoretical attention or empirical evidence, unabashed claims that complexity theory is the "next major breakthrough" abound. Given the historical frequency with which organizations have been conceived as complex, adaptive systems characterized by a wide array of dynamic behaviors, complexity theory merits our serious attention – but much work remains.

Rational-Open Systems

ECONOMICS

In mainstream economic theory, the firm observes market prices and then makes efficient choices of output quantities. All firms are alike, having complete access to the same information and technology, and the decisions they make are rational and predictable, driven by cost and demand conditions. Little attention is given to why firms might use managerial hierarchies to plan and coordinate, institutional settings and arrangements are abstracted away, and the varied character and capabilities of "real firms" are not considered. Since the mid 1950s, however, "organizational economists" have challenged this view, departing from the neoclassical view of the firm.

Adhering closely to neoclassical economic assumptions about firm homogeneity, Joe Bain's (1956) "structure-conduct-performance" (SCP) framework in industrial organization economics sought to explain how market processes direct firms in meeting consumer demand, how market processes break down and result in socially wasteful "monopoly profits," and how these processes adjust (or can be adjusted) to improve economic performance. Harold Demsetz (1973) and George Stigler (1968) challenged Bain's view of strategies such as collusion to create entry barriers as necessarily anti-competitive, instead viewing the principal managerial objective as profit maximization through development of specialized, high-quality resources and capabilities. The role of the manager implied in this view was a key point of departure for Richard Caves and Michael Porter's (1977) – also see Porter (1979) – rewriting the SCP causal chain as "conduct-structure-performance" to explain firm conduct and performance. Although this inverted framework had little to say about how managers organize and direct particular firms, it has been used widely to define and explain the strategies available to firms in their search for profits.

There were also departures from rational-choice neoclassical microeconomics. Resource-based theory (Barney, 1991) and evolutionary economics (Nelson and Winter, 1982) emerged from dissatisfaction with the ability of the neoclassical theory of the firm to handle real-world management problems outside an equilibrium context. Edith Penrose (1959, p. 31) provided an influential dynamic view of the firm as "an administrative organization and as a collection of resources" designed to explain firm growth. Building on Ronald Coase's (1937) pioneering work on firm boundaries and internal organization, and Alfred Chandler's (1962) work on the strategic growth, administrative evolution, and economic performance of large firms, Oliver Williamson's (1975, 1985, 1991) transaction cost theory explored the boundaries of markets and firms as arrangements for conducting economic activity, suggesting that "transactions" should take place within governance regimes that best economized on costs imposed by uncertainty, bounded rationality, information asymmetry and opportunism. Agency theory departs in similar ways from neoclassical theory but focuses on "agency relations" between stockholders (principles) and managers (agents) paid to act on their behalves (Jensen and Meckling, 1976), and in particular, dealing (through performance-contingent incentives, and information and control systems) with potential conflicts between them – agency problems – stemming from agents' hidden actions (or, "moral hazards") and information (or, "adverse selection") that are costly to monitor and observe.

Although clearly departing from mainstream economics in some respects, organizational discretion remains firmly disciplined by market competition in these models, ensuring individual and organizational rationality, and the efficiency of social and organizational arrangements. And, so rather than explaining decision makers' actual choices, contemporary organizational economists generally remain focused on explaining observed organizational arrangements in terms of their efficiency. As a result, many organization theorists – who have increasingly embraced a natural system view, while abandoning a rational orientation – view these developments, which do not stray too far from the neoclassical mainstream, with great skepticism, frequently challenging them with ideas about institutions, social milieu, and power. Some, harbor an even greater skepticism fearing that rational choice theory, which dominates economics, may end up "taking over" organization science (Pfeffer, 1993). These skeptics doubt the primacy of efficiency. They do not agree that bounded rationality is "an imperfect approximation of the 'unbounded' one" (Dosi, 1995, p. 5). They do not see economic practices as "givens" but as emerging in a murky world through distinctly social processes in which social networks, institutionalized rules and beliefs, and power relations play roles in the social construction and cognitive representation of certain actions as rational. And those actions may, or may not, have anything to do with "efficiency."

Organizational Epistemology and Research Methods

As James March (1996) has observed, while organization science has increasingly differentiated itself into a distinct semi-discipline with its own professional associations, journals, academic departments, and traditions, the field continues to depend heavily on more established disciplines for ideas, personnel and legitimation. Indeed, students of organization have borrowed ideas promiscuously from economics, sociology, psychology, anthropology, and biology. As a result, there is little inter-subjective agreement about what should be the foundation of explanation. This fragmentation and lack of consensus has led to pessimistic forecasts for the future of organization science. Jeffrey Pfeffer (1993: 620), for example, laments:

> without working through a set of processes or rules to resolve theoretical disputes and debates, the field of organizational science will remain ripe for either a hostile takeover from within or from outside. In either case, much of what is distinctive, and much of the pluralism that is so valued, will be irretrievably lost.

Pfeffer's invocation of Thomas Kuhn's (1962) argument that "multiparadigmaticism" is characteristic of low-status sciences is persuasive – without consistency and coherence, knowledge claims become language games. His advocacy of the development of a single "paradigm" for organization science prompted many theorists to express their views on the "problem" of multiple paradigms. A conflict, dubbed the "paradigm war," emerged between groups loosely caricatured as "positivists" (Pfeffer, 1993, 1995) and "relativists" (Van Maanen, 1995a, 1995b). Importantly, this conflict is not between competing organizational perspectives; it is a philosophical "meta-war" about whether a diversity of perspectives is good or bad for organization science (Aldrich,1992; Baum and Dobbin, 2000).

Positivists lament the plurality of perspectives and the pull in the field toward relativism and postmodernism, which assert that the foundations of normal science – prediction, falsification and generalization – cannot work for organizational phenomena because too much organizational behavior is inherently idiosyncratic. Relativists balk at formal research design, quantitative corroboration, and accumulation of empirically generated knowledge. Instead, they call for richly descriptive natural histories focused on local specifics, and appear in principle willing to entertain as many perspectives as there are socially constructed interpretations. Positivists see such an approach as fraught with subjective bias and without a means of self-correction. They claim the resulting plurality of perspectives dooms organization science to irrelevancy at best, and hostile takeover by a higher status field at worst. Thus, while positivists worry that low paradigm consensus fields are given low status in the broader scientific community and lament the number of perspectives already in use, relativists call for more!

Unfortunately, this conflict is inspired by – and promulgates – an antiquated view of philosophy of science. While philosophers' views on how best to ascertain the validity of scientific theories have been transformed dramatically over the last quarter century, none of this has had much impact on advocates for either side in the organization science debate. Does it matter that organization theorists are philosophically antiquated and uninformed? Indeed it does (McKelvey, 1997, 1999). Much of the "paradigm war" has been driven by mistaken views of positivism (e.g., that it is synonymous with quantitative methods, determinism, reification and causal laws), as well as by ignorance of philosophers' abandonment of *both* positivism and relativism as incoherent decades ago (Azevedo, this volume). The result has been the unfortunate spread and legitimation of an incorrect view of positivism, a belief in the coherence of relativism, and the idea that organization theorists are positivists and relativists when, in fact, they are *neither*. Cooler, better-informed heads might have avoided this dysfunctional altercation altogether.

Organization theorists have *never* been positivists. To positivists, science "rests on empirical inquiry rather than philosophical speculation, a view in which there is no doubt that a real objective world exists" (McKelvey, 1999, p. 385). Positivists made a strong distinction between theoretical and observable (and measurable) terms in order to ensure that scientific truth – that which is verified in objective terms – was not contaminated by meaningless assertions. That is, theoretical terms that could not be captured through first-hand sensory experience were considered *unreal* and so were theoretical explanations of causality. To test the truth of theories they therefore founded an epistemology based on axiomatic theories that clarified the language of science by eliminating all metaphysical concepts. Thus, if organization theorists were positivists, theoretical terms that are difficult to capture in operational terms, such as "organization" and "strategy," concepts such as "uncertainty" and "ambiguity," as well as the notion of a "cause-and-effect relationship," would all be meaningless.

For relativists, using external reality as the criterion for truth-testing was problematic because the external world did not exist beyond that which could be perceived and socially constructed by individuals, cultures and frameworks. What was known and believed was relative to a particular paradigm and competing paradigms were considered to be incommensurable because *truth* was relative to a specific paradigm, which possessed its own language and logic. Thus, inconsistency among paradigms could not be addressed, as discussions across perspectives were considered impossible. Consequently, organization theorists have *never* been strong relativists either. They do not believe that all paradigms are incommensurable. Incommensurability should prevent researchers from being able to communicate with or judge disputes among researchers following different paradigms, yet researchers – even those claiming to be relativists – read and write about all the so-called paradigms.

Organization theorists of all orientations appear, instead, to practice a logic-in-use that is primarily "scientific realist," one holding that there is "enough of an objective reality 'out there' that repeated attempts by various researchers, using a variety of generally approved methods of 'justification logic' eventually will discover the approximate truth of theories by successively eliminating errors" (McKelvey, 1997, p. 363). Given organization theorists' misconceptions of positivist (and relativist) epistemology, and lack of conformity to the expectations of normal science and higher status disciplines, the field is in great need of epistemological and methodological updating and direction. Scientific realism, the most widely accepted epistemology among current philosophers (Azevedo, 1997, this volume; Suppe, 1977, 1989), and the primary scientific logic-in-use in organization science, seems a good place to start.

Donald Campbell (1969, p. 328) offers a view on multiple perspectives, a "fish-scale model of omniscience," which is very much compatible with organization theorists' scientific practice:

> [the] slogan is collective comprehensiveness through overlapping patterns of unique narrownesses. Each narrowness is in this analogy a "fish scale" ... Our only hope of a comprehensive social science, or other multiscience, lies in a continuous texture of narrow specialties which overlap with other narrow specialties.

In organization science, each perspective covers a given domain of organizational life, encompassing particular phenomena and problems, which, at the boundaries, overlap with the domains of other perspectives. Although each perspective does not overlap directly with every other one, adjacent perspectives share problem domains, and frequently complement one another. To us, the organizational phenomena and problems covered in the *Companion*'s perspectives chapters suggest the "fish scale" pattern of overlaps we have drawn in Figure 0.2. Our reading indicates that while there are unmistakable demarcations among the perspectives, there are also dense interconnections and substantial overlaps among them. Although our portrayal of these overlaps may not capture their full scope, it does illustrate the wide range of opportunities for linking the narrower "specialties" – many of which, as you will soon see, are already being pursued.

Campbell (1969) recommends researchers to focus their attention mainly within a given perspective, branching out to address overlaps at its boundaries. Because perspectives

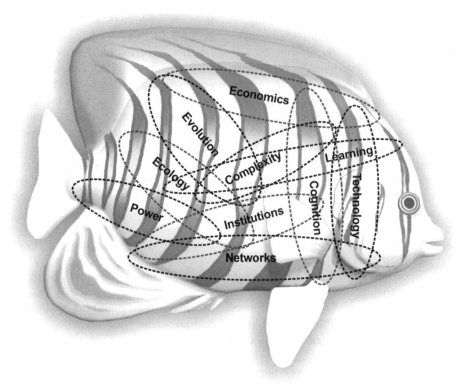

Figure 0.2 Mapping contemporary perspectives on organizations: Overlapping fish-scales

on organizations often attend to different features of related phenomena and problems, rather than phenomena and problems that are fundamentally distinct, boundary work involves *contingency studies* that beg questions:

- Under what conditions is one or another adjacent perspective better able to explain or predict a given organizational phenomenon?
- What features of a particular phenomenon does each perspective best explain or predict?
- How are processes specified within each perspective interrelated?

Research is not directly concerned with reducing the number of perspectives, either through integration or competing tests. Instead, emphasis is placed on corroboration and development of individual perspectives and conditional analyses at the boundaries of adjacent perspectives.

Of course, such a "multiscience" can only work if each of its "scales" has scientific credibility in its own right (McKelvey and Baum, 1999). Multiple perspectives (and theories comprising them) will persist (and proliferate) unproductively when a field has no means of carrying out studies leading to the incremental corroboration or refutation of key elements of the perspectives. In organization science, it is too easy for theories to stand unchallenged on the basis of speculation, intuition and *ad hoc* assumptions, rather than the prediction of novel facts and systematic empirical evidence. Unchecked, this will foster theory proliferation and impede scientific advance by hampering theoretical integration.

A diversity of perspectives need not lead to fragmentation and a lack of consensus, however. Indeed, multiple views are vital to scientific advancement and do not condemn the field to an excess of unsubstantiated assertions disguised as new theories. What is required is an epistemology capable of encompassing diverse, even seemingly contradictory, approaches. An effective multiscience thus requires an ongoing process for generating, embedding, and discarding theoretical concepts and ideas within each perspective. Coupled with the linking of those that are left into broader, more compelling understandings, such a process would result in fewer but more productive theories and perspectives on organizations having more influence and practical impact. Scientific realism thus offers both an explanation for the current diversity of perspectives on organizations, and a research model that protects against unproductive proliferation.

Scientific realism provides a credible epistemology that maintains the goal of objectivity in science, while accommodating socially constructed metaphysical conceptions of phenomena, and offering a dynamic process through which a multiscience might reduce to fewer but more compelling theories. Scientific realists believe that the world exists largely independently of our perceiving it. In contrast to relativism, there is an "out there" for us to theorize about. The job of the researcher is to improve our perceptual (measurement) processes, separate illusion from reality, and generate the most accurate possible description and understanding of the world (Hunt, 1990). While believing that our perceptions can yield knowledge about an external world, scientific realists do not believe the resulting knowledge is certain. Our observations (as well as our theories) are fallible – some are more accurate and reliable (i.e., closer to the truth) than others, the validity of knowledge claims determined, at least in part, by the way the world *is*.

Multiple perspectives and research methods are essential – consistently working within one perspective or method, no matter how powerful and fruitful, will lessen our ability to detect errors, narrow our conception of what is possible, and prompt us more easily to dogmatism. Scientific progress is a matter of generating successively more accurate approximations to the truth about both observable and unobservable phenomena. One standing proposal for a content-neutral criterion of scientific success is Imre Lakatos's (1974) idea of progressive and degenerating research programs. A research program is a series of theories. For Lakatos, new theories introduce to a research program new ways of posing problems, and transitions between theories represent *problem-shifts*. Successive theoretical transitions are *progressive* if they enable novel predictions not covered by predecessors, while retaining most previously corroborated predictions. Transitions are *conceptually progressive* if they produce new concepts with rich and simplifying structures. If the new predictions are corroborated, then the theoretical transition is also *empirically progressive*. A theory *degenerates* if its advocates merely add *ad hoc* auxiliary assumptions and hypotheses, unjustified by empirical evidence or which do not enable the prediction of novel facts, in order to rescue it.

Producing conjectures that predict novel facts, trying to refute them and modifying them in a way that is not merely *ad hoc* are important procedures in producing scientific advance without excessive theory proliferation, while, at the same time, fostering theoretical integration. It is rational, however, for some researchers to pursue degenerating theories: because both theories and tests of theories are fallible, a theory may be correct even when it appears to have been refuted. Given that a research community has the shared goal of finding true theories about the world, it is reasonable for part of the community to pursue degenerating theories; provided that most researchers pursue progressive theories, all is well (Lakatos, 1974).

Scientific realism thus supports pluralism without acceding to relativism, and provides the basis for a scientific method that can be used to select among and validate theories in perspective-neutral ways. Truthful explanation is achieved as individual researchers develop idiosyncratic interpretations of phenomena, their interpretations are socially cross-validated into a more coherent view held by the research community, which is refined over time as less accurate idiosyncratic interpretations and social constructions are weeded out. The basis for validation thus lies in inter-subjective – even cross-cultural – agreement, not in a particular theoretical or methodological approach (Campbell, 1974b).

In addition to a perspective-neutral scientific method that is up to date philosophically, several theorists also suggest that organization science needs a more explicit meta-framework to facilitate the interconnection and evaluation of theories required for an effective multiscience. Howard Aldrich (1979, 1999) and Bill McKelvey (1982), for example, suggest an evolutionary meta-framework based on Campbell's (1965) *VSR* model, which captures well the dual nature of "organization" as process and product. As described above, the three elements of the model are V) occurrence of variations – "blind," "chance," or "random" but in any event variable, S) consistent selection criteria – selective elimination of certain types of variations, and R) mechanisms for the preservation, duplication or propagation of the positively selected variants. Thus, for researchers interested in establishing such a meta-framework, the *VSR* model offers an appealing way to categorize multiple organizational perspectives based on their contributions to the evolutionary view of organizational persistence and change, as well as an explicit basis for examining the overlaps and relationships among them. We illustrate our interpretation of how contemporary perspectives on organizations might be interpreted and interrelated by adopting this evolutionary meta-framework in Figure 0.3. In the figure, we link variation, selection, and retention processes in an iterative sequence, and connect the ten perspectives to elements of the *VSR* model on which, in our view, they are most centrally focused. We do not offer this evolutionary meta-framework as the correct meta-framework, but rather as one standing proposal that enables us to interpret and connect contemporary perspectives on organizations in a meaningful way.

The Companion

To move toward a realization of Campbell's powerful vision in organization science, the *Companion* provides not only a comprehensive survey that consolidates and evaluates contemporary research perspectives on organizations, but also attends to possibilities for epistemological and methodological elaboration of the field. In Campbell's terms, then, the *Companion* aims to delineate the narrow specialties – "fish scales" – that comprise the field of organization science, evaluate their individual (and collective) scientific credibility and contributions to knowledge, and facilitate your examination of how they overlap with and relate to one another.

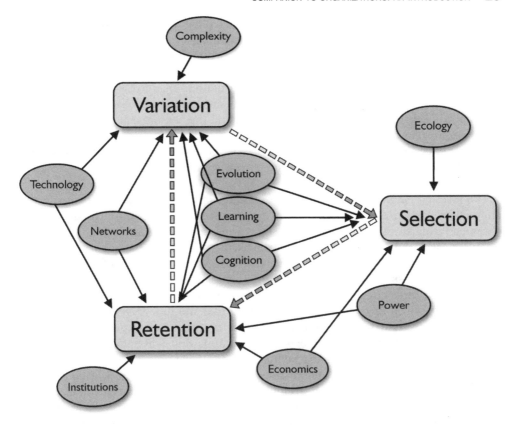

Figure 0.3 Mapping contemporary perspectives on organizations: An evolutionary meta-framework

STRUCTURE OF THE BOOK

The *Companion* is divided into four parts.

- Parts I–III give perspectives on organizations, for each level of organization: *intra*organizational, organizational and *inter*organizational.
- Part IV concentrates on organizational epistemology and research methods.

Each of Parts I–III contains ten chapters, one grounded in each of the contemporary perspectives on organizations.

To make the *Companion* easier to use and study for students, and more versatile and practical for researchers, each chapter is structured around five common elements:

- Literature review and evaluation
- Contemporary issues and debates
- Central questions that remain unanswered
- New and emerging directions for future research that appear promising
- Connections across levels of organization

Although starting from a common platform, each chapter takes on a distinctive character reflecting the unique perspective and insight of its authors. To complete their "cross-level connections," chapters were formally exchanged across levels within each perspective, resulting in a rich commentary on the connections across levels within each perspective. Many chapters were also informally exchanged across perspectives, and so you will also find many connections among the perspectives throughout the *Companion*. Table 0.1 summarizes the key topics and themes for each perspective chapter at each level of organization.

The chapters in Part IV aim to sow the seeds for a stronger future foundation for organization science. There are three chapters on epistemology and then five chapters on research methods.

The first epistemological chapter updates readers on significant developments in the philosophy of science during the past two decades. Building on the first, the second offers a critical assessment of the current state of epistemological development in organization science, and the third presents an explicit, realist organizational epistemology that is up to date in terms of recent developments in the philosophy of science and is relevant in that it specifically focuses on the epistemological peculiarities of organization science. These three chapters address the root problem of organizational epistemology: how to know which theories are more or less truthful and how to systematically move toward more truthful theories and winnow out mistakes. Accompanying them is a detailed glossary of organizational epistemology terms that will enhance your understanding as well as being a valuable source for future reference.

The five chapters on organizational research methods review and provide concrete guidance for designing and doing exemplary research on organizations in five basic modes: survey, archival, simulation, grounded theorizing, and fieldwork. Their goal is to help students to understand how researchers create knowledge about organizations, and to stimulate researchers to use methods that will be more successful in the incremental refutation or corroboration of key elements of the perspectives on organizations. Each chapter:

- outlines elements of the methodology and research design
- characterizes the method's contribution to organization science
- describes exemplar studies
- provides detailed guidelines for implementing the approach, highlighting key decision points and criteria
- delimits the kinds of research questions it is best (poorly) suited for tackling.

Conclusion

Contemporary philosophy of science demands you take a skeptical stance toward theory: No theory can be proven true or false by empirical data. And any theory can be rescued by *ad hoc* addition of assumptions to fit with existing data. Fortunately there is a vast middle ground – and it is the job of students and researchers alike to evaluate theories of organization in this middle ground. A researcher committed to a scientific realist approach to theory corroboration is committed to constant search and open argumentation, is aware that his or her resulting beliefs are fallible, and therefore provisional in

Table 0.1 Key topics and themes across perspectives and levels of organization

	Intraorganizational level	Organizational level	Interorganizational level
Cognition and interpretation	*Fiol* • Symbolic architectures • Connectionist architectures • Mental models and cognitive maps • Knowledge structures • Cognition and affect • Sensemaking • Automatic and controlled cognition • Distributed and shared cognition	*Lant* • Organization as information processors • Scanning and search • Perception and interpretation • Organizations as enactors of environments and creators of meaning • Locus of organizational cognition • Collective cognition • Situated cognition	*Porac, Ventresca, and Mishina* • Industry belief systems • Enactment of organizational communities • Product ontologies • Boundary beliefs and market identities • Industry recipes • Reputational rankings and status-ordering
Power and dependence	*Brass* • Exchange theory • Controlling critical resources • Potential power and using power • Structural sources of power • Personal sources of power • Behavioral sources of power • Group sources of power • Power potential and use • Hierarchy vs. power	*Ocasio* • Functional, structural and institutional perspectives • Political coalitions • Structural contingencies • Punctuated equilibrium • Organizational demography • Networks and social capital • Weberian, normative and political-cultural approaches	*Mizruchi and Yoo* • Co-optation • Goal displacement • Political economy • Interorganizational relationships • Competition and symbiosis • Structural autonomy • Market constraint • Network centrality • Director interlocks
Networks	*Raider and Krackhardt* • Network form and structure • Network content and relations • Dyad • Ego network • Group network • Social capital – brokerage and cohesion views • Gender and homophily	*Gulati, Dialdin, and Wang* • Strategic interdependence • Network embeddedness • Network resources and constraints • Network centrality • Network configuration • Partner profiles	*Baker and Faulkner* • Organizational dyad • Organization triad • Organization set • Organizational field • Interorganizational embeddedness • Network organizational form
Institutions	*Elsbach* • Group identities and subcultures • Sensemaking	*Palmer and Biggart* • Goal drift • Co-optation	*Strang and Sine* • Cognitive, interactive and authoritative bases of institutions

	Intraorganizational level	Organizational level	Interorganizational level
	• Mindlessness and mindfulness • Group protocols, norms and routines • Group roles and composition • Categorization processes • Symbolic leadership • Repeated negotiation and interaction • Social verification	• Imprinting and structural inertia • Loose coupling • Isomorphism • Conceptions of control • Density dependence	• State and professions as institutional entrepreneurs • Naturalistic and dialectical institutional theories of change • Performance failure and institutional rivalry theories of institutional change
Economics	*Zajac and Westphal* • Positive and normative agency theories • Incentive alignment: Symbolic management and demographic similarity • Social influence and board of directors independence • Social exchange and board of directors monitoring	*Silverman* • Transaction cost economics • Governance choices: Make or buy? • Make or ally? • Complex contracting • Resource-based view of the firm • Competence-based view of the firm • Diversification and performance	*van Witteloostuijn* • Industrial organization • Game theory • Perfect competition • Perfect contestability • Dynamic versus static efficiency • Bertrand–Cournot Nash games • Commitment and credibility
Technology	*Schilling* • Development of new technology • Impact on organizational structure, management and performance • Adoption of modular forms • Impact of information technology • Modular product and process • Interfaces and systems architecture • Role of proximity	*Tushman and Smith* • Technology cycles: Technological discontinuities, eras of ferment and dominant designs • Ambidextrous organizations • Organizational architecture • Incremental, architectural and discontinuous innovation • Innovation streams	*Stuart* • Technological structure of markets • Technological prestige • Technological crowding • Networks and structural holes • Inertia and evolution of technological systems • Technology-based competition • Technology spillovers
Learning	*Argote and Ophir* • Attention, interpretation and attribution • Distributed expertise	*Schulz* • Organizational rules and routines • Performance feedback models • Exploration and exploitation	*Ingram* • Absorptive capacity • Vicarious and congenital learning • Outcome and trait-based imitation

- Knowledge spillovers
- Interorganizational relationships
- Relational capabilities
- Learning races

- Learning under ambiguity
- Myopia and competency traps
- Learning communities
- Knowledge diffusion

- Knowledge depreciation
- Knowledge transfer
- Organizational memory and routines
- Social networks
- Team structure and dynamics

Rao
- Commensalism and symbiosis
- Community structure
- Lotka–Volterra model
- Community formation, change and collapse
- Community coherence and organization
- Institutional entrepreneurs
- Social movements

Ecology

Baum and Amburgey
- Age and size dependence
- Structural inertia
- Niche width dynamics
- Population dynamics and density dependence
- Demography of organizational founding
- Population-level learning
- Complexity in population dynamics

Galunic and Weeks
- Variation, selection and retention
- Interaction and replication processes
- Organizational routines and comps
- Competition between routines
- Complementarity between routines

Greve
- Variation, selection and retention
- Evolution of market structures
- Evolution of governance structures
- Evolution of spatial structures
- Coevolution
- Competitive interaction
- Emergence
- Path dependence

Evolution

Amburgey and Singh
- Strong and weak selection
- Adaptation and selection
- Darwinian and Lamarckian mechanisms
- Organizational speciation and extinction
- Micro- and macro-evolutionary processes
- Coevolution

Warglien
- Variation, selection and retention
- Organizational rules and routines
- Organizational genetics and replicators
- Hierarchy of evolutionary processes
- Cultural transmission in organizations
- Search and learning
- Representation and expression
- Evolution as design

Sorenson
- Interdependence
- Cellular automata
- Micro-behavior and macro-structure
- NK models
- NKC models
- Complex interorganizational dynamics
- Sensitivity to initial conditions
- Path dependence

Complexity and computation

Eisenhardt and Bhatia
- Complex adaptive systems
- Loose coupling
- NK models
- Edge of chaos
- Simple rules and complex behavior
- Emergence
- Recombination and evolution

Carley
- Complex adaptive systems
- Agents
- Decision making and problem solving
- Networks
- Information technology
- Algorithmic complexity
- Computational theorizing

nature and subject to further criticism. We challenge you to be critical consumers of organizational research, ever alert to *ad hoc* assumptions and hypotheses contained within perspectives, and to be boundary workers, seeking opportunities to refine adjacent perspectives by pursuing their interconnections. If you accept our challenge, you are sure to achieve a greater understanding of the organizational world in which we live, and you will also have helped to ensure a *progressive* future for organization science.

Acknowledgments

For helpful comments and conversations that helped us to improve this introduction, we are most grateful to Howard E. Aldrich, Martin G. Evans, and W. Richard Scott.

References

Abernathy, W. (1978): *The Productivity Dilemma*. Baltimore, MD: Johns Hopkins University Press.

Aldrich, H. E. (1979): *Organizations and Environments*. Englewood Cliffs NJ: Prentice-Hall.

Aldrich, H. E. (1992): "'Incommensurable paradigms?', Vital signs from three perspectives," in M. Reed and M. Hughes (eds), *Rethinking Organizations: New Directions in Organization Theory and Analysis*, London UK: Sage, 17–45.

Aldrich, H. E. (1999): *Organizations Evolving*. Thousand Oaks CA: Sage.

Aldrich, H. E., and Kenworthy, A. (1999): "The accidental entrepreneur: Campbellian antinomies and organizational foundings," in J. A. C. Baum and B. McKelvey (eds), *Variations in Organization Science: In Honor of Donald T. Campbell*, Thousand Oaks CA: Sage, 19–33.

Argote, L. (1999): *Organizational Learning: Creating, Retaining, and Transferring Knowledge*. Boston: Kluwer Academic Publishers.

Argote, L., and Ingram, P. (2000): "Knowledge transfer: A basis for competitive advantage in firms," *Organizational Behavior and Human Decision Processes*, 82, 150–69.

Arthur, W. B. (1989): "Competing technologies, increasing returns, and lock-in by historical events," *The Economic Journal*, 99, 116–31.

Azevedo, J. (1997): *Mapping Reality: An Evolutionary Realist Methodology for the Natural and Social Sciences*. Albany NY: SUNY Press.

Bain, J. S. (1956): *Barriers to New Competition*. Cambridge MA: Harvard University Press.

Barnard, C. I. (1938): *The Functions of Executives*. Cambridge, Mass.: Harvard University Press.

Barney, J. (1991): "Firm resources and sustained competitive advantage," *Journal of Management*, 17, 99–120.

Baum, J. A. C. and Dobbin, F. (2000): "Doing interdisciplinary research in strategic management – Without a paradigm war," in J.A.C. Baum and F. Dobbin (eds), *Economics meets Sociology in Strategic Management; Advances in Strategic Management, Vol. 17*, Stamford CT: JAI Press, 389–410.

Baum, J. A. C., and Haveman, H. A. (1997): "Love thy neighbor? Differentiation and Agglomeration in the Manhattan Hotel Industry, 1898–1990," *Administrative Science Quarterly*, 41, 304–38.

Baum, J. A. C., and McKelvey, B. (eds) (1999): *Variations in Organization Science: In Honor of Donald T. Campbell*. Thousand Oaks CA: Sage.

Baum, J. A. C., and Mezias, S. J. (1992): "Localized competition and organizational failure in the Manhattan hotel industry, 1898–1990," *Administrative Science Quarterly*, 37, 580–604.

Baum, J. A. C., and Oliver, C. (1991): "Institutional linkages and organizational mortality," *Administrative Science Quarterly*, 36, 187–218.

Baum, J. A. C., and Oliver, C. (1992): "Institutional embeddedness and the dynamics of organizational populations," *American Sociological Review,* 57, 540–59.

Baum, J. A. C., and Singh, J. V. (1994): "Organizational niches and the dynamics of organizational mortality," *American Journal of Sociology,* 100, 346–80.

Berger, P.L., and Luckmann, T. (1966): *The Social Construction of Reality: A Treatise in the Sociology of Knowledge.* Garden City NY: Doubleday.

Bijker, W., Hughes, T.P., and Pinch, T. (eds) (1987): *The Social Construction of Technological Systems: New Directions in the History of Technology.* Cambridge MA: MIT Press.

Boulding, K. E. (1956): "General systems theory: The skeleton of science," *Management Science,* 2, 197–208.

Brown, S. L., and Eisenhardt, K. M. (1998): *Competing on the Edge: Strategy as Structured Chaos.* Boston, MA: Harvard Business School Press.

Buckley, W. (1967): *Sociology and Modern Systems Theory.* Englewood Cliffs, NJ: Prentice-Hall.

Burns, T., and Stalker, G. M. (1961): *The Management of Innovation.* London: Tavistock.

Burt, R. (1980): "Models of network structure," *Annual Review of Sociology,* 6, 79–141.

Campbell, D. T. (1965): "Variation and selective retention in socio-cultural evolution," in H. R. Barringer, G. I. Blanksten, and R. W. Mack (eds), *Social Change in Developing Areas: A Reinterpretation of Evolutionary Theory,* Cambridge, MA: Schenkman, 19–48.

Campbell, D. T. (1969): "Ethnocentrism of disciplines and the fish-scale model of omniscience," in M. Sherif and C.W. Sherif (eds), *Interdisciplinary Relationships in the Social Sciences,* Chicago IL: Aldine, 328–48.

Campbell, D. T. (1974a): "Unjustified variation and selective retention in scientific discovery," in F. J. Ayala and T. Dobzhansky (eds), *Studies in the Philosophy of Biology,* London: Macmillan, 139–61.

Campbell, D.T. (1974b): "Evolutionary epistemology," in P. A. Schlipp (ed.), *The Philosophy of Karl Popper,* La Salle IL: Open Court, 413–63.

Caves, R. E., and Porter, M. E. (1977): "From entry barriers to mobility barriers: Conjectural decisions and contrived deterrence to new competition," *Quarterly Journal of Economics,* 91, 241–61.

Chandler, A. D. (1962): *Strategy and Structure: Chapters in the History of the American Industrial Enterprises.* Cambridge, MA: MIT Press.

Clegg, S. R., Hardy, C., and Nord, W. R., (eds) (1996): *Handbook of Organization Studies.* Thousand Oaks, CA: Sage.

Coase, R. H. (1937): "The nature of the firm," *Economica,* 4, 386–405.

Cyert, R. M., and March, J. G. (1963): *A Behavioral Theory of the Firm.* Englewood Cliffs, NJ: Prentice-Hall.

David, P. (1985): "CLIO and the economics of QWERTY," *Economic History,* 75, 227–332.

Davis, G. F., Diekmann, K. A., and Tinsley, C. H. (1994): "The deinstitutionalization of conglomerate firms in the 1980s," *American Sociological Review,* 59, 547–70.

Demsetz, H. (1973): "Industry structure, market rivalry and public policy," *Journal of Law and Economics,* 16, 1–9.

Dill, W. R. (1958): "Environment as an influence on managerial autonomy," *Administrative Science Quarterly,* 2, 409–43.

DiMaggio, P. J., and Powell, W. W. (1983): "The iron cage revisited: Institutional isomorphism and collective rationality in organizational fields," *American Sociological Review,* 48, 147–60.

Dosi, G. (1982): "Technological paradigms and technological trajectories: A suggested interpretation of the determinants and direction of technical change," *Research Policy,* 11, 147–62.

Dosi, G. (1995): "Hierarchies, markets, and power: Some foundational issues on the nature of contemporary economic organization," *Industrial and Corporate Change,* 4, 1–19.

Durkheim, É. (1893): *The Division of Labor in Society.* New York: Free Press, translated 1933.

Emerson, R. M. (1962): "Exchange theory, part II: Exchange relations and networks," in J. Berger, M. J. Zelditch and B. Anderson (eds), *Sociological Theories in Progress, Vol 2,* Boston MA: Houghton-

Mifflin, 58–87.

Fligstein, N. (1990): *The Transformation of Corporate Control*. Cambridge, MA: Harvard University Press.

Fligstein, N. (1996): "A political-cultural approach to market institutions," *American Sociological Review*, 61, 656–73.

Granovetter, M. (1985): "Economic action and social structure: The problem of embeddedness," *American Journal of Sociology*, 91, 481–510.

Hannan, M. T., and Freeman, J. H. (1977): "The population ecology of organizations," *American Journal of Sociology*, 82, 929–65.

Hickson, D. J., Hinings, C. R., Lee, C. A., Schneck, R. E., and Pennings, J. M. (1971): "A strategic contingencies theory of intraorganizational power," *Administrative Science Quarterly*, 16, 216–29.

Homans, G. (1950): *The Human Group*. New York: Harcourt, Brace & World Inc.

Hunt, S. D. (1990): "Truth in marketing theory and research," *Journal of Marketing*, 54, 1–15.

Jensen, M. C., and Meckling, W. H. (1976): "Theory of the firm: Managerial behavior, agency costs and ownership structure," *Journal of Financial Economics*, 3, 305–260.

Katz, D., and Kahn, R. L. ([1968} 1978): *The Social Psychology of Organizations*. New York: John Wiley.

Kauffman, S. A. (1993): *The Origins of Order: Self Organization and Selection in Evolution*. New York: Oxford University Press.

Kuhn, T. S. (1962): *The Structure of Scientific Revolutions*. Chicago IL: University of Chicago Press.

Lakatos, I. (1974): "Falsification and the methodology of scientific research programmes," in., I. Lakatos and A. Musgrave (eds), *Criticism and the Growth of Science*, Cambridge UK: Cambridge University Press, 91–196.

Lant, T. K., and Shapira, Z. (2000): *Organizational Cognition: Computation and Interpretation*. Mahwah NJ: Lawrence Erlbaum Associates.

Lawrence, P. R., and Lorsch, J. W. (1967): *Organization and Environment: Managing Differentiation and Integration*. Boston MA: Graduate School of Business Administration, Harvard University.

Levitt, B., and March, J. G. (1988): "Organization learning," *Annual Review of Sociology*, 14, 319–40.

McGuire, P., and Granovetter, M. (2001): *The Social Construction of Industry: Human Agency in the Development, Diffusion, and Institutionalization of the Electric Utility Industry*. New York: Cambridge University Press.

McKelvey, B. (1982): *Organizational Systematics: Taxonomy, Evolution, Classification*. Berkeley, CA: University of California Press.

McKelvey, B. (1997): "Quasi-natural organization science," *Organization Science*, 8, 351–80.

McKelvey, B. (1999): "Toward a Campbellian Realist Organization Science," in J. A. C. Baum and B. McKelvey (eds), *Variations in Organization Science: In Honor of Donald T. Campbell*, Thousand Oaks CA: Sage, 383–411.

McKelvey, B. (2001): "From fields to science," in R. Westwood and S. Clegg (eds), *Point/Counterpoint: Central Debates in Organization Theory*, Oxford UK: Blackwell.

McKelvey, B, and Baum, J. A. C. (1999): "Donald T. Campbell's evolving influence in organization science," in J. A. C. Baum and B. McKelvey (eds), *Variations in Organization Science: In Honor of Donald T. Campbell*, Thousand Oaks CA: Sage, 1–15.

March, J. G. (1996): "Continuity and change in theories of organizational action," *Administrative Science Quarterly*, 41, 278–87.

March, J. G., and Simon, H. A. (1958): *Organizations*. New York: John Wiley.

Marx, K. (1894): *Capital*. Moscow: Foreign Languages Publishing House, translated 1954.

Mayo, E. (1945): *The Social Problems of Industrial Civilization*. Boston MA: Graduate School of Business Administration, Harvard University.

Merton, R. K. (1957): *Social Theory and Social Structure, 2nd edn*. Glencoe IL: Free Press.

Meyer, J. W., and Rowan, B. (1977): "Institutionalized organizations: Formal structure as myth and ceremony," *American Journal of Sociology*, 83, 440–63.

Michels, R. (1911): *Political Parties*. Glencoe IL: Free Press, translated 1949.

Mills, C. W. (1956): *The Power Elite*. New York: Oxford University Press.

Mintz, B. and Schwartz, M. (1985): *The Power Structure of American Business*. Chicago: University of Chicago Press.

Nelson, R. R., and Winter, S. G. (1982): *An Evolutionary Theory of Economic Change*. Cambridge MA: Harvard University Press.

Parsons, T. (1960): *Structure and Process in Modern Society*. New York: Free Press.

Penrose, E. (1959): *The Theory of the Growth of the Firm*. Oxford UK: Oxford University Press.

Perrow, C. (1967): "A framework for comparative analysis of organizations," *American Sociological Review*, 32, 194–208.

Pfeffer, J. (1993): "Barriers to the advance of organization science: Paradigm development as a dependent variable," *Academy of Management Review*, 18, 599–620.

Pfeffer, J. (1995): "Mortality, reproducibility, and the persistence of styles of theory," *Organization Science*, 6, 681–86.

Pfeffer, J. (1997): *New Directions for Organization Theory*. New York: Oxford University Press.

Pfeffer, J., and Salancik, G. R. (1978): *The External Control of Organizations*. New York: Harper and Row.

Piore, M. J., and Sable, C. F. (1984): *The Second Industrial Divide: Possibilities for Prosperity*. New York: Basic Books.

Polanyi, K. (1944): *The Great Transformation*. New York: Holt.

Porter, M. E. (1979): "The structure within industries and companies' performance," *Review of Economics and Statistics*, 61, 214–229.

Powell, W. W. (1991): "Expanding the scope of institutional analysis," in W. W. Powell and P. J. DiMaggio (eds), *The New Institutionalism in Organizational Analysis*, Chicago IL: University of Chicago Press, 183–203.

Powell, W. W. (1996): "On the nature of institutional embeddedness: Labels vs. explanation," in J. A. C. Baum and J. E. Dutton (eds), *The Embeddedness of Strategy; Advances in Strategic Management, Vol. 13*, Greenwich CT: JAI Press, 293–300.

Roethlisberger, F. E., and Dickson, W. J. (1939): *Management and the Worker*. Cambridge MA: Harvard University Press.

Romanelli, E. (1999): "Blind (but not unconditioned) variation: Problems of copying in sociocultural evolution," in J. A. C. Baum and B. McKelvey (eds), *Variations in Organization Science: In honor of Donald T. Campbell*, Thousand Oaks CA: Sage, 79–91.

Schumpeter, J. A. ([1942] 1976): *Capitalism, Socialism and Democracy, 3rd edn*. New York: Harper and Row.

Scott, W. R. (1992): *Organizations: Rational, Natural, Open Systems, 3rd edn*. Englewood Cliffs NJ: Prentice-Hall,

Scott, W. R. (1998): *Organizations: Rational, Natural, Open Systems, 4th edn*. Englewood Cliffs NJ: Prentice-Hall.

Scott, W. R., and Meyer, J. W. (1983): "The organization of societal sectors," in J. W. Meyer and W. R. Scott (eds), *Organizational Environments: Ritual and Rationality*, Beverley Hills CA: Sage, 1–16.

Selznick, P. (1949): *TVA and the Grass Roots*. Berkeley CA: University of California Press,

Selznick, P. (1957): *Leadership in Administration*. New York: Harper and Row.

Simon, H. A. (1945): *Administrative Behavior*. New York: MacMillan.

Simon, H. A. (1991): "Organizations and markets," *Journal of Economic Perspectives*, 5(2), 25–44.

Stigler, G. (1968): *The Organization of Industry*. Chicago: University of Chicago Press.

Strang, D., and Meyer, J. W. (1993): "Institutional conditions for diffusion," *Theory and Society*, 22, 487–511.

Suppe, F. (1977): *The Structure of Scientific Theories, 2nd edn.* Urbana IL: University of Illinois Press.

Suppe, F. (1989): *The Semantic Conception of Theories and Scientific Realism.* Urbana-Champaign IL: University of Illinois Press.

Thompson, J. D. (1967): *Organizations in Action.* New York: Free Press.

Tucker, D. J., Baum, J. A. C., and Singh, J. V. (1992): "The institutional ecology of human service organizations." in Y. Hasenfeld (ed.), *Human Service Organizations,* Newbury Park, CA: Sage, 47–72.

Tushman, M. L., and Anderson, P. (1986): "Technological discontinuities and organizational environments," *Administrative Science Quarterly,* 31, 439–65.

Useem, M. (1984): *The Inner Circle.* New York: Oxford University Press.

Van Maanen, J. (1995a): "Style as theory," *Organization Science,* 6, 133–43.

Van Maanen, J. (1995b): "Fear and loathing in organization studies," *Organization Science,* 6, 687–92.

Weber, M. ([1922] 1978): *Economy and Society,* Two Volumes, G. Roth and C. Wittich (eds), Berkeley: University of California Press.

Weick, K. E. (1969): *The Social Psychology of Organizing.* Reading, MA: Addison-Wesley.

Weick, K. E. (1979): *The Social Psychology of Organizing, 2nd edn.* Reading, MA: Addison-Wesley.

Weick, K. E. (1995): *Sensemaking in Organizations.* London: Sage.

White, H. C. (1981): "Where do markets come from?" *American Journal of Sociology,* 87, 517–47.

White, H. C., Boorman, S. A., and Breiger, R. L. (1976): "Social Structure from multiple networks: 1. Blockmodels of roles and positions," *American Journal of Sociology,* 81, 730–80.

Williamson, O. E. (1975): *Markets and Hierarchies, Analysis and Antitrust Implications: A Study in the Economics of Internal Organization.* New York NY: Free Press.

Williamson, O. E. (1985): *The Economic Institutions of Capitalism: Firms, Markets, Relational Contracting.* New York: Free Press.

Williamson, O. E. (1991): "Comparative economic organization: The analysis of discrete structural alternatives," *Administrative Science Quarterly,* 36, 269–96.

Woodward, J. (1965): *Industrial Organization: Theory and Practice.* New York: Oxford University Press.

Yelle, L. E. (1979): "The learning curve: Historical review and comprehensive survey," *Decision Science,* 10, 302–28.

Zald, M. N. (1970): "Political economy: A framework for comparative analysis," in M. N. Zald (ed.), *Power in Organizations,* Nashville: Vanderbilt University Press, 221–61.

Zucker, L. (1977): "The role of institutionalization in cultural persistence," *American Sociological Review,* 42, 726–43.

Part I

Intraorganizational Level

1 Intraorganizational Institutions   37
   Kimberly D. Elsbach

2 Intraorganizational Networks   58
   Holly Raider and David J. Krackhardt

3 Intraorganizational Ecology   75
   D. Charles Galunic and John R. Weeks

4 Intraorganizational Evolution   98
   Massimo Warglien

5 Intraorganizational Cognition and Interpretation   119
   C. Marlene Fiol

6 Intraorganizational Power and Dependence   138
   Daniel J. Brass

7 Intraorganizational Technology   158
   Melissa A. Schilling

8 Intraorganizational Learning   181
   Linda Argote and Ron Ophir

9 Intraorganizational Complexity and Computation   208
   Kathleen M. Carley

10 Intraorganizational Economics   233
   Edward J. Zajac and James D. Westphal

Chapter One

Intraorganizational Institutions

KIMBERLY D. ELSBACH

Banana time followed peach time by approximately an hour. Sammy again provided the refreshments, namely, one banana. There was, however, no four way sharing of Sammy's banana. Ike would gulp it down by himself after surreptitiously extracting it from Sammy's lunch box, kept on a shelf behind Sammy's workstation. Each morning, after making the snatch, Ike would call out "Banana time!" and proceed to down his prize while Sammy made futile protests and denunciations . . . Sammy . . . never did get to eat his banana, but kept bringing one for his lunch. (From *"Banana Time": Job satisfaction and Informal Interaction*, by Donald F. Roy (1989).

Although early work on institutions examined the habituation of behavior in small groups (i.e., as with what occurred *within* the organization above) (Roy, 1989; Zucker, 1977), most subsequent organizational research on institutions has involved taken-for-granted beliefs and actions that occur at the level of industries (i.e., *across* organizations) (Tolbert and Zucker, 1983; Fligstein, 1985; Mezias, 1990). Discussion of institutions within organizations – or "intraorganizational institutions" – does not appear in the chapter on institutional theory in the recently published, *Handbook of Organizations* (Tolbert and Zucker, 1996), or in Powell and DiMaggio's (1991) review of institutional theory. Nevertheless, a closer look at organizational research suggests that institutions within organizations are common phenomena that have important consequences for organizations and their members. An explication of such taken-for-granted beliefs is the focus of this chapter.

I define intraorganizational institutions as *taken-for-granted beliefs that arise within and across organizational groups and delimit acceptable and normative behavior for members of those groups*. That is, intraorganizational institutions may also be defined as "inter-group" or "intra-group" institutions within an organization, where organizational groups may be commonly known as "departments," "teams," "subunits," "offices," or "divisions." This definition suggests that intraorganizational institutions exist, fundamentally, as shared cognitions among members of organizational groups. Such cognitions may, however, manifest themselves as observable and organizational structures, procedures, and values such as standards, customs, and routines. For example, intraorganizational institutions might include implicit norms about seating arrangements at inter-departmental meetings (e.g., engineering always sits in the back of the room), or more explicit standards about acceptable dress across departments on "casual Fridays" ("management casual" is less casual than "non-management casual").

Intraorganizational institutions are distinguished from organizational cultures by their prescriptive (vs. descriptive nature) and by their focus beliefs across organizational groups (vs. organization-wide beliefs). That is, they are beliefs about what "should" be done across groups in an organization. By contrast, culture typically refers to descriptions of what commonly "is" done in organizations (O'Reilly and Chatman, 1986), although, as I discuss later, organizational cultures or identities may become institutionalized over time. Work group cultures that become taken-for-granted might be considered a form of intraorganizational institutions.

Although a majority of research on organizational groups focuses on defining group identities and group boundaries that distinguish one group from another, a small but growing area of research focuses on how communities of groups come to share cognitions about appropriate behavior in organizations (Thompson et al., 1999).[1] This research provides the basis for much of my theory-building in this chapter and is summarized in Table 1.1.

Literature Review

Although limited research has explicitly mentioned "intraorganizational institutions," a number of related streams of research on groups, organizational cultures, and social identity have examined phenomena that fit the above definition of intraorganizational institutions. This research describes two aspects of such institutions:

1   Their forms and effects within organizations
2   The processes by which they are built

I review this literature below.

FORMS AND EFFECTS OF INTRAORGANIZATIONAL INSTITUTIONS

Institutional theorists doing research at the organizational and inter-organizational levels have typically defined institutions as conventional, standardized patterns of behavior or states of being in and across organizations (Jepperson, 1991). Common forms include organizational and industry standards, routines, and norms (Scott, 1991). Empirical research on these forms of institutions places them, roughly, into three categories:

1   Process institutions, e.g., standard operating procedures, protocols for dealing with crises
2   Structure institutions, e.g., norms about the structure of power and control, norms about output diversification
3   Value institutions, e.g., norms about organizational ideals, normative goals, pri-

Table 1.1 Selected research on intraorganizational institutions

Reference	Concepts	Variables	Findings	Contribution	Method
Literature discussing the forms and effects of intraorganizational institutions					
Elsbach (1999, 2000, 2001)	Identity management by organizational subgroups	Organizational identity, member identification	Members affirm subgroup identity thru claims and markers	Describes how intra-org. institutions are linked to organizational institutions	Qualitative field studies of legislative staffers
Jehn (1997)	Effects of group norms for cooperation, and conflict	Acceptability of intragroup conflict, group performance, and member satisfaction	Acceptability of conflict as a norm increases group performance	Shows effects of Intraorganizational institutions on performance work group of institutions	Qualitative field study of six organizational work groups
Weick (1993)	Sensemaking, role structures, and crisis reaction	Reaction to crisis when role structures fall apart	Sensemaking disintegrates when institutional role structures fall apart	Shows how role structures are a form of intraorganizational institution: Shows process of institution decline	Qualitative study of report of Mann Gulch disaster
Jermier et al. (1991)	Organizational subcultures	Personal characteristics, task exigencies, occupational specialty, values, and affirmation of subculture	Groups of detectives and patrol officers identified with one of five subcultures	Defines subcultures as type of value-institution within organizations; Describes antecedents and consequences of subcultures	Interview and questionnaire of officers in one police department
Schriber and Gutek (1987)	Temporal norms at work	Work group attitudes about time	Organizational groups develop norms about punctuality, deadlines, work pace, etc. . . .	Contributes 12 item scale of time-based institutions within organization groups	Questionnaire given to 51 work groups in 23 organizations

Literature discussing the processes of intraoganizational institution-building

Reference	Concepts	Variables	Findings	Contribution	Method
Cialdini et al. (1999)	Normative influences in organizations	Normative cues, conformity to norms	Norms are built through modeling behaviors, and by salient cues	Describes process of building and maintaining intra-organizational institutions	Review of field and lab experiments and organizational field studies
Meyerson (1994)	Organizational and departmental institutions	Organizational perspective on medicine, daily work of social workers, perceptions of burnout and ambiguity	Organizational perspective on medicine influenced the institutions of social work dept and views of burnout	Shows relationship between organizational and departmental institutions, shows how daily interactions build institutions	Qualitative study of five hospitals
Kramer (1991)	Subgroup identification and superordinate group identification in organizations	Level of categorization, intergroup competition, intergroup collaboration	Salient membership in superordinate group leads to collaboration	Shows importance of categorization processes in building institutions	Review article based on lab and field research
Pfeffer (1990)	Symbolic role of organizational management	Modeling behavior of organizational leaders, and acceptance and legitimacy of managerial values	Managers use language, ritual, and symbolism to construct shared meaning in organizations	Shows how organizational leaders can help build institutions through symbolic legitimation acts	Review article based on field research
Ashforth and Fried (1988)	Mindlessness in organizations	Organizational scripts, decision-making routines	Proliferation of scripts makes many acts mindless	Shows how scripts are a tool for institution-building	Review article

orities for use of organizational resources (Brint and Karabel, 1991; Fligstein, 1991; Galaskiewicz, 1991)

This research also suggests that these forms of institutions legitimate and dictate the processes, structures and values that organizations adopt and maintain. That is, the effects of these institutions are a routinization of behavior across organizations that fits with the prescriptions those institutions provide (DiMaggio and Powell, 1983; Scott, 1991).

INTRAORGANIZATIONAL VALUE INSTITUTIONS: GROUP IDENTITIES AND SUBCULTURES

Intraorganizational value institutions include norms about the core values and ideals of organizational subunits or groups. These values might relate to norms about the use of resources, standards for quality, or the value of a distinct organizational group. Such forms of intraorganizational institutions appear most prevalent in organizational research. In particular, a number of studies have examined how the *culture* or *identity* of an organizational group (its distinctive, central, and enduring traits – including its values and goals) is institutionalized among organization members (Jermier et al., 1991; Sackman, 1992). These subgroup identities help members to maintain positive self-concepts within organizations that may be defined by multiple and conflicting values (Elsbach, 1999).

In one study, Jermier et al. (1991) describe how groups of patrol officers and detectives in an urban police force identified with five institutionalized subcultures within the organization that were defined by their morals and goals: crime-fighting street professionals, peace-keeping moral entrepreneurs, ass-covering legalists, crime-fighting commandos, and anti-military social workers. Jermier et al. (1991, p. 171) define such organizational subcultures as

> shared understandings about the organization's mission and standards of conduct, as well as the corresponding organized practices that emerge in a group of employees.

This definition suggests that organizational subcultures are a form of intraorganizational institution. Specifically, such subcultures appear to define the taken-for-granted values that organizational groups should share. Jermier et al. (1991) also note that such values or ideals may be materialized through dress, insignia, or routine behaviors. For example, in the "crime-fighting commandos" subculture, most members affirmed their institutionalized values of traditional policing with an emphasis on rules and procedures by joining the police officers' union and rigidly saluting the shift commander. These actions symbolized the institutional nature of their subculture.

In a similar study, Sackman (1992) describes seven subcultures that evolved across three divisions of a conglomerate firm: design and control, electronics production, shop floor production, inspection, new product marketing, existing product marketing, and project coordination. These seven subcultures arose according employee's role perceptions and functional expertise, rather than to their formally defined departments or work groups. Further, values about the goals and desired behavior of each subculture were institutionalized and understood across the three firm divisions.

Finally, Elsbach (1999) describes how four separate groups of legislative staffers –

"policy wonks" concerned with idealistic law-making, "political hacks" concerned with learning the political system as a means of furthering their legislator's career, "professional staffers" concerned with the mechanics of law making, and "institutionalists" concerned with maintaining the traditions of public service – became institutionalized within the California State Legislature based on their espoused values. Legislative staff members were easily categorized as members of one of these four institutionalized values. Further, staffers found it important to distance themselves from one or more of the alternative groups. These value institutions were further expressed through physical identity markers (e.g., business cards, displayed photos or policy artifacts) and by claimed titles or self-categorizations (e.g., "political animal," "policy wonk").

In all the above examples, the existence of value institutions that defined the subcultures or sub-identities of an organization appeared to aid members in maintaining positive self-concepts and social identities with respect to their work, especially if those subcultures allowed members to express values that were counter to the "official" organization-level culture. Thus, Jermier et al. (1991) found that police officers belonging to the "anti-military social workers" subculture were the most committed members of the police force. This commitment may have been a result of these officers' belief that they were doing valuable work. As Jermier et al. (1991, p. 191) note,

> [there are] those who argue that culture is . . . the result of ordinary people resisting the hegemony of official culture and socially constructing forms that advance their own interests or reduce the stresses inherent in their daily activities (e.g., Roy, 1960, 1989; Willis, 1977). In the data analyzed here . . . resistance subcultures emerged from the practical demands of everyday working situations and officers' shared interests.

In addition, intraorganizational institutions appear to have a legitimating and rationalizing effect on perceptions of a group. As Pfeffer (1990) notes, "it is through the development of shared meaning and understanding that the cycles of interlocked behavior [e.g., routine procedures and structures within a group] become sensible and meaningful." As a consequence, Pfeffer (1990) suggests that, without shared understanding that exist as value institutions, organizational groups may be vulnerable to legitimacy threats.

INTRAORGANIZATIONAL PROCESS INSTITUTIONS: PROTOCOLS AND ROUTINES

Organizational managers are often charged with devising protocols to improve the accuracy and efficiency of functioning between groups. For example, managers commonly develop routines for monitoring cross-functional project teams (e.g., a new product development project involving engineering, marketing, and sales departments), for conducting cross-departmental training (e.g., training staff from many departments to deal with an environmental crisis), or for compiling accounting or budgeting reports on inter-departmental processes (e.g., determining additional clerical staff needed to support an additional product line). Process routines may also arise informally among members of organizational groups. For example, routines may develop concerning the degree of informal collaboration teams can expect when working on organizational projects, the use of public facilities (such as where to sit in the cafeteria, which bathrooms to use), and the expression of deference to higher status groups (such as which groups have veto power in meetings, which groups always lead project discussions). When these types of protocols or routines become the de-facto way of working across organizational groups (i.e., they become "taken-for-granted") they may be thought of as forms of intraorganizational institutions.

The organizational research on intraorganizational collaboration and conflict provides several illustrations of forms and effects of process institutions within organizations. For example, Ashforth and Fried's (1988) review of mindlessness in organizations describes how organizational scripts dictate how groups are to interact formally and informally. They note that much power-based decision making across organizational groups becomes routinized, with different factions always representing the same viewpoints (such as engineers always want more time to complete a project, while marketing managers always want to speed things up). As Ashforth and Fried (1988, p. 321) suggest

> the process of politics becomes somewhat routinized in organizations, and the outcomes, institutionalized. Once an issue is resolved it becomes taken for granted and effectively forgotten. Power and politics fade in salience and the individual comes to regard his or her distilled role as a duty, a duty which is executed without ongoing calculations of exchange (Astley, 1983).

In a similar way, Schriber and Gutek's (1987) discussion of how norms about the use of time in organizational work groups suggests that process institutions raise the areas of punctuality, work pace, synchronization and coordination of work with others, and intraorganizational time boundaries. In this way, the culture of time use becomes an institutionalized process in and across organizational groups.

Finally, Jehn's (1997) study of collaboration and conflict among and within work groups shows that the level of acceptable conflict in group meetings varies across organizations and groups within organizations. Her qualitative analysis of these intraorganizational work groups shows that groups that institutionalize the acceptance of task conflict (e.g., disagreements about work processes or goals) and discouragement of relationship conflict (e.g., conflict related to personality traits and interpersonal relations) have increased performance (i.e., higher production output, lower error rates, and increased customer satisfaction) over groups that institutionalize open relationship conflict and discourage task conflict. These results suggest that intraorganizational institutions not only have the effect of legitimating and encouraging certain types of processes, but that that they may affect the outcomes of those processes in positive or negative ways. Clearly, intraorganizational institutions represent a potentially powerful tool for managers concerned with improving group and organizational effectiveness.

INTRAORGANIZATIONAL STRUCTURE INSTITUTIONS: GROUP ROLES AND COMPOSITION

Intraorganizational structure institutions typically involve the norms about the composition of groups (e.g., demographic and training characteristics of members), and norms about status and power among and within groups (e.g., which groups are given veto power over others, which groups have an elite identity). Weick's (1993) study of the Mann Gulch fire provides an interesting example of the importance of such intraorganizational structure institutions within a "minimal organization." In his explication of the disastrous events that led to the death of 13 firefighters, Weick suggests that, when the firefighters threw away their tools in retreat of the fire, they also threw away their intraorganizational structure, i.e., their understanding of the roles of certain group members and their leadership power. In the absence of this structure, they ceased to be a coherent organization and became individuals looking out for themselves. The demise of their structure institutions (or, alternatively, the weakness of these institutions) left them with little guidance and leadership. Subsequently, only those who could function as leaders, themselves, survived. This case illustrates the power of structure institutions in crisis situations.

In a more common setting, Meyerson's (1994) analysis of institutional forces in hospital settings demonstrates how taken-for-granted beliefs about the power and status of medical departments vs. social work departments represent intraorganizational institutions that affect the daily routines of both groups. Her analysis of these two distinct intraorganizational groups across five hospitals revealed that, if a traditional medical model was in place, the status of the social work department would be relatively low compared to that of physicians and other medical professionals, and the hospital's goals and values would be consonant with this traditional medical model, e.g., curing disease, discharging patients. Alternatively, if a social work model was in place, the status of social work departments would be more equivalent to that of physicians and other medical professionals, and the hospital's goals and values would be consonant with this social work model, e.g., helping people to cope with and adapt to disease, caring for long-term clients. Meyerson's work suggests that overarching organizational value institutions can, thus, shape and support intraorganizational structure institutions. In turn, these structure institutions have real effects on how business is done, e.g., a focus on discharging patients vs. meeting their long-term care needs.

BUILDING INTRAORGANIZATIONAL INSTITUTIONS

Recent research has examined the psychological processes that lead people to institutionalize values, processes, and structures (Thompson et al., 1999). This research suggests that either *cognitive manipulation* or *social influence* is at the root of bringing specific beliefs or behaviors to the level of "taken-for-grantedness." As Meyerson (1994, p. 630) notes:

> The cognitive view suggests that organizational and individual actions and interpretations are produced through legitimated classifications, conventions, rules, interpretations, and social accounts [Berger and Luckmann (1967)]. The normative perspective relies on socialization and influence processes to explain actions and interpretations (DiMaggio and Powell, 1991).

It seems likely that similar processes may be at work at the intraorganizational level of institution building. Yet, as in the previous section, little research has been done that directly examines institution building within the organization. In the following sections, I review social psychological literature on categorization processes, symbolic management, negotiations, and social verification that appear relevant to the building of intraorganizational institutions.

CATEGORIZATION PROCESSES

Several researchers have argued that categorization processes that make salient one's status and distinctiveness *vis-à-vis* one's membership in organizational groups may be a primary factor in definitions of inter-group norms (Jermier et al., 1991; Kramer, 1991; Sackman, 1992). Interorganizational group categorization is important because it defines the boundaries of groups according to important group values and traits. As Kramer (1991, p. 203) notes:

> One consequence of categorization is that it defines the level of identification which is salient to an individual. . . . When an intergroup level is salient . . . the organization is perceived to be divided into an *ingroup* containing the self and other members of one's own group, and a set of *outgroups* containing all of the other members of the organization.

Further, categorization at the level of organizational groups may help members to meet a number of personal needs. As Kramer (1991, p. 204) suggests:

> Although the level of salient categorization is assumed to vary across situations, it is postulated here that organizational identification is defined, all else being equal, at the level of the individual's primary group in the organization [the group with which the individual most frequently interacts].

Kramer (1991) suggests that this preference for identification with one's primary work group may be explained by a number of factors, including: similarity and familiarity with group members (Mael and Ashforth, 1992), desires to be both socially distinct and affiliated (Brewer, 1991), and desires to reduce intergroup anxiety caused by interacting with members of different groups (Stephan and Stephan, 1985). Further, Elsbach's (2000) work on identification in organizations with complex, hybrid identities (i.e., organizations that are defined by multiple, competing values – such as conglomerates who make both cigarettes and cookies), shows that members may wish to identify with an intraorganizational subgroup (e.g., the cookie division) instead of the organization as a whole.

As a result of these preferences for group-level categorizations among organization members, interorganizational institutions may arise. If organization members perceive that group identifications lead to more positive outcomes (e.g., status, legitimacy, distinctiveness) than organization-level identifications, the group may come to represent the primary social affiliation for members. In these situations, the development of intraorganizational institutions helps to further enforce and define group boundaries and identities. A classic example of such institution building comes from Sherif et al.'s (1961) study of intergroup conflict and cooperation in the "Robbers Cave" boys' camp. As Sherif (1966, p. 82) notes, when athletic competitions made group-level identities salient and desirable, hostile interactions became institutionalized:

> In the Robbers Cave study, the Eagles, after defeat in a game, burned a banner left behind by the Rattlers. The next morning the Rattlers seized the Eagles' flag when they arrived on the athletic field. From that time on, name-calling, scuffling, and raids *were the rule* of the day. A large proportion of the boys in each group gave negative ratings to the character of all boys in the other. When the tournament was over, they refused to have anything more to do with members of the other group. [emphasis added]

In a more recent example, Pfeffer and Sutton (1999) describe such a process in their analysis of General Motor's, Saturn division. Because members of the Saturn division identified with this division, and appeared to disidentify with their parent organization (GM), they developed their own culture, including institutional norms that helped to underline their distinctiveness from GM and institutionalize uncooperative behavior between the divisions, e.g., they kept secret from other divisions their own best practices findings.

SYMBOLIC MANAGEMENT BY ORGANIZATIONAL LEADERS

Researchers of symbolic management practices in organizations have suggested a number of ways in which organizational leaders can manipulate perceptions of intraorganizational norms due to their unquestioned authority (Cialdini, 1984). For example, Pfeffer (1990) has suggested that management's arbitrary use of job titles and classifications might legitimate and institutionalize differences in reward levels across organizational groups. In this way, organizational leaders can make employees accept unequal pay across, what may appear to be, comparable positions. By contrast, Kramer's (1991) review of collaboration among work groups also suggests that management may encourage the development of intergroup collaboration (vs. competition) through the use of symbolic actions, such as naming intergroup projects (e.g., joint engineering–marketing ventures) or through providing rewards and resources based on intergroup output. Ashforth and Fried's work on mindlessness in organizations suggests that organizational leaders are powerful in creating institutions because employees are accustomed to organizational routines or "scripts" that call for them to accept, without question, their leaders explanations (Ashforth and Fried, 1988, p. 321):

> Leaders help create and maintain a system of interlocked behavioral and legitimating scripts, thereby institutionalizing an understanding of the content and process of organizational action.

The worth of these leadership actions are most notable when a subunit's institutional legitimacy is threatened by external events. For example, Pfeffer (1990) describes how a business school, with comparatively low salaries and resources, competed with other better-endowed schools for faculty and students. He notes that this school's leaders propagated stories and accounts that explained that this school was able to maintain a pure focus on scholarly research, without the constraints imposed by corporate donors, as well as a healthy relationship with other units on campus, because they emphasized a traditional social science approach to running the business school (vs. a more corporate orientation). As a result, Pfeffer (1990, p. 23) notes:

> The social consensus emerged that the school had a uniquely favorable intellectual environment which stimulated research and creative thought. This environment was a product of the school's unique relationship with the rest of the campus, enhanced by its comparable, low salaries, and by its emphasis on research and scholarship to the neglect of consulting and fundraising.

REPEATED NEGOTIATIONS AND INTERACTIONS

Meyerson's (1994) work on the institutionalization of a social work subculture in hospital settings suggests that everyday interactions (e.g., discharge planning) by members of the social work and medical departments can support and legitimate a set of intraorganizational institutional beliefs and values that act as guides or taken-for-granted norms about correct behavior in those departments. By repeating and negotiating normative beliefs in all aspects of work, employees bring a subculture to the level of institutionalization. As Meyerson (1994, pp. 631–2) notes:

> As people from different professional subsystems work interdependently within organizations, their ideologies and approaches come into contact. In their mundane actions and interpretations, people – with varying degrees of professional power and authority– negotiate and create an order. This order acts as a cultural constraint on actions and interpretations. Through repeated negotiations among professionals with varying degrees of power in an organization, agreements are reached about what is to be done daily and by whom, what these activities mean, and how they should be justified (Strauss et al., 1964). As behaviors, interpretations, and justifications become adopted, they create an order that constitutes the particulars of that subculture, which reconstitutes the institutional system in a particular time and context.

As noted earlier, her qualitative study of five hospital social work departments revealed that, in hospitals with a traditional organizational view of medicine and disease (e.g., people admitted were called "patients", disease was defined as a statistically abnormal condition, and medical professionals were supposed to cure patients of disease), social workers interactions with doctors led them to develop a similar subculture within their department (e.g., their goal was to help efficiently discharged cured patients) and developed a status equivalent to other medical professionals who pursued these goals. By contrast, in hospitals with a social work view of medicine and disease (e.g., people admitted were called "clients", disease was a normal part of the human condition, and the goal of medical professionals was to help clients to adapt to or accept their current condition), social workers daily interactions led them to develop a subculture in which they identified with a helping and empathetic view of medicine and bestowed a marginalized status because of their contrast with traditional medical perspectives.

Meyerson found that these two types of social work subcultures defined other intraorganizational institutions for the social work department. In particular, she found that social workers in the social work subculture viewed common social worker issues of ambiguity and burnout (i.e., a value institution) as normal or even desirable (vs. abnormal and undesirable in the traditional medicine culture). In addition, as discussed earlier, these social workers had a higher relative status than their counterparts in the traditional medical subcultures, i.e., their intraorganizational structure institutions were different.

Together, these findings suggest that intraorganizational institutions, such as the value of social work and their role in meeting organizational goals, may arise through daily negotiations and interactions with other departments and professionals in an organization. Further, these findings suggest that organization-level cultures and institutions may have a direct effect on the development of intraorganizational institutions via daily interactions and negotiations.

SOCIAL VERIFICATION AND SOCIAL PROOF

Cialdini et al.'s (1999) discourse on normative influences in organizations suggests that social influence and power play important roles in the development and maintenance of intraorganizational institutions. They subscribe to the notion of social verification (Hardin and Higgins, 1996) as a primary process in the development of such shared realities. As Cialdini et al. (1999, p.196) summarize:

> shared reality is formed and sustained for individuals when their experience and sense of reality is shared with others. This formation and transmission of reality occurs through a social verification process, which occurs when individuals receive feedback from other group members on the appropriateness of their view of reality. From this perspective, social interaction is necessary for the establishment of reality for group members.

Cialdini and his colleagues have performed numerous experiments that demonstrate the power of social verification or "social proof" as a means of establishing norms within and across groups. These studies show that, especially in situations where normative behavior is ambiguous, people will look to others for cues about what to do. These cues are especially potent if they describe "injunctive norms", i.e., norms that describe what people should do vs. what most people actually do. For example, in one study, Cialdini et al. (1991) found that when subjects entered an area where an anti-littering injunctive norm was made salient (e.g., by having a confederate litter in an area where all the litter was neatly swept into piles) those subjects littered less than if that norm was not made salient. These findings suggest that institutions within groups can be cued by messages, behavior, or leadership modeling. Other findings also suggest that the status and legitimacy of the person displaying the cue affect the social verification process (Cialdini, 1984).

Cialdini et al. (1999) note that the use of such cues may vary by organizational department or subunit. As a result, depending on the cues provided in a department, an organization-level institution may be enacted differently across intraorganizational units. As Cialdini et al. (1991, p. 201) note:

> Within one organization, norms may differ depending on the department. For example, a company might have an overall strong norm for high productivity but the content of the norm may differ within the organization (e.g., what [cues suggest] an employee needs to do to be extremely productive may vary by his or her position in the company, as well as the specific norms in his department).

Contemporary Issues and Debates

While intraorganizational institutions may help organizations to socialize and control employees, and help organizational subunits to legitimate their goals and processes, much of the more recent literature on institutions has focused on the negative or dysfunctional effects of such taken-for-granted norms, e.g., mindless acceptance of pre-existing routines, inability to implement new knowledge into existing structures, difficulties in adapting to environmental changes that conflict with existing institutions.

The following sections discuss three areas in which organizational dysfunctions appear to arise out of strong intraorganizational institutions. Future work in these areas may show how theories of intraorganizational institutions may help to remedy these dysfunctions.

THE "KNOWING–DOING GAP" AND INTRAORGANIZATIONAL INSTITUTIONS

Pfeffer and Sutton (1999, p. 4) define the "knowing–doing problem" in organizations as "the challenge of turning knowledge about how to enhance organizational performance into actions consistent with that knowledge." They suggest that many struggling or unsuccessful firms suffer – not from not knowing what to do – but from being unable to implement what they know. Organizations that consistently fail to implement what they know to be the "right" answers to management problems are said to have a "knowing–doing" gap. In their analysis of dozens of corporations facing knowing–doing problems, Pfeffer and Sutton found that mindless adherence to well-established procedures (i.e. institutions) was one of the primary causes of the persistence of knowing–doing gaps. Further, they found that knowledge management systems, which are intended to help companies to use what they know to solve problems, often exacerbate the knowing–doing gap because they are designed to access and store easily categorized and institutionalized forms of knowledge (e.g., process plans, operating procedures), but are not designed to capture the less regular and hard to institutionalized stories, myths, and anecdotes that are the essence of transferring knowledge.

Pfeffer and Sutton found that knowing–doing gap can exist at the organization level, or at the intraorganization-level. For example, at the organization level, they found that the successful computer company, Hewlett-Packard had an institutionalized culture of doing things the "HP way" (creating value and innovation through engineering). Yet, this institutionalized belief has begun to interfere with the company's need to adapt to customer needs and move to a more marketing-oriented perspective.

At the intraorganizational level, Pfeffer and Sutton found that the Saturn Division of General Motors has experienced difficulty in dealing with their parent company's management policies, and, as a result, has slowed their growth and profitability. One of their main difficulties has been shedding the notion that they are a separate company from GM and cannot operate within a large, traditional auto-manufacturing firm. As Pfeffer and Sutton (1999, p. 85) note:

> The problem is that many people at Saturn, because of its own history, are not especially interested in being part of GM. Our interviews at Saturn indicated that managers, union leaders, and employees who had a long history at Saturn often viewed themselves as being part of a company that was different and better than the rest of GM.

Pfeffer and Sutton found that this identification with one's unit (vs. the organization as whole) was rampant within GM. Employees identified with their division (e.g. Pontiac or the joint Toyota–GM venture called NUMMI) and were reluctant to work in ways that conflicted with the institutions of that unit – even if it meant concealing best practices information that would have helped the company as a whole.

These findings suggest that institutions that exist within organizations and their subunits can have a particularly strong negative effect if they constrain managers from implementing the solutions they know will solve problems. On the upside, however, understanding the institutional forces that contribute to knowing–doing gaps may help companies to close them. Pfeffer and Sutton touch on some of the institution-building processes mentioned in this chapter as means of narrowing knowing–doing gaps, e.g., categorization processes, and identification processes. Yet there are several other institution-building processes (e.g., socialization processes, symbolic management processes) that may help them to understand how to dismantle the culture that contributes to knowing–doing gaps. For example, Pfeffer and Sutton note that firms often do not implement what they know because they spend too much time talking about it in increasingly complex language. Such a focus on "smart talk" leads people to believe changes have been made, even though they have not. Further, a focus on complex language makes it hard for anyone who actually wants to implement solutions to do so. Future research might look at how the legitimacy of simple, straightforward talk might be enhanced by symbolic management tactics, such as top managers and CEOs modeling straight talk and perpetuating stories about how simple talk worked.

ORGANIZATIONAL IDENTITY AND INTRAORGANIZATIONAL INSTITUTIONS

Recent research on organizational identities suggests that defining oneself as member of a complex organization may be problematic because many such organizations seem to be defined by conflicting and evolving values (Elsbach, 2000; Elsbach and Kramer, 1996; Whetten and Godfrey, 1998). A good fit between an organization's identity and a member's self-perception today, may not exist tomorrow, e.g., working for the White House may have lost some of its luster after the Clinton–Lewinsky scandal. Further, working for an organization that merges with another or takes on new business units may change one's identification processes, e.g., how do I identify with a previously secular hospital that has been taken over by a religious organization?. These dilemmas arise, in part, because of the strong institutional beliefs and values that accompany intra-organizational groups.

Understanding the forms and effects of intraorganizational institutions may help managers to smooth the transition from one identity to another. For example, Elsbach's (2000a) study of legislative staffers coping with the hybrid identity of the California Legislature demonstrates how intraorganizational institutions (e.g., language, labels, informal interaction rules) that help to distinguish two conflicting aspects of the Legislature's identity (i.e., political and policy making) can help staffers who identify with the policy-making dimension to adapt to working for an organization that routinely (i.e., every election year) is more saliently identified with its political dimension.

More commonly, however, it appears that organizations do not attend to the need to manage the transformation from one set of institutional beliefs to another as organizations evolve. Pfeffer and Sutton (1999) describe the dysfunctional side effects of such neglect in their analysis of the evolution of GM's Saturn division as it became incorporated into its parent company. As mentioned earlier, after existing in isolation for several years, the Saturn division developed its own very strong set of value, process, and structure institutions that came to be known as "The Saturn Way." Yet, these strong institutions appear to be obstructing Saturn's evolution and continued improvement as a part of a larger, more traditional auto-manufacturing organization. As Pfeffer and Sutton (1999, p. 87) note:

> [Our] visit to the plant and our conversations suggested that [Saturn employees] would resist almost anything they saw as a fundamental change, for instance, in manufacturing processes, because it is "not the Saturn way."

In response to such a dysfunction, future research may probe deeper into the question of: "How do we help people to give up their old institutions when transitioning to a context in which new institutions better server them?"

JUSTICE AND INTRAORGANIZATIONAL INSTITUTIONS

Research on justice and equity perceptions in organizations suggests that people are more likely to accept outcomes that seem inequitable if they perceive that the procedure used to arrive at those outcomes was fair, i.e., they perceive that there was procedural justice, despite outcome injustice (Tyler, 1987). Recent research in this area has begun to delve into the question of what it takes to make decision processes appear fair (Shapiro et al., 1994). For example, proponents of the "value-expressive perspective" (Tyler, 1987; Tyler et al., 1997) suggest that individuals react positively to "having the chance to state their case, irrespective of whether their statement influences the decisions of the authorities" (Tyler, 1987, p. 333). Further, work in this area suggests that showing such consideration requires having an understanding of the social norms and expectations of the audiences involved (Elsbach, 2001).

Together, this research suggests that, to improve perceptions of fairness following decision outcomes, it is important to understand the institutions (especially the value institutions) of the parties who are affected by those decisions. Although justice research has not examined how institutions are related to decision explanations, a fruitful area for study may be examining how differences in matching explanations to intraorganizational value institutions relates to improving justice perceptions within organizations, e.g., when management is explaining a pay cut or lay-offs to employees.

Central Questions that Remain Unanswered

The literature reviewed above suggests two central questions that remain unanswered concerning intraorganizational institutions:

- Are intraorganizational institutions grounded in "hot" emotions and values vs. "cold" cognitions?
- Are intraorganizational institutions the product of individual adaptations by organizational members vs. intentional manipulation by organizational leaders?

I briefly outline these questions below.

Hot or cold intraorganizational institutions?

Neo-institutional theorists have attempted to distinguish *institutions* from more affective concepts like *values* by claiming that former are purely cognitive while the latter involve an emotional component. As DiMaggio and Powell (1991, p. 15) note:

> Not *norms and values* but taken-for-granted *scripts, rules, and classifications* are the stuff of which institutions are made. [emphasis added]

This distinction sets up the following question relevant to intraorganizational institutions: *Do intraorganizational institutions exist as cold, cognitive scripts and rules, or do they include hot, emotional attitudes and beliefs?*

On one hand, the above research on "value institutions" suggest that, when a cherished ideal or value identified with an organizational group culture becomes taken-for-granted, it might be defined as an emotion-laden intraorganizational institution. Because these institutions are linked to values they are likely to invoke emotions in people who identify or disidentify with them (Elsbach and Kramer, 1996).

On the other hand, the above research on process and structure institutions refers to taken-for-granted beliefs that are closer to purely cognitive scripts or rules. This notion falls in line with discussions of "mindlessness" in organizations (Ashforth and Fried, 1988). This research suggests that intraorganizational institutions are cold, cognitive representations that affect how people perceive their group and its roles within an organization.

Do institutions arise from individual adaptations or organizational manipulation?

A second interesting question that arises out of discussions about institution building is: *Are institutions the product of members' positive adaptations to uncontrollable environmental conditions, or are they the product of management's manipulation of organizational context?* Some of the above work appears to suggest that taken-for-granted norms among organizational groups arise as individual-level adaptations to the work environment, e.g., as a means of coping with a work environment that is unpleasant, or an organizational culture or identity that runs counter to one's own identity (Jermier et al. 1991; Sackman, 1992; Elsbach, 1999; Meyerson, 1994). As like-minded individuals adapt in similar ways over time, these responses become institutionalized at the group level within organizations. In these cases, the primary motivator of intraorganizational institutions appears to be to improve individuals' job satisfaction and self-esteem by increasing the value and status of one's social groups at work.

By contrast, some of the above researcher suggests that taken-for-granted norms among organizational groups might arise out of the purposeful actions of management. In particular, this research suggest that managers may wish to maintain norms of competition and conflict across groups as a means of improving productivity and creativity at the organizational level (Pfeffer, 1990; Jehn, 1997; Cialdini et al., 1999). In these cases, the primary motivators of intraorganizational institutions appear to be managerial control.

New and Emerging Directions for Future Research that Appear Promising

While the above literature review suggests that intraorganizational institutions have the same forms as organizational institutions – i.e., norms about group processes, structures, and values – direct study of the forms and effects of institutions within organizations is still scarce. A promising starting point for future research, therefore, might be to empirically examine the *common forms of intraorganizational institutions.* The above research on identity management in organizations, for example, suggests that intraorganizational institutions may manifest themselves as a wide range of symbols – from slogans and logos to business cards and letterhead. Such symbolic markers provide both a psychological and physical reminder of the organizations identity. Yet, the study of such symbolic markers in organizations is limited (Sundstrom and Altman, 1989). Future research might focus on how repeated use of everyday physical identity markers constitutes a form of value institutions within organization. Such a form of intraorganizational institution may be built by grassroots behavior, rather than by top management dictum.

A second area for future research might revolve around the *role of emotion in intraorganizational institutions.* The above research suggests that some forms are more emotion-laden (i.e., value institutions), while others are more cognitive (i.e. process or structure institutions). The range of institutions that arise within organizations blurs the line between cultures and rules, values and scripts. By allowing such a range to enter our models of institutions, we should be better equipped to discuss shared meaning within and between organizations. Future research may explore the relationship between taken-for-granted beliefs, emotions, and cognitions with an aim of defining how institutions are encountered, and reacted to, by organizational members.

A third area for future research concerns the *processes by which individuals build and maintain intraorganizational institutions.* The above findings suggest that both proactive manipulation and reactive adaptation may influence and direct the construction of intraorganizational institutions. It appears that, in many cases, routine adaptations arise to cope with everyday demands. Yet, in cases where those adaptations are no longer useful (but have become institutionalized), managers may nudge groups to adapt a new set of constraints. Future research may delve deeper into this issue by more directly examining when and why each type of institution building occurs, as well as when each type of institution building appears beneficial or detrimental to the groups involved.

Connections Up and Down the Hierarchical Levels

My discussion of the micro-processes used to build institutions within organizational groups can be easily transferred to the building of organization-level and interorganization-level institutions. In particular, the four methods of intraorganizational institution building defined above – categorization, repeated negotiations, symbolic management, and social proof – fit nicely with Palmer and Biggart's (this volume) discussion of acquiring institutions at birth or changing institutions after birth, and with Strang and Sine's (this volume) discussion of interorganizational institutional change.

For example, Palmer and Biggart suggest that institutions at the organization level are often formed and reinforced during the birth of new organizations. New organizations take on the structures, procedures, and values of existing and successful organizations in their industry. This process of "isomorphism" helps to reduce the liability of newness and to increase the legitimacy of newly formed organizations. From a cognitive standpoint, it appears that the processes of social proof and categorization are at work here, as I've described them at work in organizational groups. That is, when establishing routines in newly formed organizations, founders look to others for validation that their routines are normative and that they fit into identifiable categories. As a result, the same isomorphic processes that lead to dysfunctional institutions and the "knowing–doing gap" – e.g., a focus on smart-talk over action, or on analysis vs. action – can exist at both the intraorganizational level, as with the Saturn Division of General Motors, and at the organizational level, as with Hewlett-Packard.

Palmer and Biggart also propose that institutional change might occur after birth in response to trends that arise in their industry. Thus, they describe how the multi-divisional form of organizational structure appeared to take off in the late twentieth century merely because many large firms had adopted it. Palmer and Biggart suggest that this form of mimicry is driven by pressures for legitimacy. This stance fits nicely with my above discussion of institution building through symbolic management by leaders. That is, the same symbolic processes I described that lead to group norms about conflict or cooperation at the intraorganizational level, may be at work in motivating organizational norms about hierarchy and control.

In a similar fashion, Strang and Sine's discussion of institutional change at the level of organizational communities suggests that inter-organizational institutions may also develop as an symbolic response among organizations in the same industry. For example, in their studies or organizational name changes, Glynn and Abzug (1998, 2000), found that normative trends within an industry were more important than long-time corporate traditions in determining name changes among 1600 firms in the mid 1980s. Further, they found that the norms within an industry were more important than cues about that industry in determining organizational names; for example, it was more important for a manufacturing company to have a name that was normative – such as the ambiguous names Agway or Amstar – than to include words that were related to their products or processes – such as American Sugar.

Conclusion

In this chapter, I have examined how intraorganizational institutions are manifest, built, and effective in the daily routines of organizations and their members. This examination reveals that, although not discussed explicitly by institutional theorists (who tend to focus on organization or interorganization level institutions), such taken-for-granted beliefs within and across organizational groups are prevalent and powerful in shaping organizational life. Further, this analysis suggests that a focus on intraorganizational institutions may reveal a new perspective on old problems, such as organizational change and adaptation, organizational justice, and the implementation of organizational knowledge and technology. As a result, it is my hope that this chapter serves as a catalyst for pushing institutional theorists to increase the level of magnification of their research microscopes, and to study how organizational groups relate to the institutional values, processes, and structures that define and constrain their behavior.

Note

1 It is important to note that this chapter is grounded, primarily, in *organizational* research on groups. Although much of this organizational research is based on social psychological theory, this chapter does not provide a comprehensive review of the extensive psychological litera- ture on intergroup relations and intergroup conflict. This focus highlights field observations about intraorganizational institutions, which commonly involve on-site research of real-life organizational groups in action. By contrast, much of the psychological research on groups is based in laboratory studies.

References

Ashforth, B. E., and Fried, Y. (1988): "The mindlessness of organizational behaviors, "*Human Relations*, 41, 305–29.

Astley, W. G. (1983): "Political and apolitical faces of organizational power," unpublished manu- script, University of Pennsylvania.

Berger, P. L., and Luckmann, T. (1967): *The Social Construction of Reality*. Garden City, NJ: Anchor.

Brewer, M. B. (1991): "The social self: On being the same and different at the same time," *Personality and Social Psychology Bulletin*, 17, 475–82.

Brint, S., and Karabel, J. (1991): "Institutional origins and transformations: The case of American community colleges," in W. W. Powell and P. J. DiMaggio (eds), *The New Institutionalism in Organizational Analysis*, Chicago: University of Chicago Press, 337–60.

Cialdini, R. B. (1984): *Influence: The New Psychology of Modern Persuasion*. New York: Quill.

Cialdini, R. B., Bator, R. J., and Guadagno, R. E. (1999): "Normative influences in organizations," in L. L. Thompson, J. M. Levine, and D. M. Messick (eds), *Shared Cognition in Organizations, the Management of Knowledge*, Mahwah, NJ: Lawrence Erlbaum Associates, 195–211.

Cialdini, R. B., Kallgren, C. A., and Reno, R. R. (1991):"A focus theory of normative conduct: A theoretical refinement and reevaluation of the role of norms in human behavior," *Advances in Experimental Social Psychology*, 24, 201–34.

DiMaggio, P. J., and Powell, W. W. (1983): "The iron cage revisited: Institutional isomorphism and collective rationality in organizational fields," *American Sociological Review*, 48, 147–60.

DiMaggio, P. J., and Powell, W. W. (1991): "Introduction," *The New Institutionalism in Organiza- tional Analysis*. Chicago: University of Chicago Press, 1–38.

Elsbach, K. D.: (1999): "An expanded model of organizational identification," in B. M. Staw and R. I. Sutton (eds), *Research in Organizational Behavior*, Vol. 21, Greenwich, CT: JAI Press, 163– 200.

Elsbach, K. D. (2000): "Coping with hybrid organizational identities: Evidence of schizo organiza- tional identification among California legislative staff," in J. Wagner (ed.), *Advances in Qualitative Organizational Research*, Vol. 3, Greenwich, CT: JAI Press, 59–90.

Elsbach, K.D. (2001): "The architecture of legitimacy: Constructing accounts of organizational controversies", in J. M. Jost and B. A. Major (eds) *The Psychology of Legitimacy*, London: Blackwell, forthcoming.

Elsbach, K. D., and Kramer, R. M. (1996): "Members' responses to organizational identity threats: Encountering and countering the business week rankings," *Administrative Science Quarterly*, 41, 442–76.

Fligstein, N. (1985): "The spread of the multidivisional form among large firms, 1919–1979," *American Sociological Review*, 50, 377–91.

Fligstein, N. (1991): "The structural transformation of American industry: An institutional account of the causes of diversification in the largest firms, 1919–1979," in W. W. Powell and P. J. DiMaggio (eds), *The New Institutionalism in Organizational Analysis*, Chicago: University of Chicago Press, 311–36.

Galaskiewicz, J. (1991): "Making corporate actors accountable: Institution-building in Minneapolis-St. Paul," in W. W. Powell and P. J. DiMaggio (eds), *The New Institutionalism in Organizational Analysis*, Chicago: University of Chicago Press, 293–310.

Glynn, M. A., and Abzug, R. (1998): "Isomorphism and competitive differentiation in the organizational name game," in P. Shrivastava, A. S. Huff, and J. E. Dutton (eds), *Advances in Strategic Management*, Vol. 15, Greenwich, CT: JAI Press, 105–28.

Glynn, M.A., and Abzug, R. (2000): "Institutionalizing identity: Determinants and effects of symbolic isomorphism on organizational names," working paper.

Hardin, C. D., and Higgins, E. T. (1996): "Shared reality: How social verification makes the subjective objective," in R. M. Sorrentino and E. T. Higgins (eds), *Handbook of Motivation and Cognition, Volume 3: The Interpersonal Context*, New York: Guilford Press, 28–84.

Jehn, K. A. (1997): "A qualitative analysis of conflict types and dimensions in organizational groups," *Administrative Science Quarterly*, 42, 530–57.

Jepperson, R. L. (1991): "Institutions, institutional effects, and institutionalism," in W. W. Powell and P. J. DiMaggio (eds), *The New Institutionalism in Organizational Analysis*, Chicago: University of Chicago Press, 143–63.

Jermier, J. M., Slocum Jr., J. M., Fry, L. W., and Gaines, J. (1991): "Organizational subcultures in a soft bureaucracy: Resistance behind the myth and façade of an official culture, "*Organization Science*, 2, 170–94.

Kramer, R. M. (1991): "Intergroup relations and organizational dilemmas: The role of categorization processes," in B. M. Staw and L. L. Cummings (eds), *Research in Organizational Behavior*, Vol. 13, Greenwich, CT: JAI Press, 191–228.

Mael, F., and Ashforth, B. E. (1992): "Alumni and their alma mater: A partial test of the reformulated model of organizational identification," *Journal of Organizational Behavior*, 13, 103–23.

Meyerson, D. E. (1994): "Interpretations of stress in institutions: The cultural production of ambiguity and burnout," *Administrative Science Quarterly*, 39, 628–53.

Mezias, S. J. (1990): "An institutional model of organizational practice: Financial reporting at the Fortune 200," *Administrative Science Quarterly*, 35, 431–57.

O'Reilly, C., and Chatman, J. (1986): "Organizational commitment and psychological attachment: The effects of compliance, identification, and internalization on prosocial behavior", *Journal of Applied Psychology*, 71, 492–9.

Pfeffer, J. (1990): "Management as symbolic action: The creation and maintenance of organizational paradigms," in L. L. Cummings and B. M. Staw (eds), *Information and Cognition in Organizations*, Greenwich, CT: JAI Press, 1–52.

Pfeffer, J., and Sutton, R. I. (1999): *The Knowing–Doing Gap*. Boston, MA: Harvard Business School Press,

Powell, W. W., and DiMaggio, P. J. (1991): *The New Institutionalism in Organizational Analysis*. Chicago: University of Chicago Press.

Roy, D. F. (1960):"Efficiency and 'The Fix': Informal intergroup relations in a piecework machine shop," *American Journal of Sociology*, 60, 255–66.

Roy, D. F. (1989): "'Banana Time': Job satisfaction and informal interaction," in J. S. Ott (ed.) *Classic Readings in Organizational Behavior*, Belmont, CA: Brooks/Cole, 163–82.

Sackman, S. A. (1992): "Culture and subcultures: An analysis of organizational knowledge," *Administrative Science Quarterly*, 37, 140–61.

Schriber, J. B., and Gutek, B. A. 1987): "Some time dimensions of work: Measurement of an underlying aspect of organization culture." *Journal of Applied Psychology*, 72, 642–50.

Scott, W. R. (1991): "Unpacking institutional arguments," in W. W. Powell and P. J. DiMaggio (eds), *The New Institutionalism in Organizational Analysis*, Chicago: University of Chicago Press, 164–82.

Shapiro, D. L., Buttner, E. H., and Bruce, B. (1994): "Explanations: What factors enhance their perceived adequacy?" *Organizational Behavior and Human Decision Processes*, 58, 346–68.

Sherif, M. (1966): *In Common Predicament: Social Psychology of Intergroup Conflict and Cooperation.* New York: Houghton Mifflin.

Sherif, M., Harvey, O. J., White, B. J., Hood, W. R., and Sherif, C. W. (1961): *Intergroup Conflict and Cooperation: The Robber's Cave Experiment.* Norman, OK: University of Oklahoma Press.

Stephan, W. G., and Stephan, C. W. (1985): "Intergroup anxiety," *Journal of Social Issues*, 41, 157–75.

Strauss, A. L., Schatzman, R. B., Erlich, D., and Sabshin, M. (1964): *Psychiatric Ideologies and Institutions.* New York: Free Press.

Sundstrom, E., and Altman, I. (1989): "Physical environments and work-group effectiveness," in L. L. Cummings and B. M. Staw (eds), *Research in Organizational Behavior*, Vol. 11, Greenwich, CT: JAI Press, 175–209.

Thompson, L. L., Levine, J. M., and Messick, D. M. (1999): *Shared Cognitions in Organizations, The Management of Knowledge.* Mahwah, NJ: Lawrence Erlbaum.

Tolbert, P. S., and Zucker, L. G. (1983): "Institutional sources of change in the formal structure of organizations: The diffusion of civil service reform, 1880–1935," *Administrative Science Quarterly*, 28, 22–39.

Tolbert, P. S., and Zucker, L. G. (1996): "The institutionalization of institution theory," in S. R. Clegg, C. Hardy, and W. R. Nord (eds), *Handbook of Organization Studies*, Thousand Oaks, CA: Sage, 175–90.

Tyler, T. R. (1987): "Conditions leading to value expressive effects in judgments of procedural justice: A test of four models," *Journal of Personality and Social Psychology*, 52, 333–44.

Tyler, T. R., Boeckmann, R. J., Smith, H. J., and Huo, Y. J. (1997): *Social Justice in a Diverse Society Boulder.* CO: Westview Press.

Weick, K. E. (1993): "The Collapse of sensemaking in organizations: The Mann Gulch disaster," *Administrative Science Quarterly*, 38, 628–52.

Whetten, D. A., and Godfrey, P. C. (1998): *Identity in Organizations, Building Theory Through Conversations.* Thousand Oaks, CA: Sage.

Willis, P. (1977): *Learning to Labor.* New York: Columbia University Press.

Zucker, L. G. (1977): "The Role of institutionalization in cultural persistence," *American Sociological Review*, 42, 726–43.

Chapter Two

Intraorganizational Networks

HOLLY RAIDER AND DAVID J. KRACKHARDT

The adage 'its not what you know but who you know' has taken on an unfortunate ubiquity humbling the terms "network" and "networking" to broadly used buzzwords. References to networking activities abound in business periodicals, corporate newsletters and the like. We witness networking groups and mentor programs with networking intentions, the "young professional's networking group" convening interested residents of a local condominium building, and such popular press books as *Savvy Networking* (RoAne, 1993) or *Power Schmoozing* (Mandell, 1996). While there is great virtue in the message that individuals and organizations ought to be cognizant of the role networks play in organizational life, these well meaning but often cursory efforts to encourage proactive use of one's social network belie the richness of available theory and research about those networks.

We do not quibble too much with the popular adage: networks do matter and this, in fact, may be the only claim that would not engender academic debate. Empirical research accumulated over the last two decades demonstrates that social networks are associated with outcomes relevant to individuals and organizations, including what O'Reilly (1991) identifies as issues central to organization behavior studies: motivation, leadership, job design, turnover and absenteeism, and work attitudes (Krackhardt and Brass, 1994). Illustrations of these network effects include: access to labor market information (Granovetter, 1973), deal-making (Mizruchi and Stearns, 2000), career advancement (Lin 2001; Podolny and Baron, 1997), identity formation (Ibarra, 1992), trust building and cooperation (Burt, 2000; Labianca et al., 1998; Coleman 1988); commitment and retention (Krackhardt and Porter, 1986), opinions about organizations (Galaskiewicz and Burt, 1991), group and team performance (Ancona and Caldwell, 1992; Rosenthal, 1996), performance evaluations and compensation (Burt, 2000; Meyerson, 1994), and behavior at the top of the firm such as use of poison pills (Davis and Greve, 1997), to name merely a few.

This chapter is organized around the intuitions social network theory brings to bear on intraorganizational phenomenon. Work in social network theory is characterized by its emphasis on structural form (patterns and positions) or relational content (qualities of network ties), as well as by its level of analysis. These broad distinctions form the foundation of the framework for our review of the central questions addressed in this field. Key elements of central studies we highlight are summarized in Table 2.1.

Literature Review

STRUCTURE AND RELATIONS

A common sense explanation for why persons behave the way they do is to individualize. This is akin to what social psychologists refer to as the fundamental attribution error where we are likely to explain behavior in others by personality attributes rather than by situational constraints. A first step in correcting the bias is to consider people in terms of their relationships with other people. Social network theory does this by attributing behavior to the social context in which an actor is embedded. Some take a *structural* approach and focus on the pattern of relations in a social network. In this tradition, behavior, attitudes, or beliefs (outcomes) are attributed to network form: the position or location of an actor in its social network. There are essentially two kinds of mechanisms rooted in the form of the network: reach and demand.

The earliest studies focused on demand: actors differentiated by status orderings such as prestige. It was obvious – people are concerned about who has more, who is higher up. We refer to this as a demand mechanism because the differentiation among social actors is attributed to the demand on those actors – popularity – such as how many people cite them as friends. Network studies refer to this as the in-degree – the number or volume of the ties *to* a person. Early on in this research tradition, social demand was linked to esteem (Moreno, 1960) and innovativeness (Rogers, [1962] 1995). Within community structures and organizations demand is an index of power and influence (Brass, 1985, 1992; Hunter, 1953; Laumann and Pappi, 1976).

Perhaps the most elegant theoretical statement of these models is Coleman's (1990) model of prominence in exchange systems. Coleman disaggregates relationships into a definition of intertwined interest and control, where the relationship from one person to another increases with the extent to which the first person is interested in what the second person has. Once the demand structure is known in a social system, the relational structure can be imputed and an equilibrium in the system defined; see for example, Taylor and Coleman (1979). Podolny's (1993, 2000) work on status is a recent renaissance of demand models.

Demand models are distinguished from reach models by their emphasis on the actor as the object of relations; reach models are about social access. Reach models are concerned with how many people are you connected to or what sort of resources you access by virtue of those connections. Foundations in this area include Granovetter's (1973) work on weak ties; Freeman's (1977) work on betweeness centrality, and Burt's (1980 and 1992) work on autonomy and structural holes. Granovetter looks at how weak relationships access novel information (in job searches) or access external constituents (in the case of community organization). Ties can vary in their strength. Strong ties are those to people we feel closest to, see most frequently, or have known the longest. Strong ties are typically embedded in dense, overlapping networks, such that

Table 2.1 Selected studies of intraorganizational networks

Reference	Key concepts	Key variables	Key findings or predictions	Key contribution	Sample
Granovetter, 1973	Value of weak ties	Tie strength	Weak ties are entry to disparate social structures and therefore provide access to novel information	Illustrates how relational closeness or distance affects information flow in egocentric networks	100 interviews and 182 mail surveys of professional, technical, and managerial workers in Newton, MA
Freeman, 1977	Centrality	Betweeness	Centrality is associated with better access to resources, information	Illustrates how network position affects	
Burt, 1992	Structural holes	Network constraint	Low constraint networks (many holes) are a competitive advantage	Reveals how structure and network position affect outcomes such as speed of promotion and profit margins	A stratified random probability sample ($N = 284$) of the top 3305 managers in a large computer manufacturer
Podolny and Baron, 1997	Relational content	Task-advice network Strategic information network Buy-in network Mentor relation Social support network	Social capital value of structural hole networks contingent on type of network tie	For buy-in networks, closeness has a positive effect on job mobility	236 employees in a high-technology firm
Mizruchi and Stearns, 2000	Uncertainty and use of social networks Relational content Network structure	Density Hierarchy Risk Complexity	Low density deal approval networks associated with likelihood of deal closing	Networks effects predictably contingent on characteristics of transaction	91 bankers in the global banking unit of a large bank
Coleman, 1988	Social capital as cohesion and network closure	Closure	Drop out rates inversely related to social capital of student	Integration and trust emerging from network closure	Random sample of 4000 public school students
Burt, 2000	Social capital as brokerage	Autonomy	Higher rates of return (bonus compensation, job mobility) to structural hole networks	Coordination and control emerging from network brokerage	186 senior bankers in a large financial institution

weak ties more so than strong ties are portals to information or social worlds that are not already reached by one's closest friends.

Centrality refers to the extent to which an actor in the network is involved in relationships in a network. The most central person in a network is the person on the shortest path between all pairs of other positions in the network, the person the fewest steps away from reaching all persons in a network. Centrality is a mechanism for accessing resources insofar as the actor located at the crossroads of others in a network is positioned to disproportionately (and most quickly) amass information circulated in the network and to influence the network by gatekeeping the information in the network. Burt's (1992) Structural Hole theory attributes to structural positions of brokerage (ties to disconnected others) better access to information (and control of its dissemination), or control of the form of projects that connect people on other sides of a hole. These resources are linked to outcomes such as job promotions or compensation; for review, see Burt (2000).

The structural form of the network is predictive for both reach and demand models. A second broad approach within social network theory is *relational*, which emphasizes the content of relations as predictive. The emphasis in this stream of research is the content of the ties in a network. To put the distinction between these approaches another way, questions on a sociometric questionnaire that are "name generators" (e.g. List the people to whom you go for advice at work) are about the form of the network. "Name interpreters" in such questionnaires (e.g. How frequently do you talk to each of the people you named (the alters)? or data about those named contacts, such as age, education) are about the content of the network. Content-based studies look at the substance of the ties: friendship, kinship, work, advice, mentorship or at characteristics of alters in the network: demographics such as age, race, gender or education or opinions and beliefs such as commitment to the organization.

LEVELS OF ANALYSIS

One of the unique and powerful aspects of social network theory is that it is applicable at multiple levels of analysis and aggregation. It can be used to study individuals, dyads, and groups. These three levels of analysis are viable across kinds of actors: individuals, groups, and organizations, such that network theory can study, for example, the ego networks of organizations and even industry classifications (see Gulati, Dialdin, and Wang; and Baker and Faulkner, this volume). The three intraorganizational levels that are our focus are given in the rows in Table 2.2. The columns in Table 2.2 are the two approaches of network studies discussed above.

The simplest level of analysis is the dyad, a pair of actors. In dyadic network studies an important variable is some aspect of the relationship between two social actors, such as the kind of ties (friend, coworker, kin, boss, subordinate) or the strength of relationship. Studies in the alliance literature that focus on the pair of alliance partners are similarly dyadic in nature.

The second level of analysis is the network of an individual actor, referred to as an ego network or egocentric network. Here, the focal variable of study is derived from the complete network of an individual, aggregated across dyads within the network. Size, centrality, density, constraint, and range are examples of network properties used frequently in egocentric network studies.

Table 2.2 Framework of intraorganizational network studies

	Network form/Structural	Network content/Relational
Dyad	Etiology of relations	Homophily Effects of kinds of relations
Individual or ego network	Behavioral and opinion implications of variation in basic network parameters such as density, hierarchy, size	Network composition
Group	Group attitudes and behaviors	Group composition

The third level of analysis is the group as a whole, an aggregation of egocentric networks: a system of N actors yields one observed value to analyze. At this most aggregate level of analysis, the focus is on characteristics of a network as a whole, such as density (density is also used in studies of egocentric networks), connectedness, and 'averages' (summary measures to aggregate across egocentric networks, such as average constraint).

Central Questions

Central questions in intraorganizational network studies fall into one or another of the cells in Table 2.2. The columns of Table 2.2 correspond to the distinction between the structural approach of network form and the relational approach of network content. The rows of Table 2.2 correspond to the three levels of analysis. What follows here is a discussion of the theoretical ideas underlying the main questions in each of those partitions.

DYAD

Dyad studies that look at the *structure* of relations are concerned with the central question of 'where do ties come from?' The etiology of relationships has been the subject of countless studies across disciplines such as anthropology, sociology, and social psychology. Within social network studies, a prolific line of work on this topic springs from the observation that network ties tend to be between similar kinds of people, that they are homophilous. Homophily refers to the proclivity for relationships, particularly friendships, to form between people with the same gender, race, age, or occupations, for example. There are both structural form and relational content explanations for homophily.

Structural explanations focus on the contextual reasons homophilous ties form. The predominant explanation here is that colocation causes similar people to be in the same place at the same time and exposure to potential network relationships are circumscribed by this artifact. Feld (1981) takes the contextual explanation a step further and suggests that institutional constraints explain colocation. Organization demographics limit the possibilities for the kinds of networks observed (Blau, 1977). For example, in an organization comprised mostly of men, the networks of women in the organization are likely to be less homophilous than those of the men given the different proportions of the genders in the organization population. Relational content explanations for homophily include interpersonal attraction and comfort (Marsden, 1988). From this perspective, colocation is an outcome of similar or at least like-minded people selecting the same venues.

In addition to research aimed at understanding why certain kinds of ties form, *content-based* approaches to studying network dyads also consider the effects of particular kinds of ties or relational content. Examples of studies that inspect closely the content of dyadic relationships include Douthit's (2000) study of managers in financial organizations that examines whether subordinate performance is linked to qualities of the boss–subordinate relationship, and Reagans' (2000) study of how the social similarity between colleague dyads influences the performance ratings they give one another. Higgins and Kram's (2001) work on mentoring relationships calls for identifying developmental relationships, and joint consideration of tie strength and structure for understanding the role of networks on career advancement and job satisfaction.

EGOCENTRIC OR INDIVIDUAL NETWORK

Structural form approaches at the egocentric network level of analysis focus on whether, and how, characteristics of an individuals' network affect outcomes such as behavior or beliefs. Often cited examples of this stream of theory and research include the network form studies introduced in the first section of this chapter: Granovetter's ([1974] 1995) research on how weak tie networks help individuals find job faster; Burt's (1992 and 1997) studies linking manager autonomy to rate of promotion and compensation.

Granovetter ([1974] 1995) studied people who changed jobs and asked those who found their new job through a network contact how frequently they interacted with that person. Operationalizing the strength of a network tie as the frequency of seeing an alter, Granovetter reports that most – more than 80 percent – of the people who used a contact to find a job saw that person only occasionally. The theoretical implication is that people we see infrequently are an important source of unique information.

Burt's (1992) theory of Structural Holes focuses directly on the structure of networks and maintains that there is a competitive advantage (information and control benefits defined earlier) to networks where the ego is connected to disconnected others. Burt's initial empirical research on individual careers and structural holes was a study of senior managers in a large electronics and computer manufacturer; see Burt (1983) for an early incarnation of this line of work on autonomy and constraint applied at the interorganizational level. Burt's key predictor variable is the measure of network constraint, the extent to which ego is tied to alters who are themselves connected: the greater the constraint, the less the autonomy, the fewer the structural holes. The main finding is that managers are promoted more quickly when they have lower constraint networks, see Burt (2000) for review.

Egocentric studies which emphasize *network content* consider network properties similar to network-form studies, but focus on qualities of the tie rather than on structure alone. There are many studies that look at the same sorts of questions as above in network form. Podolny and Baron (1997), for example, study of the effects of networks on job mobility in a large high-technology engineering and manufacturing corporation. The authors distinguish among respondent's networks five kinds of ties – task-advice, strategic-information, buy-in, mentor, and social support – and examine whether the density of connections among kinds of alters affects job grade mobility.

Mizruchi and Stearns (2000) distinguish advice networks and approval networks in their study of deal closings in a large bank. The bankers in their study use networks to gather information from others in the organization about the client or about the financial product involved. The bank requires deals be approved by at least three officers, so each banker also needs to invoke their approval network to get the signatures necessary to close a deal. They find that managers instinctually turn to their closest contacts when gathering information (and ties among ones closest contacts are likely to be dense) yet managers with low density approval networks are more successful in closing deals. When due diligence in the approval process involves disparate, disconnected networks, there are "a diversity of views, and potential criticisms, that compel the banker to create a higher-quality product," which is likely to lead to a closed deal.

In addition to the type of tie, there is broad interest in how networks affect the transmission of beliefs or practices. So-called contagion studies look at how relationships or structures affect the diffusion of knowledge and the adoption of change (Coleman et al., 1966; Burt, 1987). For Coleman et al. (1966), the researchers were interested in predicting the prescribing of a new medication by a network of physicians. They report that the uncertainty about whether or not to prescribe the new medication was addressed via conversations with colleagues. In other words, they report that the mechanism for contagion was direct social influence, that people adopted an innovation if their "friends" had adopted it. Burt (1987), looking at the same data as Coleman et al., considered and found support for an alternate mechanism: individual physicians turn not necessarily to their close colleagues for advice, but look at the behavior of other physicians that are "like themselves" in the sense that they occupy the same position in the social structure. This is akin to mimetic processes in institutional theory.

To see how the contagion process affects organizational behavior, consider Krackhardt and Porter's (1986) study of turnover in an organization. Their analysis reveals that turnover begets turnover in patterned ways. They begin with the concern that when someone similar to you in the advice network leaves, you take that as relevant information and may leave also and their findings are consistent with this: when one person leaves, others who occupy positions in the network similar to the person who left (role equivalent people in the organization) tend to leave shortly thereafter. When someone like you leaves an organization, this is a cue to you that either the organization is inimical to persons like you, or that persons like you can find more rewarding opportunities elsewhere. This results in clusters of kinds of people leaving who are similar to each at work.

The influence of opinions and beliefs of others affects the functioning of an organization as is illustrated by Krackhardt and Porter (1985), this time looking at network content – friendship ties – to predict job satisfaction. Turning attention to the survivors (those remaining in the organization after the wave of departures) and organizational aftershocks, the authors distinguished survivors by whether or not they had friendship networks comprised mostly of people who had left the organization. Somewhat counterintuitively, they find that those who had friendship networks comprised mostly of people who left were *more* satisfied with their jobs than survivors whose friends were mostly people who had stayed. Krackhardt and Porter call this the "rotten apple theory." because friends who left were sources of negative information about the job, about the supervisor, and about the organization itself. These sources of negative information shared their negative views with their friends. Individuals with networks rife with people who eventually left had received an earful of complaints about the place ("this place stinks;" "other opportunities are more attractive;" etc.). Once those friends left, their negativity about the job left with them and one's job satisfaction increased. Those who did not have friends who left had been insulated from hearing negative views about the organization, and therefore did not experience the post-departure boost in their satisfaction.

GROUP

Studies looking at a network as a whole address the same issues, as do studies of egocentric networks. The difference here is that the researcher has data on the egocentric networks of an entire system, such as an organization or work group, and can study the relationship of the aggregate network to phenomenon of interest.

An interesting structural-form example of research at this level of analysis is Baker's study of a national securities market (Baker, 1984). Baker looks at options trading among brokers on the floor, operationalizing tie strength as the volume of trade between two brokers. Baker takes price volatility as a dependent variable and considers whether it is affected by the network structure of the brokers. When the trading floor has dense networks, he finds, there is improved communication which dampens variation in price.

To illustrate intraorganizational network studies at the group level of analysis that emphasize relational content, we turn again to Krackhardt's research (Krackhardt and Hanson, 1993). In this study, the central protagonist is a set of union organizers. Krackhardt studied the efforts of a union to organize a group of high-tech information system installers. The union used the formal authority network proscribed by the firm's organization chart and chose Hal to represent the union in the certification campaign and to lead the meetings at which unionization would be discussed. Hal, while quite vocal, even emphatic, in his support of the union, had little influence base through his network ties. His rousing rhetoric wore thin on many of his coworkers. Ultimately, the union ended up losing the certification vote by 12 to 3, an overwhelming defeat since they started with 75 percent of the people signing union interest cards.

Krackhardt gathered data on the informal social network at this firm. At the center of the friendship network in this group was Chris, who was not only an informal leader among the installers but also had strong ties to people outside of his local group of installers. Not surprisingly, given the outcome, Hal was on the periphery of this friendship network. Chris was positively disposed toward the union but not as vehemently supportive as Hal was. Chris was ignored by the union, and he kept his own thoughts to himself rather than use his influence to sway any votes in the certification campaign. Chris, who had the natural power base because of his position in the friendship network, sat idly by. Hal, whose enthusiasm for the union was second to none, had no power base in network terms. Because the union failed to elicit Chris' support and instead relied on Hal to mobilize support for the certification campaign, the campaign faced an uphill climb.

Contemporary Issues and Debate

COMPETING MECHANISMS OF BROKERAGE AND COHESION AS DEFINING SOCIAL CAPITAL

The idea of social capital is that social networks can be productive resources, much like other forms of capital (Coleman, 1988; Burt, 2000); see Lin (2001) for comparative account and critique. Social capital has been of particular interest to organizational behavior studies because it is an important resource that differentiates individuals and organizations, offering some a competitive advantage over others. What constitutes productive social capital is a point of contention within network theory. One school of thought, the Coleman School, holds that social capital occurs in networks with closure where the value of the social capital resource is communication among members of a network that both reduces information asymmetries and makes sanctions more possible because dishonorable or deviant behavior is observable. As a result, trust is less risky and therefore more likely. The other school of thought, the Burt School, holds that social capital occurs in networks without closure where the value of the social capital resource is derived from brokering information and exercising control. For Burt, information asymmetries are opportunities for individuals to build valuable social capital.

We do not resolve this debate about how social networks influence relevant outcomes but rather point out a few nuances relevant to how these perspectives are interpreted and applied. First, if usage of the term social capital is accompanied by clear meaning as to what constitutes social capital (lest it too becomes a vacuous network metaphor), we can leave the idea of social capital as "network as productive resource" without committing *by definition* to a particular kind of network structure. Second, the value of certain network structures may be context-specific. The empirical research sites in which Coleman and Burt examine their theoretical ideas could not be more different. Coleman studied the value of cohesive ties among parents and community for encouraging scholastic achievement among high school students, finding lower dropout rates when there is more social capital in the community. Burt studied the value of brokerage networks for persons working in for-profit business organizations, finding such outcomes as speed of promotion and bonus compensation. Third, the value of social capital ought to be considered at different levels of aggregation and from the perspectives of different actors in a social system. Coleman makes explicit the value of social capital as closure accrues to both individuals and the group: trust and information symmetries in closed, cohesive systems are virtues to the network and its individual constituents. Burt argues that system-wide benefits accrue from brokerage networks particularly in complex or rapidly changing organization environments because brokers access and assimilate diverse information, they are an elastic coordination mechanism unfettered by bureaucratic rigidity or the insularity of closed networks.

CONTINGENCY

At the intersection of structural and relational approaches is a growing body of research on network contingency. So-called contingency approaches take a primary network effect and demonstrate how the mechanism-to-outcome link is contingent upon ego or organizationally relevant variables. These studies establish important distinctions to the general network effects. For example, a contingency effect is a central contribution of the Podolny and Baron (1997) work on network content and job mobility. Their main finding is that for those with fate control over the respondent (the people named as necessary for "buy-in" for projects initiated by the respondent), cohesion rather than holes was associated with advancement. While the other kinds of network ties evidence effects consistent with the structural hole model, managers benefit from cohesive ties among their authority relations. Cohesion, they explain, offers "a clear and consistent set of expectations and values in order to be effective in one's role," and enable "trust and support from others that is necessary to access certain crucial resources (political aid, sensitive information, etc.) and to implement strategic initiatives" (Podolny and Baron, 1997, p. 676). They conclude that the value of the kinds of social capital is contingent on the kind of relationship at question.

Studies that look at the effects of particular kinds of ties will be about contingency to the extent they make more specific earlier research that had generalized across kinds of relationships. Other kinds of contingency applications look at demographic aspects of the ego, exemplified here by gender, and or look at aspects of the dyad, illustrated here by homophily.

GENDER

The adage "it is not what you know . . ." keeps good company with the similarly ubiquitous phrase "old boy network." There is a long historical antecedent of business organizations and economic institutions being predominately comprised of men such that business or work-related networks were also predominately populated by men (Kanter, 1977). With the demography of business organizations now including increasing proportions of women, the "old boy network" is to social network studies what the glass ceiling metaphor is to studies of career mobility and stratification. If social networks influence career success, do some people, particularly woman and minorities, have limited access to this valuable social capital? Research indicates women do have different networks in terms of homophily or instrumental effectiveness, (Brass, 1985; Ibarra, 1992, 1997) although men and women build similar kinds of networks if one looks at structural properties such as size and density (Aldrich et al., 1989; Ibarra 1997).

Burt (1998) considered gender differences in a reanalysis of his finding that low network constraint (a structural hole network) is associated with faster promotion (Burt, 1992). He found the effect holds more strongly for men in the organization studied than for woman or even for newly hired men. Burt (1998) argues that the structural hole effect is contingent on the legitimacy of the focal actors. In the firm he studied, groups with minority status (woman and newly hired men) did not experience the positive promotion effect of structural hole networks as seen for men in that organization. Rather, Burt explains, groups disadvantaged by the demography of an organization – in his data, this is women and recently recruited men, but as likely other demographic groups in different organization populations – experience a positive promotion effect if they have social networks built around a mentor who introduces the protégé to others in the organization. These protégé networks do not appear to be a structural hole network because sociometrically the tie to the mentor is a high constraint relationship.

HOMOPHILY

Apart from homophily being an interesting proclivity in how friendship choices are made, it is also thought that it engenders preferential behaviors, going out of one's way for someone like oneself. The contingent effect of network homophily is evidenced by Reagans' (2000) study in a financial organization. Using peer ratings (dyads) which determine year-end bonus compensation, Reagans looks at how the level of ratings between homophilous dyads is a function of the overall homophily in the various business units within the organization: where a dyad of similar age, or race, or gender, is embedded in a broader social structure of others of dissimilar age, or race, or gender, the peer ratings are *higher* than if the homophilous dyad were embedded in a broader social structure of similar others. Reagans concludes that the partiality expected between homophilous dyad is stronger when in minority standing and therefore salient (much like Kanter's (1977) observation that a token few will be highly visible in an organization.)

Network autocorrelation

Research in social networks is a rare case in the social sciences where the theoretical needs of researchers required the development of a specialized methodology (see also Baker and Faulkner, this volume). Along with this methodology came specialized software and lexicon.[1] Although we do not elaborate on the methodological aspects of network studies, it is worth pointing out the central methodological challenge here: the problem of network autocorrelation.

There is a fundamental difference between data observations in the majority of social sciences and the field of network analysis. In other social science studies, observations (which, once measured, become variables) are about the actor. These observations are collected into vectors, which fit neatly into econometric analysis programs. In network analysis, the basic unit of observation is the dyad, a relationship between two actors. Thus, rather than stringing observations together into vectors, each variable in network analysis is better represented as a matrix where each row and each column represent actors and the cells of the matrix represent the measured relational state between the two actors.

This basic structure of observations creates a fundamental problem for the statistical analysis of network data. The observations in standard econometric analysis are assumed to be independent of one another. More specifically, the error terms are assumed independent. But in a matrix of dyadic observations, each dyad is explicitly not independent of other dyadic observations. Some people are popular. Some women prefer to interact with other women or perhaps other people of the same age. Some people prefer to like only those who have shown affection for them. Each of these social facts is reflected in strong degrees of non-independence among cell values. Consequently, there may be strong autocorrelation among the error terms in the econometric model of these data. As such, it is risky to apply standard econometric statistical testing in such cases. Even moderate amounts of autocorrelation in network data can drastically bias hypothesis tests (Krackhardt, 1988).

One approach to address the problem is to use a test that is robust against varying degrees of autocorrelation. For example, Krackhardt (1988) suggests adapting the Quadratic Assignment Procedure (QAP) to multiple regression problems with network data. The MRQAP, as it is called, replaces the ordinary regression statistical tests with permutation-based tests of significance. Krackhardt (1988) has shown with a set of Monte Carlo simulations that these tests are unbiased under a wide variety of network autocorrelation conditions.

Another approach is to explicitly model the extent of autocorrelation in the data and proceed with more sophisticated analyses to take these parameters into account (e.g. Lincoln, 1984). Perhaps the most advanced of the specific modeling approaches is p-star, which allows a wide variety of autocorrelation parameters to be investigated (Anderson et al., 1999; Pattison et al., 2000; Crouch et al., 1998; Wasserman and Anderson, 1995; Pattison and Wasserman, 1995). P-star models are particularly attractive because they allow the researcher to answer a much larger set of statistical and modeling questions in network data than the simpler and older MRQAP. For example, while MRQAP provides significance levels for the regression coefficients, p-star allows one to calculate standard errors and confidence intervals. These p-star models work well if the model correctly matches the particular form of autocorrelation in the population. However, frequently the researcher does not know the exact form of autocorrelation that may exist in his or her data. The MRQAP test, on the other hand, has been shown to be robust against a wide variety of common network autocorrelation structures without having to model them explicitly.

Future Directions

NETWORK AND TASK FIT

A clear theme in the network literature in organizations has been that network structures themselves have predictable effects on organizational behavior. Often, however, scant attention is paid to the fact that networks do not occur in a vacuum. People who are tied together have particular tasks to do, and network effect depends in part on the relationship between the participants and the tasks they are responsible for. Initial efforts to link networks to task include Hansen et al. (2000) who attribute the speed of project completion to the match between the social structure of product teams and the uniformity of the technical problems assigned to the teams (teams with cohesive networks who are assigned more uniform problems complete projects faster, teams working on more complex problems benefit from brokerage networks). Mizruchi and Stearns (2000), in their study described earlier, find that when loans are risky, loan officers are more likely to seek advice and approval from their closest ties despite the paradox that they are more likely to get approval when they invoke disparate contacts. Similarly, but taking the firm as the focal actor, Podolny (2000) links the effectiveness of the due diligence task required of venture capital firms in IPOs to brokerage network structures. Gargiulo and Benassi (2000) juxtapose the Burt and Coleman theories of social capital and find that managers with fewer structural holes were less able to make needed adaptations in their communication networks in response to changes in task interdependencies at work.

Some people in organizations have access to more resources or to particular resources that are valuable in accomplishing tasks and therefore access to different resources moderates the network effect. Krackhardt and Carley (1998) describe a formal model for addressing these relationships. They start by noting three central domains of interest in organizations: individuals, tasks, and resources. Further, they argue, understanding organizational design amounts to understanding the relationships among the elements of these domains. The complex nature of interactions among people, tasks and resources in the organization is harnessed by a set of simple mathematical rules that can yield powerful explanations and predictions; see Carley, this volume.

TRANSLATION TO POLICY AND PRACTICE

On a final note, there is value to add by integrating social science into practice. Wayne Baker (1994, 2000) is one of the few scholars in this area who has been able to bridge this divide. The need is out there. For example, we have observed a bevy of organizations implementing mentor programs with the best of intentions to shepherd junior employees, or to better acculturate new members of the organization, to decrease employee turnover, to encourage promotion of a greater diversity of people. With the best of intentions, many programs match the mentor only by gender or race similarity. While it is productive for junior employees to learn from someone like themselves, academic research on intraorganizational networks calls into question the generality of assumptions used in the design of such programs. Homophily-based mentorship matches may not be sufficient entree to the kinds of social networks that are most beneficial to the protégé or the organization, but rather, can propagate the very stratification such mentoring programs seek to overcome.

Connections Across Levels

The three chapters in this volume illustrate consistency across the broad field of network studies. Each of the three chapters on networks recognizes that the theories and methods apply to multiple levels of analysis, distinguishes among kinds of relations, and recognizes the split between structural and relational approaches.

Baker and Faulkner emphasize the relational dimension of network studies. We use the term content or relation as a general category that encompasses what Baker and Faulkner distinguish as domains in which organizations have ties to other organizations – such as market exchange, strategic alliances, or director interlocks; and what they distinguish as populations – producers, suppliers, and buyers. From this relational springboard, however, they introduce a structural conceptualization of interlocking markets emphasizing network-form properties such as structural equivalence, position, and concentration.

Baker and Faulkner's three-dimensional depiction of organizational networks highlights the complexity of interorganizational networks, and makes this complexity tractable by breaking down the universe of those networks into populations (kinds of actors or positions), domains (kinds of ties), and reference groups (their vertical and horizontal slices). When they ask in future directions "what is an organization's network?" Baker and Faulkner remind us of an unsettled aspect of network studies: the boundary of a network. Questions about where to draw the line is reflected in methodological debate about the ideal form for network questionnaires: how many alters do we elicit from respondents? Even intraorganizational studies that include as respondents all members of the organization face a network boundary question because the ties in the social networks of the organizations' constituents are typically not limited to other members of the organization.

Gulati et al. begin with an emphasis on network-form, even defining social networks as a pattern of relations. This is what we refer to as network form or network structure. Although they focus on structure, the authors incorporate relational aspects in alliance studies when they consider "partner profiles" (characteristics of alters) or "configuration of ties" (composition of relationships). For example, the similarity between alliance partners in their innovation activities, technological distance, is analogous to the concept of homophily used in intraorganizational network studies. Lastly, Gulati et al. call for further study of the role of network content on alliances, particularly the role of relationship qualities between organizations for trust building and conflict management.

So diverse is the work in social network theory that is relevant to networks in organizations that writing this chapter was a welcomed occasion to pause and articulate a general overview of this subfield.

Conclusion

The field of intraorganizational networks is diverse: it crosscuts multiple levels of analysis, and its principles and insights are applied to a broad range of phenomena. We make this heterogeneity tractable with a framework that divides the field into levels of analysis (dyad, egocentric networks, and groups), and that distinguishes relational from structural approaches. This schematic can be both a starting point for persons newly interested in this field, and a useful springboard of reflection for those already familiar with work in this area.

Network theory and methods adroitly move across levels of analysis and kinds of actors, and the different foci of the three chapters are complementary. For example, we summarize the concept of centrality as one of the three foundations of demand models of network form, yet Gulati et al. overview different operationalizations of that same concept. We encourage readers who may be particularly interested in one or another of the levels of analysis around which the *Companion* is organized to consider the sister chapters: the three chapters on networks are complementary, their few redundancies reinforcing and their many differences enriching.

Acknowledgments

This work was supported in part by the Office of Naval Research (ONR), United States Navy Grant No. N00014-97-1-0037 and by the Center for Computational Analysis of Social and Organizational Systems (CASOS) at CMU.

Note

1   Basic software for estimating common network measures are listed at http://www.heinz.cmu.edu/project/INSNA/soft_inf.html

References

Aldrich, H., Reese, P. R., and Dubini, P. (1989): "Women on the verge of a breakthrough: Networking among entrepreneurs in the United States and Italy," *Entrepreneurship and Regional Development*, 1, 339–56.

Ancona, D. G., and Caldwell, D. F. (1992): "Bridging the boundary: External activity and performance in organizational teams," *Administrative Science Quarterly*, 37, 634–65.

Anderson, C. J., Wasserman, S., and. Crouch, B. (1999): "A p* primer: Logit models for social networks," *Social Networks*, 21, 37–66.

Baker, W. (1984): "The social structure of a national securities market," *American Journal of Sociology*, 89, 775–811.

Baker, W. (1994): *Networking Smart*. New York: McGraw Hill.

Baker, W. (2000): *Achieving Success through Social Capital*. New York: John Wiley & Sons.

Blau, P. M. (1977): *Inequality and Heterogeneity: A Primitive Theory of Social Structure*. New York: Free Press.

Brass, D. J. (1985): "Men's and women's networks: A study of interaction patterns and influence in an organization," *Academy of Management Journal*, 28, 518–39.

Brass, D. J. (1992): "Power in organizations: A social network perspective," in G. Moore and J. A. Whitt (eds), *Research in Politics and Society*, Greenwich, CT: JAI Press, 295–323.

Burt R. S (1980): "Autonomy in a social topology," *American Journal of Sociology*, 85, 892–925.

Burt, R. S. (1983): *Corporate Profits and Cooptation*. New York: Academic Press.

Burt. R. S. (1987): "Social contagion and innovation: Cohesion versus structural equivalence," *American Journal of Sociology*, 92, 1287–1335.

Burt, R. S. (1992): *Structural Holes*. Cambridge: Harvard University Press.

Burt, R. S. (1997): "The contingent value of social capital," *Administrative Science Quarterly*, 42, 339–65.

Burt, R. S. (1998): "The gender of social capital," *Rationality and Society*, 10, 5–46.

Burt, R. S. (2000): "The network structure of social capital," in R. I. Sutton and B. M. Staw (eds), *Research in Organization Behavior Research in Organizational Behavior*, Greenwich, CT: JAI Press, 345–423.

Coleman, J. S. (1988): "Social capital in the creation of human capital," *American Journal of Sociology*, 94, Supplement, s95–s120.

Coleman, J. S. (1990): *Foundations of Social Theory*. Cambridge, MA: Harvard University Press.

Coleman, J. S., Katz, E., and Menzel, H. (1966): *Medical Innovation*. New York: Bobbs-Merrill.

Crouch, B., Wasserman, S., and Contractor, N. (1998): "A practical guide to fitting social network models via logistic regression," *Connections*, 21, 87–101.

Davis, G. F., and Greve, H. R. (1997): "Corporate elite networks and the governance changes in the 1980s," *American Journal of Sociology*, 103, 1–37.

Douthit, M. W. (2000): "Supervision and social capital," dissertation, Graduate School of Business, University of Chicago.

Feld, S. L. (1981): "The focused organization of social ties," *American Journal of Sociology*, 86, 1015–35.

Freeman, L. C. (1977): "A set of measures of centrality based on betweeness," *Sociometry*, 40, 35–41.

Galaskiewicz, J., and Burt, R. S. (1991): "Interorganization contagion in corporate philanthropy," *Administrative Science Quarterly*, 36, 88–105.

Gargiulo, M., and Benassi, M. (2000): "Trapped in your own net? Network cohesion, structural holes, and the adaptation of social capital," *Organization Science*, 11, 183–96.

Granovetter, M. S. (1973): "The strength of weak ties," *American Journal of Sociology*, 78, 1360–80.

Granovetter, M. S. ([1974] 1995): *Getting a Job*. Chicago, IL: University of Chicago Press.

Hansen, M. T., Podolny, J. M., and Pfeffer, J. (2000): "So many ties, so little time: A task contingency perspective on the value of social capital in organizations," paper presented at the 2000 Organization Science Winter Conference.

Higgins, M. C., and Kram, K.E. (2001): "Reconceptualizing mentoring at work: A developmental network perspective," *Academy of Management Review*, 26, April, 264–88.

Hunter, F. (1953): *Community Power*. Chapel Hill: UNC Press.

Ibarra, H. (1992): "Homophily and differential returns: Sex differences in network structure and access in an advertising firm," *Administrative Science Quarterly*, 72, 422–47.

Ibarra, H. (1997): "Paving and alternate route: Gender differences in managerial networks," *Social Psychology Quarterly*, 60, 91–102.

Kanter, R. M. (1977): *Men and Women of the Corporation*. New York: Basic Books.

Krackhardt, D. (1988): "Predicting with networks: A multiple regression approach to analyzing dyadic data," *Social Networks*, 10, 359–81.

Krackhardt, D., and Brass, D. J.: (1994). "Intraorganizational networks," in S. Wasserman and J. Galaskiewicz (eds), *Advances in Social Network Analysis*, Thousand Oaks, CA: Sage Publications, 207–29.

Krackhardt, D., and Carley, K. M. (1998): "A PCANS model of structure in organizations," *Proceedings of the 1998 International Symposium on Command and Control Research and Technology*, Monterey, CA.

Krackhardt, D., and Hanson, J. R. (1993): "Informal networks: The company behind the chart," *Harvard Business Review*, 71, 104–11.

Krackhardt, D., and Porter, L. W. (1985): "When friends leave: A structural analysis of the relationship between turnover and stayers attitudes," *Administrative Science Quarterly*, 30, 242–61.

Krackhardt, D., and Porter, L. W. (1986): "The snowball effect: Turnover embedded in communication networks," *Journal of Applied Psychology*, 71, 50–5.

Labianca, G., Brass, D. J., and Grey, B. (1998): "Social networks and perceptions of intergroup conflict: The role of negative relationships and third parties," *Academy of Management Journal*, 41, 55–67.

Laumann, E. O., and Pappi, F. U. (1976): *Networks of Collective Action: A Perspective on Community Influence Systems*. New York: Academic Press.

Lin, N. (2001): *Social Capital: A Theory of Social Structure and Action*. Cambridge: Cambridge University Press.

Lincoln, J. R. (1984): "Analyzing relations in dyads: Problems, models, and an application to interorganizational research," *Sociological Methods and Research*, 13, 45–76.

Marsden, P. V. (1988): "Homogeneity in confiding relations," *Social Networks*, 10, 57–76.

Meyerson, E. M. (1994): "Human capital, social capital and compensation: The relative contribution of social contacts to managers' incomes," *Acta Sociologica*, 37, 383–99.

Mizruchi, M. S. and Stearns, L. B. (2000):"Getting deals done: The use of social networks in bank decision making," working paper, University of Michigan.

Moreno, J. L. (ed.) (1960): *The Sociometry Reader*. New York: Free Press.

O'Reilly C. A. (1991): "Organizational behavior: Where we've been and where we're going," *Annual Review of Psychology*, 42, 427–58.

Pattison, P., and Wasserman, S. (1995): "Constructing algebraic models for local social networks using statistical methods," *Journal of Mathematical Psychology*, 39, 57–72.

Pattison, P. E., Wasserman, S., Robins, G., and Kanfer, A. M. (2000): "Statistical evaluation of algebraic constraints for social networks," *Journal of Mathematical Psychology*, 44, December, 536–68.

Podolny, J. M. (1993):"A status-based model of market competition," *American Journal of Sociology*, 98, 829–72

Podolny, J. M. (2000): "Networks as the pipes and prisms of the market," working paper, Graduate School of Business, Stanford University.

Podolny, J. M., and Baron, J. N. (1997): "Resources and relationships: Social networks and mobility in the workplace," *American Sociological Review*, 62, 673–93.

Reagans, R. E. (2000): "The logic of social bias: Homophily bias in a hierarchical firm," working paper, Carnegie Mellon University.

Rogers, E. M. ([1962] 1995): *Diffusion of Innovations*. New York: The Free Press.

Rosenthal, E. A. (1996): "Social networks and team performance," dissertation, Graduate School of Business, University of Chicago.

Taylor, D. G., and Coleman, J. S. (1979): "Equilibrating processes in social networks, a model for conceptualization and analysis," in P. W. Holland and S. Leinhardt (eds), *Perspectives on Social Network Research*, New York: Academic Press, 257–300.

Wasserman, S., and Anderson, C. (1995): "Log-multiplicative models for valued social relations," *Sociological Methods and Research*, 24, 96–127.

Chapter Three

Intraorganizational Ecology

D. CHARLES GALUNIC AND
JOHN R. WEEKS

It still disturbs us. The thought that human behavior can be explained in the same terms as systems of flora and fauna – i.e., in the language of ecology – still provokes incredulity and irritation. The organizational ecologist is liable to be labeled reductionist, a victim of physics envy – or at least biology envy – and presumed to be incapable of, or uninterested in, understanding the more subtle complexities of human behavior and culture. Human organization, we are told, is obviously different.

A review of recent thinking in intraorganizational ecology, however, reveals such complaints as at once overestimating the rigidity and determinism of ecological theories and underestimating the degree to which the central concepts of ecology (i.e., survival of the fittest and mechanisms of variation, selection, and retention) offer a plausible and useful way to interpret the internal workings of human organizations. Rather than reducing our understanding to mechanistic laws of blind chance and Panglossian optimization, they simply suggest for our attention some important constructs (particularly organizational routines) and provide testable ideas for how these may behave (through birth, competition, complementarity, adaptation, and death). To our minds, the language of ecology is not a substitute for or retreat from the language of psychology, sociology, and the other disciplines of organization theory, but rather a companion, a platform on which organizational theorists can attempt to interpret and re-interpret existing theories. Moreover, there may be sweet irony in separating the tenets of ecological thinking from purely biological applications and applying them more generally to human organization because, we believe, we are just as likely to find places of appreciable difference between human and non-human structures as we are compelled to see their similarities.

What is "intraorganizational ecology?" Foremost, it is a view of human organization that applies ecological concepts to explain the processes occurring within organizations. Positing that taken-for-granted routines play an analogous role in organizations that genes play in biological systems, intraorganizational ecology describes organizational behavior as resulting from the interaction of these "genetic" structures and the environment. By routines we mean the regular, predictable, and discernible actions and mental processes that pattern organizational activities in domains as diverse as product development, job design, and human resource management. Like genes, they are consequential replicators: patterns that reproduce themselves and that have material impact on organizational outcomes. In general (though, as we shall discuss, there are important exceptions), those routines associated with more favorable outcomes are reproduced more often and it is in this way that adaptation proceeds.

While, in theory, we could imagine an ecology of any sort of routines – routine manners of entering the company parking lot in the morning, for example – in practice, ecological models have little to say about routines that have a trivial impact on salient organizational outcomes. The question, "Salient to whom?" is relevant here since intraorganizational ecological models make room for both blind and deliberate mechanisms of selection: routines do not reproduce themselves, they are reproduced by human agents for reasons that must be explained rather than assumed – selective breeding may be a more appropriate analogy than natural selection in many cases. Intraorganizational ecology, then, is a view of organizations as an ecology of routines.

Importantly, this ecology is described in terms of a set of evolutionary processes. Roughly speaking, we can divide these processes (see Baum and Singh, 1994) into *interaction processes* and *replication processes*. The former examine routines as ecological entities involved in mutual interactions – notably competition and complementarity – and embedded in higher-level entities (organizations, populations, communities). The latter examine routines as genealogical entities, meaning they contain some story of their history and how they have been passed along through time, and consist of the processes that cause new routines to be born and grow, existing ones to decay or die, and others to change. Correspondingly, our review of the literature will detail the interaction and replication processes surrounding organizational routines.

Literature Review: Summary of Seminal Works

Several authors serve as a good starting point for understanding intraorganizational ecology: Campbell (1969; 1975), Weick (1969), Aldrich (1979), McKelvey (1982), Nelson and Winter (1982), Burgelman (1991; 1994), and Miner (1991; 1994); see Table 3.1. Although each developed their theories within remarkably different disciplines (psychology, sociology, management theory, economics, strategy, and organizational behavior respectively), they share a similar framework in their treatment of ecological issues. The latter three works in particular establish an explicit focus on intraorganizational ecology as a theoretical domain.

Campbell (1969; 1975) produced the earliest and broadest work in this area. Campbell provided a comprehensive bridge to ecological thinking in the biological sciences. Although the connections between biology and the social sciences had already begun with the emergence of sociobiology (Wilson, 1975), Campbell's work was the first to view evolution as a generic process of variation, selection, and retention that could operate completely independently of biology. This opened the possibility of a theory of the evolution of human systems freed from the constraining assumption that genes are the only replicators. For this reason, his work, much more than earlier efforts, made a substan-

Table 3.1 Summary of the seminal works in intraorganizational ecology

Reference	Key concepts/variables	Key findings/contributions	Method and sample
Campbell (1969, 1975)	Variation-selection-retention Sociocultural evolution	One of the early attempts at bridging the biological and social sciences Biological evolution may make cultural evolution possible, but cultural evolution runs its own course.	Theoretical
Weick (1969/79)	Evolutionary metaphor for organizing	An early exposition on how the evolutionary metaphor can be of use in the study of organizations	Theoretical
Aldrich (1979)	Organizations as open systems who exhibit variation, selection, and retention	A broad and comprehensive translation of the basic principles of ecology and evolution into organizational terms	Theoretical treatise and review
McKelvey (1982)	Polythetic groupings of comps	Organizational "science" requires a classificatory scheme. Comps are natural units found within firms for the study of organizational evolution.	Theoretical treatise and review
Nelson and Winter (1982)	Selective retention and variation of routines	Firms are in essence made up of routines, whose evolution will in turn impact the survivability of the firm.	Theoretical treatise and simulation modeling
Burgelman (1983, 1991, 1994)	Internal corporate venturing and the strategy making process Strategic business exit Induced vs. autonomous process for strategy making	The selection of strategic directions and new ventures within the firm resembles an ecological process Importantly, the decision process is non-traditional, not amounting to a rational choice process made at one point in time but the consequence of variation-selection-retention processes operating across various levels of the firm	In-depth qualitative field work, focusing on one or two large firms along with a theoretical paper
Miner (1987, 1990. 1991, 1994)	Jobs as a genre of routines	The creation, adaptation and death of jobs is examined, with more general implications for routines of other sorts. Extant ecological factors operating on the evolution of jobs are well articulated.	Quantitative filed-based research along with a theoretical paper

tial impact on the study of organizations, even though this was not necessarily his goal. In particular, the application of the variation, selection, retention mechanisms of ecology that he describes to social change is by now a general, if often implied, framework in virtually all work in organizational ecology, whether at the inter or intraorganizational levels. While Campbell may not have had the organizational community in mind when writing, Weick's (1969) cogent description of these processes within human organizations provided not only a complementary treatise but also one directed at the organizations community (expanded in the 1979 edition). Indeed, most of the remaining authors, who are more explicit in their focus on intraorganizational issues, cite Campbell and Weick as important contributors to their thinking.

Aldrich's book *Organizations and Environments* (1979) was written during a time when organizational theorists were turning to consider the environment and developing what came to be known as the "open systems" view of organizations; see also Scott (1987b). Theorists were shedding their over-rationalized views of organizations and growing more comfortable with such concepts as loose-coupling, environmental variability, and organizational change. Aldrich's book is an excellent representative of the open systems school of thought and has been broadly influential in organizational theory. However, its greatest contribution was pioneering the ecological perspective for organizational theorists. Specifically, the book provides compelling translations of the basic processes of variation, selection, and retention into organizational terms, going beyond metaphor to show concretely how these processes are embedded in organizational life. Its greatest shortcoming is a consequence of its strength – the book contains so much breadth, fluidly crossing levels of analysis, that it perhaps fails to adequately specify the dynamics of intraorganizational ecologies and the unit of selection at this particular level (although chapter 5 makes useful inroads). In many ways the book was ahead of its time, laying out general concepts and issues before subfields clearly emerged and deeper discourse was conducted (typically working at a single level of analysis). It is therefore fitting that Aldrich recently published another book that looks back on the last twenty years of ecological research, again crossing levels of analysis (Aldrich, 1999).

McKelvey's book *Organizational Systematics* (1982) is as pioneering as Aldrich's book but perhaps more poignant in its message to students of organizations. McKelvey charges that organization studies can hardly be called a science if there are no attempts to systematically classify organizational forms. Without a classification system, he argues, it becomes impossible to build comprehensive and generalizable insights about organizations – we are left with either the false notion that all organizations are the same or the useless notion that all organizations are different (McKelvey and Aldrich, 1983). To his credit, McKelvey attempts the Herculean task of offering a classification method – organizations can be grouped according to their competence elements (or comps). Comps are the skills and knowledge present in the organization. In turn, organizational forms are polythetic groupings of organizations, i.e. groupings of organizations with comps that are similar and transferable between constituents (much like reproductive seeds are only transferable within the same species). While many questions arise in operationalizing this classification scheme, for our purposes comps are one of the first attempts to identify the basic ecological unit within the firm and can be considered synonymous with what we elsewhere call "routines." Although McKelvey spends much of his time at the population level of analysis, he provides a strong impetus for examining how comps (or routines) evolve, suggesting that the machinations of these basic building blocks is vital to our understanding of organizational evolution. McKelvey and Aldrich's work, therefore, create a useful platform for studying intraorganizational ecology.

The first significant attempt to outline an evolutionary theory of the firm came from Nelson and Winter (1982). Frustrated by the simplistic optimization assumptions of neoclassical economics, Nelson and Winter modeled a more realistic picture of how firms operate within an industry, borrowing freely but selectively from biology. Their work is based upon three key assumptions that have become the foundation for work in this area:

1   Routines, by which they mean essentially any regular and predictable set of business behaviors, play an analogous role in organizations to genes in biological organisms.

2   Routines are temporally defined: some are of immediate relevance and define current operating characteristics; others determine the short-to-medium term changes to current operating characteristics; and finally some routines exist that in the long run can dramatically alter the operating characteristics of the firm.

3   Various search and selection rules operate on the hierarchy of routines, altering the routines and portfolio of routines that firms hold; some rules are blind while others are deliberate and calculating; some are externally sourced while others are endogenous. Crucially, the resulting evolution of routines within firms is presented as the driving motor behind firm innovation, adaptation, and survival.

In sum, their work presents economic change as an evolutionary and ecological phenomenon. Perhaps the greatest shortcoming of the theory for our purposes is that it so heavily emphasizes *inter*organizational outcomes that the finer mechanics of *intra*organizational ecology are left underexplored, as they themselves admit (Nelson and Winter, 1982, p. 135). Nevertheless, they join Aldrich and McKelvey in having provided useful building blocks in the study of intraorganizational ecology.

Burgelman's empirical work on internal corporate venturing and strategic change (1983; 1994) and his interpretation of this process in ecological terms (1991) provides us with a more focused and detailed account of how ecological processes function within the firm. Collectively, these works make several key contributions. First, they show how the entire strategy making process can be reasonably described through the core mechanisms of variation, selection and retention – a familiar thread by now that runs through the work of Campbell and Nelson and Winter. Moreover, these mechanisms are shown to operate with different levels of intent or design: specifically, "induced" processes that begin with some retained strategic direction and, in orchestrated fashion, encourage closely related variations where the selection regime is well understood; and "autonomous" processes where variation is less planned and more emergent, where new strategies emanate from a host of lower level search routines (some of them clandestine) and where selection is made with a strong glance to the current or emergent conditions in the external environment rather than the existing strategy. This work also enriches our understanding of the relative fitness of a routine within the firm – some routines are selected out because of their performance advantages *vis-à-vis* the environment, while others are selected because they fall in line with the existing corporate mantra. Throughout his research, Burgelman also maintains that well-tuned ecological processes operating at the intraorganizational level will lead to continued survival and adaptation at the population level – a message similar to Nelson and Winter's but with data to enrich the theory. Perhaps more than any other work, therefore, Burgelman connects actual (although, as he notes, not always clearly defined) routines within firms to the full language and mechanisms of ecology.

Miner's work (1987; 1990; 1991; 1994) continues in this direction, providing an even more focused account of intraorganizational ecology. Continuing in the tradition of Campbell and Nelson and Winter, Miner maintains that the firm is fundamentally an ecological system and that the overarching processes are that of variation, selection, and retention. However, unlike these authors and the work of Burgelman, Miner focuses on one particular genre of routines – jobs – and explores in some detail how these undergo a few basic ecological processes (births, adaptation, and death). A particular strength of her work is the attention she gives to defining and measuring the factors that delineate the ecology of a firm. Thus, in relation to jobs, she uses and develops such constructs as resource uncertainty, mission ambiguity, resource variation, and a host of more demographic items (including department size and tenure of job occupants). Indeed, without such well-specified empirical work being done, intraorganizational ecology could never rise beyond the status of a quaint metaphor for complex organizational systems. Her work is also unique because it is among the first quantitative field studies of intraorganizational ecology, and so a good complement to the simulation tools of Nelson and Winter and the qualitative field studies of Burgelman.

Collectively, these works define a fledgling domain. Compared to population ecology, there is little sense of cohort or community in the development of these works, emerging as they did from different disciplines and at different periods over the last thirty years. Nonetheless, the common themes are unmistakable and the diversity in perspectives all the more enriching. Below, we turn to the wider organizational literature to examine what has been said about the two sorts of fundamental ecological processes laid down by the above authors: interaction processes (competition and complementarity) and replication processes (births, deaths, and change).

Contemporary Issues and Central Questions

INTERACTION PROCESSES

Organizations contain multiple routines in various stages of development at any point in time – it would be impossible to speak of an ecology of routines otherwise. This section considers how routines interact. Many organizational routines, of course, do not interact. For example, routines for erecting new corporate buildings and those for establishing the yearly bonus pool may not interact in any meaningful sense. The presence of interaction is an empirical question, not a strictly theoretical one, though: perhaps routines leading to very expensive buildings create in a particular organization an environment where only routines producing very small bonuses survive. In that case we would have to consider the interaction, for we focus on interactions where there is some perceptible and meaningful exchange or interdependence of ideas or resources even if it is indirect. So, routines for doing research and those for teaching, for example, although often without particularly visible links, probably contain meaningful interactions. In general, we will identify two sorts of interactions that routines may undergo: competition and complementarity.

COMPETITION BETWEEN ROUTINES

Routine competition is present whenever there is risk to the survival of one routine because of the presence of another. The endgame is usually the supplanting of one routine by another, as one routine fulfills the same objectives but with greater effectiveness, efficiency, or legitimacy, or the dominant routine simply devours scarce resources leaving no life support for others. In turn, the losing routine may face inattention, relegation to some less significant use, or death.

Several works in organization theory have shed light on routine competition. For example, Burgelman's work on Intel (Burgelman, 1994) provides a detailed account of how routines for microprocessor development were gradually selected over routines for memory development, the former gradually devouring more and more of the firm's scarce manufacturing resources and subsequently becoming Intel's definitive product. Here, the ability of middle managers to focus their attention on external conditions in making resource allocation decisions, rather than on the mantra of established corporate policy, was a key insight into how displacement of one routine by another operated. Importantly, the shift was relatively slow and conflict free, effectively a war of attrition. In this sense the competition was indirect and remarkably Darwinian – the end result of two systems gradually vying for overlapping ecological resources but without direct, head-to-head confrontation. Competition only became noticed well after both routines had existed for some time, with the decision to switch corporate strategy appearing after the shift in behavior. Similarly, Usher and Evans' (1996) study of gasoline chains in Alberta provides a rich account of how one routine for delivering gas to customers (the traditional service station) was gradually overcome by other routines (convenience stores, gas bars, and car washes).

Miner's (1991) work on job deaths similarly explores the machinations of indirect competition among routines. Although the underlying assumption is that, given resource scarcity, jobs are competing against other jobs, Miner focuses on some interesting demographical attributes of jobs in determining which ones will be displaced. For example, she finds age (younger jobs are less likely to survive than older jobs) and job founding-types (once reclassified jobs are particularly resilient while those that are opportunistic, involving newly hired talent, are not) important factors in understanding which jobs tend to survive and which ones do not. A distinguishing feature of this work is the link between individual action and these ecological processes. Miner finds that job holders with greater organizational familiarity, and so greater political resources, are less likely to see their job type disappear. This is a good example of the embeddedness of routines and individuals – while conceptually these can be parsed out, it is often difficult to cleanly separate them when examining ecological processes.

Of course, routine competition will often come in more direct and visible forms. For example, Galunic and Eisenhardt (1996) found intense competition between specific routines. In their study of a large computer corporation, entire divisions often openly competed for business charters (product-market domains of responsibility). Importantly, the competition represented a war of routines: divisions were seen, in essence, as a bundle of routines, distinguished on the basis of their unique competencies. The selection regime in this instance was based on the relative fitness of routines given the emerging market conditions. Individual actions or presence, as in Miner's work, was still important (largely through the General Manager role) but competition rested less on the merits of these individuals than the comparative quality of the routines themselves. Moreover, unlike the outcomes described by Burgelman and Miner, the losing routine-set in this instance did not die but was typically relegated to some other task (divisions were placed in charge of more suitably fitting charters, although typically less prestigious assignments). In other words, routine competition need not always lead to death.

In fact, routines will often compete simply for mind share and attention. In such cases, they may not be alternative ways to do the same thing but fundamentally two different modes of operating. March's work on exploration and exploitation is a good example (1991). Here, both routines are likely to be visible in any organization – it is hard to imagine any organization consisting completely of just exploration or exploitation routines. Nevertheless, competition does exist, and specifically a competition for the attention of the organization. Capacity devoted to exploration will mean a reduction in the capacity devoted to exploitation, and vice versa. A cyclical seesaw battle may emerge between the two, but it is unlikely that the result will be the death of one. This competition may be determined as much by the desires of organizational members to grasp and retain some legitimized identity ("innovators") as by trying to fit the demands of the environment; see also Fox-Wolfgramm et al. (1998).

Finally, work by Tushman and Anderson on dominant designs and technology cycles (Anderson and Tushman, 1990; Tushman and Anderson, 1986) provides another good account of routine competition. The distinguishing feature of these studies is the displacement of one technology or design by another (technologies here represent one or a bundle of routines). While these studies focus mostly at the interorganizational level of analysis, suggesting that novel routines often come from new organizations, incumbents are also capable of replacing their technologies endogenously. Moreover, the distinguishing feature of this displacement is the role of organizational linking mechanisms (Tushman and Murmann, 1998). The argument is that because (a) technologies often have complex linkages, and (b) changes in technological designs or requirements, and especially radical ones, require a reworking of the linkages; firms with effective organizational linkage mechanisms (whether team-based or individual) will be more likely to experience a successful transition between technological routines. In essence, effective routines for sharing information and coordinating opinion and action can help to push subsystem routines to radically change (or disappear in favor of new ones), helping the firm to evolve towards some new technological design.

COMPLEMENTARITY BETWEEN ROUTINES

As Tushman and Anderson's work suggests, routines do more than compete. Bundles of routines may compete against other bundles – the technologies in Tushman and Anderson's work – for example, but within those bundles, routines are complementing one another. More generally, a routine is complemented by another if the other's presence contributes to the focal routine's efficacy, development, and, ultimately, survival. Arguably, this is what organizations try to do: to create synergy by interweaving routines. While complementarity is bound to exist in a trivial sense (if we consider exchanges through the value chain, for example, production and marketing can be said to be complementary), complementarity can be particularly powerful and relevant where variously detailed and nuanced routines are able to coexist but with different degrees and qualities of fitness. The fact of choice in selecting and shaping routines makes complementarity a particularly important managerial issue.

Perhaps the classic work along these lines is Miller and Friesen (1984). This work argues that organizations are, in essence, tightly knit ecologies or, in their terms, configurations of underlying elements. Consistency and complementarity between elements is paramount, often dictated by the environment, and so rewarding. The resulting bonds are also powerful, as seen when tightly connected organizations require change. Often change in such organizations needs to be quantum and systemic, such that multiple elements are altered simultaneously – otherwise, change cannot occur since no single element can change and expect to survive in its altered form, having grown too dependent on neighboring elements. While they do not focus specifically on routines, the variables that they use (information processing capacities, decision making, etc.) are reasonable proxies.

Baron and Kreps (1999) provide useful insights into how complementarity functions in their work on human resource practices. First, complementarity can be technical in nature, such that the outputs of one practice or routine are useful inputs to another. So, a practice of detailed peer review could complement well an incentive scheme that seeks to reward cooperation and teamwork. Complementarity here would consist of some actual exchange between routines, such as transfers of information or knowledge. This can occur in a "steady-state mode," such that transfers are always expected and done in similar fashion (as in the example above). But this exchange can also operate in a "developmental mode," such that the data being transferred leads to the development and otherwise change of the receiving routine. A good example of the latter process is in the case of best practice transfers within large firms, where similar routines (e.g., e-commerce strategies) can be sources of comparative learning (Szulanski, 1996). Second, complementarity can also be conceptual and symbolic, such that the meaning or "message" behind a routine can resonate well with that of another. So, Hewlett-Packard's long-term employment policy resonates well with their routines for intensive and continual training, both practices sending a message of commitment to employees and exhibiting a belief in human development. In either case, the presence of one routine should improve the actual or perceived efficacy of another.

An excellent example of empirical research on routine complementarity comes from Hargadon and Sutton's study of IDEO, a product design firm (1997). Focusing specifically on organizational routines at IDEO, this work presents routines for knowledge acquisition, storage and retrieval, showing how these routines complement one another in generating a steady stream of new inventions and product innovations. Here the complementarity is both technical (acquired concepts become inputs for storage and subsequent retrieval) and conceptual (all three routines emphasize the importance of knowledge exchange and diversity).

Finally, organizations will often have a special class of routines that have a direct impact on the complementarity of other routines. We will call these meta-routines, and they function to order the interaction and exchange amongst elementary routines. A good example comes from Brown and Eisenhardt's (1997) work on continuous change in the computer industry. Arguing that change in these industries is not the result of punctuated events, they describe several ongoing and stable meta-routines that guide other underlying routines (within product development and manufacturing). One is the phenomenon of "semi-structures," which is a process of carefully prescribing links between some underlying routines while leaving other links unprescribed and open to local and temporal interpretation. Arguably, the intelligence of this (mostly cerebral or cognitive) meta-routine is in knowing what links to constrain and which ones to leave alone. A second meta-routine was for creating "links-in-time." This organizational routine attempts to align successive routines temporally as they come to bear on a project, such that a common thread of meaning can be passed along and so align and coordinate the underlying routines. Knowing when to transition and what aspects to pass along between routines was seemingly the centerpiece of this routine. This research does a good job of pointing out that change and development within firms actually depends upon stable and consistent meta-routines.

Others have also described meta-routines whose role is to reconfigure the links between existing routines and practices. Bruderer and Singh's (1996) simulation models address this issue exactly, exploring how alternatively tuned algorithms that determine the combination and quality of routines within a firm will impact organizational fitness. Similarly, in an influential work, Henderson and Clark (1990) make a strong case for understanding the meta-routines that contribute to "architectural innovation;" see also Levy (1994). Indeed, our discussion of meta-routines is not dissimilar to discussions of dynamic capabilities, whose function is largely the development of new and useful capabilities, and often done through a recombination of existing ones; see Galunic and Rodan (1998); Teece et al. (1997). Because these meta-routines are still very abstract and ill-defined, they are an important direction for further research.

SELECTION MECHANISMS

The distinguishing feature of these studies is that routines, whether indirectly and silently or directly and visibly, can put other routines at risk – the risk of being forgotten, relegated to oblivion, or simply terminated. The risk, in other words, of being selected out. There are two key issues relating to this selection: the degree to which organizational performance and the organization's environment drive selection; and the degree to which selection pressures are strong enough that we can comfortably assume that adaptation occurs. Neither is as straightforward empirically as theorists would like.

First, studies show that the selection regime can vary: sometimes the value added to organizational performance of two routines (or bundles of routines) is being compared, other times routines are selected on the basis of their fit with surrounding routines. Nelson and Winter assume a strong role for organizational performance as a selection mechanism: "Thus, profitable firms will grow and unprofitable ones will contract, and the operating characteristics of the more profitable firms therefore will account for a growing share of the industry's activity" (Nelson and Winter, 1982, p. 17). Routines, in other words, are selected on the basis of how well they contribute to organizational performance. This assumption is reflected in theoretical, empirical and modeling work such as Aldrich and Mueller (1982), Haveman (1995) and Bruderer and Singh (1996). Meyer (1994), though, has argued that this assumption is misleading. He notes that an important consequence of the different level and unit of analysis between intraorganizational ecology and its interorganizational counterpart is that internal selection mechanisms must be reckoned with as well as external mechanisms. There is no guarantee that the process of internal selection of routines leads to higher performance. A routine may be selected because it is well adapted to other routines in the organization (as in the case of complementarity within bundles). He gives examples of cases – goal displacement, for example – where the processes of internal selection of routines may lead to the maladaptation of the organization to its environment. Burgelman (1994) echoes this argument in his analysis of Intel. He argues that long-term survival depends on the fit between the internal ecological processes and the external selection pressures felt by the organization as a whole.

Miner (1994, p. 77) takes this one step further and, in so doing, ties it in to the second issue of whether selection pressures are sufficiently strong for adaptation to occur. She argues that "the manger's two primary roles are (1) to adjust the organization's relationship to higher level evolutionary processes . . . and (2) to influence the internal evolutionary process." The manager is responsible, in other words, for ensuring that requisite variety is produced and that internal selection mechanisms are consistent with external ones. It is in this way that intraorganizational ecology has brought the manager back into evolutionary thinking about organizations. Commonly, though, managers fall short in these duties as the literature on trial and error processes of organizational learning describes. Starting with the assumption that routines which are associated with positive outcomes are repeated and those associated with negative outcomes are not, this literature shows that such trial and error does not automatically lead to organizational adaptiveness because, for example, of the problems of superstitious learning (Argyris and Schon, 1978; Miner and Mezias, 1996). As Sitkin (1992) points out, without episodes of clear failure, learning is stunted as the wrong lessons are learned. Further, since organizational causes and effects are often distant in time and space, misattributions are likely (Kuwada, 1998; Senge, 1990) and, again, the wrong routines may be selected out. What's more, we know that in many cases managers are shielded from the consequences of their decisions (e.g., because of the presence of ambiguity or slack (Garud and Van de Ven, 1992)) or are able to shield their organizations from the pressures of selection (e.g., by seeking out positional advantages in the market (Barnett et al., 1994)). And, as Greenwood and Hinings (1996) note, even where a routine is identified as an "error" it will be selected out and replaced only if interests within the organization become associated with a competitive or reformative pattern. It is not enough that a routine be recognized as maladaptive; in other words, there must be an alternative to replace it and the opportunity for that replacement must be recognized. Empirically, in other words, selection pressures are often inadequate in organizations for us to assume that evolution will produce adaptation. This means, as Campbell (1969) noted early on, that organizational scholars are not free to assume that existing forms are perfectly adaptive and work backwards to discover the selection mechanism. And since we cannot assume that organizational performance is driving intraorganizational evolution, the selection mechanism must be determined independently – a much more difficult task, and one of the key challenges facing intraorganizational ecologists.

Finally, while the above research focuses on routines as the proper unit of selection, it is important to note that sometimes a bundle of complementary routines can also be the unit of selection (Aldrich, 1999). The previous section (complementarity of routines) implies as much. The implications for organizational research are significant; if routines survive preferentially because of favorable complementarities, it makes more sense to pursue the sort of research described in the previous section. It also brings intraorganizational ecology closer to organizational ecology (because the firm can be considered as effectively just one large bundle of routines).

REPLICATION PROCESSES

Given that the interaction processes described above presume the existence of a variety of routines, it is important to question where those routines, and where that variety, comes from. But we need to be careful when we talk, for example, about the birth of a routine. Biologists, after all, do not talk about the birth and death of genes. They talk about the birth and death of the organisms for which genes are a blueprint. Births are important events in biological evolution largely because they are, through the processes of crossover and mutation, the most common occasion for variation in genes and because they are the mechanism through which genes are copied. A new organism is born; existing genes are copied and possibly changed. Of course, because in the theory of intraorganizational ecology, creation and evolution are not mutually exclusive, we do consider the birth of newly created routines, but largely the issues here are how routines are reproduced and spread, how they may be altered in the course of reproduction and produce variation, how they die, and the macro-level organizational effects that these processes of reproduction with retention, variation, and selection generate.

REPRODUCTION

There are two themes in the literature concerning the reproduction of routines: that organizations have a tendency to reproduce existing routines rather than create them and that this tendency should not be taken to mean that such reproduction is trivial. In other words, reproducing existing routines is difficult, but still easier than the alternative.

The idea that organizations achieve economies of decision making and implementation by replicating routines dates back to March and Simon (1958). Organizations can more efficiently and effectively do what they have already learned through experience to do. Moreover, the more an organization becomes skilled in a routine and that routine proves itself successful, the more likely it is that the organization will replicate that routine as it becomes taken for granted as the right way of doing things (Amburgey and Miner, 1992; Schein, 1992). Specifically, a routine's chances of being replicated depend upon not just its success *per se*, but on the perceptions of organizational decision makers about its success (i.e., ease of replication and legitimacy of practice become important criteria). This has led to a concern about cases where organizational routines are reproduced even in inappropriate settings (Gersick and Hackman, 1990; Zander and Kogut, 1995). Such situations speak more to the efficiency of replication than eventual effectiveness.

While not denying these efficiencies, Nelson and Winter (1982, p. 118) make clear the importance of recognizing "replication as being a costly, time-consuming process." What makes the replication of routines difficult is first of all their largely tacit component. As Nonaka and Takeuchi (1995) and others have pointed out, following Polanyi (1966), high fidelity replication of tacit knowledge often requires knowledge transfer at the tacit level. Nelson and Winter argue that trying to articulate routines and make them explicit is not always feasible. Rather, the transfer of a routine to a new person is best accomplished by having that individual observe or be actively trained by the incumbent of the role in the old system. Given the weight of evidence that the speed with which an organization can replicate a routine depends largely on how unambiguous, articulable and observable – i.e., how codifiable – is that routine (Lippman and Rumelt, 1982; Rogers, 1983; Szulanski, 1996; Winter, 1987; Zander and Kogut, 1995), the enthusiasm among managers for "knowledge management" systems that will help to codify organizational routines is understandable, though perhaps optimistic.

If the reproduction of routines within an organization is nontrivial, the difficulties only multiply in the case of a routine reproducing itself in a new organization. It is natural that firms might target routines that seem to help other organizations to achieve desirable results such as producing a better product or producing a standard product more cheaply (Nelson and Winter, 1982). Further, institutional theorists (DiMaggio and Powell, 1983; Meyer and Rowan, 1977; Scott, 1987a) point out that organizations have a second, and often more salient, motivation for imitating routines that originate in their institutional context: legitimacy. Institutional theory, in other words, shows how "mimetic isomorphism" – or the reproduction of routines across organizations within an institutional context – is the result not only of market pressures, but also institutional pressures stemming from such sources as regulatory agencies, the state, professional bodies, and general social expectations (Greenwood and Hinings, 1996). More generally, Boyd and Richerson (1985) distinguish between various types of biases that influence which routines are imitated: direct bias (the organization imitates those routines that are most consistent with its existing routines), indirect bias (the organization imitates routines adopted by a role model organization), and frequency-dependent (the organization imitates popular routines); see also Kogut and Zander (1996).

Institutional theorist have often ignored the possibility that such imitation is non-trivial, but ecological models suggest that it is typically even more difficult than intraorganizational reproduction of routine. Researchers have studied both cases where the two firms cooperate in the reproduction process and where they do not. In the former case, so-called "learning alliances" or acquisitions are made to facilitate the reproduction of a routine from one organization to another. The operational issues of making such partnerships work are complicated (Bartlett and Ghoshal, 1995; Haspeslagh and Jemison, 1991) and the focus has been primarily on the "absorptive capacity" of the organization – its ability to "recognize the value of new, external knowledge, assimilate it, and apply it to commercial ends" (Cohen and Levinthal, 1990). The implication is that the ability to imitate routines is itself a learned ability, a meta-routine as discussed above.

Nelson and Winter (1982, p. 123) point out that what distinguishes the case of non-cooperative imitation from cooperative imitation or intraorganizational reproduction is that the "imitator's personnel cannot directly observe what goes on in the imitates'" organization. The implication of this is that it is the outputs of the routine, rather than the instructions for producing those outputs, that can be copied. Blackmore (1999) likens this difference to the difference of trying to copy an origami swan on the basis of seeing the finished product as opposed to being able to watch someone as they fold it, and she uses the biological label Lamarckian inheritance for the former case and Weismannian inheritance for the latter. Fidelity is much higher in the Weismannian case where the instructions – whether tacit or explicit – are being copied. Or, to put it another way, mutation is much more likely as an outcome in the Lamarckian case where reverse engineering is necessary.

VARIATION

Variation in routines occurs when new routines are created. "Newness" is, of course, a slippery concept. The wary consumer's question about laundry detergent applies: is a routine purporting to be "new and improved" actually new (or, for that matter, even an improvement)? It may be impossible to create an airtight boundary for newness (for the same reasons it has proven difficult to classify organizational forms). Nonetheless, this has not stopped organizational theorists from saying something about how "truly" new routines are created. New routines are created largely through modifications of existing routines or the interactions and recombinations of existing routines, i.e., through the interaction processes described above. Much of this work (e.g., Galunic and Rodan, 1998; Henderson and Clark, 1990; Teece et al., 1997) takes its lead from Schumpeter's well worn notion that invention is really a recombination of existing knowledge. These works focus largely on the secondary processes needed to nurture the development of novel routines and resources.

Authors such as Schulz (1998) and Zhou (1993), however, use ecological arguments to make predictions about the rate at which organizations will create brand new routines. Looking specifically at bureaucratic rules, Schulz found evidence against the common wisdom that "bureaucracies frantically breed rules and . . . that rule breeding intensifies as bureaucratization proceeds" (Schulz, 1998, p. 845). Instead, he found that because of the tendency for organizations to expand the scope of existing rules rather than to create new ones, the supply of organizational problems that is amenable to regulation becomes exhausted and that the rate of rule production therefore declines. Looking at the rates of creation of idiosyncratic jobs, Miner (1987) found that this form of organizational improvisation occurs even in firms with a high degree of routinization so long as mission ambiguity or resource uncertainty are present. This echoes Zhou's (1993) finding that periods of environmental turbulence tend to breed novel rules. These results parallel other studies of collective improvisation (Weick, 1998) and suggest that such improvisation can serve as the source of "random variation" in creating new routines (Moorman and Miner, 1998).

DEATH

Routines, however infrequently, do also die. In an intraorganizational setting, we mean by death the extinction of a routine in a particular organization, that it is no longer practiced there. There is relatively little direct empirical research done on the deaths of routines, a sharp contrast to population ecology where organizational deaths are highly studied. Arguably, measuring the death of routines is more complicated than measuring the deaths of organizations because many routines are tacitly held and uncodified. Nevertheless, several studies discussed above have shed some light on how routines die: Miner (1991) on the death of job types; Burgelman (1994) on the death of Intel's memory business and accompanying routines; and Usher and Evans (1996) on the death of traditional service stations in Alberta. Drawing on some of the lessons from these works, we see that to understand routine death we need to go beyond the idea explored above that death occurs through competition with other, better, routines. Specifically, we need to consider three approaches to the question of why routines die: life-cycle arguments, cognitive arguments, and institutional arguments.

Life cycle theories maintain that there is a natural duration for things and that death is simply the last phase in the existence of some entity (Van de Ven and Poole, 1995). Death, in other words, is natural, the consequence of passing time and growth and not always the outcome of competition. Applied to routines, this suggests that many routines are unlikely to enjoy indefinite attention and use but, having had their season, will be concluded. An excellent example comes from recent work by Adler (1995). Studying the life cycles of product development projects, Adler finds that the interdepartmental coordination routines are distinct across the various phases of development (pre-project, product and process design, and manufacturing). A coordination routine is generated, provides some value-added to the development process, but then passes on as the product design enters a new stage of development. In other words, routines enjoy a season but then pass away as the organization (or specific projects in this case) grow and develop new needs. Young, start-up organizations are probably the best context for this form of death. Here, routines developed at the birth of the firm (e.g., routines for soliciting venture capital monies) eventually die as the firm grows and prospers (and routines for normal finance are established).

Routines may also die because of human cognitive limitations coupled with work overload. First, recent research has found that routines are stored in our procedural memory, which is memory "for how things are done that is relatively automatic and inarticulate, and it encompasses cognitive as well as motor activities" (Cohen and Bacdayan, 1994, p. 554; Moorman and Miner, 1998). If routines are embedded in our procedural memory then cognitive overload and time pressures may deteriorate and/or extinguish certain routines. Death occurs as enough individuals are consistently squeezed for attention and cognitive bandwidth. A few abstainers is all it may take to create doubts about the routine, which generates further abstainers or delinquents, which further erodes the integrity of the routine, and so on, until the routine eventually collapses. Examples are all too common. Just think of any well-intentioned cooperative process requiring multi-actor coordination (weekly brown-bag seminars, intranet discussion forums, etc.). While these routines could die for content and competitive reasons, it is highly probable that work overload is an important source. Arguably, more minor or novel routines are likely to suffer death of this sort, as more important routines are usually backed by aids to procedural memory (fiat, sanctions, and fear).

As noted, institutional theory can also help explain deaths, or rather why routines are not likely to die even when they should. In short, routines that are highly institutionalized are less likely to die. Institutionalization here means that the routine acquires a lifelike and possibly sacred meaning (Scott, 1987a), and so even though it may no longer be appropriate to use it is likely to persist. Take, for example, the often told story of the British artillery crews during World War Two who would strangely pause several seconds before firing their motorized weapons. It took an old timer to point out that they were "holding the horses" (Morison, 1966), an act that would have been severely drummed into them in former times and a key part of their firing routine. Routine portions or entire routines without such meaning are less likely to persist under duress – they are more likely to be competed away by other routines, ignored when workload increases, forgotten, or even sensibly terminated when the context changes.

MACRO-LEVEL PATTERNS

In an evolutionary process, the result of the births, deaths, and interactions of routines is change and, in some cases, adaptation, at the organizational level. A key issue that animates the literature both in organizational and biological ecology is whether such change is incremental or punctuated. The word "evolution" is even often used to mean incremental as opposed to radical change: some indication, perhaps, of how pervasive this incrementalist assumption has become in society generally. Tushman and Romanelli (1985), Tushman and Anderson (1986), and Gersick (1991), however, challenge this orthodoxy and propose punctuated equilibrium as a new theory of evolution. Drawing on the work of natural historians such as Eldredge and Gould (1972), they claim that organizations evolve through periods of stability punctuated by reorientations, short periods of discontinuous change. The triggers for such punctuations are hypothesized to be performance pressures (Tushman and Romanelli, 1985) and internal strains or time-based transitions (Gersick, 1988; 1989). It is a measure of the success of this challenge that Brown and Eisenhardt (1997, p. 1) argue that, by proposing the possibility of incremental change, they are challenging the orthodoxy as "the punctuated equilibrium model is in the foreground of academic interest." Hannan and Freeman's (1984) structural inertia theory is largely supportive of the incrementalist camp, although only in a cynical way – they maintain that the pace of change in firm structures may be incremental but largely inadequate to the task of keeping up with the environment.

A slightly different way of viewing these different patterns of change is proposed by Miller and Friesen (1980). Accepting a view echoed by March (1981, p. 563) "organizations are continually changing, routinely, easily, and responsively, but change within them cannot ordinarily be arbitrarily controlled," they argue that the issue is not one of stability versus change or incrementalism versus punctuation, but rather one of momentum and direction. This is a point accepted by the proponents of punctuated equilibrium models: the periods of stability are marked by convergent change, not by the absence of change altogether (Tushman and Romanelli, 1985). Change occurs all the time; in other words, what are rare, and Miller and Friesen focus on, are changes in the direction of that change. Their study of organizational histories provides useful evidence of this view. We would agree with this view and encourage studies into the intelligence mechanisms of routine evolution – in other words, rather than a continued focus on whether change is incremental or punctuated; studies should examine what makes for more intelligent (successful, robust, prescient) changes to organizational routines. This gets back to the issues discussed above about the role of managerial intervention in the selection process, and it also points to an area of future research that is called for in this area. We discuss others in the next section.

Unsolved Issues and Future Research

The map of intraorganizational ecology that we provide above will be too reaching for some and incomplete for others. We believe this reflects a central problem: there is relatively little dialogue and community surrounding the domain, to the point where calling it a domain at all requires a bit of tongue-in-cheek. However exciting and novel the domain may be, it is in dire need of more conscious exchange. In other words, by far the biggest unsolved issue is the exact delineation of the domain. This chapter is a start.

The domain could also stand a fresh infusion of biological thinking, something that researchers have perhaps avoided – as we noted at the beginning of the chapter – because of the controversies surrounding mixing social and physical sciences and have perhaps felt unnecessary because of Campbell's Rule (1969) that it is a generic theory of evolution that is being applied, not a biological one; see also Aldrich (1999). But there is one development in biological evolutionary theory that is of direct relevance to theories of intraorganizational evolution: the recognition of the importance of so-called "inclusive fitness" (Hamilton, 1964) or, as Dawkins (1976) has memorably termed it, "the selfish gene." This is the idea that we take seriously the fact that the true replicators are not organisms but genes. That is, none of us creates a copy of ourselves with our children, what are copied – and more generally what are retained, selected, and varied – are our genes. While usually our genes and the bodies for which they are the blueprints are united in the evolutionary struggle of survival of the fittest, we should not be surprised by seemingly counter-intuitive exceptions such as male preying mantises who have evolved a desire to copulate with females who will decapitate them after orgasm. And we should recognize that space on the chromosome is itself a scarce resource and that genes may compete with their alleles for position (Dawkins, 1976).

For organizational theorists, this suggests considerations at two levels. First, it highlights the importance of the point raised by Meyer (1994) and others mentioned above that we should not expect that victory in the competition among routines within the organization necessarily goes to routines that enhance organizational outcomes. Enhancing organizational success or, more importantly, being seen to enhance those outcomes, is an advantage in the competition for survival, but as we have seen it is far from the only one. Legitimacy or fit with other surrounding routines may in many cases be even more important advantages. Adaptation is at the level of the routine, not necessarily at the level of the organization. Second, it suggests that it may be useful to consider the intraorganizational analog of the phenotype/genotype distinction in biology. It may be useful, in other words, to separate the particular manifestations of a routine – specific instances of routine modes and behaviors being enacted – from the informational component, the blueprint, or what has come to be called after Dawkins (1976) the "memes" of that routine. Recent work examining the possibilities of applying evolutionary frameworks to culture (Blackmore, 1999; Dawkins, 1989; Dennett, 1995) suggest that an interesting next step in the development of intraorganizational ecology may be to consider not only routines, but also their underlying memes and the dynamics of their competition of that scarcest of resources in an information age: human attention.

Within organizations, there has been some work that at least indirectly speaks to memetic issues: Kuwada's (1998) work on strategic learning via the ecology of basic assumptions, and Zander and Kogut (1995), who found that how easy an idea is to imitate is as important as its effects on whether or not it actually is imitated. Rao and Amburgey (1996) hint at an "ecology of ideas" and many people have taken the rhetorical tack when discussing evolution in organizations to frame it as March (1994) did, "The evolution of evolution." But the next step will be to pull what is known today together, to move from rhetorical flourish to empirical grounding as we investigate the implications of memes competing for such scarce commodities as human attention, air time, library shelf-space, consulting work, and course syllabi inclusion. The benefit to intraorganizational ecology will come from the assumption that being useful may not be as much of an asset for a meme in this competition as, say, being supposed to be useful, being memorable and catchy, being in the right place at the right time, or being consistent with other prevailing memes. By drawing in work about the psychology of human attention and memory, we may be able to be more systematic in our analysis of the role that perception and other subjective elements excluded by population ecology necessarily play in intraorganizational ecology. What's more, the relative speed with which memes diffuse and the fact that they inhabit the brains of many people within an organization may offer the potential for quantitative studies of intraorganizational ecology that have been impossible until now.

Finally, while the biological analogy may provide avenues for new investigation, organization theorists need to keep in mind essential differences, areas where the analogy breaks down. Far from being a problem, these are exactly the areas where research into evolutionary dynamics within organizations has the potential to inform general theories of evolution. While Lamarckian inheritance, for example, is ruled out in biological models, it is very real in the case of organizations. As Blackmore (1999) well describes, we need to consider the difference between a routine that is replicated by imitation of its manifestation and one that is replicated by diffusion of its recipe, of its memes. This is like the difference between learning a song by listening to it and trying to repeat what you have heard and learning it by being given the sheet music. The implications for copying fidelity and therefore for variation, are likely significant but have not been studied concretely. They need to be if we are to understand the possibilities and limitations of applying evolutionary models to intraorganizational phenomena.

Connections Across Levels

For all that they originate from the same starting point of a retention, selection, and variation model of change, intraorganizational ecology and population are strikingly different in almost all respects. The obvious difference is the level of analysis. Population ecologists take the individual organization as the unit of analysis (see chapters by Baum and Amburgey, and Rao in this volume). It is the phenotypic expression of a "blueprint" or set of competencies, routines, and assumptions posited to be immutable. Intraorganizational ecology takes individual competencies, routines, and assumptions as its unit of analysis. This means that selection mechanisms are different. In population ecology, it is organizational success and failure that acts to select certain blueprints. In intraorganizational ecology, organizational success and failure are still important, but it is recognized that these are relatively rare occurrences and that other, internal, forms of selection among routines are equally salient. The birth, death, changes, and interaction of routines themselves is the focus of attention.

Population ecology famously denies the importance of managerial agency at the population level. To be fair, as Baum and Amburgey's, and Rao's chapters clearly demonstrates, the field is growing remarkably concerned with entrepreneurship (or births by another name) linking these to the establishment of new organizational forms, which in turn may impact communities. It also does not deny the impact of managerial agency at the organizational level. However, it remains firm in its belief that, for existing organizations, downward causation (the impact of populations on routines) is more powerful than upward causation (the impact of routines on populations). Scholars, it claims, can look at the history of most industries and find considerable organizational 'road kill.' Intraorganizational ecology, in contrast, is explicitly shaped by managerial action at the organizational level. Managers are responsible for maintaining and directing the processes of variation, selection, and retention, and for the express purpose of staving off external selection pressures. Managers are also credited with dreaming up or significantly influencing new populations – Nokia and Hewlett-Packard are two famous examples of companies who, from modest foundations (rubber and forest products and electrical test equipment respectively) helped to craft novel industries where they are now powerful trendsetters (mobile phones and desktop printing respectively). Indeed, the current trend is for large firms to create venture capital environments within their boundaries. Population ecologists might counter, however, that Nokia's and HP's are outliers and not the norm – and there would be some truth in their claim.

Conclusion

In the final analysis, we doubt either camp will ever claim outright victory on the causation issue. More likely, the debate will continue to grow stale if un-nuanced. Indeed, if population ecology is criticized for its equivocality on agency, intraorganizational ecology is complicated by it. Perceptions of the benefits of routines and the recognition and legitimacy of variations become as important as objective characteristics of the organization and its environment for shaping the ecological process. Because of this, it is not surprising that the methods used to study intraorganizational ecology are quite different than those used in population ecology. Whereas the latter is characterized by large-scale quantitative analyses, the former is characterized by detailed and longitudinal studies of particular organizations. Some of the best qualitative work in recent years has contributed to this stream of literature. Nonetheless, the problem now for intraorganizational ecologists is to come up with more rigorous and generalizable insights into how ecological processes construct new routines and, hopefully, make impact at the population level. This is as much an issue of academic skill and ideals as focus, since it will require a modified epistemology in some cases. However, without work of this sort this domain may not be able to shed its reliance on outliers as the foundation for its causation claims.

References

Adler, P. (1995): "Interdepartmental interdependence and coordination: The case of the design/ manufacturing interface," *Organization Science*, 6(2), 147–67.

Aldrich, H. E. (1979): *Organizations and Environments*. Englewood Cliffs, NJ: Prentice-Hall.

Aldrich, H. E. (1999): *Organizations Evolving*. London, UK: Sage.

Aldrich, H. E., and Mueller, S. (1982): "The evolution of organizational forms: Technology, coordination, and control," in B. M. Staw and L. L. Cummings (eds), *Research in Organizational Behavior*, Greenwich, CT: JAI Press, 33–87.

Amburgey, T. L., and Miner, A. S (1992): "Strategic momentum: The effects of repetitive, positional, and contextual momentum on merger activity," *Strategic Management Journal*, 13, 335–48.

Anderson, P., and Tushman, M. (1990): "Technological discontinuities and dominant designs: A cyclical model of technological change," *Administrative Science Quarterly*, 35, 604–33.

Argyris, C., and Schon, D. A. (1978): *Organizational Learning: A Theory of Action Perspective*. Reading, Massachusetts: Addison-Wesley Publishing Company.

Barnett, W. P., Greve, H. R., and. Park, D. Y. (1994): "An evolutionary model of organizational performance," *Strategic Management Journal*, 15, 11–28.

Baron, J. N., and. Kreps, D. M. (1999): "Consistent human resource practices," *California Management Review*, 41(3), 29–53.

Bartlett, C. A., and. Ghoshal, S. (1995): "Changing the role of top management: Beyond systems to people," *Harvard Business Review*, May–June, 132–42.

Baum, J. A. C., and. Singh, J. V. (1994): *Evolutionary Dynamics of Organizations*. Oxford: Oxford University Press.

Blackmore, S. J. (1999): *The Meme Machine*. Oxford: Oxford University Press.

Boyd, R., and. Richerson, P. J. (1985): *Culture and the Evolutionary Process*. Chicago: University of Chicago Press.

Brown, S. L., and. Eisenhardt, K. M. (1997): "The art of continuous change: Linking complexity theory and time-paced evolution in relentlessly shifting organizations," *Administrative Science Quarterly*, 42(1), 1–34.

Bruderer, E., and Singh, J. V. (1996): "Organizational evolution, learning, and selection: A genetic-algorithm-based model," *Academy of Management Journal*, 39(5), 1322–49.

Burgelman, R. A. (1983): "A process model of internal corporate venturing in the diversified firm," *Administrative Science Quarterly*, 28, 223–44.

Burgelman, R. A. (1991: "Intraorganizational ecology of strategy making and organizational adaptation: Theory and field research," *Organizational Science*, 2(3), 239–62.

Burgelman, R. A. (1994): "Fading memories: A process theory of strategic business exit in dynamic environments," *Administrative Science Quarterly*, 39(1), 24–56.

Campbell, D. T. (1969): "Variation and selective retention in socio-cultural evolution," *General Systems*, 16, 69–85.

Campbell, D. T. (1975): "On the conflicts between biological and social evolution and between psychology and moral tradition," *American Psychologist*, 30, 1103–26.

Cohen, M. D., and Bacdayan, P. (1994): "Organizational routines are stored as procedural memory: Evidence from a laboratory study," *Organization Science*, 5(4), 554–68.

Cohen, W. M., and Levinthal, D. A. (1990): "Absorptive capacity: A new perspective on learning and innovation," *Administrative Science Quarterly*, 35, 128–52.

Dawkins, R. (1976): *The Selfish Gene*. Oxford: Oxford University Press.

Dawkins, R. (1989): *The Extended Phenotype: The Long Reach of the Gene*. Oxford: Oxford University Press.

Dennett, D. C. (1995): *Darwin's Dangerous Idea*. New York: Touchstone, Simon and Schuster.

DiMaggio, P., and Powell, W. W. (1983): "The iron cage revisited: Institutional isomorphism and collective rationality in organizational fields," *American Sociological Review*, 48, 147–60.

Eldredge, N., and Gould, S. J. (1972): "Punctuated equilibria: An alternative to phyletic gradualism," in T. J. Schopf (ed.), *Models in Paleobiology*, San Francisco: Freeman, Cooper & Co., 82–115.

Fox-Wolfgramm, S. J., Boal, K. B, and Hunt, J. G. (1998): "Organizational adaptation to institutional change: A comparative study of first order change in prospector and defender banks," *Administrative Science Quarterly*, 43, 87–126.

Galunic, D. C., and Eisenhardt K. M. (1996): "The evolution of intracorporate domains: Divisional charter losses in high technology, multidivisional corporations," *Organization Science*, 7(3), 255–82.

Galunic, D. C., and Rodan, S. (1998): "Resource recombinations in the firm: Knowledge structures and the potential for Schumpeterian innovation," *Strategic Management Journal*, 19(12), 1193–1201.

Garud, R., and Van de Ven, A. H (1992): "An empirical evaluation of the internal corporate venturing process," *Strategic Management Journal*, 13, 93–109.

Gersick, C. J. G. (1988): "Time and transition in work teams: Toward a new model of group development," *Academy of Management Journal*, 31, 9–41.

Gersick, C. J. G. (1989): "Marking time: Predictable transitions in task groups," *Academy of Management Journal*, 22, 274–310.

Gersick, C. J. G. (1991): "Revolutionary change theories: A multilevel exploration of the punctuated equilibrium paradigm," *Academy of Management Review*, 16(1), 10–36.

Gersick, C. J. G., and Hackman, J. R. (1990): "Habitual routines in task performing groups," *Organizational Behavior and Human Decision Processes*, 47, 65–97.

Greenwood, R., and Hinings, C. R. (1996): "Understanding radical organizational change: Bringing together the old and the new institutionalism," *Academy of Management Review*, 21, 1022–54.

Hamilton, W. D. (1964): "The genetical evolution of social behavior," *Theoretical Biology*, 7, 1–52.

Hannan, M. T., and Freeman, J. H. (1984): "Structural inertia and organizational change," *American Sociological Review*, 49, 149–64.

Hargadon, A., and Sutton, R. I. (1997): "Technology brokering and innovation in a product development firm," *Administrative Science Quarterly*, 42, December, 716–49.

Haspeslagh, P. C. and Jemison D. B. (1991): *Managing Corporate Diversification*. New York, NY: The Free Press.

Haveman, H. A. (1995): "The demographic metabolism of organizations: Industry dynamics, turnover, and tenure distributions," *Administrative Science Quarterly*, 40, 586–618.

Henderson, R., and Clark, K. (1990): "Architectural innovation: The reconfiguration of existing product technologies and the failure of established firms," *Administrative Science Quarterly*, 35, 9–30.

Kogut, B., and Zander, U. (1996): "What firms do? Coordination, identity, and learning," *Organization Science*, 7(5), 502–18.

Kuwada, K. (1998): "Strategic learning: The continuous side of discontinuous strategic change," *Organization Science*, 9, 719–36.

Levy, D. (1994): "Chaos theory and strategy: Theory, application, and managerial implications," *Strategic Management Journal*, 15, 167–78.

Lippman, S. A., and Rumelt, R. P. (1982): "Uncertain imitability: An analysis of interfirm differences in efficiency under competition," *Bell Journal of Economics*, 13, 418–438.

McKelvey, B. (1982): *Organizational Systematics: Taxonomy, Evolution, Classification*. Berkeley: University of California Press.

McKelvey, W., and Aldrich, H. (1983): "Populations, natural selection, and applied organizational science," *Administrative Science Quarterly*, 28, 101–28.

March, J. G. (1981): "Footnotes to organizational change," *Administrative Science Quarterly*, 26, 563–77.

March, J. G. (1991): "Exploration and exploitation in organizational learning," *Organization Science*, 2(1), 71–87.

March, J. G. (1994): "The evolution of evolution," in J. A. C. Baum and J. V. Singh (eds), *Evolutionary Dynamics of Organizations*, Oxford: Oxford University Press, 39–49.

March, J. G., and Simon, H. A. (1958): *Organizations*. New York: Wiley.

Meyer, J. W., and Rowan, B. (1977): "Institutional organizations: Formal structure as myth and ceremony," *American Journal of Sociology*, 83, 340–63.

Meyer, M. W. (1994): "Turning evolution inside the organization," in J. A. C. Baum and J. V. Singh (eds), *Evolutionary Dynamics of Organizations*, Oxford: Oxford University Press, 109–16.

Miller, D., and Friesen, P. H. (1980): "Momentum and revolution in organizational adaptation," *Academy of Management Journal*, 23, 591–614.

Miller, D., and Friesen, P. H. (1984): *Organizations: A Quantum View*. Englewood Cliffs, NJ: Prentice-Hall.

Miner, A. S. (1987): "Idiosyncratic jobs in formalized organizations," *Administrative Science Quarterly*, 32, 327–51.

Miner, A. S. (1990): "Structural evolution through idiosyncratic jobs," *Organization Science*, 1(2), 195–205.

Miner, A. S. (1991): "Organizational evolution and the social ecology of jobs," *American Sociological Review*, 56(6), 772–85.

Miner, A. S. (1994): "Seeking adaptive advantage: Evolutionary theory and managerial action," in J. A. C. Baum and J. V. Singh (eds), *Evolutionary Dynamics of Organizations*, Oxford: Oxford University Press: 76–89.

Miner, A. S., and Mezias, S. J. (1996): "Ugly duckling no more: Pasts and futures of organizational learning research," *Organization Science*, 7(1), 88–99.

Moorman, C., and Miner, A. S. (1998): "Organizational improvisation and organizational memory," *Academy of Management Review*, 23(4), 698–723.

Morison, E. E. (1966): *Men, Machines, and Modern Times*. Cambridge, MA: MIT Press.

Nelson, R. R., and Winter, S. G. (1982): *An Evolutionary Theory of Economic Change*. Cambridge, MA: The Belknap Press of Harvard University Press.

Nonaka, I., and Takeuchi, H. (1995): *The Knowledge-Creating Company*. New York, NY: Oxford Press.

Polanyi, M. (1966): *The Tacit Dimension*. New York: Doubleday.

Rao, H., and Amburgey, T. L. (1996): "Organizational ecology: Past, present, and future directions," *Academy of Management Journal*, 39(5), 1265–86.

Rogers, E. (1983): *The Diffusion of Innovation*. New York: Free Press.

Schein, E. (1992): *Organizational Culture and Leadership*. San Francisco: Jossey-Bass.

Schulz, M. (1998): "Limits to bureaucratic growth: The density dependence of organizational rule births," *Administrative Science Quarterly*, 43, 845–76.

Scott, W. R. (1987a): "The adolescence of institutional theory," *Administrative Science Quarterly*, 32, 493–511.

Scott, W. R. (1987b): *Organizations-Rational, Natural and Open Systems*, 2nd edn. Englewood Cliffs, NJ: Prentice-Hall.

Senge, P. M. (1990): *The Fifth Discipline*. New York, NY: Currency and Doubleday.

Sitkin, S. B. (1992): "Learning through failure: The strategy of small losses," *Research in Organizational Behavior*, 14, 231–66.

Szulanski, G. (1996): "Exploring internal stickiness: Impediments to the transfer of best practice within the firm," *Strategic Management Journal*, 17, Winter, 27–44.

Teece, D. J., Pisano, G., and Shuen, A. (1997): "Dynamic capabilities and strategic management," *Strategic Management Journal*, 18(7), 509–33.

Tushman, M., and Romanelli, E. (1985): "Organizational evolution: A metamorphosis model of convergence and reorientation," in B. M. Staw and R. I. Sutton (eds), *Research in Organizational Behavior*, Greenwich, CN: JAI Press, 171–222.

Tushman, M. L., and Anderson, P. (1986): "Technological discontinuities and organizational environments," *Administrative Science Quarterly*, 31, 439–65.

Tushman, M. L., and Murmann, J. P. (1998): "Dominant designs, technology cycles, and organizational outcomes," *Research in Organizational Behavior*, 20, 231–66.

Usher, J. M., and Evans, M. G. (1996): Life and death along gasoline alley: Darwinian and Lamarckian processes in a differentiating population," *Academy of Management Journal*, 39(5), 1428–66.

Van de Ven, A. H., and Poole, M. S. (1995): "Explaining development and change in organizations," *Academy of Management Review*, 20(3), 510–40.

Weick, K. E. (1969): *The Social Psychology of Organizing*. Reading, MA: Addison-Wesley.

Weick, K. E. (1979): *The Social Psychology of Organizing*, 2nd edn. New York, NY: Random House.

Weick, K. E. (1998): "Improvisation as a mindset for organizational analysis," *Organization Science*, 9, 543–55.

Wilson, E. O. (1975): *Sociobiology: The New Synthesis*. Cambridge, MA: Harvard University Press.

Winter, S. G. (1987): "Knowledge and competence as strategic assets," in D. J. Teece (ed.), *The Competitive Challenge: Strategies for Industrial Innovation and Renewal*, Cambridge: Ballinger, 159–84.

Zander, U., and B. Kogut (1995): "Knowledge and the speed of the transfer and imitation of organizational capabilities: An empirical test," *Organization Science*, 6(1), 76–92.

Zhou, X. (1993): "The dynamics of organizational rules," *American Journal of Sociology*, 98(5), 1134–66.

Chapter Four

Intraorganizational Evolution

MASSIMO WARGLIEN

Intraorganizational evolution (iOE) is a relatively new, emergent area of research. Although evolutionary metaphors have often surfaced in organization theory, attempts to analyze the evolutionary dynamics unfolding within organizations have been quite sparse and systematic only in recent years. The basic concepts and tools of iOE are thus still in the process of being shaped. As a subject of analysis, iOE is the set of processes through which intraorganizational entities of different types (e.g. routines, jobs, formal rules) reproduce and modify themselves, and change their relative frequency in populations of individuals carrying them. As a theoretical perspective, it is the attempt to apply the lens of evolutionary thinking to the observation and understanding of these processes. As it often happens, the object and the theoretical perspective are interdependent, and contribute to defining each other.

Despite its relative recentness, agreement on a core set of assumptions has quickly emerged. It would be too strong to claim that most studies on iOE fully rely on all of those postulates, but it is fair to say that they all build upon at least some of these assumptions, and are broadly consistent with the others. All these core assumptions reflect well-established ideas in the broader arena of evolutionary theories; the first two define minimal conditions allowing one to speak of an evolutionary process, while the remaining two qualify the nature of organizational evolution.

1 The "Malthusian" assumption: there are intraorganizational populations subject to selective pressures.
2 The "Darwinian" assumption: there are self-replicating entities subject to variation; fitter variants diffuse at faster rates than less fit ones.
3 The "hierarchical evolution" assumption: intraorganizational evolution is inserted in a nested hierarchy of levels of evolutionary processes.
4 The "cultural evolution" assumption: processes of replication, diffusion and variation of replicators, as well as most selective pressures, are cultural in nature.

These four assumptions serve to circumscribe the area of inquiry and distinguish it from the looser metaphorical uses of evolution so common in the organization and management literature. And, they are sufficient to foster questions and address issues that are still to a large extent open in organization science.

The Malthusian Assumption: Intraorganizational Selection

The "Malthusian" assumption is fundamental in positing that selection, one of the basic components of evolutionary processes, is at work. It focuses on ecological processes of competitive (but also potentially mutualistic) interactions within organizations.

The core concept here is that of selection, but the main operational definitions are those of population and vital events. Populations are usually defined as collections of individuals (or entities) that depend on a same environmental set of (scarce) resources. In general, it is also required that populations have a rather homogeneous character. The definition of a unitary character of the population can be rooted in the organizational "genetics" of the population (the 'Darwinian assumption'); however, most of the time purely conventional classifications prevail – an exception is McKelvey (1982). The existence of selective pressures is checked indirectly, mostly through the analysis of death and birth events within the population, as related to intra-specific variables (e.g. population density), inter-specific variables (e.g. abundance of predators) and other environmental factors (i.e. environmental change). Thus, a pragmatically useful definition of an intraorganizational population would have to include entities that have well-defined vital events (e.g. birth and death), consume (and potentially produce) resources from a common pool, and have unitary character.

There have been different attempts to define intraorganizational populations. In a sense, there is a problem of abundance. It is not difficult to single out populations of potential interest. An organization can be seen as an ecosystem that hosts an amazing variety of populations. Human populations are obvious candidates: patients accepted in psychiatric hospitals, students enrolled in universities, employees in bureaucratic organizations are all legitimate study populations: they compete for scarce organizational resources and have often clearly definable organizational life events (e.g. entry/exit). However, evolutionary research has mostly focused on other kinds of entities, usually characterized by a more proper organizational identity. Examples include populations of administrative rules (Zhou, 1993; Schulz, 1998), formal jobs (Miner, 1991), strategic initiatives (Burgelman, 1983; 1991), or development projects (Warglien, 1995). These entities define populations whose dynamics are affected by density, inter-specific competition, and other classical ecological effects.

In general, these studies provide examples of the viability of a selection perspective on intraorganizational populations. In particular, most support the existence of selective pressures, as revealed by density-dependence effects, although often mediated by the effects of different kind of heterogeneity.

THE ECOLOGY OF ORGANIZATIONAL RULES

One of the most interesting and successful attempts to study intraorganizational populations is research on populations of organizational rules (Zhou, 1993; Schulz,

1998). The study of "rule ecologies" has many appealing features, and provides an excellent illustration of intraorganizational "Malthusianism." Individuals are well-defined entities that have formal identities and formally recorded vital events. For example, a rule is born when a new rule document is put in force; it is revised when provisions are formally added or deleted from existing rules; it is suspended when it is removed and no successor takes it place. Populations are defined as collections of rules that apply to different organizational areas of activity – for example, in a University, administrative rules and academic rules. Systems of organizational rules are inherently interesting in themselves as building blocks of bureaucracy; thus, ecological properties can be plotted against the background of classic theories of bureaucracy (Weber, 1978) or more recent theories of rule-based organizational learning (Levitt and March, 1988).

Although populations of organizational rules are very neatly defined, the notion of their resource niche is less intuitive and direct. Schulz (1998) suggests that rules are bred by problems, and that the finiteness of organizational problem spaces places a limit on bureaucratic rule growth. Schulz also suggests that additional limits to rules generation operate on the "supply side": the allocation of the attention of rule makers, their jurisdictional bounds, and so on; his analysis, however, is mostly concentrated on the "demand side."

Schulz's main prediction is that rules foundings exhibit negative density-dependence: that is, that crowding of the problem space increasingly limits the rate of birth of new rules. Studying nearly a century of rule production in an important private North American University, Schulz finds that the rate of rules productions does indeed decline with the number of rules in the system. A second important prediction is that populations of rules that face different problem environments will have different ecological dynamics. In the populations of university rules studied by Schulz and Zhou, it is possible to identify and study subpopulations defined according to thematic criteria that reflect different problem environments, e.g. personnel rules, accounting rules, organization charts, etc. Schulz finds that sub-populations located at the interface between the organization and its environment experience higher founding rates, consistent with the idea that these areas are more generous in their problem supply. Other areas with high birth rates are those with diffuse agency problems (e.g. personnel rules) and those that have a heterogeneous problem-environment.

Although the characterization of the carrying capacity of the environment in terms of problem supply contributes to an explanation for why founding rates should be affected by the density of the population (saturation of the problem space), this conception of the carrying capacity for rules is not equally helpful in explaining why rules should be suspended or revised. Indeed, even after a problem disappears, many of the rules germane to that problem can survive without consuming any resource, and the main pressure they face after being born is competition from more effective solutions (i.e., rules) to a same problem. As problems disappear, so does the pressure of competing solutions, however. Thus, one may expect that rules ecologies can be more successfully studied on the side of the birth process.

The Darwinian Assumption: From Ecology to Evolution Through Replicators

Organizational genetics involves the study of self-replicating entities, whose reproduction rate is affected by selective pressure and whose replicable content is open to change over time. Defining and analyzing such 'genealogical' entities and the processes affecting their reproduction moves us from the domain of ecology into the domain of evolution.

The search for organizational replicators invariably characterizes all efforts to apply evolutionary ideas to intraorganization al phenomena. Once more, candidates abound. The most commonly studied intraorganizational replicators are listed here:

- Double interacts (Weick, 1969): behaviors of one person are contingent on the behaviors of another person – the minimal unit of collective action
- Routines (Nelson and Winter, 1982): regular, predictable, automatic collective behaviors
- Comps (McKelvey, 1982): productive and organizing competences
- Rules and procedures (Levitt and March, 1988)
- Strategies (Axelrod and Cohen, 2000): how agents in a population respond to their environment and pursue their goals

Taken together with selective dynamics, reproductive processes generate a basic cycle that Campbell (1965) referred to as the (blind) variation-selection-retention model. Of course, there are constraints in bringing together Malthusian and Darwinian processes. The most critical of these is that the units of ecological analysis be aligned with the characterization of self-reproducing genealogical entities comprising them. Individuals, populations and "genes" must be defined so that individuals in a population are carriers of genetic information, and the genetic information, in turn, provides a basis for defining the boundaries of the population. Although this may seem a rather elementary constraint, it is sufficiently stringent to make empirically interesting examples satisfying it difficult to find. As a result, ecological and evolutionary empirical studies are still quite disjoint (Baum and Singh, 1994).

To date, the "routines" at the center of Nelson and Winter's (1982) influential *Evolutionary Theory of Economic Change* represents one of the most successful attempts to capture "organizational genes," and their work provides an excellent illustration of attempts to translate evolutionary concepts into the organizational domain; see also McKelvey (1982).

What is a routine? Nelson and Winter conceptualize routines as a general term for "all regular and predictable behavioral patterns of firms" (Nelson and Winter, 1982, p. 14). The emphasis falls on the automatic, repetitive features of behavior in order to emphasize differences between routines and rationally deliberated actions. Nelson and Winter stress the tacit nature of knowledge and skills embedded in routines, providing a cognitive alternative to the explicit, calculative (neo)classical homo economicus.

In Nelson and Winter's view, the behavior of most large and complex organizations can be well approximated by the bundle of routines that they have developed and acquired. Routines tend to be stable enough to provide a good analog to the role that genes play in modern evolutionary biology (i.e., a vehicle for information transmission). The basic formulation of their theory follows a standard evolutionary scheme, in which routines are treated as stable entities that reproduce themselves across time and space at rates dependent on their relative fitness, and change through processes of recombination and mutation.

Stability is assured by organizational activities of routine control. Routine replication, however, is a process that can take shape at different levels. Simplifying, there can be both intraorganizational reproduction of routines (like in replicating the routines of an old plant in a new one) and inter-organizational reproduction (as in the case of imitation of successful routines by competitors).

Mutation is assured by control lapses in the process of reproducing routines. However, variation is also assured by processes of Schumpeterian recombination of pre-existing routines that are used as building blocks of new ones. Nelson and Winter claim that "reliable routines of well-understood scope provide the best components for new combinations" (Nelson and Winter, 1982, p. 131). In this way, past successful experience is preserved at the core of the innovation process.

Of course, Nelson and Winter are fully aware of the risks of a metaphorical abuse of the notion of organizational genes, and provide many cautions in their "user instructions" (1982, pp. 134–6). The suggestion that routines are the organizational DNA conveys the sense that routines are *the* organizational replicator, at the price of hiding the great diversity of structures undergoing reproduction in organizations and the fundamental diversity of their reproductive processes. To capture this diversity, Winter recently proposed to broaden the notion of routine by introducing a concept of "quasi-genetic traits", defined as "any trait that remains approximately constant in the organization long enough for significant feedback to accumulate at a level where outcomes are tested by an environment" (Cohen et al., 1996). Such traits encompass routines in a narrow sense, as well as rules of thumbs, heuristics and strategies, and paradigms or cognitive frameworks. It is worth noting that this articulation is mainly *cognitive*, in that it relies on the different nature of the cognitive processes underlying each kind of trait.

TACIT KNOWLEDGE AND CAPABILITIES REPLICATION

Empirical studies of routines have privileged issues related to the nature of knowledge embedded in routines. Some of the most interesting results have been obtained in laboratory research. Cohen and Bacdayan (1994) have shown how pairs of subjects could learn in the lab interlocked task performance patterns that displayed important features of organizational routines. Experimental subjects had to learn under efficiency pressure a sequence of coordinated moves in a series of similar (but not identical) card games with asymmetric information. Cohen and Bacdayan's analysis of the effects of novelty (changes in game configuration) and memory decay on learned sequences of actions support the view that routines are stored in procedural memory – that part of memory which is closely related to the tacit component of human knowledge. Replicating and extending Cohen and Bacdayan's experiment, Egidi and Narduzzo (1997), obtained analogous results and also demonstrated how routines create path-dependence and generate behavioral lock-in in novel situations (subjects tended to replicate in new task environments behavioral repertoires learned in previous rounds of the experiment, without adapting to the features of the new task).

Important results have also been achieved in field studies as well. An interesting example is the analysis by Zander and Kogut (1993, 1995) of the transfer of knowledge within multinationals. In a study on the international transfer of 44 major innovations in Swedish industrial firms, Kogut and Zander have conduced a questionnaire research, targeted on project engineers knowledgeable of the history of such major innovations. In particular, they have looked at the transfer of the capability to manufacture products as a basic process of replication of organizational "genetic information." They have tried to identify the nature of such capability and the implications of its nature for fundamental issues such as the timing of reproduction and organizational boundaries.

Zander and Kogut, drawing on Rogers (1980) and Winter (1987), have operationalized three dimensions underlying the tacitness of productive knowledge:

- *Codifiability* capturing the extent to which knowledge is captured by documents and explicit records
- *Teachability* related to the ease of teaching productive knowledge to workers
- *Complexity* defined in terms of intensity of interactions between components of an activity

On the ground of such operationalization, Zander and Kogut (1995) have shown that tacitness affects the reproduction process of manufacturing knowledge. In particular, codifiability and teachability appear to speed significantly the transfer of innovation. Since codifiability and teachability are negatively correlated to tacitness, the study confirms that tacitness implies higher levels of knowledge "stickiness".

More fundamentally, Zander and Kogut (1993) illustrate how tacitness affects organizational boundaries in the growth process. The more tacit the manufacturing knowledge, the more likely is its transfer to a wholly owned subsidiary of the innovating firm. In other words, tacit knowledge is associated to the internal growth of the firm. This provides support to Nelson and Winter's (1982) thesis that tacit knowledge tends to be at the core of the idiosyncratic capabilities that characterize an organization's competitive advantage. Zander and Kogut's studies provide a comparison of the relative effectiveness of evolutionary and transaction cost economics explanations for organizational boundaries. Although the two theories are not necessarily incompatible as far as issues of transfer of knowledge are involved, transaction costs theories clearly emphasize market failures as reasons for the internal transfer of knowledge, while evolutionary theories emphasize the nature of capability reproduction processes as the source of internalization of growth. Zander and Kogut (1993) claim that their data clearly support the second view: ownership advantages in replication processes, not market imperfections, explain organizational boundaries of the firm.

The Hierarchical Evolution Assumption: Nested Processes

Processes of organizational evolution unfold at different levels, nested into each other (Baum and Singh, 1994). The concept of a multiplicity of nested evolutionary processes is often referred to as "hierarchical evolution."

Conceiving organizational selection as hierarchical comes quite naturally. Organizations are themselves comprised of nested entities over which selection exerts its pressure. For example, in a divisional organization, new product development projects are selected within divisions (Burgelman, 1983). Divisions can be disbanded or can lose their charters (Galunic and Eisenhardt, 1996). The organization itself also constitutes an entity subject to selection (Hannan and Freeman, 1989). Furthermore, higher levels of aggregation (e.g. communities of organizations) can be considered as legitimate targets of selective processes (Barnett and Carroll, 1987).

Self-reproducing entities can also be thought as forming hierarchical structures. Nelson and Winter (1992) suggest the existence of different kinds of "metaroutines" operating on lower level ones. For example, higher level replication routines may govern the process of lower level routines reproduction and diffusion within an organization. Furthermore, entire bundles of routines may be reproduced when entire organizational units are replicated (e.g. in a manufacturing transplant).

However, this hierarchy of self-reproducing entities (Baum and Singh's, 1994 "genealogical hierarchy") need not necessarily match the hierarchy of selection levels. It can be conjectured that most replicators are to be found at the level of organizational genetics, while they are much less clearly definable at higher levels of aggregation. The simple fact that a set of competences is shared by a population of organizations (McKelvey, 1982) doesn't necessarily imply that these competences are entities of different level from competences that are more specific to a single organization – they may just be more diffused. However, a conspicuous variety of levels can be detected looking at reproductive processes instead of reproducing entities. For example, routines can be replicated within organizations (e.g. through transfer to new plants) or between organizations of a same population (e.g. through imitation) or even between organizations of different populations (e.g. again through imitation).

A central challenge of hierarchical approaches to organizational evolution is to understand how processes at different levels relate to each other. One critical theme is whether lower level entities are selected in ways that favor higher-level entities survival and reproduction. Although coherence between internal selection mechanisms and external selective pressures is clearly a goal of organizations' management (Burgelman, 1991), its achievement shouldn't be taken for granted. As the result of factors as diverse as goal displacement, agency problems, or institutional constraints, selection processes at lower levels may be on average unrelated (and occasionally dysfunctional) to higher-level evolutionary success (Meyer, 1994). From this point of view, a hierarchical framework provides an appropriate context for the classical debate on organizational adaptation vs. inertia: both properties can be more properly understood as the organization-level effect of underlying intraorganizational processes.

Furthermore, the hierarchical framework can help to reframe the debate on the continuous vs. discontinuous nature of organizational change. Discontinuous, punctuated change (Tushman and Romanelli, 1985; Sastry, 1997) at higher levels may result from the accumulation of more gradualist processes of evolution at lower hierarchical levels. Warglien (1995) explores through computer simulation how hierarchical selection generates "punctuated" change.

Hierarchical Evolution in a Population of Strategic Initiatives

Robert Burgelman's (1983, 1991) research on strategy making, internal venturing and strategic initiatives provides rich field study insight into the nesting of evolutionary processes within large corporations. Drawing on interviews, the analysis of internal organizational sources and longitudinal observation, Burgelman has observed the unfolding of new internal venturing initiatives in a major industrial organization and Intel's evolution from a memory company to a microcomputer company.

Burgelman views organizations as ecologies of strategic initiatives, struggling for the organization's resources to grow. He analyzes how processes of variation, retention and selection occurring in such ecologies shape the higher level adaptive response of organizations and redefine its strategy over time. His framework stresses the interactions between two basic intraorganizational evolutionary processes: induced and autonomous.

The induced process maintains organizational coherence by leveraging the lessons of experience. It is driven not only by an organization's strategy but also by the internal selective mechanisms that direct the allocation of resources and determine the structure of incentives. Variation is directed and channeled by the strategic and structural context inside the organization. In a detailed study of Intel, Burgelman (1991) shows how the alignment of internal selection mechanisms with the selective pressures in the environment enhances the ability of induced processes to promote organizational growth and survival.

Autonomous processes simultaneously emphasize internal variation and the exploration of new routines and environmental niches. They are not guided by the existing strategy but develop outside the induced internal selective context, and emphasize variation processes and the discovery of new opportunities for future reorientation. And, in contrast to induced processes, which benefit from the coupling of internal and environmental selection criteria, autonomous processes benefit from organizational slack (Cyert and March, 1963), loose coupling (Weick, 1976), and failures of control (Nelson and Winter, 1982). Burgelman's (1991) analysis of Intel focuses on two levels of evolutionary dynamics – the intraorganizational one (operational-level strategic initiatives) and the organizational one (organization-level strategies). His earlier work (Burgelman, 1983) on internal corporate venturing, however, shows a greater stratification of selection processes, with new internal ventures "escalating" the hierarchical ladders of the intraorganizational ecology as they grow. An important feature of organizations emerging from Burgelman's earlier work is that selection mechanisms are often quite different as one moves from lower to higher levels of the intraorganizational ecology, putting the emphasis on different performance dimensions and legitimation processes. Internal selection processes matter especially in the earlier phases, while market pressures are more crucial in subsequent phases of strategic forcing and strategic building. As a result, mortality of new ventures is often located at the transition between such different selective environments (Burgelman, 1983).

The Cultural Evolution Assumption: Artifacts, Language, and Apprenticeship

Despite the widespread use of genetic metaphors, intraorganizational evolution is a process of change in the frequencies of traits that are reproduced and transmitted in non-genetic ways – through individual learning, imitation, apprenticeship, instruction and other cultural transmission processes. Thus, organizational evolution ultimately depends on the nature of such cultural processes of reproduction and transmission. As the literature on cultural evolution has clarified (Cavalli-Sforza and Feldman, 1981; Boyd and Richerson, 1985), processes of cultural transmission show significant analogies with the mechanisms of natural evolution but may differ on substantial aspects. For example, deep analogies can be found in the similarity of the pattern of diffusion of an innovation with the diffusion of a new fitter trait in a population (Cavalli-Sforza and Feldman, 1981). At the same time, while transmission of traits in nature happens only from one generation to the following (vertical transmission), and is constrained to happen between parents and their offspring, in cultural evolution – as compared to the biological one – diffusion of traits follows different, less constrained paths, that may result in a different pace and quality of the evolutionary process. Not only cultural traits can be transmitted to non-offspring, but also diffusion may be unconstrained by generational precedence (the older can learn from the younger, or there can be intra-generational diffusion).

The emphasis on the cultural nature of organizational evolution brings naturally into focus the role of artifacts, language and apprenticeship in the transmission process – three classical objects of cultural analysis.

Cultural evolution is intimately connected to the use of artifacts as a form of social memory. Tools and objects embed in their functionality and even in their shapes and affordances useable knowledge about the world. This is recognized in the literature on organizational evolution. For example, the role of artifacts as carriers of "genetic information" is a central theme in the concept of routines: Nelson and Winter often refer to plant layouts, equipment and other physical features of the working environment as storage devices for organizational routines. Analysis of learning curves – see for example Epple et al. (1991) – confirms that manufacturing artifacts embody significant cumulative experience acquired through learning-by-doing, although clearly not all of it.

Despite the great relevance accorded by authors such as March and Simon (1958) and Arrow (1974) to organizational codes as (often organization-specific) forms of knowledge storage, little or none exists on the evolutionary role of language in intraorganizational diffusion. Despite such lack of empirical research, it is clear that language plays a key role in assuring that individual knowledge can be shared and the results of experience can be transmitted and survive its original carriers. Consider the straightforward example of the diffusion of best practices. Best-practice diffusion is built on the assumption that experience generates successful routines to be reproduced and diffused. Diffusion of such successful routines invariably requires a large effort to set up a "technology of replication" process including

(a)   learning a language within which to encode successful routines
(b)   creating cognitive artifacts that can be diffused (work-flow charts or other replicable representations)

(c) translating the high level description contained in the cognitive artifact into actual practice, generating a new routine adapted to the new context; see Hutchins and Hazelhurst (1991) for a similar conceptualization of the role of language and learning in the cultural evolution process).

All three steps clearly imply the use, creation and maintenance of language, which seems to be the most underinvestigated factor in intraorganizational diffusion.

Apprenticeship has received increasing attention as a result of ethnographic studies of organizational learning in the workplace (Orr, 1990) which reveal that cultural transmission of skills and productive knowledge in organizations occurs not through the learning of specific practices, but instead through becoming members of communities of practice (Lave and Wenger, 1991; Brown and Duguid, 1991). Howard Aldrich (1999) recently suggested an evolutionary interpretation of communities of practice as emergent entities, which are shaped by a multitude of variation and selective retention processes operating on information, cognitive schemata of members and social ties. These processes sharpen the boundaries of communities, defining their identity while at the same time creating new entities over which selection can exert its pressure.

INTRAORGANIZATIONAL DIFFUSION

Diffusion of innovations is a peculiar example of social transmission of a new cultural trait, and its analysis (Rogers, 1980) has been perhaps the single most important empirical contribution of economic disciplines to the early study of cultural evolution. However, while innovation diffusion at the inter-organizational level has been widely analyzed, research on intraorganizational diffusion is still almost lacking – notable exceptions are Attewell (1992), Leonard-Barton (1990), and Cool et al. (1997). Cool et al. (1997) suggest that the scarcity of studies reflects the assumption that intra- and inter-organizational diffusion processes are similar. However, there appear to be many conditions under which intraorganizational diffusion may be distinct. One reason for this is that agents within an organization have very different degrees of freedom in adoption (Leonard-Barton and Deschamps, 1988; Attewell, 1992). They may be differently constrained by hierarchical roles, directives, and reward systems. Furthermore, adoption processes may be very different when they are "broadcasted" from the top of the hierarchy or when they result from the aggregation of local choices distributed across the organization. Organizations charts and other organizational policies may also shape networks of diffusion.

Cool et al.'s (1997) recent study of the diffusion of electronic switching in the Bell System from 1971 to 1982, shows interesting structural features of the intraorganizational diffusion process that match well the evolutionary framework sketched in this chapter. Adopting an "ecological perspective," Cool et al. define the organization as a collection of intraorganizational entities within each of which a single process of diffusion takes place. In the Bell System case, ecological units correspond to the different Bell Operating Companies. This perspective is especially useful when the process of adoption is gradual, i.e. does not result from a single choice but from the cumulation of a long sequence of choices over time. In this case, the ecological lens focuses on different rates of adoption across different organizational units and the existence of different "critical-mass" thresholds in the process of diffusion. This allows in turn singling out two regimes in the adoption process of each unit.

Cool et al.'s (1997) findings indicate that the rate of diffusion of electronic switching in the Bell system was influenced by different factors before and after a "critical mass" or threshold of installations occurred in each unit (following Rogers (1980), critical mass was fixed at the 25 percent level). The most striking result is that before the critical mass threshold is reached, factors driving the rate of diffusion are fundamentally related to the "internal" environment of the organization ("supply-side factors", as Cool et al. label them): the cost of internal production of the switches, and the flow of resources generated by depreciation policies of the units. As the critical mass threshold is passed, the diffusion regime switches to a "demand-side" orientation, dominated by the "external" environmental variables (e.g., population density and population growth in service areas) or variable related to the interaction with the external environment (e.g., profitability of the organizational units). This result allows Cool et al. (1997) to emphasize the role of supply factors in diffusion processes, especially at the intraorganizational level.

The temporal shift from internal to external selection mechanisms has also been observed in other studies of intraorganizational processes, such as Burgelman's (1983) study of internal venturing, suggesting that such shifts may be typical of the evolution of a variety of internal processes. In general, such level shifts are related to the hierarchical nature of organizational evolution, and suggest the need for closer attention to the dynamics of diffusion in hierarchical systems as opposed to more homogeneous diffusion environments.

Summary of Empirical Results

Despite the rather homogeneous nature of their basic assumptions, evolutionary theories of intraorganizational dynamics have generated up to now a quite sparse supporting set of empirical evidence. Table 4.1 summarizes some of the key studies discussed above. The table reveals a great variety of objects of analysis and methods. This is a striking contrast with the highly structured body of evidence generated, for example, by the "population ecology of organizations" research program (see Baum and Amburgey, this volume). Variety of methods and objects is not necessarily a negative feature of a research program, particularly when divergent methods provide convergent findings, as is the case here. Nevertheless, the diversity can impede the cumulation of findings, make it more difficult to identify a core set of propositions, and develop a well-defined domain of inquiry. Exploration still dominates exploitation; if this is without doubts a sign of juvenile vitality, nevertheless it significantly exposes the field to the liabilities of newness.

Current Debates

SELECTIONISM, ADAPTATIONISM, AND INTRAORGANIZATIONAL EVOLUTION AS SEARCH AND LEARNING

The emergence of the "population ecology of organizations" research program (Hannan and Freeman, 1989; Baum and Amburgey, this volume) brought into focus a tension

Table 4.1 Synopsis of selected empirical studies on intraorganizational evolution

Reference	Object of analysis	Key variables	Key predictions and findings	Research method
Miner, 1991	Ecologies of formal jobs	Hazard rate for job death; job founding types, job characteristics	Department size, job-founding type, job novelty	Estimation of a hazard model on a formal jobs population in a major private university, over a six-year period
Schulz, 1998	Ecologies of organizational rules	Rule births	Negative density–dependence of birth rates; differential rates of growth in different sub-environments	Estimation of a model of the rule birth process in a population of organizational rules in a private university (1889–1987)
Cohen and Bacdayan, 1994	Cognitive nature of routines	Time per move, forgetting rate	Routines are stored in procedural memory.	Laboratory experimentation
Zander and Kogut, 1993, 1995	Transmission of manufacturing competences	Codifiability, teachability, complexity of competences; time of transfer and internal vs. external transfer	The timing and the organizational boundaries of transfer are affected by tacitness.	Estimation of hazard model on data from questionnaire
Burgelman, 1983, 1991	Hierarchical evolution in populations of strategic initiatives	Process variables related to the development of strategic initiatives	Two basic evolutionary processes: induced and autonomous. Higher level change is generated by lower level evolution.	Qualitative field research
Epple et al., 1991	Intra-plant transfer of knowledge	Direct labor hours per product unit	Knowledge acquired through learning-by-doing is (partially) embodied in technology.	Estimation of learning curve models
Cool et al., 1997	Diffusion of technology in intraorganizational ecologies	Adoption rate, supply-side and demand-side variables	There are two phases in the adoption process, the first driven by internal selective environment, the other by external selective pressures.	Multiple regression analysis on data from multiple documentary sources

between selectionist and adaptationst views of organizations. The tension contrasts the driving action of selection over relatively inert organizations with the role of organization-level adaptation and learning. From the viewpoint of intraorganizational evolution, however, the conceptual distinction between selection and adaptation seems more a matter of hierarchical levels than of radically different processes. Adaptation and learning at the organizational level are seen mostly as the outcome of intraorganizational ecological and Darwinian dynamics.

The intuition that a system can respond adaptively to its environment by mimicking inside itself the basic dynamics of evolutionary processes was already present in Darwin (1859); but it is mostly after the work of Holland (1975) that some basic features of evolution as a search and learning process have been clarified. Holland's central idea can be expressed in terms of problem solving. Checking a population of solutions against the problem-environment allows parallel search of the problem space; the virtues of parallel search fully blossom when processes of recombination of past solutions allow extraction from experience "schemata" or building blocks that can be assembled in new solutions. Selective pressures assure that (on average) fitter building blocks reproduce and diffuse at faster rates than less useful ones. Mutation assures that potentially useful missing information can be randomly constructed. As a result, "good" adaptive responses develop out of the Darwinian dynamics of populations of solutions.

Holland (1975) has suggested that these basic processes of "evolutionary search" are at the heart of the adaptive performance of complex systems. In two important papers, Cohen (1981, 1984) has shown how this intuition can work for modeling organizations and their adaptive responses to environments. Organizations are modeled as structures governing the interaction between multiple agents with bounded information processing resources, trying to evolve an organizational policy out of populations of building blocks for policies. An organization policy can be thought as a bundle of routines or standard procedures, and organizations essentially structure individual responsibilities, the interaction between policy makers, and define internal rewards and other governance mechanisms such as choice procedures. Computer simulations show how artificial organizations can respond to complex tasks by exploiting parallel search and recombination of policy building blocks. Cohen has also shown how different organizational structures can foster different adaptive responses, leading to the conclusion that organizational structures can be conceived as search heuristics. Furthermore, it has been possible to explore in this perspective the role of conflict in improving the performance of population search (Cohen, 1984).

While Cohen's still stands as the most systematic attempt to model organizational adaptation as parallel search, other models have delved further into the adaptive virtues of intraorganizational ecologies. Warglien (1995) has modeled the evolution of organizational competences in a population of R&D projects, using a mix of neural network machinery and Holland's ideas on evolving populations of solutions; the model reproduces phenomena such as "punctuated" adaptation, competence traps and the endogenous regulation of search efforts. Bruderer and Singh (1996), using Holland's genetic algorithm and treating organizational capacity to learn as a "gene," show how environmental selective pressures shape a population of organizations with the right "ability to learn." Although Bruderer and Singh do model evolutionary dynamics only within the population of organizations, and learning as an intraorganizational process is limited to random search, they succeed in showing how learning and evolution interact in a hierarchy of processes, and how interactions between such levels matter.

When conceptualizing intraorganizational evolution processes as search and learning, the key issue is how these processes perform two basic functions: exploitation and exploration (Holland, 1975). Exploitation refers to the ability to use the results of past experience to improve performance. Exploration refers to the search for new unexplored solutions. To stay evolvable, an organization needs to perform both functions. But exploration and exploitation involve important trade-offs in the use of resources and the allocation of risk: exploration is riskier than exploitation and absorbs in the short run resources whose return in the long run is highly uncertain. How do organizations deal with this trade-off? March (1991), in his computer model of the development and diffusion of organizational knowledge, offers a pessimistic answer, arguing that in the long run exploitation drives out exploration. His conclusions thus converge with the view that in the long run learning processes force organizations into inertia and competency traps (Levinthal, 1991). However, the picture may not be so bleak. Although there are trade-offs between exploration and exploitation – many efforts to engineer organizational evolution (March, 1994) turn out to be attempts to move the trade-off line itself, rather than reposition the organization along the line. Thus, organizations may search simultaneously for additional exploitation and exploration opportunities. The power of recombination, for example, stems from its exploitation of the wisdom of past success (the building blocks) while looking for new combinations – more exploitation and more exploration.

Unanswered Questions: Representation and Expression

Much debate on iOE often blurs the useful evolutionary distinction between representation and expression – genotype and phenotype, in the classical evolutionary vocabulary (Cohen et al., 1996). From this point of view, theories of organizational evolution tend to over-emphasize the behavioral – the concept of routine being a prominent example. In biology, there is a clear distinction between the structure that stores the genotypic information to be transmitted from individual to individual, and the phenotypic expression of such information. There seems to be no such distinction in the concept of routines. Yet, the behavioral definition of routine clearly suggests that what is reproduced is a pattern of action – a "phenotype." Yet even in nonbiological contexts it seems to make sense to keep a distinction between the ways in which "genetic" information is stored and the expression that is generated when such information is used to generate behavior. For example, there is often a neat difference between the formal definition of a job and its actual execution.

The representation/expression dualism is also helpful in defining how "genetic information" is stored and reproduced. Consider once more routines: how are they stored in organizational memories? It has been suggested (Cohen et al., 1996) that there may be different kinds of organizational supports maintaining the representation of patterns of actions. For example, production routines in a "lean" manufacturing process are "stored" in participants memories, in the physical layout of the plant, in the equipment affordances, in standard procedures constraining behavior, in other linguistic records and so on. All or part of these need to be reproduced when the routine is reproduced, say, in a new plant. The actual patterns of behavior clearly require these supports in order to be enacted, although they may differ from what is stored; for example, actual behavior may diverge form the standard procedure, but still use it as a generative resource for action (Narduzzo et al., 2000). Of course, a purely behavioral definition of routine would make these useful and important distinctions disappear.

Absent a distinction between representation and expression, the notion of replication is also problematic because it is not always clear what a "reproductive" event is. For example, when is a work routine "reproduced"? When it is just carried over time by a same work group, when the group is partially changed in its composition, or when it is used by a entirely different group of workers? This question is tied directly to the definition of the "carrying units" of the organizational genetic repertoire, and cannot been resolved until a choice is made in this respect (of course, the choice may depend on the specific context and on the goals of the analysis). Indeed, this choice coincides with the definition of what intraorganizational individuals and populations are. Here, evolutionary and ecological issues clearly intersect. However, as already remarked, a coherent joint definition of ecological units and genetic entities is still to a large extent missing in theories of iOE.

Future Directions

THE TOPOLOGY OF INTERACTION

In organizations, variation, selection and retention do not happen in homogeneous, uniform interaction spaces. Each member of an intraorganizational population belongs to multiple relational structures that define its neighborhood relations, its relative position, etc. This structure affects each element of the evolutionary process. For example, diffusion happens in networks shaped by relational structures. Variation by recombination of capabilities is considerably facilitated by the contiguity of individual bearers of different competences, as in heterogeneous design teams. And intraorganizational selection is often a process dominated by local competition (for example between development projects in a same division). Despite the importance of the topology of interactions in determining the evolutionary fate of organizations, little work has been done to advance our understanding of how the structure of local interaction affects the global behavior of intraorganizational evolving populations. As a first step in this direction, Axelrod and Cohen (2000) have suggested to distinguish two classes of interaction determinants: 'proximity,' which determines the likelihood of interaction, and 'activation factors,' which determine the sequencing of activity.

Proximity is not just physical contiguity, although the latter clearly matters in many interaction structures. Other spaces are as well relevant: for example, networks of friendship ties, the conceptual space of interaction designed by an organization chart, the neighborhood relations designed by personal positions in a community of practice. All these spaces shape the likelihood of interactions, and thus affect the flow of evolutionary events in a population. Activation patterns relate to time. It makes a difference whether processes activate interacting units in sequence (and in which sequence) or simultaneously. Much of the debate on concurrent engineering and "parallel teams" implicitly recognizes that the way competences are recombined in a design process crucially depends upon patterns of activation.

Of course, the topology of interaction is not something imposed onto intraorganizational populations (although it may to some extent be designed). To an extent, it is a self-organizing phenomenon that results from myriads of individual decisions. Axelrod and Cohen suggest several mechanisms acting on neighborhood relations in populations of agents including following another agent, copying, following signals, and tagging (developing properties detectable by other agents). Riolo (1997) has shown that allowing agents to develop tags in a population playing an iterated prisoner's dilemma facilitates the aggregation of cooperating agents, allowing the creation of subpopulations of neighboring reciprocating agents. Research on the emergence of intraorganizational networks can provide important inputs for this line of evolutionary research.

Finally, it should be remarked that as technologies of information and communication (ICT) develop and diffuse, physical constraints to the creation of conceptual spaces of interaction tend to wane; as a result, organizations are expected to considerably increase the intricacies of their patterns of interaction. From this point of view, evolutionary studies of intraorganizational dynamics will have much to gain from close interaction with research on the impact of ICT on organizational life.

EVOLUTION AS DESIGN

Since the very first pages of *The Origin of Species*, Charles Darwin (1859) directs our attention to human uses of variation and selection "under domestication." Whether he looks at domestic pigeons, horses or spaniels, he unceasingly recalls how humans have always used evolutionary processes as a design tool for improving the usefulness of domestic animals.

Recently, March (1994) has suggested that evolutionary thinking has moved from predicting history to engineering history. It is a constant theme of iOE research that a better understanding of evolutionary processes may lead to improve our ability to intervene on them, using evolution as a design tool.

One can think of "evolutionary design" as a non-obtrusive design strategy that leverages on emergent processes by tuning their parameters without trying to directly control their outcomes. Broadly speaking, "evolutionary design" has two complementary faces. On the one hand, it can try to manipulate the parameters of some basic processes, like recombination or retention. On the other hand, it can try to manipulate the fitness landscape to which intraorganizational populations adapt, e.g. designing incentive structures. Another way to frame this dual approach is to say that one can act on the population search heuristics or manipulate the problem space. Both approaches are of course complementary, and it is only a matter of conceptual convenience to separate them.

Tuning how intraorganizational populations search their problem environment is probably the most immediate way to leverage on evolutionary processes (Axelrod and Cohen, 2000). For example, organizations may alter patterns of competence recombination by manipulating the composition and mobility flows in design teams. Levels of variation can be further tuned by tightening or loosening organizational control over slack resources. Retention can be altered by personnel policies affecting employee turnover. As far as many organizational policies affect one or the other component of the evolutionary cycle, they can be thought of as potential tools for evolutionary design.

A complementary approach to evolutionary design (Levinthal and Warglien, 1999) is grounded on the observation that individuals, groups and other intraorganizational entities adapt through a variety of processes to the "fitness landscape" they confront, i.e. the payoff surfaces designed by their task environment and by task interdependencies. Drawing on Stuart Kauffman's (1993) theory of fitness landscape, Levinthal and Warglien show how the tuning of organizational interdependencies generates a continuum of fitness topographies, ranging from simple, single peaked landscapes (associated to low interdependencies) to rugged landscapes (generated by high interdependencies). Single peaked landscapes favor incremental learning and generate uniform outcomes, while rugged landscapes favor variety at the cost of coordination problems. Designing fitness landscapes allows one to engineer the context within which autonomous evolutionary dynamics take shape. Of course, this does not exclude designing the "search heuristics" governing intraorganizational evolution – quite at the opposite, different fitness surfaces may imply different strategies for searching the landscape.

Connections Across Levels of Organization

In organization theory, evolutionary arguments are often applied recursively at different levels of analysis. Thus, it is not surprising that many common threads can be found in the chapters of this *Companion* dedicated to intraorganizational, organizational and inter-organizational evolution. However, it is fair to say that most of these connections are rarely developed beyond the level of more or less deep analogies. Exploring in more systematic ways across-level connections may turn out to be a priority issue in the research agenda of evolutionary thinking in organization theory. One example is the topology of interaction. Co-location in geographic space has been shown to deeply affect inter-organizational evolution processes (Greve's chapter). At lower levels, different kinds of spatial proximity may play a prominent role; for example, both formal structure and social networks affect the frequency of interactions within organizations (Amburgey and Singh's chapter, this chapter), shaping evolutionary dynamics (e.g. diffusion patterns or aggregation processes). A better understanding of the nature of different neighborhood types is needed to go beyond simple analogies and compare interaction spatial structures at different levels; connections with network analysis may prove strategic under this respect; see Raider and Krackhardt (this volume).

Another example is the theme of path-dependence, also surfacing as the problem of inefficiency of evolutionary histories (Greve, this volume) or as the relevance of prior change histories (Amburgey and Singh, this volume). While there seems to be a diffused consensus on the proposition that evolutionary dynamics may lead to inefficient outcomes, little is known about the mechanisms explaining the emergence of inefficient solutions. Most researchers would agree that inefficiency can be explained by the presence of positive feedback in evolutionary processes, but the nature and the sources of such positive feedback are still poorly understood. In particular, little research has been conducted on how lock-in at one level may affect the dynamics of other levels: for example, lock-in phenomena at the intraorganizational level may increase inertia at the organizational level, and thus affect the balance between adaptation and selection as modes of change (Levinthal, 1991; Amburgey and Singh's chapter, this volume).

One particular theme, however, deserves privileged attention for its role in bridging levels of analysis. The concept of hierarchical evolution directly calls for a conceptual integration of different scales of interaction, and suggests that stable configurations of nested processes can emerge. Furthermore, this issue clearly connects evolutionary themes with complexity theory. Although the problem was neatly stated since Simon's classic "architecture of complexity" paper (Simon, 1962), much has still to be done in such direction. Even basic issues concerning the forms or configurations of hierarchically organized evolutionary processes, their stability over time, not to speak about their emergence, are still to a large extent virgin territories for organizational research – a notable exception is the work of Padgett (2000) on the genesis of banks in renaissance Florence. Moving from analogies to the analysis of actual connections between levels will require progress on the hierarchical structure of evolutionary processes.

Conclusion

As an emergent field of research, intraorganizational evolution is probably facing a two-sided development challenge. On the one hand, it needs to reinforce its identity, structuring its core concepts and methods and defining a shared research agenda. For instance, it is often remarked that empirical research has been biased towards the analysis of selection processes, while retention and variation have captured much less attention; see Greve (this volume) for similar considerations. However, the problem is far from being only one of empirical nature – rather, it is the expression of underlying theoretical gaps. The lack of empirical research on variation clearly reflects a lack of theoretical work, allowing one to define units of analysis and sources of variation; see Axelrod and Cohen (2000) for a first substantial step in that direction, and some examples in Amburgey and Singh (this volume). The conceptual core of intraorganizational evolution is still very partially developed, and attempts to complete it are likely to absorb much energy in years to come.

On the other hand, the impact of intraorganizational evolution research will crucially depend on its capability to establish fruitful interactions with other research perspectives. Social network analysis and complexity theory seem the most natural scientific allies, but new intellectual partnerships are worth exploring outside the traditional boundaries of organization research. One example is evolutionary game theory: interesting organizational phenomena have been shown to be tractable with its tools. For instance, the emergence of coordination can be quite accurately modeled as processes in which social learning approximates dynamics leading to evolutionary stable equilibria (Crawford, 1991). A fresh look at the evolutionary dynamics of other important phenomena, like norms and conventions, diffusion in networks, bargaining, and the evolution of contracts (Young, 1998) may result from an open dialogue between evolutionary thinking in game and organization theories.

While the need to simultaneously reinforce identity and strengthen interactions with other research streams may appear as a source of conflicting strains, it also provides an incentive for innovative work. The relative immaturity of this green research field is also its source of opportunities.

References

Aldrich, H. (1999): *Organizations Evolving.* London: Sage Publications.

Arrow, K. (1974): *The Limits of Organization.* New York: Norton.

Attewell, P. (1992): "Technology diffusion and organizational learning: The case of business computing," *Organization Science,* 3, 1–19.

Axelrod, R., and Cohen, M. D. (2000): *Harnessing Complexity.* New York: Free Press.

Barnett, W. P., and. Carroll, G. R. (1987): "Competition and mutualism among early telephone companies," *Administrative Science Quarterly,* 32, 400–21.

Baum, J. A. C., and. Singh, J. V. (1994): "Organizational hierarchies and evolutionary processes: Some reflections on a theory of organizational evolution," in J. A. C. Baum and J. V. Singh (eds), *Evolutionary Dynamics of Organizations,* New York: Oxford University Press, 3–22.

Boyd, R., and Richerson, P. J. (1985): *Culture and the Evolutionary Process.* Chicago: Chicago University Press.

Brown, J. S., and Duguid, P. (1991): "Organizational learning and communities-of-practice: Towards a unified view of working, learning and innovation," *Organization Science,* 2, 40–57.

Bruderer, E., and Singh, J. V. (1996): "Organizational evolution, learning and selection: A genetic-algorithm-based model," *Academy of Management Journal,* 39, 1322–40.

Burgelman, R. A. (1983): "A process model of internal corporate venturing in the diversified major firm," *Administrative Science Quarterly,* 28, 223–44.

Burgelman, R. A. (1991): "Intraorganizational ecology of strategy-making and organizational adaptation: Theory and field research," *Organization Science,* 2, 239–62.

Campbell, D. T. (1965): "Variation and selective retention in socio-cultural evolution," in H. R. Baringer, G. I. Blanksten, and R. Mack (eds), *Social Change in Developing Areas,* Cambridge, Mass: Schenkman, 19–49.

Cavalli-Sforza, L. L., and Feldman, M. W. (1981): *Cultural Transmission and Evolution: A Quantitative Approach.* Princeton, NJ: Princeton University Press.

Cohen, M. D. (1981): "The power of parallel thinking," *Journal of Economic Behavior and Organization,* 2, 285–386

Cohen, M. D. (1984): "Conflict and complexity: Goal diversity and organizational search effectiveness," *American Political Science Review,* 78, 435–51.

Cohen, M. D., and Bacdayan, P. (1994): "Organizational routines are stored as procedural memory: Evidence from a laboratory study," *Organization Science,* 5, 554–68.

Cohen, M. D., Burkhart, R., Dosi, G., Egidi, M., Marengo, L., Winter, S., and Warglien M. (1996): "Routines and other recurring action patterns in organizations," *Industrial and Corporate Change,* 5, 653–98.

Cool, K. O., Dierickx, I., and Szulanski, G. (1997): "Diffusion of innovations within organizations: Electronic switching in the Bell System, 1971–1982," *Organization Science,* 8, 543–59.

Crawford, V. (1991): "An evolutionary interpretation of Van Huick, Battalio and Beil's experimental results on coordination," *Games and Economic Behavior,* 3, 25–59.

Cyert, R. M., and March, J. G. (1963): *The Behavioral Theory of the Firm.* Englewood Cliffs, NJ: Prentice Hall.

Darwin, C. (1859): *On the Origins of Species by Means of Natural Selection.* London: Murray.

Egidi, M., and Narduzzo A. (1997): "The emergence of path-dependent behaviours in cooperative contexts," *International Journal of Industrial Organization,* 5, 677–709.

Epple, D., Argote, L., and Devadas, R. (1991): "Organizational learning curves: A method for investigating intra-plant transfer of knowledge acquired through learning-by-doing," *Organization Science,* 2, 58–70.

Galunic, D. C., and Eisenhart, K. M. (1996): "The evolution of intracorporate domains: Divisional charter losses in high-technology, multidivisional corporations," *Organization Science,* 7, 255–82.

Hannan, M. T., and Freeman, J. (1989): *Organizational Ecology*. Cambridge, Mass: Harvard University Press.

Holland, J. H. (1975): *Adaptation in Natural and Artificial Systems*. Ann Arbor, MI: The University of Michigan Press.

Hutchins, E., and Hazelhurst, B. (1991): "Learning in the cultural process," in C. Langton (ed.), *Artificial Life II*, Reading, Mass: Addison Wesley, 689–706.

Kauffman, S. (1993): *The Origins of Order: Self-Organization and Selection in Evolution*. New York: Oxford University Press.

Lave, J., and Wenger, E. (1991): *Situated Learning: Legitimate Peripheral Participation*. Cambridge, Mass: Cambridge University Press.

Leonard-Barton, D. (1990): "The intraorganizational environment: Point-to-point versus diffusion," in F. Williams and D. V. Gibson (eds), *Technology Transfer: A Communication Perspective*, London: Sage Publications.

Leonard-Barton, D. and Deschamps, I. (1988): "Managerial influence on the implementation of a new technology," *Management Science*, 34, 1252–65.

Levinthal, D. (1991): "Organizational adaptation and environmental selection – Interrelated processes of change," *Organization Science*, 2, 140–5.

Levinthal, D. and Warglien, M. (1999): "Landscape design: Designing for local action in complex worlds," *Organization Science*, 10, 342–57.

Levitt, B., and March, J. G. (1988): "Organizational learning," *Annual Review of Sociology*, 14, 319–40, Palo Alto CA: Annual Reviews.

McKelvey, B. (1982): *Organizational Systematics*. Berkeley, CA: University of California Press.

March, J. G. (1991): "Exploration and exploitation in organizational learning," *Organization Science*, 2, 71–87.

March, J. G. (1994): "The evolution of evolution," in J. A. C. Baum and J. V. Singh (eds), *Evolutionary Dynamics of Organizations*, New York: Oxford University Press, 39–52.

March, J. G., and Simon, H. A. (1958): *Organizations*. New York: John Wiley.

Meyer, M. W. (1994): "Turning evolution inside the organization," in J. A. C. Baum and J. V. Singh (eds), *Evolutionary Dynamics of Organizations*, New York: Oxford University Press, 109–16.

Miner, A. S. (1991): "Organizational evolution and the social ecology of jobs," *American Sociological Review*, 56, 772–85.

Narduzzo, A., Rocco, E., and Warglien, M. (2000): "Talking about routines in the field: The emergence of organizational capabilities in a new cellular phone network company," in G. Dosi, R. Nelson, and S. Winter (eds), *The Nature and Dynamics of Organizational Capabilities*, New York: Oxford University Press, 27–50.

Nelson R., and Winter, S. (1982): *An Evolutionary Theory of Economic Change*. Cambridge, Mass: Bellknap Press.

Orr, J. (1990): "Talking about machines: An ethnography of a modern job," PhD thesis, Cornell University.

Padgett, J. (2000): "Organizational genesis, identity and control: The transformation of banking in Renaissance Florence," in A. Casella and J. Rauch (eds), *Markets and Networks*, New York: Russell Sage.

Riolo, R. L. (1997): "The effects and evolution of tag-mediated selection of partners in evolving populations playing the iterated prisoner's dilemma," in T. Back (ed.), *Proceedings of the International Conference on Genetic Algorithms*, S. Francisco: Morgan Kauffman, 378–85.

Rogers, E. (1980): *Diffusion of Innovations*. New York: Free Press.

Sastry, M. (1997): "Problems and paradoxes in a model of punctuated organizational change," *Administrative Science Quarterly*, 42, 237–75.

Schulz, M. (1998): "Limits to bureaucratic growth: The density dependence of organizational rule births," *Administrative Science Quarterly*, 43, 845–76.

Simon, H. A. (1962): "The architecture of complexity," *Proceedings of the American Philosophical*

Society, 106, 467–82.

Tushman, M. L. and Romanelli, E. (1985): "Organizational evolution: A metamorphosis model of convergence and reorientation," in L. L. Cummings and B. M. Staw (eds), *Research in Organizational Behavior*, Greenwich CT: JAI Press, 171–222.

Warglien, M. (1995): "Hierarchical selection and organizational adaptation in a population of projects," *Industrial and Corporate Change*, 4, 161–86.

Weber, M. (1978): *Economy and Society*. Berkeley, CA: University of California Press.

Weick, K. (1969): *The Social Psychology of Organizing*. Reading, Mass: Addison Wesley.

Weick, K. (1976): "Educational organizations as loosely coupled systems," *Administrative Science Quarterly*, 21, 1–19.

Winter, S. (1987): "Knowledge and competence as strategic assets," in D. Teece (ed.), *The Competitive Challenge – Strategies for Industrial Innovation and Renewal*, Cambridge, Mass: Bollinger, 159–84.

Young, P. (1998): *Individual Strategy and Social Structure: An Evolutionary Theory of Institutions*. Princeton, NJ: Princeton University Press.

Zander, U. and Kogut, B. (1993): "Knowledge of the firm and the evolutionary theory of the multinational corporation," *Journal of International Business Studies*, 24, 625–45.

Zander, U. and Kogut, B. (1995): "Knowledge and the speed of the transfer and imitation of organizational capabilities: An empirical test," *Organization Science*, 6, 76–92.

Zhou, X. (1993): "The dynamics of organizational rules," *American Journal of Sociology*, 98, 1134–66.

Chapter Five

Intraorganizational Cognition and Interpretation

C. MARLENE FIOL

"This century has offered two radical solutions: ignore the mind (behaviorism) or ignore the world (cognitivism)"

(Lewis, 1992, p. 33)

In the process of developing a coherent and credible challenge to behaviorism in the past several decades, we may have created an over-simplified set of cognitive theories. A challenge as we enter the twenty-first century is to take theories of cognition to a higher level of complexity in order to better reflect two analogous revolutions that have transformed what we assume to be true about human minds and about organizational worlds. First, cognitive science is in the midst of a paradigm shift. Traditional cognitive theories, based on a computer metaphor, are symbolically oriented and concerned with conscious processes of "fetch-operate-store" cycles that are centrally controlled, much like conventional computing (Lord and Maher, 1991). This implies a fixed and limited cognitive capacity. Symbolic architectures assume that people represent the world in terms of internal mental models to which they can apply rules to form inferences across a wide array of contexts.

Limitations of this architecture to describe cognitive processes have led to a search for a new set of theories – and a new metaphor. Newer cognitive theories are focused at a neurological level and are based on a brain metaphor (Anderson, 1990). Similar to the functions of the brain, which occur among large numbers of interconnected neurons, numerous cognitive processes are thought to occur simultaneously. From this perspective, cognitive capacities are not limited to the capacities of any single process and are not centrally controlled. The whole is encoded in the parts, so that each part represents the whole.

Analogous revolutionary shifts have occurred in organizational worlds and in our assumptions about those worlds. Classical management theories, based on mechanistic models, have shaped our most basic conceptions of organization. According to these theories, organizational work involves a sequence of more or less routinized operations that are centrally controlled. Like computer models of the mind, this organizational model leads to cross-situational consistency. Organizational functions are assumed to flow from an internal set of motivations or goals. Physical assets are critical competitive resources, and an organization's physical capacity is viewed as fixed and relatively limited.

Limitations of this model to describe organizational processes have led to a search for a new set of theories – and a new metaphor. Newer theories of more flexible learning organizations are based on a brain metaphor. Like the newer neurologically based cognitive theories, these theories favor a more decentralized, distributed form of intelligence. Knowledge, rather than physical assets, is the most critical resource. And sophisticated forms of intelligence emerge from the interactions among loosely linked organizational components, thus overcoming the capacity limitations of individual units. This also implies that the most critical aspect of knowledge management is not the management of knowledge content *per se*. Rather, it has to do with creating an environment rich with knowledge cues, and managing the social processes by which organizational units interact. Here again, meanings are not imposed *a priori* from a centralized location; they emerge from the process.

SCOPE OF CHAPTER

The purpose of this chapter is to identify several key challenges as we review old assumptions and assimilate and apply the new ideas about cognition and about organizations. The newer theories about cognition and organization encourage us to embrace a number of paradoxes and to begin to provide explanations for the simultaneous existence of:

1 Knowledge as the content of internal mental models *and* knowledge accessible only through external cues
2 Interpretations as the result of cognition *and* affect
3 Automatic *and* controlled cognitive processes
4 Distributed *and* shared cognitions

I will briefly explore these four domains of intraorganizational cognition and interpretation. I conclude that it is time, as researchers, for us to stop asking "if" and "whether" apparently paradoxical cognitive processes coexist, and to begin asking "how" and "when" they occur.

I do not intend to offer global conclusions about cognition and interpretation at the end of this chapter. That would be presumptuous. The debate about the nature of both the human mind and organizations continues with intensity, and the evidence is most often inconclusive. Rather, the chapter ends with suggestions about the need for us to get off the bandwagon of passing research fads, and get on with exploring the substantive organizational issues that we feel passionate about.

Leading Paradigms in Cognition and Organization

Two cognitive architectures are thought to describe cognitive processes. Traditional theories favoring a symbolic architecture are still dominant. However, a newer breed of connectionist theories is emerging, which views cognition as a series of competing, yes/no responses from neurons in the brain. Analogous shifts are occurring in our theories of organization. After a brief review of the two architectures, I will explore some of the implications of research adhering to one or the other, or to both of them.

SYMBOLIC ARCHITECTURES

Traditional cognitive theories are symbolically oriented, concerned with conscious processes that operate on symbol structures (e.g., language) stored in long-term memory. People represent the world in terms of internal mental models or schemata from which they form inferences. The schemata are "cognitive structures that represent organized knowledge about a given concept or type of stimulus" (Fiske and Taylor, 1984, p. 140).

According to this set of theories, it is through schemata that people make sense of the world. People tend to notice schema-relevant stimuli, and they tend to understand and remember things the way they expect them to be. Schema-based cognitive processing is thought to lead to cross-situational consistency because people interpret and cognitively process input data based on an internal set of motivations or goals. According to this perspective, cognitive capacity is fixed and limited since knowledge lies in the content of a particular memory location that must be accessed.

Information processing research in the last 25 years has emphasized such explicit, conscious, symbolic processing (Lord and Maher, 1991). Symbolic architectures have also held huge appeal for organizational researchers and have been the dominant approach in organizational cognition studies to date. The Huff (1990) and Walsh (1995) works listed in Table 5.1 serve as exemplars. Huff's edited volume presents a compilation of five methods to map cognitive structures. Her belief is that such representations of mental maps are more than methodological tools: "We can hope to capture something that has the same essential characteristics as thought itself" (Huff, 1990, p. 14). Five years later, Walsh reviewed the empirical and conceptual work on cognitive content and structures in organizational studies. He noted the many different labels that organizational researchers have used to describe these mental models. Despite the diversity of labels, the research in his review has generally focused on a similar set of top-down or schema-driven information-processing constructs. As he stated at the end of his review, "we have been held captive by the computer metaphor of information processing" (Walsh, 1995, p. 308).

My chapter in the exemplar Huff volume (1990) illustrates one approach and some of the assumptions of a symbolic approach to cognitive mapping. I semiotically analyzed the Letters to Shareholders of ten chemical companies over a three-year period to derive a set of stable oppositional values underlying the cognitive structures reflected in the texts. I then linked differences in the underlying value dynamics to different organization-level choices regarding joint venture activity. Table 5.2 summarizes my research question, methodology, sample, and key assumptions in contrast to a more connectionist approach described later.

Table 5.1 Exemplar intraorganizational cognition and interpretation collections

Reference	Key concepts	Key variables	Key contributions
Symbolic architectures: Focus is on top-down serial information processing			
Huff, 1990	Cognitive maps	Mapping constructs Mapping techniques	Compilation of map types and illustrations of mapping techniques
Walsh, 1995	Knowledge structures	Knowledge structure content and structure	Historical overview and future challenges for the study of managerial and organizational cognition
Mixed architectures: Focus is on active sense making as well as top-down information processing			
Weick, 1995	Sensemaking in organizations	Belief-driven sensemaking processes Action-driven sensemaking processes	Individual and collective sensemaking defined and described
Meindl et al., 1996	Sensemaking in and between organizations	Upstream and downstream sensemaking processes	Individual and collective sensemaking defined and described
Czarniawska-Joerges, 1997	World-as-text	Stories Paradox Identities	Use of stories, serials, and themes to illustrate transformation processes
Eden and Spender, 1998	Managerial and organizational cognition	Cognition Learning Cognitive mapping	Compilation of map types and illustrations of mapping techniques

Table 5.2 Exemplar intraorganizational cognition and interpretation studies

Research question	Methodology	Sample	Key assumptions
Symbolic architectures: Focus is on top-down serial information processing			
Fiol chapter in Huff, 1990			
Role of top management thinking in the choice of strategic behaviors	Semiotic analysis of Letters to Shareholders over a period of three years	Ten chemical companies	• Meanings are rooted in a stable set of oppositions. • It is possible to capture and contrast underlying oppositional belief structures that may be unintentionally portrayed by the subject.
Mixed architectures: Focus is on active sensemaking as well as top-down information processing			
Lindell et al. chapter in Eden and Spender, 1998			
Role of top management thinking during strategic change processes	Thematic coding of in-depth interviews over a period of three years	One managing director of a hospital	• "Way-of-thinking" includes emotions, hopes, and values, as well as cognitive structures. • Action and cognition are simultaneous processes.

Top-down, serial information processing theories fit nicely with concurrent assumptions about organization. Traditional classical organizational theories emphasize independence, hierarchy, and control in a manner analogous to computer-based symbolic architectures. Even the elaboration of the systems model of organizations into a more complex contingency theory in the late 1960s is based on assumptions of rationality, objectivity, and control. Our theories of the mind and of organizations have been highly congruent, if not appropriate.

LIMITATIONS OF A SYMBOLIC APPROACH

Criticisms of a symbolic approach to cognition range from concerns that researchers' measures hold little resemblance to actual thought, to more serious questions about whether we should even bother to attempt to measure symbolic cognitive structures. Cognitive structures may be many different things. They go by many labels (Walsh, 1995) that may mean very different things to different people. They may be few or many, highly systematic or loose, affectively neutral or loaded with feeling. As a result, our analyses, at best, tend to be only loosely tied to schema-based theory and, at worst, have resulted in some distinctly un-schema-like things called schemata (Kuklinski et al., 1991). For example, organizational researchers have fine-tuned the now common technique of clustering characteristics of strategic situations as either threats or opportunities. The concern is that these factors are statistical abstractions that may have nothing to do with thoughts that research subjects actually hold within an organizational context.

Though the results of schema-based studies are generally interesting, do we really need schema theory to do the analyses? How are schemata different than much older concepts such as cognitive maps (Tolman, 1948) or personal constructs (Kelly, 1955)? Another concern is that schematic structures tend to be relatively gross and static, having little to say about their internal makeup, how they arise, or how they are changed (Kuklinski et al., 1991). Furthermore, schema-based studies tend to ignore the role of emotion, which may be critical in organizational settings that are presumably more affect-arousing than most psychological experimental settings. Finally, schema-based studies neglect social context (Walsh, 1995). Given that organizations are inherently social, this may be especially problematic for organizational studies.

The most serious concern has to do with whether we should even endeavor to measure schemata. Do people actually have such internal mental models or symbol systems of the world that guide their sensemaking? Or is this a convenient tool that we as organizational theorists have borrowed from psychology to simplify our research?

CONNECTIONIST ARCHITECTURES

Connectionist architectures are newer attempts to model human thought. They describe cognitive processing at a more micro, neurological level, in terms of the flow of activation and inhibition between networks of neuron-like processing units (Lord and Maher, 1991). Connectionist architectures use the human brain (rather than computers) as a metaphor to suggest how cognitive processes might operate. Brains consist of a very large number of interconnected neurons that can mutually excite or inhibit (Anderson, 1990). Information processing occurs through their interactions with each other, rather than by way of a central executive component.

Connectionist architectures are informing the work of a number of recent organizational researchers. Works by Weick (1995), Meindl et al. (1996), Czarniawska-Joerges (1997), and Eden and Spender (1998) are listed in Table 5.1 as exemplars. I have listed them under the heading "Mixed Architectures" in Table 5.1 because each of these authors continues to rely on some aspects of top-down schema-based theories along with a connectionist approach. For example, Weick (1995) devoted a chapter to "belief-driven" sensemaking processes; Meindl et al. (1996, ch. 9) included a study with an explicitly stated schema perspective; Czarniawska-Joerges (1997, p. 44) spoke of "accessible plots" that guide people's initial behaviors in organizations; and Eden and Spender (1998, ch. 6) included a study of relatively stable schemata in the form of success attributions. At the same time, in all of these works, the focus is also on active and real-time sensemaking and pattern matching, as well as on top-down symbol-driven choice processes.

Lindell, Melin, Gahmberg, Hellqvist, and Melander's chapter in the exemplar Eden and Spender volume (1998) illustrates one approach and some of the connectionist assumptions in studying intraorganizational cognition. They conducted numerous in-depth interviews over a three-year period with a managing director of a hospital to derive real-time accounts of his thoughts, actions, and emotions as they changed over time. Table 5.2 compares and contrasts this research with my symbolically based study in Huff's (1990) volume. The two provide a particularly useful contrast given the similarity of the research question that motivated both studies.

Connectionist, parallel information processing theories fit nicely with emerging assumptions about organization. Newer organizational theories view organizations as moving from independent competitive strategies based on a set of fixed and limited resources to collaborative strategies based on distributed knowledge; from integrated and hierarchical organizations to loosely coupled and networked forms; and from a focus on central control to autonomy and interdependence. Instead of defining managers as computing devices, researchers are beginning to define them as actors who proactively make sense of and invent their own decision possibilities (Czarniawska-Joerges, 1997; Eden and Spender, 1998; Meindl et al., 1996; Weick, 1995). The connectionist metaphor that emerges is a view of people as neurons and organization as a brain. Again, our emerging theories of the mind and of organizations remain congruent, if not appropriate.

Mixed Architectures

According to recent theorists, symbolic architectures alone seem inadequate for explaining or predicting social behavior (Lord and Maher, 1991). Connectionist architectures are emerging as alternative models. I described the last four exemplar works in Table 5.1 as incorporating both symbolic and connectionist architectures. Concerns abound as to which of these two is more appropriate than the other for explaining cognition.

The two architectures are distinct representations of human cognitive capacities and processes. They imply very different ways of processing information, and suggest different principles for explaining topics of concern to organizational theorists (Lord and Maher, 1991). Thus, they tend to be treated as competing theories.

I prefer the view that the two cognitive architectures are not competing theories. Though it is possible that they specify a different underlying nature of human cognitive processing, it may also be that they simply apply at different levels of brain activity, as Lord and Maher (1991) have suggested. Alternatively, they may reflect cognition at different stages of development for both individual and organizational systems. Figure 5.1 depicts these two ways of viewing the two architectures as complementary rather than competing. They may exist at different levels of analysis and/or at different points in time of a system's development.

Symbolic schemata are thought to be retrieved from memory in an all-or-none manner. Connectionist theories specify the microstructure underlying the schemata by filling in the gaps left in symbolic architectures. So cognition using a symbolic architecture may be influenced in part by knowledge that is activated by a connectionist architecture. The two operate at different levels. For example, schema theory explains how knowledge is retrieved from a memory location; and connectionism explains how and why that particular location was chosen over others. People may access informa-

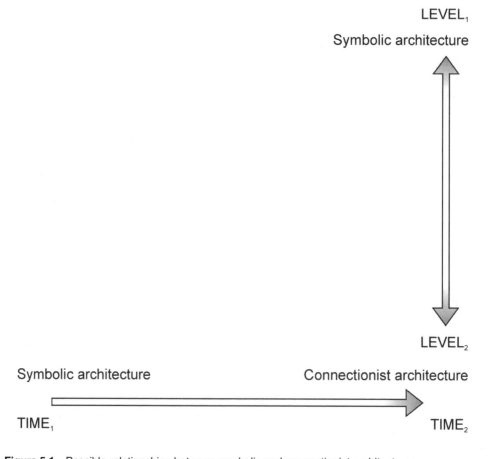

Figure 5.1 Possible relationships between symbolic and connectionist architectures

tion in memory using connectionist pattern recognition processes, thus completing partially represented symbols. As shown on the time line in Figure 5.1, the ability to recognize patterns in this way may be a developmental process, exhibited to a greater or lesser extent depending on the level of advancement of the human or organizational system.

Since organizational behavior involves the simultaneous coordination of activities at many levels, it may well require the coordination of activities involving different cognitive architectures operating in parallel. In line with this "mixed architecture" thinking, we have increasing evidence that people can learn to simultaneously process verbal and non-verbal behavior, affective cues, norms, past experiences, and attitudes without even being aware that all of these are being processed (Lord and Maher, 1991).

I will argue that a mixed cognitive architecture approach implies that we convert prior *either/or* debates into integrative *and* propositions. Below, I will touch on four such propositions:

1   Knowledge as the content of internal mental models *and* knowledge accessible only through external cues
2   Interpretations as the result of cognition *and* affect
3   Automatic *and* controlled cognitive processes
4   Distributed *and* shared cognitions

Finally, a mixed architecture approach suggests exciting opportunities for future research, which I will address in the chapter's concluding section.

The Nature of Knowledge

As has been noted, symbolic architectures represent knowledge as the content of a particular memory location that people must access. In line with this reasoning, most of the work on managerial cognition (and cognitive science in general) has focused on the content of knowledge structures or mental models (Walsh, 1995). An example is the widespread research interest in threat and opportunity schemata (Huff, 1990; Walsh, 1995). My exemplar study (Table 5.2) uncovered what I described as stable threat and opportunity orientations in the texts I analyzed. From this perspective, knowledge content is viewed as relatively fixed and homogeneous, and the capacity for storing and retrieving knowledge is inherently limited: "Human short-term memory can hold only a half dozen chunks, an act of recognition takes nearly a second, and the simplest human reactions are measured in tens and hundreds of milliseconds, rather than microseconds, nanoseconds, or picoseconds. These limits are among the most important invariants of intelligence" (Simon, 1990, p. 17). Much organizational research has focused on the implications of this limited processing capacity of decision makers.

If however, as suggested above, the brain has many sub-processors that interact when people perform complex tasks, then it should not be constrained by the limited capacity of a single processor. From a connectionist point of view, knowledge lies in connections, rather than in any one location. Consistent with this view, we know that Einstein's brain was not bigger than the average brain, though it was found to have more connections than the average brain. Knowledge is not fixed, but rather emerges at the moment it is needed from the interaction of large numbers of elements all working in concert with one another (Anderson, 1990). Based on neural or connectionist theories of cognition, knowledge content exists only in the presence of an activating source. It lies in the interactions among neurons. The content of knowledge structures is thus less important than the availability of knowledge cues and the processes by which internal and external cues interact. This assumption is reflected in the Lindell et al. (1998) exemplar study (Table 5.2), in which they attempted to capture "real-time" thinking. Meanings are not imposed *a priori* or from some centralized location; they emerge from the process. Richer cues set off more interactions, stimulating access to more knowledge. Access to knowledge is thus less limited because the system effectively bypasses short-term memory limitations.

For example, the mental capacity limitations of my university class may be due more to the fact that my learning tools tend to be visual and linguistic (symbolic), than to any inherent cognitive limitations of the class members. If I were to use multiple channels of knowledge input, attentional resources in the class might be less limiting. That is, cognitive limitations may stem from the structure of tasks and the nature of inputs, as much as from the limits of the people performing the tasks. From a developmental perspective, the mental capacity limitations of my class may also exist because our entire curriculum has revolved around honing our students' mental models of organizational worlds, with little regard for helping them develop the ability to recognize and act on emergent connections and patterns.

In sum, I suggest turning the debate about the nature of knowledge into an integrative proposition: Knowledge is located both in the content of internal mental models *and* accessible through external cues. It is time to stop asking whether symbolic *or* connectionist cognitive architectures are more appropriate. We must instead embrace the complexity of their simultaneous interactions in producing knowledge.

Cognition and Affect

Similar to the debate about whether intraorganizational institutions are "hot" or "cold" (Elsbach, in this volume), there is disagreement about whether cognitions can be affect-free. From a symbolic perspective, cognitive structures are thought to be affect-free (Lyles and Schwenk, 1992), so one can describe emotions as separate from cognition. For example, in the Huff chapter, I mapped only "cold" cognitive structures (Table 5.2), with no regard to the managers' emotional reactions to the notion of joint ventures. From a connectionist perspective, it is not the symbols that are connected, but the neuron-like units that form the basis for the symbols that are connected through multiple paths. Both emotion and thought may thus be reflected in the simultaneous operation of integrated parallel processes at this more micro level (Lord and Maher, 1991). From the latter perspective, it makes little sense to separate cognition and affect. For example, Lindell et al. (Table 5.2) noted that their subject "felt exhausted and felt that he was tearing himself apart" (Lindell et al., 1998, p. 84).

The idea that non-verbal and affective capacities for perception occur in parallel with more symbolically based cognitive capacities holds important implications for organizational behavior and outcomes. First, it renders obsolete the old arguments about whether thought precedes emotion or emotion precedes thought, or about whether or not emotions are mediating variables between cognition and action. Connectionist explanations suggest relationships between affect and cognition that reflect connections at a much deeper level than such symbolically based serial representations. This suggests that it may be unimportant where one intervenes (at the level of emotions or cognitions) to effect a change. Each will cyclically influence the other.

A second implication has to do with the need to overcome human cognitive capacity limitations. Under high-load cognitive conditions, people can overcome their cognitive limitations by placing more emphasis on nonverbal and affective processing capacities. We have long known that emotions affect cognitive interpretations because cognitive recall tends to be mood congruent (Weick, 1995). However, the idea that both emotion and thought may be reflected in the operation of integrated parallel processes suggests a much more simultaneously interactive relationship between the two than previously thought.

Until very recently, emotion has been conspicuous in its absence in organizational research. If we accept the proposition that affect may be inseparable from cognition in many decision contexts, we can no longer afford to ignore it. I agree with Walsh (1995, p. 308), who stated that "studying emotion as it relates to cognition is one of the most important new research directions the field can take." Interventions at the level of emotions must also play a more central role in organizational practice. If cognition and emotion co-exist and affect each other reciprocally, it matters less where we intervene, since the effects of cognitive intervention will spill over to emotions and vice versa. It would seem that interventions would be most powerful if they tackled both emotions and cognition simultaneously. With limited resources, however, it is important to note that interventions at either level will cyclically influence the other.

In sum, I suggest turning the hot-cold debate into an integrative proposition: Interpretations are the result of both cognition *and* affect, often operating simultaneously. It is time to stop asking "whether or not emotional elements are considered [along with cognition]" (Eden and Spender, 1998, p. 80). Instead, we must embrace the complexity of their simultaneous existence.

Automatic and Controlled Cognitive Processes

Symbolic architectures assume that people have conscious access to the operations of retrieval, transformation, and storage of symbol structures (Lord and Maher, 1991). At the same time, such internal mental models of the outside world can become well learned and routinized, thus lowering the demands for conscious control of information processing.

Mindless and routine behaviors, however, may be learned not only through cognitive analysis that is well rehearsed, but also simply by acting. This is similar to the distinction between declarative (factual) knowledge and procedural knowledge (how to do things) (Anderson, 1990). That is, people retain knowledge not only in the form of symbols expressed through language, but also as cues embedded in actions and interactions (Eden and Spender, 1998). In connectionist systems, knowledge is represented by the pattern of activation among units, not in a value stored at some specific memory location. The interrelations among the units are built up with experience, often without awareness or direct control. For example, the thought patterns of Lindell et al.'s subject

(Table 5.2) reflected new meanings as a result of what they described as interactive "chains of thinking and acting" (Lindell et al., 1998 p. 90).

Here again, the accomplishment of some tasks may occur through the simultaneous use of different architectures. For example, strategic decision makers may utilize controlled and centralized cognitive processes to retrieve well-learned schemata of their environment as threat- or opportunity-filled. An unexpected antagonistic competitor move may cause them to revise the schemata in ways that may not relate to the original schemata, and without their conscious awareness that they are doing so.

If one assumes that people have limited cognitive capacity, then mindless behavior is one way to cope under conditions of cognitive high-load. Though automatic processing may be superior to mindful behavior under business-as-usual conditions, it can lead to errors, especially under novel or problematic conditions (Fiol and Huff, 1992; Louis and Sutton, 1991). Errors occur because people do not recognize the presence of conditions in which they should switch to mindful thinking. If one assumes a connectionist architecture, cognitively busy perceivers may mindfully rely on non-verbal rather than symbolic verbal information. They may thus reduce the cognitive load by trading off one mindful cognitive resource for another, rather than risking automating the process when conditions require mindful behavior. As Simon (1990, p. 11) noted, "Problem solving by ... pattern recognition and extrapolation are examples of adaptation to complex task environments that take appropriate account of computational limitations of bounded rationality." As noted, such pattern recognition and extrapolation capabilities must be developed. Everyone may not be equally adept at trading off one mindful cognitive resource for another. To the extent that such self-regulation leads to effective individual and organizational results, we should focus on its further development.

If we accept the proposition that automatic and controlled processes operate simultaneously, the notion of "gear-switching" (Louis and Sutton, 1991) becomes obsolete, or at least of little interest. The "switches" occur so often and so quickly that it does not make sense to separate the two processes. There is no "high hill therefore low gear" mechanical connection (Czarniawska-Joerges, 1999) that makes gear-switching relevant.

Cognitive processes may thus include both automatic *and* controlled processes simultaneously. It is time to stop debating about whether the universe exists as "mindful, mindless, *or* out of our minds" (Walsh, 1995, p. 306, emphasis added). We must instead embrace the apparent paradox of their simultaneous existence.

Distributed and Shared Cognition

"Cognition belongs to individuals, not to organizations" (Eden and Spender, 1998, p. 193). Consistent with this assumption, the Lindell et al. chapter (Table 5.2) focuses on the cognitive structures of a single individual. Such a common preoccupation with individual cognition has left organizational theorists with the dilemma of how to account for cognition in groups and organizations. There continues to be significant controversy as to how to approach the study of collective cognition. Do influential individuals bring their own schema to the group, causing it to become a frame of reference for the group? Do shared schemata emerge that characterize a group mind? Should researchers examine each individual's cognitive responses and treat them as nodes in a network?

Historically, researchers studying groups and organizations have tended to view collective cognition from a symbolic perspective. For example, Lyles and Schwenk's (1992) organization-level cognitive structures represent shared symbolic schemata. Similarly, Elsbach's chapter in this volume describes intraorganizational institutions as shared cognitions across organizational members. Though fairly common (see Huff, 1990), such an approach continues to be suspect. Some of the contributors to Eden and Spender's work, for example, (1998, p. 141) found a high degree of idiosyncrasy in managers' knowledge structures about their competitive environment. They contrasted these findings to numerous prior studies that had found significant commonalties at the organizational and strategic group levels. Discounting the validity of prior findings, they concluded by arguing forcibly that cognitive data must be collected at the individual level.

The puzzle does not appear to be such a simplistic either/or puzzle, however. Both distributed and shared cognition may coexist. Sometimes shared symbolic structures do exist at the level of the collective (Staw, 1991). Often they do not. Mutual interactions in the past and desire to continue interactions in the future facilitate the conversion of individual experience into shared – or at least "equivalent" – knowledge (Weick, 1995). One would expect such shared or equivalent mental architectures to change over time, beginning with abstract and general models, and gaining increasing specificity over time through continued interactions (Klimoski and Mohammed, 1994). For example, in stable long-term teams, one would expect widespread sharing of complex mental models. Shared schemata in collectives can lead to exceptional results, as when a basketball player throws a pass at a particular spot before her teammate reaches that spot. The schemata have been well developed with lots of practice. Of course, if one of the team members is injured, or if the rules of the game change, the well-learned scripts can become a hindrance.

How do such shared or equivalent schemata develop over time in groups? Weick and Roberts (1993) argued that they were able to talk about group mind without reification because they grounded their ideas in individual actions and then treated those actions as the means by which a higher-order pattern of interrelated activities emerged. Langfield-Smith (1992) also attempted to find evidence for the development of a shared cognitive map. She found that power issues and differences in the meaning people assigned to their language got in the way of such sharing. Though components of individual cognitive maps were shared, they did not form a coherent unified map.

Both the Weick and Roberts (1993) and the Langfield-Smith (1992) studies illustrate the critical role of social interaction in the development of collective knowledge. When individual understanding is inadequate, a remaining important source of understanding is in social interaction, just as when symbolic processing leaves gaps in individual cognitive processes and the remaining knowledge resides in the neural interactions. This conceptualization of the collective mind as a pattern of interrelations of actions and actors in a social system resembles a connectionist approach.

Larson and Christensen (1993) argued that our understanding of individual cognition can be used as a basis for understanding cognition at the level of collectives. They noted that everything we know about individual cognition is inferred from observations of behavior, so cognition is at best an "explanatory fiction." They suggested expanding the fiction to help us to account for group-level processes (Larson and Christensen, 1993, p. 7).

Their "expanded fiction" draws on the following parallels between individual and collective cognition: From a symbolic perspective, groups must cope with limited cognitive resources just as individuals do. From a connectionist perspective, the way an organizational network is structured (how nodes are interconnected) affects recall and cognitive processing much like the organization of information in individual memory networks. And meta-knowledge is information about the problem-relevant information that other group members have, which is similar to mnemonic devices at the individual level. Finally, individuals lose access through loss of memory as do groups, both through individual loss of memory and through individuals leaving the group.

Collective knowledge may thus exist as highly shared symbolic schemata among members, it may exist as unevenly distributed knowledge among participants, and it may be shared or gain equivalent meanings through heedful interrelating. It is time to stop the debate about whether managerial cognitions are held at "the group *or* individual level" (Eden and Spender, 1998, p. 7, emphasis added). We must instead embrace the complexities of the two levels co-existing through interactive processes.

New and Emerging Directions for Future Research

Needless to say, the domains of managerial and organizational cognition are very imprecise. There is little agreement about what to study, how to study it, and toward what ends. To simplify and attempt to make sense of the field, we seem to have glommed onto the alluringly simple schema-based theories of cognition in organizations. The problem is that we are embracing schemata as explanations just as many psychologists appear to be backing away from them and turning to connectionist explanations of cognition.

Certainly we may continue to learn something from borrowed second-hand theoretical fads of the moment. In the process, though, we may be condemning ourselves to practicing a lagged, attenuated version of some other discipline (Kuklinski et al., 1991). And in the process, we risk becoming more and more distanced from the phenomena we want to understand. The costs of such distance are severe: It prevents us from developing a deep understanding of the issues we care about most today, and it blocks the discovery of the next level of relevant questions for future research.

What are the substantive questions about cognition in organizations that we want to better understand? We need to start with the organizational phenomena that need to be explained, and find a theory to explain them, rather than vice versa. Beginning with borrowed cognitive science theories and working back from there can take us down the wrong path because cognitive scientists and organizational researchers have different agendas. The former want to understand how the human mind functions; the latter want to understand how the human mind functions in order to understand how organizations function and how to improve their functioning. A-social, a-emotional, individual-level, conscious schemata tell us very little about cognitive processes in social, emotional, collective organizational settings. It is little wonder that organizational practitioners "rarely read us because they do not find our texts interesting" (Czarniawska-Joerges, 1997, p. 200).

How can our work on organizational cognition become more relevant, interesting, and important? I will touch on four research issues that flow from an acknowledgment of mixed cognitive architectures. First, we need to explore how knowledge transfers take place in organizations. Our current learning theories rest on old assumptions about cognition and organization. If one assumes a fixed and limited symbolic cognitive architecture and a centralized and mechanistic organizational form, learning is assumed to flow from knowledge content that is transmitted across the organization.

From a connectionist perspective, learning derives from shared experience as well as shared facts. It is a shift of focus from knowledge transmission to connection. The implications for theories of learning in organizations are significant. Explicit language-based training may actually inhibit learning. Learning mechanisms must begin to encompass interactive sense making as well as top-down sense giving.

Second, we need to better understand how symbolic and connectionist architectures interrelate. There has been very little work in cognitive science concerned with how the different cognitive architectures may interact (Lord and Maher, 1991). The research void in psychology provides an opportunity for us as organizational theorists to develop relevant insights from within organizational worlds. Weick (1995, p. 135) suggested an interesting rule of thumb: "Sensemaking involves taking whatever is clearer, whether it be a belief [e.g., symbolic schema] or an action [e.g., connectionist cue], and linking it with that which is less clear."

From a developmental perspective, individual and organizational cognitive systems may evolve at varying rates in their capacity for parallel connectionist processing. It is possible that simpler systems begin at a symbolic level and evolve over time toward connectionist approaches. Connectionism may be associated with advanced systems and superior performance. If so, learning how to learn parallel connectionist processing becomes an interesting and important avenue for future research.

Third, we need to bring contexts into the center of our theories of intraorganizational cognition and interpretation. Schema-based research sidesteps the issue of context, because internal mental models are thought to remain consistent across different contexts. From the perspective of connectionist theories, context is not simply the setting in which cognition takes place. Context is a large part of cognition itself. It is part of the process.

Finally, we need to better operationalize our constructs to capture what we think is important in cognition research. Differences between cognition and models of cognition have always existed because modeling may be quite far removed from what subjects are actually thinking. Until not too long ago, the mind was a black box for most researchers. We have begun to open the black box, mainly through the tool of symbolic mental modeling. New technologies may soon allow us to capture connectionist architectures in ways unheard of at present.

The validity of a construct is often expressed as the extent to which it measures what we think it measures, and the extent to which our conclusions are accurate according to our predictions. Instead, it may be more interesting and appropriate to ask: "Have we allowed the respondent to respond in a way which is salient and meaningful to him or her?" (Eden and Spender, 1998, p. 240). This is especially important as we attempt to measure connectionist constructs. The possibilities for accurately mapping implicit action-driven knowledge are minimal. Its tacit form means it cannot easily be made explicit through linguistic symbols. It seems to me that this makes it even more important for us, as researchers, to suspend our own well-formed mental models about our research, and allow external cues to inform us as to what is important in a research setting.

Our need for theoretical parsimony and statistical purity and simplicity seems linked to old, serial, symbolic assumptions about cognition and organization. Eden and Spender (1998, p. 206) noted that there is "a great danger of this need for numerical measures producing a form of statistical masturbation." The measures we choose may say more about us as researchers than about the subjects of our research. For example, there continue to be tensions between the cognition agendas and theories of researchers from different parts of the world. Eden and Spender (1998) argued that their volume reflected "a more European view" (p. 1). They fault contributors to the Huff (1990) (presumably more "North American") volume of "attributing similarity at every analytic level" (p. 21). Such divisions will not lead us to embrace the complexities we face. It is time to focus more on our subjects of research than on our differences as researchers.

If the field of intraorganizational cognition is imprecise today, I predict that it will only become more so as we begin to delve into the complexities reflected in the newer theories of cognition and organization. To progress as a field does not mean we will converge on consistent answers in the future. In fact, the opposite is likely to be true.

As our modeling of cognition becomes more complex, we will also need more sophisticated methods that will allow us to capture these complexities and paradoxes. I have noted the potential problems with the construct of mental models, problems with its measurement, and suggestions that perhaps no such thing as a "mental model" even exists. If we approach these issues from a paradoxical mindset, more interested in substantive issues than with our favorite research tool, we might ask: Do the measurement problems derive from situating schemata in inappropriate contexts, rather than being measurement problems *per se*? Does it matter whether or not people actually hold internal mental models? If identifying and measuring them allow us to better understand and/or predict events and behaviors in organizations, does it really matter whether or not they actually exist in the mind in the form that we say they do?

As we begin to assimilate and build on more complex theories of cognition and of organization, we must squelch our tendency for either-or thinking. It plagues most of us, even today. Though Eden and Spender (1998) represent the most recent "exemplar" on my list in Table 5.1, for example, their chapters continue to be limited by such either-or thinking: Some of them argued that cognition belongs to the individual only, and others that it is always grounded in interactions with the social world. The editors themselves continue to ask either-or questions such as "Are cognitive structures stable or continuously changing? Are managerial cognitions held at "the group or individual level?" (p. 7). To progress in our learning about intraorganizational cognition, we must begin to ask "and" rather than "or" questions.

This means that we need to embrace apparent paradox. As researchers, we tend to avoid paradoxes, or we try to untangle or resolve them. They are seen as problematic, messy, and something we need to get rid of. They violate logic; and as Van de Ven and Poole (1988) pointed out, they also violate our quest for coherent and consistent theories. Instead of embracing and making sense of paradoxes that exist in the world, we tend to engage in intricate processes of "deparadoxification" (Czarniawska, 1997, p. 173).

New metaphors can help break down old patterns of thinking. Barbara Czarniawska persuasively argued for the need for new metaphors of organization to replace old and worn out metaphors that "appear to be metaphorically deceptive" (1997, p. 4). One of the fields she turns to in search of new metaphors is literary criticism. Stories actively involve the listener and the teller in mutual construction and reconstruction. Therein lies the power of narratives in capturing the richness and the apparent paradoxes in the nature of mixed cognitive architectures. We must continue the search for new metaphors to guide us in breaking down our worn-out old schemata about organizational cognition!

Connections Across Levels

This chapter has examined *intra*organizational cognition and interpretation. How do my conclusions relate to the subsequent two chapters on organization-level and industry-level cognition and interpretation? In their discussion at the interorganizational level, Porac and Mishina point to two distinct views of cognition, reductionism and contextualism. The former relies on the primacy of individuals in cognitive activity; the latter relies on the primacy of the social context within which individuals reside. The authors suggest that researchers' intellectual predilection determines which view one holds, rather than being determined through evidence. I agree and disagree. Certainly our ontological starting point will influence which level tends to be the focus of our research. However, the arguments of this chapter suggest that reductionism and contextualism are more or less appropriate approaches, depending on the context. If knowledge in organizations exists as highly shared schemata, the collective context provides more useful information than do individual cognitive structures. If knowledge is unevenly distributed in organizations, the cognitive activity of individuals takes on more primacy.

As Lant noted in her chapter on organizational cognition, it is difficult, if not impossible, to separate the study of individual and organizational cognition and interpretation. Her discussion of organizations as information processors assumes schemata at the organizational level much like the individual mental models described in this chapter. And again similar to my arguments in this chapter, she notes that the extension from individual to organizational cognition is not straightforward. It is highly influenced by contextual factors. Porac and Mishina also note the influence of context on industry-level mindsets.

From the perspective of the connectionist theories I have described, context is an integral part of cognition, whether individual or collective. It is a process that happens through social interactions. Meaning and understanding develop through those interactions. All three chapters on cognition and interpretation are thus essentially in agreement on this point: Whether at the group, the organization, or the industry levels of analysis, cognitions emerge from the interplay of bottom-up inference processes and top-down influences and constraints over time.

Conclusion

In closing, this chapter represents a plea for us to explore a more eclectic, creative, and a more distinctively organizational "intraorganizational cognition and interpretation." To do so, we must take inspiration from both newer and older theories, not restricting ourselves to fashions of the moment. Most important, to do so, we must focus on the substantive problems that face organizations today.

Acknowledgments

Many thanks to Ed O'Connor, Joel Baum, Herman Aguinis, Karl Weick, Barbara Czarniawska-Joerges, and Thomas MacKenzie for their valuable comments on earlier versions of this chapter.

References

Anderson, J. R. (1990): *Cognitive Psychology and its Implications.* New York: Freeman.

Czarniawska-Joerges, B. (1997): *Narrating the Organization: Dramas of Institutional Identity.* Chicago, IL: The University of Chicago Press.

Czarniawska-Joerges, B. (1999): Personal communication

Eden, C., and Spender, J.-C., (eds), (1998): *Managerial and Organizational Cognition.* London: Sage.

Fiol, C. M. (1990): "Explaining strategic alliance in the chemical industry," in A. S. Huff (ed.), *Mapping Strategic Thought,* Chichester: Wiley, 227–49.

Fiol, C. M., and Huff, A. S. (1992): "Maps for managers: Where are we? Where do we go from here?" *Journal of Management Studies,* 29(3), 267–85.

Fiske, S. T., and Taylor, S. E. (1984): *Social Cognition.* Reading, MA: Addison-Wesley.

Huff, A. S. (ed.), (1990): *Mapping Strategic Thought.* Chichester: Wiley.

Kelly, G. A. (1955): *The Psychology of Personal Constructs.* New York: Norton.

Klimoski, R., and Mohammed, S. (1994): "Team mental model: Construct or metaphor?" *Journal of Management,* 20, 403–37.

Kuklinski, J. H., Luskin, R. C., and Bolland, J. (1991): "Where is the schema? Going beyond the 's' work is political psychology," *American Political Science Review,* 85, 1341–56.

Langfield-Smith, K. (1992): "Exploring the need for a shared cognitive map," *Journal of Management Studies,* 29, 349–68.

Larson, J. R., and Christensen, C. (1993): "Groups as problem-solving units: Toward a new meaning of social cognition," *British Journal of Social Psychology,* 32, 5–30.

Lewis, M. (1992): "Situated visualization: Building interfaces from the mind up," *Multimedia Review,* Spring, 23–40.

Lindell, P., Melin, L., Gahmberg, H. J., Hellqvist, A., and Melander, A. (1998): "Stability and change in a strategist's thinking," in C. Eden and J.-C. Spender (eds), *Managerial and Organizational Cognition: Theory, Methods, and Research,* Thousand Oaks, CA: Sage, 76–92.

Lord, R. G., and Maher, K. J. (1991): "Cognitive theory in industrial and organizational psychology," in M. D. Dunette and L. M. Hough (eds), *Handbook of Industrial and Organizational Psychology,* Palo Alto, CA: Consulting Psychologist Press, 1–62.

Louis, M. R., and Sutton, R. I. (1991): "Switching cognitive gears: From habits of mind to active thinking," *Human Relations,* 44, 55–76.

Lyles, M. A., and Schwenk, C. R. (1992): "Top management, strategy and organizational knowledge structures," *Journal of Management Studies,* 29(2), 155–74.

Meindl, J. R., Stubbart, C., and Porac, J. F. (eds), (1996): *Cognition Within and Between Organizations.* London: Sage.

Simon, H. A. (1990): "Invariants of human behavior," in M. Rosenzweig and L. Porter (eds), *Annual Review of Psychology,* 4, Palo Alto, CA: Annual Reviews, 1–19.

Staw, B. M. (1991): "Dressing up like an organization: When psychological theories can explain organizational action," *Journal of Management,* 17(4), 805–19.

Tolman, E. C. (1948): "Cognitive maps in rats and men," *Psychological Review,* 55, 189–208.

Van de Ven, A. H., and Poole, M. S. (1988): "Paradoxical requirements for a theory of change," in R. E. Quinn and K. S. Cameron (eds), *Paradox and Transformation: Toward a Theory of Change in Organization and Management,* Cambridge, MA: Ballinger, 19–64.

Walsh, J. P. (1995): "Managerial and organizational cognition: Notes from a trip down memory lane," *Organization Science*, 6(3), 280–321.

Weick, K. E. (1995): *Sensemaking in Organizations*. London: Sage.

Weick, K. E., and Roberts, K. H. (1993): "Collective mind in organizations: Heedful interrelating on flight decks," *Administrative Science Quarterly*, 38, 357–81.

Chapter Six

Intraorganizational Power and Dependence

DANIEL J. BRASS

"The study of power in organizations has been both plagued and blessed by the multitude of theories and approaches that have been offered" (Brass and Burkhardt, 1993, p. 441). Indeed, so much has been written about intraorganizational power, based on so little actual empirical research, that it is surprising that even a common definition of power can be distilled. Yet, it is commonly accepted that power is the ability to get others to do something that they would not otherwise do (Dahl, 1957). This simple definition is, however, not without its subtle nuances and writers have argued at length about what this definition implies. For example, does "ability" mean potential or actual use? Is resistance or conflict necessary for the exercise of power? Is power relative, situational, transitive, and perceptual? Despite these academic questions, most people in organizations seem to have an intuitive notion of power. As Salancik and Pfeffer (1977) note, most employees seem to know what power is and who has it in their organizations; members of organizations can easily nominate people that they feel have a lot of power or influence in their organizations – and they tend to agree (Brass, 1984).

This does not mean that people in organizations enjoy talking about power. As Pfeffer (1992) so often noted, power and politics are still "dirty words" in most organizations. Few organizational members prefer to see the organizational as a political arena made up of individuals or coalitions with differing interests, fighting over the best things to do or the best way to get things done. Despite the negative connotations associated with power in organizations, most employees realize that the use of power is prevalent in organizations (Gandz and Murray, 1980). Whether we view it as a good or bad thing, it is obvious that we need to study it and understand if we are to understand organizations and how they function. This chapter is an attempt to summarize what we know – and don't know – about power in organizations.

Common to many approaches to power in organizations is a reliance on exchange theory, or a dependency framework such as that offered by Emerson (1962). Power is viewed, or defined, as the opposite of dependence. The power of Actor A over Actor B is the extent to which Actor B is dependent on Actor A. Building on this framework, the strategic contingencies approach (Hickson et al., 1971) and the resource dependency approach (Salancik and Pfeffer, 1977) argue that power (the inverse of dependence) derives from control of critical resources. Control implies that other actors are dependent upon the powerful actor for the resource – they have few alternative sources for acquiring the resource. The powerful actor controls or mediates others' access to the outcome or resource. A critical resource is one that is in demand or in which another actor has a high motivational investment (Emerson, 1962). One's power increases as alternative sources of the resource diminish. Actors gain power by being irreplaceable sources of resources that are in demand. Thus, organizational actors who are able to control critical resources increase other's dependence on them and, via the exchange process, are able to acquire additional resources or bring about the outcomes they desire.

In addition to increasing others' dependence on them, actors seeking power must also decrease their dependence on others. They may increase the number of alternative sources available for acquiring the outcome, or decrease their motivational investment in the resource or outcome (Emerson, 1962). To acquire power, one must have access to critical resources that is independent, not controlled or mediated, by others. Thus, in order to acquire power, actors must do two things: increase others' dependence on them and decrease their dependence on others. In many ways, it is as simple as supply and demand. You are powerful to the extent that your control the supply of resources (few alternatives exist) that are in great demand and you are not dependent on others for the supply of resources you demand.

Because there may be a multitude and variety of resources that may be considered critical or in demand in organizations, the exchange of resources does not typically involve only one resource. Exchanges also may involve more than one transaction and occur at more than one time, but are restricted by opportunities for contact, ideological similarity, or social inertia (Marsden, 1983). For example, A may control a particular outcome that is desired by B, but B may control another, different outcome that is desired by A. A and B exchange resources, with the more powerful of the two getting the better deal.

The organization is typically more powerful than an employee (less dependent on the employee than vice versa) and gets the better of the deal – by paying the employee, the organization makes additional money over and above the cost of the employee. However, this power relationship can change if the organization becomes dependent on the employee's job completion or if the employee decreases his/her dependence on the organization by finding alternative sources of the desired resource (money).

The classic example of power/dependence relations is Crozier's (1964) study of maintenance workers in French tobacco plants. In the highly bureaucratized state-owned plants, jobs were routinized and workers paid on a piece rate system. All aspects of production were highly planned and easily controlled, except for the machinery that tended to break down. Although the maintenance works had very little formal authority, the production workers depended on the continuing smooth operation of the machines in order to earn their piece rates. Indeed the entire organization depended on the ability of the maintenance workers to keep the machines running and repair them when they broke down. Thus, the maintenance workers acquired a great deal of power by controlling one of the few critical uncertainties in the organization – the repair of the machinery. The organization could not decrease its dependence on the maintenance workers. They maintained their autonomy, status, and power by systematically avoiding any attempts by management to standardize their functions – no records of repairs were kept and no repair manuals could be found. The maintenance workers controlled the critical resource (expertise in machinery repair) and increased the organization's dependence on them by being the only ones who could provide that resource.

In addition to agreement on a power/dependence framework, researchers tend to agree that power involves a social relationship among actors, noting that the actors may be people, groups, or organizations. Because power is a social phenomenon, it is not unreasonable to assume that it is affected by perceptions. Arguments concerning the perceptual nature of power may be moot. If I perceive that another person has power over me and consequently do something that I would not otherwise do because of my perception, than, by definition, that person has power over me. Whether my perception is accurate or not makes little difference. This assumption suggests that we look not only at the sources of power but the commonly perceived indicators of power as well. Accurate perceptions of power, who has it and why, may also be critical to the successful use of power (Pettigrew, 1973; Krackhardt, 1990).

There is less agreement on whether conflict is a necessary precursor to the use of power. In defining power as the ability to make another actor(s) do something that the actor(s) would not "otherwise" do (Dahl, 1957), I suggest that there may or may not be resistance to be overcome when influencing others. When a supervisor tells a subordinate to complete a report by Monday, the subordinate may readily agree even if s/he was planning on completing the report on Tuesday. Despite the agreement, the supervisor has influenced the subordinate – made him/her do something that s/he would not otherwise do. In addition, power may be used to avoid conflicts. For example, Lukes (1974) argued that power might be used by the elite to sustain the status quo – to shape perceptions such that alternatives are not considered and existing roles are viewed as beneficial; see also Hardy and Clegg (1996). I do assume that power is more likely to be exercised and visible when conflicts exist – when actors have differing interests or preferences about either means or ends. These differences will vary in importance and more power is needed when differences exist that are important to the actors.

Researchers agree that interdependence is a necessary condition for the exercise of power. In some way, the actors must be tied together. This assumption results in very little constraint when discussing power in organizations. As Pfeffer (1992) notes, "The essence of organizations is interdependence, and it is not news that all of us need to obtain the assistance of others in order to accomplish our jobs." In cases of very low or no interdependence, there is no reason to exercise power. In cases of very high interdependence, there are incentives to avoid conflict and search for common agreement, thereby avoiding the use of power (Pfeffer, 1992). Thus, power is likely to be most often used in cases of moderate interdependence (where differences in interests exist). Neither different interests nor interdependence is, by itself, sufficient for power to be exercised.

It is often agreed that power is relative and situation, or context, specific. These assumptions lead us to conclude that an actor is not powerful in relation to all actors or all situations. For example, my doctor may be influenced by my advice about how to organize his office or handle his employees, but I will be influenced by his advice when I am ill. Despite the intuitive logic of the notion that power is relative and context specific, it is not clear that organizational members do not think of power "in general." Subordinates often defer to superiors even when contexts change (I do not want to beat my boss when playing golf). Thus, when organizational members are asked to nominate people who have a lot of influence, they seldom ask the researcher to specify the context or the specific social relationship (Brass, 1984; Salancik and Pfeffer, 1977).

Little agreement exists among researchers on the appropriate approach to the investigation of power. Three relative distinct approaches are evident in the literature. The structural approach has focused on the control of resources. In contrast, the behavioral approach has focused on the actor's ability to use resources: power tactics and bargaining skills. In addition, some sources of power are most easily associated with individual characteristics such as expertise, or personality: e.g., Machiavellianism (House, 1988); charisma (House et al., 1991); or expert and referent power (French and Raven, 1968). I refer to these as personal sources of power. Following, I review the literature on each approach.

Literature Review

Table 6.1 presents key concepts, findings, and contributions from some exemplar research studies discussed in this chapter.

STRUCTURAL SOURCES OF POWER

Pfeffer (1981) has argued that power is first and foremost a structural phenomenon. Brass (1984, p. 518) adds, "While personal attributes and strategies may have an important effect on power acquisition, . . . structure imposes the ultimate constraints on the individual." Structural sources of power reflect the properties of a social system rather than the particular attributes or behaviors of any particular individual or interaction (Astley and Sachdeva, 1984). Power results from an actor's position within the social system. Two kinds of structural position may result in power: formal (hierarchical level) and informal (network position).

The power associated with hierarchical level in an organization, often referred to as authority or legitimate power, represents the legitimated, institutionalized privilege of incumbency (Astley and Sachdeva, 1984). The power resides in the position, not the incumbent. Both supervisors and subordinates recognize and accept the power of the position (Madison et al., 1980). Because of the socially shared, institutionalized nature of hierarchical position, it is one of the strongest sources of potential power and one of the most immutable structural constraints on power. In addition, the ability to reward and punish (French and Raven, 1968) may be associated with the positions of authority in organizations.

As the classic obedience experiments illustrate (Milgram, 1965) obedience to authority is common. Subjects continued to apply perceived electrical shocks to victims when told to do so by the experimenter, disregarding cries and pleas from the supposed victim, victim's claims of heart trouble, and indicators of "Danger: Severe Shock" on the applicator dial. Milgram (1965, p. 329) concludes, "With numbing regularity good people were seen to knuckle under the demands of authority and to perform actions that were callous and severe." Although it is difficult to overestimate the power of authority in organizations, few researchers have investigated this taken-for-granted source of power; see Brass and Burkhardt (1993) for an exception. Instead, researchers have focused on informal structural sources of power such as social networks.

Table 6.1 Selected research on intraorganizational power and dependence

Reference	Key concepts	Key variables	Key predictions and findings	Key contribution	Method and sample
Brass (1984)	Social networks as structural sources of individual power	Workflow and communications network centrality, connections to dominant coalition	Network centrality, connections to dominant coalition related to reputational measures of power	Illustrates structural approach to sources of power	Regression analyses of responses to survey questionnaire of 140 non-supervisors and their supervisors in a newspaper publishing company
Kipnis and Schmidt (1988)	Upward influence styles as behavioral sources of power	Reason, friendliness, assertiveness, bargaining, appeal to high authority, and coalition formation	Four styles identified through cluster analysis; tactician style related to earnings, stress, and performance evaluation, shotgun style had negative effect	Illustrates behavioral approach to sources of power	Three studies: cluster analysis and regression of responses to survey questionnaire to 37 supervisors and their subordinates, 113 MBA students and their superiors, and 108 CEOs.
House et al. (1991)	Needs and charisma as personal sources of power	Need for power, affiliation, and achievement, activity inhibition, charisma and performance	Need for power and activity inhibition related to charisma; all three related to performance	Illustrates personal approach to sources of power	Expert coding of archival materials used in regression analysis of performance of 39 US Presidents
Salancik and Pfeffer (1974)	Power acquired by providing scarce, critical resources to organization; power affects resource allocations	Interview-based ratings, membership on research board, representation on important committees as measures of power; several determinants of power	Power related to ability to obtain outside grants and contracts, national prestige and relative size of graduate program. Power used to allocate most scarce and critical resources	Test of resource dependence theory of power at the subunit level of analysis	Regression analysis of ratings of academic departments at large Midwestern university

Study				
Hinings et al. (1974)	Power results from strategic contingencies of coping with uncertainty, workflow centrality, and nonsubstitutability	Coping with uncertainty, workflow centrality (immediacy and pervasiveness), and nonsubstitutability. Interview and questionnaire rating of subunit power	Coping with uncertainty, workflow centrality, nonsubstitutability characterized top ranked subunits	Test of strategic contingencies theory of power at the subunit level of analysis	Profile rankings of 28 subunits in 7 manufacturing organizations
Brass and Burkhardt (1993)	Potential power (structural sources) and power use (behavioral sources)	Communication network centrality, hierarchy, upward influence strategies	Structural sources of power mediated relationship between behavioral strategies and power, and vice versa	Combines structural and behavioral approaches to power	Regression analysis of questionnaire response of 75 employees at a federal agency
Burkhardt and Brass (1990)	Change in technology provides the occasion for redistribution of power	Communication network centrality, reputational measures of power	Early adopters of new technology gained centrality and power	Longitudinal study of changes in power	MANOVA analysis of power changes over four times periods for 81 employees of a federal agency

The social network approach to power has often been applied from a resource dependence framework (Emerson, 1962). Employees in central network positions have greater access to, and potential control over, critical resources than peripheral employees. Most empirical studies have found that a person's centrality in an intraorganizational network is related to power (Brass, 1984, 1985; Brass and Burkhardt, 1993; Burkhardt and Brass, 1990; Fombrun, 1983; Krackhardt 1990; Tushman and Romanelli, 1983). Centrality can be conceptualized and measured in a number of ways. From an exchange perspective, increasing one's alternatives increases one's power. Available alternatives may best be captured by the in-degree measure of power, or the number of others who choose to interact with the focal employee. Although other measures of centrality include the number of people chosen by a focal individual as well as the number of people who choose the focal individual, the in-degree measure includes only the latter (Freeman, 1979). For example, an employee may choose many others, but these others may not reciprocate the choice. The lack of reciprocation may indicate that the employee's numerous choices are not practical alternatives. In-degree measures of centrality are often used as measures of prestige on the assumption that relations are often asymmetric and that powerful actors are more often the object, rather than the source, of communication or other forms of interaction (Knoke and Burt, 1983).

Independent access to others is best tapped by the closeness measure of centrality, which is calculated by summing the lengths of the shortest paths from a focal person to all other persons in an organization. Direct links are counted as one step, with indirect links given proportionally less weight in the measure. By including indirect links, a person with only a few direct ties may be central if those few ties are direct connections to highly connected others in the network. Freeman (1979) notes that closeness centrality taps efficiency (the extent to which the focal person can reach all other persons in the shortest number of direct and indirect links). From the resource dependence perspective, closeness centrality represents access to critical resources.

Control of critical resources is best captured by the betweenness measure of centrality. Betweenness centrality measures the extent to which a focal person falls "between" any two individuals who are not themselves connected. People with high betweenness centrality act as brokers or go-betweens, bridging the "structural holes" between otherwise disconnected others. They control the flow of critical resources between these disconnected others. For example, secretaries often control access to executives – they act as powerful gatekeepers to the resources held by the higher-ups (Mechanic, 1962). Empirical evidence supports what Burt (1992) refers to as structural hole benefits (Brass, 1984; Burt, 1992; Podolny and Baron, 1997).

In a test of the structural approach to power, Brass (1984) surveyed 140 non-supervisory employees and their supervisors at a newspaper publishing company. Employees were asked to list the names of those whom they received inputs from, and sent outputs to, in the workflow (workflow network). The communication network was assessed by asking employees to list the names of those to whom they talked frequently about work-related matters. Reputational measures of power were obtained by asking non-supervisors to nominate people who are very influential in the organization, and asking supervisors to rate their subordinates on a Likert-type scale ranging from very little influence to very much influence in the organization. Significant, positive relationships were found between all three measures of centrality (degree, closeness, and betweenness) across both types of networks (workflow and communication) and reputational measures of power (Brass, 1984, 1985, 1992; Brass and Burkhardt, 1992). In addition, Brass (1984) found that connections to the dominant coalition (a group of four executives who received the most power nominations and who were themselves highly interconnected) were positively and significantly related to power.

Other social network studies have found similar results (Brass and Burkhardt, 1993, Burkhardt and Brass, 1990; Burt, 1992; Krackhardt, 1990). Although it is likely that increased power leads to higher centrality, in a longitudinal study Burkhardt and Brass (1990) found evidence that centrality tended to precede power.

Personal Sources of Power

In addition to structural sources of power, theorists have often looked at individual characteristics as potential sources of power. Individuals clearly differ in abilities, skills, and willingness to use those skills and abilities to acquire and exercise power. Prominent among the list of individual characteristics is expertise (French and Raven, 1968). Expertise implies that the knowledge held by a person is not widely distributed. The nonsubstitutable expertise creates dependence by others on the expert. For example, lower level participants in organizations, such as secretaries, may acquire power through their expertise in filing and knowing where information can be found. Information is often viewed as a critical resource in organizations and possessing information that cannot be acquired elsewhere may involve the ability to cope with critical uncertainties (Pfeffer, 1981). Organizations and people attempt to reduce uncertainty and those that can effectively do so are depended on by others. As the Crozier (1964) example illustrates, the French maintenance workers possessed expertise (how to repair machinery) that could not be acquired elsewhere.

French and Raven (1968) include referent power as one of the five bases of social power. Referent power refers to individuals identifying with and willing to be influenced by a person because of the latter's personality. As with the concept of charisma, the particular aspects of the powerful personality are difficult to identify and may be context specific, dependent on both the situation and the needs of the followers. Also, the focus on individual personality may be a result of the "fundamental attribution error" – people tend to attribute causes to people and their characteristics rather than to situational factors external to the individual. Nevertheless, charisma or referent power seems to be a rare quality that people depend on, and are willing to be influenced by.

House (1988) also has argued for the importance of other personality characteristics in the study of power. Such characteristics include dominance (the degree to which individuals are outgoing, comfortable in social settings, and willing to engage in influence attempts), McClelland's (1985) power motive (a socially learned association between the exercise of power and the experience of satisfaction), and Machiavellianism (resistance to social influence, task related rather than emotional or moral involvement with others, and a strong preference to control interactions with others and resist being controlled). All three characteristics may reflect an individual's willingness to engage in influence attempts. Mintzberg (1983) notes that all influence attempts involve the expenditure of energy. As a result, high levels of energy and physical stamina may be requisite characteristics of powerful people. Other characteristics such as self-confidence, articulateness, social adeptness, extroversion, aggressiveness, and ambition were found to be associated with power in interviews of eight-seven managers representing thirty different firms in the Southern California electronics industry (Allen et al., 1979). These managers were asked, "What are the personal characteristics of those people you feel are most effective in the use of organizational politics?" (Allen et al., 1979, p. 78). Their answers may be consistent with our stereotypes of powerful people. As such, they signal power to observers, and may be sources of influence as observers act as if the confident, articulate, outgoing person has power.

In a direct test of personal characteristics, House et al. (1991) investigated charisma and power motives among 39 US Presidents. Charismatic leaders were defined as those that "transform the needs, values, preferences, and aspirations of followers" and motivate them to "make significant personal sacrifices in the interest of some mission" rather than be motivated by self-interest (House et al., 1991, p. 364). The authors viewed charisma as a relationship between leaders and followers rather than a personality trait of the leader. Charisma was assessed by expert coding of the biographies of cabinet members, editorials from the *New York Times*, and other biographical reference works. Presidential performance was based on previously established ratings made by historians and assessment of biographies contained in encyclopedias. Measures of presidential needs for affiliation (establishing and maintaining close personal relationships), power (concern with reputation, status, and actions that affect others), achievement (concern with unique accomplishment and a standard of excellence), and activity inhibition (using power to achieve institutional rather than personal goals) were derived from a content analysis of presidents' first term inaugural addresses. Need for power and activity inhibition were significantly and positively related to charisma, while need for achievement was negatively related to charisma, and need for affiliation was not significant. Need for power, activity inhibition, and charisma were positively and significantly related to presidential performance. Although this study was a test of leadership theory, it demonstrates how the personal characteristics may be an important source of power in organizations. House (1988) cites several empirical leadership studies that indirectly support his contention that individual characteristics have a major effect on power within organizations.

BEHAVIORAL SOURCES OF POWER

Once a person has control of critical resources and the personal desire to use those resources to influence others, s/he needs to consider how to best use those resources. What are the best behavioral tactics or strategies to use to ensure that the exchange of resources is profitable? Rather than focus on the structural sources of potential power, behavioral approaches focus on power use. Using responses of power incidents from165 graduate business students, Kipnis et al. (1980) grouped influence tactics into six categories: assertiveness, ingratiation, rationality, exchange, upward appeal, and coalition formation (Kipnis and Schmidt, 1988).

Assertiveness includes such influence tactics as demanding compliance, ordering, setting deadlines, nagging, and expressing anger. Ingratiation involves behaviors such as praising, politely asking, acting humble, making the other person feel important, and acting friendly. People prefer to believe that flattery is sincere and tend to like people who provide them with praise. Interpersonal liking can be a powerful source of influence and people tend to agree with, say "yes," and do things for their friends (Cialdini, 1989). On the other hand, people do not like to be coerced. While threats can change people's behavior, they often lead to ill feelings and attempts at retaliation. The two tactics, assertiveness and ingratiation, correspond to French and Raven's coercive and reward bases of power. The theoretical rationale for the effectiveness of these two tactics lies, in part, in the principles of reinforcement theory, or operant conditioning (Thompson and Luthans, 1983). The utility of goal setting for influencing behavior, one component of assertiveness, is well established (cf. Locke, 1976).

The rationality tactic involves using reason, logic, and compromise. In addition to using rationale persuasion, which attempts to convince others that certain actions are in their own best interest, a positive image and status results from being perceived as a rational person. As Pfeffer (1981, p. 194) notes, the use of rationality is almost a religion in formal organizations. There is a widely shared belief, seldom questioned, in the effectiveness of rational analysis, planning, and decision making. Although the language of rationality can be used to justify otherwise political decisions, rationality is a highly valued, socially acceptable, legitimate means of influencing others. It is probably the most often used method of attempting to influence others.

However, the very frequent use of rational persuasion may set limits on its usefulness. At some point, we all tire of rational arguments (e.g., statistics can be used to justify any decision) and often think with our hearts rather than our heads. At these times, language, settings, and ceremonies can be effectively used to elicit emotions consistent with preferred outcomes (Pfeffer, 1992).

The exchange power tactic consists of offering to help others in exchange for reciprocal favors. Scratching each other's respective backs has long been recognized as an effective method of getting things done in governmental politics. The theoretical rationale can be found in exchange theory (Emerson, 1962) which relies heavily on reinforcement and expectancy theories. Individuals attempt to maximize their expected outcomes through the exchange of resources over time. As noted previously, the variety of possible resources in organizations makes exchange, particularly exchange over time, a very viable influence strategy. Laboratory studies (Molm, 1981) have shown that the outcomes of exchange are not a perfect linear function of power imbalance. Equity norms, previous experience, and information can each affect outcomes.

Upward appeal refers to behavioral attempts to gain support from superiors in an organization. Coalition formation involves attempts to build alliances with others. Both coalition formation and upward appeal imply that the power of persons employing these tactics may be low, so that combining resources with others or appealing to those with more power is necessary. Although few empirical studies of intraorganizational coalition formation exist (Baker and Faulkner, 1993; Eisenhardt and Bourgeois, 1988) several theoretical reviews are available (Murnighan, 1978; Murnighan and Brass, 1991; Pfeffer, 1981; Stevenson et al., 1985).

Combinations of these six upward influence tactics have been related to salary, performance evaluations and stress for managers (Kipnis and Schmidt, 1988). Research suggests that the high use of rationality and average use of the other tactics, a combination called "tactician style," may be more effective than either consistently high or consistently low use of all the tactics (Kipnis and Schmidt, 1988; Perreault and Miles, 1978).

In addition to the Kipnis list of tactics, other theorists have offered a variety of additional influence strategies. For example, Pfeffer (1992) has suggested that framing the issue or controlling the agenda can be an effective influence tactic. How things such as decisions are viewed or framed can depend on the context. As the baseball umpire noted in referring to balls and strikes, "They ain't nothing until I call them." Such framing can be particularly effective in ambiguous situations when people are struggling to make sense out of events. However, as candidates for public office have shown, even unambiguous situations such as primary wins or losses can be framed to maximize influence on others. This practice of political framing is now commonly referred to as "spin control," putting the best spin on an event.

How things are viewed depends on how they are framed – what they are compared to, if there is a committed history of action, if they are perceived as scarce. Individuals value consistent action and quickly become committed to certain courses of action. Persuading a person to take a small step (action) can quickly lead to a committed path of related actions leading to a larger goal. The person who controls the agenda controls the decisions that will be made as well as the alternatives that will be considered. Timing is also important. The order in which things are considered and the ability to delay, or, conversely, set deadlines can all affect decision making (Pfeffer, 1992).

Because power is, at least in part, perceptual, bluffing or acting as if one has power can be an effective influence tactic in some situations. Likewise, associating with someone who is considered powerful may lead to perceptions of power. When asked for a loan, the wealthy and successful Baron de Rothschild was reported to have said, "I won't give you a loan myself, but I will walk arm-in-arm with you across the floor of the Stock Exchange, and you soon shall have willing lenders to spare" (Cialdini, 1989, p. 45). Supporting this statement, Kilduff and Krackhardt (1994) found that being perceived to have a prominent friend in an organization was related to an individual's reputation as a good performer. People will often comply with influence attempts if they believe the other person has the necessary resources to exchange in the future. However, continued bluffing or associating with powerful others has its risks and can backfire if one is called on to produce the actual resources or one gains a reputation for engaging in these strategies.

GROUP SOURCES OF POWER

The above structural, personal, and behavioral sources of power have been developed for individuals in organizations. In addition, studies of the power of groups in organizations should be noted. In a study of departments in a large Midwestern university, Salancik and Pfeffer (1974) hypothesized that departments that were able to provide critical resources to the university would receive higher ratings of power by department heads on a Likert-type scale ranging from very little to a great deal of power. A second measure of subunit power was the department's representation on important university committees. Power was found to be related to a department's ability to secure outside grants and contracts, the national prestige of the department, and the relative size of the department's graduate program. They also found that power was most often used in the allocation of critical and scarce resources. The results of this study were replicated in a study of two University of California campuses (Pfeffer and Moore, 1980) in which the paradigm level of the department was also found to be related to power. Pfeffer (1981) interprets this result as an indication that consensus within a group is a relevant source of power.

In a test of strategic contingencies theory, Hinings et al. (1974) studied 28 subunits in seven manufacturing organizations in the United States and Canada. Power was hypothesized to be a function of coping with uncertainty, substitutability (ease with which a subunit's activities and personnel could be replaced), and workflow centrality (extent to which a subunit is connected with other subunits and the speed and severity with which the work of a subunit affects the outputs of the organization). Interview and questionnaire data were collected from seven chief executives and 26 department heads. To measure power, respondents were asked, "How much influence do you think each of the following departments has on problems about (list of 17 specific issues)" (Hinings et al., 1974, p. 44). The highest power rankings were for subunits with a combination of high values on coping with uncertainty, non-substitutability, and workflow centrality.

Contemporary Debates

POTENTIAL POWER VS. POWER USE

Although many approaches to power in organizations can be traced to the exchange framework of power/dependence relationships, debate has centered on the relative importance of the control of critical resources and the exchange of these resources in a skillful manner. The control of critical resources may only represent potential power. As Mintzberg (1983, p. 25) notes, actors must have the "will and skill" to actually use their potential power. Actors must be aware of the situation and have the willingness and skillfulness to translate their control of critical resources into an effective exchange. Actors who foolishly give away their resources are not likely to acquire power. On the other hand, simply being in the presence of a structurally powerful person may cause others to do things they wouldn't ordinarily do in hopes of pleasing the powerful person. Others have argued that the two components cannot be realistically separated (Mintzberg, 1983; McCall, 1979). For example, Emerson (1972, p. 67) notes, "to have a power advantage is to use it." Dahl (1957) argued that unused potential is not power.

In one of the few studies to combine structural and behavioral sources of power, Brass and Burkhardt (1993) measured network centrality and influence strategies in a questionnaire survey of 75 employees at a federal agency. Employees were asked to indicate on a 5-point Likert-type scale (from "never use this tactic" to "usually use this tactic") how frequently they used each of six behavioral tactics to influence other at work (Kipnis et al., 1980). From a roster of all agency employees, respondents were asked to circle the names of people with whom they communicate as part of the job during a typical week. For each person circled, respondents were also asked to indicate how much influence (from "very little" to "very much") the person circled has in the everyday activities of the agency.

Results indicated that certain behavioral tactics were associated with certain structural positions (assertiveness with in-degree centrality, upward appeal and coalition formation with centrality). Rationality and ingratiation appeared to be generic strategies (not associated with network measures). Network centrality and behavioral tactics were partially mediated, each by the other. Brass and Burkhardt (1993) also found that particular combinations of tactics and centrality were related to influence beyond their additive effects. These include in-degree centrality interacting with ingratiation and rationality, and betweenness centrality interacting with exchange, upward appeal and coalition formation. They concluded that skillful political activity can compensate for relatively weak resources, whereas actors in powerful positions, who control ample resources, are less dependent on their capabilities to use resources strategically than are actors who lack ample resources. Combinations of structural and behavioral sources of power can be particularly effective.

Hierarchy vs. informal sources of power

Although the legitimate authority associated with hierarchical positions in organizations is often taken for granted, most of the research and writing on power in organizations has focused on informal sources of power. Yet, it can be argued that these informal sources of power may be ineffective in the face of formal hierarchical positions, or only effective when controlling for hierarchy. As the Milgram (1965) experiments demonstrate, obedience to authority is widespread. Hierarchical rank in an organization is one of the most easily recognized and most legitimate symbols of power in organizations. Yet, we know little about the relative effects of hierarchy versus informal sources of power. Rather than simply control for hierarchy, Brass and Burkhardt (1993) included hierarchy along with other informal structural and behavioral sources of power. They found that level in the hierarchy was positively related to in-degree centrality, assertiveness, and exchange. Hierarchy accounted for roughly 25 percent of the variance in reputational measures of power, even when controlling for informal sources of power. Likewise, the informal sources of power accounted for approximately 25 percent of the variance in power when controlling for hierarchy.

Central Questions that Remain Unanswered

Most of the theory and empirical research on intraorganizational power views power from a dyadic perspective. That is, power and dependence is generally considered in relation to two actors. Actor A has power over Actor B to the extent that Actor B is dependent on Actor A. Little consideration has been given to the probability that these dyadic exchanges do not occur in isolation. Actors in organizations are embedded in a complex set of interrelationships with multiple actors. What are the effects on power of these multiple direct and indirect relationships? For example, we know that an actor can gain reputational power through association with another, more powerful actor (Kilduff and Krackhardt, 1994). Conversely, can an actor lose power through association with less powerful others? We also know that a less powerful Actor A can gain leverage over a more powerful Actor B by appealing to a third Actor C who has power over Actor B (Gargiulo, 1994). But, we know less about the transitivity of power. If Actor C has power over Actor B, and Actor B has power over Actor A, does Actor C have power over Actor A? If Actor A is dependent on Actor B for resource X, and Actor B is dependent on Actor C for resource Y, than Actor C may have power over Actor A only to the extent that resource Y can be exchanged for resource X that Actor A needs.

In such a situation, Actor B may gain power with respect to Actor C by being able to mediate the exchange between Actor C and Actor A. Actor B exchanges (at a favorable rate) some of his resource X with Actor C for some of Actor C's resource Y. Actor C obtains resource X that Actor A needs.

These multiple-actor situations can become more complicated if we consider favors and obligations. For example, instead of exchanging resources with Actor C, Actor B may request that Actor A does a favor (something Actor A would not otherwise do) for Actor C. Actor A complies with the request from Actor B and, in the process establishes a future obligation from Actor B. Actor B owes Actor A a favor in exchange for the favor that Actor A did for Actor C. In this scenario, Actor B loses power in relation to Actor A, but may gain some power in relation to Actor C (if Actor C requested that Actor B intervene with Actor A). Other possible gains and losses in power may be evident in different situations. While these examples may emphasize the notion that power is situation and relationship specific, very little research has considered the effects of multiple actors in multiple situations.

In addition to these unanswered questions about multiple actors and situations, we also have more questions than answers about integrating the multiple approaches to power, about the processes by which power changes, and about the relationship between individual power and group power within organizations. I consider each of these topics as possible new and emerging directions for future research.

New and Emerging Directions for Future Research

Integrating approaches

Although it seems reasonable to suggest that those with the will, skill, and resources will be the most powerful members of an organization, very little research has investigated combinations of structure, personality, and behavior in relation to power. Research on structural bases of power has been frequent, but research on behavioral strategies and personal sources of power has been limited, and research combining the three approaches is indeed rare. Yet, it seems imperative that we combine personal, behavioral, and structural approaches and cross levels of analysis in order to have a full understanding of power within organizations. The effects of structural sources of power will increase as the will and skill of participants decrease. Conversely, the effects of the will and skill of organizational members will increase as the effects of structural sources of power are held constant.

Future research might also consider structural, personal, and behavioral sources of power in organizations over time. Over time, the various sources of power and tactics will likely affect each other. Structure arises, becomes institutionalized, and is modified through individual interaction. For example, it is likely that such power tactics as exchange and ingratiation are instrumental in building networks; networks are helpful in building coalitions; building coalitions leads to centrality which, in turn, leads to promotions to positions of authority (Brass, 1984) and even greater centrality and power if resources are used skillfully.

CHANGES IN POWER

As Pfeffer (1981) notes, those in power tend to perpetuate their power advantage though such processes as commitment to previous decisions, institutionalization of practices, and the ability to generate additional power. Powerful people tend to get the better part of the deal when they exchange resources with less powerful others. Stability, not change, is typical of the distribution of power in most organizations. Although minor changes may occur gradually over long periods of time, the probability of a major redistribution of power may only occur when organizations experience an "exogenous shock" such as a major change in technology (Barley, 1986, p. 80). New technology provides the occasion for restructuring (Barley, 1986). When such shocks introduce uncertainty into the system, those able to cope with the new uncertainty become critical and irreplaceable and thereby gain in power.

In one of the few longitudinal studies of power, Burkhardt and Brass (1990) studied 81 employees of a federal agency prior to and following a change in technology, the introduction of a computer information system. They conducted interviews and collected questionnaire data four times over 15 months. They found that network patterns and power changed over time; early adopters of the new technology increased their centrality in the network and power to a greater degree than later adopters. Cross-lagged correlations suggested that early adopters were sought out by others, increasing their centrality, as they were able to cope with the uncertainties of the new technology. Increases in centrality were accompanied by increases in perceived power (reputational measures). Although results indicated a change in power, those who were powerful, central actors prior to the change in technology were not totally displaced by the early adopters. Interviews indicated that the previously powerful took advantage of their central positions in the organization to be the first of the later adopters to contact and learn from the early adopters. Thus, the correlation between time 1 power (three months prior to the change) and time 4 power (12 months after the change) was 0.84, indicated considerable stability.

Although this study (Burkhardt and Brass, 1990) sheds some light on changes in power over time, we still know very little about the dynamics of power. While much has been written about acquiring power, less is known about losing power. How do groups or individuals in organizations lose power over time? Citing anecdotal evidence, Pfeffer (1992) suggests that the loss of individual and group power in inevitable. Networks and sources of expertise become obsolete as circumstances change over time. "Pride, the seizure of privilege, and the lack of patience occasionally combine to cause the downfall of those in power" (Pfeffer, 1992, p. 310). The maintenance and loss of power are fruitful areas for future research.

INDIVIDUALS AND GROUPS

Although power research has separately focused on individual and groups in organizations, there has been little integration of the two. We know that individual power is affected by membership in groups; being in a powerful unit provides one with more influence. Moore and Pfeffer (1980) found that faculty in more powerful departments had a more accelerated rate of promotion than faculty in less powerful departments even when controlling for department size and academic reputation. Likewise, Ibarra (1992) and Brass (1984) found that department membership was related to individual influence. Yet, we know little about the effects of individuals on group power. Future research might investigate the effects of individual power on group power, and vice versa. Considering that power is relative both within and across groups, frog-pond effects are possible.

Frog-pond effects (Firebaugh, 1980) present some interesting twists to the possibility to investigating the same construct (power) simultaneously at different levels of analysis. Because power is a relational concept, my interpersonal power within a group depends on my relative standing in regard to other members of the group. Likewise, the group's power is relative to other groups. The group may gain (or lose) power without affecting the internal relative power hierarchy of the members. However, if a powerful individual joins the group (likely increasing the overall external perception of the power of the group), my relative interpersonal power will likely decrease within the group (another individual who is more powerful than me has been added). I become a smaller frog in a bigger pond. At the same time, it may increase my power in relation to individuals outside the group (some of the powerful individual's power accrues to the group and hence to me since I am a member of the group). If I leave the group for a less powerful group, it may decrease my external power reputation, but may increase my internal standing (I'm more powerful than most of the others in my new group). I've become a bigger frog in a smaller pond. Thus, there are some interesting complexities when considering the relative nature of intraorganizational power across levels of analysis.

Connections Across Levels

The discussion of individuals and groups within organizations can be extended to include the organizational level of analysis (Ocasio, this volume) and the interorganizational level of analysis (Mizruchi and Yoo, this volume). Much of the discussion of frog-pond effects can be extrapolated to the organizational and interorganizational levels of analysis by substituting organizations for groups. Indeed, much of the theorizing on power assumes that similar relationships hold at different levels of analysis; actors can be thought of as individuals, groups within organizations, or organizations. Theories such as resource dependence (Salancik and Pfeffer, 1974, 1977) and strategic contingencies (Hickson et al., 1971) have been applied across levels of analysis. Just as individuals depend on one another for valued resources, or strategic contingencies, so do organizations. Yet, the organization and interorganizational relations provide the context in which individual and groups vie for power within the organization. Thus, it is important that we consider these larger contexts in relation to individuals and groups.

At the intraorganizational, organizational, and interorganizational levels of analysis, there is considerable overlap between the structural perspectives. Structural approaches highlight how actors, whether they be individuals, groups, or organizations, are embedded in a structure of social relationships. These social networks provide the opportunities and constraints for acquiring, maintaining, and losing power. Considerable overlap also exists across the levels of analysis in viewing power from the functional perspective. As noted by Ocasio, functional approaches such as resource dependence and strategic contingencies argue that power arises from the need for organizations to adapt to their environments and survive. As Mizruchi and Yoo note, many researchers have viewed organizational power and survival as a function of an organization's dependence on resources held by other organizations. For individuals and groups in organizations, the resources needed to obtain power may be defined by the organization's need for survival and its interrelationships with other organizations. Individuals and groups gain power in relation to the organization by their ability to cope with uncertainty created at the interorganizational level of analysis.

The institutional perspective (Ocasio, this volume) reminds us of the importance of institutional rules, norms, and cultures in organizations. Individuals vying for power must do so within the context of formal rules, informal norms, and organizational as well as societal cultures. The taken-for-granted assumptions underlying rules, norms, and cultures can provide an almost invisible legitimization for personal, behavioral, and structural sources of power. While actors can use institutionalized rules, norms, and cultural logics to their advantage in attempting to acquire and maintain power, the institutional perspective also reminds us that such phenomena are not objective characteristics but, rather, are socially constructed. As Pfeffer (1981) notes, symbolic actions and the ability to make sense out of ambiguous events can be important determinants of power in organizations. Indeed, those who can successfully establish, or change, the rules, norms, and cultural logics have a great advantage in the power arena. Although theories and research have often been bounded by levels of analysis, a full understanding of power in organizations requires that we cross levels of analysis.

Conclusions

As noted at the beginning of this chapter, we are indeed blessed and plagued by a variety of theories and research on power in organizations. Blessed in that we have so many ideas and approaches, each with something important to say about power. Plagued in that these many theories are fragmented and so little integration has been attempted. At the intraorganizational level of analysis, research on structural bases of power has been frequent, but research on behavioral strategies and personality has been limited. Research combining the three approaches seems imperative, but is, in reality, extremely rare. Equally rare is research that considers power over time and research that crosses levels of analysis. Structure arises, becomes institutionalized, and is modified through individual interaction. As in the frog-pond example, individual power may be affected by group membership and group power may be affected by individual membership. Likewise, the organizational and interorganizational contexts affect the acquisition and use of power within organizations. Power is a complex phenomenon and it requires a complexity of approaches in order to understand fully its role in the functioning of organizations. We are plagued by the current lack of research and simultaneously blessed by the many opportunities for future research.

References

Allen, R. W., Madison, D. L., Porter, L. W., Renwick, P. A., and Mayes, B. T. (1979): "Organizational politics: Tactics and characteristics of its actors," *California Management Review*, 22, 77–83.

Astley, W. G., and Sachdeva, P. S. (1984): "Structural sources of interorganizational power: A theoretical synthesis," *Academy of Management Review*, 9, 104–13.

Baker, W. E., and Faulkner, R. R. (1993): "The social organization of conspiracy: Illegal networks in the heavy electrical equipment industry," *American Sociology Review*, 58, 837–60.

Barley, S. R. (1986): "Technology as an occasion for structuring: Evidence from observations of CT scanners and the social order of radiology departments," *Administrative Science Quarterly*, 21, 78–108.

Brass, D. J. (1984): "Being in the right place: A structural analysis of individual influence in an organization," *Administrative Science Quarterly*, 29, 518–39.

Brass, D. J. (1985): "Men's and women's networks: A study of interaction patterns and influence in an organization," *Academy of Management Journal*, 28, 327–43.

Brass, D. J. (1992): "Power in organizations: A social network perspective," in G. Moore and J. A. Whitt (eds), *Research in Politics and Society*, Greenwich, CN: JAI Press, 295–324.

Brass, D. J., and Burkhardt, M. E. (1992): "Centrality and power in organizations," in N. Nohria and R. G. Eccles (eds), *Networks and Organizations*, Boston: Harvard Business School Press, 191–215.

Brass, D. J., and Burkhardt, M. E. (1993): "Potential power and power use: An investigation of structure and behavior," *Academy of Management Journal*, 36, 441–70.

Burkhardt, M. E., and Brass, D. J. (1990): "Changing patterns or patterns of change: The effects of a change in technology on social network structure and power," *Administrative Science Quarterly*, 35, 104–127.

Burt, R. S. (1992): *Structural Holes: The Social Structure of Competition*. Cambridge, MA: Harvard University Press.

Cialdini, R. B. (1989): "Indirect tactics of image management: Beyond basking," in R. A. Giacalone and P. Rosenfeld (eds), *Impression Management in the Organization*, Hillsdale, NJ: Erlbaum, 45–56.

Crozier, M. (1964): *The Bureaucratic Phenomenon*. Chicago: University of Chicago Press.

Dahl, R. A. (1957): "The concept of power," *Behavioral Science*, 2, 201–18.

Eisenhardt, K. M., and Bourgeois, L. J. (1988): "Politics of strategic decision making in high-velocity environments: Toward a midrange theory," *Academy of Management Journal*, 31, 737–70.

Emerson, R. M. (1962): "Power-dependence relations," *American Sociological Review*, 27, 31–41.

Emerson, R. M. (1972): "Exchange theory, part I: A psychological basis for social exchange, and exchange theory, part II: Exchange relations and networks," in J. Berger, M. Zelditch, Jr., and B. Anderson (eds), *Sociological Theories in Progress*, Vol. 2, Boston: Houghton-Mifflin, 38–87.

Firebaugh, G. (1980): "Groups as contexts and frog ponds," in K. H. Roberts and L. Burstein (eds), *Issues in Aggregation – New Directions for Methodology of Social and Behavioral Science*, San Francisco: Josey-Bass, 43–52.

Fombrun, C. J. (1983): "Attributions of power across a social network," *Human Relations*, 36, 493–508.

Freeman, L. C. (1979): "Centrality in social networks: Conceptual clarification," *Social Networks*, 1, 215–39.

French, J. R. P., and Raven, B. (1968): "The bases of social power," in D. Cartwright and A. Zander (eds), *Group Dynamics*, New York: Harper and Row, 259–69.

Gandz, J. and Murray, V. V. (1980): "The experience of workplace politics," *Academy of Management Journal*, 23, 237–51.

Gargiulo, M. (1994): "Two-Step Leverage: Managing Constraint in Organizational Politics", *Administrative Science Quarterly*, 39, 1–19.

Hardy, C., and Clegg, S. R. (1996): "Some dare call it power," in S. R. Clegg, C. Hardy, and W. R. Nord (eds), *Handbook of Organization Studies*, London: Sage, 622–41.

Hickson, D. J., Hinings, C. R., Lee, C. A., Schneck, R. E., and Pennings, J. M. (1971): "A strategic contingencies theory of intraorganizational power," *Administrative Science Quarterly*, 16, 216–

29.

Hinings, C. R., Hickson, D. J., Pennings, J. M., and Schneck, R. E. (1974): "Structural conditions of intraorganizational power," *Administrative Science Quarterly*, 19, 22–44.

House, R. J. (1988): "Power and personality in complex organizations," in B. M. Staw and L. L. Cummings (eds), *Research in Organizational Behavior*, Vol. 10, Greenwich, CN: JAI Press, 305–57.

House, R. J., Spangler, W. D., and Woycke, J. (1991): "Personality and charisma in the U.S. presidency: A psychological theory of leader effectiveness," *Administrative Science Quarterly*, 36, 364–96.

Ibarra, H. (1992): "Homophily and differential returns: Sex differences in network structure and access in an advertising firm," *Administrative Science Quarterly*, 37, 422–47.

Kilduff, M., and Krackhardt, D. (1994): "Bringing the individual back in: A structural analysis of the internal market for reputation in organizations," *Academy of Management Journal*, 37, 87–108.

Kipnis, D., and Schmidt, S. M. (1988): "Upward-influence styles: Relationship with performance evaluation, salary, and stress," *Administrative Science Quarterly*, 33, 528–42.

Kipnis, D., Schmidt, S. M., and Wilkinson, I. (1980): "Intraorganizational influence tactics: Explorations in getting one's way," *Journal of Applied Psychology*, 65, 440–52.

Knoke, D., and Burt, R. S. (1983): "Prominence," in R. S. Burt and M. J. Miner (eds), *Applied Network Analysis: A Methodological Introduction*, Beverly Hills, CA: Sage, 195–222.

Krackhardt, D. (1990): "Assessing the political landscape: Structure, cognition, and power in organizations," *Administrative Science Quarterly*, 35, 342–69.

Locke, E. (1976),: "The nature and causes of job satisfaction," in M. Dunnette (ed.), *Handbook of Industrial and Organizational Psychology*, Chicago: Rand McNally, 1297–350.

Lukes, S. (1974): *Power: A Radical View*. London: Macmillan.

Madison, D. L., Allen, R. W., Porter, L. W., Renwick, P. A., and Mayes, B. T. (1980): "Organizational politics: An examination of managers' perceptions," *Human Relations*, 33, 79–100.

Marsden, P. V. (1983): "Restricted access in networks and models of power," *American Journal of Sociology*, 88, 686–717.

McCall, M. W. (1979): "Power, authority, and influence," in S. Kerr (ed.), *Organizational Behavior*, Columbus, OH: Grid, 185–206.

McClelland, D. C. (1985): *Human Motivation*. Glenview, IL: Scott Foresman.

Mechanic, D. (1962): "Sources of power of lower participants in organizations," *Administrative Science Quarterly*, 7, 349–64.

Milgram, S. (1965): "Some conditions of obedience and disobedience to authority," *Human Relations*, 18, 305–30.

Mintzberg, H. (1983): *Power In And Around Organizations*. Englewood Cliffs, NJ: Prentice Hall.

Molm, L. D. (1981): "The conversion of power imbalance to power use," *Social Psychology Quarterly*, 44, 151–63.

Moore, W. L., and Pfeffer, J. (1980): "The relationship between departmental power and faculty careers on two campuses: The case for structural effects on faculty salaries," *Research in Higher Education*, 13, 291–306.

Murnighan, J. K. (1978): "Models of coalition formation: Game theoretic, social psychological, and political perspectives," *Psychological Bulletin*, 85, 1130–53.

Murnighan, J. K., and Brass, D. J. (1991): "Intraorganizational coalitions," in M. Bazerman, B. Sheppard, and R. Lewicki (eds), *Research on Negotiations in Organizations*, Vol. 3, Greenwich, CN: JAI Press, 283–307.

Perreault, W., and Miles, R. (1978): "Influence strategy mixes in complex organizations," *Behavioral Science*, 23, 86–98.

Pettigrew, A. M. (1973): *The Politics of Organizational Decision Making*. London: Tavistock.

Pfeffer, J. (1981): *Power in Organizations*. Marshfield, MA: Pitman.

Pfeffer, J. (1992): *Managing with Power: Politics and Influence in Organizations*. Boston: Harvard Business School Press.

Pfeffer, J., and Moore, W. L. (1980): "Power and politics in university budgeting: A replication and extension," *Administrative Science Quarterly*, 25, 637–53.

Podolny, J. M., and Baron, J. N. (1997): "Resources and relationships: Social networks and mobility in the workplace," *American Sociological Review*, 62, 673–93.

Salancik, G. R., and Pfeffer, J. (1974): "The bases and uses of power in organizational decision making: The case of a university," *Administrative Science Quarterly*, 19, 453–73.

Salancik, G. R., and Pfeffer, J. (1977): "Who Gets power – and how they hold on to it: A strategic contingency model of power,, *Organizational Dynamics*, 5, 3–21.

Stevenson, W. B., Pearce, J. L., and Porter, L. W. (1985): "The concept of coalition in organization theory and research," *Academy of Management Review*, 10, 256–68.

Thompson, K. R., and Luthans, F. (1983): "A behavioral interpretation of power," in R. W. Allen and L. W. Porter (eds), *Organizational Influence Processes*, Glenview, IL: Scott, Foresman, 72–86.

Tushman, M. L., and Romanelli, E. (1983): "Uncertainty, social location and influence in decision making: A sociometric analysis," *Management Science*, 29, 12–23.

Chapter Seven

Intraorganizational Technology

MELISSA A. SCHILLING

Technology (from the Greek, techne, which means craft, or skill) refers to any manner of systematically applying knowledge or science to a practical application. As such it is one of the central factors motivating the founding, structure, and management of most organizations. Intraorganizational technology can be defined as including all forms of technology that are developed or implemented within the organization. Technology in this context is generally understood to include information technology as well as technology embodied in products, production processes, and design processes.

The management research on intraorganizational technology may be divided into two fairly distinct streams: the research on the development of new technology, and the research on the relationship between technology and the structure and management of the organization.[1] The first stream may be further subdivided into a body of descriptive work that has examined how firm size and industry structure impacts technology development, and a body of prescriptive work that seeks to identify practices firms can employ to improve the development process. The second stream, the impact of intraorganizational technology on the firm, includes such topics as how technology drives structural choice and firm boundaries, and how technology impacts performance. This area has received particularly enthusiastic attention in the last decade, as innovations in both production and information technologies have enabled dramatic transformation of many firms. A summary of some of the key empirical studies covered in this chapter is provided in Table 7.1.

Literature Review

THE DEVELOPMENT OF NEW TECHNOLOGY

There is an extensive body of research focusing on the firm as a developer of new technology. This research addresses such questions as what types of firms are more likely to be successful at developing new technologies, and how the technology development process should be managed and its performance measured.

Table 7.1 Selected studies in intraorganizational technology

Reference	Key concepts	Key variables	Key findings	Key contribution	Method and sample
Development of new technology					
Blundell et al. (1999)	The relationship between market share, market concentration, competitiveness, and innovation	Innovation (patent counts and innovation counts) Market share Market value Competitive intensity (imports, concentration, union density)	Finds that higher market share firms innovate more, and reap more gains from their innovations (consistent with Schumpeterian hypotheses) However, finds that more competitive industries innovate more on average	Reassesses the relationship between firm size and innovativeness using new estimation methods that control for unobserved firm specific heterogeneity	Dynamic count data model estimation using 3551 observations of 340 manufacturing firms listed on the London International Stock Exchange
Cooper and Kleinschmidt (1993)	Identifying the key success factors in new product development	Project success Product differentiation Synergy Order of entry Product life cycle Market attractiveness Market competitiveness	Most important determinant of development project success is product differentiation Market attractiveness and market competitiveness had little impact	Examines project level, firm level, and industry level determinants of new development project success	In-depth study of 103 projects undertaken by large chemical firms in four countries
Zirger and Maidique (1990)	Identifying the new product development strategy, process, and context attributes that determine project success	Product technical performance Product value to customer Firm's existing competencies Managerial support	In addition to product's performance and value, the integration of project with firm's existing competencies and the degree of managerial support significantly influence likelihood of success	Uses rich case study data across a large sample of projects to test often postulated drivers of development project success	Four-year field study of 330 new product development projects in the electronics industry

Reference	Key concepts	Key variables	Key findings	Key contribution	Method and sample
AMT and mass customization					
Brandyberry et al. (1999)	The impact of advanced manufacturing technology on intermediate performance outcomes	Adoption of AMT Market-oriented flexibility Organizational integration of production processes Administrative intensity	Higher levels of AMT can enhance integration of production processes However, functionally-oriented AMT can lessen market-oriented flexibility	Empirically assesses the impact of AMT on organizational integration and flexibility Identifies constraints of particular forms of AMT	Regression and MANOVA of survey data on 132 large US manufacturing firms
Kotha and Swamidass (2000)	Implementation of AMT can enhance profitability if type of AMT is matched to firm strategy	AMT: product design technologies, process technologies, logistics/ planning technologies, and information enhancement technologies Cost leadership strategy Differentiation strategy Profitability Growth	Firms implemented different types of AMT depending on their strategy The relationship between strategy and AMT types was strongest for superior performers	Demonstrates support for a contingent model of AMT adoption	Regression using survey data on 160 manufacturing firms
Firm disaggregation					
Brynjolfsson et al. (1994)	Information technology reduces internal and external coordination costs, thereby leading to smaller firms	Investment in information technology Firm size as measured by employees, sales, and value-added per firm	Investment in information technology is significantly associated with decreases in firm size Decreases are largest one to two years after investment	Demonstrates that advances in information technology may lead to smaller firms on average	Regression using data on every US manufacturing and service industry, from 1976 to 1989

Hitt (1999)	Information technology's impact on internal and external coordination costs Internal and external coordination costs as drivers of vertical integration and diversification	Information technology capital stock Vertical integration Diversification	Increased use of information technology is significantly associated with substantial decreases in vertical integration Increased use of information technology is associated with weak increases in diversification	Demonstrates the impact of information technology on internal and external coordination costs, and the consequent impact on the boundaries of the firm	8-year panel study of 549 large firms.
Schilling and Steensma (2001)	General modular systems model may be applied to the disaggregation of organizations into more modular forms Industry forces influence the likelihood of adoption of modular organizational forms	Heterogeneous inputs and demands Alliance formation Alternative work arrangements Contract manufacturing Availability of standards Rate of technological change Competitive intensity	Heterogeneity of inputs and demands encourages the adoption of modular organizational forms Relationship above moderated by the availability of standards, rate of technological change, and competitive intensity	Demonstrates applicability of general systems model Tests a predictive model about the adoption of modular organizational forms	Hierarchical moderated regression analysis of data from 330 US manufacturing industries

FIRM SIZE, R&D INVESTMENT, AND INDUSTRY STRUCTURE

In 1942, Schumpeter challenged the traditional economics antitrust orthodoxy by proposing the following two hypotheses:

1 Innovation increases more than proportionately with firm size.
2 Innovation increases with market concentration.

Schumpeter's arguments for why firm size would increase technological progress included arguments for both rate and effectiveness effects, though he did not explicitly distinguish the two. There are arguments for rate effects:

1 Capital markets are imperfect, and thus large firms have an advantage in obtaining financing for R&D projects.
2 Firms with a larger sales volume over which to spread the fixed costs of R&D experience higher returns (or lower relative costs) than firms with lower sales volume.

A third argument relating to firm size, that there are scale economies in the technology of R&D, could incorporate both rate and effectiveness effects. On the one hand, scale economies may arise because fixed investments in R&D may be amortized over a larger volume of R&D projects, thus resulting in declining marginal costs for R&D expenses. This would make a given rate of R&D investment less costly for firms with a large R&D base than for those with smaller R&D bases. However, scale economies may also arise because of experience or learning curve effects. This would imply that the firm becomes better at R&D, and should gain increases in R&D effectiveness. A fourth Schumpeterian argument, that R&D is more productive in large firms with well-developed complementary activities such as marketing and financial planning, supports the proposition that firm size increases R&D effectiveness.

These hypotheses sparked a flurry of empirical investigations, yet results remained inconclusive, encouraging substantial debate on the topic. Competing arguments were offered that suggested a negative relationship between firm size and R&D. For instance, one prominent argument is that as firms grow, efficiency in R&D decreases because of loss of managerial control (Cohen and Levin, 1989). A second, related argument is that as firms grow it becomes increasingly difficult for the individual scientist or entrepreneur to appropriate the returns of their efforts, therefore their incentives diminish. Cohen and Levin (1989) point out that even "Schumpeter (1942) himself suggested that this feature of the bureaucratization of inventive activity could undermine capitalist development" (p. 1067). Along this vein, Rotemberg and Saloner (1994) proposed that, as firms become more diversified, they are less able to provide efficient incentives for employees that allow them to innovate without suffering from conflicting goals. A fourth argument arises from the capital markets argument posited in favor of firm size; that is, small firms, who are less able to finance a large volume of R&D projects, will choose their projects more carefully, and thus have a higher proportion of successful projects. This implies that there are diminishing returns to R&D. This proposition was somewhat confirmed by Scherer (1983), and by Griliches (1990) who concludes that small firms appear to be more efficient, receiving a larger number of patents per R&D dollar (Griliches provides a well-crafted and often cited review of the work done on returns to R&D and the use of patents as a measure of innovative output for readers interested in more extensive discussion of these topics).

Contrasting results were found in a more recent study by Blundell et al. (1999). In this study, the authors use firm-level accounting data, share price information, a count of innovations, and a count of patents to test the relationship between market power and rates of innovation. Their sample includes 3551 observations from 340 British manufacturing firms. They conclude from their study that "less competitive" industries (industries with lower import penetration and higher concentration levels) innovated less overall. However, within industries, the high market share firms tended to be more effective at commercializing innovations, and tended to benefit most from innovations.

Though undoubtedly many scholars find the arguments or evidence on one side of the issue more compelling than the other, it is probably most accurate to say that the issue remains unresolved.

IMPROVING THE EFFECTIVENESS OF THE DEVELOPMENT PROCESS

Due to the extreme strategic importance of technological innovation to firm success, researchers have vigorously attempted to identify what makes some firms more success-ful at development than others. This is an extensive area of research and there are several good books and literature reviews on the topic – e.g., Clark and Wheelwright (1993), and Brown and Eisenhardt (1995) and Schilling and Hill (1998) – therefore I will simply attempt to provide a brief overview of the key themes here. Note that while much of this research has focused on new technology embodied in products, most of it is equally applicable to new technology embodied in processes; therefore little distinction will be made between the two in the current discussion.

First, there has been considerable research into how firms should choose new devel-opment projects, resulting in a number of valuation and portfolio balancing models. Development projects are often divided into categories such as radical versus incremen-tal, or platform projects (those which spawn entire families of new products) versus derivative projects. It is typically suggested that firms map their development projects by type, and seek to balance their portfolios according to their objectives and resources (Wind and Mahajan, 1988). Recent research has explored the treatment of development projects as real options, and utilizes options analysis approaches for assessing the cost and gains of undertaking a new project. This topic is discussed further in the new and emerging areas for research section.

A second major area of research has explored the role of teams and team leaders. For example, research has indicated that different types of development projects have differ-ent resource needs and management requirements. Major new projects involving break-through technologies may require full-time, collocated, cross-functional teams (Clark and Wheelwright, 1993; Johne and Snelson, 1989), sponsored by a senior executive (Zirger and Maidique, 1990; Damanpour, 1991). However, for development projects representing only a minor enhancement of an existing product or process, a full-time collocated team may be unwarranted (Schilling and Hill, 1998).

A third area has focused on the development of tools and metrics for improving and managing the development process, such as quality function deployment (Griffin and Hauser, 1992), stage-gate processes (Cooper and Kleinschmidt, 1991), and computer-aided design. Such tools can enable better identification of the match between project objectives and outcomes, enable rapid prototyping, and improve the project's likelihood of being completed on time and within budget.

Rather than being driven by a strong theoretical focus, most of the empirical research on the development process has taken an inductive approach in pursuit of identification of best practices. A prime example is Cooper and Kleinschmidt's series of studies on new product development, including studies of how new product development success should be measured (e.g., 1987) and studies that attempt to identify what makes some companies more successful than others at new product development (e.g., 1993, 1995). In their 1993 study, Cooper and Kleinschmidt find that the most important success factor of development projects was the degree of product differentiation, followed by synergies, order of entry, and stage of product life cycle. They found that market attractiveness and market competitiveness had little impact on the likelihood of project success. In their 1995 benchmarking study of how firms managed the development process, they conclude that the most successful firms

1   have a well-structured and rigorous (yet flexible) new product development process that includes extensive up-front research, tough go/kill decision points, precisely defined product requirements
2   have a well-defined new product strategy with a long-term orientation and clearly communicated new product goals
3   dedicate adequate human and capital resources to their projects, including senior-level management commitment, and
4   have high levels of R&D expenditures as a percent of sales (indicating support for an increasing returns to R&D argument).

Zirger and Maidique (1990) have also conducted a well-cited study that offers both a broad and deep examination of the drivers of development project success. They conducted a field study from 1982 to 1986 of 330 electronics product successes and failures. They conclude that, in addition to the overall quality of the research organization and the performance of the product, the likelihood of project success is significantly influenced by its fit with the firm's existing competencies (similar to Cooper and Kleinschmidt's findings regarding synergy), and the degree of managerial support during both the development and introduction stages.

THE IMPACT OF TECHNOLOGY ON ORGANIZATIONAL STRUCTURE, MANAGEMENT, AND PERFORMANCE

PRODUCTION TECHNOLOGIES: FROM THE WOODWARD TYPOLOGY TO AMT

Joan Woodward produced one of the first and most influential studies of the impact of technology on organization. Her study of one hundred manufacturing firms indicated a strong relationship between production technology and other organizational dimensions including structure, formalization, centralization, and worker skill levels. She organized the firms on a scale of technical complexity that was eventually consolidated into three technology categories: small-batch and unit production, large-batch and mass production, and continuous process production (Woodward, 1958). Woodward's findings were replicated numerous times, and her typology continues to be influential today.

However, in the late 1980s, dramatic developments in both computers and manufacturing processes enabled the introduction of a series of new technologies known collectively as advanced manufacturing technology (AMT), that were anticipated to make small-batch production as cost and time efficient as mass production. Also called computer integrated manufacturing (CIM) or flexible manufacturing systems (FMS), AMT systems utilized computerized processes to increase both the speed and flexibility of manufacturing. Computer aided design enabled rapid prototyping, while computer aided manufacturing allowed production lines to shift rapidly from one product to another. Administrative automation made the administrative control functions (such as inventory tracking and billing) more efficient. AMT systems were expected to have dramatic impacts on the structure and management of organizations, including enabling a reduction in the number of hierarchical levels, decentralization of decision making, and greater reliance on teamwork (Adler, 1988; Nemetz and Fry, 1988). Of particular importance was the potential AMT offered for making the firm more flexible (Parthasarthy and Sethi, 1992). By allowing firms to quickly alter production, AMT created strategic options for the firm to enter related markets (Lei et al., 1996).

However, empirical investigations of AMT's impact on a firm's flexibility or financial performance have been mixed (Boyer et al., 1997; Brandyberry et al., 1999; Dean et al., 1992). Kotha and Swamidass (2000) provide empirical evidence of superior performance arising from adoption of AMT – particularly when it is well integrated with the firm's strategy. They adopt an information processing perspective, and argue that AMT can enhance a firm's information processing capacity. They classify AMT into four groups: product design technologies, process technologies, logistics/planning technologies, and information exchange technologies, and then hypothesize that matching different firm strategies to appropriate types of technologies will result in superior performance. For example, they argue that the efficiency and standardization objectives of firms pursuing a low-cost leadership strategy will be best met by primarily focusing on AMT process technologies. By contrast, the greater product or market variety characterizing firms pursuing a differentiation strategy will necessitate the use of several dimensions of AMT. Using a survey of 160 US manufacturing firms, they find that firms do often match their AMT choice to their strategy, and that doing so improves performance.

Brandyberry et al. (1999) also using a survey, find mixed results. They examine the impact of different levels of AMT adoption on intermediate performance outcomes (market-oriented flexibility, integration of production processes, and administrative intensity). They conclude that while higher levels of AMT can enhance integration of production processes, some forms of AMT actually lesson market-oriented flexibility. Similarly, Lee (2000) argues that rather than uniformly increasing flexibility, many FMS systems create a set of intrinsic constraints that may hinder the firm's performance. Though there may be conflict about AMT's overall impact on firm flexibility or performance, it did give rise to an unambiguously influential manufacturing trend: mass customization.

MASS CUSTOMIZATION AND MODULARITY

Mass customization is the utilization of lean and flexible production technologies to provide high product variety and market responsiveness, while still attaining the low costs of standardized mass production (Kotha, 1995; Pine, 1993). It has been hailed as the new paradigm of production in industries as diverse as apparel manufacturing to telecommunications. One of the key ways that firms accomplish mass customization is to modularize the products or services so that some key components can be standardized and produced on a large scale, yet combined into unique configurations to enable product variety. A prime example is Sony's Walkman, which utilizes a number of standardized components within a modular architecture that enables a wide range of end configurations (Sanchez, 1999). The proliferation of end configurations based on standardized components enables Sony to closely meet heterogeneous customer requirements while still keeping costs low on the individual units.

Increasing use of modular product designs and production processes spurred a flurry of research into its causal antecedents (e.g., Schilling, 2000) and outcomes (e.g., Baldwin and Clark, 1997; Garud and Kumaraswamy, 1995; Langlois, 1992; Sanchez and Mahoney, 1996). Much of the research on product modularity has tended to examine the advantages of the adoption of modular product designs or production processes. These advantages have included being better able to meet diverse customer needs (e.g., Baldwin and Clark, 1997, 2000; Langlois, 1992; Sanchez, 1995), reap "economies of substitution" (e.g., Garud and Kumaraswamy, 1995), achieve some of the network externality advantages of a standards-based architecture, while still producing unique, proprietary components (Garud and Kumaraswamy, 1995), and creating greater strategic flexibility within the firm (e.g., Garud and Kotha, 1994; Sanchez and Mahoney, 1996). Notably, however, the research has been almost entirely theoretical, or based on anecdotal or case-study evidence. Large-sample empirical studies of product modularity have only recently begun to emerge (e.g., Worren, 2001).

The study of modularity at the product level also sparked interest in applying the concept of modularity to the organization level. Did the adoption of modular products or production processes enable the modularization of the firm? Or could the same factors that enabled increasing modularity at the product level be simultaneously enabling greater modularity at the organization level? These questions initiated a recent trend in the organizational research: explaining and predicting the adoption of modular organizational forms.

Current Trends

THE ADOPTION OF INCREASINGLY MODULAR ORGANIZATIONAL FORMS

In the past two decades, a wave of firm disaggregation surged through many industries. Many large and hierarchical firms were transformed into (or supplanted by) loosely interconnected organizational components, with semi-permeable boundaries (Ghoshal and Bartlett, 1997; Ashkenas et. al., 1995; Snow et al., 1992). The locus of production was no longer confined within the boundaries of a single firm, but occurred instead at the nexus of relationships between a variety of parties that contribute to the production function. Achrol (1997) vividly sums up this transformation: "Large-scale downsizing, vertical disaggregation and outsourcing, and elimination of layers of management have gutted the mighty multidivisional organizations of the 20th century. Replacing them are leaner, more flexible firms focused on a core technology and process, laced in a network of strategic alliances and partnerships with suppliers, distributors, and competitors" (pp. 56–7, 61). Zenger and Hesterly (1997) provide a good review of evidence that firms are downsizing, vertically disaggregating, and becoming more focused.

The phenomenon received widespread attention, though often by authors employing different terms, including "virtual organizations" (Chesbrough and Teece, 1996; Churbuck and Young, 1992; Davidow and Malone, 1992), "network organizations" (Jones et al., 1997; Miles and Snow, 1986, 1992), and "modular organizations" (Lei et al., 1996; Sanchez, 1995; Sanchez and Mahoney, 1996). While the terms were sometimes invoked in slightly different ways, they all sought to describe the supplanting of tightly integrated hierarchical organizations by "loosely coupled" networks of organizational actors (Orton and Weick, 1990).

By drawing on Simon's (1962) work on systems and "near decomposability," and Weick's (1976) ideas of "loose coupling," researchers were able to apply some of the concepts developed in the study of modular product systems to the structure of organizational systems. The terms "loose coupling" and "near decomposability" both describe systems in which components are only weakly connected to one another. In product and organizational systems, these terms typically refer to systems in which the components are relatively independent, and may be separated and recombined. Sanchez and Mahoney (1996) pointed out that the adoption of modular product designs enabled the looser coupling of production groups within the firm. The architecture of the modular product design and the standard interfaces specified therein provided a form of "embedded coordination." The standard interfaces ensured that components could be developed and produced relatively autonomously, thus the production groups responsible for them could be similarly compartmentalized. So long as the components conformed to the standard interface, compatibility was assured. This line of reasoning thus posited that much of the modularization (or disaggregation) of the production chain was the outcome of utilizing modular product designs.

Other researchers, however, argued that modular organizational forms were not simply the result of the modularization of production processes, but rather that the same forces driving the increased advantages of modularity at the product and production process level (e.g., high speed technological change, heterogeneous technological options, customer heterogeneity, the availability of standard interfaces) also acted to increase the gains from the adoption of modular organizational forms (Garud and Kumaraswamy, 1995; Schilling, 2000; Schilling and Steensma, 2001). This line of research poses that high-speed technological change can cause rapid proliferation of both diverse technological options, and diverse customer demands, thus increasing the advantages to be gained through flexible production configurations.

Furthermore, just as standards among product components reduce the specificity of components to one another, the establishment of formal or informal standards to facilitate coordination of particular organizational components can reduce any performance advantages achievable through tightly integrating those components. Standards such as ISO 9000, uniform employment policies, shared groupware platforms and the like, can enable effective loose coupling at the organizational level. Less need for integration frees firms up to pursue more flexible production configurations. For instance, firms could become more specialized by spinning off activities that could be obtained through more loosely coupled arrangements such as outsourcing. Firms could make increasing use of contingent labor or alliances to access capabilities quickly (and retain the ability to divest them quickly) rather than building such capabilities in house. All of these loosely coupled organizational forms enable more specialized components of production to be fluidly recombined into a large variety of configurations – making the entire production chain an increasingly modular system, and making the boundaries of the organization somewhat more ambiguous.

There is some empirical evidence emerging that some of the same factors that enable modularity at the product level also enable increasingly modular organizational forms. Argyres' (1999) study of the development of the B-2 "Stealth" bomber provides an in-depth look at one example of a loosely coupled production configuration, and provides rich detail of the processes used by the various firms involved. He found that the four developing companies established a shared "technical grammar." This shared technical grammar resulted in a set of social conventions that acted as a standardized interface facilitating communication and governance between the various autonomous entities involved in the bomber's development.

There is also evidence that industry-level differences in the heterogeneity of inputs and demands, availability of standards, and rate of technological change, can result in differential rates of use of alliances and alternative work arrangements across industries. Schilling and Steensma (2001) used a large sample cross-sectional study of 330 US manufacturing industries to examine whether heterogeneity in production inputs and customer demands influences the degree to which firms utilize modular organizational forms. In the study, modular organizational forms included alliance formation, use of alternative work arrangements and contract manufacturing. They found that heterogeneous inputs and demands were significantly and positively related to the use of modular organizational forms, and that the availability of standards and a high rate of technological change strengthened this relationship. This indicates support for the proposition that many of the same factors influencing the adoption of modular product forms also influence the adoption of modular organizational forms.

Many of the research arguments and results emerging from the modularity line of research are mirrored in a closely related vein of inquiry: the impact of advances in information technology on the firm.

THE IMPACT OF INFORMATION TECHNOLOGY

Though information technology has always been relevant to organization design and management, recent explosive growth in information technology, combined with the wave of firm disaggregation described earlier, motivated researchers to look at the relationship between information technology and firm boundaries with renewed vigor. Most of this research has employed either an information processing or transaction cost perspective. Though arising from different origins, both perspectives argue that advances in information technology lower the costs of coordinating activities within and across firm boundaries (Brynjolfsson, 1994; Zenger and Hesterly, 1997). The information processing perspective posits that advances in information technology can both increase a firm's capacity to process information, and lower its costs of processing information. The resulting lower cost of coordination frees the firm to pursue more structural alternatives for production than would otherwise be feasible. Similarly, trans-action-cost economists note that transaction costs are directly related to the cost of information (Alchian and Woodward, 1987). Advances in information technology can lower a firm's search costs for locating suitable partners, as well as lower the costs of monitoring performance. Thus by reducing transaction costs (which, according to trans-action cost economists, are among the primary reasons for integrating activities within the firm), advances in information technology enable the firm to make greater use of market transactions.

There is a growing body of empirical evidence in support of these arguments. For example, in the Argyres study of the development of the B-2 bomber described previously, he concludes that enhanced information technology limited the need for coordination of activities through hierarchical control. Providing broader evidence, Hitt (1999) studied 549 firms over eight years in a panel study design. Utilizing data on information technology hardware spending, firm specific financial information, and measures of firm structure, he explored the relationship between information technology, internal coordination costs, external coordination costs, vertical integration, and diversification. He found that increased use of information technology at the firm level was significantly related to decreased vertical integration, and that there appeared to be a positive relationship between use of information technology and diversification, though the evidence for this was weaker. He concludes that information technology reduces both internal and external coordination costs.

Brynjolffson et al. (1994) point out that if information technology decreases the cost of internal coordination more than external coordination, we would expect firms to grow in size (because the cost of doing more things internally decreases). Similarly, if information technology decreases the cost of external coordination more than internal coordination, we would expect the average size of firms to decrease, as firms would buy more things externally. Malone et al. (1987) argues that information technology should increase both kinds of coordination costs more than it should impact production costs, and that this will lead to more external buying. According to their argument, in general, buying externally imposes higher coordination costs (because of the need to find suppliers, negotiate contracts, etc.) but lower production costs (because external suppliers can pool the demands of multiple customers, leading to economies of scale and other cost advantages). If information technology reduces both internal and external coordination costs more than it reduces production costs, then it always impacts the balance between coordination costs and production costs the same way: in favor of buying.

Brynjolfsson et al. (1994) test the relationship between information technology and firm size using data on average number of employees per firm, sales per firm and value added per firm, and information technology investments and total capital investments for every US manufacturing and service industry, from 1976 to 1989. They found that investments in information technology were significantly related to decreasing firm size as measured by employees per establishment, employees per firm, sales per establishment, and value added per establishment. The most significant declines in size occurred one to two years after investment in information technology. Brynjolffson et al. conclude that information technology does appear to be reducing the costs of coordination, resulting in firms placing increasing reliance on market transactions.

Overall there has been a growing consensus that advances in information technology should enable a wide range of economic actors – including suppliers, customers, and rivals – to combine their activities in flexible networks of "virtual" organization (Davidow and Malone, 1992; Byrne, 1993; Zenger and Hesterly, 1997). However, this still leaves a number of important questions unanswered. To what degree will firms disaggregate? Will information technology completely eliminate the need for hierarchical relationships? This seems an unlikely scenario, but the boundary conditions for the evolution towards componentization of the firm have yet to be addressed. What structural forms will these new organizations of the future take, and how will the structure of organizations be related (or unrelated) to firm ownership? How will information technology affect the geographical distribution of organizations? These questions (and others) are discussed further in the next section.

Outstanding Questions for Future Research

Since the work on modular products and production processes, firm disaggregation and the adoption of loosely coupled organizational forms are relatively new areas of research, there is a wide array of important questions that remain to be addressed.

MODULAR PRODUCTS AND PROCESSES

Though researchers have cited advantages of modular product designs and production processes that include providing more end configurations for customers and achieving economies of substitution within the firm, there has been little work examining when firms will choose different kinds and degrees of modularity. A firm may use modular product designs within the firm that do not extend to the customer level. Such modularity enables the standardization of core components while still achieving a wide range of configurations, yet from the customer's perspective the product is not modular – it is fixed in a single configuration. The typical Sony Walkman demonstrates this type of modularity. Alternatively, firms may also employ modular designs which explicitly give configuration discretion to the customer, such as Ikea's mix-and-match shelving units, for which the customer chooses their own range of components and assembles the configuration they desire. There are also intermediate forms of product modularity, such as when the customer has some discretion over configuration, but does not typically assemble the product herself. The firm may assemble the configuration the customer desires (e.g., when a customer chooses options to be installed on a new vehicle), or there may be a market for third-party intermediaries (e.g., third-party assemblers have become common in the market for personal computing equipment). Further, modular product designs may enable the combination of components from multiple vendors (as is common in stereo componentry) or only from a single vendor (as with the Ikea shelving system mentioned earlier). When will different forms of modular product designs emerge? How will these different forms affect both customer value and firm competitiveness?

Several researchers have noted that the modularization of product systems can shift the locus of competition within an industry from the system level to the component level. Rather than producing entire product systems, firms can specialize in particular components in which they have a competitive advantage (Baldwin and Clark, 2000; Sanchez and Mahoney, 1996; Langlois, 2000). On the other hand, specializing in components rather than producing an entire product system can reduce the firm's market power or control over the system architecture (Schilling, 2000). Thus a vitally important area of research that remains to be systematically examined is how an industry-wide shift to greater reliance on modular product systems results in a reallocation of rents and competitive positioning. When will firms resist modular product designs? When will they be successful doing so? There has been some work that has speculated on these questions (e.g., Chesbrough and Christensen, 2000; Schilling, 2000), but significant empirical work has yet to emerge.

There are also a number of important questions that must be raised regarding the nature of the standard interface that enables modularity. In some modular product systems, the interface is "open" and considered a public good (Garud and Kumaraswamy, 1993; Sanchez, 1995). One could consider the electrical outlet format used in homes to be such a standard. The specifications are freely available to any vendor that wishes to produce a product that interacts with the interface. Other modular product systems are based on interfaces that are proprietary, and have degrees of "openness" (Garud and Kumaraswamy, 1993; 1995). For instance, the Window's operating system could be considered a fairly open standard, yet it is owned and controlled by Microsoft, giving Microsoft both discretion over end configurations, and ensuring that Microsoft receives rents from its use. At the other end of the spectrum, McGraw Hill's Primis modular textbook system is based on proprietary software that has very little "openness." The software enables only McGraw Hill to assemble the modular textbooks, and constrains a customer's choice of text components that may be used (it is possible, however, that publishers will migrate towards a more open interface in the future) (Venkatraman, 1997). Important research questions for the future include how the ownership and control of the interface determines its value to producers and customers, its rate of adoption, who garners the rents from its use, who controls the design of the overall system architecture, and the rate at which the architecture and interface evolve (Henderson and Clark, 1990). This is a particularly fertile area of research that is so far relatively untapped.

FIRM DISAGGREGATION AND THE ADOPTION OF MODULAR ORGANIZATIONAL FORMS

The existing research on firm disaggregation and the adoption of modular organizational forms has only begun to scratch the surface of the implications of this phenomenon. This area raises two particularly looming questions:

1   What are the limits to disaggregation?
2   To what extent does proximity still play an important role in production?

In 1965, Gordon Moore, future co-founder of Intel, estimated that transistor density would double every eighteen months. Moore turned out to be basically right, and the exponential growth rate of semiconductor performance came to be known as "Moore's

Law." This rate of increase was not expected to continue indefinitely; at the time of his original estimate Moore posited only that it would last "at least the next ten years" (Mann, 2000, p. 9). Some analysts have predicted the law will hold until 2017, others predict it will come to an end much sooner, as producers run into design constraints for which there are not yet technological solutions. Regardless, however, of the time frame or rate of deceleration, it raises obvious questions about the relationship between information technology growth and firm size and structure. If information technology advances at a rate consistent with Moore's Law, and if information technology reduces internal and external coordination costs, what implication does Moore's Law have for the rate and extent to which firm structures evolve? What are the limits to firm disaggregation? To what degree will market transactions and fluid network structures displace hierarchical control?

Furthermore, as the boundaries of production become more fluid and permeable, how will this affect the structure of property rights with respect to firm ownership? As production components become more loosely coupled in an amorphous web of relationships, and the role of hierarchical control is diminished, it becomes increasingly difficult to identify the boundaries of a single firm. In fact, it is conceivable that the whole notion of "firm" will be transformed. How will this impact ownership structure and the appropriation of rents?

Another issue arises from the joint effects of advanced manufacturing systems, the modularization of products and processes, and advances in information technology: the role of proximity. The industrial revolution and the rise of mass production systems drew human and capital production factors together into large urban centers. Economies of scale meant that there were significant increasing returns to consolidating production factors into fewer and larger establishments. Proximity between firms, suppliers, customers, and labor reduced transportation costs (Lusht and Farber, 1996), enabled better information sharing (Jaffe et al., 1993) and enabled economies of scale and scope in infrastructure development (Marshall, 1922; Romer, 1987).

From the 1950s on, however, the proliferation of private automobiles, highways, air travel, and telephones began to erode the gravitational pull of the urban center (Lusht and Farber, 1996). Metropolitan areas began to spread as both firms and families began to choose locations further from city centers. There is widespread speculation (and emerging evidence) that the rapid innovation in technology will dramatically accelerate this trend (Borja and Castells, 1997; Miller, 1998). Information technology makes distance almost irrelevant in the cost and speed of information transmission. Furthermore, the adoption of flexible manufacturing systems have significantly reduced the minimum efficient scale of production in many industries, while the modularization of products and production processes has further removed the need for proximity between factors of production. The net result is a diminishment of many of the sources of economies of integration and agglomeration.

However, there are some important advantages to proximity that technology may not overcome. Both the cost and speed of transportation for components and products will continue to be important for a large number of industries, thus leading to clustering advantages for producers and customers. Some forms of information and service exchange are greatly enhanced by physical proximity due to the complexity, richness, or interactiveness inherent in the exchange (Hansen, 1999). Notably, both the resource-based view (Barney, 1991) and the knowledge-based view (Kogut and Zander, 1992) posit that resources that are tacit in nature are more likely to give rise to a sustainable competitive advantage, and proximity may play a pivotal role in the development of and access to tacit resources. Therefore, important work remains to be done on areas that include (but need not be limited to these):

1   Identifying which sources of advantage from proximity will be impacted by changes in technology, and which are relatively immune to technology's effects
2   Whether proximity will be differentially important to different industries or different portions of the supply chain
3   Identifying the role of government in shaping the advantages of proximity through such functions as regulation, providing infrastructure or other support services for the populations that surround areas of production
4   The web of social ramifications that shifting loci of production will have on the spatial dispersion of populations, and the concomitant economic effects

New and Emerging Directions for Research

Though much of the research described here is very recent, there are some areas of research that stand out as being particularly promising for extending it, or addressing the unanswered questions posed above. Some of these areas of research are natural extensions of previous research, while others involve analogical transfer of ideas across disciplines.

CHOOSING NEW TECHNOLOGY DEVELOPMENT PROJECTS

One of the most promising new directions for research on technology development is the use of an options approach in choosing development projects. Traditional methods used to evaluate and choose investment projects range from informal to highly structured, and from entirely qualitative to strictly quantitative. Quantitative methods such as net present value (NPV) techniques provide concrete financial estimates that facilitate strategic planning and trade-off decisions. However, many authors argue that NPV may fail to capture the strategic importance of the investment decision. Recent research has emphasized the role of development projects in building and leveraging firm capabilities, and creating "options" for the future. Investments in new core technologies are investments in the organization's capabilities and learning, and create opportunities for the firm that would otherwise be unavailable (Kogut and Kulatilaka, 1994), thus standard discounted cash flow analysis has the potential to severely undervalue a development project's contribution to the firm.

Several authors have suggested that these problems might be addressed by treating new product development decisions as real options (e.g., Amram and Kulatilaka, 1999; McGrath, 2000). A firm that makes an initial investment in basic R&D or in breakthrough technologies, is buying a real call option to implement that technology later should it prove to be valuable (Hurry et al., 1992). Though there has not yet been much empirical work done in the area, several authors have developed methodologies and applications of options analysis to valuing technology development investments (e.g.,

Amran and Kulatilaka, 1999; Boer, 2000; McGrath, 2000). There has also been some evidence that an options approach does result in better technology investment decisions than a cash flow analysis approach (e.g., Benaroch and Kauffman, 2000).

Other authors, however, warn against too liberal application of the approach, pointing out that technology investment scenarios often do not conform to the same capital market assumptions upon which the approach is based (Perlitz et al., 1999). For instance, implicit in the value of options is the assumption that one can acquire or retain the option for a small price, and then wait for a signal to determine if the option should be exercised (Bowman and Hurry, 1993). In the case of a firm undertaking solo new product development, it may not be possible to secure this "option" at a small price, and in fact, it may require full investment in the technology before a firm can determine if the technology will be successful (Schilling, 1998).

STANDARD INTERFACES AND SYSTEM ARCHITECTURE

Though the organizational theory and strategy research on standard interfaces and architectures is relatively thin, there is considerable research on the topic being done by information systems researchers. Much of this research centers on the uses (and advantages) of object oriented programming (OOP). OOP is a way of encapsulating data and functions within a unit of software (an "object") in such a way that individual objects can be modified (or new objects combined) without requiring changes in the other objects. OOP makes software modular, and consequently makes expanding or upgrading software much simpler and more efficient. The development and implementation of OOP has spawned extensive research on the nature of interfaces and the implications for the architecture of software. This research may prove useful for providing direction for future studies of the modularization of other kinds of products and processes, and perhaps even firm disaggregation. The direct analog between OOP and modular manufacturing processes is already being explored, with OOP being used to simulate the componentization of manufacturing processes (e.g., Narayanan et al., 1998; Zeigler, 1990). Further integration across the information systems, operations management, organizational theory and strategic management disciplines is likely to enable quantum leaps forward in our understanding of standard interfaces, system architectures, and modularity.

THE ROLE OF PROXIMITY

Research on social networks and geographical clustering may help to provide answers to some of the questions about proximity posed above. For instance, Hansen's (1999) study of new product development projects indicated that strong ties (i.e., frequent and close contact) were necessary to transfer complex knowledge across organizational subunits. This provides evidence that the importance of proximity is to some degree a function of the nature of the information to be shared across organizational actors and other relevant stakeholders. Similarly, Nahapiet and Ghoshal (1998) posit that the density of social connections within an organization, and shared language, norms, trust, and mutual obligations, can give an organization an advantage in creating and sharing intellectual capital. Other studies have examined the importance of proximity between firms in the establishment of local relationships and their impact on resource allocation (e.g., Sorenson and Stuart, 2001). The network perspective and inter-organizational technology chapters in this volume provide further discussions of this topic.

The preceding raises an interesting paradox. Many authors have speculated that it is the information-based firms that are likely to be most impacted by advances in information technology. As the mechanisms for transferring information enable wider reach, richer content, and faster and cheaper transmission, firms whose primary business is to develop and share information should be most able to exploit any advantages achievable through disaggregation. However the area of research just described argues that information – particularly when it is complex or tacit, is precisely the kind of resource that is not easily developed or transferred through arms-length relationships. Part of the task of resolving this paradox will be disentangling some of the compound constructs we currently use. For instance, though often used interchangeably, the terms information, knowledge, and intellectual capital may represent distinct resources. Terms such as "closeness" will require parsing into different types, such as emotional, intellectual, and geographical closeness. More precision in our research may reveal, for example, that it is altogether possible to have strong ties in absence of proximity. This area of research has developed a strong following, and doubtless will progress rapidly over the next few years.

Connections Across Levels

Comparison across the three technology chapters reveals some interesting points of convergence and divergence. For example, the Tushman and Smith chapter on organizational-level technology raises an argument about organizational form and technological innovation that indicates that firm-level research on the impact of firm size or market power on rates of innovation (as discussed in the beginning of this chapter) may be futile: the firm-level of analysis obscures too much variance in the organization of innovative activity. Comparison between this chapter and Stuart's chapter on interorganizational technology also raises some interesting questions about the direction and complexity of the causal path between technology and spatial proximity.

TUSHMAN AND SMITH'S ORGANIZATION-LEVEL TECHNOLOGY

Both this chapter and Tushman and Smith's chapter on organization-level technology discuss factors influencing the efficacy of the new technology development process. While this chapter focuses on the existing economic research that has examined the relationship between technology development and firm size, R&D intensity, market power and market concentration, the chapter on organization-level technology proposes that particular organizational forms will influence the likelihood of a firm's success at technological innovation. Specifically, it is argued that ambidextrous organizations (those that have "complex organizational forms composed of multiple internally inconsistent architectures that are collectively capable of operating simultaneously for short term efficiency as well as long term innovation") are better able to avoid becoming trapped by their past competencies, and are able to simultaneously innovate incrementally and explore competence destroying innovation.

If big firms can have internal structures with the incentives and behavior of small firms, then much of the logic of the impact of firm size, R&D expenditures, or market concentration influencing technological innovation rates becomes moot. A single organization may have multiple cultures, structures, and processes within it; large firms may have entrepreneurial divisions that can both tap the greater resources of the larger corporation, yet have the incentive structures of small firms that foster the more careful choice of projects or enhance the motivation of R&D scientists. Such entrepreneurial units may be capable of developing discontinuous innovations within the large, efficiency driven organizations that tend to foster incremental innovations. This perspective provides strong justification for using multiple-level research designs that are able to capture industry-level, firm-level, division-level, and perhaps even project-level effects when exploring the drivers of new technology development success.

STUART'S INTERORGANIZATIONAL TECHNOLOGY

Both this chapter and the chapter on inter-organizational technology discuss the relationship between technology and the spatial proximity of firms, though with an interesting difference on causal direction: whereas this chapter discusses the potential impact of technology on the spatial distribution of firms, positing that technological advance may be rendering proximity less important over time, Stuart's chapter has an extensive discussion of how the spatial distribution of firms impacts the rate of technological innovation.

Stuart provides evidence of the importance of proximity, particularly in high technology industries, noting that "relations between people and organizations are bound to relatively stable spatial coordinates" and that "frequent and intensive interactions are often required in the development of technology and technology-based organizations." He points to evidence that geographical clustering has had a significant impact on the transmission of knowledge across firm boundaries, leading to agglomeration advantages in technological innovation. Both positions may ultimately be true; spatial proximity may have had a significant impact on the rate of technological spillovers and the acceleration of technological innovation through cross-fertilization, but those technological advances that enhance the richness and reach of information technology may, over time, lessen the importance of physical proximity in such spillovers or cross fertilization. This is not to say that spillovers or cross-fertilization will become less important, or that relationships between firms will become less important; rather it implies that the correlation between geography, and the density or intensity of relationships may diminish over time.

Conclusion

This chapter has examined the existing research on technology development, including work on when firms are likely to be successful at developing technology and how they can improve their development processes. It has also examined the existing and emerging work on the impact of technology on organization structure, management and performance, including the impact of advanced manufacturing technologies, modularity, and advances in information technology. This process has revealed that despite the breadth and diversity of the research that has been done in this area, we have only begun to scratch the surface. There are vast areas of unexplored research potential waiting to be tapped, and rapid technological innovation is causing those areas to expand. Furthermore, the relevance of such work to managers is irrefutable; the strategic importance of firms' ability to develop, implement and respond to technology has never been greater. It is an exciting time to be pursuing technology research.

Note

1 One could also consider the research on intraorganizational adoption and diffusion of technology as a third stream (e.g., Cool et al., 1997; Kim and Srivastava, 1998), however this body of research is fairly limited compared to the rich body of research on interorganizational technology adoption and diffusion.

References

Achrol, R. S. (1997): "Changes in the theory of interorganizational relations in marketing: Toward a network paradigm," *Academy of Marketing Science*, 25, 56–71.

Adler, P. S. (1988): "Managing flexible automation," *California Management Review*, 30(3), 34–57.

Alchian, A., and Woodward, S. (1987): "Reflections on the theory of the firm," *Journal of Institutional and Theoretical Economics*, 143, 111–136.

Amram, M., and Kulatilaka, N. (1999): *Real Options*. Boston: Harvard Business School Press.

Argyres, N. S. (1999): "The impact of information technology on coordination: Evidence from the B-2 'Stealth' bomber," *Organization Science*, 10, 162–81.

Ashkenas, R., Ulrich, D., Jick, T., and Kerr, S. (1995): *The Boundaryless Organization: Breaking the Chains of Organizational Structure*. San Francisco: Jossey-Bass Publishers.

Baldwin, C.Y., and Clark, K. (1997): "Managing in an age of modularity," *Harvard Business Review*, 75, 5, 84–94.

Baldwin, C. Y., and Clark, K. B. (2000): *Design Rules, Volume 1: The Power of Modularity*. Cambridge, MA: MIT Press.

Barney, J. B. (1991): "Firm resources and sustained competitive advantage," *Journal of Management*, 17, 99–120.

Benaroch, M., and Kauffman, R. (2000): "Justifying electronic banking network expansion using real options analysis," *MIS Quarterly*, 24, June, 70–86.

Blundell, R., Griffith, R., and Van Reenen, J. (1999): "Market share, market value, and innovation in a panel of British manufacturing firms", *The Review of Economic Studies*, 66, July 529–55.

Boer, F. P. (2000): "Valuation of technology using 'real options'," *Research Technology Management*, 43, July–August, 26–31.

Borja, J., and Castells, M. (1997): *The Local and the Global: Management of Cities in the Information Age*. London: Earthscan Publications.

Bowman, E. H., and Hurry, D. (1993): "Strategy through the option lens: An integrated view of resource investments and the incremental-choice process," *Academy of Management Review*, 18, 760–782.

Boyer, K. K., Leong, G. K., Ward, P. T., and Krajewski, L. J. (1997): "Unlocking the potential of advanced manufacturing technologies," *Journal of Operations Management*, 12, 331–47.

Brandyberry, A., Rai, A., and White, G. P. (1999): "Intermediate performance impacts of advanced manufacturing technology systems: An empirical investigation," *Decision Sciences*, 30, 993–1021.

Brown, S., and Eisenhardt, K. (1995): "Product development: Past research, present findings, and future directions," *Academy of Management Review*, 20, 343–79.

Brynjolfsson, E. (1994): "Information assets, technology, and organization," *Management Science*, 40, 1645–63.

Brynjolfsson, E., Malone, T. W., Gurbaxani, V., and Kambil, A. (1994): "Does information technology lead to smaller firms?" *Management Science*, 40, 1628–45.

Byrne, J. A. (1993): "The virtual corporation," *Business Week*, 3304, 98–104.

Chesbrough, H., and Christensen, C. M. (2000):"Technology markets, technology organization, and appropriating the returns from research," HBS working paper no 99-115, March.

Chesbrough, H., and Teece, D. (1996): "When is virtual virtuous: Organizing for innovation," *Harvard Business Review*, January–February, 65–73.

Churbuck, D., and Young, J.S. (1992): "The virtual workplace," *Forbes*, 150(12), 184–90.

Clark, K. B., and Wheelwright, S. C. (1993): *Managing New Product and Process Development*. New York: Free Press.

Cohen, W., and Levin, R. (1989): "Empirical studies of innovation and market structure," in R. Schmalensee and R. D. Willig (eds), *Handbook of Industrial Organization*, Vol. II, Elsevier Science Publishers B.V.

Cool, K. O., Dierickx, I., and Szulanski, G. (1997): "Diffusion of innovations within organizations: Electronic switching in the bell system, 1971–1982", *Organization Science*, 8, 543–59.

Cooper, R. G., and Kleinschmidt, E. J. (1987): "New products: What separates winners from losers?" *Journal of Product Innovation Management*, 4, September, 169–85.

Cooper, R. G., and Kleinschmidt, E. (1991): "New product processes and leading industrial firms," *Industrial Marketing Management*, 20(2), 137–48.

Cooper, R. G., and Kleinschmidt, E. (1993): "Major new products: What distinguishes the winners in the chemical industry?" *Journal of Product Innovation Management*, 10, March, 90–112.

Cooper, R. G., and Kleinschmidt, E. J. (1995): "Benchmarking the firm's critical success factors in new product development," *Journal of Product Innovation Management*, 12, November, 374–92.

Damanpour, F. (1991): "Organization innovation: A meta-analysis of effects of determinants and moderators," *Academy of Management Journal*, 34(3), 555–90.

Davidow, W. H., and Malone, M. S. (1992): *The Virtual Corporation*. New York: Harper Business.

Dean, J. W. Jr., Yoon, S. J., and Susman, G. I. (1992): "Advanced manufacturing technology and organization structure: Empowerment or subordination?" *Organization Science*, 3(2), 203–29.

Garud, R., and Kotha, S. (1994): "Using the brain as a metaphor to model flexible production systems," *Academy of Management Review*, 19, 671–99.

Garud, R., and Kumaraswamy, A. (1993): "Changing competitive dynamics in network industries: An exploration of Sun Microsystems' open systems strategy," *Strategic Management Journal*, 14, 351–69.

Garud, R., and Kumaraswamy, A. (1995): "Technological and organizational designs for realizing economies of substitution," *Strategic Management Journal*, 16, 93–110.

Ghoshal, S., and Bartlett, C. A.. (1997): *The Individualized Corporation*. New York: Harper Business.

Griffin, A., and Hauser, J. R. (1992): "Patterns of communication among marketing, engineering and manufacturing," *Management Science*, 38, 360–73.

Griliches, Z. (1990): "Patent statistics as economic indicators: A survey," *Journal of Economic Literature*, 18, 1661–1707.

Hansen, M. T. (1999): "The search–transfer problem: The role of weak ties in sharing knowledge across organization subunits," *Administrative Science Quarterly*, 44, 82–112.

Henderson, R., and Clark, K. B. (1990): "Architectural innovation: The reconfiguration of existing product technologies and the failure of established firms," *Administrative Science Quarterly*, 35, 9–30.

Hitt, L. M. (1999): "Information technology and firm boundaries: Evidence from panel data," *Information Systems Research*, 10(2), 134–50.

Hurry, D., Miller, A. T., and Bowman, E. H. (1992): "Calls on high-technology: Japanese exploration of venture capital investments in the United States," *Strategic Management Journal*, 13, 85–101.

Jaffe, A., Trajtenberg, M., and Henderson, R. (1993): "Geographical localization of knowledge spillovers as evidenced by patent citations," *The Quarterly Journal of Economics*, 108, 577–98.

Johne, F. A., and Snelson, P. A. (1989): "Product development approaches in established firms," *Industrial Marketing Management*, 18, 113–24.

Jones, C., Hesterly, W., and Borgatti, S. (1997): "A general theory of network governance: Exchange conditions and social mechanisms," *Academy of Management Review*, 22, 911–45.

Kim, N., and Srivastava, R. K. (1998): "Managing intraorganizational diffusion of technological innovations," *Industrial Marketing Management*, 27, 229–46.

Kogut, B., and Kulatilaka, N. (1994): "Options thinking and platform investments: Investing in opportunity," *California Management Review*, 36(2), 52–72.

Kogut, B., and Zander, U. (1992): "Knowledge of the firm, combinative capabilities, and the replication of technology," *Organization Science*, 3, 383–97.

Kotha, S. (1995): "Mass customization: Implementing the emerging paradigm for competitive advantage," *Strategic Management Journal*, 16, 21–43.

Kotha, S., and Swamidass, P. (2000): "Strategy, advanced manufacturing technology and performance: Empirical evidence from U.S. manufacturing firms," *Journal of Operations Management*, 18(3), 257–77.

Langlois, R. N. (1992): "External economies and economic progress: The case of the microcomputer industry," *Business History Review*, 66, 1–50.

Langlois, R. N. (2000): "Capabilities and vertical disintegration in process technology: The case of semiconductor fabrication equipment," in N. J. Foss, and P. L. Robertson (eds), *Resources, Technology, and Strategy*. London: Routledge, 199–206.

Lee, B. (2000): "Separating the wheat from the chaff: FMS, flexibility and socio-organizational constraints," *Technology Analysis and Strategic Management*, 12, 213–29.

Lei, D., Hitt, M. A., and Goldhar, J. D. (1996): "Advanced manufacturing technology: Organizational design and strategic flexibility," *Organization Studies*, 17, 501–24.

Lusht, K. M., and Farber, D. (1996): "Information technology and urban structure," *Real Estate Finance*, 13, 13–21.

Malone, T. W., Yates, J., and Benjamin, R. I. (1987): "Electronic markets and electronic hierarchies," *Communications of the ACM*, 30(6), June, 484–97.

Mann, C. C. (2000): "The end of Moore's Law?" *Technology Review*, 103(3), 342–49.

Marshall, A. 1922): *Principles of Economics*. London: MacMillan.

McGrath, R. T. (2000): "Assessing technology projects using real options reasoning," *Research Technology Management*, 43, July–August, 35–50.

Miles, R. E., and Snow, C. C. (1986): "Organizations: New concepts for new forms," *California Management Review*, 28(3), 62–73.

Miles, R. E., and Snow, C. C. (1992): "Causes of failures in network organizations," *California Management Review*, 34(4), 53–72.

Miller, R. (1998): "The promise of 21st-century technology," *Organization for Economic Cooperation and Development Observer*, 214, 25–8.

Nahapiet, J., and Ghoshal, S. (1998): "Social capital, intellectual capital, and the organizational advantage," *Academy of Management Review*, 23, 242–67.

Narayanan, S., Bodner, D. A., Sreekanth, U., Govindaraj, T., McGinnis, L. F., and Mitchell, C. M. (1998): "Research in object-oriented manufacturing simulations: An assessment of the state of the art," *IIE Transactions*, 30, 795–811.

Nemetz, P. L., and Fry, L. W. (1988): "Flexible manufacturing organizations: Implications for strategy and organization design," *Academy of Management Review*, 13, 627–38.

Orton, J., and Weick, K. (1990): "Loosely coupled systems: A reconceptualization," *Academy of Management Review*, 15, 203–23.

Parthasarthy, R., and Sethi, S. P. (1992): "The impact of flexible automation on business strategy and organizational structure," *Academy of Management Review*, 17, 86–111.

Perlitz, M., Peske, T., and Schrank, R. (1999): "Real options valuation: The new frontier in R&D evaluation?" *R&D Management*, 29, 255–70.

Pine II, B. J. (1993): *Mass Customization.* Boston: Harvard Business School Press.

Romer, P. (1987): "Growth based on increasing returns to specialization," *American Economic Review*, 77, 56–62.

Rotemberg, J., and Saloner, G. (1994): "Benefits of narrow business strategies," *American Economic Review*, 84, December, 1330–49.

Sanchez, R. (1995): "Strategic flexibility in product competition," *Strategic Management Journal*, 16, 135–60.

Sanchez, R. (1999): "Modular architectures in the marketing process," *Journal of Marketing*, 63, 92–112.

Sanchez, R., and Mahoney, J. (1996): "Modularity, flexibility, and knowledge management in product and organization design," *Strategic Management Journal*, 17, 63–76.

Scherer, F. M. (1983): "The propensity to patent," *International Journal of Industrial Organization*, 1, 107–28.

Schilling, M. A. (1998): "Technological lock out: An integrative model of the economic and strategic factors driving success and failure," *Academy of Management Review*, 23, 267–85.

Schilling, M. A. (2000): "Toward a general modular systems theory and its application to interfirm product modularity," *Academy of Management Review*, 25, 312–35.

Schilling, M. A., and Hill, C. W. L. (1998): "Managing the new product development process: Strategic imperatives," *Academy of Management Executive*, 12, August, 67–82.

Schilling, M. A., and Steensma, K. (2001): "The use of modular organizational forms: An industry level analysis," *Academy of Management Journal* (In press).

Schumpeter, J. (1942): *Capitalism, Socialism, and Democracy.* New York: Harper.

Simon, H. (1962): "The architecture of complexity," *Proceedings of the American Philosophical Society*, 106, 467–82.

Snow, C., Miles, R. and Coleman, H. J. (1992): "Managing 21st-century network organizations," *Organizational Dynamics*, 20(3), 5–20.

Sorenson, O., and Stuart, T. (2001): "Syndication networks and the spatial distribution of venture capital investments," *American Journal of Sociology*, (forthcoming).

Venkatraman, N. (1997):"The college textbook marketplace in the 1990s: McGraw-Hill's launch of primis," Boston University teaching case.

Ward, P. T., Leong, G. K., and Boyer, K. K. (1994): "Manufacturing proactiveness and performance," *Decision Sciences*, 25(3), 337–58

Weick, K. E. (1976): "Educational organizations as loosely coupled systems," *Administrative Science Quarterly*, 21, 1–19.

Wind, Y., and Mahajan, V. (1988): "New product development process: A perspective for reexamination," *Journal of Product Innovation Management*, 5, 304–10.

Woodward, J. (1958): *Management and Technology.* London: Her Majesty's Stationery Office.

Worren, N. (2001): "Creating dynamic capabilities: The role of modular product and process architectures," unpublished doctoral dissertation, Said Business School, Oxford University.

Zeigler, B. P. (1990): *Object-Oriented Simulation with Hierarchical Modular Models: Intelligent Agents and Endomorphic Systems.* San Diego, CA: Academic Press.

Zenger, T. R., and Hesterly, W. S. (1997): "The disaggregation of corporations: Selective intervention, high-powered incentives, and molecular units," *Organization Science*, 8, 209–23.

Zirger, B. J., and Maidique, M. A. (1990): "A model of new product development: An empirical test," *Management Science*, 36, 867–83.

Chapter Eight

Intraorganizational Learning

LINDA ARGOTE AND RON OPHIR

Intraorganizational learning involves the processes through which organizational units (e.g., groups, departments, or divisions) change as a result of experience. The units could learn from their own direct experience or from the experience of other units (Levitt and March, 1988). For example, a hospital surgical team might acquire knowledge about how to use new technology more effectively as the team gains experience (Edmondson et al., 2000). Or work groups might learn who is good at what and assign tasks to take advantage of members' expertise (Liang et al., 1995; Lewis, 2000). Or a department might benefit from the experience of another department in the firm by adopting a "best practice" it developed (Szulanski, 1996).

The main subprocesses through which intraorganizational learning occurs are creating, retaining, and transferring knowledge.[1] Creating knowledge refers to the development of new or emergent knowledge within organizations. For example, as group members gain experience working together, they might develop new knowledge or understandings that no member possessed at the start of their interactions or they might combine their previous knowledge in new ways to create a collective product (Argote et al., 2001). Retaining knowledge refers to the embedding of knowledge in various repositories so that it exhibits some persistence over time. Transferring knowledge is the process through which one organizational unit is affected by the experience of another.

Learning within organizations can manifest itself through changes in either the knowledge (e.g., see Gruenfeld et al., 2000) or the performance (e.g., see Adler and Clark, 1991) of the recipient unit. Measuring learning within organizations through assessing changes in knowledge associated with experience is challenging. A significant amount of the knowledge organizational units acquire is tacit and hence difficult to measure through the usual verbal reports typically used to assess knowledge (Berry and Broadbent, 1984, 1987; Nonaka, 1991). Further, knowledge in organizations resides in many repositories, including routines and technologies as well as individuals. Attempts to measure learning within organizations by measuring changes in knowledge must be sensitive to the non-human repositories in which some knowledge may reside. An important start on developing measures of knowledge embedded in these non-human repositories is provided by Cohen and Bacdayan (1994) who developed measures of properties of routines.

Measuring learning within organizations through measuring changes in performance associated with experience is also challenging because one must control for the many factors in addition to experience that might affect performance (Argote, 1999). Research in this tradition does not equate learning with improved performance but rather empirically examines the relationship between experience and a dimension of performance, such as unit costs (Rapping, 1965), quality (Argote, 1993), or service timeliness (Argote and Darr, 2000). Although enormous variation has been observed in the magnitude of the relationship between experience and dimensions of organizational performance, the relationship is generally positive (Argote and Epple, 1990; Dutton and Thomas, 1984).

Our focus is on learning within organizations. Thus, we focus on learning both *within* and *between* the constituent units that comprise organizations such as groups, departments, divisions, or establishments. Although we draw on findings about individual learning, reviewing that voluminous literature is beyond the scope of this chapter. Similarly, research on learning at a more macro level is beyond the scope of this chapter. Other chapters in this volume focus on learning at the level of the overall organization (Schulz) or interorganizational field (Ingram). These more macro treatments complement the micro underpinnings of organizational learning described in this chapter.

Literature Review

Empirical research on learning with organizations increased dramatically in the 1990s (Argote et al., 2001; Miner and Mezias, 1996). We organize this literature by cataloging empirical findings along two dimensions. The first dimension refers to the subprocess of organizational learning that is being analyzed: *creating*, *retaining*, or *transferring* knowledge. The second dimension that we use to organize findings about learning within organizations depicts the basic elements of organizations and the subnetworks formed by combining them. This conceptualization of organizations is based on a theoretical framework developed to characterize groups (McGrath and Argote, 2001; Arrow et al., 2000). According to the framework, the basic elements of organizations are: *members* (the human component), *tools* (the technological component), and *tasks* (the purposive component). These basic elements combine to form subnetworks. The *member–member network* is the organization's social network. The *task–task network* is the sequence of tasks or routines that the organization uses. The *tool–tool network* depicts the interrelationships among tools used by the organization. The *member–task network* is the division of labor; it maps members onto tasks. The *member–tool network* assigns members to tools. The *task–tool network* specifies which tools perform which tasks. The *member–task–tool network* identifies which members perform which tasks with which tools.

The framework posits that performance increases as the internal compatibility of the networks and their external compatibility with other networks increases (McGrath and Argote, 2001). For example, when the member–task network allocates tasks to the members most qualified to perform them, the member-task network is internally compatible and organizational performance improves. Similarly, when members have the appropriate tools to perform the tasks allocated to them, performance improves because the member–task network is compatible with the member–tool network. Thus, according to this framework, performance increases as the compatibility of the various networks increases; see also Leavitt (1961).

This "members–tool–tasks" framework developed for groups (Arrow et al., 2000) is also useful for characterizing the fundamental components of organizations. A key difference in applying the framework to organizations is that organizations typically have more levels of social systems embedded within them than groups have. For example, in an organization, an individual might belong to one or more groups that are part of departments that belong to divisions and so on. The importance of individuals' identifications may vary, such that for some purposes their membership in a group may be salient while for others their membership in a division may be more important. The conceptualization of groups can be adapted to accommodate this feature of organizations by noting that the components of social systems can occur at different levels within organizations. For example, although the component "member" refers to individuals when the framework is applied to groups, the component "member" could refer to individuals or groups or departments, when the framework is applied to organizations, depending on the level of analysis that is being used.

Another difference when one applies the framework to learning within organizations rather than to learning within groups, is that organizational performance depends on the fit of more networks. The importance of fit is especially critical when one analyzes transfer of knowledge across the constituent parts of organizations (Argote and Ingram, 2000). Knowledge is more likely to transfer from one unit to another when it fits the new context. Thus, in applying the framework to organizations rather than to groups, one must consider the fit of networks across different organizational units as well as the fit of networks within units.

As in all chapters of this companion volume, we include a list of studies that have contributed significantly to the chapter's research domain (see Table 8.1). We set two main criteria for selecting a study on learning within organizations to be included. The first criterion is that the study includes empirical evidence. The second criterion is that the study has a temporal component of learning from experience over time. We also chose the studies to represent the three major subprocesses of learning within organizations (i.e., knowledge creation, retention, and transfer) and a range of methods (e.g., archival analyses, surveys, experiments, and computer simulations).

The studies in the list include ones that focus on the creation (Lant et al., 1992; Hollenbeck et al., 1995; Paulus and Yang, 2000), the retention (Argote et al., 1990; Carley, 1992; Cohen and Bacdayan, 1994; Liang et al., 1995) and the transfer (Argote et al., 1990; Larson et al., 1996; Szulanski, 1996; Baum and Berta, 1999; Hansen, 1999; Gruenfeld et al., 2000) of knowledge within organizations. For example, Lant et al. (1992) examined the effect of top management team composition on the creation of new strategies. Argote et al. (1990) examined the retention of organizational knowledge over time. Hansen (1999) examined the impact of social networks on the transfer of knowledge between units within organizations. The studies are organized in the table according to the primary subprocess on which they focus. Several studies, however, analyze more than one subprocess of intraorganizational learning.

Table 8.1 Key empirical studies on intraorganizational learning

Reference	Key concepts	Key variables	Key predictions and findings	Key contribution	Method and sample
Creation of knowledge					
Hollenbeck et al. (1995)	Hierarchical teams – in which status differences exist among members Three core team-level constructs – team informity (availability of information cues), staff validity (degree to which members make correct assessments), hierarchical sensitivity (effective weighting of members' judgments by leader) Distributed expertise – differences in the amount of knowledge members bring to the team	Team performance was measured as decision accuracy. Study 1 – Three variables manipulated: team member familiarity (know each other before study), stability of team membership (one staff member was swapped between teams), and experience (time spent on the task). Study 2 — Independent variables included informational redundancy (number of items shared), staff member competence and team cohesiveness.	The three core variables combined have a positive effect on decision accuracy. Decision accuracy improved with experience. Much of that effect was mediated by the core variables. Instability in group membership disrupted leader's ability to effectively weight staff's input.	Presented a multilevel theory of hierarchical team decision making, suggesting that three core team-level constructs mediate the relationship between other variables and team performance.	A total of 492 students performed a simulation task of a naval command-and-control scenario. Study 1 – 21 teams that made 127 decisions. Each team included a leader and 3 staff members. Task was performed once a week for six weeks. Study 2 – 102 teams that made 24 decisions in one session only
Lant et al. (1992)	Strategic reorientation – changes in the organization's strategic course	Strategic reorientation – combination of changes in business strategy and in other key organizational dimensions Past performance – return on assets for a 5-year period.	Likelihood of strategic reorientation increased by CEO turnover, higher levels of top management team heterogeneity, poor past performance and high environmental awareness	Presented evidence that the process of strategy formulation is inherently a process of organizational learning that is affected by the organization's performance history, its members and its context	Sample included 40 furniture companies and 20 computer software firms Data gathered from the COMPUSTAT Industrial Data Base and from 10K and annual reports.

	Managerial interpretations – environmental awareness and external attributions; Turnover – CEO and top management turnover rates; Management team functional heterogeneity				
Paulus and Yang (2000)	Attention – the extent to which group members carefully process ideas exchanged; Incubation – the opportunity of group members to reflect on ideas	Group performance – total number of unique ideas generated; Group memory: total number of ideas recalled by group members; Procedures for sharing ideas (nominal pooling, brainstorming, and brainstorming with memory instructions)	Group brainstorming procedures resulted in better productivity than pooling of individual ideas	Provided initial evidence that brainstorming can actually enhance creativity and innovation in groups, under specific conditions	Idea generation in three group conditions was examined using the "brainwriting" paradigm. 30 students groups were assigned to three conditions: nominal, brainstorming, and brainstorming with memorizing ideas. Experiment included two consecutive sessions of idea generation with a recall task between them

Retention of knowledge

Argote et al. (1990)	Knowledge depreciation – occurs when organizational learning does not persist over time; Knowledge Transfer – occurs when experience acquired in one organization affects another	Learning from own production experience, measured as shipyard's cumulative output; Depreciation of knowledge; Transfer of knowledge; Additional control variables were calendar time, labor and capital inputs.	Knowledge acquired through production depreciates rapidly. Transfer of knowledge between shipyards is limited. Shipyards benefited from others' production experience prior to starting date of their production, but not thereafter	Developed procedure for estimation of knowledge depreciation; Provided early evidence for transfer of knowledge from one organization to another	Archival data analysis of data from 13 shipyards that produced Liberty Ship during World War II (Results were also applied to data on Lockheed's production of the L-1011.)

Reference	Key concepts	Key variables	Key predictions and findings	Key contribution	Method and sample
Carley (1992)	Personnel turnover – changes in the membership of organizational units Team structure – teams and hierarchies Teams defined as a set of decision makers that act autonomously (no chain of command), and hierarchies defined as a set of decision makers organized in a chain of command	Turnover – when a group member leaves and is replaced by a new one Organizational structure – centralized hierarchy and team Task complexity: 4 levels Type of task: 2 types – nondecomposable, decomposable-consensual Rate of learning – average number of decision periods until the organization increased performance by 10% Level of learning	Turnover impedes the ability of organizations to learn from experience. Teams learn faster and better than hierarchies. Hierarchies are less affected by turnover when the task is nondecomposable.	Showed in a simulation that the effect of turnover depends on group structure and the nature of the task	Simulation (Monte Carlo analysis) – 256 configurations of organizations were examined, each simulated 400 times for 2500 decision periods
Cohen and Bacdayan (1994)	Organizational routines – multi-actor, interlocking, reciprocally triggered sequences of skilled actions Procedural memory (compared to declarative memory) — relatively automatic and inarticulate memory of how things are done	Four characteristics of routines were observed: reliability, speed, repeated action sequences, and occasional suboptimality. Experimental conditions varied delay between sessions and novelty of rules used in the game.	Performance of task by dyads exhibited characteristics of organizational routines. Little decay in learning is seen over time when rules are the same. However, introduction of novel rules slows down performance.	Provided a carefully controlled examination of a complex organizational phenomenon Findings support the proposition that organizational routines are stored in individuals' procedural memory.	Thirty-two dyads playing a card game in two sessions A 2 × 2 experimental design was employed – delay between sessions and rules of the game in the second session (same or novel rules)

Study	Concepts	Measures	Findings	Interpretation	Method
Liang et al. (1995)	Transactive memory system – combination of knowledge possessed by group members and their awareness of who knows what	Transactive memory was measured based on three factors: memory differentiation, task coordination and task credibility. Social factors controlled for were task motivation, group cohesion, and social identity. Performance measures included recall of task, speed and errors made.	Groups that were trained together exhibited better recall, fewer errors, and stronger transactive memory systems than groups whose members were trained separately. Transactive memory systems mediated the relationship between training and group performance.	Transactive memory, such as develops during group training, has a positive effect on group performance (see also Moreland et al., 1998).	90 students were randomly assigned to individual or group training. One week later, subjects performed the task as a group. Data collected included performance measures, videotaping of group performance and questionnaires.

Transfer of knowledge

Study	Concepts	Measures	Findings	Interpretation	Method
Argote et al. (1990)	See above in the retention of knowledge section.				
Baum and Berta (1999)	Population-level learning Interorganizational learning (cooperative, mimetic, inferential)	Interorganizational learning – based on self report of learning events Population performance – the average profit of the firms in each industry in each learning period Independent variables include social proximity of members, firm status, firm market domain similarity, differentiation, momentum, time period, firm performance, and learning speed.	Higher performing firms, especially if they are in local non-competing populations, are likely to be sources of interorganizational learning. Likelihood of interorganizational learning is higher when firms are socially proximate and similar in market domain strategy. Firms that engaged in interorganizational learning developed a stronger learning momentum.	Examined a learning population from the inception of the industry and a range of forces that affect transfer of learning and the evolution of the industry	Longitudinal behavioral simulation, where student groups operated a medium-size functionally organized firm for 5 weeks

Reference	Key concepts	Key variables	Key predictions and findings	Key contribution	Method and sample
Gruenfeld et al. (2000)	Membership changes within organizations – when group members move from one group to another for a specified period of time	Type of group member: itinerant (members who leave the group to visit another group), indigenous (permanent members who remain within the group) Individual and group ideas – coded from essays Social influence – measured as the inclusion of members' ideas in group product Social perceptions	All members produced more unique ideas after itinerants returned to their group of origin. After returning to their group of origin, itinerant members produced more unique ideas than indigenous members did. However, itinerants' ideas were less likely to be used by the group.	Movement of members between groups may stimulate creating new ideas. It may also affect the attention to ideas produced by members who have moved between groups.	29 student groups who worked on different group tasks over a semester Longitudinal study: measures taken before, during and after membership change Data collected included essays (individual and group) written by group members after completing task, and questionnaires.
Hansen (1999)	Strength of social ties and frequency of relationships between actors	Project completion time Inter-unit tie weakness Degree of codification of transferred knowledge Knowledge dependence between units Additional variables included cohesion, structural equivalence, and reciprocity between units and controls for project, divisional and network characteristics.	Transfer of complex knowledge is facilitated by existence of strong ties, while the transfer of non-complex knowledge is facilitated by weak ties.	The impact of the strength of ties on knowledge sharing depends on the complexity of the knowledge transferred. Weak inter-unit ties facilitate search but impede the transfer of complex knowledge.	Network study of 120 new-product development projects by 41 divisions of a large electronics company Both archival and survey data were used

Larson et al. (1996)	Sharing of "unshared" information (not possessed by all group members) over time Leadership role	Frequency and timing of shared and unshared items mentioned and repeated in group discussion Group member role (medical, resident, intern, student)	Shared information was discussed more and mentioned earlier, compared to unshared information. Team leaders, who possessed more expertise, repeated (unshared) information more than other members did.	Replicated the finding that group members focus more on shared information that members hold in common than on unshared information that members possess uniquely (Stasser and Titus, 1987) in a task closer to ones found in organizations Team leaders shown to have a central role in increasing attention to unshared information	24 teams of medical personnel diagnosed two cases of patients. Each team included a resident, an intern, and a medical student.
Szulanski (1996)	Transfer of best practice – replication of a superior internal practice developed at one unit in another Internal stickiness of knowledge transfer – the difficulty of transferring knowledge within organizations	Internal stickiness measures included outcome (perceived technical success) and process (four stages of transfer process: initiation, implementation, ramp-up and integration). Independent variables included characteristics of the knowledge transferred, the source, the recipient, and the context.	Intraorganizational transfer is impeded by recipients' lack of absorptive capacity, causal ambiguity and arduous relationships between source and recipient.	Major barriers to transfer of best practices are knowledge-related factors, rather than motivational factors.	Eight companies were surveyed on 122 transfers of 38 practices.

Creating Knowledge

Research on creating knowledge within organizations has examined how characteristics of *members* affect the generation of new knowledge. Research on group composition suggests that heterogeneous groups composed of diverse members are more creative than homogeneous groups. Scientific laboratories composed of diverse members have been found to engage more in analogical reasoning and be more innovative than laboratories composed of more homogeneous members (Dunbar, 1995). Similarly, heterogeneous top management teams have been found to be more innovative than their more homogeneous counterparts (Bantel and Jackson, 1989; Lant et al., 1992; Hambrick et al., 1996). Heterogeneous new product development teams have also been found to be more innovative than homogeneous teams, especially in environments of rapid change (Eisenhardt and Tabrizi, 1995; Moorman and Miner, 1997). The dimension of heterogeneity that seems especially beneficial for innovation and performance is functional heterogeneity or diversity in members' backgrounds (Williams and O'Reilly, 1998).

A critical issue involved in managing diversity within organizations is balancing the benefits of the larger information pool diverse members provide with the costs associated with communicating with individuals from different backgrounds (Williams and O'Reilly, 1998). There is some evidence that groups are able to learn to manage their diversity as they gain experience working together: Watson et al. (1993) found that although the performance of homogeneous groups was initially superior to that of heterogeneous groups, the performance of heterogeneous groups improved at a faster rate than that of homogeneous groups until it equaled or surpassed the homogeneous groups.

Research on "divergent thinking" also points to the benefits of having diverse views represented in groups. Divergent thinking is the process of considering an issue from multiple perspectives (Nemeth, 1992). Having a minority view represented in a group has been found to stimulate divergent thinking. Groups that considered alternatives presented by a minority were more creative and performed better than groups lacking minority input (Nemeth and Wachtler, 1983; Nemeth and Kwan, 1987). A related stream of research suggests that the presence of minority views increases "integrative complexity," a more sophisticated form of information processing that involves considering multiple viewpoints and the connections and tradeoffs among them (Gruenfeld and Hollingshead, 1993; Gruenfeld, 1995). Thus, being presented with diverse views during group discussion can stimulate a group to incorporate more perspectives and viewpoints and to develop more creative solutions to problems.

Research on moving members across groups also suggests that member rotation can be a mechanism for stimulating the creation of new knowledge in groups. Gruenfeld et al. (2000) found that although moving members temporarily from one group to another did not result in knowledge being transported directly across the groups, moving members resulted in the creation of new knowledge. New knowledge was generated in groups upon their "itinerant" member's return from sojourns in other groups.

The effect of the *social networks* on the creation of knowledge has received some attention in the literature. Examining how organizations develop knowledge of their own capabilities, Rulke et al. (2000) found that relational channels, both inside and outside the organization, and internal non-relational channels (e.g., newsletters, formal training programs) contributed more to the development of new knowledge than external non-relational channels, such as trade association publications and newsletters. Thus, relationships can facilitate the creation of new knowledge.

How characteristics of the *task* or *task–task network* affect the generation of new ideas or the creation of new knowledge is also starting to receive research attention. Examining the effect of task routines on idea generation in groups, Paulus and Yang (2000) found that brainstorming groups created more novel ideas per person than individuals working alone. Their finding departs from the prevailing view that groups who use brainstorming techniques generate fewer unique ideas per person than individuals working alone (see Mullen et al., 1991, for a review) and suggests that group interactions can enhance creativity. Paulus and Yang (2000) found that procedures for interaction that exposed group members to the ideas of others while allowing them to generate ideas continuously and maintain their own identity led to the creation of more novel ideas than procedures that simply pooled the ideas of group members. Thus, when structured appropriately, group interactions can have synergistic effects on group performance and can lead to the creation of more novel ideas.

Research on how the *tool* or *tool–tool network* affects the creation of new knowledge is also relatively new. Hargadon and Sutton (1997) showed how tools can stimulate the creation of new knowledge. In their study of new product development, Hargadon and Sutton found that tools, which embody knowledge of previous products, can stimulate team members to see connections between past designs and current design problems and thereby improve the team's creativity.

In summary, research on the creation of knowledge has primarily focused on how characteristics of members, especially their diversity, affect creativity. A few recent studies have examined how characteristics of the social networks, the task network or the tool network affect creativity. We see this as a positive trend and believe that additional research on these factors will provide a more complete view of knowledge creation in organizations. Research is also needed on how the member–task network or the member–tool network affects the creation of knowledge within organizations.

Retaining Knowledge

A fundamental issue in knowledge retention is understanding where knowledge is embedded in organizations (Levitt and March, 1988; Walsh and Ungson, 1991). Knowledge can be embedded in the various components of organizations described previously. A significant component of organizational knowledge is embedded in individual *members*. For example, Engeström et al. (1990) described a medical facility where much of the knowledge was embedded in one administrator. Knowledge is especially likely to be embedded in individual members in professional service organizations, such as consulting firms or law firms (Starbuck, 1992).

To the extent that knowledge is embedded in individual members, their turnover will impair the retention of knowledge in organizations. Research has found that turnover of high-performing members adversely affected organizational knowledge retention in a production context. Based on an archival analysis of two years of data from a truck assembly plant, Argote et al. (1997) concluded that the departure of high-performing members had a negative effect on the plant's productivity. Similarly, in a laboratory study of decision making, turnover was found to hurt decision accuracy by disrupting leaders' ability to weight members' contributions appropriately (Hollenbeck et al., 1995). The effect of turnover has been found to depend on the quality of replacements and on the extent to which turnover is anticipated (Trow, 1960).

The effect of turnover has also been found to depend on characteristics of the *member–member* network, the *member–task* network, and the *member–tool* network. In a simulation study, Carley (1992) found that although teams (a set of decision makers without a chain of command) learned better and faster than hierarchies (a set of decision makers with a chain of command), hierarchies were less affected by turnover than teams. Similarly, Devadas and Argote (1995) found that structure buffered organizations from the effect of turnover. Groups with specialized roles and procedures were less affected by turnover than groups lacking specialized roles and procedures. When a member left a group that lacked specialized roles and procedures, not only was the group deprived of his or her individual knowledge and skill, the group also found its member–task network or division of labor was obsolete because it did not fit the knowledge and skills of the new member. Thus, structures with specialized roles and procedures can mitigate the effects of turnover.

The effect of turnover also depends on characteristics of the *task*. Argote et al. (1995) found that turnover was less harmful on complex tasks that involved innovation than on simple tasks that were more routine. The replacement of experienced group members by inexperienced members hurt productivity on complex tasks because some of the experienced members' knowledge was no longer relevant due to innovations that had occurred. Consistent with these results, Wells and Pelz (1966) found that turnover among scientists and engineers improved the performance of research teams. Similarly, Virany et al. (1992) found that turnover at the executive level was associated with improved organizational performance, as measured by Return on Assets, in the computer industry. Not only was turnover not disruptive in these later studies, turnover was associated with improved group and organizational performance. New members may have brought new knowledge and critical expertise with them that enabled the groups or organizations to improve their performance.

In addition to being embedded in individual members, knowledge within organizations can also be embedded in *task* sequences and routines (Cyert and March, 1963; Nelson and Winter, 1982). For example, Argote (1999) described how a more cost-effective method for painting products was embedded in an organizational routine at an automotive assembly plant. Embedding knowledge in routines makes the organization less vulnerable to the vagaries of individual participation. Once knowledge is embedded in a routine, it is no longer dependent on the individual member(s) who developed the knowledge. Knowledge that is embedded in a routine is less likely to be affected by interruptions or to depreciate than knowledge embedded in individuals (Argote, Beckman and Epple, 1990; Cohen and Bacdayan, 1994; Argote, 1999). Thus, embedding knowledge in routines or task sequences promotes its retention.

Knowledge embedded in *tools*, *tool–tool* sequences, and *task–tool* sequences is also less likely to decay than knowledge embedded in softer repositories. Hargadon and Sutton (1997) discussed how tools or artifacts can serve as repositories for past knowledge. Less knowledge depreciation has been found in firms where most of the knowledge is embedded in technology, such as automobile assembly plants, than in firms that are less technologically sophisticated, such as fast food franchises (Argote, 1999).

Knowledge can also be embedded in an organization's *member–task network*. As organizations gain experience, they learn who is good at what and assign tasks to the most qualified member (Argote, 1993). These transactive memory systems (Wegner, 1995), the combination of group members' individual knowledge and their awareness of who in the group knows what, have been found to improve group performance. Groups with well-developed transactive memory systems recall more task-related knowledge and make fewer errors than groups lacking well-developed memory systems (Liang et al., 1995; Hollingshead, 1998; Moreland et al., 1998). Similarly, groups with a well-developed "collective mind" in which members both understand that the system consists of interdependent actions and interrelate their actions in the context of the larger system have been found to make fewer errors than groups lacking such collective understandings (Weick and Roberts, 1993).

In short, research on knowledge retention is more balanced across the components of organizations than research on knowledge creation. Although considerable research has been done on knowledge embedded in members, research has also been done on knowledge embedded in other components of organizations, especially in their member–task networks (see the research on transactive memory systems). We see this as a positive trend and encourage further research on knowledge embedded in all the components of organizations.

Transferring Knowledge

Work on personnel movement suggests that moving members is powerful mechanism for transferring knowledge to other organizational units (Allen, 1977; Rothwell, 1978; Galbraith, 1990; Almeida and Kogut, 1999). When *members* are moved from one organizational unit to another, they are able to transfer tacit as well as explicit knowledge (Berry and Broadbent, 1984; 1987) and subtle understandings to the new unit. Further, members are capable of adapting knowledge to the new context (Allen, 1977). Although social psychological processes affect member's willingness to both share knowledge and be influenced by knowledge (e.g., see Gruenfeld et al., 2000), members are generally very effective knowledge conduits.

Characteristics of the units themselves also affect knowledge transfer. A unit's "absorptive capacity" or its ability to recognize and apply external information affects the success of knowledge transfer (Cohen and Levinthal, 1990; Szulanski, 1996; 2000). Similarly, previous experience in transferring knowledge affects the success of knowledge transfer attempts (Galbraith, 1990).

Characteristics of the *social network* among members (or units) have also been found to affect knowledge transfer. Early research on social networks compared the effects of various communication channels (e.g., a "wheel" in which all communication went through a central hub versus an "all-channel" network in which all members could communicate with one another) on information sharing and performance in groups. Although the wheel network was initially shown to be the best communication structure (Guetzkow and Simon, 1955; Leavitt, 1951), this effect was subsequently shown to depend on the uncertainty of the task. For routine tasks, centralized structures such as the wheel were associated with the greatest performance, whereas for nonroutine or uncertain tasks, decentralized structures such as the all-channel network, were associated with the highest performance (Heise and Miller, 1951; Macy et al., 1953; Shaw, 1954, 1964).

The effect of the communication structure on group performance has also been found to depend on properties of the *member–task* network. The member–task network interacts with the *member–member* network to affect knowledge transfer. Rulke and Galaskiewicz (2000) found that the sharing of information in "generalist" member–task networks, where groups had broadly distributed knowledge, occurred irrespective of the group's structure. However, they found that the sharing of information in "specialist" member–task networks, where each member possessed special expertise, was greater when the structure was decentralized than then it was centralized.

Other more recent studies of social networks have focused on dimensions of networks in addition to the extent of their decentralization. Having positions that bridge structural holes (Burt, 1992) has been found to be an effective mechanism for importing knowledge from other organizational units (McEvily and Zaheer, 1999). In a related vein, Hansen (1999) found that "weak ties," characterized by infrequent and distant relationships between units, facilitated the search for knowledge in other units and reduced the time to complete new product development projects when knowledge was not complex and could be codified. Allen (1977) found that having a "gatekeeper" at the boundary of a group who could communicate with internal and external constituencies improved the performance of applied research groups because these gatekeepers facilitated knowledge transfer.

The effect of the social networks on knowledge transfer within organizations has been found to depend on the nature of knowledge being transferred. Although Hansen (1999) found that "weak ties" facilitated the search for new knowledge in other units when knowledge could be codified, he found that strong ties facilitated the acquisition and interpretation of knowledge that could not be codified. The repeated interactions inherent in strong ties were critical for understanding and interpreting noncodified, tacit knowledge.

The relationship between units also affects the success of knowledge transfer (Szulanski, 1996). Knowledge transfer is greater when social contact between groups occurs (Baum and Berta, 1999). Knowledge transfers more readily across organizational units that are embedded in a superordinate relationship such as a franchise or chain than across independent units (Darr et al., 1995; Baum and Ingram, 1998; Ingram and Simons, 1999). For example, Darr et al. (1995) found that fast food stores benefited from the experience of other stores in the same franchise but not from the experience of stores in different franchises. Similarly, Baum and Ingram (1998) found that hotels benefited from the experience of other hotels in their chain up to the time they joined the chain. After the hotels joined the chain, they benefited from the experience of other local hotels in their chain but not from the experience of nonlocal hotels. Baum and Ingram suggested that routines imported from other markets after the hotel joined the chain may not have fit local conditions and thus did not benefit performance; see also Greve (1999). Thus, being embedded in a social relationship affects knowledge transfer.

Characteristics of the *task* have also been found to affect knowledge transfer. A task that is "causally ambiguous" or not well-understood is hard to transfer (Szulanski, 1996). Relatedly, a task that is easy to observe and to understand transfers more readily than a task that is difficult to observe (Meyer and Goes, 1988). How the task is framed has also been found to affect knowledge transfer among members. Framing the task as one of finding the best answer rather than one of making a consensus judgment has been found to promote the sharing of information within groups (Stasser and Stewart, 1992).

The *task–task network* also affects knowledge transfer. Knowledge that is embedded in routines transfers more readily than noncodified knowledge (Argote and Darr, 2000; Zander and Kogut, 1995). Further, a particular type of meta routine has been found to facilitate knowledge transfer to new contexts. Routines that encourage members to identify the underlying structure of problems and abstract common principles are particularly effective at promoting knowledge transfer to new contexts (Thompson et al., 2000).

The *member–task network* also affects knowledge transfer within organizations. Transactive memory systems or knowledge of who knows what (Wegner, 1986) have been found to promote the sharing of information in groups (Stewart and Stasser, 1995; Stasser et al., 2000). Groups in which members were aware of the specialized expertise each member possessed were more likely to surface unique information than groups whose members were not aware of each others' expertise. Similarly, groups with a leader who possessed greater expertise exhibited less decision-making bias because the leader repeated unique information once it was surfaced (Larson et al., 1996).

A critical predictor of whether knowledge acquired in one unit of an organization transfers to another is the extent to which the basic elements and subnetworks of one context fit the other (Argote and Ingram, 2000). Research has shown that knowledge is more likely to transfer across similar than dissimilar organizational units (Baum and Berta, 1999; Darr and Kurtzberg, 2000). Knowledge acquired in contexts that differ dramatically from each other may not be beneficial for each other's performance (Baum and Ingram, 1998; Greve, 1999).

In summary, research on knowledge transfer is more balanced across the components of organizations than research on knowledge creation or retention. We see this as a positive feature and encourage more research on how all of the components of organizations affect knowledge transfer.

Contemporary Issues and Debates

The framework we have presented points to several tensions or tradeoffs associated with learning within organizations. These tensions are now discussed.

"FIT" OR "MISFIT" OF ORGANIZATIONAL COMPONENTS

A question that the framework discussed here highlights is whether it is better, from a learning perspective, for organizational components to fit each other or to not fit. The creation of knowledge is enhanced by components that do not fit each other. As noted previously, heterogeneous groups where members have different backgrounds and information have been found to be more creative than homogeneous groups where members are similar to each other. Along similar lines, groups that entertain minority views have been found to be more creative and perform better than groups lacking exposure to minority views. Thus, having components that do not fit or are not congruent with each other can stimulate a social unit to be more creative.

By contrast, the transfer of knowledge is enhanced by organizational components that are congruent with each other. As noted previously, knowledge is more likely to transfer across units that are similar to or fit each other. Knowledge acquired in a unit that is similar to a focal unit is more likely to be relevant for the focal unit. Further, knowledge acquired in a similar unit is more likely to be interpretable and understood by the focal unit. Having components that fit or are congruent with each other increases the likelihood and success of knowledge transfer. Thus, the answer to the question of whether it better to have organizational components that fit or ones that do not fit each other depends in part on whether one is more concerned with creating or transferring knowledge.

DENSE VERSUS SPARSE SOCIAL NETWORKS

Another tension that our review reveals centers on whether it is better, from an organizational learning perspective, to have sparse social networks that are rich in structural holes or dense networks where members have many connections with each other. Some researchers have suggested that having nonredundant positions that bridge structural holes is the most effective mechanism for importing knowledge from other organizational units (McEvily and Zaheer, 1999). Others have emphasized that it is the strength of ties (and not their redundancy) that matters in knowledge transfer. Hansen (1999) found that "weak ties," characterized by distant and infrequent relationships between units, promoted knowledge transfer across units, when the knowledge was codified. By contrast, strong ties facilitated the acquisition and interpretation of knowledge that could not be codified (Hansen, 1999). Thus, the available evidence suggests that nonredundant or weak ties may be better for transferring codified knowledge and strong ties are better for transferring noncodified knowledge.

STABILITY VERSUS FLUIDITY IN MEMBERSHIP

Another tension suggested by our review is the tension between stable and fluid membership. Stable membership promotes knowledge retention and strong social identities; rotating membership promotes knowledge creation and transfer as well as weaker social identities. Under what conditions should an organizational unit aim for stable membership and under what conditions would more fluid membership be desirable?

The answer to the question of when it is better to have stable or changing membership depends in part on the subprocess of organizational learning that is most important. For organizational units that are primarily concerned with creating knowledge, such as Research and Development departments, some degree of membership change is desirable. Personnel movement has been shown to stimulate the creation of new knowledge (Gruenfeld et al., 2000) and to improve organizational performance (Wells and Pelz, 1966).

Personnel movement has also been shown to promote the transfer of knowledge across organizational units (Almeida and Kogut, 1999). Thus, when units perform similar tasks and some of the knowledge acquired by one unit is relevant for the other, personnel movement can enhance organizational performance by facilitating knowledge transfer.

On the other hand, stable group membership promotes knowledge retention. Retaining knowledge by retaining members is most likely to occur when a significant component of the organization's knowledge (e.g., tacit knowledge) is embedded in individual members and when that knowledge is not likely to become obsolete. Law firms are an example of a type of firm where much of the knowledge is embedded in individual members and where the knowledge is less likely to become obsolete than in industries where the technology is changing more rapidly. Under those conditions, we would predict that organizations would make considerable effort to retain their members and would perform better when they do.

Another effect of stable membership is the development of strong social identities. The tendency to view one's own group more positively than other groups is one of the most robust effects in social psychology (Brewer, 1979; Ashforth and Mael, 1989; Messick and Mackie, 1989; Kramer, 1991). Membership stability affects where one draws in-group versus out-group boundaries. Individuals are more likely to see members of a stable social unit as an "in-group" than they see members of a social unit whose membership is much more fluid. Thus, rotating membership is a mechanism for breaking down in-group biases and thereby improving relationships between organizational units. Knowledge transfer is more likely to occur under these conditions (Szulanski, 1996).

Unanswered Questions

The tensions or tradeoffs identified on the previous section point to unanswered questions about intraorganizational learning. These questions are likely to be answered by a "conditions-seeking approach" (Greenwald et al., 1986) – by specifying the conditions under which a particular variable relates most strongly to intraorganizational learning. For example, whether an organizational unit should be designed so that its components fit or misfit each other depends on several conditions. Organizational units in turbulent industries, performing uncertain tasks, or in the early stages of a product's life cycle may be particularly concerned with creating knowledge. Diverse components, or ones that do not fit each other, are likely to be especially beneficial under these conditions. By contrast, organizations in less turbulent environments that perform more standardized tasks may benefit more from components that fit one another and thereby facilitate knowledge transfer across them.

All organizations, however, need to both create and transfer knowledge to some degree. How organizations manage the tension between creating and transferring knowledge is an important topic for future research. This tension is related to the tension between exploring new competencies and exploiting old ones identified by March (1991). Exploring new competencies involves creating knowledge and exploiting old competencies involves standardizing and transferring knowledge. According to March, managing the tension or trade-off between exploration and exploitation is critical for organizational performance. Too much emphasis on exploration or creating new knowledge can impair the organization's ability to develop a deep and distinctive capability. By contrast, an over emphasis on exploitation can lead an organization to fall into a "competency trap" in which it continues using an approach that is no longer appropriate (Levitt and March, 1988; Lant and Mezias, 1990). How organizations manage the tension between exploration and exploitation is an important topic for future research.

Another research question suggested by the fit versus misfit tension in intraorganizational learning involves understanding exactly what is meant by "fit" and the ways organizational components can fit or fail to fit each other. There are at least two types of fit": fit as similarity and fit as complementarity. Examples of similarity can be found in discussions of knowledge transfer across contexts. In those analyses, knowledge is more likely to transfer across context that fit or are similar to each other (e.g., see Darr and Kurtzberg, 2000). By contrast, fit as complementarity implies that components fill out or complete each other. For example, a highly skilled work force could complement an organization that had few procedures or structures. Further conceptual development of the concept of fit is needed. Significant methodological advances have occurred in the assessment of fit (Edwards, 1994).

A related question suggested by our analysis of knowledge transfer is how organizational units identify "fit" and opportunities for knowledge transfer. That is, understanding how units identify similar units from whose knowledge they can benefit is an important topic for future research. Being able to ignore superficial aspects of problems or contexts and determine if their deep features are similar is critical to knowledge transfer. Individuals, however, often focus on superficial differences between problems and fail to see that the underlying features are the same and thus miss opportunities for knowledge transfer. The reverse problem may also occur: knowledge might be inappropriately applied from one context to another that it does not fit and thereby impair organizational performance. Identifying factors that facilitate an organizational unit's ability to accurately determine whether knowledge acquired in another context is likely to improve its performance is an important issue for future research.

Concerning the tension between dense versus sparse social networks, more research is needed on the relationship between properties of social networks and the extent of knowledge transfer. Particular attention should be paid to how organizations' social networks should be designed to transfer both tacit and nontacit or codified knowledge. For example, should organizations identify the predominant form of their knowledge and design their social networks around this form? Or could organizations design flexibility into their social networks and use different networks to transfer different types of knowledge? In addition to examining the relationship between social networks and knowledge transfer, research should also examine how social networks are related to knowledge creation and retention.

Concerning the tension between stable and fluid membership, research is needed on the conditions under which organizations benefit more from stable or from fluid membership. Because most organizations are concerned with creating, retaining, and transferring knowledge, research is also needed on how organizations can balance the benefits for knowledge retention associated with stable membership and the benefits for knowledge creation and transfer associated with changing membership. Organizations may manage this tension by determining the level of membership change that is optimal for their performance (e.g., see Katz, 1982). Organizations may also manage the tension by retaining members within their firms (and thereby promoting knowledge retention) but rotating members across units within the firm (and thereby promoting knowledge creation and transfer). The success of the latter strategy depends in part on the extent to which the organization knows who knows what in the firm and thus can benefit from knowledge retained in members when they are moved across social units. Knowing who knows what is more challenging when members move across social units than when they remain within the same unit (Hollenbeck et al., 1995; Moreland et al.,

1998). The success of the later strategy also depends on the extent to which new group members are motivated and able to share their ideas effectively and "recipient" groups are able and motivated to absorb the ideas.

In addition to research on the conditions that resolve the various tensions, research is also needed on the role of experience in intraorganizational learning and how experience can be structured to promote learning. Identifying the precise benefits (or costs) of experience is an important topic for future research. Several studies have shown that the ability of groups or organizations to process information improves with experience. With experience, groups became better at sharing information (Wittenbaum, 1996), identifying expertise (Liang et al., 1995; Rulke and Rau, 2000), recognizing correct solutions (Laughlin and Hollingshead, 1995) and developing more nuanced understandings of phenomena (Gruenfeld and Hollingshead, 1993). But experience can have negative effects (Gruenfeld et al., 1996) or nonmonotonic effects. For example, Katz (1982) found that the performance of R&D teams initially increased and then decreased, as the amount of time the groups worked together increased. Katz (1982) attributed the decrement in performance observed at high levels of experience to the groups becoming too inwardly focused. More research on the benefits and costs of experience is needed.

More work is also needed on how experience should be structured to promote learning. For example, is intraorganizational learning fastest when the organization's experience base is heterogeneous or homogeneous? When the experience is ambiguous or unambiguous? How can organizations learn from rare events or small amounts of experience (March et al., 1991)? Research, which is beginning on these important questions, is discussed in the next section on new and emerging directions.

New and Emerging Directions

Research on learning within organizations increased dramatically in the 1990s. While the increased incidence of empirical studies provides a body of cumulative evidence that increases our understanding of intraorganizational learning, gaps in our understanding of learning within organizations exist. The framework we used in this chapter for cataloguing studies according to the subprocess of learning they focused on (knowledge creation, retention, or transfer) and the component of organizations studied (members, tasks, tools, or their subnetworks) points to some of these gaps.

As we noted in our review, most of the work on knowledge creation has focused on how characteristics of members (especially their diversity) affect the creation of new knowledge. More research has also been done on how characteristics of members (especially the stability of their participation) affect knowledge retention. Given that members are the medium through which learning is mediated in organizations, it is fitting that more work has been done on how characteristics of members affect learning within organizations than on how characteristics of other repositories affect learning. We would like to encourage additional research on how characteristics of members affect learning within organizations, especially on the transfer of knowledge. Knowledge in the components involving members plays a critical role in learning within organizations because that knowledge is the basis for the development of distinctive capabilities and competitive advantage in firms (Argote and Ingram, 2000). Thus, we would like to strongly encourage more research on how the member–member network, the member–task network, the member-tool network, and member–task–tool network affect the creation, retention, and transfer of knowledge within organizations.

An important emerging direction for future research is the relationship between experience and intraorganizational learning. Are certain kinds of experience more likely to promote intraorganizational learning than others? Schilling et al. (2000) found that groups learned more from related experience than from identical experience. Thus, experience on tasks that were related to, but not the same as, the one the group had been performing seemed to increase the group's understanding of the problem and improve performance. The findings of Haunschild and Ni (2000) suggest that the relationship between the type of experience and intraorganizational learning is moderated by organizational form. They found that organizations that depend on a narrow range of environmental resources (specialists) tend to learn from their own heterogeneous experience. However, organizations that depend on a wide range of environmental resources (generalists) learn from their own cumulative experience, but not necessarily from their own prior experience heterogeneity.

Connections Across Levels

According to Levitt and March (1988), organizations learn from their own direct experience or from the experience of others. This important observation has had a major impact on the three chapters on learning in the current volume. Learning from one's own experience plays a somewhat larger role in the chapters on intraorganizational learning and on organizational learning than in the chapter on interorganizatonal learning. And learning from the experience of others figures prominently in the chapters on intraorganizational learning and on interorganizational learning because both of those chapters are concerned with transferring knowledge across the constituent parts of either an organization or an interorganizational field.

The three chapters identify a more fine-grained view of experience as a new direction or theme of current research on learning in organizations. Current research examines how the type of experience or characteristics of experience affect learning. For example, Miner et al. (1999) analyzed how organizations learn from failure. Current research has also examined how the similarity (Darr and Kurtzberg, 2000) or the diversity (Ophir et al., 1998; Haunschild and Ni, 2000) of experience affects learning. This more nuanced view of experience is an exciting new trend that is likely to advance our understanding of organizational learning at all levels.

The chapters on intraorganizational learning and on organizational learning differ in the likelihood they ascribe to performance improving with experience. Although the chapter on intraorganizational learning notes that learning is not equated with improved performance and describes the wide variation that has been found to characterize the relationship between experience and performance, the chapter suggests that the relationship between experience and performance is often positive. By contrast, the chapter on organizational learning suggests that performance improving with experience is a rare occurrence and describes the difficulties associated with interpreting experience. We see enormous promise in a unified treatment of organizational learning that identifies the conditions under which experience improves, harms, or has no effect on organizational performance.

All three of the chapters view the experience of others as an important source of knowledge in organizations. Learning from the experience of others can occur at all levels within and between organizations. Units can learn from other units within a firm (Szulanski, 1996); firms can learn from other firms (Powell et al., 1996). All three of the chapters emphasize the importance of relationships for learning from the experience of others. Relationships figure particularly prominently in the chapters on intraorganizational learning and on interorganizational learning. The chapters describe the forms of relationships most conducive to knowledge transfer or learning from the experience of others.

A recurring theme in the three learning chapters, especially the ones on intraorganizational and organizational learning, is that knowledge acquired through experience is embedded in various repositories, including routines (Cyert and March, 1963; Cohen and Bacdayan, 1994), rules (March et al., 2000), transactive memories (Liang et al., 1995), and technologies (Epple et al., 1996). These supra-individual repositories provide some persistence of organizational knowledge in the face of changing participation of individual members. Where knowledge is embedded has implications for knowledge transfer and for the competitive advantage of firms because knowledge in some repositories transfers more readily than knowledge in other repositories (Argote and Ingram, 2000; Schulz and Jobe, 2001).

Conclusion

Organizations vary enormously in their capability to learn. With experience, the performance of some organizations improves dramatically while the performance of others fails to improve or even deteriorates. Understanding the conditions under which organizational performance improves or fails to improve with experience is an important question for future research.

Although research has begun to identify conditions and processes that facilitate learning from experience, more research is needed on this important question. In particular, research is needed on how characteristics of experience affect an organization's ability to learn. Research is also needed on how characteristics of an organization's members, tools, tasks, and their interrelationships affect the subprocesses of organizational learning. In addition, research is needed on the tensions or tradeoffs across these subprocesses of knowledge creation, retention, and transfer. This research will enable us to understand more completely why some organizations improve with experience and others do not.

Notes

1   These subprocesses of learning within organizations are related. The subprocess of transferring knowledge might result in new knowledge being created or the organization's memory or retention system might affect its ability to create new knowledge. Although the subprocesses of organizational learning are related, they describe different aspects of organizational learning and are predicted by different factors. Thus, we feel that it is fruitful to analyze the subprocesses separately.

References

Adler, P. S., and Clark, K. B. (1991): "Behind the learning curve: A sketch of the learning process," *Management Science*, 37, 267–81.

Allen, T. J. (1977): *Managing the Flow of Technology: Technology Transfer and The Dissemination of Technological Information Within the R&D Organization*. Cambridge, MA: MIT Press.

Almeida, P., and Kogut, B. (1999): "Localization of knowledge and the mobility of engineers in regional networks," *Management Science*, 45, 905–17.

Argote, L. (1993): "Group and organizational learning curves: Individual, system and environmental components," *British Journal of Social Psychology*, 32, 31–51.

Argote, L. (1999): *Organizational Learning: Creating, Retaining, and Transferring Knowledge*. Norwell, MA: Kluwer.

Argote, L., and Darr, E. (2000): "Repositories of knowledge about productivity and timeliness in franchise organizations: Individual, structural and technological," in G. Dosi, R. Nelson and S. Winter (eds), *Nature and Dynamics of Organizational Capabilities*, Oxford: Oxford University Press, 51–68.

Argote, L., and Epple, D. (1990): "Learning curves in manufacturing," *Science*, 247, 920–24.

Argote, L., and Ingram, P. (2000): "Knowledge transfer: A basis for competitive advantage in firms," *Organizational Behavior and Human Decision Processes*, 82, 150–69.

Argote, L., Beckman, S. L., and Epple, D. (1990): "The persistence and transfer of learning in industrial settings," *Management Science*, 36, 140–54.

Argote, L., Gruenfeld, D., and Naquin, C. (2001): "Group learning in organizations," in M. E. Turner (ed.), *Groups at Work: Advances in Theory and Research*, Mahwah, NJ: Lawrence Erlbaum, 369–411.

Argote, L., Epple, D., Rao, R. D., and Murphy, K. (1997): "The acquisition and depreciation of knowledge in a manufacturing organization: Turnover and plant productivity," working paper, Graduate School of Industrial Administration, Carnegie Mellon University.

Argote, L., Insko, C. A., Yovetich, N., and Romero, A. A. (1995): "Group learning curves: The effects of turnover and task complexity on group performance," *Journal of Applied Social Psychology*, 25, 512–29.

Arrow, H., McGrath, J. E., and Berdahl, J. L. (2000): *Small Groups as Complex Systems: Formation, Coordination, Development and Adaptation*. Thousand Oaks, CA: Sage Publications.

Ashforth, B. E., and Mael, F. (1989): "Social identify theory and the organization," *Academy of Management Review*, 14, 20–39.

Bantel, K. A., and Jackson, S. E. (1989): "Top management and innovations in banking: Does the composition of the top team make a difference?" *Strategic Management Journal*, 10, Summer (special issue), 107–24.

Baum, J. A. C., and Berta, W. B. (1999): "Sources, dynamics and speed: A longitudinal behavioral simulation of interorganizational and population-level learning," *Advances in Strategic Management*, 16, 155–84.

Baum, J. A. C., and Ingram, P. (1998): "Survival-enhancing learning in the Manhattan hotel industry, 1898–1980," *Management Science*, 44, 996–1016.

Berry, D. C., and Broadbent, D. E. (1984): "On the relationship between task performance and associated verbalizable knowledge," *The Quarterly Journal of Experimental Psychology*, 36A, 209–31.

Berry, D. C., and Broadbent, D. E. (1987): "The combination of explicit and implicit learning processes in task control," *Psychological Research*, 49, 7–15.

Brewer, M. B. (1979): "In-group bias in the minimal intergroup situation: A cognitive-motivational analysis," *Psychological Bulletin*, 86, 307–24.

Burt, R. S. (1992): *Structural Holes: The Social Structure of Competition*. Cambridge, MA: Harvard University Press.

Carley, K. (1992): "Organizational learning and personnel turnover," *Organization Science*, 3, 20–46.

Cohen, M. D., and Bacdayan, P. (1994): "Organizational routines are stored as procedural memory: Evidence from a laboratory study," *Organization Science*, 5, 554–68.

Cohen, W. M., and Levinthal, D. (1990): "Absorptive capacity: A new perspective on learning and innovation," *Administrative Science Quarterly*, 35, 128–52.

Cyert, R. M., and March J. G. (1963): *A Behavioral Theory of the Firm.* Englewood Cliffs, NJ: Prentice-Hall.

Darr, E. D., and Kurtzberg, T. (2000): "An investigation of dimensions of knowledge transfer," *Organizational Behavior and Human Decision Processes*, 82, 28–44.

Darr, E., Argote, L., and Epple, D. (1995): "The acquisition, transfer and depreciation of knowledge in service organizations: Productivity in franchises," *Management Science*, 41, 1750–62.

Devadas, R., and Argote, L. (1995): "Collective learning and forgetting: The effects of turnover and group structure," paper presented at Midwestern Academy of Management Meetings, Chicago, May.

Dunbar, K. (1995): "How scientists really reason: Scientific reasoning in real-world laboratories," in R. J. Sternberg and J. E. Davidson (eds), *The Nature of Insight*, Cambridge, MA: MIT Press, 365–95.

Dutton, J. M., and Thomas, A. (1984): "Treating progress functions as a managerial opportunity," *Academy of Management Review*, 9, 235–47.

Edmondson, A. O., Bohmer, R. M. J., and Pisano, G. P. (2000): "Learning new technical and interpersonal routines in operating room teams: The case of minimally invasive cardiac surgery," in M. A. Neale, E. A. Mannix, and T. L. Griffith (eds), *Research on Managing Groups and Teams*, Vol. 3, Stamford, CT: JAI Press, 29–51.

Edwards, J. R. (1994): "The study of congruence in organizational behavior research: Critique and a proposed alternative," *Organizational Behavior and Human Decision Processes*, 58, 51–100.

Eisenhardt, K. M., and Tabrizi, B. N. (1995): "Accelerating adaptive processes: Product innovation in the global computer industry," *Administrative Science Quarterly*, 40, 84–110.

Engeström, Y., Brown, K., Engeström, R., and Koistinen, K. (1990): "Organizational forgetting: An activity theoretical perspective," in D. Middleton and D. Edwards (eds), *Collective Remembering*, London: Sage, pp. 139–68.

Epple, D., Argote, L., and Murphy, K. (1996): "An empirical investigation of the micro structure of knowledge acquisition and transfer through learning by doing," *Operations Research*, 44, 77–86.

Galbraith, C. S. (1990): "Transferring core manufacturing technologies in high technology firms," *California Management Review*, 32(4), 56–70.

Greenwald, A. G., Pratkanis, A. R., Leippe, M. R., and Baumgardner, M. H. (1986): "Under what conditions does theory obstruct research progress?" *Psychological Review*, 93, 216–29.

Greve, H. R. (1999): "Branch systems and nonlocal learning in populations," *Population-Level Learning and Industry Change, Advances in Strategic Management*, 16, 57–80.

Gruenfeld, D. H. (1995): "Status, ideology and integrative complexity on the U. S. Supreme Court: Rethinking the politics of political decision making," *Journal of Personality and Social Psychology*, 68, 5–20.

Gruenfeld, D. H., and Hollingshead, A. B. (1993): "Sociocognition in work groups: The evolution of group integrative complexity and its relation to task performance," *Small Group Research*, 24, 383–405.

Gruenfeld, D. H., Martorana, P. V., and Fan, E. T. (2000): "What do groups learn from their worldliest members? Direct and indirect influence in dynamic teams," *Organizational Behavior and Human Decision Processes*, 82, 60–74.

Gruenfeld, D. H., Mannix, E., Williams, K., and Neale, M. (1996): "Group composition and decision making: How member familiarity and information distribution affect process and performance," *Organizational Behavior and Human Decision Processes*, 67, 1–15.

Guetzkow, H., and Simon, H. A. (1955): "The impact of certain communication nets upon organization and performance in task-oriented groups." *Management Science*, 1, 233–50.

Hambrick, D. C., Cho, T. S., and Chen, M. (1996): "The influence of top management team heterogeneity on firms' competitive moves," *Administrative Science Quarterly*, 41, 659–84.

Hansen, M. (1999): "The search transfer problem: The role of weak ties in sharing knowledge across organization subunits," *Administrative Science Quarterly*, 44, 82–111.

Hargadon, A., and Sutton, R. I. (1997): "Technology brokering and innovation in a product development firm," *Administrative Science Quarterly*, 42, 716–49.

Haunschild, P. R., and Ni, B. (2000): "Learning from complexity: Effects of airline accident/incident heterogeneity on subsequent accident/incident rates," paper presented at the Academy of Management Meetings, Toronto, Canada.

Heise, G., and Miller, G. (1951): "Problem-solving by small groups using various communications nets," *Journal of Abnormal and Social Psychology*, 46, 327–35.

Hollenbeck, J. R., Ilgen, D. R., Sego, D. J., Hedlund, J., Major, D. A., and Philips, J. (1995): "Multilevel theory of team decision making: Decision performance in teams incorporating distributed expertise," *Journal of Applied Psychology*, 80, 292–316.

Hollingshead, A. B. (1998): "Group and individual training: The impact of practice on performance," *Small Group Research*, 29, 254–80.

Ingram, P., and Simons, T. (1999): "The exchange of experience in a moral economy: Embedded ties and vicarious learning in Kibbutz agriculture," in S. J. Havlovic (ed.), *Academy of Management Proceedings (Chicago)*, New York: Academy of Management. Available on CD-ROM, OMT: E1–E6.

Katz, R. (1982): "The effects of group longevity on communication and performance," *Administrative Science Quarterly*, 27, 81–104.

Kramer, R. M. (1991): "Intergroup relations and organizational dilemmas: The role of categorization processes," *Research in Organizational Behavior*, 13, 191–228.

Lant, T., and Mezias, S. J. (1990): "Managing discontinuous change: A simulation study of organizational learning and entrepreneurship," *Strategic Management Journal*, 13, 111–25.

Lant, T. K., Milliken, F. J., and Batra, B. (1992): "The role of managerial learning and interpretation in strategic persistence and reorientation: An empirical exploration," *Strategic Management Journal*, 13, 585–608.

Larson, J. R., Jr., Christensen, C., Abbott, A. S., and Franz, T. M. (1996): "Diagnosing groups: Charting the flow of information in medical decision-making teams," *Journal of Personality and Social Psychology*, 71, 315–30.

Laughlin, P. R., and Hollingshead, A. B. (1995): "A theory of collective induction," *Organizational Behavior and Human Decision Processes*, 61, 94–107.

Leavitt, H. J. (1951): "Some effects of certain communication patterns on group performance," *Journal of Abnormal and Social Psychology*, 46, 38–50.

Leavitt, H. J. (1961): "Applied organizational change in industry: Structural, technological and humanistic approaches," in J. March (ed.), *Handbook of Organizations*, Chicago: Rand McNally, 1144–70.

Levitt, B., and March, J. G. (1988): "Organizational learning," *Annual Review of Sociology*, 14, 319–40.

Lewis, K. (2000): "Is performance all in their mind(s)? The impact of transactive memory on knowledge-worker team performance," paper presented at the Academy of Management Meetings, Toronto, Canada.

Liang, D. W., Moreland, R., and Argote, L. (1995): "Group versus individual training and group performance: The mediating role of transactive memory," *Personality and Social Psychology Bulletin*, 21, 384–93.

McEvily, B., and Zaheer, A. (1999): "Bridging ties: A source of form heterogeneity in competitive capabilities," *Strategic Management Journal*, 20, 1133–56.

McGrath, J. E., and Argote, L. (2001): "Group processes in organizational contexts," in M. A. Hogg and R. S. Tindale (eds), *Blackwell Handbook of Social Psychology, Vol. 3, Group Processes,* Oxford, UK: Blackwell, 603–27.

Macy, J., Jr., Christie, L., and Luce, R. (1953): "Coding noise in a task-orientated group," *Journal of Abnormal and Social Psychology,* 48, 401–09.

March, J. G. (1991): "Exploration and exploitation in organizational learning," *Organization Science,* 2, 71–87.

March, J. G., Schulz, M., and Zhou, X. (2000): *The Dynamics of Rules: Studies of Change in Written Organizational Codes.* Stanford, CA: Stanford University Press.

March, J. G., Sproull, L. S., and Tamuz M. (1991): "Learning from samples of one or fewer," *Organization Science,* 2, 1–13.

Messick, D. M., and Mackie, D. M. (1989): "Intergroup relations," *Annual Review of Psychology,* 40, 45–81.

Meyer, A. D., and Goes, J. B. (1988): "Organizational assimilation of innovations: A multilevel contextual analysis," *Academy of Management Journal,* 31, 897–923.

Miner, A. S., and Mezias, S. J. (1996): "Ugly duckling no more: Pasts and futures of organizational learning research," *Organization Science,* 7, 88–99.

Miner, A. S., Kim, J. Y., Holzinger, I. W., and Haunschild, P. (1999): "Fruits of failure: Organizational failure and population-level learning," *Advances in Strategic Management,* 16, 187–220.

Moorman, C., and Miner, A. S. (1997): "The impact of organizational memory on new product performance and creativity," *Journal of Marketing Research,* 34, 91–106.

Moreland, R. L., Argote, L., and Krishnan, R. (1998): "Training people to work in groups," in R. S. Tindale et al. (eds), *Theory and Research on Small Groups,* New York: Plendum Press, 37–59.

Mullen, B., Johnson, C., and Salas, E. (1991): "Productivity loss in brainstorming groups: A meta-analytic integration," *Basic and Applied Social Psychology,* 12, 3–23.

Nelson, R. R., and Winter, S. G. (1982): *An Evolutionary Theory of Economic Change.* Boston: Belkman Press.

Nemeth, C. J. (1992): "Minority dissent as a stimulant to group performance," in S. Worchel, W. Wood and J. A. Simpson (eds), *Group Process and Productivity,* Newbury Park, CA: Sage, 95–111.

Nemeth, C. J., and Kwan, J. L. (1987): "Minority influence, divergent thinking and detection of correct solutions," *Journal of Applied Social Psychology,* 17, 786–97.

Nemeth, C. J., and Wachtler, J. (1983): "Creative problem solving as a result of majority and minority influence," *European Journal of Social Psychology,* 13, 45–55.

Nonaka, I. (1991): "The knowledge-creating company," *Harvard Business Review,* 69(6), 96–104.

Ophir, R., Ingram, P., and Argote, L. (1998): "The impact of demographic composition on organizational learning: An empirical investigation," paper presented at the INFORMS National Fall Conference, Seattle, WA.

Paulus, P. B., and Yang, H. (2000): "Idea generation in groups: A basis for creativity in organizations," *Organizational Behavior and Human Decision Process,* 82, 76–87.

Powell, W. W., Koput, K. W., and Smith-Doerr, L. (1996): "Interorganizational collaboration and the locus of innovation: Networks of learning in biotechnology," *Administrative Science Quarterly,* 41, 116–45.

Rapping, L. (1965): "Learning and World War II production functions," *Review of Economics and Statistics,* 47, 81–6.

Rothwell, R. (1978): "Some problems of technology transfer into industry: Examples from the textile machinery sector," *IEEE Transactions on Engineering Management,* EM-25, 15–20.

Rulke, D. L., and Galaskiewicz, J. (2000): "Distribution of knowledge, group network structure, and group performance," *Management Science,* 46, 612–25.

Rulke, D. L., and Rau, D. (2000): "Investigating the encoding process of transactive memory development in group training," *Group and Organization Management,* 25, 373–96.

Rulke, D. L., Zaheer, S., and Anderson, M. H. (2000): "Sources of managers' knowledge of organizational capabilities," *Organizational Behavior and Human Decision Processes*, 82, 134–49.

Schilling, M. A., Ployhart, R. E., Vidal, P., and Marangoni, A. (2000): "Learning by doing something else: Variation, relatedness, and organizational learning," unpublished manuscript.

Schulz, M., and Jobe, L. A. (2001): "Codification and tacitness as knowledge management strategies: An empirical exploration," *Journal Of High Technology Management Research*, forthcoming.

Shaw, M. E. (1954): "Some effects of problem complexity upon problem solution efficiency in different communication nets," *Journal of Experimental Psychology*, 48, 211–17.

Shaw, M. E. (1964): "Communication networks," in L. Berkowitz (ed.), *Advances in Experimental Social Psychology*, Vol. 1, New York: Academic Press, 111–47.

Starbuck, W. H. (1992): "Learning by knowledge-intensive firms," *Journal of Management Studies*, 29, 713–38.

Stasser, G., and Stewart, D. D. (1992): "The discovery of hidden profiles by decision making groups: Solving a problem versus making a judgment," *Journal of Personality and Social Psychology*, 63, 426–34.

Stasser, G., and Titus, W. (1987): "Effects of information load and percentage of shared information on the dissemination of unshared information during group discussion," *Journal of Personality and Social Psychology*, 53, 81–93.

Stasser, G., Vaughan, S. I., and Stewart, D. D. (2000): "Pooling unshared information: The benefits of knowing how access to information is distributed among group members," *Organizational Behavior and Human Decision Processes*, 82, 102–16.

Stewart, D. D., and Stasser, G. (1995): "Expert role assignment and information sampling during collective recall and decision making," *Journal of Personality and Social Psychology*, 69, 619–28.

Szulanski, G. (1996): "Exploring internal stickiness: Impediments to the transfer of best practice within the firm," *Strategic Management Journal*, 17, 27–43.

Szulanski, G. (2000): "The process of knowledge transfer: A diachronic analysis of stickiness," *Organizational Behavior and Human Decision Processes*, 829–27.

Thompson, L., Gentner, D., and Lowenstein, J. (2000): "Avoiding missed opportunities in managerial life: Analogical training more powerful than individual case training," *Organizational Behavior and Human Decision Processes*, 82, 60–75.

Trow, D. B. (1960): "Membership succession and team performance," *Human Relations*, 13, 259–69.

Virany, B., Tushman, M. L., and Romanelli, E. (1992): "Executive succession and organization outcomes in turbulent environments: An organizational learning approach," *Organization Science*, 3, 72–91.

Walsh, J. P., and Ungson, G. R. (1991): "Organizational memory," *Academy of Management Review*, 16, 57–91.

Watson, W. E., Kumar, K., and Michaelson, L. K. (1993): "Cultural diversity's impact on interaction process and performance: Comparing homogeneous and diverse task groups," *Academy of Management Journal*, 36, 590–602.

Wegner, D. M. (1986): "Transactive memory: A contemporary analysis of the group mind," in B. Mullen and G. R. Goethals (eds), *Theories of Group Behavior*, New York: Springer-Verlag, 185–205.

Wegner, D. M. (1995): "A computer network model of human transactive memory," *Social Cognition*, 13, 319–39.

Weick, K. E., and Roberts, K. H. (1993): "Collective mind in organizations: Heedful interrelating on flight decks," *Administrative Science Quarterly*, 38, 357–81.

Wells, W. P., and Pelz, D. C. (1966): *Scientists in Organizations*. New York: Wiley.

Williams, K. Y., and O'Reilly, C. A. (1998): "Demography and diversity in organizations: A review of 40 years of research," *Research in Organizational Behavior*, 20, 77–140.

Wittenbaum, G. M. (1996): "Information sampling in mixed-sex decision-making groups: The impact of diffuse status and task-relevant cues," unpublished doctoral dissertation, Miami University, Oxford, OH.

Zander, U., and Kogut, B. (1995): "Knowledge and the speed of the transfer and imitation of organizational capabilities: An empirical test," *Organization Science*, 6, 76–92.

Chapter Nine

Intraorganizational Complexity and Computation

KATHLEEN M. CARLEY

Organizations are complex systems. They are also information processing systems comprised of a large number of agents such as human beings. Combining these perspectives and recognizing the essential nonlinear dynamics that are at work leads to the standard nonlinear multi-agent system conclusions such as: history matters, organizational behavior and form is path dependent, complex behavior emerges from individual interaction, and change is inevitable. Such a view, while descriptive, is still far from the level of specificity and predictive richness that is necessary for organizational theory. To increase the specificity and value of our theories we will need to take into account more of the actual attributes of tasks, resources, knowledge, and human cognition. In doing so, it will be possible to achieve a more adequate description of organizations as complex computational systems. More importantly, we will also achieve a greater ability to theorize about the complexity of organizational behavior.

Intraorganizational computation and complexity is concerned with discovering, modeling, theorizing, and analyzing the fundamental nature of organizations as complex adaptive systems composed of intelligent but constrained adaptive agents. Within computational organization, science researchers search for fundamental organizational objects and the mathematical formalism with which to describe their behavior and interactions. In physics, researchers search for laws governing gravitational, electromagnetic, and other fields of force. In both cases, the aim is to discover the most reasonable basis from which, at least in principle, theories of all other processes and behaviors can be derived. In a complex process, there are typically many interacting objects (e.g. people or procedures in an organization or particles in physics) and it is rarely possible to proceed to a complete mathematical solution. Systems in which there are complex processes often exhibit nonlinear behavior, phase changes in behavior, and often reach dramatically different end states given only minor changes in initial conditions. Computational analysis, e.g., simulation or enumeration, can be used to track and analyze the detailed behavior within and among these objects (people or particles). Whether we are modeling the behavior of people, robots, organizations or atoms – computer modeling at the quantum level becomes extremely complicated as soon as more than a few of these objects are involved. Computational complexity increases and the length of time for the system to be "solved" or "simulated" on the computer increases.

Such work is carried out via formal methods – mathematical and computational reasoning. This paper describes complexity theory and computational organization theory. Then a description of organizations as complex computational systems is presented. Specific attention is paid to the role of knowledge management, network theory, computational theory, and the study of the impacts of information and tele-communication technology within organizations. Implications, limitations, and directions relative to this perspective are discussed. References are summarized in Table 9.1.

Literature Review, Summary and Evaluation

Essentially, complex systems are nonlinear systems, one sub-class of which may exhibit chaotic behavior.[1] The study of nonlinear dynamics has a long history and many books at varying level of theoretical and methodological rigor exist. Complexity theory is actually not a theory; rather, it is a paradigm, set of procedures and techniques, and an approach to complex systems. Complex systems typically have internal change, adaptation, or evolutionary mechanisms that result in behavior that on the surface might appear random but actually has an underlying order (Holland, 1995). Complex outcomes emerge from simple processes and there are multiple possible outcomes depending on input conditions and history (Kauffman, 1995), some of which may be catastrophic (McKelvey, 1999b). Order itself may be created as energy differentials dissipate (Mainzer, 1996). Complex systems have the ability to self-organize (Bak, 1996).[2] Much of the formal work in complexity is in physics, biology and chemistry; however, complex processes also occur in organizations. Complexity analysis provides us with a means for re-thinking and extending organizational theory (McKelvey, 1999a; Morel and Ramanujam, 1999) and social theory more generally (Axelrod and Cohen, 1999). The general work on complex systems extends decades of work that took either a contingency theory or information processing perspective. The result is that a number of now classic findings have emerged both computationally and empirically such as, there are multiple configurations to achieve any organizational objective, different organizational objectives require different configurations, history and order effects are critical (i.e., path dependence exists), and overall system behavior is highly nonlinear. The mathematics aside, a number of books and articles have appeared in the last decade exploring the role of complexity in the social and organizational sciences; see for example, International Symposium in Economic Theory and Econometrics (1996); Mainzer (1996); Eve et al. (1997); Cilliers (1998); Baum and McKelvey (1999), and Pines et al. (1999). Much of this work looks at complexity simply in terms of the metaphor – thus the vocabulary of emergence, holism, chaos, self-organizing, criticality, bifurcation, path dependence, etc. is used to describe organizations and their behaviors with little attention to the mathematical meaning behind those concepts. For example, in a recent issue of Emergence (Maguire and McKelvey, 1999), there were reviews of 34 such "metaphor" books. One

Table 9.1 Summary of intraorganizational complexity and computation studies

Reference	Area	Key concepts	Key contribution	Approach
Meyer and Scott, 1983	Complex systems	Size Institutions Environments Open systems	Neoinstitutional theory	Statement of theory with description Drawing on previous case studies and large scale surveys
Perrow, 1984	Complexity as metaphor	Design Coupling Errors Accidents	Accidents as inevitable	Detailed theory development drawing on case studies, ethnographies, and archival data
Epstein and Axtell, 1997	Computational organization theory	Agents Adaptation	A-life models of emergent social behavior	Computational theorizing from stylized situations Face validity Large numbers of spatially located simple adaptive agents
Burton and Obel, 1998	Computational organization theory	Design Strategy Managerial practices Processes	The Organizational Consultant: an expert system integrating the findings of contingency theory into a unified system for designing organizations	Computational theorizing about real and hypothetical organizations Validation from case studies Reasoning using rules derived from contingency theory
Harrison and Carroll, 1991	Computational organization theory	Culture Evolution Design Learning	Emergence and maintenance of distinct cultural forms in organizations	Computational theorizing about organizational culture Face validity Single parameter model of culture

Reference	Type	Model	Concepts	Description
Jin and Levitt, 1996	Computational organization theory	The virtual design team A process model combining project management, agent expertise, and organizational chart information	Design Teams Skills Agents Tasks Organization chart PERT chart Communication technology Rework	Computational theorizing about real world design teams faced with routine tasks Validation from case studies Variable number of agents varying in ability and access
Cohen et al., 1972	Computational organization theory	The Garbage Can Model: a simple model of organizational decisions resulting from personnel, solutions, and problem flows	Decisions Agents Access Salience Problems Solutions Effort	Computational theorizing about highly stylized organizational designs Face validity Small number of agents varying in ability, interests and access
Carley and Svoboda, 1996	Computational organization theory	ORGAHAD: a multi-agent model of organizational adaptation where the agents are intelligent and adaptive	Agents Knowledge Task Change strategies Access Learning	Computational theorizing about real and hypothetical organizations Strategic response as annealing process coupled with individual experiential learning Validation from experiments and case studies Variable number of agents varying in position, knowledge and task assignment

danger with the metaphor approach is that it is easy for metaphors to become fads quickly picked up and abandoned by the corporate world without necessarily advancing science and our understanding of organizations (McKelvey, 1999a).

Within organization theory, complexity and the study of complex or adaptive systems has taken on three identities – complex systems, metaphor, and computational theory building. Each of these will be described in turn and differences in the perspectives highlighted. The point here is not to gainsay the value of either the complex systems or the metaphorically based work or to exclusively laud the value of the computational work. To be sure, much can be learned via the relation between complexity and design, via reasoning from metaphors, and via reasoning from formal theory. Moreover, it may well be that some of the empirical finding about complexity and design are useful in validating the computational models. It may be that some of the "new doors" opened through metaphorical reasoning will result in simulations being constructed to do theory development relative to that topic. However, just because the terms of complexity theory and nonlinear dynamics are used does not mean that the findings or claims have a solid underlying mathematical base. Moreover, empirical results that are based on constructs derived from a metaphorical interpretation of words such as emergence, order creation, chaos, etc. may not be appropriate for testing, validating, or extending the formal theories. It is the case that all of the approaches tend to characterize complexity in terms such as number of personnel (or agents), resources, tasks, and/or the number of interconnections (network ties) among them, or number of steps in the processes used to evaluate, form, move things through or modify these networks. However, if we are to link empirical data to computational models, we need to move beyond common characterizations to actually using the same construct, e.g., complexity and all related constructs, and measuring these in the computational model and the real world in exactly the same way. Now let us consider the three areas.

COMPLEX SYSTEMS

Within organization theory more generally, the study of organizations as complex systems has a long history. Throughout the past 50 years, researchers have examined organizational complexity, in terms of the level of detail, number of objects, or degree of interconnections in the organizational or task design. This work, on organizations as complex systems, which is largely empirical, reasons about complexity using an understanding of organizational, task and process design. The goal of this work is to understand the relation between the elements of organizational design, the environment and performance. In many empirical studies, the complexity of the organization is measured in terms of perceived coupling among sub-groups, tasks, or procedures, the length of the process needed to go through to make a decision, or the number of people, resources, or constraints involved. Much of the research has looked at the fundamental nature of organizations (Etzioni, 1961), and the relation between complexity and size (Scott and Meyer, 1994), coordination (Klatzky, 1970) and formalization (Hall et al., 1967). Much of this work resulted in, or advanced, structural, contingency theory and neo-institutional theory. This work is independent of the formal work on complexity theory – although there are notable analogies. One of the major limitations in linking this work to complexity theory is the lack of agreement on how to measure complexity; e.g., is it the number of personnel or the density of the social network. Rarely is complexity measured using the metrics of complexity theory; e.g., rarely is the Lyapunov exponent calculated nor are tests for nonlinear determinism run. The Lyapunov exponent is a measure of sensitivity to initial conditions. Further, much of the empirical work on complex systems, particularly that on processes, focuses on perceived complexity, which may or may not be systematically related to actual complexity as measured in complexity theory.

An example of this approach is seen in the work of Meyer and Scott (1983). They present a neo-institutional approach in which organizations are complex systems due to their size (e.g., number of employees, number of divisions, number of processes) and are embedded in, define and respond to environments that are themselves complex (e.g., number of stake holders, legislations, institutions, and other organizations). The arguments are supported by a large number of studies many of which are based on large-scale surveys of organizations. As organizational complexity increases on one dimension, such as size, it increases on other dimensions, such as formalization of processes defining linkages. In contrast to the rational actor approaches of economics, they suggest that formal organizational structures are symbolic phenomena designed in response to the environment to demonstrate rationality rather than to achieve efficiency. Thus, complex structures and behaviors emerge from response to external events and processes for achieving legitimation. McKelvey (2000) argues that a Bénard process may underlie the emergence of complex structures from external events. Energy differentials across sites create, in McKelvey's terms, an "adaptive tension" enabling the creation of order (McKelvey, 2001). However, there has yet to be an empirical analysis examining Bénard processes within and among organizations.

COMPLEXITY AS METAPHOR

Recently, within organization science, metaphor and myth have outrun formal theory building and empirical analysis of complex systems. Most of the work in this area takes the language of complexity theory, treats it as metaphor and builds on that. For example, a complexity analogy has been used to create a revision and extension of contingency theory (Dow and Earl, 1999). The goal of the complexity theory as metaphor work seeks to open up new avenues of research, develop new theory, using analogical reasoning from complexity theory (Dow and Earl, 1999), chaos theory (Thiétart and Forgues, 1995), or biological adaptation (White et al., 1997). This body of work is less statistical than the complex systems work. Nevertheless, the research building on the complexity theory as metaphor work moves beyond discussions of the level of complexity and its relation to organizational design and performance to talk about the processes within such a system and the effects of complexity – e.g. coupling, self-organization, bifurcation, and chaos. One of the best examples of such work is Perrow's (1984) study of accidents where in-depth ethnographic and historical analysis lays the basis for arguments about complexity. In contrast to Perrow, many of the studies in this vein simply use the language of complexity and reference organizational examples.

Perrow treats complexity in terms of size (the number of individual decision makers, knowledge and tasks) and networks (the linkages between individuals, knowledge and tasks). Reasoning from in-depth case studies and archival records, he presents the argument that the processes and technologies used in high-risk situations, such as nuclear power plants, have often resulted in tightly coupled systems (many linkages). He argues that errors and accidents are perfectly normal, and indeed inevitable. Moreover, the coupling in these organizations enables the effect of errors to cascade through the organization resulting in catastrophic consequences. Small deviations can have, in a tightly coupled system, large-scale consequences.

COMPUTATIONAL THEORY BUILDING ABOUT COMPLEX SYSTEMS

Computational approaches are particularly useful in examining complex adaptive systems in general and organizations in particular. Computational approaches have been used successfully to look at the dynamics of change and complexity in a number of organizational areas: design (Jin and Levitt, 1996; Burton and Obel, 1998), innovation and evolution (March, 1991; Gibson, 1999), adaptation and change (Sastry, 1997), coordination (Carley and Prietula, 1994), emergence of hierarchy (Hummon, 1990), cooperation (Macy, 1991), organizational learning (Lant, 1994), and knowledge management (Carley and Hill, 2001). Over the past 25 years, on average, the models have become increasingly sophisticated from an algorithms perspective, increasingly grounded in empirical data, increasingly used to augment other methodological approaches, and increasingly tied to theory development. In addition, there has been an increase in the effort to link models to each other and to build on previous work.

The movement in computational organization theory is slowly leading to a new perspective on organizations. The evolving paradigm sees organizations as complex structures of agents, tasks, knowledge, and resources composed of intelligent adaptive agents (Carley and Gasser, 1999) operating under context and historical constraints, the structure of which can be designed and the behavior predicted (Burton and Obel, 1998). Through a process of synthetic adaptation, groups and organizations become more than the simple aggregate of the constituent personnel and become complex, computational and adaptive agents in their own right (Carley, 1999a). Organizations are thus intelligent, adaptive and computational agents in which learning and knowledge are distributed (Hutchins, 1995) and where ecologies of skill and strategy (Padgett, 1997) and complex social properties emerge (Epstein and Axtell, 1997). The organization and the agents within it are not simply boundedly rational information processors (March and Simon, 1958), but are cognitive agents (Carley and Newell, 1994) limited structurally, cognitively, and emotionally. Within organizations, agents, resources, knowledge and tasks are connected by, and embedded in, an ecology of evolving networks (Carley and Prietula, 1994; Carley, 1991; Krackhardt and Carley, 1998) all of which change dynamically through an ecology of learning mechanisms (Carley and Svoboda, 1996) and change processes (Sastry, 1997).

Computation is the methodology of choice in these and related areas for a variety of reasons. First, there is a general recognition that the nonlinear dynamics that characterize the system are not mathematically tractable; hence, simulation is needed. Second, there is a desire to develop empirically grounded theory – but the data with sufficient detail is ethnographic in nature and therefore consistent with the computational approach. Third, there is an interest in exploring both the short- and long-term implications of the theory as learning, adaptation, and evolution occur and computational analysis is particularly amenable to the study of emergent behavior. Finally, there is a growing concern with issues of scalability – that is, do behaviors remain the same, do our theories hold, as we move from groups of 2 or 3 to thousands? Again, through simulation, we can gain some insight into whether scale matters to the nonlinear dynamics that underlie fundamental organizational processes. This is particularly important as we move into a world where technology is making organizations of unprecedented size and distribution possible and giving people unprecedented access to larger numbers of others, ideas, technologies, and resources.

One of the earliest works the area of computational organizational theory is Cohen et al.'s (1972) Garbage Can Model of organizational choice. They present a simple information processing model of choice in which agents, solutions and tasks flow through the organization. Effort, saliency, and access link agents to tasks and solutions (resources) and so determine. Results suggest that most decisions are made by oversight. Describing the implications for various types of organizations, such as educational institutions, provides the model with face validity. This model, like others of its generation, demonstrates the potential for a simple model to generate surprising results.

Key aspects of this model that are retained in current models are the information processing approach, networks linking agents to resources and tasks, and organizational decisions resulting from individual decisions. Current models tend to be more detailed, more algorithmically complex, and to be more grounded on actual empirical data. Modern models vary in their reliance on database, artificial intelligence, and cognitive science techniques. Three models that all derived from the Garbage Can Model, and that have combined a contingency theory, information processing theory, and institutional theory perspective are VDT, ORGAHEAD and the Organizational Consultant.

The virtual design team (VDT) can be used within firms to evaluate the design of teams doing routine work (Jin and Levitt, 1996). VDT characterizes the organization in terms of agents, expertise (knowledge), tasks and the relations among these. Complex inter-connected tasks can be represented. Agents cannot learn. At a technical level, project management techniques are combined with information processing models of agents, the organization's authority relations, and the available communication technology. Actual or hypothetical project management plans and organizational charts can be entered. Changes in policies, re-designs, and re-engineered tasks can be examined by looking at the impact of such changes on various outcomes including workflow, re-work, and the speed of processing. Researchers and managers can use VDT to see how small changes in their team's structure can have dramatic effects on the outcomes for routine tasks.

ORGAHEAD (Carley and Svoboda, 1996) is a multi-agent model that can be used to examine the way in which organizations adapt to change. ORGAHEAD characterizes the organization in terms of agents, knowledge (knowledge/resources), tasks and the relations among these. Only simple choice tasks can be represented. There is a learning ecology such that agents and the organization learn, at both the knowledge and structural level. Changes in strategic redesign, HR, and re-engineering policies and personnel characteristics can be examined by looking at the impact of such changes on various outcomes including workload, performance, adaptivity, robustness, and historical trajectories. Technically, ORGAHEAD combines machine learning and optimization techniques to create a model of organizational learning and adaptation in which the strategic and tactical levels co-evolve. Actual or hypothetical authority and communication relations as well as access to resources or assignment to tasks for small to medium sized organizations can be entered. Researchers and managers can use ORGAHEAD to see how initial conditions and institutional or cognitive constraints influence adaptation.

The Organizational Consultant (Burton and Obel, 1998) is an expert system model embodying all the findings of contingency theory. The Organizational Consultant characterizes the organization in terms of features of its design (such as size) and processes (such as degree of coupling). Unlike VDT and ORGAHEAD, specific decision makers are not modeled. Rather the organization's performance, and suggestions for change, are predicted from a set of rules governing the complex ways in which the various aspects of organizational design and environment interact to effect performance. Changes in processes, structure or environment can be examined by looking at the impact of such changes on various outcomes including potential for errors and locus of problems. Technically, the Organizational Consultant combines expert system technology with case study protocols with rules derived from the literature. Actual or hypothetical descriptions of the organization's structure and processes can be entered. Researchers and managers can use the Organizational Consultant to see whether their reasoning is correct about what will happen and why given a particular organizational and environmental configuration.

Computational organization theory models vary dramatically in the level of detail used to describe and represent the agent, resources, knowledge, task, organizational structure, culture and technology. The more detailed, the more veridical these underlying models, the more precise the predictions possible from the model, the more useful the model as a managerial tool. The Garbage Can Model (Cohen et al., 1972) is simple and abstract. VDT (Jin and Levitt, 1996) and the Organizational Consultant (Burton and Obel, 1998) are more detailed and less abstract. ORGAHEAD is in between. The simpler more abstract models are typically referred to as intellective models. For these models, the central research goal is theory building: to discover general principles underlying organizational behavior. The more detailed models may allow the researcher to use the model to emulate specific organizations by entering specific authority structures and/or procedures. For these models, a key research goal is organizational engineering: to examine whether or not the performance of a specific organization will be affected by making some specific change such as re-engineering the task in a particular way or adding a new technology. In general, both the intellective and the emulative models can be used for theory building. One reason for this is that the act of building a model requires theory specification.

From the body of work in computational organization theory, which goes well beyond the examples described above, a neo-information processing paradigm has emerged. The information processing paradigm centered on the recognition that what information is available to whom when determines organizational outcomes. The neo-information processing paradigm uses recent findings from a variety of areas, including cognitive science, social networks, and distributed artificial intelligence to provide precision and specific underlying models to the general claims of information processing. Thus, the general notion of a boundedly rational agent has been replaced with exact specifications of a cognitive agent, often embodied in a general empirically grounded cognitive model such as Soar. The general notion of structural limitations on access to information has been replaced with the way in which the agents and organizations are embedded in networks influences access to information, the rate of information diffusion, and the relative power of structural positions. Collectively, the result provide a more precise understanding of the nature of information, the way in which different types of information are affected by learning processes and affect decision processes, the mechanisms for controlling the flow of information, the impact of information enablers and constraints, and so forth.

Contemporary Issues and Debates

NETWORKS

One of the linking pins that bring computational organization theory together is network analysis. As researchers in this area have moved to modeling processes – the role of networks in affecting the hiring, firing, mobility, decision-making, etc. processes has come to the fore. As researchers in this area have moved to modeling organizations as collections of agents, the role of networks in structuring and being structured by the interactions among these agents becomes critical. As researchers model interorganizational alliances, the links between organizations and the processes by which they form again become central. Networks, whether between agents, or between agents and resources or knowledge or tasks, are the glue that needs to be examined in order for computational theorizing to move beyond simple statements about individuals or dyads. The network approach is resulting in common representation schemes thus enabling data to be transferred between computational models and enabling experimental and field data to be used as input to or for validation of computational models.[3] For example, VDT (Jin and Levitt, 1996) and ORGAHEAD (Carley and Svoboda, 1996) use essentially the same network-based representation scheme for the organization's authority network and knowledge network (who knows what or has access to what resources). Since much of the computational organization theory work derives from the information processing tradition, where organizational structure and cognition constrain individual and organizational decisions, it was a natural leap to use network methodology and representation, so amenable to describing the flow of information, to describe and measure snapshots of the organization through time.

One area in which the relation between complexity, computation, and networks is emerging is in the area of power laws. Complex systems differ from random system in that they display surprising, although sometimes subtle, regularities. One that has often been referred to is the tendency of the products of complex process to follow a power law distribution. A commonly touted example is the distribution of firm sizes, which is approximately $1/f$ – i.e., a power law. Recent research is suggesting that the topology of human and organizational networks also have regularities, which can be described by power laws. For example, Faloutsos et al. (1999) found that despite the apparent randomness of the Internet, there are some surprisingly simple power-laws that describe the topology of the Internet. The power-laws they discover describe concisely skewed distributions of graph properties such as the out-degree (number of other sites linked to) associated with sites. For a complex system, the discovery of power laws is important. Power laws can be used to estimate important parameters such as the average neighborhood size. Power laws can be used to generate and select realistic topologies for computational theorizing purposes, thus enabling the development of grounded theory.

INFORMATION TECHNOLOGY

A growing recognition among computational researchers is that we cannot adequately explain, predict, or understand organizational behavior without also taking into account the information technology (IT) environment within and around the organization. From a computational perspective, a number of questions have emerged. The primary question is what is the fundamental nature of IT? How do we represent IT in these models? Research, both field, simulation, and experimental, has demonstrated that IT is both an agent and an agent enhancer. If IT is an enhancer then the reason that IT does or does not effect change is because it augments or changes the information processing capabilities of humans. For example, email is seen to effect differences in communication because its proponents of this view often predict that one of the core effects of email, the web, and various other IT will be that they will simply scale up current organizations leading to larger, more distributed, organizations and more knowledgeable, more connected individuals.

Nevertheless, new technologies have the ability to create and communicate information, make decisions and take action. In other words, modern IT is intelligent and the work in computer engineering is making it more so. Many of the databases and web-bots of the future will be agents. Theories of social change in which IT is characterized as an agent have been successfully employed to explain the effect of previous communication technologies; e.g., Kaufer and Carley (1993) use this approach to explain the impacts of print. Moreover, IT-as-agent computational theories have led to important new findings about the limitation of IT in effecting a unified and educated mass. In particular, this work suggests that IT is not a panacea equally facilitating all individuals and decreasing the socio-economic distance between disparate groups. Rather, this research suggests that since individuals who know more or know more people have more ability to learn new information, and will gravitate to IT agents, IT has the possibility of increasing the socio-economic distance between the intellectual haves and have nots (Alstyne and Brynjolfsson, 1995; Carley, 1995). Finally, the IT-as-agent approach can be used to accurately model and predict the behavior of organizations in which humans, web-bots, smart databases, robots, avatars, and so forth all work together to perform organizational and social tasks (Kaplan, 1999).

ALGORITHMIC COMPLEXITY

Algorithmic complexity is concerned with the length of the algorithm; loosely speaking, for two algorithms the one with more steps is more complex. Knowing the algorithmic complexity needed to do some task, to model some process, or to generate some organizational structure is valuable. The degree of algorithmic complexity can be used to guide development, suggest procedures for ruling out certain data as sufficient for testing certain models, determine the need for heuristic search procedures and tractability of data analysis, and enable more precise theorization. A variety of measures of algorithmic complexity, e.g., Kolmogorov-Chaitin, and a variety of proxies exist (which are often turned to for pragmatic reasons) (Lempel and Ziv, 1976). For the most part, social and organizational theorists have not attended to the role of algorithmic complexity. One advance in this area is the application of algorithmic complexity to determining the complexity of social and organizational networks (Butts, 2001). Butts argues that there is a precise correspondence between the equivalence and the structure of the social network, and the use of reduced models. For example, if a social network can be accurately characterized in terms of sets of structurally equivalent nodes and the relations among the node sets, then it is algorithmically simple. Social networks, which cannot be described in this way, are algorithmically complex. More precisely, the structure of a network is algorithmically complex to the extent that a long program is required to regenerate the structure. Thus, highly compressible structures that can be succinctly described by a set of equivalency classes of nodes and relations among the classes are algorithmically simple. Knowing the algorithmic complexity of a network provides a mathematics for reasoning about fundamental organizational constructs such as roles, power, and groups.

Algorithmic complexity can also be applied to theories of organizations that are realized in terms of grammars. A grammar can produce a series of statements or sequences describing behavior. The algorithmic complexity of these statements is related to the complexity of the grammar from which they were generated (Lindgren and Nordahl, 1988). We can take any organizational theory, or general theoretical statements, and express the theory or specific statements as a sequence. The degree complexity in these statements provides a guideline for the complexity of the grammar, which will be required to represent real-world organizational behavior. This, in turn, provides guidance in ruling out or in various proposed grammars (and associated theorem provers) purported to be adequate for the organizational behaviors they describe.

COMPARISON OF MODELS

The art of analyzing complex systems involves finding the means to extract from the computational theory no more information than we need and to map processes and results from one model onto another without sacrificing the inherent nonlinearities that define the underlying system. This means that the researcher is called upon to develop and use virtual experiments to assess core findings. The nonlinearities inherent in the underlying processes when coupled with the large number of processes, agents and variables lead to a system about which it is difficult for humans, unassisted by computation, to effectively reason about the consequences of any one action or change. Computational analysis, both enumeration and simulation, becomes an important tool for generating hypotheses about the behavior of these systems that can then be tested in the lab and field (Carley, 1999b). For each scientific method, methodologists work to develop procedures for overcoming the limitations of that methodology. In survey analysis, for example, specialized sampling procedures can be employed to increase the generalizability of the results. In computational research, one of the limitations has to do with the extent to which model specifications are driving the outcome. The assumptions made in constructing the computational model and the way in which the basic processes are characterized affect the veridicality of the model. As a trivial example, in agent-based models, the agents are segregative entities and so the models can never generate groups that contain a fraction of an agent. In contrast, when the number of actors are represented in the model using a continuous variable, groups can contain fractions of agents. In addition, the assumptions made in developing a model may, but need not, affect the generalizability of the outcomes. For example, models may represent the behavior of a specific group or company, or the more general behavior of a type of group.

Computational theorists have developed a variety of techniques for generating hypotheses, characterizing the specificity of a model, determining the veridicality of the results, and determining the generalizability of the results. These techniques include sensitivity analysis, parameter space exploration, and docking. For example, Monte Carlo techniques are used to average out assumptions about parameter values (Balci, 1994), empirical data is used to calibrate the model (Carley, 1999c) and docking (Axtell et al., 1996) is used to understand the match between two models with different core processes.

Computational models of organizations need to be built at varying levels; e.g., micro and macro, or human as actor, group as actor, organization as actor, etc. Computational models are often heralded as the means for linking the micro to the macro. To an extent, this is true. In addition, different computational models and methods can be used at multiple levels and used to reason across levels if the organization community would create a more detailed hierarchical structure for analysis. An approach, drawn from physics, is for the research community to develop a hierarchical structure of simple models each of whose function is to make possible and practical the analysis of the system being studied at that particular level of complexity. Each successive level gains in complexity. The logical relationship between contiguous levels needs to be established so that the researcher knows that the methods used at any one level are supported by the body of fact and theory gathered across all levels. This hierarchical approach can be applied at the micro level, the macro level, or both. To an extent this is being done, albeit not systematically in the area of organizational culture. Harrison and Carroll's (1991) single factor model of organizational culture and Carley's (1991) construct model of culture formation are both consistent with the body of findings regarding culture and enculturation but operate at different levels of complexity.

Central Questions That Remain Unanswered

The past decade has witnessed important recent advances in machine learning, social and organizational networks, and toolkits for computer modeling. These advances, together with the ubiquity of computing, and the growing recognition of the inherent complexity and dynamics of organizations has increased the general interest in computational modeling and theory building. As more work in this venue has appeared, a series of questions have emerged that need to be attended to for major advances in this area to occur.

REPRESENTATION

As the field of artificial intelligence has matured, researchers have came to recognize the criticality of representation; i.e., how should core elements of the model be represented. The issue of representation goes beyond empirical adequacy to computational utility. That is, several representations may be equally empirically valid (reasonable fit with the real world given the nature of the theory) but may differ in their computational utility (ability to facilitate processing, minimize algorithmic complexity, enable connections to other models, etc.). This recognition, that representation is critical, has led within the computer science community to the understanding that representation is not an art. Rather, research on how to represent model elements such as tasks, process, knowledge, resources, goals is central to the scientific enterprise. Appropriate representation schemes affect the algorithmic complexity of the model and speed of processing. They also affect the types of hypotheses and findings that can be derived from the model and the type of data needed to validate, calibrate or develop the model. As research in this area matures, common representation will be key to sharing and integrating models.

RELATIVE IMPACT OF TASK

Within the computational organization area, a number of tasks are emerging as canonical. These include the sugar production task, the binary-choice task (or its variant the radar detection task), the maze task, and the warehouse task (or its variant the web search tasks). This set does not span the space the tasks. Research using these tasks underscores the lesson from contingency theory and operations management that the nature of the task determines the effectiveness of the organizational structure and procedures. Both in the field and in virtual experiments, many critical parameters have been found to affect the value of various organizational designs. These include at least task complexity, degree of coupling or interdependence, knowledge intensity, the degree of routinization, whether resources are consumed, the speed with which the task must be completed, and the allowable error margin. Nevertheless, we do not have a comprehensive understanding of the space of tasks, how to represent tasks in general, and exactly how the various aspects of task interface with organizational goals and constraints to determine the way in which organizations are and should be designed for effective performance.

LEARNING

Organizational researchers have turned with increasing interest to the area of organizational learning. This work has highlighted that learning does occur at the organizational level and that, within the organization, there are multiple types of learning. Three types of learning commonly referred to include experiential (learning by doing), expectation based (learning by planning), and imitation (learning from others). Each of these types of learning becomes embedded in the minds of individuals, in databases, and in routines. The computational work has highlighted another type of learning – structural.

Structural learning is concerned with the embedding of knowledge in the relations connecting personnel, or organizations, or tasks. Core issues center around the relative effectiveness of the different types of learning, the interaction between learning and organizational memory, the role of IT in retaining organizational memory and enhancing learning, and the relation between learning and adaptation.

DETAIL

Perhaps the hardest issue being faced in the computational organization area is how detailed do the models need to be. Current models run from simple intellective models like the Garbage Can Model (Cohen et al., 1972) to emulative models like VDT (Jin and Levitt, 1996). A basic answer is that the level of detail depends on the way in which the model will be used, and the tradeoff between predictive and process accuracy. However, this answer does not address the core concerns, many of which have to do with the philosophy of science. On the one extreme, high predictability is expected; e.g., the results from engineering models often correlate 0.9 or better with the behavior of the systems they emulate. On the other extreme, extremely simple models are the most easily understood and replicable. At issue then is a fundamental tradeoff in the way in which research is conducted. However, the effects of detail may be more pernicious than expected. A recent study examined the impact of organizational structure on performance – while varying the level of detail (or veridicality) in the model of the agent. A key result is that the observed performance of the simulated organizations varied with structure and the level of detail in the agent model. In other words, we must carefully consider the impact of detail on the theoretical propositions derivable from the model.

EMERGENCE AND CONSTRAINT

Organizations often show an intelligence and a set of capabilities that are distinct from the intelligence and capabilities of the agents within them, or the average behavior of those agents (Macy, 1991; Kauffman, 1995; Epstein and Axtell, 1997; Padgett, 1997). Organizational behavior cannot be predicted by looking at the average behavior, or even the range of behaviors, of the ensemble members, or even that of the CEO or top management team. Rather, it is, at least in part, an emergent property of the decisions and actions taken by the set of heterogeneous agents within the organization who are in turn constrained and enabled by both their cognitive abilities and their interactions with others (Simon, 1955, 1956). The networks linking agents, knowledge, tasks, etc. affect and are affected by these agents. This web of interconnections serves to constrain and enable who takes what actions when, and the efficiency of those actions. These networks, coupled with the agents' cognitive processes, dictate what changes can occur, are likely to occur, and will have what effect (Carley and Newell, 1994). Computer modeling, because it can take into account the complexities of network dynamics and cognitive processes facilitates accurate prediction and helps us to move from saying interesting complex behaviors will emerge to saying what behaviors will emerge when. As such, a great deal of research is needed on what behaviors will emerge under what conditions and on what future scenarios are likely to occur or are infeasible given the constraints of human cognition, socio-economic policies, and the way in which the extant networks change, constrain, and enable individual behavior.

TRAINING TOOLS

One of the major difficulties in this area is the lack of adequate educational material. First, there is a lack of textbooks. The only textbooks in the area are focused just on simulation. An important exception here is Weiss (1999) *Distributed Artificial Intelligence* which is an upper-division or PhD level text. Nevertheless, what is needed is a text focused more specifically on organizations. Second, there is not an educational computational test bed filled with multiple models that students can easily use, compare, contrast, adapt, etc. in order to learn how build models and evaluate them. Third, most small intellective models have not been archived together with their results and post-processing algorithms. This makes the task of re-implementing those models and replicating earlier results non-trivial. Additional educational material is critical for the advancement of the field. Major advances in organizational research were made when statistical packages and textbooks became available. We can expect similar levels of advance when comparable educational materials become available for computational modeling, analysis, and theorizing.

New and Emerging Directions

A number of exciting and important research directions are emerging in this field. Several that promise to have sweeping consequences include the extension of the network approach, the focus on IT, mutable boundaries, the study of emotions, and the development of data archives and intelligent analysis tools. In all cases, the advances are being made possible by linking computational modeling of complex systems to other areas. Linking work on mental models and cognitive agents to work on social networks and task management facilitates the extension of the network approach. The IT work is enabled by linking work on information diffusion, learning, and discovery to work on networks, and technology. Emotions-based research is facilitated by linking work in cognitive psychology with that on learning, structural embeddedness, procedures and task performance. The new approaches to computational analysis rely on machine learning, intelligent search, and data mining techniques.

EXTENDING THE NETWORK APPROACH

As organizational theorists address issues of dynamics, increasing attention is paid to the link between knowledge, memory, procedures, learning, on the one hand and networks, tasks, personnel, technology on the other. This growing concern with the link between knowledge and interaction plays out in a number of venues – knowledge management, organizational decision making, change management, transactive memory, etc. The growing need to understand how agents and knowledge link within and among organizations is leading to new network based studies of learning, adaptation, impact of technology, and so forth. Traditional social network techniques, which have heretofore been concerned with just the relations among people, or just the relations among organizations, are being extended to look at any and all relations including the relations among information (mental models). Krackhardt and Carley (1998) suggested a meta-network scheme, PCANS, that uses networks of relations among individuals, resources, and tasks to derive organizational propositions. Carley and Hill (2001) proposed a similar approach in the area of knowledge management. A generalization of these schemes to include knowledge management issues and strategic interorganizational issues is described in table 9.2. The core concept is that webs of affiliation link agents, knowledge, resources, tasks and organizations into a giant meta-network. The advantage of a meta-network approach to knowledge management, organizational analysis, etc. is that it enables the researcher to employ the well-developed network methodology in the study of other organizational topics. Changes in policy, procedures, IT, and institutional arrangements, new discoveries, organizational births, mergers, and deaths, and personnel turnover and promotions all effect changes in this meta-network by altering the nodes and or relations. To understand such changes and to facilitate the ease of such transitions one needs to understand the impact of those changes on the meta-network. Tracking these changes, tracking this meta-network, lies at the core of being able to predict and manage such changes; i.e., it lies at the heart of knowledge management and strategic decision making.

IT FOCUS

The rapid development of new forms of information technology (IT) creates the promise of new ways of organizing and doing work. As we have moved into the realm of e-commerce, organizational researchers in general and computational organizational theorists in particular, have begun to examine the relationship between IT and fundamental organizational processes and forms. One of the most promising areas is the use of computational models to understand the impact of information technology within and among organizations. Modeling modern IT also requires modeling learning, as the IT itself is becoming intelligent and capable of learning and because organizational learning and search affect the organization's technological competence (Stuart and Podolny, 1996), Computational work on organizations and IT is facilitated by the emergent neo-information processing paradigm.

MUTABLE BOUNDARIES

One interesting notion that has emerged in the neo-information processing area is that of mutable boundaries. In most organizational research, individuals, organizations, tasks, resources, etc. are treated as entities with concrete and immutable boundaries. Thus, a task or resource moved from firm to firm retains the same configuration and remains essentially the same. However, from a neo-information processing perspective, the characteristics of these configurations depend on the information available and their information processing capabilities, including their ability to learn. A configuration is a particular combination of agents, resources, knowledge, tasks, etc. organized to meet

Table 9.2 A meta-network approach to organizational representation

Relation	People	Knowledge	Resources	Tasks	Organizations
People	**Social network** *Who knows who*	**Knowledge network** *Who knows what*	**Capabilities network** *Who has what resource*	**Assignment network** *Who does what*	**Work network** *Who works where*
Knowledge		**Information network** *What informs what*	**Skills network** *What knowledge is needed to use what resource*	**Needs network** *What knowledge is needed to do that task*	**Competency network** *What knowledge is where*
Resources			**Substitution network** *What resources can be substituted for which*	**Requirements network** *What resources are needed to do that task*	**Capital network** *What resources are where*
Tasks				**Precedence network** *Which tasks must be done before which*	**Market network** *What tasks are done where*
Organizations					**Interorganizational network** *Which organizations link with which*

some objective. Consider the objective of refilling stock in a store. The individual with pen, ink, whiteout, paper, ledger and inventory list writing a note is one configuration, and another is the web-bot sending automated email orders when a sensor in the inventory system indicates depletion is near. Boundaries are, in this sense, mutable. Since the information available to the agents in a configuration depends on the exact position of the entity in the meta-network, moving it about changes its characteristics and affects learning at the individual, group, structural and organizational level. Thus, not only are the boundaries around agents, task, etc. mutable, particularly for synthetic agents such as workgroups and organizations, but these configurations exist within an ecology of learning mechanisms which enables the organization to engage in meta-learning. Through such meta-learning, the organization develops norms and procedures which in turn become institutionalized. Such meta-learning also leads to the emergence of diversification and heterogeneous behavior at the organizational level. Advances in emergent agents and intelligent systems are enabling organizational theorists to rethink the basic nature of organizing, the mutability of boundaries, the impact of learning ecologies, and the conditions under which self-organization occurs and synthetic agents emerge. Research on the processes underlying meta-learning and institutionalization of behaviors needs to progress. Such progress is likely to blur the line between intra- and interorganizational behavior.

EMOTIONS

Most of the work in complexity and in computational organization theory, when the agents has been the focus of concern, has treated the agent as an intelligent adaptive being. However, recent work in cognitive psychology has moved beyond this to consider the role of emotions relative to cognition. Similarly, some organizational theorists are beginning to look at emotions, such as trust, and the role they play in distributed work settings within or between groups and organizations. One of the motivations is that emotions in general, and trust in particular, may play a greater role in the organizations of the future where personnel are more distributed. Essentially, there has been an implicit assumption that in organizations, since personnel know each other, see each other, etc., trust existed and emotions were kept under control or were irrelevant. However, as work is out-sourced, as more temporary workers are employed, as work is distributed geographically and temporally and as work proceeds at a faster pace (and presumably under more stress), the role of emotions may be more critical. Research needs to be directed at developing a model of the emotional-organizational agent, determining the value of emotions as a coordination mechanism, and the factors that may make the play of emotions important or irrelevant in an organizational context.

ON-LINE DATA ARCHIVES

The network approach also enables both models and data collection to proceed from the same representation base, thus facilitating docking, calibration, and validation. As more data is collected from firms using this representation scheme and stored in a common space (such as the web) multiple computational models can employ it. Web-accessible data archives, where there is a common meta-network representation, will enable more grounded theories, and make it possible for the models to serve as virtual laboratories where practitioners and scientists can conduct what-if analysis on the potential impact of policy changes, new procedures, new institutional arrangements and new IT. Such archives need to be created and research needs to proceed on how to automatically collect and maintain such data at the requisite level of detail.

INTELLIGENT ANALYSIS TOOLS

If we look back at the computational organization models of the 1970s, we find that those models tended to be exceedingly simple – only a few lines of codes, a few agents, etc. Today, many models are more complex (even algorithmically). With the models of the 1970s, it is possible to run a comprehensive analysis of the impact of all parameters built into the model. The space of outcomes can be completely simulated. Today, this is no longer possible for all models. Many models are sufficiently detailed that a complete sensitivity analysis across all parameters cannot be done in a feasible amount of time; rather, researchers often use response surface mapping techniques, experimental designs and statistical techniques to examine key aspects of the models. Thus, a key area of research is how to validate and test these highly complex models. Complex models, in which the submodels inter-related in nonlinear fashions, cannot be validated by simply validating the submodels. Another key research area is how to use intelligent agents to automatically navigate the parameter space and run virtual experiments.

Synopsis

Computational analysis and theorizing is playing an increasingly important role in the development of organizational theory. In part, this is due to the growing recognition that social and organizational processes are complex, dynamic, adaptive, and nonlinear, that organizational and social behavior emerges from interactions within and between ecologies of agents, resources, knowledge, tasks, and other organizations and that the relationships among and within these entities are critical constraints on, and enablers of individual and organizational decision making and action. In part, the computational movement is due to the recognition that organizations are inherently computational since they have a need to scan and observe their environment, store information and procedures, communicate, and transform information through human or artificial agents. Computational theories are providing the organizational research with both a new toolkit for examining organizations and new insights into the fundamental nature of organizations. Computational models have value beyond theory building. They can also be used for experimental and survey refinement, the comprehension and visualization of dynamics, and the comprehension and visualization of complexity.

Connections Across Levels

There are several important avenues for multi-level research that can be facilitated by taking a computational approach to complex systems. These include, but are not limited to, new organizational forms, organizational learning, organizational errors, and meta-learning. One of the key goals should be to move beyond metaphor and to determine ways to empirically map information on real organizations to the formal computational theories.

Consider the notion that organizations might want to operate on the edge of chaos and manage chaos as the energy differentials and tensions present at that point should make possible new discoveries, new organizational forms, new opportunities for profit, etc. This idea has captured the imagination of academician and manager. So far, it is little more than a metaphor providing a new vocabulary to describe the potential for change. However, if we are to move to a greater understanding of organizations and change, empirical measures of chaos need to be developed, that can be validated and used both in the models and in field and/or experimental settings. Further, scales need to be developed to determine how close to the edge of chaos the organization is operating. One issue is whether such measures and scales could be "context free"; that is, valid within and among organizations operating in different industries. Finally, if the edge of chaos is where change is possible, then this should be where entities lose and reform boundaries. Thus, another issue is can we recognize and measure the point at which boundaries become mutable?

A second set of research questions centers around coupling and organizational learning. Eisenhardt and Bahtia (this volume) argue that the degree of coupling determines the effectiveness with which organizations will evolve. Sorenson (this volume) goes on to argue that the orderliness underlying the founding and failures of new firms is related to the degree of coupling. At issue is – what is coupled? Eisenhardt and Bahtia (this volume) note that knowledge flows through ties at the intra- and interorganizational level thus suggesting that the coupling is occurring between people and between organizations. Sorenson (this volume) and Levinthal (1997) look at R&D and organizational learning suggesting that the coupling is occurring between bits of knowledge or patents, or between organizations and knowledge. The meta-network approach (table 9.2) suggests that coupling occurs simultaneously within and among sets of agents, resources, knowledge, tasks, and organizations. Movement of personnel and information within and among firms leads to changes in the degree of coupling, the location of the coupling, and the degree of variance in the coupling (which can be measured as variance in degree) in any of the sub-networks and the system of the whole. An issue that transcends levels is whether the learning processes, as we move from individual, to group, to organization, or from subtask, to task, to meta-task does, result in the pattern of errors, innovation, exceptions, etc, being a fractal. In other words, which of these patterns scale? Another issue for consideration is the way in which coupling is related to organizational adaptation. For example, does successful adaptation require a certain level of coupling across the board in all the networks in the meta-network or can tight coupling in one network be traded for low coupling in another? Is there a level of coupling that is too high?

A third set of questions has to do with tipping points. It is generally recognized that the coordination and communication mechanisms, characteristic behaviors, and mechanisms for retaining information depend in some sense on the size of the organization. For example, coordination and communication mechanisms admitting rapid information diffusion, consensus formation, resource allocation, and task assignment appear to be different for organizations comprised of 5, 25, 200, 5000 or more people. Are there formal tipping points, particular sizes or degrees of complexity, where changeovers in coordination mechanisms are required? Does the tipping point depend on the degree of coupling in the meta-network?

Conclusion

Computational analysis and theorizing is playing an increasingly important role in science. The use of computational models to reason about organizations is leading to advances in a plethora of topics ranging from social capital to e-commerce, from knowledge management to entrepreneurship, from organizational culture to interorganizational alliance. Computational analysis provides us with a way of developing and characterizing theories and extending and analyzing data that is uniquely suited to understanding organizations. Simulation techniques in general, and multi-agent systems in particular, enable the researcher to reason about complex, dynamic, and information processing systems in which agents work collectively and individually in both cooperative and competitive situations. As such, the set of procedures and techniques that comprise complexity theory will certainly have a role to play in characterizing and evaluating organizations – either virtual or real – as new computational theories and large scale organizational databases are developed.

Acknowledgments

This work was supported in part by the Office of Naval Research (ONR), United States Navy Grant Nos ITI9633662, KDI IIS-9980109, and NSF IGERT CASOS. The views and conclusions contained in this document are those of the author and should not be interpreted as representing the official policies, either expressed or implied, of the Office of Naval Research, the National Science Foundation, or the U.S. government. The author thanks the following people for their comments on this and related works: Carter Butts, Ju-Sung Lee, Bill McKelvey, Benoit Morel and Ranga Ramanujam.

Notes

1   Actually, the term chaos does not refer to a class of systems, but to the dynamic behavior of many nonlinear systems. The behavior of concern is high sensitivity to initial conditions. Complex systems need not be chaotic and "chaos cannot explain complexity" (Bak, 1996, p.31).

2   The edited volume by Kiel and Elliot (1996) provides base models and measures, as does the review by Mathews et al. (1999). Standard information on the nature of chaos, dynamical systems and approaches for measuring the Lyapunov exponent are also provided. There are also a number of very useful websites in this area:
    http://www.calresco.force9.co.uk/sos/sosfaq.htm
    http://views.vcu.edu/complex/
    http://views.vcu.edu/~mikuleck/ON%20COMPLEXITY.html
    http://www.casos.ece.cmu.edu
    http://necsi.org
    http://www.santafe.edu/
    http://www.soc.surrey.ac.uk/research/simsoc/simsoc.html

3   An example here is the A2C2 project funded by ONR, where a network representation

scheme of the organization's architecture is used to represent all relations among personnel, tasks, and resources. The same representation scheme is used in the petri-net models at George Mason, the excel models at University of Connecticut, the ORGAHEAD simulations at Carnegie Mellon University, and the experiment data collection efforts at the Naval Post Graduate School. This facilitated direct comparison of the output of the three models and the experimental data.

References

Alstyne, M. V., and Brynjolfsson, E. (1995): "Communication networks and the rise of an information elite – Does communication help the rich get richer?" paper presented at the International Conference on Information Systems, Amsterdam.

Axelrod, R. M., and Cohen, M. D. (1999): *Harnessing Complexity: Organizational Implications of a Scientific Frontier.* New York: Free Press.

Axtell, R., Axelrod, R., Epstein, J. M., and Cohen, M. D. (1996): "Aligning simulation models: A case study and results," *Computational and Mathematical Organization Theory,* 1(2), 123–42.

Bak, P. (1996): *How Nature Works: The Science of Self-Organized Criticality.* New York, NY: Copernicus.

Balci, O. (1994): "Validation, verification, and testing techniques throughout the life cycle of a simulation study," *Annals of Operations Research,* 53, 121–73.

Baum, J. A., and McKelvey, B. (eds.) (1999): *Variations in Organizations: In Honor of Donald T. Campbell.* Thousand Oaks, CA: Sage.

Burton, R. M., and Obel, B. (1998): *Strategic Organizational Design: Developing Theory for Application.* Norwell, MA: Kluwer Academic Publishers.

Butts, C. (2001): "The complexity of social networks: Theoretical and empirical findings," *Social Networks,* 23, 31–71.

Carley, K. M. (1991): "A theory of group stability," *American Sociological Review,* 56(3), 331–54.

Carley, K. M. (1995): "Communication technologies and their effect on cultural homogeneity, consensus, and the diffusion of new ideas," *Sociological Perspectives,* 38(4), 547–71.

Carley, K. M. (1999a): "On the evolution of social and organizational networks," in Steven B. Andrews and David Knoke (eds), *Research in the Sociology of Organizations, Vol. 16: Networks In and Around Organizations,* Stamford, CT: JAI Press, 3–30.

Carley, K. M. (1999b): "On generating hypotheses using computer simulations," *Systems Engineering,* 2(2), 69–77.

Carley, K. M. (1999c): "Validating computational models," CASOS working paper, CMU.

Carley, K. M., and Gasser, L. (1999): "Computational organization theory," in G. Weiss (ed.), *Distributed Artificial Intelligence,* Cambridge, MA: MIT Press.

Carley, K. M., and Hill, V. (2001): "Structural change and learning within organizations," in A. Lomi (ed.), *Dynamics of Organizational Societies: Models, Theories and Methods,* Cambridge, MA: MIT Press/AAAI Press/Live Oak, (forthcoming).

Carley, K. M., and Newell, A. (1994): "The nature of the social agent," *Journal of Mathematical Sociology,* 19(4), 221–62.

Carley, K. M., and Prietula, M. (1994): "ACTS theory: Extending the model of bounded rationality," in K. M. Carley and M. Prietula (eds), *Computational Organization Theory,* Hillsdale, NJ: Lawrence Earlbaum Associates, 55–87.

Carley, K. M., and Svoboda, D. M. (1996): "Modeling organizational adaptation as a simulated annealing process," *Sociological Methods and Research,* 25(1), 138–68.

Cilliers, P. (1998): *Complexity and Postmodernism: Understanding Complex Systems.* New York: Routledge.

Cohen, M. D., March, J. G., and Olsen, J. P. (1972): "A garbage can model of organizational choice," *Administrative Sciences Quarterly,* 17(1), 1–25.

Dow, S. C., and Earl, P. E. (eds) (1999): *Contingency, Complexity and the Theory of the Firm.* Cheltenham: Edward Elgar.

Epstein, J., and Axtell, R. (1997): *Growing Artificial Societies.* Boston, MA: MIT Press.

Etzioni, A. (ed.) (1961): *Complex Organizations: A Sociological Reader.* New York: Holt, Rinehart & Winston,

Eve, R. A., Horsfall, S., and Lee. M. E., (eds) (1997): *Chaos, Complexity, and Sociology: Myths, Models, and Theories.*Thousand Oaks, CA: Sage Publications.

Faloutsos, M., Faloutsos, P., and Faloutsos, C. (1999): "On power–law relationships of the internet topology," *Proceedings of the Association for Computing Machinery SIGCOMM Conference,* Cambridge MA: Association for Computing Machinery, 251–62.

Gibson, D. (1999): "Mapping the dynamics of change: A complexity theory analysis of innovation in five Vermont high schools," PhD dissertation, University of Vermont.

Hall, R., Haas, J. Johnson, E., and Norman, J. (1967): "Organizational size, complexity, and formalization," *American Sociological Review,* 32(6), 903–12.

Harrison J.R., and Carroll, G.R. (1991): "Keeping the faith: A model of cultural transmission in formal organizations," *Administrative Science Quarterly,* 36, 552–82.

Holland, J. (1995): *Hidden Order: How Adaptation Builds Complexity.* Cambridge MA: Perseus Publishing, Helix Book Series.

Hummon, N. P. (1990): "Organizational structures and network processes," *The Journal of Mathematical Sociology,* 15(2), 149–61.

Hutchins, E.: (1995): *Cognition in the Wild.* Cambridge, MA: MIT Press.

International Symposium in Economic Theory and Econometrics Commerce, Complexity, and Evolution (1996): "Topics in economics, finance, marketing, and management," Proceedings of the Twelfth International Symposium in Economic Theory and Econometrics, University of New South Wales.

Jin Y., and Levitt, R.) (1996): "The virtual design team: A computational model of project organizations," *Computational and Mathematical Organization Theory,* 2(3), 171–96.

Kaplan, D. (1999): "The STAR system: A unified multi-agent simulation model of structure, task, agent, and resource," unpublished PhD thesis, Heinz School of Public Policy and Management, Carnegie Mellon University.

Kaufer, D. S., and Carley, K. M. (1993): *Communication at a Distance: The Effect of Print on Socio-Cultural Organization and Change.* Hillsdale, NJ: Lawrence Erlbaum Associates.

Kauffman, S, A. (1995): *At Home in the Universe: The Search for Laws of Self-Organization and Complexity.* New York, NY: Oxford University Press.

Kiel, D, and Elliott, E. (eds) (1996): *Chaos Theory in the Social Sciences: Foundations and Applications.* Ann Arbor, MI: University of Michigan Press.

Klatzky, S. R. (1970): "Relationship of organizational size to complexity and coordination," *Administrative Science Quarterly,* 15(4), 428–38.

Krackhardt, D., and Carley, K. M. (1998): "A PCANS model of structure in organization," *Proceedings of the 1998 International Symposium on Command and Control Research and Technology,* Monterray, CA, June, 113–19.

Lant, T. (1994): "Computer simulations of organizations as experiential learning systems: Implications for organizational theory," in K. M. Carley and M. Prietula (eds), *Computational Organization Theory,* Hillsdale, NJ: Lawrence Erlbaum Associates, Ch. 9.

Lempel, A., and Ziv, J. (1976): "On the complexity of finite sequences," *IEEE Transactions on Information Theory,* 22, 75.

Levinthal, D. (1997): "Adaptation on rugged landscapes," *Management Science,* 43, 934–50.

Lindgren, K., and Nordahl, M. (1988): "Complexity measures and cellular automata," *Complex Systems,* 2, 409–40.

McKelvey, B. (1999a): "Complexity theory in organization science: Seizing the promise or becoming a fad," *Emergence,* 1, 5–32.

McKelvey, B. (1999b): "Avoiding complexity catastrophe in coevolutionary pockets: Strategies for rugged landscapes," *Organization Science,* 10, 294–321.

McKelvey, B. (2000): "Improving corporate IQ," *Proceedings, 3rd Intangibles Conference on Knowledge*, New York: Ross Institute of Accounting Research, Stern School, NYU, May.

McKelvey, B. (2001): "Dynamics of new science leadership: Strategy, microcoevolution, distributed intelligence, complexity," in A. Y. Lewin and H. Volberda (eds), *Mobilizing the Self-Renewing Organization*, Thousand Oaks, CA: Sage, forthcoming

Macy, M. W. (1991): "Chains of cooperation: Threshold effects in collective action," *American Sociological Review*, 56(6), 730–47.

Maguire, S. and McKelvey, B. (1999): "Complexity and management: Moving from fad to firm foundations," *Emergence*, 1, 19–61.

Mainzer, K. (1996): *Thinking in Complexity: The Complex Dynamics of Matter, Mind, and Mankind.* New York: Springer.

March, J. G. (1991): "Exploration and exploitation in organizational learning," *Organizational Science*, 2, 71–87.

March, J. G., and Simon, H.A. (1958): *Organizations.* New York, NY: Wiley.

Mathews, K. M., White, M. C., and Long, R. G. (1999): "Why study the complexity sciences in the social sciences?" *Human Relations*, 52(4), 439–62.

Meyer, J. W., and Scott, W. R. (1983): *Organizational Environments.* Newbury Park, CA: Sage.

Morel, B., and Ramanujam, R. (1999): "Through the looking glass of complexity: The dynamics of organizations as adaptive and evolving systems," *Organization Science*, 10(3), 278–93.

Padgett, J. F. (1997): "The emergence of simple ecologies of skill," in B. Arthur, S. Durlauf, and D. Lane (eds), *The Economy as an Evolving Complex System II*, Vol. XXVII, Reading MA: Addison-Wesley, 199–222.

Perrow, C. (1984): *Normal Accidents: Living with High-Risk Technologies.* New York: Basic Books.

Pines, D., Cowan, G., and Meltzer, D. (eds) (1999): *Complexity: Metaphors, Models, and Reality.* Reading, MA: Addison-Wesley, Santa Fe Institute series.

Sastry, M. (1997): "Problems and paradoxes in a model of punctuated organizational change," *Administrative Science Quarterly*, 42(2), June, 237–75.

Scott, W. R., and Meyer, J. W. (1994): *Institutional Environments and Organizations: Structural Complexity and Individualism.* Thousand Oaks, CA: Sage Publications.

Simon, H. (1955): "A behavioral model of rational choice," *Quarterly Journal of Economics*, 69, 99–118.

Simon, H. (1956): "Rational choice and the structure of the environment," *Psychological Review*, 63, 129–38.

Stuart, T. E., and Podolny, J. M. (1996): "Local search and the evolution of technological capabilities," *Strategic Management Journal*, 17, 21–38.

Thiétart, R. A., and Forgues, B. (1995): "Chaos theory and organization," *Organization Science*, 6, 19–31.

Weiss, G. (ed.) (1999): *Multiagent Systems: A Modern Approach to Distributed Artificial Intelligence.* Cambridge, MA: MIT Press.

White, M. C., Marin, D. B., Brazeal, D. V., and Friedman, W. H. (1997): "The evolution of organizations: Suggestions from complexity theory about the interplay between natural selection and adaptation," *Human Relations*, 50(11), 1383–401.

Chapter Ten

Intraorganizational Economics

EDWARD J. ZAJAC AND JAMES D. WESTPHAL

Agency theory has had and will likely continue to have a significant influence on intraorganizational economics research, particularly in the domain of corporate governance. While the agency perspective is typically seen as having its origins in the 1970s (Ross, 1973; Jensen and Meckling, 1976), its roots can be traced back to Berle and Means' (1932) influential statement about self-interested managers in large US corporations, highlighting problems emerging from the growing separation of ownership and control. This theme of concern for aligning managers' and owners' interests later blossomed briefly with the so-called managerialist school within economics (Marris, 1964; Williamson, 1964), which held that top managers pursue personal goals that are incongruent with profit maximization for the firm. However, after a short period of debate and research in the economics literature in the early to mid-1960s on whether firms were unitary, profit-maximizing entities or devices through which managers pursue their own goals, mainstream economists largely abandoned this question without having resolved it.

Ironically, the idea of goal incongruence in the managerialist school in the 1960s represented an early (and somewhat unfulfilled) opportunity for linkages between economists and a growing community of organizational theorists taking a behavioral science perspective, who had come to understand and accept two related facts. First, the presence of intraorganizational politics is the rule, rather than the exception in most formal organizations (Cyert and March, 1963), and second, economists' assumption of the firm behaving as a unitary actor was largely a convenient fiction. It was *convenient* in the sense that it enabled economists to focus on modeling the industry-level and market-level processes that interested them the most; it was a *fiction* in the sense that behavior in most formal organizations could be shown to be significantly affected by intraorganizational political and/or bureaucratic processes (Allison, 1971). One can therefore imagine the strong pressures among mainstream economists at that time (and even today) to cling to the assumption of the firm as a unitary rational actor, given the field's primary interest and deep investment in modeling the competitive interplay of rational organizational actors in an industry; for an example of competitive interactions among boundedly rational players in an industry, see Zajac and Bazerman (1991).

What intraorganizational economics needed was a way to acknowledge the existence of intraorganizational politics without having to relax the assumption that organizations behave "as if" they are fully rational in their competitive interactions. A theory that could show how incentives could be optimally structured to address divergent intraorganizational interests would be most helpful in this regard, and agency theory's popularity is due in part to its ability to serve this role. What is now called agency theory emerged in the early/mid-1970s from more abstract formalized analyses of principal–agent relationships and the basic problem of delegation (Ross, 1973). This stream of the agency research, sometimes referred to as the normative agency literature, is interested in formal modeling approaches to designing the optimal principal–agent contract (Milgrom and Roberts, 1992).

This literature focused on efficient risk bearing, and in particular, the trade-off between incentives and insurance, and in some cases the trade-off between incentives and monitoring. Although it had obvious organizational implications, the normative agency literature has had little impact on organizational research. This is likely attributable to the fact that research in this stream was not focused on organizational issues *per se* (much of the literature focused on examples such as sharecropping), and its more mathematical orientation has been less accessible to organizational researchers (Eisenhardt, 1989).

The implications of agency theory became more central with the emergence of a second, more empirical-oriented research stream, sometimes referred to as the positive agency literature, which sought to explain the existence of certain contractual structures and organizational governance arrangements. Jensen and Meckling's (1976) classic statement of the agency problem and their discussion of ways to minimize agency costs in corporations is in many ways a natural extension of Berle and Means (1932). This variant of agency theory, developed almost independently of the normative approach, examines the problems – and partial contractual solutions – that arise as firms grow and move away from owner-entrepreneur control, and toward making greater use of professional managers who exercise considerable control over corporate decision making without facing the full risks of ownership.

A substantial literature drawing from positive agency theory has developed in the area of top management incentives, as well as the monitoring function of boards of directors (Fama and Jensen, 1983). Much of this positive agency-based literature on executive compensation resembles that of the traditional managerialist school, but rather than focusing on whether or not firms maximize profits, the primary emphasis is on establishing if and/or where incentive or monitoring problems reside within organizations and how to address them. Jensen and Murphy's (1990) widely cited study can, for example, be viewed as a descriptive managerialist study that searches – with little success – for evidence of a CEO-pay-for-firm-performance relationship in large US corporations. Such unsuccessful searches are often accompanied by more or less explicit calls for an increase in the pay-for-performance component of compensation contracts, or in some cases, greater regulation or reform of executive compensation practices. Again, given organizational researchers' long-standing acceptance of goal incongruence in organizational life (Pfeffer, 1981; Mintzberg, 1983), the influence of the positive agency literature on organizational analysis seems understandable.

In sum, agency theory has raised organizational researchers' sensitivity to the importance of managerial incentives, board of director monitoring, and efficient risk bearing.

Although some of these issues were already understood in the organizational literature, others were new and different. Specifically, agency-based research has brought at least two significant issues to the study of corporate governance and CEO/board relations in intraorganizational economics. First, the normative literature has highlighted the potential importance of managerial risk aversion as affecting the choice of an optimal incentive arrangement. Second, the positive literature has focused attention on the need to establish ways to improve the managerial pay-for-performance relationship, and on the possibility of substituting board control for incentive compensation. Although this agency-based literature has fostered the convergence of economic and behavioral perspectives on organizational governance, intraorganizational economics researchers have sought further, more explicit integration of these perspectives as a defining quality of their work.

Our focused review of intraorganizational economics research first shows how positive and normative versions of agency theory can be connected. Then, we examine the two main approaches to combining economic and behavioral perspectives in intraorganizational economics, which we refer to as *aggregative* and *integrative*. Table 10.1 summarizes the illustrative studies that we survey in our review.

Literature Review

CONNECTING POSITIVE AND NORMATIVE AGENCY THEORIES

Integrating fragmented streams of research on positive and normative agency theory has yielded important new insights and predictions. Although the positive agency literature typically extols the virtues of high-powered incentive compensation in organizations, studies in this stream have tended to neglect potentially important organizational factors derived from normative agency theory that might explain the variation in observed compensation contracts (i.e., where there is a decreased emphasis on incentives).

For example, while positive agency research highlights the value of placing greater amounts of managerial compensation and managerial wealth at risk by tying it closer to firm performance, normative agency researchers stress the need to consider the potential *disadvantages* of forcing managers to bear excessive compensation risk (Beatty and Zajac, 1994). This intersection of positive and normative agency predictions highlights the possibility that while contingent compensation may have desirable incentive/motivational properties relative to non-contingent forms of compensation, it may also has undesirable risk-bearing properties. Consequently, linking a manager's compensation too closely to firm wealth might lead to risk-avoiding behavior on the part of the agent.

Nobel laureate in economics Myron Scholes explained this tension succinctly in a roundtable debate on the question of whether or not there should be a tightening of the pay-for-performance contingency for top management (*Journal of Applied Corporate Finance*, 1992, p. 123):

> Managers are more likely to attach significantly more value to a given level of cash than to the same expected level in stock or options because they can use that cash to buy a diversified portfolio of common stocks, bonds, or whatever. But, as you force managers to reduce their cash compensation while making a larger investment in their own firm, you're

Table 10.1 Research on intraorganizational economics

Reference	Key concepts	Key variables	Key predictions/findings	Key contribution	Method and sample
Connecting positive and normative agency theories					
Beatty and Zajac (1994)	Incentive alignment, firm risk, and monitoring capacity	CEO long-term incentives, beta, board independence from management	Higher levels of firm risk would decrease the level of compensation risk in CEO compensation contracts	Applied agency theory to explain empirical finding from behavioral research that CEO pay is often not strongly tied to firm performance	Longitudinal analyses of archival data on incentives, risk, and board independence for sample of IPOs, 1984
Zajac and Westphal (1994)	Incentive alignment, firm risk, monitoring capacity, strategic complexity	CEO long-term incentives, beta, board independence from management, firm diversification	U-shaped relationship between strategic complexity and monitoring capacity	Showed that monitoring capacity is limited by decision-making complexity	Longitudinal analyses of archival data on incentives and board independence for *Fortune 500* companies, 1987–91
Theoretical aggregation					
Kosnik (1990)	Board independence, incentives, and corporate greenmail	Board compensation, director ownership, and greenmail	Board independence interacts with variance in director incentives to predict greenmail	Suggested that effects of board monitoring on governance is contingent on social relationship between directors	Analysis of greenmail decisions by large companies from 1979–83
Davis (1991)	Board independence, interlock ties and poison pill adoption	Ratio of outside to inside directors, board ties to poison pill adopters, board centrality, poison pill adoption	Board interlock ties affect poison pill adoption, but board independence (monitoring capacity) does not	Showed that social structural factors predict adoption of takeover defenses but agency factors do not	Longitudinal analysis of poison pill adoption among *Fortune 500* companies, 1984–9
Boeker (1992)	Board power, agency costs, and governance	Board independence from management, firm performance, CEO dismissal	Board independence and poor performance will predict CEO dismissal	Showed that both agency factors and political factors predict corporate governance	Longitudinal analyses of CEO dismissals at semiconductor producers from 1968 to 1989

Theoretical integration

Porac et al. (1999)	Power, political interests, and selective comparisons in determining CEO compensation	Shareholder power, CEO pay, firm/industry performance, the choice of peers in CEO pay comparisons	Powerful managers made normatively acceptable pay comparisons when shareholders are powerful	Provided evidence that governance practices (the determination of CEO pay) are defined by political interests, and subject to social constraints	Content analysis of CEO pay comparisons for S&P 500 companies, 1992–3
Westphal and Zajac (1994)	Power and institutional decoupling	Board independence from management, adoption and (non) implementation of executive incentive plans	Powerful managers favor formal adoption of executive incentive plans, while decoupling actual compensation from formal plans.	Shows how internal power relationships can lead to symbolic use of compensation contracts	Longitudinal analysis of adoption and implementation of executive incentive plans for Fortune 500 companies, 1972–90
Zajac and Westphal (1995)	Explanations to shareholders for CEO incentive compensation	Indicators of CEO power and demography, time of incentive plan adoption, types of explanations (agency vs. human resource)	CEO power, demography, and time of incentive plan adoption predict which explanations firms give for new CEO incentive plans.	Shows that the purpose of incentive alignment is subjective and can be explained by political, psychological, and institutional factors	Content analysis of explanations for long-term incentive plans in proxy statements by Fortune 500 companies, 1976–90
Westphal and Zajac (1995)	Power, CEO/board similarity, and CEO compensation	Board independence, demographic similarity, level and risk of CEO compensation	Powerful CEOs favor appointment of demographically similar directors, which leads to generous compensation contracts.	Addresses how social psychological biases mediate effects of power on compensation contracts	Longitudinal analysis of demographic similarity and CEO compensation for Fortune 500 companies, 1986–91
Belliveau et al. (1996)	Social capital and CEO compensation	CEO board appointments, trusteeships, memberships in social clubs, and prestige of educational institution attended, and CEO compensation	CEO social capital influences CEO pay independently of firm performance.	Shows that CEOs are rewarded in part for their social status, independently of their performance	Regression analyses of CEO compensation for large companies listed in 1985 Business Week Survey of Executive Compensation

Reference	Key concepts	Key variables	Key predictions/findings	Key contribution	Method and sample
Westphal and Zajac (1998)	Institutional decoupling, impression management, and stock market reaction to incentive plans	Decoupling of incentive plans, verbal explanations for plans, abnormal returns following plan adoption	Stock market reacts favorably to adoption of incentive plans with an "agency" explanation, whether or not plans implemented	Provides quantitative evidence for benefits from symbolic management of corporate governance practices	Event study of market reactions to adoption of incentive plans by *Fortune 500* companies, 1982–92
Westphal and Zajac (1997)	Social exchange and CEO/board power	Board interlock ties, change in board independence and CEO pay	Change in social exchange relationships between managers of differerent firms triggers change in CEO/board relationships within firms.	Linked macro-structure of interlocking directorates with micro-level power relationships	Longitudinal analyses of change in board independence and CEO pay at *Fortune/Forbes 500* companies, 1982–92
Westphal (1998)	Structural power, interpersonal influence. CEO compensation and corporate strategy	Structural board independence from management, CEO ingratiation and persuasion, CEO compensation level and risk, firm diversification	CEO influence tactics offset the effects of structural board independence on CEO compensation and change in corporate strategy.	Showed how micro-social processes change macro-level relationships between structural power and economic constructs such as incentive alignment	LISREL analysis of archival measures of structural power, survey measures of CEO influence, and measures of compensation and diversification for *Fortune/Forbes 500* companies; data from 1993–97
Westphal (1999)	CEO/board social ties, monitoring, advice-seeking, and firm performance	Survey measures of monitoring, advice-seeking, and social ties, firm profitability and market-to-book value	CEO/board social ties increase cooperation between CEO and board, which leads to subsequent performance gains.	Showed how lack of board independence had unexpected benefits for corporate governance	Regression analysis of CEO advice-seeking, board monitoring, and firm performance for *Fortune/Forbes 500* companies; data from 1993–97

| Gulati and Westphal (1999) | Firm interlock ties, CEO/board cooperation, monitoring, and alliance formation | Survey measures of monitoring, advice-seeking, and trust, alliance formation and interlock ties. | Effect of board interlock ties on alliance formation is contingent on behavioral processes that underlie the tie. | Showed that board monitoring can have unanticipated side effects on corporate strategy, in area of alliance formation | Analysis of alliance formation for *Fortune/Forbes 500* companies; survey data from 1995, alliance data from 1970–96 |

asking them to bear more risk – risk that cannot be diversified away by holding other stocks and bonds. And because that risk cannot be diversified, companies will be forced to pay their executives disproportionately more in total compensation to compensate them for bearing this nondiversifiable risk

As Beatty and Zajac point out, the key issue here is not whether, in an absolute sense, the incentive benefits outweigh the risk-sharing costs of incentive-based compensation but, rather, the need to recognize the potential trade-off between incentives and risk sharing, and begin to identify contingencies affecting that trade-off. Notably, while there is a substantial body of economic research that seeks to find strong correlations between managerial compensation and firm performance, there is little corresponding empirical research that examines the question of managerial incentives and risk aversion.

Beatty and Zajac (1994) examined this question empirically in a large-sample study of US firms undertaking an initial public offering in 1984. They suggest that there is a need to recognize explicitly the potential *costs* – not just benefits – of using incentives, and start to identify the organizational and individual contingencies that could affect the consideration of the incentive cost/benefit tradeoff. They focus on one such organizational contingency – firm risk – that may increase the riskiness of incentive compensation contracts, and therefore may make managers particularly reluctant to accept them. Consistent with their argument, Beatty and Zajac find that riskier firms face greater difficulties, and thus greater costs, when using incentive compensation contracts, given the risk-aversion of top managers, and as a result, are less likely to emphasize incentive compensation. They also find that firms undertaking an initial public offerings generally respond to this problem of inadequate incentive compensation by structuring boards of directors to provide greater levels of monitoring. These findings indicate that incentives, monitoring, and risk-bearing are important factors shaping the structure of firms' executive compensation contracts, ownership, and boards of directors.

Zajac and Westphal (1994) report similar results using a longitudinal data set on a sample of over 400 of the largest US corporations from 1987 to 1991. They develop and test a contingency cost/benefit perspective on governance decisions as resource allocation decisions to explain how and why the observed levels of managerial incentives and monitoring vary across organizations and over time. Their study is unique in attempting to address explicitly the likely costs of monitoring top management – and how that cost may differ – depending on the complexity of organizations' strategies. They also advance the idea that there may be salience threshold levels for managers, and thus considerable diminishing "behavioral returns" to increases in incentive compensation. Their findings suggest that the contingent relationships proposed by Beatty and Zajac (1994) may be more logarithmic than linear: while incentives that reward managers for shareholder returns can shift managerial attention toward shareholder interests, this cognitive shift is achieved at relatively low levels of incentive compensation; higher levels increase compensation risk with smaller motivational benefit.

Agency theory and the organizational literature that has developed from it have raised researchers' sensitivity to the importance of managerial incentives, board of director monitoring, and efficient risk bearing. The normative literature has highlighted the potential importance of managerial risk aversion as affecting the choice of an optimal incentive arrangement, while the positive literature has focused attention on the need to establish ways to improve the managerial pay-for-performance relationship, and on substituting board control for incentive compensation. Organizational researchers have contributed by showing specific ways in which the two separate streams of agency research can be linked.

THEORETICAL AGGREGATION

One useful approach to integrating economic and behavioral perspectives, and perhaps the most common approach in intraorganizational economics, involves aggregating different perspectives to explain a given phenomenon. Several examples of this approach can be found in the literature on CEO succession. A simple agency perspective on succession would predict, for instance, that poor firm performance should increase the likelihood of CEO succession. Boards monitor firm performance on behalf of shareholders, and replace top managers in response to evidence that CEOs are not promoting shareholder welfare *vis-à-vis* its competitors. Behavioral studies of CEO succession routinely hypothesize such a relationship between firm performance and CEO succession as a sort of baseline, agency prediction (e.g., Dalton and Kesner, 1985; Boeker, 1992). Studies adopting this approach then complicate the agency perspective by adding hypotheses rooted in behavioral perspectives. Several studies, for example, predict and find that the power of the board of directors affects the likelihood of succession, or change in CEO characteristics, controlling for firm performance (e.g., Boeker, 1992; Cannella and Lubatkin, 1993; Zajac and Westphal, 1996).

Another example of theoretical aggregation in governance research is Kosnik's (1990) study on corporate greenmail by large companies from 1979 to 83. Kosnik first developed agency hypotheses predicting that incentives and board independence from management would predict corporate greenmail. Further hypotheses applied theoretical perspectives on small group decision making to consider how variance in incentives among directors could influence the likelihood of greenmail by affecting the level of social cohesion and debate among board members. In another example, Davis (1991) aggregates agency theory with a sociological perspective on boards of directors. In his study of poison pill adoptions, Davis again captured agency predictions with measures of board independence from management, while developing entirely separate theoretical arguments and hypotheses, rooted in the sociological literature to predict the effects of social networks on poison pill adoption.

Several aggregation studies have posited interactions between economic and behavioral variables on governance outcomes. Boeker (1992), for example, examined the interaction between firm performance and board power on CEO succession among semiconductor producers from 1968 to 1989; see also Cannella and Lubatkin (1993). Although Boeker's study moves beyond pure aggregation in its analysis, the theoretical arguments are not fully integrated. While stating that CEO succession is more likely in poor performing firms when boards are relatively powerful, for example, Boeker does not specify *how*, theoretically, economic factors amplify board power or vice versa. As is often the case in interdisciplinary research, while formal hypotheses and empirical tests are based on a multiplicative model that includes interactions between economic and behavioral factors, the theoretical arguments are primarily additive.

THEORETICAL INTEGRATION

SYMBOLIC MANAGEMENT AND INCENTIVE ALIGNMENT

One approach to theoretical integration of behavioral and economic perspectives adopted by intraorganizational economists draws on sociological perspectives to situate economic constructs or phenomena in a larger social context. In a series of studies, Zajac and Westphal have explored how corporate governance policies such as executive incentive plans can be viewed as symbolic phenomena. In one study, Westphal and Zajac (1994) examined *how* and *when* firms adopt formal executive incentive plans to symbolize commitment to shareholder interests, rather than to change the firm's substantive compensation arrangements. Their findings, based on data for a large sample of firms over a 20-year period (1972–90), showed that internal political factors and external institutional forces systematically predict the likelihood of such symbolic action. Firms with powerful CEOs were more likely to adopt, but not implement, long-term incentive plans that increase compensation risk for top executives, and the rate of such decoupling increased over time.

In a second study, Zajac and Westphal (1995) further developed their symbolic management perspective on corporate governance by examining the verbal explanations that firms provide for new executive incentive plans adopted by Fortune 500 companies from 1976 to 1990. They found that different justification logics were invoked by corporate leaders to explain similar incentive plans, and that institutional, political, and social psychological factors systematically predict the particular logic that firms use in explaining the plans to shareholders. Over time, the sample firms increasingly justified their new incentive plans by invoking an "agency" logic emphasizing the role of incentive plans as a *control mechanism* that aligned executive pay with shareholder interests. Earlier in the study period, however, such plans were more often justified by a "human resource" logic, describing incentives as a *reward mechanism* that helped to attract and retain scarce leadership talent. Over time, agency-based perspectives on corporate governance thus appear to have acquired symbolic value as an appropriate account for CEO compensation and related governance practices.

Zajac and Westphal (1995) also showed that firms with powerful CEOs were more likely to use a human resource explanation for incentive plans, while firms with powerful boards of directors were more likely to use an agency explanation. Thus, while agency theory implicitly assumes that incentives have a consistent, objective meaning to organizational participants, Zajac and Westphal's research indicates that the purpose of incentives is socially and politically constructed, and that the very meaning of incentives cannot be understood without reference to the social context.

Further extending this theme, Westphal and Zajac (1998) examined the consequences of symbolic management in corporate governance, finding that the symbolic adoption of CEO incentive plans generated positive stock market returns. Based on an event study of market reactions to CEO incentive plans adopted between 1982 and 1992, they found that the stock market reacted favorably to the adoption of such plans even when they were not actually implemented, and the reaction was more positive to the extent that firms offered legitimate explanations for them. These findings are particularly striking in reference to a large literature in financial economics on stock market reactions to executive incentive plans, which has interpreted positive market reactions to such plans (particularly long-term performance plans) as evidence for their economic efficiency. Westphal and Zajac's findings suggest, instead, that market reactions reflect prevailing assumptions, or socially constructed beliefs about the benefits of executive incentive plans, and that those assumptions could be further influenced by corporate communications about the plans.

In a study of CEO pay comparisons for S&P companies from 1992 to 1993, Porac et al. (1999) showed how powerful CEOs made pay comparisons to other top managers that served to justify higher levels of compensation. Given that these comparisons are displayed in proxy statements, they represent a kind of impression management by CEOs, providing further evidence that compensation contracts are not simply objective instruments of incentive alignment, but are subjective instruments of power.

These studies introduce a new, more social perspective on executive compensation to the corporate governance literature, by theorizing and demonstrating empirically how the use (or non-use) of an economic control mechanism (i.e., long-term incentives) is affected by the macro-social context. And, in doing so, introducing a new class of determinants of a core theoretical construct in agency theory. Indeed, the conclusion from this research for agency theory is not merely that economic perspectives on intraorganizational phenomena are incomplete, but that they are specified incorrectly, and risk providing inaccurate conclusions, unless social explanations are incorporated within the analysis.

DEMOGRAPHIC SIMILARITY AND INCENTIVE ALIGNMENT

In addition to situating economic constructs within a larger social context, another approach to theoretical integration involves examining micro-social factors shaping these constructs, or factors mediating their determinants and consequences. Adopting such an approach, Westphal and Zajac (1995) applied social psychological theories on demographic similarity and intergroup relations to explain how powerful CEOs perpetuate their control over economic outcomes (e.g., compensation amount and risk) by favoring the appointment of demographically similar outside directors. This approach complements agency and political models of executive compensation focused on economic and structural determinants of governance policies, by identifying the roles of social psychological factors in mediating the effects of power on decision making outcomes. Their sample for this study included Fortune 500 companies from 1986 to 1991. Westphal and Zajac show how the use of compensation contracts as an economic control mechanism is systematically biased by demographic similarity in CEO/board relationships, and how powerful CEOs reinforce this bias by selecting demographically similar director candidates.

Similarly, Belliveau et al. (1996), in a study of large companies listed in the 1985 *Business Week* survey of executive compensation, showed how CEO compensation contracts are influenced by the CEO's social capital or prestige, independently of firm performance. They suggest that social capital can be captured by indicating the number of board appointments and trusteeships held by the CEO, memberships in social clubs, and the prestige of educational institutions attended by the CEO.

SOCIAL INFLUENCE AND BOARD INDEPENDENCE

Westphal (1998) combined data from a survey of CEOs and outside directors at large Fortune/Forbes 500 companies in 1995, with archival data on board structure, CEO compensation and corporate strategy in order to examine further how micro-social processes in CEO/board relationships mediate the effects of board structure on decision making outcomes. As noted earlier, a central hypothesis in recent research on boards of directors – rooted in agency theory – is that structural board independence from management increases the board's tendency to control management decision making on behalf of shareholders. Westphal found that increases in structural board independence prompted CEOs to engage in interpersonal influence tactics such as ingratiation and persuasion that offset the effect of increased independence on corporate strategy and CEO compensation policy. The findings show how considering the role of micro-social processes that occur inside the "black box" of board behavior can fundamentally change our understanding of macro-level relationships posited by agency theorists in substantive and unexpected ways.

In a follow-up study using the same dataset, Westphal (1999) examined how a lack of structural board independence from management might also lead to unexpected benefits by encouraging cooperation between CEOs and outside directors in the strategic decision-making process. Whereas strict agency assumptions suggest that board independence should promote shareholder interests by enhancing the board's capacity to engage in independent control, by integrating micro-social perspectives on cooperation and politics into an analysis of board independence, Westphal arrived at a very different conclusion about the performance consequences of board structure.

SOCIAL EXCHANGE AND BOARD MONITORING

A more comprehensive form of integration in intraorganizational economics research involves incorporating *both* micro- and macro-social processes into an analysis of corporate control mechanisms. In one study in this genre, Westphal and Zajac (1997) drew on social exchange theory and research on norms of reciprocity to advance a multilevel theoretical explanation of how change in CEO/board relationships that involve greater board independence from management may have diffused through a network of interlocking directorates among Fortune/Forbes 500 companies from 1982 to 1992. Specific findings suggested that CEO-directors (i.e., directors who serve as CEO at another firm) were more likely to support CEO leadership at the focal firm, but that when such directors experienced greater board independence at their home firm they were more likely to "defect" from the network of mutually supportive CEOs by promoting greater board independence from management at the focal firm. Thus, boards of directors' propensity to engage in control were influenced by a social mechanism that involves both macro-social ties among firms (i.e., board interlock ties), and micro-social exchange relationships within firms. Change in social exchange relationships at other, tied-to firms leads to similar change at the focal firm, and these changes critically determine a board's propensity to engage in independent control over its management.

While the research reviewed on symbolic management suggests that economic incentives cannot be understood without considering the larger social context through which corporate leaders interpret them, Westphal and Zajac's (1997) study of social exchange and board monitoring suggests that another basic construct in information economics – performance monitoring – is ultimately given meaning by social relationships. The agency theory rationale for executive incentives is to control agency costs by aligning incentives with shareholder interests, and, similarly, the explicit rationale for increased board independence is to control agency costs by exercising objective oversight with respect to managerial behavior and decision making. The assumption underlying such controls is that managers, if left to their own devices, will pursue courses of action that threaten shareholder interests.

Westphal and Zajac's (1997) findings indicate that this agency explanation does not explain the exercise of these controls. When outside directors initiate greater board independence, do they make this change because they believe that top managers would otherwise pursue actions that benefit themselves at the expense of shareholders, as assumed by agency theorists? This seems unlikely given that a majority of outside directors are themselves top managers at other large companies, as well as qualitative evidence that top managers do not feel that independent board control is necessary or desirable (Lorsch and MacIver, 1989). Westphal and Zajac's research suggests instead that increased board control reflects changes in social exchange relationships, and that the agency explanation that such changes reflect the need to reduce agency costs resulting from interest misalignment serves primarily as a legitimate rationale for change, rather than as a change driver. Put more strongly, the agency explanation provides a superficial rationale for actions that have social causes.

STRATEGIC SIDE-EFFECTS OF BOARD MONITORING

In a second recent example of multilevel integration, Gulati and Westphal (1999) examined how board ties between firms affect the likelihood of alliance formation, depending on the content of relationships between CEOs and outside directors. This research combined survey data on CEO/board relationships at Fortune/Forbes 500 companies collected in 1995 (discussed above) with archival data on alliances between these companies from 1970 to 1996. This study is notable for its attempt to combine a quite comprehensive, social psychological perspective on trust in CEO/board relationships, together with a sociological perspective on the formation of interorganizational relationships, in order to explain more fully the consequences of an intraorganizational economic control mechanism (i.e., board control over management).

Drawing on ideas from intergroup relations theory about how the level of control and cooperation affects trust in relationships, they argued that cooperation between CEOs and directors in the strategic decision making process would provide a foundation for strategic cooperation between a focal firm and the home companies of directors on the board (i.e., companies where directors serve as top manager). Conversely, they argued that independent board control would decrease the likelihood of strategic cooperation between firms by reducing the level of trust between managers of different firms. Indirect network ties between firms, they predicted, would amplify these relationships; CEO/board relationships characterized by control rather than cooperation, for example, would have a stronger negative influence on alliance formation if CEO and directors were also linked by indirect ties. Supporting these hypotheses, Gulati and Westphal's findings clearly illustrate how micro-social relationships between managers and directors can affect interorganizational relationships. Their integrative perspective on governance shows how the independent board control advocated by agency theorists can have unintended side effects by reducing the level of trust in CEO/board relationships, which in turn may have important strategic consequences for firms.

Although few other studies have examined the effect of agency control mechanisms on strategic cooperation, there is evidence that independent board control does not necessarily improve the quality of strategic decision making or, ultimately, firm performance (Black, 1998). The reason, perhaps, is that economic analyses of control neglect the side effects that these control mechanisms may have on social relationships, which in turn affect the range of strategic options available to firms.

Contemporary Issues and Debates

THE AMBIGUITY OF CEO PERFORMANCE

An emerging debate in intraorganizational economics concerns the conceptualization and measurement of performance. The construct of incentive alignment is composed of two facets: performance, and a corresponding reward. Although a great deal of research has focused on different kinds of rewards for a given level of performance, until recently little research has considered different kinds of performance that might be rewarded.

Zajac and Westphal (2000) argue that despite an explosion of empirical research on executive compensation, the positive agency predictions regarding the power of organizational incentives for senior management have not been fully tested. Specifically, they argue that most economic and behavioral research neglects the fact that firms don't use the same performance criteria when assessing their CEOs, that more than one criterion is often used, and that the weights assigned to such criteria differ across firms. Zajac and Westphal (2000) suggest that, in fact, incentives may work well, insofar as affecting CEO behavior to maximize the indicator that firms have chosen, but that this may have negative consequences for other important indicators. They invoke goal setting theory to highlight the parallelism in the agency and behavioral science predictions regarding the unwieldy power of incentives and the tradeoffs inherent in the choice of fewer versus more performance indicators. Empirically, they use unique survey data and longitudinal archival data to demonstrate that firms do get what they reward, but at the expense of other performance criteria. This research calls attention to the limits of incentive alignment: where firms have multiple performance criteria that are not perfectly correlated, they face opportunity costs in rewarding a given criterion.

ISOLATIONISM AS AN IMPEDIMENT TO INTERDISCIPLINARY RESEARCH

This paper has focused on interdisciplinary research that involves integrating sociological and social psychological perspectives together with economic constructs to explain organizational phenomena. Other varieties of interdisciplinary research are possible, and have recently been pursed by organizational scholars. For instance, a simpler, but still useful form of integration involves weaving together closely related theories from different disciplines that lead to similar predictions about an outcome. As an example of this approach, Westphal and Seidel (2000) consider how different sources of social information could affect the attitudes of CEOs toward their boards by drawing eclectically from psychological research on social information processing, as well as research on framing in sociology and political science.

All three of these literatures offer compatible but subtly different perspectives on how social information affects attitudes and relationships, yet they have developed in almost complete isolation from one another. Studies that integrate compatible theories from different disciplines in this way can help answer Pfeffer's call (1994) for greater unification in organizational theories, while still enriching our theoretical understanding of economic constructs. In this way, it is possible to capture social complexity of behavioral perspectives without losing the parsimony and elegance of economic perspectives. Without such theoretical integration, the interdisciplinary approach advocated here runs the risk of fragmenting research on corporate governance and organizational control.

Is intraorganizational economics "economics"?

Although the theoretical perspectives developed in the corporate governance literature are complex, they are also clearly consistent across multiple studies that examine disparate governance phenomena. Such consistency is possible because a truly integrated multidisciplinary framework can be usefully applied to explain a wide range of organizational outcomes. Thus, in addition to making contributions to multiple literatures, another advantage of the interdisciplinary approach advocated in this study is that it offers more theoretical power, allowing researchers to maintain a more unified theoretical approach in explaining a variety of organizational phenomena.

It might appear that our approach to interdisciplinary research assigns a relatively small role to economic perspectives. However, economic theories – in this case information economics – essentially provide a point of departure and a focal point for our interdisciplinary approach. Central constructs of agency theory, including incentive alignment, performance monitoring and control, and (to a lesser extent) information asymmetry, figure prominently in our theoretical perspective. Information economics provides the skeleton, and sociological, socio-political, and social psychological theories provide the flesh of this perspective. However, in enriching economic constructs with behavioral perspectives, our approach changes the very meaning of the constructs. Incentive alignment becomes a vehicle of impression management. Performance monitoring becomes a reflection of social exchange relationships. And information asymmetry becomes an indicator in disparate knowledge and experience resulting from social network ties. Accordingly, the interdisciplinary approach advocated here can be considered "intraorganizational economics" that captures the social and political complexity of organizations, or it can be considered "organizational theory" that builds on key constructs from economic theories of organizational control. The label is perhaps less important than achieving a substantive theoretical integration.

Questions that Remain Unanswered

DIRECTOR EXPERIENCE AND INFORMATION ASYMMETRY

One issue in intraorganizational economics that has received little research attention is how the experience of principals (e.g., corporate directors) can affect information asymmetry in control relationships. In a recent study of social networks and corporate governance, Carpenter and Westphal (2001) examined the effect of director network ties to other firms on the ability of directors to monitor strategic decision making. It was hypothesized, and found empirically, that while the simple number of director ties to other boards has no effect on director involvement in monitoring activity, network ties that provide directors with relevant strategic knowledge and perspective do predict such involvement. This study developed a socio-cognitive perspective on the effects of board interlock ties on director monitoring activity, again integrating social psychological and sociological (i.e., social structural) perspectives to explain the effectiveness of the board as a corporate control mechanism.

Economic perspectives on control in organizational research provide only limited insight into variation in the capability of principals to exercise control over agents effectively. The notion of information asymmetry pertains to an inherent problem in any principal-agent relationship. In the context of board control over management, information asymmetry refers to the disparity in knowledge between directors and managers about what managers are actually doing (Jensen and Meckling, 1976). It does not address knowledge disparities that result from variation in experience with different strategic alternatives. The latter knowledge disparity would seem to be more critical than information asymmetry, as defined by agency theorists, in determining the effectiveness of boards in monitoring management.

Alternatively, one might suggest that the construct of information asymmetry is under-specified theoretically, just as our earlier research suggested that the constructs of incentive alignment and performance monitoring are under-specified. Again, this specification problem arises from failing to incorporate the larger social context. Part of the problem is that the social context can provide information and knowledge that may enhance the ability of principals to exercise control over agents. More importantly, however, our perspective recognizes that board control is not simply, or even primarily, about reducing agency costs. Instead, it involves providing additional input that may help to correct for the knowledge limitations or behavioral commitments of top managers, and director experience on other boards can enhance the effectiveness of boards in correcting for these managerial limitations.

MONITORING WHEN THE PRINCIPAL IS A GROUP

Another limitation of information economics perspective on performance monitoring is that it typically assumes that monitoring is exercised by an individual, and thus does not consider the process losses (or gains) that could occur when monitoring is exercised by groups. Thus, applications of agency theory to corporate boards tend to assume that the board is a unitary actor. This provides a variety of research opportunities for organizational scholars to integrate theory and research on small group processes into economic perspectives on control. Westphal and Milton (2000), for instance, examine variation in the influence of individual directors over board decision making. In particular, they consider how the influence of demographic minorities on boards is contingent on their prior experience in a minority vs. majority role on other boards, as well as their social network ties to majority directors through common board memberships. Where minority status indicates that directors have unique knowledge or perspective to contribute to the decision-making process (e.g., as would be the case if the director has a marketing background, while all other directors have a finance background), a simple revision of the agency perspective would suggest that minority status should enhance the director's contribution to the decision-making process (i.e., involvement should be commensurate with the director's potential contribution). At the same time, social psychological perspectives on minority influence and intergroup relations would suggest that the involvement of such directors can be limited by out-group biases directed at the minority. Westphal and Milton (2000) showed, however, that demographic minorities could avoid out-group biases that would otherwise minimize their influence when they have prior experience on other boards or network ties to other directors that enable them to create the perception of similarity with the majority. For instance, minority directors who have relatively extensive prior experience in a minority role on other boards (on the same or different characteristics), or common appointments on other boards with majority directors, tend to be more influential than majority directors in the decision-making process.

This study incorporates micro-social and macro-social complexity into an economic analysis of corporate control. An individual director's ability to contribute to corporate control is not strictly determined by their knowledge base, but also by the learned ability to communicate that knowledge (i.e., by virtue of their prior experience in a minority role), and social network ties that ameliorate the biases of others. This theoretical analysis explains an individual's involvement in corporate control by developing a theoretical framework that integrates inter-group relations theory (at a micro-social level) and perspectives on social embeddedness (at a macro-social level) to explain monitoring in corporate control (Granovetter, 1985; Turner, 1987). While an agency perspective on control tends to assume that the principal is a unitary actor, a behavioral perspective that accounts for micro-social and macro-social complexity can explain why a group principal may be more or less effective than an individual.

POWER, EXPERIENCE, AND AGENCY COSTS

While we have discussed the potential to use behavioral perspectives to shed new light on specific constructs from agency theory, such as incentive alignment and monitoring, there are also opportunities to conduct further research that develops an interdisciplinary perspective on agency costs, broadly conceived.

In an extension of our earlier work on institutional decoupling, for instance, Westphal and Zajac (2001) examine how another corporate governance policy that has typically been examined from a strict economics perspective – stock repurchase plans – can also be explained by an interdisciplinary approach that incorporates macro-social perspectives. Past research in financial economics had viewed stock repurchase plans from an agency perspective: when firms adopt these plans, they return free cash flow to investors rather than allowing management to waste cash on empire building projects that benefit managers more than shareholders. Since repurchase plans reduce agency costs in this way, they should be favorably received in the stock market. And in fact, many studies have shown that in recent years, the market reacts favorably to stock repurchase plans. Our findings suggested, however, that many firms formally adopted repurchase plans without subsequently implementing the plans. In seeking to explain such decoupling, Westphal and Zajac (2001) developed a theoretical framework that integrated micro-political factors with experiential factors. In particular, we suggested that powerful CEOs had an interest in avoiding implementation of repurchase plans, to preserve their discretion over the allocation of free cash flow, while independent boards had an interest in implementing the plans to control agency costs on behalf of shareholders. Thus, CEO power over the board should predict the likelihood of decoupling repurchase plans. At the same time, this effect should be amplified when firms have experience with decoupling, either through board network ties to other firms that have engaged in decoupling, or through prior experience with decoupling at the focal firm. These hypotheses were supported, showing again how an economic construct (free cash flow, as an indicator of agency costs), is affected by a combination of micro-social factors (i.e., political dynamics in the CEO/board relationship) and macro-social factors (board network ties to other decoupling firms).

Promising Directions for Future Research

HOW DID AGENCY THEORY EMERGE AS A DOMINANT IDEOLOGY?

One unanswered question in intraorganizational economics has to do with the rise in the popularity and influence of the agency perspective (particularly the positive agency literature). While the theory is typically seen as time-invariant and addressing fundamental and enduring problems related to the delegating and contracting of work, it is not obvious that the significant growth of the theory can be explained primarily in terms of its theoretical power or compelling internal logic. Rather, research could begin to examine more closely the important historical factors also that can help to explain why agency theory became so popular in the USA starting in the 1980s. Such research would likely point to growing dissatisfaction with the economic performance of large US corporations in the prior decade of the 1970s, and the criticisms of corporate managers that accompanied this dissatisfaction (Hayes and Abernathy, 1980). US corporations were at that time perceived as having become globally uncompetitive, particularly when compared with Japanese firms, and the accused culprits were top US managers, who were seen as having grown their firms excessively in terms of scale and scope. This historical setting provided fertile ground for the rise of a theoretical orientation that viewed top managers less as providing the solutions to poor organizational performance, and more as being a significant part of the problem. Future research that documents the micro-mechanisms behind the explosion in agency theory during this time would be valuable in also identifying the historical conditions under which agency theory might find a less favorable reception.

Zajac and Westphal (2001) address this in their study of the consequences of the rise of agency theory as an ideology. Drawing from both sociological perspectives on institutionalization and economic perspectives on learning, they suggest that financial markets' conceptualization of particular corporate governance practices (e.g., stock buybacks), is less a function of the inherent efficiency or inefficiency of such practices, and more a function of the dominance of a particular ideology (e.g., agency theory) and the institutionalization of the practice through cumulative adoption. They first propose that an ideological shift toward an agency perspective on corporate governance led the market to reverse its interpretation of stock buybacks in the USA from the late 1970s to the mid-1990s. They argue further that the emergence of such a dominant ideology also increases the incidence of institutional decoupling over time (i.e., whereby firms announce stock buybacks but do not implement them), but that contrary to market learning arguments, institutionalization processes limit the extent to which markets are sensitive to observable instances of decoupling. Based on their supportive findings using extensive longitudinal data on announced stock buybacks over a fifteen-year time span, they conclude that markets can be "taught" by active attempts to establish a dominant ideology that will influence collective perceptions, but that such efforts may paradoxically limit a market's opportunity for subsequent learning.

In fact, in addition to examining the periodicity of agency theory's influence, one could also examine the degree to which it is accepted in alternative contemporaneous contexts, e.g., across cultures. In one such study, Zajac and Fiss (2000) present evidence suggesting that the transfer of agency theory ideas into the corporate governance practices of firms in other modern economies, such as Germany, will likely need to be modified in both substantive and symbolic ways to deal with deeply rooted cultural differences. Specifically, they show that shareholder value maximization, as emphasized by agency theory, is far from universally accepted indicator of corporate performance, and that large German corporations, after initially embracing shareholder value maximization as a concept, have recently created new hybrid concepts that are more consonant with German cultural values.

WHAT'S EFFICIENT ABOUT POWER (AND VICE VERSA)?

Another arena for future research contributions in intraorganizational economics involves examining more deeply the relationship between power and efficiency in agency theory. Agency theorists typically conceptualize their research as promoting the efficiency features of the voluntary contractual relationship between principal and agent. In this way, the concept of power is not at all central to agency theory, yet the theory is often used to describe and analyze superior/subordinate relationships within organizations. Clearly, subordinates are not only contractual partners with their organizational superiors for the execution of some work-related tasks, but also social exchange partners in a power/dependence relationship. Research that would examine how principal–agent relationships differ – either descriptively or normatively – when embedded in different power/dependence situations could help to contextualize the contractual solutions that agency theory can offer.

In addition, agency theory could begin to consider how alternatives in contract design, such as incentives vs. monitoring, may have implications not only for the efficiency of the contract, but also the extent to which power differences exist in the relationship. For example, the use of monitoring can create a contracting context that places a greater perceived emphasis on power and control, whereby the use of incentives may be perceived as promoting greater agent autonomy and discretion in the execution of a delegated task.

The connection between power and efficiency can and should be more carefully explored in other economics-based theories that could be considered intraorganizational. For example, we intentionally did not address Williamson's (1975) transaction costs perspective, since Silverman (this volume) devotes significant attention to it elsewhere in this volume. However, we believe researchers should more explicitly recognize that Williamson's discussion of the advantage of "fiat" in locating transactions inside organizations is essentially about the efficient use of power in organizations. In other words, while power and efficiency are often unfortunately viewed as competing explanations, intraorganizational economics research can easily discuss more seriously the efficiency implications of power relationships in organizations, and the power implications of an efficiency orientation in organizations.

Connections Across Levels

Given the extensive body of research on corporate governance, it is surprising to note how few studies have considered multilevel relationships in developing economic perspectives on corporate governance. One approach might be to link levels using a single theoretical perspective, e.g., economics. We suggest, however, that such a narrow theoretical approach is unlikely to be successful, as economists have themselves begun to realize. As Gibbons (1998) states in a recent essay, work in economics on incentives has been extremely narrow in focus. He suggests that ignoring the political, sociological, and social psychological realities of organizations could led economists to propose models of incentives that are incomplete at best, and dangerous at worst. Holmstrom and Roberts (1998) reach a similar conclusion in their critique of transaction cost and property rights analyses of what activities should be located within organizations.

Thus, we suggest that a more fruitful approach to developing a multilevel perspective on organizations involves integrating theory and research on micro-social processes in the firm with firm- and inter-firm-level economic constructs. This approach is consistent with van Witteloostuijn's (this volume) view that organizational economics would be enriched by meaningfully integrating the behavioral complexity that has been observed in organizational research with economic models of inter-firm relationships. We suggest, however, that such research should go beyond adjusting the assumptions of economic models to accommodate greater behavioral complexity, such as nonprofit-maximizing behavior. While this is an important and useful beginning, we propose that researchers also begin to examine the actual relationships between behavioral constructs and economic constructs.

For instance, in the context of interfirm relationships, as Silverman (this volume) proposes, researchers might examine how social network ties between managers of collaborating firms affect alliance performance by raising or lowering transaction costs in the relationship (Gulati and Westphal, 1999). Similarly, researchers might explore how network ties and other behavioral processes that enhance social control in relationships substitute for mutual economic incentives in reducing opportunism in interfirm relationships (Zajac and Olsen, 1993). As van Witteloostuijn (this volume) suggests, however, examining such research questions will require economists to incorporate new, field-based research methods, including the more sophisticated approaches to measurement generally used in the organizational sciences, as well as incorporating behavioral theories into their models. Conversely, organizational researchers with an interest in multilevel research must learn to integrate the use of econometric analyses of archival data with field-based and survey methods.

Conclusion

In this chapter, we have argued that the future progress of intraorganizational economics, and agency theory in particular, may depend on developing theoretical perspectives that incorporate social processes into economic constructs. Such primary constructs as incentive alignment, monitoring and risk can be enriched and in some ways reinterpreted by examining their relationship to such behavioral constructs as social influence processes, political processes, institutional processes, and social networks. To extend Pfeffer's (1994) proposition regarding the benefits of a unified organizational theory, a meaningful integration of economics with sociological and psychological theories of organizational behavior would enhance the unity of the social sciences, thereby enhancing its impact on the larger community.

References

Allison, G. T. (1971): *Essence of Decision: Explaining the Cuban Missile Crisis*. Boston: Little, Brown & Co.

Beatty, R. P., and Zajac, E. J. (1994): "Managerial incentives, monitoring, and risk-bearing: A study of executive compensation, ownership, and board structure in initial public offerings," *Administrative Science Quarterly*, 39, 313–35.

Belliveau, M. A., O Reilly, C. A. III, and Wade, J. B. (1996): "Social capital at the top: Effects of social similarity and status on CEO compensation," *Academy of Management Journal*, 39, 1568–93.

Berle, A., and Means, G.C. (1932): *The Modern Corporation and Private Property*. New York: Macmillan.

Black, B. S. (1998): "Shareholder activism and corporate governance in the United States," in P. Newman (ed.), *The New Palgrave Dictionary of Economics and the Law*, New York: Groves Dictionaries.

Boeker, W. (1992): "Power and managerial dismissal: Scapegoating at the top," *Administrative Science Quarterly*, 37, 400–21.

Cannella, A. A. Jr., and Lubatkin, M. (1993): "Succession as a sociopolitical process: Internal impediments to outsider selection," *Academy of Management Journal*, 36, 763–93.

Carpenter, M., and Westphal, J.D. (2001): "The strategic context of social network ties: Examining the impact of director appointments on board involvement in strategic decision making," *Academy of Management Journal*, (forthcoming).

Cyert, R. M., and March, J. G. (1963): *A Behavioral Theory of the Firm*. Englewood Cliffs, NJ: Prentice-Hall.

Dalton, D. R., and Kesner, I. F. (1985): "Organizational performance as an antecedent of inside/outside chief executive succession: An empirical assessment," *Academy of Management Journal*, 28, 749–62.

Davis, G. F. (1991): "Agents without principles? The spread of the poison pill through the intercorporate network," *Administrative Science Quarterly*, 36, 583–613.

Eisenhardt, K. M. (1989): "Agency theory: An assessment and review," *Academy of Management Review*, 14, 57–74.

Fama, E. F., and Jensen, M. C. (1983): "The separation of ownership and control," *Journal of Law and Economics*, 26, 301–25.

Gibbons, R. (1998): "Incentives in organizations," *Journal of Economic Perspectives*, 12, 115–32.

Granovetter, M. (1985): "Economic action and social structure: A theory of embeddedness," *American Journal of Sociology*, 91, 481–510.

Gulati, R. and Westphal, J. D. (1999): "The dark side of embeddedness: An examination of the influence of board interlocks, CEO/board relationships, and third-party ties for interfirm alliances," *Administrative Science Quarterly*, 44, 473–506.

Hayes, R. H., and Abernathy, W. J. (1980): "Managing our way to economic decline," *Harvard Business Review*, 58, 67–77.

Holmstrom, B., and Roberts, J. (1998): "The boundaries of the firm revisited," *Journal of Economic Perspectives*, 12, 73-94.

Jensen, M. C., and Meckling, W. H. (1976): Theory of the firm: Managerial behavior, agency costs, and ownership structure," *Journal of Financial Economics*, 3, 305–50.

Jensen, M. C., and Murphy, K. J. (1990): "Performance pay and top-management incentives," *Journal of Political Economy*, 98, 225–63.

Journal of Applied Corporate Finance (1992): "Stern Stewart roundtable on management incentive compensation and shareholder value," 5, 110–30.

Kosnik, R. D. (1990): "Effects of board demography and directors' incentives on corporate greenmail decisions," *Academy of Management Journal*, 33, 129–50.

Lorsch, J. W., and MacIver, E. (1989): *Pawns or Potentates: The Reality of America's Corporate Boards*. Boston: Harvard Business School Press.

Marris, R. L. (1964): *The Economic Theory of Managerial Capitalism*. London: Macmillan.

Milgrom, P., and Roberts, J. (1992): *Economics, Organization and Management*. Englewood Cliffs, NJ: Prentice-Hall.

Mintzberg, H. (1983): *Power In and Around Organizations*. Englewood Cliffs, NJ: Prentice-Hall.

Pfeffer, J. (1981): *Power in Organizations*. Cambridge: Harper and Row.

Pfeffer, J. (1994): "Barriers to the advance of organizational science: paradigm development as a dependent variable," *Academy of Management Review*, 18, 599–620.

Porac, J. F., Wade, J. B., and Pollock, T. G. (1999): "Industry categories and the politics of the comparable firm in CEO compensation," *Administrative Science Quarterly*, 44, 112–44.

Ross, S. (1973): "The economic theory of agency: The principal's problem," *American Economic Review*, 63, 134–39.

Turner, J. C. 1987: *Rediscovering the Social Group: A Self-Categorization Theory*. Oxford: Blackwell.

Westphal, J. D. (1998): "Board games: How CEOs adapt to increases in structural board independence from management," *Administrative Science Quarterly*, 43, 511–37.

Westphal, J. D. (1999): "Collaboration in the boardroom: The consequences of social ties in the CEO/board relationship," *Academy of Management Journal*, 42, 7–24.

Westphal, J. D., and Milton, L. (2000): "Avoiding social barriers: How experience and social network ties affect the influence of demographic minorities on corporate boards," *Administrative Science Quarterly*, 45, 366–98.

Westphal, J. D., and Seidel, M-D. (2000): "How do social network surveys affect social network ties?" working paper, University of Texas at Austin.

Westphal, J. D., and Zajac, E. J. (1994): "Substance and symbolism in CEOs' long-term incentive plans," *Administrative Science Quarterly*, 39, 367–90.

Westphal, J. D., and Zajac, E. J. (1995): "Who shall govern? CEO/board power, demographic Similarity, and New Director Selection", *Administrative Science Quarterly*, 40, 60–83.

Westphal, J. D., and Zajac, E. J. (1997): "Defections from the Inner Circle: Social Exchange, reciprocity, and the diffusion of board independence in U.S. corporations," *Administrative Science Quarterly*, 42, 161–83.

Westphal, J. D., and Zajac, E. J. (1998): "The symbolic management of stockholders: Corporate governance reforms and shareholder reactions," *Administrative Science Quarterly*, 43, 127–53.

Westphal, J. D., and Zajac, E. J. (2001): "Explaining institutional decoupling: The case of stock repurchase programs," *Administrative Science Quarterly*, (forthcoming).

Williamson, O. E. (1964): *The Economics of Discretionary Behavior: Managerial Objectives in a Theory of the Firm*. Englewood Cliffs, NJ: Prentice-Hall.

Williamson, O. E. 1975: *Markets and Hierarchies: Analysis and Antitrust Implications*. New York: Free Press.

Zajac, E. J., and Bazerman, M. H. (1991): "Blind spots in industry and competitor analysis: The implications of interfirm (mis)perceptions for strategic decisions," *Academy of Management Review*, 16, 37–56.

Zajac, E. J., and Fiss, P. (2000): "Corporate governance and contested terrain: The rise of the shareholder value orientation in Germany," working paper, Northwestern University

Zajac, E. J., and Olsen, C. P. (1993): "From transaction costs to transactional value analysis: Implications for the study of interorganizational strategies," *Journal of Management Studies*, 30, 131–45.

Zajac, E. J., and Westphal, J. D. (1994): "The costs and benefits of managerial incentives and monitoring in the largest U.S. corporations: When is more not better?" *Strategic Management Journal*, 15, 121–42.

Zajac, E. J., and Westphal, J. D. (1995): "Accounting for the explanations of CEO compensation: Substance and symbolism," *Administrative Science Quarterly*, 40, 283–308.

Zajac, E. J., and Westphal, J. D. (1996): "Who shall rule after a CEO succession? Predicting the likelihood and direction of changes in CEO characteristics," *Academy of Management Journal*, 39, 64–90.

Zajac, E. J., and Westphal, J. D. (2000): "Do firms get what they pay for? How alternative performance criteria affect the CEO pay-for-performance relationship," working paper, Northwestern University.

Zajac, E. J. and Westphal, J. D. (2001): "Do markets learn? The institutionalization of stock buybacks," working paper, Northwestern University.

11 Organizational Institutions   259
    Donald A. Palmer and Nicole Woolsey Biggart

12 Organizational Networks   281
    Ranjay Gulati, Dania A. Dialdin, and Lihua Wang

13 Organizational Ecology   304
    Joel A. C. Baum and Terry L. Amburgey

14 Organizational Evolution   327
    Terry L. Amburgey and Jitendra V. Singh

15 Organizational Cognition and Interpretation   344
    Theresa K. Lant

16 Organizational Power and Dependence   363
    William Ocasio

17 Organizational Technology   386
    Michael L. Tushman and Wendy Smith

18 Organizational Learning   415
    Martin Schulz

19 Organizational Complexity and Computation   442
    Kathleen M. Eisenhardt and Mahesh M. Bhatia

20 Organizational Economics   467
    Brian S. Silverman

Chapter Eleven

Organizational Institutions

DONALD A. PALMER AND
NICOLE WOOLSEY BIGGART

In this chapter, we examine research on the institutional environment of organizations – the regulative, normative, and cognitive structures that are the sources of order shaping behavior in firms and other types of organizations. The institutional environment is the meaning system in which organizations reside.

ORGANIZATIONS IN INSTITUTIONAL ENVIRONMENTS

In the institutional approach, organizational environments are conceptualized as "fields" within which interacting organizations are constrained by regulative, normative, and cognitive structures. Organizational fields also consist of organizational forms that are consistent with, and thus legitimated by, the broader system of constraints. Regulative structures are rules regarding permitted behavior, including laws and law-like procedures. Normative structures are expectations about acceptable behavior, and cognitive structures are theories-in-use that stipulate the way to achieve efficient and effective behavior (which may or may not in fact be efficient or effective). The hallmark of the old institutionalism in organizational analysis, largely work done until the 1980s, was its attention to regulative and normative structures. The hallmark of the new institutionalism is its attention to cognitive structures (Scott, 1995).

Institutionalized forms proliferate and are adopted by organizations through three mechanisms. They may spread through coercive pressures, in which organizations comply with powerful actors' requirements to avoid punishments. They may proliferate through normative processes, in which organizations conform to other actors' expectations to obtain their approval. Finally, forms may proliferate through mimetic processes, in which organizations mimic practices assumed to be successful (DiMaggio and Powell, 1983). Regulative structures are associated in the literature with coercive pressures, normative structures with normative pressures, and cognitive structures associated with mimetic processes. In practice, though, a one-to-one correspondence between types of institutional structures and mechanisms of diffusion does not exist.

Early in the development of the new institutional perspective, scholars characterized organizational environments as varying in the extent to which they are subject to institutional forces. At one extreme were technical environments, in which organizations were evaluated on the basis of the efficiency and effectiveness of their processes, as judged by the cost and quality of their outputs. For-profit organizations operating in highly competitive markets fell into this category. At the other extreme were institutional environments, in which organizations were evaluated on the basis of the legitimacy of their processes, as judged by the conformity of their structures to accepted criteria. Not-for-profit organizations operating in non-market contexts fell into this category. Thus, Meyer and Rowan (1977) used educational organizations to illustrate the operation of institutional processes in their foundational statement of the new institutional perspective.

This approach has been progressively abandoned; perhaps because it limits the scope of institutional theory to organizations in non-market environments or to those in which there are clearly identified legitimated forms and performance measures. Orrú, Biggart and Hamilton (1997) argue, too, that conceptualizing environments as being composed of separate technical and institutional environments may be a false dichotomy based on dualistic Western assumptions. They argue that in the case of Japanese business groups at least "It is not despite their institutional isomorphism that Japanese enterprise groups are economically fit, but because of the incorporation of institutional elements in their organizations that they [were] so successful" (1997, p. 376).

Literature Review

Research on the institutional environments of organizations has largely focused on three questions: Where do institutional constraints *come from?* What *effects* do institutional structures have on organizations? How does *change* in institutional environments come about and diffuse? Table 11.1 offers an overview of key works addressing these issues.

WHERE DO INSTITUTIONAL CONSTRAINTS COME FROM?

Supra-organizational forms, of which the state and its agencies are penultimate, are generally assumed to be the principal originators and carriers of institutional structures, particularly regulative structures. The laws of the state and the administrative routines of its agencies define constraints, such as laws of incorporation, within which organizational actions are constructed (North, 1981). The state also creates normative structures as government agencies develop ways of organizing that serve as models for other organizations (Baron et al., 1986). Other supra-organizations, which are sometimes legitimated by or even connected to the state, such as industry associations, can provide state-like functions for organizations in specialized domains. These supra-organizations, though, differ from the state in their inability to call upon the legitimate use of force to obtain compliance (Ingram and Simmons, 2000). These supra-organizations embody institutional structures that are predominately normative in character.

Table 11.1 Selected research on organizational institutions

Reference	Key concepts	Key variables	Key predictions and findings	Key contribution	Method
Selznick, [1949] 1966	Goal drift, cooptation	Interorganizational dependence	Institutional structures in which organizations are embedded determine the goals that organizations can legitimately pursue.	Analyzes how institutional structures influence organizational goals	Historical case study
Stinchcombe, 1965	Structural inertia, founding conditions	Density of inter-organizational linkages in which organization is embedded	Institutional structures characterizing organizational fields determine the character of organizations that enter the field subsequently.	Analyzes how institutional structures influence organizational form at birth	Historical case study
Meyer and Rowan, 1977	Loose coupling	Persistence	Organizational and interorganizational structures tend to take on a life of their own, valued for themselves rather than for the outcomes to which they lead.	Outlines the institutional framework for organizational analysis	Theory construction
DiMaggio and Powell, 1983	Isomorphism	Coercive, regulative, and normative processes	Organizations in a field will tend to adopt the same forms and practices in response to institutional pressures.	Differentiates three institutional change processes	Theory construction
Dobbin et al., 1988	Evolution of institutional practice	Organizational charter (public/private) and presence of personnel departments and labor lawyers	State policy establishes norms and professions develop cognitive frameworks that give rise to new institutional elements.	Analyzes where institutional constraints/elements come from	Quantitative empirical

Reference	Key concepts	Key variables	Key predictions and findings	Key contribution	Method
Fligstein, 1990	Conceptions of control	Functional background of top managers and prevalence of new forms in organizational field	Normative and mimetic pressures influence the diffusion of new innovations.	Analyzes how institutional structures influence organizational change after birth	Historical and quantitative empirical
Palmer et al., 1993	Mimetic, normative, and coercive pressures	Competitor and interlock partner form. CEO functional and educational background, and bank ownership	Mimetic, normative, and coercive pressures shape the diffusion of innovations, although sometimes in unexpected ways.	Simultaneously considers multiple dimensions of all three of the proposed mechanisms through which organizations become isomorphic	Quantitative empirical
Hannan et al., 1995	Density dependent selection	Number of other similar organizations that are alive at the time	Density dependence increases birth and survival rates at low levels but decreases birth and survival rates at high level.	Analyzes how institutional structures influence birth rates of organizations with different forms	Quantitative empirical
Ingram and Simmons, 2000	Transaction	State formation	State formation establishes institutional structures that make organizational forms possible.	Analyzes how institutional structures influence organizational survival	Quantitative empirical
Biggart and Guillén, 1999	Historical origins of institutional structures	Organization of elites, ideology, social structures	Economic development path shaped by institutions.	Development strategy should take account of institutional structure of society	Comparative-historical case comparison

Professions sometimes emerge with the development of supra-organizations and serve as independent sources of institutional material. The professions define normative and cognitive structures such as standards of practice, interpretive frames, and exclusionary jargon. Professional schools, such as graduate schools of business, socialize students to embrace norms, values, and beliefs conducive to their performance of professional roles (Schein, 1961). They also develop and disseminate ways of conceptualizing problems and solutions (Espeland and Hirsch, 1990). Hirsch (1986) examined changes in discourse that characterized the hostile takeover of corporations. He showed how business professionals changed their interpretations of takeover events, over time justifying and reframing positively unfriendly acquisitions of other firms. DiMaggio (1991), in an archival analysis, shows how the professionalization of museum officials at the beginning of the twentieth century reinterpreted the role of museums from that of collection and conservation by connoisseurs, to exhibition and interpretation for the general public. Professionals, allied with foundation officials, created new normative and cognitive structures that continue to shape the structure and functioning of museums.

Dobbin, Edelman, Sutton, and associates (Dobbin et al., 1988; Edelman, 1990; Dobbin et al., 1993; Sutton et al., 1994) show how different carriers of institutions together produced related regulative, normative, and cognitive structures that led to the legalization of the workplace. According to their analyses, state mandates created regulative structures that defined certain policies and outcomes as discriminatory and thus illegal. However, because these mandates did not prescribe specific non-discriminatory policies, the state created generalized normative pressures to create legal guarantees in the workplace and developed models of employee governance that organizations might emulate. Pressures were interpreted and specific models observed by members of the developing personnel profession. The interpretation entailed the development of new cognitive elements, such as new conceptions of the individual as having equal rights (in keeping with broader societal developments) and new conceptions of efficiency. Personnel professionals proselytized their cognitive framework and championed specific practices.

Economic and political innovations also originate and carry institutional structures. Meyer and Rowan (1977), in a restatement of Weber's Iron Cage, maintain that bureaucratic forms emerge as efficient technical solutions to organizational problems. However, once in place, they come to take on a life of their own and proliferate regardless of their efficiency. Tolbert and Zucker (1983) have formalized this argument further. They characterize the process of institutionalization as a three-stage process. In the first stage, actors experiment with solutions to problems of adaptation to the internal or external environment. In the second stage, superior solutions proliferate as other actors learn, albeit imperfectly as the result of limited search, of their technical attributes. In the third stage, widely diffused solutions acquire legitimacy and are taken for granted as the most appropriate way to conduct organizational behavior, regardless of their potentially eroding technical merit. In fact, it is the increasingly non-rational basis of a structure's durability that testifies to its institutionalization. Institutional structures persist because they are valued as things in themselves, rather than for their economic or political utility. This is the pattern suggested by research on the spread of the city manager form of government in the USA (Tolbert and Zucker, 1983).

What effects do institutional structures have on organizations?

FORM AT BIRTH

Institutional structures shape the kinds of administrative forms organizations establish when founded. According to the institutional perspective, organizations are assembled from available institutionalized forms and within existing institutional constraints. Therefore, they are not entirely "new," but constituted from existing institutional patterns and conceivable ways of being in a state of organization. Typically, there is a range of institutionalized forms available to choose from, and institutional constraints are often somewhat loose, so new organizations entering a population of like organizations, for example schools or hospitals, often exhibit considerable structural and behavioral variation.

Concern about efficiency and effectiveness though, cause organizations to progressively adopt similar forms, either through incremental change (adaptation) or because some forms fail (are "selected out"). Uncertainty about the characteristics of alternative forms generates a social comparison process with other like organizations, and eventually there is convergence around a dominant form, a "safe bet," in a process called isomorphism. Further, structural inertia, difficulty in changing already existing forms, leads organizations to retain their initial forms as they age. Finally, uncertainty about the efficiency and effectiveness of possible alternatives, as well as the promise of legitimacy that conformity brings, leads newer organizations to employ forms already in use. As a result, organizations tend to reflect the institutional structure of the time in which their field was established, regardless of when they were founded.

For example, when the construction industry was forming, informal labor contracting was the primary form of employment contract. This was the most efficient form of organizing for the construction industry at the time. However, years later, construction firms continued to employ labor contracting. This is because this form of selecting workers was assumed to be appropriate in the industry and was thus viewed as legitimate (Stinchcombe, 1965). Similarly, when the organizers of the TVA began to implement their programs, they incorporated elements of the existing institutional environment. Specifically, they employed University Extension agents and their networks to educate and organize farmers to facilitate the implementation of programs. The cognitive orientation of these professionals came to define the grassroots philosophy (Selznick, 1966).

BIRTH RATES OF ORGANIZATIONS EMPLOYING DIFFERENT FORMS

If the institutional environment determines the form organizations take at birth, then it follows that the institutional environment influences the birth rates of organizations employing different forms. A growing number of scholars examine birthrates from an institutional perspective, appropriating a dependent variable popularized by population ecologists. Several studies examine the impact the state has on the birth rates of organizations of different kinds. For example, Dobbin and Dowd (1997) demonstrate that state policies that regulated the availability of capital and determined the legality of cartels shaped the structure of competition and thus the rate at which railroads were formed in Massachusetts in the late nineteenth and early twentieth century. During periods when the state provided capital for the creation of new railroads and the preservation of existing railroads, and during periods when cartels were encouraged and competition mitigated, railroad founding rates increased. However, during periods when cartels were discouraged and thus competition was great, founding rates declined.

A raft of studies focusing on a wide variety of organizations (including restaurants, newspapers, labor unions, semi-conductor producers, and automobile manufacturers) examines the relationship between the prevalence of organizations of a specific type and the birth rate of organizations of that type. This "density dependence" research shows that as the number of organizations of a particular type grows, the rate at which organizations of this type are born increases. Researchers reason that the number of pre-existing organizations of a particular type is an indicator of the extent to which organizations of that type are institutionalized – in particular, the extent to which the form they employ is cognitively legitimate. The more legitimate a form is, the more likely organizations employing that form will be born. When there are many organizations of a particular type in a field, though, increasing density leads birthrates to decline. Researchers presume that large numbers of similar organizations generate competitive pressures and discourage the founding of new organizations in their field (Carroll and Hannan, 1989a; Hannan and Carroll, 1992). Recent research has more precisely specified the relationship between organizational density and birth rates. It indicates that institutional processes, captured by the initial stimulating effect of increasing organizational density on birth rates, operate at higher levels of analysis (e.g., international as opposed to the national level) than competitive processes, captured by the later depressing effect of density (Hannan et al., 1995).

ORGANIZATIONAL SURVIVAL

If the institutional environment influences organizational birth rates, then it follows that this environment also influences organizational mortality rates. Ingram and Simons (2000) examine the impact of state structures on organizational life chances. They show that the formation of the Israeli state both reduced the mortality rate of worker cooperatives in Israel and depressed the stimulating effect that affiliation with the Israeli labor party (the Histadrut) had on cooperative survival chances. The vast majority of research on the impact of institutional structures on organization life chances, though, focuses on the impact that the increasing numbers of organizations of a particular type has on the survival chances of organizations of that type. This research has produced findings that mimic the findings on organizational birth rates. It indicates that organizational life chances increase as organizational density increases – presumably because increasing density is associated with (as cause or consequence of) increasing cognitive legitimacy. However, at high-density levels, survival rates decline – presumably because increasing density is associated with increasing competitive pressures (Carroll and Hannan, 1989a).

GOAL DRIFT

The earliest practitioners of the institutional approach identified a potential trade-off to the increased legitimacy and life chances produced by incorporating institutionalized elements. In a process dubbed "goal drift," organizations modify their goals in order to obtain legitimacy associated with the incorporation of institutionalized elements. For example, in order to acquire needed legitimacy from Congress, the TVA brought rich landowners into their leadership structure. This led to abandonment of the grassroots approach in general and plans for cooperative fertilizer production more specifically (Selznick, [1949] 1966).

At some point, the desire to ensure the survival of their organizations can cause leaders to abandon their goals altogether. Because institutional structures often have a normative dimension, organizations that adopt institutionalized structures become expressions of social values. These social values may override the instrumental goals that motivated an organization's formation. Organizations themselves become institutions whose survival is warranted on the basis of their structure and process, rather than on the basis of their outputs. Hence, Gusfield (1955) showed that the Women's' Christian Temperance Movement shifted from cause to cause as its successive objectives were achieved.

HOW DOES CHANGE IN INSTITUTIONAL ENVIRONMENTS COME ABOUT AND DIFFUSE?

Perhaps the largest body of new institutional scholarship focuses on the diffusion of institutionalized elements to organizations after birth. This scholarship examines a large variety of organizational structures, strategies, and behaviors. Among large corporations alone, it considers adoption of the multidivisional form, the pursuit of diversifying acquisitions, the pricing of acquisition targets, the announcement and implementation of stock repurchase programs, and the replacement of top managers. According to the literature three agents are responsible for much institutional change.

The state is a critical source of institutional change. It establishes regulative structures that create opportunities and constraints for organizational action. For example, Dobbin and Dowd (2000) demonstrate that changes in antitrust law and enforcement at the turn of the century changed both the volume and reasons for acquisition activity in the railroad industry. The Interstate Commerce Act of 1887 and the Sherman Antitrust Act of 1890 prohibited firms from forming pools, cartels, and trusts with other firms in their industry. The passage of these acts precipitated aggressive merger and acquisition campaigns in many industries, as firms scrambled to cope with the resulting competitive uncertainties. Further, they transformed increasing industry concentration, which previously was largely irrelevant, into a stimulant of acquisition behavior. As we noted, the state also provides models that other organizations can copy. For example, Sutton et al. (1994) maintain that the US federal government's own personnel practice reforms provided models for other organizations to mimic as they responded to generalized normative pressures to legalize the workplace in the 1960s. They show that public sector organizations, which they maintain had the greatest exposure to these models, were particularly quick to adopt due process and grievance procedures believed consistent with these models.

Professionalization is another important source of institutional change. Individuals who have been socialized to view particular organizational forms as appropriate champion these forms at work and to acquaintances in collegial bodies. Thus organizations embrace new forms in proportion to the extent their members are affiliated with professional schools or associations through which assumptions, values, beliefs and theories about innovations are disseminated. For example, Fligstein (1990) maintains that in the

1960s CEOs trained in finance were more likely to embrace the "finance conception of control," which favored diversification and the structures (MDF) and tactics (acquisitions) that facilitate it. In a parallel argument, Espeland and Hirsch (1990) maintain that CEOs who attended elite business schools were steeped in the "firm as portfolio model," which favored the same strategies, structures, and tactics. Thus, several studies have shown that firms run by CEOs with finance backgrounds and elite business school degrees were more likely to diversify, adopt the MDF, and pursue acquisitions (Fligstein, 1985, 1991; Fligstein and Brantley, 1992; Palmer et al., 1993; Palmer and Barber, 2001).

Organizations also embrace new forms in proportion to their prevalence in the environment, regardless of the forms' origin. Pressures driving this mimicry process are assumed to be primarily cognitive in character. A form's prevalence is thought to be a cause or consequence, and thus an indicator, of its legitimacy. Organizations copy prevalent structures because they take for granted that prevalent forms are appropriate. Normative pressures, though, can also be involved. Organizations may infer that other constituents of their field prefer prevalent structures. The use of widely accepted forms cloaks organizations in the mantel of legitimacy necessary for survival. For example, several studies show that the likelihood that large corporations adopted the multidivisional form in the latter part of the twentieth century depended on the number of other large firms that had already adopted this form in their industry (Fligstein, 1985; Palmer et al., 1993).

Prospective adopters differ in the extent to which they are aware of other organizations employing institutionalized forms. Centrality in inter-organizational networks can provide organizations with information about new forms. Linkages to organizations that have already adopted a new form, a condition dubbed "cohesion," can provide organizations with even more detailed information about the new forms and expose organizations to normative pressures to adopt them. Haunschild (1993) shows that corporations whose directors sit on the boards of directors ("interlock" with) many other firms, especially firms that had recently engaged in acquisitions, were more likely to complete acquisitions themselves.

Organizations employing an institutionalized form differ in the extent to which they are considered appropriate objects of mimicry by prospective adopters. For example, Haunschild and Beckman (1998) demonstrate that corporations are most likely to mimic the acquisition behavior of the other firms to which they are interlocked when those other firms are similar to them with respect to primary industry location. Galaskiewicz and Burt (1991) show that corporate philanthropy officers are likely to give donations to non-profit social welfare organizations that receive money from other corporations that occupy similar positions in the philanthropy officer social networks – a condition called "structural equivalence."

Of course, if organizations knew which structures were efficient and effective, they would not have to scrutinize the behavior of other organizations in an attempt to determine acceptable forms. Thus the search for signs of legitimate structures in the behavior of fellow field and industry constituents is particularly intense under conditions of uncertainty. Haunschild (1994) demonstrates that corporations are most likely to pay premiums similar to those paid by the other firms to which they are interlocked, when there is uncertainty regarding the appropriate purchase price of a target. Davis and Greve (1997) integrate these insights, and analyze the likelihood that firms will adopt two innovations, golden parachutes and poison pills, as a function of their connection to prior adopters, the contagiousness of prior adopters, and their susceptibility to infection.

Coercive, normative, and mimetic mechanisms of institutional change have been theorized to work hand in hand. For example, Fligstein (1990) assumes that changes in antitrust law and enforcement precluded the pursuit of horizontal and vertical acquisitions beginning in the early 1950s. This restricted firms interested in pursuing acquisitions to enact diversifying acquisitions in the great merger wave of the 1960s and provided an opportunity for finance CEOs to rise to the top of the organization. Finance CEOs brought with them norms and cognitive frameworks and championed strategies (diversification) and structures (the MDF) consistent with these norms and cognitions. The increasing proliferation of strategies, structures, and tactics associated with the new norms and cognitive framework reinforced the diffusion of each in turn. Finally, in response to these developments in the real world, prescriptive models of the conglomerate firm were developed in business schools (albeit too late to have much of an effect).

Current Issues and Debates

INSTITUTIONAL THEORY: AN OVERSOCIALIZED VIEW OF ORGANIZATIONS?

Many institutional analyses assume that organizations passively adapt to institutional constraints and incorporate institutionalized elements in their environments after birth. For example, Fligstein (1990) assumes that large firms relatively quickly abandoned horizontal and vertical acquisitions in favor of diversifying acquisitions in response to changing antitrust law and enforcement in the 1950s and 1960s. Dobbin and Dowd (2000) attribute agency to economic elites, but only insofar as they reacted without protest to environmental changes. When confronted with new state mandates corporate elites experimented with a range of potential responses. After one of these responses became accepted as superior to the others, it diffused rapidly via mimicry. Corporate elites did not challenge, alter, or circumvent state mandates according to their explanation.

Not all institutional theorists believe that actors, both individuals and organizations, are inescapably caught up in pressures to conform. Hirsch (1997) has argued against this presupposition – see also Perrow (1985) – contending that there is much evidence for strategic and purposive action among organizations, and attempts to resist norms and regulations. To assume otherwise is to assume away the role of power and interest as explanatory factors. Certainly there are organizations that fail to incorporate institutionalized elements. For instance, organizations sometimes violate the law, contest enforcement actions, and even escape prosecution and penalty (McCaffrey, 1982). To make Perrow and Hirsch's criticisms significant, though, one has to demonstrate that attempts to flaunt institutional constraints are numerous, successful, and consequential. Preliminary research (Maher and Palmer, 2000) indicates that while one-tenth of the firms making acquisitions in the 1960 ran afoul of either the Justice Department or the Federal Trade Commission, about half of these firms eventually completed their contested acquisitions. Moreover, the Justice Department and Federal Trade Commission attempted to resolve most of these cases through negotiation with the firms involved.

This suggests that it is inaccurate to represent US antitrust policy in this period as exogenous to corporate action and imposed upon firms with complete success, as some implicitly do.

Some institutional theorists have acknowledged the failure of institutional theory to adequately take into account interest and agency (DiMaggio, 1988). A few institutional theorists have even begun to develop the implications of this critique (Oliver, 1991, 1992). For example, Fligstein (1987), drawing on the insights of the resource dependence perspective (Pfeffer and Salancik, 1978) and its precursors (Perrow, 1970) has elaborated what he calls a "political cultural" model of organizational change. Managers acquire power to the extent that they can make credible claims to possess resources needed to cope with the critical contingencies that face their organizations. Once they obtain power, however, they seek to entrench it by promulgating rules, telegraphing norms, and championing cognitive frameworks. They allocate responsibilities to subunits from which they came, communicate norms about how to reach the top and champion ways of conceptualizing the organization's critical issues. Ocasio and Kim (1999) build on these ideas to analyze the changing nature of CEO functional backgrounds in the1980s. Fligstein implies that CEOs with finance backgrounds developed and disseminated the finance conception of control because it bolstered their positions of power in the firm (1990). It is of course possible to conceive of institutional entrepreneurs as being situated in other structures. Palmer and Barber (2001) attempt to understand the proliferation of innovative corporate acquisition strategies in the 1960s partly as a function of the class position of the top managers of large firms in the period.

Institutional theory has taken on an even more active cast in the management science literature, presumably because its constituencies value knowledge that can support pro-active managerial behavior. In the management science version of institutional theory, managers are characterized as actively scanning their environments for institutional elements that, if adopted, can provide their organizations with legitimacy and thus a strategic advantage. Further, in some formulations, managers are assumed to adopt institutionalized elements in a decidedly disingenuous fashion. This is the case in Zajac and Westfall's (2000) analysis of stock repurchase programs that are announced but not consummated.

INSTITUTIONAL CHANGE: SUBSTANCE OR CEREMONY?

There is a tension within the institutional approach between the old instititutionalism, which tends to view institutional processes as giving rise to substantive change and the new institutionalism, which tends to view these pressures as giving rise to ceremonial gestures (Tolbert and Zucker, 1996). The old institutionalist orientation is reflected in the analysis of goal drift, discussed above. The new institutionalist orientation is reflected in their analysis of loose coupling.

In their charter statement of the new institutional perspective, Meyer and Rowan (1977) observed that the legitimacy benefits and survival advantages of adopting institutionalized elements can paradoxically generate inefficient routines that inhibit performance. For example, the adoption of formalized procedures in public schools covered the educational process with a patina of rationality while simultaneously threatening to encumber teachers with added tasks that contributed little to their students' education.

When confronted with such a threat, organizations have a tendency to isolate institutional elements from technical ones. They conform in a ceremonial fashion to institutional structures, without changing the core technical processes of day-to-day business.

In recent studies, Westphal and Zajac (1994) and Zajac and Westphal (2000) have examined the conditions under which organizations engage in ceremonial as opposed to substantive compliance with institutional rules, norms, and cognitive frameworks. Their analyses of long-term incentive plans and stock buyback programs offer a way to chart a middle ground between the old and new institutionalists on this issue, by viewing loose coupling as a variable phenomenon.

INTEGRATION OF INSTITUTIONAL AND POPULATION ECOLOGY THEORY: UNEASY SYMBIOSIS?

In the late 1980s, researchers began to synthesize institutional and ecological theory to study the impact of institutional structures on organizational founding or failure rates. As noted above, researchers used institutional theory to account for the curvilinear relationship between organizational density and organizational birth and death rates. In this account, the number of organizations employing a form early in a population's history was considered an indicator of the cognitive legitimacy of that form at the time. Researchers also used institutional theory to account for the generally positive relationship between organizational age and survival. In this account, the age of an organization was considered an indicator of the institutionalization of organizational routines and interorganizational relations. But these inferences have been challenged. In particular, critics maintain that the prevalence of organizations employing a particular form might be related to other institutional factors that actually stimulate birth rates and depress death rates (Singh, 1993). For example, increasing density of organizations following the establishment of a population might reflect the creation of government mandates or the diffusion of norms favoring creation of organizations of a particular type (Baum and Powell, 1995). In fact, density might be related to non-institutional factors that regulate organizational vital rates. For example, the initial increase in organizational density in a population might be associated with technological innovations that give rise to spurts of organizational founding (Zucker, 1989).

Partly in response to these critiques, scholars have attempted to measure density-related legitimacy more directly. Baum and Oliver (1992) have shown that that the increasing founding rate and decreasing death rate that accompanies increasing density in a population of childcare service organizations (CCSOs) in Toronto was largely the result of the increasing density of "institutional linkages" between CCSOs and other legitimate organizations in the city. As the number of service agreements granted to CCSOs by city government increased and the number of site sharing arrangements CCSOs established with public schools, churches, and similar organizations in the community grew, more CCSOs were formed and fewer died. Further, the effect of density on founding and death rates was eliminated when the density of these institutional linkages was taken into account. Singh et al. (1986) show that being listed in a community directory, obtaining tax exempt status from the state, and possessing a large board of directors accounts for the increasing survival rate that voluntary social service organizations experience as they age. These studies, then, not only validate the early claims of population ecologists that organizational density (and age) is (are) associated with or-ganizational legitimacy but also indicate how basic ecological processes might be driven by institutional dynamics.

Ruef and Scott (1998) and Scott et al. (2000) take this research one step further. They show that the impact of legitimacy on survival rates can vary over time, depend-ing on the criteria by which organizations are awarded legitimacy. The authors exam-ine the impact that certification by two kinds of professional oversight bodies had on the life chances of hospitals in the San Francisco Bay Area between 1945 and 1990: asso-ciations that evaluate hospitals according to technical criteria and associations that evaluate them on managerial grounds. They find that the mortality rate of hospitals was relatively independent of both kinds of normative legitimacy in the immediate post-World War II period, a period characterized by local independent physician control. Technical legitimacy regulated mortality rates between 1966 and 1982, a period marked by increasing federal government financing of health care. Finally, managerial legiti-macy has come to regulate hospital life chances in recent years, as the health care industry has become increasingly competitive and dominated by managed care arrange-ments. Legitimacy was assumed to improve hospital survival chances in the latter two periods by reducing uncertainty about hospital technical and managerial adequacy.

Hannan and Carroll (Carroll and Hannan, 1989b; Hannan and Carroll, 1995), though, question the wisdom of attempting to measure density-related legitimacy directly. On the one hand, they believe that critics overestimate the theoretical importance of some of the proposed alternative predictors of rising organizational founding rates. As they put it, "it is hard to think of a relevant theory in any of the social sciences that is inconsistent with the view that regulation directed at an organizational population affects its evolution" (Hannan and Carroll, 1995, p. 540). On the other hand, they think their critics underestimate the methodological difficulty of separating out the impacts of increasing organizational density and the institutional processes believed to underpin its effect on founding rates. Specifically, they point out that increasing organizational den-sity is likely to be both cause and consequence of many of the developments envisioned to be the true cause of increasing founding rates, such as increases in media attention and government regulation.

Hannan and Carroll dismiss alternative explanations for density related legitimacy as unlikely to be theoretically important, and as methodologically difficult to isolate. We agree that few theories deny that state regulation influences organizational evolution. However, we think that theorizing the relationship between state structure (and institu-tional structures more generally) and organizational evolution is far from complete. We also agree that it is difficult to isolate institutional from ecological effects on organiza-tional evolution, but difficulty is not a reason to abandon the search for the social relationships that underpin organizational change, even if the results uncovered are partial or ambiguous. All social processes, including institutional and ecological ones, are interrelated, and to limit inquiry to easily measured indicators (e.g. the number of similar and different organizations in an environment) is to limit the possibility of more nuanced and rich understandings.

For example, Haveman and Rao (1997) have conducted research that simultaneously substantiates Carroll and Hannan's claim that institutional and ecological dynamics are intimately intertwined and refutes their implicit assumption that for this reason the mutual impact of each on the other cannot be studied. In their study of the US savings and loan industry, Haveman and Rao maintain that aspects of the institutional environment shaped the birth and death of thrift organizations of different types. Further, they argue that the influence of institutions on organizational vital rates was reciprocated by the impact of population dynamics on institutions in this field. Specifically, they show that the first US thrifts were modeled after pre-existing thrifts in the UK. This model was associated with a variety of normative elements, especially the value of cooperation and disciplined savings. A variety of "technical" factors (e.g. immigration, employment instability) necessitated changes in this model in the USA. However, the tendency of institutionalized action to persist over time slowed the pace of this change. Further, the institutional character of the environment shaped the specific character of these changes. Haveman and Rao identify the Progressive Movement as a primary source of the norms (voluntarism) and cognitive frameworks (association of efficiency with bureaucracy) that favored the rise of the new model of thrift organization. However, the authors assert that some of the institutional elements that shaped the incipient thrift industry were eroded by the death of old and birth of new types of thrifts. Thus ecological processes shaped the development of institutions as much as institutional developments shaped ecological processes in the thrift field.

Remaining Questions

WHAT ARE THE MECHANISMS LINKING INCORPORATION OF INSTITUTIONAL ELEMENTS TO ORGANIZATIONAL SURVIVAL?

Conformity to institutional constraints and adoption of institutionalized forms cloaks organizations in the mantle of legitimacy. Legitimacy can enhance an organization's ability to obtain and utilize resources, which can enhance its performance, which in turn can improve its survival chances. But increased access to resources provided by legitimacy can have a direct impact on organizational survival chances, regardless of its impact on performance. This presumed relationship is the cornerstone of the resource dependence perspective. Indeed, legitimacy has been theorized to increase organizational survival chances, regardless of any impact on performance. Long ago, Stinchcombe (1965) noted that legitimate organizations sometimes survive because stakeholders view their survival as appropriate, even in the face of gross inefficiency. From the standpoint of the new institutional perspective, organizations conform to institutional constraints and incorporate institutionalized forms because they assume that they are appropriate, regardless of their actual and potentially changing efficiency and effectiveness characteristics (Meyer and Rowan, 1977).

Few have examined the relationship between conformity to institutional constraints or the incorporation of institutionalized forms and the possession of legitimacy; but see Deephouse (1996). A few preliminary studies have examined the impact of conformity to institutionalized constraints on organizational performance. They demonstrate that adoption of forms legitimated by the state in emerging capitalist economies provides firms with performance advantages (Park et al., 2000). No one whom we are aware of, though, has examined the impact of conformity to institutionalized constraints or the incorporation of institutionalized forms and the acquisition of resources. Does conforming with institutionalized expectations lead to greater legitimacy and increased access to resources? The vast majority of research, reviewed above, instead focuses on the relationship between the conformity to institutional constraints, or incorporation of institutionalized forms, and organizational survival.

CAN THE NEW INSTITUTIONALISM OVERCOME MEASUREMENT PROBLEMS?

A number of measurement problems plague the elaboration and evaluation of the new institutionalism in organizational analysis; see Schneiberg and Clemens (2001) for an extensive review. New institutionalists often fail to clearly delineate the specific character of the regulative, normative, or cognitive structures in questions, and fail to identify which structures effect the organizations in question. As a result, new institutional analyses often fail to acknowledge the existence of multiple competing bases of organization legitimacy. Ruef and Scott's (1998) and Scott et al.'s (2000) study of San Francisco Bay Area hospital survival rates are exceptions in this regard.

Second, new institutional analyses sometimes fail to directly assess the extent to which structures are institutionalized and thus constrained by institutional pressures. This problem is particularly the case with cognitive structures. For example, Ocasio (1999) captures the presence of formal rules covering top manager succession by measuring the number of other high-ranking executives (presidents, chief operating officers, and vice chairman) in top management. He captures the presence of informal rules covering succession by measuring the extent to which previous succession events involved the appointment of either an insider or outsider. He finds that organizations that have many internal candidates to chose from and who have chosen internal candidates in the past are more likely to chose internal candidates when replacing their CEO. He argues that this is evidence of an institutionalized pattern, but these patterns might be the consequence of simple probability and unobserved heterogeneity. Hybels and Ryan's (1997) examination of the biotechnology industry is a notable exception in this regard.

Finally, new institutional research often is imprecise in its characterization of the specific processes through which institutions are transmitted. More often than not, statistical associations between the adoption of a form by an organization and the institutionalization of the form in its field are taken to be indicative of more than one process. For example, the impact of a form's prevalence and the likelihood of its subsequent adoption are taken to be indicative of both normative and cognitive processes. Separate attention to coercive processes is particularly lacking (Mizruchi and Fein, 1999).

HAS INSTITUTIONAL THEORY OVERSTEPPED ITS INTELLECTUAL BOUNDS?

As new theories develop, they have a tendency to expand in scope: a theory's proponents have an interest in staking as wide a theoretical and empirical claim as possible to enhance their theory's apparent utility, and they must answer the challenges of critics who suggest alternative explanations. Incorporating alternative explanations under the rubric of one's theory is one way to blunt criticism. The expansion of theories in this way can enhance their realism and utility, and we have seen this in the new institutionalism. At the outset, institutional theorists limited their arguments to organizations in particular kinds of environments – so called institutional environments. Increasingly, though, they have progressively expanded their focus to include organizations in all types of environments, including so-called technical environments (Mezias, 1990). In addition, they have attempted to answer critics by incorporating concepts of interest and agency (Thornton and Ocasio, 1999). Both of these developments have extended institutional theory to good effect.

The expansion of theories resulting from imperialistic or defensive tendencies, however, sometimes runs the risk of re-labeling existing concepts without adding to the current store of knowledge. For example, several new institutional analyses of the impact of state action on organizational change attribute importance to the state's selective creation and distribution of resources needed by organizations for survival. Researchers have argued that state-provided capital stimulated the founding of new railroads in the USA (Dobbin and Dowd, 1997) and reduced the death rates of producer cooperatives in Israel (Ingram and Simmons, 2000). However, the state's role as creator and distributor of resources has long been conceptualized within the population ecology, resource dependence, and political economy perspectives.

Similarly, institutional analyses of the impact of prior adoptions on new adoptions of innovations theorize the process as an instance of mimetic isomorphism. This research maintains that under conditions of uncertainty, organizations view other organizations in their field as potential models of appropriate behavior. Those models that are most prevalent are assumed most appropriate and legitimate. However, models might be prevalent because they are efficient and effective. Institutional theorists tend not to distinguish between these two possibilities, viewing both as representative of institutional processes. Learning theories, however, have long presumed that organizations learn by copying other organizations that have successfully adopted new innovations. Modeling economizes on search costs and the resulting savings outweigh the benefits that might accrue from more thorough searches. Again, it is unclear whether much is gained by including this process under the umbrella of institutional theory labeled as mimetic isomorphism. Indeed, Haunschild and her colleagues are beginning to take research on the diffusion of innovations further by departing from the institutional framework and embracing a more explicit learning focus (Haunschild and Miner, 1997).

The expansion of theories resulting from imperialistic or defensive tendencies also runs the risk of limiting or distorting the utility of a theory. The potentially detrimental effect of expanding a theory to take into account critiques is particularly worrisome in connection with attempts to incorporate political dynamics into institutional theory, especially as this has occurred in the management literature. Critics of institutional theory have called for greater attention to matters of interest, strategic activity, and power and some, in particular management scholars, have responded. However, while adopting a more strategic standpoint, management scholars have eroded core features of the institutional perspective by trivializing them. Institutionalized elements are implicitly assumed to be superficial, described as essentially cosmetic and not actually shaping organizational behavior. Managers are assumed to stand apart from the institutional environment, selecting which institutional elements to use to dress up their organizations for some external audience. Finally, legitimacy implicitly is a commodity rather than a relation, a quantity to be obtained rather than a quality to be emulated. As such, the institutional perspective becomes indistinguishable from the resource dependence perspective, as legitimacy is conceptualized as a resource to manage (Pfeffer and Salancik, 1978). As a result, in the hands of management scholars, the new institutionalism loses its unique attributes, such as the recognition that apparently rational action sometimes produces unintentional consequences such as goal drift.

New Directions

We see two new directions in which institutional analysis might go – one substantive, the other methodological. Most institutional analyses focus on large-scale institutional environments such as nations or intra-national states to examine the effects of constraints and institutional predisposition on organizational structure and performance. The concern has largely been with finding variation: Why do this country's organizations look different from that country's? Why do this state's firms behave differently from that state's? Many of these studies have demonstrated the power of institutions, both at the level of cognitive and regulative structures, to shape organizational action.

An important direction for research, we believe, is to examine the conditions under which institutional differences might begin to merge or to remain resolutely parochial even when there is pressure for convergence. The development of global economic activity, both in financial and commodity markets, is increasingly placing actors who come from different institutional settings together as strategic allies and customers. Regional economic organizations such as that formed by the North American Free Trade Act (NAFTA), the Association of South East Asian Nations (ASEAN) and the European Economic Community (EEC) are attempts to create rules and conventions that will be mutually understandable and legitimate to subordinate organizational actors. Multinational enterprises have divisions in different institutional settings. What are the areas where institutions converge, and in what areas of action does this fail? This line of research has important empirical consequences for international policy organizations and multinational enterprises. It is also an exciting way in which to discover the limits of institutions when confronted by market forces or political pressures. Are some institutional settings flexible, and others more entrenched? When pressured by market forces and local institutions, how do organizations of various types, in various places, respond?

Most new institutional studies rely on a statistical analysis to investigate institutional processes. We think that the new institutionalism would be enriched by the use of the growing insights of qualitative work on organizations. We believe that this will begin to address issues that are left open by statistical approaches to understanding, for example the sources of legitimate forms, and the processes by which they effect organizations. One recent approach deserves the attention of institutional theorists: the French Conventions School. This school of thought, which embraces both economists and sociologists in France, assumes that actors want to be effective and "efficient." Somewhat like symbolic interactionists, and (like Selznick and his contemporaries) having roots in the American pragmatism of William James and John Dewey, the Conventions School examines the situational resources – tools, persons, institutions, physical environments, cognitive frames – that actors use to construct a strategy of gain. These scholars argue that because economic action is collective, situations must be interpreted iteratively in mutually intelligible ways, therefore developing and utilizing institutionalized conventions. "[The] points of reference for evaluating a situation and coordinating with other actors are essentially established by conventions between persons. Conventions emerge both as responses to and as definitions of uncertainty; they are attempts to order the economic process in a way that allows production and exchange to take place according to expectations which define efficiency" (Storper and Salais, 1997, p. 16).

The Conventions School sees the critical economic conundrum to be coordination, not exchange or transaction costs, although both are clearly involved. They do close observation of economic settings where conventional points of reference and everyday practice are ruptured or likely to be contested, for example, negotiations taking place in the European Economic Union; see Wilkinson (1997) for a review. This is similar in spirit to work done by earlier institutionalists, but also similar to Barley's (1990) examination of the development of new frames and relations in a hospital setting in response to technology changes. Studying conventions as they are formed and institutionalized, and then asking what difference they make in labor organizations, product markets, organizational form and practice adoption, and other types of organized economic activity, will give observational grounding to an approach that recently has relied primarily on statistical association. The development of a more micro and fieldwork tradition in the institutional analysis of organizations will extend and develop its insights. It will give us another way to think about the impact of organizational fields, and offer a perspective on questions about where institutions come from, the meanings they have for actors, and how they effect relations of power within and between organizations.

Connections Across Levels

We see at least two ways in which questions about institutional forces can better be understood by examining organizational processes across levels. Connecting the insights of research done at each level of analysis can answer questions, or generate understandings, not possible when working within a single level of analysis (Biggart, 1991). First, we believe that research on institutionalized group norms and identity might help us to understand how and why new structural forms are created. Second, we see an opportunity to understand the relationship between micro, meso, and macro forms within an organizational field, society, or other social aggregation.

Institutional theorists are largely concerned with structures – forms and activities – that become taken-for-granted aspects of organized life. They have been far less concerned with the origin of forms as the product of ongoing interaction. There is, however, the more macro approach to historical origins of forms. Bendix, ([1956] 1974) and Dore (1973) demonstrate the emergence of Western and Japanese economic institutions from pre-industrial social organization. More recently, Biggart and Guillén (1999) show the impact of institutional structure on a society's possible economic development strategies. Nonetheless, there has been relatively little concern with the origin of institutions outside of large-scale historical studies.

As Elsbach's chapter discusses, intra-organizational institutions such as values and routines may be deeply held understandings embedded in group and individual identities. The intra-organization studies that led to the "discovery" of these elements of institutional structure are largely based on fieldwork methods and allowed researchers access to the cognitive frames and legitimating beliefs of actors who develop and maintain these micro-institutional structures. Although not a primary object of this research, the intra-organizational level of analysis, we believe, holds promise for revealing the ways in which institutional structures are formed and developed in ongoing interaction. This is a crucial step to understanding structural origins and would be particularly useful in examining emerging institutions in, for example, the Internet economy.

Similarly, we see an opportunity to examine the relationship between structures at various levels of analysis. How are patterns of organization related across levels of a social system? Are patterns of organization reproduced across levels? For example, a family structure may be reproduced in a family-owned business, which may be in turn reproduced in a family-like set of relations between a mother company and affiliated firms, and finally in a family-like arrangement between the state and the business sector. Institutional theory sensitive to research at different levels of analysis can begin to get at issues of causation and reproduction of form and potentially to the ease or intractability of forms when pressured to change.

Conclusion

This is an exciting time to be an institutional theorist. Marketization of traditional economies, globalization of exchange, widespread migration, cultural diffusion via mass media, a new informational economy, the growth of regional trading blocs, are all conditions that would appear to challenge provincial institutional organization patterns. Institutional theorists are well positioned to analyze which organizational patterns will emerge, which will remain and diffuse, and to what effect?

References

Barley, S. R. (1990): "The alignment of technology and structure through roles and networks," *Administrative Science Quarterly*, 35, 61–103.

Baron, J. N., Dobbin, F. R., and Jennings, P. D. (1986): "War and peace: The evolution of modern personnel administration in US industry," *American Journal of Sociology*, 92, 350–83.

Baum, J. A. C., and Oliver, C. (1992): "Institutional embeddedness and the dynamics of organizational populations," *American Sociological Review*, 57, 540–60.

Baum, J. A. C., and Powell, W. W. (1995): "Cultivating an institutional ecology of organizations: Comment on Hannan, Carroll, Dundon, and Torres," *American Sociological Review*, 60, 529–39.

Bendix, R. ([1956] 1974): *Work and Authority in Industry: Ideologies of Management in the Course of Industrialization*. Berkeley: University of California Press.

Biggart, N. W. (1991): "Explaining Asian economic organization: Toward a Weberian institutional perspective," *Theory and Society*, 20, 199–232.

Biggart, N. W., and Guillén, M. (1999): "Developing difference: social organization and the rise of the auto industries of South Korea, Taiwan, Spain and Argentina," *American Sociological Review*, 64, 722–47.

Carroll, G. R., Hannan, M. T. (1989a): "Density dependence in the evolution of populations of newspaper organizations," *American Sociological Review*, 54, 524–41.

Carroll, G. R., and Hannan, M. T. (1989b): "On using institutional theory in studying organizational populations," *American Sociological Review*, 54, 545–48.

Davis, G. F., and Greve, H. R. (1997): "Corporate elite networks and governance changes in the 1980s," *American Journal of Sociology*, 103, 1–37.

Deephouse, D. L. (1996): "Does isomorphism legitimate?" *Academy of Management Journal*, 39, 1024–39.

DiMaggio, P. J. (1988): "Interest and agency in institutional theory," in L. G. Zucker (ed.), *Institutional Patterns and Organizations: Culture and Environment*, Cambridge, MA: Ballinger, 3–21.

DiMaggio, P. J. (1991): "Constructing an organizational field as a professional project: US art museums, 1920-1940," in W. W. Powell and P. J. DiMaggio (eds), *The New Institutionalism in Organizational Analysis*, Chicago: University of Chicago Press, 267–92.

DiMaggio, P. J., and Powell, W. W. (1983): "The iron cage revisited: Institutional isomorphism and collective rationality in organizational fields," *American Sociological Review*, 48, 147–60.

Dobbin, F. R., and Dowd, T. J. (1997): "How policy shapes competition: Early railroad foundings in Massachusetts," *Administrative Science Quarterly*, 42, 501–29.

Dobbin, F. R., and Dowd, T. J. (2000): "Antitrust and the market for corporate control: Railroading, 1825–1922," *American Sociological Review*, 65, 635–57

Dobbin, F. R., Edelman, L., Meyer, J. W., Scott, W. R., and Swidler, A. (1988): "The expansion of due process in organization," in L. G. Zucker (ed.), *Institutional Patterns and Organizations: Culture and Environment*, Cambridge, MA: Ballinger, 71–98.

Dobbin, F. R., Sutton, J., Meyer, J. W., and Scott, W. R. (1993): "Equal opportunity law and the construction of internal labor markets," *American Journal of Sociology*, 99, 396–427.

Dore, R. (1973): *British Factory–Japanese Factory: The Origins of National Diversity in Industrial Relations*. Berkeley: University of California Press.

Edelman, L.B. (1990): "Legal environments and organizational governance: The expansion of due process in the American workplace," *American Journal of Sociology*, 95, 1401–40.

Espeland, W. N., and Hirsch, P. M. (1990): "Ownership changes, accounting practice, and the redefinition of the corporation," *Accounting, Organizations, and Society*, 15, 77–96.

Fligstein, N. (1985): "The spread of the multidivisional form among large firms, 1919–1979," *American Sociological Review*, 50, 377–91.

Fligstein, N. (1987): "The intraorganizational power struggle: the rise of finance personnel to top leadership in large corporations, 1919–1979," *American Sociological Review*, 52, 44–58.

Fligstein, N. (1990): *The Transformation of Corporate Control*. Cambridge, MA: Harvard University Press.

Fligstein, N. (1991): "The structural transformation of American industry: An institutional account of the causes of diversification in the largest firms, 1919–1979," in W. W. Powell and P. J. DiMaggio (eds), *The New Institutionalism in Organizational Analysis*, Chicago: University of Chicago Press, 311–36.

Fligstein, N., and Brantley, P. (1992): "Bank control, owner control, or organizational dynamics: Who controls the large modern corporation?" *American Journal Sociology*, 98, 280–307.

Galaskiewicz, J., and Burt, R. S. (1991): "Interorganizational contagion in corporate philanthropy," *Administrative Science Quarterly*, 36, 88–105.

Gusfield, J. R. (1955): "Social structure and moral reform: A study of the Women's Christian Temperance Union," *American Journal of Sociology*, 61, 221–32.

Hannan, M. T., and Carroll, G. R. (1992): *Dynamics of Organizational Populations: Density, Legitimation, and Competition*. New York: Oxford University Press.

Hannan, M. T., and Carroll, G. R. (1995): "Theory building and cheap talk about legitimation: Reply to Baum and Powell," *American Sociological Review*, 60, 539–44.

Hannan, M. T., Carroll, G. R., Dundon, E. A., and Torres, J. C. (1995): "Organizational evolution in a multinational context: Entries of automobile manufacturers in Belgium, Britain, France, Germany, and Italy," *American Sociological Review*, 60, 509–28.

Haunschild, P. R. (1993): "Interorganizational imitation: The impact of interlocks on corporate acquisition activity," *Administrative Science Quarterly*, 38, 564–92.

Haunschild, P. R. (1994): "How much is that company worth? Interorganizational relationships, uncertainty, and acquisition premiums," *Administrative Science Quarterly*, 39, 391–411.

Haunschild, P. R., and Beckman, C. M. (1998): "When do interlocks matter? Alternative sources of information and interlock influence," *Administrative Science Quarterly*, 43, 815–18.

Haunschild, P. R., and Miner, A. S. (1997): "Modes of interorganizational imitation: The effects of outcome salience and uncertainty," *Administrative Science Quarterly*, 42, 472–501.

Haveman, H. A., and Rao, H. (1997): "Structuring a theory of moral sentiments: Institutional and organizational coevolution in the early thrift industry," *American Journal of Sociology*, 102, 1606–52.

Hirsch, P. M. (1986): "From ambushes to golden parachutes: Corporate takeovers as an instance of cultural framing and institutional integration," *American Journal of Sociology*, 91, 800–37.

Hirsch, P. M. (1997): "Sociology without social structure: Neoinstitutional theory meets brave new world," *American Journal of Sociology*, 102, 1702–23.

Hybels, R., and Ryan, A. (1997): "Entrepreneurship in US commercial biotechnology from 1974–1989: An empirical test of the legitimation dynamic in density dependence theory," unpublished manuscript, University of Alberta.

Ingram, P., and Simmons, T. (2000): "State formation, ideological competition, and the ecology of Israeli workers' cooperatives, 1920–1992," *Administrative Science Quarterly*, 45, 25–53.

McCaffrey, D. P. (1982): *OSHA and the Politics of Health Regulation*. New York: Plenum Publishing.

Maher, M., and Palmer, D. (2000): "Illegal corporate acquisitions in the 1960s," unpublished manuscript, Graduate School of Management, University of California, Davis.

Meyer, J. W., and Rowan, B. (1977): "Institutional organizations: Formal structure as myth and ceremony," *American Journal of Sociology*, 83, 340–63.

Mezias, S. J. (1990): "An institutional model of organizational practice: Financial reporting at the Fortune 200," *Administrative Science Quarterly*, 35, 431–57.

Mizruchi, M. S., and Fein, L. C. (1999): "The social construction of organizational knowledge: A study of the uses of coercive, mimetic, and isomorphism," *Administrative Science Quarterly*, 44, 653–83

North, D. C. (1981): *Structure and Change in Economic History*. New York: Norton.

Ocasio, W. (1999): "Institutionalized action and corporate governance: The reliance on rules of CEO succession," *Administrative Science Quarterly*, 44, 384–416.

Ocasio, W., and Kim, H. (1999): "The circulation of corporate control: Selection of functional backgrounds of new CEOs in large US manufacturing firms, 1981–1992," *Administrative Science Quarterly*, 44, 532–62.

Oliver, C. (1991): "Strategic responses to institutional processes," *Academy of Management Review*, 16, 145–79.

Oliver, C. (1992): "The antecedents of deinstitutionalization," *Organization Studies*, 13, 563–88.

Orrú, M., Biggart, N. W., and Hamilton, G. G. (1997): *The Economic Organization of East Asian Capitalism*. Thousand Oaks, CA: Sage Publications.

Palmer, D., and Barber, B. (2001): "Challengers, established elites, and innovation in the market for corporate control: Diversifying acquisitions of large US corporations in the 1960s," *Administrative Science Quarterly*, 46, 87–120.

Palmer, D. A., Jennings, D. P., and Zhou, X. (1993): "Late adoption of the multidivisional form by large US corporations: Institutional, political, and economic accounts," *Administrative Science Quarterly*, 38, 100–32.

Park, S. H., Li, S., and Tse, D. K. (2000): "Determinants of firm performance in a transitional economy: Institutional vs. economic effects in China," unpublished manuscript, Department of Organization Management, Rutgers University.

Perrow, C. (1970): "Departmental power and perspectives in industrial firms," in M. N. Zald (ed.), *Power in Organizations*, Nashville: Vanderbilt University Press, 59–89.

Perrow, C. (1985): "Overboard with myth and symbols," *American Journal of Sociology*, 91, 151–55.

Pfeffer, J., and Salancik, G. R. (1978): *The External Control of Organizations: A Resource Dependence Perspective*. New York: Harper & Row.

Ruef, M., and Scott, W. R. (1998): "A multidimensional model of organizational legitimacy: Hospital survival in changing institutional environments," *Administrative Science Quarterly*, 43,

877–904.

Schein, E. (1961): "Management development as a process of influence," *Industrial Management Review*, 2, 59–77.

Schneiberg, M., and Clemens, E. (2001): "The typical tools for the job: Research strategies in institutional analysis," in W. W. Powell and D. L. Jones (eds), *How Institutions Change*, Chicago: University of Chicago Press.

Scott, W. R. (1995): *Institutions and Organizations*. Thousand Oaks, CA: Sage Publications.

Scott, W. R., Ruef, M., Mendel, P. J., and Caronna, C. A. (2000): *Institutional Change and Healthcare Organizations: From Professional Dominance to Managed Care*. Chicago: University of Chicago Press.

Selznick, P. ([1949] 1966): *TVA and the Grass Roots: A Study in the Sociology of Formal Organization*. New York: Harper and Row.

Singh, J. V. (1993): "Review essay: Density dependence theory-current issues, future promise," *American Journal of Sociology*, 99, 464–73.

Singh, J. V., Tucker, D. J., and House, R. J. (1986): "Organizational legitimacy and the liability of newness," *Administrative Science Quarterly*, 31, 171–93.

Stinchcombe, A. L. (1965): "Social structure and organizations," in J. G. March (ed.), *Handbook of Organizations*, Chicago: Rand McNally, 142–93.

Stinchcombe, A. L. (1968): *Constructing Social Theories*. Chicago: University of Chicago Press.

Storper, M., and Salais, R. (1997): *Worlds of Production: The Action Frameworks of the Economy*. Cambridge, MA: Harvard University Press.

Sutton, J. R., Dobbin, F., Meyer, J. W., and Scott, W. R. (1994): "The legalization of the workplace," *American Journal of Sociology*, 99, 944–71.

Thornton, P. H., and Ocasio, W. (1999): "Institutional logics and the historical contingency of power in organizations: Executive succession in the higher education publishing industry, 1958–1990," *American Journal of Sociology*, 105, 801–43

Tolbert, P. S., and Zucker, L. G. (1983): "Institutional sources of change in the formal structure of organizations: The diffusion of civil service reform, 1880–1935," *Administrative Science Quarterly*, 28, 22–39.

Tolbert, P. S., and Zucker, L. G. (1996): "Institutional analyses of organizations: Legitimate but not institutionalized," in S. Clegg, C. Hardy and W. Nord (eds), *Handbook of Organization Studies*, London: Sage Publications.

Westphal, J. D., and Zajac, E. J. (1994): "Substance and symbolism in CEOs' long-term incentive plans," *Administrative Science Quarterly*, 39, 367–90.

Wilkinson, J. (1997): "A new paradigm for economic analysis?" *Economy and Society*, 26, 305–39.

Zajac, E. J, and Westphal, J. D. (2000): "The political and social determinants of stock buybacks," unpublished manuscript.

Zucker, L. G. (1977): "The role of institutionalization in cultural persistence," *American Sociological Review*, 42, 726–43.

Zucker, L. G. (1989): "Combining institutional theory and population ecology: No legitimacy, no history (comment on Carroll–Hannan, ASR, August 1989)," *American Sociological Review*, 54, 542–45.

Chapter Twelve

Organizational Networks

RANJAY GULATI, DANIA A. DIALDIN, AND
LIHUA WANG

If the maxim "networks matter" was discounted during a period dominated by economic theories of firms, considerable theoretical research and empirical evidence has since infiltrated the scholarly consciousness. If scholars previously modeled and encapsulated the environment within measures of competitiveness in product or supplier markets, we know now that the organization's environment is much broader encompassing its social network of external contacts. We also know that these external contacts have implications for the organization's survival and livelihood. For example, we know that firms organized in networks have higher survival chances and that prestigious partners help firms go to IPO faster and gain higher valuations at IPOs than firms which do not have these partnerships.

Network perspectives build on the general notion that economic action does not take place in a barren social context but is instead embedded in a social network of relationships. A social network can be defined as a "set of nodes (e.g., persons, organizations) linked by a set of social relationships (e.g., friendship, transfer of funds, overlapping membership) of a specified type" (Laumann et al., 1978, p. 458). While the original focus of network research was on understanding how the embeddedness of individuals influences their behavior, a similar argument has been extended to organizations (Burt, 1982; Walker, 1988; Mizruchi, 1992; Gulati, 1998). Organizations can be interconnected with other organizations through a wide array of social and economic relationships, each of which can constitute a social network. These include supplier relationships, resource flows, trade association memberships, interlocking directorates, relationships among individual employees, and prior strategic alliances.

We focus on organizational networks: the focal organization's pattern of relationships with other organizations in the same network. Specifically, the organization's egocentric network consists of the focal organization (called ego), a set of organizations (called alters) who have ties with ego, the ties between ego and alters, and the ties between alters (Wasserman and Faust, 1994). The egocentric organizational network is a channel through which the focal organization obtains resources and information from the environment that is quality-controlled in both its content and credibility.

Scholarship on egocentric organizational networks has focused primarily either on their effects on firm behavior such as new alliance formation and partner selection (Gulati, 1995a; 1995b; 1998), or on the effects of specific types of ties, such as cohesive ties or bridging ties, on information benefits (e.g., Stuart, 2000; Anand and Khanna, 1995). Recently, scholars have extended these ideas and begun to examine

1   how social networks are created, and
2   how adopting a network lens can lead to a deeper understanding of differences in firm performance (Gulati, Nohria, and Zaheer, 2000).

In this chapter, we move from reviewing the impact of social networks on *behavior* to studying their formation and their implication for *firm performance*. Table 12.1 summarizes the key research themes we address and identifies key studies we consider within each theme.

Literature Review, Summary, and Evaluation

FORMING ORGANIZATIONAL NETWORKS

Until recently, scholars had viewed the creation of egocentric organizational networks as driven largely by exogenous factors such as the distribution of resources and the social structure of resource dependence (e.g., Aiken and Hage, 1968; Pfeffer and Salancik, 1978; Burt, 1983). The resource dependence perspective suggests that firms will create ties with those whom they share the greatest interdependence (Pfeffer and Nowak, 1976). Although the resource dependence perspective sheds light on the critical contingencies guiding the creation of new ties, one drawback of this perspective is that it assumes an atomistic environment in which information about other organizations is widely available and freely accessible to all.

Network scholars have extended the resource dependence perspective and focused on the role of the social context, primarily, the cumulation of prior ties between firms for the formation of new organizational networks (Gulati, 1995b; Gulati and Gargiulo, 1999). They suggest that prior inter-firm ties create a social network in which most firms are embedded and that this network shapes the flow of valuable information about new tie opportunities and the reliability, capabilities, and trustworthiness of these potential partners. The informational advantages to firms from such a social network can enable the creation of new ties by three distinct means: access, timing, and referrals (Burt, 1992). Access refers to information about current or potential partners as to their capabilities and trustworthiness. Timing entails having informational benefits about potential partners at the right time. Referrals can be particularly important in tie formation, as a firm's existing partners may refer other firms to it for partnering or to enter three-way partnerships.

Recently, Gulati and Gargiulo (1999) have suggested that network formation results from a dynamic process driven both by these exogenous interdependencies that prompt organizations to seek cooperation and by endogenous network embeddedness mechanisms that help them determine with whom to build partnerships. The network emerges as a result of an iterative process in which new partnerships modify the previous social

Table 12.1 Selected studies of organizational networks

Reference	Key concepts	Key variables	Key predictions and findings	Key contribution	Sample and method
Baum et al. (2000)	• Network configuration (vertical and horizontal ties; strong and weak ties)	• Network size at founding • Network efficiency at founding • Innovative capabilities of potential rivals	Organizational alliance network should be configured to provide efficient access to diverse information and capabilities with minimum redundancy, conflict and complexity. In addition, the firm should ally with rivals who provide more opportunity for learning but less risk of intra-alliance rivalry.	Reveals how the network configuration of start-ups affects their performance	• 142 Canadian biotech start-up firms that began operations (1991–6) • Random effect GLS model
Dyer and Nobeoka (2000)	• Knowledge sharing • Network identity • Dynamic learning capability		A highly interconnected network benefits all network members by facilitating knowledge sharing and learning and increasing productivity of the members.	Evaluates why some firms' networks provide their member more benefits than the networks of other firms	• Toyota's vertical network • Exploratory multi-method case study: interview, archival, and survey
Gulati (1999)	• Network resources • Firm capability	• Cliques • Closeness • Experience	Both time-varying network resources and a firm's alliance formation capability increases the likelihood of a firm entering further alliances.	Illustrates how network resources and firm capability affect a firm's decision to enter new alliances	• 166 largest firms in three worldwide sectors: new materials, industrial automation, and automotive products (1981–9) • Panel probit model

Reference	Key concepts	Key variables	Key predictions and findings	Key contribution	Sample and method
Gulati and Gargiulo (1999)	• Interdependence • Prior alliances • Common third parties • Joint centrality	• Interdependence • Structural differentiation • Repeated ties • Common ties • Joint centrality	The probability of a new alliance between specific organizations increases with their interdependence and also with their prior mutual alliances, common third parties and joint centrality in the alliance network. Also, the differentiation of the emerging network structure mitigates the effect of interdependence and enhances the effect of joint centrality on new alliance formation.	Demonstrates the significance of the social network in shaping firm behavior of alliance formation	• Same sample as Gulati (1999) • Cross-sectional time series panel design (1970–89) • Level of analysis is the dyad • Random-effects panel probit estimates
Ingram and Baum (1997)	Network benefits and constraints	• Local experience • Non-local experience • Local market power • Reputation • Competitive dynamics	Firms increase their survival chances by participating in a network because the network provides the advantages of knowledge transfer and learning, scale economies, access to resources, market	Assesses the effect of participating in a chain network on firm survival	• 558 transient hotels operated in Manhattan (1898–1980) • Piecewise exponential model of hazard rate

Study	Concepts	Propositions	Variables	Data and methods
Rowley et al. (2000)	Exploration and exploitation	power, and reputation. But the firm may also suffer from strategic constraints. Whether the firm benefits from the membership depends on which predominate. Firms in dense local network and/or having environmental requirement of exploration should favor weak ties.	• Strength of the ties • Density of local network • Industry environmental requirement	Illustrates how network configuration and an industry's environment interact with each other to affect firm performance • Semiconductor network and steel industry network (1990–7) • Number of ties is 132 in semiconductor industry; 138 in steel industry
Stuart et al. (1999)	• Status transfer • Prominence of partners	Young firms with prominent partners go to IPO faster and earn greater valuations at IPO than firms that lack such connections. These benefits are amplified when the uncertainty about the quality of the young firms' product increases.	• The rate of IPO and the market capitalization at IPO • Prominence of affiliates • Prominence of investing banks • Firm attributes • Environmental conditions	Shows how partner profiles in a firm's network affects its performance • 301 biotechnology firms specializing in the development of human diagnostics and therapeutics, and funded by venture capital firms (1978–91) • Models: Hazard rates, piecewise exponential, OLS regression

network, which then shapes the formation of future cooperative ties. The authors, however, found that the influence of interdependence and network factors on the formation of organizational networks was not constant over time. The effect of these factors is moderated by the level of the social system's structural differentiation: the extent to which organizations occupy an identifiable set of network positions and a proxy for the amount of information available in the emerging network. The higher the structural differentiation of the network, the lower the effect of interdependence, and the greater the effect of endogenous variables will be on the likelihood of tie formation. Underlying these findings is the idea that existing ties enable organizations to decide with whom to build new partnerships. These new ties increase the amount of information available that in turn enhances the potential to shape future partnerships.

NETWORK RESOURCES AND CONSTRAINTS AND THEIR IMPLICATION FOR FIRM PERFORMANCE

Participating in a network benefits members by providing opportunities for the sharing of various kinds of resources. Several recent studies of network effects on firms have indicated that these resources may include financial (Ingram and Inman, 1996; Keister, 1998), institutional (Baum and Oliver, 1991), knowledge and information resources, as well as a host of other resources in the network (Ingram and Inman, 1996). On the one hand, the structured opportunity for resource sharing may benefit members by improving their financial performance (Berg et al., 1982; Keister, 1998), increasing their survival chances (Baum and Oliver, 1992; Ingram and Inman, 1996; Ingram and Baum, 1997) and enhancing their innovative/learning capability (Gemser et al., 1996; Dyer and Nobeoka, 2000). On the other hand, membership in a network in and of itself may limit members from discovering opportunities and information outside the network and may limit the local adaptability of the firms (Ingram and Baum, 1997). As a consequence, these ties may negatively influence firm performance. Networks giveth; networks taketh away.

FINANCIAL RESOURCES

In some instances, networks enable firms to gain access to capital necessary to sustain firm operations and invest in firm growth. One specific instance in which this may occur is when networks substitute for formal financial systems and give firms access to otherwise scarce resources and unaffordable business opportunities (Keister, 1998). Rather than, or in complement to, relying on banks for capital, members can take advantage of the opportunity to share financial resources in their own network of firms. Because financial resources are shared within the network, where firms have more information about each other, transaction costs are likely to be lower (Khanna and Rivkin, 2001). Financial resources are especially relevant in emerging markets where formal financial infrastructures are not well established (Khanna and Palepu, 1999). For example, evidence from 40 of the largest Chinese business groups and their 535 members indicates that members reported higher financial performance and productivity when informal financial arrangements were made for them to share financial resources (Keister, 1998).

INSTITUTIONAL RESOURCES

Institutional resources result from the legitimacy and status of the organizational network as a whole. By association, members are accorded the legitimacy and status of the network to which they belong. For example, a consumer's uncertainty about a new product's quality may be mitigated if the consumer learns that a member of a highly reputable network produces this product. These resources can help increase the survival chance as well as the financial performance of the members (Khanna and Palepu, 1999). For example, Ingram and Baum's (1997) study of chain affiliation of Manhattan hotels during 1898-1980 suggests that a hotel that joins a high-status hotel chain signals its high status. As a consequence, consumers' uncertainty about the quality of the hotel's service is reduced and the survival chances of the hotel are increased.

KNOWLEDGE AND INFORMATION RESOURCES

Knowledge and information resources of a network refer to the collective knowledge owned by all firms within the network. The network connections can be a conduit for disseminating both existing and newly acquired knowledge so that all members can quickly access it. In a study of diffusion of Total Quality Management (TQM) practices, Westphal et al. (1997) found that hospital networks were an important medium for the transmission and diffusion of TQM practices among hospitals. As a result of such diffusion networks, the learning/innovative capability of the members was enhanced. Ingram and Baum (1997) also found that hotel chain networks facilitate knowledge transfer and learning among members and increase the survival chances of the members. Similar effects have also been reported in supplier networks of automobile companies such as Toyota (Dyer and Nobeoka, 2000). In Toyota's vertical network, common identity and strongly interconnected ties between Toyota and its suppliers as well as among suppliers themselves facilitate knowledge sharing and learning providing its members learning and productivity advantages over non-members.

Although networks provide opportunities for firms to share various resources, they may also constrain members and contribute to their negative performance. First, being a member of a network may lock a firm into the existing relationships (Nohria and Garcia-Pont, 1991; Gomes-Casseres, 1994) and prevent it from joining another network. Second, network membership may expose the firm to the risk of unwittingly transferring valuable knowledge and proprietary information to competitor firms in the network (Doz and Hamel, 1998; McEvily and Zaheer, 1999). Third, being a member of a network may compel a firm to adhere to norms and practices that meet the lowest common need of the firms. These practices and strategies may not be the most suitable ones for every member's circumstance (Ingram and Baum, 1997; Westphal et al., 1997).

FIRM NETWORK CHARACTERISTICS AND THEIR IMPLICATION FOR FIRM PERFORMANCE

Scholarship on the effects of a firm's network characteristics – the pattern of relationships a focal firm has with other firms – has focused primarily either on their effects on firm behavior such as new alliance formation and partner selection (Gulati, 1995a; 1995b; 1998), or on the effects of specific type of ties characteristics, such as cohesive ties or bridging ties, on information benefits (Anand and Khanna, 1995; Stuart, 2000). Less attention has been paid to whether and how the structural characteristics of organizational networks account for the performance differences among firms and the performance of those ties themselves (Gulati and Lawrence, 2000; Gulati and Wang, 2000). Further, there have been few efforts to link the structural characteristics of the organizational network of a firm with other organizational characteristics (e.g., size, age, overall strategies) and with other competitive and institutional environments to explain the performance differences among firms.

Three dimensions of an organization's network – centrality within the overall network, structural configuration of ties, and partner profiles – affect the value it derives from that network. As a result, a focal firm's performance depends on its ability to position itself and configure its ties (e.g., weak versus strong, bridging versus cohesive) in a way that optimizes both its access to information and its ability to exert control over others in its organizational network. A firm's performance is further influenced by its ability to construct ties with partners through whom it will gain status and knowledge, and from whom it is able to capture network resource spillovers. We discuss each of the three dimensions of an organization's network and their implications for firm performance.

NETWORK CENTRALITY OF A FIRM IN THE OVERALL NETWORK

A firm's network centrality refers to the degree to which the firm has a strategically important position in the network (Freeman, 1979). Being central in a network provides a focal firm various information advantages (in the form of access, timing and referral), control benefits (i.e. power) and learning (Gulati, 1999). The three most widely used centrality indicators – degree, closeness, and betweenness centrality – capture different ways in which a firm is able to extract value from its organizational network. Degree centrality refers to the extent to which a firm is involved in the network and is measured by the number of the firm's direct ties (Freeman, 1979). High degree centrality makes a firm more visible to other firms in the network and increases its chance of being reached by other firms for new rewarding opportunities. As a result, high degree centrality is likely to facilitate the magnitude of value the firm extracts from its network and to lead to positive performance consequences. At the same time, degree centrality also reflects the total experience of the focal firm in cooperating with other firms. Researchers have found that prior experience facilitates value creation through learning. The lessons include not only managerial capabilities associated with interfirm alliances, but also the capability to create new alliances (Dyer and Singh, 1998; Lyles, 1988; Gulati, 1999). Therefore, the higher a firm's degree centrality, the more cooperative experience the focal firm has and the more capabilities it has to extract value from these alliances.

Although degree centrality may provide firms with information and learning benefits, it is at best an incomplete indicator of firm centrality. By only counting the number of ties in which a focal firm is involved, degree centrality assumes the homogeneity of the ties in providing the firm with information and learning benefits. It does not tell us where these ties are positioned in the whole network. In fact, the empirical evidence on the linkage between degree centrality and firm performance is very limited and mixed. For example, Shan et al. (1994) found that the number of ties between start-up firms and established firms is positively related to innovative output in biotechnology industry. Gulati (1999) found that the number of alliances formed by the focal firm affects its capability to form new alliances in the future. Stuart (2000), however, found that a simple count of the number of alliances does not affect firm performance as measured by rate of innovation and rate of sales growth. While the relationship between degree centrality and firm performance has yet to be disentangled, other centrality indicators are clearly necessary to illustrate how firm centrality is related to the value created by a firm from its organizational network.

The other two frequently used centrality indicators are closeness centrality and betweenness centrality. Closeness centrality indicates how closely connected a firm is to the rest of the firms in the network, both directly and indirectly. It is computed as the shortest path distance of each actor from others in the network (Freeman, 1979). A central firm can interact with other firms quickly and access information more rapidly (Wasserman and Faust; 1994; Gulati, 1999). This information may include the knowledge of new business opportunities as well as information about valuable innovations. In addition, high closeness centrality reveals that the focal firm is more easily accessed by other firms in the network and thus is more likely to be referred by other firms when rewarding opportunities are available.

Betweenness centrality is the extent to which a firm lies between other firms in the network. It is computed as the frequency with which an actor falls between two other actors on the shortest paths connecting them (Freeman, 1979). The importance of betweenness centrality has been documented in various communication networks and interlocking directories (Mizruchi, 1982; Mintz and Schwartz, 1985). The basic argument is that an actor who lies between two other nonadjacent actors occupies an important strategic position by having greater control of the interactions between them in terms of both information and resource flow (Freeman, 1979). Furthermore, it may also gain favorable terms in negotiations by playing the two unconnected firms against each other (Burt, 1992). Therefore, high betweenness centrality may allow a focal firm to extract more value from its network through its powerful position in the network.

CONFIGURATION OF TIES IN THE FIRM'S NETWORK

Another dimension of the firm's network is its structural configuration of ties: the composition and positioning of different types of ties. The importance of the ties' structural configuration arises from the varied benefits a firm can extract from the different types of ties (Baker, 1990). There are many ways to categorize inter-firm ties, such as strong versus weak ties, cohesive versus bridging ties, horizontal versus vertical ties, and institutional versus non-institutional ties. We focus on two configurations of ties in the network: cohesive versus bridging ties and strong versus weak ties.

A cohesive tie is one that connects a focal firm with another firm which is also connected with at least one another partner of the focal firm. A bridging tie within a focal firm's egocentric network is a tie that connects the focal firm with another firm that is not connected with any partner of the focal firm. For example, in the network of Firm *A* (Figure 12.1), *AB*, *AC*, and *AD* are all cohesive ties while *AE* and *AF*

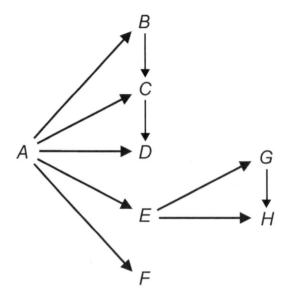

Figure 12.1   Example of an organizational network

are bridging ties. A strong tie in a focal firm's network connects the focal firm and another firm with which the focal firm has intensive interaction. Weak ties, on the other hand, consist of the focal firm and another firm with which the focal firm only has very few interactions.

Strong versus weak ties emphasize dyadic properties and do not consider other ties in the network. Cohesive versus bridging ties, however, concern broader aspects of the egocentric network representing the extent to which a particular tie is embedded in both prior ties between the two parties and in third party ties. For example, a firm's organizational network that is rich in cohesive ties may also contain many connections between this firm and other firms but there will also be many connections among its partners. A firm's network that is rich in strong ties, however, means that the firm has many strong direct ties with other firms, but provides no information about the connection between its partners. Although, empirically, strong ties tend to be cohesive ties and weak ties tend to be bridging ties (Burt, 1992), this is not necessarily always the case. Bridging ties could be either strong or weak depending on the intensity of interaction between the focal firm and another firm with whom the focal firm ties (Burt, 1992; McEvily and Zaheer, 1999).

- **Cohesive ties versus bridging ties**   In different ways, both cohesive ties and bridging ties benefit firms. Cohesive ties reduce both transaction and coordination costs through social norms and sanctions that facilitate trust and cooperative exchange (Coleman, 1988; Gulati and Singh, 1998). Bridging ties provide information and control benefits (Burt, 1992) for the focal firm in the form of access, timing, and referral to information and learning opportunities. Just as they benefit firms, however, cohesive and bridging ties can also harm them. For example, cohesive ties may prevent firms from obtaining new non-redundant information. Similarly, a firm with bridging ties assumes the risk of partnering with firms with whom it has limited prior cooperative experiences (Gulati, 1999; Gulati and Wang, 2000).

Given the complexity of benefits and constraints provided by cohesive ties and bridging ties, the question is less about which ties are better because a firm's network usually consists of both types of ties. The more relevant question is: How do firms configure the two types of ties in a way that maximizes the benefits of both safety and opportunity as well as minimizing the risks involved in the cooperative relationship? In a recent study, Baum et al. (2000) found that startups in the biotechnology industry enjoy greater performance advantages when their networks are configured in a way that provide efficient access to diverse information and capabilities, more opportunity for learning, and less risk of inter-alliance rivalry.

- **Strong ties versus weak ties**   Another way to think about the structural configuration of ties in a firm's egocentric network is by examining how strong ties and weak ties are configured (Uzzi, 1996; Baker, 1990). Strong ties promote trust and reciprocity and facilitate the transfer of private information and critical resources at the dyadic level. A firm with many strong ties and few weak ties, however, trades with a confined set of partners and may seal itself off from the market. It will, as a consequence, receive less new information about opportunities in the market. It may also develop resource dependence on the partners with whom the firm has strong ties. Weak ties, on the other hand, provide the firm with new information and opportunities in the market (Granovetter, 1985). It may also reduce the resource dependence of the firm on its strong partners (Baker, 1990). Therefore, a firm should configure its network in a way that fits its strategic needs for both information and resources. Baker (1990), for example, found that firms usually develop a combination of strong and weak ties with their investment banks to exploit the benefits of both types of ties yet avoid their disadvantages.

Although both cohesive ties and strong ties create trust between a firm and its associated partners, a cohesive ties argument emphasizes that trust emerges from the firm's embeddedness in a social network beyond the dyad, while a strong ties argument proposes that trust comes from the intensive interaction within the dyad. By the same token, although both bridging ties and weak ties bring new information and opportunities to the focal firm, a bridging ties argument focuses more on the fact that the focal firm and the bridging partner connect two disparate networks (thus two distinctive sets of information sources). Conversely, a weak ties argument focuses more on the fact that new information comes from sources with whom the focal firm does not frequently interact.

Ultimately, the appropriate tie configuration may depend on the context in which firms are situated. A focal firm situated in a dense network may benefit more from an egocentric network rich in bridging ties and weak ties because the social context already provides the benefits that it might otherwise receive from cohesive ties and strong ties (McEvily and Zaheer, 1999; Rowley et al., 2000). Strong ties may be favored in a stable exploitative environment such as the steel industry while weak ties may be favored in an uncertain or an exploration environment such as the semiconductor industry (Rowley et al., 2000).

The design of the egocentric network may also depend on the information and resource needs of the focal firm. For example, if a firm's strategic objective and overall survival requires access to reliable sources of information, then the firm may want to develop more cohesive ties. In contrast, if the strategic objectives necessitate acquiring novel information and continuous learning, then an egocentric network rich in bridging ties may be more beneficial to the firm. Ultimately we need a more contingent model of the relationship between network configuration and firm success.

PARTNER PROFILES

Partner profiles refer to the traits of a focal firm's partners. We discuss how three aspects of partner profiles – partner's status, technological distance from focal firms, and its network characteristics – affect the focal firm performance.

Recent research suggests that the status of a focal firm's partners is positively related to the focal firm's performance (Stuart, 2000). The underlying mechanism is status transfer between the partners. As a result, strategic alliances with high-status firms can enhance the status of a focal firm. The public markets are likely to view the gaining of a prestigious alliance partner as an endorsement of a focal firm's quality. This is especially true for small and young firms when the uncertainty about the quality of the firm's product is high (Stuart et al., 1999). For example, Higgins and Gulati (2000) found that the greater the number of top management team ties to prominent biotechnology organizations and pharmaceutical and/or healthcare organizations, the greater the prestige of the firm's investment bank. They also find a positive relationship between these ties and IPO success.

A second partner attribute that may affect firm performance is the technology distance between the focal firm and its alliance partners. Researchers have suggested that this distance positively affects a firm's innovative outputs, its ability to adapt to its technological position, and its ability to overcome organizational inertia (Stuart and Podolny, 1999). Two firms are proximate in technological network if their innovative activities are similar. When a focal firm forms an alliance with another technologically distant firm, novel technological innovations are more likely, resulting from combining complementary but distinctive sets of innovative capabilities from the two firms. In addition, such an alliance also provides potential opportunities for the focal firm to acquire new knowledge from its partners and thus extend its knowledge base into new and unrelated areas away from their core business area. Alliances with technologically distant partners, as a result, represent a potentially effective way to overcome organizational inertia and adapt to new technological areas critical to a focal firm's success.

Finally, focal firms can benefit by capturing spillovers of their partners' network connections. By connecting to a partner with rich network resources, a focal firm increases its prospects of accessing information from its partner's network. In a recent study, Gulati (1999) showed how the amount of network resources available to firms affects their proclivity to enter new alliances. This argument could easily be extended to consider the impact of network resources for firm performance. Furthermore, it would also be possible to consider the extent to which the partners of central firms benefit directly and indirectly from allying with them.

Contemporary Issues and Debates

MEASURING FIRM PERFORMANCE

The recent efforts to understand the performance implications of strategic networks raise the practical debate of how best to capture and measure these effects. One approach to estimating the performance of firms would be to measure how much value the public markets attributed to each network member from participating in that particular network. For example, several alliance researchers have conducted event study analyses on the stock market effects of alliance announcements (McConnell and Nantell, 1985; Mohanram and Nanda, 1997; Anand and Khanna, 2000). To the extent that stock market reactions predict the likely future outcomes from alliances, these results provide evidence on the consequences of alliances for firms. Another method of measuring firm performance involves estimating the extent to which firms are embedded in alliances and the likelihood of their survival. Thus, survival is considered a proxy for performance (Baum and Oliver, 1991, 1992; Mitchell and Singh, 1996).

In a related line of research, scholars have looked at the factors that contribute to an alliance's success and not just to firm success (Heide and Miner, 1992; Parkhe, 1993; Gulati and Lawrence, 2000). Although these researchers looked at the performance of individual alliances, their measurement approach merits emulation in examining network effects on firm performance. Rather than relying solely on archival measures, these researchers collected more substantive information with surveys and in-depth interviews with individual alliance members. It would be fruitful to examine the role of the antecedents of alliance success on the success of firms entering those alliances.

Another issue regarding the study of performance concerns the fact that the majority of studies examining the performance implications of a firm's egocentric network characteristics focus on a few industries. Among these are the semiconductor (Anand and Khanna, 1995; Stuart and Podolny, 1999; Rowley et al., 2000; Stuart, 2000), computer (Anand and Khanna, 1995), and biotechnology industries (Shan et al., 1994; Baum et al., 2000). These are all high technology industries, and therefore the results may reflect idiosyncratic findings specific only to firms in such industries and not to wider trends. In addition, most studies only look at one industry at a time yet industry characteristics are important in determining whether certain networks are effective or not (Berg et al., 1982; Gemser et al., 1996). As a result, there is a need for cross-industry analyses that would allow the development of more contingent models of network effects.

MICRO-LEVEL INFLUENCES ON PERFORMANCE

In this chapter, we have adopted primarily a macro-network perspective; however, there are also micro-network concerns that have implications for organizational behavior and performance. One example is the role of social psychological processes in egocentric organizational network formation. Whereas most research avoids these processes, such an orientation obscures the complexity of human interaction, and thus the social psychological process that directs such behavior (Zajac and Olsen, 1993; Ring and Van de

Ven, 1994; Doz and Hamel, 1998; Kale et al., 2000b). Adopting a perspective that emphasizes the behavioral aspects of organizational life as well could add significantly to our understanding of network formation and firm performance.

An important behavioral concept that has been much studied for interfirm alliances is trust (Barney and Hansen, 1994). Scholars have incorporated this affective dimension of trust to demonstrate its importance in influencing behavior and outcomes in alliances (Dyer and Singh, 1998; Dyer and Nobeoka, 2000). In one study, Zaheer et al. (1998) demonstrate how interorganizational trust reduces both the costs of negotiation between partners and conflict between them as well as directly influencing firm performance. Similarly, Kale et al. (2000b) indicate how the management of conflict between network partners is key to enabling partners to share information and know-how, developing trust, and ultimately, to foster learning.

Another social psychological process with potential implications for firm performance in strategic alliances is that of procedural justice. This process suggests that people evaluate the fairness of dispute resolution and allocation processes in terms of the procedures used to carry them out. The application of procedural justice is evident in studies that stress the relational value of "voice" in partnerships (Helper, 1991). These studies suggest that partners will be more satisfied with their relationship to the extent that each allows the other symbolic opportunities to contribute to the whole design, production, and marketing process even if some of these inputs do not ultimately influence the outcomes which result.

Central Questions that Remain Unanswered

ARE THE EFFECTS OF THE ORGANIZATIONAL NETWORK ON FIRM PERFORMANCE INVARIANT?

We believe that network effects on firms are likely to vary systematically with the context in which they occur. Two such contingent factors include the characteristics of the firm and the industry characteristics of which the firm is a part. In empirical terms this indicates a possible interaction between industry and firm characteristics with measures of a firm's network such as centrality, tie configuration, and partner profiles.

There is suggestive evidence that organizational performance may vary with the interactive effect of firm or industry characteristics and network characteristics. For example, two related firm characteristics that have been extensively studied are organizational age and size. It is quite likely that young and small firms often obtain more benefits from their networks than their larger and older counterparts because of status transfer, enhanced legitimacy, and access to resources (Baum and Oliver, 1991). With respect to industry characteristics, in an exploitation environment, where firms are out to exploit their existing technologies, skill, or information (March, 1991), a firm belonging to a network characterized mainly by strong ties is likely to perform better. In an exploration environment, however, where firms are out to explore for new innovations and opportunities, a firm belonging to a network characterized mainly by weak ties is likely to perform better (Rowley et al., 2000). It is also possible that in highly institutionalized environments, new firms may have greater pressure to connect with high status firms to gain legitimacy. In environments that are not highly institutionalized, however, firms may consider connecting with firms that provide them increased efficiency (Westphal et al., 1997).

WHAT ARE THE COMPARATIVE EFFECTS OF MULTIPLE NETWORKS ON FIRM PERFORMANCE?

The array of organizations with which a focal firm interacts constitutes an "organizational set" (Evan, 1966). This organizational set situates a focal firm into multiple types of networks. For example, a firm may maintain a horizontal network with its competitors, a vertical network with its suppliers, an institutional network with government agencies, and an interlocking directorate network with other firms. Although it is important to consider the effect of the overall configuration of all types of ties in a focal firm's "organizational set", the current network literature on inter-organizational relationships rarely takes more than one network into consideration (Gulati, 1998). How these different networks interact may affect firm performance (Blau, 1994). Gulati and Westphal (1999), for example, found that board interlock ties (one network) increased or decreased the likelihood of alliance formation depending on the content of relationship between CEOs and outside directors (a second network). In another study, Podolny et al. (1996) investigated how the positioning of firms in their product and status networks affects firm survival chances. They found that the life chances of a firm in an uncrowded niche increased monotonically with its status but the positive effect of status on an organization's life chance declined with the crowding of its niche. Taken together, these studies highlight the importance of future research examining the impact of multiple networks on firm performance.

HOW DOES THE CONTENT OF THE ORGANIZATIONAL NETWORK, AND NOT MERELY ITS STRUCTURAL CHARACTERISTICS, AFFECT FIRM PERFORMANCE?

The current literature mostly focuses on the structural characteristics of a firm's network while ignoring the content of information flowing through the network. In research on interpersonal networks, the content of networks (such as friendship networks, task-advice networks, strategic information networks, etc) is explicitly assessed and found to interact with the structural characteristics of these networks to affect an individual's outcomes (Podolny and Baron, 1997). This logic can easily be extended to organizational network research. As we have already pointed out, organizations typically participate in various networks such as interlocking networks, alliance networks, and trade-association networks. It is possible that each of these networks has a different effect on firms depending upon the information they transmit. It could also be the case that the ties in each network are heterogeneous. For example, whereas research on interlocking directorates typically emphasizes the positive information benefits of the network for the focal firm, Gulati and Westphal (1999) found that some of these network ties negatively affect focal firms. When the board of directors exerted higher levels of independent control over management, challenging the CEO on strategic issues and monitoring CEO performance, the likelihood that an alliance would form between them decreased. Conversely, when the relationship between the CEO and the board of directors was cooperative the likelihood that the two firms would form an alliance increased.

New and Emerging Directions for Future Research

Incorporating relational accounts into traditional strategic management perspectives allows for a deeper understanding of the sources of interfirm differences in profitability. In this section, we focus on one inchoate and promising research area that blends together a network perspective with a more traditional strategic management perspective – the resource-based view of the firm (RBV). This view emphasizes how firms are able to combine rare and unique collection of resources within a single firm to create synergies and achieve a competitive advantage over competing firms (Barney, 1991; Dierickx and Cool, 1989; Rumelt, 1984; Wernerfelt, 1984). By exclusively focusing on the firm, researchers have paid scant attention to firms' external environments and, specifically, to how firms use their networks to develop and capitalize on these capabilities (Gulati, Nohria and Zaheer, 2000).

We propose that rents accrue to firms due to both their unique resource endowments and to the organizational network to which they belong. These unique resource endowments, or capabilities, specify the potential range of behavior and actions that firms may take. How these capabilities are developed and to what extent they can be leveraged, however, depends on the resources and constraints that the network environment provides. Some of these organizational ties may enable firms to take advantage of their capabilities and increase the firm's performance while other ties may inhibit the use of the firm's capabilities and decrease its performance (Gulati and Dialdin, 2001).

To illustrate our argument, we examine two possible arenas, or capabilities, for inquiry: absorptive capacity and relational management and demonstrate how the effect of each for firm performance may be moderated in important ways by network factors. We chose only two capabilities in an effort to be illustrative and concise. We believe that network effects may moderate the influence of a number of other capabilities on firm performance as well.

ABSORPTIVE CAPACITY

Absorptive capacity describes the ability of a firm to recognize the value of new, external information, assimilate it, and leverage it to its economic advantage (Cohen and Levinthal, 1990). The underlying premise of absorptive capacity is that the ability of firms to recognize valuable information and make use of it largely depends on the level of prior related knowledge. Absorptive capacity of a firm may also depend on the level of communication between its internal units, and on the interface of the units with the external environment (Cohen and Levinthal, 1990).

The concept of absorptive capacity is easily extended to the study of firms and their alliances. Without access to reliable sources of information even firms with the most developed routines for absorbing knowledge are hindered in their effort to appropriate value from their partnerships. However, by accessing their organizational network ties, firms are presented with a plethora of information sources about potential partners. For example, by tapping in to this network, a firm can gain access to credible information about the "transparency" of potential partners, i.e. "the learning opportunity that each partner affords the other" (Doz and Hamel, 1998, p. 207). Also, firms can gauge the level of the other firm's absorptive capacity by the presence of a dedicated alliance function that coordinates all alliance-related activity (Kale et al., 2000a). Thus, the network serves as a screening mechanism for firms in their search for partners and as a mechanism to limit search costs for potential partners.

Other informational advantages bestowed by networks relate to the trustworthiness of potential partners. Networks of prior alliances can enhance trust both by providing information to partners about each other's reliability and by reinforcing a concern for reputation (Gulati, 1995a; Gulati, 1999; Burt and Knez, 1995). In particular, firms are weary of potential partners who have a reputation of being "learning racers." By identifying "good partners," firms are more likely to attain higher returns for their absorptive capacities than if they partnered with "learning racers."

RELATIONAL CAPABILITIES

Relational management refers to the ability to coordinate alliance activities, manage conflict, foster trust, and encourage information exchange between partners. It is an important capability given the intrinsic dependencies that exist among partners and the possibility of conflict between them. Poor conflict management skills obstruct the pursuit of integrative goals, destroy the relationship, and may ultimately dissolve the alliance (Kale et al., 2000b).

Well-developed relational management skills afford firms the capability to pursue integrative agreements. Firms with such capabilities are adept at searching for differences and interests in order to trade-off on these differences and create a larger pie. Developing routines for managing relationships notwithstanding, partnerships with firms that are incompatible in their relational management capabilities renders the capability itself useless (Gulati, Kumar, and Zajac, 2000; Gulati and Lawrence, 2000). For example, firms that prefer to settle conflicts through mediators may concede financial value to their partners who prefer settling disputes through expensive lawsuits. Thus, identifying partners with well-developed *and* compatible relational management capabilities is key.

As previously discussed, a network of prior ties can serve as a screening mechanism for firms in their search for partners and as a mechanism to limit search costs for potential partners. Information from both current and prior ties identifies the range of relational management styles that are available. By providing firms with the ability to screen those partners whose conflict management style is most compatible, focal firms can better make partnering decisions. Thus, the information that the network provides can be instrumental in shaping firms' choice of partners and the formation of new alliances (cf. Gulati, 1995b; Gulati and Gargiulo, 1999).

Networks can also confer information about the trustworthiness of potential partners. Such a priori trust can facilitate the coordination of interdependent activities of alliances – a feature of relational management capabilities. Without the development of trust, the higher the interdependence (and consequently, the more activities to coordinate), the higher the expected coordination costs (Gulati, 1995a; Gulati and Singh,

1998). Entering alliances with partners who one trusts can also significantly alleviate concerns about coordination costs. Firms that trust each other are likely to have a greater awareness, or a willingness to become aware, of the rules, routines, and procedures each follows. Thus, trusting firms may have greater competence in transacting with each other, which makes the interface between them easier to manage.

An additional source of benefit that networks of prior ties can provide is information on "best-practices" with respect to managing relationships. Through its indirect ties, firms can learn about normative practices and appropriate behavior (Davis and Greve, 1997; Haunschild and Miner, 1997), generally, and about managing relationships, specifically. Westphal et al. (1997) for example, illustrate how firms can learn about Total Quality Management (TQM) practices through social network ties. They found that for early adopters of TQM, social networks help decision makers to identify which practices promote the firm's (in this case, the hospital's) strategic objectives. Similarly, firms in strategic alliances may refine their relational management skills by learning about the other firm's respective skills.

Connections Across Levels

While our focus was specifically on the organizational-level networks, the versatility of a network perspective and its implications for behavior in and of organizations is illustrated in the combined effort of the three network chapters in this volume (Baker and Faulkner, and Raider and Krackhardt). Baker and Faulkner, for example, introduce the interorganizational network box where multiple relationships between focal organizations, producers, and suppliers are arranged forming horizontal and vertical planes that correspond to organizational sets and organizational fields, respectively. In our chapter, we consider one type of network for an organization, such as its vertical or its horizontal network. Baker and Faulkner, however, may provide us with a framework for aggregating "up" from one type of network in which the organization is involved to a horizontal plane in which multiple networks intersect and which afford organizations with various forms of financial, institutional and information resources.

Raider and Krackhardt explore similar questions to ours but at a lower level of aggregation. For example, they explore how individual ties originate and what benefits accrue to network actors within organizations. While they emphasize both structural and relational (content) explanations on whether and how an individual's network affects his or her behaviors and beliefs, we concentrate on structural factors only. We do, however, highlight that more research is needed in explaining how the content of ties in a network affects behavior and performance.

Two factors that are important at the organizational, interorganizational, and the intraorganizational levels of analysis are the relational content and the structural form of the respective networks. The relational aspects of a network include the content of the ties and the information and resources that flow through them. In contrast, the structural facets of a network focus on the position of the actor in the overall network and the benefits that are associated with such a position. The dyadic relationship of a focal actor with any other actor comprises the relational aspects of the network. This dyadic relationship as well as the other dyadic relationships of the same actor is the basic unit that forms the organizational network of the actor. While the relational aspects highlight the importance of the content of ties, they do not provide information on how these dyadic ties relate to one another. Conversely, structural aspects of the egocentric network address how multiple dyadic relationships are patterned in aggregate but do not necessarily examine the content of those ties. Ultimately, the influence of networks depends on the independent and interactive influence of both their relational and structural aspects. This is evident from prior research which suggests that strong dyadic connections and a cohesive network provide fine-grained information and facilitate trust, while weak dyadic ties and a network rich in structural holes provide unique information and opportunities for focal actors. Relational and structural aspects might also be complementary such that in a structurally cohesive environment, weak ties may be more desirable than strong ties, whereas in a network rich in structural holes, strong ties may be more desirable.

Another possible linkage between the different levels of analysis is the tension between the interests of the individual actors and those of the organization. For example, interlocking networks are simultaneously interpersonal and interorganizational. Interlocks provide benefits to organizations while also furthering the interests of the managers. It is likely that these two interests may conflict and therefore a problem of agency may arise. Self-serving managers may compromise the effectiveness of the organization's interlock network. Social and organizational control mechanisms could be developed to prevent individual actors from pursuing their interests at the expense of the larger organization or society. The three chapters on networks in this volume together provide some valuable clues into the arena of multi-level networks, which remains a fertile terrain for future research.

Conclusion

Over the past two decades there have been exciting theoretical and methodological developments for the study of networks at many levels of analysis. This chapter has focused on the organizational network. While some of the earlier network research focused on examining how organizational networks influence the behavior of organizations, such as tie formation, we have suggested that to truly comprehend the process of value creation through networks, we must understand how the different aspects of the network (e.g. centrality, configuration of ties in a firm's network and partner profiles) independently and simultaneously impact firm behavior and outcomes. The next wave of organizational network research should also continue to explore the boundary conditions of network effects by studying the contingencies under which they vary. By discovering these contingencies, or as Kuhn (1962) would put it, anomalies, the next generation of network scholars are likely to make exciting contributions to the advancement of a network perspective of organizations.

References

Aiken, M., and Hage, J. (1968): "Organizational interdependence and intraorganizational structure," *American Sociological Review*, 33, 912–30.

Anand, B. N., and Khanna, T. (1995): "On the market valuation of inter-firm agreements: The computer and telecommunications industries, 1990–1993," working paper of NBER Summer Industrial Organization Workshop, Cambridge.

Anand, B. N., and Khanna, T. (2000): "Do firms learn to create value? The case of alliances," *Strategic Management Journal*, 21, 295–315.

Baker, W. E. (1990): "Market networks and corporate behavior," *American Journal of Sociology*, 96, 589–625.

Barney, J. B. (1991): "Firm resources and sustained competitive advantage," *Journal of Management*, 17, 99–120.

Barney, J. B., and Hansen, M. H. (1994): "Trustworthiness as a source of competitive advantage," *Strategic Management Journal*, 15, 175–90.

Baum, J. A. C., and Oliver, C. (1991): "Institutional linkages and organizational mortality," *Administrative Science Quarterly*, 36, 187–218.

Baum, J. A. C., and Oliver, C. (1992): "Institutional embeddedness and the dynamics of organizational populations," *American Sociological Review*, 57, 540–59.

Baum, J. A. C., Calabrese, T., and Silverman, B. S. (2000): "Don't go it alone: Alliance network composition and startups' performance in Canadian biotechnology," *Strategic Management Journal*, 21, 267–94.

Berg, S. V., Duncan, J., and Friedman, P. (1982): *Joint Venture Strategies and Corporate Innovation*. Cambridge, MA: Oelgeschlager.

Blau, P. M. (1994): *Structural Contexts of Opportunities*. Chicago, IL: University of Chicago Press.

Burt, R. (1982): *Toward a Structural Theory of Action*. New York: Academic Press.

Burt, R. (1983): *Corporate Profits and Cooptation: Networks of Market Constraints and Directorate Ties in the American Economy*. New York: Academic Press,

Burt, R. (1992): *Structural Holes: The Social Structure of Competition*. Cambridge, MA: Harvard University Press,

Burt, R., and Knez, M. (1995): "Kinds of third-party effects on trust," *Rationality and Society*, 7, 225–92.

Cohen, W. M., and Levinthal, D. A. (1990): "Absorptive capacity: A new perspective on learning and innovation," *Administrative Science Quarterly*, 35, 128–52.

Coleman, J. S. (1988): "Social capital in the creation of human capital," *American Journal of Sociology*, 94, supplement S95–120.

Davis, G. F., and Greve, H. R. (1997): "Corporate elite networks and governance changes in the 1980s," *American Journal of Sociology*, 103, 1–37.

Dierickx, I., and Cool, K. (1989): "Asset stock accumulation and sustainability of competitive advantage," *Management Science*, 35, 1504–13.

Doz, Y. L., and Hamel, G. (1998): *Alliance Advantage: The Art of Creating Value Through Partnering*. Boston, MA: Harvard Business School,.

Dyer, J. H., and Nobeoka, K. (2000): "Creating and managing a high performance knowledge-sharing network: The Toyota case," *Strategic Management Journal*, 21, 345–67.

Dyer, J. H., and Singh, H. (1998): "The relational view: Cooperative strategy and sources of interorganizational competitive advantage," *Academy of Management Journal*, 23, 660–79.

Evan, W. M. (1966): "The organization-set: Toward a theory of interorganizational relations," in J. D. Thompson (ed.), *Approaches to Organizational Design*, Pittsburgh, PA: University of Pittsburgh Press 173–91.

Freeman, L. C. (1979): "Centrality in social networks: Conceptual clarification," *Social Networks*, 1, 215–39.

Gemser, G., Leenders, M. A., and Wijnberg, N. M. (1996): "The dynamics of inter-firm networks in the course of the industrial life cycle: The role of appropriability," *Technology Analysis and Strategic Management*, 8, 439–53.

Gomes-Casseres, B.: "Group versus group: How alliance networks compete," *Harvard Business Review*, 72 (1994), 62–74.

Granovetter, M. (1985): "Economic action and social structure: The problem of embeddedness," *American Journal of Sociology*, 91(1985), 481–510.

Gulati, R. (1995a): "Does familiarity breed trust? The implications of repeated ties for contractual choice in alliances," *Academy of Management Journal*, 38, 85–112.

Gulati, R. (1995b): "Social structure and alliance formation pattern: A longitudinal analysis," *Administrative Science Quarterly*, 40, 619–52.

Gulati, R. (1998): "Alliances and networks," *Strategic Management Journal*, 19, 293–317.

Gulati, R. (1999): "Network location and learning: The influence of network resources and firm capabilities on alliance formation," *Strategic Management Journal*, 20, 397–420.

Gulati, R., and Dialdin, D. (2001): "Firm capabilities, network characteristics, and firm performance," working paper, Kellogg Graduate School of Management.

Gulati, R., and Gargiulo, M. (1999): "Where do interorganizational networks come from?" *American Journal of Sociology*, 104, 1439–93.

Gulati, R., and Lawrence, P. (2000): "Organizing vertical networks: a design perspective," working paper, Kellogg Graduate School of Management.

Gulati, R., and Singh, H. (1998): "The architecture of cooperation: Managing coordination costs and appropriation concerns in strategic alliances," *Administrative Science Quarterly*, 43, 781–814.

Gulati, R., and Wang, L. (2000): "Tie characteristics and stock market reaction to the announcement of joint ventures," working paper, Kellogg Graduate School of Management, Northwestern University.

Gulati, R., and Westphal, J. (1999): "Cooperative or controlling? The effects of CEO–board relations and the content of interlocks on the formation of joint ventures," *Administrative Science Quarterly*, 44, 473–506.

Gulati, R., Kumar, N., and Zajac, E. (2000): "Interorganizational dynamics and their impact on alliance performance and stability," working paper, Kellogg Graduate School of Management.

Gulati, R., Nohria, N., and Zaheer, A. (2000): "Strategic networks," *Strategic Management Journal*, 21, 203–15.

Haunschild, P. R., and Miner, A. S. (1997): "Modes of interorganizational imitation: The effects of outcome salience and uncertainty," *Administrative Science Quarterly*, 42, 472–500.

Heide, J. B., and Miner, A. S. (1992): "The shadow of the future: Effects of anticipated interaction and frequency of contact of buyer-seller cooperation," *Academy of Management Journal*, 35, 265–91.

Helper, S. (1991): "Strategy and irreversibility in supplier relations: The case of the U.S. automobile industry," *Business History Review*, 65, 781–824.

Higgins, M. C., and Gulati, R. (2000): "Getting off to a good start: The effects of upper echelon affiliations on interorganizational endorsements," working paper, Harvard Business School.

Ingram, P., and Baum, J. A. C. (1997): "Chain affiliation and the failure of Manhattan hotels, 1898–1980," *Administrative Science Quarterly*, 42, 68-102.

Ingram, P., and Inman, C. (1996): "Institutions, inter-group competition, and the evolution of hotel populations around Niagara Falls," *Administrative Science Quarterly*, 41, 629–58.

Kale, P. J., Dyer, J., and Singh, H. (2000a): "Alliance capability, stock market reaction, and long-term success," Paper presented at the Academy of Management Meeting, Toronto.

Kale, P., Singh, H., and Perlmutter, H. (2000b): "Learning and protection of proprietary assets in strategic alliances: Building relation specific capital," *Strategic Management Journal*, 21, 217–37.

Keister, L. A. (1998): "Engineering growth: Business group structure and firm performance in China's transition economy," *American Journal of Sociology*, 104, 404–40.

Khanna, T., and Palepu, K. (1999): "The right way to restructure conglomerates in emerging markets," *Harvard Business Review*, 77, 125–34.

Khanna, T., and Rivkin, J. (2001): "Estimating the performance effects of networks in emerging markets," *Strategic Management Journal*, 22, 45–74.

Kuhn, T. S. (1962): *The Structure of Scientific Revolutions.* Chicago, IL: University of Chicago Press.

Laumann, E. O., Galaskiewicz, J., and Marsden, P. V. (1978): "Community structure as interorganizational linkages," *Annual Review of Sociology,* 4, 455–84.

Lyles, M. A. (1988): "Learning among joint venture-sophisticated firms," in F. K. Contractor and P. Lorange (eds), *Cooperative Strategies in International Business,* Lexington, KY: Lexington Press, 301–16.

McConnell, J. J., and Nantell, T. J. (1985): "Corporate combinations and common stock returns: The case of joint ventures," *Journal of Finance,* 40, 519–36.

McEvily, B., and Zaheer, A. (1999): "Bridging ties: A source of firm heterogeneity in competitive capabilities," *Strategic Management Journal,* 20, 1133–56.

March, J. G. (1991): "Exploration and exploitation in organizational learning," *Organization Science,* 2, 71–87.

Mintz, B., and Schwartz, M. (1985): *The Power Structure of American Business.* Chicago, IL: University of Chicago Press.

Mitchell, W., and Singh, K. (1996): "Survival of businesses using collaborative relationships to commercialize complex goods," *Strategic Management Journal,* 17, 169–95.

Mizruchi, M. S. (1982): *The American Corporate Network, 1904–1974.* Beverly Hills, CA: Sage Publications.

Mizruchi, M. S. (1992): *The Structure of Corporate Political Action.* Cambridge, MA: Harvard University.

Mohanram, P., and Nanda, A. (1997): "When do joint ventures create value?" working paper, Harvard Business School, 96–128.

Nohria, N., and Garcia-Pont, C. (1991): "Global strategic linkages and industry structure," *Strategic Management Journal,* 12, 105–24.

Parkhe, A. (1993): "Strategic alliance structuring: A game theoretic and transaction cost examination of interfirm cooperation," *Academy of Management Journal,* 36, 794–829.

Pfeffer, J., and Nowak, P. (1976): "Joint venture and interorganizational interdependence," *Administrative Science Quarterly,* 21, 398–418.

Pfeffer J., and Salancik, G. R. (1978): *The External Control of Organizations.* New York: Harper and Row.

Podolny, J. M., and Baron, J. N. (1997): "Resources and relationships: Social networks and mobility in the workplace," *American Sociological Review,* 62, 673–93.

Podolny, J. M., Stuart, T. E. and Hannan, M. T. (1996): "Networks, knowledge, and niches: Competition in the worldwide semiconductor industry, 1984–1991," *American Journal of Sociology,* 102, 65989.

Ring, P. S., and Van de Ven, A. (1994): "Developmental processes of cooperative interorganizational relationships," *Academy of Management Review,* 19, 90–118.

Rowley, T., Behrens, D., and Krackhardt, D. (2000): "Redundant governance structures: An analysis of structural and relational embeddedness in the steel and semiconductor industries," *Strategic Management Journal,* 21, 369–86.

Rumelt, R. P. (1984): "Towards a strategic theory of the firm," in R. B. Lamb (ed.), *Competitive Strategic Management,* Englewood Cliffs, NJ: Prentice-Hall, 556–71.

Shan, W., Walker, G., and Kogut, B. (1994): "Interfirm cooperation and startup innovation in the biotechnology industry," *Strategic Management Journal,* 15, 387–94.

Stuart, T. E. (2000): "Interorganizational alliances and the performance of firms: A study of growth and innovation rates in a high-technology industry," *Strategic Management Journal,* 21, 791–811.

Stuart, T. E., and Podolny, J. M. (1999): "Positional consequences of strategic alliances in the semiconductor industry," *Research in Sociology of Organizations,* 16, 161–182.

Stuart, T. E., Hoang, H., and Hybels, R. (1999): "Interorganizational endorsements and the performance of entrepreneurial ventures," *Administrative Science Quarterly,* 44, 315–49.

Uzzi, B. (1996): "The sources and consequences of embeddedness for the economic performance of organizations: The network effect," *American Sociological Review*, 61, 674–98.

Walker, G. (1988): "Network analysis for cooperative interfirm relationships," in F. K. Contractor and P. Lorange (eds), *Cooperative Strategies in International Business*, Lexington, KY: Lexington Press, 227–40.

Wasserman, S., and Faust, K. (1994): *Social Network Analysis: Methods and Applications*. Cambridge, UK: Cambridge University Press.

Wernerfelt, B. (1984): "A resource based view of the firm," *Strategic Management Journal*, 5, 171–80.

Westphal, J., Gulati, R., and Shortell, S. M. (1997): "Customization or conformity? An institutional and network perspective on the content and consequences of TQM adoption," *Administrative Science Quarterly*, 42, 366–94.

Zaheer, A., McEvily, B., and Perrone, V. (1998): "Does trust matter? Exploring the effects of interorganizational and interpersonal trust on performance," *Organization Science*, 9, 141–59.

Zajac, E. J., and Olsen, C. P. (1993): "From transaction cost to transactional value analysis: Implications for the study of interorganizational strategies," *Journal of Management Studies*, 30, 131–45.

Chapter Thirteen

Organizational Ecology

JOEL A. C. BAUM AND TERRY L. AMBURGEY

Organizational ecology aims to explain how social, economic and political conditions affect the relative abundance and diversity of organizations and to account for their changing composition over time. Research in organizational ecology is grounded in three observations. First, aggregates of organizations exhibit diversity. Second organizations' have difficulty devising and executing changes fast enough to meet the demands of uncertain, changing environments. And, third, organizations arise and disappear continually. Given these observations, ecological analyses formulate organizational change and variability at the population level, highlighting differential creation of new and demise of old organizations and populations with heterogeneous attributes. This formulation contrasts adaptation approaches, which explain organizational diversity in terms of ongoing organizations' leaders cumulative strategic choices.

Changes in organizational populations reflect the operation of four basic processes: *variation, selection, retention,* and *competition* (Aldrich, 1979; Campbell, 1965; McKelvey, 1982). Variations result from human behavior. Any kind of change, intentional or blind, is a variation. Individuals produce variations continuously in their efforts to adjust their behavior to others in the organization and to adjust the organization's relationship to the environment. The centrality of issues of coordination and control in organization theory is a testament to the commonness of variation inside organizations. Organizational variations provide the raw material for selection processes. Some variations prove more beneficial to organizations than others in acquiring resources in a competitive environment and are thus selected positively by managers inside organizations. Similarly, investors, customers, and government regulators in the resource environment select among the variations in place among organizations competing for resources.

When successful variations are known, or when environmental trends are identifiable, individuals can attempt to copy and implement these successful variations in their own organization, or they can attempt to forecast, anticipate, plan, and implement policies in the context of the predictable trends. But when successful variations are unknown, because, for example, the behavior of consumers and competitors is unpredictable, the probability of choosing the correct variation and implementing it successfully is low. Even when effective variations are identifiable, ambiguity in the *causes* of success may frustrate attempts at implementation and imitation. Under such conditions, variations can be viewed as experimental trials, some of which are consciously planned and some of which are accidental, some of which succeed and some of which fail. Whether or not they are known, over time, successful variations are *retained* as surviving organizations come to be characterized by them.

If the survival odds are low for organizations with a particular variant, it does not mean that these organizations are destined to fail. Rather, it means the capacity of individuals to *change* their organizations successfully is of great importance. Ecological approaches do not remove individuals from responsibility for or influence over their organization's success and survival – *individuals do matter*. Why have there been so many claims to the contrary? One important part of the confusion is that *determinism* is mistakenly contrasted with *voluntarism* rather than with *probabilism*. Leaving aside whether their actions are intelligent or foolish, planned or improvised, individuals can clearly influence their organizations' futures. Under conditions of uncertainty and ambiguity, however, there are severe constraints on the ability of boundedly rational individuals to consistently conceive and implement changes that improve organizational success and survival chances in the face of competition. Thus, "in a world of high uncertainty, adaptive efforts ... turn out to be essentially random with respect to future value" (Hannan and Freeman, 1984, p. 150). At its inception, organizational ecology focused more on differential rates of organizational failure than to differential rates of entry, largely for reasons of methodological tractability. Although this shortcoming has been largely addressed, organizational ecology is still viewed – inaccurately – as a theory of organizational failure. Organizational founding and failure figure prominently in organizational ecology because they affect the relative abundance and diversity of organizations. Ecological approaches to organizational founding and failure constitute a radical departure from traditional approaches to entrepreneurship and business failure, which focused primarily on individual initiative, skills, and abilities. By concentrating on the traits of entrepreneurs and managers, these approaches deflect attention away from the volatile nature of organizational populations. Ecological approaches, by comparison, emphasize contextual causes that produce variations in organizational founding and failure rates over time by influencing opportunity structures that confront potential organizational founders and resource constraints that face existing organizations.

The focus of organizational ecology research continues to change rapidly, however, as researchers turn their attention to processes of organization-level change and tests of structural inertia theory, revealing the role of organization-level change for understanding what organizations do as individuals, populations, and communities.

Literature Review

In broad terms, theory and research in organizational ecology focuses on two themes summarized in Table 13.1: *demographic processes* and *ecological processes*.

Table 13.1 Selected studies in organizational ecology

Reference	Key concepts	Key variables	Key findings and predictions	Key contribution	Method and sample
Demographic processes: Age and size dependence					
Ranger-Moore, 1997	Senescence Obsolescence	Age Size Environmental stability	Liability of aging is driven by obsolescence	Age and size effects moderated by environmental stability	Event history analysis Life insurance companies
Henderson, 1999	Technology strategy	Proprietary and standards-based strategies	Trade-off between growth and risk	Technology strategy moderates age effects	Event history analysis Computer firms
Demographic processes: Rates of change					
Amburgey et al., 1993	Organizational momentum Change history	Organizational change Failure	Relationship between change and failure is duration dependent and moderated by age	Structural inertia includes both resistance to change and momentum for change	Event history analysis Newspapers
Demographic processes: Consequences of change					
Baum and Singh, 1996	Niche change Competitive intensity	Overlap and nonoverlap density	Competitive intensity increases niche expansions but decreases contractions	Effect of change on failure moderated by competitive intensity	Event history analysis Day care centers
Greve, 1999	Structural inertia Regression to the mean	Size	Effect of change is moderated by size and performance level	Performance is a function of both systematic and random components	Nonlinear least-squares Radio stations
Ecological processes: Niche width					
Swaminathan, 1995	Resource partitioning	Concentration of mass producers	Founding of specialist wineries is stimulated by concentration among mass producers	Supports resource partitioning model while controlling for alternative processes	Negative binomial regression Farm wineries
Ecological processes: Density dependence					
Hannan et. al., 1995	Density dependent legitimation and competition	Population density	Legitimation effects are broader in scope than competitive effects	Effects of density vary by geographic scope	Event count analysis Automobile firms

Demographic processes

Whereas founding processes are typically conceived as attributes of a population since no organization exists prior to founding, change and failure processes occur at organizational and population levels – existing organizations have histories and structures that influence their rates of change and failure. Studying organizational failure and change is thus complicated by the need to consider processes at both levels. Demographic analysis examines the effects of organization-level characteristics on rates of organizational change and failure.

AGE AND SIZE DEPENDENCE

A central line of inquiry in demographic processes is the effect of organizational aging on failure. Until recently, the predominant view was the *liability of newness* (Stinchcombe, 1965), which proposes that, because they have to learn new social roles, create new organizational routines, and lack endorsements and exchange relationships at a time when resources are stretched to the limit, young organizations will have higher failure rates. A complementary viewpoint is that selection processes favor structurally inert organizations capable of demonstrating reliability and accountability, which requires high reproducibility. Since reproducibility, achieved through institutionalization and routinization, increases with age, older organizations should be less likely to fail (Hannan and Freeman, 1984).

A related line of research examines how organizational size influences failure. Small organizations' propensity to fail results from several *liabilities of smallness*, including problems raising capital, recruiting and training a workforce, paying higher interest rates and handling costs of regulatory compliance (Aldrich and Auster, 1986). Moreover, as organizations grow, they increasingly emphasize predictability, formalization and control, demonstrating greater reliability and accountability and consequently less vulnerability to failure. The significance of the liability of smallness stems in part from its relation to the liability of newness: Since new organizations tend to be small, if small organizations have higher failure rates, empirical evidence of a liability of newness may actually reflect specification error. With few exceptions, studies support the liability of smallness prediction that organizational failure rates decline with increased size. In contrast, however, although early studies consistently found a liability of newness, more recent studies controlling for time-varying size generally do not, and this has prompted formulation of alternative theoretical perspectives on age dependence.

The *liability of adolescence* (Fichman and Levinthal, 1991) predicts a ∩-shaped relationship between age and failure. New organizations begin with a stock of assets (e.g., goodwill, positive beliefs, commitment, resources) that buffers them during an initial "honeymoon period" even if early outcomes are unfavorable. The larger the initial stock, the longer the organization is buffered. As initial endowments are depleted, organizations unable to meet ongoing resource needs because, for example, they are unable to establish effective routines or stable exchange relations, are increasingly likely to fail.

Liabilities of newness and adolescence provide divergent accounts of age dependence for young organizations, but both imply a monotonic decline in failure for older organizations. Yet, processes underlying these models occur early in organizational lifetimes and have limited implications for older organizations. The *liability of aging* (Baum, 1989; Barron et al., 1994; Ranger-Moore, 1997) identifies processes affecting older organizations and predicts that failure increases with aging. The liability of aging begins with another insight from Stinchcombe's essay: "the organizational inventions that can be made at a time in history depend on the social technology available at that time" (1965, p. 153). Organizations reflect their founding environment. As environments change, however, bounded rationality and structural inertia make it difficult for individuals to keep their organizations aligned with environmental demands. Encountering a series of environmental changes may thus expose aging organizations to a risk of *obsolescence*. Aging may also bring about *senescence*: an accumulation of internal friction, precedent and political pacts that impede action and reliable performance, lowering organizational performance – and survival chances – even in a stable environment. Obsolescence and senescence pose separate risks: senescence is a direct effect of aging; obsolescence a result of environmental change.

Ranger-Moore (1997) recently examined age dependence in an archival, event history study of 154 New York life insurance companies during 1813–1985. First, he attempted to show the sensitivity of age dependence in organizational failure to the inclusion of time-varying measures of organizational size. Second, he examined patterns of age dependence of life insurance companies for evidence of senescence and obsolescence. Based on the conceptual distinction between these processes, he suggested that positive age dependence in failure rates reflects a liability of senescence in a stable environment, whereas in a turbulent environment, positive age-dependence greater than that in stable environments reflects combined liabilities of senescence and obsolescence. To test these ideas, Ranger-Moore compared estimates of age dependence across several, more or less stable, historical periods. Results supported global hypotheses for size and age, showing age dependence to be sensitive to inclusion of time-varying size and in particular that a spurious liability of newness appeared without size controlled. However, the liability of aging exhibited by life insurance companies (after controlling for size) suggested only a liability of obsolescence; there was no liability of aging during stable historical periods.

More generally, divergent age dependence results might reflect variation in age dependence across populations or subpopulations (Baum, 1996). In this view, newness, adolescence, and obsolescence are complementary rather than competing models, only one of which is correct. To address this possibility, research must test alternative age dependence models' mediating variables directly rather than using age as a surrogate for all underlying constructs. Henderson (1999) recently conducted such a study in which he hypothesized contingent age dependence effects dependent on an organization's technology strategy. *Proprietary strategists* explore new technologies by engaging in search, variation, and experimentation; the growth potential is large but so is the risk of failure. *Standards strategists* emphasize the refinement of existing technologies, forgoing future growth opportunities for risk reduction. Proprietary strategists take longer to develop a stable and reproducible set of organizational routines and capabilities and may also experience lower legitimacy than standards strategists. This, coupled with lower initial growth, should produce more initial failure of proprietary strategists. Moreover, proprietary strategists' reliance on internal technology makes adaptation to external changes difficult. Standards strategists, in contrast, should readily absorb external innovations, particularly from other standards strategists. Henderson's partial adjustment models of sales growth and event history models of failure among 649 US personal computer manufacturers during 1975–92 provided strong support for his contingency view. One exception was that proprietary strategists did not exhibit a liability of newness. Henderson's results demonstrate how multiple patterns of age dependence can operate simultaneously in a single population. His study also reveals important tradeoffs between growth and the risk of failure resulting from the joint effects of age and strategy.

ORGANIZATIONAL CHANGE

Most research on organizational change concentrates on *content*: A change to a more (less) advantageous configuration is considered adaptive (detrimental) (Amburgey et al., 1993). Complementing this focus, *structural inertia theory* (Hannan and Freeman, 1984) emphasizes *change process*. While content effects of change center on the difference between the performance consequences of organizational attributes before and after change, process effects focus on disruptions to internal routines and external exchange relationships. Structural inertia theory raises two questions.

How changeable are organizations?

The *structure* in structural inertia theory refers only to core organizational features (goals, forms of authority, core technology and market strategy) related to "the claims used to mobilize resources for beginning an organization and the strategies and structures used to maintain flows of scarce resources" (Hannan and Freeman, 1984, p. 156). *Peripheral* features buffer an organization's core from uncertainty. Core features exhibit greater inertia than peripheral features, but the claim is not that they never change. Instead, inertia is defined relative to environmental change: "the speed of reorganization is much lower than the rate at which environmental conditions change" (Hannan and Freeman, 1984, p. 151). Inertia also varies with organizational *age* and *size*. Because older organizations have more formalized structures, standardized routines, institutionalized power distributions, dependencies and commitments, inertia should increase with age. Moreover, as organizations grow, they increasingly emphasize predictability, formalization and control, becoming more predictable and inflexible. Large size, by buffering organizations from environments, may also reduce the impetus for change.

Although not included in structural inertia theory, a complete understanding of organizational change requires consideration of organizations' *change histories* (Amburgey et al., 1993). The more experienced an organization becomes with a particular change, the more likely it is to repeat it. If the change becomes causally linked with success in decision makers' minds – regardless of whether such a link exists – repetition is even more likely. The change process may thus itself become routinized and subject to inertial forces, creating *organizational momentum* – the tendency to maintain direction and emphasis of prior actions in current behavior. To reconcile momentum with commonly observed periods of organizational inactivity, Amburgey et al. (1993) propose that local organizational search processes (Cyert and March, 1963) produce momentum that is strongest immediately after a change occurs, but declines over time.

In an event history analysis of 1011 Finnish newspapers' change and failure over a 193-year period, Amburgey et al. (1993) find substantial support for a combined structural inertia and momentum model. Rates of change in newspaper content and publication frequency both declined with organizational age, but at the same time displayed momentum, increasing with the number of prior changes of the same type, and also endogenous decay, with recently experienced changes most likely to reoccur, and the likelihood declining with time since the change. Research offers substantial empirical evidence of momentum in actions including strategic and organizational change (Kelly and Amburgey, 1991), mergers and acquisitions (Amburgey and Miner, 1992; Ginsberg and Baum, 1994), technological choices (Christensen and Bower, 1996; Noda and Bower, 1996; Stuart and Podolny, 1996), strategic alliance formation (Gulati, 1995; Gulati and Gargiulo, 1999), and foreign market entry (Mitchell et al., 1994; Chang, 1995). Tests of age and size dependence in rates of organizational change have yielded mixed results, however, and taken together provide little systematic support for structural inertia theory's key predictions (Baum, 1996).

Overall, research indicates that, while momentum – and sometimes inertia – constrains organizations, they do initiate substantial change in response to environmental shifts (Baum, 1996). Of course, inertia and momentum are not necessarily harmful: In addition to promoting performance reliability and accountability, they can keep organizations from responding too quickly and frequently to uncertain environmental change. Ultimately, whether inertia and momentum are adaptive depends on the *hazardousness* of change.

Is organizational change beneficial?

When viewed dynamically, organizational change can be both adaptive and disruptive. According to structural inertia theory, core change destroys or renders obsolete established routines, disrupts exchange relations and undermines organizational legitimacy by impairing performance reliability and accountability. If organizations' stakeholders favor reliability and accountability, then organizations may often fail precisely as a result of their attempts to survive – even attempts that might, ultimately, have proved adaptive. Because their structures, routines and linkages are more institutionalized, older organizations are especially likely to experience disruption following core change. In contrast, large organizations may be buffered from core change disruption by, for example, maintaining both old and new routines during transition or overcoming deprivations and competitive challenges accompanying the change. If an organization survives the short-run hazard, its failure rate is predicted to decline over time as its reliability, exchange relations, and legitimacy are re-established. Only if the rate of decline is faster than before the change, however, will the organization ultimately benefit from taking the short-term risk.

Baum and Singh (1996) examined the interaction of adaptation and selection in a population of 789 daycare centers in Toronto during 1971–89. Adaptation was defined as alteration of the organization's niche in response to competition, selection as differential failure. They focused on "organizational niche changes," core changes that involve alterations (both expansion and contraction) in the ages of children daycares are licensed to enroll. They measured competition for each daycare as "overlap density," the sum of the overlaps between each center's niche and those of all others. They proposed that greater overlap density leads to more change and that changes that increase (decrease) an organization's overlap density raises (lowers) its risk of failure. Their event analysis revealed that competition increased rates of organizational niche expansion but not contraction. Support for the disruptive effects was mixed for expansion, but strong for contraction, which proved hazardous, particularly immediately after they change, and for smaller and older daycares. Niche expansion and contraction were both, however, significantly more (less) life threatening if they increased (decreased) the level of competition a center faced. Notably, while Baum and Singh found that daycare centers could change their niches in survival enhancing ways, on average, it turns out, they did not.

In another innovative study, Greve (1999) modeled effects of changes in organizations' market positions on their market share to study performance consequences of core change, and also to clarify the moderating role of organizational size in structural inertia theory. If larger size leads to greater structural inertia, larger organizations should suffer more severe declines in performance. If, however, larger organizations have greater resource endowments that buffer them from disruptive effects of change, they should experience performance decline after change but not an increased risk of failure. Since branches of multiunit organizations should experience the inertial effects of large size combined with benefits of market power, they offer an ideal arena for separating inertia and resource endowment effects. For branches of large multiunits, performance decline after a core change should be greater (or lesser) than for unitary organizations. Because regression to the mean tends to produce improvement after poor performance, a pattern of making changes when performance is low can make changes appear successful. Only by comparing organizations that change, with poor performers that do not, can increased performance due to regression and change be distinguished. Greve analyzed data on 2490 radio stations in 160 US radio markets during 1984–92. Market positions are defined as the format of the radio station, and changes in format are taken as core changes. Nonlinear least-squares estimates indicated that large and high-performing organizations experienced greater audience share losses following changes.

These and other empirical studies indicate that while core change is not necessarily disruptive in the short run, organizations do not necessarily improve their survival chances in the long run either (Baum, 1996). Two research design problems seem likely to produce systematic *underestimates* of the hazardousness of change, however. First, annual data typically available may not detect the deadliest changes – those proving fatal within a year. Second, because organizations founded before a study period are not observed when they are youngest, smallest, and most likely and vulnerable to change their inclusion likely biases downward estimates of the risk of change.

ECOLOGICAL PROCESSES

NICHE WIDTH DYNAMICS

Niche width theory (Hannan and Freeman, 1977) focuses on two aspects of *environmental variability* to explain differential survival of *specialists*, which possess few slack resources and concentrate exploiting a narrow range of customers, and *generalists*, which appeal to the mass market and exhibit tolerance for more varied environments. *Variability* refers to environmental fluctuations about the mean over time. *Grain* refers to the patchiness of these fluctuations with frequent variations termed *fine-grained* and periodic termed *coarse-grained*. The key prediction is that in fine-grained environments, with large magnitude variations relative to organizational tolerances, specialists outcompete generalists regardless of environmental uncertainty. Specialists ride out the fluctuations;

generalists are unable to respond quickly enough to operate efficiently. Thus, niche-width theory challenges the classical contingency theory prediction that uncertain environments always favor generalists that spread their risk.

In contrast to niche width theory, which predicts that for a given population one optimal strategy exists, Carroll (1985) proposes that, in environments characterized by economies of scale, competition among generalists to occupy the center of the market frees peripheral resources that are most likely to be used by specialists. He refers to the process generating this outcome as *resource partitioning*. His model implies that in concentrated markets with a few generalists, specialists can exploit more of the available resources without engaging in direct competition with generalists. This yields the prediction that increasing market concentration increases the failure rate of generalists and lowers the failure rate of specialists. Resource-partitioning theory is supported in studies of newspaper organization failure (Carroll, 1985, 1987) as well as several more recent studies of founding and failure of American breweries (Carroll and Swaminathan, 1992), and founding of Rural Cooperative Banks in Italy (Freeman and Lomi, 1994) and US farm wineries (Swaminathan, 1995), which each offer partial support. Swaminathan (1995), for example, analyzed founding rates of specialist, farm wineries over a 50-year period starting shortly after the end of Prohibition. Although results showed that farm winery foundings were lower in states with higher numbers of mass-production wineries, suggesting localized competition between these two organizational forms, consistent with resource partitioning theory, increasing concentration of generalist mass-producers increased the founding rate of farm wineries.

Although the specialist–generalist distinction is common in ecological research, tests of niche-width and resource-partitioning theories' predictions are limited, and do not explicitly contrast niche-width and resource-partitioning predictions. Recent studies frequently examine *spatial* and *temporal* environmental variation without reference to niche width, pointing to the need to elaborate niche-width models to encompass spatial as well as temporal environmental variation.

POPULATION DYNAMICS AND DENSITY DEPENDENCE

Research on founding and failure in organizational ecology has paid considerable attention to endogenous *population dynamics* and *density dependence* processes. Previous population dynamics – patterns of founding and failure – shape current founding rates (Delacroix and Carroll, 1983). Initially, prior foundings signal opportunity to entrepreneurs, encouraging founding. But as foundings increase further, resource competition increases, discouraging founding. Prior failures have analogous effects. At first, failures release resources that can be reassembled into new organizations. But further failures signal a hostile environment, discouraging founding. Resources freed by prior failures may also enhance the viability of established organizations, lowering failures in the next period (Carroll and Delacroix, 1982).

Density-dependent explanations for founding and failure are similar though not identical. Initial increases in the number of organizations can increase the institutional legitimacy of a population, enhancing the capacity of its members to acquire resources. However, as a population continues to grow, competition with others for scarce common intensifies. Combined, the mutualistic and competitive effects suggest a ∩-shaped relationship between density and founding and a ∪-shaped relationship with failure

(Hannan and Carroll, 1992). Hannan et al.'s (1995) multilevel analysis of density dependence in the entry of automobile firms in Europe is among the latest in this stream. The primary hypothesis in this study is that the legitimizing effects of density operate on a wider geographic scale than its competitive effects. While most studies analyze density dependence at a single level, Hannan and his colleagues modeled legitimacy and competition effects of organizational density at different levels of analysis, and in particular, casting legitimacy at a higher level (Europe) than competition (country). The key idea is that cultural images and frames cross social boundaries more easily than material resources used to build and sustain organizations. As a consequence, competitive environments should be more local than institutional environments. Archival data on founding of 2,520 automobile manufacturers in five European countries for the period 1886–1981 were used to estimate event count models of density effects at different levels. Results of the analysis support the idea that European density has a positive effect on entry rates but country-specific density has a negative effect for only two of the five countries (France and Italy, but not Belgium, Germany, or the UK).

Studies of wide variety of organizational populations provide empirical support for density-dependent founding and failure. By comparison, population dynamics findings are mixed and, when modeled together with population density, population dynamics effects are weaker and less robust. Even Delacroix and Carroll's (1983) original findings do not hold up when density is introduced in a reanalysis of their data (Carroll and Hannan, 1989a); but see Delacroix et al. (1989). One explanation for the dominance of density dependence over population dynamics is the more systematic character of density relative to the changes in density produced by founding and failure. A related explanation is the greater sensitivity of rate dependence estimates to outliers. These issues need to be examined more thoroughly before population dynamics is abandoned, which has been the trend in recent research.

Contemporary Issues and Debates

RESPECIFYING DENSITY DEPENDENCE

Although support for density dependence is quite strong, it has received critical attention for its proposed integration of ecological and institutional perspectives, assumption that each organization influences and is influenced by competition equally, and inability to explain the concentration common to older populations. Several innovative respecifications of the original formulation have been advanced to address these limitations (Table 13.2). Although Hannan and Carroll frequently challenge such efforts (e.g., 1992; 1995), they nevertheless promise to improve substantive interpretation and realism of the original model. We briefly consider three of these respecifications.

DENSITY AND INSTITUTIONAL PROCESSES

Organizational ecologists distinguish between cognitive and sociopolitical legitimacy. An organizational form is cognitively legitimated when there is little question in the minds of actors that it serves as the natural way to effect some kind of collective action.

Table 13.2 Elaborations of the density dependence model

Model	Critiques*	Elaboration	References
Density delay	3	Incorporates imprinting effect of density at founding	Carroll and Hannan (1989b)
Mass dependence	2, 3	Weights each organization's competitive effect by its size	Barnett and Amburgey (1990)
Multiform models	2	Estimates intrapopulation microstructures and interpopulation (community) macrostructures	Barnett (1990)
Level of analysis	2	Estimates variation in density dependence across level of geographic aggregation (city, state, region, nation)	Carroll and Hannan (1989a); Carroll and Wade (1991); Hannan et al. (1995)
Institutional embeddedness	1	Estimates population legitimation with relational density (endorsements by powerful actors and organizations)	Baum and Oliver (1992)
Nondensity measures	1	Estimates population legitimation with nondensity measures (certification contests, media content measures)	Rao (1994)
Localized competition	2, 3	Weights competitive effects of organizations on each other by their proximity (size, price, location)	Baum and Mezias (1992); Baum and Haveman (1997)
Organizational niche overlap	1, 2	Disaggregates population density for each organization based on resource (non)overlaps with other organizations	Baum and Singh (1994a; 1994b)
Location dependence	2	Incorporates information on spatial structure of organizational population	Lomi (1995)
Time-variation	1, 3	Distinguishes effects of low density early and in a population's history	Baum (1995)
Changing basis of competition/ Dynamic selection	2, 3	Incorporates variation in the strength competitive processes over a population's life cycle	Baum (1995); Barron (1999)
Competitive intensity	2, 3	Weights each organization's competitive strength by its age and/or competitive experience	Barnett et al. (1994); Barnett (1997)

Notes: * Critiques addressed by elaboration: 1 = proposed integration of ecological and institutional perspectives; 2 = assumption that each organization influences and is influenced by competition equally; 3 = inability to explain the concentration common to older populations.

Embeddedness in relational and normative contexts influences an organizational form's sociopolitical legitimacy by signaling conformity to social and institutional expectations. Institutionalist theorists consider these two facets fundamentally interrelated – while cognitive legitimacy may be achieved without sociopolitical approval, sociopolitical legitimacy is a vital source of, or impediment to, cognitive legitimacy. Density dependence theory emphasizes *only* cognitive legitimacy (Hannan et al., 1995).

Density dependence theorists defend their exclusive focus with a series of interrelated arguments. The main claim is that legitimacy defies direct measurement: "[R]econstructing the exact details of changing levels of legitimation . . . attention to all of the unique features of that population . . . learning what fraction of relevant individuals take a particular organizational form for granted . . . [thus] theories of legitimation and competition can be studied systematically and comparatively *only* by testing their implications for the relationships between other observables" (Hannan and Carroll, 1992, pp. 37–9). This "indirect" approach is criticized because conforming findings may proxy for a wide range of possible effects and reveal little about the theoretical explanations designed to account for them (Zucker, 1989; Delacroix and Rao, 1994; Baum and Powell, 1995). These critiques are countered by the density-as-process argument, in which legitimation is not a variable to be measured but a process that relates density to founding and failure: "growth in density *controls* . . . [legitimation] processes – it does not reflect them" (Hannan and Carroll, 1992, p.69).

Proxy and process views suggest different effects of adding covariates to empirical models. If density is a proxy, measuring legitimation more directly should attenuate or eliminate density's legitimacy effect; the density-as-process view implies a strengthening of density's legitimation effect after including such covariates (Hannan and Carroll, 1992, pp.70–1). Baum and Oliver (1992) provide a test of the proxy-versus-process prediction. They conceive sociopolitical legitimacy in terms of institutional embeddedness – interconnections between the population and its institutional environment. More interconnections between a population its institutional environment signals greater conformity with normative expectations and worthiness for support (DiMaggio and Powell, 1983). Institutional embeddedness is measured with *relational density*, defined as the number of formal relations between the population and key institutions (e.g., government agencies, community organizations). Although initial estimates supported density dependence for both founding and failure of Toronto daycare centers, supporting the density-as-proxy view, legitimacy effects of initial increases in organizational density disappeared after inclusion of relational density, and the effects of organizational density became purely competitive. Relational density, in contrast, exhibited predicted mutualistic effects at low levels; see also Hybels et al. (1994).

DENSITY AND COMPETITIVE PROCESSES

Density dependence theory assumes that all members of a population are equivalent, with each member assumed to compete for the same scarce resources and to contribute to and experience competition equally. Yet, theory in organizational ecology suggests that the intensity of competition between organizations in a population is a function of their similarity in resource requirements: the more similar the resource requirements, the greater the potential for intense competition – see, for example McPherson (1983), Baum and Singh (1994a, b). Hannan and Freeman (1977, pp. 945–6), for example, propose that organizations of different sizes use different strategies and structures. As a result, although engaged in similar activities, large and small-sized organizations in a population depend on different resource mixes, and so similarly sized organizations should compete most intensely. Although such "size-localized" competition did not initially receive empirical attention, studies in settings including Manhattan banks (Banaszak-Holl, 1992), US credit unions (Amburgey et al., 1994), Manhattan hotels (Baum and Mezias, 1992), US health maintenance organizations (Wholey et al., 1992), and New York State life insurance companies (Ranger-Moore et al., 1995) provide evidence of size-localized competition. These findings demonstrate that the intensity of competition faced by organizations in a population depends not only on the number (i.e., density) of organizations in a population, but on their relative sizes as well. Baum and Mezias (1992) generalize the model showing organizations similar in size, product price, and geographic locations compete more intensely.

Research on localized competition also offers important insights into the dynamics of organizational diversity. Localized competition models imply a pattern of disruptive or segregating selection (Amburgey et al., 1994) in which competition for finite resources leads eventually to differentiation. This mode of selection, which has not been emphasized in the ecological literature, tends to increase organizational diversity by producing gaps rather than smooth, continuous variation in the distribution of the members of a population along some organizational dimension.

ACCOUNTING FOR CONCENTRATION

Organizational populations appear to follow a common growth path: The number of organizations grows slowly initially, then increasing rapidly to a peak. Once the peak is reached, the number of organizations decline and concentration increases. Since, in the original density dependence model, each organization is assumed to contribute to and experience competition equally, no organization or group of organizations can dominate. Consequently, the model predicts logistic population growth to an equilibrium level, but cannot account for the decline or concentration. This limitation has received considerable attention (see Table 13.2). The most recent is Barron's (1999) "dynamic selection" model, a variant of Baum's (1995) earlier "changing basis of competition" model that emphasizes the organizational size distribution of a population.

In Barron's version, as organizations grow in scale they may be able to take deliberate steps to prevent the formation of new competitors. And, even if they do not, the fact that they already have well-established exchange networks, reputations, customer loyalties, and staff expertise makes it more difficult for new entrants. Therefore, as the size distribution of a population shifts to the right, Barron predicts that the founding rate will decline. He tests this prediction using the mean of the log size distribution, which is approximately symmetric. For failure, Barron's argument is somewhat different. In the early years of a population, when density is low, the failure rate is high because the legitimacy of the organizational form is also low. However, competition is also weak. Under early low-density conditions, therefore, he proposes that failures are distributed randomly, with no organizations heavily disadvantaged relative to any other. As density increases further, however, competition increases, and organizations best able to withstand the more intense competition should have an increasing advantage in terms of survival chances. Thus, the gap in survival chances of robust and frail organizations should widen as the density increases. Barron uses size to differentiate robust and frail organizations, and thus predicts that as the total number of organizations in the population increases, the survival benefits of large size should increase. He tested and corroborated the model in an analysis of founding and failure of New York State credit unions during 1914–90.

Central Questions

DEMOGRAPHY OF ORGANIZATIONAL FOUNDING

Although organizational founding is an important theme in organizational ecology, foundings have typically been treated as identical additions to homogenous populations. The absence of organization-specific factors in founding studies contrasts sharply with ecological analyses of failure and change where issues of organizational heterogeneity have long been conspicuous. Studying heterogeneity in founding is complicated because attributes that might be used as explanatory variables cannot be observed for organizations that do not yet exist. As a result, the organization itself cannot be the focal point of study. Ecological researchers initially sidestepped this complication by treating the population as the unit experiencing foundings, but if founding rates vary with organizational attributes or local environmental features, this heterogeneity will result in specification bias. Some progress has been made on this problem by specifying more fine-grained population substructures (i.e., subpopulations based on location, profit orientation, or strategy) into which organizations are differentially founded. Unfortunately, this approach suffers operational problems (e.g., artificial, arbitrary and numerous subpopulations, ambiguous risk-set definition) that can undermine efforts to operationalize the approach empirically. Consequently, subpopulation entry studies typically provide either descriptive accounts of organizational niches that were actually filled or estimate empirical models that are potentially seriously misspecified. Two alternatives have recently appeared that make it possible to examine how differentiation within populations and variation in their environments affect the details of the founding process.

The first involves derivation of empirical corrections for unobservable region-specific variance in founding of particular organizational forms (Lomi, 1995). In this approach, organizational populations are not subdivided on the basis of abstract, a priori categories, but based on categories estimated directly from the data. Lomi's analysis of founding of Italian cooperative banks using this approach yields three main findings. First, level of analysis is an important factor in specifying founding processes. Models of cooperative bank founding are better specified at the regional than national level. Second, models neglecting unobserved heterogeneity tend to overestimate the importance of ecological processes (e.g., density dependence, resource partitioning). Indeed, after controlling for unobserved heterogeneity across regions organizational density loses statistical significance. Third, the analysis revealed the existence of two distinct heterogeneous segments within the population. When the founding rate was allowed to vary *between* segments, effects of density become statistically weaker but maintain the predicted direction. When the rate was allowed to vary *within* segments, evidence of heterogeneous response to general population processes was found.

Complementing standard ecological analyses that ask *when* foundings occur – by any kind of organization in any location in a population's niche – the second approach, introduced by Baum and Haveman (1997) takes organizational foundings as given and ask *what kinds* of organizations are founded and *where?* Their approach is relational, focusing on organizations' positions relative to each other in the resource space, and so does not require specification of subpopulations where foundings can occur. Given that a new organization appears, they examine how similar in product (size and price) and geographic space it is to neighboring organizations. Their analysis of Manhattan hotels during 1898–1990 reveals some of the complexity of founding processes in a multidimensional resource space. Size-localized competition prompted hoteliers to differentiate new hotels from incumbents in geographic location and price. Geographically localized competition influenced new entrants' size differentiation in the same way. Price-based agglomeration economies, however, led hoteliers to cluster their new entries both in terms of geography and size, and geography-based economies led to clustering in terms of price. Overall, Manhattan hotel founders appear willing to trade-off differences in size for similarity in price.

Aggregates and Ensembles

Our review highlights some of the pitfalls associated with treating members of an organizational population as homogenous. Although density dependence respecifications designed to address this have been an important advance (see Table 13.2), the result is typically a respecification of the population as a set of aggregates rather than a single aggregate; organizational ecology has yet to incorporate the rapidly growing literature on organizational networks and ensembles. Ensembles, unlike aggregates, are structured. The analytic categories that have developed within organizational ecology provide little insight into the (potential) internal structure of a population because they focus primarily on attributes rather than relationships. This is not to say that relationships have been entirely absent within ecological work, but rather that relationships have been incorporated primarily at the organizational level as an attribute and that the scope of relationships has been narrowly specified.

Miner et al. (1990), treated formal interorganizational relationships as an organizational attribute that reduces organizational failure rates by providing a resource buffer against environmental shocks. Baum and Oliver's (1992) relational density measure specifies formal relations between organizations and key institutions at the organizational level and then aggregates them. The resource partitioning model specifies a relationship between categories within a population (large generalists and small specialists) rather than at the organizational level but like most ecological work to date it provides a narrow set of possible relationships: competition or mutualism. This narrow approach to relationships is also adopted in studies of competitive relationships. Baum and his colleagues (Baum and Mezias, 1992; Baum and Haveman, 1997), for example, view competition among firms as a function of their positions relative to each other in the resource space.

Research on organizational networks and ensembles (see chapters by Gulati et al., and Baker and Faulkner, this volume) indicates that the development and evolution of populations' internal structures may be vital to their dynamics. Whether or not demographic and ecological processes affect and are affected by such population structures is a question that cannot be answered without theoretical elaboration within organizational ecology and with network researchers.

Emerging Directions

POPULATION-LEVEL LEARNING

Recently, a stream of research on population-level learning (Miner and Haunschild, 1995; Miner and Anderson, 1999) has emerged to tackle some important aspects of organizational variation. While evidence of organizations' *reliance* on the experience of others is copious, evidence on the *importance* of vicarious learning from others is not extensive. Research on population-level learning explores the possibility that organizations benefit vicariously from the experiences of others. Experience at the population level may generate learning benefits for individual organizations without requiring the specific investments or risk exposure that may prove fatal for organizations.

Although individual organizations may tend toward inertia, populations of organizations may still produce substantial variation and knowledge that individual organizations can acquire. At the population level, a lack of cohesion and authority structures may allow the proliferation of new ideas and routines. By observing their population, organizations can potentially learn the strategies, practices, and technologies employed by other successful organizations. Even recklessly innovative organizations that quickly fail can generate new knowledge that adds to the experience of the population. So, the best strategy for individual organizations may often be to emphasize exploitation of others successful explorations (Levinthal and March, 1993).

Population experience takes many forms. Other organizations' operating experience may contribute to internal efficiency in a similar way to an organization's own cumulative operating experience. By observing other organizations' operations, reading about them in trade journals, listening to lectures about them, or by hiring their employees, an organization can gain ideas about managing its own operations. Moreover, just as an organization can observe consumers' responses to it, it can observe their responses to other organizations (White, 1981). Organizations also need a model of competitors. Population operating experience can generate part of what is necessary for a model of competitors by locating them in the niche space (White, 1981). Organizational failures may provide a particularly valuable opportunity to learn about competing (Ingram and Baum, 1997). Managers (and the media) naturally attend to failures, and since failing organizations no longer try to protect a competitive future, the details of their experience may be more accessible. By looking at failures, organizations can learn what not to do; by looking at failures' successful rivals they can learn what competitive moves are effective. People employed by the failed organization also disseminate its experience when they join other organizations.

Baum and Ingram (1998) found that the stock of population operating experience at the time of founding played a much larger role in lowering failures of Manhattan hotels than operating experience the population accumulated after their founding. Ingram and Baum's (1997) study of US hotel chains replicated this finding, and also found, in contrast, that for competitive experience, only failures after founding benefited organizations. These findings suggest that organizations are capable of "survival-enhancing" learning from competitive population experience, but not population operating experience – successive generations of new organizations exploit their population's operating experience at the time they are founded, but unable to take advantage of subsequent advances.

COMPLEXITY IN POPULATION DYNAMICS

There has been a great deal of interest recently in the application of complexity theory to a variety of real-world, time-dependent systems driven by the promise of this new branch of mathematics to untangle and bring forth order from seeming disorder; see chapters by Carley et al. (this volume). Many natural and social systems – including biological (Kauffman, 1993), economic (Anderson et al., 1988), and organizational (Cheng and Van de Ven, 1996; Brown and Eisenhardt, 1998; McKelvey, 1998; 1999) – are now recognized to exhibit chaotic or nonlinear behavior, the complexity of which is so great that they were previously considered random. Research suggests complex systems tend not to gravitate toward random or highly ordered behavior but rather toward an intermediate level of (dis)order "at the edge of chaos" that lies between randomness and order. This complexity enables the systems to maximize benefits of stability while retaining a capacity to change (Kauffman, 1993).

Population dynamics research in organizational ecology has strong, but largely unexplored, ties to complexity theory. Among the oldest and most famous examples of simple deterministic nonlinear equations that produce complex behavior are the Logistic and Lotka–Volterra equations, which were originally conceived as models of population growth, and from which the density dependence model is derived. Complexity theory provides a rich theoretical framework as well as techniques for detecting nonlinear dynamics that can describe – and potentially help to account for – the dynamics of founding and failure in organizational populations. Baum and Silverman (1999) analyzed founding and failure time series for 12 populations using these techniques.[1] Among the 24 founding and failure series they analyzed, 7 (29 percent) were classified as orderly, 3 (13 percent) as random, and 13 (54 percent) as complex. Their results provide the first empirical assessment of the extent to which orderly, random, or complex behavior characterizes organizational population dynamics.

If organizational populations tend to gravitate toward "the edge of chaos," this poses a challenge for organizational ecologists because analytic approaches typically employed in organizational ecology are not well suited to modeling complex dynamical systems (Morrison, 1991; Dooley, 1994). Modeling complexity increases with data complexity (Dooley, 1994). Organizational populations that yield time series with a high degree of order (linear deterministic) or disorder (random) are easy to model. Those having a moderate degree of disorder can be modeled with linear differential or difference models. Systems with intermediate values of (dis)order are the most difficult to model. Once we know this, however, we have a better idea of what models to apply to understand the dynamics: use stochastic models to explain random processes, linear deterministic models to explain orderly behavior, and nonlinear dynamic modeling to explain complex processes (Morrison, 1991).

Connection Across Levels

UPWARD AND DOWNWARD CAUSATION

The focus of organizational ecology research has transformed dramatically since Hannan and Freeman's original theoretical statement. Researchers increasingly focus their attention on processes of organization-level change and tests of structural inertia theory (Barnett and Carroll, 1995). This research reveals some of the potential significance of organization-level change for understanding what organizations do as individuals, as populations, and as communities. But, it also points to a potential clash of selectionist causal paths in organizational ecology. Is emergent order in an organizational population – the kinds of organizations surviving – the result of the ecological selection of populations? Organizations? Or among individuals and ideas within organizations that combine to create successful organizations?

The prevalent view appears to be that "order" is the result of a multilevel interplay between downward and upward causation: the order that is favorably selected ecologically is the result of ecological processes inside organizations (Campbell, 1965; Baum and Singh, 1994c; McKelvey, 1997; Aldrich, 1999). The implication of this view is that organizational ecologists can best study change by examining how social and environmental conditions and interactions within and among organizations and organizational populations jointly influence the rates at which new organizations and new populations are created, existing organizations and organizational forms die out, and individual organizations change. As our review, along with its companion intraorganizational and interorganizational ecology chapters, demonstrates this is clearly the trend in recent research.

Together the three organizational ecology chapters point to a hierarchical set of ecological processes. The hierarchies relevant to organizational ecology are *inclusive* with levels are nested one within the other. Wholes are composed of parts at lower levels of organization, and are themselves parts of more extensive wholes. Organizational communities, are composed of populations of organizational forms, which themselves are composed of organizations, which are in turn composed of work groups, and so on. The nesting of entities into larger entities at a higher level of organization creates a system of levels. Each level constitutes a "node of selection" at which organizational entities are either retained or eliminated (Baum and Singh, 1994c).[2]

Dynamic interactions at each hierarchical level constitute entities at the next-higher level of this nested ecological hierarchy. As is clear from Galunic and Weeks' chapter, interactions among jobs bind workgroups together, which in turn bind organizations together. Interactions among organizations of the same form constitute populations. Competition, mutualism, collective action, collective learning, and other ecological processes at this level are the characteristic phenomena responsible for producing the variables most frequently studied at the organizational level – organizational density, rates of founding, failure, and change. When we become concerned with the interactions of populations of different organizational forms, as Rao's chapter explains, we have moved up to the community level. Populations, not organizations, interact to shape communities. Ecological processes at this level include inter-population competition, symbiotic interactions, institutional entrepreneurship and social movements related to new organizational forms, and changes in environmental carrying capacities. Processes at each level of each level of organization, then, each represent only a part of the overall ecological process.

There are also interactions among levels. Although there is a degree of autonomy of event and process at each hierarchical level, there is also both upward and downward causation (Campbell, 1990). Interactions across different levels constrain the kinds of processes that can occur at a given level and regulate those that do occur. Upward causation means that features of each level constrain what emerges at the next higher level. People's understanding of and beliefs about organizations help shape the decisions from which organizations are formed (Galunic and Weeks, this volume). These decisions are then launched into the higher level of the population, where processes such as competition and entrepreneurship take over. Downward causation means that selection among higher-level organizational entities shapes and constrains subsequent lower-level ecological processes. As a result, ecological processes at one level affect the nature and variability of organizational entities at lower levels. Thus, what goes on at one level of the ecological hierarchy shapes processes and events at other levels, with dynamics connected most strongly at adjacent lower and upper levels. Organizational ecology must become fundamentally concerned with all these coupled interactions.

Conclusion

While organizational ecologists would like their theories to maximize *generality* across organizations, *realism* of context, and *precision* in measurement, no theory can do all these at the same time (McGrath, 1982). Theories must sacrifice on some dimensions to maximize others. Realistic theories, for example, may apply to only a limited domain, while general theories may be inaccurate or misleading in specific cases. Historically, organizational ecologists appear to have favored a trade-off of precision and realism for generality in their theories (Singh, 1993). Precision and realism are clearly sacrificed for generality in density dependence and in structural inertia theories, for example. On the one hand, this strategy has proven to be a key strength: Organizational ecologists have accumulated a wealth of empirical evidence from diverse organizational settings unparalleled in organization science. On the other hand, it is also a major weakness: Accumulated empirical estimates for such variables as organizational age, size, and density reveal little about theoretical explanations underlying the empirical regularities. This fosters skepticism regarding the veracity of inferred processes because supportive findings cannot be interpreted precisely, and contradictory findings are difficult to account for on theoretical grounds. The studies we presented in this chapter all share in common the tendency to yield some generality in the interest of improved realism and precision. Altering the ecological research orientation in this way is an important step toward resolving organizational ecology's conceptual and empirical problems, and realizing more of its great potential contribution to theory, research and practice in organization science.

Notes

1   These included Manhattan hotels, 1898–1990; Manhattan banks, 1761–1980; New York City Newspapers, 1725–1989; San Francisco newspapers, 1845–1975; US labor unions,

1835–1985; US trade associations, 1900–82; Massachusetts railroads, 1822–1925.

2 Baum and Singh (1994c) present a hierarchical conception of *evolutionary* processes that encompasses ecological processes of "interaction" as well as historical processes of "replication"; see also Galunic and Weeks, and Warglien (this volume).

References

Aldrich, H. E. (1979): *Organizations and Environments.* Englewood Cliffs, NJ: Prentice-Hall.

Aldrich, H. E. (1999): *Organizations Evolving.* Thousand Oaks, CA: Sage.

Aldrich, H. E., and Auster, E. R. (1986): "Even dwarfs started small: Liabilities of age and size and their strategic implications," in B. Staw and L. Cummings *Research in Organizational Behavior,* Volume 8, Greenwich, CT: JAI Press, 165–98.

Amburgey, T. L., and Miner, A. S. (1992): "Strategic momentum: The effects of repetitive, positional, and contextual momentum on merger activity," *Strategic Management Journal,* 13, 335–48.

Amburgey, T. L., Dacin, T., and Kelly D. (1994): "Disruptive selection and population segmentation: Interpopulation competition as a segregating process," in J. A. C. Baum and J. V. Singh (eds), *Evolutionary Dynamics of Organizations,* New York: Oxford University Press, 240–54.

Amburgey, T. L., Kelly, D., and Barnett W. P. (1993): "Resetting the clock: The dynamics of organizational change and failure," *Administrative Science Quarterly,* 38, 51–73.

Anderson, P. W., Arrow, K. J., and Pines, D. (eds) (1988): *The Economy as an Evolving Complex System.* Redwood City, CA: Addison-Wesley.

Banaszak-Holl, J. (1992): "Historical trends in rates of Manhattan bank mergers, acquisitions, and failures," unpublished manuscript, Center for Health Care Research, Brown University.

Barnett, W. P. (1990): "The organizational ecology of a technological system," *Administrative Science Quarterly,* 35, 31–60.

Barnett, W. P. (1997): "The dynamics of competitive intensity," *Administrative Science Quarterly,* 42, 128–60.

Barnett, W. P., and Amburgey, T. L. (1990): "Do larger organizations generate stronger competition?" in J. V. Singh (ed.), *Organizational Evolution: New Directions,* Newbury Park, CA: Sage, 78–102.

Barnett, W. P., and Carroll, G. R. (1995): "Modeling internal organizational change," *Annual Review of Sociology,* 21, 217–36.

Barnett, W. P., Greve, H. R., and Park, D. Y. (1994): "An evolutionary model of organizational performance," *Strategic Management Journal,* 15, 11–28.

Barron, D. N. (1999): "The structuring of organizational populations," *American Sociological Review,* 64, 421–45.

Barron, D. N., West, E., Hannan, M. T. (1994): "A time to grow and a time to die: Growth and mortality of credit unions in New York City, 1914-1990," *American Journal of Sociology,* 100, 381–421.

Baum, J. A. C. (1989): "Liabilities of newness, adolescence, and obsolescence: Exploring age dependence in the dissolution of organizational relationships and organizations," *Proceedings of the Administrative Sciences Association of Canada,* 10(5), 1–10.

Baum, J. A. C. (1995): "The changing basis of competition in organizational populations: Evidence from the Manhattan hotel industry, 1898–1990," *Social Forces,* 74, 177–205.

Baum, J. A. C. (1996): "Organizational ecology," in S. Clegg, C. Hardy, and W. Nord (eds), *Handbook of Organization Studies,* London: Sage, 77–114.

Baum, J. A. C., and Haveman, H. A. (1997): "Love thy Neighbor? Differentiation and agglomeration in the Manhattan hotel industry," *Administrative Science Quarterly,* 42, 304–38.

Baum, J. A. C., and Ingram, P. (1998): "Survival-enhancing learning in the Manhattan hotel industry, 1898–1990," *Management Science,* 44, 996–1016.

Baum, J. A. C., and Mezias, S. J. (1992): "Localized competition and organizational failure in the

Manhattan hotel industry, 1898–1990," *Administrative Science Quarterly*, 37, 580–604.

Baum, J. A. C., and Oliver, C. (1992): "Institutional embeddedness and the dynamics of organizational populations," *American Sociological Review*, 57, 540–59.

Baum, J. A. C., and Powell, W. W. (1995): "Cultivating an institutional ecology of organizations: Comment on Hannan, Carroll, Dundon, and Torres," *American Sociological Review*, 60, 529–38.

Baum, J. A. C., and. Silverman, B. S. (1999): "Complexity in the dynamics of organizational founding and failure," in M. Lissack and H. Gunz (eds), *Managing Complexity in Organizations: A View from Many Directions*, New York: Quorum Press, 292–312

Baum, J. A. C., and Singh, J. V. (1994a): "Organizational niche overlap and the dynamics of organizational mortality," *American Journal of Sociology*, 100, 346–80.

Baum, J. A. C., and Singh, J. V. (1994b): "Organizational niche overlap and the dynamics of organizational founding," *Organization Science*, 5, 483–501.

Baum, .J. A. C., and Singh, J. V. (eds) (1994c): *Evolutionary Dynamics of Organizations*. New York: Oxford University Press.

Baum, J. A. C., and Singh, J. V. (1996): "Dynamics of organizational responses to competition," *Social Forces*, 74, 1261–97.

Brown, S. L., and Eisenhardt, K. M. (1998): *Competing on the Edge*. Boston: Harvard Business School Press.

Campbell, D. T. (1965): "Variation and selective retention in socio-cultural evolution," in H. R. Barringer, G. I. Blanksten, and R. W. Mack (eds), *Social Change in Developing Areas: A Reinterpretation of Evolutionary Theory*, Cambridge, MA: Schenkman, 19–48.

Campbell, D. T. (1990): "Levels of organization, downward causation, and the selection-theory approach to evolutionary epistemology," in G. Greenberg and E. Tobach (eds), *Theories of the Evolution of Knowing*, Hillsdale, NJ: Lawrence Erlbaum Associates, 1–17.

Carroll, G. R. (1985): "Concentration and specialization: Dynamics of niche width in populations of organizations," *American Journal of Sociology*, 90, 1262–83.

Carroll, G. R. (1987): *Publish and Perish: The Organizational Ecology of Newspaper Industries*. Greenwich, CT: JAI Press.

Carroll, G. R., and Delacroix, J. (1982): "Organizational mortality in the newspaper industries of Argentina and Ireland: An ecological approach," *Administrative Science Quarterly*, 27, 169–98.

Carroll, G. R., and Hannan, M. T. (1989a): "Density delay in the evolution of organizational population: A model and five empirical tests," *Administrative Science Quarterly*, 34, 411–30.

Carroll, G. R., and Hannan, M. T. (1989b): "Density dependence in the evolution of newspapers organizations," *American Sociological Review*, 54, 524–41.

Carroll, G. R., and Swaminathan, A. (1992): "The organizational ecology of strategic groups in the American brewing industry from 1975–1990," *Corporate and Industrial Change*, 1, 65–97.

Carroll, G. R., and Wade, J. B. (1991): "Density dependence in the evolution of the American brewing industry across different levels of analysis," *Social Science Research*, 20, 271–302.

Chang, S-J. (1995): "International expansion strategy of Japanese firms: Capability building through sequential entry," *Academy of Management Journal*, 38, 383–407.

Cheng, Y-T., and Van de Ven, A. H. (1996): "Learning the innovation journey: Order out of chaos?" *Organization Science*, 7, 593–614.

Christensen, C. M., and Bower, J. L. (1996): "Customer power, strategic investment, and the failure of leading firms," *Strategic Management Journal*, 17, 197–218.

Cyert, R. M., and March, J. G. (1963): *A Behavioral Theory of the Firm*. Englewood Cliffs NJ: Prentice Hall.

Delacroix, J., and Carroll, G. R. (1983): "Organizational foundings: An ecological study of the newspaper industries of Argentina and Ireland," *Administrative Science Quarterly*, 28, 274–91.

Delacroix, J., and Rao, H. (1994): "Externalities and ecological theory: Unbundling density dependence," in J. A. C. Baum and J. V. Singh (eds), *Evolutionary Dynamics of Organizations*, New York: Oxford University Press, 255–68.

Delacroix, J., Swaminathan, A., and Solt, M. E. (1989): "Density dependence versus population dynamics: An ecological study of failings in the California wine industry," *American Sociological Review*, 54, 245–62.

DiMaggio, P. J., and Powell, W. W. (1983): "The iron cage revisited: Institutional isomorphism and collective rationality in organizational fields," *American Sociological Review*, 48, 147–60.

Dooley, K. (1994): "Complexity in time series modeling." *Society for Chaos Theory in Psychology and the Life Sciences*, 2, 1–3.

Fichman, M., and Levinthal, D. A. (1991): "Honeymoons and the liability of adolescence: A new perspective on duration dependence in social and organizational relationships," *Academy of Management Review*, 16, 442–68.

Freeman, J., and Lomi, A. (1994): "Resource partitioning and foundings of banking cooperative in Italy," in J. A. C. Baum and J. V. Singh (eds), *Evolutionary Dynamics of Organizations*, New York: Oxford University Press, 269–93.

Ginsberg, A., and Baum, J. A. C. (1994): "Evolutionary processes and patterns of core business change," in J. A. C. Baum and J. V. Singh (eds), *Evolutionary Dynamics of Organizations*, New York: Oxford University Press, 127–51.

Greve, H. R. (1999): "The Effect of Core Change on Performance: Inertia and Regression toward the Mean," *Administrative Science Quarterly*, 44, 590–614.

Gulati, R. (1995): "Social structure and alliance formation patterns: A longitudinal analysis," *Administrative Science Quarterly*, 40, 619–52.

Gulati, R., and Gargiulo, M. (1999): "Where do interorganizational networks come from?" *American Journal of Sociology*, 104, 1439–93.

Hannan, M. T., and Carroll, G. R. (1992): *Dynamics of Organizational Populations: Density, Competition, and Legitimation*. New York, Oxford University Press.

Hannan, M. T., and Carroll, G. R. (1995): "Theory building and cheap talk about legitimation: Reply to Baum and Powell," *American Sociological Review*, 60, 539–44.

Hannan, M. T., and Freeman, J. (1977): "The population ecology of organizations," *American Journal of Sociology*, 83, 929–84.

Hannan, M. T., and Freeman, J. (1984): "Structural inertia and organizational change," *American Sociological Review*, 49, 149–164.

Hannan, M. T., Carroll, G. R., Dundon, E. A., and Torres, J. C. (1995): "Organizational evolution in a multinational context: Entries of automobile manufacturers in Belgium, Britain, France, Germany and Italy," *American Sociological Review*, 60, 509–28.

Henderson, A. D. (1999): "Firm strategy and age dependence: A contingent view of the liabilities of newness, adolescence, and obsolescence," *Administrative Science Quarterly*, 44, 281–314.

Hybels, R. C., Ryan, A. R., and Barley, S. R. (1994): "Alliances, legitimation, and founding rates in the U.S. biotechnology field, 1971–1989," paper presented at the Academy of Management national meetings, Dallas TX.

Ingram, P., and Baum, J. A. C. (1997): "Opportunity and constraint: Organizations' learning from the operating and competitive experience of industries," *Strategic Management Journal*, 18, (Summer Special Issue), 75–98.

Kauffman, S. A. (1993): *Origins of Order: Self-organization and Selection in Evolution*. Oxford: Oxford University Press.

Kelly, D., and Amburgey, T. L. (1991): "Organizational inertia and momentum: A dynamic model of strategic change," *Academy of Management Journal*, 34, 591–612.

Levinthal, D. A., and March, J. G. (1993): "The myopia of learning," *Strategic Management Journal*, 14, 94–112.

Lomi, A. (1995): "The population ecology of organizational founding: Location dependence and unobserved heterogeneity," *Administrative Science Quarterly*, 40, 111–44.

McGrath, J. E. (1982): "Dilemmatics: The study of research choices and dilemmas," in J. E.

McGrath, J. Martin, and R. A. Kulka (eds), *Judgement Calls in Research*, Beverly Hills, CA: Sage, 69–102.

McKelvey, B. (1982): *Organizational Systematics*. Berkeley, CA: University of California Press.

McKelvey, B. (1997): "Quasi-natural organization science," *Organization Science*, 8, 352–80.

McKelvey, B. (1998): "Complexity vs. selection among coevolutionary microstates in firms: Complexity effects on strategic organizing," *Comportamento Organizacional E Gestão*, 4, 17–59.

McKelvey, B. (1999): "Toward a Campbellian realist organization science," in J. A. C. Baum and B. McKelvey (eds), *Variations in Organization Science: In Honor of Donald T. Campbell*, Thousand Oaks, CA: Sage, 383–411.

McPherson, J. M. (1983): "An ecology of affiliation," *American Sociological Review*, 48, 519–32.

Miner, A. S., and Anderson, P. (eds) (1999): *Population Level Learning and Industry Change (Advances in Strategic Management, Vol. 16)*, Stamford, CT: JAI Press.

Miner, A. S., and Haunschild, P. R. (1995): "Population level learning," in B. Staw and L. Cummings (eds), *Research in Organizational Behavior, Volume 17*, Greenwich, CT: JAI Press, 115–66.

Miner, A. S., Amburgey, T. L., and Stearns, T. (1990): "Interorganizational linkages and population dynamics: Buffering and transformational shields," *Administrative Science Quarterly*, 35, 689–713.

Mitchell, W., Shaver, J. M., and Yeung, B. (1994): "Foreign entrant survival and foreign market share: Canadian companies' experience in United States medical sector markets," *Strategic Management Journal*, 15, 555–67.

Morrison, F. (1991): *The Art of Modeling Dynamic Systems*. New York: Wiley.

Noda, T., and Bower, J. L. (1996): "Strategy making as iterated processes of resource allocation," *Strategic Management Journal*, 17, (Summer Special Issue), 159–92.

Ranger-Moore, J. (1997): "Bigger may be better but is older wiser? Organizational age and size in the New York life insurance industry," *American Sociological Review*, 62, 903–20.

Ranger-Moore, J., Breckenridge, R. S., and Jones, D. L. (1995): "Patterns of growth and size-localized competition in the New York state life insurance industry, 1860–1985," *Social Forces*, 73, 1027–50.

Rao, H. (1994): "The social construction of reputation: Certification contests, legitimation and the survival of organizations in the American automobile industry; 1895–1912," *Strategic Management Journal*, 15, (Winter Special Issue), 29–44.

Singh, J. V. (1993): "Review essay: Density dependence theory – Current issues, future promise," *American Journal of Sociology*, 99, 464–73.

Stinchcombe, A L (1965): "Social structure and organizations." in J. G. March (ed.), *Handbook of Organizations*, Chicago, IL: Rand McNally, 153–93.

Stuart, T. E., and Podolny, J. M. (1996): "Local search and the evolution of technological capabilities," *Strategic Management Journal*, 17, (Summer Special Issue), 21–38.

Swaminathan, A. (1995): "The proliferation of specialist organizations in the American wine industry: 1941–1990," *Administrative Science Quarterly*, 40, 653–80.

White, H. C. (1981): "Where do markets come from?" *American Journal of Sociology*, 87, 517–47.

Wholey, D. R., Christianson, J. B., and Sanchez, S. M. (1992): "Organizational size and failure among health maintenance organizations," *American Sociological Review*, 57, 829–42.

Zucker, L. G. (1989): "Combining institutional theory and population ecology: No legitimacy, no history," *American Sociological Review*, 54, 542–45.

Chapter Fourteen

Organizational Evolution

TERRY L. AMBURGEY AND
JITENDRA V. SINGH

The intellectual tension between questions of stability and questions of change permeate the social sciences in general and organizational theory in particular. After a substantial period of time when the central questions were devoted to issues such as optimal processes and the maintenance of stable organizational relationships, interest in developmental processes and organizational change have reemerged. An examination of organizational evolution is broadly informative to organizational scholars interested in change and development. Evolutionary change is also of interest to decision-makers interested in adapting their organizations to changing circumstances. Moreover, the ubiquity of organizations in modern societies suggests that change in many aspects of social life will be intimately linked with change in the nature and functioning of organizations.

We conceptualize organizational evolution as a process that involves the following features: dynamic change over time, a dependence of present and future trends on prior history (path dependence), multiple levels of analysis, and the interplay of modification and replacement. All views of organizational evolution involve, by definition, change over time. Many evolutionary theories propose that change itself is dynamic, that the nature of change processes is different across historical time or developmental stages. As a consequence, history or path dependent change has emerged as a central construct in many evolutionary theories. To the extent that organizational outcomes at one point in time depend on the prior occurrence and timing of specific events, evolutionary theories become more complex but also more informative.

Although a focus on change is common to all theories of evolution, the level of analysis used is a point of divergence. Historically, evolutionary theories have focused on particular levels so that we have theories of intraorganizational evolution, organizational evolution, population evolution, and community or institutional evolution. One of the most profound changes in evolutionary thinking is the recognition that evolutionary change typically involves simultaneous and interdependent changes across multiple levels. As a consequence, evolutionary models devoted to a single level of analysis are increasingly viewed as providing incomplete descriptions and explanations. Similarly, different evolutionary theories have been based on different causal mechanisms; more specifically the modification of existing entities or the replacement of existing entities.

A second major change in evolutionary thinking is the recognition that not only do both causal mechanisms operate but that they are fundamentally interdependent. We suggest that although questions of organizational evolution have drawn more attention in recent years with the relative fecundity of theory and research in organizational ecology, their scope is broader. Indeed, organizational evolution is a central question in the study of organizations. Various theories of organizations (such as institutional theory, organizational ecology, organizational learning, and evolutionary economics) can be used to specify the processes by which organizational evolution takes place.

We review and frame the literature in terms of five key shifts that have led to the emergent evolutionary synthesis in organization studies. Some of these are:

- A shift from strong to weak selection. Early formulations argued that adaptation was the predominant mode of change. Later, ecological theory emerged suggesting that selection mechanisms predominated. The burden of empirical evidence from numerous studies better supports a view in which selection plays an important role but occurs together with adaptive change in organizations. Thus, adaptation and selection are not opposing forces; they act in complementary ways (Amburgey et al., 1993; Halliday et al., 1993).
- A shift from a focus primarily on Darwinian mechanisms to a focus on both Darwinian and Lamarckian mechanisms, such that organizational features can be transmitted between organizations over time (both through adaptation and the entry of new organizations). Whereas it is clear that Darwinian selection does operate, it is increasingly evident that Lamarckian selection is an important component of intraorganizational and higher order change. Thus, in addition to an examination of entities in their respective ecological contexts, there is also an interest in their genealogical lines of descent (Bruderer and Singh, 1996; Stark, 1996; Rao, 1998).
- A shift from viewing institutional and selection views as antithetical, to the view that institutional contexts, whether the state or changing social beliefs and values, often provide the selection context, highlighting their complementarity (Davis et al., 1994; Stark, 1996; Rao, 1998).
- A shift from focusing primarily on macrostructure of organizational populations to a simultaneous focus of micro and macrostructure, involving the simultaneous study of nested levels of analysis, in particular their nested, hierarchical nature (Lomi and Larson, 1996; McPherson and Rotolo, 1996).
- A shift from viewing environmental context as exogenous to endogenous environmental contexts, leading to coevolution (Barnett and Hansen, 1996; McPherson and Rotolo, 1996).

In choosing which pieces of work to review, we adopted three guidelines. First, we included only research published as articles in peer reviewed journals. Although important contributions have been made in book chapters and books (Aldrich, 1999), we believe journal articles best represent the state of affairs in evolutionary theory. Second, we included only articles published within the last decade. Although foundation or classic articles provide a sense of where evolutionary theory has come from we want to illustrate where it is and where it is likely to go. In other words, we want to illustrate not just the current state of affairs but also the state of the art. Finally, we chose articles that exemplified one or more or the shifts that we see in evolutionary theory. Our conceptualization of evolutionary thinking is that research on organizational evolution constitutes a polythetic group; the attributes we've identified characterize the field as a whole, but individual theories or studies will generally have some subset of the features. We've grouped the studies by the shifts we think they exemplify even though most of the studies could be placed in multiple categories. A summary description of the studies is contained in Table 14.1.

Literature Review

EVOLUTIONARY TRANSFORMATION: FROM STRONG TO WEAK SELECTION

One of the most pronounced shifts in theorizing about organizational evolution is the consolidation or blending of transformation and selection processes. We have labeled that synthesis as a shift from strong (selection only) to weak (both selection and transformation) selection in theories of organizational evolution. Two studies stood out to us as highlighting evolutionary transformation.

Halliday et al. (1993) examined transformation of a population of organizations in terms of shifts in relative embeddedness in markets and states, alternative solutions to the problems of obtaining resources, managing competition and constructing legitimacy. They show how resource dependency and institutional factors led to a segmentation of state bar associations into a form relying on the market and a form relying on the state. Their research relies on both historical qualitative description and quantitative analysis of transformations to examine factors associated with organizations maintaining the original form or adopting the new form.

Halliday and colleagues argue that while all organizations are embedded within both state and market environments, they can be characterized in terms of their primary institutional locus. The institutional locus of a population can become problematic when major ideological shifts occur that affect the legitimacy of different institutional positions or when changing interests or market conditions alter the availability of resources. The locus of institutional embeddedness results from the relative efficacy of the market and the state in ensuring resource flows, managing competition and providing legitimacy. A shift from reliance on the market to reliance on the state increases as the organization's ability to obtain resources and legitimacy decreases, and as the competition for market resources increases. As a consequence, organizations are more likely to seek reliance on the state if they are younger and less well established and if a previous attempt at unification failed. Some 50 years after the initial creation of bar associations relying on market resources an alternative form, which relies on the state, was initiated. The legitimation of the new form was not accompanied by the delegitimation of the old form; the initial form retained legitimacy and coexists with the new. The segmentation of professional associations into market-dependent and state-dependent forms indicated that evolution in organizational forms does not necessarily follow a sequential pattern where one form replaces another.

Halliday et al. (1993) place primary emphasis on the environmental determinants

Table 14.1 Summary of organizational evolution studies

Reference	Key concepts	Key variables	Key predictions and findings	Key contribution	Method and sample
Evolutionary transformation					
Halliday et al., 1993	Institutional locus	Market performance State efficacy and willingness to solve problems Organizational history	Market performance and state traits increases unification attempts. Younger, less well established associations have a higher probability of transformations.	The locus of institutional embeddedness results from the relative efficacy of the market and the state in ensuring resource flows, managing competition and providing legitimacy.	State bar associations Event history analysis of unification attempts, logistic regression of unification success
Amburgey et al., 1993	Structural inertia, organizational momentum, change history	Organizational change in newspaper frequency and content, organizational failure	Relationship between change and failure is duration dependent and moderated by age.	Structural inertia includes both resistance to change and momentum for change.	Event history analysis of change and failure 1011 Finnish newspapers from 1770 to 1963
Speciation and extinction					
Rao, 1998	Cultural frames Institutional entrepreneurs	Advertising, product choices and consumer expenditures	Institutional entrepreneurs mobilize resources through the use of frames and theories that justify an organizational form by specifying its characteristics as indispensable, valid, and appropriate.	Cultural frames are constructed through the recombination of existing cultural elements.	Archival and public sources, census statistics, newspaper articles, and the writings of participants
Stark, 1996	Recombinant property Decentralized assets Centralized liabilities Multiplicity of legitimizing principles	Ownership	Property transformation occurred without conventional privatization.	Ability to maneuver among disparate evaluative principles and to produce multiple accountings is a form of organizational hedging.	220 largest enterprises and banks in Hungary 1989–94 Archival analysis of enterprise ownership

Davis et al., 1994	Model of appropriate corporate practice	Diversification Acquisition	Substantial decline in the prevalence of the firm-as-portfolio model	Appropriate placement of organizational boundaries have changed through time although a consistent principle has been growth.	Fortune 500 firms Event history analysis of corporate acquisitions
Bruderer and Singh, 1996	Organizational learning Fitness landscapes		Learning produces a region of intermediate fitness around a fitness spike.	Learning only shortens the time required for optimal forms to be realized with a spike-like fitness landscape.	Genetic algorithm computer simulation
Linking micro- and macro- processes					
McPherson and Rotolo, 1996	Affiliation carrying capacity Transient curve	Transient curve gradient Niche location and width	The nature of the gradients of the transient fluctuation curve determine the nature of niche shifts.	The transient curve drives the movement of organizational niches and in turn, is affected by shifts in niches so that the transient deviations return to the long run carrying capacity. Thus the model involves an endogenous source of change.	Membership histories of 1050 individuals 1974–89 Pooled cross-section time series regression
Lomi and Larsen, 1996	Spatial structure of organizational interactions	Local organizational population density	Effects of density vary with distance.	Global effects of density arise from simple processes of local interaction linking micro- and macro-processes.	Cellular automata computer simulation
Endogenous Evolutionary Change					
Barnett and Hansen, 1996	Competitive history	Mean and variance in the durations of an organization's competitive relationships	Recent competitive experience is beneficial while more distant experience is not.	Competition and constrained adaptation are sources of disequilibrium and evolutionary change in organizational populations.	Event history analysis of failure rates among 2970 Illinois banks from 1900 to 1990

leading to a shift of institutional locus, but also included organizational attributes such as age or a prior failed attempt. Amburgey et al. (1993) examined organizational change from a very different perspective, examining the relationship between organizational change and failure and momentum for change. They proposed that organizational change could be both adaptive and disruptive, arguing that it had two distinct effects: process effects and content effects. Process effects of organizational change increase the likelihood of failure through the disruption of internal routines and external interactions although the disruption is more severe for older organizations and becomes attenuated with the passage of time. Content effects of change depend on the performance of the organization before and after the change. The net effect of change on an organization is thus conceived a combination of the content of the change, the age of the organization at the time of the change and the elapsed time since the change. As a consequence, the transformation of organizations in a population is a mixture of both adaptation and selection.

Amburgey et al. (1993) argued that complete understanding of organizational change requires consideration of the likelihood of change and organizations' *change histories*. The more experienced an organization becomes with a particular change, the more likely it is to repeat it. The change process may thus itself become routinized and subject to inertial forces, creating *organizational momentum* – the maintenance of direction and emphasis of prior actions in current and future actions. To reconcile momentum with commonly observed periods of organizational inactivity, the authors propose that local organizational search processes (Cyert and March, 1963) produce momentum that is strongest immediately after a change occurs, but declines over time. In their analysis of Finish newspapers from 1770 to 1963, Amburgey et al. (1993) supported their combined structural inertia and momentum model. Rates of change in newspaper content and publication frequency both declined with organizational age, but at the same time displayed momentum, increasing with the number of prior changes of the same type, and also endogenous decay, with recently experienced changes most likely to reoccur, and the likelihood declining with time since the change.

Both Halliday et al. (1993) and Amburgey et al. (1993) find consistent relationships between age and change histories on the likelihood of change. They also demonstrate that substantial change in the composition of a population can occur through transformation as well as the entry and exit processes of selection. However, the two studies place emphasis on very different factors; Halliday et al. (1993) utilize institutional theory and place their emphasis on the environment while Amburgey et al. (1993) utilize structural inertia theory and place their emphasis on factors internal to the organization.

Speciation and extinction

Rao (1998) adopts a very different approach to organizational evolution. Rather than examine transformation or selection processes within an existing population, he examined the creation of new organization forms, where form indicates an organizational population rather than an organizational variant within a population. Since new organizational forms embody beliefs, values and norms the emergence of a form necessitates the constitution of the form as a cultural object. Rao contrasts three perspectives on variations in organizational forms: the random variation, constrained variation, and cultural-frame perspectives. The study examines the initial period when consumer watchdog organizations were being created since the early history of a new organizational form is a period when existing institutional arrangements are delegitimated and new norms and beliefs are constructed.

The random variation perspective argues that variations in organizational forms arise randomly as the result of modifications in the routines of existing organizations or the isolation of a small group of organizations that share competencies in a favorable resource environment. The constrained variation perspective argues that environmental conditions predictably produce variations in organizational forms through the production of resource spaces not occupied by existing organizations. The cultural-frame institutional perspective argues that new organizational forms are created when actors with sufficient resources see a new form as an opportunity to realize highly valued interests. A core feature of this perspective is that the creation of a new form requires that institutional entrepreneurs legitimize the theory and values embodied in the form.

New forms can arise from either organized politics or social movements, but in either case the rules and interests of actors are not fixed, and the rules governing interaction are contested. In contrast to the constrained variation model, the cultural-frame model asserts that new organizational forms do not necessarily arise in an open resource space; a new form has to be constructed from existing cultural materials by institutional entrepreneurs. Institutional entrepreneurs are activists who combine previously unconnected beliefs and norms into an organizational solution to a problem, thereby mobilizing legitimacy and material resources. Institutional entrepreneurs mobilize resources through the use of frames; theories, which justify an organizational form by specifying its characteristics as indispensable, valid, and appropriate. These cultural frames are constructed through the recombination of existing cultural elements.

Another contrast to the constrained resource perspective is that the cultural-frame model allows for the possibility that new forms arise in resource spaces that are occupied by existing organizations. In this case institutional entrepreneurs construct an open niche by appropriating resources from existing uses.

Standards and testing organizations were an organizational precursor to nonprofit consumer watchdog organizations. Another precursor form of organization was a consumer league. Consumer leagues were modeled on trade unions and relied on the threat of boycotts to establish lower prices and improved standards of living. Just as standards and testing organizations were linked to commercial entities, consumer leagues were associated with women's groups and trade unions. A resource space for nonprofit consumer watchdog groups developed as a result of increases in advertising, product choices and consumer expenditures coupled with a lack of product liability rules. Institutional entrepreneurs responded to the opening resource space with rival cultural frames for nonprofit consumer watchdog groups, each related to precursor groups. One frame constituted an organization similar to standards and testing groups but with consumers as the constituency. The other frame was more diversified in goals, technologies and constituencies and was related to consumer leagues.

The frame defining consumer watchdog organizations as impartial testing agencies servicing consumers acting as rational decision makers was used as the foundation for a follow-on organization while the diversified frame garnered less support and engendered no further creations. Hostility from vested interests forced the consumer watchdog organization using a diversified consumer-as-worker frame to drop labor-related activism and emphasize testing. Thus a contest over the identity of the consumer delineated the boundaries of the form.

Stark (1996) also examines the emergence of a new organizational form. He examined the emergence of recombinant property, a form of organizational hedging where actors respond to uncertainty by diversifying assets and redefining and recombining resources in an attempt to justify the organization on the basis of multiple legitimizing principles. The transformation of property in post-socialist Hungary involved the decentralized reorganization of assets and the centralized management of liabilities. This led to the blending of public and private property, organizational boundaries and justificatory principles. The organizational forms, routines and practices, and social networks in existence persisted and provided the basis for the emergence of new organizational forms through improvisation and recombination. Existing forms also provided assets, resources, and the basis for credible commitments and coordinated actions. Actors strategically exploited the ambiguities created by a multiplicity of legitimating principles. Private property emerged inside extent socialist firms rather than being embodied in separate organizations producing hybrid, mixed property forms. Property transformation occurred without conventional privatization.

Recombinant property is an attempt to hold resources that can be justified or assessed by more than one standard. Decentralized reorganization of assets produced inter-enterprise ownership networks while centralized management of liabilities transformed private debt into public debt. An exemplar of recombinant property is a limited-liability company owned by private individuals, by private ventures, and by other limited-liability companies owned in turn by joint stock companies, banks, and large public enterprises owned by the state. These metamorphic networks blur the boundaries between enterprises as well as the boundary between public and private. The government put in place a two-stage strategy of recapitalizing banks and using banks to collect enterprise debt. The recapitalization made the state the dominant shareholder of the large commercial banks. The debt consolidation induced the enterprise networks to engage in risk shedding through the organizational separation of assets and liabilities.

Stark (1996) argued that to survive and thrive, an organization must first identify the relevant system of accounting in which something can exist as a resource, since assets and liabilities have value in relation to legitimizing principles. Regrouping assets (and liabilities) involves making new associations by rearranging social ties among persons and by drawing on diverse justificatory principles. The ability to maneuver among disparate evaluative principles and to produce multiple accountings is a form of organizational hedging. This hedging process led to the development of a new organizational form that blended aspects of precursor forms.

Both Rao (1998) and Stark (1996) examined the emergence of new organizational forms, the process of organizational *speciation*. Davis et al. (1994) examined the disappearance of an organizational form, the process of *extinction*. They investigated the process of deconglomeration using an institutionalist interpretation of how corporate practices and rhetoric co-evolved. They provide, in essence, a case study of an organizational field documenting the widespread abandonment of practices associated with the firm-as-portfolio model of appropriate corporate practice. The "firm-as-portfolio" model of appropriate corporate practice was the basis of a growth strategy utilizing diversification. By 1980 the diversification strategy was the dominant growth strategy and the diversified firm was the dominant organizational form. The next decade, however, saw massive restructuring and a shift back towards corporate specialization.

An institution is a convention that has become legitimized. Conventions arise when actors with a common interest in a rule or arrangement coordinate their actions and conventions are legitimized when they are able to withstand challenges on instrumental grounds. Legitimated conventions parallel other aspects of the "way the world works" and is therefore "natural." Ideas about the appropriate placement of organizational boundaries have changed through time although a consistent principle has been growth – expansion of boundaries is an appropriate end to pursue. Prior models of appropriate corporate practice involved growth through horizontal or vertical expansion. The most recent model is growth through diversification and the structural form of a conglomerate, the firm-as-portfolio model. The widespread use of the firm-as-portfolio model in the absence of good evidence that the model promoted profitability suggests that the spread of the model was due to institutional factors.

Several factors were proposed as leading to the shift. The regulatory regime supporting the model had changed, financial barriers to external challengers were lowered and the "conglomerate discount" had weakened corporate financial performance. One factor was economic perspectives casting doubt on the efficacy of the form. Financial theory, suggesting that investors should diversify not firms, led to a conglomerate discount in financial markets and poor stock price performance. Inherent in the firm-as-portfolio model is that activities both inside and outside the boundaries of the firm should be subject to the same market tests and that decisions about the appropriateness of activities is not the sole province of the managers of the firm but revocable by capital markets.

A second factor was the construction of a market for corporate control through innovation in financing supported by a shift away from strong antitrust regulatory policy. Reductions in anti-trust enforcement made it easier for parts of conglomerate could be sold to buyers in the same industry. Legal barriers to hostile takeovers also fell. Innovations in takeover financing emerged that facilitated bust-up takeovers by making it easier for small firms or even individuals to buy much larger firms.

The work of Rao (1998), Stark (1996), and Davis et al. (1994) demonstrate the intimate relationship between the creation and disappearance of organizational forms and the institutional environment, and more specifically, legitimizing principles. The authors differ, however, in several important respects. One important difference is the extent to which legitimizing principles are exclusive or can be blended. Another is the role of human agency; for example Rao (1998) emphasizes the role of institutional entrepreneurs while Stark et al. (1996) and Davis et al. (1994) emphasize organizational or collective action. Finally, the authors vary in their assessment of the role of precursor forms of organization, Rao (1998) and Stark (1996) describe a process where precursor forms of organizations provide the foundation of a new form, while Davis et al. (1994) describe more of an antithetical relationship between forms.

In a related integrative study, Bruderer and Singh (1996) combine the adaptation and selection focus of Halliday et al. (1993) and Amburgey et al. (1993) with the speciation and extinction focus of Rao (1998), Stark (1996) and Davis et al. (1994). Bruderer and Singh use a genetic algorithm simulation to examine variation, adaptation, and selection of organizational routines. The basic premise behind their simulation was that organizational learning guides and accelerates the process of organizational evolution and that the capacity for learning is an organizational trait itself subject to selection pressures. Organizational forms are defined as high-level routines specifying strategy and structure. The match between the form of the organization and the demands of the environment defines organizational fitness. A fitness landscape contains all possible forms along one dimension and the corresponding level of fitness along another. The simulation specifies organizational form as a sequence of 20 routines each with 3 possible values (0, 1, ?). A value of 1 is "correctly" specified, a value of 0 is incorrectly specified, and a value of '?' has unknown effect and is open to learning. The fitness landscape was defined first as flat with a single spike such that an organization is highly successful only if all key routines exactly match environmental demands. The second specification was with a hill-like landscape with intermediate levels of fitness.

The model implements three evolutionary processes: variation in the creation of new forms, the exit of organizations, and learning as an example of adaptation. New forms were specified as a recombination of existing forms. Organizational learning was specified as a number of random learning trials for the "unknown" elements of the organization's routines. The fitness returns of learning were a function of the time required to learn the correct form (if ever learned). The primary result of the simulations is that learning significantly shortens the time required for optimal forms to be realized with a spike-like fitness landscape. In a hill-like landscape, populations with relatively inert members can reach optimality through selection quickly. Another important implication is that learning constructs a region of intermediate fitness around a fitness spike, thus transforming it into a hill-like landscape. As a consequence, the simulation shows how organizational attributes can alter an exogenous fitness regime.

LINKING MICRO- AND MACRO-PROCESSES

Much of the work in organizational evolution has been driven by dichotomies such as adaptation and selection or speciation and extinction. Another dichotomy extent in the literature is the micro- and macro- distinction. McPherson and Rotolo (1996) developed and tested a model of the changes in the social composition and heterogeneity of voluntary groups. They ask the question: what determines the composition of voluntary groups? A specific goal of their research is to show how the dynamics of recruitment and loss at the individual level produce systematic effects at the organizational, population, and community levels. The study also emphasizes the variation of organizational types in the voluntary sector, where types refer to a population with distinctive memberships and activities.

McPherson and Rotolo define the niche as the area that the organization occupies along a resource dimension, in this case the dimension is the sociodemographic dimension of education. Voluntary groups create and maintain their niches through the homophilous social networks that tie individuals together. The mean and standard deviation of sociodemographic characteristics define each niche, where the mean defines the center of the niche and the standard deviation the width of the niche. They restricted their attention to a niche space defined by education because it is the most widely studied variable in research on affiliation and shows the most consistent relationship to affiliation.

The carrying capacity of voluntary organizations along the educational dimension is defined by the authors as the average number of affiliations associated with a given level of education. Individuals have finite resources (including time). When the resource demands on an individual exceed the resource "budget" one or more affiliation will be dropped. Short-term fluctuations around the carrying capacity drive the dynamics of the model. When transient fluctuations in the affiliation rate of a region raises the number of affiliations above the carrying capacity then memberships will be created more slowly and terminated more quickly

The transient curve measures the current variation of the affiliation rate around the long-term carrying capacity and indicates the intensity of competition from members that drive niche movement along a sociodemographic dimension. When a voluntary group's niche spans a region of increasing or decreasing gradient in the transient fluctuation, the group will experience a shift of niche. The nature of the gradients of the transient fluctuation curve will determine the nature of the niche shift. A single gradient will produce a directional shift since groups experiencing greater competitive pressure on one edge of their niche along a sociodemographic dimension will shift their niches away from that pressure. When the transient curve is convex upward (inverted U-shaped) the group will gain more members at the edge of the niche than the center and increase diversity of membership. When the transient curve is concave up (U-shaped), the group will gain more members in the center than the edges of the niche and decrease the diversity of membership. Moreover, the transient curve determines which areas in the resource space are likely to see the creation of new organizations (negative transient fluctuations) and which are not (positive transient fluctuations). The transient curve not only drives the movement of organizational niches but it is, in turn, affected by shifts in group niches so that the transient deviations return to the long-run carrying capacity. Thus the model involves an endogenous source of change.

Lomi and Larsen (1996) also examine the coupling of micro- and macro- levels, albeit within density dependence theory, which posits curvilinear relationships between the number of organizations in a population and the vital rates of entry and exit. As new organizations enter a new population the increased numbers legitimate the population and as a result increased density raises entry rates and reduces exit rates. However a point is reached where the competitive effects of crowding outweigh any legitimation produced by higher population density. Above this level of density further increases in density lower entry rates and raise exit rates.

The density dependence model of organizational ecology has been specified at a variety of levels of analysis ranging from the city to the country or even the continent; see Baum and Amburgey (this volume). The variety of levels specified for the relationship between density and vital rates represents an assumption of homogenous mixing and interaction among members. Understanding the relationship between localized structures of interaction and vital rates is an important step in understanding population dynamics. Lomi and Larsen (1996) point out that spatial structure is important because the activities of organizations are defined in and by time and space. Moreover, the recurrence of spatial concentration across industries and societies suggests that spatial structure is a general factor influencing the ecological dynamics of organizational populations. But how can populations with widely varying local conditions consistently display regular aggregate patterns of density? What micro-level processes of interaction are consistent with the regularity of growth in density so widely observed?

The computational model used by Lomi and Larsen (1996) specifies that the behavior of an organization has a direct impact on other organizations in the immediate neighborhood and a diffuse effect on organizations farther away. Neighborhoods have partial overlap and share only some of their members. The computational model of population dynamics shows how the global dynamics of population density arise from simple rules of local interaction among individual organizations. The key finding is that standard specifications of density dependence are consistent with a wide variety of micro-processes regulating the entry, survival, and exit of individual organizations although the population-level between density and vital rates is highly sensitive to the local rules of interaction. Density is regulated by the extent to which interaction is localized; the broader the neighborhood, the smaller the equilibrium level of density. Also, the dynamics of organizational populations are constrained much more by legitimacy than competition.

Lomi and Larsen (1996) and McPherson and Rotolo (1996) examine the micro–macro-linkage but define the levels of analysis very differently between the two sets of authors. For McPherson and Rotolo (1996) micro- refers to the behavior of individual human beings. Lomi and Larsen (1996) utilize micro- to refer to small-scale spatial locations and individual organizations. However, taken together the two studies illustrate how phenomena at different levels of analysis have both "horizontal" and "vertical" effects.

ENDOGENOUS EVOLUTIONARY CHANGE

A particular form of horizontal effect is *co-evolution*, a process in which the sets of organizations evolve interactively. Barnett and Hansen (1996) examine the evolutionary consequences of competitive interaction with learning. The authors assume that an organization facing competition engages in localized search and satisficing that allows adaptation. This adaptive response then in turn triggers adaptive responses on the part of competitors, which ultimately increases the competitive pressure on the firm thus producing a self-reinforcing escalation of competitive intensity known as the "Red Queen" effect (Van Valen, 1973). Barnett and Hansen (1996) propose that the strategies of firms develop under uncertain conditions and that organizations possess limited *ex ante* rationality so that the realized strategies emerge over time as the accumulation of incremental adjustments in response to externally triggered shortfalls in performance. The viability of a focal firm is then a function of its own competitive history as well as the competitive histories of its rivals. When shortfalls in performance are produced by competition with other organizations rather than exogenous shocks the Red Queen effect can operate.

Whether or not the Red Queen effect is adaptive or maladaptive depends on the relative costs and benefits of change. One constraint affecting the relative costs/benefits is timing. Recent competitive experience is argued to be beneficial while more distant experience is not. A longer mean duration of an organization's competitive relationships in recent times increases its viability while a similar duration in the more distant past decreases its viability.

The experience of its competitors has the opposite effect, a longer mean duration of the competitive relationships experienced by an organization's rivals in recent times decreases the organization's viability while similar experience in the distant past increases the organization's viability. A second constraint is the multiplicity of co-evolutionary processes. Organizations facing multiple cohorts of rivals face multiple conflicting demands and reduced viability. This implies that the variance of competitive experiences will have an effect distinct from the mean duration. As a consequence, organizations experiencing a greater variance in the duration of its competitive relationships will suffer a lower viability.

SUMMARY

Although the studies reviewed here come from a variety of disciplines and utilize a variety of methods, they demonstrate the substantial shifts that have occurred in thinking about organizational evolution. Not all of the shifts are equally pronounced. The view that institutional contexts provide the context for evolutionary processes (Davis et al., 1994; Stark, 1996; Rao, 1998) is particularly strong. Institutional theory is arguably one of the most active areas within organizational theory; the contribution to evolutionary theory is correspondingly strong. Similarly, the shift from strong selection to weak selection is substantial, so that an examination of only transformation or entry/exit processes is rare. Those elements of population ecology dealing with organizational change (i.e. structural inertia theory) have largely accepted the shift from strong to weak selection mechanisms. A simultaneous examination of micro and macrostructure or an examination of endogenous change processes is still relatively rare. We believe this is partly due to disciplinary isolation and partly due to the empirical and methodological hurdles that must be overcome to do this type of research.

Contemporary Issues and Debates

FROM EX POST DESCRIPTION TO EX ANTE PREDICTION

If, as Rao (1998) points, rival institutional entrepreneurs construct incompatible cultural frames that vie for dominance, what determines success? Rao points to the success of collective action and the endorsement of powerful actors. Similarly, if entrepreneurs construct frames by recombination of preexisting organizational models, which aspects of which models act as raw material? Is there a systematic pattern of the most successful elements of successful models being chosen? Are the most visible elements chosen? Similarly, when and how incompatible cultural frames can coexist is not clear. Davis et al. (1994) describes what seems to be a winner-take-all context for corporate cultural frames while Stark (1996) describes a context where competing frames not only co-exist but also are used simultaneously by organizations.

VIRTUAL REALISM IN VIRTUAL REALITIES

Bruderer and Singh (1996) and Lomi and Larsen (1996) made simplifying assumptions in constructing their simulation. While simple models are useful starting points, they point out the desirability of increasing the richness of the model by modifying its assumptions. While increasing the reality of simulation models is undoubtedly desirable, the nature of the empirical reality to be used is not clear. For example, Bruderer and Singh (1996) justify their use of recombination of existing forms to specify new forms as empirically grounded. But which (and how many) predecessors will act as sources? Should elements be chosen at random or systematically? Unfortunately, the current state of empirical work provides little systematic guidance.

Central Questions

Substantial changes have occurred in our thinking about organizational evolution in the past decade and some very good research has propelled the field. Nonetheless, a number of important questions remain. We have singled out two of these central questions for attention.

The first centers on relative effects. Although theorizing about organizational evolution has seen a synthesis of transformation and selection processes it seems unlikely that the two processes will generally have the same magnitude of effect on evolutionary change. What factors lead to transformation or selection as dominant evolutionary mechanisms? The societal sectors within which organizations operate clearly make a difference. Halliday et al. (1993) examined State Bar Associations while Amburgey et al. (1993) examined newspapers. In the medium term it seems unlikely that attorneys will forgo a professional association while newspapers come and go. While it is sensible to expect that transformation will play a greater role in the evolution of Bar Associations than selection, distinguishing organizations that seek economic rents and from those that don't doesn't substantially advance the state of theory.

A second outstanding question involves organizational imitation or transfer. The transfer of characteristics or attributes from one organization to another is a central feature of organizational evolution. Rao (1998), Stark (1996), and Bruderer and Singh (1996) utilize it extensively and explicitly. However, theories of organizational evolution have not developed any systematic explanation of when different mechanisms of transfer will occur. For example, research on the adoption of innovation distinguishes between contagion mechanisms wherein one organization transfers something directly to another from broadcast mechanisms wherein external actors disseminate the innovation without direct contact. Bruderer and Singh (1996) adopt the contagion mechanism of direct transfer while Stark (1996) implies that cultural elements of organizations are widely available.

New Directions

STRUCTURAL EVOLUTION

Organizational evolution has yet to incorporate the rapidly growing literature on organizational networks. Empirical analyses of organizational networks have provided valuable insights into the nature and effects of structural characteristics, such as the relative efficiency of information flow through networks with different structures. This is particularly true when *multiplex* networks are examined, networks comprised of a variety of different types of relationships. However, network analyses *per se* have been static, and even when information over time has been available, the temporal component has been set aside (Barley et al., 1992). The evolution of multiplex inter-organizational networks will involve integration of both organization-level and network-level processes and a dynamic consideration of both levels of analysis. It also involves a consideration of a variety of relationships. Assessment of the evolution of network structures and the evolution of organizations' structural position will enrich both evolutionary theory and network analysis. How transformation and selection processes affect and are affected by population structure is a question that cannot be answered without theoretical elaboration within evolutionary theory, but we believe the future will see such work.

THEORETICAL CONVERGENCE AND METHODOLOGICAL VARIETY

Evolutionary theories have a central focus on change, and as a consequence empirical work necessarily involves longitudinal information of some kind. However, a wide variety of approaches are not only possible but also desirable; large sample statistical analyses and qualitative case analysis shed light on different phenomena and act in a complementary way. Similarly, simulation techniques play an important role in providing a way to test the implications of theories devoted to community level evolution. The data necessary to study the coevolution of multiple populations of organizations makes empirical analyses of these processes very difficult. Well-constructed simulation models provide a way to study the workings of these processes. Finally, laboratory experiments provide a way to study certain micro-level processes involved in intraorganizational and certain organizational level theories of evolution

Although methodological variety is desirable, progress in evolutionary thinking will require greater integration of theories. Consider, for example, networks and strategic alliances. Much of the recent work on inter-organizational relationships focuses on the organizational networks that result from the formation of formal alliances, while another stream of work emphasizes relationships as a strategic choice of individual firms (Barley et al., 1992). Unfortunately, neither stream of work substantially informs the other. Work combining network-level and organization-level phenomena has been rare and it typically has focused on the effect of network related attributes of organizations on the actions of organizations.

EVOLUTION AND CO-EVOLUTION

A third new direction in thinking about organization evolution is an emerging emphasis on co-evolution, the coupled evolution of multiple populations or forms. Organization theory is showing an increased appreciation of the fact that organizational populations or forms are embedded within organizational fields. Organizational fields consist of organizations in an institutional arena, and important stakeholders such as customers, suppliers, regulators, and organizations in closely related areas. As a consequence, organizations and populations do not evolve in isolation; changes reverberate throughout the field as a number of the reviewed studies indicate. Co-evolution involves a sophisticated appreciation of dynamic processes as the work of Barnett and Hansen (1996) indicates. Moreover, the empirical requirements of studying co-evolution are truly gargantuan. The analysis of co-evolutionary processes is a likely candidate for the use of simulation models.

Connections across levels

A basic premise of our approach to evolutionary thinking in organizational theory is that evolutionary mechanisms operate at multiple levels of analysis and that evolutionary processes at different levels are interrelated. Both Warglien's chapter on intraorganizational evolution and Greve's chapter on interorganizational evolution corroborate this premise and provide a window on what is likely to be the future of evolutionary analysis in organization theory.

A number of potentially fruitful areas of interchange across the three levels are evident in the chapters – two strike us as particularly profitable. The first is a synthesis of the work on the evolution of rule systems within organizations exemplified by Schulz (1998) and the genetic algorithm simulation examination of variation, adaptation, and selection of organizational routines exemplified by Bruderer and Singh (1996). An informed specification of the internal dynamics of organizational rule systems would substantially enrich the modeling beyond the specification of learning as a process of random search. Similarly, work on the internal dynamics of rule systems can be enriched by refining problem space definitions to reflect variations in the fitness landscapes faced by organizations.

A second area of interchange involves work on the evolution and devolution of markets and work on institutional evolution. As Greve (this volume) points out, "A special and important market evolution is the transformation of corporations as actors with undisputed boundaries and authority relations to marketable goods that can be bought without their own consent, combined with others, or split and sold." This area is enriched by work on organizations as cultural objects (Stark, 1996; Rao, 1998).

Conclusion

We believe that organization theory itself is subject to evolution, that it exhibits dynamic change over time, a dependence of present and future trends on prior history (path dependence), multiple levels of analysis, and the interplay of modification and replacement. Although we are hardly objective observers, we believe that the (near term) future of organization theory is evolutionary theory in its variegated forms.

References

Aldrich, H. E. (1999): *Organizations Evolving.* London: Sage Publications.
Amburgey, T. L., Kelly, D., and Barnett, W. P. (1993): "Resetting the clock: The dynamics of organizational change and failure," *Administrative Science Quarterly*, 38, 51–73.
Barley, S. R., Freeman, J., and Hybels, R. C. (1992): "Strategic alliances in commercial biotechnology," in N. Nohria and R. Eccles (eds), *Networks and Organizations*, Boston: Harvard University Press, 311–47.
Barnett, W. P., and Hansen, M. T. (1996): "The red queen in organizational evolution," *Strategic Management Journal*, 17, 139–58.

Bruderer, E., and Singh, J. V. (1996): "Organizational evolution, learning and selection: A genetic algorithm based model," *Academy of Management Review,* 39, 1322–49.

Cyert, R. M., and March, J. G. (1963): *A Behavioral Theory of the Firm.* Englewood Cliffs, NJ: Prentice-Hall.

Davis, G. F., Diekmann, K. A., and Tinsley, C. H. (1994): "The decline and fall of the conglomerate firm in the 1980s: The deinstitutionalization of an organizational form," *American Sociological Review,* 59, 547–70.

Halliday, T. C., Powell, M. J., and Granfors, M. W. (1993): "After minimalism: Transformations of state bar associations from market dependence to state reliance, 1918–1950," *American Sociological Review,* 58, 515–35.

Lomi, A., and Larsen, E. R. (1996): "Interacting locally but evolving globally – A computational approach to the dynamics of organizational populations," *Academy of Management Journal,* 39, 1287–321.

McPherson, J. M., and Rotolo, T. (1996): "Testing a dynamic model of social composition: Diversity and change in voluntary groups," *American Sociological Review,* 61, 179–202.

Rao, H. (1998): "Caveat Emptor: The construction of nonprofit consumer watchdog organizations," *American Journal of Sociology,* 103, 912–61.

Schulz, M. (1998): "Limits to bureaucratic growth: The density dependence of organizational rule births," *Administrative Science Quarterly,* 43, 845-76.

Stark, D. (1996): "Recombinant property in East European capitalism," *American Journal of Sociology,* 101, 993–1027.

Van Valen, L. (1973): "A new evolutionary law," *Evolutionary Theory,* 1, 1–30.

Chapter Fifteen

Organizational Cognition and Interpretation

THERESA K. LANT

The application of cognitive concepts to theories of organization traces its roots to an open system, information-processing view of the firm (e.g. March and Simon, 1958; Cyert and March, 1963). The major questions addressed by this view include how an organization obtains information about its environment and its prior experience, and how it uses this information to make decisions and take action.

It is a difficult, perhaps impossible task to classify the work on organizational cognition separate from work on individual level cognition and interorganizational cognition. Cognition, by definition, has to do with the "act or process of knowing" (Random House dictionary). Research that has applied cognitive theory to organizations has struggled, and continues to struggle, with the dilemma of moving from the individual process of knowing to the organizational process of knowing. Further, individuals know both more and less than what is "contained" in the organizations within which they work.

I define organizational cognition and interpretation as pertaining to cognitive phenomena in and by organizations that impact the organization as a whole. This includes the organization's strategy, mission, adaptation to the environment, and major decisions that impact the organization's relationship with its environment.

An Historical Framing: Organizations as Information Processing Systems Versus Systems of Meaning Creation

The role of cognition in organizations has been seen differently, depending on whether one views organizations as systems of *information* or systems of *meaning* (Lant and Shapira, 2000). March and Simon (1958) viewed organizations as information processing systems consisting of embedded routines through which information is stored and enacted. Some researchers have taken this to mean that organizations are systems that process and code information in a *computational* manner. That is, the problem that organizations face is one of searching and processing relevant information when such search is costly and decision makers are boundedly rational. Other researchers interpret March and Simon to mean that organizations are social entities that enact their world. Some see in these words the elements of collective mind (Sandelands and Stablein, 1987.) These two views represent distinct branches of cognition research in organizations, the computational approach and the interpretive approach. The computational stream of research examines the processes by which managers and organizations *process information* and make decisions. The interpretive approach investigates how *meaning* is created around information in a social context.

Organizations as Information Processing Entities

The fundamental argument in this stream of thought is that individuals, and thus organizations, have limited information processing abilities. Once researchers accepted the argument that individuals are boundedly rational (Simon, 1957), then information search and the decisions based on limited search and cognitive processing became interesting research questions. One could no longer assume that organizations in the same environment would behave in the same way. It was likely that information scanning activities would differ, and that interpretations of information would differ across organizations. This being the case, it became important to study what organizations paid attention to and how they interpreted the information that they gathered (March and Simon, 1958; Cyert and March, 1963). The role of managers as information processors also became a focus of this research. The initial research focused on the scanning and search activity of firms. Following this work, there emerged a concern for how information from the environment is perceived and interpreted by managers.

SCANNING AND SEARCH

Issues of organizational scanning and search were explored by researchers in systems theory (Bonini, 1963), organizational design (Galbraith, 1973), and management practice (Aguilar, 1967). The key contribution of these studies was to recognize organizations as open systems that process information, and the recognition that organizations scan their environment and process gathered information in different ways. Little attention was paid to the cognitive processes that underlay information processing. Rather, these models developed stylized rules for how information was gathered and processed, and then drew implications for organizational design and decisions.

PERCEPTION AND INTERPRETATION

Attention eventually turned to addressing the phenomenon of subjective perception. This was a significant step, in that it explicitly recognized the subjectivity of perceptions in the processing of information by organizations. Although information processing limitations had been recognized in earlier work, the idea that the information that is available could be perceived and interpreted differently by different individuals and groups was a new idea. Child (1972) argued that managers played a critical role in positioning their organizations within their environment through strategic choice. Duncan's (1972) empirical study of perceived environmental uncertainty was a major step that examined how decision-making groups within organizations perceived their environment. Starbuck (1976, p. 1081) made the important observation that organizations "tend to crystallize and preserve their existing states of knowledge whenever they set up systems to routinely collect, aggregate, and analyze information."

Thus, by the mid 1970s the field had recognized the critical role of managers in firms, and at the same time, had recognized that assessing and reacting to the organization's environment was not an unambiguous process. This combination of conceptual arguments lay the groundwork for extending research on individual cognition in order to draw implications for organizations.

Throughout the 1980s a series of important studies were conducted that elaborated the empirical evidence and theoretical explanations for the fact that managers play a critical role in steering their organizations, but that they are likely to perceive their organization's environment differently. Meyer (1982) demonstrated that even for clearly observable events of great significance, different organizations perceived and interpreted these events in different ways, and these differing interpretations led to different strategies. Kiesler and Sproull (1982) drew from research on individual level social cognition on problem sensing, scanning, noticing, and interpreting stimuli to develop a set of propositions for why managers see things differently.

During this time, we also see a transition from viewing organizations as quasi-rational (albeit boundedly rational) information processing systems to seeing organizations as systems of interpretation. By drawing on the theoretical assumptions of the several decades of work described above, Daft and Weick (1984) developed a comprehensive model of organizations as interpretation systems. The intellectual history of their model can be seen from their four basic assumptions. First, organizations are complex, open systems that process information from the environment. This assumption derives from the general systems theory work that developed around the same time as organization theory (Boulding, 1956) and the general approach to organizations as information processing entities. Second, they assume that organizations have cognitive systems and memories that transcend those of the individuals that populate organizations. Embedded within this assumption is recognition that individuals may have differing perceptions of the same stimuli (Starbuck, 1976), but that the act of organizing demonstrates some possibility of convergence of interpretations and chosen actions (Weick, 1979). Third, they assume that top-level managers are the key mechanisms of organizational interpretations. This assumption reflects the primacy of the dominant coalition construct developed in Cyert and March (1963). Fourth, organizations vary in the ways they come to know and interpret their environment. Daft and Weick (1984) describe four basic modes based on two dimensions – how active or passive scanning is and whether the environment is assumed to be analyzable or incomprehensible. These two dimensions imply differences in the way organizations scan their environment, interpret the information they acquire, and take action based on these interpretations. Another key contribution of this work was to underscore the reciprocal processes of scanning, interpretation, and action.

Daft and Weick (1984) provided an important comprehensive model for directing future work. Their assumptions were generally accepted and drove a significant body of work in the late 1980's and early 1990's that strove to understand organizational interpretation processes in a more fine-grained way.

KEY STUDIES OF INFORMATION PROCESSING AND INTERPRETATION

The initial attempts to understand organizational interpretation processes revolved around applying individual information processing characteristics that had been discovered in the areas of social psychology and cognitive psychology (Table 15.1). Jackson and Dutton's (1988) study applied categorization theory to managerial interpretations of strategic issues. Categorization theory holds that in order for individuals to make sense of their world, they form categories in their minds under which experiences can be classified and thus understood. Cognitive categorization appears to be a fundamental requirement for learning. Just as children learn to classify experiences as dangerous or safe, managers learn to classify experiences as threats or opportunities. Jackson and Dutton set out to demonstrate that managers would categorize strategic issues as potential threats or opportunities. They also attempted to discover the issue characteristics that influence how a manager classifies issues one way or another. Their evidence suggests that managers did use this categorization scheme and viewed threats as negative and opportunities as positive. Threats and opportunities also elicited different emotions.

Their findings were somewhat surprising in that it was not entirely clear how issue characteristics mapped on to these two categories. Managers seemed to have a negative (threat) bias. That is, they were more likely to interpret issues as threats rather than opportunities. However, issues that were ambiguous might be interpreted as either a threat or an opportunity. The more control a manager thought they had over their environment, the more likely they were to see an ambiguous issue as an opportunity. Although the basic tenants of categorization theory were applicable to managers' issue classification, it was apparent that the interpretations of managers were complex, and that more work was needed to determine the factors that influence their interpretations.

One possible explanation for the ambiguity in managerial issue interpretation was that managers' interpretations were influenced by their past experience, not just current stimuli. Walsh (1988) examined whether managerial belief structures that develop from past work experience would bias information processing. He was attempting to extend the findings of Dearborn and Simon (1958) that managers with experience in one functional area would selectively perceive and interpret information consistent with the belief structures of that function. Walsh (1988) found no such simple relationship between belief structures and prior work experience. He found that "the dominant dimensions of managers' belief structures did not constrain their information processing" (p. 887). Again, managerial interpretations were proving to be complex and explaining them still elusive.

Thomas and McDaniel (1990) studied the impact of top management team structure on interpretations. This was one of the first studies of managerial interpretations to examine the influence of contextual factors. They found that top management teams that were structured so as to process large amounts of information were more likely to label strategic issues positively (i.e. as opportunities). Such team structures were also related to higher degrees of information usage and higher perceptions of control over issues. This finding reinforces Jackson and Dutton's finding that managers who perceived more control over their environment were more likely to perceive issues positively. The Thomas and McDaniel study related the structure of the management team to the labeling of strategic issues. This relationship seemed to work through the

Table 15.1 Key empirical studies: Information processing perspective

Reference:	Key concepts	Key variables	Key predictions and findings	Key contribution	Method and sample
Jackson and Dutton, 1988	Issue identification • Threat • Opportunity	Perceived issue characteristics (threat vs. opportunity)	Perceptions of threat vs. opportunity influenced by characteristics of issues described Some issue characteristics ambiguous; some distinctively associated with threat or opportunity Threats and opportunities eliciting different feelings	Issue perceptions biased toward seeing threats; but interpretations of issue characteristics are not simple categorizations.	Study 1: Managers enrolled in executive education (questionnaire) Study 2: MBA alumni (scenario responses)
Walsh, 1988	Selective perception, belief structures	Belief structures, work history, problem identification, information use, requests for information	Work experience predicted to influence belief structures, and belief structures predicted to influence information processing of ambiguous situations No simple relationship between work experience and belief structures No simple relationship between belief structures and information use	The impact of past experience on perception and information processing is complex, not simple categorization or narrow filtering.	Managers enrolled in executive education (sorting task, case analysis)
Thomas and McDaniel, 1990	Strategic issue interpretation	Issue labels, information usage, information processing structure of top management team, organizational strategy	Higher information processing capacity of top management team expected to lead to more positive labeling of strategic issues, more information usage, and higher perceptions of control Findings support predictions	Predicted and confirmed the importance of decision makers' context in influencing interpretations	Hospital CEOs, archival data from trade publications (questionnaires, scenarios)

Study		Variables	Findings		Sample
Milliken, 1990	Interpretation of environmental change, state uncertainty associated with scanning task, effect uncertainty associated with interpretation task, and response uncertainty associated with response task	State, interpretation, and response uncertainty, resource dependence, organizational effectiveness, organizational identity, extent of decentralization	Resource dependence moderates relationship between state and effect uncertainty Organizational effectiveness, decentralization and organizational identity negatively related to perceptions of uncertainty	Perceptions of uncertainty are multidimensional. Uncertainty regarding the occurrence of an environmental change, the perception of the change as negative or positive, and uncertainty regarding how to respond are distinct, and influenced differently by resource dependencies and organizational characteristics.	University administrators (questionnaire)
Thomas et al., 1993	Linking strategic sensemaking (scanning, interpretation, action) with performance outcomes	Scanning, interpretation, strategic changes, performance	High levels of scanning and information use associated with positive interpretations and perceptions of control regarding strategic issues Positive labeling of strategic issues and perceptions of control related to strategic change Strategic change associated with higher performance	Links cognitions to actions and performance	Hospital CEOs (questionnaires, case scenarios)

processing of large amounts of information and perceiving control over the environment. Taken together, these findings suggest that managers who are able to process information readily (i.e. are not overwhelmed) felt more control over their environment and, thus, perceived strategic issues as possible opportunities for action, not threats. The strength of the effects of context in this study versus the strength of findings found in the Walsh and Jackson and Dutton studies suggested that contextual factors play a critical role in determining how managers process information and interpret this information.

Also in 1990, Milliken studied the impact of environmental context as well as organizational context on managerial interpretations. She explored the impact of different types of environmental uncertainty on interpretations. Her findings also suggest a high degree of complexity in interpretations. Perceptions of environmental uncertainty were multidimensional. These dimensions mapped on to the three stages of managerial information processing and interpretation – scanning, interpreting, and acting. These stages in the process were also affected differently by organizational contextual factors, such as the degree of resource dependence. For example, dependency on resources that might become scarce caused managers to *interpret* this issue as a threat, but did not influence whether or not they *noticed* the issue or how they would *respond* to the issue. Managers' perceptions of their organizational context influenced both interpretations of how an issue would affect the organization and beliefs about how to respond. For instance, managers who perceived their organizations as effective and having a strong identity believed that the changing environment would not have a large impact on them and that they would respond effectively.

Thomas et al. (1993) performed an empirical study that linked the constructs of organizational scanning, interpretation, action, and outcomes. The distinct contribution of their work is that it builds a theoretically meaningful framework from the historical body of thought about cognition in organizations, and conducts a comprehensive study to document whether the predicted relationships hold empirically. Their study extended the exploration of and explanation for managerial interpretations to ask the questions – do these interpretations influence strategic change and performance? Similar to prior studies, they found that high levels of scanning and information usage were associated with positive interpretations and perceptions of control regarding strategic issues. These positive interpretations and perceptions of control, in turn, were associated with strategic change, which in turn was associated with higher performance.

We learn some important lessons from this progression of key empirical studies in the information processing tradition. First, the extension of individual information processing to information processing in organizational settings is not straightforward. Managerial cognitions appear to be complex and highly influenced by contextual factors. Information processing capability tended to influence perceptions of control, which in turn influenced how issues were interpreted. Interpretations also appear to influence and be influenced by change – both organizational and environmental. Furthermore, associations among cognition, organizational action, and performance appear to exist, though the findings thus far are tentative.

Organizations as Enactors of Environments and Creators of Meaning

Weick's (1979) book, *The Social Psychology of Organizing*, was not inconsistent with the information processing view of organizations, but did offer a different view of the inter-pretation process at work. It shared the open systems view, acknowledged that organi-zational cognition transcends individual level cognition, and allowed for varying interpretations of the environment. There were two fundamental arguments in this book, however, that encouraged the development of a different approach to understand-ing organizational cognition.

First, Weick offered a distinct rationale for why interpretations of similar stimuli differ. Weick suggested that interpretations differ because all organizations fundamentally face different environments. They do so because environments are enacted, not interpreted. The term *interpretation* suggests that a phenomenon exists that is being perceived. The term also connotes that phenomena exist in some objective sense. For example, markets for publicly traded securities can be described by an average value at the end of each trading day. This valuation exists in an objective sense. My interpretations of the mean-ing and implications of that value may vary from other individuals, but they do not change that objective valuation. The term *enactment* suggests that the phenomenon being interpreted by the perceiver is also created by the perceiver. My interpretations of the stock market valuation will influence my investment actions, and these investment actions, in aggregate, influence the market valuation. My interpretations of this valua-tion are also embedded in a history of my own investment decisions. Thus, from an enactment perspective, the stock market valuation that I interpret is, in fact, different from the valuation as experienced by every other investor. The concept of enactment encouraged a distinct stream of work that assumed that reality is not so much perceived as constructed (Berger and Luckmann, 1967).

The second of Weick's arguments was a departure from the focus on top managers as the most important "interpreters" in the organization. Weick viewed the way in which "reality" is constructed as a social interaction process. That is, interpretation does not occur within the heads of top managers, but rather is a social process that occurs through interaction throughout an organization. Much of the substance of organized activity that gets interpreted is created by the actions and interactions of individuals within organizations. When individuals act and interact in predictable ways, we call these actions standard operating procedures. Many of these procedures affect an organi-zation's interaction with elements in its environment, such as interactions with custom-ers and suppliers. These interorganizational interactions can also take on a regular pattern. This view of organizational cognition suggests a web of social interaction that creates patterns of understanding and activity among actors both within and without the organization. The top management interpretation view is more focused on the perceptions of the external environment by key decision makers. Managers might differ in the way in which they perceived the environment, due to differences in their past experience, the way their teams were structured, etc, but there was an objective refer-ent.

This distinction led to a substantively different body of work, in which symbolism became as important as substance. This work sees organizations as systems of meaning creation. Pfeffer (1981) suggested that managers influence interpretations through their symbolic acts. He argued that managers' interpretations of the environment and subsequent strategic choices – the critical aspects of the information processing view – have little impact on organizational outcomes due to the power of external control. Where managers do have a powerful impact is in shaping the interpretations of others through symbolic language and action. Smircich and Stubbart (1985) agreed, adding that in order to see how organizations come to an understanding of the world around them, one must recognize how managers help to create this world through their actions and symbolic language. Feldman and March (1981) proposed that much of the information that is gathered and analyzed by organizations is done for purely symbolic reasons. The content of the information is decoupled from the belief structures of the organization, rather than being the source of these belief structures. Gioia and Chittipeddi (1991) found empirical evidence of this viewpoint in their study of organizational change in an academic environment. They found that cycles of sensemaking and sensegiving by organizational leaders and members created the reality that was experienced by other organizational members.

KEY STUDIES OF ENACTMENT AND MEANING CREATION

Bartunek's (1984) study of ideological and structural change in a religious order is a powerful example of how symbolic reframing by organizational leaders can lead to fundamental, substantive organizational change (Table 15.2). She documents the changes in interpretive schemes within this organization and the relationship between interpretive change and organizational restructuring. She found that although leadership and environmental events are key triggers to organizational change, the influence of these factors is moderated by the interpretive scheme of the organization. She found that where leaders have the most impact is on these interpretive schemes. By providing alternative schemes, they facilitate change in these schemes and subsequent organizational change.

Donnellon et al. (1986) were also interested in documenting the role of shared meaning in creating organized action. They expected that shared meaning would be a precondition to organized action. They explored how communication behaviors can produce shared meanings. They found, to their surprise, that groups could engage in organized action without having developed shared beliefs about taking the action. Communication mechanisms were critical to achieving collective action. Such action took place even when organizational members held different beliefs, so long as their beliefs were consistent with the same organized action.

Weick and Roberts' (1993) study of aircraft carriers also uncovered interesting implications for collective action. They found that groups can perform activities that make it appear as though all members share the same knowledge and beliefs, even when they do not. What they actually share, however, is a set of rules about how to relate to each other in order to produce organized action. Thus, Weick and Roberts' description of collective mind is not the same as shared beliefs. The collective mind of a group exists in the interrelations of their social activity. Sharing the same beliefs is not a precursor to organized action. Meaning and understanding, even shared beliefs, develops as a result of these social interactions.

Table 15.2 Key empirical studies: Enactment perspective

Reference	Key concepts	Key variables	Key predictions and findings	Key contribution	Method and sample
Bartunek, 1984	Shared interpretive schemes	Interpretive schemes Environmental changes Emotional reactions Member actions Organizational leadership	Describing second-order change in interpretive schemes, exploring the relationships between change in interpretive schemes and organizational restructuring, and the role of the environment and leadership in these processes	Although leadership and environmental events influence organizational change, their influence is moderated by the interpretive scheme of the organization. Leaders have profound impact on organizational interpretive schemes.	Case study of an international women's Roman Catholic religious order Data consist of documents and interviews.
Donnellon et al., 1986	Communication acts Equifinal meaning Organized action	Metaphor Logical argument Affect modulation Linguistic indirection	Identify communication behavior associated with shared meaning (resulting in organized action). Results indicate that shared meaning was not a necessary precondition of organized action. Equifinal meaning is achieved, post action, via four communication mechanisms (key variables).	Organized action can result from disparate meanings that have the same behavioral implications. Shared meaning is not a precondition for organized action.	Undergraduate students, videotaped behavioral simulation Discourse analysis
Weick and Roberts, 1993	Collective mind Heedful interrelating	Mindfulness Group performance Interrelating	Group performance is the outcome of four defining properties: creation of social forces, contribution, representation, and subordination of action; the creation of a joint situation of interrelations among activities; degree of heed and degree of coupling.	Collective mind is embodied in the interrelating of social activities; meaning and understanding is created in the interactions among individuals, not just in the individual mind.	Observation of flight deck operations, anecdotal illustrations of concepts

Reference	Key concepts	Key variables	Key predictions and findings	Key contribution	Method and sample
Fiol, 1994	Collective learning Content consensus Framing consensus	Judgmental content Objective content Rigidity of frame Breadth of frame	Convergence around a broad frame of interpretations provides the common understanding needed to move toward collective action despite the persistence of divergent content of interpretations.	Group consensus is multidimensional. Consensus on framing is necessary for group action, but not consensus on content of interpretations.	Linguistic analysis of communication log of new venture team in financial institution
Gioia et al., 1994	Symbolism Strategic change Influence	Sensemaking Influence	Discovered emergent stages of strategic change: interpretation (identity definition), definition of strategic issues, legitimation of change agents, and institutionalization of change. Pervasive use of symbols and metaphors used in sensemaking and in navigating power structures in order to have influence.	Highlights strategic change as more than change in fit with environment; represents change in cognitive perspective – shift in organizational belief structure, value system, and identity Highlights importance of symbolic interaction in achieving strategic change Symbolism as a language for understanding change.	Interpretive study of university undergoing strategic change; researchers roles were actor–observer (insider) and multiple outsiders. Data gathered from field notes, tapes and transcripts of task force meetings, interviews, and documentation

Fiol (1994) further explored whether "consensus" or shared beliefs is a necessary condition for organized action. She found that the concept of consensus is multidimensional; consensus on the framing of issues is necessary for group action, but not consensus on the content of interpretations. These findings seem to mirror those found by Donnellon et al. Symbolic agreement facilitates action; it is not necessary, or perhaps even possible, to achieve full agreement on the meaning and reasons for taking an action. Gioia et al. (1994) also found that managing symbolic language was crucial to the enactment of strategic change. They found, as did Bartunek, that organizational change requires changes in belief structures, identity, and values. The multitude of individuals necessary to implement organizational change is unlikely to ever agree on the substantive aspects of the change. However, symbolism can be used as a language for understanding change, and symbols and metaphor can be used to navigate power structures and varying beliefs.

These five studies of organizational cognition from the enactment perspective have yielded noteworthy lessons. Collective action does not require shared cognitions and belief structures. Organized action or strategic change can be driven by shared understanding of rules of interaction and the symbolic meaning of the action. They also seem to suggest that symbol *is* substance and metaphor *is* meaning.

Debates about the Locus and Essence of Organizational Cognition

An obvious distinction between the studies from the information processing perspective and those from the enactment perspective is the method used. The information processing studies tended to elicit individual responses to questionnaires or scenarios. The stimulus used to trigger responses was organizational, but the interpretations were individual. In contrast, the enactment studies investigated collective beliefs and actions by using case studies, direct observation of interactions, and linguistic analysis. Thus, an implicit distinction between these two perspectives is "where the action is." In the information processing perspective, the cognitive action takes place in the heads of individuals. In the enactment perspective, the cognitive action takes place among individuals engaged in collective activity. This distinction has led to a recent debate about the locus of cognition.

Although research continues that is consistent with either the information processing view or meaning creation view, there is a growing recognition that organizations are both systems that process information and systems that create meaning. An adequate understanding of organizational cognition requires an acknowledgement of both elements of organizations. Organizations will always face both the dilemma of *ignorance* and the dilemma of *ambiguity* (March, 2000). Ignorance is a problem of *computation*. Intelligent action requires information and prediction. In a world where information is difficult and costly to obtain, and future states are uncertain, intelligent action is problematic. Ambiguity, on the other hand, is a problem of *interpretation*. In order to assess the intelligence of actions, one has to know what outcomes are desired, and know when outcomes have been achieved. The definition of preferences turns out to be a very sticky problem, and one that, in organizations, is played out in a social domain. As March (1997) noted, decision making in organizations can be viewed at times as rational and computational in nature at times and as retrospective sensemaking processes at other times. In different social contexts computational cognition is facilitated or inhibited. Enactment processes influence the boundaries and categories that determine what is computed and what is not; what is important and what is not. Neither dilemma can be subsumed under the other. Systems of meaning cannot be reduced to systems of information processing, and vice versa. We need meaning and interpretation in order to set our goals; determining which goals are important to us is an interpretive process (Lant and Shapira, 2000).

Collective Cognition: Aggregation or Interaction?

Another issue that has not been resolved is the question of how individual cognition combines to produce collective cognition in organizations. Indeed, much work in social cognition assumes that collective cognition can be reduced to an aggregation of individual cognition. Much of the work on organizational cognition has not even dealt with the aggregation issue. Rather, it has relied on the notion that a dominant coalition (top management team) embodies the cognition of the organization.

A few articles have attempted to deal with the levels of analysis issue either theoretically (Glynn et al., 1993) or empirically (Thomas et al., 1994). Some have argued that cognition in organizations should not be viewed as the mere aggregation of individual cognition (Lant, 1999; Lant and Phelps, 1999; Walsh, 1995). The interaction among individuals may lead to higher (or lower) levels of knowledge creation, as is the case in group problem solving where interactions among individuals may lead to either synergism or groupthink phenomena (Maier, 1967).

Recently, skepticism about purely collective thought has ebbed (Walsh, 1995, p. 294). Walsh notes that some theorists remain tethered to the dominant computer metaphor and examine the distributional aspects of organizational mind, while others look to social processes as the substrate for the organizational mind and argue that once we move to the collective level of analysis, cognition goes beyond individual minds (Sandelands and Stablein, 1987; Glynn et al., 1993; Weick and Roberts, 1993). An important related issue is how we should view organizations as repositories of knowledge. Is knowledge (i.e. previous cognition) simply encoded in rules and routines? Or is knowledge in organizations somehow recreated and reinterpreted with use? If we have learned anything from the studies discussed in this chapter, it is that organizational cognition as not the simple aggregation of individual cognition (Walsh, 1995; Lant and Phelps, 1999).

Potential Frames to Move Us Forward

The perspective of situated cognition may provide a mechanism with which we can traverse levels of analysis without resorting to aggregation from individual to organization and from organization to collective (Brown and Duguid, 1991). In taking a situated cognition perspective on how distributed knowledge develops among collectives of individuals or organizations, one can apply the assumptions of situated cognition theory (also referred to as situativity theory or situated action theory) (Greeno and Moore, 1993). "The central claim of situativity theory is that cognitive activities should be understood primarily as interactions between agents and physical systems and with other people" (Greeno and Moore, 1993, p. 49). This perspective is in contrast to the more widely held view of cognition and knowledge as residing in the minds of individuals, where it guides perception and interpretation, and from which it can be shared or transferred (communicated) to others. On the face of it, it is difficult for us to consider how cognitions could reside anywhere else but the mind. The theory of situated action, however, turns this fundamental assumption on its head.

The essentials of the argument are that human thought, cognition, or knowledge is situated within a cultural system, including artifacts and practices, which is itself made up of prior thoughts and knowledge. Knowledge is embedded in these systems, which reach out across time and space, and our own thoughts are enabled and constrained by this embedded knowledge. As Pea (1993) articulates, our own knowledge cannot be separated from the contextual knowledge that frames it:

> Knowledge is commonly socially constructed, through collaborative efforts toward shared objectives or by dialogues and challenges brought about by differences in persons' perspectives. Intelligence may also be distributed for use in designed artifacts as diverse as physical tools, representations such as diagrams, and computer-user interfaces to complex tasks . . . These ubiquitous mediating structures that both organize and constrain activity include not only designed objects such as tools, control instruments, and symbolic representations like graphs, diagrams, text, plans, and pictures, but people in social relations, as well as features and landmarks in the physical environment. Imagine the absence of the following resources and the detrimental effects of that absence on the activities to which they may contribute intelligence: keyboard letters, labels on instrument controls, everyday notes, well placed questions, the use of space to organize piles of materials on a desktop, the emergent text in a written composition one is constructing. These everyday cases show the active and evolving structuring of the material and social environments to make them a repository of action mediators (Pea, 1993, pp. 48–9).

Situated action views learning as occurring perpetually with ongoing activity by an actor. With each act of coordination, whether physical, mental, or linguistic, an actor is composing, changing, or reinforcing neural connections. Knowledge is created through this learning process, and can become embedded not just in an actor's mind, but in how the actor's environment becomes structured as a result of activity. As a result, knowledge is distributed across space and time, not just within individual minds; it resides in people, practices, artifacts, and symbols. These components constitute organizations as well as society at large.

A Research Agenda for the Study of Situated Cognition

The adaptive sensemaking perspective suggested by Bogner and Barr (2000) is an example of the type of theoretical framework that moves us toward studies of cognition that highlight the dynamic interaction among actors as opposed to the static content of their minds. Bogner and Barr argue that in hypercompetitive environments the cognitive frameworks developed by managers focus more on process than content. That is, managers come to know their environments through dynamic interactions with other actors in the context of certain events (e.g. new technologies). The form of this collective knowledge is an understanding of the process of how, for instance, new technologies will impact the competitive actions of firms. It is knowledge about *how* rather than *what*. Although this study is a useful framework for encouraging process oriented empirical study, it does not solve the problem of how to study the emergence of collective cognition through the process of interaction.

The challenges of tracing social interaction processes have always been significant. Interaction does not often leave traces; people often do not recall the interactions that led to the development of certain beliefs. Just as the physical sciences have gone a long way to discover the means of tracing interaction, so the behavioral sciences must follow. Thinking about the popular children's experiment of mixing baking soda and vinegar to produce bubbling, oozing lava from a volcano, we get a powerful image of how two innocuous and common substances can create a surprising outcome that could not have existed without their interaction. Through experimental chemistry, the underlying chemical process that creates the bubbling outcome has been determined.

Methods of tracing social interaction as a source of social cognition and social structure have not yet met with this kind of success. There are many reasons for this. Humans are more unpredictable than chemical elements. If you mix baking soda and vinegar you will always get pretend lava. If you observe the interaction of the same two individuals in the same context discussing the same issues you are likely to get different outcomes each time. Baking soda is always baking soda. Humans, on the other hand, are learning entities. Since they learn from experience, humans are never entirely the same person from one experience to the next. Once you multiple this variability by the number of individuals in an organization and grasp the combinatorial possibilities of their interaction, the notion of tracing human interaction in organizations quickly becomes overwhelming. However, this should not stop us from trying! We have seen beautiful case study examples that trace the evolution of social cognition in organizations. The more such case studies we can encourage, the more likely we are to discover patterns. A key question remains, however, whether interaction can be studied in large scale, or whether interaction studies are destined to remain in the domain of case studies. With the evolution of digital communication technology, we may discover creative ways of tracing interaction on a larger scale. Electronic mail is an example of how interaction among individuals can be traced. Valuable studies are underway about collectives that interact primarily via email (Moon and Sproull, 2000). Still, email is only one form of human interaction. As more and more interaction occurs via ubiquitous wireless technology, another opportunity for tracing interaction may present itself. We must continue to think of creative ways to leverage new technologies to study the ways in which people interact, and how this interaction evolves into the social cognition that drives the behavior of organizations.

Connections Across Levels

As I stated at the start of this chapter, it is difficult to separate the work on organizational cognition from that of individual level cognition and inter-organizational cognition. The parallels between the key constructs, questions, and dilemmas can be seen in all three of the cognition chapters in this volume. Fiol's chapter sheds light on the debate I describe above regarding the locus and essence of cognition. Fiol's discussion of the two paradigms of individual cognition – symbolic and connectionist – parallel the paradigms discussed in this chapter – information processing versus meaning creation. The perspective of organizations as information processing systems is based on the individual level models of symbolic processing, in which individuals interpret stimuli by using pre-existing mental knowledge structures. The perspective of organizations as systems of meaning creation shares the same assumptions as connectionist models of individual cognition, in which the interactions among actors are the key process by which interpretations are made and meaning is created.

Fiol and I come to similar conclusions regarding the future of these two paradigm debates. We both argue against an either/or determination, and encourage a recognition that both paradigms are simultaneously correct. Fiol suggests that the two cognitive architectures, symbolic and connectionist, operate at different levels of brain activity. I argue in this chapter and elsewhere (Lant and Shapira, 2000) that organizations are both systems of information processing and systems of meaning creation depending on the type of activity.

> Although we recognize the utility of modeling organizations as symbolic representational systems (Vera and Simon, 1993), we agree with Searle (1990) that the manipulation of symbols is not sufficient to explain the *meaning* that these symbols connote to actors. We also differ from those who would argue that symbols mean whatever we want them to mean. Bougon (1992, p. 381) suggests that "there is no underlying or deeper reality to be discovered. The socially constructed reality of a system of cognitive maps . . . is the social reality." We take the position that *social* reality is constructed, but also that the symbolic representation of basic rules and mechanisms is important. We suggest that symbolic representation and meaning creation are interdependent, not mutually exclusive.
>
> We need meaning and interpretation in order to set our goals; determining what types of outcomes are important to us is an interpretive process. We also need meaning and interpretation in order to make sense of the outcomes and events that occur (for instance, is this a normal event or a cause for concern?). In order to take volitional action, though, actors must, at least for certain period of time, fix their goals and decide on a certain interpretation of outcomes (Lant and Shapira, 2000, p. 369).

The Porac et al. chapter on inter-organizational cognition is relevant to the debate I describe above regarding whether collective cognition is the aggregation of individual cognition or the outcome of interactive, social processes. The Porac chapter relates the issue of belief homogeneity with the existence of collective cognition. Much of the interorganizational cognition research discussed in that chapter takes cognitive homogeneity among members of a collective as evidence of collective cognition. As Porac warns, however, such a litmus test for the existence of collective cognition quickly results in quagmire of threshold judgments about how much consensus is enough to claim a collective belief system exists. The research summarized in this chapter on organizational level cognition may help us to avoid this quagmire. As discovered by Bartunek (1984), Donnellon et al. (1986), and Weick and Roberts (1993), shared beliefs were not a necessary condition for collective action! Once collective action occurs, it may or may not lead to increased commonality in beliefs. Further, as Fiol (1994) discovered, consensus is multidimensional. Collective action may require some agreement on the overall framework for taking collective action, but variance in underlying beliefs about why to take action and the meaning of these actions does not prevent collective action from taking place.

My sentiments regarding the collective cognition debate are similar to those I hold regarding the symbolic versus connectionist architecture debate. The cognitions of individual members of a collective are important, but their primary importance lies in the way they influence interaction with other members of the collective. The level of consensus in a collective should be viewed as an outcome of a social interaction process. This process can yield a high level of consensus or dissensus. A lack of consensus does not negate the existence of a collective whose actions are guided by a set of principles of interaction. As Fiol has also argued, we need to move away from a fixation on either/or debates to an emphasis on discovering the underlying factors that lead to differing levels of shared meaning and collective action among members of organizations and other collectives.

Conclusion

After reviewing the past two decades of research on organizational cognition and studying the two complementary chapters in this volume, I am struck by the importance of pursuing two promising avenues for exploring cognitive phenomena in and among organizations. First, if we are to deepen our understanding of organizational cognition, we need to understand the relationships between cognition and social interaction. Second, the parallels between the dilemmas described in all three cognition chapters in this volume cry out for breaking down the artificial distinctions between levels of analysis.

The fundamental issues that arise when reading these chapters are the nature of human mind, the way in which the human mind is embedded in and shaped by social context, and the nature of collective action and belief. These issues are critical to all "levels" of organizational cognition. In fact, these levels may be an artifact of the structure of our scientific inquiry. Organization theory has taken the organization as a boundary object that delineates activities within and without. Cognitive science has taken the brain as a similar boundary object. The more we understand both the human mind and organizations as inextricably embedded in context, rather than contained within artificial but convenient containers, the more we will be able to escape the levels of analysis trap. The more we understand the complexities of human cognition and collective cognition, the better able we will be to avoid the paradigm pitfalls that have plagued this area of inquiry.

Acknowledgments

I would like to thank Joel Baum for his patience, insight, and support while I was writing this chapter. I would also like to thank Joel for introducing me and my children to the baking soda and vinegar volcano experiment years ago, which has turned out to be quite useful for this chapter!

References

Aguilar, F. (1967): *Scanning The Business Environment.* Reading, MA: Addison-Wesley.
Bartunek, J. (1984): "Changing interpretive schemes and organizational restructuring: The example of a religious order," *Administrative Science Quarterly*, 29, 355–72.

Berger, P. L., and Luckmann, T., (1967): *The Social Construction of Reality: A Treatise in the Sociology of Knowledge*. New York: Bantam Doubleday Bell Publishing Group.

Bogner, W. C., and Barr, P. (2000): "Making sense in hypercompetitive environments: A cognitive explanation for the persistence of high velocity competition," *Organization Science*, 11, 212–26.

Bonini, C. (1963): *Simulation of Information and Decision Systems in the Firm*. Englewood Cliffs, NJ: Prentice Hall.

Bougon, M. G. (1992): "Congregate cognitive maps: A unified dynamic theory of organization and strategy," *Journal of Management Studies*, 29, 369–89.

Boulding, K. E. (1956): "General systems theory: The skeleton of science," *Management Science*, 2, 197–207.

Brown, J. S., and Duguid, P. (1991): "Organizational learning and communities of practice: Toward a unified view of working, learning, and innovation," *Organization Science*, 2, 40–57.

Child, J. (1972): "Organizational structure, environment, and performance: The role of strategic choice," *Sociology*, 6, 1–22.

Cyert, R. M., and March J. G. (1963): *A Behavioral Theory Of The Firm*. Englewood Cliffs, N.J.: Prentice-Hall.

Daft, R. L., and Weick, K. E. (1984): "Toward a model of organizations as interpretation systems," *Academy of Management Review*, 9, 284–95.

Dearborn, D. C., and Simon, H. A. (1958): "Selective perception: A note on the department identifications of executives," *Sociometry*, 21, 284–95

Donnellon, A., Gray, B., and Bougon, M. G. (1986): "Communication, meaning, and organized action," *Administrative Science Quarterly*, 31, 43–55.

Duncan, R. B. (1972): "Characteristics of organizational environments and perceived environmental uncertainty," *Administrative Science Quarterly*, 17, 313–27.

Feldman, M. S. and March, J. G. (1981): "Information in organizations as signal and symbol," *Administrative Science Quarterly*, 26, 171–86.

Fiol, C. M. (1994): "Consensus, diversity, and learning in organizations," *Organization Science*, 5, 403–20.

Galbraith, J. R. (1973): *Designing Complex Organizations*. Reading, MA: Addison-Wesley.

Gioia, D., and Chittipeddi, K. (1991): "Sensemaking and sensegiving in strategic change initiation," *Strategic Management Journal*, 12, 443–48

Gioia, D., Thomas, J., Clark, S. and Chittipeddi, K. (1994): "Symbolism and strategic change in academia: The dynamics of sensemaking and influence," *Organization Science*, 5, 363–83.

Glynn, M. A., Lant, T., and Milliken, F. (1993): "Mapping learning processes in organizations: A multi-level framework linking learning and organizing," in C. Stubbart, J. Meindl, and J. Porac (eds), *Advances in Managerial Cognition and Organizational Information Processing, Vol. 5*, Greenwich, CT: JAI Press, 43–84.

Greeno, J. G., and Moore, J. L. (1993): "Situativity and Symbols: Response to Vera and Simon," *Cognitive Science*, 17, 49–60.

Jackson, S. E., and Dutton, J. E. (1988): "Discerning threats and opportunities," *Administrative Science Quarterly*, 33, 370–87.

Kiesler, S., and Sproull, L. (1982): "Managerial responses to changing environments: Perspectives on problem sensing from social cognition," *Administrative Science Quarterly*, 27, 548–70.

Lant, T. K. (1999): "A situated learning perspective on the emergence of knowledge and identity in cognitive communities," in J. Porac and R. Garud (eds), *Advances in Managerial Cognition and Organizational Information Processing, Vol. 6*, 171–94.

Lant, T. K., and Phelps, C. (1999): "Strategic groups: A situated learning perspective," in A. Miner and P. Anderson (eds), *Advances in Strategic Management, Vol. 16*, 221–47.

Lant, T. K., and Shapira, Z. (2000): *Organizational Cognition: Computation and Interpretation*. Mahwah, NJ: Lawrence Erlbaum Associates.

Maier, N. F. (1967): "Assets and liabilities in group problem solving: The need for an integrative function," *Psychological Review*, 74, 239–49.

March, J. G. (1997): "Understanding how decisions happen in organizations," in Z. Shapira (ed.), *Organizational Decision Making*, Cambridge, UK: Cambridge University Press, 9–32.

March, J. G. (2000): "The pursuit of intelligence in organizations," in T. Lant and Z. Shapira (eds), *Organizational Cognition: Computation and Interpretation*, Mahwah, NJ: Lawrence Erlbaum Associates, 61–71.

March, J. G., and Simon, H. (1958): *Organizations*. New York: Wiley.

Meyer, A. "Adapting to environmental jolts," *Administrative Science Quarterly*, 27, (1982): 515–37.

Milliken, F. J. (1990): "Perceiving and interpreting environmental change: An examination of college administrators' interpretations of changing demographics," *Academy of Management Journal*, 33, 42–63.

Moon, J. Y., and Sproull, L. (2000): "Essence of distributed work: The case of the Linux Kernel," *FirstMonday*, 11. Also available at www.firstmonday.org/issues/issue5_11/moon/index.html

Pea, R. D. (1993): "Practices of distributed intelligence and designs for education," in G. Solomon (ed.), *Distributed Cognitions: Psychological and Educational Considerations*, Cambridge: Cambridge University Press, 47–87.

Pfeffer, J. (1981): "Management as symbolic action: The creation and maintenance of organizational paradigms," in B. M. Staw and L. L. Cummings (eds), *Research in Organizational Behavior, Vol. 3*, Greenwich, CT: JAI Press, 1–52.

Sandelands, L. E., and Stablein, R. E. (1987): "The concept of organization mind," in S. Bacharach and N. Ditimaso (eds), *Research in the Sociology of Organizations*, Vol. 5. Greenwich, CT: JAI Press, 135–61.

Searle, J. R. (1990): "Is the brain's mind a computer program?" *Scientific American*, 262(1), 26–31.

Simon, H. (1957): "A behavioral model of rational choice," in H. A. Simon (ed.), *Models of Man*, New York: John Wiley, 241–60.

Smircich, L., and Stubbart, C. (1985): "Strategic management in an enacted world," *Academy of Management Review*, 10, 724–36.

Starbuck, W. H. (1976): "Organizations and their environments," in M. D. Dunnette (ed.), *Handbook of Organizations*, Chicago, IL: Rand McNally College Publishing, 1069–124.

Thomas, J. B., and McDaniel, R. (1990): "Interpreting strategic issues: Effects of strategy and information processing structure of top management teams," *Academy of Management Journal*, 33, 286–306.

Thomas, J. B., Clark, S. M., and Gioia, D. A. (1993): "Strategic sensemaking and organizational performance: Linkages among scanning, interpretation, action, and outcomes," *Academy of Management Journal*, 36, 239–70.

Thomas, J. B., Shankster, L. J. and Mathieu, J. E. (1994): "Antecedents to organizational issue interpretation: The roles of single-level, cross-level, and content cues," *Academy of Management Journal*, 37, 1252–84.

Vera, A. H., and Simon, H. A. (1993): "Situated action: A symbolic interpretation," *Cognitive Science*, 17, 7–48.

Walsh, J. P. (1988): "Selectivity and selective perception: An investigation of managers' belief structures and information processing," *Academy of Management Review*, 31, 873–96.

Walsh, J. (1995): "Managerial and organizational cognition: Notes from a trip down memory lane," *Organization Science*, 6, 280–319.

Weick, K. E. (1979): *The Social Psychology of Organizing*. Reading, MA: Addison-Wesley.

Weick, K., and Roberts, K. (1993): Collective mind in organizations: Heedful interrelating on flight decks. *Administrative Science Quarterly*, 38, 357–81.

Chapter Sixteen

Organizational Power and Dependence

WILLIAM OCASIO

> *Organizations generate power; it is the inescapable accompaniment of the production of goods and services; it comes in many forms from many sources; it is contested; and it is certainly used.*
>
> **Perrow (1986, p. 265)**

Ranging from Weber's ([1922] 1968) ideal-typical analysis of bureaucratic domination to Burt's (1992) structural hole theory, the analysis of the determinants and consequences of power have played an important role in organization theory. Research in organizational power and dependence follows, however, not a single line of development but disparate and at times contradictory approaches. These include views of power as emerging from bureaucratic structures (Gouldner, 1954; Crozier, 1964), shifting political coalitions (Cyert and March, 1963), structural contingencies and resource dependencies (Hickson et al., 1971; Pfeffer and Salancik, 1978), organizational demography (Kanter, 1977), institutional logics (Jackall, 1988; Thornton and Ocasio, 1999), and organizational networks (Burt, 1992, 1997). These multiple approaches have not come together into a unified understanding of power and dependence, but reflect instead an organized anarchy of diverse research problems and theoretical solutions all identifying the ubiquity and criticality of organizational power, but relying on different mechanisms to explain its determinants and consequences.

Given the view that power is context or relationship specific (Pfeffer, 1981a), organizational power and dependence relates to the power of individuals and groups relative to their relationship with and their dependence on organization. Consequently, adapting Weber's ([1922] 1968) definition of power to the organizational level, I define organizational power as the ability of individuals and groups to affect organizational actions and outcomes, despite resistance.

To make sense of the multiple theories of organizational power and dependence, I classify the various approaches into three broad perspectives: functional, structural, and institutional. While potentially complementary, these three perspectives on organizational power and dependence hold different underlying assumptions on the nature of organizations and the sources and consequences of power. Functional theories of power highlight how the power of individuals and groups within organizations results from the need for organizations to survive and adapt to their environments. Structural theories highlight how the allocation of power within organizations is embedded in the structure of social relationships within and outside organizations. Institutional theories stress how organizational power is embedded in the formal rules, normative commitments, and cultural logics that characterize the organization and its institutional environment. These three perspectives are best understood as ideal types, as individual theories and research studies classified within the three perspectives often combine assumptions and mechanisms from the other two approaches.

Literature Review

Table 16. 1 presents key concepts, findings, and contributions from some of the exemplar theories and research studies discussed in this chapter, organized according to the three perspectives.

FUNCTIONAL PERSPECTIVES

Functional perspectives on organizational power and dependence view organizations as social systems seeking to adapt to their environments. As social systems, organizations are constituted by coalitions of interest groups and organizational subunits, with varying goals, interests, and capabilities. According to functionalist perspectives, the power of individuals and groups is determined by their *contributions* to organizational performance and survival and their ability to solve objectively defined organizational problems. Three variants are identified and reviewed here:

1   Theories of political coalitions (March and Simon, 1958; Cyert and March, 1963)
2   Structural contingency and resource dependence theories (Hickson et al., 1971; Pfeffer and Salancik, 1978
3   Punctuated equilibrium theory (Tushman and Romanelli, 1985)

Although no longer dominant, functional theories remain central to our understanding of the determinants and consequences of power and dependence in organizations and continue to inspire additional theoretical development and empirical research.

ORGANIZATIONS AS POLITICAL COALITIONS

A key contribution of the Carnegie School tradition in organization theory (March and Simon, 1958; Cyert and March, 1963) is the view of organizations as shifting political coalitions, characterized by heterogeneity of goals and organizational conflict. This perspective challenges unitary actor models of organizational action and presents instead a theory of organizations where members of the coalition are participants in political structures of mutual dependence and interdependence. The Carnegie School was more directly concerned, however, with explaining the importance of political processes in the

Table 16.1 Selected research on organizational power and dependence

Reference	Concepts	Variables	Findings	Contribution	Method
Functional perspectives					
Cyert and March (1963)	Political coalitions, organizational slack	Standard operating procedures, resources, search and attention rules	Sequential attention to goals of coalition members leads to quasi-resolution of conflict	Integrates view of firm as political coalition with bounded rationality as alternative to economic theory	Theoretical analysis, case studies, computer simulations
Hickson et al. (1971)	Structural contingencies	Uncertainty, criticality, non-substitutability subunit power	Subunit power is a multiplicative function of ability, criticality, and uniqueness in control of uncertainty	Extends power-dependence theory to subunit control over organizational uncertainties, contingencies	Theoretical analysis
Pfeffer and Salancik (1978)	Resource dependencies, enacted environment, organizational effectiveness	Environmental effects, power-dependencies, succession	Power determined by environmental contingencies; succession leads to organizational adaptation	Provides comprehensive power-dependence theory to adaptation to environmental contingencies	Theoretical analysis supported by quantitative empirical studies
Tushman and Romanelli (1985)	Punctuated change, convergence, inertia, power relationships	Perceived performance strategic reorientation, executive succession	Strategic reorientation under performance leads to succession and transformation	Develops punctuated equilibrium of succession and transformation	Theoretical analysis
Structural perspectives					
Kanter (1977)	Demography, homophily, informal networks	Sponsors, alliances, opportunities, alliances, demographic proportion	Homosocial reproduction of managers leads to men having greater power than women	Demonstrates importance of demography, structural determinants of power and outcomes	Ethnography of industrial corporation, theory development
Ocasio (1994)	Circulation, obsolescence, contestation	Executive tenure, board structure, succession	Obsolescence and contestation limit executive power	Develops and tests new models of circulation of power as alternative to model of entrenchment	Hazard rate model of CEO succession in US industrial corporations
Westphal and Zajac (1997)	Social exchange, generalized reciprocity, board control	CEO/board power, diversification, contingent, compensation	Diffusion of board control through social exchange	Develops and tests model of generalized reciprocity as alternative to dominant model of elite cohesion	Hazard rate model of adoption of contingent compensation, changes in diversification in Fortune 50

Reference	Concepts	Variables	Findings	Contribution	Method
Burt (1997)	Social capital, structural ecology, networks	Structural holes, peers, early promotion, bonuses	Returns to structural holes higher with limited number of peers	Shows that value of social capital on promotions and compensation is contingent on competitors	Network and regression analysis of 170 men in senior positions in major corporations
Institutional perspectives					
Selznick (1957)	Institutionalization, organizational character, mission, and purpose	Commitments, roles, interest groups, elite autonomy, dependence, stratification	Institutionalization is embodied through leadership, social and political structures	Links institutionalization social and political structures	Theoretical analysis
Crozier (1964)	Bureaucracy, bounded rationality, dependence	Uncertainty, discretion, rationalization	Power relationships and discretion cannot be suppressed with bureaucratic rationalization	Demonstrates operation of power relationships in bureaucracies	Ethnographic analysis of two bireaucratic agencies
Jackall (1988)	Patrimonial bureaucracy, institutional logics	Fealty, managerial circles, ideology, vocabularies, managerial success	Upheavals and political struggles endemic; conflict hidden behind organizational rhetoric	Shows that patrimonial bureaucracy links contests for formal position with fealty relations with superiors	Ethnographic analysis in three organizations of manager's rules for survival and success
Fligstein (1990)	Conceptions of control	Functional backgrounds, structural contingencies, org, strategy and structure	Changes in institutions of the state lead to transformations in corporate control, rise in finance conception	Develops and tests nonfunctional theory of power determined by state, conceptions of control	Historical analysis combined with multinomial logistic regressions of executive selection, strategy
Thornton and Ocasio (1999)	Institutional logics, organizational attention	Editorial and market logics, competition, acquisition, succession	Historical changes in institutional logics lead to change in determinants, of executive succession	Shows that executive power is historically contingent, embedded in institutional logics	Interviews, historical analysis and hazard rate modeling of succession in publishing

generation of organizational subgoals and the determination of organizational stability and change, than in elucidating the determinants of organizational power. It emphasized, however, the importance of the contributions made by members of the organization's coalition to organizational survival, and this focus served as a foundation for subsequent work on organizational power and dependence both from structural contingency and resource dependence theories.

March and Simon's (1958) classic theoretical treatise, *Organizations*, presents an alternative to consensus-based theories of organizational behavior and highlights the importance of negotiations, politics, and conflict within organizations. The treatise does not present a unified theory of organizations, but instead provides a series of propositions on a wide variety of organizational topics, many of which have had lasting influence on our understanding of power and dependence in organizations, including the analysis of participation, conflict, bargaining, and uncertainty absorption.

Organizations' functional orientation is most directly reflected in its extension of Barnard's (1938) inducement-contribution theory of organizational participation. For March and Simon (1958) organizations are settings in which groups and individuals with varying goals participate in the organization by providing contributions in exchange for the inducements they receive. Organizational survival is predicated on the ability of organizations to generate sufficient inducements to its coalitions of employees, managers, suppliers, distributors, and customers. Unlike Barnard (1938), which stresses that inducements lead to organizational cooperation and consensus, March and Simon (1958) argue that given uncertainty and incomplete contracts, conflicts of interest persist among members of the organization's coalition and consensus among organizational actors is never attained. Given goal heterogeneity, they posit that intergroup conflicts among members of the coalition will increase with task interdependence among coalition members, difference in goals, and difference in perceptions about the organization and its environment. With the existence of intergroup conflict, bargaining and politics are likely to emerge as solutions to organizational conflict. They further posit that uncertainty provides opportunities for coalition members to increase their power, as control over uncertainty allows individuals and groups who absorb and interpret the uncertainty to increase their power and influence over other coalition members.

In *The Behavioral Theory of the Firm*, Cyert and March (1963) further developed the view of organizations as shifting political coalitions. The theory was based on and developed through both case studies and computer simulations of organizational decision making. A key assumption of the theory is that organizations do not have a stable or consistent set of goals or preferences. Cyert and March posit instead that organizational goals are a set of more or less independent constraints imposed on the organization through a process of bargaining among coalition members. As in March and Simon's (1958) formulation, contributions and inducement of the members of the coalition determine the allocation of resources (and at least implicitly, power) to coalition members. Cyert and March highlight the importance of slack resources in the continuing political bargaining process. Organizational slack provides a cushion for side payments for coalition members and a mechanism for restoring equilibrium in the organization's coalition.

In Cyert and March's (1963) formulation of the political bargaining process, organizations develop a set of mechanisms to allocate power and resolve conflicts among coalition members:

1 The reliance on the budget as a mechanism for generating inducements and side payments
2 The allocation of discretion to coalition members through the division of labor and specialization
3 The standardization of procedures where past decisions become policy constraints for future bargaining and negotiation.

These mechanisms combined result in a quasi-resolution of conflict through sequential attention to goals. Organizations resolve conflict by attending to goals of members of the coalition at different times and in different contexts. The resulting time buffer between goals permits the organization to solve one problem at a time, attending to one goal at a time and leading to loose coupling in organizational actions and decisions. Organizational goals are subject to change, however, as aspiration levels are not met. In the long run, changes in organizational goals reflect the adaptation of goals to changes in the structure of the political coalition.

STRUCTURAL CONTINGENCIES AND RESOURCE DEPENDENCIES

Structural contingency and resource dependency theory build and extend the Carnegie School's view that power and politics in organizations is determined by the process of bargaining and economic exchange among participants in the organization's political coalition. By applying Emerson's (1962) theory of power and dependence to the organizational level, they provide a more explicit elaboration of the determinants of organizational power and dependence within organizational coalitions.

A direct application of Emerson's power-dependence framework is found in Thompson's (1967) theoretical treatment on organizational structure and action. Through a series of propositions, he examines how individuals deal with dependency relationships in organizations:

1 Individuals in highly discretionary jobs seek to maintain power equal to or greater than their dependence on others.
2 When individual power is less than their dependence, people seek coalitions with people in the external environment that may increase their power.
3 The more sources of uncertainty for the organization, the more bases for their power, and the greater the number of political positions in the organization.

Hickson et al. (1971) articulate a functional perspective on organizational power and dependence in their structural contingencies theory that builds on and extends Emerson (1962) and Thompson (1967), as well as March and Simon (1958) and Crozier (1964; see Institutional Perspectives below). They posit that the most critical organizational function or the source of the most important organizational uncertainty determines which subunits gain power within organization. They present a multiplicative model of power, where subunit power is the product of three factors:

1 The ability of the subunit to cope with critical organizational uncertainties or contingencies

2   The uniqueness, or non-substitutability of their capabilities
3   The pervasiveness or importance of the contingency to the organization

Hinings et al. (1974) directly tested the theory in an empirical study of the power of twenty-eight subunits in seven companies. Consistent with their theory, they find that coping with uncertainty alone is not sufficient to explain organizational power, but uncertainty most be accompanied by workflow centrality and low substitutability.

Pfeffer and Salancik (1978) extend and generalize the structural contingency theory in their resource dependence theory of organizational and interorganizational power. They argue that organizations, as open social systems, require a continuing provision of resources – personnel, money, social legitimacy, customers, and a variety of technological and material inputs – to survive and continue to function within their environments. Those individuals and subunits that provide the most critical and non-substitutable resources will come to have organizational power, rise to positions of executive leadership, and exert their influence over organizational decisions, structures, and outcomes. While executives controlling the dominant coalition attempt to buffer the organization from environmental change, executive succession and selection is a primary mechanism for organizational adaptation and change (Pfeffer and Salancik, 1978, p. 229), and for restoring equilibrium between the organization and the critical resource dependencies in its environment.

Several studies provide empirical support for a resource dependence theory of organizational power. In studies of departmental power in universities (Salancik and Pfeffer, 1974; Pfeffer and Moore, 1980) resources dependencies were found to be of the significant determinants of power. In a research-oriented university, the most critical contingencies were research money and academic prestige. Consequently, the proportion of outside funding, the department's national status in academic rankings, and the size of their graduate programs best predicted departmental power. The resource dependence perspective has also served to explain the structure and composition of boards of directors, (Pfeffer, 1972, 1973, 1974). For example, bankers are brought into boards of firms facing financial contingencies (Pfeffer, 1972), while representatives of the media are more likely to be members of public utilities (Pfeffer, 1974).

PUNCTUATED EQUILIBRIUM THEORY

While resource dependence and structural contingency theories view political struggles within organizations as important mechanisms for organizational adaptation, population ecologists originally posited organizational power as a source of organizational inertia (Hannan and Freeman, 1977). This view is particularly congruent with the institutionalization of power perspective. To resolve the contradiction between power as a source of inertia, and power as a source of organizational adaptation and change, Tushman and Romanelli (1985) develop a punctuated equilibrium model of organizational change and transformation. This model combines organizational inertia associated with a continuation of executive leadership and executive succession triggering organizational adaptation.

Several empirical studies have supported the punctuated equilibrium model of political re-orientation and organizational transformation. Virany et al. (1992) found two modes of organizational adaptation in turbulent environments. The most typical mode combines CEO succession, sweeping executive-team changes, and strategic reorientations. A more rare, and over the long-term more effective, adaptational mode involves strategic reorientation and executive-team change, but no succession of the CEO. Similarly, Tushman and Rosenkopf (1996) examine the effects of both CEO and executive team succession on both organizational change and subsequent firm performance. They find those while simple CEO succession without executive team change enhances incremental organization change the combination of CEO succession with executive team change triggers discontinuous change.

STRUCTURAL PERSPECTIVES

A key assumption of structural perspectives on organizational power and dependence is that individuals and groups in organizations are embedded in a structure of social relationships (Granovetter, 1985). Structural perspectives typically view the social determinants of power as complementary to human capital sources identified by functional perspectives. While recognizing the importance of economic production and exchange in the generation of organizational power, structural perspectives view social relationships as having autonomous influence, with the use of power directed towards satisfying the interests and goals of powerful individuals and groups, rather than the functional needs of the organization. Three variants of the structural perspective are influential in contemporary research on organizational power:

1   Organizational demography
2   Networks and social capital
3   Managerial elite theories

ORGANIZATIONAL DEMOGRAPHY

Kanter's (1977) *Men and Women of the Corporation* presents an ethnographic account of the structural determinants of behavior in organizations. The book provides a seminal contribution to the study of organizational demography and highlights the centrality of power in explaining organizational actions and outcomes. Kanter begins her analysis of power by recognizing the contributions of the functionalist perspective, stressing the importance of organizational performance, criticality, and control over resource dependencies and structural contingencies. But Kanter goes beyond functional approaches by stressing the importance of informal social networks and alliances with sponsors, peers, and subordinates in the determination of power. Furthermore, Kanter stresses how the power within organizations is a function of the structures of opportunities for career mobility and the demographic similarity with other individuals and groups in positions of high power. One of Kanter's (1977) key contributions is the proposition of homosocial reproduction of managers, as homophily or demographic similarity is a key determinant of whether managers get promoted to positions of formal authority. Furthermore, her analysis and findings of her research show how demographic similarity is a determinant of the likelihood to join informal networks, obtain sponsorship from powerful executives, form peer alliances and learn the rules of the game from peers.

Building on Kanter's theory, and combining it with social network perspectives, Ibarra

(1992) used a network analysis of men and women's interaction patterns to study gender inequalities in the organizational distribution of power. She found two mechanisms that create and reinforce inequality: sex differences in homophily (i.e., preference for similar others) and in the ability to convert individual and structural resources into network advantages. Men were found to gain greater network returns from similar individual and positional resources, as well as from homophilous relationships.

Many other applications of organizational demography, while not directly focusing on organizational power, have important implications for how demography affects the ability of individuals and groups to achieve organizational success. For example, Cohen et al. (1998) examined how the organizational sex composition influences the intraorganizational mobility of male and female managers. They found that the impact of sex composition depends on hierarchical level: Women are more likely to be hired and promoted into a particular job level when a higher proportion of women is already there.

NETWORKS AND SOCIAL CAPITAL

Network analysis, for the most part, builds on the power-dependence relationships originally identified by Emerson (1962) and Blau (1964), which also underlie functionalist variants of resource dependence theory (Thompson, 1967; Pfeffer and Salancik, 1978). What distinguishes structural variants of social exchange from functional perspectives is their focus on social commitments (Cook and Emerson, 1978). Social commitments involve loyalty and long-term social relationships that persist independent of the economic benefits and involve irrationality in the short-run sense of ignoring better alternatives in favor of maintaining preexisting social relationships. Given social commitments and obligations, power in organizational networks reflects not only resource dependence resulting from economic exchange but from the resources and constraints derived from long term social relationships.

Burt's (1992) structural hole theory emphasizes the constraints that social commitments impose on social relationships both within and between organizations. Structural hole theory defines organizational power in terms of the information and control advantage of being the broker in relationships between actors otherwise disconnected in social networks. Disconnected actors create a structural hole in the social structure and provide opportunities to broker the flow of information between actors in the network and to exert power over activities involving disconnected actors. The power that flows to brokers of structural holes results, at the organizational level, in greater promotion opportunities and economic returns.

In a subsequent empirical analysis of managers in an electronic and computing equipment firm, Burt (1997) extends and reformulates the concept of structural holes in terms of social capital. Burt defines and measures social capital in terms of network constraints, where greater constraint means fewer structural holes. Burt finds that, on average, a negative association between network constraint and compensation bonuses and early promotion. The value of social capital from bridging structural holes was found, however, to be contingent on the number of other managers at the same organizational level. This suggests that the value of social capital is higher for managers at senior level of the organization, who face a smaller number of peers.

While Burt (1992, 1997) defines social capital in terms of freedom from network constraint and brokering structural holes, other organizational researchers employ a different perspective, defining social capital in terms of density and centrality in the network of social relationships. For example, Belliveau et al. (1996) view social ties as a form of social resource and social capital in organizations. They compare the effects of social capital, measured both absolutely and relatively, on CEO-compensation in a sample of 61 CEO compensation committee chairperson dyads. They find a chair's absolute social capital and a CEO's social capital relative to his or her chair's significantly increased executive compensation

MANAGERIAL ELITES

One of the most active areas of research on organizational power and dependence is the study of the determinants and consequences of the power of managerial elites (Pettigrew, 1993). Managerial elite theories focus on the structural relationships between senior executives and managers in top management groups (Hambrick and Mason, 1984) and corporate boards of directors (Useem, 1984).

Hambrick and Mason's (1984) upper echelon perspective has triggered a stream of research on the power of top management groups. They view the top management group as the dominant political coalition within organizations (Cyert and March, 1963) with structural perspectives on organizational demography and its emphasis on social similarity among group members. Using a top management team perspective and employing an inductive qualitative analysis of eight top management teams, Eisenhardt and Bourgeois (1988) found that the more powerful the CEO the greater the tendency among remaining executives to consolidate power and engage in alliance and political insurgencies. Building on both functional and structural perspectives, Finkelstein (1992) identified three power dimensions in top management groups: structural, ownership, and expertise. He relies on data from a group of 1763 top managers in three industries to assess the validity and reliability of these three power dimensions.

Much research has been done on power within corporate boards of directors. For example, Finkelstein and D'Aveni (1994) explored the effects of CEOs with dual position as chairman of the board. They found that duality was less common when CEOs had high informal power and when firm performance was high. Westphal and Zajac (1995) using a longitudinal design of Fortune 500 companies, examined CEO influence in the board of director selection process and found that powerful CEOs seek to use their power within the board to appoint new board members who are demographically similar. Boeker (1992) found that CEOs who had power over their boards displace blame for poor performance onto their subordinates, and the top managers of the organization are subsequently replaced, while the CEO remains.

While most early research on power in managerial elites focused on the effects of intraelite cohesion, top management groups are also characterized by conflict and competition among group members (Hambrick, 1994). For example, Ocasio (1994), combining structural perspectives with political coalitional approaches (Cyert and March, 1963) emphasizes the role of competition and conflict in the model of circulation of power. Two mechanisms were identified that led to power circulation: obsolescence and contestation among executives. Executives were posited to be subject to obsolescence with increased executive tenure and limits to their ability to adapt to environmental contingencies.

INSTITUTIONAL PERSPECTIVES

Institutional perspectives view organizational power as embedded in institutions – the system of formal rules, normative commitments, and cultural logics that enable and constrain organizational decisions and actions. Institutional perspectives view material explanations of the sources and consequences of power as insufficient. Critical contingencies, resource dependencies, and formal and informal structures are seen not as objective properties of organizations and their environments, but as themselves shaped by prevailing institutional rules, norms, and logics within organizations and organizational fields (Palmer and Biggart, this volume). Early institutional perspectives focused on the interplay between formal rules, normative commitments, and organizational power (Selznick, 1949, 1957; Gouldner, 1954; Crozier, 1964). More recent institutional approaches (Brown, 1978, Jackall, 1988, Fligstein, 1990) view the sources and uses of organizational power as socially constructed properties of social grouping and institutions (Berger and Luckmann, 1967). While the 1990s has seen an increase in research from a institutional perspective, this approach serves not to deny the importance of both the effects of economic and social structural determinants of power, but to show how these effects are moderated by the impact of culture and institutions. Within the institutionalist perspective I will review three broad variants: Weberian theories, normative theories, and political-cultural theories.

WEBERIAN THEORIES

Weber's sociology of domination ([1922] 1968) presents a departing point for the study of power in bureaucratic structures. His ideal-typical comparative analysis of bureaucratic-rational control, patrimonial authority, and charismatic authority have all been influential to the study of organizations. Weberian perspectives on power and dependence highlight the interplay between formal bureaucratic rules and the structures of organizational power. The focus of this perspective has been to show how in its empirical manifestation, power within formal organizations departs from the ideal-typical model of rationalized bureaucratic control developed by Weber ([1922] 1968). Much of this research has been conducted through detailed case studies and organizational ethnographies. While Weber stressed the functionality of bureaucracy, neo-Weberian perspectives have typically emphasized how powerful individuals and groups exert control over bureaucratic structures in unanticipated ways that depart from their rational design. More recent research highlights departures from the bureaucratic ideal type through culture and informal controls. This research suggests that informal and cultural control rather than increasing the power of individuals and groups within organizations, limits their discretion and increases their dependence on the organization.

Gouldner's (1954) ethnographic account of leadership succession in a gypsum mine and factor examines the transition from a more consensus form of bureaucratic control to one of punitive control. Gouldner views bureaucracy as a man-made instrument, constructed by individuals in proportion to their power in a given situation. He posits that organizational rules may be used by supervisors and subordinates alike, taking advantage of them for punitive purposes and as a bargaining tool. With different interests and values among groups, bureaucratic rules are adopted to establish control over subordinates. Gouldner's view of bureaucratic institutions highlights their role in determining the relative power of supervisors over subordinates.

Crozier (1964), in his book *The Bureaucratic Phenomenon*, highlights the importance of power relationships between groups and individuals in explaining bureaucratic structures and patterns of action. Crozier's book is primarily remembered and cited for his observations that maintenance workers held considerable power because they were capable of dealing with machine breakdowns – a major source of organizational uncertainty in the highly mechanized French tobacco monopolist that he studied. Through his penetrating analysis, Crozier identified control over uncertainty as a key source of power and posited that the power of A over B depends on A's ability to predict B's behavior and on the uncertainty of B about A's behavior. Crozier's analysis was highly influential in the development of the structural contingency theory of power, described above.

But Crozier's more general contributions to our understanding of organizational power, while less well remembered, focus on the development of discretion, within a bureaucratic system of rules designed to limit such discretion. Despite the rationalization of control in bureaucracy, power relationships and discretion can never be completely suppressed, as it is impossible to eliminate uncertainty in the context of bounded rationality. For Crozier, uncertainty results, however, not just from the task itself, as highlighted by subsequent interpretations of his work by structural contingency theorists (Hickson et al., 1971), but also from political struggles between individuals and groups attempting to increase their own discretion and limiting the ability of others to control their actions. Unlike most subsequent interpretations of his work, Crozier views the stable equilibrium of power observed in the tobacco monopolists as an unusual case, with more dynamic systems of power likely where there are several sources of uncertainty, where political coalitions are less permanent, and where environmental change creates greater instability.

Following the Weberian tradition a series of ethnographic and field research studies have examined the dependence of both managers and employees on prevailing control systems in organizations. Jackall (1988), in a brilliant ethnography of managerial rules for survival and success, argues that hidden behind the bureaucratic veneer of formal rules and control, power in American corporation is characterized by a patrimonial systems of fealty, loyalty, and obligation. In this patrimonial bureaucracy the rhetoric of teams and cooperation belies an ongoing political struggle and contest for promotion and success. Jackall (1988) combines a Weberian approach with a cultural, phenomenological perspective. Jackall relies on the concept of institutional logic to characterize the formal and informal rules and codes of conduct that provide guidance for executives in their quest for power and control. In Jackall's analysis both strong social relationships with those in positions of formal power and authority, and the skilled use of institutional logics provide managers with effective power sources.

While Jackall (1988) approaches power relationships in traditional divisional, bureaucratic organizations, other studies from a Weberian perspective have emphasized the rise of formal and informal controls in organizations. Barker (1993) provides an ethnographic account of how an organization evolves from the hierarchical control of bureaucracy to the concertive control of self-managing teams. Individuals within teams were increasingly dependent on value-based normative rules and concertive control appeared to constrain the organization's members more powerfully than bureaucratic control. Similarly, Adler (1992) finds that the organizational control that results from a "learning bureaucracy" in NUMMI, the joint venture between Toyota and General Motors, while increasing productivity and efficiency, also increases dependence of organizational members on the prevailing productive system.

NORMATIVE THEORIES

Selznick (1949) provided an early normative account of power and dependence in organizations. He presents an institutionalist analysis of the unanticipated consequence of administrative or bureaucratic control his classic study in *TVA and the Grass Roots: A Study of Politics and Organization*. Like the functionalist perspective Selznick views organizations as adaptive social structures seeking to adapt to their environments. But unlike functional views on power, Selznick stresses the political processes that arise not from means–ends relationships in the production of goods and services, but from the unanticipated consequences of organizational commitments. In adapting to their environments, informal and unanticipated social structures and centers of power arise that limit the autonomy of the organizations and its managers to accomplish their formal objectives. For Selznick, an organization's commitments are a critical mechanism in explaining how informal structures of power are generated. For the TVA its commitment to become a successful business and to its official doctrine of grass roots participation took precedence over its formal goal as a conservation agency. This commitment was enforced both by interorganizational dependencies with land-grant colleges and influential local agricultural groups hostile to the New Deal's conservation policies, as well as by internal agricultural leadership that was recruited within the TVA and which constituted its personnel. Both interorganizational and intraorganizational dependencies on powerful agricultural interests limited the ability of its formal policies to take hold. With his focus on formal and informal cooptation as mechanisms by which the balance of power between different interests groups takes hold, Selznick presaged later view of organizations as political coalitions, as well as open systems perspectives on interorganizational power and dependencies (Mizruchi and Yoo, this volume).

Selznick's (1957) focus on institutionalization as a determinant of power and politics in organizations is further developed and articulated in his treatise, *Leadership in Administration*. Selznick posits that organizations become institutionalized as they are infused with value beyond the functional requirements of the task at hand. Institutions develop a set of normative commitments that define organizational character, mission, purpose, and distinctive competence. The organization's social and political structures form a complex system of relations among persons and groups that embody the organization's purpose and commitments. The six elements of the social and political structure identified by Selznick are (1) formal roles; (2) internal interest groups; (3) social stratification; (4) cultural beliefs; (5) participation in decision making; and, (6) dependencies on resources and information. According to Selznick, the development and use of power in the organization's social structure serves to communicate, spontaneously protect and advance the organization's purpose. Selznick's institutional view of power and politics is functionalist, but the functions supported and maintained are defined not of economic means–ends relationships, but of organizational values and normative commitments.

Selznick's normative approach to institutionalization is reflected in contemporary approaches to institutions that highlight the operation of organizational identities and the logic of appropriateness (March and Olsen, 1989). In the organizational literature, this perspective has been followed by Ocasio (1999) to explain insider versus outsider succession in large industrial corporations. Ocasio posits that succession is guided both by formal rules and normative precedents, and that rules both enable and constrain board decision making.

POLITICAL–CULTURAL APPROACHES

Brown (1978) presents a version of a political–cultural approach through his theoretical development of a political phenomenology of organizations. For Brown (1978) organizational power is shaped by organizational paradigms – the inter-subjectively agreed upon set of assumptions and commitments that define the nature and meaning of that which the organization is. Brown posits that organizational paradigms shape power as they "provide roles to be enacted in particular ways, in particular settings, and in particular relation to other roles." Paradigms also affect the utilization of power by defining the definition of organizational problems, leadership, and the structure of selective attention and inattention in organizations. According to Brown, organizational power is most strategically deployed not in making decisions but over political struggles over the design of paradigmatic frameworks that constitute the meaning of organizational actions and decisions. Paradigms structure organizational agendas and shape what can be negotiated or not negotiated.

While Brown's conceptualization of a political phenomenology of organizations has not led to a separate school or line of research, it has influenced a variety of scholars and researchers who have emphasized the importance of cultural logics and frames in the determination and use of power. For example Brown (1978) directly influenced Pfeffer's (1981b) symbolic management perspective on organizations. Pfeffer (1981b) like Brown (1978) employs the concept of organizational paradigm and examines the determinants and consequences of organizational rhetoric. But Pfeffer's approach remains less directly constructivist, as he sees organizational paradigms and symbolic management as ideological practices decoupled from a material world that is shaped by resource dependencies (Pfeffer and Salancik, 1978). Symbols and paradigms are nevertheless consequential for the deployment and use of organizational power.

The symbolic management perspective has led to a variety of empirical studies on the use of symbols, language, and rituals in the exercise of organizational power. For example, Morrill (1991) employs a symbolic approach in his ethnography of conflict resolution at a toy manufacturing company. He identifies how changes in management structure from a strict hierarchy to a matrix management organization led to structural conditions conducive to a highly ritualized conflict management, culturally and linguistically framed as a code of honor. Reputation and honor ceremonies were found to be sources of control and information of top managers over their subordinates. Morrill stresses the interplay between cultural and structural forces in the management of conflict and political dynamics among executives.

While Brown (1978) and Pfeffer's (1981b) approaches are developed at the organizational level, neo-institutional theory (Meyer and Rowan, 1977; DiMaggio and Powell, 1983) has influenced political-cultural perspectives by bringing the institutional environment directly into the determination of the determinants and consequences of organizational power and dependence. Fligstein's (1985, 1987, 1990) analysis of the transformation of large US corporations and driven by the rise and fall of various functional backgrounds in the organizational power struggle and their associated conceptions of control is perhaps the most influential example of such an approach.

Through a series of empirical articles (Fligstein, 1985, 1987) and in his book (Fligstein, 1990), *The Transformation of Corporate Control*, Fligstein examines the rise and fall to power of various functional backgrounds to positions of dominance and authority in large US corporations. Fligstein views power struggles as closely tied to cultural struggles, as the various functional backgrounds each represent distinct cultural conceptions of how to run large corporations and to control competition. Fligstein (1987) examines the rise of finance personnel and the finance conception of control to the top in the 1960s and the 1970s. The finance conception views the corporation as a portfolio of assets, with an increased prevalence of mergers and acquisitions, diversification, and the rise of the multidivisional form (Fligstein, 1985). In his book, Fligstein (1990) combines statistical analysis of the determinants and consequences of executive power with historical analysis of the role of the state, in particular, changes in antitrust law and implementation in determining the dominance of distinct conceptions of control.

Ocasio and Kim (1999) refine and extend Fligstein's approach in an analysis of selection of functional backgrounds of new CEOs in the 1980s and early 1990s. They find evidence of an ideological and political obsolescence of financial CEOs and a change in the strategic contingencies that previously favored finance and the financial conception of control. Their results suggest that conceptions of control are best understood as styles, rather than institutions, as these conceptions are neither taken for granted nor isomorphic across industries or the manufacturing sector, but are subject to sectoral variation, contestation, and change.

Thornton and Ocasio (1999) extend an institutional perspective on organizational power and dependence by examining executive succession in the higher education publishing industry. They examine the effects of institutional transformation from an editorial logic to a market logic with a resulting change in the determinants of executive organizational power. They posit that institutional logics structure organizational attention (Ocasio, 1997) making some determinants of power more salient than others. Combining qualitative, historical analysis of the two logics, editorial and market, with hazard rate models of succession, they find that while positional determinants of power are stronger under an editorial logic, economic determinants are stronger under a market logic. They conclude that the determinants of executive power are historically contingent, as shaped by the prevailing institutional logic.

Contemporary Issues and Debates

As evidenced by the literature review above, the study of organizational power and dependence remains highly fragmented. Rather than engaging in general debates across perspectives, researchers focus their attention on a set of specific issues and problem areas. Two issue areas, however, have been the recent focus of researchers across perspectives:

1 The effects of economic performance on organizational power
2 The determination of cohesion versus conflict in the organization's dominant political coalition

EFFECTS OF ECONOMIC PERFORMANCE

Perhaps the central tenet of a functional perspective on organizational power is the proposition that changes in organizational performance lead to changes in the distribution of power and in the alignment of the organization with the environment (Cyert and March, 1963; Pfeffer and Salancik, 1978; Tushman and Romanelli, 1985). Researchers from both structural and institutional perspectives have challenged this proposition and have proposed modifications to this view. While the evidence supports the functionalist view that changes in organizational power are more likely under conditions of poor performance, these effects have neither been found to be particularly large nor robust, but subject to structural and institutional contingencies. The nature and extent of these contingencies remains an active subject of debate in contemporary research.

ENTRENCHMENT VERSUS CONTESTATION

Pfeffer (1981a) modified the earlier functionalist perspective on succession as a mechanism for adaptation by proposing that powerful individuals and groups are likely to entrench themselves and institutionalize their organizational power. Salancik and Pfeffer (1977) term this perspective the institutionalization of power. Although they rely on taken-for-grantedness as a mechanism for entrenchment, this perspective is best understood as primarily structural, rather than institutional. They rely on two key propositions of a structural perspective on organizational power:

1   Organizational power is a function of social commitments and obligations incurred in social relationships
2   The effects of social relationships on the allocation and distribution of organizational power occurs independently of their contribution to organizational performance.

This perspective has received empirical support by Boeker (1989, 1992) and Cannella, and Lubatkin (1993).

Ocasio (1994) proposed political contestation as an alternative mechanism for organizational responses to poor economic performance. He posits that poor performance leads to a restructuring of the dominant political coalition and that political contests for power will emerge within the organization. He found evidence of contestation moderating the effects of performance on executive succession. In particular Ocasio (1994) found that the greater the number of inside board members under conditions of poor performance, the higher the rate of CEO succession. This suggests that insiders are potential rivals to the power of the CEO and this rivalry is likely to lead to decreased entrenchment under poor economic performance. Ocasio's model has been further supported and extended by Ocasio and Kim (1999) who find that the effects of performance on the selection of functional backgrounds of new CEOs is moderated by political contests among different styles or conceptions of control.

DECOUPLING

Using a symbolic management perspective, Westphal and Zajac (1994, 1998) posit that organizations and their boards of directors are likely to respond by symbolic responses favored by financial markets, but that these responses are decoupled from their actual implementation. Westphal and Zajac (1994) employ a symbolic management perspective in their empirical analysis of the separation of substance and symbolism in CEO compensation. They find that a substantial number of firms are likely to adopt but not actually use, or only limitedly use, long-term incentive compensation, suggesting a decoupling of use from their rhetoric. Furthermore, they find that this decoupling is particularly prevalent in firms with powerful CEOs. Westphal and Zajac (1998) found similar evidence of decoupling in a study of stock buybacks; firms were likely to announce stock buybacks but not actually undertake them.

RULES AND LOGICS

Institutional perspectives on organizational power posit that the effects of economic performance on the determinants and consequences of power are shaped by the prevailing rules and logic in the organization and the organizational field (Ocasio, 1995). Ocasio (1999) found empirical support for this proposition in his study of insider versus outsider CEO succession. While Ocasio found a main effect of performance on outsider succession, this effect was moderated by past experience of the organization with both insider and outsider succession. This suggests that power is embedded in organizational rules and that, under poor economic performance, organizations are likely to increasingly rely on the institutionalized rules, rather than change their rules as suggested by more functional perspectives (Cyert and March, 1963).

COHESION AND CONFLICT IN DOMINANT POLITICAL COALITIONS

Another area of contemporary debate is the extent of cohesion versus conflict in the organization's dominant coalition. While functional perspectives of power tend to support a view of shifting political coalitions and intraelite conflict, both structural and institutional perspectives are divided in the extent of intraelite cohesion and conflict found within organizations. While the upper echelons perspective (Hambrick and Mason, 1984) has been interpreted as emphasizing a cohesive top management group, others have suggested that contestation and conflict within top management is common (Hambrick, 1994; Ocasio, 1994). Westphal and Zajac (1997) examine the limits to elite cohesion in corporate boards of directors in a longitudinal study of the diffusion of contingent compensation and changes in diversification in Fortune 500 firms. They find that CEO-directors typically support fellow CEOs by impeding increased board control over management but that CEO-directors may also foster an increase in board activism and control over the CEO if they have experienced it in their own corporation. Drawing on social exchange theory, they find that CEO-directors experience a reversal in the basis for generalized social exchange with other top managers from one of deference and support to one of independence and control.

Social capital perspectives also differ on their emphasis on cohesion (Coleman, 1988) versus conflict. Structural hole theories (Burt, 1992, 1997) focus on entrepreneurial opportunities to bridge differences among organizational executives as determinants of power. Institutional perspectives also differ on the degree of cohesion in organizational fields with Fligstein (1990) positing the dominance of singular perspectives in a particular time period, while Ocasio and Kim (1999) suggest instead the prevalence of conflict and political contestation among elites within an organizational field.

Critical Unresolved Questions

Given the widely varied theories and research finding on organizational power and dependence, the question of how to integrate the various perspective remains. The literature reviewed supports the view that organizational power is multi-dimensional, and that economic, social, and cultural factors interact to determine the various sources and uses of organizational power (Thornton and Ocasio, 1999). While no integrative perspective exists, the concept of political capital provides a potential unifying concept to elucidate the various power sources available to individuals and groups in organizations. I define political capital as the variety of economic, social, and cultural resources available to individuals and groups to influence organizational decisions and actions. The sources of political capital in organizations include: human capital (Hickson et al., 1971); financial capital (Cyert and March, 1963; Pfeffer and Salancik, 1978), social capital (Kanter, 1977; Burt, 1997), institutional capital (Selznick, 1957), and cultural capital (Jackall, 1988; Fligstein, 1990).

Given the variety of sources of power and political capital available to individuals and groups, the allocation and use of organizational power is inherently unstable. Organizations are constituted by shifting political coalitions (Cyert and March, 1963), and power is subject to contestation (Jackall, 1988; Ocasio, 1994) and intraelite conflict and change (Westphal and Zajac, 1997). A key challenge for future research is determining how the various sources of political capital change over time, both to reflect organizational-level changes (Pfeffer and Salancik, 1978; Jackall, 1988; Ocasio, 1994) or changes in the organizational field (Fligstein, 1990; Westphal and Zajac, 1997; Thornton and Ocasio, 1999).

Promising Area of Research

A promising area of research is to determine the particular contingencies that affect organizational power. While various sources of political capital exist in organizations, not all these sources will be equally important to the organization and its dominant coalition. Given this variation, recent research has moved away from identifying universal determinants of organizational power to establishing the contingent economic, structural, and institutional factors underlying organizational power. For example, Burt (1997) has shown that the value of political capital is contingent on both the demographic distribution of social capital within the organization, as bridging structural holes is a critical at high levels of the organizations, where managers face limited numbers of competitors, but not at lower levels. Similarly, Burt (1998) explores the differential consequences of social capital for men and women in corporations, as they face different networks and demographic structures.

From an institutional perspective, Thornton and Ocasio (1999) show how the determinants of executive power are historically contingent on the prevailing institutional logics. As higher education publishing firms shifted from a professional or editorial logic to a market logic, the determinants of organizational power shifted from positional determinants of power to market forces. This research further suggests that determining the contingencies in the value of political capital is a key research challenge, and helps explain the low level of replicability of findings across research studies.

Connections Up and Down the Hierarchical Levels

The study of power and dependence has clear links across levels of analysis: intraorganizational, organizational, and interorganizational. Some perspectives, particularly resource dependence theory, in both its functional and structural variants, have clear applications and serves as a multi-level theory that applies across all levels of analysis (Emerson, 1962; Pfeffer and Salancik, 1978). Cross-level issues and links can also serve to deepen our understanding of the determinants and outcomes of organizational power.

Westphal's (1998) study of the behavior CEOs in corporate boards is an important example of how intraorganizational power affects organizational-level outcomes. Following Brass and Burkhardt (1993) – see also Brass (this volume) – Westphal examined the relationship between behavioral and structural sources of power in corporate boards, a central topic of concern at the managerial level. In his analysis, Westphal focuses on the operation of mechanisms at the social psychological and intraorganizational levels. He found that changes in board structure that increase the board's independence from management are associated with higher levels of CEO behavioral strategies of ingratiation and persuasion toward board members, and that such influence behaviors offset the effect of increased structural board independence on corporate strategy and CEO compensation policy.

The effects of interorganizational power on the organizational level are most directly evident in neo-institutional approaches to power (Fligstein, 1990; Thornton and Ocasio, 1999). Structural perspectives at the interorganizational level can also be readily applied to examine the determinants and consequences of organizational power and dependence (Mizruchi and Yoo, this volume). The work on interlocking boards of directors provides a prime example as interlocks affect organizational-level decisions by corporate boards of directors (Davis, 1991; Mizruchi, 1992; Westphal and Zajac, 1997). General changes at the interorganizational level in corporate governance, for example, the rise in institutional investors (Davis and Thompson, 1994; Useem, 1996).

Conclusions

In this chapter I examined the myriad approaches to the study of organizational power and dependence and have classified them into three general, albeit sometimes overlapping perspectives: functional, structural, and institutional. The theoretical fragmentation observed in the study of organizational power is reflective of a similar fragmentation in organizational theory and research. This fragmentation presents both an opportunity and a challenge for organizational scholars. The exploitation of within perspective research trajectories, for example the study of social capital, decoupling, and institutional logics should continue to provide research opportunities that deepen our understanding of organizational power. The greater and more difficult challenge is to bridge, if not integrate the varied perspectives. Given the centrality and ubiquity of power, successful efforts at integration are likely to yield benefits not only for understanding organizational power and dependence, but also for organizational theory as a whole.

References

Adler, P. S. (1992): "The learning bureaucracy: New United Motors Manufacturing, Inc.," in L. L. Cummings and B. M. Staw (eds), *Research in Organizational Behavior*, 15, 111–94.

Barker, J. R. (1993): "Tightening the iron cage: Concertive control in self-managing teams," *Administrative Science Quarterly*, 39, 408–37.

Barnard, C. I. (1938): *The Functions of the Executive*. Cambridge, MA: Harvard University Press.

Belliveau M. A., O'Reilly C. A, and Wade J. B. (1996): "Social capital at the top: Effects of social similarity and status on CEO compensation," *Academy of Management Journal*, 39, 1568–93.

Berger, P. L., and Luckmann, T. (1967): *The Social Construction of Reality*. New York: Doubleday.

Blau, P. M. (1964): *Exchange and Power in Social Life*. New York: John Wiley & Sons.

Boeker, W. (1989): "The development and institutionalization of subunit power in organizations," *Administrative Science Quarterly*, 34, 388–410.

Boeker, W. (1992): "Power and managerial dismissal: Scapegoating at the top," *Administrative Science Quarterly*, 37, 400–21.

Brass, D. J., and Burkhardt, M. E. (1993): "Potential power and power use: An investigation of structure and behavior," *Academy of Management Journal*, 36, 441–70.

Brown, R. H. (1978): "Bureaucracy as praxis: Towards a political phenomenology of organizations," *Administrative Science Quarterly*, 23, 365–82.

Burt, R. S. (1992): *Structural Holes: The Social Structure of Competition*. Cambridge, MA: Harvard University Press.

Burt, R. S. (1997): "The contingent value of social capital," *Administrative Science Quarterly*, 42, 339–65.

Burt, R. S. (1998): "The gender of social capital," *Rationality and Society*, 10, 5–46.

Cannella, A. A., and Lubatkin M. (1993),.: "Succession as a sociopolitical process: Internal impediments to outsider succession," *Academy of Management Journal*, 36, 763–93.

Cohen L. E., Broschak J. P., and Haveman H. A(1998): "And then there were more? The effect of organizational sex composition on the hiring and promotion of managers, " *American Sociological Review*, 63, 711–27.

Coleman, J. S. (1988): "Social capital in the creation of human-capital," *American Journal of Sociology*, 94, S95–S120.

Cook, K. S., and Emerson, R. M. (1978): "Power, equity, and commitment in exchange networks," *American Sociological Review*, 43, 721–39.

Crozier, M. (1964): *The Bureaucratic Phenomena*. Chicago: University of Chicago Press.

Cyert, R. M., and March, J. G. (1963): *A Behavioral Theory of the Firm*. Englewood Cliffs, NJ: Prentice-Hall.

Davis, G. F. (1991): "Agents without principles? The spread of the poison pill through the intercorporate network," *Administrative Science Quarterly*, 35, 141–73.

Davis, G. F and Thompson, T. (1994): "A social movement perspective on corporate control," *Administrative Science Quarterly*, 39, 285–312.

DiMaggio, P. J., and Powell, W. W. (1983): "The iron cage revisited: Institutional isomorphism and collective rationality in organizational fields," *American Sociological Review*, 48, 147–60.

Eisenhardt, K. M., and Bourgeois L. J. (1988): "Politics of strategic decision-making in high-velocity environments – Toward a midrange theory," *Academy of Management Journal*, 31, 737–40.

Emerson, R. M. (1962): "Power-dependence relations," *American Sociological Review*, 27, 31–41.

Finkelstein, S. (1992): "Power in top management teams: Dimensions, measurement, and validation," *Academy of Management Journal*, 35, 505–38.

Finkelstein, S., and D'Aveni, R. A. (1994): "CEO duality as a double-edged-sword: How boards of directors balance entrenchment avoidance and unity of command," *Academy of Management Journal*, 37, 1079–108.

Fligstein, N. (1985): "The spread of the multidivisional form among large firms, 1919–1979," *American Sociological Review*, 50, 377–91.

Fligstein, N. (1987): "The intraorganizational power struggle: Rise of finance presidents in large firms, 1919–1979," *American Sociological Review*, 52, 44–58.

Fligstein, N. (1990): *The Transformation of Corporate Control*. Cambridge, MA: Harvard University Press.

Gouldner, A. (1954): *Patterns of Industrial Bureaucracy*. Glencoe, IL: Free Press.

Granovetter, M. (1985): "Economic action and social structure: The problem of embeddedness," *American Journal of Sociology*, 91, 481–510.

Hambrick, D. C. (1994): "Top management groups: A conceptual integration and reconsideration of the 'team' label," in B. M. Staw and L. L. Cummings (eds), *Research in Organizational Behavior*, 16, 171–94.

Hambrick, D. C., and Mason, P. A. (1984): "Upper echelons: The organization as a reflection of its top managers," *Academy of Management Review*, 9, 193–206.

Hannan, M. T., and Freeman, J. (1977): "The population ecology of organizations," *American Journal of Sociology*, 82, 929–64.

Hickson, D. J., Hinings, C. R., Lee, C. A., Schneck, R. E., and Pennings, J. M. (1971): "A strategic contingencies theory of intraorganizational power," *Administrative Science Quarterly*, 16, 216–29.

Hinings, C. R., Hickson, D. J., Pennings, J. M., and Schneck, R. E. (1974): "Structural conditions of intraorganizational power," *Administrative Science Quarterly*, 19, 22–44.

Ibarra, H. (1992): "Homophily and differential returns: Sex-differences in network structure and access in an advertising firm," *Administrative Science Quarterly*, 37, 422–47.

Jackall, R. (1988): *Moral Mazes: The World of Corporate Managers*. New York: Oxford University Press.

Kanter, R. M. (1977): *Men and Women of the Corporation*. New York: Basic Books.

March, J. G., and Olsen, J. P. (1989): *Rediscovering Institutions: The Organizational Basis of Politics*. New York: Free Press.

March, J. G., and Simon, H. A. (1958): *Organizations*. New York: John Wiley & Sons.

Meyer, J. W. and Rowan, B. (1977), "Institutionalized organizations: Formal structure as myth and ceremony," *American Journal of Sociology*, 83, 340–63.

Mizruchi, M. S. (1992): *The Structure of Corporate Political Action*. Cambridge, MA: Harvard University Press.

Morrill, C. (1991): "Conflict management, honor, and organizational change," *American Journal of Sociology*, 97, 585–621.

Ocasio, W. (1994): "Political dynamics and the circulation of power: CEO succession in large U.S. industrial corporations, 1960–1990," *Administrative Science Quarterly*, 39, 285–312.

Ocasio, W. (1995): "The enactment of economic adversity: A reconciliation of theories of failure-induced change and threat-rigidity," in L. L. Cummings and B. M. Staw, (eds), *Research in Organizational Behavior*, 17, 287–331.

Ocasio, W. (1997): "Towards an attention-based view of the firm," *Strategic Management Journal*, 18, 187–206.

Ocasio, W. (1999): "Institutionalized action and corporate governance: The reliance on rules of CEO succession," *Administrative Science Quarterly*, 44, 384–416

Ocasio, W., and Kim, H. (1999): "The circulation of corporate control: Selection of functional backgrounds of new CEOs in large US manufacturing firms, 1981–1992," *Administrative Science Quarterly*, 44, 532–62

Perrow, C. (1986): *Complex Organizations: A Critical Essay*, 3rd edn. New York: McGraw Hill.

Pettigrew, A. M. (1993): "On studying managerial elites," *Strategic Management Journal*, 13, 163–82.

Pfeffer, J. (1972): "Size and composition of corporate boards of directors," *Administrative Science Quarterly*, 17, 218–28.

Pfeffer, J. (1973): "Size, composition and function of hospital board of directors," *Administrative Science Quarterly*, 18, 349–64.

Pfeffer, J. (1974): "Cooptation and the composition of hospital board of directors," *Pacific Sociological Review*, 17, 333–63.

Pfeffer, J. (1981a): *Power in Organizations*. Marshfield, MA: Pittman.

Pfeffer, J. (1981b): "Management as symbolic action: The creation and maintenance of organizational paradigm," in L. L. Cummings and B. M. Staw, (eds), *Research in Organizational Behavior*, 3, 1–52.

Pfeffer, J., and Moore, W. (1980): "Power in university budgeting: A replication and extension," *Administrative Science Quarterly*, 25, 637–53.

Pfeffer, J., and Salancik, G. (1978): *The External Control of Organizations: A Resource Dependence Perspective*. New York: Harper and Row.

Salancik, G., and Pfeffer, J. (1974): "The bases and uses of power in organizational decision making: The case of a university," *Administrative Science Quarterly*, 19, 453–73.

Salancik, G., and Pfeffer, J. (1977): "Who gets power – and how they hold on to it: A strategic-contingency model of power," *Organizational Dynamics*, 5, 3–21.

Selznick, P. (1949): *TVA and the Grass Roots: A Study of Politics and Organization*. Berkeley, CA: University of California Press.

Selznick, P. (1957): *Leadership in Administration*. New York: Harper and Row.

Thompson, J. D. (1967): *Organizations in Action*. New York: McGraw Hill.

Thornton, P. H., and Ocasio, W. (1999): "Institutional logics and the historical contingency of power in organizations: Executive succession in the higher education publishing industry, 1958–1990," *American Journal of Sociology*, 105, 801–43.

Tushman, M. L., and Romanelli, E. (1985): "Organizational evolution: A metamorphosis model of convergence and reorientation," in L. L. Cummings and B. M. Staw, (eds), *Research in Organizational Behavior*, 7, 171–222.

Tushman, M. L., and Rosenkopf, L. (1996): "Executive succession, strategic reorientation and performance growth: A longitudinal study in the US cement industry," *Management Science*, 42, 939–53.

Useem, M. (1984): *The Inner Circle*. New York: Oxford University Press.

Useem, M. (1996): *Investor Capitalism: How Money Managers Are Changing the Face of Corporate America*. New York: Basic.

Virany, B., Tushman, M. L., and Romanelli, E. (1992): "Executive succession and organization outcomes in turbulent environments: An organization learning approach," *Organization Science*, 3, 72–91.

Weber, M. ([1922] 1968): *Economy and Society: An Interpretive Sociology*. New York: Bedminister Press.

Westphal J. D. (1998): "Board games: How CEOs adapt to increases in structural board independence from management," *Administrative Science Quarterly*, 43, 511–37.

Westphal J. D., and Zajac E. J. (1994): "Substance and symbolism in CEOs long-term incentive plans," *Administrative Science Quarterly*, 39, 367–90.

Westphal J. D., and Zajac E. J. (1995): "Who shall govern: CEO/board power, demographic similarity, and new director selection." *Administrative Science Quarterly*, 40, 60–83.

Westphal J. D., and Zajac E. J. (1997): "Defections from the inner circle: Social exchange, reciprocity, and the diffusion of board independence in US corporations," *Administrative Science Quarterly*, 42, 161–83.

Westphal, J. D., and Zajac, E. J. (1998): "The symbolic management of stockholders: Corporate governance reforms and shareholder reactions," *Administrative Science Quarterly*, 43, 127–53.

Chapter Seventeen

Organizational Technology

MICHAEL L. TUSHMAN AND WENDY SMITH

Technological Change, Ambidextrous Organizations and Organizational Evolution

Technical change is one of the core drivers of organizational fates (Tushman and Nelson, 1990; Nelson, 1995). While technological change accentuates organizational failure rates, there is substantial heterogeneity in organizational life chances (Barnett and Carroll, 1995). Some firms thrive during eras of ferment, other firms proactively destabilize their product class with technological discontinuities, even as most firms are swept away during Schumpeterian gales of creative destruction (Morone, 1993; Carroll and Teo, 1996; Grove, 1996; Sorensen and Stuart, 2000). The stream of research on organizational technology is interested in how organizations shape and are, in turn, shaped by technological change. This literature sheds substantial light on how organizational architectures, capabilities and senior teams affect both a firm's ability to shape technological change and to effectively compete when technologies change.

Technology and resource rich firms often fail to sustain their competitiveness at technology transitions. Consider SSIH, the Swiss watch consortium, Goodyear Tire, Polaroid, and Oticon, the Danish hearing aid firm. These organizations dominated their respective worldwide markets, SSIH and Goodyear through the 1970s and Polaroid and Oticon through the early 1990s. Each developed new technologies that had the capabilities to re-create their markets (e.g., quartz movements, radial tires, digital imaging, and in-the-ear [ITE] volume and tone control). But although SSIH, Goodyear, Polaroid and Oticon had the technology and the resources to innovate, it was smaller, more aggressive firms that initiated new technology in these four industries. SSIH, Goodyear, Polaroid and Oticon prospered until new industry standards – what we will call dominant designs – rapidly destroyed their market positions (Glassmier, 1991, Sull, 1999, Tripsas and Gavetti, 2000). Similar liabilities of success have been found in disk drives (Christensen and Bower, 1996), business equipment (Rosenbloom, 2000), photolithography (Henderson and Clark, 1990), typesetting (Tripsas, 1999), among others (Miller, 1994; Tushman and O'Reilly, 1997).

In the watch, tire, photography and hearing aid markets, it was not new technology that led to the demise of the Swiss, Americans or the Danes; indeed, SSIH, Goodyear, Polaroid and Oticon were technology leaders. Nor was the rapid loss in market share due to lack of financial resources or to governmental regulations. Rather, the rapid demise of SSIH and Goodyear and the losses at Polaroid and Oticon were rooted in organizational complacency and inertia. These pathologies of sustained success stunted their ability to renew themselves. This success syndrome is particularly paradoxical in that each of these firms had the competencies, resources and technologies to proactively drive innovation streams. Innovation streams are patterns of innovations; some that build on and extend prior products (e.g., mechanical watches, bias ply tires, and behind-the-ear [BTE] hearing aids), while others destroy those very products that account for a firm's historical success (e.g. analog to digital imaging). Innovation streams focus theoretical and empirical attention away from isolated innovations and toward patterns of innovation over time.

This paradoxical pattern in which winners, with all their competencies and assets, become losers is found across industries and countries (Hamel and Prahalad, 1994; Utterback, 1994; Christensen, 1998). It seems that building core competencies and managing through continuous improvement are not sufficient for sustained competitive advantage. Worse, building on core competencies (e.g., for the Swiss, precision mechanics) and engaging in continuous incremental improvement actually traps the organization in its past and leads to catastrophic failure as technologies and markets shift. Core competencies often turn into rigidities (Leonard-Barton, 1992; Benner and Tushman, 2000). Those firms caught by historically anchored inertia are unable to build, extend, or destroy their existing competencies in order to develop innovations that would create new markets (as Starkey did with ITE hearing aids) or rewrite the competitive rules in existing markets (as Seiko and Michelin did with quartz watches and radial tires). These inertial firms get selected out of their competitive arenas by basic ecological dynamics (Levinthal, 1997; Carroll and Hannan, 2000; Sorensen and Stuart, 2000).

But liabilities of success are not deterministic; core competencies need not become core rigidities. Some organizations are capable of proactively shifting bases of competition through streams of innovation (Tushman and O'Reilly, 1997; Brown and Eisenhardt, 1998). These firms are able to develop incremental innovation as well as innovations that alter industry standards, substitute for existing products, and/or reconfigure products to fundamentally different markets. For example, in the watch industry, Seiko not only was able to compete in mechanical watches, but was also willing to experiment with quartz and tuning fork movements. Based on these technological options, Seiko managers made the decision to substitute quartz movements for their existing mechanical movements. In retrospect, the switch to the quartz movement led to fundamentally different competitive rules in the watch industry. Similarly, Starkey (a US hearing aid company) was able to move beyond BTE hearing aids to ITE hearing aids by simply reconfiguring existing hearing aid components. This seemingly minor architectural innovation led to a new industry standard and to different industry rules anchored on sound quality and fashion.

Dynamic capabilities are rooted in driving streams of innovation. Firms that survive technological transitions compete through patterns of innovation over time: incremental, competence-enhancing innovation (e.g., thinner mechanical watches); architectural innovation (e.g., Starkey's ITE hearing aid); taking existing technologies to new customer segments, and fundamentally new, often competence-destroying, innovation (e.g., Seiko's quartz movement). By driving streams of innovation, senior teams increase the probability that their firm will be able to shape industry standards, take advantage of new markets for existing technology, and proactively introduce substitute products that, as they cannibalize existing products, create new markets and competitive rules (Hurst, 1995; Burgelman and Grove1996; Teece,1996; Brown and Eisenhardt, 1998).

These dynamic capabilities are rooted in a firm's ability to be ambidextrous – to both learn and incrementally build on its past even as it simultaneously creates technological options from which senior teams make strategic bets (Duncan, 1976; Tushman and O'Reilly, 1997). Because of powerful inertial processes accentuated in those most successful firms, these strategic bets must be coupled with discontinuous organizational changes (Romanelli and Tushman, 1994; Sastry, 1997; Gavetti and Levinthal, 2000). We discuss the topics of technology cycles, innovation streams, ambidextrous organizations, senior teams, and discontinuous organizational change in turn.

Technology Cycles and Dominant Designs

Technology cycles are composed of technological discontinuities (for example, quartz and tuning fork movements in watches) that trigger periods of technological and competitive ferment. During eras of ferment, rival technologies compete with each other and with the existing technological regime. These turbulent innovation periods close with the emergence of an industry standard or dominant design (Anderson and Tushman, 1990; Utterback, 1994). For example, in early radio transmission, continuous-wave transmission was a technological discontinuity that threatened to replace spark-gap transmission. Continuous-wave transmission initiated competition not only between this new innovation and spark-gap transmission but also among three variants of the innovation: alternating-wave, arc, and vacuum tube transmission. This period of technological ferment led to vacuum tube transmission as the dominant design in radio transmission (Aitken, 1985; Rosenkopf and Tushman, 1994). The emergence of a dominant design ushers in a period of incremental as well as architectural technological change, a period that is broken at some point by the next substitute product. The subsequent technological discontinuity then triggers the next wave of technological variation, selection, and retention (Figure 17.1).

Technology cycles are seen most directly in nonassembled or simple products (e.g., glass, chemicals, skis, tennis racquets). For example, in crop fungicides, Ciba-Geigy's Tilt (propiconazol) was a new chemical entity that challenged Bayer's and BASF's products. Tilt triggered competition between chemical entities as well as between a vast number of propiconazol formulations. Ciba eventually created its EC 250 version, which became the industry standard in crop fungicides. Ciba's Crop Protection Division then initiated several product substitutes (including genetically engineered seeds) to cannibalize and replace propiconazol. These fundamentally new crop protection products initiated the next technology cycle in the crop protection market (Rosenkopf and Tushman, 1994).

In more complex assembled products (e.g., computers or watches) and systems (e.g., radio or voice mail), technology cycles apply at the subsystem level. David Landes (1983) and Thomas Hughes (1983) provide rich historically anchored detail on the

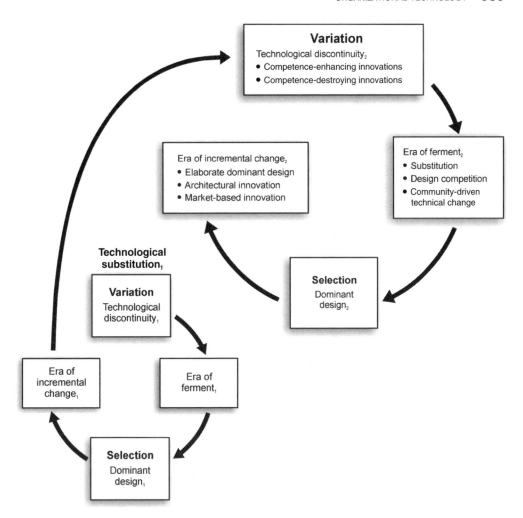

Figure 17.1 Technology cycles over time
(adapted from Rosenkopf and Tushman, 1994)

watch and electric power industries from their respective births (Table 17.1). These comprehensive histories illustrate the interplay between technology, organizations and communities. Watches, for example, are assembled products made up of at least four subsystems: energy source, oscillation device, transmission, and display. Each of these subsystems has its own technology cycle. In watch oscillation, the pin-lever escapement became the dominant design in the late nineteenth century. Escapements became better and better through incremental changes in the same fundamental design until the late 1960s. Between 1968 and 1972, escapements were threatened by both tuning fork and quartz oscillation. This period of technological competition among escapements, tuning fork oscillation, and quartz movement ended with the emergence of quartz oscillation as the dominant design in the subsystem. As with mechanical escapements, the emergence of quartz movements as the dominant design led, in turn, to numerous incremental

Table 17.1 Technology cycles and dominant designs

Reference	Key concepts	Variables	Predictions and findings	Contributions	Method and sample
Landes (1983), Hughes (1983)	Dominant designs Technological change Organizations and communities	Detailed historical analyses	Historical analyses from beginnings of time telling and energy systems	Deep understanding of interplay between technological change, organizations, and the contexts within competition takes place.	Historical analyses
Cusumano et al. (1992)	Dominant designs Social construction of technology	Market leadership Strategic alignment Position to market	VHS beat BETA in the marketplace because: • VHS established as alliance with Japanese competitor Matshushita rather than Sony (Beta) b/c Sony was not willing to wait to distribute their product before firms decided that they were the industry standard • Sony poorly managed the relationships with allied companies • Matshushita helped get JVC into the US market quicker	Demonstrates that dominant designs are shaped by socio-political forces as well as technological innovation Indicates that first mover status does not always determine the winner	Historical case study using archival data: videocassetter recording industry
Tripsas (1999)	Creative destruction Dominant designs	Incumbent vs. New firms Technological experience Complementary assets Competition/segment growth First product of a generation	Incumbent typesetter maintained market share when the new generations of products used their existing complementary assets (ie, font libraries, sales network, and manufacturing capabilities. Incumbent firms were more successful in the market place than new firms if they were still able to utilize their core capabilities. Incumbent firms invested in new generation technology before new firms. New firms were able to create more technologically superior products (ie, better print quality) much quicker than incumbent firms.	Demonstrates that core assets became core rigidities as new firms were able to innovate quicker and with greater technological capabilities than incumbents Suggests that incumbent firms can be handicapped by their core assets as they often attempt to adapt their competencies to new innovations instead of building out new ones; firms more successful when their old assets were applicable	Archival data: 1886–1990 42 firms of typesetting industry

improvements in the quartz movement and sharp decreases in innovation in tuning fork and escapement oscillation devices.

Not all subsystems are equivalent. Rather, products are composed of hierarchically ordered subsystems that are coupled together by linking mechanisms that are as crucial to the product's performance as are the subsystems themselves (Clark, 1985; Henderson and Clark, 1990; Baldwin and Clark, 2000). Those more core subsystems are either tightly coupled to other subsystems or are strategic bottlenecks (Hughes, 1983; Tushman and Murmann, 1998; Schilling, 2000). In contrast, peripheral subsystems are weakly connected to other subsystems. Shifts in core subsystems have cascading effects on other more peripheral subsystems (Ulrich and Eppinger, 1995). Further, subsystems shift in relative strategic importance as the industry evolves. In watches, oscillation was the key strategic battlefield through the early 1970s; then, once the quartz movement became the dominant design, the locus of strategic innovation shifted to the face, energy, and transmission subsystems. Similar dynamics of subsystem and linkage technology cycles have been documented in a variety of industries (Hughes, 1983; Van de Ven and Garud, 1994; Baum et al., 1995).

The technological discontinuities that initiate technology cycles are relatively rare, unpredictable events triggered by scientific advance (e.g., battery technology for watches) or through a recombining of existing technology (e.g., Sony's Walkman or continuous aim gunfire) (Morison, 1966; Sanderson and Uzumeri, 1995). Technological discontinuities rupture existing incremental innovation patterns and spawn periods of technological ferment that are confusing, uncertain, and costly to customers, suppliers, vendors, and regulatory agencies. Absent governmental regulation, a single dominant design emerges from periods of variation, or eras of technological ferment (Noble, 1984, Anderson and Tushman, 1990; Cusumano et al, 1992). During windows of opportunity at the emergence of dominant designs, competing firms must switch to the new standard or risk getting locked out of the market (Christensen et al., 1998; Tegarden et al., 1999).

How do dominant designs emerge? Except for the most simple nonassembled products, the closing on a dominant design is not technologically driven because no technology can dominate on all possible dimensions of merit. Nor does the closing on a dominant design take place through the invisible hand of the market (Noble, 1984; Pinch and Bijker, 1987). Rather, it occurs through social, political, and organizational competition among the alternative technological variants (Hughes, 1983; Tushman and Rosenkopf, 1992; Baum et al., 1995; Cusumano and Yoffee, 1998). Dominant designs emerge out of the struggle between alternative technological trajectories initiated and pushed by competitors, alliance groups, and governmental regulators – each with their own political, social, and economic agendas. This social construction of technology has been thoroughly documented in a range of industries (Bijker et al., 1987). In an unusually rich process oriented case study, Van de Ven et al. (1988) provide detail on the complex regulatory, organizational, and physician dynamics in the evolution of industry standards in the cochlear implant industry. This case not only describes the evolution of standards at the subsystem level, it also describes how one firm, 3M, worked outside its boundaries to shape industry standards.

Similarly, the emergence of the VHS over Beta as a dominant design in the videocassette recorder industry illustrates the process of technology cycles, and the social and political influences on this process. Cusumano et al. (1992) used historical data on technological capabilities, mass market demands, and organizational strategies for six key companies developing videocassette recorders between 1975 and 1988. They demonstrated that though initially Beta was more technologically advanced (tapes held greater amount of information with a higher resolution, etc.) and initially captured more of the market, JVC was able to beat Sony through proactive alliances with strong producers and distributors.

Dominant designs are watershed events in a technology cycle. Before a dominant design emerges, technological progress is driven by competition between alternative technologies. After a dominant design emerges, subsequent technological change is driven by the logic of the selected technology itself (Figure 17.1). The closing on a dominant design shifts innovation from major product variation to major process innovation and, in turn, to incremental innovation – to building on, extending, and continuously improving the selected variant. These periods of incremental innovation lead to profound advances in the now standard product (Hollander, 1965; Myers and Marquis, 1969; Abernathy, 1978). In contrast, the consequences of betting on the wrong design are devastating – particularly if that design is a core subsystem (e.g., IBM's losing control of the microprocessor and operating system in PCs to Intel and Microsoft).

Technology cycles apply both for product subsystems and for linking technologies, and they apply across product classes – the only difference between high-tech (e.g., disk drive) and low-tech (e.g., concrete) industries is the length of time between the emergence of a dominant design and the subsequent discontinuity. Technology cycles highlight the points at which senior teams have substantial impact on firm and product class evolution versus where they only have minor impacts (Finkelstein and Hambrick, 1996; Christensen et al, 1998). During eras of ferment, actions by senior teams affect both the nature of technical change as well as organizational fates. During eras of incremental change, however, managerial influence on technical progress in the existing trajectory is sharply limited. Senior teams can, however, destabilize their product class by initiating different types of innovation— by driving innovation streams.

Innovation Types and Innovation Streams

For complex products the locus of innovation occurs both within subsystems and with those technologies that link subsystems together (Baldwin and Clark, 2000; Schilling, 2000). Decomposing products into components and linking mechanisms and clarifying target markets/customers helps untangle incremental, architectural, discontinuous, and market innovation types (Henderson and Clark, 1990; Christensen, 1998; Tushman and Murmann, 1998) (see Figure 17.2).

INCREMENTAL INNOVATIONS

These are innovations that push the existing technological trajectory for existing subsystem and linking mechanisms. Such innovations are associated with significant product improvement and enhanced customer satisfaction over time (Hollander, 1965; Myers and Marquis, 1969).

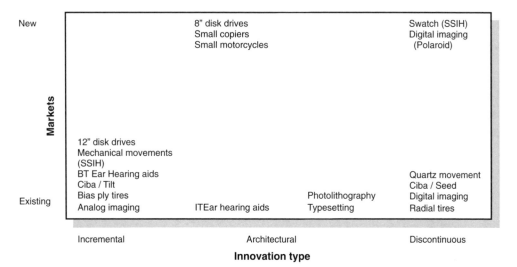

	Incremental	Architectural	Discontinuous
New	8" disk drives Small copiers Small motorcycles		Swatch (SSIH) Digital imaging (Polaroid)
Existing	12" disk drives Mechanical movements (SSIH) BT Ear Hearing aids Ciba / Tilt Bias ply tires Analog imaging	ITEar hearing aids	Photolithography Typesetting	Quartz movement Ciba / Seed Digital imaging Radial tires

Markets — Innovation type

Figure 17.2 Innovation streams
(adapted from Tushman and O'Reilly, 1997)

ARCHITECTURAL INNOVATIONS

These involve shifts in subsystems and/or linking mechanisms (Henderson and Clark, 1990). These relatively simple innovation types are often initially targeted to new markets. Henderson and Clark (1990) identified architectural and modular innovation and explored their impacts on firms in the photolithography industry (Table 17.2). Archival data and extensive interviews with the senior management teams of incumbents and new entrants indicated that the contact aligner and its successor, the proximity aligner, were exactly the same in their component subsystems, but altered the way that these subsystems interacted with one another. Over four such architectural innovations, incumbents treated the innovation as if it were an incremental innovation. Established organizations either failed to recognize the need to restructure their organization, to seek new markets, or to alter their production processes. In each case, incumbents failed to adapt to seemingly minor technical change. Similarly, Starkey's move into the fashion hearing aid market, Honda's early move to smaller motorcycles, the migration of disk drive technology from mainframes to personal computers, and Canon's smaller copiers are examples of architectural innovations that transformed their product classes. While these innovations were technologically simple, in each case incumbents fumbled their future (Kearns and Nadler, 1992; Henderson, 1995; Christensen, 1998).

DISCONTINUOUS INNOVATION

This involves discontinuous technological change in a core subsystem. Such technical shifts trigger cascading changes in other less core subsystems and linking mechanisms (Tushman and Murmann, 1998). For example, in the photography industry, digital imaging was a competence destroying change in the camera's core subsystem. Tripsas

Table 17.2 Innovation types and innovation streams

Reference	Key concepts	Variables	Predictions and findings	Contributions	Method and sample
Henderson and Clark (1990)	Innovation characteristics Architectural innovation	Technological characteristics Commercial impact of innovation Organizational change	Innovations in photolithography from contact aligners to proximity aligners did not alter any of the subsystems, but rather the way the subsystems interacted. Established producers of semi-conductor aligners were unable to alter their organization to adopt the new aligners.	Introduces concept of architectural innovation, which is unique from other innovations in that it alters linkages between subsystems, and not the subsystems themselves. Demonstrates that architectural innovation requires subsequent organizational restructuring and knowledge acquisition, which often go unnoticed by established firms.	Field study, archival data and interviews Photolithography industry Over 100 interviews
Sanderson and Uzumeri (1995)	Innovation types Product families	Type of innovation Product price Number of models in product line	Sony market dominance is linked to its first mover status, ability to design products to the customer preferences of different markets, and managerial commitment to constant innovation. New technologies were based on a consistent dominant design, with constant incremental and generational innovation to meet new customer demands.	Demonstrates technology cycles at the firm level, suggesting that companies committed to innovation create a series of incremental, generational, etc. improvements, into what they identify as a product family. Product families were managed through the creation of dedicated design teams, committed to creating new products in response to customer feedback.	Archival data interviews Personal stereo market, Sony walkman 1979–88
Christensen (1998)	Technological trajectories Value networks Disruptive technologies	Technical change Customer change Organizational fate	Incumbants cede new customer segments to new entrants. These new entrants then proceed to move up market and disrupt incumbants.	Clearly documents in a variety of industries the inability of incumbents to switch value networks at their considerable peril. Documents how difficult it is for incumbents to go down market.	Census of disk drive producers 1974–90

and Gavetti (2000) document via interviews and industry data how Polaroid, a leading incumbent, was able to generate the technological know-how, but was unable to go to market with digital cameras due to profound organizational inertia and stunted senior team cognitive models. Sull et al. (1997) and Sull's (1999) historical analysis of the tire industry demonstrates how difficult it is for incumbents to initiate discontinuous innovation even when they have all the requisite technical competencies.

Where incremental, architectural, and discontinuous innovations are defined by their technological impact on subsystems and/or linking mechanisms, *market* based innovations are those innovations that are targeted to new markets or customer segments. These often technically simple innovations are frequently missed by incumbents, at their considerable peril. Christensen (1998) conducted a census of all disk drive produces from 1974–90. He found that in the transitions from 14" to 3.5" disk drives, in every case incumbents were displaced by new players. Each of these architectural innovations was initially most useful to newer, less demanding customers from the incumbents' perspective. In every case, incumbents ceded these new markets to new players and, in every case, these new players proceeded to subsequently move up market. Christensen (1998) observes that these technologically simple innovations are disruptive to an incumbent's existing organizational architectures (note that they are not technologically disruptive).

Building on products as composed of subsystems and linking mechanisms, Sanderson and Uzumeri (1995) developed the notion of product platforms and families. A platform is a set of core subsystems; a product family is a set of products built from the same platform. These product families share traits, architecture, components, and interface standards. For example, once Sony closed on the WM-20 platform for their Walkman, they were then able to generate more than 30 incremental versions within the same family. Over a ten-year period, Sony was able to develop four Walkman product families and more than 160 incremental versions of those four families. Devoting sustained attention to technological discontinuities at the subsystem level (e.g., the flat motor and the miniature battery), closing on a few standard platforms, and generating incremental product proliferation helped Sony to control industry standards and outperform their Japanese, American, and European competitors in this product class (Sanderson and Uzumeri, 1995).

Thus lying behind S-shaped product life cycle curves are fundamentally different innovation dynamics (Klepper, 1996). Eras of ferment are associated with discontinuous product variants. Dominant designs are associated with fundamental process innovation. After dominant designs emerge, the subsequent eras of incremental change are associated with product modularization and are fertile periods for incremental, architectural, discontinuous, and market based innovation. Given the nature of technology cycles, then, the roots of sustained competitive advantage may lie in a firm's ability to proactively initiate multiple innovation types – to initiate streams of innovation. Yet the external push for innovation streams runs counter to internal inertial forces. Incumbents, even when armed with technological capabilities, are held hostage to their successful pasts. It seems to be difficult for incumbents to develop the diverse competencies and organizational capabilities to shape and take advantage of dominant designs, to shape architectural innovation, to move to less demanding markets, or to introduce substitute products before the competition.

Ambidextrous Organizations

A firm's dynamic capabilities are rooted in its ability to drive innovation streams – to simultaneously create incremental, architectural, market and discontinuous innovations (Tushman and O'Reilly, 1997; Teece, 1996). Ambidextrous organizations are complex organizational forms composed of multiple internally inconsistent architectures that are collectively capable of operating simultaneously for short-term efficiency as well as long-term innovation (Duncan, 1976; Weick, 1979; Bradach, 1997). Such heterogeneous organizational forms build in the experimentation, improvisation, and luck associated with small organizations, along with the efficiency, consistency, and reliability associated with larger organizations (Imai et al., 1985; Eisenhardt and Tabrizi, 1995).

Organizational architectures for incremental innovation are fundamentally different from those for all other innovation types. Continuous incremental improvement in products and processes and high-volume throughput are associated with organizations with relatively formalized roles and linking mechanisms, centralized procedures and processes, efficiency-oriented cultures and highly engineered work processes (Burns and Stalker, 1961; Eisenhardt and Tabrizi, 1995; Nadler and Tushman, 1997). Efficiency-oriented units drive continuous improvement, exploitation, and the elimination of variability and have relatively short time horizons (Levitt and March, 1988; Levinthal, 1997). Such units are often relatively large and old, with highly ingrained, taken-for-granted assumptions and knowledge systems (Milliken and Lant, 1991) (see Figure 17.3).

In contrast to incremental innovation, discontinuous innovation emerges from entrepreneurial organizational architectures. Entrepreneurial units/organizations are relatively small; they have loose, decentralized product structures, experimental cultures, loose work processes, strong entrepreneurial and technical competencies, and relatively young and heterogeneous human resource profiles (McGrath and MacMillan, 2000). These units generate the experiments/options from which the organization's senior team can learn about the future (Levitt and March, 1988; Leonard-Barton, 1995; McGrath, 1999). These units build new experience bases, knowledge systems, and networks to break from the larger organization's history. They generate variants from which the senior team can make bets on possible dominant designs, new customer segments, and technological discontinuities (Nonaka, 1988; Burgelman, 1994). In contrast to the larger, more mature, efficiency-oriented units, these small entrepreneurial units are inefficient and rarely profitable and have no established histories (Figure 17.3). These entrepreneurial units may be created internally or acquired externally through acquisition, contract research, joint ventures or alliances (Roberts and Berry, 1985; Teece, 1996; Silverman, 1999).

Architectural innovations take existing technologies and link these technologies in novel ways; they are built not on new technological breakthroughs, but rather on integrating competencies from both the efficiency oriented as well as the entrepreneurial subunits. While technologically simple, architectural innovations require fundamentally different linking structures, incentives, competencies and cultures from the existing architecture (Iansiti and Clark, 1994). Because of the difficulties of building linkage capabilities in the context of incremental innovation, architectural innovations are often not initiated by incumbent industry leaders (Brown and Eisenhardt, 1995; Henderson,

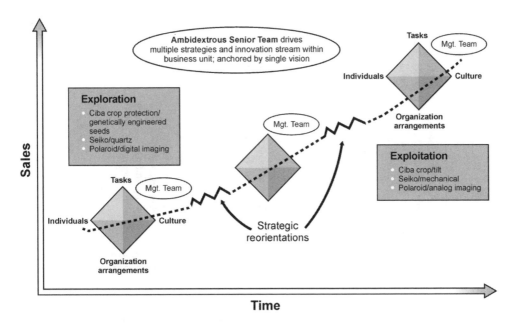

Figure 17.3 Ambidextrous organizations: Exploitation and exploration within business units

1995). Similarly, taking existing products to new markets must deal with the resistance of a firm's current customers and existing resource allocation processes. These sources of inertia often hold successful incumbents hostage to their pasts (Rosenbloom and Christensen, 1994; Christensen, 1998).

While incremental, architectural, and discontinuous innovations require fundamentally different organizational architectures, to drive streams of innovation these contrasting architectures must reside in within a single business unit. Senior management's challenge is to build into a single organization multiple internally consistent organizational architectures that are themselves inconsistent from each other (Figure 17.3). In ambidextrous organizations, single organizations host multiple cultures, structures, processes, management teams, and human resource capabilities in order to be incrementally innovative while at the same time creating products that may make the existing product line obsolete (Duncan, 1976; Bradach, 1997; Tushman and O'Reilly, 1997).

Ambidextrous organizational forms build in organizational capabilities to simultaneously explore and exploit, to decrease variance as well as to increase variance at the same time. March (1991) suggests that organizational learning is accentuated when there is both the exploitation and exploration simultaneously (Table 17.3). Exploitation of knowledge extends existing knowledge resulting in predictable, positive returns (at least in the short term.) In contrast, exploration is inherently experimental and often inconsistent with previous knowledge. Exploration accentuates variation, which in the short term is risky. Using a computer simulation that includes the internal strategic pressure and external competitive pressure, March demonstrates the survival value of balancing these inconsistent learning modes.

Table 17.3 Ambidextrous organizations

Reference	Key concepts	Variables	Predictions and findings	Contributions	Method and sample
Burgelman (1991)	Intraorganizational processes Organizational evolution Ambidextrous decision making	Product introduction Revenue by product Senior team commitment to new products	Intel strategic shift from memory chips (DRAM) to microprocessors products was driven mostly by the resource allocation process to follow more high margin products. The strategic shift from being a primarily memory focused company to a processor focused company was much more challenging and required a product champion to demonstrate the necessity to a skeptical senior management team.	Demonstrates the differentiation of incremental change and radical change in terms of senior team commitment, and change in team firm cognitions Suggests the effect of inertial forces even in a high velocity environment	Field study with interview and archival data Intel 1972–88
Tripsas and Gavetti (2000)	Organizational inertia Organizational cognition Core capabilities Senior management teams	Organizational and senior management team beliefs and cognition Product success New product introduction Organizational structures	Polariod's senior management provided resources for constant R&D and new product development. After committing to the instant photo, new products were congruent with the organizational and strategic management team beliefs of this focus. Top management teams were able to manage across several innovations when there was cognitive congruence among products. Political tension among managers resulting from incongruent organizational cognition resulted in lagging digital products.	Shows how innovation across an innovation stream requires structures that are separated from one another, yet has linkages at level of senior management and strategic decision making. Further adds the component of organizational cognition–belief systems in organizations, as uniting factors in linking organizational innovations	Field study with interviews and archival data Polaroid company

| March (1991) | Organizational learning Exploration and exploitation | External factors (competition) Internal factors (strategy) Learning speed | Exploitation strategies (expand on existing information) ensure increased congruence between individual and organizational learning, expands existing competencies and has greater organizational certainty. Exploration (finding new information) expands organizational variability and alternatives and has uncertain returns. The balance between exploration and exploitation was influenced by competitive factors and strategic action. | Organizational learning through balancing opposing processes | Computer simulation |

Similarly, Burgelman (1991) identified contrasting learning modes in his field study of innovation at Intel. Induced strategic processes involve the continuation of current organizational strategy. These tended to be incremental changes, such as the continued development of memory chips. In contrast, autonomous strategic processes, which created the possibility of new products often to different customers, were typically outside the scope of the extant strategic initiative. Intel's senior team was less enthusiastic about funding these ventures because the uncertainty for market success was higher. Burgelman's analyses document how innovation streams require fundamentally different learning modes operating in parallel.

Ambidextrous organizations build in cultural, structural, and demographic contradictions. These internal contradictions are necessary if the organization is to be able to produce streams of innovations. Yet these contradictions create instability and conflict between the different organization units – between those historically profitable, large, efficient, older, cash-generating units and the young, entrepreneurial, experimental, cash-absorbing units. Because the power, resources, and traditions of organizations are usually anchored in the older, more traditional units, these units usually work to ignore, sabotage, or otherwise trample entrepreneurial units (Cooper and Smith, 1992; Leonard-Barton, 1992; Morone, 1993; Hamel and Prahalad, 1994; Miller, 1994). Ambidextrous organizations require subunits that are highly differentiated, weakly linked internally, but tightly integrated through the senior team (Tushman and O'Reilly, 1997).

The certainty of today's incremental advance often works to destroy the potential of tomorrow's architectural, market, or discontinuous advance. For example, Tripsas and Gavetti's (2000) inductive analysis of Polaroid's experience with digital cameras documents the senior team difficulties in building these complex organizational forms. As the market leader in the instant photography industry, Polaroid developed incremental innovations of their hallmark SX-70 instant camera (eg. improving the photo quality subsystem), while at the same time seeking new markets with digital imaging cameras. Such a discontinuous innovation had the potential to disrupt their exiting film/analog franchise. The incremental improvements in the instant camera occurred within an existing organizational structure, while the development of the digital camera technology occurred in its own separate laboratory, with 90 percent of its employees hired new for this project. While the products and technology were available, Polaroid's senior team was unable to take the strategic actions to capitalize on their digital investments. As Polaroid's senior team was unable to change their organizational, strategic and cognitive models, Polaroid remained trapped in its historically rooted analog market.

Given the inertial, defensive, and political dynamics that exist in successful organizations, senior management teams must not only separate, protect and legitimize entrepreneurial units, they must also make the strategic and organizational decisions to take advantage of this internal and/or external experimentation. While ambidextrous organizational forms can enhance dynamic organizational capabilities, they are difficult to implement. In industry after industry, either exploitation drives out exploration or today's customer trumps tomorrow's. To drive innovation streams, senior teams must build in and sustain internally inconsistent architectures even as they are the locus of strategic integration.

Ambidextrous Senior Management Teams

Strategic integration across innovation streams is anchored in a senior team's understanding of these innovation and organizational dynamics and their symbolic and substantive actions (Pfeffer, 1981; Tripsas and Gavetti, 2000). Internal structural heterogeneity provides the senior team with the ability to improvise in the present even as it experiments for the future (Iansiti and Clark, 1994; Brown and Eisenhardt, 1998; Gavetti and Levinthal, 2000). If these diverse capabilities can be integrated, they permit the organization to innovate for both today and tomorrow; but without integration, the potential of an ambidextrous organization is lost.

A clear, emotionally engaging vision provides a strategic anchor from which senior teams can balance the contrasting requirements of innovation streams (Collins and Porras, 1994; Hamel and Prahalad, 1994). Simple, direct competitive visions create a point of clarity within which an organization can simultaneously host incremental and discontinuous innovations (Nonaka, 1988; Hurst, 1995). Sustained, consistent commitment to a unit's vision, even as strategies and objectives change, reinforces that vision. Commitment is further reinforced by senior management continuity and by their consistent behaviors in support of the vision (Pfeffer and Sutton, 2000). Through such clarity and consistency of vision, the senior team can support the internally contradictory organizational architectures associated with ambidextrous organizations and still be seen as consistent and credible. For example in Ciba's Crop Protection Division, the senior team's aspiration of "keeping crops healthy" permitted the division to simultaneously work on chemical and biological technical trajectories.

The senior team's composition and demography and its ways of working together are also powerful tools for achieving integration in ambidextrous organizations (Hambrick, 1998). A study of the top management teams in 24 firms in the electronic industry suggested that homogeneity in age and tenure but heterogeneity in expertise in top management teams lead to more positive team dynamics and increased ability to make adaptive changes (O'Reilly et al., 1993). While there are benefits in senior management continuity, there are also benefits in creating highly heterogeneous, demographically young senior teams. Such teams have the benefit of consistency in vision from the top along with the ability to import new team members with different competencies and expertise (Virany et al., 1992; Smith et al., 1994). For example, as Microsoft grew, Bill Gates broadened his senior team with managers from outside Microsoft with marketing, organizational, and technical skills (Cusumano and Selby, 1995).

Highly effective senior teams have diverse competencies to handle the contrasting innovation demands of ambidextrous organizations. In contrast, senior teams that are demographically old and homogeneous are typically dominated by historically anchored perspectives and simple cognitive models (Milliken and Lant, 1991; Miller, 1994). Inertial senior teams get stuck in routinized processes and are unable to deal with the contrasting demands imposed by innovation streams (Hambrick and D'Aveni, 1988; Boeker, 1989; Louis and Sutton, 1989). Organizations can develop diverse senior team competencies by importing executives from outside the firm, by creating diverse career experiences internally, by building heterogeneous teams within the organization, and often by executive team turnover (Hambrick, 1994, 1998; Zajac and Westphal, 1996).

Effective senior teams are also able to work together in a way that takes advantage of their internal differences. Effective senior teams have internal processes that enable them to handle greater information and decision alternatives and to deal with diverse points of view and contrasting opinions (Edmondson, 1999; Eisenhardt, 1989). In a survey of 53 management teams, Smith et al. (1994) demonstrate that senior team processes such as formal communication, informal communication, and social integration have an impact upon successful team performance independent of senior team demography (Table 17.4). Diverse, self-critical senior teams with effective group processes not only get their own work accomplished but model appropriate ways to deal with conflict and cross-cutting priorities in the larger organization. In contrast, senior teams that send mixed messages, that cannot resolve their own conflicts, and that do not collaborate internally create highly unstable, politically chaotic organizations (Williams and O'Reilly, 1998; Pfeffer and Sutton, 2000).

Finally, senior management teams can create formal roles, structures, processes, and rewards to facilitate strategic integration. Particularly for architectural innovation, the development roles and formal linking mechanisms encourage integration within the senior team and across diverse parts of the organization. Team-based rewards that measure and value diverse types of innovation and collaborative team behaviors motivate team members to work together (Iansiti and Clark, 1994; Brown and Eisenhardt, 1995; Nadler and Tushman, 1997).

Innovation Streams and Discontinuous Organization Change

Within ambidextrous organizations, entrepreneurial units provide learning-by-doing data, variation, and luck to drive possible new dominant designs, architectural innovations, and/or product substitutions. Whether done internally, through alliances or acquisitions, the senior team can learn about alternative futures from these entrepreneurial units. In contrast, those more mature units drive sustained incremental innovation and short-term learning. The senior management team can then draw upon these diverse types of innovation and learning to make strategic decisions – when to initiate a dominant design, when to move on new customers, what product variant to bet on, when to initiate an architectural innovation, and/or when to introduce a product substitute.

The success of strategic choices of dominant designs, new customers, architectural innovation, and/or product substitutes are only known after the fact. Through building ambidextrous organizational capabilities, the senior management team maximizes the probability that they will have both the expertise and the luck from which to make industry-shaping decisions proactively rather than reactively. Ambidextrous organizations create options from which the senior team makes informed bets on the future (Burgelman and Grove, 1996; McGrath, 1999). While correct strategic bets can be known only in retrospect, managerial action within the firm – and with collaborators, alliance partners, and governmental agencies – can affect the ultimate closing on an industry standard or the success of a product substitute (Teece, 1987; Cusumano and Yoffee, 1998; Rosenkopf and Tushman, 1998).

At the closing of a dominant design, the strategic innovation requirements within the firm shifts from a focus on major product variation to major process innovation and then to sustained incremental innovation (Abernathy and Clark, 1985; Utterback, 1994). At product substitution events, for architectural innovations, and/or for taking an exist-

Table 17.4 Senior teams

Reference	Key concepts	Variables	Predictions and findings	Contributions	Method and sample
Smith, K. et al. (1994)	Senior management teams Demography Social processes	Team demography (size, tenure, heterogeneity) Team process (social integration, informal communication, communication frequency) Performance (ROI, sales growth)	Heterogeneity of TMT detracts from success in high velocity environments. Successful socialization process for TMT in high velocity environments include strong informal communication, but limited formal communication.	Process variables (communication, etc.) are as important in understanding the functioning of TMT as structural variables (demographics, etc.).	Survey data: 53 firms in high velocity environments (Single business unit)
O'Reilly et al. (1993)	Senior management team Demography Organizational change	TMT demography (tenure, age) TMT dynamics (balance of responsibility, trust among members, etc.) Turnover Organizational change Performance	Increased homogeneity of team tenure leads to increased positive team dynamics, less turnover, and increased ability to make adaptive changes. No evidence to support the hypothesis that positive team dynamics decreased the turnover of team members, or increased the ability to make adaptive changes.	Suggests the limited effect of homogeneity, and the need to support both homogeneity and heterogeneity simultaneously to achieve a balance between efficiency and innovation	Survey: 24 firms in electronics industry

Reference	Key concepts	Variables	Predictions and findings	Contributions	Method and sample
Virany et al. (1992)	Senior management teams CEO succession Turnover	Succession Executive team change Organizational performance (ROA)	In turbulent environments, CEO succession and senior team turnover were associated with increased organizational performance. Low performing firms had less executive team change, and CEO change. Historically high performing firms had fewer CEO successions and less executive team succession, though the same number of reorientations.	Suggests that the impact of CEO succession and senior team change is contingent on the firm's context Suggests that turnover increases the amount of learning and thus contributes to change Differentiates between CEO succession and executive team turnover	Archival data: 59 minicomputer firms
Sastry (1997)	Punctuated equilibrium Macro change model	Strategic reorientation Inertia Perceived performance Pressure for change Time for change	Cycles of organizational change involved two distinct period – convergence and reorganization. To ensure that newly developed competencies are not destroyed, organizations need time to integrate their competencies. In developing reorientations, organizations must evaluate a strategic move based upon organizational-environmental fit.	Determined the feasibility of the punctuated equilibrium model Demonstrates the conditions under which strategic reorientations are most effective in an organization	Computer simulation: systems dynamics model

ing product to new markets, strategic management shifts from incremental innovation to major product, market or architectural innovation. As strategic innovation requirements shift at these junctures, so too must the dominant organizational capabilities (Sorensen and Stuart, 2000). Those organizational architectures, those structures, roles, cultures, processes, and competencies, appropriate during eras of ferment are no longer appropriate during eras of incremental change. Similarly, those organizational architectures appropriate during eras of incremental change are no longer appropriate during eras of ferment (Foster, 1987; Benner and Tushman, 2000).

Because structural and social inertia are so powerful, managers can attempt to rewrite their industry's rules only if they are willing to rewrite their organization's rules. At these strategic junctures, shifts in a firm's innovation stream can be executed only through discontinuous organizational change (Tushman and Romanelli, 1985; Greenwood and Hinings, 1993; Miller, 1994; Rosenbloom, 2000). For example, IBM's 360 decision in mainframes was coupled with sweeping shifts in IBM's structure, controls, systems, and culture. In contrast, bold strategic moves or great technology uncoupled from organizational capabilities leads to underperformance (Virany et al., 1992; Tripsas and Gavetti, 2000). Similarly, Sony's superior Beta technology format was to unable to counter JVC's combination of an adequate VHS technology coupled with brilliant organizational capabilities and strategic alliances (Cusumano et al., 1992). Innovation streams are, then, rooted as much in reconfigured organizational architectures as in technological prowess (Rosenbloom and Christensen, 1994; Sull, 1999; Rosenbloom, 2000).

Innovation streams and the associated frame-breaking organizational changes are often initiated by transformed senior teams (Ancona, 1990; Meyer et al., 1990; Virany et al., 1992; Romanelli and Tushman, 1994). While reorientations are risky and often done incompetently (Henderson, 1993; Carroll and Teo, 1996), persistence in the face of a changing innovation stream is even more so. Further, if strategic reorientations are not done proactively, they have to be done reactively – as with Burroughs in mainframes, SSIH in watches, Polaroid in digital cameras, and Oticon in hearing aids. Reactive reorientations (turnarounds) are more risky than proactive reorientations because they must be implemented under crisis conditions and under considerable time pressure (Hambrick et al., 1998).

Senior management's challenge in leading discontinuous change is fundamentally different from that in leading incremental change (Weick and Quinn, 1999). Senior teams must build the capabilities to manage both, if they are to effectively manage across an innovation stream (Barnett and Carroll, 1995; Nadler et al., 1995). Those more effective discontinuous changes are initiated and directed by the senior team, are shaped by an integrated change agenda, and are rapidly implemented – driven by the senior team's vision and consistent actions (Nadler, 1998). These challenges are often associated with shifts in the senior team and within middle management (Pettigrew, 1985; Kanter et al., 1992).

If implemented through incremental change methods, reorientations run the risk of being sabotaged by the politics, structures, and competencies of the status quo (Kearns and Nadler, 1992; Virany et al., 1992). For example, in Ciba's Crop Protection Division, the transition from fundamentally different fungicides to EC-50 (their bet on a dominant design) was executed through sweeping changes in the division and through a new fungicide team. In contrast, breakthrough innovation at Xerox in the late 1970s and early 1980s and Polaroid in the 1990s were not coupled with corresponding organizational shifts. The politics of stability held Xerox and Polaroid hostage to their pasts (Smith and Alexander, 1990; Tripsas and Gavetti, 2000).

Managing innovation streams is about managing internal paradoxes in the context of innovation streams: managing efficiency *and* innovation, tactical *and* strategic, incremental *and* discontinuous, today *and* tomorrow (Quinn and Cameron, 1988; Brown and Eisenhardt, 1998; Gavetti and Levinthal, 2000). Managing innovation streams is about consistency and control as well as variability, learning by doing, and the cultivation of luck. It is the crucial role of the senior team to embrace these contradictions and take advantage of the tensions and synergies that emerge from juggling multiple competencies simultaneously (Van de Ven et al., 1988; Hurst, 1995; Tushman and O'Reilly, 1997). It is the senior team's role to bind these paradoxical requirements together through their substantive and symbolic actions.

Contemporary Issues and Debates

While innovation streams may well be at the root of dynamic capabilities, there is much debate on the notion of technology cycles. There is controversy on units of analysis, definitions of concepts, causal mechanisms, and the boundary conditions of dominant designs (Tushman and Murmann, 1998). There are also differences in defining and measuring the different types of innovation (e.g. architectural vs disruptive) as well as the impact of innovation types on organizational competencies (Tushman and Anderson, 1986; Henderson and Clark, 1990; Christensen, 1998). These theoretical and methodological confusions are an impediment to our field's progress in understanding the nature of technological change and as such reflect major theoretical and empirical opportunities (Ehrenberg, 1995; Gatignon et al. 2000).

While we have taken a point of view here, there is much debate and controversy on the nature and dynamics of organizational change (Rajagopalan and Spreitzer, 1997; Weick and Quinn, 1999), and the appropriate unit of analysis to study change (Galunic and Eisenhardt, 1994). The field needs greater clarity on the locus of innovation and at what level of analysis to study these processes. Though we have argued for the discontinuous change as innovation streams shift, others have argued for more incremental, time paced change (Brown and Eisenhardt, 1995). The conditions under which punctuated, incremental, and selectional approaches to change are appropriate is an area ripe for theoretical and empirical investigation; see also Barnett and Carroll (1995).

There are also substantial differences in how to effectively implement ambidextrous structures. Ambidextrous structures require strategic coordination to ensure the integration of an innovation into the firm's innovation stream and to leverage strategic capabilities (Tushman and O'Reilly, 1997). While we have argued that the linkages must be within the senior team to ensure strategic control of the innovation stream, other models suggest that the entrepreneurial units must be completely separated or spun out from the business unit (Christensen and Overdorf, 2000; Klepper and Sleeper, 2000). Research is required to shed light on the issue of strategic integration – when and under what conditions must highly differentiated units be integrated vs split out from the business unit.

Unanswered Questions and Emerging Questions

Senior teams are clearly vital in creating and sustaining ambidextrous organizations and innovation streams. Yet much work remains to be done. Important areas to explore include the nature and impact of founders and/or charismatic leaders on complex organizational forms (House et al., 1991; Kets de Vries, 1998; Burton, 2001), and the impact of senior team and CEO turnover on strategic integration (Gavetti and Levinthal, 1997; Hambrick, 1998). Further, much work remains to be done in exploring the tradeoffs of homogeneity versus heterogeneity in senior team composition and in exploring differential senior team processes associated with operating in multiple modes simultaneously (Williams and O'Reilly, 1998; Edmondson, 1999). Finally, the exploration of culture and core values in sustaining ambidextrous designs is an area ripe for investigation (Chatman and Barsad, 1995).

Another emerging research area is in exploring the role of managerial cognition as an important aspect of dynamic organizational capabilities. How senior teams conceptualize environmental threat/opportunities, how they switch cognitive gears, and how they attend to and deal with and balance the multiple time frames associated with ambidextrous organizational forms are crucial unanswered questions. While there is a set of initial ideas on managerial cognition, much work remains to be done (Garud et al., 1997; Louis and Sutton, 1989; Milliken and Lant, 1991;Tripsas and Gavetti, 2000)

Comparative institutional conditions impact innovation and dynamic capabilities (Nelson, 1995). Yet there is very little empirical work on the impact of institutional differences on innovation streams and organizational forms. This is clearly an important emerging domain. For example, West (2000) and Chesbrough's (1999) research in the semiconductor and disk drive industries finds that institutional conditions differ greatly between the USA and Japan, and that these institutional conditions are associated with fundamentally contrasting organizational approaches to innovation. Building comparative theory and research that integrates institutional differences and organizational characteristics as they differentially impact dynamic capabilities is an important research opportunity.

Another emerging research opportunity is the locus of technological variation. While some argue for internal entrepreneurship (Burgelman, 1994; Tushman and O'Reilly, 1997), others argue that sources of variation must either be kept separate from the business unit or accessed through acquisition, alliances, contract research or joint ventures (Christensen, 1998; Silverman, 1999). An important research opportunity is to untangle the performance implications of different generators of technical variation as well as the alternative loci of organizational boundaries and methods of strategic integration.

Finally, another crucial research opportunity relates to service innovation. While services represent more and more of a firm's value added, we know very little about how firms create service innovation (Quinn, 1992 for an exception). The literature on innovation and organizations is firmly anchored in product innovation. As there is no compelling reason that the underlying dynamic of service innovation should be similar to product innovation, directly exploring the dynamics of service innovation is an important emerging topic.

Connections Across Levels

This review has taken a business unit centric view of technology and innovation streams. We have taken technical change as an exogenous characteristic that the business unit can shape during eras of ferment and at technological transitions. An important cross-level research perspective treats technical change as an outcome of community level dynamics (Hunt and Aldrich, 1998; Aldrich, 1999). This co-evolutionary approach treats technical change as a result of the interactions of between institutions, competitors, community organizations, and customers (Nelson, 1994; Stuart, this volume). From this community perspective, technological change is driven by the interplay of multiple actors with differing levels of power and by know-how trading within community organizations/networks (Podolny and Stuart, 1995; Rosenkopf and Tushman, 1998; Stuart, 1999). This community approach puts a premium on understanding community networks and boundary spanning dynamics (Rosenkopf and Nerkar, 2001; Powell et al., 1996).

Consistent with this coevolutionary approach, much technical variation is generated by entrepreneurial action (Romanelli and Schoonhoven, 2001). An important cross level research opportunity is to connect organizational learning to population/community level learning (Miner and Haunschild, 1995; Hunt and Aldrich, 1998). As entrepreneurial actions are sources of variation, connection to this community's successes and failures is a source of survival value to incumbents (Baum et al., 2000; Rosenkopf and Nerkar, 2001). Finally, the linkages between institutional forces for process intensity and innovation outcomes has been largely unexplored (Benner and Tushman, 2000)

Within multidivisional firms, the linkage between the product's form and organizational architecture is an important research opportunity that builds on the organizational design literature rooted on strategic grouping and linking (Schilling, this volume; Nadler and Tushman, 1997). What has been less studied is the issue of organization design, linking mechanisms, and organizational boundary shifting to drive innovation across multi-divisional firms (Galunic and Eisenhardt, 1994). Finally, the linkages between senior team demography and processes and organizational learning is an important cross-level research opportunity (Williams and O'Reilly, 1998; Edmondson, 1999).

Conclusion

Even if periods of incremental change do build organizational inertia, organizations can create and shape innovation streams. Through building ambidextrous organizational forms and creating options from which the senior team initiates proactive strategic change, organizations can manage the rhythm by which each expiring strength gives birth to its successor. Prior organizational competencies provide a platform so that the next phase of an organization's evolution does not start from ground zero; evolution involves, then, learning as well as unlearning (Weick, 1979). Organizations can, then, renew themselves through a series of proactive strategic reorientations anchored by a common vision. Like a dying vine, the prior period of incremental change provides the compost for its own seeds, its own variants, to thrive following a reorientation in the subsequent period of incremental change.

In this review we have taken a strong point of view on organizational evolution. As dynamic capabilities are not rooted in technology cycles, organizational architectures, senior teams, or change dynamics alone, our understanding of the nature of dynamic capabilities must be rooted in deeply understanding these modules of evolution and how they interact with each other. Yet each module is open to much debate – the nature of technology cycles, the nature of organizational architecture, the role of senior teams, and the nature of organizational change are all contested domains. Yet this energy is well founded, for these issues are both professionally interesting as well as managerially crucial. There is significant opportunity, therefore, in digging deeply into those controversies in technology cycles, organizational architectures, senior teams and change, and perhaps even more so in building integrative theory and research across these interdependent domains.

Acknowledgments

We thank Lori Rosenkopf, Mary Tripsas and Joel Baum for their reviews and critical comments.

References

Abernathy, W. (1978): *The Productivity Dilemma.* Baltimore: Johns Hopkins University Press.

Abernathy, W., and Clark, K. (1985): "Innovation: Mapping the winds of creative destruction." *Research Policy*, 14, 3–22.

Aitken, H. (1985): *The Continuous Wave.* Princeton: Princeton University Press.

Aldrich, H. (1999): *Organizations Evolving.* London: Sage Publications.

Ancona, D. (1990): "Top management teams: Preparing for the revolution," in J. Carroll (ed.), *Applied Social Psychology and Organizational Settings*, Hillsdale, NJ: L. Erlbaum Assoc., 99–128.

Anderson, P., and Tushman, M. (1990): "Technological discontinuities and dominant designs: A cyclical model of technological change," *Administrative Science Quarterly*, 35, 604–33.

Baldwin, C., and Clark, K. (2000): *Design Rules: The Power of Modularity.* Cambridge, MA: MIT Press.

Barnett, W., and Carroll, G. R. (1995): "Modeling internal organization change," *American Review of Sociology*, 21: 217–36.

Baum, J., Calabrese, T., and Silverman, B. S. (2000): "Don't go it alone: Alliance networks and startup performance in Canadian biotechnology," *Strategic Management Journal*, 21(3), 267–294.

Baum, J., Korn, H. and Kotha, S. (1995): "Dominant designs and population dynamics in telecommunications services," *Social Science Research*, 24, 97–135.

Benner, M., and Tushman, M. (2000): "Process management and organizational adaptation: The productivity dilemma revisited." working paper, Harvard Business School.

Bijker, W., Hughes, T., and Pinch, T. (1987): *The Social Construction of Technological Systems.* Cambridge, MA: MIT Press.

Boeker, W. (1989): "Strategic change: Effects of founding and history," *Academy of Management Journal*, 32, 489–515.

Bradach, J. (1997): "Using the plural form in the management of restaurant chains," *Administrative Science Quarterly*, 42, 276–303.

Brown, S., and Eisenhardt, K. (1995): "Product development: Past research, present findings and future directions," *Academy of Management Review*, 20, 343–378.

Brown, S., and Eisenhardt, K. (1998): *Competing on the Edge: Strategy as Structured Chaos.* Boston, MA: Harvard Business School Press.

Burgelman, R. (1991): "Intraorganizational ecology of strategy making and organizational adaptation," *Organization Science*, 2(3), 239–62.

Burgelman, R. (1994): "Fading memories: A process theory of strategic business exit," *Administrative Science Quarterly*, 39, 24–56.

Burgelman, R., and Grove, A. (1996): "Strategic dissonance," *California Management Review*, 38, 8–28.

Burns, T., and Stalker, G. (1961): *The Management of Innovation*. London: Tavistock.

Burton, M. D. (2001): "The company they keep: Founders' models for high technology firms," in K. Schoonhoven and E. Romanelli (eds), *The Entrepreneurship Dynamic: The Origins of Entrepreneurship and its Role in Industry Evolution*, Palo Alto: Stanford University Press, forthcoming.

Carroll, G., and Hannan, M. (2000): *The Demography of Corporations and Industries*. Princeton: Princeton University Press.

Carroll, G., and Teo, A. (1996): "Creative self destruction among organizations: An empirical study of technical innovation and organizational failure in the American automobile industry, 1885–1981," *Industrial and Corporate Change*, 5(2), 619–43.

Chatman, J., and Barsad, S. (1995): "Personality organization culture, and cooperation," *Administrative Science Quarterly*, 40, 423–43.

Chesbrough, H. (1999): "The organizational impact of technological change: A comparative theory of national factors," *Industrial and Corporate Change*, 8(3), 447–85.

Christensen, C. (1998):*The Innovator's Dilemma*. Boston, MA: Harvard Business School Press.

Christensen, C., and Bower, J. (1996): "Customer power, strategic investment, and the failure of leading firms," *Strategic Management Journal*, 17, 197–218.

Christensen, C., and Overdorf, M. (2000): "Meeting the challenge of disruptive change," *Harvard Business Review*, March–April, 66–77.

Christensen, C., Suarez, F., and Utterback, J. (1998): "Strategies for survival in fast-changing industries," *Management Science*, 44(12), S207–S220.

Clark, K. (1985):"The interaction of design hierarchies and market concepts on technological evolution," *Research Policy*, 14, 235–51.

Collins, J., and Porras, J. (1994): *Built to Last*. New York: Harper Business.

Cooper, A., and Smith, C. (1992):"How established firms respond to threatening technologies," *Academy of Management Executive*, 6(2), 55–70.

Cusumano, M., and Selby, R. (1995): *Microsoft Secrets*. New York: Free Press.

Cusumano, M., and Yoffee, D. (1998): *Competing on Internet Time*. New York: Free Press.

Cusumano, M., Mylonadis, Y., and Rosenbloom, R. (1992): "Strategic maneuvering and mass market dynamics: The triumph of VHS over Beta," *Business History Review*, 51–93.

Duncan, R. (1976): "The ambidextrous organization: Designing dual structures for innovation," in R. Kilman and L. Pondy (eds), *The Management of Organizational Design*, New York: North Holland, 167–88.

Edmondson, A. (1999): "Psychological Safety and learning behavior in work teams," *Administrative Science Quarterly*, 44(4), 350–83.

Ehrenberg, E. (1995): "On the definition and measurement of technological discontinuities," *Technomation*, 5, 437–52.

Eisenhardt, K. (1989): "Making fast strategic decisions in high velocity environments," *Academy of Management Journal*, 32, 543–76.

Eisenhardt, K., and Tabrizi, B. (1995): "Acceleration adaptive processes," *Administrative Science Quarterly*, 40, 84–110.

Finkelstein, S., and Hambrick, D. (1996): *Strategic Leadership: Top Executives and Their Effect on Organizations*. New York: West.

Foster, R. (1987): *Innovation: The Attacker's Advantage*. New York: Summit Books,

Galunic, D. C., and Eisenhardt, K. (1994): "Reviewing the strategy–structures–performance paradigm," in B. Staw and L. Cummings (eds), *Research in Organization Behavior*, Greenwich, CT: JAI Press, 255–82.

Garud, R., and Ahlstrom, D. (1997): "Technology assessment: A socio-cognitive perspective," *Journal of Engineering and Technology Management*, 14(1), 25–50.

Gatignon, H., Tushman, M., Anderson P., and Smith, W. (2000): "A structural approach to measuring innovation," working paper, Harvard Business School.

Gavetti, G., and Levinthal, D. (2000): "Looking forward and looking backward: Cognitive and experiential search," *Administrative Science Quarterly*, 45, 113–37.

Glassmier, A. (1991): "Technological discontinuities and flexible production networks: The case of Switzerland and the world watch industry," *Research Policy*, 20, 469–85.

Greenwood, R., and Hinings, C. R. (1993): "Understanding strategic change," *Academy of Management Journal*, 6, 1052–81.

Grove, A. (1996): *Only the Paranoid Survive: How to Exploit the Crisis Points That Challenge Every Company and Career*. New York: Currency Doubleday.

Hambrick, D. (1994): "Top management groups: A reconsideration of the team label," in B. Staw and L. Cummings (eds), *Research in Organizational Behavior*, Greenwich, CT: JAI Press, 171–214.

Hambrick, D. (1998): "Corporate coherence and the top team," in D. Hambrick, D. Nadler and M. Tushman (eds), *Navigating Change*, Boston, MA: Harvard Business School Press, 123–40.

Hambrick, D., and D'Aveni, R. (1988): "Large corporate failures as downward spirals," *Administrative Science Quarterly*, 33, 1–23.

Hambrick, D., Nadler, D., and Tushman, M. (eds) (1998): *Navigating Change*. Boston, MA: Harvard Business School Press.

Hamel, G., and Prahalad, C. (1994): *Competing for the Future*. Boston, MA: Harvard Business School Press.

Henderson, R. (1993): "Underinvestment and incompetence as responses to radical innovation: Evidence from the photolithographic alignment equipment industry," *Rand Journal of Economics*, 24, 248–69.

Henderson, R. (1995): "Of life cycles real and imaginary: The unexpectedly long old age of optical lithography," *Research Policy*, 631–43.

Henderson, R., and Clark, K. (1990): "Architectural innovation: The reconfiguration of existing product technologies and the failure of established firms," *Administrative Science Quarterly*, 35, 9–30.

Hollander, S. (1965): *Sources of Efficiency*. Cambridge, MA: MIT Press.

House, R., Spangler, W., and Wyocke, J. (1991): "Personality and charisma in the U.S. presidency," *Administrative Science Quarterly*, 36, 364–96.

Hughes, T. (1983): *Networks of Power*. Baltimore: Johns Hopkins Press.

Hunt, C., and Aldrich, H. (1998): "The second ecology: The creation and evolution of organizational communities in the world wide web," in B. Staw and L. Cummings (eds), *Research in Organizational Behavior*, Volume 20, Greenwich, CT: JAI Press, 267–302.

Hurst, D. (1995): *Crisis and Renewal*. Boston, MA: Harvard Business School Press.

Iansiti, M., and Clark, K. (1994): "Integration and dynamic capability," *Industry and Corporation Change*, 3, 557–606.

Imai, K., Nonaka, I., and Takeuchi, H. (1985): "Managing the new product development process: How Japanese firms learn and unlearn," in K. Clark, R. Hayes and C. Lorenz (eds), *The Uneasy Alliance*, Boston, MA: Harvard Business School Press, 337–76.

Kanter, R., Stein, B., and Jick, T. (1992): *The Challenge of Organizational Change*. New York: Free Press.

Kearns, D., and Nadler, D. (1992): *Prophets in the Dark*. New York: Harper.

Kets de Vries, M. (1998): "Vicissitudes of leadership," in D. Hambrick, D. Nadler and M. Tushman (eds), *Navigating Change*, Boston, MA: Harvard Business School Press, 38–69.

Klepper, S. (1996): "Entry, exit, growth, and innovation over the product life cycle," *American Economic Review*, 86, 562–83.

Klepper, S., and Sleeper, S. (2000): "Entry by spinoffs," working paper, Carnegie Mellon.

Landes, D. (1983): *Revolution in Time.* Cambridge, MA: Harvard University Press.

Leonard-Barton, D. (1992): "Core capabilities and core rigidities: A paradox in managing new product development," *Strategic Management Journal*, 13, 111–25.

Leonard-Barton, D. (1995): *Wellsprings of Knowledge.* Boston, MA: Harvard Business School Press.

Levinthal, D. (1997): "Three faces of organizational learning: Wisdom, inertia and discovery," in R. Garud, P. Nayyar, and Z. Shapira (eds), *Technological Innovation: Oversights and Foresights*, Cambridge, UK: Cambridge University Press, 167–80.

Levitt, B., and March, J. (1988): "Organization learning," *American Review of Sociology*, 14, 319–40.

Louis, M., and Sutton, R. (1989): "Switching cognitive gears: From habits of mind to active thinking," in S. Bacharach (ed.), *Advances in Organizational Sociology*, Greenwich, CT: JAI Press, 55–76.

March, J. (1991): "Exploration and exploitation in organizational learning," *Organization Science*, 2, 71–87.

McGrath, R. (1999): "Falling forward: Real options reasoning and entrepreneurial failure," *Academy of Management Review*, 24, 13–30.

McGrath, R., and MacMillan, I. (2000): *The Entrepreneurial Mindset: Strategies for Continuously Creating Opportunity in an Age of Uncertainty.* Boston, MA: Harvard Business School Press.

Meyer, A., Brooks, G., and Goes, J. (1990): "Environmental jolts and industry revolutions," *Strategic Management Journal*, 11, 93–110.

Miller, D. (1994): "What happens after success: The perils of excellence," *Journal of Management Studies*, 31(3) 325–58.

Milliken, F., and Lant, T. (1991): "The effect of an organization's recent history on strategic persistence and change," in J. Dutton, A. Huff and P. Shrivastava (eds), *Advances in Strategic Management*, Vol. 7, Greenwich, CT: JAI Press, 129–56.

Miner, A., and Haunschild, P. (1995): "Population level learning," in B. Staw and L. Cummings (eds), *Research in Organization Behavior*, Greenwich, CT: JAI Press, 115–66.

Morison, E. (1966): *Men, Machines, and Modern Times.* Cambridge, MA: MIT Press.

Morone, J. (1993): *Winning in High Tech Markets.* Boston, MA: Harvard Business School Press.

Myers, S., and Marquis, D. (1969): *Successful Industrial Innovation.* Washington, DC: NSF.

Nadler, D. (1998): *Champions of Change.* San Francisco, CA: Jossey Bass.

Nadler, D., and Tushman, M. (1997): *Competing by Design: The Power of Organizational Architectures.* New York: Oxford University Press.

Nadler, D., Shaw, R., and Walton, E. (1995): *Discontinuous Change.* San Francisco: Jossey Bass.

Nelson, R. (1994): "The co-evolution of technology, industrial structure, and supporting institutions," *Industrial and Corporate Change*, 3, 47–63.

Nelson, R. (1995): "Recent evolutionary theorizing about economic change," *Journal of Economic Literature*, 33, 48–90.

Noble, D. (1984): *Forces of Production.* New York: Knopf.

Nonaka, I. (1988): "Creating order out of chaos: Self-renewal in Japanese firms," *California Management Review*, 3, 57–73.

O'Reilly, C., Snyder R., and Booth, J. (1993): "Effects of executive team demography and organizational change," in G. Huber and W. Glick (eds), *Organizational Design and Change*, New York: Oxford University Press, 147–75.

Pettigrew, A. (1985): *The Awakening Giant: Continuity and Change at ICI.* Oxford, UK: Blackwell.

Pinch, T., and Bijker, W. (1987): "The social construction of facts and artifacts," in W. Bijker, T. Hughes and T. Pinch (eds), *The Social Construction of Technological Systems*, Cambridge, MA: MIT Press, 17–50.

Pfeffer, J. (1981): "Management as symbolic action," in L. Cummings, and B. Staw (eds), *Research in Organizational Behavior*, Vol. 3, 1–52.

Pfeffer, J., and Sutton, R. (2000): *The Knowing-Doing Gap*. Boston, MA: Harvard Business School Press.

Podolny, J., and Stuart, T. (1995): "A role-based ecology of technological change," *American Journal of Sociology*, 100(50) 1224–60.

Powell, W., Koput, K. W., and Smith-Doerr, L. (1996): "Interorganizational collaboration and the locus of Innovation," *Administrative Science Quarterly*, 41, 116–45.

Quinn, J. B. (1992): *Intellegent Enterprise*. New York: Free Press.

Quinn, R., and Cameron, K. (1988): *Paradox and Transformation*. Cambridge, MA: Ballinger Publications.

Rajagopalan, N., and Spreitzer, G. (1997): "Toward a theory of strategic change," *Academy of Management Review*, 22(1), 48–79.

Roberts, E., and Berry, C. (1985): "Entering new businesses: Selecting strategies for success," *Sloan Management Review*, (Spring), 3–17.

Romanelli, E., and Schoonhoven, K. (eds) (2001): *The Entrepreneurship Dynamic: The Origins of Entrepreneurship in Its Role in Industry Evolution*. Stanford: Stanford University Press.

Romanelli, E., and Tushman, M. (1994): "Organization transformation as punctuated equilibrium," *Academy of Management Journal*, 37, 1141–66.

Rosenbloom, R. (2000): "Leadership, capabilities, and technological change: The transformation of NCR," *Strategic Management Journal*, 1083–103.

Rosenbloom, D., and Christensen, C. (1994): "Technological discontinuities, organization capabilities, and strategic commitments," *Industry and Corporate Change*, 3, 655–86.

Rosenkopf, L., and Nerkar, A. (2001): "Beyond local search: Boundary-spanning, exploration, and impact in the optical disc industry," *Strategic Management Journal*, (forthcoming).

Rosenkopf, L., and Tushman, M. (1994): "The coevolution of technology and organization," in J. Baum and J. Singh (eds), *Evolutionary Dynamics of Organizations*, New York: Oxford University Press, 403–24

Rosenkopf, L., and Tushman, M. (1998): "The co-evolution of community networks and technology: Lessons from the flight simulation industry," *Industrial and Corporate Change*, 7, 311–46.

Sanderson, S., and Uzumeri, M. (1995): "Product platforms and dominant designs: The case of Sony's Walkman," *Research Policy*, 24, 583–607.

Sastry, A. (1997): "Problems and paradoxes in a model of punctuated organizational change," *Administrative Science Quarterly*, 42(2), 237–77.

Schilling, M. (2000): "Toward a general modular systems theory and its application to interfirm product modularity," *Academy of Management Review*, 25, 312–34.

Silverman, B. S. (1999): "Technological resources and the direction of corporate diversification: Toward an integration of the resource-based view and transaction cost economics," *Management Science*, 45(8), 1109–24.

Smith, D., and Alexander, R. (1990): *Fumbling the Future*. New York: Harper.

Smith, K., Olian, J., Sims, H., and Scully, J. (1994): "Top management team demography and process," *Administrative Science Quarterly*, 49, 412–38.

Sorensen, J., and Stuart, T. (2000): "Aging, obsolescence and organizational innovation," *Administrative Science Quarterly*, 45, 81–112.

Stuart, T. (1999): "A structural perspective on organizational innovation," *Industrial and Corporate Change*, 8, 745–75.

Sull, D. (1999): "The dynamics of standing still: Firestone and the radial revolution," *Business History Review*, 73, 430–64.

Sull, D., Tedlow, R., and Rosenbloom, R. (1997): "Managerial commitments and technology change in the U.S. tire industry," *Industrial and Corporate Change*, 6, 461–500.

Teece, D. (1987): "Profiting from technological innovation," in D. Teece (ed.), *The Competitive*

Challenge, New York: Harper & Row, 185–219.

Teece, D. (1996): "Firm organization, industrial structure and technological innovation," *Journal of Economic Behavior and Organizations*, 31, 193–224.

Tegarden L., Hatfield, D., and Echols, A. (1999): "Doomed from the start: What is the value of selecting a future dominant design?" *Strategic Management Journal*, 20, 495–518.

Tripsas, M. (1999): "Unraveling the process of creative destruction: Complementary assets and incumbent survival in the typesetter industry," *Strategic Management Journal*, 20, 119–42.

Tripsas, M., and Gavetti, G. (2000): "Capabilities, cognition and inertia: Evidence from digital imaging," *Strategic Management. Journal*, 21, 1147–61.

Tushman, M., and Anderson, P. (1986): "Technological discontinuities and organization environments," *Administrative Science Quarterly*, 31, 439–65.

Tushman, M., and Murmann, J. (1998): "Dominant designs, technology cycles, and organizational outcomes," *Research in Organizational Behavior* 20, 213–66.

Tushman, M., and Nelson, R. (1990): "Technology, organizations and innovation: An introduction," *Administrative Science Quarterly*, 35, 1–8.

Tushman M., and O'Reilly, C. (1997): *Winning Through Innovation*. Boston, MA: Harvard Business School Press.

Tushman, M., and Romanelli, E. (1985): "Organizational evolution: A metamorphosis model of convergence and reorientation," in B. Staw and L. Cummings (eds), *Research in Organizational Behavior*, Vol. 7, Greenwich, CT: JAI Press, 171–222.

Tushman, M., and Rosenkopf, L. (1992): "On the organizational determinants of technological change: Towards a sociology of technological evolution," in B. Staw and L. Cummings (eds), *Research in Organizational Behavior*, Vol. 14, Greenwich, CT: JAI Press, 311–47.

Ulrich, K., and Eppinger, S. (1995): *Product Design and Development*. New York: McGraw Hill.

Utterback, J. (1994): *Mastering the Dynamics of Innovation*. Boston, MA: Harvard Business School Press.

Van de Ven A., and Garud, R. (1994): "The coevolution of technical and institutional events in the development of an innovation," in J. Baum and J. Singh (eds), *Evolutionary Dynamics of Organization*. New York: Oxford University Press, 425–43.

Van de Ven, A., Angle, H., and Poole, M. (1988): *Research on the Management of Innovation*. New York: Harper.

Virany, B., Tushman, M., and Romanelli, E. (1992): "Executive succession and organization outcomes in turbulent environments," *Organization Science*, 3, 72–92.

Weick, K. (1979): *The Social Psychology of Organizing*. Reading, MA: Addison-Wesley.

Weick, K., and Quinn, R. (1999): "Organizational change and development," *Annual Review of Psychology*, 50, 361–86.

West, J. (2000): "Institutions, information processing and organization structure in R&D," *Research Policy*, 29, 349–73.

Williams, K., and O'Reilly, C. (1998): "Demography and diversity in organizations: A review of forty years of research," *Research in Organizational Behavior*, 20, 77–140.

Zajac, E., and Westphal, J. (1996): "Who shall succeed? How CEO board preferences affect the choice of new CPOs," *Academy of Management Journal*, 39, 64–90.

Chapter Eighteen

Organizational Learning

M ARTIN S CHULZ

Organizational learning denotes a change in organizational knowledge. Organizational learning typically adds to, transforms, or reduces organizational knowledge. Theories of organizational learning attempt to understand the processes that lead to (or prevent) changes in organizational knowledge, as well as the effects of learning and knowledge on behaviors and organizational outcomes.

Organizational learning draws much of its appeal from the presumption that organizations are capable of intelligent behavior, and that learning is a tool for intelligence, though sometimes an intriguingly unreliable one. The basic model is that organizations collect experiences, draw inferences, and encode inferences in repositories of organizational knowledge, such as formal rules and informal practices. In this view, organizations are shaped by complex learning processes that combine current experiences with lessons learned in the past.

Current approaches to organizational learning emphasize routines as repositories of knowledge and conceptualize learning as making and updating routines in response to experiences (Levitt and March, 1988). Routines are regarded as recurrent sequences of action that span multiple organizational actors and assets. Examples of organizational routines include organizational rules, roles, conventions, strategies, structures, technologies, cultural practices and capabilities. In this view, organizational routines function as the primary form of organizational knowledge. The focus on routines in organizational learning theories establishes a supra-individual basis of organizational learning. Organizational routines are independent from the individual actors who make and execute them and they frequently persist even after their creators have left the organization. Routine-based learning is thus located on an organizational level, above the level of individual learning.

Literature Review, Summary and Evaluation

ORIGINS OF ORGANIZATIONAL LEARNING

Notions of organizational learning gained prominence in the 1950s when they were thrown into an ongoing debate between behaviorists and economists. Economic models of the firm had become dominant during and after the Second World War, yet many researchers, especially those with a behaviorist orientation, were dissatisfied with those models. Behaviorists such as March, Simon, and Cyert attacked the classical economic theory of the firm on the grounds that its models were overly simplistic and contradicted empirical evidence.

In *Organizations*, March and Simon (1958) refuted the claim of economic models that organizational decision outcomes are uniquely determined by environmental constraints. March and Simon argued that organizational behavior depends on complex organizational processes which introduce massive unpredictability into organizational decision making. They evoked (among others) several organizational learning ideas to support their claim, and, in the course of that argumentation, pioneered a remarkable number of themes that proved central to subsequent learning research. Organizations, they suggested, experience recurrent decision situations, and, in response, develop performance programs – highly complex, organized sets of responses. The main occasion for program adaptation arises when performance declines below aspiration levels. Aspiration levels themselves, however, adapt to many things including past performance and performance of reference groups. As a consequence, program adaptation may result from purely random encounters with improvement opportunities.

The focus on organizational learning was sharpened in the *Behavioral Theory of the Firm* (Cyert and March, 1963). In it, they conceived the firm as a complex, adaptive system – a system that, due to its internal complexity, was able to display considerable autonomy because it could produce outcomes not uniquely determined by external constraints. Organizational learning was captured in a "learning cycle" in which organizations responded to external shocks by adjusting the likelihood of reusing specific operating procedures (SOPs), a concept essentially equivalent to March and Simon's performance programs. SOPs that lead to preferred outcomes were subsequently used more frequently. Cyert and March envisioned a multilevel hierarchy of procedures that accomplished organizational adaptation. SOPs guided change in organizational behavior in response to short-run feedback, while more slowly changing higher-level procedures guided change in lower-level SOPs in response to long-run feedback.

These early conceptions of organizational learning conveyed a tension between two images of adaptation. On the one hand, learning could be seen as a rational organizational trait, compatible with rationalistic assumptions of economic theories: Organizations were directed toward performance improvement, and, in the long run, could result in an improved match between organizational arrangements and environmental constraints. On the other hand, learning could be seen as contributing to nonrational outcomes: Adaptation processes were complex and slow and sensitive to small variations in organizational parameters – characteristics more compatible with notions of limited rationality (Simon, 1955), or even its absence.

March and Olsen (1975) argued that the rational adaptation assumption inherent in learning models was unrealistic. Instead, ambiguity prevails – goals are ambiguous or in conflict, experience can be misleading, and interpretations are problematic. The authors explored four situations in which ambiguity enters the learning cycle portrayed in Figure 18.1:

1 In *role-constrained learning*, individual role definitions prevent individuals from bringing their learning to bear on their actions, when, for example, rigid bureaucratic rules inhibit changes of individual behavior. The outcome is inertia.
2 In *superstitious learning* (Lave and March, 1975) the connection between organizational action and environmental response is severed. In this situation the organization learns from an apparent environmental response even though it was not caused by the organization.
3 In *audience learning* the connection between individual action and organizational action becomes problematic, when, for example, individuals in a staff unit develop new, powerful solutions that, however, are not implemented due to cultural inertia.
4 In *learning under ambiguity* – it is not clear what happened or why it happened – individuals develop interpretations about causal connections on the basis of insufficient or inaccurate information about the environment, and instead draw on myths, illusions, or ideology.

Together, these four possible "disconnects" suggest that improvement is not a necessary outcome of learning, even though learning is intendedly adaptive. Instead, when ambiguity is present, beliefs, trust, and perceptions determine what happens. Levinthal and March (1981) introduced a formalized learning model that incorporates learning under ambiguity that illustrates some implications of learning under ambiguity. In their model, which focused on the search for new technologies, ambiguity enters at two

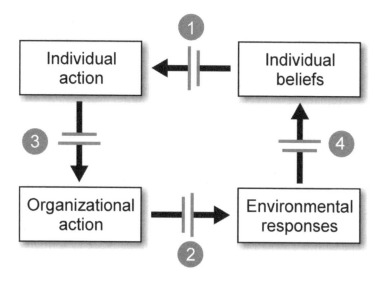

Figure 18.1 Four possible disconnects in the learning cycle

places. First, the effect of an adopted technology on performance was considered uncertain. Second, adopted technologies were seen as evolving – they could improve or decay over time. Simulations of the model showed that returns from search depend on the time horizon, that in ambiguous environments, identical organizations will learn to specialize on a search strategy, and that organizational technology trajectories were intensely path dependent. In addition, they found that fast learners adapted quickly to both correct and false signals. Conversely, slow learners were not as easily be confused by false signals, but they were also slow to respond to correct ones.

CONTEMPORARY RESEARCH

Although a steady stream of research on organizational learning was produced during the 1960s, 1970s, and 1980s, it has intensified considerably since the late 1980s. The number of publications increased dramatically, a special issue of *Organization Science* (2(1), 1991) was published on organizational learning, and new empirical research programs were begun. While uneven development of organizational learning research makes it difficult to cast its recent history as a continuous succession of dominant ideas, several distinct themes can serve as anchors for a review of the field. Table 18.1 presents a summary of the studies selected for review.

PRODUCTION AND ADAPTATION OF RULES AND ROUTINES

Organizational routines have moved into the forefront of organizational learning research since Levitt and March (1988) advanced the notion of organizational learning as the encoding of lessons in routines. A remarkable aspect of this conceptualization was the relative autonomy granted to routines. Routines are seen as capable of surviving considerable turnover of rule makers and rule users. Routines appeared as disembodied imprints of history – they make the lessons of history (but not the history itself) accessible to members who have not themselves experienced the history. The notion of encoding in semi-autonomous routines clearly established a supra-individual basis of organizational learning, retained notions of both limited-rational and rational adaptation, and invited linkages to bureaucracy theory (Schulz, 1998a), evolutionary models (Nelson and Winter, 1982; Miner, 1990), theories of culture (Weick, 1991; Cook and Yanow, 1993), and later, knowledge based theories of the firm (Grant, 1996).

Miner (1987, 1991) conducted the first set of studies on routine-based learning. She focused on a special kind of routines, organizational jobs. Organizations, she suggested, could adapt to environments by creating jobs at specific occasions, for specific people, or for specific purposes, by retaining these jobs if they produce satisfying outcomes, and by eliminating jobs when they cease serving a useful purpose. In her 1991 study, for example, Miner explored rates of job death in a private university. She found that jobs in large departments have lower death rates, perhaps because they lack the capacity to monitor the value of jobs. She also found that novelty increases the likelihood of job death, consistent with her view that novel jobs are more likely to contain "bad ideas."

The intensified focus on routines also gave rise to a research program on organizational rules. Organizational rules can be regarded as formalized routines, and rule production and change can be regarded as outcomes of organizational learning processes.

Table 18.1 Selected organizational learning studies

Reference	Key concepts	Key variables	Key predictions and findings	Key contribution	Method and sample
Origins of organizational learning March and Simon, 1958	Performance programs Aspiration levels		Environmental change induces change of performance programs. Performance change leads to adaptation of aspiration levels.	Organizational behavior is not uniquely determined by the context, but depends in important ways on organizational learning.	Theory development
Cyert and March, 1963	Standard operating procedures Hierarchies of rules Adaptation of goals Problemistic search		SOPs which lead to preferred outcomes are more likely to be used subsequently. General rules adapt less readily and less rapidly than more specific rules. Goals are determined by past experiences, experience of reference groups, past goals, and bargaining. Slack stabilizes the system. Negative slack leads to change.	The firm is an adaptive system. Organizational structure and practices affect the development of goals and expectations and the execution of choice.	Theory development Case studies Experiments Simulation
March and Olsen, 1975	Ambiguity Broken learning cycles Superstitious learning Audience learning Role-constrained learning Learning under ambiguity		Ambiguity introduces disconnects in learning cycles. Development of beliefs depends on intense interaction between perceptions, preferences, trust and alienation.	Improvement is not a necessary outcome of learning, even if learning is intendedly adaptive.	Theory development
Levinthal and March, 1981	Technologies Refinement search Innovation search Slack search Search competencies		Search strategies adapt to performance. Refinement depletes pool of opportunities. Search competencies increase (with decreasing increments) with search experience.	Path dependence of learning Learning in stochastically driven environments can lead to substantial differentiation among identical organizations.	Theory development Simulation

Reference	*Key concepts*	*Key variables*	*Key predictions and findings*	*Key contribution*	*Method and sample*
Contemporary research on organizational learning: Production and adaptation of rules and routines					
Levitt and March, 1988	Routines Encoding Competency traps		Competencies can inhibit adaptation. Outcomes of adaptation in ecologies of learners are hard to predict.	Learning as encoding of inferences in routines	Theory development
Miner, 1991	Social ecology of jobs	Death rates of jobs	Department characteristics affect job death rates. Job characteristics affect job death rates.	Organizational evolution as an outcome of the turnover of routines The turnover of routines depends on characteristics of context and content of routines.	Quantitative analysis of hazard rates of job death Hazard rate models
Schulz, 1992	Assets (such as organizational knowledge, goodwill, etc.) Depletion of assets	Rates of rule change	Depletion of organizational knowledge encoded in rules creates obsolescence. Depletion of normal distributed assets creates positive duration dependence.	Obsolescence can be seen as a result of learning where experiences deplete support for encoded knowledge.	Simulation theory development
Zhou, 1993	External crises Attention allocation	Rule birth rates Rule change rates	Negative effect of rule age on rates of rule change Positive effect of prior changes on rates of rule change Positive effect of attention to rules on rule births and on rule changes	Rule births are affected by crises or external shocks, while rule changes are affected by internal learning processes.	Quantitative analysis of rule births and changes in a university Poisson regression and hazard rate models
Schulz, 1998a	Bureaucratic proliferation Rule populations Problem supply, absorption, recycling, and sorting	Rule birth rates Rule density Rule suspension rates	Negative density dependence of rule birth rates Positive effect of rule suspensions on rule birth rate	Organizations learn by making rules, but rule proliferation inhibits organizational learning and thereby inhibits further rule production. The second law of bureaucracies: the number of bureaucratic rules increases with shrinking increments.	Quantitative analysis of time series data of rule births of a university Fixed effects Poisson regression models

March et al., 2000	Rule dynamics Rule histories	Rates of rule birth and rule change	Rule dynamics is driven by three groups of factors: 1 Generation and recognition of problems 2 Rule ecologies 3 Accumulation of competencies	Rules are carriers of knowledge. Rule dynamics reflect knowledge evolution. Rule histories are inefficient and path dependent. Rules track environmental changes, but the tracking is imprecise and the match between rules and current conditions is attenuated. Rules are traces of history.	Quantitative and qualitative exploration of rule births and changes in a university Poisson regression and hazard rate models

Contemporary research on organizational learning: Performance feedback

Lant, 1992	Aspiration level updating Attainment discrepancy models Rational expectation models	Aspiration level Performance	$Y(t) = \alpha_0 + \alpha_1 Y(t-1) + \alpha_2[Z(t-1) - Y(t-1)] + \varepsilon$, where $Y(t)$ is the aspiration level in time period t, and $Z(t)$ is the performance at t, and $\alpha_1..\alpha_3$ are parameters. Predictions: $\alpha_1 > 0, \alpha_2 > 0, \alpha_3 > 0$.	Aspirations adapt to past performance and past aspirations. Optimistic bias: aspirations are set above expectations.	Experiments with US MBA students (using the Markstrat game) Regression models
Lant et al., 1992	Organizational reorientation and convergence	Organizational changes Past performance Top management team characteristics	Poor past performance increases the likelihood of reorientation. Awareness of managers about environmental changes increases the likelihood of reorientation. Heterogeneity of top management teams increases the likelihood of reorientation.	Past performance, environmental turbulence, and characteristics of top management teams affect strategic reorientation of organizations.	Poisson regression models of counts of organizational changes of firms in the US furniture and computer software industries.
March, 1988	Fixed versus variable risk preferences Adaptive aspirations Random walks	Risk preference Wealth level Aspiration level	Increases in wealth levels decrease risk seeking. Increases in aspiration levels increase risk seeking. Slow adaptation of aspiration levels makes risk taking sensitive to the past performance history.	Risk taking depends on aspirations, and aspirations adapt to experiences. When aspirations adapt to past performance, a smoothing of behavior results.	Theory development Simulation

Reference	Key concepts	Key variables	Key predictions and findings	Key contribution	Method and sample
Lant and Mezias, 1992	Organizational change Convergence and reorientation	Adaptive changes	Adaptive search routines make organizations more responsive to environmental changes. High performing firms exhibit fewer changes. Ambiguity attenuates adaptation.	Most organizational change is produced by conventional, routine activities. The same processes which lead to convergence can also lead to reorientation.	Theory development Simulation
Greve, 1998	Organizational performance Organizational change Historical and social aspiration levels Slack search	Format changes of radio broadcasting stations Market share	As performance relative to social and historical aspiration levels increases, the likelihood of organizational change decreases. The effect is stronger above aspiration levels than below.	Organizational change depends on performance relative to social and historical aspiration levels. Failure increases the probability of change much more slowly than success decreases it.	Quantitative analysis of data from radio stations in 160 US radio markets Logit regression models

Contemporary research on organizational learning: Limits of learning (myopia)

Reference	Key concepts	Key variables	Key predictions and findings	Key contribution	Method and sample
March, 1991	Exploration and exploitation	Quality of organizational knowledge Primacy (coming out first among competitors)	Diversity facilitates exploration and thereby improves organizational knowledge. In competition for primacy, exploration increases the chances to come out first. Learning strategies which increase the reliability of performance reduce chances to come out first.	Exploitation tends to drive out exploration. Learning which increases diversity can benefit organizations.	Theory development Simulation

Contemporary research on organizational learning: Communities of learners

Barnett et al., 1994	Forbearance Exposure to competitors (density as a form of experience) Multiunit strategy vs single unit strategy	Return on average assets (ROAA) Density	Subunits of multi-unit banks are buffered from competition through mutual forbearance. This impedes learning and retains poor performing units. In contrast, single-unit banks develop into better performers when exposed to competition. Learning during regulated, protected times creates competency traps.	Organizations can learn from exposure to competition. Learning is crippled when multi-unit organizations buffer subunits from selection pressures of the market.	Quantitative analysis of time series and event history data about retail banks in Illinois 1987–93 Partial adjustment models, hazard rate models
Brown and Duguid, 1991	Communities of practice Canonical vs non-canonical practice		Communities of practice are the main locus of learning.	Informal learning Soft depositories of knowledge (stories)	Theory development

Contemporary research on organizational learning: Dissemination of organizational knowledge

Schulz, 2001	Interunit knowledge flows Relevance of knowledge Uncertain relevance of new knowledge Production of new knowledge, encoding of knowledge, recombining existing knowledge	Outflows of knowledge from subunits of MNCs	Collecting new knowledge intensifies vertical outflows to supervising subunits Knowledge codification intensifies outflows of knowledge Combining old knowledge affects mainly horizontal outflows to peer units	Production of knowledge affects the dissemination of knowledge. Relevance discovery: Sending new knowledge with uncertain relevance vertically upwards provides faster exposure of the new knowledge to a wider range of remote and different knowledge, and thereby facilitate a faster and more comprehensive assessment of its relevance.	Quantitative analysis Survey data from subsidiaries of MNCs in the US and Denmark Regression models

In an early study, Schulz (1992) developed a depletion of assets model of rule change. Following Fichman and Levinthal (1991), he assumed that organizational rules vary in initial assets – goodwill and belief of rule makers plus compatibility with current conditions. Over time these assets become depleted as problems are discovered, the environment changes, and commitment and goodwill of rule makers erode. In a simulation study, Schulz explored how such a depletion of assets affects the duration dependence of hazard rates of rule change. He found that the distribution of initial assets and the rate of depletion of assets determined whether a rule's hazard rate increases or decreases over time. Thus, while knowledge encoded in rules decays – becoming obsolete as the organization encounters experiences contradicting the rules – the decay can be delayed (and rules stabilized) when the processes of generating and processing of contradicting experiences are slowed by learning curves, or ignoring of experience.

Zhou (1993) explored births and changes of academic rules of Stanford University. He found that rule births and rule changes follow different processes. Rule births were affected by crises or external shocks (and so fluctuated across historical time periods), while rule changes were, in contrast, affected more by internal learning processes. In a second study of rule births, Schulz (1998a) explored the role of *rule density* – the number of rules in a given rule population, comparing arguments from bureaucracy, organizational learning, and population ecology theories. Bureaucracy theory (at least its more radical versions) predicts that rules breed more rules – a positive density dependence of the rule birth rate. In contrast, organizational learning theory and population ecology suggest that rule making is subject to limited resources (e.g., unsolved problems) which would be absorbed as the rule apparatus grows, leaving less resources for new rules – resulting in a negative effect of rule density on rule birth rates. Empirical analysis of university rules indicated strong negative density dependence of birth rates, supporting the notion that learning is self-limiting. Schulz concluded that Weber's "iron law of bureaucratic proliferation" must be amended with a second law specifying that the number of bureaucratic rules of a system increases in shrinking increments.

March et al.'s (2000) recent study of organizational rules integrates and expands prior work, presenting a broad theoretical frame in which the dynamics of organizational rules are driven by three main factors.

1 *Generation and recognition of problems* Rules and rule changes depend on experience with problems, and on processes which control the supply of problems and their recognition by organizational actors (e.g., organizational attention, problem absorption, and external crises).
2 *Rule ecologies* Rules are also interdependent with other rules – competing for scarce resources (such as attention and problems) or connected by functional dependence (when rules build on other rules).
3 *Accumulation of competence* Rules develop competencies with problems, rule users develop competencies with rules, and rule makers develop competencies with rule making and changing. Competencies of rules and rule users reduce incentives for change and thereby stabilize rules, while rule maker's competencies would intensify rule changes.

Follow-up research by Schulz and Beck (2000) comparing rule changes in a German bank to those of Stanford University found that rule change patterns were very similar in these two very different contexts, corroborating the idea that rule change is guided by a general set of principles.

PERFORMANCE FEEDBACK

Several models have been proposed to explain how organizational learning is induced. Performance feedback models are based on the idea that organizations learn when they experience problems. In these models, organizations encounter problems, initiate a problematic search for solutions (Cyert and March, 1963), adopt solutions that solve problems, and retain good solutions for future use. Problems are conceptualized as performance shortfalls – situations in which (actual or anticipated) performance would fall below aspiration levels. A key assumption of this model is that aspiration levels adapt to past performance, which breaks with the orthodox economic postulate of exogenous, stable aspirations of decision makers. As a result, performance feedback models treat organizational learning as a two-stage process. In the first stage, organizations adapt their behavior when performance falls short of aspirations, and in the second stage, they would adapt their aspirations to achieved performance. Not surprisingly, research on performance feedback evolved into two branches.

The first branch – aspiration level adjustment – describes how targets of organizations (and of individuals) adjust to past experiences and experiences of reference groups. Early formulations of aspiration level adjustment were introduced by Cyert and March (1963) and Levinthal and March (1981), as described above. More recently, Lant (1992) compared several models of aspiration level updating empirically by means of experiments. The experimental setup consisted of recurrent cycles during which teams of American MBA students would set aspiration levels on the basis of feedback they received about their performance. She found that groups consistently set aspirations above past performance, suggesting that subjects were persistently optimistic about what they could achieve, or perhaps challenging themselves to perform better.

The second branch – behavioral adjustment – explores whether and how divergence between achieved performance and aspiration levels, or performance gaps, affects organizational change, search, and risk taking. The main assumption of these approaches is that behavioral adjustment intensifies when performance falls short of aspirations, and that it subsides when performance exceeds aspirations. Lant et al.'s (1992) analysis of data taken from 10K reports of firms operating in the furniture and computer software industries suggested that poor past performance (relative to industry performance) leads to strategic reorientation. The authors also found that performance feedback had weaker effects in the more turbulent computer software industry. Thus, the signaling value of past performance is weaker in turbulent environments, thereby rendering organizational learning less effective.

Several studies have explored how behavioral adjustment interacts with aspiration level adaptation. March (1988), for example, explored the effect of adaptive aspiration levels on risk taking by means of modeling. He found that when aspirations adapt to past performance, a smoothing of behavior results – organizations become less sensitive to variations in performance. In subsequent work (March and Shapira, 1992), the model has been elaborated by incorporating slack search (an increase of risk taking above the aspiration level) and a survival point at which resources are exhausted and risk aversion predominates.

Behavioral adjustment in the context of organizational change was modeled in Lant and Mezias's (1992) simulation study comparing convergence and reorientation (i.e., incremental and radical change). While prior work emphasized different causes of these two modes of change, specifically that top managers would create and implement radically new routines in response to substandard performance (Tushman and Romanelli, 1985), Lant and Mezias showed that the processes leading to convergence can also lead to reorientation.

Greve (1998) explored the effect of performance gaps on organizational change of radio broadcasting stations in the USA. Two kinds of aspiration levels were considered: Historical aspiration levels were modeled as a moving average of past performance (market share), and social aspiration levels were modeled as average share of all stations in a given market. Greve found that organizational changes (in broadcasting format or production) declined when a station's performance exceeded aspiration levels, and increased when performance fell short of aspiration levels, thus broadly supporting the performance feedback model. He also found that effects of performance gaps were stronger above than below aspiration levels, suggesting that decision makers used different adaptation rules above and below their aspiration levels, and that the effect of performance gaps on changes depended on the type of change, for example, performance below aspiration levels intensified innovative, but not routine changes.

LIMITS OF LEARNING (MYOPIA)

The conception of organizational learning as a self-limiting process is prevalent. A prototypical self-limiting learning process is the competency trap (Levitt and March, 1988), in which organizations develop competencies with routines and thereby improve performance, while also becoming trapped by their own competencies when returns from using a routine are sufficiently large to prevent experimentation with alternatives.

In his influential study of the self-limiting nature of organizational learning March (1991), distinguished two modes of adaptation, "exploration" and "exploitation." Exploration captures experimentation, risk taking, and innovation, while exploitation captures the re-use of existing knowledge and its incremental adjustment. March argued that organizations face a trade-off between the two learning modes. Systems that engaged in exploration to the exclusion of exploitation suffered the costs of experimentation without gaining many of its benefits, and systems that engaged in exploitation to the exclusion of exploration were prone to becoming trapped in suboptimal, stable equilibria. Exploitation, however, tends to drive out exploration because exploitation has higher certainty, speed, proximity, and clarity of feedback, making it more attractive to decision makers than the slow, imprecise, and uncertain feedback from exploration. In the study, March explored how the quality of organizational knowledge and the chances of winning against competitors are improved by cultural diversity and reduced by organizational efforts to increase the reliability of performance.

Subsequent research in this vein has explored processes that cause limits to learning, in particular, how specialization and simplification lead to myopia (Levinthal and March, 1993), and also expanded the competency trap idea to other kinds of traps, including "failure traps," an escalation of increasingly futile and increasingly desperate change efforts (Levinthal and March, 1993), and "codification traps," which occur when the extension and habitual application of old rules to new problems eliminate the perceived need to create new rules (Schulz, 1998a).

COMMUNITIES OF LEARNERS

Most organizational learning is situated in environments consisting of other learners (Herriott et al., 1985; Levitt and March, 1988). Mutual adaptation of multiple learners creates unpredictability, and reduces the chances that each learner fully understand what is going on. When learners compete, surprising imbalances can result. Weaker firms, for example, may become competent in coping with the dominant firms, while dominant firms, by virtue of their capability to ignore their competition, will not develop such competencies. Barnett et al. (1994) have explored empirically some implications of such a situation. In their study, they compared single unit banks with branch system banks. They found that single unit banks gained strength through exposure to competition, while multiunit banks did not because they could mollify competitive pressures through mutual forbearance, and thereby survive without learning how to compete from the market.

Learning communities also reside within organizations. Rule ecologies (Schulz, 1998a; March et al., 2000) are a case in point. Individual rules are seen as learning units that form communities, compete for scarce resources, and infect each other with change. Another example is communities of practice (Brown and Duguid, 1991), which evolve as "noncanonical practice" around formal work processes. These communities learn when their members interpolate between formal directives and demands of the situation. Lessons learned are captured in stories about problems and their causes. Stories thus function as informal repositories of accumulated, collective wisdom that play an important role for innovation.

DISSEMINATION OF ORGANIZATIONAL KNOWLEDGE

Processes that distribute organizational knowledge within or between organizations are an important part of organizational learning. Between organizations, the concept of "absorptive capacity" – organizational capabilities to assess, assimilate, and exploit external knowledge – plays a central role (Cohen and Levinthal, 1990). Although the concept was originally introduced to understand why firms invest in knowledge resources, subsequent research has applied the concept to intraorganizational knowledge transfer, where a lack of absorptive capacity was seen as contributing to "stickiness" of knowledge (Szulanski, 1996).

Recently, Schulz (2001) has explored how knowledge production in subunits affects knowledge dissemination between subunits of multinational corporations. He found that learning which produces new, non-routine knowledge stimulated vertical flows to supervising units, while production of old, incremental knowledge intensified horizontal flows to peer subunits. Schulz's interpretation focused on the uncertain relevance of new, non-routine knowledge. Sending new, non-routine knowledge vertically upwards would provide faster exposure of new knowledge to a wider range of remote and different knowledge, and thereby facilitate a faster and more comprehensive assessment of its relevance.

Summary and Evaluation

Organizational learning theory started in the 1950s with a shot across the bow of orthodox economic theory, challenging its simplistic and rationalistic assumptions. As research has grown and branched out in new directions, it has kept its rebellious spirit, maintaining – even broadening – its claim that organizations need to be considered as causally autonomous. Organizational learning is neither a rational adaptation to environmental constraints, nor reducible to individual behavior. It resides on its own level of emergence, following a complex, perhaps stochastic, eigendynamics. Yet it is also displays a significant level of fragmentation and lack of integration that makes it difficult to draw an unambiguous map of its topology.

Several themes stand out in the forgoing review. One is a focus on dynamics. Organizational learning research is saturated with dynamic notions – behavior is adaptive, and so are aspirations, routines, and organizational knowledge. Even change is time varying and path dependent, following different trajectories from iteration to iteration. Indeed, stability is regarded as a curious outcome of perverse, myopic learning processes. This focus makes organizational learning a primary contender for explanations of social and organizational change and stability. A second theme is a focus on models. A large proportion of work on organizational learning is based either on simulation models or on analysis of longitudinal data with complex statistical models. To some degree, this reflects the efforts of learning researchers to capture the complexity of learning with appropriate symbolic representations. This modeling trait has contributed greatly to sharpening theoretical concepts, but, in the case of simulation-based research, can border on model solipsism (Miner and Mezias, 1996). The third theme is the continuous and inspired leadership of James G. March, whose playful, evocative, and powerful ideas have profoundly affected organizational learning research from the beginning.

Contemporary Issues and Debates

Organizational learning theory is fragmented. A key ingredient to the fragmentation is the lack of a singular, well-defined dependent variable. Is the main focus on exploring the sources of organizational learning, is it on different forms of learning, or is it on the outcomes of organizational learning? It appears that organizational learning is about all three. At the root of the fragmentation and ambiguities are divergent conceptions of learning and divergent ideas about the sources of learning.

Conceptions of learning

LEARNING AS IMPROVING

An elementary notion of learning focuses on improvement of outcome measures such as performance, success, or precision. Organizations are assumed to increase behavior that results in favorable outcomes and decrease behavior that results in unfavorable outcomes, a notion similar to stimulus response models (Lave and March, 1975). Such adaptation leads to a positive effect of experience on favorable outcomes, a relationship typically captured in learning curves (Lieberman, 1987; Argote and Epple, 1990; Adler and Clark, 1991; Epple et al., 1991; Argote, 1996). The improvement notion is especially prevalent in applied work, where it has led to the widespread assumption that learning automatically benefits organizations (Stata, 1989; Senge, 1990; Garvin, 1993; Probst and Buchel, 1997; Fulmer, et al., 1998). In contrast to the applied literature, the academic literature on learning is less confident about its benefits and more attentive to obstacles, complexities, hazards and "non-traditional qualities" of learning (Weick, 1991). Nevertheless, improvement could be regarded as the null hypothesis of organizational learning that can be compared to more complex and less traditional models.

Research on organizational learning has explored a number of alternatives to the simple improvement model. One is adaptation of the environment. If the environment adapts to a focal unit, its match with environmental conditions improves, even if the unit does not learn, e.g., when small competitors adapt to a dominant company which then does not need to adapt (Barnett et al., 1994), or when rule users develop competencies with rules and thereby stabilize the rules without improving them (March et al., 2000). A second complication arises from unobserved heterogeneity. It can create the appearance of improvement even though the units have not changed (Schulz, 1992). A number of additional complications have been discussed, including adaptation of aspiration levels (March and Simon, 1958; Cyert and March, 1963; Mezias, 1988; Lant, 1992), scarce experiences (March et al., 1991), exhaustion of improvement opportunities (Levinthal and March, 1981; Schulz, 1992; 1998a), myopia (Levinthal and March, 1993), competency traps (Levitt and March, 1988), noise (Lant and Mezias, 1992; Lant et al., 1992), superstitious learning (Lave and March, 1975), nested learning (Levitt and March, 1988), and advantages of slow learning (Lounamaa and March 1987).

LEARNING AS RECORDING

More recent work on learning has increasingly understood organizational learning as recording of organizational knowledge. The basic idea is that organizations make experiences, draw inferences, and encode the inferences into organizational routines, such as rules, procedures, conventions, technologies, strategies (Levitt and March, 1988). By encoding knowledge in routines, organizations can retain, share, and re-use solutions found in the past. Routines thereby can provide organizations with efficiency and reliability. They can even help to repair cognitive limitations of individuals (Heath et al., 1998). Implicit in this recording notion is a "process" instead of an "outcome" perspective on learning. Recording of knowledge is seen as a learning activity, regardless of the benefits it might entail for the organization. Some encoding might even be detrimental: Old lessons retained can be inappropriate for new situations (Barnett et al., 1994), and their mindless application can contribute to escalation (Allison, 1971). Likewise, the encoding of valuable lessons in tangible depositories incurs the risk of involuntary transfer of strategically important knowledge to competitors (Winter, 1987; Zander and Kogut, 1995), although the risks appear to depend on the type of knowledge involved, the form of codification used, and the strategic context of the organization (Schulz and Jobe, 2001).

The recording of knowledge perspective is intensely historical. Learning inscribes lessons drawn from history onto the organization. Organizations thereby appear as "residue of history" (March et al., 2000). Yet, the encoding of lessons is not likely to be an immediate, continuous and complete mapping of history onto routines. Encoding takes a fair amount of organizational effort and absorbs scarce organizational attention (Zhou, 1993). Organizational agencies in charge of encoding tend to have limited resources and capacities (Schulz, 1998a). The outcome is a discontinuous, delayed, and incomplete mapping of lessons. As a result, the match between current routines and current conditions is attenuated (March et al., 2000). On the level of formal rules, the discontinuity of the encoding process leads to a complex interplay between knowledge encoded and knowledge not yet encoded in rules. Knowledge encoded captures experiences that have been accumulated in the past history of a rule, while knowledge not yet encoded captures experiences made since the most recent revision of a rule. Both kinds of knowledge evolve differently and have different effects. Empirical studies suggest that knowledge encoded stabilizes rules, while knowledge not yet encoded destabilizes rules (Schulz, 1998b; March et al., 2000; Schulz and Beck, 2000).

LEARNING AS EVOLUTION OF KNOWLEDGE

The evolutionary perspective on learning is related to the recording of knowledge notion, but takes a broader focus centered on processes that bring about change in organizational knowledge, including changing the stock of knowledge, its character, and its distribution over subunits. In contrast to the recording notion, change of organizational knowledge is also seen as systemic and self-induced, or even as accidental, chaotic, and non-intended (Mezias and Glynn, 1993). Work in this tradition has frequently a distinctive cognitive flavor (Duncan and Weiss, 1979; Weick, 1979; Sandelands and Stablein, 1987; Weick and Roberts, 1993), and empirical studies have explored cognitive structures (Carley, 1990) and knowledge networks of organizations (Klimecki and Lassleben, 1994, 1998; Hansen, 1999). The evolution notion also plays an important role in models of knowledge combination (Buckley and Carter, 1998; Nahapiet and Ghoshal, 1998), knowledge creation (Hedlund and Nonaka, 1993; Nonaka, 1994), and organizational communication (Szulanski 1996; West and Meyer, 1997). It even resonates with approaches to cultural meaning development within organizations (Cook and Yanow, 1993).

A core assumption of the evolutionary approach is that knowledge evolution depends in important ways on actual and potential connections between knowledge elements. Organizational knowledge does not consist of a collection of isolated kernels. Rather, individual pieces of knowledge are embedded in an interconnected network of other pieces that provide an ecological context for changes in knowledge. Changes in some parts of the knowledge structure tend to trigger changes in other, related, or similar parts (March et al., 2000). Growth of the organizational knowledge base depends on establishing connections between prior knowledge and new knowledge. The recognition of such connections can be greatly aided by the degree to which prior knowledge helps organizations to assess, assimilate and exploit new, external knowledge (Cohen and Levinthal, 1990), and frequently this involves connecting to related knowledge domains in order to access new knowledge domains (Lane and Lubatkin, 1998). For the establishment of connections between knowledge elements, it appears that recognizing the relevance of knowledge plays an important role (Schulz, 2000), and that organizational subunits send knowledge with uncertain relevance to supervising units in order to explore potential connections with other knowledge of the organization (Schulz, 2001).

Establishing connections between knowledge elements is likely also one of the most important sources of innovation in organizations (Nelson and Winter, 1982). In this regard, work in the knowledge-based view has explored how firms can derive competitive advantage from knowledge combination (Buckley and Carter, 1998; Nahapiet and Ghoshal, 1998), and how firms can use knowledge combination to deter imitation by competitors (Kogut and Zander, 1992).

Sources of Learning

What do organizations learn from? A wide variety of sources are considered in the literature, including own past experiences (March and Olsen, 1976; Covington, 1985; Huber, 1991), experiences of others (Iwai, 1984; Cohen and Levinthal, 1989; Jensen, 1988), thinking (Weick, 1979; Sandelands and Stablein, 1987; Pisano, 1994), knowledge recombination (Kogut and Zander, 1992), small losses (Sitkin, 1992), and experimentation (Comfort, 1985; Levitt and March, 1988; Huber, 1991). Most of these sources play two roles in organizational learning – they provide impetus for learning (e.g., initiate search for solutions) and they can provide the raw materials (experiences, ideas, etc.) from which organizations derive lessons. Perhaps because the two roles are empirically correlated, work on learning does not generally distinguish the two.

OWN AND OTHERS EXPERIENCE

A primary source of learning is experience. A distinction can be made between learning from own experience and learning from experience of others (Levitt and March, 1988). The two are likely to involve different mechanisms. Collecting direct experiences can be very costly, yet is likely to produce more unique outcomes, while learning from experiences of others usually involves less cost, but tends to produce less unique outcomes. Learning from direct experience depends critically on organizational processes that generate experiences – e.g., stimulate experimentation, or intensify the problem supply (Schulz, 1998a) – the movement of "problem instigators" between activity domains (March et al., 2000), or investment in search activities (Levinthal and March, 1981; Mezias and Glynn, 1993). In contrast, learning from others depends on mechanisms that give access to, or generate exposure to experiences of others, such as networks and institutional mechanisms (Levitt and March, 1988; Hansen, 1999).

QUALITY OF EXPERIENCE

A related debate concerns the quality of experience. While applied and economic approaches frequently take experience at face value, academic and behavioral approaches emphasize that experience is confounded by ambiguity and thereby disrupts learning cycles (March and Olsen, 1975). Numerous causes of ambiguity are discussed. In the presence of noise in the stream of experience, learning degrades (Lant and Mezias, 1992; Carley and Lin 1997), or even gives rise to superstition (March and Olsen, 1975). Feedback from actions taken tends to be delayed and remote (March, 1991; Lomi et al., 1997), and frequently is biased by post-decision surprises (Harrison and March, 1984). Learning from experience in one part of the organization is often confounded by simultaneous adaptation in other parts (Levinthal and March, 1993; Lounamaa and March 1987).

ENDOGENOUS EXPERIENCE

Finally, experiences are frequently not exogenous. Experiences can become endogenous when outcomes of past learning determine what the organization experiences subsequently. Frequently, this narrows the range of alternatives considered. Competency traps (Levitt and March, 1988) are a prominent case in point, because they inhibit collecting of new experiences with alternative technologies. Similar cases include learning substitution (Levinthal and March, 1993), codification traps (Schulz, 1998a) and coercive bureaucracies (Adler and Borys, 1996; Shrivastava, 1983). Yet, prior learning can also broaden the range of organizational experiences and stimulate learning, for example, by increasing absorptive capacity (Cohen and Levinthal, 1990), by leading to new rules which entail new experiences with them (March et al., 2000), or by establishing search rules (Levinthal and March, 1981; Hey, 1981, 1982) or change routines (Mezias and Glynn, 1993). In either case, when experiences become endogenous, organizational learning becomes path dependent. Although such path dependencies can benefit organizations by limiting the chances of competitors to imitate a focal organization (Cohen and Levinthal, 1990), they can also hurt organizations by severely constraining their capabilities to adapt to new situations.

Central Questions That Remain Unanswered

FORMAL RULES

A large number of questions emerge from the relatively young research program on organizational rules. One set of questions concerns the internal composition of rules. Rules usually consist of a number of related provisions. How does the homogeneity and relatedness of rule provisions affect rule changes? Perhaps internal homogeneity stabilizes rules, because such rules offer a narrower target for emerging problems and challenges. Perhaps a high level of interdependence between component provisions impedes incremental changes and thereby entails radical changes. A second question regards rule implementation. It is conceivable that strict rather than lax implementation generates more experiences that can induce rule changes. How does rule implementation and use affect rule changes? A third area concerns the effects of knowledge not yet encoded in rules. Although the basic proposition is that knowledge not yet encoded destabilizes rules, rules can become increasingly stable when knowledge not yet encoded is not monitored. What determines the degree to which rules are monitored? How does monitoring of rules affect their propensity to change incrementally or radically? How does the organizational context affect the level of monitoring of rules?

PRIOR LEARNING

Organizational learning frequently builds on what has been learned in the past. Although relations between prior and later learning have found some attention, the underlying mechanisms are poorly understood so far. One important mechanism is refinement, where successive changes of organizational knowledge or behavior lead to improvements which reduce the need for further changes. Yet, empirical studies appear to disconfirm such refinement effects. Instead, they consistently find a positive effect of prior changes on subsequent changes, both for rule revisions (Zhou, 1993) and for organizational changes (Amburgey et al., 1993). In response, researchers have developed a number of learning interpretations, including tinkering (March et al., 2000), repetitive momentum (Amburgey et al., 1993), and notoriety (Schulz and Beck, 2000). Empirically, it appears difficult to disentangle such mechanisms because they confound each other. What statistical techniques and types of data would allow us to reliably decompose these effects? Under what conditions does organizational learning produce convergent trajectories of change, and when does it produce acceleration of change? When does learning invite more learning, and when does it obviate or inhibit further learning? How does prior learning direct, constrain, and enable subsequent learning?

DISPERSED LEARNING AND ASPIRATIONS

Learning in organization occurs simultaneously, in many places, on different subjects, and with different speeds. How does dispersed learning affect the distribution of knowledge in organizations? How do organizations manage this distributed knowledge production process, and how do they derive strategic advantage from it? A related question is: How does dispersed learning aggregate to induce larger changes (e.g., of strategies or structures)? The result is not necessarily a random jumble. When learning processes are interdependent, external shocks can trigger cascades of learning that can aggregate to form large waves of change. Even when learning processes are independent, large external shocks can start cohorts of simultaneous learning processes which subsequently can intensify rates of change (Schulz, 1992), and thereby produce escalations of change events (the mechanism is similar to a set of flashlights running out of battery power). Research in this area is in very early stages, and much work remains to be done.

Closely related is the issue of dispersed aspirations. Most research on performance feedback is based on organization-level aspirations. Very limited attention has been paid to situations in which aspirations are dispersed and heterogeneous. How do aspirations of subgroups or individuals aggregate to form organizational aspirations? Organizations are typically not democracies; so simple majority rules will not suffice to adequately model organizational aspiration formation. It is possible that such models could make good use of ideas borrowed from theories of coalition formation, social networks, institutional contagion, and status expectations (Greve, 1998). Furthermore, when individual and organizational aspirations differ, it is conceivable that members with deviant aspirations become frustrated and decide to leave, while members with conforming aspirations stay – a vicious cycle of conformity. It is not entirely clear that such a narrowing of the distribution of aspirations is beneficial. On one hand, it might create stronger consensus, stronger cultures, or improved coordination, but on the other hand, it is likely to drive out innovation.

New and Emerging Directions

INFORMAL ROUTINES

Routine-based notions of organizational learning have stimulated a fair amount of research on written rules, but much less research on informal and tacit routines. Yet, informal routines are important for organizations because they tend to be less imitable, and because they sometimes complement or even substitute formal rules. A few empirical approaches to exploring informal routines have emerged. One approach examines routines in laboratory studies, exploring connections between organizational and psychological models of procedural and declarative memory (Cohen, 1991; Walsh and Ungson, 1991; Cohen and Bacdayan, 1994). Another promising approach identifies the grammars underlying the sequential patterns of action that make up routines (Pentland and Reuter, 1994). Although the role of routines is widely acknowledged in economic (Axelrod, 1984; Kreps, 1990), evolutionary (Nelson and Winter, 1982; Hannan and Freeman, 1984), and cultural (Douglas, 1986) work, little quantitative research has explored how informal routines are formed, changed, replicated, abandoned, and recombined with other routines. It is possible, but not necessary that routines follow patterns similar to those found in formal rules. Hopefully, future research will shed some light on these issues.

FORMAL RULES

Several new directions have emerged in research on formal rules. One is the comparative study of rule making and changing, e.g., comparing rule change in different organizational and societal contexts, and comparing different kinds of rule change (e.g., Schulz and Beck, 2000). A second direction is related to the legal context of organizational rule making (Edelman, 1990; Sutton and Dobbin, 1996; Sitkin and Bies, 1994).

DIVERSITY OF EXPERIENCE

Apparently, diversity is beneficial to learning – at least up to a point (Fiol and Lyles, 1985). Barkema and Vermeulen (1998) explored how product diversity and multinational diversity affect the mode of foreign entry (startup or acquisition) of Dutch companies. Using data on foreign ventures of 25 large non-financial Dutch firms from 1966 to 1994, they found that multinational diversity had a positive linear effect on the propensity of firms to expand through startups, but that product diversity had a non-linear inverted U-shaped effect. Thus while diverse multinational experiences contributed to the development of technological capabilities, making startups more attractive than acquisitions, high levels of product diversity exceeded the information processing capabilities of management teams lowering the propensity to startup.

Diversity also affects how organizations learn, with diverse experiences appearing to stimulate exploration learning (Moorman and Miner, 1998; Luo and Peng, 1999). At the same time, learning from diverse experience may require matching organizational capacities to interpret, assess and assimilate diverse experiences (Cohen and Levinthal, 1990; Lane and Lubatkin, 1998). This suggests that diversity of experiences is positively related to the diversity of organizational knowledge. However, how these two exactly interact is not well understood. Nor do we know how diversity of organizational knowledge translates into organizational performance, although simulation-based research suggests that there might be a positive effect (March, 1991).

TRANSACTIVE MEMORY

Transactive memory captures group members' awareness of the range of knowledge available within the group and which members are experts in specific domains (Wegner, 1987). Although the concept has been applied mainly to knowledge sharing in small groups (Liang et al., 1995; Rulke et al., 1998; Rulke and Rau, 2000), transactive memory may also play a role in organizational learning. As Kieser and Koch (2000) have pointed out, when organizations make or change rules, they face the problem of efficiently integrating across dispersed, specialized knowledge bases related to a rule proposal. How do organizations identify specialized relevant knowledge and incorporate it into rules? Clearly, even for moderately sized organizations, pooling the knowledge of all organizational participants is not an option. Instead, it appears that organizational rule making processes rely extensively on "directory specialists" (Wegner 1995) who know which departments would be affected by a rule change and where the relevant experts are located (Kieser and Koch, 2000). Kieser and Koch's study establishes a very promising connection between notions of organizational knowledge and rule-based notions of organizational learning. At the same time, however, it raises a number of new and intriguing questions. How do organizations appoint directory specialists? How do directory specialists stay up to date? How do organizations identify or anticipate serendipitous interactions between dispersed knowledge domains? How do organizational cultures, hierarchies, and politics modify the link between transactive memory and rule making?

Connections Across Levels

Learning is a multilevel phenomenon. In organizations, learning on one level almost always constrains or enables learning on other levels. For example, rule users develop competencies with rules, while rules adjust to technical and political problems encountered by the organization. Both learning processes can clash, for example, when rule changes destroy user competencies or when rule users resist rule changes (March et al., 2000). At the same time, the organization adjusts its rule making procedures to the requirements of its environment, which, in turn, is populated by learning organizations. Clearly, such cross-level connections can have complex and surprising outcomes (Levitt and March, 1988), and the resulting unpredictability could well be taken as grounds to accord considerable causal autonomy to organizations, notwithstanding reductionist and contextualist approaches which see organizations as reducible to environmental constraints or characteristics of its members.

Connections between organizational learning and intraorganizational learning give rise to a number of interesting research opportunities. Of particular importance is the relation between organizational rules and intraorganizational networks of actors, tasks, and tools. Although a fair amount of research has explored effects of such intraorganizational networks on learning within organizations (Argote, this volume), much less research has explored how learning affects the emergence and development of actor-task-tool networks. Yet, it appears that most such network ties (e.g., which actors perform which tasks) are established and regulated by organizational rules (e.g., job descriptions, rules about reporting relations, schedules). Because rules are produced and adapted by organizational learning, it is quite possible that actor-task-tool networks are themselves the outcome of organization-level learning processes. From this perspective, it might be worthwhile for future research to explore how the organizational rule dynamics affects actor-task-tool networks, for example, how rule adaptation impacts the erosion or improvement of network consistency, how standardization and specialization contribute to the emergence of structural holes, and how knowledge capture and encoding practices affect the chances that fluid actors co-produce, share, and combine knowledge they derive from fleeting experiences.

A closely related, but more abstract question is, how do organizations assure that their rules partition their actor-task-tool networks into sub-networks in ways that minimize the need to transfer knowledge between parts (Simon, 1965; Grant, 1996), while at the same time facilitating effective knowledge production and exploitation? Perhaps future research in this direction can develop a new, learning based theory of organization design that illuminates how organizations dynamically adapt their structures to experiences. Such a theory would hopefully be able to complement or even replace the antiquated notions of information processing which currently dominate the design field.

A second set of research questions arises from connections between organizational learning and interorganizational learning (Ingram, this volume). Clearly, interorganizational learning depends critically on the knowledge and learning of other organizations – for interorganizational learning to succeed something to be learned needs to exist. Consequently, a primary question is, how does knowledge production in some organizations encourage or limit interorganizational learning (or even interorganizational espionage) of others? For example, does the type of the knowledge produced (e.g., rare, basic, applied, volatile) or the form of production (planned, accidental, exploration) affect interorganizational learning?

It may be equally important to understand how knowledge differentials emerge and persist between organizations, even if (or especially when) knowledge is articulated and thus comparatively fluid. This raises questions about the role of secrecy, how rules of secrecy inhibit interorganizational learning. Why do some organizations and actors benefit more than others from bridging interorganizational knowledge differentials and from circumventing secrecy rules? Another set of issues is related to interorganizational learning of relevant knowledge. Presumably, organizations benefit more by retrieving from others knowledge that is relevant (rather than irrelevant). Yet, how do organizations develop and adapt conceptions of relevance? How do they identify relevant sources of knowledge? Does use of a knowledge channel reinforce itself akin to a competency trap? And most importantly, how can organizations find knowledge that is sufficiently related to be relevant for their purposes but at the same time so serendipitous that it provides at least temporary competitive advantage? Baum et al. (2000) and Greve (2000) attempt to provide some early answers to these questions.

Conclusion

Many questions, few answers. Is this a sign of weakness of the field of organizational learning? Not at all! The paucity of answers and the abundance of questions in the field is an indicator of its youthful vitality and its enormous future potential. Clearly, organizational learning is a complex, multifaceted and multilevel phenomenon. This is both a liability and an asset. On the one hand, the complexity of research problems imposes intimidating data and modeling requirements, including the collection of longitudinal and multilevel datasets and the development of new mathematical and statistical models. On the other hand, it offers a wealth of exciting research opportunities and the potential to uncover comparatively deep principles of organizational or even social change and stability. The road ahead might be a difficult one to travel, but it is guaranteed to lead through spectacular terrain.

References

Adler, P. S., and Borys, B. (1996): "Two types of bureaucracy: Enabling and coercive," *Administrative Science Quarterly*, 41, 61–89.

Adler, P. S., and Clark, K. B. (1991): "Behind the learning curve: A sketch of the learning process," *Management Science*, 37, 267–81.

Allison, G. T. (1971): *Essence of Decision: Explaining the Cuban Missile Crisis*. Boston: Little, Brown.

Amburgey, T. L., Kelly, D., and Barnett, W. P. (1993): "Resetting the clock: The dynamics of organizational change and failure," *Administrative Science Quarterly*, 38, 51–73.

Argote, L. (1996): "Organizational learning curves: Persistence, transfer and turnover," *International Journal of Technology Management*, 11, 759–69.

Argote, L., and Epple, D. (1990): "Learning curves in manufacturing," *Science*, 247, 920–24.

Axelrod, R. (1984): *The Evolution of Cooperation*. New York: Basic Books.

Barkema, H. G., and Vermeulen, F. (1998): "International expansion through start–up or acquisition: A learning perspective," *Academy of Management Journal*, 41, 7–26.

Barnett, W. P., Greve, H. R., and Park, D. Y. (1994): "An evolutionary model of organizational performance," *Strategic Management Journal*, 15, 11–28.

Baum, J. A. C., Li, S. X., and Usher, J. M. (2000): "Making the next move: Influences of experiential and vicarious learning and strategy on the spatial evolution of chains," *Administrative Science Quarterly*, 45, 766–801.

Brown, J. S., and Duguid, P. (1991): "Organizational learning and communities of practice: Toward a unified view of working, learning, and innovation," *Organization Science*, 2, 40–57.

Buckley, P. J., and Carter, M. J. (1998): "Managing cross border complementary knowledge: The business process approach to knowledge management in multinational firms," working paper 98–2, Carnegie Bosch Institute. Also available at http://cbi.gsia.cmu.edu/buckley/buckley.html.

Carley, K. M. (1990): "Group stability: A socio-cognitive approach," *Advances in Group Processes*, 7, 1–44.

Carley, K. M., and Lin, Z. (1997): "A theoretical study of organizational performance under information distortion," *Management Science*, 43, 1–22.

Cohen, M. D. (1991): "Individual learning and organizational routine: Emerging connections,"

Organization Science, 2, 135–39.

Cohen M. D., and Bacdayan P. (1994): "Organizational routines are stored as procedural memory – Evidence from a laboratory study," *Organization Science*, 5, 554–68.

Cohen, W. M., and Levinthal, D. A. (1989): "Innovation and learning: The two faces of R&D," *The Economic Journal*, 99, 569–96.

Cohen, W. M., and Levinthal, D. A. (1990): "Absorptive capacity: A new perspective on learning and innovation," *Administrative Science Quarterly*, 35, 128–52.

Comfort, L. K. (1985): "Action research: A model for organizational learning," *Journal of Policy Analysis and Management*, 5, 100–118.

Cook, S. D. N., and Yanow, D. (1993): "Culture and organizational learning," *Journal of Management Inquiry*, 2, 373–90.

Covington, C. R. (1985): "Development of organizational memory in presidential agencies," *Administration & Society*, 17, 171–96.

Cyert, R., and March, J. G. 1963): *A Behavioral Theory of the Firm*. Englewood Cliffs, NJ: Prentice-Hall.

Douglas, M. (1986): *How Institutions Think*. Syracuse, NY: Syracuse University Press.

Duncan, R., and Weiss, A. (1979): "Organizational learning: Implications for organizational design," *Research in Organizational Behavior*, 1, 75–123.

Edelman, L. B. (1990): "Legal environments and organizational governance: The expansion of due process in the American workplace," *American Journal of Sociology*, 95, 1401–40.

Epple, D., Argote, L., and Devadas, R. (1991): "Organizational learning curves: A method for investigating intra-plant transfer of knowledge acquired through learning by doing," *Organization Science*, 2, 58–70.

Fichman, M., and Levinthal, D. A. (1991): "Honeymoons and the liability of adolescence: A new perspective on duration dependence in social and organizational relationships," *Academy of Management Review*, 16, 442–68.

Fiol, C. M., and Lyles, M. A. (1985): "Organizational learning," *Academy of Management Review*, 10, 803–13.

Fulmer, R. M., Gibbs, P., and Keys, J. B. (1998): "The second generation learning organizations: New tools for sustaining competitive advantage," *Organizational Dynamics*, 27, 6–20.

Garvin, D. A. (1993): "Building a learning organization," *Harvard Business Review*, 74, 78–91.

Grant, R. M. (1996): "Toward a knowledge based theory of the firm," *Strategic Management Journal*, 17, (Winter Special Issue), 109–22.

Greve, H. R. (1998): "Performance, aspirations, and risky organizational change," *Administrative Science Quarterly*, 43, 58–86.

Greve, H. R. (2000): "Market niche entry decisions: Competition, learning, and strategy in Tokyo banking, 1894–1936," *Academy of Management Journal*, 43, 816–36.

Hannan, M. T., and Freeman J. (1984): "Structural inertia and organizational change," *American Sociological Review*, 49, 149–64.

Hansen, M. T. (1999): "The search–transfer problem: The role of weak ties in sharing knowledge across organization subunits," *Administrative Science Quarterly*, 44, 82–111.

Harrison, J. R., and March, J. G. (1984): "Decision making and postdecision surprises," *Administrative Science Quarterly*, 29, 26–42.

Heath C., Larrick R. P., and Klayman J. (1998): "Cognitive repairs: How organizational practices can compensate for individual shortcomings," *Research in Organizational Behavior*, 20, 1–37.

Hedlund, G., and Nonaka, I. (1993): "Models of knowledge management in the West and Japan," in P. Lorange, B. Chakravarthy, J. Roos and A. Van de Ven (eds), *Implementing Strategic Processes, Change, Learning and Co-operation*, Oxford: Basil Blackwell, 117–44.

Herriott, S. R., Levinthal, D., and March, J. G. (1985): "Learning from experience in organizations," *American Economic Review*, 75, 298–302.

Hey, J. D. (1981): "Are optimal search rules reasonable? And vice versa? (And does it matter anyway?)," *Journal of Economic Behavior and Organization*, 2, 47–70.

Hey, J. D. (1982): "Search for Rules for Search," *Journal of Economic Behavior and Organization*, 3, 65–81.

Huber, G. P. (1991): "Organizational learning: The contributing processes and the literatures," *Organization Science*, 2, 88–115.

Iwai, K. (1984): "Schumpeterian dynamics: An evolutionary model of innovation and imitation," *Journal of Economic Behavior and Organization*, 5, 159–90.

Jensen, R. (1988): "Information capacity and innovation adoption," *International Journal of Industrial Organization*, 6, 33550.

Kieser, A., and Koch, U. (2000): "Organizational Learning as Rule Construction," manuscript presented at the AoM Symposium on Organizational Rules – New Approaches to Bureaucracies and Organizational Learning, Academy of Management Meetings, Toronto.

Klimecki, R. G., and Lassleben, H. (1994): "Exploring the process of organizational learning: An empirical study using cognitive maps and network analysis," paper presented at the Second IFSAM Conference in Dallas, August 18.

Klimecki, R., and Lassleben, H. (1998): "Modes of organizational learning: Indications from an empirical study," *Management Learning*, 29, 405–30.

Kogut, B., and Zander, U.: (1992), "Knowledge of the firm, combinative capabilities, and the replication of technology," *Organization Science*, 3, 383–97.

Kreps, D.M. (1990): "Corporate culture and economic theory," in J. E. Alt and K. A. Shepsle (eds), *Perspectives on Positive Political Economy*, Cambridge: Cambridge University Press, 90–143.

Lane, P. J., and Lubatkin, M. (1998): "Relative absorptive capacity and interorganizational learning," *Strategic Management Journal*, 19, 461–77.

Lant, T. K. (1992): "Aspiration level adaptation: An empirical exploration," *Management Science*, 38, 623–44.

Lant, T., and Mezias, S. J. (1992): "An organizational learning model of convergence and reorientation," *Organization Science*, 3, 47–71.

Lant T. K., Milliken F. J., and Batra B. (1992): "The role of managerial learning and interpretation in strategic persistence and reorientation: An empirical exploration," *Strategic Management Journal*, 13, 585–608.

Lave, C. A., and March, J. G. (1975): *An Introduction to Models in the Social Science*. New York: Harper and Row.

Levinthal, D., and March, J. G. (1981): "A model of adaptive organizational search," *Journal of Economic Behavior and Organization*, 2, 307–33.

Levinthal, D. A., and March, J. G. (1993): "The myopia of learning," *Strategic Management Journal*, 14, 95–112.

Levitt, B., and March, J. G. (1988): "Organizational learning," *Annual Review of Sociology*, 14, 319–40.

Liang, D. W., Moreland, R., and Argote, L. (1995): "Group versus individual training and group performance: The mediating role of transactive memory," *Personality and Social Psychology Bulletin*, 21, 384–93.

Lieberman, M. B. (1987): "The learning curve, diffusion, and competitive strategy," *Strategic Management Journal*, 8, 441–52.

Lomi, A., Larsen, E. R., and Ginsberg, A. (1997): "Adaptive learning in organizations: A system dynamics-based exploration," *Journal of Management*, 23, 561–82.

Lounamaa, P. H., and March, J. G. (1987): "Adaptive coordination of a learning team," *Management Science*, 33, 107–23.

Luo, Y., and Peng, M. W. (1999): "Learning to compete in a transition economy: Experience, environment, and performance," *Journal of International Business Studies*, 30, 269–96.

March, J. G. (1988): "Variable risk preferences and adaptive aspirations," *Journal of Economic Behavior and Organization*, 9, 5–24.

March, J. G. (1991): "Exploration and exploitation in organizational learning," *Organization Science*, 2, 71–87.

March, J. G., and Olsen, J. P. (1975): "The uncertainty of the past. Organizational learning under ambiguity," *European Journal of Political Research*, 3, 147–71.

March, J. G., and Olsen, J. P. (1976): "Organizational learning and the ambiguity of the past," in J. G. March and J. P. Olsen (eds), *Ambiguity and Choice in Organizations*, Bergen: Unversitetsforlaget, 54–68.

March, J. G., and Shapira, Z. (1992): "Variable risk preferences and the focus of attention," *Psychological Review*, 99, 172–83.

March, J. G., and Simon, H. A. (1958): *Organizations*. New York: John Wiley.

March, J. G., Schulz, M., and Zhou, X. (2000): *The Dynamics of Rules: Change in Written Organizational Codes*. Stanford: Stanford University Press.

March, J. G., Sproull, L., and Tamuz, M. (1991): "Learning from samples of one or fewer," *Organization Science*, 2, 1–13.

Mezias, S. J. (1988): "Aspiration level effects: An empirical study," *Journal of Economic Behavior and Organization*, 10, 389-400.

Mezias S. J., and Glynn M. A. (1993): "The 3 faces of corporate renewal - Institution, revolution, and evolution," *Strategic Management Journal*, 14, 77–101.

Miner, A. S. (1987): "Idiosyncratic jobs in formalized organizations," *Administrative Science Quarterly*, 32, 327–51.

Miner, A. S. (1990): "Structural evolution through idiosyncratic jobs: The potential for unplanned learning," *Organization Science*, 1, 195–210.

Miner, A. S. (1991): "Organizational evolution and the social ecology of jobs," *American Sociological Review*, 56, 772–85.

Miner, A. S., and Mezias, S. J. (1996): "Ugly ducking no more: Past and futures of organizational learning research," *Organization Science*, 7, 88–99.

Moorman, C., and Miner, A. S. (1998): "The convergence of planning and execution: Improvisation in new product development," *Journal of Marketing*, 62, 1–20.

Nahapiet, J., and Ghoshal, S. (1998): "Social capital, intellectual capital, and the organizational advantage," *Academy of Management Review*, 23, 242–66.

Nelson, R. R. and Winter, S. G. (1982): *An Evolutionary Theory of Economic Change*. Cambridge: Belknap.

Nonaka, I. (1994): "A dynamic theory of organizational knowledge creation," *Organization Science*, 5, 14–37.

Pentland, B. T., and Reuter, H. H. (1994): "Organizational routines as grammars of action," *Administrative Science Quarterly*, 39, 484–511.

Pisano, G. P. (1994): "Knowledge, integration, and the locus of learning - An empirical analysis of process development," *Strategic Management Journal*, 15, (Winter Special Issue), 85–100.

Probst, G., and Buchel, B. (1997): *Organizational Learning: The Competitive Advantage of the Future*. New York: Prentice Hall.

Rulke, D. L., and Rau, D. (2000): "Investigating the encoding process of transactive memory development in group training," *Group & Organization Management*, 25, 373–96.

Rulke, D. L., Zaheer, S., and Anderson, M. H. (1998): "Transactive knowledge and performance," manuscript presented at the Academy of Management Annual Meeting in San Diego.

Sandelands, L. E., and Stablein, R. E. (1987): "The concept of organization mind," *Research in Organizational Behavior*, 5, 135–61.

Schulz, M. (1992): "A depletion of assets model of organizational learning," *Journal of Mathematical Sociology*, 17, 145–73.

Schulz, M. (1998a): "Limits to bureaucratic growth: The density dependence of organizational rule births," *Administrative Science Quarterly*, 43, 845–76.

Schulz, M. (1998b): "A model of organizational rule obsolescence," *Journal of Computational and*

Mathematical Organization Theory, 4, 241–66.

Schulz, M. (2000): "Pathways of relevance: Exploring inflows of knowledge into subunits of MNCs," working paper, Department of Management and Organization, University of Washington.

Schulz, M. (2001): "The uncertain relevance of newness: Organizational learning and knowledge flows," *Academy of Management Journal*, 44, forthcoming.

Schulz, M., and Beck, N. (2000): "Iron laws of bureaucracy – Comparing incremental and radical change of organizational rules in the U.S. and in Germany," working paper, Department of Management and Organization, University of Washington.

Schulz, M., and Jobe, L. A. (2001): "Codification and tacitness as knowledge management strategies: An empirical exploration," *Journal of High Technology Management Research*, 12, 139–65.

Senge, P. M. (1990): *The Fifth Discipline. The Art and Practice of The Learning Organization*. New York: Doubleday.

Shrivastava, P. (1983): "A typology of organizational learning systems," *Journal of Management Studies*, 20, 7–28.

Simon, H. A. (1955): "A behavioral model of rational choice," *Quarterly Journal of Economics*, 69, 99–118.

Simon, H. A. (1965): "The architecture of complexity," *General Systems Yearbook*, 10, 63–76.

Sitkin, S. B. (1992): "Learning through failure – The strategy of small losses," *Research in Organizational Behavior*, 14, 231–66.

Sitkin, S. B., and Bies, R. J. (1994): *The Legalistic Organization*. Thousand Oaks, CA: Sage.

Stata, R. (1989): "Organizational learning – The key to management innovation," *Sloan Management Review*, 30, 63–74.

Sutton, J. R., and Dobbin, F. (1996): "The two faces of governance: Responses to legal uncertainty in US firms, 1955–1985," *American Sociological Review*, 61, 794–811.

Szulanski, G. (1996): "Exploring internal stickiness: Impediments to the transfer of best practices within the firm," *Strategic Management Journal*, 17, (Winter Special Issue), 27–43.

Tushman, M. and Romanelli, E. (1985): "Organizational evolution: A metamorphosis model of convergence and reorientation," *Research in Organizational Behavior*, 7, 171–222.

Walsh, J. P., and Ungson, G. R. (1991): "Organizational memory," *Academy of Management Review*, 16, 57–91.

Wegner, D. M. (1987): "Transactive memory: A contemporary analysis of the group mind," in B. Mullen and G. R. Goethals (eds), *Theories of Group Behavior*, New York, Springer Verlag, 185–208.

Wegner, D. M. (1995): "A computer network of human transactive memory," *Social Cognition*, 13, 319–39.

Weick K. E. (1979): *The Social Psychology of Organizing*. Reading, Mass: Addison Wesley.

Weick, K. E. (1991): "The nontraditional quality of organizational learning," *Organization Science*, 2, 116–24.

Weick, K. E., and Roberts, K. H. (1993): "Collective mind in organizations: Heedful interrelating on flight decks," *Administrative Science Quarterly*, 38, 357–81.

West, G. P., III, and Meyer, G. D. (1997): "Communicated knowledge as a learning foundation," *International Journal of Organizational Analysis*, 5, 25–58.

Winter, S. G. (1987): "Knowledge and competence as strategic assets," in D. J. Teece (ed.), *The Competitive Challenge: Strategies for Industrial Innovation and Renewal*, Cambridge, MA: Ballinger, 159–84.

Zander, U., and Kogut, B. (1995): "Knowledge and the speed of the transfer and imitation of organizational capabilities: An empirical test, *Organization Science*, 6, 76–92.

Zhou, X. (1993): "The dynamics of organizational rules," *American Journal of Sociology*, 98, 1134–66.

Chapter Nineteen

Organizational Complexity and Computation

KATHLEEN M. EISENHARDT AND
MAHESH M. BHATIA

Significant theories of organization pose fundamental questions about the nature of organizations. Transaction cost theory, for example, asks, "Why do organizations exist?" (Coase, 1937; Williamson, 1975), while ecology queries, "Why are there so many kinds of organizations?" (Hannan and Freeman, 1977). Although complexity theory is among the newest organization theories, it nonetheless poses a fundamental question that is equally central: Why do some organizations adapt? In particular, complexity theory seeks to explain how organizations adapt, especially in high-velocity (i.e., ambiguous, fast-paced, and uncertain) environments (Brown and Eisenhardt, 1998). As such, the theory complements evolutionary theories of adaptation (Kauffman, 1993, McKelvey, 1999) and provides a particularly promising avenue for understanding the coevolutionary interplay of adaptation and selection among and within organizations (Lewin and Volberda, 1999).

Complexity theory is a part of a major paradigm shift within the scientific community from Newtonian models that dominated nineteenth- and twentieth-century science to newer, often biologically based models that deal with growth and emphasize unpredictability, nonlinearity, and loss of control. Complexity theory's intellectual roots can be partially traced to general systems theory (von Bertalanffy, 1968) and deterministic approaches such as chaos theory, catastrophe theory, and nonlinear dynamical systems (Epstein, 1997; Dooley and Van de Ven, 1999; Thiétart and Forgues, 1995). As significant, its roots are also in biology where evolutionary biologist, Stuart Kauffman (1993, 1995), has probably become the most influential contributor. Strikingly, however, insights have also come from a variety of scholarly disciplines, including chemistry (Prigogine and Stengers, 1984), computer science (Holland, 1975, 1995, 1999; Simon, 1996), physics (Gell-Mann, 1994; Bar-Yam, 1997), entomology (Gordon, 1999), organization theory (Carley and Svoboda, 1996; Boisot and Child, 1999, McKelvey, 1999), political science (Axelrod, 1981; Padgett, 1998), economics (Anderson et al., 1988; Arthur, 1989), and strategy (Levinthal, 1997; Brown and Eisenhardt, 1998; Macintosh and MacLean, 1999; Rivkin, 2000). The agenda of these researchers includes identifying how a wide variety of physical, biological, and social systems evolve and grow (Fontana and Ballati, 1999).

The term "complexity" refers to the complicated (i.e., orderly enough to have some stability, and yet adaptive, even surprising) behavior that emerges from complex adaptive systems, not to the complexity of the system itself (Gell-Mann, 1994). These behaviors are deemed "complex" because they are lengthy to describe. As Gell-Mann (1994) notes, "The complexity of a system can be described mathematically by the length of the schema needed to describe the properties of its data stream". The outcomes of more structured systems can be described briefly because they operate like well-behaved machines with predictable, well-ordered outcomes. The outcomes of less-structured systems can be simply described as well because they are random, a readily defined property in mathematics. In contrast, at the edge of chaos, the system-level behavior is an unpredictable mix of outcomes that are neither completely structured nor random.

The central argument of complexity theory is that when the agents constituting the system are partially connected, the system adapts. But, when those agents are over-connected, they become gridlocked and so the system cannot adapt (i.e., the so-called complexity catastrophe). Similarly, when the agents are under-connected, the system becomes too disorganized to adapt (i.e., the so-called error catastrophe). In contrast, the partial connection among the agents allows them to coevolve with one another and their environment. The result is the emergence of adaptive, sometimes surprising, and occasionally abrupt macro-level systemic behavior from the micro-level interactions among the agents. Thus, complexity theory focuses on the interdependence among agents within a system. That system is often described using the terminology of "NK" modeling, where "N" is the number of agents and "K" is the number of connections between them (Anderson, 1999; Kauffman, 1995). The counter-intuitive insight is that complex (i.e., surprising, ordered, adaptive, stable) behavior emerges from simply connected systems.

Complexity theory deals with a general class of problems that can be modeled as a system of multiple, unique, partially connected agents – i.e., complex adaptive system – seeking to adapt or grow. The interaction of these agents produces outcomes at the system level (Holland and Miller, 1991). Unique agents enhance the possibility of innovation over that likely when the agents are identical (Axelrod and Cohen, 1999). A greater number of agents increases opportunities for innovative combinations as well (Galunic and Eisenhardt, 2001). Multi-functional top management teams of strategic business units (SBUs) that are focused on adapting their organizations to changing markets can be modeled as complex adaptive systems. Jazz bands in which multiple musicians playing different instruments create adaptive music can as well. Corporations with multiple businesses and alliance networks among distinct firms are also illustrations. In the biological world, ant colonies, for example, exhibit distinct roles (e.g., workers, queens, etc.) and can also be modeled as complex adaptive systems (Gordon, 1999).

A central concept of complexity theory is the edge of chaos. In the context of biological evolution, Kauffman (1995) describes the edge of chaos as "the natural state between order and chaos, a grand compromise between structure and surprise". In the natural world, the edge of chaos is a transition point or zone such as the ecosystem around undersea heat vents. Very rich life forms and emergence of unusual, complicated physical outcomes characterize such transitions. In the organizational world, the edge of chaos is where apparently paradoxical behaviors such as innovation and efficiency, self- and collective-interest, and exploitation and exploration simultaneously exist (Brown and Eisenhardt, 1998; Anderson, 1999; Lewin and Volberda, 1999). Berliner (1994), for example, describes the jazz band as "thinking in motion and creating art at the edge of certainty and surprise." Lewin and Volberda (1999) observe that the edge of chaos is where organizations optimize the benefits of stability, while retaining the capacity to change.

Literature Summary, Review, and Evaluation

In this section, we review and evaluate the organizational research on complexity theory. Given that complexity theory is relatively new, we have included research in which the authors do not explicitly mention complexity theory, but do use a similar problem structure. We have also noted linkages to well-known topics in organization theory in order to highlight what is "old" and what is "new" about complexity theory. In the course of our review, we also touch upon several computational methods (e.g., NK, agent-based, and cellular automata models) that are particularly effective in examining complexity theory. Sorenson (this volume) provides an excellent overview of the concepts, advantages, and disadvantages of applying cellular automata and NK models in studying organizational phenomena. Given that complexity theory is inherently multi-level such that the interactions at one level of analysis produce outcomes at the next level, we include empirical studies in which either intraorganizational actions produce organizational outcomes or organizational interactions yield interorganizational outcomes. The section is organized around five fundamental concepts: loose coupling, edge of chaos, simple schemata, emergence of order, and recombination.

LOOSE COUPLING AND NK PHENOMENA

A fundamental argument in complexity theory is that partially connected systems of agents will adapt more effectively than ones that are highly coupled (high K relative to N) or highly decoupled (low K relative to N), an idea closely related to the notion of loosely coupled systems (Weick, 1976). Like complex adaptive systems, loosely coupled systems maintain the identity, uniqueness and separateness of constituent elements. Weick (1976) argues that such systems can potentially retain a greater number of possible recombinations, mutations, and novel solutions than would be the case with a tightly coupled system. Although tightly coupled systems may be more efficient, loosely coupled ones adapt more effectively to changing conditions. Further, loosely coupled systems have many independent sensing elements that "know" their environment better than tightly coupled systems that have fewer externally constrained and independent elements. Therefore, a loosely coupled system can "sense" when and where to change with greater skill than a tightly coupled system. There are several studies that have addressed this key proposition – some explicitly, others more implicitly (Table 19.1).

In one such study of adaptability among firms in the typesetter industry, Tripsas (1997) found that Mergenthaler Linotype, a firm founded in 1886 and still leading the market in 1990, had survived three revolutions of rapid, competence-destroying technological change. She partly attributes the firm's adaptability to its geographically distributed research sites, which appear to constitute a loosely coupled system of unique agents. Competition among these distinct research sites spurred innovation, and helped to overcome organizational inertia by allowing development of different technology generations. Multiple locations also provided a source of variation, enabling the firm to leverage differences in local environments. In contrast, less adaptive organizations had more tightly controlled and centralized research activities.

In a similar study of adaptation, Bradach (1997) found that partial connection among agents (in this study, restaurants in large US chains) led to superior adaptability. Moreover, the distribution of connections within the chain was not uniform. Clumps of tightly coupled company stores that were closely linked by standards and daily data exchange were inter-mixed with loosely coupled franchise stores. The loose connections of the franchise units to other parts of the chain permitted extensive experimentation with new ways of doing business. The closely coupled company stores provided a means to rapidly spread the most promising innovations throughout the chain as well as to foster efficient operations. Neither form alone would be as effective. As the author writes, "The processes of the plural form may enable organizations to escape their natural tendency to ossify over time by creating a built-in constructive tension between parts that keeps the organization receptive to new influences, yet in control" (Bradach, 1997, p. 301).

Chandler's (1962) study of strategy and structure provides a different lens on NK phenomena. In the face of rapid industry change, monolithic DuPont was broken up into a number of loosely coupled, modular business units that then enabled the firm to become more innovative and grow. At roughly the same time (i.e., from the 1920s to the early 1930s), Alfred Sloan conversely aggregated a set of previously decoupled carmakers in the formation of General Motors – a corporation that then went on to become the largest automotive company in the world. The point illustrated is that the managers at both DuPont and GM enabled adaptation by organizing their firms as complex adaptive systems, but from different directions (i.e., over-connected at DuPont, under-connected at GM). Ironically, however, both companies ossified over time (i.e., from the post-World War II era to the late 1980s), rather than continuing to evolve as systems on the edge of chaos.

Social network studies provide particularly useful insights into NK phenomena. Although such studies usually take the perspective of a focal actor, not the system as in complexity theory, they often carefully explore the interactions (i.e., strength, content, and number of ties) among agents that lead to the finding that loosely connected networks are most adaptive (Stearns and Mizruchi, 1986; Hansen, 1999; Rowley et al., 2000). For example, Uzzi's (1997) study of 23 firms in the garment industry is typical of such studies. Uzzi found that firms that had a mix of strong and weak ties with other firms (i.e., partially interconnected systems of firms) were flexible and responsive to changes in their environments. By contrast, firms with more ties had difficulty adapting to new situations because novelty was limited. Firms with fewer ties also adapted less well because of their inability to engage in rapid and informal coordination with partnering

Table 19.1 Selected empirical studies illustrating loose coupling and NK phenomena

Reference	Industry, research context, and method	Relevant findings
Tripsas (1997)	• Typesetter industry • Field based research supplemented with secondary and archival data	Geographically distributed, loosely connected research sites of a firm, induced sufficient variation to help it adapt to three competence-destroying technological changes.
Bradach (1997)	• Five large US restaurant chains • Qualitative field research	Loosely coupled franchise units permitted experimentation. Closely coupled company stores diffused innovations and fostered efficient operations. Partial connection among agents led to superior adaptability.
Uzzi (1997)	• 23 entrepreneurial garment firms • Qualitative and quantitative study of inter-firm relationships	Firms with a mix of strong and weak ties with other firms in their network enjoy adaptive flexibility. In a network of interconnected agents, the motivation of agents is neither completely selfish nor cooperative *ex-ante*, but is an emergent property of the social structure.
Saxenian (1994)	• Semiconductor memories, workstations and personal computers • Field research in the Silicon Valley and Boston's route 128 region	Open culture and interconnectedness of Silicon Valley firms helped them adapt. The stand-alone, closed and vertically integrated firms of Boston route-128 region could not adapt to changes in their business environment.
Levinthal (1997)	• NK model simulations	"K" is a powerful driver of adaptability in a system of interconnected agents. When there are extreme (high or low) values of "K" especially relative to "N", adaptation becomes much less efficient.

firms. As significant, Uzzi's work explored the nature of ties among firms, revealing the economies of time, integrative agreements, and Pareto improvements in allocatable efficiency of strong ties between firms.

Finally, Saxenian (1994) implicitly used an NK perspective to explain differences in regional adaptation. On the one hand, the partial interconnectedness (K) through open cultures and employee transfer among firms (N) in Silicon Valley (NK-system) helped that region to adapt to the Japanese attack on the semiconductor memory market in the 1980s. On the other hand, Boston's route-128 region (NK-system) failed to adapt effectively to the arrival of workstations and personal computers in the computer industry because the minicomputer makers (N) within the region consisted mainly of stand-alone (K), vertically integrated organizations.

Many of the real-world studies that we describe above examine agents in systems remaining adaptive within changing environments. Drawing from Wright (1931), Kauffman (1995) has pioneered the application of computational models in complexity theory research that reverse this perspective. These models allow a system described in terms of N (number of nodes) and K (number of interconnections) to evolve to a "fitness peak" on a "landscape" that is usually fixed (largely due to the analytic challenges of a continuously moving landscape). Various combinations of N and K are simulated to determine the emergent properties of the system (Carley, 1995; McKelvey, 1999; Rivkin, 2000). So, unlike real-world studies, these computational simulations fix the environment (or, occasionally permit an environmental "jolt"), and then let the system evolve to an optimal point. Yet, despite the difference in perspective, the implications for organizations are the same, namely that partially connected systems of agents adapt more effectively. Moreover, although these models lack close connection with real-world phenomena, they can be powerful in revealing multi-level and nonlinear effects, and in simulating systems with different patterns of connection among multiple agents. In particular, they have been effective in modeling the challenge of climbing to "high fitness peaks" on "rugged landscapes" (Rivkin, 2000).

Levinthal's (1997) study effectively illustrates many of these points. Using computer simulations, he varied the degree of interconnectedness (K) within organizations, and found a positive relationship between persistence of organizational form and interconnectedness. Further, when he introduced an environmental jolt, tightly coupled organizations were subject to higher failure rates. Those tightly coupled organizations that did succeed often relied on "long jumps" to launch successful major reorientations. By contrast, loosely coupled organizations adapted more readily to environmental change.

EDGE OF CHAOS

Complexity theory is not only consistent with loose coupling, but also extends it by proposing an edge of chaos between disorder and order. This contrasts with the dichotomy between tight vs. loose coupling (Weick, 1976) and between the earlier mechanistic vs. organic organization (Burns and Stalker, 1966; Lawrence and Lorsch, 1967). In the natural world, the edge of chaos is a transition point or zone, characterized by rich life forms and emergence of complicated phenomena. Examples include the tidal area between sea and land, the transition zone at 32°F between water and ice, the area around underwater heat vents, and the transition zone between the laminar flow of a placid stream and turbulent flow. In the organizational world, the edge of chaos is also a transition point where inherently paradoxical behaviors such as both innovation and execution, and exploration and exploitation coexist (Brown and Eisenhardt, 1998). Organizations at the edge of chaos create just enough structure to maintain basic order, but keep structural interdependencies at a minimum (Lewin and Volberda, 1999).

The edge of chaos is not a stable equilibrium, but rather a "far-from-equilibrium" state (Kauffman, 1995). Specifically, the edge of chaos is "dissipative," meaning that it takes energy to maintain (Prigogine and Stengers, 1984). In the physical world, when water comes out of a tap at a rate that is fast enough to create a swirling pattern, but not so fast as to have no pattern, the water forms a dissipative structure. It requires energy in the form of continued addition of water to maintain the swirl. In organizations, the edge of chaos is also dissipative in that it requires constant managerial attention to stay poised in simultaneously paradoxical states of order and disorder.

The edge of chaos is also characterized by frequent mistakes (Brown and Eisenhardt, 1998). These mistakes are so prevalent that improvjazz, a musical form of complex adaptive systems, has a name for them, "trainwrecks." A key organizational skill, therefore, is not mistake avoidance, but rather quick recovery while errors are still small. Dissipative structure and the related proclivity to err imply that complex adaptive systems are vulnerable not only to the usual selection pressures of the external environment, but also to the ease with which such systems fall away from the edge of chaos. The micro-economic interpretation of being poised at the edge of chaos is, therefore, pushing out the efficient frontier between innovation and efficiency to a more optimal point, but to a point that is also inherently unstable.

At the edge of chaos, the scale of change is distributed as an inverse power law (i.e., the scale of change is distributed as many small ones, a few mid-sized ones, and the occasional large one). Small changes in behavior at time t can be followed by small, medium or large changes in outcomes at time $t + 1$, rendering the outcome of the system unpredictable in terms of scale and direction of change (Morel and Ramanujam, 1999). The term, "self-organized criticality," is often used to describe systems poised in this state (Bak, 1996). A frequently mentioned example of self-organized criticality is a sand pile. Trickling sand onto the pile triggers avalanches with scale distributed as an inverse power law (Waldrop, 1992). Change according to an inverse power law distribution contrasts with a punctuated equilibrium distribution (Tushman and Anderson, 1986), where rare periods of massive change interrupt long stretches of stability within overly structured, inertial systems. Complexity theory, therefore, provides an alternative explanation to inertia for large-scale change (McKelvey, 1999).

At the organizational level of analysis, two empirical studies begin to describe what happens in organizations at the "edge" (Table 19.2). They indicate the rich interplay among actors as they balance paradoxical tensions such as between innovation and efficiency, and self- and collective-interest. One such study is Mintzberg and McHugh's (1985) longitudinal examination of the emergence of strategy at National Film Board (NFB) of Canada that covered almost four decades. The Film Board was organized as a loosely coupled "adhocracy" in which highly fragmented movie projects were linked within the corporation through simple rules around innovation. The NFB was highly paradoxical – achieving direction without being directed, relying on emergent strategies while being proactive, cycling between convergence and divergence, finding order in disorder. Peripheral movies were tolerated, even as there were pressures for focused

Table 19.2 Selected empirical studies illustrating the edge of chaos

Reference	Industry, research context, and method	Relevant findings
Mintzberg and McHugh (1985)	• National Film Board of Canada (NFBC) • Longitudinal case study of the emergence of strategy	Describes an organizational view of the edge of chaos. For four decades, NFBC balanced various organizational paradoxes, while responding to its environment and "doing its own thing". Staying at the edge of chaos without over- or under-managing was a crucial managerial challenge.
Brown and Eisenhardt (1997)	• Computer industry, 9 firms • Inductive multiple case study of multiple product development in nine SBUs across nine firms	High-performing SBUs had organizational semi-structures which helped them stay at the edge of chaos and helped their design teams to repeatedly innovate in a timely manner.

thematic directions in filmmaking. The organization paradoxically was responsive to the environment and yet "did its own thing" (Mintzberg and McHugh, 1985, p. 191). Actions could come from anywhere and spread throughout the organization. Staying at the edge of chaos without over- or under-managing the organization was a crucial managerial challenge. Indeed NFB very often veered off into chaos.

In a second study that illuminates the edge of chaos, Brown and Eisenhardt (1997) examined adaptation via multi-product innovation in nine computing businesses. They found that SBUs, which produced adaptive product flows, had organizational semi-structures (i.e. limited structure around responsibilities and priorities with extensive communication and design freedom) that provided the frame in which design teams could fluidly tradeoff between efficiency and innovation. In contrast, less adaptive organizations were either more tightly structured or less. But, tensions around maintaining just a few priorities, limited structure, and organized probes into the future revealed the difficulties involved in staying at the edge of chaos. One manager described this fragility as follows: "We do things on the fly . . . I'm not comfortable with the lack of structure but I hate to mess with what is working" (Brown and Eisenhardt, 1997, p. 28).

The edge of chaos is a fundamental concept in complexity theory. But, there are few empirical studies of the edge of chaos in organizations. Rather, the concept has often been vividly described in discussions of "the edge of certainty and surprise" (Berliner, 1994, p. 220) within jazz bands, product teams, Marine fire units, and basketball squads (Berliner, 1994; Hatch and Weick, 1998; Moorman and Miner, 1998; Weick, 1998). Further, we know of no studies of the inverse power law of change in an organizational context. Nonetheless, such studies will probably appear in the future and have a profound impact on understanding of adaptation and growth, complementing the dominant change paradigm of punctuated equilibrium.

SIMPLE SCHEMATA, COMPLEX BEHAVIOR

To this point, we have focused on the interconnections among agents. Now we turn to the agents themselves. Complexity theory assumes agents act locally in accordance with simple rules or more formally "schemata" that partially structure their behavior. Schemata are cognitive structures that determine what action the agent takes given its perception of the immediate environment.

Agents in a complex adaptive system can be guided either by the same schemata or unique ones (Anderson, 1999). Schemata may specify the boundary conditions of actions, priorities, timing, or "how to" rules within which agents act (Eisenhardt and Sull, 2001). The most effective rules are simple because they allow for agents to act in complicated (i.e., ordered, innovative, and yet surprising) ways without sinking into chaos (Eisenhardt and Martin, 2000; Sastry and Lee, 2000). The counterintuitive insight is, therefore, that a few simple rules, like loose coupling, generate the complicated (i.e., adaptive, stable, ordered, surprising) behavior that occurs at the edge of chaos.

Since each agent responds to its local context according to its schemata, there is no "lead" agent or central coordinator (Axelrod and Cohen, 1999). Yet, by following their schemata, the interactions of agents cause orderly patterns to emerge at the global or collective level (Maguire and McKelvey, 1999; Okhuysen and Eisenhardt, 2002). A well-known example of emergent patterns is the computer simulation of autonomous, bird-like agents or "boids" that interact in an on-screen environment with moving obstacles (Waldrop, 1992). The behavior of each boid is governed by three rules:

1 Maintain a minimum distance from the other boids.
2 Match the velocity of nearby boids.
3 Move to the center of mass of the boids.

The startling result is that, independent of starting position, boids always end up in a flock. That flock moves as a natural flock of birds would, fluidly flying around obstacles. They divide and reform when they reach an obstacle. If a boid runs into an obstacle, it recovers and catches up. This complex behavior emerges despite there being no leader and no rule that says, "form a flock."

Several studies that examine the interaction of agent schemata and their effects on emergent system behavior have been reported (Table 19.3). For example, Axelrod (1981) demonstrated the emergence of cooperative behavior in the context of simple rules in a very well known study. Using game theory techniques, he showed how cooperative behavior could emerge in a group of self-interested agents, without any central control, by starting with a cluster of individuals who rely on the rule of reciprocity (or the "tit-for-tat" rule) in their one-on-one interactions.

In a more complicated organizational example, Burgelman (1994) documented how Intel's simple rule to allocate scarce manufacturing capacity in plants, "maximize the margins-per-wafer-start" (Burgelman, 1994, p. 43), led to highly adaptive behavior at the organizational level. As margins for memory products declined and those for microprocessors increased, the independent actions at the manufacturing plants led to a shift of the entire company into microprocessors from memories, without being explicitly intended by the senior corporate executives.

Eisenhardt and Sull (2001) have described how simple rules among firms operating in high-velocity markets yield adaptive strategies to capture fleeting opportunities and create high growth. For example, Yahoo!'s successful alliancing strategy is largely unstructured, consisting of a small number of rules for managers (the agents in this case) wishing to form alliances: no exclusive deals, no deals longer than a year, and the basic service provided by the deal is always free. These rules set the boundary conditions within which Yahoo! managers have wide latitude for making a variety of alliance deals that constantly help them flexibly adapt their own businesses and collectively, grow the corporation.

The effects of simple rules on adaptation also appear at the interorganizational level. For example, Axelrod et al. (1995) examined standard setting for the Unix operating system. In this and similar industry contexts, the mating rule – "avoid cooperation with near rivals" – was indicated. From this simple rule, the authors showed that the individual cooperative decisions among agents (i.e. firms) generated a distinctive structure over time, with two groups formed around competing standards.

Kogut (2000) described the Toyota Production System, a system of relationships between Toyota and its key suppliers, using data from a study by Fruin and Nishiguchi (1993). Toyota's inter-supplier networks did not emerge out of conscious design, but rather from an emergent process guided by several simple rules including: Toyota should transfer relevant knowledge competencies to suppliers, and suppliers must prove, codify,

Table 19.3 Selected empirical studies illustrating simple schemata, complex behavior

Reference	Industry, research context, and method	Relevant findings
Axelrod (1981)	• Computer and experimental simulations	Cooperative behavior emerges among agents using a tit-for-tat rule to guide their interactions.
Burgelman (1994)	• Semiconductor industry • Longitudinal case studies at Intel Corporation	Intel's rule to maximize margins-per-wafer-start in allocating scarce manufacturing capacity led to its shifting into making microprocessors from memories, without it being explicitly intended by corporate managers.
Axelrod et al. (1995)	• Choices of nine computer companies to join one of two competing alliances • Economic modeling of Nash equilibrium outcomes	The simple rule of "avoid cooperation with near rivals" among industry competitors generated two groups around competing standards for the UNIX operating system.
Kogut (2000)	• Automobile industry • Draws on field research at Toyota by Fruin and Nishiguchi (1993)	Structure of organizational networks is an emergent outcome generated by rules that guide the cooperative decisions of firms in competitive markets. The emergence of Toyota's inter-supplier networks was guided by three simple rules, which, themselves, were emergent in nature.
Gulati and Gargiulo (1999)	• New materials, industrial automation and automotive products industries • Panel data on strategic alliances over a twenty-year period in a sample of 166 American, European and Japanese organizations	Interorganizational networks are macro-level phenomena emerging out of micro-level decisions of organizations seeking to access resources.
Lomi and Larsen (1996)	• Cellular automata simulation model with $n = 100$ and varying k	Global dynamics at the level of an organizational population emerge from the simple rules of local interaction among individual organizations.

and share their knowledge with other suppliers. While these rules themselves were emergent in nature, later intentional adherence to these rules suggested that Toyota executives gained an explicit understanding of the value of these rules in structuring an adaptive network of relationships within the Toyota family of companies.

This emergence of system-level structure from the interactions of agents is similar to the emergence of macro-behavior from micro-interactions, which has a long tradition within organization theory. Early scholars such as Barnard (1938) and Blau (1955) have recognized how organizational structures emerge from the repeated interactions of organizational members. Granovetter (1973) demonstrated how the nature of interactions such as the strength of interpersonal ties could explain a variety of macro-level phenomena like diffusion, social mobility, and political organization. Similarly, Giddens (1979) observed that the interaction among actors gives rise to an emergent structure which, in turn, affects subsequent interactions and sets up a recursive dynamic. Through generative rules and resources, the system is produced and re-produced by the interaction among agents that yields often unintended, system-level outcomes. Complexity theory extends this thinking with an explicit focus on the types of schemata and the mechanisms by which interactions among agents are structured.

Gulati and Gargiulo (1999) provide an illustration. They used longitudinal data on strategic alliances in a sample of American, European, and Japanese organizations in three industries over a twenty-year period to study the emergence of interorganizational networks. Their model portrays the social structure of interorganizational relations as a "macro" phenomenon emerging out of the "micro" decisions of an organization seeking to gain access to resources and trying to minimize the uncertainty associated with choosing alliance partners. Further, as the emergence of a network structure increases the information available to organizations, it also limits the effective range of potential partners that organizations are likely to consider.

In an elaborate computational simulation, Lomi and Larsen (1996) used a cellular automata model to simulate the interactions between organizations. They explored the link between the local micro-behavior of individual organizations and evolutionary patterns of organizational populations. By changing the rules surrounding the number of other organizations with which a focal organization interacted and the nature of that interaction, they demonstrated how the patterns within organizational populations emerged from the simple rules of local interaction among individual organizations. In particular, they found that rules at the organizational-level about the size of a neighborhood, defined as the number of competitors directly affecting and being affected by a focal organization, had a powerful effect on the adaptation patterns of organizational populations.

EMERGENCE OF COMPLEX ADAPTIVE SYSTEMS

Previously, we have described the complex adaptive behavior that emerges both from partially connected systems of agents and from agents operating with simple schemata. We now turn to how these complex adaptive systems emerge. Several studies demonstrate that, when agents interact extensively with one another, they will evolve into a complex adaptive system (Table 19.4). In other words, they will self-organize (Kauffman, 1995) into modular structures of agents with distinct roles.

Table 19.4 Selected empirical studies illustrating emergence of complex adaptive systems

Reference	Industry, research context, and method	Relevant findings
Brown and Eisenhardt (1998)	• 12 firms in the computing industry • Inductive multiple case study of adaptation and performance	With repeated interactions among heads of SBUs in a company, the SBUs took on a role structure that allowed them to compete in the market place as a team. This emergent order enabled managers to capture synergies from their multiple businesses. SBUs in firms with autocratic senior managers or with business heads who had few interactions did not self-organize.
Mowery et al. (1996)	• Patent data from 792 alliances in the CATI database • Trace the changes in the technological portfolio of firms as a result of alliances	Partners in many alliances took on increasingly unique roles that transformed the alliance into a complex adaptive system of partially connected, specialized partners.
Lorenzoni and Lipparini (1999)	• Italian packaging machine industry • Longitudinal analysis of three inter-firm alliance-networks • Qualitative research based on interviews and secondary sources	The firms in each network coevolved to a position of specialized technological competence, thus resembling a complex adaptive system, in which firms integrated knowledge more as they became less similar.

For example, Brown and Eisenhardt's (1998) study of adaptation and performance in 12 computing firms revealed some of the conditions under which self-organization occurred. The authors found that when business heads have repeated interactions, they take on a role structure that allows the group of businesses to compete in the market place as team. In the case of one company, one of its businesses became the golden goose, another became the scout for next products, and a third protected the low end of the product line from attack. As a result of this emergent order, the managers were able to capture the synergies from their multiple businesses. In contrast, businesses in firms with autocratic senior managers or with business heads who had few interactions did not self-organize.

There is also evidence from interorganizational studies of alliances that reveal the emergence of ordered roles among interacting alliance partners. Mowery et al. (1996) used patent data to trace the changes in the technological portfolio of firms as a result of alliances. Using data from 792 alliances, the authors found that the partners in a substantial subset of the alliances exhibited technological divergence. This result contrasted sharply with the anticipated technological convergence that would occur if alliances were geared toward knowledge acquisition. That is, the partners in many alliances took on increasingly unique roles that transformed the alliance into a complex adaptive system of partially connected, specialized partners.

A similar pattern of evolution of firms into increasingly specialized positions in a self-organizing system also appeared in a longitudinal analysis of three inter-firm alliance networks in the Italian packaging machine industry (Lorenzoni and Lipparini, 1999). These firms engaged in co-design and co-manufacturing processes, and exchanged goods on a daily basis. Between 1988 and 1995, the firms in each network coevolved to positions of specialized technological competence, thus resembling a complex adaptive system in which firms integrated knowledge more as they became less similar.

RECOMBINATION AND EVOLUTION

Each component of a complex adaptive system (i.e., agents, their schemata, and the number, nature and strength of connections among agents) can change over time (Anderson, 1999; Axelrod and Cohen, 1999). New agents, schemata, and connections can appear. Old ones can exit. Existing ones may evolve into new ones. Indeed, adaptation at the edge of chaos is a combination of path-dependence and path-creation. So, for example, new rules can evolve to guide the behavior of agents, while old ones die off. Agents can coevolve by reconnecting in fresh ways with one another to create new system-wide synergies (Lewin and Volberda, 1999; McKelvey, 1999; Eisenhardt and Galunic, 2000). In a process termed "patching" (Kauffman, 1995; Eisenhardt and Brown, 1999), agents can come into the system, exit, split into two agents, or combine with other agents. Recombinations of existing agents through patching or the coevolution of the connections among agents can provide a particularly rapid and lower risk adaptation path (Henderson and Clark, 1990; Ciborra, 1996; Levinthal and Warglien, 1999; Galunic and Eisenhardt, 2002).

The optimal amount of structure for effective evolution of complex adaptive systems varies with the dynamism of the environment. As velocity increases, the scale or "patch size" of agents (e.g., business units in a corporation) often becomes smaller as the need for agility comes to dominate efficiency (Kauffman, 1995). Also in such markets, the number of connections between agents frequently decreases as the need for independent, not collective, action becomes greater, while the number of schemata guiding agents becomes fewer (thus reducing constraints) as the need for innovation increases relative to efficiency. Despite these seemingly natural extensions of the theory, however, there are only a few empirical studies regarding this aspect of complexity theory (Table 19.5).

In two related studies, Galunic and Eisenhardt (1996, 2002) used a grounded theory building approach to study the adaptation of a multi-business corporation to changing product market conditions through patching. The authors characterized the organization as a complex adaptive system, termed a "dynamic community", with distinct strategic business units as its constituting agents. The authors found that this dynamic community could achieve significant adaptation by recombining businesses and their match with charters (i.e., product-market opportunities) as the environment changed. The large number of related businesses created organization-level adaptation, even though the businesses themselves (in this case, the agents) changed more slowly. As important, the authors noted that the patching process combined economic (i.e., most fit business unit wins) and social (i.e., business units that need help win) simple rules to guide managers.

At a higher level of analysis, Stark (1996) gives an account of the post-socialist Hungarian society that is suggestive of a complex adaptive system, with organizations within the society as the interconnected agents. He described the asset recombination strategy being used, which, despite countering the norms of Western capitalism (e.g. clearly defined property rights), appears to ensure adaptability at the societal level in the Hungarian context. Using enterprise-level data on the ownership structures of Hungary's 220 largest enterprises, the author demonstrated how ownership interconnections between publicly-owned and privately-owned organizations acted as an organizational hedging strategy in an uncertain institutional environment and permitted the recombination of assets as the environment changed. Thus, the author concluded that post-socialist societies face their greatest challenge not in finding the right mix of public and private, but in finding the right organization of that diversity (i.e., interconnections between public and private assets) such that recombinations that yield both adaptability and accountability can occur.

SUMMARY AND EVALUATION

The principle ideas of complexity theory are supported in a range of organizational studies. When brought together in close interaction, agents will often form complex adaptive systems (Mowery et al., 1996; Brown and Eisenhardt, 1998; Lorenzoni and Lipparini, 1999) in which the agents become distinct from one another through the course of interaction. In other words, they self-organize. Complex adaptive systems of partially interacting agents are more adaptive than either more tightly coupled or more loosely coupled ones (Saxenian, 1994; Bradach, 1997; Tripsas, 1997; Uzzi, 1997). In particular, at the transition zone of the edge of chaos, agents cope with paradoxical tensions that make such zones rich arenas for complex behavior to emerge (Mintzberg and McHugh, 1985; Brown and Eisenhardt, 1997). Simple rules governing the behavior

Table 19.5 Selected empirical studies illustrating recombination and evolution

Reference	Industry, research context, and method	Relevant findings
Galunic and Eisenhardt (1996, 2002)	• Electronics, computing, telecommunications industry • Inductive multiple case study of charter-change in ten business units within a large corporation	An organization with many related SBUs can adapt to changing markets by rematching SBUs with product-market domains or charters.
Stark (1996)	• Hungary's 220 largest enterprises • Qualitative enterprise-level field research and data on ownership structures	Asset recombination through interconnections between public and private firms may help societal adaptation in an uncertain institutional environment.

of agents yield emergent and complicated patterns of behavior that are adaptive over time (Axelrod, 1981; Burgelman, 1994; Axelrod et al., 1995; Koput and Powell, 2000; Sastry and Lee, 2000; Eisenhardt and Sull, 2001). Recently, studies in which complex adaptive systems evolve over time through the evolution of individual agents, the coevolution of the connections among the agents (Brown and Eisenhardt, 1998), and their recombination are beginning to appear (Stark, 1996; Galunic and Eisenhardt, 1996; 2002). Taken together, these studies support the central ideas of complexity theory and reveal the conditions under which systems are adaptive. They also indicate the value of triangulating computational models, case studies, and traditional deductive studies using data from organizations to produce a richer view of the theory.

Contemporary Issues and Debates

The most controversial issue to date in complexity theory is the meaning of the term, "complexity." Indeed, the inability of complexity researchers to resolve this issue has been a convenient point of attack for some of the theory's harshest critics (Horgan, 1995). As an example, Johnson (1997) describes how one scholar compiled a list of how scientists have used the word, "complexity." The good news is that there were only a few underlying dimensions to the different definitions of complexity. The bad news is that there were, nonetheless, about three-dozen different definitions.

The debate for students of organizations centers on two competing definitions that have more to do to with "where the complexity lies" than with the meaning of "being complex." Simon (1996), for example, defined a complex system as one made up of a large number of parts that have many interactions. Therefore, complexity is defined in terms of the number of connections and agents within the system. In contrast, Gell-Mann (1994) defined a complex system as one in which the length of the schema needed to describe the properties of its outcomes is long. In other words, complexity is defined in terms of the outcome of the system.

On the one hand, defining complexity in terms of a highly structured system suggests organizations with predictable outcomes. This view of complexity seems interesting in stable environments, where the traditional laws of organization that emphasize stability, predictability and linearity would apply, or in situations where systems reliability is paramount. On the other hand, defining complexity in terms of complex (i.e., surprising, innovative, effective) behavior suggests a simple organization. The latter view of complexity strikes us as suggestive of organizations that are more organic, counter-intuitive and relevant in dynamic environments, where adaptability, not reliability, is the key, and where mistakes are tolerated. So in our view, the competing definitions describe different types of systems that fit different contexts. Nonetheless, the debate continues.

A second debate centers on appropriate research methods. One position is that research on complexity theory must rely on mathematically proven or computationally justified facts (Morel and Ramanujam, 1999). Therefore, computational methods such as various kinds of simulation models, including genetic algorithms, cellular automata, agent-based modeling and related NK modeling, are uniquely appropriate. A related position is that research must take into account the multi-level and embedded nature, multidirectional causalities, path dependence, and nonlinearities inherent in complex adaptive systems (Lewin and Volberda, 1999). The implication is again drawn that research should take on a longitudinal and quantitative style. A third position (and the one that we hold) is that computational approaches are simply methods. They are not theories, and they are not necessarily uniquely applied to complexity theory. Rather, we take the view that significant theories of organization should be accessible from many methodological perspectives.

In exploring this debate, we can draw useful lessons from the literature on historical institutionalism wherein nonlinear and multi-directional phenomena of path dependence, critical junctures, and policy feedback loops have been widely studied using a variety of methods (Thelen, 1999). Multiple-case study methods can be particularly revealing and yet also rigorous (Campbell, 1975) for studying the linkages between micro-level interactions among individuals and the emergent macro-level behavior. The literature on self-organizing communities of practice in organizations is a good example of such methods (Brown and Duguid, 1991) as are several research studies described above (e.g. Mintzberg and McHugh, 1985; Tripsas, 1997).

Taken together, these observations suggest the appropriateness of a multi-method view. Clearly, computational methods allow more precise revelation of systemic properties and crucial nonlinearities within complex adaptive systems. Yet, rigorous case study research in actual organizations is likely to reveal the rich nuances underlying novel concepts like the edge of chaos or fitness landscape. More conventional, deductive studies with data from organizations provide a third lens that is more systematic than case research and more closely tied to organizations than computational methods. So, we think that multi-method research is appropriate. Nonetheless, it is also true that methodological advances can provide tools that enable researchers to accelerate the advancement of theory much as blockmodels (White et al., 1976) and event history analysis (Tuma and Hannan, 1984) did for social network and ecology theories, respectively. Similarly, methodological improvements, notably in computational modeling, have the potential to attract scholars and hasten the advancement of complexity theory.

Central Unanswered Questions

The most intriguing and unanswered question in complexity theory centers on the edge of chaos. Scholars agree that the edge of chaos is the state between order and disorder where optimal adaptation can occur. In fact, Kauffman's (1995) rather poetic definition of the edge of chaos as "a natural state between order and chaos, a grand compromise between structure and surprise" is commonly accepted. Further, the edge of chaos has interesting properties such as prevalence of errors, the existence of change distributed as an inverse power law, and the emergence of complicated, combinatorial behavior. Although these properties are not clearly conceptualized as is typical in early-stage theory, they are not deeply controversial either.

Rather, the debate centers on the stability of systems at the edge of chaos. Kauffman (1995), on the one hand, argues that systems naturally evolve to the edge of chaos. Brown and Eisenhardt (1998), on the other hand, describe the edge of chaos as a paradoxical state that involves simultaneous presence of opposing states. They argue that complex adaptive systems tend to fall away from the edge into either too much order or too much disorder.

One reason for the difference may be the choice of problems and contexts. Kauffman's

(1995) interest is in the emergence of order from a highly disordered state at the birth of the biological world. Perhaps as well, biological systems naturally survive at the edge of chaos. By contrast, Brown and Eisenhardt (1998) study established social systems in which organizations can be over- or under-structured. So the difference in views may be due to biological vs. social systems, emphasis on the birth of systems vs. their ongoing adaptability, or both. As of now, we do not see a clear resolution to this question and so it is an important direction for future research as noted below. It, however, may well be one of those constructs for which complexity theory plays out differently in particular domains. As Gell-Mann (1994) observes, a principal research challenge for complexity theory, broadly defined, is to sharpen its concepts and propositions for the particular physical, biological, or social context of interest.

Directions for Future Research

Since the edge of chaos is perhaps the most intriguing and debated concept within complexity theory (Macintosh and MacLean, 1999), one direction for future research explores the paradox inherent at the edge of chaos, and the related schemata that guide the interaction of agents at the "edge". How do people simultaneously hold innovation and efficiency as goals? What kinds of schemata are relevant? Another intriguing path is to explore mistakes. How do they happen? How do people recover from them? Does the scale of the mistake matter? The distribution of change at the edge of chaos is a third potential path. Is the scale of change distributed as an inverse power law or as punctuated equilibrium? In high-velocity environments, is an inverse power law distribution more adaptive than punctuated equilibrium?

A second direction of research is to link complexity theory more explicitly with social network and knowledge theories. For example, although there are differences in point of view (actor within the system vs. system) and emphasis on social processes (status and power vs. flexibility and adaptation) between social network and complexity theories, concepts such as structural holes and the strength of weak ties are closely related to the adaptability of systems at the edge of chaos. Considering the insights from social network studies on the nature of ties (Uzzi, 1997; Rowley et al., 2000;) and the effects of structural holes (Burt, 1992) on adaptation might lead to increased understanding of complex adaptive systems. Similarly, while complexity is a structural theory, knowledge is flowing through the connections among agents, suggesting a duality between the two theories (Eisenhardt and Santos, 2002). Indeed, a number of studies of knowledge describe how knowledge is effectively transferred along intraorganizational and interorganizational ties (Zander and Kogut, 1995; Szulanski, 1996; Lane and Lubatkin, 1998; Simonin, 1999). Greater understanding of how structural properties affect knowledge flows might benefit both perspectives (Okhuysen and Eisenhardt, 2002).

A third path is leadership. Complex adaptive systems are, in theory, leaderless. But, organizations are usually not. Indeed, a central distinction between biological and organizational models is that organizations involve people who can influence their systems in a conscious way. Therefore, leadership is one research direction in which organizational researchers can uniquely take the theory beyond its natural science origins into more precise specification for human social systems.

There is, of course, some understanding of leadership in complex adaptive systems.

For example, a key insight is that, since self-organizing processes depend upon the context within which they arise, leaders can indirectly affect the dynamics of the process by manipulating its context (Levinthal and Warglien, 1999). As an example, Eisenhardt and Galunic (2000) have discussed that when corporations act as complex adaptive systems of interconnected SBUs, corporate managers set the context for the creation of synergies while the managers of SBUs actually find them. Moreover, there is a venerable tradition in strategy research advocating the role of leaders to set the context, recognize emergent strategies, and intervene only on rare occasions, rather than develop deliberate strategies (Quinn, 1980; Mintzberg and McHugh, 1985).

Yet, while there is convergent thinking about leadership, there is also room for more clarity (Stacey, 1995). How does leadership operate when managers may be able to choose, plan, and control the next interventions, but cannot predict their long-term outcomes? What skills are involved in managing paradox at the edge of chaos? How do the various levels of hierarchy interact?

Connections Across Levels

In this chapter, we focus on complexity theory at the organizational level of analysis. Complexity theory is, however, inherently multi-level – i.e., the interactions of agents at one level of analysis produce outcomes at the next higher level. Therefore, our chapter bridges the others by including studies in which intraorganizational actions lead to organizational outcomes (Mintzberg and McHugh, 1985; Bradach, 1997; Tripsas, 1997) and organizational actions lead to interorganizational outcomes (Saxenian, 1994; Stark 1996).

Consistent with Carley's and Sorenson's intra- and interorganizational complexity and computation chapters in this volume, we observe complexity theory's central focus on the interdependence among agents within so-called "complex adaptive systems." Like the others, we also note the importance of nonlinearities, dynamics, and the links between complexity and social network approaches. We agree that the term "complexity" has too many meanings. Yet, there are also differences in our approaches. Some of these differences are to be expected given the different levels of analysis. For example, Sorenson's interorganizational chapter naturally includes greater emphasis on competitive strategy among firms within markets. By contrast, our chapter is more centered on the adaptation of individual organizations. Other differences, however, reflect cleavage in our points of view.

On the one hand, given our perspective that computation is more a method than a theory and our colleagues' outstanding efforts in covering this terrain, we say little about computation per se. Indeed, we are more concerned that an over-emphasis on computational techniques may retard the development of complexity theory. On the other hand, we say much more about the constructs and propositions of complexity theory, its basis in extant empirical research, and linkages with other organizational theories. In other words, we view complexity as a theory of organization, albeit a new and under-developed one. We are also willing to deal in metaphor, recognizing the importance of metaphors – from "nexus of contracts" to "garbage can" to "iron cage" – within organizational theory. Our approach is to try to advance complexity theory by beginning to ground the metaphor in rough constructs and propositions, which can be explored with a variety of multi-level research methods including computation (Klein and Kozlowski, 2000). Taken together, the collection of chapters gives readers a multi-faceted view of one of the frontiers of organization theory.

Conclusion

This chapter discusses complexity theory at the organizational level of analysis, and touches upon computational methods, an approach well suited to exploring complexity theory (Carley, 1995, Levinthal, 1997). We observe that complexity theory follows in the tradition of loose coupling (Weick, 1976, Mintzberg and McHugh, 1985), the emergence of macro-behavior from micro-level social interactions (Granovetter, 1973, Giddens, 1979), and well-known network phenomena such as structural holes (Burt, 1992) and the structure of social ties (Uzzi, 1997). It also relates to recent interest in modularity (Baldwin and Clark, 1999; Schilling, 2000) and knowledge-based thinking (Zander and Kogut, 1995).

Complexity theory also covers new ground. Constructs like the edge of chaos and agent schemata, and processes like self-organization and patching provide fresh organizational perspectives. The central insight of complexity theory that partially connected agents operating within simple rules drive complicated, adaptive behavior at the system level is fundamental to understanding organizations. Equally fundamental is the observation that the price of that adaptability is the loss of control, unpredictability, and the relentless demands for managerial attention within dissipative structures. From a managerial standpoint, complexity theory provides counter-intuitive advice: fewer ties can create more synergies, simple rules can produce complicated outcomes, and managing scale, not just focus, of organizational units is important.

Ultimately, the most significant value of complexity theory within organizational thinking is in providing an explanation of how organizations adapt and grow, especially in high-velocity environments where pace, ambiguity, and uncertainty reign. Thus, complexity theory fills a fundamental gap within the organization theory tool kit as a complementary change perspective to slower-paced evolutionary theory. Complexity theory is the theory of organization that treats change as routine. It is at the cutting-edge of science, broadly defined, where organizational theorists can contribute and not just borrow. As significant, it is extraordinarily relevant to the organization of firms engaged in highly dynamic environments where adaptation and growth are key organizational outcomes.

Acknowledgments

We appreciate the helpful comments of Joel Baum, Fabrizio Ferraro, Jeffrey Martin, Kelley Porter, and Filipe Santos.

References

Anderson, P. (1999): "Complexity theory and organization science," *Organization Science*, 10, 216–32.
Anderson, P. W., Arrow, K. J. and Pines, D. (1988): *The Economy as an Evolving Complex System.*

Redwood City, CA: Santa Fe Institute Studies in the Sciences of Complexity.

Arthur, W. B. (1989): "Positive Feedbacks in the Economy," *Scientific American*, 262, 92.

Axelrod, R. (1981): "The emergence of cooperation among egoists," *The American Political Science Review*, 75, 306–18.

Axelrod, R., and Cohen, M. D., (1999): *Harnessing Complexity: Organizational Implications of a Scientific Frontier*. New York, NY: The Free Press.

Axelrod, R., Mitchell, W., Thomas, R., Bennett, D. S., and Bruderer, E. (1995): "Coalition formation in standard-setting alliances," *Management Science*, 41, 1493–1508.

Bak, P. (1996): *How Nature Works: The Science of Self-Organized Criticality*. New York: Copernicus.

Baldwin, C., and Clark, K. (1999): *Design Rules: The Power of Modularity*. Cambridge, MA: MIT Press.

Barnard, C. I. (1938): *The Functions of the Executive*. Cambridge, MA: Harvard University Press.

Bar-Yam, Y. (1997): *Dynamics of Complex Systems*. Reading, MA: Addison-Wesley.

Berliner, P. F. (1994): *Thinking in Jazz: The Infinite Art of Improvisation*. Chicago, IL: University of Chicago.

Blau, P. M. (1955): *Dynamics of Bureaucracy*. Chicago, IL: University of Chicago Press, Ch. 7.

Boisot, M., and Child, J. (1999): "Organizations as adaptive systems in complex environments: The case of China," *Organization Science*, 10, 237–52.

Bradach, J. L. (1997): "Using the plural form in the management of restaurant chains," *Administrative Science Quarterly*, 42, 276–303.

Brown, J. S., and Duguid, P. (1991): "Organizational learning and communities of practice: Toward a unified view of working, learning and innovation," *Organization Science*, 2, 40–57.

Brown, S. L., and Eisenhardt, K. M. (1997): "The art of continuous change: Linking complexity theory and time-paced evolution in relentlessly shifting organizations," *Administrative Science Quarterly*, 42, 1–34.

Brown, S. L., and Eisenhardt, K. M (1998): *"Competing on the Edge: Strategy as Structured Chaos*. Boston, MA: Harvard Business School Press.

Burgelman, R. A. (1994): "Fading memories: A process theory of strategic business exit in dynamic environments," *Administrative Science Quarterly*, 39, 24–56.

Burns, T., and Stalker, G. M. (1966): *The Management of Innovation*. London: Tavistock.

Burt, R., (1992): *Structural Holes.*, Cambridge, MA: Harvard University Press.

Campbell, D. T. (1975): "'Degrees of freedom' and the case-study," *Comparative Political Studies*, 8, 178–93.

Carley, K. M. (1995): "Computational and mathematical organization theory: Perspective and directions," *Computational and Mathematical Organization Theory*, 1, 39–56.

Carley, K. M., and Svoboda, D. M. (1996): "Modeling organizational adaptation as a simulated annealing process," *Sociological Methods and Research*, 25, 138–68.

Chandler, A. D. (1962): *Strategy and Structure: Chapters in the History of the Industrial Enterprise*. Cambridge, MA: MIT Press.

Ciborra, C. U. (1996): "The platform organization: Recombining strategies, structures and surprises," *Organization Science*, 7, 103–18.

Coase, R. (1937): "The nature of the firm," *Economica*, 4, 386–405.

Dooley, K. J., and Van de Ven, A. (1999): "Explaining complex organizational dynamics," *Organization Science*, 10, 358–72.

Eisenhardt, K. M., and Brown, S. L. (1999): "Patching: Restitching business portfolios in dynamic markets," *Harvard Business Review*, 77, 72–82.

Eisenhardt, K. M. and Galunic, D. C. (2000): "Coevolving: At last, a way to make synergies work," *Harvard Business Review*, 78, 91–101.

Eisenhardt, K. M., and Martin, J. A. (2000): "Dynamic capabilities: What are they?" *Strategic Management Journal*, 21, 1105–21.

Eisenhardt, K. M., and.Santos, F. M. (2001): "Knowledge-based view: A new theory of strategy?"

in A. Pettigrew, H. Thomas and R. Whittington (eds), *Handbook of Strategy and Management*, Thousand Oaks CA: Sage Publications, (forthcoming).

Eisenhardt, K. M., and Sull, D. (2001): "Strategy as simple rules," *Harvard Business Review*, January, 3–12.

Epstein, J. M. (1997): *Nonlinear Dynamics, Mathematical Biology, and Social Sciences*. Reading, MA: Addison-Wesley.

Fontana, W., and Ballati, S. (1999): "Complexity," *Complexity*, 4, 14–16.

Fruin, M., and. Nishiguchi, T (1993): "Supplying the Toyota production system: Intercorporate organizational evolution and supplier subsystems," in B. Kogut (ed.), *Country Competitiveness: Technology and the Organizing of Work*, New York: Oxford University Press.

Galunic, D. C., and Eisenhardt, K. M. (1996): "The evolution of intracorporate domains: Divisional charter losses in high-technology, multidivisional corporations," *Organization Science*, 7, 255–82.

Galunic, D. C., and Eisenhardt, K. M. (2002): "Architectural innovation and modular corporate forms," *Academy of Management Journal, Special Issue on New and Evolving Organizational Forms*, forthcoming.

Gell-Mann, M. (1994): *The Quark and the Jaguar: Adventures in the Simple and the Complex*. New York: W. H. Freeman.

Giddens, A. (1979): *"Agency, Structure", Central Problems in Social Theory*. Cambridge, MA: Cambridge University Press.

Gordon, D. M. (1999): *Ants at Work: How an Insect Society is Organized*. New York, NY: The Free Press.

Granovetter, M. S. (1973): "The strength of weak ties," *American Journal of Sociology*, 78, 1360–80.

Gulati, R., and Gargiulo, M. (1999): "Where do interorganizational networks come from?" *American Journal of Sociology*, 104, 1439–93.

Hannan, M., and Freeman, J. (1977): "The population ecology of organizations," *American Journal of Sociology*, 82, 929–63.

Hansen, M. T. (1999): "The search-transfer problem: The role of weak ties in sharing knowledge across organizational subunits," *Administrative Science Quarterly*, 44, 82–111.

Hatch, M. J., and Weick, K. E. (1998): "Critical resistance to the jazz metaphor," *Organization Science*, 9, 600–04.

Henderson, R. M., and Clark, K. B. (1990): "Architectural innovation: The reconfiguration of existing product technologies and the failure of established firms," *Administrative Science Quarterly*, 35, 9–30.

Holland, J. H. (1975): *Adaptation in Natural and Artificial Systems: An Introductory Analysis with Applications to Biology, Control and Artificial Intelligence*. Ann Arbor: University of Michigan Press.

Holland, J. H. (1995): *Hidden Order: How Adaptation Builds Complexity*. Reading, MA: Addison-Wesley.

Holland, J. H. (1999): *Emergence: From Chaos to Order*. Reading, MA: Addison-Wesley.

Holland, J. H., and Miller, J. H. (1991): "Artificial adaptive agents in economic theory," *American Economic Review Papers and Proceedings*, 81, 365–70.

Horgan, J. (1995): "From complexity to perplexity," *Scientific American*, 272, 104.

Johnson, G. (1997): "Researchers on complexity ponder what it's all about," *New York Times*, May 6.

Kauffman, S. A. (1993): *The Origins of Order: Self Organization and Selection in Evolution*. New York: Oxford University Press.

Kauffman, S. A. (1995): *At Home in the Universe: The Search for Laws of Self-Organization and Complexity*. New York: Oxford University Press.

Klein, K. J., and Kozlowski, S. W. J. (2000): *Multilevel Theory, Research, and Methods in Organiza-*

tions: Foundations, Extensions, and New Directions. San Francisco: Jossey-Bass.

Kogut, B. (2000): "The network as knowledge: Generative rules and the emergence of structure," *Strategic Management Journal*, 21, 405–25.

Koput, K., and Powell, W. W. (2000): "Not your stepping stone: Collaboration and the dynamics of industry evolution in biotechnology," working paper.

Lane, P. J., and Lubatkin, M. (1998): "Relative absorptive capacity and interorganizational learning," *Strategic Management Journal*, 19, 461–77.

Lawrence, P. R., and Lorsch, J.W. (1967): *Organization and Environment: Managing Differentiation and Integration.* Boston, MA: Division of Research, Graduate School of Business Administration, Harvard University.

Levinthal, D. A. (1997): "Adaptation on rugged landscapes," *Management Science*, 43, 934–50.

Levinthal, D. A., and Warglien, M. (1999): "Landscape design: Designing for local action in complex worlds", *Organization Science*, 10, 342–57.

Lewin, A. Y., and Volberda, H. W. (1999): "Prolegomena on coevolution: A framework for research on strategy and new organizational forms," *Organization Science*, 10, 519–34.

Lomi, A., and Larsen, E. R. (1996): "Interacting locally and evolving globally: A computational approach to the dynamics of organizational populations," *Academy of Management Journal*, 39, 1287–321.

Lorenzoni, G., and Lipparini, A. (1999): "The leveraging of interfirm relationships as a distinctive organizational capability: A longitudinal study," *Strategic Management Journal*, 20, 317–38.

Macintosh, R., and MacLean, D. (1999): "Conditioned emergence: A dissipative structures approach to transformation," *Strategic Management Journal*, 20, 297–316.

McKelvey, B. (1999): "Avoiding complexity catastrophe in coevolutionary pockets: Strategies for rugged landscapes," *Organization Science*, 10, 294–321.

Maguire, S., and McKelvey, B. (1999): "Complexity and management: Moving from fad to firm foundations," *Emergence*, 1, 19–61.

Mintzberg, H., and McHugh, A. "(1985): Strategy formation in an adhocracy," *Administrative Science Quarterly*, 30, 160–97.

Moorman, C., and Miner, A. (1998): "Organizational improvisation and organizational memory," *Academy of Management Review*, 23, 698–723.

Morel, B., and Ramanujam, R. (1999): "Through the looking glass of complexity: The dynamics of organizations as adaptive and evolving systems," *Organization Science*, 10, 278–93.

Mowery, D. C., Oxley, J., and Silverman, B. (1996): "Strategic alliances and interfirm knowledge transfer," *Strategic Management Journal*, 17, 77–91.

Okhuysen, G.A., and Eisenhardt, K. M. (2002): "Integrating knowledge in groups: How simple formal interventions help", *Organization Science*, forthcoming.

Padgett, J. F. (1998): "Organizational genesis, identity and control: The transformation of banking in Renaissance Florence," working paper,

Prigogine, I., and Stengers, I. (1984): *Order Out of Chaos: Man's New Dialog With Nature.* New York: Bantam Books.

Quinn, J. B. (1980): *Strategies for Change: Logical Incrementalism.* Homewood, IL: Irwin.

Rivkin, J. W. (2000): "Imitation of complex strategies," *Management Science*, 46, 824–44.

Rowley, T., Behrens, D., and Krackhardt, D. (2000): "Redundant governance structures: An analysis of structural and relational embeddedness in the steel and semiconductor industries," *Strategic Management Journal*, 21, 369–86.

Sastry, A., and Lee, F. (2000): "Pairing stability with change: Rules, operations and structures in an enduring organization," working paper, University of Michigan, School of Business.

Saxenian, A. (1994): "Lessons from Silicon Valley," *Technology Review*, July, 42–51.

Schilling, M. A. (2000): "Towards a general modular systems theory and its application to interfirm product modularity," *The Academy of Management Review*, 25, 312–34.

Simon, H. A. (1996): *The Sciences of the Artificial.* Cambridge, MA: MIT Press.

Simonin, B.L. (1999): "Ambiguity and the process of knowledge transfer in strategic alliances," *Strategic Management Journal*, 20, 595–623.

Sorenson, O. (2001): "Interorganizational complexity and computation," in J. A. C. Baum (ed.), *The Blackwell Companion to Organizations*, Oxford, UK: Blackwells.

Stacey, R. D. (1995): "The science of complexity: An alternative perspective for strategic change processes," *Strategic Management Journal*, 16, 477–95.

Stark, D. (1996): "Recombinant property in East European capitalism", *American Journal of Sociology*, 101, 993–1027.

Stearns, L., and Mizruchi, M. (1986): "Broken-tie reconstitution and the functions of interorganization interlocks: A reexamination," *Administrative Science Quarterly*, 31, 522–39.

Szulanski, G. (1996): "Exploring internal stickiness: Impediments to the transfer of best practice within the firm," *Strategic Management Journal*, 17, 27–43.

Thelen, K. (1999): "Historical institutionalism in comparative politics," *Annual Review of Political Science*, 2, 369–404.

Thiétart, R. A., and Forgues, B. (1995): "Chaos theory and organization," *Organization Science*, 6, 19–31.

Tripsas, M. (1997): "Surviving radical technological change through dynamic capability: Evidence from the typesetter industry," *Industrial and Corporate Change*, 6, 341–77.

Tuma, N. B., and Hannan, M. T. (1984): *Social Dynamics: Models and Methods*. Orlando, USA: Academic Press.

Tushman, M. L., and Anderson, P. (1986): "Technological discontinuities and organizational environments," *Administrative Science Quarterly*, 31, 439–65.

Uzzi, B. (1997): "Social structure and competition in interfirm networks: The paradox of embeddedness," *Administrative Science Quarterly*, 42, 36–67.

von Bertalanffy, L. (1968): *General Systems Theory: Foundations, Development and Applications*. New York: G. Braziller.

Waldrop, M. M. (1992): *Complexity: The Emerging Science at the Edge of Order and Chaos*. New York: Simon and Schuster.

Weick, K. E. (1976): "Educational organizations as loosely coupled systems," *Administrative Science Quarterly*, 21, 1–19.

Weick, K. E. (1998): "Improvisation as a mindset for organizational analysis," *Organization Science*, 9, 543–55.

White, H. C., Boorman, S. A. and Breiger, R. L. (1976): "Social structure from multiple networks: Blockmodels of roles and positions," *American Journal of Sociology*, 81, 730–79.

Williamson, O. E. (1975): *Markets and Hierarchies: Analysis and Antitrust Implications*. New York: Free Press.

Wright, S. (1931): "Evolution in Mendelian populations," *Genetics*, 16, 97–159.

Zander, U., and Kogut, B. (1995): "Knowledge and the speed of the transfer and imitation of organizational capabilities: An empirical test," *Organizations Science*, 6, 76–92.

Chapter Twenty

Organizational Economics

BRIAN S. SILVERMAN

Organizational economics has thrived as a field of study for nearly three decades. Although Barney and Hesterly (1996) note exceptions, the field of organizational economics can generally be distinguished from other fields within organization theory by its assumption that managers attempt to maximize profits, its reliance on rationality (bounded or perfect), and its emphasis on competition as a discipliner of wayward organizations. As such, organizational economists tend to favor efficiency explanations for organization, believing that many non-efficiency issues highlighted by other organization theorists are likely to be resolved through the price mechanism (for example, see the discussion of resource dependence below).

Neoclassical economic theory highlights the profound ability of markets to efficiently allocate resources to production of desired goods, yet leaves a limited role for firms, which serve as "black box" production functions that frictionlessly convert a set of inputs into a set of outputs. It was left to Coase (1937) to ask the twin questions: If markets are so effective, then why do firms ever exist? And, if firms exist because they are in fact better than the market at allocating resources, then why is the economy not organized into a single huge firm? Coase's answer was that firms and markets differ in their ability to manage economic exchange, and that those activities for which firms provide less costly management will be organized within firms, and vice versa. Coase's work thus placed transaction costs at the center of the market-hierarchy choice. However, lacking a proposal for operationalizing transaction costs, his work was "frequently cited, but little used" for 35 years (Coase, 1972, p. 63).

In the early 1970s, a number of economic theorists returned to the comparative analysis of organizations and markets with renewed vigor. Among their efforts, Williamson's (1975) conception of transaction cost economics has become perhaps the most widely known.[1] Resting on the behavioral assumptions of bounded rationality and opportunism, transaction cost economics asserts that transactions will be organized within governance structures based on a set of observable characteristics correlated with transaction costs of organizing. In the mid-1980s a second wave of theorists, drawing on Penrose (1959), Schumpeter (1942), and Demsetz (1973), introduced the resource-based view of the firm, in which the firm is conceived as a bundle of idiosyncratic resources and capabilities. For these scholars, who invoke a particularly bounded form of rationality, organizations exist to combine productive resources in ways that markets cannot.[2]

Organizational Economics – Theory and Evidence

TRANSACTION COST ECONOMICS (TCE)

Building on Coase (1937), Commons (1934), Barnard (1938), and Hayek (1945), among others, and conceptualizing markets and firms as alternative structures for governing economic activity, transaction cost economics (TCE) proposes that economic actors "align transactions, which differ in their attributes, with governance structures, the costs and competencies of which differ, in a discriminating, mainly, transaction cost economizing, way" (Williamson, 1991, p. 270). Resting on the behavioral assumptions of bounded rationality and opportunism, transaction cost economics asserts that transactions will be located in governance structures based on their characteristics – chiefly uncertainty, frequency, asset-specificity (Williamson 1985) and appropriability (Teece, 1986).

Why bounded rationality and opportunism? If rationality were not bounded – that is, "intendedly rational, but limitedly so" (Simon, 1947, p. xxiv) – then economic actors could write complete contracts specifying appropriate responses to any potential event. Organization plays no role in a world in which complete contracting is possible. Similarly, in the absence of opportunism – defined as a propensity for self-interest seeking with guile, or, more colloquially, the propensity to take advantage of a situation for one's own benefit – actors could simply agree to "work things out" as future events unfold. Again, organization plays no role in a world in which all people can be relied upon to selflessly cooperate at all times.[3] Given bounded rationality and opportunism, however, economic exchange can be hazardous to one's health. Consequently, transacting parties seek governance forms that will cost-effectively mitigate potential problems in exchange. Hierarchical governance is typically more effective than markets at mitigating high levels of transactional hazard and at managing coordinated adaptation, but this comes at a cost of higher fixed setup costs and weaker incentives (Williamson, 1975).

TCE illuminates those characteristics of a transaction, defined as any actual or potential exchange across a technologically separable interface, that are likely to create exchange hazards. It also illuminates characteristics of governance structures that are likely to attenuate these hazards. Most important is the degree of specific investment required to support a transaction, termed "asset-specificity." An asset is specific to a particular transaction if its value in its next-best use (i.e., in a transaction with a different party) is less than its use in this transaction. The greater the difference between the value of an asset in its first-best and its next-best use, the more specific that asset is to the transaction (Klein et al., 1978; Williamson, 1979). If a transaction is supported by generic assets, then breakdown in exchange is not problematic; each party may seek out new exchange partners with no loss in value of its assets. However, if a transaction is supported by specific assets, then breakdown in exchange imposes a loss of value on the owner of the transaction-specific assets. More importantly, once a party to an exchange has made an investment in specific assets, its exchange partner may be tempted to renege on the exchange agreement to extract a better deal. Since the first party's assets are worth less in their next-best use, the party is willing to pay up to the difference in its first-best and next-best use to the second party. Specific assets arise in the form of physical asset specificity (e.g., a machine that is tailored to serve only one customer), human asset specificity, site specificity, dedicated assets, or temporal specificity (e.g., a need for timely response).

Consider an example based loosely on Joskow's (1985) study of coal mine contracts and an illustration from Barney (1997, ch. 10). Imagine a coalmine owner, *A*, whose riverside mine currently relies on barges to transport its coal. Suppose mine owner *A* and railroad *B* are negotiating a deal under which *B* will build a rail spur to *A*'s mine and then carry some specified portion of *A*'s coal at some specified price. Once *B* has built the rail spur, however, *A* has an incentive to reopen negotiations over price. Since the already-built rail spur has little value for *B* in any other transaction, *B* would be willing to take a lower price ex post than it agreed to ex ante. Thus, exchange between *A* and *B* is fraught with ex post hazard for *B*. This phenomenon, by which pre-investment bargaining conditions are transformed post-investment, is often termed the "fundamental transformation" (Williamson, 1985, pp. 61–3). Anticipating this, *B* will only agree to a deal that includes sufficient safeguards for its investment. In contrast, the contract between mine owner *A* and barge firm *C* is likely to be characterized by lower degree of hazard, since *C*'s assets can be relocated without as substantial a loss of value.

Increased environmental uncertainty surrounding a transaction is also predicted to increase the level of hazard, since such uncertainty increases the difficulty of ex ante contracting. Put differently, in a world devoid of uncertainty, even boundedly rational parties could anticipate perfectly how a transaction would evolve in the future. In such a world, railroad *B* and mine owner *A* could write cheaply and enforce easily a contract specifying price and quantity to be transported. However, uncertainty introduces the likelihood that unforeseen events will lead to (or provide a pretext for) contractual breakdown. Thus, increased uncertainty – when coupled with asset-specificity – leads to increased exchange hazards.

Appropriability, or the ability to appropriate returns from investments, is a relevant attribute of transactions, particularly transactions related to innovation (Teece, 1986; Oxley, 1997). The presence of a weak "appropriability regime" (Teece, 1986) increases the risk that proprietary technological knowledge will leak from one party to another during the course of an economic exchange. Finally, the frequency with which a transaction occurs is predicted to increase the likelihood of hierarchical governance, essentially due to scale economies of bureaucracy (e.g., the cost associated with setting up a personnel office can be amortized across many employment decisions). Of the transaction attributes discussed by Williamson (1975, 1985), frequency is perhaps the least frequently tested.

When exchange hazards are negligible – broadly, when assets supporting a transaction are generic – spot markets offer the lowest-cost form of governance. Market discipline provides strong incentives for effort, and parties incur few set-up costs for governing spot market transactions. Reliance on generic assets allows parties to adapt autonomously to subsequent environmental changes, and disputes arising between transacting parties can be nearly costlessly resolved by exiting the relationship. As the level of asset-specificity in a transaction increases, along with the attendant hazards, parties will prefer intermediate governance forms such as long-term contracts, franchises, and alliances. Although these entail higher bureaucratic costs and weaker incentives than spot markets, such forms provide additional safeguards (e.g., minimum volume purchase guarantees; extended property rights) that protect investment in specialized assets and that may encourage coordinated adaptation efforts. At high levels of hazard – when assets are extremely transaction-specific – the costs of markets and of intermediate forms exceed that of hierarchy. Although hierarchy further mutes incentives and incurs additional fixed set-up costs, these are outweighed by savings associated with managing the exchange. Within a hierarchy, disagreements can be resolved by authority rather than through legal recourse, providing sharper control over specific investments. These different governance arrangements are supported by different legal regimes, ranging from classical contract law for market governance to "forebearance" law for hierarchy (Masten, 1988; Williamson, 1991; Rubin, 1995).

Over the years, TCE has evolved in numerous respects. One of these relates to the development of appreciation for credible commitments in supporting exchange. In its original formulation, TCE highlighted the problem of bilateral dependence – that is, when both parties to a transaction are dependent on the other – as the most hazardous form of transaction (Williamson, 1975). Yet this raises a question: if I am as dependent on my exchange partner as she is on me, then what incentive do I have to upset our exchange relationship? In the coal mine-railroad example, it does not appear that the relationship would be less stable if the mine owner had no recourse to barge carriage. Research in the 1980s indicated that such bilateral dependence might actually be more stable than unilateral dependence, and that one way to support a market-based exchange relationship that requires specific investments by one party is to increase the level of specific investment made by the other party (Williamson, 1983). With both parties at risk of loss if the exchange relationship breaks down, the relationship may be stronger. A second area of development relates to the institutional environment. Although early TCE theory was generally silent about macro-level institutions, recent research has explicitly incorporated institutional features such as legal regimes and norms (Williamson, 1991).

EMPIRICAL RESEARCH

As recently as 1991, TCE was occasionally derided as a theory without empirical support (Simon 1991). Yet today there are more than 600 empirical studies whose results are consistent with transaction cost principles (Boerner and Macher, 2000). These encompass qualitative studies, small sample survey-based research, and large-scale econometric studies relying on secondary-source data. Table 20.1 summarizes the studies selected for review.

The transaction cost lens was used initially to examine make-or-buy phenomena, including backward integration in automobile components (Monteverde and Teece, 1982a) and aerospace system construction (Masten, 1984), forward integration into an in-house sales force (Anderson and Schmittlein, 1984), and product or geographic diversification (Teece, 1980; Hennart, 1982; Henisz, 2000). Elaborations on this framework have been applied to numerous arrangements other than the polar modes of market and hierarchy. These include the "lending" of idiosyncratic assets to exchange partners (Monteverde and Teece, 1982b), long-term contracts (Joskow, 1987), take-or-pay con-

Table 20.1 Transaction cost economics: Representative empirical studies

Reference	Key concepts	Key variables	Key predictions/findings	Key contribution	Method; sample
Classic make-or-buy					
Monteverde and Teece, 1982a	Make-or-buy decision is a function of asset-specificity.	DV: make-or-buy input IV: asset-specificity	Asset-specificity is positively associated with internal sourcing.	Pioneering study of vertical integration through TCE lens	Probit; 133 automobile component sourcing decisions by GM and Ford Used expert ratings to code asset-specificity
Masten, 1984	Make-or-buy decision is a function of asset-specificity and uncertainty.	DV: make-or-buy input IV: asset specificity; uncertainty (complexity)	Asset-specificity and uncertainty are positively associated with internal sourcing. The interaction between these further increases the likelihood of internal sourcing.	Pioneering study of vertical integration as function of both asset-specificity and uncertainty	Probit; 1,887 aircraft component sourcing decisions Used survey methods to code specificity and complexity variables
Contracting					
Joskow, 1987	Contract duration is a function of asset-specificity.	DV: contract duration IV: asset-specificity	Asset-specificity is positively associated with contract duration.	Pioneering study of relational contracting through TCE lens	OLS and MLE; 277 contracts between coal suppliers and electric plants
Alliances					
Pisano, 1990	Make-or-ally choice is a function of contractual hazards.	DV: make-or-ally for R&D IV: asset-specificity; appropriability	Asset-specificity and appropriability concerns are positively associated with in-house R&D.	Pioneering study of alliances through TCE lens	Probit; 92 biotechnology R&D projects undertaken by pharmaceutical firms
Oxley, 1997, 1999	Alliance structure is a function of appropriability hazards.	DV: degree of equity IV: appropriability hazard; strength of intellectual property rights	Appropriability concerns are positively associated with equity stakes in alliances	Pioneering study of appropriability effects on alliance structure.	Probit, ordered probit; 165 alliances undertaken by US firms; 727 international alliances

Reference	Key concepts	Key variables	Key predictions/findings	Key contribution	Method; sample
Other					
Spiller, 1985	Vertical mergers are rewarded for increasing efficiency, and not for increasing market power.	DV: abnormal stock market returns upon announce-ment of merger IV: asset-specificity; market power	Asset-specificity is positively associated with stock market gains from merger announcement; market power is not associated with gains.	Pioneering study of mergers through TCE lens; pioneering study to test conflicting hypotheses derived from competing theories of the firm	System of equations; studied 29 mergers in the US
Gatignon and Anderson, 1988	Mode of foreign direct investment is a function of asset-specificity.	DV: Degree of equity ownership IV: asset-specificity; uncertainty	Behavioral uncertainty (environmental uncertainty) is positively (negatively) related to degree of equity ownership. These effects are exacerbated in the presence of asset-specificity.	Pioneering study of mode choice of foreign direct investment	Multinomial logit; 1,267 foreign subsidiaries of US firms
Masten et al., 1991	Direct measurement of transaction costs	DV: cost of internal organization IV: asset specificity; uncertainty	Asset specificity and uncertainty reduce costs of internal organization, rather than increasing costs of market organization.	Pioneering study that measures directly transaction costs	2SLS; studied 74 components in naval shipbuilding. Used survey to obtain and code data.
Silverman et al., 1997	Proper transactional alignment should have measurable performance consequences.	DV: firm failure (exit) IV: misalignment in governance of 1) driver employ-ment relation; 2) capital structure	Firms whose key transactions are properly aligned will enjoy superior survival rates than firms whose key transactions are not properly aligned.	Pioneering study of link between governance and economic performance	Hazard rate models based on population of several thousand large motor carriers, 1977–89

Note: DV = dependent variable; IV = independent variable.

tract provisions (Masten and Crocker, 1985), franchising (Lafontaine, 1992), the exchange of offsetting specific investments (Heide and John, 1988), and alliances (Pisano, 1990; Oxley, 1997). TCE logic has also been extended to such traditionally non-economic phenomena as the internal organization of political bodies (Weingast and Marshall, 1988; Moe, 1990), relations among lobster fishermen (Acheson, 1985), and even the rise in popularity of engagement rings (Brinig, 1990).

Empirical studies typically identify the governance of a particular type of transaction, either within a single firm or across many firms, and measure those characteristics of a transaction that are hypothesized to affect the governance decision. Quantitative studies then typically use statistical techniques to test whether transaction characteristics are associated as predicted with governance choices.

Monteverde and Teece (1982a) is paradigmatic of many transaction cost studies in its identification of a single type of transaction, its use of survey data to collect otherwise elusive measures of asset-specificity, and its reliance on binary estimation models. Noting that US automobile manufacturers produced some components in-house and sourced other components externally, the authors hypothesize that an automaker's decision to make or buy a given component turned on the degree to which the production process for that component generated specialized know-how. They identify 133 automotive components with the help of executives at one auto assembler, and obtain from General Motors and Ford information on the extent to which each component was sourced or produced in-house. They next survey industry experts to obtain Likert scale response data on the degree to which each component required significant design engineering investment, and was specific to a particular manufacturer, make and model of vehicle. Finally, they estimate a probit regression of governance on component attributes and find that, as predicted, component engineering investment (interpreted as a measure of specialized know-how) and component specificity are positively associated with vertical integration of component production. In subsequent studies of the automobile industry, Walker and Weber (1984, 1987) use similar survey techniques to measure uncertainty in component volume demand and in a component's technological stability. They find that increased volume uncertainty is associated with vertical integration – but only when the competition to supply that component is "thin" (i.e., when asset-specificity is high).

An alternate empirical approach that obviates the need for survey data is to identify observable characteristics of transactions that permit an ex ante ordinal ranking of the transactions' asset-specificity. In a study of coal-burning power plants, Joskow (1985) divides plants into several different categories, one of which is "mine-mouth." In contrast to "typical" plants built to use coal from multiple mines, a mine-mouth plant is located directly next to a mine and is designed to burn coal of the quality found in that mine. Joskow deduces that mine-mouth plants are characterized by more asset-specificity than typical plants, and consequently that such plants and their coal sources are more likely to be vertically integrated than are typical plants and their coal sources. He finds evidence consistent with this prediction.

More recent empirical research has explored phenomena between markets and hierarchies, while also incorporating more explicitly institutional features. For example, Oxley (1999) explores the impact of alliance characteristics and institutional environment on the structure of alliances. Using the CATI database of alliance announcements (Hagedoorn and Schackenraad, 1994), Oxley codes the governance structure of each alliance (equity vs. non-equity) as well as alliance features that are presumed correlated with technology leakage concerns, such as alliance scope – commercialization only, design only, or design and commercialization. Using CATI's identification of alliance partners' nationality, she then employs published ratings of countries' intellectual property systems to measure the strength of the "appropriability regime" surrounding each alliance. Oxley finds that increased likelihood of technology leakage and weaker appropriability regimes are associated with reliance on the more hierarchical equity joint venture form.

Although TCE predicts that governance choice depends on attendant transaction costs, empirical research typically eschews direct measurement of such costs in favor of reduced form estimation. This reliance on reduced form estimation, which is common throughout strategy and organization research, occurs for two reasons.[4] Although some scholars have made bold attempts to measure transaction costs (Dyer, 1997), their measurement is extraordinarily difficult, particularly for contracting costs. As Masten et al. (1991, p. 3) note, "many hazards of exchange, such as inflexibility in response to changing circumstances ... are either implicit or latent to the transaction." Put differently, it is difficult to construct measures of expectations of costs – particularly for market exchanges where potential costs arise from events such as a supplier's attempt to renegotiate a contract. Estimation of comparative costs of governance is also hampered by standard selection problems: how can we obtain information on the cost of the governance mode not selected?

Building on the structural modeling boom in the late 1980s (Bresnahan, 1989), Masten et al. (1991) address these obstacles in a study of 74 transactions undertaken by a large naval shipbuilder. Through a survey, the authors obtain data similar to that of Monteverde and Teece (1982a), and further obtain data on the costs of internal organization – measured as the number of hours management spent planning, directing, and supervising a particular transaction (multiplied by the average hourly management wage rate) – for the 43 transactions performed in-house. They then estimate a two-stage model in which the second stage estimates the cost of organizing those in-house transactions, correcting for selection bias. Masten et al. thus estimate the costs of organizing transactions in-house, and, more importantly, the costs that would be incurred had these transactions mistakenly been organized through the market or had the market-based transactions mistakenly been organized in-house. The numbers are substantial: organization costs totaled roughly 14 percent of production costs, and reliance on the wrong governance mode would more than double organization costs on average.

TCE thus offers a framework involving comparative institutional analysis to infer which mode of organization – market, hierarchy, or hybrid – will best govern a given transaction and what contractual provisions are likely to support exchange. By considering the firm in terms of both production and organization technologies, TCE illuminates organizational issues in ways beyond the scope of neoclassical economics. By applying an efficiency criterion and a relatively sparse parameterization of human behavior, TCE generates a wide set of refutable predictions concerning organization form. Although these have been framed most frequently in the make-or-buy context, a wide range of economic, political, and social institutions have proven amenable to TCE reasoning. Further, the last two decades have witnessed the development of a substantial body of empirical evidence consistent with TCE predictions of organizational form.

Resource-based view of the firm (RBV)

Although the resource-based view offers an approach to understanding organization form, it initially arose in response to the prevailing structure-conduct-performance (SCP) theory of firm performance in economics (Bain, 1956; Caves and Porter, 1977) and strategic management (Porter, 1980). Adhering closely to neoclassical assumptions about firm homogeneity, SCP attributes most variation in firm performance to differences across industries or strategic groups. Yet scholars in the early 1980s voiced concern that such a view ignored important within-firm features. The early RBV emphasized how variation in firms' access to key factor inputs (Wernerfelt, 1984; Barney, 1986), and/or impediments to firms' ability to imitate one another (Rumelt, 1984) could lead to variation in firm performance within an industry, and to variation in the attractiveness of a particular industry for a particular firm. A firm's ability to succeed in a given product market is thus predicated on its access to necessary factor inputs or entrepreneurial insight – resources – relevant to that product market. For example, if resource X is crucial to success in product market Y, then a firm that owns X and competes in market Y will earn greater profits than its market Y rival that does not own X, all else equal. Further, market Y will represent a more attractive opportunity for a potential entrant that owns X than for one that does not (Rumelt, 1984; Wernerfelt, 1984).

This framework rests on the assumption that resource profiles vary persistently across firms (Dierickx and Cool, 1989; Barney, 1991, Peteraf, 1993). Although neoclassical economics assumes that most resource advantages erode over time, Lippman and Rumelt (1982) provide a formal model in which uncertain imitability discourages rivals from attempting to copy a firm's resource-based advantage. As Mahoney and Pandian (1992) relate in their overview of the resource-based literature, scholars have identified a wide range of "isolating mechanisms" (Rumelt, 1984) to explain persistence of resource heterogeneity.

A second branch of the resource-based view focuses on a firm's capabilities – its ability to combine inputs (Teece et al., 1997). This branch, which draws on routine-based evolutionary theory proposed by Nelson and Winter (1982), focuses almost exclusively on the role of knowledge – particularly tacit knowledge – in explaining firm behavior. In the 1990s, this competence-based branch has devoted most of its attention to explaining how knowledge affects organization structure, rather than how it affects variation in firm performance. As such, the competence-based branch positions itself in reaction to transaction cost economics far more than to the SCP model (Langlois and Foss, 1997).

The competence-based branch proposes that firms embody different capabilities and that firm boundaries are determined by the nature of what firms can do particularly well. Predicated on strong assumptions of bounded rationality and cognitive limitations, a firm that has unique strengths and weaknesses in its productive capability, is expected to internalize those activities that are complementary to its unique features. Given variability in productive capabilities, identity matters more in the competence-based branch than in transaction cost economics.

In the competence-based branch, bounded rationality not only precludes the writing of complete contracts, but also implies that tacit knowledge about production is likely to vary across economic actors; see also Williamson (1975, pp. 31–7). Further, bounded rationality prevents two actors from communicating their needs to each other, even if both are acting in good faith: "thus, members of one firm may quite literally not understand what another firm wants from them" (Langlois and Foss, 1997). In such a world, costs incurred in market exchange are not associated with opportunism, but with information processing problems attendant on communication and coordination (Gulati and Singh, 1998). As such, this view is related as much to the information processing view of Galbraith (1977) and to coordination costs (Thompson, 1967) as to concern over contractual hazards. Firms are assumed more efficient than markets at combining and diffusing key knowledge to the appropriate individuals. Rather than focusing on hazard-inducing transaction attributes such as asset specificity, the focus is thus on coordination-sensitive attributes of routines such as the degree of interdependence, the degree of tacit knowledge that must be circulated, and the consequent need for coordination under uncertainty (Conner, 1991).

Whereas the "canonical transaction" for TCE was explicitly vertical integration, the implicit canonical transaction for the early RBV was diversification. This prototypical transaction draws on Teece's (1982) discussion of multiproduct firms. The RBV has also devoted attention to interfirm collaboration, focusing in particular on predicting which firms are likely to select each other as alliance partners. In this view, generic absorptive capacity (Cohen and Levinthal, 1990) is less important than dyad-specific absorptive capacity (Dyer and Singh, 1998; Mowery et al., 1998); hence, a firm faces a distinct cost-benefit profile for each potential alliance partner. In addition, Kogut (1988) and Teece (1992) have focused on the ally-or-make-or-buy decision, proposing that alliances are undertaken when economic actors need to obtain rapid access to new resources or capabilities. Thus, alliances are used not in response to intermediate levels of asset specificity but in response to

1   the gap between existing capabilities and desired capabilities, and
2   the time frame over which this gap must be closed.

EMPIRICAL RESEARCH

A relatively young theoretical approach, the resource-based view has a briefer empirical history than does transaction cost economics. Although much empirical support comes from reinterpretation of studies predating the RBV (Gort, 1962; Rumelt, 1974), the theory boasts qualitative case studies, small sample survey-based research, and large-sample estimation relying on secondary-source data. Although initial theoretical work emphasized single-business issues, the locus of empirical resource-based research shifted rapidly to the issue of diversification, where it has had perhaps its most sustained impact. Table 20.2 summarizes the studies selected for review.

Like many resource-based studies of diversification, Montgomery and Hariharan (1991) rely on published data to support large-sample econometric tests. The authors use FTC Line of Business data, collected from large US firms between 1974 and 1977, to explore diversification choices. The FTC database records information on the industries (at 3- or 4-digit SIC level) in which each reporting firm operates as well as the firm's sales, R&D expenditures, advertising expenditures, and the like. The authors perform a logit estimation of the likelihood that firm j diversifies into industry k, finding that a firm is more

Table 20.2 Resource-based view: Representative empirical studies

Reference	Key concepts	Key predictions/findings	Key variables	Key contribution	Method/sample
Diversification					
Montgomery and Hariharan, 1991	Diversification is a function of a firm's resource profile.	Resource similarity is positively associated with entry.	DV: diversifying entry IV: resource similarity	Comprehensive study of diversification direction through RBV lens	Logit; 1,120 entry decisions by 350 large US firms
Performance					
Montgomery and Wernerfelt, 1988	Firm performance is a function of "appropriate" diversification.	The relatedness of a firm's diversification is positively associated with its value.	DV: Tobin's *q* IV: diversification relatedness	Comprehensive study of diversification-performance relationship through RBV lens	OLS; 126 large, publicly traded US firms
Rumelt, 1991	Within-industry variation in performance exceeds inter-industry variation.	Business unit effects account for at least as much variance in performance as do industry effects.	DV: business unit profitability IV: industry, firm, and business unit effects	Pioneering study of intra- vs. inter-industry performance differences	Variance components model; 2,810 business units operated by 463 large US corporations over a four-year period
Alliances					
Mowery et al., 1996	Alliance partner selection is a function of partner-specific technological overlap.	Technological overlap has an inverted-U relationship with partner selection.	DV: alliance partner choice IV: technological overlap	Early study of alliance partner selection in the RBV	OLS and logit; 160 alliance decisions; matched control sample
Capabilities					
Henderson and Cockburn, 1994	A firm's research productivity is a function of its technical competence.	A firm's commitment to a pro-pub policy is positively associated with its patenting output, as is R&D resource allocation by committee (as opposed to a "dictator").	DV: patents IV: "pro-pub" – importance of scientific publication to promotion; other research-friendly firm features	Pioneering operationalization of organizational competence	Poisson, negative binomial, non-linear least squares; 3,210 research program-year observations from 10 pharmaceutical firms over 30-year period

Reference	Key concepts	Key variables	Key predictions/findings	Key contribution	Method/sample
Joint RBV-TCE					
Argyres, 1996	Make-or-buy decision is a function of asset-specificity and differential firm capabilities.	DV: make-or-buy input IV: asset-specificity; productive capabilities	Asset-specificity is positively associated with internal sourcing; superior internal capabilities are positively associated with internal sourcing.	Pioneering case study integrating RBV and TCE	Case study of 13 transactions in large US electrical component firm
Poppo and Zenger, 1998	Distinguish between TCE and RBV by effect of asset specificity on costs of exchange • TCE: market performance degrades as asset specificity increases. • RBV: hierarchy performance improves as asset specificity increases.	DV: exchange performance IV: firm-specific assets; measurement difficulty; technological uncertainty; expertise	Asset-specificity is negatively associated (not associated) with performance of market-based transactions (internalized transactions); other IVs also demonstrate different effects on performance of market exchange than on hierarchy.	Pioneering study examining conflicting hypotheses of TCE and RBV	2SLS; 1,368 information systems transactions undertaken by 152 Fortune 500 firms Used survey responses to code performance
Silverman, 1999	Diversification is a function of a firm's resource profile and of contractual hazards.	DV: entry IV: resource similarity; contractual hazards	Resource similarity is positively associated, and appropriability is negatively associated, with entry.	Pioneering study integrating RBV and TCE in diversification; operationalization of technological resources	Logit; 2,416 entry decisions by 436 large US firms

Note: DV = dependent variable; IV = independent variable.

likely to diversify into an industry the more similar are the industry's R&D intensity (i.e., the ratio of R&D spending to sales), advertising intensity, and capital expenditure intensity to those of the firm. To the extent that these intensity measures proxy for technological, marketing, and project management resources, respectively, these results are consistent with the proposition that firms diversify in directions that enable them to exploit existing resources.

Related research has explored the effect of diversification on firm performance. Montgomery and Wernerfelt (1988) and Wernerfelt and Montgomery (1988) use secondary source data on public firms to estimate the relationship between the extent of a firm's diversification and its stock market value. The authors find that more "related" diversification – measured by proximity of the firm's businesses in the SIC system (Caves et al., 1980) – is associated with higher Tobin's q, which, as the ratio of a firm's market value to the replacement cost of its assets, is a conventional measure of a firm's expected future profits. Relatedly, using FTC categorizations of acquisitions as "related" or "unrelated," Singh and Montgomery (1987) find that stock market gains associated with acquisition announcements are higher for related than for unrelated acquisitions.

How well do the measures used in these studies proxy for resources? Intensity measures appear far removed from the actual resources they are intended to measure. Further, whereas theory proposes that a key resource is valuable in only a narrow range of applications, reliance on R&D intensity implies a high degree of fungibility of technological resources. Similarly, proximity of two industries in the SIC numbering system may not map sufficiently closely to similarity in terms of the resource profiles needed to compete successfully in those industries. Recent research has, however, begun to develop more fine-grained measures of resources, both through published data and through surveys. In a study of technology-driven diversification by large US firms, for example, Silverman (1999) links each firm's patent portfolio to specific industries in which its patents are likely to provide value, thus developing a measure of technological resources that is more industry-specific and less fungible than R&D intensity. He finds that addition of such resource measures significantly improves the explanatory power of models predicting the direction of corporate diversification. Patent-based measures of resources have also expanded the scope of alliance research, which indicates that the technological resource overlap of firms affects both the selection of alliance partners and the outcome of alliances (Mowery et al., 1996, 1998).

Combining survey and published data, Henderson and Cockburn (1994) explore the effect of R&D competence on the research productivity of ten pharmaceutical firms. Granted access to the archives of these firms, the authors are able to identify R&D inputs by research program (e.g., all of Merck's research projects related to hypertension) for up to 30 years. Separately, they identify patents awarded to these firms and match them to the relevant research program. Finally, they augment this with surveys at each firm that yield, among other items, Likert-scale responses to questions about organizational practices hypothesized to influence the development of research competence. Henderson and Cockburn use Poisson estimation to relate firms' patent productivity to measures of research competence, finding evidence of both firm-specific heterogeneity in research productivity and systematic competence-based effects on research productivity. Zander and Kogut (1995) have also employed survey data to characterize manufacturing knowledge or capabilities to explore how these characteristics affect the speed of intrafirm transfer and interfirm imitation.

Thus, the RBV offers an approach to infer which mode of organization will best govern a given resource. Perhaps because research in this area is unusually context-bound – there are few general rules regarding which resources will matter for a given firm or industry – the RBV still must address several basic questions to define its explanatory framework (Williamson, 1999), including: When is a resource crucial? Are more resources always better than less? It remains unclear how quickly this approach will mature, and whether it will ultimately serve as rival or complement to TCE. Nevertheless, the RBV continues to generate excitement among organizational economists and strategy scholars: four of the papers honored as "Best Paper" in *Strategic Management Journal* over the last eight years have been contributions to the resource-based view (Wernerfelt, 1984; Rumelt, 1991; Amit and Schoemaker, 1993; Peteraf, 1993).

Current Issues and Debates

OPPORTUNISM

A number of scholars have taken issue with TCE's emphasis on the opportunistic nature of human actors. On occasion this appears to stem from moral repugnance for the idea of opportunism as much as from concerns over the predictive power of the theory (Donaldson, 1990; Ghoshal and Moran, 1996).[5] However, resource-based critics have generally argued that opportunism is simply an unnecessary assumption for a theory of organization (Conner and Prahalad, 1996). Others have also proposed that "trust" may obviate concerns about opportunistic behavior (Ring and Van de Ven, 1992).

In response to the RBV's dismissal of opportunism, TCE adherents propose the following thought experiment: take a firm as described by the RBV, where people located in close proximity to each other have repeated contact and the expectation of continued repeated contact. Now, imagine that everything were to remain the same, with the exception that hierarchical governance is removed – that is, all of these people still interact as before, but their federation is governed by market agreements rather than by hierarchy (not unlike the "putting out" system common in the 1800s (Williamson, 1975)). Why in the absence of opportunism is this market arrangement any less capable than the firm (Foss, 1996)?[6]

This debate remains central to the broader conversation between TCE and RBV, and between TCE and organization theory at large. The debate will likely continue, in part because it is exceedingly difficult to disentangle opportunism, bounded rationality, and trust empirically (or theoretically); see Craswell (1993) and Williamson (1993a, b). For example, while RBV scholars argue that tacit knowledge encourages hierarchy due to coordination costs entirely independent of opportunism, TCE predicts that tacit knowledge will be positively associated with hierarchy due in part to concerns over opportunism. Unless the RBV lens can generate conflicting hypotheses, or researchers can find a way to measure directly variables such as opportunism, RBV faces the difficult task of challenging an established theory without compelling empirical evidence.

Firm heterogeneity and path dependence

The debate over heterogeneity and path dependence in a model of organization can be conceived as a debate between parsimony and operationalization on one side and realism on the other. Critics charge that, by assuming that firms generally have access to the same production functions, TCE assumes away differences in productive abilities that might shape firm boundaries (Langlois and Foss, 1997), leading to a focus on minimizing governance costs to the exclusion of increasing productive value (Rindfleisch and Heide, 1997). By throwing off such constraints, the RBV emphasizes the responsibility of economic actors to create and exploit specialized, rent-generating assets under conditions of uncertainty (Barney and Hesterly, 1996). In response, Williamson (1999) and others have noted that although RBV's embrace of heterogeneity along multiple dimensions may enhance its list of the factors affecting organization, this embrace in turn complicates the development of a rigorous operationalization of relevant resource attributes. Put differently, as long as everything is heterogeneous, the RBV is vulnerable to charges of tautology similar to those that afflicted TCE before the 1970s.

"You're both wrong!" – Sociological critiques

Sociology-based organization theorists often criticize organizational economics for underemphasizing the impact of social processes on the nature of economic activity (Perrow, 1981). Three criticisms stand out. First, resource dependence adherents argue that the predictions of TCE and RBV are strikingly similar to those arising from resource dependence – specifically, that firms integrate to "manage" their dependence on their environment – and that integration in the presence of "key resources" is driven in fact by power relations rather than efficiency (Pfeffer and Salancik, 1978). Second, social network scholars argue that the atomistic, calculative approach embodied in organizational economics ignores the fact that transactions are embedded in a rich social context (Granovetter, 1985). Consequently, organizational economists ignore key attributes of transactions such as social relations between transactors. More generally, TCE's emphasis on dyadic ties lead it to underemphasize the contextual effect that an actor's social network may have on governance (Podolny, 1994; Uzzi, 1997), and on the range of transaction opportunities facing that actor (Burt, 1992). Third, institutional theorists argue that organizational economists should consider norms and other institutional pressures in addition to formal legal regimes (Oliver, 1997; Roberts and Greenwood, 1997).

Is organizational economics just wrong-minded resource dependence? I suggest not, for three reasons. First, resource dependence assumes a peculiarly myopic view of economic behavior (Williamson, 1985). Actors muddle along without much forethought, suddenly find themselves dependent on an outside party, and only then rush to "manage" this relationship. In contrast, organizational economists assume that economic actors at least try to anticipate future developments. This suggests an empirical test to distinguish between the two theories: look at the evolution of exchange relationships over a period of time. Second, organizational economics offers far sharper predictions than does resource dependence. For example, Pfeffer and Salancik (1978) note the "power" that General Motors has over its suppliers, and credit this power with GM's ability to dictate terms to its suppliers. Although likely, this offers no insight into why GM chooses to make some components and purchase others. In contrast, TCE offers a discriminating and empirically supported prediction of this decision. Third, for organizational economists, the notion that GM has power relative to its suppliers does not negate an efficiency explanation of organization. Assume that GM does dictate terms to its supplier. Presumably GM offers a price that enables the supplier to barely break even, thus taking all profits for itself. Given that GM is going to gain all of the profits, what governance structure will GM want to impose? Presumably, GM will want to impose that structure that will maximize profits. Which structure will maximize profits? The most efficient structure will do so, by definition. More generally, organizational economists frequently see power relations playing out in prices, and so having limited impact on organization form.

Regarding the "embeddedness" argument, some RBV scholars explicitly incorporate social context into their work. Kogut and Zander (1992, 1996) invoke the social nature of a firm as the basis of its coordination advantages vs. the market. TCE research has not embraced social structure arguments as warmly. To a TCE adherent, a social tie looks suspiciously similar to a hostage or credible commitment: it involves a relationship-specific investment that is of no value should the relationship terminate. One exception that points toward benefits of incorporating social structure is Jones et al. (1997), who attempt a synthesis between TCE and embeddedness, proposing that in some circumstances embeddedness may safeguard against opportunism by diffusing information about reputations and by facilitating collective sanctions.

At the same time, organizational economists' insight may inform social network theory. For example, although network theorists have prescribed that firms should attempt to develop ties with high-status organizations (Stuart et al., 1999), organizational economics raises concerns about the price of such ties. Suppose that biotech firm A can ally with pharmaceutical firm B or C, which are identical except that B is of higher status than C. Firm A would prefer to ally with B in order to obtain status conferral benefits. But presumably B, being cognizant of its status advantage, will charge A a higher alliance price than will C (this could be a cash transfer, more favorable contractual terms regarding future drug products, etc.). In fact, if the price premium charged by B doesn't exactly equal the incremental benefit A gets from allying with B rather than with C, then B is leaving money on the table. Hence, if we take into account the different costs to biotech firm A of allying with each potential partner, A should be indifferent between the two allies. Generally, to the extent that network position is something that firms invest in and exploit (Podolny and Phillips, 1996), the logic of organizational economics should be able to inform network research as much as network research will inform organizational economics.

Finally, with respect to institutional theory, several organizational economics studies incorporate the role of norms. Ellickson's (1989) study of whaling and Acheson's (1985) study of lobstering both ascribe transaction cost efficiency properties to norms developed over time in these communities. Argyres and Liebeskind (1998) argue that biotechnology startups arose to take advantage of institutional norms that constrained universities' ability to delineate property rights over academic biotechnology research. In turn, it is likely that an efficiency approach to institutions offers powerful insights that can inform institutional theory. For example, although institutional theorists often imply that state-enforced institutions dominate private institutions (Ingram and Clay, 2000), some TCE studies indicate that efficiency seeking may be so powerful as to encourage private norms that overwhelm inefficient state institutions. Palay (1985) highlights the use of informal efficiency-enhancing "contracts" between railroads and shippers even though these rules, which explicitly violated the mandate of the Interstate Commerce Commission, could not be legally enforced. In sum, it is clear that further integration of background institutions (Davis and North, 1971; Meyer and Rowan, 1977, North, 1990) and transaction-level governance – with particular emphasis on ways that firms organize to influence background institutions (de Figueiredo and Tiller, 2001) – is a fruitful area for further research.

Future Avenues for Research

INTEGRATION OF TCE AND RBV

Although adherents of TCE and RBV each offer criticisms of the other, they also note strong complementarities between the two lenses. Adherents of both approaches (Langlois and Foss, 1997; Williamson, 1999) propose that joint application of the approaches may provide a more comprehensive analysis of organizations. Thus, where the RBV identifies which assets or activities ought to be combined to generate rents, TCE can provide insight as to how this combination should be governed (Chi, 1994). Silverman (1999), for example, studies the effect of firms' *ex ante* technological resource base and of contracting hazards on diversification. He finds that although a firm is more likely to diversify into an industry the more applicable its *ex ante* technological resource base is to that industry, the presence of feasible technology licensing markets in an industry reduces the likelihood of diversifying entry. This suggests that there are circumstances in which firms exploit their technological resources through contractual means, which in turn offers one way in which TCE and RBV can be intertwined.

Analogously, where TCE acknowledges that variation in firms' production technologies may affect governance choice, the RBV may provide direction as to when and where such variation is likely to arise. Argyres's (1996) study of several vertical integration decisions in a Fortune 500 company demonstrates how such variation, in conjunction with transaction cost concerns, affects governance decisions. To the extent that the RBV points out which assets should be joined to create value, and TCE points out how these assets should best be governed, a joint TCE-RBV approach may enrich strategic management as well as organization theory. Recent efforts to combine TCE, RBV and strategic management (Nickerson, 1997; Ghosh and John, 1999; Nickerson et al., 2001) provide first steps in this ambitious agenda.

Finally, recent attempts to incorporate history into governance choice may facilitate integration of TCE and RBV. In response to criticisms that TCE has not adequately incorporated history into current governance decisions, several researchers have begun to explore ways of relaxing the standard TCE assumption that each transaction should be analyzed in isolation. If interdependence across transactions is allowed, then governance of a focal transaction can depend on investments that support other, related transactions and on prior governance decisions. Argyres and Liebeskind (1999) propose the concept of "governance inseparability," according to which an actor's governance choice for a new transaction is shaped by unanticipated consequences of its past governance choices. For example, a firm that accepts collective bargaining for one group of employees may find that its decisions regarding scope of activities or subsequent relations with other employees are constrained. Relatedly, Nickerson (1997) and Nickerson and Silverman (1998, 1999) propose the concept of "transaction interdependence," in which investments made to support one transaction can introduce hazards for other transactions as well; see also Bercovitz (2000). For example, an investment in firm-specific reputation to support a motor carrier-customer transaction can be tarnished by poor driver (supplier) performance, and thus introduces a hazard into the carrier-driver transaction that leads to the use of company drivers rather than owner-operators.

Each of these ideas requires operational refinement. As Argyres and Liebeskind acknowledge, the fact that a firm's actions are constrained at time $t + 1$ due to commitments made at t may demonstrate the proper functioning of TCE, whereby an actor constrains his actions in $t + 1$ to ensure that a desired action goes through in t. Thus, it can be difficult to distinguish empirically whether ex post constraints are due to farsighted contracting or to unanticipated shocks. As for transaction interdependence, unless precise conditions under which interdependence matters are spelled out, then any governance form can be "explained" by simply expanding the range of allegedly related transactions until finding one that accounts for the observed governance arrangement. Recognition of relations among transactions may nevertheless allow TCE to incorporate a stronger dose of historicity and path dependence. And, because resources might fruitfully be operationalized as "clusters" of transactions (Williamson 1999), approaches that consider multiple transactions through some form of interdependence or inseparability may facilitate the integration of TCE and RBV.

PERFORMANCE CONSEQUENCES OF TCE AND RBV: STRATEGY, ORGANIZATION STRUCTURE, AND PERFORMANCE

What happens to an economic actor whose transactions are not aligned with appropriate governance structures? TCE presumes that such an actor will suffer adverse performance consequences. Actors whose transactions are misaligned are presumed more likely to display poor financial performance and to fail (or adapt) than those whose transactions are properly aligned. TCE research has been generally silent on the issue of performance consequences.[7] Indeed, some contend that the lack of research on the performance-alignment relationship is a weakness of TCE (Gulati, 1998; Winter, 1990). Thus a useful future direction for TCE research is to explore the performance effects of misalignment: Does misalignment in fact harm performance? Under what conditions? Do misaligned firms attempt to change governance structures so as to reduce this misalignment?

Studying performance effects of organizations' decisions is quite difficult for economists (Masten, 1993). Since economic actors are presumed to behave as boundedly rational profit maximizers, it follows that each firm makes optimal governance decisions, conditional on its own idiosyncrasies. Given this presumption, what should a researcher conclude when she sees that (a) firms whose transactions have similar attributes vary in their governance decisions and (b) firms whose governance choices vary from those prescribed by TCE also have lower performance? Absent other information, she must conclude that for those firms that are "misaligned," being misaligned is optimal due to some unobserved firm or transaction characteristics (which may also affect performance). Anything else would be hubris.

One way to overcome this is to correct for selection bias via Masten et al.'s (1991) structural modeling approach. An alternate method is to conduct quasi-experiments on firms that undergo an environmental "shock." Silverman et al. (1997) and Nickerson and Silverman (2000) take advantage of the 1980 deregulation of US interstate trucking to study performance effects of misalignment among motor carriers. They find that misaligned carriers incur lower profitability and higher failure rates than their appropriately aligned rivals. They further find that misaligned carriers attempt to realign their transactions, but that such adaptation occurs slowly and is subject to adjustment costs.

Relatedly, a great deal of empirical resource-based research has studied performance effects of resource heterogeneity, in particular performance effects associated with different types of diversification. However, much of this research has ignored the unobserved heterogeneity issue noted above. (See also Shaver's (1998) critique of the foreign direct investment literature.) Future RBV research would benefit from more careful consideration of unobserved heterogeneity. Effort devoted to surmounting these issues is well spent; investigating how firm strategy and organization form interact to affect firm performance presents one of the most exciting frontiers of research in strategy and organization theory today.

ORGANIZATIONAL ECONOMICS AND SOCIOLOGY-BASED ORGANIZATION THEORY

Organizational economics will likely progress through greater consideration of social and political features and processes. Organizational economists are likely to incorporate these features as "shift parameters" (Williamson, 1991; Oxley, 1999) that operate in the background of economic action, changing governance choices on the margins but not substantively altering the basic logic of organizational economics. For other organization theorists interested in this area, research that can demonstrate where, how, and under what circumstances such features actually alter this logic would make a substantial contribution to organizational economics.

As noted above, however, insights from organizational economics may also be fruitfully extended to other branches of organization theory: An efficiency lens and an appreciation of prices can enhance research on perspectives including social networks, institutions, and power and dependence.

Connections Across Levels

Van Witteloostuijn (this volume) notes that interorganizational economics emphasizes the strategic motivations of firms. Insights from interorganizational economics may prove particularly fruitful for introducing firms' strategic motivations to organizational economics, and consequently enhancing our understanding of the linkages between firms' strategizing and economizing impulses. For example, the literature on vertical foreclosure (Hart and Tirole, 1990), in which a firm vertically integrates to deny its rivals access to key assets, may provide additional context to efficiency-motivated vertical integration decisions in TCE and the RBV. Similarly, the literature on multimarket contact (Bernheim and Whinston, 1990), which assesses the effect on competitive intensity of meeting the same rival in multiple markets, may provide additional context to efficiency-motivated diversification decisions from organizational economics.

Further, many of the effects in van Wittleoostuijn's "eight-effects" model of interorganizational economics affect the context in which organizational choices are made. Although these contextual effects are typically included in organizational economics studies, additional attention to the sources of these effects – perhaps possible through explicit integration of interorganizational economics concepts – may yield more insight. For example, organizational economics provides strong prescriptions for governance of assets such as brand names, but provides little insight into circumstances in which investment in such assets is likely to occur. Interorganizational economics provides insight into this latter question (Sutton, 1991).

Just as interorganizational economics may provide deeper contextual background for organizational economics, organizational economics may do so for intraorganizational economics. Zajac and Westphal (this volume) describe research on the monitoring and incentive system for a firm's senior managers. Such research typically takes as given the set of activities inside an organization. The fundamental question of organizational economics – which transactions or activities should be performed within the organization and which through the market – raises issues concerning exactly what changes when, say, two firms are merged such that one becomes a subsidiary of the other. At the very least, this question suggests a need for intraorganizational studies of mid-level managers. It also suggests the benefits of comparative institutional analysis even in considering intraorganizational issues. Of course, any intraorganizational research that sheds more light on the motivation and coordination of managers will inform organizational economics' continued exploration of make-or-buy decisions.

Conclusion

In this chapter, I have surveyed transaction cost economics and the resource-based view of the firm, two prominent strands of organizational economics. Although the two approaches are at different stages of maturity, each has a bright future. I encourage organization theorists to explore the research on which they are based, and to conduct research that pushes forward the frontiers of organizational economics and bridges it more concretely to other perspectives within organization theory.

Acknowledgments

Thanks to Raffi Amit, Nick Argyres, Joel Baum, Bill Hesterly, Peter Klein, Jackson Nickerson, Anita McGahan, Joanne Oxley, and Oliver Williamson for comments on earlier drafts.

Notes

1   Alternatives include Alchian and Demsetz (1972), who view the firm as a "nexus of contracts" that can efficiently overcome problems in monitoring team production; Jensen and Meckling (1976), who view the firm as a mechanism to overcome agency problems; and

Grossman and Hart (1986) and Hart and Moore (1990), who view the firm as a collection of property rights over physical assets that can efficiently motivate individuals through allocation of residual claims.

2 The field of organizational economics has benefited from several thoughtful surveys by Shelanski and Klein (1995), Barney and Hesterly (1996), Rindfleisch and Heide (1997), and Klein (1999) as well as theoretical critiques (Williamson, 1999). I highly recommend these to interested readers.

3 Acknowledging opportunism does not imply that all people are always opportunistic. The mere fact that some individuals will behave opportunistically under some circumstances, and that this propensity cannot be observed ex ante, is sufficient to create contractual frictions such that organization form matters.

4 For example, organizational ecologists theorize about legitimation and competition, but measure these indirectly through density counts; resource dependence scholars theorize about power, but instead measure interdependence.

5 Yet opportunism arises in organization theories such as resource dependence, where managers selectively pass information to advance their own interests (Pfeffer, 1978, p. 18–19), and bureaucracy, which purportedly ameliorates featherbedding (Perrow 1972). (Thanks to Bill Hesterly for raising this point.)

6 In a sense, this argument stands Teece (1982) on its head. Teece argues that, in the absence of transaction costs, the mere fact that an asset can be used to produce for two different product markets does not imply that the same firm has to produce in both markets – the firm could contract out the asset's use in one market. The above argument states that the mere fact that two assets should be joined together to produce for a product market does not imply that the same firm has to own both assets – unless there are hazards that preclude contracting.

7 A few cross-sectional TCE studies have investigated alignment and negotiation costs (Walker and Poppo, 1991) or customer satisfaction levels (Goodman et al., 1995; Poppo and Zenger, 1998).

References

Acheson, J. A. (1985): "The Maine lobster market: Between market and hierarchy," *Journal of Law, Economics and Organization*, 1, 385–98.

Alchian, A. A., and Demsetz, H. (1972): "Production, information costs, and economic organization," *American Economic Review*, 62, 777–95.

Amit, R., and Schoemaker, P. (1993): "Strategic assets and organizational rent," *Strategic Management Journal*, 14, 33–46.

Anderson, E., and Schmittlein, D. (1984): "Integration of the sales force: An empirical examination," *Rand Journal of Economics*, 15, 385–95.

Argyres, N. S. (1996): "Evidence on the role of firm capabilities in vertical integration decisions," *Strategic Management Journal*, 17, 129–50.

Argyres, N. S., and Liebeskind, J. P. (1998): "Privatizing the intellectual commons: Universities and the commercialization of biotechnology," *Journal of Economic Behavior & Organization*, 35, 427–74.

Argyres, N. S., and Liebeskind, J. P. (1999): "Contractual commitments, bargaining power, and governance inseparability: Incorporating history into transaction cost theory," *Academy of Management Review*, 24, 49–63.

Bain, J. S. (1956): *Barriers to New Competition*. Cambridge, MA: Harvard University Press.

Barnard, C. A. (1938): *The Functions of the Executive*. Cambridge, MA: Harvard University Press.

Barney, J. B. (1986): "Strategic factor markets: Expectations, luck, and business strategy," *Management Science*, 42, 1231–41.

Barney, J. B. (1991): "Firm resources and sustained competitive advantage," *Journal of Management*, 17, 99–120.

Barney, J. B. (1997): *Gaining and Sustaining Competitive Advantage*. Reading, MA: Addison Wesley.

Barney, J. B., and Hesterly, W. (1996): "Organizational economics: Understanding the relationship between organizations and economic analysis," in S. Clegg, C. Hardy and W. R. Nord (eds), *Handbook of Organization Studies*, London: Sage Publications.

Bercovitz, J. E. L. (2000): "The structure of franchise contracts," unpublished dissertation, Haas School of Business, University of California, Berkeley.

Bernheim, B. D., and Whinston, M. D. (1990): "Multimarket contact and collusive behavior," *Rand Journal of Economics*, 21, 1–26.

Boerner, C., and Macher, J. (2000): "Transaction cost economics: A review and assessment of the empirical literature," unpublished manuscript, Haas School of Business, University of California, Berkeley.

Bresnahan, T. (1989): "Empirical studies of industries with market power," in R. Schmalensee and R. Willig (eds), *Handbook of Industrial Organization*, New York: North Holland.

Brinig, M. (1990): "Rings and promises," *Journal of Law, Economics and Organization*, 6, 203–15.

Burt, R. S. (1992): *Structural Holes: The Social Structure of Competition*. Cambridge, MA: Harvard University Press.

Caves, R. M., and Porter, M. E. (1977): "From entry barriers to mobility barriers: Conjectural decisions and contrived deterrence to new competition," *Quarterly Journal of Economics*, 91, 241–61.

Caves, R. M., Porter, M. E., and Spence, A. M. (1980): *Competition in the Open Economy: A Model Applied to Canada*. Cambridge, MA: Harvard University Press.

Chi, T. (1994): "Trading in strategic resources: Necessary conditions, transaction cost problems, and choice of exchange structure," *Strategic Management Journal*, 15, 271–90.

Coase, R. H. (1937): "The nature of the firm," *Economica*, 4, 386–405.

Coase, R. H. (1972): "Industrial organization: A proposal for research," in V. R. Fuchs (ed.), *Policy Issues and Research Opportunities in Industrial Organization*, New York: National Bureau of Economic Research.

Cohen, W. M., and Levinthal, D. A. (1990): "Absorptive capacity: A new perspective on learning and innovation," *Administrative Science Quarterly*, 35, 128-152.

Commons, J. R. (1934): *Institutional Economics*. Madison WI: University of Wisconsin Press.

Conner, K. R. (1991): "A historical comparison of resource-based theory and five schools of thought within industrial organization economics: Do we have a new theory of the firm?" *Journal of Management*, 17, 121–54.

Conner, K. R., and Prahalad, C. K. (1996): "A resource-based theory of the firm: Knowledge versus opportunism," *Organization Science*, 7, 477–501.

Craswell, R. (1993): "On the uses of 'trust': Comment [Calculativeness, trust, and economic organization]," *Journal of Law and Economics*, 36, 487–500.

Davis, L. E., and North, D. C. (1971): *Institutional Change and American Economic Growth*. Cambridge: Cambridge University Press.

De Figueiredo, J. M., and Tiller, E. H. (2001): "The structure and conduct of corporate lobbying: How firms lobby the Federal Communications Commission," *Journal of Economics and Management Strategy*, 10, 91–122.

Demsetz, H. (1973): "Industrial structure, market rivalry, and public policy," *Journal of Law and Economics*, 16, 1–13.

Dierickx, I., and Cool, K. (1989): "Asset stock accumulation and sustainability of competitive advantage," *Management Science*, 35, 1504–11.

Donaldson, L. (1990): "The ethereal hand: Organizational economics and management," *Academy of Management Review*, 15, 369–81.

Dyer, J. (1997): "Effective interfirm collaboration: How firms minimize transaction costs and maximize transaction value," *Strategic Management Journal*, 18, 535–56.

Dyer, J., and Singh, H. (1998): "The relational view: Cooperative strategy and sources of interorganizational competitive advantage," *Academy of Management Review*, 23, 660–79.

Ellickson, R. C. (1989): "A hypothesis of wealth-maximizing norms: Evidence from the whaling industry," *Journal of Law, Economics and Organization*, 5, 83–97.

Foss, N. J. (1996): "Knowledge-based approaches to the theory of the firm: Some critical comments," *Organization Science*, 7, 470–76.

Galbraith, J. R. (1977): *Organization Design*. Reading, MA: Addison Wesley.

Gatignon, H., and Anderson, E. (1988): "The multinational's degree of control over foreign subsidiaries: An empirical test of a transaction cost explanation," *Journal of Law, Economics and Organization*, 4, 305–36.

Ghosh, M., and John, G. (1999): "Governance value analysis and marketing strategy," *Journal of Marketing*, 63, (Special issue) 131–45.

Ghoshal, S., and Moran, P. (1996): "Bad for practice: A critique of the transaction cost theory," *Academy of Management Review*, 21, 13–48.

Goodman, P., Fichman, M., Lerch, J., and Snyder, P. (1995): "Customer–firm relationships, involvement, and customer satisfaction," *Academy of Management Journal*, 38, 1310–24.

Gort, M. (1962): *Diversification and Integration in American Industry*. Princeton: Princeton University Press.

Granovetter, M. (1985): "Economic action and social structure," *American Journal of Sociology*, 91, 481–510.

Grossman, S. J., and Hart, O. (1986): "The costs and benefits of ownership: A theory of vertical and lateral integration," *Journal of Political Economy*, 94, 691–719.

Gulati, R. (1998): "Alliances and networks," *Strategic Management Journal*, 19, 293–317.

Gulati, R., and Singh, H. (1998): "The architecture of cooperation: Managing coordination costs and appropriation concerns in strategic alliances," *Administrative Science Quarterly*, 43, 781–814.

Hagedoorn, J., and Schakenraad, J. (1994): "The effect of strategic technology alliances on company performance," *Strategic Management Journal*, 15, 291–309.

Hart, O., and Moore, J. (1990): "Property rights and the nature of the firm," *Journal of Political Economy*, 98, 1119–58.

Hart, O., and Tirole, J. (1990): "Vertical integration and market foreclosure," *Brookings Papers on Economic Activity*, (Special Issue), 205–86.

Hayek, F. (1945): "The use of knowledge in society," *American Economic Review*, 35, 519–30.

Heide, J. B., and John, G. (1988): "The role of dependence balancing in safeguarding transaction-specific assets," *Journal of Marketing*, 52, 20–35.

Henderson, R. M., and Cockburn, I. (1994): "Measuring competence? Exploring firm effects in pharmaceutical research," *Strategic Management Journal*, 15, Winter, 63–84.

Henisz, W. J. (2000): "The institutional environment for multinational investment," *Journal of Law, Economics and Organization*, 16, 334–64.

Hennart, J. F. (1982): *A Theory of Multinational Enterprise*. Ann Arbor: University of Michigan Press.

Ingram, P., and Clay, K. (2000): "The choice-within-constraints new institutionalism and implications for sociology," *Annual Review of Sociology*, 26, 525–46.

Jensen, M. C., and Meckling, W. H. (1976): "Theory of the firm: Managerial behavior, agency costs and ownership structure," *Journal of Financial Economics*, 3, 305–60.

Jones, C., Hesterly, W. S., and Borgatti, S. P. (1997): "A general theory of network governance: Exchange conditions and social mechanisms," *Academy of Management Review*, 22, 911–45.

Joskow, P. L. (1985): "Vertical integration and long-term contract: The case of coal-burning electric generating plants," *Journal of Law, Economics and Organization*, 1, 33–80.

Joskow, P. L. (1987): "Contract duration and relationship-specific investments: Empirical evidence from coal markets," *American Economic Review*, 77, 168–85.

Klein, B., Crawford, R. A., and Alchian, A. A. (1978): "Vertical integration, appropriable rents, and the competitive contracting process," *Journal of Law and Economics*, 21, 297–326.

Klein, P. (1999): "New institutional economics," unpublished manuscript, University of Georgia.

Kogut, B. (1988): "Joint ventures: Theoretical and empirical perspectives," *Strategic Management Journal*, 9, 319–32.

Kogut, B., and Zander, U. (1992): "Knowledge of the firm, combinative capabilities, and the replication of technology," *Organization Science*, 3, 383–97.

Kogut, B., and Zander, U. (1996): "What firms do: Coordination, identity, and learning," *Organization Science*, 7, 502–18.

Lafontaine, F. (1992): "Agency theory and franchising: Some empirical results," *Rand Journal of Economics*, 23, 263–83.

Langlois, R. N., and Foss, N. J. (1997): "Capabilities and governance: The rebirth of production in the theory of economic organization,2 DRUID working paper 97-2, Danish Research Unit for Industrial Dynamics.

Lippman, S., and Rumelt, R. P. (1982): "Uncertain imitability: An analysis of interfirm differences in efficiency under competition," *Bell Journal of Economics*, 13, 418–38.

Mahoney, J. T., and Pandian, J. (1992): "The resource-based view within the conversation of strategic management," *Strategic Management Journal*, 13, 363–80.

Masten, S. E. (1984): "The organization of production: Evidence from the aerospace industry," *Journal of Law and Economics*, 27, 403–17.

Masten, S. E. (1988): "A legal basis for the firm," *Journal of Law, Economics and Organization*, 4, 181–98.

Masten, S. E. (1993): "Transaction costs, mistakes, and performance: Assessing the importance of governance," *Managerial and Decision Economics*, 14, 119–29.

Masten, S. E., and Crocker, K. J. (1985): "Efficient adaptation in long-term contracts: Take-or-pay provisions for natural gas," *American Economic Review*, 75, 1083–93.

Masten, S. E., Meehan, J. W., and Snyder, E. A. (1991): "The costs of organization," *Journal of Law, Economics and Organization*, 12, 1–25.

Meyer, J. W., and Rowan, B. (1977): Institutionalized organizations: Formal structure as myth and ceremony," *American Journal of Sociology*, 83, 340–63.

Moe, T. (1990): "Political institutions: The neglected side of the story," *Journal of Law, Economics and Organization*, 6, 213–53.

Monteverde, K., and Teece, D. J. (1982a): "Supplier switching costs and vertical integration in the automobile industry," *Bell Journal of Economics*, 13, 206–13.

Monteverde, K., and Teece, D .J. (1982b): "Appropriable rents and quasi-vertical integration," *Journal of Law and Economics*, 25, 321–28.

Montgomery, C. A., and Hariharan, S. (1991): "Diversified expansion by large established firms," *Journal of Economics, Behavior and Organization*, 15, 71–89.

Montgomery, C. A., and Wernerfelt, B. (1988): "Diversification, Ricardian rents, and Tobin's q," *Rand Journal of Economics*, 19, 623–32.

Mowery, D. C., Oxley, J. E., and Silverman, B. S. (1996): "Strategic alliances and interfirm knowledge transfer," *Strategic Management Journal*, 17, Winter, 77–91.

Mowery, D. C., Oxley, J. E., and Silverman, B. S. (1998): "Technological overlap and interfirm cooperation: Implications for the resource-based view of the firm," *Research Policy*, 27, 507–23.

Nelson, R. R., and Winter, S. G. (1982): *An Evolutionary Theory of Economic Change*. Cambridge, MA: Harvard University Press.

Nickerson, J. A. (1997): Toward An economizing theory of strategy: The choice of strategic position, assets, and organizational form," unpublished PhD dissertation, Haas School of Business, University of California, Berkeley.

Nickerson, J. A. and Silverman, B. S. (1998): "Transactional interdependencies, resources, and path dependence: Firm heterogeneity within transaction cost economics," working paper, Washington University in St. Louis.

Nickerson, J. A. and Silverman, B. S. (1999): "Why aren't all truck drivers owner-operators? Asset ownership and the employment relation in interstate for-hire trucking," Harvard Business School working paper, no 00-015.

Nickerson, J. A. and Silverman, B. S. (2000): "Why firms want to organize efficiently and what keeps them from doing so: Evidence from the for-hire interstate trucking industry," manuscript, Harvard Business School.

Nickerson, J. A., Hamilton, B., and Wada, T. (2001): "Strategy, hazards, and governance: A study of overnight package delivery in Japan," *Strategic Management Journal*, 22, (forthcoming).

North, D. C. (1990): *Institutions, Institutional Change, and Economic Performance*. Cambridge: Cambridge University Press.

Oliver, C. (1997): "Sustainable competitive advantage: Combining institutional and resource-based views," *Strategic Management Journal*, 18, 697–714.

Oxley, J. E. (1997): "Appropriability hazards and governance in strategic alliances: A transaction cost approach," *Journal of Law, Economics and Organization*, 13, 387–409.

Oxley, J. E. (1999): "Institutional environment and the mechanisms of governance: The impact of intellectual property protection on the structure of inter-firm alliances," *Journal of Economic Behavior and Organization*, 38, 283–309.

Palay, T. (1985): "Avoiding regulatory constraints: The use of informal contract," *Journal of Law, Economics, and Organization*, 1, 155–75.

Penrose, E. T. (1959): *The Theory of the Growth of the Firm*. Oxford: Oxford University Press.

Perrow, C. (1972): *Complex Organizations: A Critical Essay*. Glenview, IL: Scott, Foresman.

Perrow, C. (1981): "Markets, hierarchies, and hegemony: A critique of Chandler and Williamson," in A. Van de Ven and J. Joyce (eds), *Perspectives on Organization Design and Behavior*, New York: Wiley.

Peteraf, M. A. (1993): "The cornerstones of competitive advantage: A resource-based view," *Strategic Management Journal*, 14, 179–92.

Pfeffer, J. (1978): *Organizational Design*. Arlington Heights, IL: AHM Publishing.

Pfeffer, J., and Salancik, G. (1978): The External Control of Organizations: A Resource-Dependence Perspective (New York: Harper & Row,

Pisano, G. P. (1990): "The R&D boundaries Of the firm: An empirical analysis," *Administrative Science Quarterly*, 35, 153–76.

Podolny, J. M. (1994): "Market uncertainty and the social character of economic exchange," *Administrative Science Quarterly*, 39, 458–83.

Podolny, J. M., and Philips, D. J. (1996): "The dynamics of organizational status," *Industrial and Corporate Change*, 5, 453–71.

Poppo, L., and Zenger, T. R. (1998): Testing alternative theories of the firm: Transaction cost, knowledge-based, and measurement explanations for make-or-buy decisions in information services," *Strategic Management Journal*, 19, 853–77

Porter, M. E. (1980): *Competitive Strategy*. New York: Free Press.

Rindfleisch, A., and Heide, J. B. (1997): "Transaction cost analysis: Past, present and future applications," *Journal of Marketing*, 61, 30–54.

Ring, P. S., and Van de Ven, A. (1992): "Structuring cooperative relationships between organizations," *Strategic Management Journal*, 13, 483–98.

Roberts, P. W., and Greenwood, R. (1997): "Integrating transaction cost and institutional theories: Toward a constrained-efficiency framework for understanding organizational design adoption," *Academy of Management Review*, 22, 346–73.

Rubin, E. L. (1995): "The non-judicial life of contract," *Northwestern University Law Review*, 90, 107–31.

Rumelt, R. P. (1974): *Strategy, Structure, and Economic Performance.* Boston: Harvard Business School Press.

Rumelt, R. P. (1984): "Towards a strategic theory of the firm," in R. B Lamb (ed.), *Competitive Strategic Management,* Upper Saddle River, NJ: Prentice Hall.

Rumelt, R. P. (1991): "How much does industry matter?" *Strategic Management Journal,* 12, 167–86.

Schumpeter, J. A. (1942): *Capitalism, Socialism, and Democracy.* New York: Harper & Bros.

Shaver, J. M. (1998): "Accounting for endogeneity when assessing strategy performance: Does entry mode choice affect FDI survival?" *Management Science,* 44, 571–85.

Shelanski, H. A., and Klein, P. G. (1995): "Empirical research in transaction cost economics: A review and assessment," *Journal of Law, Economics and Organization,* 11, 335–61.

Silverman, B. S. (1999): "Technological resources and the direction of corporate diversification: Toward an integration of transaction cost economics and the resource-based view," *Management Science,* 45, 1109–24.

Silverman, B. S., Nickerson, J. A., and Freeman, J. (1997): "Profitability, transactional alignment, and organizational mortality in the U.S. trucking industry," *Strategic Management Journal,* 18, Summer, 31–52.

Simon, H. A. (1947): *Administrative Behavior.* New York: MacMillan.

Simon, H. A. (1991): "Organizations and markets," *Journal of Economic Perspectives,* 5, 25–44.

Singh, H., and Montgomery, C. A. (1987): "Corporate acquisition strategies and economic performance," *Strategic Management Journal,* 8, 377–86.

Spiller, P. T. (1985): "On vertical mergers," *Journal of Law, Economics and Organization,* 1, 285–312.

Stuart, T. E., Hoang, H., and Hybels, R. (1999): "Interorganizational endorsements and the performance of entrepreneurial ventures," *Administrative Science Quarterly,* 44, 315–49.

Sutton, J. (1991): *Sunk Costs and Market Structure.* Cambridge, MA: MIT Press.

Teece, D. J. (1980): "Economies of scope and the scope of the enterprise," *Journal of Economic Behavior and Organization,* 1, 223–47.

Teece, D. J. (1982): "Towards an economic theory of the multi-product firm," *Journal of Economic Behavior and Organization,* 3, 39–64.

Teece, D. J. (1986): "Profiting from technological innovation: Implications for integration, collaboration, licensing, and public policy," *Research Policy,* 285–305.

Teece, D. J. (1992): "Competition, cooperation, and innovation: Organizational arrangements for regimes of rapid technological progress," *Journal of Economic Behavior and Organization,* 18, 1–25.

Teece, D. J., Pisano, G. P., and Shuen, A. (1997): "Dynamic capabilities and strategic management," *Strategic Management Journal,* 18, 509–33.

Thompson, J. D. (1967): *Organizations in Action.* New York: McGraw-Hill.

Uzzi, B. (1997): "Social structure and competition in interfirm networks: The paradox of embeddedness," *Administrative Science Quarterly,* 42, 35–67.

Walker, G., and Poppo, L. (1991): "Profit centers, single-source suppliers, and transaction costs," *Administrative Science Quarterly,* 36, 66–87.

Walker, G., and Weber, D. (1984): "A transaction cost approach to make-or-buy decisions," *Administrative Science Quarterly,* 29, 373–91.

Walker, G., and Weber, D. (1987): "Supplier competition, uncertainty, and make-or-buy decisions," *Academy of Management Journal,* 30, 589–96.

Weingast, B. R., and Marshall, W. J. (1988): "The industrial organization of Congress; or why legislatures, like firms, are not organized as markets," *Journal of Political Economy,* 96, 132–63.

Wernerfelt, B. (1984): "A resource-based view of the firm," *Strategic Management Journal,* 5, 171–80.

Wernerfelt, B., and Montgomery, C. A. (1988): "Tobin's q and the importance of focus in firm performance," *American Economic Review,* 78, 246–50.

Williamson, O. E. (1975): *Markets and Hierarchies: Analysis and Antitrust Implications.* New York:

Free Press.

Williamson, O. E. (1979): "Transaction-cost economics: The governance of contractual relations," *Journal of Law and Economics*, 22, 3–61.

Williamson, O. E. (1983): "Credible commitments: Using hostages to support exchange," *American Economic Review*, 73, 519–40.

Williamson, O. E. (1985): *The Economic Institutions of Capitalism*. New York: Free Press.

Williamson, O. E. (1991): "Comparative economic organization: The analysis of discrete structural alternatives," *Administrative Science Quarterly*, 36, 269–96.

Williamson, O. E. (1993a): "Calculativeness, trust, and economic organization," *Journal of Law and Economics*, 36, 453–86.

Williamson, O. E. (1993b): "Calculativeness, trust, and economic organization: Reply," *Journal of Law and Economics*, 36, 501–05.

Williamson, O. E. (1999): "Governance-based vs. competence-based theories of the firm," *Strategic Management Journal*, 20, 1087–108.

Winter, S. G. (1990): "Survival, selection, and inheritance in evolutionary theories of organization," in J. V. Singh (ed.), *Organizational Evolution: New Directions*, Newbury Park, CA: Sage Publications.

Zander, U., and Kogut, B. (1995): "Knowledge and the speed of the transfer and imitation of organizational capabilities: An empirical test," *Organization Science*, 6, 76–91.

Part III

Interorganizational Level

21 Interorganizational Institutions   497
       David Strang and Wesley D. Sine

22 Interorganizational Networks   520
       Wayne E. Baker and Robert R. Faulkner

23 Interorganizational Ecology   541
       Hayagreeva Rao

24 Interorganizational Evolution   557
       Henrich R. Greve

25 Interorganizational Cognition and Interpretation   579
       Joseph F. Porac, Marc J. Ventresca, and Yuri Mishina

26 Interorganizational Power and Dependence   599
       Mark Mizruchi and Mina Yoo

27 Interorganizational Technology   621
       Toby E. Stuart

28 Interorganizational Learning   642
       Paul Ingram

29 Interorganizational Complexity and Computation   664
       Olav Sorenson

30 Interorganizational Economics   686
       Arjen Van Witteloostuijn

Chapter Twenty-one

Interorganizational Institutions

DAVID STRANG AND WESLEY D. SINE

Institutional approaches to the study of organizations provide an active and fruitful line of organizational research. Seminal theoretical statements include Meyer and Rowan (1977), DiMaggio and Powell (1983); for reviews see Scott (1987, 1995) and DiMaggio and Powell 1991). Unlike Selznick's (1949) inquiry into how organizations become institutions, contemporary work asks how organizations are influenced by institutionalized rules and institutional environments – forces that operate above and across organizations. Much research documents institutional effects on organizational practices, performance, and life chances. Substantive attention focuses mainly on the impact of the state and the professions on organizations, and on tracing the diffusion of new organizational practices and forms.

While we know much about how organizations are molded by institutional forces, the sources of institutions and institutional change are relatively neglected. Brint and Karabel (1991) contend that a muscular "sociology of institutional forms" needs to be complemented by an under-developed "sociology of institutional change." DiMaggio (1988) argues that "institutional theory tells us relatively little about 'institutionalization' as an unfinished process ... even less about deinstitutionalization: why and how institutionalized forms and practices fall into disuse." And Hirsch (1997) contends that prevailing institutionalisms suggest a *Brave New World* where harmony and order reign supreme.

These silences are especially important given concern that institutional accounts cannot provide a coherent analysis of change. The foundational notion of an "institution" emphasizes permanence and stability. Theoretical commitments leave little room for the usual drivers of change. Interests and purposes are viewed as socially constructed, diminishing the prospects of action in opposition to institutionalized rules. And while institutions have been interpreted as systems of opportunity as well as of constraint, the relevant opportunities involve not systemic change but skillful performance along conventional lines – those seized by Joe DiMaggio or Marilyn Monroe, not Che Guevara or Sid Vicious.

Powerful critiques from "within" as well as "outside" the institutional perspective contend that core theoretical positions need to be rethought if institutional change is to be grappled with effectively. DiMaggio (1988) and Brint and Karabel (1991) seek to bring power and interest back in. Zucker (1989) develops ideas about entropy and the contagion of legitimacy. Oliver (1991, 1992) argues for a more strategic institutionalism, Clemens and Cook (1999) for the mutability of schemas, and Powell (1991) for explicit models of path dependency. Stinchcombe (1997) points to the strengths of an "old institutionalism" that treated institutions as organizations manned by people committed to substantive values, and Greenwood and Hinings (1996) combine its insights with contemporary approaches to develop models of change.

This chapter focuses on neo-institutional and related lines of research that address macro-institutional change. While we agree that fundamental theoretical positions must be reworked if institutional change is to be better explained, we also think that review of empirical work provides useful insight into the logic of institutional accounts, and can suggest lessons for theoretical and empirical progress.

CONCEPTIONS OF INSTITUTIONS AND INSTITUTIONAL EFFECTS

Neo-institutional analysis in organizational studies makes up one wing of a larger "institutional turn" in the social sciences. Choice-theoretic studies of institutions in economics and analyses of decision-making structures in political science form two related streams of thought; see Hall and Taylor (1996) for a review. Campbell and Pedersen (2001) demonstrate connections and complementarities among different institutional traditions. Despite fundamental diversity, these perspectives share a common opponent in reductionist approaches that view the preferences and capacities of individual actors as directly generating complex social outcomes. Institutional theories posit instead a two-level model of social action, where individual action is constrained and shaped by an institutional context. All institutional theories thus argue that particular practices or outcomes can become "built in" to the social order – occurring without substantial effort or mobilization, and resistant to counter-mobilization (Jepperson, 1991).

What sorts of factors can be taken as strongly shaping but relatively unresponsive to social action? Here the variety of institutionalisms part company. Institutions can be identified with "rules of the game" that bound everyday politics. Or institutions can be identified with the way organizational edifices and routines structure behavior. Or institutions can be identified with culture: the categories and understandings that shape how actors understand themselves and the lines of action they are able to formulate.

In organizational research, institutionalists have generally taken the third road. Organizational neo-institutionalists describe forms, practices and routines as institutionalized when they are invested with social meaning. Selznick describes a practice as institutionalized when it is "infused with value beyond the technical requirements of the task at hand" (1957, p. 17). Meyer, Boli and Thomas (1987, p. 13) see institutions as "cultural rules giving collective meaning and value to particular entities and activities, integrating them into larger schemes." Scott (1995) points to three types of institutional supports: the regulative (formal rules and incentives constructed by the state and other empowered agents of the collective good), normative (informal rules associated with values and explicit moral commitments), and cognitive (abstract rules associated with the structure of cognitive distinctions and taken-for-granted understandings).

There is important variety even within these "pillars" or "bases" of institutionalization (Sine, 1999). Practices may be cognitively institutionalized because they are *taken-for-granted* on a pre-conscious level and escape critical scrutiny. Or practices may be cognitively institutionalized because they have perceived *efficacy* within self-conscious models for behavior. Practices may be normatively institutionalized because they reflect deeply felt *values* (see Elsbach's discussion in this volume of "hot" and "cold" cognitions). Or they may be normatively institutionalized because they are *prevalent* and *integrated* into other activities. Practices may be regulatively institutionalized because they are *authorized* by agents of the collectivity, or because defections are *penalized* by powerful actors.

If institutional "pillars" co-varied strongly, institutional change would be exceedingly rare. But different institutional supports may be weakly correlated with each other, and even in tension. For example, it is often easier to legitimate non-existent practices than established ones, whose blemishes are all too obvious. And where cognitive, normative, and regulative supports are not well aligned, they provide resources that different actors can employ for different ends.

Consider an exemplar of social theory, Max Weber's *The Protestant Ethic and the Spirit of Capitalism*. Weber conceptualizes that spirit as a culturally distinctive orientation, where individuals conceive it their duty to accumulate wealth through sober, law-abiding, rational effort, and to re-invest rather than enjoy the fruits of their labors. This orientation emerged (in Weber's account) out of the evolution of religious doctrine, as the idea of predestination led Calvinists to search for indirect evidence of their salvation. But Weber also argues that capitalism outlived its religious sources:

> "The Puritan wanted to work in a calling; we are forced to do so. For when asceticism was carried out of the monastic cells into everyday life, and began to dominate worldly morality, it did its part in building the tremendous cosmos of the modern economic order. This order is now bound to the technical and economic conditions of machine production which today determine the lives of all the individuals who are born into this mechanism ..." (Weber, 1958, p. 180).

Weber's argument is thus about institutional change. Cultural movements can produce new lines of action that are later institutionalized. And institutional structures can shake their cultural roots, as puritanical entrepreneurs give birth to trapped organization men and fun-loving hedonists.

Literature Review

Theoretical blinders aside, institutional research routinely studies substantial historical change (see Table 21.1 for some key studies). It does so in a search for theoretically meaningful variation. After all, institutional accounts often imply that organizations are affected in the same way, or even homogenized by, a common institutional environment. This sort of argument suggests comparison of organizations operating within different institutional environments. And a main way of observing different institutional environments is by examining a sector undergoing dramatic historical transformation.

Table 21.1 Selected research on interorganizational institutions and institutional change

Reference	Key concepts	Key variables	Key predictions and findings	Key contribution	Method and sample
Cole, 1989	Comparative diffusion across nations	Strength of professional associations; roles of management and labor	Institutionalization of new practice requires strong professional infrastructure and links to powerful actors.	Organizational analysis of professions	Examination of spread of small group activities in the USA, Japan, and Sweden
Davis and Greve, 1997	Comparative diffusion across practices	Characteristics of innovation adopters and their social networks	Legitimate innovations diffuse by weaker ties than do illegitimate innovations.	Links cognitive and relational treatments of legitimacy	Diffusion of poison pills and golden parachutes among American corporations
Davis et al., 1994	Demise of a dominant corporate form	Characteristics of acquired and acquiring firms	Conglomerates acquired by outsiders due to economic inefficiency; lost legitimacy due to changing conceptions of the firm	Demonstrates joint role of performance failure and cultural change in deinstitutionalization	Bust-up takeovers of conglomerates, 1980s
DiMaggio and Powell, 1983	Institutional isomorphism in organizational fields	Coercive, mimetic, and normative processes	Organizational fields tend to become isomorphic.	Conceptualizes general institutional processes promoting isomorphism	Theoretical analysis of mechanisms underlying change in different industries
Dobbin et al., 1993; Edelman et al., 1999	Adoption of formal organizational policies	Policies creating internal labor markets; period effects and proximity to state sector; legal logics	Unintended impact of state policy on organizational structure	Details reciprocal interpretive activity of state and professions	Event history and qualitative analyses of personnel practices, 1970–90s
Fligstein, 1990	Corporate conceptions of control	Regulatory regimes; organizational background of CEOs	Corporations shift to new models of control due principally to change in state policy.	Identifies variation in corporate structures and their link to state policy	Historical analysis of US corporations in the twentieth century

Hirsch, 1986	Institutionalization of a deviant innovation	Images employed in describing takeovers; frequency of takeovers over time	Intertwined changes in social action (who conducts takeovers) and collective representations	Describes framing as a collective activity and its link to organizational communities	Reports on hostile takeovers appearing in the *Wall Street Journal*, 1970–80s
Haveman and Rao, 1997	Organizational forms as embodying theories of moral sentiments	Typology of thrifts; founding and failure rates	Industry change involves organizational selection based on institutional linkages.	Builds connections between ecological and institutional arguments	Event history analysis of the life chances of California thrifts, 1890–1928
Leblebici et al., 1991	Industry systems as ways of solving public goods problems; marginal and central actors	Periodization of radio systems; identity of innovators; precipitants of system change	Movement between radio broadcasting systems occurs at points of institutional crisis or completion; innovators are marginals.	Develops endogenous account of institutional change	Historical account of radio broadcasting industry
Meyer and Rowan, 1977	Institutional rules; organizational myth and ceremony	Formal *vs* behavioral structure; institutional rules and environment	Institutional rules spur formation and elaboration of rationalized organizations.	Charter statement for institutional analysis in organizational studies; neo-Weberian model of the emergence and functioning of formal organization	Theoretical analysis of educational organizations

NATURALISTIC ACCOUNTS OF INSTITUTIONALIZATION

A core dynamic within institutional imagery is institutionalization itself as a natural and undirected process. Berger and Luckmann (1967) argue that institutions build up naturally in any social situation. As people act jointly towards some end, activities are habitualized and reciprocally interpreted. "There I go again" becomes "there we go again" becomes "this activity involves these sorts of roles and behaviors." Socially constructed interpretations are nascent institutions that "harden" and "deepen" as they are transmitted to others (particularly the next generation) as objective facts about the world rather than contingent agreements. For Berger and Luckmann, social interaction naturally crystallizes in institutional form, and purposive "action" is needed not to form but to transform institutions.

Much work follows these insights in detailing the cultural legitimation of new practices. Hirsch (1986) sensitively portrays changing social understandings in an analysis of business press reports on hostile takeovers. Early takeovers were understood as meaningless violations of the social order, on a par with drive-by shootings. As takeovers accelerated in scope and began to be executed by insiders as well as outsiders, more complex imageries of "cowboys and Indians" and "princesses and knights" developed. Hirsch argues that this new discourse normalized takeovers, providing both winners and losers with a script and roles to play. A crime had become a game.

Hannan and Freeman's (1989) model of the endogenous population dynamics provides a simple formal model of institutionalization. They argue that legitimacy should increase with the number of instances of an organizational form presently in operation. "When numbers are small, those who attempt to create a form must fight for legitimacy: they must argue both for the special purposes of a proposed organization and for the design of the form. Once many instances of the form exist, the need for elaborate justifications diminishes" (1989, p. 132). Legitimacy leads to more organizational foundings and fewer organizational failures, which leads to population growth, which generates even more legitimacy.

Other work treats legitimacy as a product of relational embeddedness where organizations gain standing through ties to other organizations. Baum and Oliver (1992) find that the life chances of child care organizations in Toronto improved with the volume of relationships to city government, schools, churches, and other community organizations. Ritti and Silver (1986) discuss the way a new governmental watch-dog group strategically developed relationships with other public and private organizations. And most famously, Selznick (1949) examined how the Tennessee Valley Authority built ties to local actors and interests, improving its life chances while altering its initial goals.

Diffusion studies stress the interdependent roles of both cognitive "sense-making" and social networks in the transmission of new ideas and behaviors (Strang and Soule, 1998). For example, Davis and Greve (1997) examine the spread of two different practices, the poison pill and the golden parachute. They argue that the two innovations were channeled by different network structures because one was legitimate and the other illegitimate. The poison pill (legitimated as a defense for shareholders) diffused through the relatively thin ties of board overlaps, while the golden parachute (delegitimated as a reward for incompetent managers) diffused more slowly through the relatively thick ties of local business communities.

CHANGE AGENT

Different institutional accounts of change view different actors as central. We consider three sets of "institutional entrepreneurs" or "change agents":

● States and professions who lead institutional reform movements "from the top"
● Marginals and outsiders who innovate
● Mobilized groups who push for institutions that reflect their concerns and interests.

INSTITUTIONAL REFORMERS AT THE TOP

Much work treats the state and the professions as key institutional entrepreneurs. The state directly regulates business and other organizations, can offer incentives, and is a sufficiently large exchange partner that it often impacts other organizations in unanticipated ways. Professions can carve out areas of autonomy, induce occupational cultures that affect organizations in similar ways, and often rise to the fore as interpreters and mediators of state policies.

Fligstein (1990) treats shifting patterns of antitrust law as promoting change in corporate "conceptions of control" (dominant models of corporate strategy and structure). For example, the Sherman Anti-Trust Act concluded an era of "direct control," where firms sought to destroy competitors or to collude with them to partition markets. In the 1960s, prohibition of mergers that increased market concentration obliged leading firms to experiment with new strategies and to construct new structures (such as the financially-administered conglomerate) that fit within the constraints of federal policy.

Much work demonstrates the impact of the state on organizational employment practices. Baron et al. (1986) find that the federal government's active management of the economy during World War II promoted formalization of employment, as wartime agencies constructed job categories to slow turnover and firms used them to communicate their manpower needs. The more recent evolution of human resource practices is also linked to state policy, particularly through the unintended effects of equal rights law. By requiring firms to make (and demonstrate to the satisfaction of third parties that they had made) race-blind hiring and promotion decisions, EEO law generated not only affirmative action officers but also performance testing (Edelman, 1990, 1992; Dobbin et al., 1993).

Strang and Bradburn (2001) note that the state also constructs organizational forms. In the early 1970s, the Nixon administration diagnosed rising health costs as a product of fee-for-service arrangements, where third party insurance footed the bill while physicians made decisions about what care should be provided. Their solution was to conceptualize a new organizational form, the health maintenance organization (HMO), which would better align incentives and capabilities by integrating health insurance and delivery. This new form was then sponsored by the federal government, which held out carrots to potential HMO founders and eliminated restrictive professional practices.

Hamilton and Biggart (1988) argue that differences in industrial structure in Japan, Korea, and Taiwan result from the problems faced by states and their consequent legitimating strategies. In Japan, a post-war state with little centralized power facilitated the re-emergence of fief-like *zaibatsu* that could organize economic sectors and take on substantial welfare and identity-creating roles. In Korea, a state torn by civil war sought to direct economic activity by creating large, hierarchically structured *chaebol* that could be managed by state planning agencies. And in Taiwan, Chang Kai-shek's regime supported family-oriented business while studiously avoiding favoritism, an approach that helped win acceptance among indigenous Taiwanese. Hamilton and Biggart emphasize that while legitimating strategies draw on prior models of the relationship between state and society, they rework those models to fit new problems.

Discussions of the state's role as an institutional entrepreneur reveal two different sorts of arguments. In part, attention to the state permits a cultural analysis of the social, political, and professional understandings that direct state action. For example, Strang and Bradburn (2001) emphasize that state legislators and health analysts found market models more sensible than arguments about professional discipline or bureaucratic regulation. Dobbin (1994) demonstrates that policy models show great variation across national contexts and great stability over time.

A more structural argument is also made about the state. Because it is such a large organizational actor, the state's entry into an organizational field often directly restructures behavior. As a large, formal organization the state promotes the formalization of local, associational arrangements (Meyer, Scott and Strang, 1987). Baron et al. (1986) emphasize that the state's early impact on employment practices was less informed by a theory of personnel standards and more by wartime exigencies and the unanticipated impact of coordinated national production.

The professions form a second class of collective actors whose roles are emphasized within institutional accounts of change. In some contexts, of course, professionals play highly conservative parts – particularly where they defend their traditional privileges and autonomy (Starr, 1982). But professionals also act as organizational reformers. Shenhav (1999) describes the efforts of industrial engineers like Taylor to rationalize production and systematize the practice of management, emphasizing their conflict with not only workers but managers as well. McKenna (1999) reports how McKinsey consultants invented the notion of corporate culture in a response to declining interest in their long-standing remedy of decentralization.

The accounts of state-driven change described above rely heavily on the creative roles of the professions as well as the visible hand of government regulation. For example, Dobbin et al.'s (1993) analysis of the impact of EEO law on employment practices provides only half the story, since legislation imposes abstract requirements rather than concrete procedures that firms must follow. Lawyers and human resource professionals then elaborate responses that they argue will be acceptable to the courts and improve organizational productivity to boot. Edelman et al. (1999) demonstrate that court decisions were actively influenced by the logics developed by these professionals.

Weaker professional projects may produce a "dynamics without change" where new approaches gain substantial followings but then lose credibility rather than becoming institutionalized. For example, the human relations and organizational development movements have promoted participatory management for several decades while remaining a "loyal opposition" to the traditions of line management. Similarly, quality engineers have generated a series of change initiatives, like quality circles and TQM, which have gained prominence as dramatic techniques of organizational improvement without becoming highly institutionalized.

Cole (1989) underscores the importance of professional organization in a comparison of the spread of small group activities in the USA, Japan, and Sweden. Japanese quality engineers worked through a well-established professional organization (the Japanese Union of Scientists and Engineers) and won the support of key executives in major industries. Swedish work reforms were sponsored by powerful trade union and employer federations. By contrast, American quality circle proponents were independent consultants with no organizational base and weak ties to top-level managers and major unions. The result was rapid turnover among rival "quality fads" in the United States, a quite different result from substantial growth of small group activities in Sweden and their institutionalization in Japan.

CHALLENGERS AS INSTITUTIONAL INNOVATORS

While institutional theorists have generally emphasized the ability of the state and the professions to construct new institutions, others concerned with institutional change have pointed in the opposite direction: to marginal actors, to newcomers and outsiders, and to under-performers. It is here where the motivation for change is most palpable, where institutionalized "rules of the game" appear as constraints rather than the basis of success, and where actors have the least to lose.

Leblebici et al. (1991) argue that system-transforming practices in radio broadcasting were developed by marginal actors. "New practices were introduced by . . . shady traders, small independent stations, renegade record producers, weaker networks, or enterprising advertising agencies" (1991, p. 358). For example, hucksters introduced on-air advertising that generated a market for radio stations rather than radio manufacturers, and small stations responded to the rise of television with format experimentation that led to the demise of the major network shows and the emergence of local deejays as radio personalities.

Stearns and Allan (1996) argue that "challengers" rather than established elites were the innovators in all four of the major merger waves of the last century. Corporate raiders were cultural outsiders with little experience in Fortune 500 firms. And the techniques developed to finance takeovers of the big by the small were developed not by major financial institutions, but by peripheral traders like KKR and Michael Milken. Davis et al. (1994) point out that "bust-up" takeovers during the 1980s "were done to core players, not by them."

Weaker and more vulnerable organizations may be particularly likely to trade institutional scripts for new opportunities. Kraatz and Zajac (1996) find that smaller, financially insecure colleges have abandoned purist notions of a liberal education to add cash-generating professional programs. Tolbert and Sine (1999) show that the same sorts of colleges have moved most rapidly in adding non-tenured, part-time, and temporary faculty. While professional programs and temporary employment conflict with traditional institutional ideals of a liberal education and the "academic freedom" protected by tenure, inconsistency is endurable when organizational survival is at stake.

THE MOBILIZATION OF SOCIAL GROUPS

A third main class of "institutional entrepreneurs" are social groups with common interests and well developed organizational capacity. The role of such groups is pointed to directly by Stinchcombe (1965, p. 107), for whom an institution is "a structure in which powerful people are committed to some value or interest." Institutional change then arises when the values of the powerful change, when the distribution of power changes, or when groups mobilize to more effectively act upon their interests.

Marx provides the classic analysis of institutional change driven by conflict and mobilization. The groups who count are classes defined in oppositional terms: the capitalists who control the means of production and the proletariat who lack capital and thus need to sell their labor power. Marx's political analysis is then concerned with the conditions under which an analytically defined class will become conscious of itself as a group with common interests and a common enemy. While Marx compared the French peasantry to "a sack of potatoes" due to the weakness of relations transcending the family farm, he argued that the working class would become revolutionary as it became concentrated in factories owned by fewer and fewer capitalists.

Edwards (1979) and Jacoby (1985) apply this perspective to the shift in industrial production from direct shop floor supervision to bureaucratic controls and protections. The "drive system" was defended by foreman, production managers, and plant superintendents who wanted to get product out cheaply and retain flexibility in dealing with the workforce. It was attacked by unions seeking to protect their members (as well as social reformers and personnel professionals motivated by a positive-sum view of labor relations). Regulated internal labor markets emerged out of the post-World War II settlement, a period where American union organization stood at an all-time high (Guillén, 1994).

Elites may act as institutional entrepreneurs as well. Brint and Karabel (1991) point to the role of administrative leaders in initiating change in the niche occupied by American community colleges. Junior colleges were founded in the shadow of an established academic system, traditionally cast in the role of "feeder schools" preparing students to transfer into four-year programs. Brint and Karabel describe junior college administrators as actively seeking a less subordinated niche. They argue that elites identified vocational education for white-collar work as that niche and actively repositioned junior colleges prior to the softening labor market of the 1970s, which eroded student opposition and permitted substantial organizational change.

Greenwood and Hinings (1996; Hinings et al., 1991) describe struggle between organizational coalitions over "organizational templates." For example, professional organizations can be structured as partnerships or corporations; public agencies can adopt a bureaucratic or a customer service logic; management–worker relations may be defined as solidary or as oppositional. In an analysis reminiscent of Marxist accounts of revolutionary change, Hinings et al., (1991) argue that institutional templates may change when an emerging coalition finds the existing template inimical to its interests, has a sense of itself as a mobilized group, and has an alternative to offer. They note the case of Arthur Andersen, whose management consulting division increased in size and revenue generating capacity but not in power. Consultants identified Arthur Andersen's partnership structure as marginalizing their position, and pushed to reorganize around a corporate model.

Attention to the way organizational leaders and coalitions craft organizational missions recalls the insights of the "old institutionalism" of Selznick. What is involved is more a marriage than a replay of these ideas, however. Rather than treating organizations as inventing and developing distinctive missions, recent work emphasizes public choices among well-defined institutional frames and collective efforts. Greenwood and Hinings (1996) thus argue that organizational coalitions select templates from a larger institutional menu. And Brint and Karabel (1991) see community college leaders as moving collectively rather than individually towards vocational programs.

TRIGGERS OF INSTITUTIONAL CHANGE

Change agents are often ushered onto the stage by "triggering" conditions. These often take the form of a problem or crisis that motivates a search for alternatives. For radio broadcasting this might be the advent of television; for health care it might be spiraling costs; for employment practices it might be wartime mobilization.

Triggering conditions are undertheorized within the institutional perspective. They appear as exogenous conditions that weaken institutional supports and precipitate efforts at reform or innovation. It is difficult even in principle to incorporate such conditions into an institutional theory of change, since crises should be less likely to be recognized as such within successfully institutionalized domains. By attending to triggering conditions, institutional accounts implicitly assume that existing practice is not institutionalized but instead primordial and unorganized.

Perhaps the most common triggering condition is performance failure. Institutionalized practices are threatened when they fail to deliver the goods. For example, Kuhn (1962) argues that most science consists of puzzle solving within a dominant paradigm. Over time, however, anomalies appear that are resistant to satisfactory solution. Failure to resolve anomalies then leads toward paradigm change. For instance, efforts by medieval astronomers to predict planetary orbits within the Platonic system led to great improvement in astronomical observation and calculation. But these improvements only highlighted the anomalies that continued to appear as astronomers interpreted planetary movements as circular and geocentric. Growing dissatisfaction with Platonism laid the foundation for Copernicus and Kepler to successfully forward a heliocentric model of the solar system where planets followed elliptical orbits.

In organizational research, analyses of top-down institutional reform often start from performance failures that falsify established theories of effective action. For example, Sine (2000) finds that the oil crisis of the 1970s motivated scrutiny of industry structure. Since the 1930s, the utility industry had been organized into regional monopolies, an approach legitimated by economic theories of increasing returns to scale. But heightened scrutiny led a variety of economists to make the case that utilities were not natural monopolies. Legislators then drew on the expert literature to make the case for deregulation and to counter stakeholders within the industry.

Performance failure motivates other sorts of institutional innovators as well. Davis et al. (1994) note that the "bust up" takeovers of the 1980s were preceded by a track record of relative economic failure. Since the 1960s, conglomerates were out-performed by randomly selected portfolios of companies operating in the same industry (Davis et al., 1994, p. 55). By the 1980s, the managers who had built conglomerates were seen as having made a "colossal mistake" as public discussions of failure spurred takeover artists to acquire and bust up corporations.

Performance failure provides only one possible trigger of institutional change, however; see Oliver (1992) for a detailed discussion of sources of deinstitutionalization. For example, Haveman and Rao (1997) relate the life chances of institutional models to broad social structural change. Early thrifts were built around principles of mutuality and individual effort that worked well given the strength and stability of local communities. After the turn of the century, however, these plans were increasingly displaced by alternative schemes that added bureaucratic roles, alternative forms of membership, and freer entry and exit. Haveman and Rao describe this shift as flowing from the modernization of American society, as immigration and urbanization turned an America of small towns and close-knit groups into a society of strangers.

LEGITIMATING CHANGE

What role do cultural materials play in institutional change? Interpretive schemes can delegitimate existing arrangements as inefficient, dysfunctional, or backward, and simultaneously promote an alternative practice as optimal and progressive. In addition to social structural change, for example, Haveman and Rao (1997) suggest that the Progressivist emphasis on predictability and expertise supplied ideological supports for new types of thrifts.

Strang and Bradburn (2001) emphasize the power of market models in the state's conceptualization of health maintenance organizations. Prepaid plans had historically been interpreted as steps toward direct consumer control or as enhanced teamwork among physicians. But the reframing of HMOs as economizing vehicles that "got the incentives right" proved a powerful rhetorical weapon in legislative and regulatory decision making. Close examination of the legislative process (Brown, 1983) indicates how powerfully the new argument for HMOs dominated debate.

Davis et al. (1994) point to shifting organizational understandings in explaining the deinstitutionalization of the conglomerate in the 1980s. While arguing that takeovers were conducted by outsiders in response to performance failure, Davis et al. push the analysis one step further to ask why elites were unable to defend themselves. They argue that the conglomerate was made vulnerable by a re-conceptualization of the firm as a "nexus of contracts." What might have been resisted as the ghoulish dismembering of the nation's largest corporations was instead understood as the belated but necessary restructuring of corporate monstrosities.

Of course, existing institutional arrangements possess cultural backing as well. Davis et al. (1994) note that the conglomerate had been theorized via a "firm as portfolio" model that touted the ability of top management teams to make discerning investment decisions. Strang and Bradburn describe the health sector as organized around a model of "professional sovereignty" vested in the expertise and integrity of the physician.

But the frames that legitimate dominant practices can lose credibility. Performance failure can accomplish this discrediting, most powerfully when failures occur that are anomalous and inexplicable within the frame. Frames also lose credibility when they evolve in internally inconsistent or outlandish ways. Davis et al. (1994) explain that the "firm as portfolio" model strained deeper understandings of the firm as an organic collectivity. If firms were like portfolios consisting of manifestly unrelated activities, then they could be broken up into their independent parts. And conversely, if "portfolios with smokestacks" were not organic wholes, then perhaps the fundamental notion of firms as naturally bounded collectivities was mistaken. Davis et al. thus argue that conglomerates themselves helped sponsor the "nexus of contracts" model, and its own evolution into ideas about core competence, virtual firms, and even "Moebius strip organizations."

Attention to cultural sources of change emphasizes that institutional arguments need not assume over-socialized actors. Friedland and Alford (1991) argue that different "societal spheres" embody different characteristic logics: that of self-interested action in the economic sphere, representation and democracy in the political sphere, love, and commitment in the sphere of the family, and so on. Institutional entrepreneurs are then able to legitimate new projects by importing alternative logics. Radical feminists can re-interpret the family within a frame of individual rights to argue for a household contract, while health care analysts can re-interpret doctors as profit-maximizers within a "health care industry" that should be treated like any other market.

We can see the impact of compelling re-interpretations of organizational problems by observing what happens in their absence. In one such case, Tolbert and Sine (1999) examine the deinstitutionalization of tenure-based university employment. While tenure is fundamental to much university employment and supported by the efforts of the American Association of University Professors (AAUP), increased cost pressures in the 1970s resulted in heavy scrutiny of all wage costs. Universities responded in various ways, with a small number doing away with tenure altogether (or seeking to do so). A much more important but less visible response, however, was to incrementally increase the number of part-time, temporary, and adjunct positions, so that rules about tenure remained unchanged but came to cover fewer positions.

When institutional reform is culturally foreclosed, a characteristic form of deinstitutionalization tends to occur. Institutions are not transformed but adulterated through the introduction of new, opposing practices. Symbolic values and behavior are decoupled, so organizations celebrate traditional practices while quietly pursuing others as well. Institutional adulteration also diffuses in a particular way: divergence from institutional rules occurs in peripheral and vulnerable organizations rather than central and leading ones, and adulteration tends not to be contagious. Finally, adulteration can even be seen to protect and preserve the (now more delimited) institution. For example, tenure for some remains robust, in part, because poorly paid temporary and part-time faculty can be hired.

Current Issues and Debates

We note two measurement issues for institutional research in general and the study of institutional change in particular. First, better methods of assessing the abandonment and transformation of organizational practices are needed. Most research focuses on the initial adoption of novel practices, which are generally positive acts recorded by the state or relevant associations. By contrast, abandonment is frequently a non-event where material support for a practice is quietly withdrawn. New data collection methods that identify "organizational histories" linking adoptions, abandonments, and transformations are needed; see Easton and Jarrell (1998) for an exemplary study in this direction.

A second challenge is to better assess legitimacy. Ecological models of density dependence have stimulated sharp criticism as culturally and relationally uninformed. For example, Zucker (1989) points out that protesters throw blood on fur coats not because they are unused to seeing mink, but because they are concerned with animal cruelty and loss of ecological diversity. Baum and Powell (1995) argue for direct inspection of the media communications that promote new practices and industries (Hybels and Ryan, 1996). Hannan and Carroll (1995) defend density counts as highly general and parsimonious relative to culturally specific measures.

This debate generates two lines of research. First, it promotes efforts to devise rich direct measures of legitimacy. For example, Ruef and Scott (1998) examine different forms of hospital accreditation and how these affect organizational survival and Hybels and Ryan (1996) directly measure media sources of legitimacy and their influence on organizational foundings. Second, the generality of density dependence studies can be exploited by probing variation across organizational populations. If critics like Zucker are right, some populations are "born legitimate" while others face a heavy struggle against powerful opponents and entrenched public opinion. Comparative analysis of patterns of density dependence across different organizational populations can probe cultural and political sources of variability in legitimacy.

Questions That Remain Unanswered

INSTITUTIONALIZATION AND INSTITUTIONAL DECLINE

Haveman (2000) argues that the lack of agreement about central constructs is an impediment to progress in the institutional research tradition. The most fundamental unanswered question is when is an organizational practice or form an institution? Without consensus on this point, the concept of "institution" is extremely imprecise, a "you know it when you see it" phenomenon. Most institutional work agrees that organizational practices and forms are fully institutionalized when they are adopted by most of the organizations within an institutional field (Tolbert and Zucker, 1996). Yet, there is little theoretical or empirical work that develops enough precision to differentiate between the pre-institutionalized, semi-institutionalized, and fully institutionalized stages of an organizational form or practice (Tolbert and Zucker, 1996).

Similar ambiguity about the nature of an institution exists at the organizational level, where empirical research often treats institutionalization as a dichotomous variable; for exceptions see Sine (2000) and Tolbert and Sine (1999). For example, CEO decisions to adopt a popular management practice may be counted as institutionalizing it even though the practice is not viewed as legitimate to or taken for granted by the majority of employees at the firm. This imprecision is largely a result of ambiguity about the characteristics that differentiate the institutionalized from the uninstitutionalized.

A second unanswered question that follows the first is at what point of abandonment is an organizational process or form undergoing deinstitutionalization? The lack of paradigmatic consensus and imprecision impedes researchers collective ability to propose and test hypotheses (Haveman, 2000) about institutional decline, and is reflected in the paucity of literature on the topics. Critical questions about the life cycle of institutions cannot be approached without theoretical tools that enable researchers to examine fluctuations in degrees of institutionalization (Schneiberg and Clemens, 1998). Fluctuations in usage, discourse, and relational embeddedness are common, but without a clearly defined measure of institutionalization it is difficult to address their causes and consequences (Sine, 1999).

Paradigmatic confusion is not new to the institutional research tradition. Early tautological conceptions of institutionalization defined institutions as patterned actions that persist (Zucker, 1987). From this perspective, institutions could not change for if they did, then they would not be "persisting" and not an institution. Zucker (1987, p. 444) explained that contemporary institutional theories avoid this trap by "treating institutionalization as a variable and by separating its causes from its major consequence." Effective discussion of institutional change is aided by an underlying theoretical understanding of institutionalization as a matter of degree rather than a defined state (Tolbert and Zucker, 1996).

Empirical research on institutional change requires clear explanations about those institutional qualities that enable organizational behaviors and forms to resist change and endure. Discussions of institutional change would be advanced by an index based on observable dimensions of institutional resistance to change. Such an index might include cognitive measures of taken for grantedness developed through discourse analysis, normative measures of density of usage from associational records or organizational surveys, and regulatory measures of formal mandates promulgated by governments, professions, and trade associations (Sine, 1999).

LEGITIMACY VS. STATUS

Legitimacy has been seen by institutional theorists as fundamental to the explanation of why some practices and organizational forms are more prevalent than others (Suchman, 1995). Often cited definitions of legitimacy include the "generalized perception or assumption" that certain practices or forms are appropriate. Thus, institutionalists argue that organizations may strategically adopt certain practices in order to increase their legitimacy and thereby improve their chances for survival and enhanced performance (Oliver, 1991; Meyer and Rowan, 1977) or that they adopt practices that are so legitimate that they are taken for granted (Berger and Luckmann, 1967). This argument implies a stratification of organizations, practices, and forms along a continuum of legitimacy. At one end of the continuum are less accepted organizations and practices and at the other end are organizational practices and forms that are congruent with commonly accepted norms and values (Suchman, 1995).

This view of stratification is limited in its power to explain choices among legitimate alternatives. For example, the fact that Harvard Business School curricula are more likely to be disseminated than are the curricula of entirely legitimate "third tier" universities cannot be understood simply by reference to legitimacy. The traditional sociological concept of status is useful here. Numerous sociologists have argued that organizations and institutions are stratified and some are more prestigious than others (Parsons, 1949; Perrow, 1961, Stinchcombe, 1965; Merton, 1968). Status influences organizational and intraorganizational practices such as exchange relations (Thye, 2000), interorganzational affiliations (Podolny, 1993; Benjamin and Podolny, 1999), citation patterns (Crane, 1972), resource allocation (Perrow, 1961), internal labor markets (Merton, 1968), and technology adoption (Shane and Sine, 2000). More attention is needed to its role in the creation, diffusion, and decline of institutions.

New and Emerging Directions

RESEARCH DESIGN

Institutional research furthers an understanding of change when it examines contexts where institutions are incomplete or collapsing, or where multiple institutional frames are in competition. Such contexts are not rare but ubiquitous. For example, many efforts at organizational change appeal to fundamental cultural values, like "scientific management," "workplace democracy," and "personal development." But the actors who promote these ideas and whose interests are directly bound up in their acceptance are often located outside the organization altogether (consultants and researchers) or in oppositional or peripheral organizational roles (unions, quality control engineers, personnel/human resource professionals). These settings provide an opportunity to examine under what conditions cultural backing can be translated into institutional change, and to observe what happens when it is not.

Institutional research increasingly studies these sorts of contested settings. For example, Rao (1998) portrays competition between alternative ways of framing consumer watchdog groups. *Consumer Reports* was formed around a technocratic ideal, treating the consumer as a rational actor in need of product evaluation by neutral scientists. By contrast, *Consumers Union* was formed around notions of working-class solidarity, where the watchdog organization reported on consumer goods but also on labor practices and the health of working communities. *Consumer Reports* was able to dominate the competition, leading its rival to move towards a more socially neutral, scientific role.

A second trend is towards longer-term analyses of institutional change. Analyses over short time periods tend to portray institutions as unchanging, and even those that examine a key turning point can argue that the "ancient regime" was not quite institutionalized enough. But work that describes the rise and fall of institutions (more adequately than studies of the "fall and rise") must address endogenous sources of change. Much historically informed scholarship provides exemplars here, as do expansive organizational analyses like Fligstein (1990) and Guillén (1994). For example, Starr's (1982) magisterial analysis of American health system documents the rise of the medical profession, the consequent ability of physicians to ward off efforts at national health care and to expand the financial base of the system, and the "coming of the corporation" via for-profit hospital chains, HMOs, and managed care. The continuities in Starr's account allow one to see how physician dominance and organizational growth ultimately undercut professional claims to autonomy, leading the health care field to move from an institutional structure of professional sovereignty to one centered on health care corporations.

MAKING IT DYNAMIC

Endogenous dynamics are rare in accounts of institutional change. The state intervenes in personnel decisions affairs due to shifts in the political arena (like the Civil Rights movement and its roots in migration patterns and party realignments) that are not produced by firms or human resource administrators. Colleges respond to shifting student career orientations that are not generated by the schools themselves. These arguments point to important drivers of change, but are theoretically incomplete because causal loops are not closed. We note several lines of analysis that begin to redress this problem.

John Meyer and colleagues (Meyer and Rowan, 1977; Meyer, Boli and Thomas, 1987) offer an endogenous dynamic of rationalization. They view Western culture as defining individuals as moral, rational agents whose actions should realize progress and equality. This cultural project underwrites the construction of professions, state agencies, and social reformers. But as more activities come under the inspection of expert "others" (Meyer and Jepperson 2000), more inequities and opportunities for rationalization are discovered. These discoveries support further professional expansion, which identify even more problems to be rectified. Rationalization is here a positive feedback system, where cultural attention to "social problems" produces reformers and reformers produce social problems.

This argument can be reworked to identify more contradictory dynamics, where newly authorized actors turn out to have goals that are different from those of their creators. DiMaggio (1991) argues that while social elites supported professionalization as part of building museums that responded to their vision, museum professionals then gravitated to a reform movement aimed at educating the general public. Museum professionals were deferential to the desires of upper class trustees and donors when wearing "organizational hats," but their national associations promoted branch museums and a more inclusive model of the museum.

A second core problem is whether ideas about the crystallization of institutions can be "run backward" to model decay as well as growth. Zucker (1988) suggests attention to entropy, where laboriously constructed institutions are lost through transmission errors and disuse. Abrahamson (1996; Abrahamson and Fairchild 1999) draws attention to management fashions, arguing that popularity provides no guarantees in sectors oriented to rhetorics of progress and novelty. Strang and Macy (2000) find that weak assumptions about abandonment lead imitative processes of the type described by DiMaggio and Powell (1983) to produce faddish cycles rather than institutional stability.

Other lines of argument see "completed institutions" as particularly unstable. If a population of organizations adopts the same model or practice, they draw on the same, increasingly scarce resources. Competitive pressure will thus tend to intensify, and organizations will perceive less opportunity for extraordinary success. Leblebici et al. (1991) argue that it is under these conditions that core organizations adopt innovations developed on the periphery, provoking large-scale institutional change. Greenwood and Hinings (1996) suggest that these are also the conditions under which risk-seeking organizations embrace new institutional templates. While new approaches may provide lower average returns than institutionalized templates, they offer the only chance of outdistancing the field.

Finally, institutional crisis and change can be endogenized by treating the opposing groups as constituting each other. Marx's model of class struggle is an exemplar here. At one level his model involves rivalry between differing institutions, each carried by a social class (so the bourgeoisie carries capitalism and the working class, socialism). But these classes are not groups that happen to come into contact – they construct each other, and their conflict is fundamental to their identities. Further, the resolution of this conflict is seen by Marx as occurring at a point of institutional completion. Socialism becomes imminent as capitalism concentrates ownership of the means of production, driving petty capitalists into the ranks of the workers, promoting class-based mobilization, and driving down the rate of profit. In several senses, Marx thus portrays an endogenous dynamic of institutional change.

Connections Across Levels

Structures of meaning inhabit every level of analysis. Yet following Meyer and Rowan's (1977) powerful notion of societal myths, organizational researchers have treated institutions as residing at interorganizational and supra-organizational (i.e., societal) levels. This conception supplanted that of the "old institutionalists," which treated organizations as emergent institutions with distinctive traditions and modes of adaptation (Selznick, 1949; Clark, 1970). It is notable (but not surprising) that all three of the reviews of the institutional perspective in this volume take the externality of institutions to organizations as a starting point.

Given this scheme, causes within the institutional perspective flow down from contexts rather than up from actors. Mimetic, normative, and coercive pressures involving inter- and supra-organizational relations lead to adoption, implementation, adaptation, and maintenance decisions by organizations (DiMaggio and Powell, 1983; Westney, 1987). Organizational actions then shape the problems and opportunities faced by groups and units within organizations.

It seems clear that the research community is moving towards more reciprocal formulations. As Elsbach (this volume) details, institutional analyses at the intraorganizational level are developing rapidly. And while there remains little theorization of "organizational institutions," much recent work views organizational responses to larger institutions as strategic (Westphal et al., 1997; Tolbert and Sine, 1999). Organizational variability is linked to action orientations (like Westphal et al's discussion of customization) rather than vulnerability to institutional mandates (like that induced by dependence on the state for funds or accreditation). While external pressures and opportunities are of great consequence as is abundantly clear in Palmer and Biggart's chapter, new practices also bubble up from the actions of organizations and their subunits.

For example, in the late 1980s, Motorola responded to competitive threats from Japan by adopting an aggressive quality management program. While the policies it adopted were shaped by evolving approaches to organizational change and quality control in American business as a whole, Motorola's program moved from formal initiative to a self-reinforcing system of small group innovation. Motorola capitalized on its success by marketing its approach to other corporations, who sent their staff to Motorola's training facility (Motorola University), hired Motorola consultants, and sometimes poached Motorola's quality managers to reproduce the "Motorola approach to quality." In this case we see a cycle in which broad interorganizational conditions stimulated the adoption of management innovations at the organizational level, formal programs catalyzed institutional transformation at the intraorganizational level, and the resulting package then diffused to other organizations.

In general, institutional analysis can treat both the isomorphic and the constitutive nature of institutional processes. Organizational and interorganizational research commonly emphasizes the importance of isomorphic pressures on the adoption and maintenance of organizational forms and processes (DiMaggio and Powell, 1983; Tolbert and Zucker, 1983; Baron et al., 1986). Intraorganizational research often examines emergent institutional processes such as the creation and adaptation of scripts and roles (Barley, 1986; Ashforth and Fried, 1988). While in this review we have considered models of interorganizational institutional change, multilevel analyses may offer the firmest ground for theoretical and empirical advance.

Conclusion

The study of substantial institutional change is a common subject of institutional research, and empirical research develops real insights into change agents, triggering conditions, and legitimating models. But institutional accounts of change are not theories because they point to proximate conditions rather than endogenous dynamics, and do not address institutional change because they treat established arrangements as uninstitutionalized. Much recent conceptual and empirical work addresses these limitations by attending to the variety of institutional resources that actors can access, and by treating actors as creative institutional entrepreneurs rather than conforming dopes.

References

Abrahamson, E. (1996): "Management fashion," *Academy of Management Review*, 21, 254–85.

Abrahamson, E., and Fairchild, G. (1999): "Management fashion: lifecycles, triggers, and collective learning processes," *Administrative Science Quarterly*, 44, 708–40.

Ashforth, B. E., and Fried, Y. (1988): "The mindlessness of organizational behaviors," *Human Relations*, 41, 305–329.

Barley, S. R. (1986): "Technology as an occasion for structuring: Evidence from observations of CT scanners and the social order of radiology departments," *Administrative Science Quarterly*, 31, 78–108.

Baron, J. N., Dobbin, F., and Jennings, P. D. (1986): "War and peace: The evolution of modern personnel administration in US industry," *American Journal of Sociology*, 92, 350–83.

Baum, J. A. C., and Oliver C. (1992): "Institutional embeddedness and the dynamics of organizational population," *American Sociological Review*, 57, 540–59.

Baum, J. A. C., and Powell, W. W. (1995): "Cultivating an institutional ecology: Comment on Hannan, Carroll, Dundon, and Torres," *American Sociological Review*, 60, 529–38.

Benjamin, B. A., and Podolny, J. M. (1999): "Status, quality, and social order in the California wine industry," *Administrative Science Quarterly*, 44, 563–89.

Berger, P. L., and Luckmann, T. (1967): *The Social Construction of Reality*. New York: Doubleday.

Brint, S., and Karabel, J. (1991): "Institutional origins and transformations: The case of American community colleges," in W. W. Powell and P. J. DiMaggio (eds), *The New Institutionalism in Organizational Analysis*, Chicago: University of Chicago Press, 337–60.

Brown, L. D. (1983): *Politics and Health Care Organization*. Washington, DC: Brookings.

Campbell, J. L., and Pedersen, O. K. (eds) (2001): *The Second Movement in Institutional Analysis: Neoliberalism in Perspective*. Princeton: Princeton University Press.

Clark, B. (1970): *The Distinctive College: Antioch, Reed, and Swarthmore*. New York: Aldine.

Clemens, E. S., and Cook, J. M. (1999): "Politics and institutionalism: Explaining durability and change," *Annual Review of Sociology*, 25, 441–66.

Cole, R. E. (1989): *Strategies for Learning*. Berkeley: University of California Press.

Crane, D. (1972): *Invisible Colleges: Diffusion of Knowledge in Scientific Communities*. Chicago: University of Chicago Press.

Davis, G. F., Diekmann, K. A., and Tinsley, C. H. (1994): "The decline and fall of the conglomerate firm in the 1980s: The deinstitutionalization of an organizational form," *American Sociological Review*, 59, 547–70.

Davis, G. F., and Greve, H. R. (1997): "Corporate elite networks and governance changes in the 1980s," *American Journal of Sociology*, 103, 1–37.

DiMaggio, P. J. (1988): "Interest and agency in institutional theory," in L. G. Zucker (ed.), *Institutional Patterns and Organizations*, Cambridge, Mass: Ballinger, 3–22.

DiMaggio, P. J. (1991) "Constructing an organizational field as a professional project: US Art Museums, 1920–1940," in W. W. Powell and P. J. DiMaggio (eds), *The New Institutionalism in Organizational Analysis*, Chicago: University of Chicago Press, 267–92.

DiMaggio, P. J., and Powell, W. W. (1983): "The iron cage revisited: Institutional isomorphism and collective rationality in organizational fields," *American Sociological Review*, 48, 147–60.

DiMaggio, P. J., and Powell, W. W. (1991): "Introduction," in W. W. Powell and P. J. DiMaggio (eds), *The New Institutionalism in Organizational Analysis*, Chicago: University of Chicago Press, 1–38.

Dobbin, F. (1994): *Forging Industrial Policy: The United States, Britain and France in the Railway Age*. New York: Cambridge University Press.

Dobbin, F., Sutton, J. R., Meyer, J. W., and Scott, W. R. (1993): "Equal opportunity law and the construction of internal labor markets," *American Journal of Sociology*, 99, 396–427.

Easton, G., and Jarrell, S. (1998): "The effects of total quality management on corporate performance: An empirical investigation," *Journal of Business*, 71, 253–307.

Edelman, L. B. (1990): "Legal environments and organizational governance: The expansion of due process in the American workplace," *American Journal of Sociology*, 95, 1401–40.

Edelman, L. B. (1992): "Legal ambiguity and symbolic structures: Organizational mediation of civil rights law," *American Journal of Sociology*, 97, 1531–76.

Edelman, L. B., Uggen, C., and Erlanger, H. S. (1999): "The endogeneity of legal regulation: Grievance procedures as rational myth," *American Journal of Sociology*, 105, 406–54.

Edwards, R. (1979): *Contested Terrain: The Transformation of the Workplace in the Twentieth Century*. New York: Basic Books.

Fligstein, N. (1990): *The Transformation of Corporate Control*. Cambridge, Mass: Harvard University Press.

Friedland, R., and Alford, R. R. (1991): "Bringing society back in: Symbols, practices, and institutional contradictions," in W. W. Powell and P. J. DiMaggio (eds), *The New Institutionalism in Organizational Analysis*, Chicago: University of Chicago Press, 232–63.

Greenwood, R., and Hinings, C. R. (1996): "Understanding radical organizational change: Bringing together the old and new institutionalism," *Academy of Management Review*, 21, 1022–54.

Guillén, M. F. (1994): *Models of Management*. Chicago: University of Chicago Press.

Hall, P. A., and Taylor, R. (1996): "Political science and the three new institutionalisms," *Political Studies*, 44, 936–58.

Hamilton, G. G., and Biggart, N. W. (1988): "Market, culture, and authority: A comparative analysis of management and organization in the Far East," *American Journal of Sociology*, 94, S52–94.

Hannan, M. T., and Carroll, G. R. (1995): "Theory building and cheap talk about legitimation: Reply to Baum and Powell," *American Sociological Review*, 60, 539–44.

Hannan, M. T., and Freeman, J. (1989): *Organizational Ecology*. Cambridge Mass: Harvard University Press.

Haveman, H. A. (2000): "The future of organizational sociology: forging ties among paradigms," *Contemporary Sociology*, 29, 476–86.

Haveman, H. A., and Rao, H. (1997): "Structuring a theory of moral sentiments: Institutional and organizational coevolution in the early thrift industry," *American Journal of Sociology*, 102, 1606–51.

Hinings, C. R., Brown, J. L., and Greenwood, R. (1991): "Change in an autonomous professional organization," *Journal of Management Studies*, 28, 375–93.

Hirsch, P. M. (1986): "From ambushes to golden parachutes: Corporate takeovers as an instance of cultural framing and institutional integration," *American Journal of Sociology*, 91, 800–37.

Hirsch, P. M. (1997): "Sociology without social structure: Neoinstitutional theory meets Brave New World," *American Journal of Sociology*, 102, 1702–23.

Hybels, R. C., and Ryan, A. R. (1996): "Entrepreneurship in U.S. commercial biotechnology from 1974 to 1989: An empirical test of the legitimation dynamic in density dependence theory," working paper, University of Illinois.

Jacoby, S. (1985): *Employing Bureaucracy: Managers, Unions, and the Transformation of Work in American Industry, 1900–1945*. New York: Columbia University Press.

Jepperson, R. L. (1991): "Institutions, institutional effects, and institutionalism," in W. W. Powell and P. J. DiMaggio (eds), *The New Institutionalism in Organizational Analysis*, 143–163.

Kraatz, M. S., and Zajac, E. J. (1996): "Exploring the limits of the new institutionalism: The causes and consequences of illegitimate organizational change," *American Sociological Review*, 61, 812–36.

Kuhn, T. S. (1962): *The Structure of Scientific Revolutions*. Chicago: University of Chicago Press.

Leblebici, H., Salancik, G. R., Copay, A., and King, T. (1991): "Institutional change and the transformation of interorganizational fields: An organizational history of the U.S. radio broadcasting industry," *Administrative Science Quarterly*, 36, 333–63.

McKenna, C. (1999): "The world's newest profession: The rise of management consulting in the twentieth century," PhD thesis, The Johns Hopkins University.

Merton, R. K. (1968): "The Matthew effect in science," *Science*, 159, 56–63.

Meyer, J. W., and Jepperson, R. L. (2000): "The 'actors' of modern society: The cultural construction of social agency," *Sociological Theory*, 18, 100–20.

Meyer, J. W., and Rowan, B. (1977): "Institutionalized organizations: Formal structure as myth and ceremony," *American Journal of Sociology*, 83, 440–63.

Meyer, J. W., Boli, J., and Thomas, G. M. (1987): "Ontology and rationalization in the western cultural account," in G. M. Thomas, J. W. Meyer, F. O. Ramirez, and J. Boli (eds), *Institutional Structure*, Newbury Park, CA: Sage, 12–38.

Meyer, J. W., Scott, W. R., and Strang, D. (1987): "Centralization, fragmentation, and school district complexity," *Administrative Science Quarterly*, 32, 186–201.

Oliver, C. (1991): "Strategic responses to institutional processes," *Academy of Management Review*, 16, 145–79.

Oliver, C. (1992): "The antecedents of deinstitutionalization," *Organization Studies*, 13, 563–88.

Parsons, T. (1949): *Essays in Sociological Theory*. Glencoe, IL: The Free Press.

Perrow, C. (1961): "Organizational prestige: Some functions and dysfunctions," *American Journal of Sociology*, 66, 335–41.

Podolny, J. M. (1993): "A status-based model of market competition," *American Journal of Sociology*, 98, 829–72.

Powell, W. W. (1991): "Expanding the scope of institutional analysis," in W. W. Powell and P. J. DiMaggio (eds), *The New Institutionalism in Organizational Analysis*, Chicago: University of Chicago Press, 183–203.

Rao, H. (1998): "Caveat emptor: The construction of nonprofit consumer watchdog organizations," *American Journal of Sociology*, 103, 912–61.

Ritti, R. R., and Silver, J. H. (1986): "Early processes of institutionalization: The dramaturgy of exchange in interorganizational relations," *Administrative Science Quarterly*, 31, 25–42.

Ruef, M., and Scott, W. R. (1998): "A multidimensional model of organizational legitimacy: Hospital survival in changing institutional environments," *Administrative Science Quarterly*, 43, 877–904.

Schneiberg, M., and Clemens, E. S. (1998): "The typical tools for the job: research strategies in institutional analysis," unpublished working paper, prepared for W. W. Powell and D. L. Jones (eds), *Bending the Bars of the Iron Cage*.

Scott, W. R. (1987): "The adolescence of institutional theory," *Administrative Science Quarterly*, 32, 493–511.

Scott, W. R. (1995): *Institutions and Organizations*. Thousand Oaks, CA: Sage.

Selznick, P. (1949): *TVA and the Grass Roots*. Berkeley, CA: University of California Press.

Selznick, P. (1957): *Leadership in Administration*. Berkeley, CA: University of California Press.

Shane, S. and Sine, W. D. (2000): "Organizational status and the commercialization of knowledge," working paper, University of Maryland – College Park.

Shenhav, Y. (1999): *Manufacturing Rationality*. Oxford: Oxford University Press.

Sine, W. D. (1999): "Paths to deinstitutionalization: Forms, processes, and outcomes," paper presented at the annual meetings of the American Sociological Association, Chicago.

Sine, W. D. (2000): "From hierarchies to markets: The deregulation of the U.S. electric utility industry," paper presented at the annual meetings of the American Sociological Association, Washington DC.

Starr, P. (1982): *The Social Transformation of American Medicine*. New York: Basic Books.

Stearns, L. B., and Allan, K. D. (1996): "Economic behavior in institutional environments: The corporate merger wave of the 1980s," *American Sociological Review*, 61, 699–718.

Stinchcombe, A. L. (1965): "Social structure and organizations," in J. G. March (ed.) *Handbook of Organizations*, Chicago: Rand McNally, 142–93.

Stinchcombe, A. L. (1997): "On the virtues of the old institutionalism," *Annual Review of Sociology*, 23, 1–18.

Strang, D., and Bradburn, E. M. (2001): "Theorizing legitimacy or legitimating theory? Neoliberal discourse and HMO policy," in J. Campbell and O. K. Pedersen (eds), *The Second Movement in Institutional Analysis: Neoliberalism in Perspective*, Princeton: Princeton University Press.

Strang, D., and Macy, M. W.(2000): "'In search of excellence': Fads, success stories, and communication bias," *American Journal of Sociology*.

Strang, D., and Soule, S. A. (1998): "Diffusion in organizations and social movements: From hybrid corn to poison pills," *Annual Review of Sociology*, 24, 265–90.

Suchman, M. C. (1995): "Managing legitimacy: strategic and institutional approaches," *The Academy of Management Review*, 20, 571–610.

Thye, S. R. (2000): "A status value theory of power in exchange relations," *American Sociological Review*, 65, 407–32.

Tolbert, P. S., and Sine, W. D. (1999): "Determinants of organizational compliance with institutional pressures: The employment of non-tenure-track faculty in institutions of higher education," paper presented at the annual meetings of the Academy of Management, Chicago.

Tolbert, P. S., and Zucker, L. G. (1983): "Institutional sources of change in the formal structure of organizations: The diffusion of civil service reform," *Administrative Science Quarterly*, 28, 22–39.

Tolbert, P. S., and Zucker, L. G. (1996): "The institutionalization of institutional theory," in S. R. Clegg, C. Hardy, and W. R. Nord (eds), *Handbook of Organization Studies*, Thousand Oaks, CA: Saga, 175–90.

Weber, M. (1958): *The Protestant Ethic and the Spirit of Capitalism*. New York: Scribner's.

Westney, D. E. (1987): *Imitation and Innovation: The Transfer of Western Organizational Patterns to Meiji Japan*. Cambridge, MA: Harvard University Press.

Westphal, J. D., Gulati, R., and Shortell, S. M. (1997): "Customization or conformity? An institutional and network perspective on the content and consequences of TQM adoption," *Administrative Science Quarterly*, 42, 366–94.

Zucker, L. G. (1987): "Institutional theories of organizations," *Annual Review of Sociology*, 13, 443–64.

Zucker, L. G. (1988): "Where do institutional patterns come from? Organizations as actors in social systems," in L. G. Zucker (ed.) *Institutional Patterns and Organizations,* Cambridge, Mass: Ballinger, 23–49.

Zucker, L. G. (1989): "Combining institutional theory and population ecology: No legitimacy, no history," *American Sociological Review,* 54, 542–5.

Chapter Twenty-two

Interorganizational Networks

WAYNE E. BAKER AND ROBERT R. FAULKNER

Interorganizational networks (ION) are a venerable subject in sociology and organizational theory. Recently, however, the concept of the "network" has become even more popular, as pundits, management consultants, and organizational theorists promote the "network" as the interorganizational form of the future (Powell, 1987; Powell and Smith-Doerr, 1994) and even the emerging form of society (Pescosolido and Rubin, 2000) This popularity has not brought clarity to a subject that is already broad and eclectic. For example, the "network organization" means many things to many people, as DiMaggio (2001) discusses. Different researchers examine different aspects of the network organization, and different consultants put different features of it into practice. Given the broad and fragmented field of interorganizational networks our goal in this chapter is sensemaking: We propose a way to structure this field in a way that imposes order on it, captures contemporary debates and issues, highlights unanswered questions, and points to some new and emerging directions for future research.

We offer the concept of the interorganizational network or ION "box," a three-dimensional array that captures the main concepts in the field. We show, for example, how different foci – dyads, triads, organization set, organizational field, and interorganizational network – fit into this framework. We illustrate these components of the ION box by reviewing key studies in the field of interorganizational networks. We discuss three categories of contemporary debates – embeddedness, institutionalization, and the rise of the network organizational form. Finally, we offer new directions for study, showing that our structuring of the field suggests new avenues of research even for old questions about interorganizational networks:

- What is an organization's network?
- What is interorganizational embeddedness?
- What are the conjoint activities of organizations?

We conclude with a shift of perspective from a view of interorganizational networks of as a "network of interlocking organizations" to a "network of interlocking domains."

Structuring the Field of Interorganizational Networks

The field of research on ION draws from a diverse array of theories and spans levels of analysis from microstructures (Laumann and Marsden, 1982) to organizational fields (DiMaggio, 1991) and the entire economy (Burt, 1992). To structure this eclecticism, we propose a framework we call the interorganizational network or ION "box," a versatile three-dimensional rectangular matrix of organizations and activities. This ION box is inspired by developments in network theory and analysis, such as three-dimensional blockmodeling (Baker, 1986).

A simple illustration of the ION box is shown in Figure 22.1. This box arrays the interrelationships of three populations – producers, suppliers, and buyers – across domains. Suppliers and customers can be thought of as specific organizations or segments. Some of the major domains identified in the field of interorganizational studies include

1 market exchange, e.g., Baker (1990)
2 strategic alliances, e.g., Gulati (1995)
3 joint participation in an underwriting syndicate, e.g., Podolny (1993)
4 director interlocks, e.g., Mizruchi (1996)
5 political action, e.g., Neustadl and Clawson (1988) and Mizruchi (1989)
6 family ties, e.g., Zeitlin et al. (1974)
7 illegal activities, such as price-fixing conspiracies (e.g., Baker and Faulkner 1993).

These domains of activities occupy what we call *k*-space in the ION box. Like an accordion, the ION box can be expanded or contracted to change levels of analysis, units of observation, or range of activity domains. For example, many other domains could be added to our Figure 22.1. And, a single domain in our illustration could be expanded. For example, the market domain could be elaborated into multiple markets.

The ION box is divided into three main blocks. The middle block contains a set of focal organizations; these are principal subjects of the analysis.[1] In this illustration, we consider these focal organizations to be producers. The left block contains the suppliers (upstream) and the right block contains the customers (downstream). In the middle block, we assign each producer to a row (n) and corresponding column (m) for each relation (k). Figure 22.1 shows five types of relations (k), chosen to illustrate the diversity of interorganizational ties (business, interlocks, political action, family, and illegal activities). Of course, additional or different k relations could be included. In the middle block, each k matrix is square, because a single population of producers is arrayed on both the rows and columns. In Figure 22.1, each i, j, k entry represents the relationship between producer i and producer j for relation k. An i, j, k entry could be binary, indicating the presence or absence of a relationship, such as the presence of an interlock between two producers, or an i, j, k entry could be continuous, indicating a quantity or quality associated with the relationship, such as the quantity of goods manufactured in a joint venture between two producers.

The left block contains organizations that supply the middle block. We assign the suppliers to the columns, and the producers to the rows, of each k matrix in the left block. Unlike k-matrices the middle block, which are square because a single population is arrayed along the rows and columns, the k-matrices in the left block are rectangular,

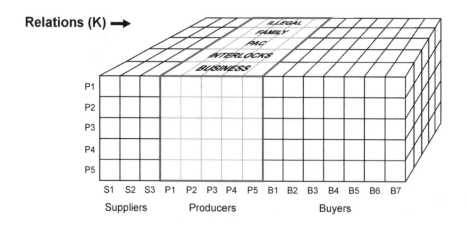

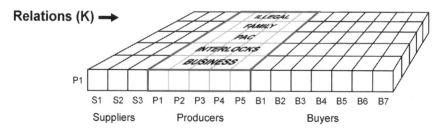

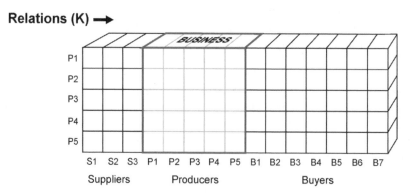

Figure 22.1 The ION box

because two populations are arrayed along the rows (producers) and the columns (suppliers). The right block contains the customers of the middle block. We construct the right block in a way similar to the left block. We assign the customers to the columns, and the producers to the rows, of each k matrix in the right block. Like k-matrices the left block, k-matrices in the right block are rectangular, because two populations are arrayed along the rows (producers) and the columns (customers).

Our following review shows how the ION box captures commonly used interorganizational concepts, as it suggests new areas of research. We organize this review according to units of analysis: dyad, triad, organization set, and organization field. Key studies are summarized in Table 22.1.

DYAD

It is a truism to say that a dyad – a pair of interacting organizations – is the basic unit of analysis in interorganizational research. But the dyad is not as simple as it may seem. For example, our ION box captures six types of dyads. An i, j, k cell in the middle block represents a dyad of producers for a particular domain. If we consider all k for the pair, however, we have a dyad set: the multiple relationships between two producers. Similarly, an i, j, k cell in the left block represents a dyad composed of a producer and a supplier for a particular domain. If we consider all k for the producer-supplier pair, however, we have another type of dyad set: the multiple relationships between a producer and a supplier. Finally, an i, j, k cell in the right block represents a dyad composed of a producer and a customer for a particular domain. If we consider all k for the producer-customer pair, we have the third type of dyad set: the multiple relationships between a producer and a customer.

In-depth studies of dyads help to make sense of interorganizational relations by learning "what flows across the links, who decides on those flows in the light of what interests, and what collective or corporate action flows from the organization of links" (Stinchcombe, 1990, p. 381). A study of dyads focuses tightly on the contents of a single dyad or dyad set in the ION box, such as Larson's (1992) informant and respondent centered ethnographic study of the exchange relationship between an entrepreneurial firm and its partnered organization. Observations of four entrepreneurial firms and seven dyadic ties to key upstream suppliers and downstream customers show how alliances were forged, strengthened, and sustained. The industries represented were telephone equipment, clothing, computer hardware, and environmental systems. Repeated interfirm dyadic exchanges lead to interdependencies. Social partnership emerges as a primary mechanism for governing business-to-business transactions. Social orientations are tucked into market relationships; reciprocity weighs as much as competitive pricing tactics. Eventually informal understandings replace formal contracts. Mutual obligations and strategic interests converge, slowly and cautiously at first, followed by a rapid upturn in perceived interdependence. The operations of a pair intertwine and one's success is dependent on the other's. Managers speak of "co-destiny," a phrase used by one firm's vice president in talking about the thick alliance-like behaviors with a supplier. The informal convention was "no suprises." This meant that both parties would share information, graciously offer disclosures about order flows, frankly discuss pricing, and willingly provide early warnings about potentially costly contingencies.

Interfirm alliances and "co-destiny" cultures demonstrate just how complex and interesting governance arrangements between firms can be across the i, j, k spaces. Close inspection of pricing practices in a dozen or so manufacturing firms would be an ideal laboratory for beginning to understand how organizations behave as both suppliers and buyers, the heart of the exchanges in the i, j, k matrix. Complications arise when a business unit transacts with firms in the market and also has business relations "inside" its own firm, transacting with other divisions. Thus, the single i, j, k dyad could also

Table 22.1 Key studies of interorganizational networks

ION space domains	Studies	Methods	Outcomes	Contribution
	Candidates			Lead concepts
Dyads	Larson, 1992	IXX/16	Coordination/trust	Cooperative relations
	Eccles and White, 1988	IXA/13	Costs/dilemmas	In(ex)ternal markets
	Zuckerman, 1999	XXA/K	(Il)legitimacy/penalty	Coverage/reviews
Triads	Gargiulo, 1993	n.a.	Counter controls	Co-optation
	Baker and Obstfeld, 1999	XXA/K	Social capital	(Dis)union designs
	Della Porta and Vannucci, 1999	IXA/<H	Corruption	Iron triangle
	Davis, 1979	n.a.	Network toolbox	Triadic census
Organization set	Evan, 1966	n.a.	Focal firm's linkages	Sensitizing concept
	Baker, 1990	IXA/>K	Autonomy/robustness	Hybrid/interface
	Uzzi, 1999	IOA/23	Survival/firm	Embeddedness/mix
	Baker et al., 1998	IXA/>K	Survival/relationship	Hazards/dissolution
	Baker and Faulkner, 1993	XXA/24	Secrecy/verdict/penalty	Conspiracy/collusion
Organization field	DiMaggio and Powell, 1983	n.a.	Isomorphism	Sensitizing concept
	Laumann and Knoke, 1987	IXA/K	Power/leverage	Policy in action
	Suchman, 1998	IXA/H	Pollination/capital	Structuration/venture
	Powell et al., 1996	IOA/<H	Learning/synergies	Collaboration
	Scott et al., 2000	IXA/H	Discourse/strategies	Reform/markets

Notes:
Methods: I = *interview*, O = *observation*, A = *archives*. X = this method of data collection was *not* used in the design and implementation of the interorganizational study.

N = number of organizations and/or representatives of organizations employed as units of observation and analysis in the empirical study: H=hundreds, K=thousands.

Interviews may be either "respondent" or "informant" based. Observations may be either "systematic" or "ethnographic." Systematic observation of interorganizational networks is typically "tightly" structured. The aim of data collection is to standardize the way in which ION connections are observed by the investigator *and* to tightly control the way in which they are recorded. This facilitates reliability and matrix analysis. Fieldwork, on the other hand, explores organizational domains and interorganizational connections in an open-system and multi-method fashion. Explicitly qualitative work is by design "loosely" administered. One aim is to capture the "richness" of the interplay within the *i, j, k* domains. The other aim is to discover unanticipated connections and linkages across the domains. Students of organizations and IONs have underutilized multi-method research. Multi-method contrasts with much organizational research, in which archives and documents appear to embody all the information that is relevant to the ION, somewhat like the role that "price" plays in economic theory (where price embodies all the information that is relevant to the transaction).

represent an intraorganizational transfer between divisions of a single firm. In an observation, interview, and archival study, Eccles and White (1988) show that "firms" operate in a market but also in a hierarchy. Fieldwork in three chemical companies showed that the imperatives of the market might only partially align with the imperatives of the firm. A divisional pricing policy that dictates or mandates "full cost pricing," requires divisions to do business with their "home" firm. Market considerations, such as price, take a secondary role because top level divisional chiefs set the target goals. Dyadic relations between firms are thereby shaped by policies internal to each firm. Interfirm outcomes in the ION box for dyads are shaped by intrafirm requirements.

TRIAD

Our ION box captures twelve types of triads. The first six consider sets of three for one domain: three producers, three suppliers, three customers, two producers and a supplier, two producers and a customer, and the producer–supplier–customer triad. As we consider all k for the triads, we get six triad sets: the multiple relationships for three producers, three suppliers, three customers, two producers and a supplier, two producers and a customer, and for the producer–supplier–customer triad.

Triads analysis has a long and rich history in network analysis – see, for example, Davis's (1979) review of the Davis/Holland/Leinhardt studies – but most work has focused on interpersonal ties, not interorganizational networks. The few exceptions are Laumann, et al.'s (1978) microstructural analysis of networks of community organizations, Burt's (1992) theory of structural holes, Gargiulo's (1993) concept of two-step leverage, Baker and Obstfeld's (1999) triads census of six types of alliances in the global automobile industry, and Della Porta and Vannucci (1999) study of the illegal exchanges between the government, business, and the Mafia – the so-called iron triangle – see also Gambetta (1993).

Two logics drive interorganizational triads, according to Baker and Obstfeld (1999). A "union logic" drives the *selection* of ties; a "disunion" logic drives the *avoidance* of ties. For example, Corning employs the union strategy when it closes a structural hole between two of its alliance partners, introducing them to each other and encouraging them to create their own alliance. General Motors' long-term avoidance of Ford Motor Company's main investment bank, Goldman Sachs, reveals a disunion logic used to maintain a structural hole. Baker and Obstfeld (1999) quantify these logics by taking a complete triads census of six types of alliances in the global automobile industry: joint ventures, manufacturing/assembly, technology sharing, supplier relationships, marketing/distribution, and equity investments. The use of union and disunion logics varies by type of alliance. For example, disunion triads occur more often than by chance in joint ventures, technology sharing, and manufacturing/assembly. Union triads occur more often than by chance in supplier ties, marketing/distribution, and equity investments. This study shows that the statistical analysis of triads can yield new insights into interorganizational networks. The triads approach to the analysis of interorganizational networks is a fruitful area of future research, especially when one considers the essential nature of market competition as a triad: two (or more) sellers vying "for opportunities of exchange" with a buyer (Weber, ([1922] 1978; p. 635; Swedberg, 1994, p. 271); see, also, Simmel (1950, pp. 154–62).

ORGANIZATION SET

The ION box indicates several types of organization sets for a single relation (k): a producer's set of ties to other producers, a producer's set of suppliers, a producer's set of customers, and – putting them all together – a producer's combined set of ties to other producers, suppliers, and customers. As we consider all k for all sets, we get a *horizontal plane* of organizational sets: a producer's set of ties to other producers, suppliers, and customers across all domains; see Figure 22.1, middle, for an illustration.

The organization set is a venerable concept in research on interorganizational networks. Some of the classic case studies of organizations include analyses of an organization and its suppliers or customers, such the Tennessee Valley Authority and its relations with suppliers and governmental bodies (Selznick, 1949). Such studies foreshadowed the concept of the organization set, but Evan (1966) formalized it. Since then, organizational researchers have examined various types of organizations sets. For example, Baker (1990) analyzed the cross-sectional relationships between each of 1530 corporations and their organization sets of investment banks. Uzzi (1999) considered the financial k-space from the other side of the exchange, examining the ties between commercial banks and their organization sets of corporate customers.

Baker et al. (1998) examined the dynamics of organizations sets, analyzing the continuity and dissolution of ties between 398 corporations and 1644 advertising agencies from 1971 to 1993. Using event-history methods, they found that the continuity and dissolution of market ties was a function of three forces: competition, power, and institutional forces. Competition was the weakest force; institutional forces were the strongest. Competition always increased the risk of dissolution of market ties. Power could raise or lower the risk of dissolution: when agencies had more power, market ties tended to last; when clients had more power, market ties tended to dissolve. Most institutional forces reduced the risk of dissolution. This study illustrates trends in the sociological study of markets and interorganizational networks: a shift from cross-sectional data to longitudinal data, and a movement from single theories to multiple theoretical perspectives.

ORGANIZATIONAL FIELD

An organizational field comprises the "organizations that, in the aggregate, constitute a recognized area of institutional life: key suppliers, resource and product consumers . . . and other organizations that produce similar services and products" (DiMaggio and Powell, 1983, p. 148); see, also, Aldrich (1999, pp. 49–50). This concept is captured as a *vertical plane* in our ION box, indicating the set of producers, suppliers, and customers involved in a particular domain of activity; see Figure 22.1, bottom, for illustration. Examples of research on organizational fields include DiMaggio's (1991) study of US art museums, Laumann and Knoke's (1987) network analysis of the organizations involved in energy and healthcare national policy making, and Suchman's (1998) investigation of law and finance in Silicon Valley.

The task of explaining how viable organizational communities coalesce over time poses a challenge to the analysis of organizational fields. It also offers a solution to the "structuration puzzle" or the process through which coherent and consistent social relations – shared meanings and stable role enactments – emerge within a group of previously isolated firms. Suchman (1998) gathered a range of qualitative data (informant interviews) and quantitative data (content analysis of 100 actual venture capital financing contracts) to explore the culture and structure of interorganizational relations between venture capital firms, law firms, and emerging growth companies in Silicon Valley. Various financing practices blossom but then solidify or center around a limited repertoire of contractual archetypes, driven mostly by the tightening organization-to-organization activities in the community's legal and financial services sectors. From 1975 to 1990, Silicon Valley developed a tightly scripted set of standardized financing archetypes. The choice of contract archetype in any given firm-to-firm transaction was made largely on features of historical timing and interorganizational network embeddedness.

The discussion of dyads, triads, organization sets, and organization fields highlights the various component parts of interorganizational networks. Together, they constitute interorganizational networks: the entire set of relationships among producers, suppliers, and customers across all k domains. The ION box itself represents interorganizational networks; see Figure 22.1, top. Few studies have attempted to capture interorganizational networks as a whole. A partial exception is Burt's (1983) analysis of economic transactions, captured in the form of input-output tables of exchanges between producers, suppliers, and customers, and director interlocks, but this study considers only two of the many domains that exist in the k-space: business transactions and interlocks. Obviously, this is an area where more work needs to be done.

Contemporary Issues and Debates

Issues and debates about interorganizational networks have changed over time. Here we highlight three major categories of contemporary concern: embeddedness, institutionalization, and the rise of the network organizational form.

EMBEDDEDNESS

The theoretical proposition encapsulated in the term "embeddedness" has captured and fired the imagination of interorganizational researchers. Early on, economic anthropologist Polanyi (1957) described the extent to which economic institutions are enmeshed and embedded in political and social institutions. But it was Granovetter's (1985) theoretical development of the idea that vivified research on the relationships across the k-space in our ION box. For example, Uzzi has produced a stream of research documenting and specifying the effects of social structure on economic transactions. For example, he shows that the extent of embeddedness influences the survival rates of contractor firms in the New York garment industry; this relationship is curvilinear, where the highest survival rates are achieved by firms located between the extremes of arm's-length ties and fully embedded ties (Uzzi, 1996, 1997). Similarly, he documents a curvilinear effect in relationships between commercial lenders and small business customers: The customers who pay the lowest interest rates are located between the same extremes (Uzzi, 1999; Uzzi and Gillespie, 1999).

Extant research on embeddedness in interorganizational networks generally considers a small range of possibilities captured in the ION box, though Dacin et al. (1999) demonstrate the virtues of thinking about embeddedness in a wider and broader way. For example, Uzzi's structural foci are only the dyad and the organization set. The original formulations of the embeddedness proposition (Polanyi 1957; Granovetter 1985), however, imply the need to study a wider range of embeddedness phenomena. Framed according to the ION box, embeddedness could mean the correlation of k-matrices among producers (the middle block of Figure 22.1), among suppliers in terms of their relationships to producers (the left block), among customers in terms of their relationships to producers (the right block), or even the correlation of k-matrices involving suppliers, producers, and customers. Studies outside the field of interorganizational research, such as Padgett and Ansell's (1993) network analysis of Florentine merchants, bankers, and families, highlights the promise of enlarging the field of analysis of embeddedness in interorganizational networks.

INSTITUTIONALIZATION

Contemporary organizational theorists draw heavily on institutional theory to understand many aspects of organizational life. DiMaggio and Powell (1983) developed the seminal statement, delineating three mechanisms of institutionalization: mimetic, normative, and coercive. Isomorphism of the organizational field of U.S. art museums, for example, is largely shaped by conformity to the requirements of federal funding agencies (DiMaggio, 1991). Lawyers in Silicon Valley, through the process of developing standardized venture capital financing contracts, stabilize and routinize the relationships between venture capital firms and start-up technology firms (Suchman, 1998). Mimetic forces influence patterns of corporate gift giving to nonprofit organizations (Galaskiewicz and Wasserman, 1989). Mimetic isomorphism drove the adoption of the "poison pill" hostile takeover defense, as executives learned about such tactics through their director interlocks (Davis, 1991). Mimetic isomorphism itself can be divided into different types of interorganizational behaviors, such as "trait imitation," "outcome imitation," and "frequency imitation" (Haunschild and Miner, 1997).

Recently, organizational scholars have raised some cautions about the ease with which institutional theory is invoked to explain interorganizational processes. "Most often," Scott (1995, pp. 64–90) argues, "a process argument is little more than a historical account – a narrative frequently consisting of 'stage-naming' concepts that provide a description of a sequence of events." Mizruchi and Fein (1999) argue that the DiMaggio and Powell (1983) article is often merely an honorific citation in organizational studies, and that in practice it is difficult to distinguish between the three isomorphic processes. Baker et al. (1998) note that other forces play major roles in interorganizational networks. They show that the hazard of dissolution of an interorganizational tie is a function of power dynamics and competition, as well as institutional forces. The inclusion of power as a force reminds us of the importance of resource dependence (Pfeffer and Salancik, 1978), and the inclusion of competition reminds us that market forces also drive the dynamics of interorganizational relations. Sometimes the basic fact that competition forms the context of interorganizational networks appears to be lost or forgotten. The role of the state in shaping interorganizational relations is more often assumed than studied, though Fligstein (1996) reminds us that markets are politics; see, also, Schumpeter's (1942) call for a "fiscal sociology." We agree with Powell's (1991) call for an "expanded institutionalism" that views competitive and institutional forces as variables that coexist in all social institutions.

RISE OF THE NETWORK ORGANIZATIONAL FORM

Organizational theorists have charted the demography of organizational forms, such as the rise of the multidivisional form (Fligstein 1985) and the decline and deinstitutionalization of conglomerate firms (Davis et al., 1994). Since the late 1980s, observers of organizations have noted the rise of a new form: the network organization. Some emphasized its internal organizational features (Baker, 1992), while others stressed its super-organizational structure (Powell, 1990), but it is clear that this form is a set of both internal and external networks (Baker 1994). The network form is consistent with, and supported by, the emerging social network model of society (Pescosolido and Rubin, 2000). The diffusion of this organizational form is now so widespread that DiMaggio (2001) has coined the term "the network conception of control."

The rise of this form has clear implications for interorganizational research, because interorganizational networks and permeable boundaries are some of its defining and constituent features. Researchers have studied important parts of the external networks associated with this organizational form. For example, Powell and associates (Powell, 1990; Powell et al., 1996) focus on collaborative ties between biotechnology startups and large pharmaceutical companies. Gulati (1995) studied alliance dyads, showing how past alliances beget new alliances; see, also, Gulati and Singh (1998). Such studies of parts of the network organizational advance our understanding of this new organizational form, but no study has yet attempted to study the "whole" of it – as represented by the ION box.

Unanswered Questions and New Directions

Contemporary issues and debates illustrate what has long plagued the field of interorganizational networks: its vast and fragmented nature (Oliver, 1990). What the field needs is completeness: a more comprehensive view of interorganizational networks, a broader and wider perspective that takes in more of the phenomena than can be revealed by studies of dyads, triads, organizational sets, or even organizational fields. Our comparison of the foci of existing studies with the ION box shows that enormous tracts of the ION territory are unexplored and uncharted. Our following discussion offers some directions for exploring these tracts.

WHAT IS AN ORGANIZATION'S NETWORK?

This question has been answered by focusing on parts of an organization's network, but not the whole. For example, interorganizational researchers may focus on a producer's alliances with other producers, but ignore its market ties to suppliers and customers. Clearly, these market ties influence patterns of alliance formation among producers, and should be included in the analysis. The study of an organization's market ties is often relegated to the fields of marketing and strategy. We need to bring the market back in, and not cede this territory to other disciplines. The ION box shows that a producer's network includes its market ties to suppliers and to customers as well as its links to other producers. Of course, an organization's network includes its ties across the complete k space of domains. An organization's network, therefore, is an entire horizontal plane in the ION box, as shown in Figure 22.1 (middle).

A single horizontal plane represents a producer's interorganizational form. A network organization, for example, would exhibit an expansive set of ties to suppliers, customers, and other producers, across the k domains. This suggests that the extent to which a producer has adopted and implemented the network model could be quantified; see Baker (1992). Two organizations with similar horizontal planes have implemented the same interorganizational model. The comparison of multiple horizontal planes in the ION box would reveal the various forces at work in structuring interorganizational networks. For example, a leader-follower pattern would be shown by one horizontal plane (the follower) becoming more and more like another horizontal plane (the leader).

Indeed, the similarities and dissimilarities of organizations' networks, observed by comparing horizontal planes, would reveal the underlying "shared rules" or "institutions," such as rules of exchange, governance structures, and conceptions of control (Fligstein, 1996, p. 658). Competitive rules of exchange, for example, discourage producers from using the same suppliers (often referred to as conflicts of interest). If such rules were in effect, we would expect to see high levels of disagreement between the horizontal planes, such as a negative correlation of the two matrices. (Network analysis provides several measures, in addition to the correlation, that could be used to evaluate structural similarity, e.g., Wasserman and Faust (1994). Because the purpose of our chapter is not methodological, we do not address the issue of measurement. Rather, we use the correlation as a means of describing the intuition of our argument.) Prior to institutionalization, however, we would expect to observe a correlation close to zero. The emergence phase of a market (Fligstein, 1996), for example, is the period of greatest fluidity because roles, rules of exchange, governance structures, and other aspects of the social structure and culture of the market are not yet solidified (Fligstein, 1996, p. 664).

WHAT IS INTERORGANIZATIONAL EMBEDDEDNESS?

Like the first question, this one has been answered by focusing on parts of an organization's network and subsets of its k space, but not the whole. Typically, relations between only two populations are studied, such as supplier-producer ties, or producer-customer ties; and, only two k domains are examined at a time, such as bank lending relationships and personal ties (Uzzi, 1999; Uzzi and Gillespie, 1999), interlocks and investment banking services (Baker, 1990), or interlocks and contributions to political action committees (Mizruchi, 1989). It is quite likely that these studies are underspecified; unmeasured domains may cause the observed correlation of the two k spaces. A comprehensive study of interorganizational embeddedness would extend the typical analysis in two ways. It would include more of an organization's network (ties to suppliers, producers, and customers), and it would include more domains of activity. In Figure 22.1, this is the correlation of vertical planes (k relations) from front to back in the ION box.

WHAT ARE THE CONJOINT EXCHANGE ACTIVITIES OF ORGANIZATIONS?

This is a view of the ION box from its sides. For example, each "slice" of the right block represents a buyer's organizational set *vis-à-vis* producers across k domains. Two customers with similar "slices" are structurally equivalent in their networks of relationships to producers. For example, high correlations across these "slices" would indicate the extent to which the *downstream* market is structured by its ties to producers. Similarly, each "slice" of the left block represents a supplier's organizational set *vis-à-vis* producers across k domains. Two suppliers with similar "slices" are structurally equivalent in their networks of relationships to producers. High correlations across these "slices" would indicate the extent to which the *upstream* market is structured by its ties to producers. One could even compare slices between suppliers and customers, which would indicate the extent of institutionalization across the upstream and downstream populations.

Domains are interrelated through the conjoined exchange activities of a population of organizations. The ION box with its k space facilitates this shift in perspective. From this vantage point, we see corporate actors engaged in several markets simultaneously. They watch each other (White 1981; Baum and Haveman 1997), spend considerable time and energy on devising strategies for taking investment "positions" in multiple markets, and develop solutions to the problems of managing their resources in the face of competition. At times they compete, squaring off against one another in markets. At other times they cooperate in alliances, or engage in illegal collective action (Baker and Faulkner, 1993). The introduction of new and novel instruments of trade or technologies prod organizations into action, sometimes disrupting the status quo, at other times resulting in the diversion or shifting of resources across k domains. Whatever the range of activities and the magnitude of resource allocation, the market economy can be viewed as a *network of interlocking markets* as well as a network of interlocking organizations.

Paradoxically, the "network of interlocking organizations" appears to prevail in organizational theory and research, while the "network of interlocking markets" has only begun to emerge in economic sociology. While it is recognized that socio-economic behavior of firms result in "positions" in markets, it is less well appreciated that these "positions" may be conceptualized as the "behavioral k linkages" across markets themselves. For example, finance strategy advises risk-averse organizations (as investors) to diversify their portfolios of investments. Accordingly, the organization will take positions in multiple financial markets. These positions are the concrete linkages or threads across the markets. From an elevated view of the ION box, the interrelationships of markets are formed by the collective behavioral linkages of a population of organizations as market actors. The result is an observable *intermarket structure*. Examining only one market and its organizational participants asserts that action occurs on a single plane in the k space. Examining only a pair of markets, as is typically done in economics, forces the assumption that other markets do not substantially influence the pair under study. Examining only a pair of markets also glosses over the domains and how other contexts of interorganizational behavior (i.e., political, cultural, familial-kinship, illegal) influence economic behavior.

Recent developments in organizational ecology examine the interactions of organizations across multiple markets. In this perspective, populations are comprised of heterogeneous micro-niches in which organizations interact, both competitively and cooperatively (Baum and Singh, 1994; Baum and Haveman, 1997). These multi-market ecology models do not incorporate networks directly. Thus, the marriage of multi-market ecology models and network models would produce enormous breakthroughs in the understanding of markets as social institutions.

Networks of Interlocking Markets

Some initial definitions provide the foundation for what is to follow. The k space in the ION box (Figure 22.1) denotes specific markets. For simplicity, four markets are the k relations for our illustration. A *market* is a set of exchanges involving a specific product or service. Examples from the financial sector include the markets for US Treasury bills, GNMA mortgages, and foreign currencies (Baker, 1987). *Trader* refers to an organization as a market actor. A *trader population* refers to all organizations that participate in one or more market domains. *Trader participation* refers to the "open positions" a trader has in a given market. An open position is the number of contracts held by a given trader in a given market at a specified point in time. *Inter-temporal* exchanges of traders in domains and the consequences of new domains for traders are of considerable importance (we will postpone a discussion of this for now). *Type of participation* refers to the economic purpose of a position.

A vector represents each trader's participation in a set of markets. An entry in a vector corresponds to a trader's open position in multiple markets. We use binary data for simplification in the examples to follow. A "1" in the vector represents the presence of an open position in a market. A "0" represents the absence of an open position in a market. For example, consider the market positions (or organization market set) for the hypothetical organization W, represented by the following vector:

MARKETS

	A	B	C	D
TRADER W:	1	0	1	1

This vector shows that trader W holds open positions in three markets (A, C, and D) and has no position in a fourth market (B).

Add market participation vectors for three more traders. These four vectors now form a matrix in the ION box. This is a "two-mode" matrix (Wasserman and Faust, 1994). Each row corresponds to a trader's participation in four k spaces or markets; each column corresponds to all the positions the trader population holds in an individual market. This *trader by market* matrix is arrayed as follows:

MARKETS

	A	B	C	D
TRADER W:	1	0	1	1
X:	0	1	0	0
Y:	1	0	1	1
Z:	0	1	0	0

In its present form, this trader by market matrix does not reveal any intrinsic pattern(s). But if the rows and columns are rearranged so that similar vectors are grouped together, a distinct pattern emerges. First, row vectors are rearranged, preserving the order of column vectors. The matrix now appears as:

MARKETS

	A	B	C	D
TRADER W:	1	0	1	1
Y:	1	0	1	1
X:	0	1	0	0
Z:	0	1	0	0

Trader W and trader Y are clustered together because they have similar (in this case, identical) vectors. Trader X and trader Z are clustered because they also have similar (in this case, identical) vectors. (The horizontal line represents the partition between the two subsets of traders.)

By clustering traders who have similar vectors, subsets of traders are identified in which each subset is comprised of traders who participate in the market system in similar ways. Traders with similar patterns of participation are structurally equivalent across markets. Traders in *k* space are structurally equivalent if they have very similar vectors (or patterns of participation) across domains (the four hypothetical markets, A, B, C, and D).

This partitions the trader population (rows) into discrete subsets of market actors. Each subset of structurally equivalent traders may be viewed as a single *class* of traders. In the matrix above, two classes of traders are now identified: the subset (W, Y) and the subset (X, Z). The first subset is referred to as trader class [A], and the second subset is referred to as trader class [B].

The columns of the matrix also may be rearranged according to the same rule of structural equivalence. The *trader by market* matrix now looks like this.

MARKETS

	B	A	C	D
TRADER W:	0	1	1	1
Y:	0	1	1	1
X:	1	0	0	0
Z:	1	0	0	0

Thus markets A, C, and D are grouped together because they have similar vectors; and market B stands alone. (A vertical line could be drawn to represent the partition between the subsets of markets).

By clustering similar columns, we identify structurally similar market domains. Two or more markets are structurally equivalent, of course, when traders use them in the same or similar ways. Therefore, markets A, C, and D are equivalent because they are based on similar patterns of organizational or trader behavior (domain participation). Market B, however, is not similarly participated in; traders use market B in a different way than the other three markets. Each subset of markets forms a single *class* of markets. Market B constitutes a single class of markets (referred to as market class "A," and markets A, C, and D constitute another class of markets (referred to as market class "B").

Now that the rows and columns of the matrix have been reordered so that traders are grouped together and markets are grouped together, the intrinsic structure of this market system is cast into sharp relief. The partitions derived by applying the rule of structural equivalence to the traders (rows) and to the markets (columns) divide the trader by market matrix into four distinct patterns. We have now rearranged the market box to reveal an interorganizational and intermarket structure. By coding the submatrices containing all "1" entries as "1" and the submatrices containing all "0" entries as "0," the newly partitioned matrix can be reduced to a smaller matrix that shows the market system at a more aggregate level. At this level, the individual organization (the trader) and the distinct domain (the market) are ignored. The market system is viewed on the level of trader classes and market classes. The resulting matrix (or image) appears as:

MARKET CLASS

		"A"	"B"
TRADER CLASS	[A]	0	1
	[B]	1	0

In this market box image, a "**1**" indicates the participation of a *class* of traders in a class of markets. A "**0**" indicates that a *class* of traders does not participate in a class of markets. Each "**1**" on the collective level represents a *position* in the market system. There are two positions in this hypothetical market system. The position of trader class [A] in market class "B," and the position of trader class [B] in market class "A."

A position represents an area of high *intermarket concentration* in the market domain. Some conceptualizations of intermarket concentration focus on a single large trader's position in one or more markets. While this approach is useful in exploring how a trader's attributes (size, endowment, capabilities) affects market participation and power, the approach is deficient since intermarket concentration may involve a subset of structurally equivalent traders who trade heavily in more than one market. The ION box and *k* spaces developed in this chapter can be used to examine the position of a single trader in one or more markets, and more importantly, to discover the aggregate positions of a subset of traders (i.e., a trader class) who are similarly concentrated in a subset of financial markets.

The overall configuration of an image reveals important features of the structure of the market as a system. In the example used above, there are two *mutually exclusive market centers* represented by the two positions. Since trader. class [A] trades *only* in market class "B," and trader class [B] trades only in market class "A," the market system is shown to be divided into non-overlapping subsets of markets.

Many other overall configurations are possible. Consider the intermarket structures represented by the following 2×2 images:

A. 0 0   B. 1 1   C. 1 0   D. 1 0   E. 1 0   F. 1 0   G. 1 1
   0 0   1 1   0 0   0 1   1 0   1 1   0 0

Each of these hypothetical images represents a characteristic structure of *organizations as classes of traders* in markets and, at the same time, markets as interrelated through the conjoint activities of their organizations. Images *A* and *B* represent two possible intermarket structures: The former indicates no trading takes place in the market system, while the latter indicates that all traders participate in all markets. Image *C* depicts a *single market center*: One trader class uses one market class, but the other trader class does not trade at all. Image *D* represents the *exclusive market centers* discussed above. Image *E* indicates that both trader classes hold positions in the same class of markets, but neither trader class participates in the other market class. Consequently, the market class in which both trader classes participate contains the *core markets* in the market system. Image F indicates that both trader classes take positions in one market class (the "core") while only one trader class uses the other subset of markets. The class of markets in which only a single trader class participates contains the *peripheral markets.* Hence, image *F* represents a *core-and-periphery* intermarket structure. Image G represents a *unified market structure*: One trader class holds positions in both market classes, but the other trader class is comprised of nonparticipants.

In contrast to the conventional economic view of the market as an abstract and generalized market mechanism, we propose that the market may be conceptualized and modeled as a social network of interlocking markets. A market economy is a "structure of social structures" (Baker, 1983, 1987; Faulkner, 1983; White, 1992). In contrast to the conventional sociological view of the market as a matrix of relations among concrete organizations, we propose that the market may be seen as a social network of interlocking trader classes. Interorganizational behavior shorn from its anchoring in work activity or domain participation is the sociological equivalent of neo-classical abstraction. From the perspective of this chapter, the critical issue is not measurement of organizational networks as much as how to think about a matrix – the ION box of organizations and domains. The empirical study of interorganizational networks has long been impeded by lack of an adequately conceptualized model of the *k* domain space across which organizations and organizational classes participate. A single domain or single market cannot make up an economy. Any market economy is more that a single set of relationships around a single object. We have illustrated briefly how an economic domain (*k* space with markets *A, B, C,* and *D*) is a set of sets – a grouping of multiple markets.

If markets (and by implication, other domains) are interconnected by the conjoint exchange activities of actors across the set of constituent domains, then the ION box and the images we have described and illustrated may be used to evaluate intertemporal changes in the behavior of organizations across domains. For example, it may be applied to answer many of the pressing questions about new domains opening up or shutting down, represented by the accordion-like expansion and contraction of the *k*-space of our ION box.

Connections Across Levels

The three network chapters cover a broad sweep of network phenomena, ranging from interpersonal networks inside organizations (Raider and Krackhardt) to (inter)organization sets (Gulati, Dialdin, and Wang) to interorganizational networks (Baker and Faulkner). These chapters fit like Chinese boxes, one inside the other: the intraorganizational network is contained in the egocentric network of organizations which fits, in turn, inside the ION box we propose in this chapter. They illustrate that network theory is robust; the network concepts that apply to interpersonal networks also apply to interorganizational relations. For example, the "ego" in an egocentric network can be a person or an organization, while the "alters" can be other people or other organizations (Raider and Krackhardt versus Gulati, Dialdin, and Wang, respectively). Indeed, the chapters show that the entire network toolkit can be used to study organizational networks, no matter what the level of analysis may be.

The ease with which network concepts can be generalized across levels and units of analysis is a liability as much as a benefit for research on organizational networks. Organizational theory has always suffered from a tendency to treat an organization as if it were a person. Network theory makes this fallacy even easier to commit. For example, when the concept of "ego" is used to represent a corporate actor instead of a natural person, we nearly forget that a legal fiction does not have drives, motives, interests, and values. It is difficult – if not impossible – to impute the goal or purpose of human behavior (Black, 2000). Confusing humans and organizations makes it even more difficult.

Raider and Krackhardt operate under the radar of the other two chapters. By looking inside a "node" in an interorganizational network, they remind us that an organization is a form of collective action. For example, the observed configuration of an organization set – or, as Gulati, Dialdin, and Wang call it, the egocentric network – is as much the result of the intraorganizational power struggle as the attempt to manage resource dependence or reduce transaction costs. An organization is not as free to choose its alters as Gulati, Dialdin, and Wang imply; competition, power, and institutional forces all influence the configuration of an organization set (Baker et al., 1998). The ION box attempts to capture some of the larger forces that shape interorganizational relations.

Conclusion

The three network chapters suggest two different but complementary angles of attack. Taken together, the three chapters show the need to integrate across levels, examining the interplay of intraorganizational networks, the (inter)organization set, and interorganizational networks (e.g., the ION box). Integration across levels in research on interorganizational networks is a specific instance of a general problem in social theory: the micro-to-macro problem in explanations of system behavior (Coleman 1990). This problem plagues social theory but it is particularly acute in research on interorganizational networks. Few studies have tried to examine, for example, how the internal power politics of an organization are played out in decisions about the composition of an organization set, and in turn how the macrostructure of interorganizational networks constrains the possible organization sets to choose from, though there is some work on this problem (Baker et al., 1998).

Our chapter presents a macro-level research problem: the concrete analysis of interorganizational networks and interlocking domains as a complete social system. We lay the foundation for an exploration of interorganizational networks in domains and domains across networks. Organizational sociology has accumulated an impressive array of technical tools for the analysis of interorganizational networks. But we need new conceptual equipment for our toolkit. Our main conceptual framework is the interorganizational network or ION box. We used the ION box to structure the eclectic, fragmented field of research on interorganizational networks. This three-dimensional array captures the main concepts in the field – dyads, triads, organization set, organizational field, and interorganizational network – as it suggest new avenues of research. For example, the ION box shows that an organization's network extends far beyond the usual boundaries imposed by most research. It also provides an expanded view of the concept of interorganizational embeddedness. Finally, by providing a comprehensive conceptualization of interorganizational networks, we shift from the view of interorganizational networks of as a "network of interlocking organizations" to a "network of interlocking domains." This shifts the emphasis of research from organizations to networks of domains.

Notes

1   A focal organization can be a firm, establishment, or line of business. At one level of analysis, for example, the organization could be a corporation itself; at a lower level, it could represent the divisions of a corporation. For simplicity, we consider the focal organization as a "firm."

References

Aldrich, H. (1999): *Organizations Evolving*. Thousand Oaks, CA: Sage.

Baker, W. E. (1983): "Intermarket structures: Modeling the interrelationships of markets and traders," paper presented at the 1983 annual meetings of the American Sociological Association.

Baker, W. E. (1986): "Three-dimensional blockmodels," *Journal of Mathematical Sociology*, 12, 191–223.

Baker, W. E. (1987): "What is money? A social structural interpretation," in M. S. Mizruchi and M. Schwartz (eds), *Intercorporate Relations: The Structural Analysis of Business*, Cambridge: Cambridge University Press, 109–44.

Baker, W. E. (1990): "Market networks and corporate behavior," *American Journal of Sociology*, 96 589–625.

Baker, W. E. (1992): "The network organization in theory and practice," in N. Nohria and R. G. Eccles (eds), *Networks and Organizations: Structure, Form, and Action*, Boston, MA: Harvard Business School Press, 397–429.

Baker, W. E. (1994): *Networking Smart*. New York: McGraw-Hill

Baker, W. E., and Faulkner, R. R. (1993): "The social organization of conspiracy: illegal networks in the heavy electrical equipment industry," *American Sociological Review*, 58, 837–60.

Baker, W. E., and Obstfeld, D. (1999): "Social capital by design: structures, strategies and institutional context," in R. T. A. J. Leenders and S. Gabbay (eds), *Corporate Social Capital and Liability*, Norwell, MA: Kluwer Academic, 88–105.

Baker, W. E., Faulkner, R. R., and Fisher, G. A. (1998): "Hazards of the market: The continuity and dissolution of interorganizational market relationships," *American Sociological Review*, 63, 147–77.

Baum, J. A. C., and Haveman, H. A. (1997): "Love thy neighbor? Differentiation and agglomeration in the Manhattan hotel industry," *Administrative Science Quarterly*, 42, 304–38.

Baum, J. A. C., and Singh, J. V. (1994): "Organizational niches and the dynamics of organizational mortality," *American Journal of Sociology*, 100, 346–80.

Black, D. (2000): "Dreams of pure sociology," *Sociological Theory*, 18, 343–67.

Burt, R. S. (1983): *Corporate Profits and Cooptation*. New York: Academic Press.

Burt, R. S. (1992): *Structural Holes: The Social Structure of Competition*. Cambridge: Harvard University Press.

Coleman, J. S. (1990): *Foundations of Social Theory*. Cambridge: Harvard University Press.

Dacin, M. T., Ventresca, M. J., and Beal, B. D. (1999): "The embeddedness of organizations:

dialogue and directions," *Journal of Management* 25, 317–56.

Davis, G. F. (1991): "Agents without principles? The spread of the poison pill through the intercorporate network," *Administrative Science Quarterly*, 36, 583–613.

Davis, G. F., Diekmann, K. A. and Tinsley, C. H. (1994): "The decline and fall of the conglomerate firm in the 1980s: The deinstitutionalization of an organizational form," *American Sociological Review*, 59, 547–70.

Davis, J. A. (1979): "The Davis/Holland/Leinhardt studies: An overview," in P. W. Holland and S. Leinhardt (eds), *Perspectives on Social Network Research*, New York: Academic Press, 51–62.

Della Porta, D., and Vannucci, A. (1999): *Corrupt Exchanges*. New York: Aldine de Gruyter.

DiMaggio, P. J. (1991): "Constructing an organizational field as a professional project: U.S. art museums, 1920-1940," in W. W. Powell and P. J. DiMaggio (eds), *The New Institutionalism in Organizational Analysis*, Chicago: University of Chicago Press, 267–92.

DiMaggio, P. J. (2001): "Conclusion: Change, paradox and the futures of business organization," in P. J. DiMaggio (ed.), *The Twenty-First Century Firm: Changing Economic Organization in International Perspective*, Princeton: Princeton University Press, forthcoming.

DiMaggio, P. J., and Powell, W. W. (1983): "The iron cage revisited: institutional isomorphism and collective rationality in organizational fields," *American Sociological Review*, 48, 147–60.

Eccles, R., and White, H. (1988): "Price and authority in inter-profit center transactions," *American Journal of Sociology*, Supplement 94, S17–S51.

Evan, W. M. (1966): "The organization-set: Toward a theory of interorganizational relations," in J. D. Thompson (ed.), *Approaches to Organizational Design*, Pittsburgh: University of Pittsburgh Press, 173–88.

Faulkner, R. R. (1983): *Music on Demand*. Rutgers, NJ: Transaction Books.

Fligstein, N. (1985): "The spread of the multi-divisional form among large firms, 1919–1979," *American Sociological Review*, 50, 377–91.

Fligstein, N. (1996): "Markets as politics: a political-cultural approach to market institutions," *American Sociological Review*, 61, 656–73.

Galaskiewicz, J., and Wasserman, S. (1989): "Mimetic processes within an interorganizational field: an empirical test," *Administrative Science Quarterly*, 34, 454–79.

Gambetta, D. (1993): *The Sicilian Mafia: The Business of Private Protection*. Cambridge, MA: Harvard University Press.

Gargiulo, M. (1993): "Two-step leverage: managing constraint in organizational politics," *Administrative Science Quarterly*, 38, 1–19.

Gulati, R. (1995): "Social structure and alliance formation patterns: A longitudinal analysis," *Administrative Science Quarterly*, 40, 619–52.

Gulati, R., and Singh, H. (1998): "The architecture of cooperation: Managing coordination uncertainty and interdependence in strategic alliances," *Administrative Science Quarterly*, 43, 781–814.

Granovetter, M. (1985): "Economic action and social structure: A theory of embeddedness," *American Journal of Sociology*, 91, 481–510.

Haunschild, P. R., and Miner, A. S. (1997): "Modes of interorganizational imitation: The effects of outcome salience and uncertainty," *Administrative Science Quarterly*, 42, 472–500.

Larson, A. (1992): "Network dyads in entrepreneurial settings: A study of the governance of exchange relationships," *Administrative Science Quarterly*, 37, 76–104.

Laumann, E. O., and Knoke, D. (1987): *The Organizational State*. Madison, WI: University of Wisconsin Press.

Laumann, E. O., and Marsden, P. V. (1982): "Microstructural analysis in interorganizational systems," *Social Networks*, 4, 329–48.

Laumann, E. O., Galaskiewicz, J., and Marsden, P. V. (1978): "Community structures as interorganizational linkages," *Annual Review of Sociology*, 4, 455–84.

Mizruchi, M. S. (1989): "Similarity of political behavior among large American corporations,"

American Journal of Sociology, 95, 401–24.

Mizruchi, M. S. (1996): "What do interlocks do? An analysis, critique and assessment of research on interlocking directorates," *Annual Review of Sociology,* 22, 271–98.

Mizruchi, M. S., and Fein, L. C. (1999): "The social construction of organizational knowledge: A study of the use of coercive, mimetic, and normative isomorphism," *Administrative Science Quarterly,* 44, 653–83.

Neustadtl, A., and Clawson, D. (1988): "Corporate political groupings: Does ideology unify business political behavior?" *American Sociological Review,* 53, 172–90.

Oliver, C. (1990): "Determinants of interorganizational relationships: Integration and future directions," *Academy of Management Review,* 15, 241–65.

Padgett, J. F., and. Ansell, C. K. (1993): "Robust action and the rise of the Medici: 1400–1434," *American Journal of Sociology,* 98, 1259–319.

Pescosolido, B. A., and Rubin, B. A. (2000): "The web of group affiliations revisited: Social life, postmodernism and sociology," *American Sociological Review,* 65, 52–76.

Pfeffer, J., and Salancik, G. (1978): *The External Control of Organizations: A Resource Dependence Perspective.* New York: Harper & Row.

Podolny, J. M. (1993): "A status-based model of market competition," *American Journal of Sociology,* 98, 829–72.

Polanyi, K. (1957): "The economy as instituted process," in K. Polanyi, C. Arensberg and H. Pearson (eds), *Trade and Market in the Early Empires: Economies in History and Theory,* Chicago: Henry Regnery Co., 243–70.

Powell, W. W. (1987): "Hybrid organizational arrangements: New form or transitional development?" *California Management Review,* 30, 67–87.

Powell, W. W. (1990): "Neither market nor hierarchy: Network forms of organization," *Research in Organizational Behavior,* 12, 295–336.

Powell, W. W. (1991): "Expanding the scope of institutional analysis," in W. W. Powell and P. J. DiMaggio (eds), *The New Institutionalism in Organizational Analysis,* Chicago: University of Chicago Press, 183–203.

Powell, W. W., and Smith-Doerr, L. (1994): "Networks and economic life," in N. J. Smelser and R. Swedberg (eds), *The Handbook of Economic Sociology,* Princeton, NJ: Princeton University Press, 368–402.

Powell, W. W., Koput, K. W., and Smith-Doerr, L. (1996): "Interorganizational collaboration and the locus of innovation: Networks of learning in biotechnology," *Administrative Science Quarterly,* 41, 116–45.

Schumpeter, J. A. ([1942] 1975): *Capitalism, Socialism and Democracy.* New York: Harper & Row.

Scott, W. R. (1995): *Institutions and Organizations.* Thousand Oaks, CA: Sage.

Scott, W. R., Ruef, M., Mendel, P., and Caronna, C. (eds) (2000): *Institutional Change and Healthcare Organizations: From Professional Dominance to Managed Care.* Chicago: University of Chicago Press.

Selznick, P. (1949): *TVA and the Grass Roots.* Berkeley: University of California Press.

Simmel, G. (1950): *The Sociology of Georg Simmel,* K. H. Wolff, (ed.), trans., New York: The Free Press.

Stinchcombe, A. L. (1990): "Organizations, occupations and markets: Weak structural data," *Contemporary Sociology,* 19, 380–82.

Suchman, M. C. (1998): "The contracting universe: Notes on the evolution of standardized venture capital financing contracts in Silicon Valley," a version of this paper was presented at the 1999 annual meetings of the Academy of Management, Chicago, Illinois.

Swedberg, R. (1994): "Markets as social structures," in N. J. Smelser and R. Swedberg (eds), *The Handbook of Economic Sociology,* Princeton, NJ: Princeton University Press, 255–82.

Uzzi, B. (1996): "The sources and consequences of embeddedness for the economic performance of organizations: the network effect," *American Sociological Review,* 61, 674–98.

Uzzi, B. (1997): "Social structure and competition in interfirm networks: The paradox of embeddedness," *Administrative Science Quarterly*, 42, 35–67.

Uzzi, B. (1999): "Embeddedness in the making of financial capital: How social relations and networks benefit firms seeking financing," *American Sociological Review*, 64, 481–505.

Uzzi, B., and Gillespie, J. J. (1999): "Corporate social capital and the cost of financial capital: An embeddedness approach," in R. T. A. J. Leenders and S. M. Gabbay (eds), *Corporate Social Capital and Liability*, Boston: Kluwer, pp. 446–59.

Wasserman, S., and Faust, K. (1994): *Social Network Analysis: Methods and Applications*. Cambridge: Cambridge University Press.

Weber, M. ([1922] 1978): *Economy and Society: An Outline of Interpretive Sociology*, G. Roth and C. Wittich (eds), E. Fischoff et al., trans., Berkeley, CA: University of California Press.

White, H. C. (1981): "Where do markets come from?" *American Journal of Sociology*, 87, 517–47.

White, H. C. (1992): *Identity and Control: A Structural Theory of Action*. Princeton, NJ: Princeton University Press.

Zeitlin, M., Ewen, L. A., Ratcliff, R. E. (1974): "New princes for old? The large corporation and the capitalist class in Chile," *American Journal of Sociology*, 80, 87–123.

Zuckerman, E. W. 1999. "The categorical imperative: Securities analysts and the illegitimacy discount," *American Journal of Sociology*, 104, 1398–1438.

Chapter Twenty-three

Interorganizational Ecology

HAYAGREEVA RAO

Interorganizational ecology is the study how similar and dissimilar populations that comprise communities interact with each other and how they collectively adapt to the environment. An organizational community is a group of populations bound by ecological ties of commensalism and symbiosis that consequently, coevolve with each other and their environment. *Symbiosis* involves mutual "inter-dependence of unlike forms, i.e. units of dissimilar functions" (Hawley, 1950, p. 209), and implies that populations occupying different niches benefit from each other's presence. *Commensalism*, in contrast, involves the "co-action of like forms, i.e. units of similar functions" (Hawley, 1950, p. 209) and entails potential competition between interacting populations. The degree of competition between populations depends on the degree of similarity or overlap of the niches they occupy.

The group of populations may be delimited to a restricted geographic area (e.g., Silicon Valley), but can encompass a national, regional, or global economic system, depending on the technical or institutional core (e.g., the telecommunications community). In general, organizational communities consist of a mosaic of semi-isolated patches. In such cases, they can be geographically localized as in the case of North Carolina's Research Triangle or the German Machine-Tool District, or have wider scope if they are built around a shared core technology or standard such as the Wintel Community or ApplePC community in recent years.

Irrespective of whether a community is geographically localized or dispersed, the outcomes for organizations in any one population are fundamentally intertwined with those of organizations in other populations that belong to the same community system. Therefore, the study of community dynamics devolves into an analysis of the processes that underlie the creation and demise of organizational populations, and thereby affect the stability of the community as a whole.

Literature Review and Evaluation

COMMUNITY DEFINITION

Populations are the key constituents of communities and are equated with distinct organizational forms. However, there is substantial divergence of opinion on how to define organizational populations and organizational forms: multiple definitions premised on different approaches to organizational classification have been discussed in the literature (Aldrich, 1999; Baum, 1989; Hannan and Freeman, 1989; McKelvey, 1982, pp35–65; Rao and Singh, 1999; Rich, 1992; Romanelli, 1989). In view of these taxonomical hurdles and cul-de-sacs, organizational ecologists have defined populations as commonsense categorizations used by actors to understand discontinuities in social identity. For example, ecologists have treated craft and industrial trade unions, and different categories of newspapers (daily vs. weekly). Recently, Polos et al. (1999) have formalized the linkage between organizational forms and identity, and argued that an organizational form is a social identity that is enforced by insiders or outsiders, and therefore, premised on a genetic and a penal code. By implication, a population is a set of organizations defined by an enforced social identity. Thus, beer producers may be sorted into multiple populations such as industrial brewers, brewpubs, microbrewers, and craft brewers because each grouping entails a socially enforceable identity. This conceptualization of populations is akin to the strategic group concept literature in industrial economics: firms in an industry cluster into strategic groups on the basis of shared attributes, and mobility barriers impede crossovers from one group to another and can impair legitimacy and performance.

Just as there are discordant views on what constitutes a population, there is also heterogeneity in the definition of a community. Community ecologists have anchored on different dimensions of the core characteristics of organizations to define communities. Hannan and Freeman (1984) proposed a distinction between the core and peripheral attributes of organizations. Core organizational features include

(a) *stated goals*, the basis on which legitimacy and other resources are mobilized
(b) *authority relations*, the basis of exchange within the organization and between the organization and its members (including governance structures)
(c) *core technology*, as encoded in capital investment, infrastructure, and the skills and knowledge of employees and
(d) *market strategy*, the kinds of clients or customers to which the organization orients its production, and the ways in which it attracts resources from the environment.

Peripheral features (e.g., number and sizes of subunits, number of levels in authority structures, span of control, patterns of communication, interlocking directorates, strategic alliances), refer to all other attributes (Hannan and Freeman, 1984, p. 157).

In practice, community ecologists have used each of the four core dimensions suggested by Hannan and Freeman (1984) to define communities. Thus, communities have been defined in terms of a primary goal such as education (Nielsen and Hannan, 1977; Caroll, 1981), strategy (Brittain and Wholey, 1988, Boeker, 1991), authority structures in the savings and loan industry (Haveman and Rao, 1997), core technologies such as telephony (Barnett and Carroll, 1987, Barnett 1990), and market distinctions among day care organizations (Baum and Singh 1994b). Researchers have defined community at different levels of analysis, and, by implication, covered more diverse and less diverse communities. For example, Baum and Korn (1994) and Korn and Baum (1994) defined "community" at the level of a national economy in Canada, rather than among closely related populations in a region such as Silicon Valley (Saxenian, 1994), or a single industry like semi-conductors (Brittain and Wholey, 1988) or a combination of a single region and industry such Iowa and Pennsylvania phone companies (Barnett and Carroll, 1987).

OVERVIEW OF COMMUNITY EVOLUTION

Community evolution consists of three sub-processes: variation embodied in new populations and forms, selection shaped by symbiotic and commensalistic relations between constituent populations, and the retention of established populations (Baum and Singh, 1994b; Hunt and Aldrich, 1998; Baum and Rao, 2001). New organizational forms are constructed in organizational communities by entrepreneurs seeking to exploit technological discontinuities and institutional shocks that disrupt the prevalent social order (Astley, 1985; Oliver, 1992). Community dynamics have much in common with processes of organizational field (de)structuration and DiMaggio and Powell (1983, p. 148) describe organizational fields as "those organizations that, in aggregate, constitute a recognized area of institutional life: key suppliers, resource and product consumers, regulatory agencies, and other organizations that produce similar services or products." Scott (1994, pp. 207–8, 1995) notes that "the notion of a field connotes the existence of a community of organizations that partakes of a common meaning system and whose participants interact more frequently and fatefully with one another than with actors outside of the field." The primary difference appears to be one of levels, with organizational fields frequently constituted by multiple local organizational communities that vary in their degree and form of functional integration (Baum and Rao, 2001).

Commensalistic and symbiotic relations within and among constituent populations exert pressure on a community's constituent units, and generate a hierarchical order over time. Hawley (1950, p. 221) proposed that functional differentiation led to inequality because "certain functions are by their nature more influential than others; they are strategically placed in the division of labor and thus impinge directly upon a larger number of other functions." Populations occupying central locations are well positioned to play coordinating roles (Aldrich, 1979, pp. 327–40). For instance, the literature on bank control holds that banks consolidate their dominance in organizational communities through director interlocks to shape the flow of resources between organizations and owners or top executives (Mintz and Schwartz, 1985); but see Davis and Mizruchi (1999). Over time, organizational communities become functionally integrated systems of interacting populations that secure autonomy as members of the community come to exchange resources more with each other than directly with the environment (Astley, 1985). As a result, outcomes for organizations of any one form may be fundamentally intertwined with those of organizations of other forms residing in the same community. A population is affected not only by *direct* interactions with other populations, but also by *indirect* interactions and feedback processes (Hannan and Freeman, 1989). In Silicon Valley, for example, symbiotic relationships that flourished among entrepreneurs, educators, venture capitalists, and law firms promoted "collective learning and flexible adjustment among specialist producers of a complex of related technologies" (Saxenian, 1994, p. 2).

As a community's internal structure is elaborated, it approximates a closed system featuring a restricted number of possible niches within its boundary that are progressively saturated, and competition impedes the rise of new organizational forms. No new population can be added without affecting the functional integration of the system for better or for worse, and the size of each population is balanced against the needs of other populations in the community. Thus, the approach of community closure coincides with competitive saturation within its constituent populations.

But tight internal coupling among component populations also creates conditions that presage community collapse. When complex systems experience disturbances beyond a certain threshold level, they may disintegrate due to domino-like effects. Thus, tightly coupled community systems can be fragile and prone to collapse and simplification when confronted with disturbances that upset their equilibrium, and although they may be reestablished though ecological succession – they also may not rebound (Pimm, 1991; Kauffman, 1993).

As relationships within a community become progressively integrated, competition may shift from the population to the community level: competition between populations may be supplanted by rivalry between communities (Baum and Rao, 2001). The performance of organizations in populations can affect the abundance of all organizations in the local community as a unit. When multiple local communities exist that vary in their population composition, routines and repertoires may diffuse to the extent they confer advantages on the local community *relative* to others. In such cases, the social structure of organizational communities can be seen as the outcome of adaptations that have evolved over time due to inter-community competition (Sober and Wilson, 1998).

COMMUNITY STRUCTURE

Since data on actual interconnections between organizations in a community are rare, organizational ecologists have primarily relied on indirect evidence obtained by the effects of population density on vital rates. In general, they have employed a variant of the Lotka–Volterra model from bio-ecology to study community structure in sectors and industries (Hannan and Freeman, 1989).

The starting point for organizational ecologists is a logistic population growth function to model competitive selection acting on the growth of a single population:[1]

$$\frac{dN}{dt} = rN(1 - \frac{N}{K})$$

When a population interacts with other populations as part of a community, it is necessary to consider its relationships with those other populations. The single-population formulation can be extended to encompass a population's linkages with other populations in the same community. Consider the simple case of a two-population community:

$$\frac{dN_A}{dt} = rN_A(1 - \frac{N_A}{K_A} - \alpha_{AB}\frac{N_B}{K_A})$$

$$\frac{dN_B}{dt} = rN_B(1 - \frac{N_B}{K_B} - \alpha_{BA}\frac{N_A}{K_B})$$

The community represented by this pair of equations is composed of two populations, A and B, which affect each other's growth rates through their interdependence. The second equation is the mirror of the first. The terms a_{AB} and a_{BA} are coefficients representing the interdependence of populations A and B. These coefficients represent the proportional effect each member in one population has on the carrying capacity of the other. Thus the presence of a member of population A (B) reduces by the fraction α_{AB} (α_{BA}) the resources available for population B (A). The two-population model can be generalized to a community of n populations as:

$$\frac{dt}{dt} = rN_i(1 - \frac{\Sigma\alpha_{ij}N_j - N_i}{K_i}), \ \Sigma\alpha_{ij} = 1$$

Symbiotic relations involve mutual "inter-dependence of unlike forms, i.e. units of dissimilar functions" (Hawley, 1950, p. 209), and imply that populations occupying different niches benefit from each other's presence (i.e., $a_{AB}>0$, $a_{BA}>0$). For instance, interacting populations of 'complementors' abound in the Wintel community (Shapiro and Varian, 1999). The populations of software vendors and original equipment manufacturers each producing and selling one component of the 'Wintel' PC standard is perhaps the most visible example. Commensalism, in contrast, involves "co-action of like forms, i.e. units of similar functions" (Hawley, 1950, p. 209) and implies potential competition between interacting populations. The degree of competition between populations depends on the degree of similarity or overlap of the niches they occupy. Aldrich (1999, p. 302) has identified six scenarios of commensalisms; see also Baum (1996, pp. 91–2) and Brittain and Wholey (1988):

- *Full competition* (i.e., $\alpha_{AB} < 0$, $\alpha_{BA} < 0$) Growth in each population leads to a decline in the other because their niches overlap.
- *Partial competition* (i.e., $\alpha_{AB} < 0$, $\alpha_{BA} = 0$) Inter-population relations are asymmetric, with only one having a negative effect on the other.
- *Predatory competition* (i.e., $\alpha_{AB} < 0$, $\alpha_{BA} > 0$) one population expands at the expense of another.
- *Partial mutualism* (i.e., $\alpha_{AB} > 0$, $\alpha_{BA} = 0$) Obtains when inter-population relations are asymmetric, with only one population benefiting from the presence of the other.
- *Full mutualism* (i.e., $\alpha_{AB} > 0$, $\alpha_{BA} > 0$) means that two populations are in overlapping niches and benefit from the presence of the other.
- *Neutrality* (i.e., $\alpha_{AB} = 0$, $\alpha_{BA} = 0$) means that two populations have no influence on each other, although they do affect other populations in the community.

Table 23.1 summarizes the salient studies of community structure. Quantitative stud-

Table 23.1 Select studies in interorganizational ecology

Reference	Key concepts	Key variables	Key findings	Key contribution	Method and sample
Nielsen and Hannan, 1977	Commensalism Symbiosis	Expansion rate Inter-sectoral dependence	Positive interdependence across sectors	Positive serial interdependence	Time series US education system
Carroll, 1981	Commensalism Symbiosis	Expansion rate Inter-sectoral dependence	Web of mutualistic and competitive relations	Nonlinear specification of interpopulation relationships	Time series analyses US educational system
Barnett and Carroll, 1987	Commensalism Symbiosis	Death rates Local, non-local Commerical, mutual densities	Mutualism between forms and non-local competition	Symbiosis between forms	Event history models US phone industry
Brittain and Wholey, 1988	Commensalism Symbiosis	Death, birth and growth rates of r and K- strategists	Web of mutualism and competition	Relations among market strategists	Event history models, growth rate models Electronic components industry
Barnett, 1990	Ecology of a technical system	Vital rates of firms belonging to different technical orders	Mutualism and competition in network industries	Technological complementarity and incompatibility	Event history models US phone industry
Wholey et al., 1993	Professional interests and communities	Entry rates of group and IPA forms	First and late mover patterns	Corporate and professional interests in HMO founding	Event history models HMO industry
Saxenian, 1994	Symbiosis	Alliances and partnerships	Collaboration and segmentalism	Comparative analyses of communities	Case study Silicon Valley and Route 128
Suchman, 1995	Symbiosis	Linking pin roles	Law firms and the reduction of uncertainty	Mediating populations	Case study Silicon Valley

ies of community structure have looked at the effects of population densities on vital rates such as foundings, growth or failure. In a pioneering study, Nielsen and Hannan (1977) defined all organizations committed to the goal of education as a community and analyzed the effect of interactions among populations in the primary, secondary, and tertiary educational sectors on the expansion of the national education systems they comprised. They reported a mutualistic pattern of hierarchical interdependence within national education systems: enrollment in primary education had positively effects on secondary enrollment, and enrollment in primary and secondary education had a positive impact on the expansion of tertiary enrollment. Carroll (1981) contended that since the expansion of one population may lead to a contraction of resources for other populations, a model of community dynamics should include relations with all possible interacting populations. His study demonstrated that populations of primary, secondary, and tertiary education organizations were linked by a complex web of competitive and mutualistic relationships. These results suggested that when organizational communities are analyzed in terms of single dyadic relationships, the potential for specification bias is large.

Other pioneering studies have investigated the birth and death rates of populations in a community created around a technical core. Barnett and Carroll (1987) studied the mortality of telephone companies based on different authority structures and found that whether mutualism or competition obtained between neighboring firms was contingent on their organizational form. Firms in separate geographical locations were discovered to be competitive with each other, regardless of organizational form. They concluded that the mutual and commercial forms apparently flourished in separate niches and were symbiotically related. Barnett (1990) investigated the mortality of firms in the telephone industry and reported that mutualism obtained among both advanced and primitive firms if they were technologically standardized and differentiated. Competition existed when organizations were technologically incompatible or noncomplementary. Brittain and Wholey (1988) studied the dynamics of r and K strategist populations in the US electronics components manufacturing industry and showed that a complex system of competitive, mutualistic, and asymmetric relationships influenced the birth, death, and growth of firms in the strategic populations comprising the industry.

Other studies have looked at communities cohering around institutional linkages and looked at the birth rates and death rates of firms embodying different authority structures. Wholey et al. (1993) analyzed the relationship between two types of HMOs (health maintenance organizations) – Groups and Independent Practice Associations (IPAs). They found that Groups were more likely than IPAs to be the first HMO to enter a community because the collaborative structure of Groups may have enabled them to defuse resistance from medical associations. However, once HMOs had entered a community, IPAs entered rapidly because their less tightly coupled organizational structure allowed them to be assembled easily. In an innovative study, Baum and Singh (19964b) and Baum and Oliver (1996) investigated the death and birth rates of for-profit and non-profit day care firms in the Toronto area and dimensionalized population interactions using the constructs of overlap and non-overlap density and found that both types of density constrained birth and death rates.

If quantitative studies rely on the Lotka–Volterra model to account for community dynamics, qualitative studies using interviews and archival data have emphasized how communities cohere around common cultural cores. Saxenian (1994) compared the

Silicon Valley community with the Route 128 community because both had similar origins and technologies but found that the two communities had evolved differently. Silicon Valley had a regional network system that fostered collective learning, strategic alliances and flexible adjustment among companies that made specialty products within a broad range of related technologies. In contrast, the Route 128 region was based on a small number of relatively vertically integrated corporations with few crosscutting ties. Suchman (1995) also studied Silicon Valley and chronicled how law firms played an important role in standardizing governance structures, and reducing uncertainty for venture capitalists and entrepreneurs and universities by developing legal conventions, templates, and protocols that speeded up entrepreneurial activity and reduced constraints on capital mobilization.

COMMUNITY FORMATION, CHANGE AND COLLAPSE

Technical and institutional discontinuities (new laws, new norms and beliefs) spawn opportunities for entrepreneurs to initiate transformations in existing populations or to establish new organizational forms. In turn, commensalism and symbiosis may sort the affected populations into distinct niches and bind the populations into a community sharing a common fate.

Hunt and Aldrich (1998) showed how technological change was instrumental in the elaboration of a commercial community built around the world-wide web (WWW). They discussed how a standardized browser technology constituted the technical core that attracted infrastructural populations (hardware, telecommunications, internet service providers, search engine firms), usage promoters (web guides and web consultants and web page designers), and commercial users (firms doing business on through the web). They also pointed out that consortia such as the WWW consortium and governmental agencies such as the NSF played an important role in legitimating the community.

Some studies have looked at community-level change. Haveman and Rao (1997) studied the thrift industry and chronicled how new logics of saving emerged due to the foundings of new firms based on new savings plans rather than the adaptations of existing firms. They also described how entrepreneurs blended plans to constitute hybrid plans and thereby, modified the boundaries of populations in the thrift industry. In a detailed study of the California health care community, Scott et al. (1999, pp. 24–5) proposed that community change could be triggered by the birth of new logics motivating the behavior of actors, the advent of new collective actors, the crystallization of new meanings associated with behaviors of actors, the formation of new relationships among actors, and the modification of population and community boundaries.

Organizational researchers have devoted little attention to how catastrophes trigger the collapse of communities (Hawley, 1986). However, economic historians have chronicled the effects of catastrophes such as the Great Panic of 1907 or the Great Depression on regions and industries. Moen and Tallman (1992) investigated the effects of the Great Panic of 1907 in the New York banking community and found that trust companies experienced the contraction of loans and deposits but state banks and national banks were cushioned from these effects. Wheelock (1995) reported that the Great Depression did not exert a uniform effect on the collapse of banks and other financial intermediaries but noted that state policies accounted for inter-state variations in the death rates of financial institutions. Thus, institutional policies can amplify or buffer communities from the effect of catastrophes.

Contemporary Issues and Debates

Despite the impressive accumulation of empirical research on community level processes, key debates and controversies linger in the literature about the coherence of communities, and the organization of communities.

COHERENCE OF COMMUNITIES

Organizational theorists have disagreed about the composition and coherence of communities (Baum and Rao, 2001). DiMaggio (1994) questioned whether populations were the right unit of analysis and asked whether community studies over-privileged formal organizations. He argued that populations might not be the right unit of analysis because social processes efface population boundaries, many communities consisted of tiny populations, and population models were not suited to capture the effects of collective action. He pointed out that an overemphasis on formal organizations led researchers to gloss over how technologies competed with each other and professions were locked in competition. In response, Barnett (1994) suggested that a community be defined as populations of organizations united through bonds of symbiosis or commensalism, and argued that overly broad conceptualization of communities would mean that community ecology would degenerate into a study of economy and society where organizational sociologists would lose their comparative advantage. My own view is that that populations of organizations are a useful unit of analysis but that models of community dynamics must explicitly consider the effects of professional mobilization and formal and informal networks. Thus, informal ethnic networks can play a powerful role in recruiting potential founders and accelerating the rate of growth of a population such as budget motels in the community of organizational populations that make up the hospitality industry. Similarly, an analysis of the development of the community of organizational populations that comprise the legal services industry would be incomplete if it ignored the professional mobilization that was a precursor to establishment of the alternative dispute resolution mechanisms.

A related issue hinges around whether organizational communities have sufficient coherence as entities to be selected as entire units (Baum and Singh, 1994b; Campbell, 1974) in organization theory. Recently, Aldrich (1999) suggested that selection at the organizational community level depends upon the existence of a very tight coupling among populations, a condition most likely requiring strong centralized dominance by political authorities, as in authoritarian political regimes. An alternative view is that when selection is viewed as operating at multiple levels, strong coupling is not required for community-level selection (Sober and Wilson, 1998).

ORGANIZATION OF COMMUNITIES

A third controversy has swirled around the 'functional' organization of a community (Baum and Rao, 2001). Discussions of organizational communities equate higher-level functional organization with evidence of strong ecological interactions and dynamic equilibria. However, strong interdependence and dynamic equilibria are properties of many chemical, physical, biological, and social systems and do not imply functional organization. An organizational population can have a carrying capacity, regardless of whether it manages or overexploits its resources. Even the most dysfunctional communities can be stable, responding in ways that resist perturbation – stability at the community level occurs when the overall system of interpopulation interactions is characterized by negative feedback (Puccia and Levins, 1985). Moreover, although mutualism certainly plays an important role in community-level functional organization, and may be more common in functional than dysfunctional organizational communities, the proportion of interactions in a community that are mutualistic says little about its functional organization. Functional community-level organization can involve competition and predation, in addition to mutualism. Indeed, mutualism is an inevitable byproduct of indirect effects and will exist even in highly dysfunctional communities (Baum and Korn, 1994).[2] Some writers claim that complex system dynamics can produce higher level functional organization in the absence of natural selection (Kauffman, 1993; McKelvey, 1998, 1999). Although it is certainly true that complex systems dynamics can produce striking patterns in the absence of natural selection, similar to the often-striking "strange attractor" patterns that can be generated by complex systems of equations, *pattern* is not the same as *functional organization*.

A subsidiary issue concerns the commonness of "neutral" relationships between populations. Aldrich (1999) suggested that this was a consequence of observing mostly loosely coupled social systems because evolutionary selection forces favor them. Since communities survive when their various subparts can adapt autonomously, gaps exist even in complex communities with many interconnected populations. In such cases, when we attempt to detect competition in a community structure that contains the effects of competition (e.g., reduced number of populations, balanced population sizes) we fail to detect competition. In other words, neutrality is not an absence of interactions but an evolved set of interactions that eliminates competitive effects that might otherwise occur. Another possibility is coevolution, wherein, "the joint evolution of two (or more) [populations] that have close ecological relationships but do not exchange genes and in which reciprocal selective pressures operate to make the evolution of either [population] partially dependent on the evolution of the other" (Pianka, 1994, p. 329). Although coevolution has become an umbrella term for a variety of processes and outcomes of reciprocal evolutionary change, it is important to distinguish between the *reciprocal evolution* of coevolution from the simultaneously changing *mutual causation* of systems theory and ecology. This basic difference sets up a tension between coevolution and ecological interaction that can account for observing neutrality. Given similar resource requirements (ecological similarity), but *absent coevolution* among populations, one population in a predator/prey interaction will win out in the race toward competitive exclusion—the inferior population either migrates to a different niche or becomes extinct. But *with coevolution*, organizations within two ecologically similar populations might evolve toward different niches such that the inferior population would survive. Thus, "rapid-coevolution" can alter nature of ecological interactions (McKelvey, 1999).

Directions for Future Research

An important avenue for future research concerns how the boundaries of populations are created and effaced through social movement processes. Recent versions of cultural frame-institutionalism suggest that the creation of new organizational forms entails an institutionalization project, wherein institutional entrepreneurs actively define, justify, and push the theory and values underpinning a new form. In this line of argument, activists construct boundaries around activities and validate these boundaries such that a new category of organizations emerges. Because such activities often exhibit purposive goals and structured roles, some researchers liken such institutional projects to social movements (Fligstein, 1996; Swaminathan and Wade, 2001; Rao et al., 2001). Social movements are likely to be the mechanism through which population boundaries are created in very hierarchically organized communities. In such cases, central actors have vested interests in preserving the social order, and innovations originate in the periphery. Since peripheral actors possess little influence, social movements are the vehicles of collective action by which new forms become established. Such social movements typically assume a "conflict-oriented" character in the sense that conflict arises when organized attempts to modify the prevalent institutional order encounter opposition from interest groups opposed to the change. For example, the craft-brewing form arose as a reaction to industrial brewing and was powered by a social movement in which authenticity and tradition were valued in beer making (Carroll and Swaminathan, 2000). Equally importantly, when rival coalitions of organization builders champion different organizational models, the boundaries of an organizational form become questions of politics rather than efficiency. In such cases, the boundaries of a new organizational form become established when there is a truce among the constituents of the community about which model will be used to organize activities. Rao (1998) showed how the boundaries of non-profit consumer watchdogs embodied a truce amongst newspapers, Congress, and rival camps espousing different definitions of consumers. An important task for ecological researchers is to dimensionalize how communities spawn social movements, and are in turn, shaped by them.

Second, future research needs to be attentive to how alliances, partnerships and interlocking directorates cut across population boundaries and transform inter-population relations. In an early paper, Astley and Fombrun (1983) argued that communities were characterized by diagonal interdependence between firms located in different industries and pointed out that network organizations played an important coordinating role in organizational communities. A key issue for ecological researchers is to discern the community-level antecedents of network organizations and the community-level consequences of these coordinating structures.

Finally, future research also needs to be more attentive to the role of professions in organizational communities. In many instances, problems or issues persistently spill over from one profession to another (Abbott, 1988), thereby, creating conflicts between professions and promoting the birth of new organizational forms. Morrill (2001) chronicles how alternative dispute resolution (ADR) arose at the interstices of the legal and social work professions, and documents how attempts to professionalize ADR were instrumental in establishing boundaries around the form. A central challenge for ecological researchers is to delineate how conflict among the professions shapes the evolution of communities.

Connections Up and Down Hierarchical Levels

Populations in communities, organizations in populations, and routines within organizations comprise an ecological hierarchy (Baum and Singh, 1994a). Dynamic interactions within each level bind entities together at the next-higher level of the nested ecological hierarchy. Thus, interactions among jobs bind workgroups together, which in turn bind organizations together, and interactions among organizations of the same form constitute populations, and in turn, linkages among populations constitute communities. Variation, selection and retention (VSR) processes operate within each level of analysis. Systems of this type, hierarchical structures with feedback in which underlying components comprise and react to the overall organization, are termed *heterarchies* (Hofstader, 1979).

Each level may be seen as operating quasi-independently with some degree of autonomy of event and process, but there is also upward and downward causation within the entire hierarchy (Campbell, 1974, 1990). Arguably, interactions across different levels limit the range of processes that can unfold at a given level, and constrain the processes that do occur. Entities at one level can function as "environment" or context for entities at another level. In downward causation, VSR at higher levels limits VSR processes at lower levels, whereas, upward causation denotes that persistent features of the previous level constrain what emerges at the next level. Such cross-level interactions are likely to be strongest across contiguous levels with their significance declining as the levels involved become increasingly remote.

Campbell (1990, p.4) prophetically emphasized downward causation, and stated that "all processes at the lower levels of a hierarchy are restrained by, and act in conformity the laws of the higher levels." One implication is that the persistence, or continued replication, of lower level units is crucially dependent on the maintenance of the organized unit interfacing with the habitat. Thus, the selection of populations within communities constrains the life chances of organizations, and by implication, routines within organizations; see Galunic and Weeks (this volume). For example, the delegitimation of tobacco by the anti-smoking movement have impaired the growth rates of individual cigarette producers, and influenced the mix of routines within tobacco firms. New populations may migrate from one community to another, and thereby, change the mix of organizations and routines inherent in a community. For example, the entry of cable companies into the telecommunications community has brought in new organizations, and new sets of jobs.

Conversely, upward causation means that persistent features of the lower level constrain what emerges at the next level. Thus, organizations in a population can imitate routines situated in other populations in local environments, and such interorganizational imitation may in turn, create homogeneity and change the structure of commensalism within communities. For instance, credit unions can imitate commercial banks and intensify competition between both. Alternately, Baum and Amburgey, this volume, imply that organizations in one population may establish linkages with targets in another population, and such interorganizational linkages, in turn, may change the structure of symbiosis in organizational communities. For instance, hotels and airline companies are now bound together through a web of frequent-flyer programs.

An important consequence of hierarchical selection in ecological hierarchies is that selection pressures may often be conflicting: adaptations that are beneficial at one level may by deleterious at another level. For instance, union power may enable some classes of jobs to be retained through industry-wide agreements, but jeopardize the fates of individual organizations and the overall population. Another consequence of multi-level selection is that cooperation and competition may be exhibited at multiple levels. For example, firms within populations may band together into effective trade associations to ward off competitive incursions from other areas, but at the cost of great competition within the population.

Thus far, this chapter has focused on the potential range of interactions within the ecological hierarchy consisting of populations, organizations, and routines. Baum and Singh (1994a) also point to the existence of a genealogical hierarchy composed of organizational forms, organizations, and competences. If the accent in the ecological hierarchy is on interaction, the emphasis in the genealogical hierarchy is on replication. Organizations feature in both hierarchies because they are interactors and replicators. Just as there is multi-level causation in the ecological hierarchy, there is also multi-level causation in the genealogical hierarchy, and cross-causation across both hierarchies. Arguably, retention of organizational forms and competences is affected by processes in the ecological hierarchy responsible for the changing composition of ecological entities over time. In turn, however, what is retained also influences interactions within the ecological hierarchy. Neither hierarchy as causally prior to the other; both are necessary for a theory of organizational evolution.

Conclusion

Any study of how organizations affect society requires that we study communities of organizational populations. An emphasis on community ecology implies that we understand both the causes and consequences of organizational diversity across sets of populations. Research into how new organizational forms are created is sorely needed to understand how technological innovations are themselves organizational outcomes. Inter-population relationships may affect the patterns of mobility and inequality in societies. The study of these and related issues provides organizational ecologists to engage themselves with public policy questions and thereby, balance rigor with relevance.

Acknowledgments

I am grateful to Joel Baum for his thoughtful editorial suggestions.

Notes

1   Recall that K is the carrying capacity of the population's environment, r is the natural

growth rate of the population, N is population density—the number of organizations in the population, and t is a time interval.

2 For example, competition between two populations, A and B, which benefits a third population, C, because it also competes with B, would appear as mutualism between populations A and C even if A and C did not interact directly.

References

Abbott, A. (1988): *The System of Professions: An Essay on the Division of Expert Labor.* Chicago: University of Chicago Press.

Aldrich, H. E. (1979): *Organizations and Environments.* Englewood Cliffs, NJ: Prentice-Hall.

Aldrich, H. E. (1999): *Organizations Evolving.* London: Sage.

Astley, W. G. (1985): "The two ecologies: Population and community perspectives on organizational evolution," *Administrative Science Quarterly*, 30, 224–41.

Astley, W. G., and Fombrun, C. J. (1983): "Collective strategy: Social ecology of organizational environments," *Academy of Management Review*, 8, 576–87.

Barnett, W. P. (1990): "The organizational ecology of a technological system," *Administrative Science Quarterly*, 35, 31–60.

Barnett, W. P. (1994): "The liability of collective action: Growth and change among early American telephone companies," in J. A. C. Baum and J. V. Singh (eds.) *Evolutionary Dynamics of Organizations*, New York: Oxford University Press, 337–54

Barnett, W. P., and Carroll, G. R. (1987): "Competition and mutualism among early telephone companies," *Administrative Science Quarterly*, 32, 400–21.

Baum, J. A. C. (1989): "A population perspective on organizations: A study of diversity and transformation in child care service organizations," unpublished PhD dissertation, University of Toronto.

Baum, J. A. C. (1996): "Organizational ecology," in S. Clegg, C. Hardy and W. Nord (eds), *Handbook of Organization Studies*, London: Sage, 77–114.

Baum, J. A. C., and Korn, H. J. (1994): "The community ecology of large Canadian companies, 1984–1991," *Canadian Journal of Administrative Sciences*, 11, 277–94.

Baum, J. A. C., and Oliver, C. (1996): "The institutional ecology of organizational founding," *Academy of Management Journal*, 39, 1378–1427.

Baum, J. A. C., and Rao, H. (2001): "Evolutionary dynamics of organizational populations and communities," in M. S. Poole and A. Van de Ven (eds), *Handbook of Organizational Change and Development*, New York: Oxford University Press, forthcoming.

Baum, J. A. C., and Singh, J. V. (1994a): "Organizational hierarchies and evolutionary processes: Some reflections on a theory of organizational evolution," in J. A. C. Baum and J. V. Singh (eds), *Evolutionary Dynamics of Organizations*, New York: Oxford University Press, 3–20.

Baum, J. A. C., and Singh, J. V. (1994b): "Organizational niche overlap and the dynamics of organizational founding," *Organization Science*, 5, 483–501.

Boeker, W. (1991): "Organizational strategy: An ecological perspective," *Academy of Management Journal*, 34, 613–35.

Brittain, J. W., and Wholey, D. H. (1988): "Competition and coexistence in organizational communities: Population dynamics in electronics components manufacturing," in G. R. Carroll (ed.), *Ecological Models of Organizations*, Cambridge, MA: Ballinger, 195–222.

Campbell, D. T. (1974): "Evolutionary Epistemology," in P. A. Schlipp (ed.), *The Philosophy of Karl Popper*, London: MacMillan, 413–63.

Campbell, D. T. (1990): "Levels of organization, downward causation, and the selection-theory approach to evolutionary epistemology," in G. Greenberg and E. Tobach (eds), *Theories of the Evolution of Knowing*, Hillsdale, NJ: Lawrence Erlbaum Associates, 1–17.

Carroll, G. R. (1981): "Dynamics of organizational expansion in national systems of education,"

American Sociological Review, 46, 585–99.

Carroll, G. R., and Swaminathan, A. (2000): "Why the microbrewery movement? Organizational dynamics of resource partitioning in the American brewing industry after Prohibition," *American Journal of Sociology*, 106, 715–62.

Davis, G. F., and Mizruchi, M. S. (1999): "The money center cannot hold: Commercial banks in the U.S. system of governance," *Administrative Science Quarterly*, 44, 215–39.

DiMaggio, P. (1994): "The challenge of community evolution," in J. A. C. Baum and J. Singh (eds), *Evolutionary Dynamics of Organizations*, New York: Oxford University Press, 444–50.

DiMaggio, P. J., and Powell, W. W. (1983):"The iron cage revisited: Institutional isomorphism and collective rationality in organizational fields," *American Sociological Review*, 48,147–60.

Fligstein, N. (1996): "Markets as politics: A political cultural approach to market institutions," *American Sociological Review*, 61, 656–73.

Hannan, M. T., and Freeman, J. H. (1984): "Structural inertia and organizational change," *American Sociological Review*, 49, 149–64.

Hannan, M. T., and Freeman, J. H. (1989): *Organizational Ecology*. Cambridge, MA: Harvard University Press.

Haveman, H. A., and Rao, H. (1997): "Structuring a theory of moral sentiments: Institutional and organizational co-evolution in the early thrift industry," *American Journal of Sociology*, 102, 1606–51.

Hawley, A. H. (1950): *Human Ecology*. New York: Ronald.

Hawley, A. H. (1986): *Human Ecology*. Chicago: University of Chicago Press.

Hofstader, D. R. (1979): *Gödel, Escher, Bach: An Eternal Golden Braid*. New York: Basic Books.

Hunt, C. S., and Aldrich, H. E. (1998): The second ecology: Creation and evolution of organizational communities," in B. Staw and L. L. Cummings (eds), *Research in Organizational Behavior*, Greenwich, CT: JAI Press, 267–302.

Kauffman, S. A. (1993): *The Origins of Order: Self-Organization and Selection in Evolution*. New York: Oxford University Press.

Korn, H. J., and Baum, J. A. C. (1994): "Community ecology and employment dynamics: A study of large Canadian companies, 1985–1991," *Social Forces*, 73, 1–31.

McKelvey, B. (1982): *Organizational Systematics*. Los Angeles, CA: University of California Press.

McKelvey, B. (1998): "Complexity vs. selection among co-evolutionary firms: Factors affecting Nash equilibrium fitness levels," *Comportamento Organizacional E Gestão*, 4, 17–59.

McKelvey, B. (1999): Dynamics of new science leadership: An OB theory of the firm, strategy, and distributed intelligence," working paper, Anderson School at UCLA.

Mintz, B., and Schwartz, M. (1985): *The Power Structure of American Business*. Chicago: University of Chicago Press.

Moen, J., and Tallman, E. (1992): "The bank panic of 1907: The role of trust companies," *Journal of Economic History*, 52, 611–30.

Morrill, C. (2001):: "Institutional change and interstitial emergence: The growth of alternative dispute resolution in American law, 1965–1995," in W. W. Powell and D. L. Jones (eds), *Bending the Bars of the Iron Cage: Institutional Dynamics and Processes*, Chicago: University of Chicago Press, forthcoming.

Nielsen, E., and Hannan, M. T. (1977): "The expansion of national education systems: Tests of a population ecology model," *American Sociological Review*, 41, 479–90.

Oliver, C. (1992): "The antecedents of deinstitutionalization," *Organization Studies*, 13, 563–88.

Pianka, E. R. (1994): *Evolutionary Ecology*, 5th edn. New York: HarperCollins.

Pimm, S. L. (1991): *Balance of Nature?* Chicago: University of Chicago Press.

Polos, L., Hannan, M, and Carroll, G. (1999): "Forms and identities: On the structure of organizational forms," working paper Nagymoros Group.

Puccia, C. J., and Levins, R. (1985): *Qualitative Modeling of Complex Systems*. Cambridge, MA: Harvard University Press.

Rao, H. (1998): "Caveat emptor: The construction of non-profit consumer watchdog organizations," *American Journal of Sociology*, 103, 912–61.

Rao H., and J. V. Singh (1999): "Types of variation in organizational populations: The speciation of new organizational forms," in J. A. C. Baum and B. McKelvey (eds), *Variations in Organization Science: In Honor of Donald T. Campbell*, Thousand Oaks, CA: Sage, 63–77.

Rao, H., Morrill, C., and Zald, M. (2001): "Power plays: How social movements and collective action create new organizational forms," in B. Staw and R. Sutton (eds), *Research in Organizational Behavior, vol 22*, Greenwich CT: JAI Press, 237–82.

Rich, P. (1992): "The organizational taxonomy: Definition and design," *Academy of Management Review*, 17, 758–81.

Romanelli, E. (1989): "Organizational birth and population variety: A community perspective on origins," in B. Staw and L. L. Cummings (eds), *Research in Organizational Behavior*, Greenwich, CT: JAI Press, 211–246.

Saxenian, A. (1994): *Regional Advantage: Culture and Competition in Silicon Valley and Route 128*. Cambridge, MA: Harvard University Press.

Scott, W. R. (1994): "Conceptualizing organizational fields: Linking organizations and societal systems," in H-U. Derlien, U. Gerhardt, and F. W. Scharpf (eds), *Systemrationalität und Partialinteresse [Systems Rationality and Partial Interests]*, Baden, Germany: Nomos Velagsgesellschaft, 203–21.

Scott, W. R. (1995): *Institutions and Organizations*. Thousand Oaks, CA: Sage.

Scott, W. R., Ruef, M., Mendel, P. J., and Caronna, C. A. (1999): *Institutional Change and Organizations*. Chicago: University of Chicago Press.

Shapiro, C., and Varian, H. (1999): *Information Rules*. Boston: Harvard Business School Press.

Sober, E., and Wilson, D. S. (1998): *Unto Others: The Evolution and Psychology of Unselfish Behavior*. Cambridge, MA: Harvard University Press.

Suchman, M. C. (1995): "Localism and globalism in institutional analysis: The emergence of contractual norms in venture finance," in W. R. Scott and S. Christensen (eds), *The Institutional Construction of Organizations*, Thousand Oaks, CA: Sage, 39–63.

Swaminathan, A., and Wade, J. (2001): "Social movements and new organizational forms," in K. Schoonhoven and E. Romanelli (eds), *The New Entrepreneurial Dynamic*, Stanford, CA: Stanford University Press, forthcoming.

Wheelock, D. C. (1995): "Market structure and bank failures during the Great Depression," *Federal Reserve Bank of St. Louis Review*, 77, 27–38.

Wholey, D. R., Christiansen, J. B., and Sanchez, S. (1993): "Professional reorganization: The effect of physician and corporate interests on the formation of Health Maintenance Organizations," *American Journal of Sociology*, 99, 175–211.

Chapter Twenty-four

Interorganizational Evolution

HENRICH R. GREVE

Interorganizational evolution is the process of cumulative change in social structures composed of or affecting multiple organizations. Theory of interorganizational evolution specifies mutual and path dependent influences between organizations and their environment so that small differences in initial conditions can lead to large differences in the subsequent evolutionary path. Interorganizational evolution takes place at the level of the interorganizational field (DiMaggio and Powell, 1983), population (Hannan and Freeman, 1977), or community (Astley, 1985). Interorganizational structures and behaviors are found in many arenas of organizational activity, and evolutionary arguments have been made in several areas of interorganizational inquiry. The work is joined by a common interest in the evolution of procedures and structures that define the organization's relation with other actors (ecological structures); see Baum and Singh (1994).

I will give a brief description of the main theoretical components of evolutionary arguments before turning to applications. I will review evolutionary work on the origin and change of market structures (Haveman and Rao, 1997), policy arenas (Frank, 1997; Hoffman, 1999), industrial districts (Carroll and Harrison, 1994; Saxenian, 1994), and cross-national differences in management and governance (Orrú et al., 1991; Guillén, 1994; Hollingsworth et al., 1994). Readers interested in evolutionary theory should also consult the chapters on networks, institutions, and technology of this book and recent reviews on institutions (Scott, 1995), markets (Swedberg, 1994; Lie, 1997), law (Edelman and Suchman, 1997), and organizational evolution (Aldrich, 1999). This review covers work after the review by Aldrich (1979) with an emphasis on work done in the 1990s. Papers have been selected for review based on whether they contain evolutionary reasoning, and includes some work that is not self-described as evolutionary.

Evolutionary Theory

To show the structure of an evolutionary theory of interorganizational structure, consider the classic "War and peace: The evolution of modern personnel practice in US industry" (Baron et al., 1986). This historical study of the origin of important personnel management practices becomes an evolutionary paper because of its balanced discussion of the historically unique features of this process, such as the wartime manpower reporting and classification required by the state, and the general evolutionary processes, such as the retention of these wartime practices in the large firms originally subjected to them and the diffusion of similar practices to smaller firms. Thus, the two distinctive features of evolutionary theory (Gould, 1989, pp. 284–91) are present in the paper: First, part of the explanation for current conditions is historical contingency, that is, early events such as wartime labor controls are consequential for the subsequent evolution and to some degree arbitrary. Second, the mechanisms of evolution are systematic and consequential, since diffusion processes predictably cause practices to spread throughout a population. This balance between specific contingencies and general mechanisms distinguishes evolutionary theory from pure description on the one hand and "just-so" explanations of why the current conditions are efficient on the other (Aldrich, 1999).

Evolutionary research can be analyzed following the conceptual scheme of variation, selection, and retention (Campbell, 1965), where variation generates practices that are differentially selected and retained in the social system. Variation in interorganizational structures is generated when new organizational forms are assembled (Rao and Singh, 1999) or when existing organizational forms make innovations that rearrange their relations with other organizations. Innovations can be made by rearranging existing structures or importing existing structures into a new context, so variation can be generated either by transferring practices or by creating radically new ones. Variation-generating processes have seen little attention so far, probably because much variation comes under the category of historical contingency – it is the work of technological, organizational, and institutional entrepreneurs and innovators, and is seen as less amenable to systematic study than the systematic mechanisms of evolution.

Selection means that the frequency of behaviors is changed by some mechanism. Interorganizational selection is created by inter- and intra-organizational imitation (Rogers, 1995; Strang and Soule, 1998), organizational founding and failure (Carroll and Hannan, 2000), and coercion by powerful actors (DiMaggio and Powell, 1983). These are processes that interest organizational theorists and are amenable to systematic study, so selection processes have seen considerable study. Most studies reviewed here concern selection.

Retention simply means that a structure and behavior is maintained over time. In organizational inquiry, the process of retention is often viewed as unproblematic since organizations are highly effective retention systems (this is the same as saying that they exhibit structural inertia, Hannan and Freeman, 1984). In research on interorganizational evolution, retention is more tenuous since it relies on the continued contributions of multiple autonomous organizations engaged in exchange or governance. Retention thus requires collective action over time (Moe, 1990), which means that either that the individual interests that support a given interorganizational structure must remain or that actors must fail to exploit opportunities to change. Retention may be easier in old organizational populations since they develop differentiated role structures that reduce the ability of any single organization to affect changes (Hannan, 1997).

Interorganizational Origins and Change

MARKET STRUCTURES

The fundamental feature of markets is exchange of goods or services for money among buyers and sellers. Work on the evolution of such patterns of exchange is rare, but fortunately not totally absent. Leblebici et al. (1991) examined how the radio broadcasting industry from 1920 to 1960 evolved from its initial pattern of exchange through an intermediate stage into the current pattern where commercial radio stations broadcast advertisements paid for by firms, and where the audience of each radio station is estimated by a ratings agency which is paid by subscribing stations. Thus the radio industry, which appears to offer a free product (the program), is economically based on an exchange of "ears for money" between radio stations and advertisers. Leblebici et al. show that the early economic arrangements differed from the present and were replaced when innovations by marginal actors in the industry were imitated and eventually adopted widely. The process of imitation was systematic and driven by the superior economic performance of the new patterns of exchange, but was also contingent in that the succession of old arrangements by new ones halted as soon as an economically viable market form had been found.

A similar process of market transformation was found in the early history of thrift associations (1890–1928) (Haveman and Rao, 1997). Competition among different plans (which defined, simultaneously, the governance structure of the organization and the savings and loans products it offered) led to a nearly complete succession of the oldest plans by newer plans more suitable for the loosely knit communities with mobile members that were becoming the norm in the USA. This evolution was largely driven by organizational founding and failure and was closely tied with broader social mores. This latter link provided an important contingency in the evolutionary process, as the forms that eventually prevailed were originally vilified as contrary to the mutualist moral code of the thrifts, but later rose through their links to the rational-bureaucratic ideals of the progressivism movement. These links with larger social forces are not surprising given the central role of banking in modern society and its susceptibility to regulation based on broader social goals.

Another important evolutionary process is the creation of new markets or absorption of old markets. Sometimes the market structure can evolve although the production process does not, as organizations can absorb exchanges previously done in the market or externalize intra-organizational exchanges to the market. Here Lazerson (1993, 1995) – see also Lorenzoni and Ornati (1988) – has studied how the old system of "putting-out" steps in textile production to subcontractors recently has reemerged in the Italian textiles and clothing industry. Underlying this process is an economic incentive through tax breaks for small businesses, but the problems of making such a production system responsive and reliable have led to the evolution of geographically localized networks of exchange around a closely knit group of actors. Thus an economic exchange structure is created by market incentives and shaped by preexisting social relations. How social ties influence the creation and maintenance of new economic actors and exchanges is clearly described by Uzzi's (1996; 1997) study of New York's apparel industry, where some of the noneconomic motives behind the exchanges were reflected in prosocial (even when not individually rational) behavior and exchange networks. Others have discovered similar close exchanges that appear to be inefficient for the overall exchange network (Provan and Sebastian, 1998).

A special and important market evolution is the transformation of corporations as actors with undisputed boundaries and authority relations to marketable goods that can be bought without their own consent, combined with others, or split and sold. Thus a new interorganizational structure, the market for corporate control, has in recent decades emerged through a complex evolutionary process. The diffusion of new ideologies had an important supporting role, as the concept of the corporation as a financial and contractual concept gained in importance, replacing the earlier metaphor of the corporation as an organism (Davis et al., 1994; Fligstein, 1990). The main tool of corporate buyers, the unsolicited takeover offer, went the usual route from an innovation used by outsiders and viewed as threatening by established actors to becoming a highly legitimate tool of the elite (Hirsch, 1986; Palmer, Barber, Zhou, and Soysal, 1995; Stearns and Allan, 1996). Corporations resisted this commodification process both by adopting individual countermeasures (Davis and Greve, 1997) and by collective action towards state governments (Davis and Thompson, 1994). Proponents of a free market for corporations also used collective action, however, and ultimately prevailed through the much stronger economic interests on their side. Besides demonstrating the roles of ideology, collective action, and individual opportunism in this evolutionary process, scholars have held a lively debate on the relative importance of these factors (Fligstein, 1995; Palmer, Barber, and Zhou, 1995).

Market structures often gain additional structure from the establishment of durable exchange relations between pairs of actors. The existence of such fixed patterns of exchange is sometimes used to argue against perfect markets (Granovetter, 1985), and their evolution is a matter of considerable interest. Research on the number of transaction partners (Baker, 1990) and the selection of partner identity (Podolny, 1993; 1994) in 1980's investment banking shows a highly differentiated market where the statuses of clients and banks guide who will deal with whom. Podolny (1994) compared the selection of co-managers in the market for traditional investment grade securities and the more recent market for noninvestment grade securities, showing that both markets were structured by the uncertainty-reducing strategies of firms. The form of uncertainty reduction differed, however, as banks chose familiar partners in the traditional investment grade market, but relied more on overall status in the highly uncertain market of noninvestment grade securities. Both mechanisms retain the existing structure of interorganizational trades. Podolny (1994) also showed that the status matching mechanism became weaker as the banks gained familiarity with the noninvestment grade market, suggesting a transition to matching by familiarity as the market stabilized.

Another market structure is created by organizational specialist strategies that let organizations contest only a small portion of the market demand. This is the consumer market equivalent to the transaction partner selection described above, and is done by tailoring the product to fit a niche of the potential customer population. The process of generating variation by innovating niches has seen little study, but we know a fair amount about how niches are selected. Concentrated markets are structurally ripe for niche strategies and give specialist organizations higher founding rates and survival chances (Carroll, 1985; Lomi, 1995; Swaminathan, 1995; Wade, 1995). Niche structures also evolve through the mimetic adoption of innovative niche strategies by existing organizations. In industries with multiple markets, newly discovered niches are transferred among markets by a process of imitation where organizations with branches in multiple markets are particularly active, as they transfer strategies that they have seen or done elsewhere to a focal market (Greve, 1996; 1998). Large and successful organizations are also influential, as they are watched and imitated by others (Haveman, 1993). The opposite process of abandoning old niches also involves imitation, which is particularly strong within corporate structures (Greve, 1995). Thus markets obtain their niche structure by selection through imitation and differential founding and failure. Contingency affects this process through the order in which niche strategies are innovated, as the mimetic adoption of each strategy fills resource space that similar strategies could have exploited. This causes the set of niches that will rise to be contingent and unpredictable even though the rise of some sort of niche structure is highly predictable.

Standard economic theory takes the boundaries and actors of a market as given, and some organizational theorists make the same assumption. By contrast, evolutionary work has shown that every aspect of markets is subject to path-dependent cumulative change. The organizational forms involved in a market, their roles in the exchange, specific exchange dyads, and niche structures are determined by variation, selection, and retention driven by local economic incentives. Since economic exchanges require participation of buyers and sellers, construction of radically new forms of exchange is more difficult to achieve through an evolutionary process than elaboration of old. Variation and selection processes are strong enough to substantially change markets over a time span of about a decade, but over shorter time periods retention processes appear to dominate.

GOVERNANCE STRUCTURES

Many actors-organizations and individuals-seek to govern interorganizational fields, and they are in turn targets of influence attempts by organizations in the fields. Recent work has taken resource dependence ideas of interorganizational control (Pfeffer and Salancik, 1978) into an evolutionary direction by showing how control attempts cumulatively shape an interorganizational field (DiMaggio, 1991; Holm, 1995). Important actors are the state, the judiciary, the core organizational population, advocacy organizations, and professionals. Because of the many actors showing active interest and agency and the multiple routes of influence and governance, the evolution of governance systems is a very complex process. The state affects organizations through direct influence and by setting premises for the evolution of the interorganizational field (Dobbin, 1995). The core organizations of an interorganizational field often seek to influence the state directly or through corporatist organizations (Holm, 1995; Hooks, 1990). Advocacy organizations seek to influence the core organizations directly or through the state (Hoffman, 1999; Rao, 1998). Professionals working inside the organization or consulting with it intercept influence attempts from the environment and make their own interpretation of the demands and required compliance (Sutton and Dobbin, 1996). Though this list of important relations in interorganizational governance suggests that a model of evolution driven by multiple, interrelated processes is needed at some point, the best contributions so far have simplified the analysis by concentrating on one or two of these relations at a time.

The state is often seen as an influence target or dispute solver, but it is important to remember that it also has interests, such as the goals of the party controlling the legislature or executive branch. The railroad industry in nineteenth-century USA (Dobbin, 1995) showed considerable influence of the state on business structure and behavior. Legislative and judicial activity closely tracked the current political agenda, going through phases of local development with state financial support, state support of price agreements, and a policy reversal leading to suppression of price agreements but tacit approval of mergers and monopolistic pricing. These policies could largely be treated as external influences on the industry, which led to complete transformations of its structure and behavior according to the incentives given by each policy regime. There were also feedback effects, however, as the interorganizational price agreements caused fears of power concentration that, along with similar agreements in other industries, eventually spawned the policy change towards suppression of price agreements. An important contingency was provided by the Supreme Court, whose support of the free-market reforms eventually caused the industry to give up any hope of introducing modified forms of price controls.

The law has a special role in the field of governance because of its potential permanence and often-ambiguous meaning. Legal changes force organizations to make sense of the new rules and their consequences, and this process of social construction of meaning is influenced by professional agendas and interorganizational imitation (Edelman, 1990; Sutton et al., 1994; Stearns and Allan, 1996; Sutton and Dobbin, 1996). It is also influenced by advocacy groups, who see the power vested in the courts as a tempting target of influence and use the legal system to deter against unwanted corporate behaviors. These actors are active participants in the evolution of governance who systematically learn the rules of the field by trial and error, but their participation is also determined by contingencies such as the precedence set by early decisions and the actions of current policy makers (Hoffman, 1999).

An interesting case of the interaction of organizations and law is the field of bankruptcy law. Delaney (1992) showed in several case studies that corporations have during the 1980s exploited legal ambiguity and pro-business judges to significantly extend the situations in which bankruptcy can be used by the organizations against claimants such as other organizations, unions, or class-action plaintiffs. Law evolves by accretion, as decisions are made by extending, modifying, and occasionally reversing previous decisions, and the accretion leads to strong path dependence and historical contingency. The specialized nature of bankruptcy law favors large corporations that can use specialist law firms, causing bankruptcy law to become a nearly closed system heavily influenced by a small group of law firms and their corporate clients (Delaney, 1999).

Advocacy organizations have governance of other organizations as their goal, and have an important role in interorganizational evolution. They are themselves subject to selection based on how well their agenda and rhetoric fits public interest (Minkoff, 1994; Rao, 1998). Rao (1998) studied consumer watchdog organizations, whose sheer number, membership, and ability to influence consumer decisions may make them the pre-eminent form of advocacy organization affecting firm behavior in the USA. He found that the pioneer watchdog organizations in the early twentieth century faced strong pressures from business and politicians, and went through a lengthy process of adjusting their goals and methods to achieve legitimacy and protection against attacks. This adjustment made the field of watchdog organizations isomorphic, as an early split between product-testing organizations and organizations whose agenda included labor conditions collapsed into the current model of science-based testing of products. Important contingencies were provided by the small number of prominent organizations and leading individuals, making the initial choice of agenda (product testing) a focal point around which subsequent founding attempts focused, either in conformity or opposition. Arguably a larger or less transparent field of organizations could have accommodated more variation in the organizational form.

Governance structures get strong path dependence from their links with broader social forces and with entrenchment of powerful actors. Variation is still provided by governance entrepreneurs who either oppose or seek to exploit the current system, and large-scale change is possible. Since change in governance structures is done through mobilization of actors opposed to the status quo, it often seems to occur as sudden swings when the forces in opposition overwhelm the forces of conservation. This pendulum motion differs from the process of elaboration and differentiation seen in market structures.

SPATIAL STRUCTURES

The spatial distribution of organizations is important in itself and as a contributing factor to the evolution of organizational fields, and has recently gained popularity in organization theory. The history of such research traces back to human ecology (Hawley, 1950), however, and is part of a broader movement towards the study of space in sociology (Kono et al., 1998) and economics (Krugman, 1992). The current interest can be traced to work documenting the widespread existence of industrial districts, which are local agglomerations of organizations doing related forms of business, and the claim that organizations in such districts jointly develop competitive advantages relative to organizations located outside (Porter, 1990). Related work in economics has involved disputes between scholars favoring evolutionary explanations (Krugman, 1992) versus scholars sticking to traditional (for economics) static efficiency arguments (Kim, 1995) and scholars favoring more historical explanations (Martin and Sunley, 1996). In organization theory, the evolutionary perspective dominates this line of research.

Saxenian's (1994) comparative analysis of the computer industry districts in the Silicon Valley and around Route 128 during the 1980s shows two consequences of such spatial agglomeration. First, the spatial proximity of firms produced homogeneity in corporate cultures and interorganizational interaction patterns in both regions. Second, the interaction differed sharply across regions. Silicon Valley developed a fluid labor and knowledge market where social connections and knowledge exchange among firms were frequent and to some extent unmanageable, since they rose out of preexisting social relations such as past school or coworker ties and norms of openness and knowledge sharing. It also had high organizational specialization with well-developed factor markets. In Route 128, interorganizational interaction remained rare and in conflict with an emphasis on loyalty to the firm, consistent with the influence of the older and more regimented firms that formed the core of this region. Organizations internalized their procurement, resulting in poorer factor markets. These differences underlines the potential for divergent evolution based on different initial conditions, and is an important counterexample to the claim that collaborative relations are a necessary consequence of spatial proximity. The norm of reciprocity cuts both ways, so a secretive organization can suppress interorganizational interaction just as effectively as an open organization can promote it. Factor markets can be destroyed by self-contained organizations, just as they can be created by specialist organizations.

In some contexts, advantages of agglomeration are well documented. As noted earlier, Lazerson (1993; 1995) showed the rise of new intermediate markets for textile products in Italy and showed that the localized structure of these exchange structures made them as responsive to disturbances as an integrated organization. The need for such responsiveness becomes an important retention mechanism, as it would be difficult for any single organization to leave the region without incurring communication and logistic problems that would make the intermediate markets less useful for it. However, Harrison (1997) cautioned that the retention of such industrial districts is problematic, and presented case evidence that the small and financially weak organizations in such districts are easy acquisition targets. Large firms have moved into the Italian industrial districts at will, acquiring small firms and rearranging their exchange relations in a more hierarchical and centralized fashion. This restructuring of exchanges does not directly lead to the collapse of the district, but the propensity of large corporations to buy their inputs from widely dispersed suppliers can gradually weaken the local supplier structure, causing difficulty for the remaining small firms that need nearby suppliers. Thus, while spatial aggregation is important in some industries and locales, the capacity of the modern corporation for managing dispersed activities implies that advantages of aggregation should not be taken for granted. Harrison's discussion of how large corporations weakened industrial districts in Italy resembles Saxenian's critique of their role in Route 128, suggesting a general conflict between locales and large corporations.

A different warning is given by Sorenson and Audia (2000), who found that both founding and failure rates were higher inside the northeastern industrial district of shoemaking in the US than elsewhere, and interpreted this as showing that spatial proximity leads to advantages in the founding process, but also to greater competition among organizations. Proximate competition has also been found in populations of hotels (Baum and Mezias, 1992; Ingram and Inman, 1996), banks (Lomi, 1995), and brewers (Wade et al., 1998), supporting the claim that nearby organizations of the same form increase mortality rates. Thus it seems reasonable to separate the effects of being in an industrial district into effects on the founding process and effects on the life expectancy, and carefully test where the retention of industrial district structures comes from.

Strong path dependencies in the organizational founding process suggest that agglomeration can occur without agglomeration advantages. Greve (2000) found weak competitive effects in the founding of bank branches in early twentieth-century Tokyo banking, but strong mimetic effects from large banks and strong momentum from the bank's own earlier decisions. Thus the spatial structures of individual banks and the population as a whole became more localized than the structure of the market justified. Such other- and self-mimetic processes are both systematic and strongly contingent on initial conditions, as the population will center around whatever point initially had most organizations. For Tokyo banks, the initial center was determined by the spatial distribution of a predecessor financial institution much less dependent on contact with the general public than bank branches are, and the path-dependent founding created a population that stayed somewhat aloof of its customers.

The spatial dimension is interrelated with other aspects of the firm operations. Manhattan hotels appeared to prefer locations near other hotels provided these followed different pricing strategies, thus producing clusters in the spatial dimension but dispersion in the pricing dimension (Baum and Haveman, 1997). Expectations of competitive intensity may also come into play. It is well documented that large corporations compete selectively, choosing to mutually forbear against competitors met in multiple markets while competing fully against those met in a single market (Barnett et al., 1994; Evans and Kessides, 1994; Gimeno and Woo, 1996; Gimeno, 1999). This, in turn, has been shown to influence the choice of markets to enter for California commuter airlines (Baum and Korn, 1999), but not for Tokyo banks (Greve, 2000).

In the evolution of spatial structures, selection processes often appear to overwhelm variation processes. There appears to be little room for experimentation before the location decisions and local forms of interaction become specialized, making the initial moves highly influential for the subsequent process. Whether retention processes are strong enough to make spatial agglomerations stable is a controversial issue, however, since they are weakened by localized competition and attract large firms who hollow out their self-reinforcing structure. Spatial structures seem to offer an important opportunity to study the balance of selection and retention mechanisms.

COMPARATIVE STUDIES

An important and under-developed area is comparative research on inter-organizational evolution. There are good reasons for this neglect, as comparison of different interorganizational fields over time is a complex effort that easily becomes a book-length contribution. Nevertheless, important studies have been done. Saxenian's comparison of two high-tech regions in the USA has already been mentioned, and Guillén (1994) compared the evolution of scientific management, human relations, and structural analysis management practices in the USA and three European nations. He showed that these evolutionary processes received similar inputs in the form of ideologies and techniques of management, but evolved differently due to the interdependence with organizational structures, workplace relations, and general politics and culture. Interesting common patterns are the dependence of all three practices on large and complex organizations and the strong link from labor conflict to the adoption of human relations practices. Significant differences in the timing and depth of adoption are also shown and partly explained by how wide support these practices had in each nation, especially from the state, the unions, and professionals. The explanation leaves a substantial role for pure contingency, as the adoption of practices with such broad ideological and technical implications as management system necessarily has more determinants than even a four-nation study can fully sort out. Guillén's (1994) call for further analysis from other nations (such as the Soviet Union and Japan) should be answered.

Hollingsworth et al. (1994) is a collection of comparative studies of industrial governance, often with an interest in governmental or interorganizational influences on firm behavior and outcomes. Notable for its evolutionary orientation is Herrigel's (1994) comparison of the machine tool industries in the USA and Germany from the nineteenth century to the 1980s. In the late period, his conclusions resemble those of Saxenian: An industry composed of large, self-contained and distrustful organizations (USA) had greater difficulty adapting to environmental changes than one with small, specialized and collaborating organizations (Germany). An important extension is provided by the documentation of how initial conditions affected the evolution of the industry. The main reason for the large size of the US machine tool firms was that their industry was born just as mass manufacturing started in the US, while the German firms remained small because regional differences in economy and markets precluded mass manufacturing. Herrigel (1994) also notes that mechanisms for mutual governance and collaboration were deliberately put in place in Germany through the establishment of an industry association, and this association also proved useful when the German industry initially missed the importance of computer numerical control equipment and had to do joint research to catch up with Japan.

A remarkable monograph on innovation in the Japanese electronics industry contributes to two neglected research themes by being a comparative (USA and Japan) study of variation (innovation and new technologies) (Johnstone, 1999). By tracing the process from innovation to commercialization of several technologies in the electronics industry, Johnstone (1999) shows that small and medium-size firms with high technological competence were pioneers in refining and commercializing new technologies, explicitly rejecting an effective role of government guidance of technology development in Japan and weakening the argument for special Japanese forms of knowledge management. He shows that large Japanese firms missed opportunities just as readily as large US firms did, and that most innovative R&D laboratories in Japan revolved around the work of one person. The innovative Japanese electronics firms were small, entrepreneurial, and risk-taking, and thus were more similar to Silicon Valley firms than to large Japanese firms.

SUMMARY

Table 24.1 shows a selection of studies on interorganizational evolution, and clearly illustrates the wide range of research themes and approaches present in this field. Research on interorganizational evolution is currently in a fermentation stage, where a multitude of theories and empirical approaches is pursued and some very exciting findings are made. Less desirably, it has modest communication among the different research efforts and formalization of theory and research approaches. The high tolerance of experimentation makes this an exciting time to participate in such research, and has helped lay a wide foundation for future research. Since evolutionary theory encompasses models of quite different substance, such as competition, institutionalization, power, and learning, there is low expectation of or need for a reduction in the diversity of approaches. What is needed, however, is more communication among approaches and among studies in each approach. A common forum (i.e., a Journal of Organizational Evolution) would improve the communication. Studies employing explicitly stated hypotheses and formal hypothesis testing would also increase communication, as the

Table 24.1 Summary of key interorganizational evolution studies

Reference	Key concepts	Key variables	Key findings	Key contribution	Method and sample
Baron et al., 1986	Emergence and retention of new organizational activity	Adoption of personnel management practices	Effect of wartime personnel controls on current formal personnel management	Balance of systematic process and contingency	Historical analysis of US corporations in the twentieth century
Haveman and Rao, 1997	Market evolution through the competition of organizational forms	Founding, failure, change of thrifts	Founding and failure is main evolutionary process, societal norms provided selection pressures.	Compared selection processes and studied both process and outcome.	Hazard rate analysis of founding, failure, change of thrifts in the USA, 1890–1928
Podolny, 1994	Retention of status order in markets	Selection of co-manager bank in security issues	Status matching of investment banks under conditions of uncertainty	Retention system based on individual incentives to maintain existing collective order	Logit analysis of firm pairings in securities offerings in the USA, 1981–7
Dobbin, 1995	Public policy and industry coevolution	Structure and behavior of industry	Major phases in industry structure tracked legal changes.	Economic and managerial principles are specific to a given governance regime.	Historical analysis of US railroad industry, 1825–1906
Delaney, 1992, 1999	Law evolving through corporate initiative	Change in interpretation of law and users of law	Wider interpretation of bankruptcy eligibility followed initiatives of corporations and law firms.	Differential access to key actors of a governance system can shift power in favor of high-access actors.	Case studies of US bankruptcies 1980s and 90s
Saxenian, 1994	Interfirm interaction norms and competitiveness	Differential behaviors and competitiveness of firms in Silicon Valley and Route 128	High interorganizational communication and specialization gave better responsiveness to competitive challenges.	Change potential embedded in interfirm interaction patterns as well as in behavior of each firm and selection of firms	Comparative analysis of two US high-tech districts in the 1980s
Greve, 2000	Path-dependent spatial structure of new industry	Branch entry location choices	Momentum within firms and imitation between firms stronger than competitive forces	Spatial agglomeration arises from organizational decision-making routines.	Decision analysis of bank branch entries in Tokyo, 1894–1936
Guillen, 1994	Comparison of evolutionary processes	Management practices in US and European states	Evolutionary processes diverge due to structural, political, and other environmental contingencies.	Embeddedness of management practice in societal context	Comparative historical study of USA, Germany, Great Britain, and Spain

common methodological ground of such studies allows replication, comparison, and disproof. Integrative studies addressing issues from multiple approaches will also be useful once each approach has accumulated a stable set of findings.

Contemporary Issues and Debates

Organizational scholars often incorporate evolutionary arguments into other theoretical perspectives, which has given evolutionary theory a position of being used frequently in a subsidiary role but rarely as a main theory. This has weakened its identity, and it is often not viewed as a distinct theoretical perspective. Important evolutionary papers are classified under other perspectives. For example, "War and Peace" (Baron et al., 1986) is usually viewed as an institutional paper. This classification is partially correct, since the paper describes the genesis of an institution, but it is incomplete since it is an *evolutionary* paper on institutions and thus different from the many non-evolutionary papers on institutions. Ironically, this is a common fate of evolutionary papers because evolutionary arguments are uncontroversial in organization theory and thus do not need to be presented polemically.

The ill-defined boundary of evolutionary theory has also led to something like a free-for-all where researchers can use the word evolution without adopting its main implications. Some advocates of static efficiency as a primary mode of explanation invoke evolution as a mechanism for making efficient things happen (Williamson, 1981), ignoring the historical contingency of evolutionary arguments. Sometimes, evolution seems to be a fancy way of saying change, as the word inexplicably occurs in studies that contain no evolutionary theory. A study of evolution should be very clear about the subject that evolves, the mechanisms of evolution, and what (if any) historical contingencies are involved. Students of evolution should not take the presence of the word evolution as a sign that a paper contains evolutionary theory, or its absence as a sign that it does not. The issue of delineating and defining evolutionary work is the single most important problem of current evolutionary theory (Aldrich, 1999).

Other issues also need attention. In evolutionary processes where multiple causes are at work, as in the rise of the market for corporations discussed above, debates sometimes erupt about which evolutionary process is most important. While such debates can provide important insights into a particular sequence of events, the generalizability of the conclusions is seriously circumscribed. The contingencies of evolutionary processes enable the apparent order of importance of causal factors to differ even among evolutionary processes that have similar causes, making conclusions about the relative importance very precarious. An important special case of such "causal primacy" debates is the classical graduate school debate on the role of environmental selection versus individual adaptation in evolutionary processes. This discussion no longer excites scholars to the degree it used to, and recently position papers have been replaced by innovative comparisons of the strength of these processes in given contexts (Haveman and Rao, 1997). Again, the contingent nature of evolutionary processes suggests caution in drawing general conclusions from any single study, but comparison of multiple processes seems likely to be a productive approach to answering questions of causal primacy.

An important question in evolutionary theory is whether evolutionary processes produce outcomes that are efficient for the actors or for society (March, 1994). These questions (individual and societal efficiency are different) cannot be addressed directly because they involve comparison of an actual evolutionary path with hypothetical paths, but strong indirect tests can be provided by closer analysis of the implications of plausible models. Recent work has used analytical and simulation methods to show that some mechanisms of evolution can fail to reach efficient outcomes (Lomi and Larsen, 2001). Density-dependent organizational founding and failure can lead to more efficient organizational forms failing to succeed existing organizational forms (Carroll and Harrison, 1994), and imitation can cause inefficient practices to spread in uncertain environments (Bikhchandani et al., 1992; Strang and Macy, 1999). Such studies are valuable because they challenge the assumption that evolution causes efficient outcomes, and thus show how true evolutionary arguments differ from "just-so" explanations.

Remaining Questions

It is perhaps only a natural reaction to (and rejection of) a past of static, cross-sectional studies that organizational scholars have become very adept at studying evolutionary *processes*. The causes of imitation, founding, failure, collective action, and legal change are studied with considerable sophistication and will continue to yield important findings. The full benefit of these insights will not be realized, however, unless attention is also turned to evolutionary *outcomes*. Here, many evolutionary studies display considerable lack of caution by drawing conclusions about the direction of evolutionary processes based on analysis of selection processes alone. Evidence that selection processes drive the population in one direction cannot establish that this is the evolutionary path, as lack of retention or high variation can cause it to vary from the direction of the selection pressure. Careful evolutionary studies show the direction of the selection pressure and the aggregate change in population characteristics (Davis et al., 1994; Haveman and Rao, 1997).

A second remaining question is the role of contingency in interorganizational evolutionary processes. Contingencies are difficult to prove, but this task must be done, as it is on the tension between mechanism and contingency that evolutionary arguments thrive and demonstrate their importance to organization theory (Aldrich, 1999, pp. 196–222). Here, comparative work is very valuable. An important contribution of Guillén's (1994) study of management systems in the USA and Europe is the finding that similar sets of management practices were adopted and practiced differently because contextual differences formed contingencies whose effects accumulated over time. Similarly, Aldrich (1999, pp. 213–15) argued that the corporate deconglomeration movement in the USA is based on local cultural and ideological contingencies, and thus it is not surprising that it has failed to spread to Asian nations such as Thailand. Comparative studies can discover contingencies that escape notice in single-context studies (Orrú et al., 1991; Hollingsworth et al., 1994).

New Directions for Research

Coevolution, which recently has been given some theoretical and empirical attention (Van de Ven and Garud, 1994; Haveman and Rao, 1997; Lewin et al., 1999), can be defined as an evolutionary process involving two or more organizational forms that influence the fitness of each other (see Kauffman, 1993, p. 238). This definition excludes evolutionary processes where forms do not influence each other and is thus somewhat restrictive, but this is needed for the "co" to be meaningful. Studies of how evolutionary paths are affected by institutional differences have been called coevolutionary, but are actually comparative studies of evolution. Important coevolutionary outcomes are "Red Queen" races where competing organizational forms simultaneous increase their individual fitness at similar rates, yielding no net advantage, and "Frozen Equilibria" where organizational forms develop mutual adaptations that create selection pressures against any variations that disrupt the mutualistic relation (Kauffman, 1993, ch. 6).

Though evidence is currently scarce, both processes may be found in inter-organizational evolution. Red Queens may cause "hypercompetition," that is, markets with a persistently high rate of product change and competitive maneuvering (D'Aveni, 1994). Barnett and Hansen (1996) developed a theory of Red Queen coevolution resulting from mutual competitive responses and learning-by-doing in an organizational population. These processes let organizations adapt to competitors similar to themselves, which are likely to be competitors founded at the same time as them (Stinchcombe, 1965). The hypotheses were supported by showing greater failure rates among organizations with little experience and with a high variance of founding dates among the competitors. Similarly, frozen equilibria have been predicted from specialization and mutual adaptation within organizational populations, and have been shown for telephone firms and automobile makers (Barnett, 1994; Hannan, 1997).

Coevolutionary processes have interesting implications. Red Queens force organizations to spend considerable effort changing without reaping any comparative advantage. Such processes can contribute to economic development when they take the form of innovation or productivity races, but for the organization they are a form of social trap that requires more costly competitive actions than what would have been optimal. Frozen equilibria may contribute to organizational inertia, since a selection regime against organizational variations away from the mutualistic equilibrium will eliminate organizations that attempt to change when there are many mutualistic adaptations. Mutualistic adaptations are likely in technologies with linked components (Rosenkopf and Tushman, 1994), production systems with exchanges among organizational forms (Barnett, 1994; Hannan, 1997), and regulatory regimes with tight relations between regulators and regulated organizations (Haveman and Rao, 1997). Frozen equilibria do not change endogenously, but can be replaced through competition from an alternative community of mutually adapted organizations. The well-known cycles of technological ferment and dominant design (Utterback and Abernathy, 1975; Rosenkopf and Tushman, 1994) may be caused by frozen equilibria melting down as a result of competition from another community.

Variation and *retention* have been studied considerably less than selection, with some undesirable consequences. Neglect of variation mechanisms can create the impression of orderly and historically efficient evolution, eroding the perceived need for evolutionary arguments (Aldrich, 1999, pp. 223–58). Important questions of variation are how new organizational forms (Rao and Singh, 1999) and routines (Suchman, 1995) are generated. Inattention to retention mechanisms can cause analysts to draw incorrect inferences from studies of selection processes in contexts where retention mechanisms affect the evolution. Arguably the retention of interorganizational structures is more problematic than the retention of intraorganizational structures, since interorganizational structures involve multiple actors and fall into disuse more easily through the lack of a single decision-making structure. It is promising that some scholars have recently studied variation (Baum and McKelvey, 1999; Rura-Polley, 1999) and retention (Podolny, 1994; Harrison, 1997).

A problem in developing the study of variation and retention is the lack of accepted methods for studying these mechanisms. Here, some creativity is needed. For students of retention it is useful to note that when population ecologists were faced with the question of whether founding and failure processes would lead to stable population structures, simulation methods were used to give an affirmative answer (Hannan and Carroll, 1992; Carroll and Harrison, 1994). This is a nice example of using an indirect proof of the retention properties of an evolutionary system when direct proof is not available, and similar methods can be used to study the properties of the mimetic processes often encountered by students of evolution (Strang and Macy, 1999). Too many studies view the suggestion that imitation will lead to organizational isomorphism (DiMaggio and Powell, 1983) as an axiom rather than a hypothesis, and equate a mimetic process with an isomorphic population at some future time. The study of variation might benefit from new approaches such as optimal matching algorithms, which allow extraction of commonalties and divergence from paths of event sequences (Stovel et al., 1996; Blair-Loy, 1999). These approaches allow the researcher to pin down that variation means, allowing tests of its determinants and consequences.

Connections across Levels of Evolution

Evolutionary processes typically involve causal relations across levels of analysis (Amburgey and Singh, this volume), and some evolutionary research concentrates on cross-level causation. This is an outstanding feature of evolutionary work, as many other theoretical traditions clearly separate the levels of analysis. Evolutionary theory has analyzed the properties of multi-level evolutionary processes (Baum and Singh, 1994; Warglien, 1995), and empirical studies have explored organizational effects on population processes (Holm, 1995), field effects on organizational processes (Rao, 1998), intra-organizational effects on organizational processes (Burgelman, 1994), and organizational effects on intra-organizational processes (Schulz, 1998). Additional examples are provided in the other evolutionary chapters (Amburgey and Singh, this volume; Warglien, this volume). Cross-level work seems to move towards a debate on whether evolutionary processes can be reduced to theories of unit-level organizational behavior and rules for their interaction or whether macro-level processes unfold independently and later affect the micro behavior. The issue poses a problem for the integration of population ecology and institutional theory, as ecologists often aggregate population-level processes from organization-level properties (Lomi and Larsen, 1996; Barnett, 1997) while many institutionalists stress field-level constraints on organization-level behavior (Dobbin, 1995). The debate is thus likely to bring out differences between perspectives that share important assumptions.

Some phenomena change character when seen through the lens of cross-level evolution, as the connections across levels provide additional explanatory variables or clarify the change processes. Sometimes a step down one level of analysis gives new insights.

Abrupt ("punctuated") organizational change of strategy has been found to stem from gradual search and selection processes internally in the organization (Burgelman, 1983) and abrupt industrial change of technological standard has been attributed to gradual search and selection by key actors in the organizational field (Garud and Rappa, 1994; Levinthal, 1998). A step up one level of analysis also helps explain some phenomena. From a field-level view, the process of strategic change looks less analytical than some strategic theories envision and more like a form of conformity (Fiegenbaum and Thomas, 1995; Greve, 1998) or a gradual movement towards resource-rich places in the environment (McPherson et al., 1992; Ruef, 1997). Both kinds of cross-level theory benefit from evolutionary theorizing, as the classic evolutionary concerns with processes that unfold over time and contain path dependencies help push cross-level explanations beyond trivial reduction or aggregation. Still, cross-level reinterpretations are often contested by researchers who prefer within-level explanations, and the resulting discussion and research helps advance evolutionary work on organizations.

CONNECTIONS WITH OTHER INTERORGANIZATIONAL PERSPECTIVES

Evolutionary theory occupies a central place in interorganizational theory since evolutionary arguments are so widespread in current organizational theory and since non-evolutionary mechanisms often have evolutionary consequences. This leads to frequent connections between interorganizational evolution and other perspectives, and only the most important of these can be covered here. Interorganizational ecology is the theory of communities of organizations, and is largely based on evolutionary reasoning (Rao, this volume). It contains in-depth studies of the coevolutionary processes of multiple organizational populations and the founding phases of new markets and technologies. Research on institutional change also provides insights into important processes of interorganizational evolution (Strang and Sine, this volume). An important insight drawn from this research is the multiple processes that contribute to change in how organizations interact: institutional change can be driven by its own path-dependent dynamics, but interventions by organized parties such as professions and consultants also influence the direction.

Research relevant to the mechanisms of evolution is found in the chapter on interorganizational power and dependence (Mizruchi and Yoo, this volume). Many studies of power have followed an organizational field over time, showing how cooptation and attempts to control resource dependence have consequences for organizational patterns of control and exchange. Learning among organizations is another important mechanism of evolution (Ingram, this volume), and findings suggesting local knowledge spillovers of various kinds provide important clues to how spatial agglomeration processes can become irreversible. Both power and learning can create path-dependent evolutionary processes, and the details of how these mechanisms shape interorganizational evolution will not be known without more investigation.

Conclusion

The position of evolutionary theory on interorganizational phenomena seems secure, as it fits the subject of organizations and the theorizing style of organizational scholars very well. It provides a way of thinking about phenomena and analyzing social change that yields important insights. Every theoretical mechanism of interest to organizational scholars comes with qualifications on the importance of initial conditions for future events, and evolutionary theory provides a framework for analyzing such relations. The main doubt about its future is whether evolutionary reasoning will continue to exist as a strong undercurrent in other theoretical research programs or whether it will emerge as a research program in itself. While there are advantages to an emergence as a separate research program, it should also be remembered that much of the substance of evolutionary studies is furnished by theories such as competition, institutionalization, and learning, and the excitement in evolutionary research is provided by the meeting of a given theoretical mechanism with an evolutionary approach to modeling. There are thus some advantages to a continued overlap of evolution and other theories.

Although many topics currently addressed by evolutionary theory have seen study since the 1970s, evolutionary theory still has many unanswered questions and understudied applications. Studies conducted now are likely to become influential both by setting the agenda for which topics should be addressed and which theoretical mechanisms to emphasize, and by constituting examples for how evolutionary studies can be conducted. It is likely that quantitative studies will become more frequent, and will lead to some tension between work emphasizing the contingency and multi-causality of evolutionary processes and work making simplifications to model important evolutionary processes. This is a healthy tension, as the tendency to emphasize complexity and the tendency to simplify both need to be kept in check in order to maintain a dual focus on systematic processes and historical contingency. Interorganizational evolution is still a free-for-all that accommodates a wide range of research questions and approaches, and is an area of opportunity for researchers who seek to shape the future of organization theory.

Acknowledgments

I am grateful for suggestions from Howard Aldrich, William P. Barnett, Joel A. C. Baum, William Ocasio, and Hayagreeva Rao.

References

Aldrich, H. (1979): *Organizations and Environments*. Englewood Cliffs, NJ: Prentice-Hall.

Aldrich, H. (1999): *Organizations Evolving*. Thousand Oaks, CA: Sage.

Astley, W. G. (1985): "The two ecologies: Population and community perspectives on organizational evolution," *Administrative Science Quarterly*, 30, 224–41.

Baker, W. E. (1990): "Market networks and corporate behavior," *American Journal of Sociology*, 96, 589–625.

Barnett, W. P. (1994): "The liability of collective action: Growth and change among early telephone companies," in J. A. C. Baum and J. V. Singh (eds), *Evolutionary Dynamics of Organizations*, New York: Oxford University Press, 337–54.

Barnett, W. P. (1997): "The dynamics of competitive intensity," *Administrative Science Quarterly*, 42, 128–60.

Barnett, W. P., and Hansen, M. T. (1996): "The Red Queen in organizational evolution," *Strategic Management Journal*, 17, Summer Special Issue, 139–57.

Barnett, W. P., Greve, H. R., and Park, D. Y. (1994): "An evolutionary model of organizational performance," *Strategic Management Journal*, 15, Summer, 11–28.

Baron, J. N., Dobbin, F., and Jennings, P. D. (1986): "War and peace: The evolution of modern personnel practice in US industry," *American Journal of Sociology*, 92, 250–83.

Baum, J. A. C., and Haveman, H. (1997): "Love thy neighbor? Differentiation and agglomeration in the Manhattan hotel industry, 1898–1990," *Administrative Science Quarterly*, 42, 304–38.

Baum, J. A. C., and Korn, H. J. (1999): "Chance, imitative, and strategic antecedents of multimarket contact," *Academy of Management Journal*, 42, 171–93.

Baum, J. A. C., and McKelvey, B. (1999): *Variations in Organization Science: In Honor of Donald T. Campbell*. Thousand Oaks, CA: Sage.

Baum, J. A. C., and Mezias, S. (1992): "Localized competition and organizational failure in the Manhattan hotel industry, 1898–1990," *Administrative Science Quarterly*, 36, 187–218.

Baum, J. A. C., and Singh, J. V. (1994): "Organizational hierarchies and evolutionary processes: Some reflections on a theory of organizational evolution," in J. A. C. Baum and J. V. Singh (eds), *Evolutionary Dynamics of Organizations*, New York: Oxford University Press, 3–20.

Bikhchandani, S., Hirshleifer, D., and Welch, I. (1992): "A theory of fads, fashion, custom, and cultural change as informational cascades," *Journal of Political Economy*, 100, 992–1026.

Blair-Loy, M. (1999): "Career patterns of executive women in finance: An optimal matching analysis," *American Journal of Sociology*, 104, 1346–97.

Burgelman, R. A. (1983): "A process model of internal corporate venturing in the diversified major firm," *Administrative Science Quarterly*, 28, 223–44.

Burgelman, R. A. (1994): "Fading memories: A process theory of strategic business exit in dynamic environments," *Administrative Science Quarterly*, 39, 24–56.

Campbell, D. T. (1965): "Variation and selective retention in socio-cultural evolution," in H. R. Barringer, G. I. Blanksten, and R. Mack (eds), *Social Change in Developing Areas*, Cambridge, MA: Schenkman, 19–49.

Carroll, G. R. (1985): "Concentration and specialization: Dynamics of niche width in populations of organizations," *American Journal of Sociology*, 90, 1262–83.

Carroll, G. R., and Hannan, M. T. (2000): *The Demography of Corporations and Industries*. Princeton: Princeton University Press.

Carroll, G. R., and Harrison, J. R. (1994): "On the historical efficiency of competition between organizational populations," *American Journal of Sociology*, 100, 720–49.

D'Aveni, R. A. (1994): *Hypercompetition: Managing the Dynamics of Strategic Maneuvering*. New York: Free Press.

Davis, G. F., and Greve, H. R. (1997): "Corporate elite networks and governance changes in the 1980s," *American Journal of Sociology*, 103, 1–37.

Davis, G. F., and Thompson, T. A. (1994):"A social movement perspective on corporate control," *Administrative Science Quarterly*, 39, 141–73.

Davis, G. F., Diekmann, K. A., and Tinsley, C. H. (1994): "The decline and fall of the conglomerate firm in the 1980s: The deinstitutionalization of an organizational form," *American Sociological Review*, 59, 547–70.

Delaney, K. J. (1992): *Strategic Bankruptcy: How Corporations and Creditors use Chapter 11 to Their Advantage*. Berkeley: University of California Press.

Delaney, K. J. (1999): "Veiled politics: Bankruptcy as a structured organizational field." in H. K. Anheier (ed.), *When Things Go Wrong: Organizational Failures and Breakdowns*, Thousand Oaks, CA: Sage, 105–22.

DiMaggio, P. J. (1991): "Constructing an organizational field as a professional project: U.S. art museums, 1920–1940," in W. W. Powell and P. J. DiMaggio (eds), *The New Institutionalism in Organizational Analysis*, Chicago: University of Chicago Press, 267–92.

DiMaggio, P. J., and Powell, W. W. (1983): "The iron cage revisited: Institutional isomorphism and collective rationality in organizational fields," *American Sociological Review*, 48, 147–60.

Dobbin, F. (1995): "The origins of economic principles: Railway entrepreneurs and public policy in the 19th-century America," in W. R. Scott and S. Christensen (eds), *The Institutional Construction of Organizations: International and Longitudinal Studies*, Thousand Oaks, CA: Sage, 277–301.

Edelman, L. B. (1990): "Legal environments and organizational governance: The expansion of due process in the American workplace," *American Journal of Sociology*, 95, 1401–40.

Edelman, L. B., and Suchman, M. C. (1997): "The legal environments of organizations," in J. Hagan and K. S. Cook (eds), *Annual Review of Sociology, vol. 23*, Palo Alto: Annual Reviews, 479–515.

Evans, W. N., and Kessides, I. N. (1994): "Living by the 'Golden Rule': Multimarket contact in the U.S. airline industry," *Quarterly Journal of Economics*, 109, 341–66.

Fiegenbaum, A., and Thomas, H. (1995): "Strategic groups as reference groups: Theory, modeling and empirical examination of industry and competitive strategy," *Strategic Management Journal*, 16, 461–76.

Fligstein, N. (1990): *The Transformation of Corporate Control*. Cambridge, MA: Harvard University Press.

Fligstein, N. (1995): "Networks of power or the finance conception of control? Comment on Palmer, Barber, Zhou, and Soysal," *American Sociological Review*, 60, 500–3.

Frank, D. J. (1997):"Science, nature, and the globalization of the environment, 1870–1990," *Social Forces*, 76, 409–437.

Garud, R. and Rappa, M. E. (1994): "A socio-cognitive model of technology evolution: The case of cochlear implants," *Organization Science*, 5, 344–62.

Gimeno, J. (1999): "Reciprocal threats in multimarket rivalry: Staking out 'spheres of influence' in the U. S. airline industry," *Strategic Management Journal*, 20, 101–28.

Gimeno, J., and Woo, C. Y. (1996): "Hypercompetition in a multimarket environment: The role of strategic similarity and multimarket contact in competitive de-escalation," *Organization Science*, 7, 322–41.

Gould, S. J. (1989): *Wonderful Life*. New York: Norton.

Granovetter, M. (1985): "Economic action and social structure: The problem of embeddedness," *American Journal of Sociology*, 91, 481–510.

Greve, H. R. (1995): "Jumping ship: The diffusion of strategy abandonment," *Administrative Science Quarterly*, 40, 444–73.

Greve, H. R. (1996): "Patterns of competition: The diffusion of a market position in radio broadcasting," *Administrative Science Quarterly*, 41, 29–60.

Greve, H. R. (1998): "Managerial cognition and the mimetic adoption of market positions: What you see is what you do," *Strategic Management Journal*, 19, 967–88.

Greve, H. R. (2000): "Market niche entry decisions: Competition, learning, and strategy in Tokyo banking, 1894–1936," *Academy of Management Journal*, 43, 816–36.

Guillén, M. F. (1994); *Models of Management: Work, Authority, and Organization in a Comparative Perspective*. Chicago: University of Chicago Press.

Hannan, M. T. (1997): "Inertia, density, and the structure of organizational populations: Entries in European automobile industries, 1886–1981," *Organization Studies*, 18, 193–228.

Hannan, M. T., and Carroll, G. R. (1992): *Dynamics of Organizational Populations*. Oxford: Oxford University Press.

Hannan, M. T., and Freeman, J. (1977): "The population ecology of organizations," *American Journal of Sociology*, 82, 929–964.

Hannan, M. T., and Freeman, J. (1984): "Structural inertia and organizational change," *American Sociological Review*, 49, 149–164.

Harrison, B. (1997): *Lean and Mean: Why Large Corporations Will Continue to Dominate the Global Economy*. New York: The Guilford Press.

Haveman, H. A. (1993): "Follow the leader: Mimetic isomorphism and entry into new markets," *Administrative Science Quarterly*, 38, 593–627.

Haveman, H. A., and Rao, M. V. H. (1997): "Structuring a theory of moral sentiments: Institutional and organizational coevolution in the early Thrift industry," *American Journal of Sociology*, 102, 1606–51.

Hawley, A. H. (1950): *Human Ecology: A Theory of Community Structure*. New York: Ronald.

Herrigel, G. (1994): "Industry as a form of order: A comparison of the historical development of the machine tool industries in the United States and Germany." in J. R. Hollingsworth, P. C. Schmitter, and W. Streeck (eds), *Governing Capitalist Economies: Performance and Control of Economic Sectors*, New York: Oxford University Press, 97–128.

Hirsch, P. M. (1986): "From ambushes to golden parachutes: Corporate takeovers as an instance of cultural framing and institutional integration," *American Journal of Sociology*, 91, 800–37.

Hoffman, A. J. (1999): "Institutional evolution and change: Environmentalism and the U.S. chemical industry," *Academy of Management Journal*, 42, 351–71.

Hollingsworth, J. R., Schmitter, P. C., and Streeck, W. (1994): *Governing Capitalist Economies: Performance and Control of Economic Sectors*. New York: Oxford University Press.

Holm, P. (1995): "The dynamics of institutionalization: Transformation processes in Norwegian fisheries," *Administrative Science Quarterly*, 40, 398–422.

Hooks, G. (1990): "From an autonomous to a captured state agency: The decline of the new deal in agriculture," *American Sociological Review*, 55, 29–43.

Ingram, P., and Inman, C. (1996),: "Institutions, intergroup competition, and the evolution of hotel populations around Niagara Falls," *Administrative Science Quarterly*, 41, 629–58.

Johnstone, B. (1999): *We Were Burning: Japanese Entrepreneurs and the Forging of the Electronic Age*. New York: Basic Books.

Kauffman, S. A. (1993): *The Origins of Order: Self-Organization and Selection in Evolution*. Oxford: Oxford University Press.

Kim, S. (1995): "Expansion of markets and the geographic distribution of economic activities: The trends in U.S. regional manufacturing structure, 1860–1987," *Quarterly Journal of Economics*, 110, 881–908.

Kono, C., Palmer, D., Friedland, R., and Zafonte, M. (1998): "Lost in space: The geography of corporate interlocking directorates," *American Journal of Sociology*, 103, 863–911.

Krugman, P. (1992): *Development, Geography, and Economic Theory*. Cambridge, MA: MIT Press.

Lazerson, M. (1993): "Future alternatives of work reflected in the past: Putting-out production in Modena." in R. Swedberg (ed.), *Explorations in Economic Sociology*, New York: Russell Sage Foundation, 403–27.

Lazerson, M. (1995): "A new phoenix? Modern putting-out in the Modena knitwear industry," *Administrative Science Quarterly*, 40, 34–59.

Leblebici, H., Salancik, G. R., Copay, A., and King, T. (1991): "Institutional change and the transformation of interorganizational fields: An organizational history of the U.S. radio broadcasting industry," *Administrative Science Quarterly*, 36, September, 333–63.

Levinthal, D. A. (1998): "The slow pace of rapid technological change: Gradualism and punctuation in technological change," *Industrial and Corporate Change*, 7, 217–47.

Lewin, A. Y., Long, C. P., and Carroll, T. N. (1999): "The coevolution of new organizational forms," *Organization Science*, 10, 535–50.

Lie, J. (1997): "Sociology of markets," in J. Hagan and K. S. Cook (eds), *Annual Review of Sociology, vol. 23*, Palo Alto: Annual Reviews, 341–60.

Lomi, A. (1995): "The population ecology of organizational founding: Location dependence and unobserved heterogeneity," *Administrative Science Quarterly*, 40, 111–44.

Lomi, A. and Larsen, E. R. (1996): "Interacting locally and evolving globally: A computational approach to the dynamics of organizational populations," *Academy of Management Journal*, 39, 1265–87.

Lomi, A., and Larsen, E. R. (2001): *Dynamics of Organizational Societies: Models, Theories, and Methods*. Menlo Park, CA and Cambridge, MA: AAAI Press and MIT Press, forthcoming.

Lorenzoni, G., and Ornati, O. (1988): "Constellations of firms and new ventures," *Journal of Business Venturing*, 3, 41–58.

March, J. G. (1994): "The evolution of evolution." in J. A. C. Baum and J. V. Singh (eds), *Evolutionary Dynamics of Organizations*, New York: Oxford University Press, 39–49.

Martin, R., and Sunley, P. (1996): "Paul Krugman's geographical economics and its implications for regional development theory: A critical assessment," *Economic Geography*, 74, 259–92.

McPherson, J. M., Popielarz, P. A., and Drobnic, S. (1992): "Social networks and organizational dynamics," *American Sociological Review*, 57, 153–70.

Minkoff, D. C. (1994): "From service provision to institutional advocacy: The shifting legitimacy of organizational forms," *Social Forces*, 72, 943–69.

Moe, T. (1990): *The Organization of Interests*. Chicago: University of Chicago Press.

Orrú, M., Biggart, N. W., and Hamilton, G. G. (1991): "Organizational isomorphism in East Asia," in W. W. Powell and P. J. DiMaggio (eds), *The New Institutionalism in Organizational Analysis*, Chicago: University of Chicago Press, 361–89.

Palmer, D., Barber, B. M., and Zhou, X. (1995): "The finance conception of control – 'The theory that ate New York?' Reply to Fligstein," *American Sociological Review*, 60, 504–8.

Palmer, D., Barber, B. M., Zhou, X., and Soysal, Y. (1995):" The friendly and predatory acquisition of large U.S. corporations in the 1960s: The other contested terrain," *American Sociological Review*, 60, 469–99.

Pfeffer, J., and Salancik, G. R. (1978): *The External Control of Organizations*. New York: Harper and Row.

Podolny, J. M. (1993): "A status-based model of market competition," *American Journal of Sociology*, 98, 829–72.

Podolny, J. M. (1994): "Market uncertainty and the social character of economic exchange," *Administrative Science Quarterly*, 39, 458–83.

Porter, M. E. (1990): *The Competitive Advantage of Nations*. New York: Free Press.

Provan, K. G., and Sebastian, J. G. (1998): "Networks within networks: Service link overlap, organizational cliques, and network effectiveness," *Academy of Management Journal*, 41, 453–63.

Rao, H. (1998): "Caveat emptor: The construction of nonprofit consumer watchdog organizations," *American Journal of Sociology*, 103, 912–61.

Rao, H., and Singh, J. V. (1999): "Types of variation in organizational populations: The speciation of organizational forms," in J. A. C. Baum and B. McKelvey (eds), *Variations in Organization Science*, Thousand Oaks, CA: Sage, 63–7.

Rogers, E. M. (1995): *Diffusion of Innovations*, 4th edn. New York: Free Press.

Rosenkopf, L., and Tushman, M. L. (1994): "The coevolution of technology and organization," in J. A. C. Baum and J. V. Singh (eds), *Evolutionary Dynamics of Organizations*, New York: Oxford University Press, 403–24.

Ruef, M. (1997): "Assessing organizational fit on a dynamic landscape: An empirical test of the relative inertia thesis," *Strategic Management Journal*, 18, 837–53.

Rura-Polley, T. (1999): "Constructing variation: Insights from an emerging organizational field." in A. Miner and P. Anderson (eds), *Advances in Strategic Management vol. 16*, Greenwich, CT: JAI Press, 249–75.

Saxenian, A. (1994): *Regional Advantage: Culture and Competition in Silicon Valley and Route 128*. Cambridge, MA: Harvard.

Schulz, M. (1998): "Limits to bureaucratic growth: The density dependence of organizational rule births," *Administrative Science Quarterly*, 43, 845–76.

Scott, W. R. (1995): *Institutions and Organizations*. Thousand Oaks, CA: Sage.

Sorenson, O., and Audia, G. (2000): "The social structure of entrepreneurial activity: Geographic concentration of footwear production in the U.S., 1940–1989" *American Journal of Sociology*, 106, 424–62.

Stearns, L. B., and Allan, K. D. (1996): "Economic behavior in institutional environments: The corporate merger wave of the 1980s," *American Sociological Review*, 61, 699–718.

Stinchcombe, A. L. (1965): "Social structure and organizations," in J. G. March (ed.), *Handbook of Organizations*, Chicago: Rand McNally, 142–93.

Stovel, K., Savage, M., and Bearman, P. (1996): "Ascription into achievement: Models of career systems at Lloyd's Bank, 1890–1970," *American Journal of Sociology*, 102, 358–99.

Strang, D., and Macy, M. W. (1999): "'In search of excellence': Fads, success stories, and communication bias," *Academy of Management Best Paper Proceedings CD-ROM*, Chicago: Academy of Management Association.

Strang, D., and Soule, S. A. (1998): "Diffusion in organizations and social movements: From hybrid corn to poison pills," *Annual Review of Sociology*, 24, 265–90.

Suchman, M. (1995): "Localism and globalism in institutional analysis: The emergence of contractual norms in venture finance." in W. R. Scott and S. Christensen (eds), *The Institutional Construction of Organizations: International and Longitudinal Studies*, Thousand Oaks: Sage, 39–63.

Sutton, J. R., and Dobbin, F. (1996): "The two faces of governance: Responses to legal uncertainty in U.S. firms, 1955 to 1985," *American Sociological Review*, 61, 794–811.

Sutton, J. R., Dobbin, F., Meyer, J. W., and Scott, W. R. (1994): "The legalization of the workplace," *American Journal of Sociology*, 99, 944–71.

Swaminathan, A. (1995): "The proliferation of specialist organizations in the American wine industry, 1941–1990," *Administrative Science Quarterly*, 40, 653–80.

Swedberg, R. (1994): "Markets as social structures," in N. J. Smelser and R. Swedberg (eds), *The Handbook of Economic Sociology*, Princeton: Princeton University Press, 255–82.

Utterback, J., and Abernathy, W. (1975): "A dynamic model of product and process innovation," *Omega*, 33, 639–56.

Uzzi, B. (1996): "The sources and consequences of embeddedness for the economic performance of organizations: The network effect," *American Sociological Review*, 61, 674–98.

Uzzi, B. (1997): "Social structure and competition in interfirm networks: The paradox of embeddedness," *Administrative Science Quarterly*, 42, 35–67.

Van de Ven, A., and Garud, R. (1994),: "The coevolution of technical and institutional events in the development of an innovation." in J. A. C. Baum and J. V. Singh (eds), *Evolutionary Dynamics of Organizations*, New York: Oxford University Press, 403–24.

Wade, J. (1995): "Dynamics of organizational communities and technological bandwagons: An empirical investigation of community evolution in the microprocessor market," *Strategic Management Journal*, 16, 111–33.

Wade, J. B., Swaminathan, A., and Saxon, M. S. (1998): "Normative and resource flow consequences of local regulations in the American brewing industry, 1845–1918," *Administrative Science Quarterly*, 43, 905–35.

Warglien, M. (1995): "Hierarchical selection and organizational adaptation in a population of projects," *Industrial and Corporate Change*, 4, 1–19.

Williamson, O. E. (1981): "The economics of organization: The transaction cost approach," *American Journal of Sociology*, 87, 548–77.

Chapter Twenty-five

Interorganizational Cognition and Interpretation

JOSEPH F. PORAC, MARC J. VENTRESCA,
AND YURI MISHINA

March and Simon (1958) proposed that organizations can be understood as cognitive phenomena that derive from, and in turn influence, the mental models, frames-of-reference, and routinized knowledge structures of their participants. In its emphasis on knowledge representations as the basis for organizing, the Carnegie School preceded by almost twenty years a general cognitive turn that has been evident across the social sciences as a whole. Although this cognitive perspective has been elaborated and debated, it has remained fundamental to organizational theory for the past half century and has triggered robust research literatures on such topics as administrative decision-making, strategy formulation, organizational learning, and organization-environment relationships. Indeed, fueled by the growth of cognitive science, the cognitive perspective on organizations has become one generative root of modern organizational theory.

Cognitive organizational theorists assume that an individual's behavior toward external stimuli is mediated by his or her cognitive representations of those stimuli. At least since Dill (1958), scholars have recognized that this core assumption implies that how organizations respond to their environments is contingent on the environmental interpretations of key participants who are responsible for monitoring, sensing, and interacting with external constituents and trends. Research suggests that the mental models of participants shape their environmental scanning proclivities (Daft and Weick, 1984), influence what they do and do not notice about the environment (Starbuck and Milliken, 1988), affect their interpretations of environmental opportunities and threats (Dutton and Jackson, 1987), and determine their assessments of the costs and benefits of alternative competitive strategies (Porac and Rosa, 1996). Extending this argument even further, if organizations and their environments are viewed as mutually constitutive, as enacted (Weick, 1979; 1995), then the mental models of organizational participants actively shape the environmental spaces in which organizations exist. Since these environmental spaces are largely composed of other organizations, interorganizational landscapes are defined, in part, by the mental models of participants as well. This active and cognitivist view of interorganizational dynamics is the subject we explore in this chapter.

Most modern approaches to research at the interorganizational level recognize the fundamental role of cognitive representations in the dynamics of organizational communities. This is especially vivid in the literatures on interorganizational learning (Ingram, this volume) and institutions (Strang and Sine, this volume), but cognitive perspectives are present in most other contemporary approaches because current interorganizational research typically focuses on the strategic choices and interactions that occur among organizations in competitive contexts. Even in ecological models (Rao, this volume), which tend to downplay the explanatory role of strategic choice, the distinctly cognitive concept of "legitimacy" plays a central explanatory role.

So if it is not "cognition" *per se* that differentiates interpretive from other approaches to interorganizational phenomena, what does mark this boundary? We believe that the key distinguishing characteristic of interorganizational cognition and interpretation research is an explicit focus on conceptualizing and describing the collective cognitive structures underlying interorganizational relations. Researchers have not been content with using cognitive constructs as unobservable intervening variables to explain interorganizational actions and outcomes. Instead, they have explicitly theorized about the nature of interorganizational cognitive structures and, more importantly, have measured collective cognitive constructs empirically using a variety of methods. This explicit dual focus on theorizing about and measuring the cognitive bases of interorganizational phenomena is the essential feature of research in this domain.

We begin this review by first situating interorganizational relationships within the cognitive micro-processes of market-making and the development of what we will term industry belief systems. We focus our review on studies of market actors and contexts, primarily on the interorganizational beliefs underlying market relationships (e.g., competitor to competitor, supplier to buyer, etc.). Moreover, as organizational theorists, we are particularly interested in belief systems on the supply side of markets – that is, the collective beliefs that influence the interpretations and actions of organizations competing within particular industry segments. To this end, we will first introduce four types of industry beliefs: product ontologies, definitions of market structures, industry recipes, and organizational reputations. We will then discuss the enactment processes that link these belief types together and that connect beliefs with actions. These enactment processes will be the basis for a more specific discussion of research on each belief type. Table 25.1 provides a summary of the key studies that we include in our review. We will end the chapter with contemporary conceptual and methodological issues, future research directions, and cross-level opportunities.

Table 25.1 Summary of key interorganizational cognition and interpretation studies and findings

Reference	Key concepts	Key variables	Predictions and findings	Key contribution	Method and sample
Petroski (1993)	Practical problems of fastening paper	Design problem solving	Fasteners evolved to "holding by embracing".	Shows the underlying metaphors that subserve product ontologies	Historical records and patent records
Pinch and Bijker, 1987	User groups and the bicycle	Problem solving for each group of riders	Bicycle closed around a modern type as problems were resolved.	Shows how ontological evolution is a social process	Historical record and product brochures
Garud and Rappa, 1994	Ontological debate	Standards, beliefs, and communities of believers	FDA intervened to force ontological closure.	Shows how ontological evolution is often a contest	Historical records, interviews, observations
Reger and Huff, 1993	Cognitive strategic groups	Perceived strategic groups and performance	Consensual cognitive groups existed.	Shows that industries are cognitively stratified	Structured interviews with Chicago bankers
Porac et al., 1995	Industry models and rivalry networks	Product/organizational characteristics, rivalry	Rivalry networks will be organized by industry models.	Shows a link between rivalry and cognitive stratification	Surveys of Scottish knitwear managers
Hodgkinson and Johnson, 1994	Cognitive taxonomy	Organizational position and competitive beliefs	Organizational position influences boundary beliefs.	Shows that boundary beliefs are variable within organizations	Interviews with British grocery managers

Reference	Key concepts	Key variables	Predictions and findings	Key contribution	Method and sample
Phillips, 1994	Industry culture	Basic industry beliefs about the world	Differences will exist across industries in their cultural assumptions.	Shows how industries are environments for specific cultures	Interviews in the museum and California wine industries
Porac et al., 1989	Industries as cognitive communities	Competitive identities and causal beliefs	Strategic enactment across a value chain is self reinforcing.	Shows how a specific industry recipe is maintained via sensemaking	Interviews with Scottish knitwear managers
Abrahamson and Fairchild, 1999	Change in quality circle discourse over time	Counts of articles about quality circles	The quality circle movement has a definite life cycle.	Shows how some industry beliefs are quite transient	Counts of articles over a 15-year period
Fombrun and Shanley, 1990	Organizational reputation	Organizational size, advertising, risk, profitability, and *Fortune* ranking	*Fortune* reputations are predicted from various organizational attributes.	Shows that organizational reputations are predictably constructed	Archival and survey data from firms in the *Fortune* rankings
Benjamin and Podolny, 1999	Organizational reputation and status	Reputation, status, and product prices	Higher status and more reputable firms will obtain higher prices for their products.	Shows one important economic effect (price) is affected by reputation	Archival data on wineries in the California wine industry

Industry Belief Systems and the Enactment of Organizational Communities

KINDS OF INDUSTRY BELIEFS

The study of collective beliefs in market contexts must be anchored in a micro theory of market relationships and market making. Because most cognitive researchers take an interpretive, and actor-centered, perspective on market beliefs, a useful micro theory would be one that assumes that markets are social constructions that emerge from the interplay of cognition and action over time. In this regard, work by White (1981; 1992; 2001) is particularly relevant. White suggests that producer markets are networks of actors who are bound together in equivocal transactions that are stabilized by shared assumptions and frames-of-reference. Market networks can be further subdivided on the basis of two identity constructs – a "producer" community and a "buyer" community. A market network evolves around activities and artifacts that are traded across these two communities. Activities and artifacts are not stable "things out there," but instead are sets of informational cues that attach to definitions and interpretations that become commonly accepted and taken-for-granted. Over time, as social interactions occur within and between producer and buyer communities, an explicit and articulable market nomenclature evolves to capture typical aspects of what is being traded, the terms of trade, and the competitive regime controlling strategic choices among the actors involved. It is these nomenclatures, and their associated cognitive structures, that we call *industry belief systems*. We identify four types of such beliefs.

First, a product "ontology" links usage conditions, product cues, and buyer/seller profiles into a nomenclature that distinguishes one product market from another. For example, minivans have come to be defined as an array of such attributes as "car-like handling," "front-wheel drive," "cupholders," "low step in height," "passenger side air bag," and "storage space large enough for a 4×8 piece of plywood" (Rosa et al., 1999). As these beliefs have formed over time, they have shaped the commonsense definition of minivans and have created a product specific nomenclature, or ontology, that distinguishes minivans from other vehicle types and, indeed, other product types. To the extent that a singular constellation of attributes becomes recognized as the defining features of a product domain, one can say that an ontology has "closed" around a particular product definition (Pinch and Bijker, 1987).

Product ontologies are the basis for shared mental models delimiting which organizations are participants in the same market, and thus are competitors, and which are not. These mental models about the boundaries of competition are the second component of market belief systems and influence the attentional patterns of market actors by orienting them toward some actors and away from others. Attentional clusters define sets of rivals, and buyers of rival products, by creating "frames of comparability" (Leifer, 1985; Levin and Espeland, 2001) that establish the boundaries of a market space. Such frames exist at multiple levels of inclusiveness, and together form a "cognitive taxonomy" of organizational forms (Porac and Thomas, 1990). Very specific categorical labels, such as minivan or truck manufacturer, summarize the more restricted range of comparabilities that comprise the primary networks of rivalry and competition in specific product markets. More abstract labels such as vehicle manufacturer, or simply manufacturer, summarize organizational communities that are knitted together by a wider array of comparabilities cross-cutting several market networks. These broader sets are often considered to be industries.

Stable and consensually defined boundaries delimiting producer communities allow industry beliefs to evolve into yet a third set of cognitive representations that shape the strategies of organizations competing within those boundaries by imprinting fundamental logics of action. These elaborated cognitive representations have been variously termed industry "macro-cultures" (Abrahamson and Fombrun, 1994), "mindsets" (Phillips, 1994), "recipes" (Spender, 1989), and collective "strategic concepts" (Huff, 1982). Industry recipes, in part, consist of very fundamental assumptions about time and space, the nature of work relationships within an industry, and the relationship between an industry and its environment (Phillips, 1994; Lacey, 2000). Other aspects of industry recipes form a set of constructs and causal beliefs for thinking through strategic problems and the nature of long-run competitive advantage (Porac et al., 1989; Spender, 1989). Still other components of recipes are transient fads that come and go according to the current fashion (Barley and Kunda, 1992; Abrahamson and Fairchild, 1999).

Finally, the relative success of firms in operationalizing a strategic recipe provides information to market participants, and to the interorganizational community at large, about an organization's competencies and reliability. Generalized opinions about competencies are the informal basis for reputational rankings among organizations within an industry, rankings that are fueled through formal and informal assessments by the business press, market analysts, and various rating agencies (Elsbach and Kramer, 1996; Fombrun, 1996; Zuckerman, 1999; Greve and Taylor, 2000). As Fombrun (1996) notes, although reputational orderings are abstracted from the actions and outcomes of market behavior, they are more than mere effects of markets because they create evaluative overlays that shape the expectations and choices of market participants. These overlays motivate both corrective actions when organizations occupy disadvantaged positions in the reputational order as well as protective actions that are designed to reinforce any positional advantages.

MARKET STORIES AND THE ENACTMENT OF THE BELIEF HIERARCHY

Each of the four elements of industry belief systems is created and shared among market actors by means of stories. Stories are critical sensemaking tools among participants in social systems (White, 1992; Weick, 1995). In dialogues among and between buyers, producers, and other industry actors (e.g., journalists, stock analysts, etc.), stories externalize internal cognitive representations and put them into play as public interpretations of industry events and conditions that can be either accepted or contested. Stories build product ontologies by establishing and explaining the linkages between an artifact, its understood attributes, and its usage conditions (Rosa et. al., 1999). Stories shape competitive boundaries by isolating and labeling the comparabilities that define similar and dissimilar organizational forms (Porac et al., 1989). Stories diffuse industry recipes by championing certain practices and assumptions while devaluing others (Hirsch, 1986; Barley and Kunda, 1992; Abrahamson and Fairchild, 1999). Finally, stories crystallize reputational rankings by encouraging the use of certain performance metrics at the expense of others, and by deploying these metrics to highlight organizational accomplishments and to disparage organizational failures (Fombrun, 1996). It is for this reason that scholars mapping the structure and dynamics of industry belief systems have focused a great deal of their attention on the analysis of industry rhetorics.

The story-based nature of market sensemaking implies that industry belief systems are accomplishments that are fashioned, maintained, and transformed over time via public and private discourse. This fact places constraints on the durability and stability of industry beliefs because such beliefs are continuously evolving and changing. Since industry belief systems are always contestable and subject to revision, they are dynamic interpretive systems that reflect the tug and pull of new contingencies and new participants trying to disrupt the existing conceptual order.

This dynamic tension between stability and instability in industry belief systems is a result of the multi-level enactment processes that bind together the beliefs and actions of organizations over time. The four elements of industry beliefs form an ordered hierarchical enactment system with reciprocal cognition-action relationships between elements. This ordered system is depicted in Figure 25.1. The elements are positioned in the figure according to how fundamental they are to the enactment process, with elements positioned at the bottom of the figure being prerequisites to elements positioned toward the top. This ordering proposes asymmetrical relationships among types of beliefs. A coherent product ontology, for example, must exist for organizations to be judged comparable and members of the same market. Similarly, stable boundary beliefs and market categorizations must exist before industry specific recipes can evolve to guide strategic sensemaking among member organizations. Finally, recipes must form, and be agreed upon, before performance metrics can be created and reputational rankings using such

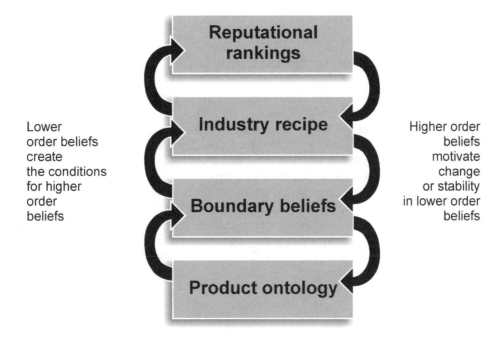

Figure 25.1   The enactment of industry belief systems

metrics implemented. Thus, moving from bottom to top in Figure 25.1, each element embodies the more fundamental beliefs within an organizational community that are assembled by organizational and other field actors.

This bottom-up inference process, however, is counterbalanced by top-down influences and constraints on the enactment of belief elements over time. Starting from top to bottom in Figure 25.1, reputational rankings motivate organizations to enact, extend, and sometimes modify industry recipes in order to reinforce or alter their position in ranking tournaments. The enactment or replacement of industry recipes in this way influences the understood boundaries of industries by either reinforcing the existing industry categories or by creating new logics of action that suggest alternative categorizations (Thornton and Ventresca, 2001). These boundary developments obviously have implications for the base product ontologies that are at the core of an industry since they affect the degree of closure around a particular set of product beliefs. The heterogeneity of the enactment order under conditions of industry emergence and change (Ventresca and Lacey, 1999) is an open research topic, something we return to in our discussion of unanswered questions and future research directions.

This framework is general and abstracted from the details of local industry circumstances and the idiosyncratic beliefs that make a particular organizational community different from others. We advance the framework here, however, to help make sense of the diversity of the literature that we will introduce in the remainder of this chapter. Studies of industry belief systems very much form a subdiscipline of social and organizational research that one might call "industry ethnography." Industry ethnographers have used a variety of empirical methods, both quantitative and qualitative, to directly describe the product ontologies, boundary beliefs, strategic recipes, and reputational structures of industry communities. It is to specific examples of such ethnography that we now turn.

Product Ontologies as Market Cores

We defined product ontologies as cognitive representations that link attributes, usage conditions, and buyer characteristics into a definition of a product or service that is exchanged in market transactions. The notion of a product ontology has its roots in social constructionist views of markets in which the object of exchange is not taken as a "given" but instead is viewed as an outcome of a socio-cognitive project of interaction, struggle, negotiation, and learning between buyers and sellers (Bijker et al., 1987). In this view, much of what consumers and producers know of product markets resides in the knowledge structures, or product ontologies, shared by these two parties, and their joint understanding of products evolves as these knowledge structures change over time. This evolution is driven by active experimentation with different attribute configurations, and the resulting learning process is quite open-ended until producers and consumers converge, at least temporarily, on a common understanding of the product or service being exchanged.

Work that has explicitly mapped this cognitive convergence comes mainly from two sources. The first is research by historians who have traced the social foundations of a variety of common products. Excellent exemplars of this work include Petroski's studies of the pencil (1992) and paper clip (1993), Friedel's (1994) history of the zipper, and

Vincenti's (1993) exploration of aircraft design. Petroski's work is particularly interesting given his careful attention to tracing the collective thought processes underlying product conceptualizations. Petroski suggests that product evolution results from ongoing efforts within a community of producers to resolve collectively recognized deficiencies in existing designs. In his study of the paper clip, for example, Petroski (1993) examined historical records and patent applications to show that prior to the mid-1800s the dominant product for binding sheets of paper together was the straight pin. The pin, according to Petroski, was embedded within a product ontology that emphasized "holding by piercing," and brought with it certain disadvantages such as holes in the paper that eventually became ragged, pin points that could prick fingers or get snagged with other pages, and rust marks that accumulated in humid environments. Efforts to overcome these disadvantages led to a number of fastener variations during the latter part of the nineteenth century, but a true breakthrough did not occur until the base product ontology shifted from a "holding by piercing" to a "holding by embracing" conceptualization of fasteners in the late 1800s and early 1900s. This "holding by embracing" ontology eventually produced the rounded GEM paper "clip" that can be found in almost every office today.

Ontological convergence motivated by design problem solving has also been studied by social constructionists exploring technological change. Pinch and Bijker (1987) report one particularly relevant study that detailed the early development of the bicycle and showed how different bicycle variations (e.g., the Singer Xtraordinary, Lawson Bicyclette, and the American Star) were created in order to resolve usage problems encountered by different groups of riders (e.g., women, racers, etc.). Through a qualitative examination of historical records from the bicycle industry, Pinch and Bijker observe that after a period of "interpretive flexibility," where producers experimented with a variety of product designs depending on the problems being resolved, the bicycle ontology eventually closed around the modern conception of bicycles as a constellation of attributes that includes a low front wheel, diamond shaped frame, rear chain drive, and pneumatic tires.

Similar ontological closure was observed by Garud and Rappa (1994) in their qualitative study of cochlear implant technology. In the case of implants, closure came only after emotional debates had fractured producing organizations into competing ontological communities. Cochlear implants are small electronic amplifiers that are directly embedded in the ear of the hearing impaired to facilitate sound reception. The first implants were "single channel" devices that amplified only one sound frequency. These were small devices that could be easily inserted and removed without serious damage to the inner ear. Later developments in implant technology produced "multi channel" devices that amplified multiple sound frequencies, but were larger, more difficult to insert, and permanently damaged the cochlea upon removal. With the development of these latter devices, an emotionally charged public discussion occurred between advocates of the safer, but less effective, single channel implant logic and proponents of the more effective, but physically invasive, multi channel logic. Eventually, the Federal Drug Administration (FDA) intervened and anointed the multi channel device as the implant of choice, essentially creating ontological convergence by fiat.

Together, these and other studies (Rosa et. al., 1999; Sirsi et al., 1996) suggest a number of conclusions about the initialization and time course of product ontologies. First, new ontologies are results of an inventor, or inventing organization, questioning the dominant ontology and attempting to solve product problems that have not been solved before. As Petroski (1993) suggests, inventors must be ontological "critics" before they can change the world through their ideas. Second, once a nascent product ontology has formed, it evolves as the interests of buyers, sellers, and other key market actors motivate design problem solving. Finally, ontologies are externalized and reflected in market stories, texts, and documents. Thus, to map ontologies, one must spend time deciphering market discourse of varying types.

Boundary Beliefs as Market Identities

Closure in a product ontology stimulates the congealing of a producer network around a set of common beliefs about market structure. As White (1981) suggests, a market is a small numbers social construction produced when firms observe each others' actions and define unique product positions *vis-à-vis* each other. The key market-making task is to collectively establish a "frame of comparability" (Leifer, 1985) that defines some producers to be members of the market while excluding others. Frames of comparability are often evident in statements of identity such as "We're a knitwear producer" (Porac et al., 1995) or "We're in the grocery business" (Hodgkinson and Johnson, 1994). To be meaningful, these identity statements require stable product ontologies that define the concepts of "knitwear" and "grocery." As Garud and Lant (1998) show in their study of New York City's "Silicon Alley," without stable product ontologies, industries are cha- otic or, in their words, "kaleidoscopic." Given that any single producer "defines its role in terms of the similarities and differences it has with respect to other producers" (White and Eccles, 1987, p. 984), boundary beliefs must emerge around stable product ontologies to lock in inter-firm comparisons and create a reproducible competitive order.

That such beliefs do, in fact, emerge within interorganizational communities has been well established in a number of empirical studies; see Hodgkinson (1997) for a complete review. One well-known example of this research is Reger and Huff's (1993) investiga- tion of "cognitive strategic groups" within the Chicago banking community. The notion of strategic group emerged in the management literature to recognize that industries tend to be stratified into multiple sets of firms whose members pursue similar business strategies. Slanting their study in a cognitive direction, Reger and Huff (1993) mapped the similarities and differences among eighteen Chicago banks as perceived by key strategists in the industry. Through structured interviews, Reger and Huff asked twenty- three executives from six of these banks to compare each of the eighteen banks with each other and to specify the strategic dimensions along which the banks were similar or different. The results suggested that bank executives parsed the local banking indus- try into three separable groups of firms: large money center banks concentrating on wholesale and commercial activities in a national or global market, regional mid-market banks that focused on local small businesses and consumers, and a miscellaneous group that included banks of different kinds that were hard to categorize.

Reger and Huff's results are consistent with the claim that boundary beliefs emerge within industries to segment firms into market networks. At the same time, however, Reger and Huff did not examine whether banks within each consensually understood group in the Chicago banking community actually perceived other group members as rivals embedded within the same product ontology. More direct evidence for this latter attentional structuring comes from Porac et al.'s (1995) study of Scottish knitwear producers. Using material collected from qualitative interviews, Porac et al. constructed a questionnaire that asked eighty-nine knitwear executives to rate their firms on a number of relevant product dimensions. Respondents were also asked to check off from an exhaustive list of industry members those knitwear firms that they considered competitors and regularly monitored. Porac et al. then clustered the firms on the basis of their product attributes and uncovered six distinct clusters of attributes that suggested six different product ontologies existed in the industry. These six ontologies were associated with distinct "rivalry networks" in the sense that producers embedded within a given ontology tended to view each other as rivals and paid little attention to the firms in the other product groups. Firms rarely cited more than five to nine competitors, and these competitors were almost always firms within their own product category. Porac et al. concluded that the rivalry networks they observed in the industry seemed to be stable cognitive orderings that structured competition in the industry.

Although these and other studies have uncovered substantial evidence supporting the existence and importance of boundary beliefs in structuring markets, research by Johnson and his colleagues (Bowman and Johnson, 1992; Calori et al., 1992; De Chernatony et al., 1993; Hodgkinson and Johnson, 1994; Daniels et al., 1995) provides a useful counterpoint in suggesting that boundary disagreements often exist among managers within and between organizations, even in old line and stable industries such as groceries and pump manufacturing. Hodgkinson and Johnson (1994), for example, interviewed twenty-three managers in two grocery firms in England and elicited detailed cognitive taxonomies of the grocery industry from each respondent. Although the categories of grocery competitors were generally similar across managers, differences existed from manager to manager in the number of levels and categories reported within their individual mental models. One interesting result was that managers who had broader strategic responsibilities within their firm seemed to have significantly more elaborate cognitive representations of the industry. Hodgkinson and Johnson concluded that a manager's job responsibilities conditioned his or her ability to gather information about organizational variation in the industry.

Taken as a whole, research thus suggests that boundary beliefs form around distinctive product ontologies within an industry. Experienced managers possess quite detailed cognitive representations of market boundaries while less experienced managers conceive of competitive boundaries in simpler and more holistic ways. This variability aside, research suggests that, at least in mature and stable industries, boundary representations are not completely idiosyncratic to individual managers, but seem to be derived from a collective "industry model" (Porac et al., 1995) that is partially shared with others in the same organizational community. Industry models channel the attentional patterns of actors toward firms that are embedded within the same product space such that rivalry networks are denser within understood market boundaries than they are across boundaries. Moreover, research supports White's (1981) contention that markets are small numbers social constructions in the sense that actors rarely report more than a handful of rivals in their own market network.

Industry Recipes as Logics for Market Action

By channeling the attentional focus of organizations toward comparable peers, strong boundary beliefs create the conditions for the development of industry-specific logics for action *vis-à-vis* competitors, suppliers, customers, the capital markets, and regulatory agencies. Following Spender (1989), we label these logics industry "recipes" to reflect the fact that such beliefs constitute rule systems for reasoning through strategic problems and justifying organizational action.

Differences in the emphasis on the generative logics that frame problems and strategic choices within industry contexts distinguish interpretive approaches to interorganizational relationships from institutional (Strang and Sine, this volume) and learning (Ingram, this volume) perspectives. Interpretive, institutional, and learning theorists have all identified characteristic mechanisms within bounded organizational communities that foster structural sameness of forms and practices, and all three make substantial use of cognitive constructs in their explanatory accounts, e.g., "the collective rationality of organizational fields" as a prior condition for specific mechanisms of isomorphism (DiMaggio and Powell, 1983). Both institutional and learning research highlight the ways organizations appropriate from a stock of available "models" or, in more recent empirical work, how organizational imitation promotes the diffusion of practices across firms in an industry; but see Westney (1987) for an important corrective to the overly efficient conception of imitation dominant in much empirical research. These research approaches typically employ such cognitive constructs as omnibus background assumptions (e.g., organizational environments are assumed to be highly "uncertain," fields are "structured") or impute such constructs from patterns of organizational practices.

While interpretivists accept the role of imitation, the demands of central authority and complex legal environments, and expertise organized into professions in stabilizing industry recipes, they problematize the linkage between collective belief systems and collective action. Interpretivist research treats the link between how industry participants "think" and how they "act" as an empirical problem rather than as an unexamined assumption, and organizational practices are not accepted as one-to-one indicators of cognitive representations among industry participants. This stance provides interpretivists with useful analytic license to theorize explicitly about, and explore empirically, the structure, content, and patterning of industry recipes in an organized community qua cognitive phenomena. In doing so, interpretivists attempt to discern the multiple layers of intersubjective meaning that underlie, and justify, industry practices.

In this regard, some researchers view industries as cultural milieus and study the stable and fundamental cultural assumptions that shape the worldview of industry members. A good example of this type of research is Phillips' (1994) study of wineries and art museums. Through unstructured ethnographic interviews with a variety of employees from firms within each industry, Phillips assessed industry differences in assumptions about the relationship between the industry and the environment, the origins of truth, the nature of time and space, the nature of innate human qualities, the purpose of work, and work relationships. Her results suggest that employees in the museum industry orient towards an evangelical educational mission with respect to their constituents, emphasize formal education rather than experience as a basis for expertise, and desire collaborative and egalitarian work relationships. Wineries, on the other hand, identify more with a geographical region, consider experience more important than formal education, and prefer work relationships to be organized hierarchically along distinct chains of command.

While Phillips chose to study industry variation in deep seated conceptions of time, space, professional identifications, and work relationships, other interpretivists explore middle range beliefs about the cause-effect relationships influencing business outcomes (Porac et al., 1989; Spender, 1989). Porac et al. (1989), for example, studied the small subset of Scottish knitwear producers that manufacture very expensive cashmere garments for sale at exclusive retail shops around the world. These firms are bound together by a very stable product ontology and collective identity as purveyors of "classically elegant" knitwear. Porac et al. found evidence for a consensual business model that emphasizes production expertise and manufacturing flexibility over high fashion design. This model locks these firms into producing certain types of garments that are then sold to particular kinds of high-end retail shops that cater to wealthy consumers preferring classic clothing designs. Porac et al. suggest that this industry recipe is self-reinforcing and taken-for-granted, and is contested only by outsiders who come into the industry with different business logics and beliefs about knitwear production, design, and marketing.

Both Phillips (1994) and Porac et al. (1989) studied the relatively enduring components of industry recipes that create bedrock justifications for organizational action over time. Abrahamson (1991; 1996; 1997; Abrahamson and Fairchild, 1999) has shown, however, that certain elements of industry beliefs are in constant flux, and that transient logics come and go according to the fads and fashions of the time. Abrahamson and Fairchild (1999), for example, studied the rise and decline of the quality circle logic during the period from 1974 to 1995. These researchers argued that managerial fads are generated through market stories passed along by consultants, the popular press, and academic journals. Using counts of articles written about quality circles as their dependent variable, Abrahamson and Fairchild traced the pattern of quality circle discourse over time. Their results suggest that after a quiet period of gestation during the late 1970s, the quality circle logic exploded into the consciousness of American management in the early 1980s. After peaking in 1983, however, discussions about quality circles entered a decade-long decline until, by 1995, the frequency of topical stories had returned to the levels evident in the 1970s. Abrahamson and Fairchild provide evidence that this popularity curve in quality circle discourse reflects the transient acceptance and subsequent rejection of the logic over time.

Reputational Rankings as Market Status Orders

A stable product ontology, consensual market boundaries, and taken-for-granted strategic recipes together create the conditions for measuring and evaluating the performance of firms within an industry. These evaluations take place at different levels and encompass different metrics. At the level of face-to-face interactions, informal assessments of product quality permeate most industries, and industry insiders usually have well-articulated nomenclatures, and implicit status rankings, for judging one organization's outputs against another's. In the Scottish knitwear industry, for example, Porac et al. (1995) report that managers have finely calibrated mental models for comparing the products of their firms. What appear to be identical garments to a novice are in fact easily identified by managers as having been manufactured by two different firms in the industry, each with their own technical proclivities and competencies. Similarly, Benjamin and Podolny (1999) note the subtleties of California wine appellations as quality markers among producers and wine connoisseurs. These informal technical metrics are consistent with White's (1981) claim that producers in a market eventually structure themselves into role positions that reflect an implied quality ordering. This ordering, and the attentional interlocks that support it, are the defining features of a producer's market from an interpretivist's perspective.

Insider quality assessments, however, are only weak signals to outsiders such as customers, financial investors, and government regulators who are often not privy to the specialized technical nomenclatures of an industry. As Fombrun (1996) notes, the informational needs of these outsiders have provided the impetus for a multibillion-dollar information infrastructure that amplifies and refracts weak quality signals for broader public consumption. Rating agencies, consumer testing laboratories, enthusiast magazines, securities analysts, and news agencies all play a role in this refraction process (Zuckerman, 1999; Taylor and Clement, 2001). These evaluators provide alternative assessments of firm quality using metrics constructed for their own purposes. To the extent that these metrics attract publicity and widespread public appeal, however, firms within an industry must recognize the reality of the resulting reputational order and respond accordingly. Some may even incorporate these alternative metrics into their own internalized quality assessments.

Research on reputation and status orderings within industries has been steadily accumulating in recent years – see Fombrun (1996) for a review – as organizational scholars explore both their causes and consequences. A good example of research examining the former is Fombrun and Shanley (1990). Each year *Fortune* magazine solicits ratings of corporate quality from outside directors, executives, and securities analysts familiar with different industries. These ratings are then summarized by ranking companies in different business sectors. Using data from *Fortune's* 1985 rankings, as well as company information obtained from the COMPUSTAT database, Fombrun and Shanley sought to account for reputational differences among the 119 firms in their sample. Their results suggest that firms with better public reputations are more profitable, have lower market risk indicators, spend more on advertising, and are larger in size than less reputable firms. Fombrun and Shanley concluded that both economic (profitability, market risk) and non-economic (visibility) factors are involved in shaping a firm's perceived status among informed observers.

A study of California wine producers by Benjamin and Podolny (1999) is a good example of research examining the consequences of an industry's reputational order. Benjamin and Podolny reason that a firm's reputation in an industry is more than an epiphenomenon generated through public appraisals, that it has implications for the opportunities available to the firm and, in particular, for the prices that the firm can charge for its products. They distinguish between the quality of a firm's wines, as indexed by the judgments of wine experts, and a firm's status, which they suggest is a function of a wine's appellation linking it to a particular growing region in the state. Quality, status, and price data for a ten-year period were collected from various guides to California wines and from the US government. After controlling for a number of non-reputational variables such as the age and size of the producing winery and the cost of the varietal grapes in the bottle, Benjamin and Podolny found that wines of higher perceived quality and status garner higher prices in the marketplace. They conclude that a winery's position in the reputational hierarchy of the industry influences the amount of attention given to its wines and the general regard that consumers and wine experts have for these products. Because they command more attention in the marketplace, and their wines are more highly prized, reputable wineries are able to command a higher price for their outputs.

Contemporary Issues and Debates

Interorganizational research on cognition and interpretation has begun to congeal around a set of phenomena, theoretical frameworks, and methods of analysis. Researchers studying industry belief systems explicitly argue that interorganizational fields are not simply collections of tangible assets that accumulate over time, nor merely patterns of action directed toward utilizing such assets in productive ways. Instead, these researchers suggest that industries are enacted fields that are knitted together by collective beliefs about desirable product attributes, market structures, appropriate ways of doing business, and the relative quality of member firms. These beliefs are externalized through discourse within the industry and are operationalized through their influence on the strategic choices of industry actors. Over time, through enactment processes, they become embedded within the resource patterns of the industry. Cognitive researchers have set themselves to the task of discovering how this occurs.

In doing so, interorganizational interpretivists have stepped away from early concerns with the information processing, or computational, models characteristic of the Carnegie tradition and toward the focus on social construction and enactment characteristic of Weick and others (Lant, this volume). This changing emphasis brings with it, however, two issues that percolate through the published work in this area. The first, and perhaps most important, issue concerns the theoretical status of collective cognitive representations; see Thompson and Fine (1999) for excellent multi-disciplinary review of this issue. One view is that the notion of a collective representation is inherently meaningless because only individuals think, not groups, nor organizations, nor industries (Nonaka and Takeuchi, 1995). This reductionist view challenges the notion of industry belief system on the grounds that collective cognition is, at best, a metaphorical construct that extends individual psychology in problematic ways to the collective context. On the other hand, there is a long history of argument in sociology (Mannheim, 1985), social psychology (Moscovici and Duveen, 2001), and anthropology (Douglas, 1986; D'Andrade, 1995) suggesting just the opposite, that individual minds are essentially *tabula rasas* until filled with symbolic content residing at a collective level. In this latter view, collective representations, and the social processes that create, reinforce, and destroy them, are the primary loci for meaning in any given social context.

The second issue intertwined with this line of research pits homogeneity against pluralism in industry beliefs. Even if the construct of collective beliefs is theoretically meaningful, some have suggested that industry contexts are too pluralistic and too fragmented for a collective belief system to emerge. This is essentially the criticism of Johnson and his colleagues regarding research on industry models and boundary beliefs (see our earlier discussion of this research). Johnson suggests that differences in organizational circumstances, job position within organizations, industry experience, and any number of other demographic and competitive factors may undermine the consensus that models of industry belief systems assume. To some extent this issue involves the criterion that one employs to label a belief collective or not. Is perfect consensus required? Fifty percent consensus? Thirty percent? At the same time, Johnson's point is well taken. If one looks for consensus, one is likely to find it. The problem with a more pluralistic view of industry beliefs, however, is that such a view does not explain how markets are stabilized and congeal around a set of actors. If consensual beliefs are not binding firms and their customers together, what is?

These two issues are not likely to be resolved in the near future. The theoretical status of the concept of collective belief is really not an empirical question and is, instead, a question of one's ontological starting point. Does one assume the primacy of the individual or the primacy of the collective in shaping the contents of cognitive representations? This starting point is a matter of one's intellectual predilections and training more than it is something that can be decided on the basis of evidence. The second issue, however, is much more empirical and involves the measurement of belief systems across firms in an industry within and across time periods. If one can find pockets of belief consensus within an industry, and show that this consensus waxes and wanes in systematic ways over time, one has begun to build the case for the existence of industry belief systems and their importance as elements assembled into the coherent and resilient activity systems we call markets. This shift, from expecting a stable and consensual belief system to order a market, to instead identifying a constellation of belief elements and the variable linkages among them which can be associated with more or less resilient activity spaces over time joins directly with research on connectionist directions in cognition studies (Fiol, this volume), studies of narrative (Czarniawska, 1997) and accounts/stories (White, 2001), and more general efforts to conceptualize and measure meaning in non-reductive ways (Mohr, 1998). Furthermore, Thompson and Fine review work on such "socially shared meanings" to identify at least three meanings for "shared" that may reframe this research puzzle: shared as "in agreement," or the consensus model; but also "experienced or held in common," as in overlapping mental models; and finally "divided up into portions," related to notions of distributed cognition and transactive systems of knowledge (1999, p. 280).

Unanswered Questions and Future Research Directions

The consensus/dissensus tension can energize a good deal of future research in this area if we incorporate the insights of cognition research at the individual (Fiol, this volume) and organizational (Lant, this volume) levels. Rather than continued efforts to document consensus or dissensus in a static way, we propose a modified activity systems view that incorporates time-dependent analyses and links form and type of consensus or dissensus to market processes over time.

The basic research technologies are available. There are a number of entry points for attacking the problem empirically. One strategy is to work with cross-sectional cognitive data and map the topology of beliefs within an industry. Once a topology is understood, it should be possible to uncover key relationships that predict the position of actors within this belief space. This is the sort of work that has been done already by Johnson and his colleagues in their focus on the demographic predictors of belief heterogeneity in an industry, but there is more work to be done in ferreting out interesting patterns of relationships. For example, markets may cohere around particular ontologies, boundary beliefs, recipes, and reputational orderings, but industries usually contain more than one market so defined. Does this mean that an industry is really a collection of semi-modular market cultures, each with their own unique element? Porac et al. (1995) hint at the possibility of this being the case in the Scottish knitwear industry, but a good deal more work is needed to understand how market-level beliefs become embedded within industry-level beliefs, and how industry-level beliefs are formed through the aggregation of market modules.

It is possible to extend this strategy by examining belief topologies over time. This is essentially the strategy of Abrahamson and Fairchild, Petroski, Garud and Rappa, and Pinch and Bijker. These researchers show how diachronic studies can inform the consensus-dissensus issue and turn what appears to be a contradiction into a useful theoretical rapprochement. In all of these studies, belief consensus was an emergent process that evolved as actors within an industry played out their strategic games. In the case of Abrahamson and Fairchild, a well-published consensus around the useful-ness of quality circles emerged after a long gestation period, but quickly transformed into a period of questioning, qualification, and skepticism about the circle concept. In Petroski's study of the paper clip, consensus around the ontology of "holding by piercing" was slowly replaced by the concept of "holding by embracing." In Pinch and Bijker's study, dissensus about the attributes of the ideal bicycle eventually coalesced into the consensual ontology for the modern type. These are three different patterns of consensus-dissensus evolution, and there are still many questions left unanswered about what pattern is likely to emerge under what circumstances and time periods. Moreover, research such as this injects politics and stratification into the study of interorganizational cognition in very useful ways in the sense that belief evolution is driven by the interests of social groups competing for interpretive dominance (Heimer, 1996; Carlile, 2001). We suspect that the intersection of interests and cognition will be a fertile ground for future study.

Connections Across Levels

The three "Cognition and Interpretation" chapters in this volume sketch out common tensions between computational information processing views of cognition and views of cognition as the enactment of meaning over time. They offer caveats and counsel for further research directions. First, we should reduce our analytic reliance on assump-tions about cognition as stable, content-full, and necessarily complete at the level of individual actors. Second, we should move from the prevailing empirical work on the content of knowledge structures or mental models that prevail in studies of managerial cognition to knowledge in action and the enactment of beliefs over time. All three chapters develop the concept of cognitive systems rather than cognition per se, and each places emphasis on belief dynamics that are embedded in social contexts such as groups, organizations, or markets. Each dissents from the formal reductionist goals of cognitive psychology by arguing for more grounded research into the problems of cognizing and interpreting in, among, and by organizational actors. Finally, we should move from the notion of "shared" cognition as an overlap of knowledge representations to "sharing" cognition as a dynamic phenomenon that is situated in concrete circumstances.

Conclusions

Interorganizational cognition and interpretation happens "in the rough" – in distributed, collective, though not necessarily consensual, situated social practices. These practices generate information that is multivocal, and the stratification among available interpretive logics is central. The broader knowledge structures and belief systems of industry and market participants as well as other field actors both reflect and refract these systems of meaning. Mapping these, recognizing their dynamism, and at the same time how they enable stable interaction is the challenge for the next generation of research.

References

Abrahamson, E. (1991): "Managerial fads and fashions: The diffusion and rejection of innovations," *Academy of Management Review*, 16, 586–612.

Abrahamson, E. (1996): "Management fashion," *Academy of Management Review*, 21, 254–85.

Abrahamson, E. (1997): "The emergence and prevalence of employee management rhetorics: The effects of long waves, labor unions, and turnover, 1875 to 1992," *Academy of Management Journal*, 40, 491–533.

Abrahamson, E., and Fairchild, G. (1999): "Management fashion: Lifecycles, triggers, and collective learning processes," *Administrative Science Quarterly*, 44, 708–40.

Abrahamson, E., and Fombrun, C. J. (1994): "Macrocultures: Determinants and consequences," *Academy of Management Review*, 19, 728–55.

Barley, S. R., and Kunda, G. (1992): "Design and devotion: Surges of rational and normative ideologies of control in managerial discourse," *Administrative Science Quarterly*, 37, 363–99.

Benjamin, B. A., and Podolny, J. M. (1999): "Status, quality, and social order in the California wine industry," *Administrative Science Quarterly*, 44, 563–89.

Bijker, W., Hughes, T. P., and Pinch, T. (1987): *The Social Construction of Technological Systems*. Cambridge, MA: MIT Press.

Bowman, C., and Johnson, G. (1992): "Surfacing competitive strategies," *European Management Journal*, 10, 210–19.

Calori, R., Johnson, G., and Sarnin, P. (1992): "French and British top managers' understanding of the structure and the dynamics of their industries: A cognitive analysis and comparison," *British Journal of Management*, 3, 61–78.

Carlile, P. R. (2001): "A pragmatic view of knowledge and boundaries: Boundary objects in new product development," *Organization Science*, in press.

Czarniawska, B. (1997): *Narrating the Organization: Dramas of Institutional Identity*. Chicago: University of Chicago Press.

Daft, R. L., and Weick, K. E. (1984): "Toward a model of organizations as interpretation systems," *Academy of Management Review*, 9, 284–95.

D'Andrade, R. G. (1995): *The Development of Cognitive Anthropology*. Cambridge: Cambridge University Press.

Daniels, K., De Chernatony, L., and Johnson, G. (1995): "Validating a method for mapping managers' mental models of competitive industry structures," *Human Relations*, 48, 975–91.

De Chernatony, L., Daniels, K., and Johnson, G. (1993): "A cognitive perspective on managers' perceptions of competition," *Journal of Marketing Management*, 9, 373–81.

Dill, W. R. (1958): "Environment as an influence on managerial activity," *Administrative Science Quarterly*, 2, 409–43.

DiMaggio, P. J., and Powell, W. W. (1983): "The iron cage revisited: Institutional isomorphism and collective rationality in organizational fields," *American Sociological Review*, 48, 147–60.

Douglas, M. (1986): *How Institutions Think*. Syracuse, NY: Syracuse University Press.

Dutton, J. E., and Jackson, S. E. (1987): "Categorizing strategic issues: Links to organizational action," *Academy of Management Review*, 12, 76–90.

Elsbach, K. D., and Kramer, R. M. (1996): "Members' responses to organizational identity threats: Encountering and countering the *Business Week* rankings," *Administrative Science Quarterly*, 41, 442–76.

Fombrun, C. J. (1996): *Reputation: Realizing Value from the Corporate Image*. Boston, MA: Harvard Business School Press.

Fombrun, C. J., and Shanley, M. (1990): "What's in a name? Reputation building and corporate strategy," *Academy of Management Journal*, 33, 233–58.

Friedel, R. (1994): "The history of the zipper," *American Heritage of Invention and Technology*, 10, 8–16.

Garud, R., and Lant, T. (1998): "Navigating Silicon Alley: Kaleidoscopic experiences," working paper, New York University.

Garud, R., and Rappa, M. A. (1994): "A socio-cognitive model of technology evolution: The case of cochlear implants," *Organization Science*, 5, 344–62.

Greve, H. R., and Taylor, A. (2000): "Innovations as catalysts for organizational change: Shifts in organizational cognition and search," *Administrative Science Quarterly*, 45, 54–80.

Heimer, C. (1996): "Explaining variation in the impacts in the law: Organizations, institutions, and professions," *Studies in Law, Politics, and Society*, 15, 29–59.

Hirsch, P. M. (1986): "From ambushes to golden parachutes: Corporate takeovers as an instance of cultural framing and institutional integration," *American Journal of Sociology*, 91, 800–37.

Hodgkinson, G. P. (1997): "Cognitive inertia in a turbulent market: The case of UK residential estate agents," *Journal of Management Studies*, 34, 921–45.

Hodgkinson, G. P., and Johnson, G. (1994): "Exploring the mental models of competitive strategists: The case for a processual approach," *Journal of Management Studies*, 31, 525–51.

Huff, A. S. (1982): "Industry influences on strategy reformulation," *Strategic Management Journal*, 3, 119–31.

Lacey, R. (2000): "Institutional tension and organizational change in the U.S. software industry," working paper, University of Florida.

Leifer, E. M. (1985): "Markets As mechanisms: Using a role structure," *Social Forces*, 64, 442–72.

Levin, P., and Espeland, W. N. (2001): "Pollution futures: Commensuration, commodification, and the market for air," in A. J. Hoffman and M. J. Ventresca (eds), *Organizations, Policy, and the Natural Environment*, Stanford, CA: Stanford University Press, in press.

Mannheim, K. (1985): *Ideology and Utopia: An Introduction to the Sociology of Knowledge*. New York: Harcourt Brace.

March, J. G., and Simon, H. (1958): *Organizations*. New York: Wiley.

Mohr, J. (1998): "Measuring meaning structures," *Annual Review of Sociology*, 24, 345–70.

Moscovici, S., and Duveen, G., (eds) (2001): *Social Representations: Studies in Social Psychology*. London: Polity Press.

Nonaka, I., and Takeuchi, H. (1995): *The Knowledge-Creating Company: How Japanese Companies Create the Dynamics of Innovation*. New York: Oxford University Press.

Petroski, H. (1992): *To Engineer is Human: The Role of Failure in Successful Design*. New York: Vintage Books.

Petroski, H. (1993): *The Evolution of Useful Things*. New York: Knopf.

Phillips, M. E. (1994): "Industry mindsets: Exploring the cultures of two macro-organizational settings," *Organization Science*, 5, 384–402.

Pinch, T., and Bijker, W. (1987): "The social construction of facts and artifacts: Or how the sociology of science and the sociology of technology might benefit each other," in W. Bijker, T. P. Hughes, and T. Pinch (eds), *The Social Construction of Technological Systems*, Cambridge, MA: MIT Press, 17–50.

Porac, J. F., and Rosa, J. A. (1996): "Rivalry, industry models, and the cognitive embeddedness of the comparable firm," in J. E. Dutton and J. A. C. Baum (eds), *Advances in Strategic Management*, vol. 13, Greenwich, CT: JAI Press, 363–88.

Porac, J. F., and Thomas, H. (1990): "Taxonomic mental models in competitor definition," *Academy of Management Review*, 15, 224–40.

Porac, J. F., Thomas, H., and Baden-Fuller, C. (1989): "Competitive groups as cognitive communities: The case of Scottish knitwear manufacturers," *Journal of Management Studies*, 26, 397–416.

Porac, J. F., Thomas, H., Wilson, F., Paton, D., and Kanfer, A. (1995): "Rivalry and the industry model of Scottish knitwear producers," *Administrative Science Quarterly*, 40, 203–27.

Reger, R. K., and Huff, A. S. (1993): "Strategic groups: A cognitive perspective," *Strategic Management Journal*, 14, 103–24.

Rosa, J. A., Porac, J. F., Runser-Spanjol, J., and Saxon, M. S. (1999): "Sociocognitive dynamics in a product market," *Journal of Marketing*, 63, 64–77.

Sirsi, A. K., Ward, J., and Reingen, P. (1996): "Microcultural analysis of variation in sharing of causal reasoning about behavior," *Journal of Consumer Research*, 22, 345–72.

Spender, J. C. (1989): *Industry Recipes: An Enquiry into the Nature and Sources of Managerial Judgement*. New York: Blackwell.

Starbuck, W. H., and Milliken, F. J. (1988): "Challenger: Fine-tuning the odds until something breaks," *Journal of Management Studies*, 25, 319–40.

Taylor, A. H., and Clement, M. (2001): "Cognitive rationing: Informational influences on accuracy and risk taking of financial analysts." working paper, Tuck School of Business at Dartmouth College.

Thompson, L., and Fine, G. A. (1999): "Socially shared cognition, affect, and behavior: A review and integration," *Personality and Social Psychology Review*, 3, 278–302.

Thornton, P. H., and Ventresca, M. J. (2001): "Entrepreneurial strategies and boundary redefinition in organizations, markets, and industries: An actor-based method to study institutional change," in M. J. Ventresca and J. Porac (eds), *Constructing Markets and Industries*, London: Elsevier Science, Ltd.

Ventresca, M. J. and Lacey, R. (1999): "Industry entrepreneur origins and activities in the emergence of U.S. online database industry, 1969–1982." working paper, Kellogg Graduate School of Management.

Vincenti, W. G. (1993): *What Engineers Know and How They Know It: Analytical Studies from Aeronautical History*. Baltimore, MD: Johns Hopkins Press.

Weick, K. E. (1979): *The Social Psychology of Organizing*. Reading, MA: Addison-Wesley.

Weick, K. E. (1995): *Sensemaking in Organizations*. London: Sage.

Westney, D. E. (1987): *Imitation and Innovation: The Transfer of Western Organizational Patterns to Meiji Japan*. Cambridge, MA: Harvard University Press.

White, H. C. (1981): "Where do markets come from?" *American Journal of Sociology*, 87, 517–47.

White, H. C. (1992): *Identity and Control: A Structural Theory of Social Action*. Princeton, NJ: Princeton University Press.

White, H. C. (2001): *Networks in Markets*. Princeton, NJ: Princeton University Press, forthcoming.

White, H. C., and Eccles, R. (1987): "Producers' markets," in J. Eatwell, M. Milgate and P. K. Newman (eds), *The New Palgrave: A Dictionary of Economics*, 3, London: MacMillan, 984–6.

Zuckerman, E. (1999): "The categorical imperative: Securities analysts and the illegitimacy discount," *American Journal of Sociology*, 104, 1398–1438.

Chapter Twenty-six

Interorganizational Power and Dependence

MARK S. MIZRUCHI AND MINA YOO

Whether they are for-profit corporations that manufacture consumer goods, private, non-profit organizations that rely on grants and donations, or government agencies that rely on public support, organizations must respond to the concerns of environmental constituents. This need to respond constitutes a form of dependence. And the external constituents who represent the source of this dependence are often other organizations. An organization on which other organizations are dependent may as a consequence gain power over them.

The issue of interorganizational power and dependence goes back as far as Max Weber's writings in *Economy and Society* and has been addressed by organizational theorists for more than half a century. It is only since the mid-1970s that this issue has played a major role in organizational analysis, however. In this chapter we briefly trace the history of research on interorganizational power and dependence, focusing on a few representative works. We then discuss the flood of research on interorganizational dependence that has emerged since the late 1970s. In treating this work, we present examples from a range of theoretical perspectives, including the "old" and the "new" institutional theory, the resource dependence model, and political sociology. After providing a critical review of this literature, we address a series of unanswered questions and identify several areas for future research.

The study of interorganizational power and dependence has its roots in three different schools of thought: the classical sociological theories of Marx and Weber, responses to closed-system approaches within organizational theory, and social exchange theory in social psychology. Although Marx never developed a systematic model of organizations, his writings in *Capital* (Marx, 1967) contained an implicit view of bureaucracy as a means by which capitalists controlled workers. This view formed a foundation on which a group of sociologists beginning in the 1970s analyzed organizations within the larger capitalist political economy. Weber too viewed organizations within a broader societal context. The rise of bureaucracy was a specific manifestation of the growing rationalization of Western societies. This approach has played a prominent role in contemporary work on interorganizational relations. A second important perspective on interorganizational power and dependence arose as a response to the organizational theory that predominated in the post-World War II USA, which had become increasingly focused on the internal workings of organizations (Perrow, 1986). Dissatisfied with this "closed-system" model, researchers drew on works in what is now called the "old" institutional theory as well as a series of early works on interorganizational relations, and began to call for a greater focus on the environments within which organizations operate (Zald, 1970). The third perspective, social exchange theory, gained prominence as many of the researchers who began to focus on organizational environments found themselves operating at the interorganizational level of analysis. Drawing on formulations by Emerson (1962) and Blau (1964), organizational theorists began to examine interorganizational power as a function of organizations' dependence on the resources held by other organizations. This led to the development of the resource dependence model, one of the most influential approaches to interorganizational analysis.

Before continuing, our use of the term "power" requires some discussion. Power can be conceived in terms of an ability to accomplish one's goals despite resistance (Weber, 1968), to coerce desired behavior out of others (Dahl, 1957, pp. 202–3), to set the boundaries within which discussion and/or decision making takes place (Bachrach and Baratz, 1962), or to convince others to believe what one wants them to believe (Lukes, 1974). Any or all of these conceptions of power could be viewed as a function of one actor's dependence on another. To the extent that actors are aware of this dependence, as most organizations are assumed to be in the interorganizational literature, then the first three conceptions of power are likely to be more relevant to our discussion than the fourth. But even the latter is not incompatible with arguments based on resource dependence. We therefore assume the relevance of all four conceptions in the discussion that follows.

Early Research: 1949–70

Any discussion of interorganizational power and dependence must begin with Selznick's classic study of the Tennessee Valley Authority, *TVA and the Grass Roots* (1949). Developed during the 1930s as a cornerstone of Franklin Roosevelt's New Deal, the TVA was the largest public works project ever established in the USA, bringing electricity and advanced agricultural technology to the rural South. Finding itself dependent on the local elites of the South, the TVA absorbed them into its decision-making structure, a process Selznick termed "co-optation." Although co-optation may result in power sharing with the co-opted actors, it can also be a primarily symbolic strategy. In its fertilizer test-demonstration program, for example, the TVA depended on local soil improvement associations, which selected farmers for the program and distributed TVA phosphates, to maintain the program's required status as educational. By co-opting these associations, the TVA was also able to insulate itself from accusations of favoritism in the selection of participants. The TVA also reversed its earlier policy of using public ownership of land as a conservation measure, a position that had threatened to alienate local agricultural interests. This example illustrates an ambiguity in the concept of co-optation: at what point does co-optation change from a process involving a powerful organization absorbing potential threats to its existence to that of a vulnerable organization whose dependence on another makes it a captive? The relative balance of power between organizations involved in co-optation has been a major source of controversy in interorganizational analysis. We address this issue in detail later in the chapter.

It was nearly a decade before sociologists followed up Selznick's study with a major theoretical statement. In a 1958 article, Thompson and McEwen identified three types of cooperative relations among organizations, coalition (involving alliances such as joint ventures), bargaining (including negotiation of contracts), and co-optation (defined, following Selznick, as absorption of potentially disruptive elements into an organization's decision making apparatus). As an example of co-optation, Thompson and McEwen noted that, "[t]he acceptance on a corporation's board of directors of representatives of banks or other financial institutions is a time-honored custom among firms that have large financial obligations or that may in the future want access to financial resources" (1958, p. 27). In a major 1967 statement, Thompson built on the earlier paper to develop a comprehensive power-dependence model of organizations. Drawing on Emerson (1962) and Blau (1964) and using Dill's (1958) concept of task environment, which includes customers, suppliers, competitors, and regulatory groups, Thompson proposed that the dependence of an organization on another is proportional to the organization's need for resources or services that the other organization can provide and inversely proportional to the ability of alternative organizations to provide the same resource or service. In response to the predicament created by the organization's potential subservience to others and by the variable availability of alternatives, Thompson argued that dependent organizations placed considerable importance on boundary-spanning units, such as their board of directors, which protect the organization's technical core by engaging in competitive and cooperative strategies with the organizations on which they are dependent.

Along these lines, Zald (1970) introduced a "political economy" perspective. Although Zald's primary purpose was to account for the direction and processes of organizational change, this approach focused on political structures both inside and outside the organization. Consistent with Thompson's model, the focal organization's autonomy is reduced as control over resources (and the accompanying sanctions) is held by the other party. To deal with this, organizations enter into formal or informal alliances, both horizontal and vertical, with these alters. Horizontal alliances, which include legal devices such as mergers and illegal ones such as price setting, occur among participants in the same markets. Vertical alliances, which can include mergers and joint ventures as well as joint directorships, occur among customers, suppliers, and distributors. Zald suggested that organizations will use both formal and informal means to influence one another. One such example is the lobbying of state officials. The American steel industry's historic quest for protective tariffs on imported steel was a means by which its members attempted to influence the policies of the industry's major customers such as automobile manufacturers (Prechel, 1990).

Theoretical and Empirical Advances: The 1970s and 1980s

The above works went far toward moving organizational analysis away from a closed-system model, but it was only in the 1970s that the emphasis moved more explicitly toward an interorganizational level of analysis. Several key early works built on the theories discussed above, most notably articles by Pfeffer (1972a; 1972b) and Allen (1974). Although there were other important formulations during this period (Jacobs, 1974; Cook, 1977), the most comprehensive theoretical statement on interorganizational power and dependence was a 1978 book by Pfeffer and Salancik, which presented a detailed theoretical discussion as well as the results of a number of the authors' earlier empirical works. Pfeffer and Salancik began with four key premises: organizations are first and foremost concerned with survival; in order to survive they require resources, which they often cannot generate internally; as a consequence, organizations must interact with elements in the environment on which they depend, which often include other organizations; survival is therefore based on an organization's ability to manage its relations with other organizations. Because organizations depend on elements in their environment for resources, those groups can make claims on them, and organizations may find themselves attempting to satisfy the concerns of these environmental constituencies. According to Pfeffer and Salancik, there are three crucial factors that determine the extent to which one organization depends on another: the importance of the resource to the organization's survival, the extent to which a particular group inside or outside the organization has access to or discretion over use of the resource, and the extent to which alternative sources of the resource exist. If an organization is greatly in need of specialized knowledge, if that knowledge is scarce within the organization, and if few alternative sources of that knowledge exist, then the focal organization will be heavily dependent on organizations that possess this knowledge (1978, pp. 45–6).

One important feature of Pfeffer and Salancik's discussion is their point that dependence can be mutual. Just as one organization can depend on another, two organizations can simultaneously depend on one another. Power becomes unequal when one organization's dependence exceeds the other's. Drawing on Hawley's work on human ecology (1950), Pfeffer and Salancik distinguished competitive interdependence (characteristic of organizations operating in the same market) from symbiotic interdependence (characteristic of organizations that exchange resources vital to the existence of each). Organizations can adopt a number of strategies to deal with their interdependencies. These strategies include mergers and acquisitions, joint ventures and other types of alliances, and appointment of organizational representatives to the firm's decision-making body through mechanisms such as interlocking directorates. A significant stream of research, much of it by Pfeffer, has examined the extent to which organizations adopt these various strategies under conditions of dependence.

In two early articles, Pfeffer focused on mergers and board of director appointments respectively as mechanisms of absorption. In the first study, Pfeffer (1972a) found, in an examination of 854 mergers between 1948 and 1969, that nearly 50 percent of the variation in acquisitions across industries could be accounted for by three variables: percent of sales made to other industries, percent of purchases made from other industries, and total transactions between the industries. In a second study (1972b), Pfeffer examined the boards of 80 randomly selected US nonfinancial corporations in 1969, hypothesizing that firms with high dependence on external capital (as indicated by a high debt/equity ratio) would attempt to co-opt representatives of financial institutions that controlled the valued resource. Despite the admitted crudity of his measures, Pfeffer found a positive association between the firm's debt/equity ratio and the proportion of its outside directors.

Except for studies by Pfeffer and his colleagues (Pfeffer, 1972a; Pfeffer and Nowak,

1976) that focused on mergers and joint ventures, most empirical studies within the resource dependence model focused on interlocking directorates. In a study of 250 large US manufacturing corporations in 1935 and 1970, Allen tested Thompson and McEwen's suggestion that firms that were heavily indebted to a particular bank would be likely to co-opt representatives of the bank onto their board of directors. Although, as in Pfeffer's case, Allen did not have data on direct transactions between firms and particular banks, he found that a firm's capital intensity was unrelated to its number of interlocks with financial institutions and that its debt ratio was *negatively* related, contrary to his hypothesis.

A major study of the causes and consequences of director interlocks by Pennings (1980) also yielded equivocal support for the resource dependence argument. Pennings examined several measures of capital dependence, including capital intensity, current debt, current ratio (current assets/current liabilities), debt-equity ratio, and long-term debt and six different measures of financial interlocking and found a wide range of results, some consistent with the resource dependence hypothesis and some contrary to it.

Subsequent to the Allen and Pennings studies, researchers have generated more consistent support for the idea that organizations will co-opt representatives of organizations that control resources on which they depend. Burt (1983) advanced a "structural autonomy" model to account for co-optation and firm performance. Drawing on Simmel as well as Pfeffer and Salancik, Burt argued that actors in social networks will benefit to the extent that they avoid dependence on others, occupy relatively sparse (non-competitive) positions in social structures, and are depended on by those that occupy relatively crowded positions. Applied to industries, Burt suggested that an industry will be profitable to the extent that it is concentrated (that is, its members occupy a relatively sparse position), other industries depend heavily on it for sales and/or purchases, and those industries on which it depends for sales and purchases are competitive (that is, its members occupy relatively crowded positions). Burt showed that industries with these characteristics, that is, with high structural autonomy, earn higher profits than industries with low structural autonomy. Conversely, to the extent that an industry is heavily dependent on a highly concentrated industry, the latter can be said to exercise constraint over the former. Using interlocks as his indicator of co-optation, he found, consistent with his hypothesis, that industries will attempt to co-opt members of industries that exercise constraint over them. More recent studies by Richardson (1987), Mizruchi and Stearns (1988), and Lang and Lockhart (1990) have found further support for the hypothesis that organizations will interlock with those that hold resources on which they are dependent, although some studies have failed to support this view (Galaskiewicz et al., 1985; Palmer, Friedland, and Singh, 1986).

A study by Baker (1990) provided a more specific look at the ways in which firms manage their resource dependence relations with other firms. Virtually unique among studies within the resource dependence tradition, Baker's study examined direct relations between firms and their investment banks. Baker hypothesized that when firms faced high dependence on an investment bank for capital and market information, they would tend to stay in long-term relations with those banks. When dependence was low, he suggested that relations would be more short-lived and episodic. Baker found that most firms engaged in a range of relations with investment banks, in which one main bank was used for a disproportionate volume of transactions while rival banks were used on a transaction-by-transaction basis. This study moved beyond the earlier studies of dependence and co-optation by showing the ways in which firms actively managed their relations with firms that controlled crucial resources. Supporting Baker's findings, in a study of acquisitions during the 1960s, Palmer et al. (1995) showed that firms that had interlocks with commercial and investment banks were more likely than were firms without such ties to be acquired in a friendly rather than predatory fashion. This may indicate that social ties to elites protect a firm from hostile takeovers. It also is consistent with the idea that co-optation of these elites can be effective in averting environmental threats.

Recent Trends

Recent works have increasingly highlighted processes of influence flowing across organizations. This research, which is in part a descendant of the resource dependence model and in part an outgrowth of recent work within social network and new institutional theories, has spawned several studies that have shown the diffusion of firm behaviors through social network ties.

In a series of studies of contributions by Twin Cities corporations to local non-profit organizations, Galaskiewicz (1985; Galaskiewicz and Wasserman, 1989; Galaskiewicz and Burt, 1991) showed that firms were especially susceptible to being influenced by high-status opinion leaders if the latter were in direct contact with the firm's executives while soliciting contributions for particular causes. Galaskiewicz and Burt (1991) showed that firms tended to mimic the contribution patterns of other firms with which they were structurally equivalent in interfirm networks, that is, firms that were tied through social connections of their executives to the same third parties. In addition to his focus on economic interdependence, Mizruchi (1989; 1992) showed that firms that were socially tied through director interlocks were more likely than non-connected firms to engage in similar political behavior. Mizruchi also found that structurally equivalent firms (those with interlocks with the same third parties) were especially likely to display similar behavior. Davis (1991) showed that firms that were interlocked with firms that had recently adopted "poison pill" takeover defense policies were more likely to adopt such policies themselves. And Haunschild (1993) showed that firms whose directors sat on the boards of firms that had recently engaged in acquisitions were more likely than firms without such ties to make acquisitions themselves.

This increasing attention to the spread of behavior across interfirm networks suggests a movement away from concerns with interorganizational power. Although the language of power is often missing from these studies, however, the processes the authors describe are often similar. Firms whose interlock partners engage in similar behavior are not necessarily actively attempting to coerce this behavior. But the outcome of such processes often operates as if that were the case. This is especially evident in a range of works within the new institutional theory, in which organizations conform to dominant conceptions of appropriate behavior in response to actual or anticipated pressures and gain legitimacy. Covaleski and Dirsmith (1988) examined the ways in which a large state university was forced into conforming to the state government's budgeting procedures. This was done as a means of currying favor with the state government in an attempt to increase its allocations. Fligstein (1990) showed that legislation by the state restricting firms' ability to engage in vertical integration (the Celler–Kefauver Act of 1950) had the unanticipated consequence of precipitating a wave of diversification into unrelated industries.

The role of power between organizations is also evident in Baron et al.'s (1986) study of the institutionalization of personnel administration by the end of World War II. The authors showed how state and federal governments, through employment-stabilization plans, War Labor Board (WLB) rulings, and War Production Board (WPB) publications, provided models of employment. Government policies designed to control turnover and wages during wartime labor shortages encouraged firms to adopt bureaucratic practices in order to document their labor needs to the satisfaction of the national stabilization plans by classifying jobs and wage categories, implementing personnel departments, job analysis and evaluation systems, and analyzing wage surveys and manpower. In a study of financial reporting practices among *Fortune* 200 firms, Mezias (1990) examined the adoption by firms of the flow-through method (FTM), an accounting technique adopted by the vast majority of the largest US firms in the early 1960s. He showed that firms subject to regulations by the Interstate Commerce Commission were more likely to adopt the FTM than were non-regulated firms. Levitt and Nass (1989) showed that differences in the homogeneity of textbooks in physics and sociology reflected the coercive, mimetic, and normative processes described by DiMaggio and Powell. Coercive and normative pressures from members of the academic disciplines accounted in part for the homogeneity in physics texts (since the pressures tended to be similar) and the heterogeneity in sociology texts (because of the diversity of the field). Mimetic isomorphism occurred, Levitt and Nass showed, in cases in which editors copied other successful texts: To the extent that certain texts defined the standards for other texts, mimetic isomorphism in this case can be seen as influence. Palmer et al. (1993), in a study of "late" adoption of the multidivisional form (during the 1960s), showed that the number of prior adopters in the firm's industry, the firm's dependence on financial institutions (measured by its debt-equity ratio), whether the firm's CEO attended an elite business school (an indicator of elite cohesion, as suggested in Zeitlin's argument (1974), as well as of normative isomorphism), and the firm's number of non-officer interlocks (but not officer interlocks) with other late adopters were all positively associated with its likelihood of adopting. Han (1994) showed that the means by and extent to which firms mimic their peers in choosing accounting firms is heavily affected by their status in the industry. The largest firms in an industry attempt to differentiate themselves from one another. Medium-sized firms attempt to mimic the high-status firms. Low-status firms are either unable or do not feel it necessary to mimic either the high or medium-status firms. The influence of the larger firms on the mid-sized ones does not appear to be deliberate. But that makes its force no less genuine.

Attention to resource dependence and the exercise of interfirm power have not entirely disappeared from recent literature. In a study of relations between advertising firms and their clients, Baker et al. (1998) suggested that the continuity and dissolution of interorganizational ties were affected jointly by competition, power, and institutional forces. In testing the role of power and dependence on market tie continuity and dissolution, Baker et al. suggested that corporations were dependent on agencies not only for advertisements, information, and access to advertising buyers but also for downside insurance, while the agencies depended on the clients for products and services to be advertised. Although corporate clients can reduce their dependence (and increase their power) by dissolving their relationship with their agencies, the reverse rarely happens. Consistent with the resource dependence model, the size and the financial status of the client were found to be negatively associated with the dissolution of a tie. Agency status (based on the firm's number of clients weighted by the client's sales) and centrality (in the network of transactions) as well as an improvement in the client's sales (perceived advertising effectiveness) were also found to be negatively associated with dissolution.

Challenges to the Resource Dependence Approach

The resource dependence model did not go unchallenged. In a major theoretical statement and a response to a critique by Allen, Zeitlin (1974; 1976) argued that the organization is not the appropriate unit of analysis for understanding corporate power. Instead, he suggested that corporations in capitalist societies are most appropriately viewed as tools by which members of a dominant social class accumulate capital. In Zeitlin's view, this class is a socially cohesive group of wealthy individuals held together through kinship and other types of social ties. This group maintains its privileges, according to Zeitlin, through common schooling and socialization experiences in exclusive arenas, marriage of offspring, and restrictive social policies. Corporations should not be viewed as independent entities with their own set of interests, Zeitlin suggested, but rather as means by which members of this elite group extract profits from labor. The dominant segment of this class is a group that Zeitlin referred to as finance capitalists. These are individuals whose interests span those of individual firms, often reflected in their positions on multiple boards of directors. They are "[n]either 'financiers' extracting interest at the expense of industrial profits nor 'bankers' controlling corporations, but finance capitalists on the boards of the largest banks *and* corporations, [who] preside over the banks' investments as creditors *and* shareholders" (1976, p. 900, emphasis in the original). In this view, interlocks between corporations represent not responses to interorganizational power and dependence but rather the dominance of a social class whose power is based not in, but outside of, the organizations on whose boards they sit.

   Zeitlin's formulation generated a considerable amount of empirical research. Ratcliff, (1980) for example, in a study of the lending behavior of 77 St. Louis area banks, found that banks with large numbers of interlocks and ties to upper-class social clubs were more likely than banks without these characteristics to lend to other corporations and capitalists for profit-seeking investments as opposed to individuals for home mortgages. These effects held even when the size of the banks was controlled. A second stream of research was developed as a direct test of the resource dependence argument (Koenig et al., 1979; Ornstein, 1980; Palmer, 1983). These researchers reasoned that if director interlocks were primarily reflections of interorganizational resource dependence, then when an interlock between two firms was accidentally broken through death or retirement of the individual connecting the organizations, the tie should be replaced within a suitably brief period. To the extent that accidentally broken ties are not replaced, these researchers argued, it would suggest that the interlocks reflected social relations among the individuals across firm boundaries rather than ties between the specific organizations. Such a finding, they suggested, would be more consistent with Zeitlin's class model than the resource dependence model. All of these studies, especially those by Koenig et al. and Palmer that were based on data from the USA, found that the vast majority of broken ties were not reconstituted within four years. This raised questions for the view that interlocks were primarily reflections of interorganizational co-optation.

The broken ties studies themselves were subject to criticism. First, it is possible that some ties that were originally formed based on resource dependence no longer reflected these relations by the time they were broken. Stearns and Mizruchi (1986) also noted that a firm that is dependent on a particular resource might reconstitute a tie by linking with another organization in the same industry, a process they called "functional" reconstitution. In a study of 255 broken ties among 22 US firms over a 30-year period, Stearns and Mizruchi found that taking functional reconstitutions into account increased the rate of reconstitution by nearly 50 percent, to nearly half of all broken ties. Other broken ties studies focused more on the determinants of reconstitution than on their frequency (Ornstein, 1984; Palmer et al., 1986).

The weight of the evidence from these studies suggests that director interlocks among firms reflect resource dependence, social ties among elites, and a range of other factors; see Mizruchi (1996) for a review of the interlock literature. What remains unclear from these works, both among resource dependence theorists and their critics, is the source of interorganizational power.

The Sources of Interorganizational Power

Critics of the resource dependence model discussed above were sensitive to the possibility that organizations were subject to external control. The sources of external control for Zeitlin and proponents of his social class theory were not other organizations, but members of a dominant social class. But as we have suggested, organizations may be subject to the power of other organizations as well as controlling ownership interests.

Based on its roots in social exchange theory, the resource dependence model assumes that control over resources on which other organizations depend gives power to an organization. This means that power in an interorganizational relation is inversely related to the degree of dependence of one organization on the other. Unfortunately, and paradoxically, resource dependence theorists' emphasis on co-optation has led to an underemphasis on the exercise of interorganizational power. In Selznick's initial discussion, co-optation was a means by which an already powerful organization absorbed potential threats. Selznick acknowledged that it was the TVA's dependence on local agricultural interests and land grant colleges that compelled the organization to co-opt them. The assumption here was that of a powerful organization acting in a strategic manner. The resource dependence theorists who descended from Selznick continued to treat co-optation as an essentially voluntary strategy. The studies by Allen, Pfeffer, Pennings, and Burt all assumed that firms made a decision to co-opt firms on whose resources they depended. But if we take the resource dependence argument seriously, it is not clear that co-optation is a voluntary strategy of the co-opter. Selznick acknowledged, importantly, that the process of co-optation actually forced the TVA to diverge from its intended policies in order to accommodate the local interests. To that extent, one could say that the local groups' control over resources critical to the TVA gave them power over it.

If an organization, through its control over crucial resources, holds power over other organizations, would it not be possible for this organization to actively exercise that power? Why not use this power to coerce desired behavior from dependent organizations? Rather than being co-opted by these dependent organizations, perhaps what is actually occurring is that the powerful organizations are infiltrating those that depend on them. Consider the Thompson and McEwen example of the firm that is heavily dependent on capital and co-opts a banker onto its board. An alternative interpretation is that the bank, realizing the firms' dependence on it, actively installs itself into the firm's decision-making structure by demanding board representation as a price for its resource. As Aldrich (1979, p. 296) suggested, "the term 'co-optation' may involve too much voluntarism in some cases, such as when taking on a director from a bank is the price a firm pays for having its corporate bonds underwritten."

A close reading of the resource dependence literature indicates that these theorists are in fact aware of this issue. Pfeffer (1972b, p. 222) noted that co-optation "involves exchanging some degree of control and privacy of information for some commitment for continued support from the external organization." Pfeffer and Salancik (1978, p. 164) argued that "[b]y appointing persons to the organization's governing board, particularly those with initially incompatible interests, the organization becomes susceptible to the influence of these individuals." Citing Selznick's study of the TVA, Pfeffer and Salancik added that "[w]hile support may be achieved, the original aims of the organization may be diverted" (p. 165). Pennings (1980, p. 24) went even further, suggesting that "[w]hen the direction of an interlocking directorate originates from the donor organization, the linkage may be an attempt at coercion."

Despite these theorists' awareness that control over resources can give power to an organization, virtually no research within this model has examined the role of interorganizational power from the perspective of organizations that control crucial resources, as Zald (1970) had called for in his important theoretical statement and that Aldrich (1999) has called for in a recent comprehensive synthesis. A partial exception is a stream of research on organizations' political activities, centered around works by Laumann and Pappi (1976), Galaskiewicz (1979), and Laumann and Knoke (1987). These studies showed that organizations with high centrality in resource exchange networks had both higher levels of reputed power and greater degrees of success in political conflicts than did less central organizations. This research focused less on the direct exercise of power between organizations, however, and more on how organizations used their power to accomplish their political goals. Burt's structural autonomy model moved further in the direction of examining the exercise of interorganizational power, although his analysis was at the level of interindustry rather than interfirm relations. As noted above, Burt (1983) argued, and demonstrated, that an industry's ability to constrain dependent industries is positively associated with its profitability. Burt stopped short of saying that these structurally autonomous industries are exercising power; as he noted, autonomy, the ability to achieve one's goals without constraint, is distinct from power, the ability to achieve one's goals despite constraint. Yet the exercise of power remains implicit in Burt's model. If firm A is heavily dependent on members of industry X and industry X is highly concentrated, A will have few alternative partners with which to do business should it be dissatisfied with a given firm. To that extent, the firm in industry X can take advantage of its leverage to extract concessions from firm A. This could be viewed as an exercise of power.

Two Illustrations of the Exercise of Interorganizational Power

The works discussed in the previous sections all dealt with the issue of interorganizational power. The exercise of power was not always the authors' primary concern, however, so their treatments of the topic were sometimes more implicit than explicit. In this section we describe works in which authors explicitly focused on the issue of interorganizational power.

THE ROLE OF FINANCIAL INSTITUTIONS

One of the most explicit attempts to address the issue of interorganizational power was the study by Mintz and Schwartz (1985). Although not overtly framed within the resource dependence literature, Mintz and Schwartz resuscitated a tradition that went back to the early twentieth century by arguing that major banks and insurance companies held a disproportionate share of power in intercorporate relations through their control of capital, the universal resource on which the vast majority of nonfinancial corporations depend. Unlike studies in an earlier tradition of bank control arguments, Mintz and Schwartz did not suggest that banks directly controlled nonfinancial firms. Rather, through their decisions about where capital will be allocated, the banks were assumed to exercise an overall hegemony, setting the broad parameters within which nonfinancial firms operate. Banks exercised this hegemony in a number of ways. In some (but by no means a majority of) cases, banks installed their representatives on companies' boards. This was most likely to occur in situations in which the latter were experiencing financial difficulty (Richardson, 1987; Mizruchi and Stearns, 1988). Banks are not legally allowed to own stock in nonfinancial corporations in the USA but their trust departments often manage company pension funds through which they purchase stock in a range of companies. As far back as the 1960s, more than 30 percent of the largest US nonfinancials had a single bank that controlled more than five percent of the company's stock. The prevalence of these institutional stockholdings has continued to increase in recent years (Useem, 1996), although the concentration of voting by individual banks has not. Still, according to Mintz and Schwartz, the primary mechanism of financial power was not their stock ownership but their control over capital allocation.

Because they viewed financial hegemony as a general phenomenon rather than a relationship between two particular firms, Mintz and Schwartz argued that most director interlocks do not reflect lending relations between particular banks and nonfinancials. A majority of bank interlocks involve officers of nonfinancial corporations sitting on bank boards, as opposed to bank officers sitting on the boards of nonfinancials. The prevalence of nonfinancial officers on bank boards, Mintz and Schwartz suggest, represents an attempt by banks to acquire information from leading members of a range of industries. Bank boards thus become arenas for general discussions about the state of the economy. But the centrality of banks in the interlock network is still a function of their control over the most highly demanded resource in the economy.

Mintz and Schwartz's study, although published in 1985, was based primarily on data from the 1960s. As Davis and Mizruchi (1999) have shown, the economic dominance of large US commercial banks declined significantly from the early-1980s through the mid-1990s. Theoretically, however, Mintz and Schwartz's argument, that bank power was associated with their control over capital, remains a major contribution. Rather than disproving the Mintz and Schwartz thesis, Davis and Mizruchi's finding that the banks' centrality in corporate interlock networks has declined in response to the proliferation of alternative sources of capital actually provide further support for it. When capital was controlled almost exclusively by commercial banks, they were the most central organizations in the interfirm network. As alternative sources of capital developed and commercial banks lost their leverage, their position in the interfirm network declined as well. Part of this decline, according to Davis and Mizruchi, was due to the banks' own decision to reduce the size of their boards, an adaptation to their changing role in the economy. Other studies during this period provided further examples of organizations using their control over resources to exercise power over other organizations. In a study of corporate responses to mass-transit propositions in California, Whitt (1982) found that financial institutions reversed their earlier policy of supporting mass-transit proposals when pressured by oil companies on which they were dependent for business. Although this example, involving nonfinancial corporations exercising power over financials, runs counter to Mintz and Schwartz's argument, the theoretical principle, that firms can use their economic leverage to coerce desired behavior out of other firms, is consistent with it. In a study of corporate political campaign contributions, Clawson et al. (1992) similarly reported an example of a firm that contributed to a liberal Congressman against its own wishes because it had been pressured to do so by a major customer. DiMaggio and Powell (1983) theorized that organizations would often conform in both structures and strategies to organizations on which they are dependent, a process they refer to as coercive isomorphism.

INTERFIRM POLITICAL BEHAVIOR

Based on the findings that firms that control highly valued resources take advantage of the consequent dependence by exercising power over those firms, Mizruchi (1989; 1992) has developed what he called an interorganizational model of cohesion. One process in which interorganizational cohesion occurs, Mizruchi suggested, is in corporate political behavior. Mizruchi noted that left to their own devices, there are industries and sectors in which firms are likely to have opposing interests on political issues. As noted above, members of the steel industry in the USA have for years advocated protective tariffs on imported steel, which prevents foreign producers from selling steel to US steel consumers at reduced prices. Auto companies, which purchase large amounts of steel, have historically opposed these tariffs because they increase the price of domestic steel.

Using this example, as well as those such as that from Whitt's study described above, Mizruchi argued that members of industries that were economically interdependent would tend to contribute to the same political candidates and take the same positions in their Congressional testimony. A firm that was highly dependent (for purchases and/or sales) on firms in a particular industry would be more likely to display similar political behavior to firms in the latter than would less dependent firms. But Mizruchi also argued that similarity of political behavior would be high even when interdependence was relatively symmetric. Following an argument by Emerson (1962, pp. 33–4), Mizruchi suggested that to the extent that each firm had few alternatives with which to do business, both would have a stake in maintaining a smooth relationship.

This formulation suggested three hypotheses: firms with high levels of interdependence will exhibit high similarity of political behavior; the level of asymmetry of dependence should have no effect on similarity of behavior; and the effect of the total level of interdependence on similarity should be constant across levels of asymmetry. Examining the 1,596 dyadic relations among 57 large US manufacturing firms, Mizruchi found support for all three hypotheses. He concluded that power results in solidarity among actors under conditions favorable to the powerful actor.

Unanswered Questions

Table 26.1 presents a summary of the key findings and contributions of some of the studies we have discussed. The table is not comprehensive, but focuses instead on the works that dealt explicitly with dependence and the exercise of interorganizational power. These studies, along with the others reviewed here, provide considerable evidence for a relation between resource dependence and interorganizational power. Corporations often establish formal or informal relations with firms on which they are dependent. This may involve voluntary co-optation by the focal firm or it may represent an attempt by one firm to take advantage of another firm that depends on it by infiltrating its decision-making apparatus. As several authors have conceded, it may represent both processes simultaneously. Regardless, the evidence of the co-optation studies as well as the study by Baker (1990) on the ways in which firms manage their relations with their investment banks suggests that firms must take into account those on which they are dependent. Consistent with this work, Burt (1983) has shown how members of industries that are able to exercise market constraint over other industries achieve relatively high profits. This finding suggests that firms with high levels of economic leverage over other firms will take advantage of this leverage by charging higher prices to their customers or demanding lower prices from their suppliers.

As we have seen, a number of scholars have criticized the notion that the constraints faced by corporations are imposed primarily by other organizations. Rather, they argue that a dominant social class whose interests transcend those of particular firms exercises simultaneous control over groups of corporations. Given the number of hostile takeovers during the 1980s and the apparent growth of stockholder activism that reappeared during that period (Useem, 1993; 1996), this view is not without empirical support. Still, even if some corporations remain under the influence of families or other stockholder groups, these corporations must continue to do business with other corporations. Although some of these corporations may be those under the control of the same ownership groups, few of the largest US firms retain individual stockholders with a greater than five percent holding.

Acknowledging the continuing importance of organizations, Mintz and Schwartz (1985) theorized that banks and insurance companies, through their control of capital, were able to maintain a broad level of hegemony over nonfinancial firms. As Davis and Mizruchi (1999) have shown, this view is less applicable in more recent years than in earlier decades, but Mintz and Schwartz's theoretical argument, that control over a crucial resource was the source of bank power, is consistent with evidence that bank

Table 26.1 Summary of key interorganizational power and dependence studies

Reference	Key concepts/variables	Key findings/contributions	Method/sample
Selznick, 1949	Formal and informal co-optation, goal displacement, institutionalization	Organization diverted its original goals to pacify local elites. Shows organizations adapt to their environment by absorbing potentially disruptive elements	Historical case study of TVA
Thompson, 1967	Domain, task environments, constraint, contingency, interdependence	Organizations seek to reduce dependence on other organizations by maintaining alternatives. Organizations increase their power by seeking status and through contracting, co-opting, and coalescing.	Theoretical model
Zald, 1970	Political economy, coalitional alliance, horizontal and vertical interorganizational relationships	Organizational autonomy is reduced by dependence. Organizations develop alliances to counter dependence.	Theoretical model
Pfeffer and Salancik, 1978	Resource dependence, competitive and symbiotic interdependence	Organizations establish formal ties with organizations on which they depend for resources. Comprehensive presentation of and empirical support for the resource dependence model	Theoretical statement and series of empirical studies
Burt, 1983	Structural autonomy, market constraint, director interlocks, profits	Industries with high structural autonomy have higher profits. Industries establish formal ties with those by which they are constrained. Shows economy as a network of interdependent relations and how network position affects profits and strategies	Network models, empirical illustrations and tests using major US industries
Mintz and Schwartz, 1985	Financial hegemony, discretion, network centrality, interlocking directorates	Major financial institutions, through their control of capital, exercised broad hegemony over the American economy in the post-WWII period. Shows power of network analysis in analyzing interlocking directorates and demonstrates how centrality can be used to capture actors' power	Network models and historical case studies of large US corporations

Mizruchi, 1992	Cohesion, interorganizational model of corporate political unity and conflict, market constraint, director interlocks	Firms that are economically interdependent and socially tied are more likely to engage in similar political behavior. Shows behavioral and political consequences of interfirm relations	Network analysis of dyadic relations between large US corporations
Baker, 1990	Relationship, transaction, and hybrid organization-market interface; intensity and asymmetry of power; criticality of resource	Organizations maintain hybrid market interfaces, with both relationship (long-term) and transaction (episodic) orientations. Shows organizations manipulate their market relations to reduce dependence and gain power	Field interviews and regression analyses of corporations with market value > $50 million

capital is no longer as crucial as it was during the period of Mintz and Schwartz's study. Moving to the political arena, Mizruchi (1992) showed that interdependent firms tend to engage in similar political behavior, suggesting that interdependence allows firms to coerce, either overtly or covertly, desired political behavior out of dependent customers and/or suppliers.

Despite a considerable amount of evidence in support of view that interorganizational power follows dependence relations, most of this evidence comes from data in highly aggregated form. Despite considerable anecdotal evidence, we have little knowledge of the means by which organizations actually use the dependence of others to exercise power over them. While we have shown that the processes analyzed by recent studies within the network and institutional frameworks are similar to the exercise of interorganizational power, the question is whether this new emphasis has led organizational analysts to neglect important aspects of interorganizational relations. Although we are strongly supportive of this new literature, we are also concerned that researchers have abandoned an area of continued relevance. In a study of articles that operationalized concepts from DiMaggio and Powell's classic article on institutional isomorphism, Mizruchi and Fein (1999) found that in virtually every case in which researchers operationalized variables for mimetic and normative isomorphism, the same measures could have been used as indicators of coercive isomorphism. They argued that this reflected a trend among organizational researchers to de-emphasize interorganizational power and coercion. The overarching power of major US commercial banks may have declined in recent years. But this does not mean that organizations no longer exercise power over other organizations.

Future Directions: Who Controls?

This last point raises a question that has received virtually no attention since Mintz and Schwartz's study more than a decade ago: If bank power has declined, what, if anything, has taken its place? Where is the locus of power in the corporate world at the turn of the twenty-first century? Because this topic has gone almost unstudied, in this conclusion we shall briefly review the few arguments that have been made, evaluate their plausibility, and suggest an agenda for future research.

There are four arguments of which we are aware that can account for the locus of power in the contemporary US and global business community. The first, associated most prominently with Domhoff (1998), suggests that the locus of power has changed little since the early 1980s. In this view, the US economy is still dominated by a relatively small group of generally cohesive elites. What has changed is simply the individuals involved. Instead of the scions of the older wealthy families such as the Rockefellers and Mellons, Domhoff suggested, the elite is now dominated by a later generation of individuals, most of who continue to have relatively privileged origins. The general character of the system, one in which this small group, through its business and policy organizations, advances its interests through infiltration and control of the state, remains intact. Although they did not claim that the corporate elite is composed of a cohesive band of privileged scions, Davis et al. (2000), in a study of the structure of the interlock network among *Fortune* 1000 firms, have drawn attention to the stability of the corporate elite. They found that despite significant changes in the governance of corporations between 1982 and 1999, the structure of the network has remained largely unchanged.

A second view, advanced most prominently by Michael Useem (1996), is that institutional stockholders have become the dominant center of power in US business. This is a result of the continued increase in their holdings over the past three decades but also because as the sizes of their holdings increase, the ability to display their dissatisfaction with corporate policy by exiting (selling) becomes more limited. As a consequence, Useem suggested that institutional investors have become increasingly active in attempting to directly influence corporate policies. Whether these institutionals constitute anything approaching the cohesive elite described by Domhoff or even the "inner circle" described by Useem himself in an earlier work (1984) is unclear, however. As Useem noted, although some leading institutional investors represent long-standing, powerful, and connected firms such as Citigroup and Bankers Trust, those who manage company pension funds are increasingly tied to professional rather than intraclass networks (1996, pp. 267–9).

A third, related, argument has been suggested by Davis (1999). Drawing on the Davis and Mizruchi (1999) study that documented a decline in the centrality of leading financial institutions in the US economy, Davis suggested that there is no longer a single, identifiable group of dominant economic actors in the US economy. Rather, pressures for both firms and the state to conform emanate directly from the capital market, whose influence has increased markedly since the early 1980s. Firms are as subject to external influence and control now as they ever were. In fact, one could argue that corporate managers have less autonomy now than during the heyday of managerialism in the 1950s and early 1960s. The difference is that there is now no single, consciously organized interest that oversees business as a whole in the way that Mintz and Schwartz argued that the leading banks did. This argument is similar to Useem's in that it acknowledged pressures from the capital market while stopping short of identifying a self-conscious group of cohesive, powerful actors. But Davis placed less weight on institutional investors as a specifically influential group.

Finally, a fourth possible argument is that the locus of business power has become internationalized, to the point that it no longer makes sense to try to identify a particular national business community, at least in the USA. This argument may be difficult to sustain because it remains relatively tractable to identify the national (or, in the case of Europe, regional) business communities outside the USA.

At the current stage, all of these arguments remain at the level of speculation. A full investigation would likely take researchers somewhat far afield from the traditional terrain of organizational analysis. Yet an understanding of the rapid changes in the environments within which corporations operate, in the USA and abroad, is essential if we are to fully address the issue of interorganizational power and dependence in the contemporary world.

Connections Across Levels

Two of the other chapters in this volume, Brass's essay on "Intraorganizational Power and Dependence," and Ocasio's essay on "Organizational Power and Dependence," address issues very similar to those of our chapter but at different levels of analysis. In this section, we point to some of the similarities between our chapter and theirs as well as some of the ways in which phenomena at one level influence related phenomena at another.

There are several points at which the three chapters intersect. All of them draw heavily on social exchange theory, especially the formulations of Blau and Emerson, in which power in an interaction is viewed as inversely related to one actor's dependence on the other. Ocasio invokes both Blau and Emerson while discussing the determinants of power and dependence within organizational coalitions, a component of what he calls functional perspectives, which treat organizations as adaptive to their environments. Brass relies on Emerson's definition of power throughout his review of structural, personal, and behavioral sources of power, which he suggests comprise the three distinct approaches that research on intraorganizational power and dependence has taken. A second source of similarity is the use of network theory. One of the great strengths of network theory is its tenet that a given structure of relations will have certain behavioral consequences, regardless of the level of analysis. A five-actor network with a given structure is assumed to lead to similar outcomes, whether the actors are individuals within an organizational subunit, different wings of the organization, different organizations themselves, or even larger units such as nation-states. Although he distinguishes power from social capital and from resource dependence by highlighting the long-term commitment aspect of social capital, Ocasio emphasizes the advantages garnered through the creation and maintenance of what Burt (1992) calls "structural holes" (defined as sparse personal networks). Burt showed that managers who occupy structural holes are more likely than non-hole occupants to earn rapid promotions, while industries that occupy structural holes in inter-industry exchange networks are more likely than non-hole occupants to earn high profits. Similarly, Brass points to individuals' centrality and its impact on their control over the flow of resources, a finding that, as we have seen, is consistent with outcomes in interorganizational networks as well. Finally, both Ocasio, with his attention to norms, assumptions, and commitments, and Brass, with his discussion of the institutionalization of power structures, invoke, either explicitly or implicitly, the new institutional theory. As we have suggested, power struggles among organizations both affect, and are affected by, the quest for legitimacy.

Despite the obvious similarities in the processes of power and dependence that operate across levels of analysis, there are phenomena at certain levels that have specific effects on those at other levels. Pfeffer and Salancik's resource dependence model is a macro-level version of social exchange theory, in which an organization's power in an interorganizational relation is a function of the degree to which other organizations depend on it for valued resources. A key tenet of the theory, however, is the view that what goes on inside an organization can be understood only by reference to an organization's relation with its environment. Both Brass and Ocasio acknowledge this point, and focus considerable attention on the internal forces that are affected by external conditions. Both authors, for example, refer to the idea that the individuals and subunits that most effectively manage environmental contingencies will gain power.

At the same time, there are forms of interorganizational activity that can be more fully understood by considering forces internal to the firm. Interlocking directorates, for example, which are assumed to result in part from an organization's dependence on other organizations, are also in part a consequence of internal organizational processes. One means by which a leader inside an organization gains power and legitimacy is by establishing relations with those outside the organization. The process of sitting on multiple boards may be one means of accomplishing this goal. Similarly, a CEO may consolidate his or her power inside the firm by appointing loyal outsiders. Even the range of organizational activities that diffuse through interorganizational networks, such as adoption of the multidivisional form, mergers and acquisitions, and takeover defense policies, may have originated in power struggles internal to various organizations. As with most organizational phenomena, therefore, power and dependence operate at multiple levels, and the operation at one level is likely to influence that at other levels as well.

Researchers studying interorganizational relations would benefit from considering theories that are useful at both the organizational and intraorganizational levels. The use of concepts such as trust and reciprocity in theorizing about the "network form of organizing" (Powell, 1990), for example, reflects the transfer of individual level theories of influence to the interorganizational level. Similarly, since researchers have found demographic characteristics to affect patterns of power and dependence at the intraorganizational and organizational levels, it is also useful to consider the extent to which the demographic characteristics of organizational leaders either reflect, or influence, an organization's power with respect to its environment (Davis et al., 2000).

Conclusion

Although we have identified a number of studies in which authors focus on the direct exercise of interorganizational power, we have also seen that a number of authors who do not explicitly invoke the concepts of power and dependence actually do so implicitly through their discussion of interorganizational influence. We believe that it would be of great value for researchers to work to more consciously identify the sources, the means, and the effects of interorganizational power and dependence. As Perrow (1991) has noted, we live in a society of organizations. In such a society, it is alarming that the interest in how organizations are coerced, cajoled, or otherwise influenced to behave in certain ways by other organizations has not received more attention. It is essential that we reconsider the role of power and coercion in organizational life, not only within, but also among, organizations.

Acknowledgments

Research for the paper was supported in part by the University of Michigan Business School. Please address correspondence to Mark S. Mizruchi, Department of Sociology, University of Michigan, Ann Arbor, MI, 48109-1382, phone: (734) 764-7444; FAX: (734) 763-6887. Electronic mail can be sent to mizruchi@umich.edu.

References

Aldrich, H. E. (1979): *Organizations and Environments*. Englewood Cliffs, N.J.: Prentice-Hall.
Aldrich, H. E. (1999): *Organizations Evolving*. London: Sage Publications.
Allen, M. P. (1974): "The structure of interorganizational elite co-optation: Interlocking corporate directorates," *American Sociological Review*, 39, 393–406.

Bachrach, P., and Baratz, M. S. (1962): "The two faces of power," *American Political Science Review*, 56, 947–52.

Baker, W. E. (1990): "Market networks and corporate behavior," *American Journal of Sociology*, 96, 589–625.

Baker, W. E., Faulkner, R. R., and Fisher, G. A. (1998): "Hazards of the market: The continuity and dissolution of interorganizational market relationships," *American Sociological Review*, 63, 147–77.

Baron, J. N., Dobbin, F. R., and Jennings, P. D. (1986): "War and peace: The evolution of modern personnel administration in U.S. industry," *American Journal of Sociology*, 92, 350–83.

Blau, P. M. (1964): *Exchange and Power in Social Life*. New York: John Wiley and Sons.

Burt, R. S. (1983): *Corporate Profits and Cooptation: Networks of Market Constraints and Directorate Ties in the American Economy*. New York: Academic Press.

Burt, R. S. (1992): *Structural Holes: The Social Structure of Competition*. Cambridge, MA: Harvard University Press.

Clawson, D., Neustadtl, A., and Scott, D. (1992): *Money Talks: Corporate PACs and Political Influence*. New York: Basic Books.

Cook, K. S. (1977): "Exchange and power in networks of interorganizational relations," *Sociological Quarterly*, 18, 62–82.

Covaleski, M. A., and Dirsmith, M. W. (1988): "An institutional perspective on the rise, social transformation, and fall of a university budget category," *Administrative Science Quarterly*, 33, 562–87.

Dahl, R. A. (1957): "The concept of power," *Behavioral Science*, 2, 201–15.

Davis, G. F. (1991): "Agents without principles? The spread of the poison pill through the intercorporate network," *Administrative Science Quarterly*, 36, 583–613.

Davis, G. F. (1999): "Financial markets and classes in late capitalism," paper presented at the Annual Meeting of the Academy of Management, Chicago.

Davis, G. F., and Mizruchi, M. S. (1999): "The money center cannot hold: Commercial banks in the U.S. system of corporate governance," *Administrative Science Quarterly*, 44, 215–39.

Davis, G. F., Yoo, M., and Baker, W. E. (2000): "The small world of the corporate elite," working paper, Department of Organizational Behavior, University of Michigan.

Dill, W. R. (1958): "Environment as an influence on managerial autonomy," *Administrative Science Quarterly*, 3, 409–43.

DiMaggio, P. J., and Powell, W. W. (1983): "The iron cage revisited: Institutional isomorphism and collective rationality in organizational fields," *American Sociological Review*, 48, 147–60.

Domhoff, G. W. (1998): *Who Rules America? Power and Politics in the Year 2000*, 3rd edn. Mountainview, CA: Mayfield.

Emerson, R. M. (1962): "Power-dependence relations," *American Sociological Review*, 27, 31–41.

Fligstein, N. (1990): *The Transformation of Corporate Control*. Cambridge, MA: Harvard University Press.

Galaskiewicz, J. (1979): *Exchange Networks and Community Politics*. Beverly Hills, CA: Sage Publications.

Galaskiewicz, J. (1985): *Social Organization of an Urban Grants Economy*. Orlando, Fla.: Academic Press.

Galaskiewicz, J., and Burt, R. S. (1991): "Interorganization contagion in corporate philanthropy," *Administrative Science Quarterly*, 36, 88–105.

Galaskiewicz, J., and Wasserman, S. (1989): "Mimetic processes within an interorganizational field: An empirical test," *Administrative Science Quarterly*, 34, 454–79.

Galaskiewicz, J., Wasserman, S., Rauschenbach, B., Bielefeld, W., and Mullaney, P. (1985): "The impact of corporate power, social status, and market position on corporate interlocks in a regional network," *Social Forces*, 64, 403–31.

Han, S.-K. (1994): "Mimetic isomorphism and its effect on the audit services market," *Social Forces,* 73, 637–63.

Haunschild, P. R. (1993): "Interorganizational imitation: The impact of interlocks on corporate acquisition activity," *Administrative Science Quarterly,* 38, 564–92.

Hawley, A. H. (1950): *Human Ecology.* New York: Ronald Press.

Jacobs, D. (1974): "Dependency and vulnerability: An exchange approach to the control of organizations," *Administrative Science Quarterly,* 19, 45–59.

Koenig, T., Gogel, R., and Sonquist, J. (1979): "Models of the significance of interlocking corporate directorates," *American Journal of Economics and Sociology,* 38, 173–86.

Laumann, E. O., and Knoke, D. (1987): *The Organizational State: Social Choice in National Policy Domains.* Madison: University of Wisconsin Press.

Laumann, E. O., and Pappi, F. U. (1976): *Networks of Collective Action: A Perspective on Community Influence Systems.* New York: Academic Press.

Lang, J. R., and Lockhart, D. E. (1990): "Increased environmental uncertainty and changes in board linkage patterns," *Academy of Management Journal,* 33, 106–28.

Levitt, B., and Nass, C. (1989): "The lid on the garbage can: Institutional constraints on decision making in the technical core of college-text publishers," *Administrative Science Quarterly,* 34, 190–207.

Lukes, S. (1974): *Power: A Radical View.* New York: Macmillan.

Marx, K. (1967): *Capital: A Critique of Political Economy.* New York: International Publishers.

Mezias, S. J. (1990): "An institutional model of organizational practice: Financial reporting at the Fortune 200," *Administrative Science Quarterly,* 35, 431–57.

Mintz, B., and Schwartz, M. (1985): *The Power Structure of American Business.* Chicago: University of Chicago Press.

Mizruchi, M. S. (1989): "Similarity of political behavior among large American corporations," *American Journal of Sociology* 95, 401–24.

Mizruchi, M. S. (1992): *The Structure of Corporate Political Action.* Cambridge, MA: Harvard University Press.

Mizruchi, M. S. (1996): "What do interlocks do? An analysis, critique, and assessment of research on interlocking directorates," *Annual Review of Sociology,* 22, 271–98.

Mizruchi, M. S., and Fein, L. C. (1999): "The social construction of organizational knowledge: A study of the uses of coercive, mimetic, and normative isomorphism," *Administrative Science Quarterly,* 44, 653–83.

Mizruchi, M. S., and Stearns, L. B. (1988): "A longitudinal study of the formation of interlocking directorates," *Administrative Science Quarterly,* 33, 194–210.

Ornstein, M. D. (1980): "Assessing the meaning of corporate interlocks: Canadian evidence," *Social Science Research,* 9, 287–306.

Ornstein, M. D. (1984),: "Interlocking directorates in Canada: Intercorporate or class alliance?" *Administrative Science Quarterly,* 29, 210–31.

Palmer, D. (1983): "Broken ties: Interlocking directorates and intercorporate coordination," *Administrative Science Quarterly,* 28, 40–55.

Palmer, D., Barber, B. M., Zhou, X., and Soysal, Y. (1995): "The friendly and predatory acquisition of large U.S. corporations in the 1960s: The other contested terrain," *American Sociological Review,* 60, 469–99.

Palmer, D., Friedland, R., and Singh, J. V. (1986): "The ties that bind: Organizational and class bases of stability in a corporate interlock network," *American Sociological Review,* 51, 781–96.

Palmer, D. A., Jennings, P. D., and Zhou, X. (1993): "Late adoption of the multidivisional form by large U.S. corporations: Institutional, political and economic accounts," *Administrative Science Quarterly,* 38, 100–32.

Pennings, J. M. (1980): *Interlocking Directorates.* San Francisco: Jossey-Bass.

Perrow, C. (1986): *Complex Organizations: A Critical Essay,* 3rd edn. New York: McGraw-Hill.

Perrow, C. (1991): "A society of organizations," *Theory and Society*, 20, 725–62.

Pfeffer, J. (1972a): "Merger as a response to organizational interdependence," *Administrative Science Quarterly*, 17, 382–94.

Pfeffer, J. (1972b): "Size and composition of corporate boards of directors," *Administrative Science Quarterly*, 17, 218–28.

Pfeffer, J., and Nowak, P. (1976): "Joint ventures and interorganizational interdependence," *Administrative Science Quarterly*, 21, 398–418.

Pfeffer, J., and Salancik, G. (1978): *The External Control of Organizations: A Resource Dependence Perspective*. New York: Harper and Row.

Powell, W. W. (1990): "Neither market nor hierarchy: Network forms of organization," in B. Staw and L. Cummings (eds), *Research in Organizational Behavior, vol. 12*, Greenwich, CT: JAI Press, 295–336.

Prechel, H. (1990): "Steel and the state: Industry, politics, and business policy formation, 1940–1989," *American Sociological Review*, 55, 648–68.

Ratcliff, R. E. (1980): "Banks and corporate lending: An analysis of the impact of the internal structure of the capitalist class on the lending behavior of banks," *American Sociological Review*, 45, 553–70.

Richardson, R. J. (1987): "Directorship interlocks and corporate profitability," *Administrative Science Quarterly*, 32, 367–86.

Selznick, P. (1949): *TVA and the Grass Roots: A Study in the Sociology of Formal Organization*. Berkeley: University of California Press.

Stearns, L. B., and Mizruchi, M. S. (1986): "Broken-tie reconstitution and the functions of interorganizational interlocks: A reexamination," *Administrative Science Quarterly*, 31, 522–38.

Thompson, J. D. (1967): *Organizations in Action*. New York: McGraw-Hill.

Thompson, J. D., and McEwen, W. J. (1958): "Organizational goals and environment: Goal-setting as an interaction process," *American Sociological Review*, 23, 23–31.

Useem, M. (1984): *The Inner Circle*. New York: Oxford University Press.

Useem, M. (1993): *Executive Defense: Shareholder Power and Corporate Reorganization*. Cambridge, MA: Harvard University Press.

Useem, M. (1996): *Investor Capitalism: How Money Managers Are Changing the Face of Corporate America*. New York: Basic.

Weber, M. (1968): *Economy and Society: An Interpretive Sociology*, 3 vols. New York: Bedminster Press.

Whitt, J. A. (1982): *Urban Elites and Mass Transportation*. Princeton: Princeton University Press.

Zald, M. N., (ed.) (1970): *Power and Organizations*. Nashville: Vanderbilt University Press.

Zeitlin, M. (1974): "Corporate ownership and control: The large corporation and the capitalist class," *American Journal of Sociology*, 79, 1073–1119.

Zeitlin, M. (1976): "On class theory of the large corporation: Response to Allen," *American Journal of Sociology*, 81, 894–904.

Chapter Twenty-seven

Interorganizational Technology

TOBY E. STUART

It is hard to imagine a more significant topic in today's economy than "interorganizational technology." The business press is laden with reports of technology-driven strategic partnerships and corporate combinations, the diffusion of ecommerce and other technology-based initiatives throughout the corporate community, the growth in venture capital dispersions to high tech startups, and the waging of intercorporate intellectual property disputes. These phenomena are inherently about interorganizational technology; they relate to the structure of intercorporate relations in technology-based industries, or to the influence of supra-organizational structures on the evolution of technology.

Given the significance of the topic in the present day, it is heartening to observe resurgence in organizational theorists' interest in the multifaceted relationships between technology, technical change, and the organizational context. Although organizational scholars historically conceived of technology as an exogenous force, its role in shaping organizational structure was taken as a, if not the, central question in the discipline when contingency theory was the dominant paradigm in organizational sociology (Woodward, 1958). However, technology fell from its prominent position in the literature as the contemporary open systems perspective – spearheaded by resource dependence theory, organizational ecology, and institutional theory – gradually supplanted contingency theory as the preferred orientation for understanding and modeling organizational behavior. Fortunately, led by the development and refinement of the network, evolutionary, and learning theory perspectives on the organization-environment interface, this situation has begun to reverse. Moreover, those who have developed these viewpoints have reawakened interest in technology while maintaining the fundamental insight of the open systems perspective: organizations reside in and are shaped by a nexus of relationships with their environments.

The literature on interorganizational technology can be parsed into four areas:

(i)   Work addressing the impact of technological change on the emergence, differential success, and demise of different types of organizations

(ii) The study of how the social structure of a market influences the diffusion of innovations through communities of users

(iii) Research explaining the influence of the (geographic and organizational) structure of organizational fields on the development of technology

(iv) The study of how the technological structure of a market affects the formation of concrete interorganizational relations (e.g., strategic alliances)

Evolutionary theorists have for the most part developed area (i), while network analysts and those interested in organizational learning have led the progress in areas (ii), (iii), and (iv).

The first area consists of the literature on incremental, radical, and architectural innovation (and the related work on eras of technological ferment, dominant designs, and modularity), and the implications of these broad patterns of technological change for organizational dynamics; exemplars include Abernathy (1978), Tushman and Anderson (1986), and Henderson and Clark (1990). The second area, the study of the diffusion of innovations, specifies the social influence processes that affect individuals' and organizations' decisions to adopt new technologies. This research documents the social processes that individuals and organizations employ to resolve uncertainty about the quality and attributes of innovations, and thus to make informed decisions about whether or not to adopt a technology; Strang and Soule (1998) offer a recent review of the diffusion literature.

This chapter will focus on areas (iii) and (iv) of the literature on interorganizational technology: I will describe the work on the interdependencies between the structure of organizational fields and the rate and direction of technological change, as well as highlight some of the findings of the few studies examining how the structure of technological fields influence the formation of concrete interorganizational relations. Table 27.1 summarizes some of the significant studies in these areas of research. Although the sociological literature on interorganizational technology is relatively undeveloped, it contains extensive work on the basic social *mechanisms* that will ultimately help us to understand how the characteristics of and relations among producers affect innovation behaviors. These mechanisms include structural properties of organizations' positions in their markets, most notably status and competition. In addition, organizational inertia (sometimes known as 'local search' when referring to innovation-related activity) is thought by many to be a fundamental property of organizations. Although local search is an organization-level phenomenon, its presence among the members of a population of firms has implications for the structure of technological fields and the pattern of interorganizational relations in those fields.

Technology Structure as an Ecology of Organizational Positions

Since Hannan and Freeman's (1977) programmatic article on population ecology, White's (1981) publication of a sociologically-informed market model, and Burt's (1982) analysis of the network structure of the input-output tables for the US economy, the concept of position (and the roles associated with different positions) has united much of the research on interorganizational relations in economic sociology and organization theory.

Table 27.1 Summary of selected interorganizational technology studies

Reference	Key concepts	Key variables	Key findings	Key contribution	Method and sample
Podolny and Stuart, 1995	The direction of technological change	Technological prestige	High status innovators direct technical change by lending status to uncertain endeavors.	Network-based conceptualization of technological fields	Analysis of the rate at which semiconductor patents are cited
Stuart et al., 1999	The social underpinnings of entrepreneurial activity in high tech industries	Technological prestige	Early-stage companies with high-status backers are quicker to IPO.	The role of inter-organizational networks in development of startups	Hazard rate analysis of IPOs in the biotechnology industry
Powell et al., 1996	Distributed competencies in high tech industries	Centrality in alliance networks	Alliances lead to firm growth.	The importance of alliance networks to the growth of biotech firms	Growth rates of large sample of biotech firms
Ahuja, 2000	Structural holes and innovation	The configuration of egocentric alliance networks	Firms with structural holes in alliance networks innovate at high rates.	Relationship between firm performance and structure of alliance networks	Patent rate in sample of large chemical companies
Barnett, 1990	Community structure in complex technical systems	Densities of different types of organizations	Mutualistic relationship between organizations in different populations in technical system	Applying community ecology to modeling the evolution of complex technical system	Mortality rates of early telephone companies
Podolny et al., 1996	Relational conception of inter-firm competition in technical fields	Technological crowding	Crowding around firms' technological activities reduces firm growth.	The influence of differentiation in innovative activity on firm outcomes	Growth rates in large sample of semiconductor firms

Reference	Key concepts	Key variables	Key findings	Key contribution	Method and sample
Kogut et al., 1995	Entry induction; technical standards	Firm entry	Competition among incumbents creates "entry induction".	Entry is related to alliance availability.	Analysis of entry in sample of semiconductor firms
Sorensen and Stuart, 2000	Geographic reach of inter-firm exchange relations	Positions in inter-firm exchange network	Well networked VC firms less likely to invest in spatially proximate target companies	Reach of information networks determines spatial boundaries of interfirm exchange.	"Dyad" model of probability that VC firm invests in startup
Jaffe et al., 1993	Geographic reach of technological spillovers	Spatial distance between citing–cited patent	Technological spillovers are geographically localized.	Despite ease of communication, technical knowledge remains spatially concentrated.	Probability that one patent cites another

An actor's position (or, equivalently, its "niche") in a social or market structure is the location it occupies in a recurrent structure of latent or concrete, direct or diffuse relationships. The niche or positional structure of a market thus refers to the implicit or formal relationships among types of actors in the system. Conceptually, the reason to delineate organizational positions is to identify the incentive and opportunity structures that govern organizational behavior and to classify the constraints inhibiting different activities, including the creation of new technologies or the initiation of innovation-related, inter-organizational relationships. In general, organizational sociologists hope that precisely casting the positions of producers in a market according to their locations in role structures, status orderings, and market niches, will lead to an understanding of the structural antecedents of corporate action.

Economic sociology's distinctive contribution to the study of market organization and its consequences is the theoretical and empirical work on organizational positions, including how positions are defined, how they emerge and why and how they influence organizational behavior net of firm attributes. The potential of organizational sociology to enlighten the linkages between the technological environment and organizational behavior will therefore emerge as researchers explicate the behavioral consequences of organizational positions in high technology contexts. While the broader literature on organizational environments identifies a number of empirical regularities driven by attributes of organizations' positions (such as the competitive intensity or status of a niche), the challenge for research on interorganizational technology is to empirically distill sufficiently fine-grained properties of organizations' positions to explain innovation-related behaviors and outcomes. This is an emerging area of research with great potential to contribute to our understanding of high technology firms and markets.

One approach to identifying positions is for the analyst to immerse himself in the particulars of any given context to develop a classification of producer roles (for example, a catalog of the technological specializations of the members of an organizational population); a related and more practical approach is to limit attention to contexts in which a third party, such as a consulting firm, government agency, or data vendor, has created a reliable taxonomy of an industry and classified producers according to it. One example of large-sample empirical research employing this tactic is Barnett's (1990) study of early US telephone companies, which develops a community ecology framework to explain variable survival rates among producers specializing in different niches in a multi-firm technical system. Barnett's analysis of mortality rates among turn-of-the-century telephone companies in Pennsylvania and Iowa shows that technological mutualism across differentiated producer roles (i.e., complementarities between different types of telephone companies) influences firm survival rates. Wade's (1995) study of microprocessor producers also uses a community ecology approach to explain organizations' differential adoption rates of competing microprocessor standards. A third study employing this approach is Baum et al.'s (2000) study of patenting and alliancing in the Canadian biotechnology industry; this article sorts producers into categories (e.g., diagnostics, agriculture biotechnology, etc.) to examine competitive and mutualistic relations between firms within and across technological segments.

Joel Podolny and I have collaborated on a series of papers that develop a context-independent approach to delineating producer positions. This method does not require an a priori classification of producers by type to distinguishing among organizations' positions in high technology contexts. Instead, it relies on the fact that when actors create technological advances, they implicitly link their initiatives to those of their predecessors. Historians, evolutionary theorists, and sociologists of technology have noted that, for the most part, technology evolves along coherent trajectories – new technologies emerge from and extend pre-existing discoveries (Hughes 1983; Tushman and Anderson, 1986; Latour, 1987; Basalla, 1988). When organizations are the agents of innovation, we know from a number of studies that they draw their ideas for new technologies from sources (customers, universities, competitors, and the like) beyond their immediate boundaries, and that these ideas always represent improvements to inventions developed by external actors (Utterback, 1974; von Hippel, 1988; Rosenkopf and Nerkar, 2001). Therefore, organizational innovators develop externally generated ideas to improve previously made discoveries.

The cornerstone of our work is the observation that the cumulative nature of technical change occasions implicit connections between the actors participating in the development of a technological area, which can be used to delineate the organizational context of innovation. In particular, all new innovations connect to specific elements in the established body of technological knowledge by extending those elements (Podolny and Stuart, 1995; Podolny, Stuart, and Hannan, 1996; Stuart and Podolny, 1996; Stuart, 1998; Stuart, 2000). We view these latent connections between the developments of different actors as the ties in a "technological network," which serves as the ecosystem in which organizational innovation is situated. Thus, if we can map the links between "discrete" inventions, technological areas (for example, the collection of technologies in domains such as optical disks, genomics, semiconductor memories, and the like) can be viewed as evolving networks in which each node is an invention and ties are the inter-invention ideational links stringing together the nodes. Innovation occurs when new nodes (inventions) extend the frontier of the existing network.

Absent the ability to observe the technological network, the concept would be useful only for informing case studies, simulations, or theoretical conjectures about how the structure of the network might affect technological evolution. For example, there is a small but growing community of sociologists interested in the social construction of technology. Researchers in this area rely heavily on the metaphor of a network or "web" of linkages between actors and technical artifacts, but the evidence offered in support of the theory has been limited to case studies, and even these have been restricted to historical accounts of the development of technologies in relatively small communities of actors.

Fortunately, researchers may utilize at least one data source – patents – to systematically measure technological networks in all areas in which economic actors routinely patent their discoveries. As a condition for issuing a patent, the US Patent Office requires that applicants must acknowledge previously granted patents that had made technological contributions similar to those claimed in their applications. Thus, patents are published with bibliographies, in the form of citations, that highlight the links between the ideas embodied in the current and antecedent inventions. Using citations as patent-to-patent ties, researchers can create a network of all patents in a technological area and detail the time-changing positions of the organizations that work in that domain. This is possible if we accept the set of assumptions necessary to reach the conclusion that attributes of firms' positions can be accurately described by composite measures computed over the individual patents in their portfolios.[1]

The following sections describe three attributes of organizations' positions, competitive intensity, status, and inertia, and how these positional characteristics affect a variety of organizational behaviors and outcomes. I focus on these three attributes because sociologists have developed general theories describing their effects on economic actors, and I believe that these general insights will inform the specific questions of the determinants of the rate and direction of innovation and the structure of intercorporate relations in high technology.

STATUS AND POWER IN ORGANIZATIONAL SYSTEMS

Status distinctions emerge from asymmetric flows of deference (or at least asymmetric attributions of merit) among the actors in a social system. The opportunities and constraints associated with the occupancy of different status positions has been a topic of general interest in organizational sociology (Podolny, 1993; Hannan, 1998; Stuart et al., 1999). Although there is very little work on status dynamics in high technology, prestige distinctions likely play a particularly significant part in the evolution of markets characterized by rampant uncertainty – a characteristic that is generally found in technology-based industries (Tushman and Rosenkopf, 1992). The reason for this is that, by its very nature, uncertainty – when users and innovators must make non-obvious choices between competing options – hinders actors' abilities to adjudicate between competing products, services, or solutions. Prestige dynamics come into play in high technology settings precisely because it is not possible to evaluate inventions or technical approaches strictly on their own merits. Given the obstacles to using purely technical criteria for deciding between competing alternatives, decision makers are likely to use other pieces of information, such as the statuses of the producers and users associated with a product or service, to guide their assessments about the quality of competing choices (Merton, 1973).[2]

One of the interesting results of the uncertainty in technology-based markets, recognized even in the efficiency-orientated economics literature, is that the "best" technologies do not always win in the marketplace (Katz and Shapiro, 1985). Moreover, historians of technology inform us of many instances of multiple and competing technical approaches (Merton, 1973; Hughes, 1983; Pinch and Bijker, 1987): given any technical problem, there may be many suitable technical solutions, and ex ante there is often considerable ambiguity about which of the alternatives is the superior choice. Podolny and Stuart (1995) offer a sociological explanation for the process according to which particular technological solutions are selected from the entries in a technological competition. This paper asserts that the collection of technologies in a domain compete for the attention of innovators and users. The winners in this competition are the technologies accepted by the market and chosen as candidates for elaboration by many members of the community of innovators; the losers are relegated to the heap of technological dead ends.

Podolny and Stuart (1995) argue that status dynamics play an important role in resolving the contest for attention among competing innovations. This paper analyzes the rate at which thousands of semiconductor patents are cited in future patents (a measure of the adoption rate of a technology by subsequent innovators) as a function of the statuses of the organizations associated with the patent (specifically, the innovator and the previous adopters of the technology). We measure firm status using the patent citation network; because patent citations implicitly involve a leader (the owner of the antecedent patent) and a follower (the developer of the consequent patent), organizations that have recently produced many highly cited patents are considered to have high status. We find that, even after controlling for observable measures of the quality of an innovation, the statuses of the organizations associated with different innovations affect the appeal of the technologies to potential adopters. When a high status organization sponsors a technology, it is more likely to receive attention and elaboration from users and other innovators. Moreover, because technologies are refined in the process of use and elaboration, those that are selected may appear to be superior ex post even if they may not have been ex ante. This argument is empirically confirmed in the analysis of the development of semiconductor technologies.

Stuart et al. (1999) show that the same sponsorship process can explain differential performance levels across the young firms in technology industries (similar evidence is reported in Stuart, 2000, and Baum et al., 2000). Because the prior accomplishments of an entrepreneurial venture are rarely sufficient to resolve the uncertainty about its quality, Stuart et al. argue that one of the factors that evaluators use to estimate the worth of young companies is the prestige of their exchange partners – including alliance partners, the venture capitalists who invest in them, and lead customers. The Stuart et al. (1999) paper analyzes the population of US-based, venture capital-backed biotechnology firms, presenting an empirical analysis of the hazard of IPO and the market value of a company conditional on a public offering. Stuart et al. finds that startup biotech firms with high status alliance partners and equity investors experience IPOs sooner and garner higher market values than new entrants that lack prestigious sponsors. Moreover, consistent with the view that the status of a firm's affiliates matters most when there is uncertainty about the firm's quality, the paper shows that the effect of having high status affiliates increases in the level of uncertainty surrounding the quality of the startups in the population.

Status dynamics are likely to play a particularly significant role in the evolution of markets with standards (i.e., sets of coordinated product designs enabling the components of a technical system work together), which are typically characterized by increasing returns. Examples of markets in which standards are central to industry evolution include certain segments of the software business (such as operating systems and electronic mail routing tools), telecommunications, and video games. Prestige distinctions have an amplified influence on the developmental trajectories of standards-based industries because of the high probability that these industries will be dominated by a single standard. This in turn is explained by the fact that the advantage of using a particular standard is an increasing function of the number of others who have adopted it, and thus early gains in the installed base of users yields a snowballing advantage for that platform (Katz and Shapiro, 1985). Prestige differences influence the path to market dominance because high status organizations benefit both from attributions of (high) quality and from the expectation among potential adopters that they will out-compete less recognized rivals. As a result, early adopters are likely to favor the technology standard sponsored by (or at least affiliated with) high status organizations, and when a standard begins to gain market share against a rival approach, it tends to quickly accrue additional momentum until it occupies the major share of the market.

Although the social dynamics may be less interesting, powerful organizations and those with regulatory authority also influence the direction of technological change and the structure of interorganizational relationships in technology-based markets. For example, studies of the machine tool and aircraft industries describe the multifaceted influence of the military on technological development in those contexts (Mowery and Rosenberg, 1981). Similarly, government agencies can also spur the adoption of certain organizational practices. For example, due to the strategic importance of microelectronics to the military in the 1950s, the Department of Defense mandated that all chip producers with DoD contracts would need to recruit "second sources" (i.e., alternate suppliers licensed to produce and sell the relevant device) for all devices under contract. This practice became a standard component of buyer-supplier contracts throughout the industry as a whole (Tilton, 1971).

INERTIA AND INTERORGANIZATIONAL EVOLUTION

Organizational ecologists, and evolutionary and learning theorists typically assume that organizations change slowly and search locally. Inertia is rooted in part in the stable standard operating procedures that initiate and govern organizational action (Cyert and March, 1963). Other structural and individual-level factors contributing to local search include: individual decision makers within organizations are boundedly rational and heavily anchored on past experiences when they evaluate alternative courses of action; current staff members typically have developed expertise specific to the area(s) in which an organization has previously focused, and therefore often favor continuance in their employer's activities, particularly if their expertise is of little value to other organizations; and, to preserve their privileged positions, dominant political coalitions inside the firm often use their influence to adopt policies that favor the status quo (Burgelman, 1994). Even if these internal forces could be easily modified to shift the direction of the firm, external constituencies often pressure organizations to behave reliably and in ways that approximate the organization's past activities (Hannan and Freeman, 1984). Similarly, the focus organizations require to service existing customers often hampers their ability to perceive and pursue emerging market opportunities (Rosenbloom and Christensen, 1994).

Evolutionary theorists, recognizing the many inertial pressures that act upon organizations, posit a Markovian conception of organizational adaptation in which organizational change is the product of searches for new practices initiated in the neighborhood of an organization's existing routines (Cyert and March, 1963; Nelson and Winter, 1982; Cohen and Levinthal, 1990; Stuart and Podolny, 1996). As Nelson and Winter (1982, p. 211) describe it, "for any firm engaging in exploration, search is 'local' in the sense that the probability distribution of what is found is concentrated on techniques close to current ones." This assumption about search behavior is supported by a number of case studies demonstrating that technology firms practice local search (Burgelman, 1994). Much of this work has illuminated the difficulties that established organizations experience when attempting to adapt to significant technological shifts; see Tushman and Anderson (1986) for a discussion of the extreme case of radical technological change, and Henderson and Clark (1990) for a discussion of the organizational challenges posed by architectural innovations. There are also a few large sample studies, all relying on patent data, which demonstrate that organizations typically innovate within the areas of their established expertise (Stuart and Podolny, 1996; Sorensen and Stuart, 2000; Rosenkopf and Nerkar, 2001).

Although inertia is obviously an organization-level phenomenon and the domain of this chapter is interorganizational technology, I discuss it because the existence of an ecology of local searchers has a number of implications for interorganizational relations and market dynamics within populations of high technology firms. First, if organizations search within the areas of their established competencies, the folk wisdom about the dynamism and adaptability of high technology organizations likely belies a stable structure of organizational niches when an area of technology is viewed from the market or population level (Stuart and Podolny, 1996; Sorensen and Stuart, 2000). Related to this point, Kim and Kogut (1996) show that certain core technologies serve as platforms that naturally branch into new directions. This suggests that although firms may appear to be moving into new (with respect to the focus of their past initiatives) areas of activity, patterns of firm diversification may simply reflect local search-driven branching processes in underlying technologies. If firm niches are defined relative to those of other producers, then branching processes will shift the foci of sets of organizations in similar directions. Thus, the existence of platform technologies raises the intriguing possibility that there are significant "absolute" changes in firms' innovative activities but few "relative" (i.e., compared to other producers) shifts. In other words, the industry-wide niche structure may be stable even in areas experiencing rapid technological change.

Inertial forces in organizational search trajectories have opposing implications for the inception of horizontal interorganizational relationships (e.g., licensing agreements, R&D alliances, and other forms of strategic partnering). On one hand, because an organization's routines and knowledge base are contingent on its areas of technological focus, firms that work in similar niches develop similarities in their operating assumptions and knowledge bases. This relates to alliance formation because firms that share an understanding of technologies and market segments are better equipped to exchange or jointly develop new technology (Cohen and Levinthal, 1990). On the other hand, the constraints on an organization's ability to broaden its search activities suggest the need for cooperative strategies that bridge technological areas when there is a high potential for synergistic combinations among the technical skills residing in non-overlapping neighborhoods (Burt, 1992; Stuart and Podolny, 1999; Ahuja, 2000); see Fleming (2001) for the role of recombination in generating important new discoveries. This suggests that alliances that span technological gaps may be particularly significant when they succeed, but that the obstacles to successful collaboration are likely to be greatest in just this situation.

Although empirical evidence is relatively scant, two sets of studies report evidence suggesting that technology-based alliances are more common among firms with overlapping innovation trajectories: Stuart (1995; 1998) and Mowery et al. (1996). Both of these studies utilize patent citation data to gauge the level of overlap in the niches of producers: a pair of firms has high technological overlap when the members of the pair are issued patents that cite the same set of existing patents (stated in terms of the technological network framework discussed above, the two firms are "structurally equivalent" in the patent citation network). Employing network dyad models in which the probability that two firms establish an alliance is treated as a dependent variable, both studies show that alliances are more likely among pairs of firms with overlapping technological niches.

THE ECOLOGY OF TECHNOLOGY-BASED COMPETITION

Economic sociologists posit that actors compete when they are redundant. In network-based models of the structure of the relations in a group of actors, redundancy is evinced when it is possible to substitute one of the nodes in a network for others without significantly altering the structure of relations in the network; this argument is developed in an interorganizational context in DiMaggio (1986), Burt (1992), Baum and Singh (1994) and Podolny et al. (1996). Competition as lack of differentiation is also a central premise in ecological models of the competitive intensity of the organizational niche (McPherson, 1983).

Although the organizations literature has not explored the question of how the competitive structure of high technology markets affects the dynamics of innovation generation (Tushman and Nelson, 1990), there are a large number of empirical studies in industrial organization economics evaluating the relationship between market structure, the rate of firm innovation, and the level of corporate R&D spending. This work is motivated by Schumpeter's (1942) assertion that highly competitive market structures attenuate firms' incentives to invest in innovation. Schumpeter's reasoning was that only firms with market power are able to appropriate a significant fraction of the returns from innovation; in markets that even approximately conform to the ideal typical definition of a competitive structure, too large a fraction of the rents accruing to innovations dissipate through competitive imitation. However, a number of authors have noted that the Schumpeterian literature has produced conflicting findings across studies, calling into question the extent to which the large body of empirical work supports any causal statements about the relationships between market concentration, R&D spending, and the rate of innovation (Cohen et al., 1987). Of course, the erratic findings in the Schumpeterian literature suggest the need for alternative approaches.

In one of the few sociological studies addressing the form of the competition-innovation link, Stuart (2000) posits that firms in highly competitive market positions actually invest more in innovation than comparable firms occupying less competitive niches. Using the patent network framework, this paper employs "structural equivalence" (Lorrain and White, 1971) – a measure of relational redundancy – to determine the level of differentiation of the technological position of any given organization with respect to all of its competitors. Thus, each firm is assigned to a firm-specific niche of varying levels of competitive intensity. My core assertion in this paper is that high crowding leads producers to attempt to distinguish their activities from the initiatives of technologically adjacent organizations. This pursuit of differentiation assumes the form of heavy investments in the development of technology (i.e., high R&D spending). The paper finds that firms in highly competitive niches both invest more in R&D and innovate (patent) at higher rates than otherwise comparable firms.

Kogut et al. (1995) present another paper that employs network-based arguments to elucidate the competition-innovation relationship. This paper shows that the competition among incumbents for technological dominance induces the entry of startups into new market segments. "Entry induction" occurs as established firms recruit startups to be new users and additional producers of their technologies. The mechanism by which entry is induced is that established firms offer startups access to their technologies through strategic alliances. Thus, the Kogut et al. paper proposes that entry patterns are linked to the competitive structure of a market. While the competition-entry relationship has been discussed at length in industrial organization economics, the Kogut et al. paper proposes a different explanation for the relationship with distinct empirical implications.

Current Areas of Interest

In the work on interorganizational technology, an area of increasing interest concerns how organizations' participation in strategic alliances affects innovative behavior. The importance of this topic is underscored by historical and case-based research documenting many examples of the impact of organizational coalitions on technical evolution in different fields. For example, in the middle 1970s the Ministry of International Trade in Japan sponsored the VLSI research consortium among the nation's largest semiconductor producers, which is widely cited as the catalyst that enabled Japanese firms to dominate the semiconductor memory business throughout the 1980s.

It stands to reason that because technology-based alliances are forums for the exchange of ideas and for the joint development of new knowledge, they will influence the path of advancement of technology in the contexts in which firms frequently partner to develop technology. There are now a few empirical studies that support this view. Once again, these studies utilize patents as innovation indices. Stuart (2000) shows that a focal semiconductor firm with partnerships with particularly successful semiconductor innovators enjoys higher rates of innovation than otherwise comparable firms. This study generalizes a standard social influence model, analyzing firms' patent rates as a function of a set of control variables and a composite "influence variable" that is computed by post-multiplying a matrix representation of the alliances in an industry by a vector of the patent counts of the firms in the industry.[3]

Applying Burt's (1992) structural holes argument to an interfirm alliance network, Ahuja (2000) shows that firms which establish structurally diverse egocentric alliance networks experience higher rates of innovation. Ahuja analyzes firms' rate of patenting in the chemicals industry over a 10-year period. He finds that firms with many structural holes – alliances with structurally non-redundant contacts – in their egocentric partnership networks patent at a higher rate. In a related study but one that explores how technology alliances affect the *direction* of corporate innovation, Stuart and Podolny (1999) find that alliances with technologically proximate firms tend to reinforce organizations' tendencies to produce innovations in the neighborhood of their previous endeavors, but alliances that bridge two firms in technologically differentiated niches promote the production of non-local innovations. Mowery et al. (1996) also shows that alliance activity increases the overlap in partnering firms' innovation profiles, particularly in deals that include equity participation.

In a similar vein, there is growing interest in how technological change affects intercorporate partnering. Powell et al. (1996), for example, argue that the torrid pace of advance in an array of technological areas, such as the life sciences, has been one of the central drivers of intercorporate partnering. In this particular context, recent developments in areas such as combinatorial chemistry, ultra-high-throughput screening, and bioinformatics have paved the way for fundamental advances in the drug discovery process. Powell et al. argue that because science has advanced so quickly and on so many different fronts, no single organization possesses the full complement of skills to capitalize on the breadth of biotechnological advances. Their view of the biotech industry is one in which competencies are dispersed across industry participants, and alliances have therefore been used as tools to facilitate organizational learning and to expand the scope and depth of the knowledge base of the firm.

Another recent and promising avenue of research is Lee Fleming's work analyzing the characteristics and antecedents of important inventions. Most of the large sample research on the organizational consequences of technological change has treated the arrival of significant (often referred to as "radical") inventions as random occurrences that are exogenous to the population under analysis. This treatment of radical innovations partly reflects the difficulty of identifying the underlying factors that produce path-breaking insights; it also reflects the often-noted empirical fact that many of the watershed technical changes that catapult a technological area into upheaval emerge from sources beyond the area's boundary (Abernathy and Utterback, 1978). Fleming's (2001) research views technological novelty as an outcome of the blending of existing technical factors in new combinations. Fleming's work analyzes the rate at which patents are cited in future patents, but is unique in that it employs a relatively new estimation procedure to focus on both the mean and variance of the citation distribution. He argues that employing novel combinations of antecedent ideas increases the variance of the importance of new technologies – although most previously unexplored combinations will yield insignificant results, some will produce radical breakthroughs. With the use of patent data, his research aims to document the characteristics of significant discoveries and identify the organizational antecedents of such discoveries.

Outstanding Questions

Based upon the early stage of the literature in the domain of interorganizational technology, there are many more unanswered questions than compelling empirical findings concerning the relationships between market organization and innovation outcomes. I will use the remainder of the chapter to address one area of research in which organization theorists can contribute significantly to our understanding of interorganizational technology: the spatial organization of economic activity in high technology. In short, the reason why this is a promising area for research is that social networks are enormously important in many activities performed in the process of developing new technologies. Because social networks implicitly exist in space (i.e., relations are between people and organizations that are bound to relatively stable spatial coordinates) and frequent and intensive interactions are often required in the development of technology and technology-based organizations, network-analytic approaches can offer many insights into the spatial organization of high technology.

This view is at least casually supported in ethnographic accounts and case studies of the geographic concentration of technology firms in different regions, which emphasize the role of networks in producing a multitude of outcomes, ranging from company foundings to the diffusion of information on technologies and market opportunities across corporate boundaries; for example, see Saxenian's (1994) comparison of the evolution of Silicon Valley and Route 128 regions. In fact, even the economic explanations of geographic clustering (Jaffe et al., 1993) ascribe a role to social networks in the transmission of technical knowledge across firm boundaries. Moreover, many histories of Silicon Valley highlight the direct and multiplex, mutualistic relationships in the region's community ecology; in particular, accounts of the dynamism of the region describe the influence of the deep-seated interactions among startups, universities, venture capital partnerships and law firms. Thus, many scholars argue that inter-personal and inter-organizational networks of varying types contribute to the emergence and sustenance of technology-based geographic clusters (Almeida and Kogut, 1999).

I believe that network-based theories of the transmission of entrepreneurship-relevant information may generate testable predictions regarding the spatial distribution of entrepreneurial activity, and how this distribution changes over time. There is an enormous literature in sociology on the role of networks in the movement of information of different types and qualities, for example, Granovetter (1973) and Burt (1992). For two reasons, information transfer is a central issue in the geography of entrepreneurial activity:

1   The ability to transfer credible and reliable information is essential in entrepreneurial contexts because there are severe information problems in the new venture creation and fundraising process – most notably, uncertainty about new venture quality and information asymmetries (Gompers and Lerner, 1999).

2   Social and professional relationships are known to be spatially concentrated (Festinger et al., 1950; Kono et al., 1998).

To the extent that established social relationships help solve the information transfer problem, the most fecund geographic areas for entrepreneurial activity are those in which would-be entrepreneurs have broad and dense personal and professional networks. By the same reasoning, potential entrepreneurs will find it very difficult to amass resources to launch new organizations in areas in which they lack a rich set of social ties. This argument is outlined in greater detail below.

Sociologists have argued that pre-existing relations between the parties involved in economic exchanges, as well as the past participation of those agents in exchanges with common third parties and other members of an integrated social system, help to overcome information and incentive problems in inter-actor exchanges. When any particular inter-actor exchange is embedded in a temporal sequence of transactions between the same actors, or is a component of a broader network of ongoing exchanges, the incentives of the parties in the transaction to behave opportunistically in the focal exchange are tempered by the knowledge that their reputations will suffer if their counterparty and / or other members of the social system discover that they behaved opportunistically. Regardless of whether they are individuals or organizations, counterparties in embedded exchanges are therefore less likely than strangers to refrain from potentially beneficial transactions because of information problems.

In the realm of technology-based entrepreneurship, the observation that information problems inhibit resource-based exchanges among actors who are unknown to one another is reflected in adages such as, "it's not what you know, it's who you know." Phrases such as this express the common wisdom that personal connections are a (if not *the*) essential catalysts of the organization startup process. This observation is consistent with the growing body of empirical evidence that shows that social capital is a critical resource in efforts to build organizations of all types; see, for example, Aldrich and

Auster (1986), Stuart et al. (1999) and Shane and Stuart (2001) for an analysis in a high technology context. One explanation for why having many contacts is so important in the entrepreneurial process is that embedded transactions reduce the risk of opportunistic behavior; thus, all other things equal, an entrepreneur is much more likely to close a deal if it is with a counterparty who knows (or knows of) the entrepreneur.

The fact that uncertain transactions are easier to execute among individuals and organizations in the same social circles will influence the geographic distribution of entrepreneurial activity if individuals and their social networks are unevenly distributed through space. The obstacles to securing resources and commitments for the purpose of starting a new firm from skeptical investors, risk averse job seekers, and cautious customers may be impossible to overcome in the absence of pre-existing relationships between the principals of a startup and these resource holders. One implication of this is a region in which social structures are created by high rates of interfirm job mobility or high concentrations of firms in the same technology-based industries are likely to experience more company starts than other areas. This would occur because individuals in high mobility geographic regions are inevitably exposed to a series of contacts in their areas of professional specialization. Whereas economists assert that the presence of increasing returns (often labeled, "agglomeration economies") leads entrepreneurs to establish new technology-based firms in close proximity to existing enterprises of the same kind, a competing, sociological explanation for this phenomenon would be that industries exhibit spatial clustering because the social networks of would-be entrepreneurs are broader and deeper in areas with established populations of particular types of firms.

This line of reasoning also suggests that, to the extent that individuals and organizations vary in the spatial range of their contacts networks, they will be more or less constrained in the geography of their economic activities. For instance, Sorensen and Stuart (2001) show that venture firms have higher probabilities of investing in geographically distant startups if they have a pre-established relationship within another VC firm that is spatially close to the startup and chooses to invest in it. Similarly, within any context, there is likely to be variance across time in the geographic localization of entrepreneurship-relevant social relationships. In particular, the geographic scope of individuals' social networks in new areas of technology are likely to expand over time as trade associations, and technical, industry, and investment conferences are established. This would suggest that, in any given area of technology, the network-based constraints on the geography of economic activities are likely to decline (Zucker et al., 1997, present suggestive evidence in the case of biotechnology).

In a related vein, there has not been any work in organizational sociology fleshing out the relationship between geographic concentration and the creation of formal interorganizational relations. For example, we are unaware whether strategic alliances exhibit evidence of spatial clustering net of what would be expected based upon the spatial distribution of technological specialties. Recent research suggests that board interlocks are spatially localized (Kono et al., 1998); whether formal interorganizational relations (strategic alliances, buyer–supplier ties, mergers) have spatial antecedents remains an open question. Based upon the ethnographic work illuminating high rates of intra-region mobility among technologists in some technology clusters, one might anticipate that formal organizational relations are often launched by interpersonal relationships that span organizational boundaries.[4]

The possible connections between geographic location and formal interorganizational relationships is one component of a much broader set of likely "proximity" effects that may arise as research on interorganizational technology progresses. Given the apparent spatial concentration of high technology firms, the influential role of a cadre of leading venture capital firms in financing many of the most successful technology companies, the existence of serial entrepreneurs who establish a sequence of startups in the same general area, the extraordinarily high rates of interfirm mobility among technologists and managers in some of the technology clusters, and the seemingly ubiquitous use of interfirm alliances in high technology, it is likely that there are dense and rich connections between high tech firms at multiple levels of these organizations (e.g., many organizations share equity holders, board members, technology sharing agreements, informal friendships among organizational members, and the like). The extent to which these kinds of intercorporate ties,

(i)   exhibit spatial patterns
(ii)   amalgamate into coherent structures at the organizational field level
(iii) reveal the influence of central, powerful actors, and
(iv)   display predictable patterns of network evolution

remain unexplored questions.

Connections Across Levels

The hallmark of open systems understandings of organizational behavior is that intricate connections intertwine organizations and their environments. In view of the dynamism of high technology environments and the diversity in the organizational forms that participate in advancing technology, the linkages between extra- and intra-organizational processes are likely to be especially myriad and profound in this domain. It is therefore to be anticipated that the themes of Shilling's (this volume) chapter on intraorganizational technology and Tushman and Smith's (this volume) chapter on organizational technology overlap with the points of emphasis in this chapter and raise intriguing opportunities for research at the boundaries of these analytic levels.

One promising area for research would be to ground the study of technology-related interorganizational relationships in models of the internal technology development process. Such models might take many different forms; for example, they might focus on how an organization's decision to enter an alliance may be influenced by incentive issues (e.g., the incentives for R&D personnel to participate in an inter- versus intra-firm technology development project), commitment problems (e.g., the credibility of the commitment of an R&D director to support a researcher with a radical or high variance product development idea), and internal political processes (e.g., the support of the marketing function and the opposition of the manufacturing function to an interfirm product development project). Developing models along these lines will improve our understanding of when firms establish alliances and how these deals perform. Moreover, the evolutionary processes discussed by Tushman and Smith (this volume) are particularly germane to the issue of how internal organizational dilemmas affect the formation and performance of intercorporate partnerships. The salience and severity of incentive, commitment, and political dilemmas almost surely vary in a predictable manner over the technology cycle.

Many of the studies of intercorporate technology alliances metaphorically view these agreements as technological bridges connecting organizations. For example, Ahuja (2000) and Mowery et al. (1996) assert that alliances act as pathways that ferry innovation-related knowledge between allied firms. Yet, in light of the mobility levels in technology-based industries, the individuals that occupy key liaison positions between a high tech firm and its alliance partners may be tantamount to limited term employees. As White (1970) observed, internal job ladders possess the defining features of vacancy chains; the occupants of managerial positions are constantly shifting as a vacancy at a high level in an employment system generates a series of mobility events below. In technology, the mobility in managerial ranks driven by internal promotions may pale in comparison to that which is created by interfirm mobility. Indeed, due to high rates of organizational founding, growth, decline, and failure, interfirm mobility rates in technology are extraordinarily high, and technical workers' allegiance to their professions often supersedes their commitment to their employers. These conditions lead to a second opportunity for cross-level research: how is the stability, the incidence, and the pattern of interorganizational relationships affected by the high rates of inter- and intrafirm mobility of managers? To the extent that the strength of interfirm ties rests in the personal relationships among individual managers, high mobility may lead to the dissipation of the relational capital between organizations.

A third, high potential area for cross-level research concerns the relationships between intra-firm environments and rates of new firm creation. As organizational ecologists have frequently observed, the employment rosters of existing organizations comprise the individuals who are at greatest risk of starting new companies of like kind (Phillips, 2001). It is almost certainly the case that conditions within "parent firms," the incumbents in a high technology industry at any given time, affect the likelihood that some of the employees of these organizations will depart to establish new (and often competing) ventures. Intraorganizational conditions such as typical rates of promotion and stock option appreciation, the level of bureaucratization, the abilities of individuals to appropriate some of the returns produced by their technology development successes, the terms of workers' employment contracts, and the level of organizational growth, are all probable predictors of the hazard that employees depart to start new organizations. Moreover, functional areas within parent firms almost surely differ in their propensities to produce founders of new companies, and these differences also likely covary with the technology cycle. Thus, cross-level research promises to contribute significantly to our understanding of the entrepreneurial process in high technology.

Conclusion

This is an exciting time for research on interorganizational technology. This subject is centrally important to how the economy functions and how industries and organizations flourish. It is essential to the prosperity of the discipline that organizational theorists develop theory and evidence that inform the structure and dynamics of technology-based industries. As a result, this will be a rewarding area for young scholars to make a claim to a territory in the discipline's intellectual space.

Acknowledgments

Author is Fred A. Steingraber-A.T. Kearney Professor of Organizations and Strategy at the Graduate School of Business, University of Chicago. I would like to acknowledge the financial support of the Graduate School of Business, University of Chicago, and a research grant from the Kauffman Center for Entrepreneurial Leadership.

Notes

1   In particular, one must make an assumption about the weight assigned to each patent in computing firm-level positioning measures. The simplest approach would be to treat each patent equally, but many more complex schemes can be implemented: allowing older patents to decay; weighting individual patents in proportion to the number of citations they receive, and so on.

2   Asch (1951) is the seminal work establishing that social influence processes mold subjective assessments, even when there is only very modest uncertainty associated with a judgement. In a review of the diffusion literature, Strang and Soule (1998) observe that the diffusion of innovations has been studied so frequently precisely because the decision to adopt an innovation is subject to uncertainty. The risk that inheres in the adoption decision is the attribute of an innovation that creates interesting social dynamics around the spread of the innovation; since potential adopters are often unable to confidently assess the quality of an innovation, social influence processes determine adoption rates.

3   There is a general class of social influence models of the form: $y = \rho W y + x\beta + e$. In these models, y refers to an attitude or opinion held by the actors in a network, W is often known as a structure matrix because each of its elements (the w_{ij}) measures the influence that the opinion of actor j has on the opinion of actor i, and x is an $n \times k$ matrix of k covariates. (In the case of an alliance network, **W** would typically be a binary matrix indicating the presence or absence of a strategic partnership between firms i and j.) In other words, in addition to the effects of a set of exogenous influences, the value of yi is assumed to be influenced by a weighted combination of the opinions (yj) of other actors. Substituting an alliance matrix for W and a vector of patent counts for y, the model expresses the patent rate as a function of the alliance-weighted influence of the patent totals of firms' alliance partners.

4   Gilson (1999) offers the intriguing hypothesis that state-level differences in the legal code and enforcement of trade secrets and non-compete laws explain the success of Silicon Valley relative Boston's Route 128.

References

Abernathy, W. J. (1978): *The Productivity Dilemma*. Baltimore, MD: The Johns Hopkins Press.

Abernathy, W. J., and Utterback, J. M. (1978): "Patterns of industrial innovation," *Technology Review*, June/July, 41–47.

Ahuja, G. (2000): "Collaboration networks, structural holes, and innovation: A longitudinal study," *Administrative Science Quarterly*, 45, 425–55.

Aldrich, H., and Auster, E. R. (1986),: "Even dwarfs started small: Liabilities of age and size and their strategic implications," *Research in Organizational Behavior*, 8, 165–98.

Almeida, P., and Kogut, B. (1999): "Localization of knowledge and the mobility of engineers in regional networks," *Management Science*, 45, 905–17.

Asch, S. E. (1951): "Effects of group pressure upon the modification and distortion of judgement" in M. H. Guertzkow (ed.), *Groups, Leadership and Men*, Pittsburgh: Carnegie Press, 117–90.

Barnett, W. P.: "The organizational ecology of a technological system," *Administrative Science Quarterly*, 35 (1990), 31–60.

Basalla, G. (1988): *The Evolution of Technology*. New York: Cambridge University Press.

Baum, J. A. C., and Singh, J. V. (1994): "Organizational niches and the dynamics of organizational mortality," *American Journal of Sociology*, 100, 346–80.

Baum, J. A. C., Calabrese, T., and Silverman, B. S. (2000): "Don't go it alone: Alliance network composition and startups' performance in Canadian biotechnology," *Strategic Management Journal*, 21, (Special Issue), 267–94.

Burgelman, R. A. (1994): "Fading memories: A process theory of strategic business exit in dynamic environments," *Administrative Science Quarterly*, 39, 24–56.

Burt, R. S. (1982): *Toward a Structural Theory of Action*. New York: Academic Press.

Burt, R. S. (1992): *Structural Holes: The Social Structure of Competition*. Cambridge, MA: Harvard University Press.

Cohen, W. M., and Levinthal, D. A. (1990): "Absorptive capacity: A new perspective on learning and innovation," *Administrative Science Quarterly*, 35, 128–52.

Cohen, W. M., Levin, R. C., and Mowery, D. C. (1987): "Firm size and R&D intensity: A reexamination," *The Journal of Industrial Economics*, 35, 543–65.

Cyert, R., and March, J. G. (1963): *A Behavioral Theory of the Firm*. Englewood Cliffs, N.J.: Prentice-Hall.

DiMaggio, P. (1986): "Structural analysis of organizational fields: A blockmodel approach," *Research in Organizational Behavior*, 8, 335–70.

Festinger, L., Schachter, S., and Back, K. W. (1950): *Social Pressure in Informal Groups*. New York: Harper.

Fleming, L. (2001): "Recombinant uncertainty in technological search," *Management Science*, 47, 117–32.

Gilson, R. J. (1999): "The legal infrastructure of high technology industrial districts: Silicon Valley, Route 128, and covenants not to compete," *New York University Law Review*, 74, 575–629.

Gompers, P. A., and Lerner, J. (1999): *The Venture Capital Cycle*. Cambridge, MA: MIT Press.

Granovetter, M. S. (1973): "The strength of weak ties," *American Journal of Sociology*, 78, 1360–80.

Hannan, M. T. (1998): "Rethinking age dependence in organizational mortality: Logical formalizations," *American Journal of Sociology*, 104, 126–64.

Hannan, M. T., and Freeman, J. H. (1977): "The population ecology of organizations," *American Journal of Sociology*, 82, 929–64.

Hannan, M. T., and Freeman, J. H. (1984): "Structural inertia and organizational change," *American Sociological Review*, 49, 149–64.

Henderson, R. M., and Clark, K. B. (1990): "Architectural innovation: The reconfiguration of existing product technology and the failure of established firms," *Administrative Science Quarterly*, 35, 9–31.

Hughes, T. (1983): *Networks of Power: Electrification in Western Society*. Baltimore: Johns Hopkins University Press.

Jaffe, A., Trajtenberg, M., and Henderson, R. (1993): "Geographic localization of knowledge spillovers, as evidence by patent citations," *Quarterly Journal of Economics*, 108, 577–98.

Katz, M. L., and Shapiro, C. (1985): "Network externalities, competition, and compatibility," *American Economic Review*, 75, 424–40.

Kim, D.-J., and Kogut, B. (1996): "Technological platforms and diversification," *Organization Science*, 7, 283–301.

Kogut, B., Walker, G., and Kim, D. J. (1995): "Cooperation and entry induction as an extension of technological rivalry," *Research Policy*, 24, 77–95.

Kono, C., Palmer, D., Friedland, R., and Zafonte, M. (1998): "Lost in space: The geography of corporate interlocking directorates," *American Journal of Sociology*, 103, 863–911.

Latour, B. (1987): *Science in Action*. Cambridge, MA: Harvard University Press.

Lorrain, F., and White, H. C. (1971): "Structural equivalence of individuals in social networks," *Journal of Mathematical Sociology*, 1, 49–80.

McPherson, J. M. (1983): "An ecology of affiliation," *American Sociological Review*, 48, 519–32.

Merton, R. C. (1973): "The Matthew effect in science," in N. W. Storer (ed.), *The Sociology of Science*, Chicago: University of Chicago Press.

Mowery, D. C., and Rosenberg, N. (1981): "Technical change in the commercial aircraft industry, 1925–1975," *Technology Forecasting and Social Change*, 20, 347–58.

Mowery, D. C., Oxley, J. E., and Silverman, B. S. (1996): "Technological overlap and interfirm cooperation: Implications for the resource-based view of the firm," *Research Policy*, 27, 507–23.

Nelson, R. R., and Winter, S. G. (1982): *An Evolutionary Theory of Economic Change*. Cambridge, MA: The Belknap Press.

Phillips, D. J. (2001): "The parent–progeny transfer and organizational mortality: The case of Silicon Valley law firms, 1946–1996," working paper, University of Chicago.

Pinch, T. J., and Bijker, W. E. (1987): "The social construction of facts and artifacts," in W. E. Bijker, T. P. Hughes and T. J. Pinch, (eds), *The Social Construction of Technological Systems*, Cambridge: MIT Press.

Podolny, J. M. (1993): "A status-based model of market competition," *American Journal of Sociology*, 98, 829–72.

Podolny, J. M., and Stuart, T. E. (1995): "A role-based ecology of technological change," *American Journal of Sociology*, 100, 1224–60.

Podolny, J. M., Stuart, T. E., and Hannan, M. T. (1996): "Networks, knowledge, and niches: Competition in the worldwide semiconductor industry, 1984–1991," *American Journal of Sociology*, 102, 659–89.

Powell, W. W., Koput, K. W., and Smith-Doerr, L. (1996): "Interorganizational collaboration and the locus of innovation: Networks of learning in biotechnology," *Administrative Science Quarterly*, 41, 116–45.

Rosenbloom, R. S., and Christensen, C. M. (1994): "Technological discontinuities, organizational capabilities, and strategic commitments," *Industrial and Corporate Change*, 3, 655–85.

Rosenkopf, L., and Nerkar, A. (2001): "Beyond local search: Boundary-spanning, exploration, and impact in the optical disc industry," *Strategic Management Journal*, 22, 287–306.

Saxenian, A. (1994): *Regional Advantage: Culture and Competition in Silicon Valley and Route 128*. Cambridge, MA: Harvard University Press.

Schumpeter, J. A. (1942): *Capitalism, Socialism and Democracy*. New York: Harper.

Shane, S., and Stuart, T. E. (2001): "Organizational endowments and the performance of university-based startups," *Management Science*, forthcoming.

Sorenson, J. B., and Stuart, T. E. (2000): "Aging, obsolescence, and organizational innovation," *Administrative Science Quarterly*, 45, 81–112.

Sorenson, O., and Stuart, T. E. (2001): "Syndication networks and spatial distribution of venture capital investments," *American Journal of Sociology*, forthcoming.

Strang, D., and Soule, S. A. (1998): "Diffusion in organizations and social movements: From hybrid corn to poison pills," *Annual Review of Sociology*, 24, 265–90.

Stuart, T. E. (1995): "Technological positions, strategic alliances, and the rate of innovation in the worldwide semiconductor industry," unpublished dissertation, Graduate School of Business, Stanford University.

Stuart, T. E. (1998): "Network positions and propensities to collaborate: An investigation of strategic alliance formation in a high-technology industry," *Administrative Science Quarterly*, 43, 668–98.

Stuart, T. E. (2000): "Interorganizational alliances and the performance of firms: A study of growth and innovation rates in a high-technology industry," *Strategic Management Journal*, 21, 791–811.

Stuart, T. E., and Podolny, J. M. (1996): "Local search and the evolution of technological capabilities," *Strategic Management Journal*, 17, 21–38.

Stuart, T. E., and Podolny, J. M. (1999): "Positional consequences of strategic alliances in the semiconductor industry," *Research in the Sociology of Organizations*, 16, 161–82.

Stuart, T. E., Hoang, H., and Hybels, R. (1999): "Interorganizational endorsements and the performance of entrepreneurial ventures," *Administrative Science Quarterly*, 44, 315–49.

Tilton, J. E. (1971): *International Diffusion of Technology: The Case of Semiconductors*. Washington, D.C.: The Brookings Institute.

Tushman, M. L., and Anderson, P. (1986): "Technological discontinuities and organizational environments," *Administrative Science Quarterly*, 31, 439–65.

Tushman, M. L., and Nelson, R. R. (1990): "Introduction: Technology, organizations, and innovations," *Administrative Science Quarterly*, 35, 1–8.

Tushman, M. L., and Rosenkopf, L. (1992): "Organizational determinants of technological change: Toward a sociology of technological evolution," *Research in Organizational Behavior*, 14, 311–47.

Utterback, J. M. (1974): "Innovation in industry: A study of the origination and development of ideas for new scientific instruments," *Science*, 183, 620–26.

Von Hippel, E. (1988): *Sources of Innovation*. New York: Oxford University Press.

Wade, J. (1995): "Dynamics of organizational communities and technological bandwagons: An empirical investigation of community evolution in the microprocessor market," *Strategic Management Journal*, 16, 111–33.

White, H. C. (1970): *Chains of Opportunity: System Models of Mobility in Organizations*. Cambridge, MA: Harvard University Press.

White, H. C. (1981): "Where do markets come from?" *American Journal of Sociology*, 87, 517–47.

Woodward, J. (1958): *Management and Technology*. London: H.M.S.O.

Zucker, L. G., Darby, M. R., and Brewer, M. B. (1997): "Intellectual human capital and the birth of U.S. biotechnology enterprises," *The American Economic Review*, 88, 290–306.

Chapter Twenty-eight

Interorganizational Learning

PAUL INGRAM

Interorganizational learning occurs when one organization causes a change in the capacities of another, either through experience sharing, or by somehow stimulating innovation. Interorganizational learning may be intentional, or unintentional. As the idea that knowledge is key to the performance of organizations has become more influential, attention to processes of interorganizational learning has increased. Interorganizational learning is seen as one of the most important routes by which organizations can develop competitive advantage. Consequently, the topic has received substantial recent research interest. Relatedly, managers are actively working to improve their organizations' interorganizational learning.

A leaping-off point for research on interorganizational learning is the massive literature on organizations' learning from their own experience (Yelle, 1979; Argote, 1999). Typically, that literature finds that as organizations gain experience by, for example, producing more of a given output, their cost and/or time to produce decreases at a decreasing rate. This robust phenomenon is called the learning curve. An analogous phenomenon forms the basis of the literature we examine here. A typical study evidencing interorganizational learning is a regression where the focal organization's cost to produce is the dependent variable, modeled as a function of other organizations' cumulative production (e.g. total units produced in past periods), and control variables such as the focal organization's own cumulative production, and current scale of production (Irwin and Klenow, 1994; Darr et al., 1995).

While the interorganizational learning curve forms the archetype for research in this area, there are two distinct subclasses of research approaches that can be used to frame the literature. These correspond to the broad types of organizational learning activities, experiential learning, and innovative learning from research or experimentation. Experiential learning, exemplified by the classic learning curve, is the marginal refinement of existing practices as experience accrues. Innovative learning yields more radical improvements, often in the creation of new products and processes, and emerges from more far-reaching search, experimentation and recombination of existing knowledge. March (1991) explains that firms may prefer either of these types of learning (that he calls exploitive and explorative) depending on their approach to risk, but that there is a general bias towards the more certain experiential learning. Firms may also pursue experiential and innovative learning simultaneously.

For both experiential and innovative learning, the abstract interorganizational learning process can be broken down to identify key components. Interorganizational learning requires that a "sender" organization does something that stimulates learning in a "receiver" organization. The relationship between the sender and receiver is also important: Are they joined in a joint venture? Do they compete with each other? Keys to understanding interorganizational learning, then, are to understand how the nature of the sender, receiver, and the relationship between them affect the process, and what actions by the sender cause what learning responses in the receiver. The literature includes important papers that have examined these questions for experiential and innovative learning.

The most recent research on the topic is to examine the implications of interorganizational learning in a competitive context, and to determine the significance of a range of interorganizational relationships for learning. While that work is answering key questions about the context and conditions for interorganizational learning, outstanding questions remain. The most pressing concerns the mechanisms through which interorganizational learning happens. Most research has taken a birds-eye view, relating experience or other organizational characteristics to learning outcomes, without examining the mechanisms that link them.

Literature Review

LEARNING-ACTIONS

Ingram and Baum (1997a) is a useful paper to illustrate experiential interorganizational learning, because it demonstrates the types of experience and types of organizational performance that may be related through interorganizational learning (Table 28.1). The paper examines the failure rate of US hotel chains from 1896 to 1985. It has a family resemblance to traditional learning-curve research, in that it relates experience to performance, but it is somewhat atypical because the performance measure is not cost or time to produce, but rather the risk of organizational failure. Ingram and Baum reasoned that industry experience could influence an organization in many ways beyond reduction in production cost. For example, industry experience may indicate which product configurations are attractive to the market, which would result in higher obtained prices, rather than lower costs. The risk of organizational failure is a comprehensive measure of performance that reflects the many ways experience may be beneficial. Ingram and Baum measured industry operating-experience (with a service-industry analog of cumulative production), which mirrors the traditional learning-curve operationalization of experience. Ingram and Baum also measured competitive experience, which is the cumulative number of other organizations' failures that the focal organization has observed. Competitive experience can be a source of learning regarding competition and strategic maneuvering.

The findings indicated benefits of both industry operating and industry competitive experience. Industry operating experience that accumulates during the focal chain's

Table 28.1 Selected interorganizational learning studies

Reference	Key concepts	Key variables	Key predictions and findings	Key contribution	Method and sample
Ingram and Baum, 1997a	Vicarious learning from industry experience Congenital learning from industry experience before founding	Industry operating experience (before and since the focal organization's founding) Industry competitive experience (before and since the focal organization's founding)	Industry operating experience before and since the focal organization's founding reduces its risk of failure. Industry operating experience since the focal organization's founding reduces its risk of failure.	Illustrates the experiential form of interorganizational learning by demonstrating that two types of industry experience improve the performance of organizations	Hazard-rate study of the failure rate of all US hotel chains, 1896–1985
Henderson and Cockburn, 1996	Knowledge spillovers in the form of improvements to the focal organization's R&D productivity as a function of competitors productivity in related research programs	Significant patents Competitors' research productivity	From 1960 to 1978 research productivity is enhanced by competitors' productivity in the same (but not in similar) research program. From 1979 to 1988 research productivity is enhanced by competitors productivity in similar (but not the same) research programs.	Illustrates the innovative form of interorganizational learning by demonstrating that research productivity of one organization spills over to other organizations in its industry	Event-count models of significant patents for 10 pharmaceutical companies, 1960–88
Podolny and Stuart, 1995	Status of knowledge creator as an influence on whether others use the knowledge	Egocentric niche of a patent defined by the patents it cites and those that cite it Technological status of an organization as a function of the proportion of all patent citations it receives	A 'Matthew Effect' exists, where patents that are introduced by high status firms, and which cite and are cited by patents of high status firms, receive more citations.	Indicates the significance of the knowledge sender's status to make it influential in others' learning	Hazard models of the likelihood that one US semiconductor patent will be cited by another, 1976–91

	Concepts	Constructs/Variables	Propositions	Contribution	Method/Data
Haunschild and Miner, 1997	Trait imitation as the likelihood that organizations with certain traits are more likely to be imitated. Outcome imitation as the likelihood that extreme and positive outcomes increase imitation	Likelihood that a decision by an organization will be imitated by others. Organization traits such as size and profitability. History of past decision outcomes	Large, profitable organizations are more likely to be imitated by others. Extreme outcomes are more likely to encourage (if positive) or discourage (if negative) imitation than are less extreme outcomes.	Demonstrates key elements of the influence of knowledge senders as a function of what they are and do	Logistic regressions of likelihood to choose an investment banker as an advisor, all acquisitions in which both organizations were public, US based companies, 1 January 1896 to 15 July 1993
Cohen and Levinthal, 1990	Absorptive capacity as the readiness of a firm to recognize and integrate knowledge in its environment. R&D produces absorptive capacity in addition to innovations	R&D intensity (expenditure/sales). Environmental conditions that create an incentive to build absorptive capacity	Firms make R&D expenditures partly to build and maintain their absorptive capacity.	Introduces a key idea about which organizations will benefit from interorganizational learning, and outlines the dynamics that lead to absorptive capacity	Regression of R&D intensity of a sample of business units, 1975–77
Hamel, 1991	Interorganizational learning is the result of design rather than default	The learning intent of organizations as they approach an alliance. The receptivity of organizations to learn	Organizations that approach an alliance with the intent to internalize their partner's skills learn more. Organizations that are receptive to learning will learn more.	Emphasizes that success at interorganizational learning is dependent on the motivation and strategy that the organization brings to the process	Detailed case studies of nine international alliances, including many interviews with participants

Reference	Key concepts	Key variables	Key predictions and findings	Key contribution	Method and sample
Darr et al., 1995	The distinction between the experience of others that are related to the focal organization and the experience of unrelated others	Cost of production Experience of the organization, related organizations, and unrelated organizations	Organizations experience a learning benefit in the form of reduced cost of production from the experience of others they are related to. No learning benefit is obtained from the experience of unrelated others.	Provides strong empirical evidence for the significance of interorganizational relationships to facilitate interorganizational learning	Learning-curve studies of 36 stores of a pizza franchise in western Pennsylvania. 1 January 1989 to 15 June 1990
Powell et al., 1996	Network organizations as the cradle of innovation in fast-moving industries R&D alliances as the source of relational capabilities that lead to more ties, and organizational growth	Organizational growth R&D alliances Network centrality and diversity of ties	Support is found for a dynamic model of relational capabilities, where R&D alliances lead to network diversity, centrality and experience, and eventually to organizational growth.	Documents the dynamics and significance of a network arrangement to promote innovation	Qualitative observations and regressions relating network ties and growth for bio-technology firms. 1990–94

lifetime reduces its risk of failure. A similar reduction in failure comes from competitive experience during the focal chain's lifetime. So, the focal chain becomes more robust as a function of others' experience. Ingram and Baum also looked for an effect of industry experience before the focal chain's founding, what could be called congenital experience. Congenital experience may be particularly useful because it is available when an organization is in the process of design. They reasoned that it is at the design stage, before organizational structure and routine takes hold, that organizations may benefit most from others' experience, and found a large benefit of industry operating experience (but not competitive experience) before the focal chain's founding. Among the many other examples of experiential interorganizational learning are studies of semiconductor production (Irwin and Klenow, 1994), US pizza stores (Darr et al., 1995), Manhattan hotels (Baum and Ingram, 1998), Israeli kibbutzim (Ingram and Simons, 1999), and British pizza stores (Darr and Kurtzburg, 2000).

Henderson and Cockburn (1996) illustrate innovative interorganizational learning in a study of the R&D productivity of pharmaceutical companies from 1960 to 1988. Their dependent variable was the number of "significant patents" (patents registered in at least two of the USA, Japan, and the European Community) for a given research program of a given pharmaceutical firm. Each pharmaceutical firm (there were 10 in the study, accounting for 25 percent of all pharmaceutical R&D) will typically have ten to fifteen distinct research programs, each targeted to discovering therapies for a particular disease area (e.g. hypertension or depression). Significant patents were predicted by a number of characteristics of the firms and the research programs. Important results on these influences included that there were economies of scale and scope for research productivity. Firms that had larger R&D expenditures, and conducted R&D in more research programs, produced more patents in their programs.

Another important part of this study was to look for interorganizational learning in the form of spillovers from one firm's research productivity to another's. Such spillovers are indicated if a competitor's patents (in the focal research program, or in a related program) increase the predicted productivity of the focal firm's research program. Henderson and Cockburn's analysis indicates that they do: "At the mean, for example, a program whose competitors' programs in the same and in related fields are roughly 10% more productive will be approximately 2% more productive itself." The authors of this study also find that the nature of spillovers in the pharmaceutical industry changed over time. This is likely because the nature of research in the industry changed. Other examples of innovative interorganizational learning include studies of patenting in US biotechnology (Podolny and Stuart, 1995), strategic alliances worldwide (Mowery et al., 1996), and US semiconductors (Almeida and Kogut, 1999).

SENDERS

Podolny and Stuart (1995) contribute significantly to the idea that it is not just (or even primarily) the quality of new knowledge, but also characteristics of the knowledge sender, which determine whether others will take the knowledge and apply it. They start with the recognition that technologies that are best in terms of performance criteria are not always the most influential in terms of market outcomes, and subsequent evolution of knowledge. Podolny and Stuart argue that attributes of the innovating organization partly account for the significance of an innovation. Their particular focus is on status. They adapt the "Matthew Effect" argument that Merton (1968) used to explain the success of academic innovations. The importance of an innovation is difficult to determine when it is new; it depends on its adoption and application by others, and that takes time. So, how does the public initially decide which innovations to adopt or to apply? Partly, they decide based on the status of the innovator, giving more attention to those with high status. For example, controlling for the quality of two academic papers, the paper with an author of higher status is likely to receive more initial attention. This initial attention helps the paper become "important," certainly more important than the equal-quality paper from a lower status author. The linking of status and attention may be quite sensible, because status often derives partly from the quality of past output, and may therefore signal the quality of future output.

Empirically, Podolny and Stuart examine patenting in the semiconductor industry, from 1976 to 1991. Their unit of analysis is the individual patent, and their dependent variable is the likelihood that a subsequent patent will cite the focal patent. So the analysis is more precisely on whether one patent will learn from another, rather than on whether one organization will learn from another. But of course, the patents are produced by organizations, and it is the status of the producing organization (the sender) that is expected to influence subsequent citations. An organization's status at any time was measured as the proportion of all semiconductor patent citations from the previous twelve months that had been to the organization's patents. The findings are that the status of the patenting organization affects the likelihood that a patent will be cited. Further, the status of organizations whose patents cite a focal patent, or whose patents are cited by the focal patent, both increase the focal patent's likelihood of citation. For interorganizational learning, the implication is that innovations of a high-status organization are more likely to be attended to and applied, in other words, learned from. Rowley et al. (2000) consider yet another characteristic of the sender, its network of contacts to other firms. They argue that senders with diverse networks offer more in industries where innovative learning is key; see also Dyer and Nobeoka (2000).

Haunschild and Miner (1997) consider the influence of a broader set of sender-characteristics on interorganizatonal learning. They argue that the size and profitability of an organization, and its success with a given action, will influence other organizations to imitate its actions. They study this in the context of choices of which investment bankers to use as advisors in all acquisitions between public companies in the USA between 1986 and 1993. They use logistic regression to predict the likelihood of an acquirer's use of an investment banking firm as a function of

1   the frequency with which other firms used a given banker
2   traits of those other firms, and
3   premiums paid by those other firms.

They find that frequent investment banker choices are likely to be imitated, as are the choices of large and successful firms. Size and success appear to make knowledge senders more influential. They also find that extreme results in terms of premiums paid by past acquisitions using a particular investment banker influence the likelihood of imitation, probably because of the salience of extreme outcomes. Other evidence linking sender characteristics to experiential interorganizational learning comes from studies of new product offerings of savings and loan organizations (Haveman, 1993), and the adoption of matrix structures by hospitals (Burns and Wholey, 1993).

RECEIVERS

What characteristics of an organization make it more or less likely to learn from others? Part of the explanation is the preparedness of the organization to absorb external knowledge, what Cohen and Levinthal (1990) have called its absorptive capacity. Building on research regarding learning processes of individuals, those authors argue that organizations need the right type of prior knowledge to benefit from new knowledge presented by their environments: "The premise of the notion of absorptive capacity is that the organization needs prior related knowledge to assimilate and use new knowledge" (p. 129). The justification for this argument begins with individual psychology, and the recognition that individual learning is much more effective with prior experience in a problem area. But absorptive capacity of the organization is not just an aggregation of individual absorptive capacities. Organizations are better able to cull knowledge from their environments if they have "boundary spanning" members that are able to understand that knowledge and direct it to the appropriate part of the organization. Prior knowledge also helps an organization to know "who knows what" in their environment, producing the interorganizational equivalent of the transactive memory that facilitates learning in groups of individuals (Argote, this volume).

The significance of prior related knowledge to future learning creates strong path-dependency in the knowledge trajectories of organizations. If organizations do not make early investments to acquire knowledge in a quickly moving field, they may be locked out of that field because they do not have the absorptive capacity to recognize opportunities or to integrate new knowledge. Cohen and Levinthal apply the absorptive capacity argument to derive predictions regarding organizations' expenditures on research and development (R&D). They claim that R&D expenditures have two key effects, the familiar one of directly contributing to the organization's innovation, and an indirect effect of increasing the organization's absorptive capacity, and thereby facilitating their learning from others. R&D expenditures, according to Cohen and Levinthal, should be understood in light of these two opportunities. Their analysis is based on a large cross-sectional analysis at the level of the business unit in their sample. They surveyed business unit managers as to the appropriability and technological opportunity conditions they faced, and supplemented that with the Federal Trade Commission's Line of Business Program data on business unit sales and R&D expenditures. Their dependent variable is a business unit's R&D intensity (R&D expenditures/sales), and they find empirical support for specific arguments about which learning environments offer greater incentives for absorptive capacity and therefore R&D investment. A number of subsequent studies have shown that absorptive capacity of the receiver firm increases its learning from others (Liebeskind et al., 1996; Barkema and Vermuelen, 1998; Gupta and Govindarajan, 2000).

Hamel (1991) denotes a number of other receiver characteristics that affect interorganizational learning, particularly in the context of strategic alliances. His study induces theory from detailed qualitative analysis of nine international alliances. His findings imply that interorganizational learning occurs by design rather than default.

He highlights two receiver characteristics that affect learning in the face of a given learning opportunity: intent, which establishes the desire to learn, and receptivity, which creates the capacity to learn. Some firms approach an alliance with a *substitution* intent, and may be satisfied by simply substituting their partner's capability in a particular skill area for their own deficiency. This is to be compared with an *internalization* intent, which is to explicitly internalize the skills of the partner. Internalization is much more likely to lead to interorganizational learning than substitution. The relative advantage of the internalization approach is seen in this comment by a project manager whose firm had an internalization intent, and a record of success at interorganizational learning: "We wanted to make learning an automatic discipline. We asked the staff every day, 'What did you learn from [our partner] today?' Learning was carefully monitored and recorded (p. 91)."

Receptivity is the openness to accept knowledge from the partner, and requires humility and enthusiasm for learning. Firms differ in receptivity, with some approaching an alliance from the deferential position of students, and others demanding the position of teachers, which may have higher status, but presents lower potential for learning. Some firms had low receptivity because they viewed the alliance as a confirmation of the firm's failure to maintain its competitiveness on its own. Others had structural inhibitions to change and learning, what is often called structural inertia. Consistent with this qualitative observation, quantitative analyses have found that interorganizational learning decreases as organizational structures become more firmly established (Argote et al., 1990; Baum and Ingram, 1998). Quantitative research has also shown that the receiver's motivation to learn contributes positively to interorganizational learning (Gupta and Govindarajan, 2000).

RELATIONSHIPS

The specific consideration of the relationships between organizations that learn from each other is one of the most important developments in the recent study of interorganizational learning. The emerging position is that a relationship between organizations greatly facilitates learning between them. This is in contrast to the previously dominant idea, that significant amounts of knowledge simply spill over the boundaries of organizations, to be consumed by any other organization in the environment.

Darr et al. (1995) present evidence of the significance of interorganizational relationships for transfer of learning in a learning-curve study of the productivity of pizza stores, finding that transfer is greater between stores owned by the same franchisee. They describe three mechanisms that facilitate the transfer of learning between organizations, and which are more likely between stores with a common owner. Regular communication between organizations increases the opportunity to share knowledge, and was more common among pizza stores with common owners, which would regularly report data to each other. Personal acquaintances between the members of different organizations create levels of empathy, familiarity and trust which smooth the exchange of information (Uzzi, 1996; Ingram and Simons, 1999; Ingram and Roberts, 2000). Personal acquaintances develop between pizza stores with common membership through physical proximity and meetings. Meetings provide a direct opportunity to share experience by creating face-to-face contact, and by causing managers to explicitly focus on problems, and discuss solutions. Members of pizza stores with common ownership met at least once a week, while stores without common ownership (which were all part of the same franchise system) met only once per month.

The analysis and empirical findings of Darr et al. (1995) are particularly strong. The study used three types of experience to predict the cost of production for each of 36 stores. Self-learning was captured by the focal store's own experience (measured in cumulative pizzas produced). Learning from others was captured with two measures, the experience of stores related to the focal store through common ownership, and the experience of other stores in the franchise system that were in the same geographic region, but unrelated to the focal store. The analysis included weekly observations for each store over an 18-month period. Learning in a study of this type is evidenced by a positive relationship between experience and performance, in this case, cost-efficiency of production. Given the large learning-curve literature it is not surprising that costs were found to decrease with the store's own experience. There was also strong evidence of knowledge transfer between stores with common owners. So, as a given store gained experience, other stores with the same owner enjoyed a decrease in their costs of production. Such interorganizational learning was not evident, however, from the experience of unrelated stores. Absent joint ownership, others' experience had no effect on efficiency. In this pizza industry, there was evidence of interorganizational learning through the relationship of common ownership, but no evidence of spillovers of experience to unrelated organizations.

Related work demonstrating experiential interorganizational learning through relationships is of two types. The first is interorganizational learning curve studies which, like Darr et al. (1995) relate experience of related others to performance. Examples come from US hotel chains (Ingram and Baum, 1997b), Manhattan hotels (Baum and Ingram, 1998), US radio stations (Greve, 1999), Israeli kibbutzim (Ingram and Simons, 1999), and British pizza stores (Darr and Kurtzburg, 2000). The second type examines the adoption of practices through interorganizational networks. Examples include studies of large corporations (Davis, 1991), hospitals (Burns and Wholey, 1993), and liberal arts colleges (Kraatz, 1997).

Powell et al. (1996) show the role of relationships for a different type of interorganizational learning, innovation based on R&D. They study the biotechnology industry in the early 1990s, and document a network form of organization with a particular competence for spurring innovation. In the biotechnology industry there is a web of interconnections (joint ventures, research agreements, minority equity investments, licensing and other kinds of partnerships) between firms. Apparently, these arrangements allow "network organizations" to develop and apply competencies that no one firm appears able to manage internally. The power of these networks is seen when they are compared to the large pharmaceutical firms that dominated more traditional forms of drug discovery. Those firms have not been able to match the rate and quality of innovations produced by biotechnology networks.

The specific arguments made by Powell et al. (1996) may be seen as an application of the absorptive capacity argument (Cohen and Levinthal, 1990) with specific recognition of the role of relationships for learning. The heart of the argument is that prior relationships affect the subsequent network position, which leads to favorable outcomes, such as growth for the organization. Their empirical findings support this position. R&D

alliances appear central in their model, making the organizations that have them central, and allowing them to form other (non-R&D) ties. Those other ties further improve the organization's network position as they create experience managing network ties, and a diversity of resources that the firm is connected to through relationships. The centrality and network experience of the organization lead to its subsequent growth. These results are reinforced by a later study that indicated that start-up firms in Canadian biotechnology performed better if they were allied with other firms with strong capabilities for innovation (Baum et al., 2000). Dyer and Nobeoka (2000) provide further insight as to how network structures promote learning with their case study of the highly successful Toyota production network.

Contemporary Issues and Debates

LEARNING AND COMPETITION

With the recognition that interorganizational learning is a route to competitive advantage, attention is turning to models of the interplay between competition and learning. The effort here is to describe the relevance of interorganizational competition to interorganizational learning, and even more, to document the impact of learning on competitive outcomes. The relevance of competition to interorganizational learning stems from the view that similarity between organizations makes those organizations more intense competitors (Baum and Mezias, 1992). At the same time, similarity between organizations increases the opportunity for certain types of interorganizational learning. For example, Darr and Kurtzburg (2000) found, in a learning-curve study of English pizza stores, that interorganizational learning occurred only between stores that employed the same strategy. Henderson and Cockburn (1996) produced a related result – that spillovers between the research knowledge of pharmaceutical firms were within similar research programs. Other research has shown that spillovers in worldwide semiconductor production were only within families of related chip-designs (Irwin and Klenow, 1994). These findings suggest that organizations have the most to learn from their closest competitors (Ingram and Roberts, 2000).

Beyond its influence on who can learn from whom, competition also affects incentives to learn, and outcomes of learning. Two related areas of research, referred to as the Red Queen effect, and learning races, explore the dynamics between competition and learning.

RED QUEEN EFFECT

Competition creates a disincentive against interorganizational learning. Knowledge that transfers from the focal organization to its competitor can harm the focal organization – as the competitor gets stronger, the focal organization's relative standing worsens, as does its performance. This indirect negative effect of competitors' learning has been dubbed the "Red Queen effect" after the Red Queen's advice to Alice that in a world that changes rapidly, one must move quickly just to keep up. Barnett and Hanson (1996) apply a model based on the Red Queen to explain the failures of Illinois banks from 1900 to 1993. They begin with the view that when organizations face performance shortfalls on a particular dimension they search for solutions, and when performance is restored to an acceptable level, they suspend search (March, 1981; Nelson and Winter, 1982). They suggest a competitive dynamic that sees one firm's superior performance trigger a search for improvements by its rival. If improvements are found and the second firm's competitive position improves, the first firm will suffer in the face of its rival's renewed potency, and will begin its own search for improvements. They find support for their theory with results that indicates that the focal firm's own competitive experience (operationalized by years of contact with competitors) reduces its risk of failure, while its rivals' aggregate competitive experience increases its risk of failure. The first result captures the learning advantage of being pushed to improve by rivals, while the second result captures the competitive cost of facing rivals that have themselves improved.

Other evidence of the Red Queen comes from Ingram and Simons (1999). That study examined the implication of other organizations' operating experience on the profitability of kibbutz agriculture. It included all kibbutzim from 1954 to 1965. The analysis categorized others' experience as to whether the other was related (via co-membership in a formal organizational group) or unrelated to the focal organization. Following the logic outlined above that relationships facilitate learning, Ingram and Simons predicted that related experience would have a greater benefit to profitability than unrelated experience, which it did. Unrelated experience, in fact, decreased the profitability of the focal kibbutz. That is, the kibbutz became less profitable as those that competed with it but were not related to it accrued experience. The best explanation for this is that others' learning impacted negatively on the focal organization by increasing the level of competition.

LEARNING RACES

Learning races occur when there are winner-take-all implications of learning or innovation, for example, if there were very large first-mover effects, such that the introduction of a new product greatly damages the viability of others. Henderson and Cockburn (1996) examine such a situation when they introduce the idea of "exhaustion effects" into their study of spillovers in pharmaceutical research. Their idea is that innovations by one firm may dampen innovation by another, by exhausting the commercial potential for innovations of a certain kind. Henderson and Cockburn find that in the 1979–88 period, competitors' innovations in a given research program reduce the likelihood that the focal firm will have innovations in that program.

"Winner-take-all" learning situations also have fundamental implications for the dynamics of strategic alliances. Khanna et al. (1998) propose a theory that applies to all strategic alliances with interorganizational learning as a product. The theory rests on the distinction between public and private benefits of strategic alliances. Public benefits accrue to all members of the alliance, and only when each member has contributed sufficiently to realize them. Private benefits, by contrast, accrue to one partner, regardless of the benefits achieved by other partners (and may even be at the cost of other partners). Khanna et al. argue that private benefits create an incentive for participants in alliances to race to learning by contributing resources to achieve their own private benefits, and then stopping contributions before public benefits are achieved. This dynamic helps explain why dissatisfaction and perceptions of exploitation are sometimes the outcome of alliances formed to promote interorganizational learning; see also Baum et al. (2000).

INTERORGANIZATIONAL RELATIONSHIPS AND INTERORGANIZATIONAL LEARNING

Research such as Darr et al. (1995) recommends a privileged position for interorganizational relations, and current research is following up on this important topic. Key efforts are to determine the relative importance of relationships for learning, and the types of relationships that lead to learning.

RELATIVE IMPORTANCE OF RELATIONSHIPS

Work to date weighs heavily in favor of interorganizational learning through relationships as opposed to arm's-length learning. I am aware of only four learning-curve studies that categorize others' experience as to whether those others are related or unrelated to the focal organization (Darr et al., 1995; Baum and Ingram, 1998; Ingram and Simons, 1999; Darr and Kurtzburg, 2000). These studies examine different industries and a range of relationships, but all four yield the same key result: interorganizational learning occurs between related organizations, but not between those that are unrelated.

Consistent with the premise that relationships facilitate knowledge transfer, research on joint ventures has found that closer, more hierarchical arrangements between firms (such as joint equity investments) produces more knowledge transfer than arrangements that are closer to arm's length (such as contracts; Kogut, 1988; Mowery et al., 1996). Other studies appear to demonstrate interorganizational learning at arm's length (e.g., Irwin and Klenow, 1994; Henderson and Cockburn, 1996; Ingram and Baum, 1997a). But none of those studies differentiate between the experience of other organizations that are related or unrelated to the focal organization. By lumping all others' experience together, these studies may confound interorganizational learning through relationships with weak or non-existent interorganizational learning at arm's length.

TYPES OF INTERORGANIZATIONAL RELATIONSHIPS

Of course, all interorganizational relationships are not the same, and another stream of current research delineates the significance of various types of relationships. One of the most interesting topics here is the close interpersonal relationships that may develop between members of different organizations. Uzzi (1996, p. 678) argues that when interorganizational relationships are embedded in social relationships, information exchange is enhanced. Social relationships create trust, empathy, and reciprocity, which are necessary to transfer complex, or tacit, knowledge between organizations (Kogut and Zander, 1992). Evidence that interpersonal connections between managers leads to similar behavior by their firms comes from such diverse contexts as corporate philanthropy (Galaskiewicz and Wasserman, 1989) and the strategic behavior of large and small organizations (Geletkanycz and Hambrick, 1997; Ingram and Roberts, 2000).

Board interlocks are probably the most researched relationship for interorganizational learning. A board interlock exists between two organizations when a member of the board of directors of one is also on the board of the other. Presumably, that board member can access knowledge at one organization, and take it to the other. A number of studies have found that firms with board interlocks are more likely to exhibit similar behavior (Davis, 1991; Haunschild, 1993; Palmer et al., 1993).

Other contemporary research is examining what could be considered the dark side of relationships for interorganizational learning. Particularly when the relationship implies hierarchical authority, organizations may adopt the practices of relational-partners without full consideration of their appropriateness. Ingram and Baum (1997b) find this among Manhattan hotels, which benefit from the experience of their chains in Manhattan, but are actually harmed by the chain's experience outside of Manhattan, probably because of chain-wide standardization of practices that are inappropriate for Manhattan. Greve (1999) replicates this result in a study of the US radio broadcasting industry.

Mowery et al. (1996) also find a non-obvious implication of dissimilarity between partners in a learning relationship. They study joint ventures, and find that sometimes, the partners to a venture grow more dissimilar in terms of their knowledge. Instead of learning from each other, they appear to do the opposite, applying what Hamel (1991) called the substitution intent to pursue distinct knowledge resources. Mowery et al. explain that sometimes the partners to a joint venture co-specialize, relying on each other to provide necessary knowledge inputs to the joint venture, without actually transferring knowledge between the organizations.

Central Questions that Remain Unanswered

There is no doubt that the central question yet unanswered regarding interorganizational learning is "just how does it happen?" To be sure, there is much yet to be discovered about the structural conditions that facilitate interorganizational learning, and the organizational and competitive outcomes that result. But, the missing link is to relate R&D and experiential spillovers to specific mechanisms via which organizations tap into the knowledge available in their environments. Discovering this would have key implications for managing organizations. For example, managers might be advised as to which practices and structures will best position their organizations to remain on the frontier of valuable new knowledge in their industry.

Research into the mechanisms by which interorganizational learning occurs necessitates a balance between rich sources of data that accurately capture the day-to-day activities of interorganizational learners, and sensitivity to theory and past research so as to avoid the temptation to merely describe interorganizational learning efforts. Appleyard (1996) provides a good early example of the type of research that is needed. She theorizes that the use of specific interorganizational mechanisms will depend on characteristics of the industry and the broader institutional environment. For example, she uses a learning-race logic to argue that a fast-pace of technological change in an industry will discourage private knowledge sharing. She also compares the Japanese and US institutional systems with regard to knowledge, and hypothesizes that private knowledge sharing mechanisms will be less common in Japan due to a first-to-patent system of intellectual property, and weaker networks connecting scientists in different organizations. She finds support for these ideas in a survey of knowledge sharing activities of Japanese and US participants in the steel and integrated circuit industries.

One of Appleyard's core assertions, that the nature of competition in an industry affects the mechanisms of interorganizational learning, seems useful to explain a surprising feature of one of the industries I've studied in detail, the US hospitality industry. I was struck, after reading decades of trade journals of that industry, that hotel managers seemed very willing to reveal their trade secrets – it appeared to me that they felt compelled to trumpet every good idea they discovered in the most public sources. Why should this be so in a competitive industry, where good ideas adopted by rivals may hurt the originating organization through a Red-Queen mechanism? Perhaps it is because competition in the hospitality industry is localized, with hotels competing only with a few others that are physically close to them, and similar in level of luxury and other attributes (Baum and Mezias, 1992). Under these conditions, many of the beneficiaries of a hotel manager's journal article on, say, "banquet management," would be hotels that do not compete with the author. And even if the author's small set of competitors read the article and adopted its wisdom, the resulting Red-Queen penalty to the author might be offset by the rewards of admiration and professional standing administered by thousands of non-competitor readers.

Another exciting study that examines in detail the mechanisms of interorganizational learning is Rulke et al. (2000). This study advances beyond Appleyard (1996) by not only asking managers directly how they learn, but also relating their answers to measures of their organization's knowledge. Effectively, this puts a check on managers' perceptions, and allows insight into which managerial efforts yield useful interorganizational learning. The results are notable, particularly for their correspondence with other research that indicated the significance of interorganizational relationships to facilitate learning. The study relies on a survey of the managers of chain-grocery stores. The survey included measures of each manager's organization's knowledge, as well as the manager's perception of the importance of various learning channels. The learning channels were internal and external, with the external being most relevant here. The external-relational channel included attendance at conference presentations, communication with manufacturers and wholesalers, and personal contacts at competing firms. The external non-relational channel included arm's-length mechanisms such as trade journals and trade-association newsletters. The results indicate that the relational channel improved the organization's knowledge, but the non-relational channel did not.

Almeida and Kogut (1999) evidence another important mechanism for interorganizational learning in the form of employees who move from one organization to another, carrying knowledge in their heads or briefcases. Almeida and Kogut use this idea to explain the very important differences between the research productivity of geographic regions in the US semiconductor industry. They claim that part of the reason that more innovations occur in Silicon Valley than, say, Arizona, is the pattern of intra-regional mobility. For every 100 researcher-years, the Arizona semiconductor industry experiences 0.55 intra-regional moves (from one firm in the Arizona semiconductor industry to another). The comparable figure for the Silicon Valley semiconductor industry experiences is 10.13 intra-regional moves. That is to say, moves from one semiconductor firm to another in the same region are about twenty times as likely in Silicon Valley as they are in Arizona (by contrast, inter-regional moves are equally likely for the two regions). In fact, such moves are more than twice as likely in Silicon Valley than in any other region in the country. Almeida and Kogut argue that this pattern of researcher mobility creates a pattern of knowledge sharing that greatly enhances innovation. For example, an engineer that moves to a new firm can combine her new employer's knowledge with that of her old firm. This combination is possible because social networks persist after job changes – in Silicon Valley, the engineer may still carpool with her old colleagues (Saxenian, 1994). Almeida and Kogut show that the level of intra-regional mobility is an important predictor of the number of important semicon-ductor patents in a region.

New and Emerging Directions for Future Research that Appear Promising

Interorganizational learning is a relatively new field of study, so almost all of the work reviewed here could be considered new and emerging. I call attention to two additional topics in the field that are likely to produce interesting and useful results. The first is the expansion of the category of experiences that are understood to be the source of interorganizational learning. The second is to explicitly incorporate uncertainty into theories of interorganizational learning.

TYPES OF EXPERIENCE

In the learning-curve literature, experience is most often taken as operating experience. Similar treatment has occurred in the subset of learning-curve studies that examine interorganizational learning (Argote et al., 1990; Irwin and Klenow, 1994; Darr et al., 1995; Baum and Ingram, 1998; Ingram and Simons, 1999). However, operating experience is not the only source of learning or interorganizational learning, just as operations is not the only skill that contributes significantly to organizational performance. A number of other forms of experience have been studied less frequently, such as collaborative experience (Simonin and Helleloid, 1993; Powell et al., 1996) and foreign-entry experience (Barkema et al., 1996). Recent studies have explored the impact of sources of experience that have been previously overlooked, such as organizational failure (Ingram and Baum, 1997a; Kim, 1999; Miner et al., 1999).

The possibility of further delineating the types of experience that lead to interorganizational learning presents great opportunities for scholarship and management practice. No doubt there are virgin avenues for learning to be discovered. Every organizational activity, whether good or bad, is a potential source of experience, and therefore, interorganizational learning. Research on these other types of experience, however, is not just a matter of making new recognitions as to what it is that organizations accumulate experience on. For starters, research on different types of experience will only flourish when the paucity of knowledge on mechanisms for interorganizational learning is redressed. Until we know how experience is transferred, we will be limited in efforts to discover what experience is transferred and when, because there are interdependencies between types of experience and the mechanisms of transfer. For example, legally-sensitive experience such as dealing with racial discrimination charges will probably only transfer through close, face-to-face relationships. The experience of a failed organization may be particularly likely to diffuse through employee mobility as participants in the failure go to new jobs. I suspect that as the mechanisms of transfer are more fully described, new types of experiential learning will be discovered simply by asking, "what could pass through this mechanism?"

Empirical work on other types of experience will require careful attention to operationalization. The approach so far has been to follow the common practice for measuring operating experience and simply count occurrences of the experience-generating event (joint-ventures participated in, organizational failures observed, foreign-direct investments made, etc.). This approach has been taken because of convenience. Guidance as to how to properly operationalize other types of experience will have to come from new theory. The traditional learning curve, with its operating experience, rests on an old and robust psychological theory of reinforcement learning through repetition (Thorndike, 1906). It should not be automatically assumed that learning from very different types of experience works the same way. Critical questions are "what is salient about the experience?" and "what is the pattern of reinforcement for learning?" Essentially, the cognitive processes that link experience to learning must be theorized. For example, is it only extreme outcomes, or perhaps the heterogeneity of a given type of experience, that leads to learning (Haunschild and Miner, 1997; Haunschild and Beckman, 1999)?

Uncertainty

The idea that uncertainty affects organizational learning has been seminal (Cyert and March, 1963). It is also an idea that cuts across the disciplines, particularly economics and sociology, which contributes to the study of interorganizational learning. The branch of information economics known as herd theory offers formal models that indicate that, under uncertainty, it may be optimal to mimic others (Scharfstein and Stein, 1990; Banerjee, 1992; Bala and Goyal, 1998). These models rest on the premise that as long as there is some chance that others have better information than the focal decision maker, it may be rational to do what those others do. This dynamic creates herd behavior, where many decision makers converge on the same decision. Empirical evidence does indicate that interorganizational mimicry is greater under conditions of uncertainty (Haunschild and Miner, 1997). Another intriguing stream of empirical research demonstrates an enhanced significance of interorganizational endorsements (a sign of quality) under uncertainty (Stuart et al., 1999).

A challenge to moving research on learning under uncertainty forward is the definition and operationalization of uncertainty. The studies cited above had to do with valuations of companies and could rely on financial measures and estimates to operationalize uncertainty. In many other learning circumstances there are no accessible measures for uncertainty. How for example can a receiver firm be certain that a practice employed by a sender firm is worth implementing? There may be some indications of the efficacy of the practice, but such indications are seldom definitive, and even so, there is the question of whether the practice will work in the second firm. Again, the first step is theory to define risk and link it to learning. And again, the starting point is cognition, although what we know already suggests that this task will be difficult.

While uncertainty presents empirical and theoretical challenges, it also presents opportunities. One of the most exciting concerns the apparent cultural differences in risk and risk taking (Weber et al., 1998). If members of different cultures perceive and respond to risk differently, it may be that uncertainty differentially affects interorganizational learning in different countries. The intersection of risk, uncertainty and culture suggests traps that managers should be aware of, and the possibility to affect interorganizational learning by changing the demographics of the firm.

Linkages to Other Levels

The connections between the topic of interorganizational learning, and learning at the sub-organizational and organizational levels are strong. The research presented in the chapters by Argote and Ophir, and Schulz forms the micro-theory that is necessary to understand interorganizational learning.

The members–tools–tasks framework presented in the Argote and Ophir chapter is very useful for answering one of the most pressing questions for those who attempt interorganizational learning: Will knowledge from one organization effectively transfer to another? That framework recognizes the basic elements of organizations as members, tools and tasks, and characterizes knowledge as residing in those elements, and in the networks between them. This perspective helps the analyst to better understand the implications of transferring something that contains knowledge from one organization to another. For example, consider an attempt to transfer knowledge between organizations by moving an apparently knowledgeable employee from one organization to the other. This type of action takes place all the time, as when a firm hires a key engineer away from a competitor. The members-tools-tasks framework indicates that a first test as to whether such a transfer will be successful is whether the new member fits with the members, tools and tasks in the new organization. That congruence is a first requirement for organizational effectiveness. But even more problematic for the transfer of knowledge are issues surrounding the networks in which knowledge may be embedded. It is possible that the member's knowledge at the original organization was not completely contained in the member, but rather embedded in the member-tool, member-member, or member-task networks. For example, perhaps the member relied on knowledge of who in the original organization knew what (contained in the member-member network) or who did what tasks (member-task network). Knowledge embedded in the networks between organizational elements will be much more difficult to transfer – it will not be enough simply to move an element (member, task or tool) from one organization to another.

Another contribution of Argote and Ophir's discussion of intraorganizational learning and the interorganizational level concerns the possibility that processes of knowledge storage and transfer in groups of individuals have analogs in groups of organizations. Here I am thinking specifically of the concept of transactive memory. As Argote and Ophir explain, this is the knowledge of who in a group knows what and can do what. Groups with better transactive memories perform better on various group tasks. It seems possible that groups of organizations might also have transactive memories. At the level of the organizational group, transactive memory would be an awareness of the capabilities of organizations in the group. Such awareness could promote group performance by smoothing transactions between organizations in the group. It would seem to be necessary for the effective functioning of "network organizations" that form systems of flexible production (Lazerson, 1995).

Similarly, the processes of organizational learning described by Schulz surely operate at the interorganizational level. A legitimate starting position is the hypothesis that aspirations, performance and feedback work similarly to condition interorganizational learning as they do organizational learning. More refined theory could be developed to predict when organizations will look to other organizations experience instead of their own, and how the two types of experience may evoke different responses from organizations. It is also true that one of Shulz's key points, that experience does not always produce positive results for organizations, is clearly demonstrated at the interorganizational level. My own preference is to avoid calling both good and bad results of experience "learning." My fear is that employing that labeling, as Schulz and many others do, will eventually result in an erosion of the term learning, as it will apply to too many things (almost all instances of interdependence between organizations are somehow dependent on experience and therefore subject to the loose application of "learning"). Labeling issues aside, there are many instances where interorganizational transfer of experience produces negative results. The Red Queen effect is a prime example I have already discussed. In many other instances, experience may be applied to organizations where it is inappropriate (Ingram and Baum, 1997b; Greve, 1999).

Conclusion

Interorganizational learning sometimes seems like a boon to organizational performance. It seems to promise the best of both worlds – the benefit of accumulating knowledge without the cost of accumulating experience. In this chapter I have organized the literature on interorganizational learning as to dealing with experiential or innovative learning, and focusing on characteristics of the sender or receiver of knowledge, or on the relationship between them. Beyond simply organizing the literature, I have argued that interorganizational learning is not as easy, or as riskless, as it is generally portrayed to be. Risks come from the fact that interorganizational learning is often a race between competitors, and organizations may lose relative ground even as they learn. Another risk is that others' experience will be misapplied, causing organizations to adopt practices that are not appropriate for their specific conditions. The difficulty of interorganizational learning is such that close relationships between senders and receivers of knowledge are necessary for effective transfers to occur – there is little in the way of cheap and easy learning from arm's-length others. And finally, there are severe problems associated with the fact that we know little about the actual organizational practices that result in interorganizational learning. This last shortcoming is the most pressing in the literature, and presents a substantial barrier to generating scholarly advice that can be expected to improve organizational practice.

References

Almeida, P., and Kogut, B. (1999): "Localization of knowledge and the mobility of engineers in regional networks," *Management Science*, 45, 905–17.
Appleyard, M. (1996): "How does knowledge flow? Interfirm patterns in the semiconductor industry," *Strategic Management Journal*, 17, (Winter special issue), 137–54.
Argote, L. (1999): *Organizational Learning: Creating, Retaining and Transferring Knowledge*. Boston: Kluwer.
Argote, L., Beckman, S. L., and Epple, D. (1990): "The persistence and transfer of learning in industrial settings," *Management Science*, 36, 140–54.
Bala, V., and Goyal, S. (1998): "Learning from neighbors," *Review of Economic Studies*, 65, 595–621.
Banerjee, A. V. (1992):"A simple model of herd behavior," *Quarterly Journal of Economics*, 107,

797–817.

Barkema, H. G., and Vermuelen, F. (1998): "International expansion through start-up or acquisition: A learning perspective," *Academy of Management Journal*, 41, 7–26.

Barkema, H. G., Bell, J. H. J., and Pennings, J. M. (1996): "Foreign entry, cultural barriers, and learning," *Strategic Management Journal*, 17, 151–66.

Barnett, W. P., and Hansen, M. T. (1996): "The Red Queen in organizational evolution," *Strategic Management Journal*, 17, (Summer special issue), 139–57.

Baum, J. A. C., and Ingram, P. (1998): "Survival-enhancing learning in the Manhattan hotel industry, 1898-1980," *Management Science*, 44, 996–1016.

Baum, J. A. C., and Mezias, S. (1992): "Localized competition and organizational failure in the Manhattan hotel industry, 1898-1990," *Administrative Science Quarterly*, 37, 580–604.

Baum, J. A. C., Calabrese, T., and Silverman, B. S. (2000): "Don't go it alone: Alliance networks and startups' performance in Canadian biotechnology, 1991–97," *Strategic Management Journal*, 21, 267–94.

Burns, L., and Wholey, D. (1993): "Adoption and abandonment of matrix management programs: Effects of organizational characteristics and interorganizational networks," *Academy of Management Journal*, 36, 106–38.

Cohen, W. M., and Levinthal, D. A. (1990): "Absorptive capacity: A new perspective on learning and innovation," *Administrative Science Quarterly*, 35, 128–52.

Cyert, R. M., and March, J. G. (1963): *A Behavioral Theory of the Firm*. Englewood Cliffs, NJ: Prentice-Hall.

Darr, E., and Kurtzburg, T. (2000): "Selecting knowledge transfer partners: An investigation of strategic similarity and difference," *Organizational Behavior and Human Decision Processes*, 64, 28–44.

Darr, E., Argote, L., and Epple, D. (1995): "The acquisition, transfer and depreciation of knowledge in service organizations: Productivity in franchises," *Management Science*, 41, 147–60.

Davis, G.F. (1991): "Agents without principles? The spread of the poison pill through the intercorporate network," *Administrative Science Quarterly*, 36, 583–613.

Dyer, J. H., and Nobeoka, K. (2000): "Creating and managing a high-performance knowledge-sharing network: The Toyota case," *Strategic Management Journal*, 21, 345–67.

Galaskiewicz, J., and Wasserman, S. (1989): "Mimetic processes within an interorganizational field: An empirical test," *Administrative Science Quarterly*, 34, 454–79.

Geletkanycz, M. A., and Hambrick, D. C. (1997): "The external ties of top executives: Implications for strategic choice and performance," *Administrative Science Quarterly*, 42, 654–81.

Greve, H. R. (1999): "Branch systems and nonlocal learning in organizational populations," *Advances in Strategic Management*, 16, 57–80.

Gupta, A. K., and Govindarajan, V. (2000): "Knowledge flows within multinational corporations," *Strategic Management Journal*, 21, 473–96.

Hamel, G. (1991): "Competition for competence and interpartner learning within international strategic alliances," *Strategic Management Journal*, 12, 83–103

Haunschild, P. R. (1993): "Interorganizational imitation: The impact of interlocks on corporate acquisition activity," *Administrative Science Quarterly*, 38, 564–92.

Haunschild, P. R., and Beckman, C. M. (1999): "Learning through networks: Effects of partner experience on acquisition premiums," paper presented at the Annual Meetings of the Academy of Management, Chicago, August.

Haunschild, P. R., and Miner, A. S. (1997): "Modes of interorganizational imitation: The effects of outcome salience and uncertainty," *Administrative Science Quarterly*, 42, 472–500.

Haveman, H. A. (1993): "Follow the leader: Mimetic isomorphism and entry into new markets," *Administrative Science Quarterly*, 38, 593–627.

Henderson, R., and Cockburn, I. (1996): "Scale, scope and spillovers: The determinants of research productivity in drug discovery," *The Rand Journal of Economics*, 27, 32–59.

Ingram, P., and Baum, J. A. C. (1997a): "Opportunity and constraint: Organizations' learning from the operating and competitive experience of industries," *Strategic Management Journal*, 18, (Summer Special edition), 75–98.

Ingram, P., and Baum, J. A. C. (1997b): "Chain affiliation and the failure of Manhattan hotels, 1898–1980," *Administrative Science Quarterly*, 42, 68–102.

Ingram, P., and Roberts, P. R. (2000): "Friendships among competitors in the Sydney hotel industry," *American Journal of Sociology*, 106, 387–423.

Ingram, P., and Simons, T. (1999): "The exchange of experience in a moral economy: Thick ties and vicarious learning in kibbutz agriculture," in S. J. Havlovic (ed.), *Best Paper Proceedings*, Chicago IL: Academy of Management, OMT E1–E6.

Irwin, D. A., and Klenow, P. J. (1994): "Learning-by-doing spillovers in the semiconductor industry," *Journal of Political Economy*, 102, 1200–27.

Khanna, T., Gulati, R., and Nohria, N. (1998): "The dynamics of learning alliances: Competition, cooperation and relative scope," *Strategic Management Journal*, 19, 193–210.

Kim, J. Y. (1999): "Crash test without dummies: Interorganizational learning from failure experience in the U.S. commercial banking industry, 1894–1998," working paper, University of Wisconsin at Madison.

Kogut, B. (1988): "Joint ventures: Theoretical and empirical perspectives," *Strategic Management Journal*, 9, 319–32.

Kogut, B., and Zander, U. (1992): "Knowledge of the firm, combinative capabilities, and the replication of technology," *Organization Science*, 3, 383–97.

Kraatz, M. S. (1997): "Learning by association? Interorganizational networks and adaptation to environmental change," *Academy of Management Journal*, 41, 621–43.

Lazerson, M. (1995): "A new phoenix: Modern putting-out in the Modena knitwear industry," *Administrative Science Quarterly*, 40, 34–59.

Liebeskind, J. P., Oliver, A. L., Zucker L., and Brewer, M. (1996): "Social networks, learning, and flexibility: Sourcing scientific knowledge in new biotechnology firms," *Organization Science*, 7, 428–43.

March, J. G. (1981): "Footnotes to organizational change," *Administrative Science Quarterly*, 26, 563–77.

March, J. G. (1991): "Exploration and exploitation in organizational learning," *Organization Science*, 2, 71–81.

Merton, R. K. (1968): "The Matthew effect in science," *Science*, 159, 56–63.

Miner, A. S., Kim, J. Y., Holzinger, I. W., and Haunschild, P. R. (1999): "Fruits of failure: Organizational failure and population-level learning," *Advances in Strategic Management*, 16, 187–220.

Mowery, D. C., Oxley, J. E. and Silverman, B. S. (1996): "Strategic alliances and knowledge transfer," *Strategic Management Journal*, 17, (Winter special issue), 77–91.

Nelson, R. R., and Winter, S. G. (1982): *An Evolutionary Theory of Economic Change*. Cambridge, MA: Harvard University Press.

Palmer, D. A., Jennings, D., and Zhou, X. (1993): "Late adoption of the multidivisional form by large U.S. corporations: Institutional, political and economic accounts," *Administrative Science Quarterly*, 38, 100–31.

Podolny, J. M., and Stuart, T. E. (1995): "A role-based ecology of technological change," *American Journal of Sociology*, 100, 1224–60.

Powell, W. W., Koput, K. W., and Smith-Doerr, L. (1996): "Interorganizational collaboration and the locus of innovation: Networks of learning in biotechnology," *Administrative Science Quarterly*, 41, 116–45.

Rowley, T. J., Behrens, D., and Krackhardt, D. (2000): "Redundant governance structures: An analysis of structural and relational embeddedness in steel and semiconductor industries," *Strategic Management Journal*, 21, 369–86.

Rulke, D. L., Zaheer, S., and Anderson, M. H. (2000): "Sources of managers' knowledge of organizational capabilities," *Organizational Behavior and Human Decision Processes*, 64, 134–49.

Saxenian, A. (1994): *Regional Advantage*. Cambridge, MA: Harvard University Press.

Scharfstein, D., and Stein, J. (1990): "Herd behavior and investment," *American Economic Review*, 80, 465–79.

Simonin, B. L., and Helleloid, D. (1993): "Do organizations learn? An empirical test of organizational learning in international strategic alliances," in D. Moore (ed.), *Best Paper Proceedings*, Madison, WI: Academy of Management, 222–6.

Stuart, T. E., Hoang, H., and Hybels, R. C. (1999): "Interorganizational endorsements and the performance of entrepreneurial ventures," *Administrative Science Quarterly*, 44, 315–49.

Thorndike, E. L. (1906): *Principles of Teaching*. New York: A. G. Seiler.

Uzzi, B. (1996): "The sources and consequences of embeddedness for the economic performance of organizations: The network effect," *American Sociological Review*, 61, 674–98.

Weber, E. U., Hsee, C. K., and Sokolowski, J. (1998): "What folklore tells us about risk and risk taking: Cross-cultural comparisons of American, German, and Chinese proverbs," *Organizational Behavior and Human Decision Processes*, 75, 165–70.

Yelle, L. E. (1979): "The learning curve: Historical review and comprehensive survey," *Decision Sciences*, 10, 302–38.

Chapter Twenty-nine

Interorganizational Complexity and Computation

Olav Sorenson

In order to be able to understand the great complexity of life and to understand what the universe is doing, the first word to learn is synergy.

R. Buckminster Fuller

Complexity 'theory' refers to a closely related set of ideas and approaches for understanding the effects of intermediate levels of interdependence between components in a dynamic system. One might usefully question what 'interdependence' means in this context. Thompson (1967) divides interdependence into three categories. Pooled interdependence links independent entities. A Chamber of Commerce, for example, might provide this function. Sequential interdependence refers to a serial relationship between two components. If firm *A* affects *B*'s output, but not vice versa, we would say that the pair exhibit sequential interdependence, such as what one might find between a buyer and its supplier. Finally, reciprocal interdependence covers cases where firm *A* affects *B*'s output and *B* affects *A*'s output. Complexity primarily focuses on the behavior generated by this last type: reciprocal interdependence. Because this type of interdependence often generates models that stymie mathematical analysis, researchers rely on computational methods (i.e., computer simulation) to understand the theoretical implications of a set of assumptions. However, computational models do not necessarily imply complexity, and researchers can use complexity concepts without resorting to simulation.

Interdependence across firms drives the interest in complexity and computational approaches at the interorganizational level. In this sense, complexity and computation follow an established sociological tradition in the study of organizations. Whereas classical economics typically treats firms as operating without regard for the actions of other individual firms, sociological approaches to organizations consider these interactions explicitly (Granovetter, 1985). Indeed, all open systems approaches to organizations (Scott 1998, pp. 82–100) deal explicitly with interdependencies between firms, whether with buyers and suppliers (Pfeffer and Salancik, 1978), with institutional actors (Meyer and Rowan, 1977) or with rivals (Hannan and Freeman, 1977). Following this tradition, the ideas and models that underlie complexity and computational approaches share a focus on the interactions between firms.

Complexity and computation move beyond traditional open systems theories, however, by combining an explicit consideration of the interactions between organizations with a dynamic perspective. Although a variety of organizational theories recognize that organizations change over time and that they interact with the environment, the difficulty of analyzing these dynamic systems has limited their systematic study. Dynamic systems can generate three types of behavior: orderly, chaotic and random. Orderly systems repeat the same behavior or cycle of behaviors with complete predictability, whereas random systems exhibit no behavioral patterns over time. Chaotic systems, or complex systems, also repeat behaviors, but in an unpredictable fashion, making them particularly difficult to analyze. Recent advances in computing now make it possible to study these chaotic dynamic interactions through simulation. Since these dynamic systems generate orderly system-level behavior that observers find difficult to anticipate from the rules governing the systems' individual components – in this case the firms – some classify models as belonging to complexity if they exhibit such emergent properties; Anderson (1999) and Lichtenstein (2001) develop good reviews from this perspective.

Despite the clear fit with existing open systems perspectives, inter-organizational level research in complexity and computation remains sparse. Interest in organizational applications of complexity theory and computational methods has spawned several research centers, at least two new journals (*Computational and Mathematical Organization Theory* and *Emergence*), multiple special issues of existing journals (*Organization Science*, 10(3); *Journal of Business and Entrepreneurship*, 11, special issue; Research Policy, 29 (7–8) and numerous books, e.g., Eve et al. (1997) and Axelrod and Cohen (2000). Even with this recent flurry of research and interest in the application of complexity theory and computational methods to organizations, relatively little of this work addresses issues at the inter-organizational level of analysis. The paucity of work at this level of analysis should surprise us because these perspectives offer useful tools for considering seriously interactions between firms.

Literature Review

Research on interorganizational complexity and computation addresses a wide variety of issues with a relatively small set of models (Table 29.1). The fact that a small set of models can address an extended range of organizational problems suggests that some common fundamental properties may underlie these issues. Since two models in particular show broad applicability – cellular automata and NK models – I will organize my review around them. Nonetheless, I will also cover other approaches at the end of this section.

Table 29.1 Selected interorganizational complexity and computational studies

Reference	Key concepts	Key variables	Key predictions and findings	Key contribution	Method and sample
Lomi and Larsen, 1996	Micro-level interactions between firms generate macro-level population dynamics.	Neighborhood radius (inter-firm interdependence) Solitude (legitimation) Suffocation (competition)	Firms spread as the range of interaction increases. Legitimation leads to clustering in space.	Demonstrates the application of cellular automata to the evolution of industries	2-dimensional cellular automata (simulation)
Levinthal, 1997	Interdependence within organizations in a population affects the nature of industry evolution.	K = interdependence internal to firms	Interdependence can allow multiple organizational forms to co-exist. Interdependent firms cannot adapt to change in the environment.	Illustrates a direct application of the NK-model	NK-model (simulation)
Rivkin, 2000	Strategic complexity provides a barrier to imitation.	N = number of firm policies K = degree of interdependence between those policies in determining firm performance	With even a small degree of error in imitation, moderate levels of complexity prevent successful imitation.	Shows the potential for moving beyond the basic NK-model to more realistic search behaviors	Modified NK-model (simulation)
Carroll and Harrison, 1994	Competition does not necessarily select the most efficient organizational form.	Likelihood that a decision by an organization will be imitated by others Organization traits such as size and profitability History of past decision outcomes	Large, profitable organizations are more likely to be imitated by others. Extreme outcomes are more likely to encourage (if positive) or discourage (if negative) imitation than are less extreme outcomes.	Illustrates the use of a simulation outside the cellular automata or NK framework	Simulated differential equation system

David, 1992	Individual actors can influence the path of history at key moments.		Shows that qualitative accounts can also rigorously apply complexity concepts	Historical examination of the competition between AC and DC electricity standards
Sorenson, 1997, 2003	Vertical integration limits organizational adaptability. Environmental volatility limits the returns to adapting.	K = vertical integration (internal interdependence) Environmental volatility (measured as autocorrelation in products and technologies)	Over time, vertically integrated firms will perform progressively worse vs. less-integrated rivals. Environmental volatility mitigates this disadvantage.	Demonstrates moving from a model to hypotheses on to empirical corroboration	NK-model Hazard models of the likelihood of market exit and growth rate models of sales in the computer workstation industry, 1980–96

CELLULAR AUTOMATA

The primary strength of cellular automata models is in the structured nature of interactions between firms. Each organization interacts with other organizations that lie in close proximity to it. Empirical research verifies that firms compete locally on a variety of dimensions including: geographic location (Carroll and Wade, 1991; Sorenson and Audia, 2000), size (Baum and Mezias, 1992; Ranger-Moore et al., 1995), product strategy (Sorenson, 2000), factor markets (Sørensen, 1999) and technological position (Podolny et al., 1996). Thus, it seems reasonable to assume that most of the interdependence between firms occurs among neighbors on these and other dimensions. By examining these localized interactions with cellular automata, organizational researchers can hopefully learn more about how organizational dynamics unfold in space. Though much of the use of cellular automata in the social sciences focuses on individual-level behavior and interactions, researchers have applied cellular automata at the interorganizational level to investigate pricing behavior (Keenan and O'Brian, 1993), the geographic distribution of firms (Lomi and Larsen 1996), strategic imitation and profitability (Larsen and Markides, 1997), the evolution of strategy (Lomi and Larsen, 1997), density delay (Lomi and Larsen, 1998) and the relationship between firm age and performance (Lomi and Larsen, 2001).

Allesandro Lomi and Erik Reimer Larsen, two European researchers, offer the best example of the use of cellular automata to study organizational interactions. Although cellular automata can take a variety of shapes and sizes, Lomi and Larsen use a two-dimensional variant partitioned into squares. Imagine a chessboard with dozens of squares on each side. Each square represents a potential niche that a single organization can occupy. Figure 29.1 illustrates such a two-dimensional world with 25 potential niches and 7 firms (the shaded squares). Interdependence enters the model through organizations interacting with their neighbors. When an organization resides in a particular square, it interrelates with the other firms in its neighborhood – the adjacent positions within some radius. For example, if the neighborhood radius equals one, then each organization interacts with the eight squares surrounding the one in which it resides (equivalent to the potential moves for a king in chess). Increasing the radius to two units expands the neighborhood to include 24 squares, and so forth.

A simple set of rules governs the dynamics of this simulated population. To understand these rules, let us examine the dynamics of one round using figure 29.1, assuming a neighborhood radius of one. Initially, Lomi and Larsen seed the space with randomly placed firms. In each subsequent period, two forces determine the birth and death of firms. Drawing on the idea of legitimation from organizational ecology, firms need neighbors because they cooperate to some degree by sharing common suppliers, employee training costs and the task of convincing others of the value of their activities (Hannan and Freeman, 1977). When too few firms occupy the neighboring squares, the firm dies of solitude. If firms in our example need at least two neighbors to avoid death by solitude, the firm occupying niche 1 will die in this round because only one firm (at square 3) sits adjacent to it. On the other hand, organizations in the same population compete with each other for vital resources. When too many organizations encircle the niche, it expires from suffocation – or insufficient resources. If firms can have no more than four neighbors before resources become too scarce to support them all, then the

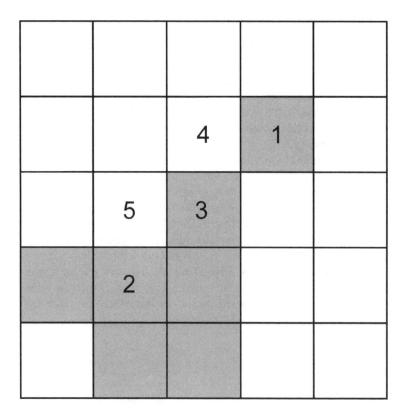

Figure 29.1 2-dimensional cellular automata

firm in niche 2 will die of suffocation because it has five neighbors. Lomi and Larsen refer to the range between these two limits as the "survival band" – the firm in niche 3, for example, lies in this range and hence will continue into the next round. Assuming a delicate balance between cooperation and competition, Lomi and Larsen only allow firms to enter an unoccupied niche when a specific number, and only that quantity, of neighbors surround it. For example, if an unoccupied niche needed two adjacent firms to generate a birth, then a new firm will appear in niche 4, but not in niche 5 (because too many existing firms neighbor it). These simple rules generate complex simulated dynamics that mimic the behavior of real organizational populations.

Using this simulation, Lomi and Larsen examine a variety of organizational issues. One interesting result that they find pertains to the distribution of firms in the space (Lomi and Larsen, 1996). Specifically, their simulations demonstrate that the degree of spatial differentiation increases as the radius of the neighborhood expands; as firms interact with more distant rivals, those that survive end up further and further apart. This finding suggests that one might expect industries to diffuse geographically as they mature. If space represents dimensions of product characteristics, as one commonly sees in marketing and economics, the results imply that firms within industries likely spread into distinct product niches over time. Lomi and Larsen also find that increases in the legitimation effect – the minimum number of neighbors necessary for survival – amplify the degree to which the population clusters, as opposed to spreading evenly across the grid.

Another recent paper investigates how differences in the dynamics of organizational populations, in turn, affect organizational events. Much as Durkheim (1952 [1897]) viewed suicide as an indicator of societal cohesion rather than an individual trait, Lomi and Larsen (2001) argue that the relationship between mortality rates and organizational age may arise from the structure of the industry. Following Stinchcombe (1965), most organizational theory argues that firms change as they mature. Because these changes affect organizational functions, these theories posit a relationship between firm age and performance (Hannan, 1998). Lomi and Larsen suggest, instead, that changes in performance as organizations mature may arise from the local structure of organizational relations. In particular, they can generate increasing mortality rates with age by changing either of two parameters in their models. First, when the minimum number of neighbors that firms need to survive increases, failure rates become increasingly positive with organizational age. Second, as the radius of the neighborhood expands, age dependence becomes more and more positive. Thus, as industries become ever more global, one might expect old firms to become increasingly disadvantaged relative to their younger rivals. Both parameters appear to intensify the degree to which failures ripple through the population causing cascades of failure.

NK MODELS

Stuart Kauffman, a medical doctor associated with the Santa Fe Institute, developed the *NK*-model to simulate the evolution of biological systems. His work provides a method for using fitness landscapes to model evolution. Fitness landscapes conceptualize evolution as a process of searching for higher elevations on a terrain, like trying to navigate one's way up a mountain range. Higher points on the landscape correspond to superior fitness levels. Wright (1931, 1932) first introduced fitness landscapes as a conceptual tool, but Kauffman dramatically increased the usefulness of this heuristic device by formulating the *NK*-model to link interdependence to the topography of these landscapes. His book, *The Origins of Order* (1993), describes the *NK*-model in detail and shows its applicability to and implications for a variety of biological problems.

The *NK* model generates fitness landscapes by varying two parameters: N and K. Figures 29.2 and 29.3 illustrate the construction of these landscapes. N represents the number of components comprising a system. For simplicity, Kauffman considers these components to take one of two possible values, 0 or 1, thereby using a binary string to represent the characteristics of an organism. K represents the degree of interdependence in the system. Specifically, K denotes the number of these components that jointly determine the value of each component's contribution to the system's overall fitness (epistatic interactions in the genetic context). Kauffman generates these contributions by taking different draws from a unit [0,1] uniform distribution depending on both the value of the focal element and the values of the K elements with which it interacts. The fitness of the system overall comes from averaging the contributions of each of these components. Therefore, the impact of changing one element increases as K rises.

Consider the extremes. When $K = 0$, each component independently determines a

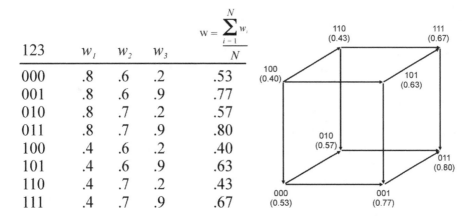

123	w_1	w_2	w_3	$W = \dfrac{\sum\limits_{i=1}^{N} w_i}{N}$
000	.8	.6	.2	.53
001	.8	.6	.9	.77
010	.8	.7	.2	.57
011	.8	.7	.9	.80
100	.4	.6	.2	.40
101	.4	.6	.9	.63
110	.4	.7	.2	.43
111	.4	.7	.9	.67

Figure 29.2 Landscape without interdependence ($N = 3$, $K = 0$)

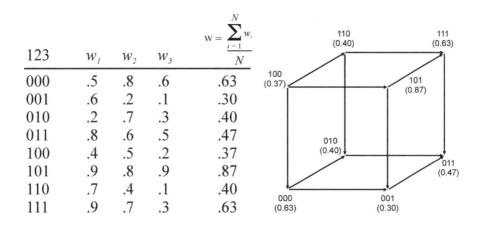

123	w_1	w_2	w_3	$W = \dfrac{\sum\limits_{i=1}^{N} w_i}{N}$
000	.5	.8	.6	.63
001	.6	.2	.1	.30
010	.2	.7	.3	.40
011	.8	.6	.5	.47
100	.4	.5	.2	.37
101	.9	.8	.9	.87
110	.7	.4	.1	.40
111	.9	.7	.3	.63

Figure 29.3 Landscape with maximal interdependence ($N = 3$, $K = 2$)

small fraction ($1/N$) of the system's fitness. In figure 29.2, each component contributes an independent value to the overall fitness. For example, component 2 adds 0.6 when it takes a value of 0 and 0.7 when it takes a value of 1. Averaged with components 1 and 3, the fitness of this system when all these components take a value of zero is 0.53 ($=[0.8 + 0.6 + 0.2]/3$). As we can see by moving from one vertex to the next on the adjacent cube, values change gradually on these landscapes.

At the upper limit, when $K = N - 1$, each component's contribution depends on the level of every other element. Thus, the amount that component 2 adds to the fitness changes depending on the values of the other two components (see figure 29.3). Also, the values of those components change with the value of component 2. At this extreme, changing one part of the system can completely alter the system's overall fitness. Consequently, fitness shifts abruptly between adjacent vertices in figure 29.3.

To model evolution, Kauffman combines these landscapes with a search process. Agents improve their fitness levels by incrementally moving up hills – representing regions of higher fitness – on the landscape. At each step, the agent samples the neighboring positions on the landscapes (i.e., those that would require a change in the value of only one of the system's N components). If one of those positions offers a higher fitness level than it currently has, the agent moves to that position by changing one of its elements. The arrows in figures 29.2 and 29.3 show potential moves from each point. When the agent reaches a peak – a point surrounded only by positions with lower fitness levels – search stops. Like a hiker climbing in a dense fog, these searchers can only see the portion of the landscape that immediately surrounds their current position. Thus, they do not know whether they found the only peak or whether an even higher mountain lies just past an adjacent valley. When $K = 0$, the landscape only contains one peak and any incremental walk will find it (e.g., 011 in figure 29.2). However, as the degree of interdependence, K, intensifies, the number of peaks multiplies and the likelihood that a searcher will get stuck on a sub-optimal peak rises. For example, in figure 29.3, a local searcher could get stranded at the coordinates 000, even though 101 corresponds to the highest fitness level.

The NK model offers researchers several advantages. First, social scientists appear to find it easier to translate this model into an organizational setting than many other models imported from the physical and biological sciences. Second, the model allows us to see quite clearly the relationship between interdependence and processes of interest. Third, in addition to the copious investigations of Kauffman and his colleagues (Kauffman and Levin, 1987; Kauffman, 1993), a number of other researchers have contributed to our understanding of the properties of the NK model (Macken et al., 1991; Weinberger, 1991; Solow et al., 1999b).

Daniel Levinthal's (1997) investigation of the variety of strategies that different organizations pursue within the same industry provides a nice example of the application of the NK model at the interfirm level. He considers N and K attributes of the organization, concentrating on K – the degree of internal interdependence among the organization's routines. Using this framework, he argues that both changes internal to the firm (adaptation) and the death and replacement of heterogeneous firms (selection) reduce the range of strategies used in an industry over time. The degree to which these processes reduce diversity depends on the degree of internal interdependence. When firms exhibit a high degree of interdependence, a multitude of strategies can operate successfully within the same industry because firms that vary somewhat in initial conditions diverge as they make incremental improvements to their routines. For example, he suggests that the diverse histories of Federal Express and UPS have led each to address the need for timely shipping in a very different manner. On the other hand, when relatively few opportunities for synergy exist, a single dominant form – a collection of best practices – tends to emerge. He further argues that the degree of interdependence also affects competition between organizational populations. While industries populated by firms with low levels of interdependence can adapt to environmental conditions, industries inhabited by tightly coupled organizations fall prey to Schumpeterian competition, adapting through the extinction and replacement of firms.

Jan Rivkin (2000) employs the NK model to answer a very different question. He argues that strategic complexity can generate sustainable rents by creating barriers to imitation. In his application, N indicates the number of policies that a firm might employ (e.g., incentives, inventory practices, etc.) and K represents the degree of interdependence among these policies in determining the effectiveness of the firm's operations. By allowing a population of would-be imitators to search the NK landscape in an attempt to beat the best strategy identified in 100 previous searches, Rivkin examines the likelihood of successful imitation. He shows that rivals will find it nearly impossible to match the leading firm's performance when a high degree of interdependence connects policies. Interestingly, he moves beyond Kauffman's model, allowing rivals to search the landscape by observing and implementing the policies of the industry leader. One might expect this process to increase dramatically the likelihood that an imitator could match the leader's performance; however, Rivkin (2000) shows that even small errors in these observations confound the copying of highly complex strategies. This conclusion suggests that complexity may then also preclude firms from replicating their own success. Elsewhere, Rivkin (2001) demonstrates that intermediate levels of complexity (strategic interdependence) can allow the focal firm to replicate their advantage in new markets while still preventing rivals from successfully imitating these operations. So, intermediate levels of complexity might allow firms to compete successfully by managing the balance between the demand for transferring know-how internally and the threat of competence diffusing externally.

OTHER COMPUTATIONAL APPROACHES

Not all computational approaches fall under the rubric of cellular automata or NK models. For example, Hannan and Carroll (1992) develop a simulation to model the dynamics of organizational populations. This population ecology simulator, based on the differential equations of density dependence and parameters estimated from empirical studies of actual organizational populations, allows researchers to understand how various ecological processes affect system-level characteristics (e.g., the total number of firms in the population). Theoretical biologists and mathematicians have also addressed this problem analytically – e.g., May (1974) – but to gain mathematical tractability they must make a host of assumptions that remove much of the realism from the density dependence model. Using this simulation, Hannan and Carroll (1992) discover two interesting system-level properties of the density-dependent model. First, the timing of the rapid expansion typically found in the early stage of an industry appears largely unpredictable because it results from the amplification of random events through positive feedback loops. Second, density delay – the idea that the density at the time of the organization's founding has lasting effects on mortality rates – generates cycling in the size of the population.

Other researchers have adapted this simulation to consider new issues in organizational ecology. Carroll and Harrison (1994) extend it to examine whether the most efficient organizational forms typically survive competition. Since the simulation allows them to define the organization's fitness in isolation, they can avoid the problem faced in empirical research of differentiating the intrinsic organizational strength from the specifics of a particular industry history. Interestingly, they find that competition among organizational populations only generates a modest tendency to eliminate the weaker firms in favor of the stronger ones. Density dependence also appears to create a type of first mover advantage that disadvantages more efficient firms when they arise subsequent to an inferior firm type in the same niche. Similarly, positive feedback can lead to the success of inferior technologies (David 1985) and the adoption of less efficient theories (Kuhn, 1962; Sterman and Wittenberg, 1999). This research calls into question a large body of empirical economics research that assumes that the mere existence of an organizational or industry structure indicates its superiority (e.g., Monteverde and Teece, 1982). Barron (1999) further extends this simulation to include organizational growth processes. He shows that tradeoffs in the growth of industries through the expansion of existing firms versus through the founding of new organizations may drive the decline from peak density typically seen in organizational populations. Though not framed as complexity-based research per se, these simulations show the usefulness of computational methods in more established research domains.

OTHER COMPLEXITY APPROACHES

Complexity applications that do not incorporate explicit formal models fall into two categories. On one side, a large number of popular publications oriented toward managers primarily use complexity as a metaphor. These articles and books adopt the language of complexity without implementing its technology. Thus, they add little to our understanding of organizations. The other set consists of serious interpretations of historical accounts of the evolution of organizations and industries. Though qualitative in nature, these studies provide detailed insight into the interactions between organizations.

David (1992) provides a classic example of this type of historical research in his study of the competition between alternating current (AC) and direct current (DC) power. He argues that the actions of individuals can profoundly affect future events when feedback mechanisms magnify the amplitude of their actions. Because of these positive feedback loops, competitions between opposing 'standards' can react sensitively to individual actions. To provide evidence of this sensitivity, David presents a detailed account of the events surrounding the competition between AC and DC. Early in this standards race, DC appeared to lead both technologically and in the size of its installed base. Though AC caught up by the mid-1880s, David presents a strong case that DC power could still have prevailed with the proper strategic moves and continued investments in technological development. Nevertheless, his narrative points to Thomas Edison's effective withdrawal from the industry due to short-term capital constraints as the catalyst that allowed AC to become the dominant standard.

These complex interorganizational dynamics also appear in Kirsch's (2000) interesting account of the evolution of the automobile industry. He asks why internal combustion engines, rather than electric motors, power our cars today. In the early years of the century, electric cars actually offered a more economical means of urban transportation. Though certain events contributed to the demise of the electric car – such as World War I increasing the demand for vehicles with a long range – Kirsch argues that positive feedback processes primarily drove the adoption of petrol-based engines. Small initial differences in performance attracted more development dollars to the internal combustion engine. In turn, those investments magnified the initial performance advantages of gasoline engines, creating a virtuous cycle that led to the dominance of petrol engines. Detailed historical accounts of a variety of other industries – including typewriter manufacturers (David, 1985), computer disk array providers (McKendrick and Carroll, 2001), the Danish wind turbine industry (Karnøe and Garud, 2001) and others – also take qualitative approaches that complement complexity and computational perspectives.

Contemporary Issues and Debates

MODEL REALISM

Though complexity and computational approaches have begun to enhance our understanding of organizations, the models remain somewhat unrealistic in relation to our empirical understanding of firms. This lack of realism comes in large part from applying without modification models originally intended for the biological and physical sciences to the study of organizations. Thus, each class of models brings with it some limitations.

Cellular automata, and the particular variants used by Lomi and Larsen, include several shortcomings. First, these models hold constant the dimensionality – typically to one or two dimensions – and the scope of interactions between organizations. Limiting the number of dimensions may generate unrealistic models of the world as it dramatically limits the richness of competitive interactions between firms. For example, increases in the variety of competitive arenas heighten the opportunity for niche strategies, even in the center of the market (Péli and Nooteboom, 1999). More importantly, fixing the degree of interaction (neighborhood radius) handicaps the ability of this approach to yield information on the dynamics of embedded behavior because the degree of interdependence does not vary. Second, some of the assumptions made by Lomi and Larsen do not fit well with the findings of empirical research. For example, ecological research observes that competition operates more locally than legitimation (Hannan et al., 1995). Nevertheless, Lomi and Larsen always model these two processes using the same neighborhood radius. Also, whereas they model foundings as a fixed entry rate in the locations at risk, research on the geography of foundings finds that local density increases founding rates (Sorenson and Audia, 2000). However, future research can presumably tune these parameters to match empirical evidence.

When applied to the social sciences, the NK model also has clear limitations. First, the NK model offers a very simple, and probably unrealistic, representation of firm-level behavior. Kauffman's simulations model actors – in his case genes – as though they either sample locations on the landscape at random or as though they climb hills by moving to adjacent points that offer higher fitness levels. Nevertheless, intelligent actors, such as the people that inhabit organizations, may develop more sophisticated search algorithms. People can learn from experience. They can continue to search even when positioned at a local peak (March, 1988). They may even develop cognitive maps of the landscapes they search (Gavetti and Levinthal, 2000). Second, the NK model's construction limits each member of the network (i.e. firm) to interacting with exactly the same number of other network members. In contrast, a huge body of sociological research tells us that firms occupy very different positions from one another and that these positions importantly affect firm behavior and outcomes. For example, prominent firms interact with a much larger number of alters than more peripheral firms and higher rents appear to accrue to these central positions (Podolny, 1993). Thus, though this assumption might provide a useful baseline, one must wonder how well the results of the model apply to networks with varied degrees of interaction.

GOING MULTILEVEL

Some recent research now seeks to merge inter-firm level interactions with the internal structure of the organization. To varying degrees, the studies above treat organizations as homogenous black boxes. However, recent research extends these models to include intra-organizational dynamics. For example, studies by both Sorenson (1997, 2003) and McKelvey (1999) use the NK model to consider both intra- and inter-firm level interdependencies. Interestingly, these studies arrive at similar conclusions, though the explanations for these findings differ substantially.

My own research (Sorenson 1997, 2003) examines the interaction between interdependence and environmental volatility. Applying Kauffman's model to the issue, I translate N as the number of stages of the value chain required to produce a particular good. K corresponds to the degree of interdependence in the firm's activities. Using this translation, Kauffman's simulations tell us that firms should become increasingly rigid as their internal interdependence rises. To relate this rigidity to environmental conditions, I extend Kauffman's framework by allowing the topography of the landscape to shift at random. While loosely coupled organizations find it easiest to improve efficiency through adaptation, their advantage declines as the degree of environmental volatility rises. When the rate of environmental change becomes exceedingly high, adaptation becomes worthless and tightly coupled organizations outperform their more adaptive rivals.

Some find this conclusion – that inert organizations outperform adaptive firms in highly volatile environments – counter-intuitive. This dissonance stems from viewing environmental change as a discrete event. If organizations adapt to one environment that undergoes a major shift (e.g., deregulation), then flexible organizations will most quickly adapt to the new environment. However, when the environment continuously changes, adaptive organizations only outperform their less flexible rivals if they can change more quickly than the environment. At sufficiently high levels of volatility, firms simply cannot adapt faster than the environment changes, making their modifications worthless. To the extent that these adaptive efforts divert scarce resources from other activities, flexible organizations end up paying a price for adaptations that fail to generate any positive returns.

Though not common in the complexity literature, I move from the model to empirical corroboration using data on the American computer workstation industry. The degree of internal production (vertical integration) provides important information regarding the likely degree of interdependence between these production processes. Firms that internalize two processes probably tailor their operations to each other more than when these stages take place across firm boundaries. Therefore, the extent of vertical integration provides a proxy for the degree on interdependence in firm operations. Two measures capture different aspects of environmental volatility. Technological uncertainty proxies the difficulty of determining a standard technology among manufacturers by measuring the degree of divergence in the processors and operating systems used across firms. Market instability, the yearly change in same product sales, captures volatility in consumer preferences. When firms first integrate, it increases their performance, but as expected, non-integrated firms outperform vertically integrated firms over the long run in stable environments, both in terms of increased sales growth and reduced mortality rates. As either technological uncertainty or market instability increases, however, vertically integrated firms hold their advantage for longer and longer periods. In the most volatile periods, integrated firms never lose their competitive advantage relative to firms that simply assemble components to make workstations (Sorenson, 1997, 2003).

McKelvey (1999) attacks the same fundamental issue within Kauffman's own framework. Kauffman provides an extension of the NK model, the NKC model, which allows one to model explicitly the interactions between entities. McKelvey adopts this framework to generate hypotheses about the interaction between organizational structure and the intensity of competition. One can think of the NKC model as two NK landscapes that interact at C of their components. McKelvey translates this model to organizations by considering N the stages of the value chain within which an organization operates, K the degree of interdependence between these stages and C the number stages in which the firm's performance depends on either competitive or cooperative interaction with its rival. Using this framing, McKelvey derives several hypotheses for the performance of organizations. For example, firms with a slightly lower level of interdependence generally outperform more tightly coupled rivals. Less intuitively, the model also predicts that firms should try to match the levels of their internal and external interdependencies. In other words, firms that depend on the actions of rivals in many domains do better when they couple their own internal operations more tightly.

Interestingly, McKelvey's use of the NKC-model makes the same prediction that I found support for in the computer workstation industry – but based on a very different rationale. High C corresponds to a volatile landscape. In the workstation industry, vertically integrated firms do better as the volatility of the environment rises. Although I interpret this contingency effect as the result of changes in the value of adaptation, McKelvey's treatment suggests a different explanation: The shifting landscapes prevent tightly coupled organizations from getting locked into local peaks, thereby allowing highly interdependent internal structures to continue adapting. Resolving these two possibilities will require more detailed information on organizational actions. Nonetheless, linking the internal structure of the firm to the external environment provides an important and largely untapped arena for future research.

Central Questions Unanswered

EMPIRICAL CORROBORATION

The central unanswered question in this domain asks simply whether these results improve our understanding of organizations. One can derive most of the hypotheses generated by the computation and complexity literature using traditional organizational theories. Spatial economics (Marshall, 1922; Lörsch, 1954) predicts the same geographic configurations as Lomi and Larsen's (1996) cellular automata. Systems theory (Simon, 1962), resource dependence theory (Pfeffer and Salancik, 1978) and organizational ecology (Hannan and Freeman, 1984) can all build cases for the relationship between the firm's internal structure, environmental volatility and firm performance found in Sorenson (1997, 2003) and McKelvey (1999). Rivkin's explanation for sustainable advantage comes very close to that of Lippman and Rumelt (1982).

Given this potential for alternative explanation and the almost complete lack of empirical verification of the expectations generated by complexity theory and computational models, some researchers wonder whether we will one day consider this body of work a short-lived fad (Cohen, 1999; Baum and Silverman, 2001). To date, complexity and computation largely offer a means of explicitly considering the interactions between firms when describing organizational behavior. Although explaining the same phenomena as existing theory forms a necessary condition for theoretical progress, science moves forward when new theories offer novel predictions (Popper 1977 [1934]). These new predictions allow researchers to develop critical tests to determine whether the new theory really does improve our understanding of the world. In the short run, the research community may wish to let complexity and computation proceed without this corroboration in the interest of allowing it to develop without being prematurely eradicated by the lack of empirical evidence. Nevertheless, the contribution of the perspective to our understanding of organizations will ultimately determine its longevity.

At the interorganizational level, empirical evidence remains sparse. Baum and Silverman (2000) analyze the dynamics of organizational foundings and failures. Their analyses of multiple organizational populations indicate that orderly or chaotic processes underlie the dynamics of most of these populations. Only a few appear to exhibit random behavior. Their results support complexity and computational approaches because they suggest that dynamic systems with intermediate levels of interdependence govern these industry vital rates. Nevertheless, although their research validates this class of models, it does not point to the usefulness of one particular complexity or computational approach over another.

Research at another level of analysis provides some hope that empirical research might venerate complexity and computation. In research with Lee Fleming, I use the *NK* model to understand better the process of technological invention (Fleming and Sorenson, 2001). We frame the process of invention as one in which inventors search unknown landscapes for useful recombinations of technological components, a perspective that harkens back to the classics in the field (Gilfillan, 1935; Schumpeter, 1939). In this application, N denotes the number of technological components being combined and K indicates the degree of interdependence between these components. According to this framing, highly interdependent components (high K or the inverse of modularity) generate rugged landscapes that defy inventors' best efforts to search for useful new configurations. Our examination of nearly 20,000 patents confirms this expectation. Patents recombining highly interdependent components receive fewer citations, an indicator of invention quality in the patent literature. Patents using components with an intermediate level of interdependence receive the most citations. Though taking a different approach, Baum and Silverman (2001) also find that a deterministic – though high dimensional – process appears to underlie technological evolution.

Although this research provides some prima facie evidence for the applicability of the *NK* model, some subsequent analysis offers even stronger support for the value of this theoretical approach. The *NK* model generates the "complexity catastrophe" – the difficulty of finding good combinations on highly interdependent landscapes – by using algorithms that assume searchers do not understand the topography of the underlying landscape. Nevertheless, humans appear to violate this assumption sometimes. For example, basic science might provide inventors with an understanding of the technologies they use, allowing them to predict roughly the usefulness of many new configurations without trying them. We investigate this possibility in a second paper by categorizing patents according to whether the patent cites a scientific article or not (Fleming and Sorenson, 2004). Indeed, patents that cite science show no noticeable "complexity catastrophe" as they combine increasingly interdependent components; in fact, the usefulness of invention (patent citations) rises with interdependence. Meanwhile, the negative effects of interdependence become even more pronounced in the patents that do not cite science. These results offer even stronger support for the applicability of the *NK* model because they demonstrate that the model does not hold under conditions that violate its assumptions.

SYNCHRONOUS OR ASYNCHRONOUS

Another important unanswered – and generally unasked – question regards the timing of actions in these simulations. By and large, the simulations above use synchronous updating: at each period every agent makes decisions based on the state of the world in the previous period. This framework assumes simultaneity of action, an unlikely event in the real world. At the other extreme, one could create a simulation such that only one agent acts in each period (called asynchronous updating). Here, agents need not worry about the unknown actions of other agents because each takes its own turn. This seemingly minor issue can dramatically impact the results generated by the simulation. For example, in a simulation using synchronous updating Nowak and May (1992) show that cooperators form a stable proportion of the population in a cellular automata based on the Prisoner's Dilemma game. In a version with asynchronous updating, however, Huberman and Glance (1993) show that defection becomes the dominant outcome.

The information available to the actor making a decision crucially differentiates these two approaches. With synchronous updating, each actor does not know the decisions of other actors until after their decision has been made because these other agents make simultaneous decisions. In contrast, the actor knows the actions of every other agent when making a decision in asynchronous simulations. However, neither of these cases fits well with reality. Although actors almost never make decisions simultaneously (to the extent that has any meaning in a relativistic world), they do often make decisions before they receive information revealing the other agents' actions. When actors must make their decisions before they know what others did, they effectively operate in a synchronous updating world. Interestingly, Huberman and Glance (1993) note that the behavior of their asynchronous cellular automata does converge on the synchronous models as they slow the speed of information diffusion across actors.

New and Emerging Directions of Future Research

Most early applications of complexity theory took models from the hard sciences and applied them largely without modification to organizational problems. Though these efforts generated interesting perspectives on the topics they tackled and fueled excitement for this theoretical approach, as indicated in the discussion of 'model realism', it remains unclear whether the results would hold if the model assumptions fit more closely our understanding of organizations. Emerging research addresses this question by tailoring the models to our knowledge of organizational processes.

Search Processes

Though the NK model includes an (often) unlikely assumption of blind search, researchers have begun to elaborate this model to include more realistic search algorithms. For example, as described above, Jan Rivkin allows firms to search the strategic landscape by (imperfectly) imitating more successful rivals. This expansion adds realism to the model by linking it to social learning theory (Bandura, 1986) and institutional theory (Meyer and Rowan, 1977), which both argue that firms imitate their peers. Firms that use this type of learning experience roughly the same outcomes as the local searchers that inhabit Kauffman's original model (Rivkin, 2000). By adding costs to change, Mezias and Lant (1994) show that imitation may actually hurt firms engaging in it. Though this learning process apparently does not affect the NK model greatly, understanding the impact of more realistic search algorithms and decision-making processes remains an important issue in applying complexity and computation to organizations.

Gavetti and Levinthal (2000) expand Kauffman's model in a different direction by allowing managers to use cognitive maps to navigate the landscape. Like roadmaps, these cognitive maps lack the detail of the actual landscape, but provide managers with a rough picture of its topography. Not surprisingly, these maps enable managers to find higher fitness peaks (better strategies) when they accurately reflect the underlying fitness landscape. It comes as a surprise, however, that cognitive maps improve search outcomes even when they do not represent the landscape well. The intuition for this finding lies in the search process itself. When managers lack a cognitive representation of the landscape, they must stop searching when they reach a local peak. Thinking that better alternatives exist elsewhere, however, managers that follow a cognitive map can continue searching even when that search requires them to endure a period of poor performance before finding another good strategy. Interestingly, this work suggests that management gurus, regardless of the veracity of their claims, may serve a useful purpose by giving managers the confidence to implement painful changes.

Though this work begins to examine how different search processes react to complex environments, it leaves unexamined a broad range of search behaviors. For example, can organizations effectively learn from the experience of other firms if they employ more sophisticated algorithms than simply follow-the-leader? One might imagine a variety of imitative rules ranging from following the crowd to a regression-like decomposition of the relationships between strategic choices and organizational performance. Also, future research should consider the effectiveness of decentralized learning. Most organizations delegate responsibility across a range of decision makers. Therefore, an aggregation of several independent searches might represent the search behavior of organizations more accurately than a model that treats the firm as though some central manager controls all of its actions. Considering a more realistic range of search behaviors offers fertile territory for future research in complexity and computation.

Structured Landscapes

Researchers can also make the NK model more realistic with regard to the types of interactions modeled. Though no published work to date deals with these issues, a substantial body of sociological work on inter-organizational networks can inform future investigations along these lines (see Baker and Faulkner's chapter in this volume for a review). Thus, researchers might usefully consider how the properties of a system change when agents contribute differentially to the overall system fitness. Solow et al. (1999a) offer some initial investigations along these lines in a biological context, but these ideas have yet to move into the organizational realm. For example, they demonstrate that when one component contributes sufficiently more than the others to system fitness that local search finds the highest fitness when that component interacts with a large number of other components (i.e., high K). Thus, when actors differ sufficiently in importance, even highly interdependent systems can avert the "complexity catastrophe."

Organization theorists could also investigate the importance of differences in the number and pattern of connections between firms. To some degree, organizations can manage the extent and shape of their connections to other firms. For example, they can often choose to source a component from a single supplier or from multiple providers. How do these choices affect the firm's ability to maximize performance? How do they impact the efficiency of the economy as a whole? Understanding the importance of these different structures presents another important area for future investigation.

Eventually, this research may allow organizational theorists to make recommendations to practitioners. This advice will likely center around two types of managerial action: search design and organization design. By investigating the success of various search algorithms, researchers may identify which types of learning behaviors best handle different environmental conditions. Alternately, organizational theorists might develop a better understanding of how organizational design can allow the organization to adapt more effectively. Ultimately, research needs to investigate both of these factors together to determine whether search processes and organizational design characteristics operate as complements or contradictions. Nevertheless, before any recommendations can be made, researchers must validate these expectations with empirical research.

Connections Across Levels

Looking at more micro-level applications of complexity and computation both suggests new directions for intraorganizational work in this field and hints at how the experience of macro-level researchers might inform research at these lower levels of analysis.

Level of model detail offers one dimension on which the lessons go both ways. In contrast to the models used at the macro-level, many of the simulations developed to investigate intraorganizational processes include a tremendous amount of detail. As Carley (this volume) describes, these simulations include information on the reporting structures and information flows within the firm, as well as models of the cognitive processes the actors within the firm follow. Interorganizational researchers could dramatically increase the realism of their models by following this lead in basing their models on well-developed theories of psychological and organizational processes. Moreover, one could even imagine building models of interacting firms by creating ecologies of adaptive organizational simulators, such as ORGAHEAD (Carley and Svoboda, 1996). Though these highly detailed simulations might more closely match reality, moving to these more realistic representations also exacts a price: understanding the key drivers of these complicated models can prove nearly impossible. The highly abstract models found at the interorganizational level have the advantage of allowing researchers to understand more clearly which factors critically drive the behavior of the system. In this sense, micro-level researchers might consider following the example of their macro-level counterparts in trying to develop models that capture the essence of a problem without drowning in the intricacies of the situation.

Particularly at the organizational level, as Eisenhardt and Bhatia's chapter illustrates, researchers have focused on the emergent properties of complex systems more than the underlying system characteristics that produce these properties. For example, the "edge of chaos" – a poetic term for the inflection point at which the level of interdependence in the system maximizes its rate of adaptation – occupies a central position in this research stream. Kauffman (1993) suggests that systems naturally adapt to this inflection point of maximal adaptability. Nevertheless, as Brown and Eisenhardt (1998) assert, the tensions underlying this state make it inherently unstable. Fleming and Sorenson (2001) show empirical support for this proposition by finding that inventors systematically err on the side of too much order when designing new technologies. Though one should approach these issues with caution, organizational researchers at all levels can find a much richer set of dependent variables to investigate both theoretically and empirically by looking at this work on emergent properties.

Conclusion

Complexity and computation offer powerful new tools for thinking about organizational processes. This fledgling perspective on organizations should excite students of organizations because it opens a vast range of virgin territory for future study. Researchers can contribute substantially by investigating the importance of different search processes or the role of structure in adaptive processes. They can also play a significant role by improving the realism of these models or by infusing intra-organizational models with micro-level representations of independent adaptive agents. Nevertheless, I would particularly encourage researchers to take the road less traveled. Ultimately, complexity and computation's ability to predict real world outcomes will determine the fate of this perspective. The development of theory already outpaces empirical work corroborating these models and investigating where they diverge from the actual behavior of organizations. Thus, those that provide these empirical tests will play a critical role in its development.

Acknowledgments

Thanks go out to Joel Baum, Lee Fleming, Benyamin Lichtenstein, Bill McKelvey and Sue McEvily for comments on this review. Any errors or oversights remain my own.

References

Anderson, P. (1999): "Complexity theory and organization science," *Organization Science*, 10, 216–32.
Axelrod, R., and Cohen, M. (2000): *Harnessing Complexity*. New York: Free Press.

Bandura, A. (1986): *Social Foundations of Thought and Action: A Social Cognitive Theory*. Englewood Cliffs, NJ: Prentice Hall.

Barron, D. (1999): "The structuring of organizational populations," *American Sociological Review*, 64, 421–45.

Baum, J. A. C., and Mezias, S. (1992): "Localized competition and organizational failure in the Manhattan hotel industry, 1898–1990," *Administrative Science Quarterly*, 37, 580–604.

Baum, J. A. C. and Silverman, B. S. (2000): "Complexity in the dynamics of organizational founding and failure," in M. Lissack and H. Gunz, (eds), *Managing Complexity in Organizations*, New York: Quorum Press, 292–312.

Baum, J. A. C., and Silverman, B. S. (2001): "Complexity, (strange) attractors, and path dependence in innovation trajectories," in R. Garud and P. Karnøe (eds), *Path Dependence and Creation*, Hillsdale NJ: Lawrence Erlbaum Associates, 169–209.

Brown, S., and Eisenhardt, K. (1998): *Competing on the Edge*. Boston: Harvard Business School Press.

Carley, K., and Svoboda, D. (1996): "Modeling organizational adaptation as a simulated annealing process," *Sociological Methods and Research*, 25, 138–68.

Carroll, G., and Harrison, R. (1994): "On the historical efficiency of competition between organizational populations," *American Journal of Sociology*, 100, 720–49.

Carroll, G., and Wade, J. (1991): "Density dependence in the organizational evolution of the American brewing industry across different levels of analysis," *Social Science Research*, 20, 217–302.

Cohen, M. (1999): "Commentary on the *Organization Science* special issue on complexity," *Organization Science*, 10, 373–76.

David, P. (1985): "Clio and the economics of QWERTY," *American Economic Review*, 75, 332–37.

David, P. (1992): "Heroes, herds and hysteresis in technological history: Thomas Edison and 'the battle of the systems' reconsidered," *Industrial and Corporate Change*, 1, 129–80.

Durkheim, E. ([1897] 1952): *Suicide*. London: Routledge.

Eve, R., Horsfall, S., and Lee, M., (eds) (1997): *Chaos, Complexity and Sociology*. Thousand Oaks, CA: Sage.

Fleming, L., and Sorenson, O. (2004): "Science as a map in technological search," *Strategic Management Journal*, 25, 909–28.

Fleming, L., and Sorenson, O. (2001): "Technology as a complex adaptive system: Evidence from patent data," *Research Policy*, 30, 1019–39.

Gavetti, G., and Levinthal, D. (2000): "Looking forward and looking backward: Cognitive and experiential search," *Administrative Science Quarterly*, 45, 113–37.

Gilfillan, S. (1935): *Inventing the Ship*. Chicago: Follett Publishing.

Granovetter, M. (1985): "Economic action and social structure: The problem of embeddedness," *American Journal of Sociology*, 91, 481–510.

Hannan, M. (1998): "Rethinking age dependence in organizational mortality: Logical formalizations," *American Journal of Sociology*, 104, 126–64.

Hannan, M., and Carroll, G. (1992): *Dynamics of Organizational Populations*. New York: Oxford University Press.

Hannan, M., and Freeman, J.: "The population ecology of organizations," *American Journal of Sociology*, 82, (1977), 929–64.

Hannan, M., and Freeman, J. (1984): "Structural inertia and organizational change," *American Sociological Review*, 49, 149–64.

Hannan, M., Carroll, G., Dundon, E., and Torres, J. (1995): "Organizational evolution in a multinational context: Entries of automobile manufacturers in Belgium, Britain, France, Germany, and Italy," *American Sociological Review*, 60, 509–28.

Huberman, B., and Glance, N. (1993): "Evolutionary games and computer simulations," *Proceedings of the National Academy of Sciences USA*, 90, 7716–18.

Karnøe, P., and Garud R. (2001): "Path creation and dependence in the Danish wind turbine field," in J. Porac and M. Ventresca (eds), *Constructing Industries and Markets*, New York: Pergamon Press, in press.

Kauffman, S. (1993): *The Origins of Order: Self-Organization and Selection in Evolution*. New York: Oxford University Press.

Kauffman, S., and Levin, S. (1987): "Toward a general theory of adaptive walks on rugged landscapes," *Journal of Theoretical Biology*, 128, 11–45.

Keenan, D. and O'Brian, M. (1993): "Competition, collusion and chaos," *Journal of Economic Dynamics and Control*, 17, 327–53.

Kirsch, D. (2000): *The Electric Vehicle and the Burden of History*. New Brunswick, NJ: Rutgers University Press.

Kuhn, T. (1962): *The Structure of Scientific Revolutions*. Chicago: University of Chicago Press.

Larsen, E., and Markides, C. (1997): "Imitation and the sustainability of competitive advantage," working paper, London Business School.

Levinthal, D. (1997): "Adaptation on rugged landscapes," *Management Science*, 43, 934–50.

Lichtenstein, B. (2001): "The matrix of complexity: A multi-disciplinary approach to studying emergence," in A. Lewin and H. Voldberda (eds), *Mobilizing the Self-Renewing Organization; The Coevolution Advantage*, London: Sage, forthcoming.

Lippman, S., and Rumelt, R. (1982): "Uncertain imitability: An analysis of interfirm differences in efficiency under competition," *Bell Journal of Economics*, 13, 418–38.

Lomi, A., and Larsen, E. (1996): "Interacting locally and evolving globally: A computational approach to the dynamics of organizational populations," *Academy of Management Journal*, 39, 1287–1321.

Lomi, A., and Larsen, E. (1997): "A computational approach to the evolution of competitive strategy," *Journal of Mathematical Sociology*, 22, 151–76.

Lomi, A., and Larsen, E. (1998): "Density delay and organizational survival: Computational models and empirical comparisons," *Journal of Computational and Mathematical Organization Theory*, 3, 219–47.

Lomi, A., and Larsen, E. (2001): "Age dependence in organizational mortality rates: Computational models and empirical comparisons," in A. Lomi and E. Larsen (eds.), *The Dynamics of Organizations: Computational Modeling and Organizational Theories*, Menlo Park, CA: AAAI/MIT Press, 296–306.

Lörsch, A. (1954): *The Economics of Location*. New Haven, CT: Yale University Press.

Macken, C., Hagan, P. and Perelson, A. (1991): "Evolutionary walks on rugged landscapes," *SIAM Journal of Mathematics*, 51, 799–827.

March, J. (1988): *Decisions and Organizations*. Oxford: Basil Blackwell.

Marshall, A. (1922): *Principles of Economics*, 8th edn. London: MacMillan.

May, R. (1974): *Stability and Complexity in Model Ecosystems*, 2nd edn. Princeton, NJ: Princeton University Press.

McKelvey, B. (1999): "Avoiding complexity catastrophe in coevolutionary pockets: Strategies for rugged landscapes," *Organization Science*, 10, 294–321.

McKendrick, D., and Carroll, G. (2001): "On the genesis of organizational forms: Evidence from the market for disk arrays," *Organization Science*, 12, 661–82.

Meyer, J., and Rowan, B. (1977): "Institutionalized organizations: Formal structure as myth and ceremony," *American Journal of Sociology*, 83, 340–63.

Mezias, S., and Lant, T. (1994): "Mimetic learning and the evolution of organizational populations," in J. Baum and J. Singh (eds), *Evolutionary Dynamics of Organizations*, New York: Oxford, 179–98.

Monteverde, K., and Teece, D. (1982): "Supplier switching costs and vertical integration," *Bell Journal of Economics*, 13, 206–13.

Nowak, M., and May, R. (1992): "Evolutionary games and spatial chaos," *Nature*, 359, 826–29.

Péli, G., and Nooteboom, B. (1999): "Market partitioning and the geometry of the resource space," *American Journal of Sociology*, 104, 1132–53.

Pfeffer, J., and Salancik, G. (1978): *The External Control of Organizations*. New York: Harper & Row.

Podolny, J. (1993): "A status-based model of market competition," *American Journal of Sociology*, 98, 829–72.

Podolny, J., Stuart, T., and Hannan, M. (1996): "Networks, knowledge, and niches: Competition in the worldwide semiconductor industry, 1984–1991," *American Journal of Sociology*, 102, 659–89.

Popper, K. ([1934] 1977): *The Logic of Scientific Discovery*. London: Routledge.

Ranger-Moore, J., Breckenridge, R., and Jones, D. (1995): "Patterns of growth and size-localized competition in the New York life insurance industry, 1860–1985," *Social Forces*, 73, 1027–50.

Rivkin, J. (2000): "Imitation of complex strategies," *Management Science*, 46, 824–44.

Rivkin, J. (2001): "Imitation, replication and complexity," *Organization Science*, 12, 274–93.

Schumpeter, J. (1939): *Business Cycles*. New York: McGraw-Hill.

Scott, W. (1998): *Organizations: Rational, Natural and Open Systems*, 4th edn. Englewood Cliffs, NJ: Prentice-Hall.

Simon, H. (1962): "The architecture of complexity," *Proceedings of the American Philosophical Society*, 106, 467–82.

Solow, D., Burnetas, A., Roeder, T. and Greenspan, N. (1999a): "Evolutionary consequences of selected locus-specific variations in epistasis and fitness contributions in Kauffman's NK model," *Journal of Theoretical Biology*, 196, 181–96.

Solow, D., Burnetas, A., Tsai, M., and Greenspan, N. (1999b): "Understanding and attenuating the complexity catastrophe in Kauffman's *NK* model of genome evolution," *Complexity*, 5, 53–66.

Sørensen, J. (1999): "Executive migration and interorganizational competition," *Social Science Research*, 28, 289–315.

Sorenson, O. (1997): "The complexity catastrophe in the computer industry: Interdependence and adaptability in organizational evolution," unpublished PhD dissertation, Stanford University.

Sorenson, O. (2000): "Letting the market work for you: An evolutionary perspective on product strategy," *Strategic Management Journal*, 21, 277–92.

Sorenson, O. (2003): "Interdependence and adaptability: Organizational learning and the long-term effect of integration," *Management Science*, 49, 446–63.

Sorenson, O., and Audia, G. P. (2000): "The social structure of entrepreneurial activity: Geographic concentration of footwear production in the US, 1940–1989," *American Journal of Sociology*, 106, 424–62.

Sterman, J., and Wittenberg, J. (1999): "Path dependence, competition and succession in the dynamics of scientific revolution," *Organization Science*, 10, 322–41.

Stinchcombe, A. (1965): "Social structure and organizations," in J. G. March (ed.), *Handbook of Organizations*, Chicago: Rand McNally, 142–93.

Thompson, J. (1967): *Organizations in Action*. New York: McGraw-Hill.

Weinberger, E. (1991): "Local properties of Kauffman's N-k model: A tunably rugged energy landscape," *Physical Review A*, 44, 6399–413.

Wright, S. (1931): "Evolution in Mendelian populations," *Genetics*, 16, 97–159.

Wright, S. (1932): "The roles of mutation, inbreeding, crossbreeding and selection in evolution," *Proceedings of the XI International Congress of Genetics*, 1, 356–66.

Chapter Thirty

Interorganizational Economics

ARJEN VAN WITTELOOSTUIJN

Organizations do not operate in an environmental vacuum. To the contrary: on a daily basis, organizations interact with a large number of outsiders, varying from clients and suppliers to governmental bodies and competitive rivals. Interorganizational economics focuses analysis on the organizational and societal consequences of organizations' direct and indirect contacts with other organizations in the market place. The economics of interorganizational contact is the domain of industrial organization (IO).[1] Traditionally, IO focused on the consequences of the market firms' conduct for market functioning and societal welfare. In the 1980s, however, IO-business strategy linkages gained prominence (Shapiro, 1989), and many highly regarded IO economists, including Harvard's Michael Porter, now hold appointments in business schools.

In this chapter, I present an 'eight-effect' model of market performance to organize the IO literature into an overarching framework. I combine ideas from IO economics' empirical and theoretical study of firm strategy and market behavior with ideas from organization science (OS), a multidisciplinary field interested in the functioning of organizations in their environments, broadly defined. I develop what I call the IO–OS cross-fertilization circle that combines both perspectives' strengths, and conclude that IO's theory of the firm and market can and must be "humanized." I put forward examples from my own work of a "humanized" IO, and as evidence of the value of IO–OS cross-fertilization.

In IO, the *homo sapiens* of flesh and blood is virtually absent. IO's core, the game theory of competitive rivalry, exploits an abstract notion of the firm as an information-effective (discounted) expected profit-maximizing production function. This abstraction continues to be refined in sophisticated analyses of different information regimes and principal-agent linkages (Tirole, 1988). However, even then the firm's CEO, top management team and personnel are not recognizable. In OS, in contrast, firm-specific human resources are omnipresent. In the upper echelon tradition, for example, the characteristics of CEOs and top management teams are seen as central to firm strategy and performance (Finkelstein and Hambrick, 1996). However, IO's strength is also OS's weakness – OS lacks IO's theoretical power. Merging IO's theoretical apparatus with OS's rich empirical tradition is likely to open up challenging avenues for future work.

Literature Review, Summary and Evaluation

IO's history can be broken down roughly into three stages. Before World War I, IO was inextricably bound up with the (micro)economics of (im)perfect competition, forming a natural part of general (Walras, [1874] 1954) or partial (Marshall, 1920) equilibrium perspectives. Subsequently, 50 years of empirical work (Mason, 1939) established IO as a distinct meso-level (i.e., industry-level) subdiscipline within economics focused on market structure, conduct and performance linkages (Scherer, 1980). Finally, since the mid-1970s, the so-called 'modern' IO mounted an agenda of game-theoretic model building (Tirole, 1988), reviving the seminal contributions of Bertrand, Cournot, Hotelling and Stackelberg, among others. Currently IO appears to be entering a fourth stage oriented toward closing the gap between empirical and theoretical research (Sutton, 1991, 1998). It is in this context that OS's empirical richness can fold into IO's theory development agenda.

With the widespread diffusion of game theory in IO, the production of modeling bits and pieces has accelerated to unprecedented rates. Specialized IO journals such as the *International Journal of Industrial Organization*, the *Journal of Industrial Economics* and the *RAND Journal of Economics* publish dozens of modeling exercises that add to the already massive stock. These theoretical models commonly share three basic building blocks. The major dependent variable is market performance, which is primarily determined by the market structure and firm conduct. Market performance pertains to such society-relevant issues as overall (i.e., industry-level) employment, innovativeness and profitability. Market structure relates to the pre-conditioned demand and supply-side features in terms of, for example, price elasticity and firm density that follow from the industry's fundamental client utility and production technology characteristics. Firm conduct reflects the behavioral repertoire of market participants in the short run (e.g., price setting) and the long run (e.g., R&D investment).

Figure 30.1's scheme presents an eight-effect framework of market performance. The scheme recasts IO's basic structure-conduct-performance framework (Scherer and Ross, 1990) in a more fine-grained eight-effect typology. Although the framework originates from gameless 'Bainian' times (Bain, 1956), the scheme puts modern IO's game theory into clear view as well (Tirole, 1988).

Although the core of IO agrees with the causality suggested by the structure-conduct-performance framework, IO also attends to obvious reciprocal causalities. This produces an eight-effect typology if a 'residual' environmental effect category is included.

1 **Window effect** IO's starting point is a market's structure, which reveals an industry's basic characteristics in terms of the demand side's utility pattern and the supply side's technology set. Firms' behavioral repertoires are determined largely by features of market structures. For example, if the demand side is not interested in product variety (as in the case of salt, for example), then product differentiation is not an issue. So, market structure features define the window of strategy opportunities open to firms. This window effect is reflected in any game

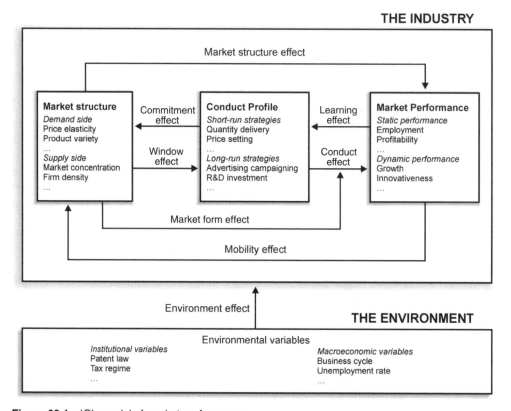

Figure 30.1   IO's model of market performance

model's assumption base. Put differently, the market structure features define the boundaries of the firms' competitive arsenal. For instance, with product homogeneity and diseconomies of scale, firms' conduct profile is dominated by price-taking behavior. An example is the classic case of perfect competition (Novshek and Sonnenschein, 1987).

2 **Conduct effect**   The interplay of firms' short- and long-run strategies determines market performance. Since Smithian times (Smith, ([1776] 1974), the static *versus* dynamic efficiency dilemma has generated much theorizing. Static efficiency refers to average cost pricing; dynamic efficiency is associated with an "optimal" level of innovativeness. Historically, this tension reflects a tradeoff (Schumpeter, 1943): faced with the prospect of a zero profit (i.e., average cost pricing), firms do not invest in R&D. In IO, this tradeoff is captured by determining the effect of firm conduct on societal welfare (typically proxied by the sum of the consumers' and producers' surplus). Building on Baumol et al.'s (1982) work on perfect contestability, solutions to this dilemma have been explored in cases with a multimarket entry threat (van Witteloostuijn, 1992).

3 **Market structure effect**   Market structure can have a direct effect on market performance. A key argument in antitrust law is, for instance, that high market

concentration produces welfare-reducing market power because of the potential to exploit the demand side (Stigler, 1968). Another example relates to the search for an "optimal" innovation-enhancing market structure (Kamien and Schwartz, 1982). Market structure–market performance hypotheses have induced a thriving stream of empirical research. For example, the idea that market concentration (firm density) is positively (negatively) associated with market-level profitability has been examined, with equivocal results (Schmalensee, 1989).

4 **Market form effect**   Together, market structure and firm conduct interact to define the market's form – roughly, the rules of the competitive game. Traditionally, IO distinguishes four ideal-type market forms:

(i)   perfect competition
(ii)   monopolistic competition
(iii) oligopoly, and
(iv)   monopoly.

Particularly through the application of game theory, modern IO has developed many subforms of monopolistic competition (Eaton and Lipsey, 1989) and oligopoly rivalry (Stiglitz, 1989). For example, the Bertrand–Cournot oligopoly distinction is commonplace, where Bertrand refers to price competition and Cournot to quantity rivalry. In a two-stage game setting, however, Bertrand (second-stage price rivalry) and Cournot (first-stage capacity installment) competition can be merged (Kreps and Scheinkman, 1983).

5 **Commitment effect**   Investment behavior is a key dimension of firm conduct. The sunk nature of irreversible investments is crucial in understanding competition (Baumol, 1982). The irreversibility of investment may radically change the rules of the game by shifting the firms' reaction curves (Dixit, 1982) through the credible signaling nature of the commitment (Ghemawat, 1991). This, in turn, feeds into the market's structure, influencing market concentration and firm density. In investment-prone industries, for example, large-scale market leaders invest heavily in advertising or R&D, relegating the small-scale followers to market niches. The result is a dual market structure (Sutton, 1991). Additionally, any sunk investment cost erects an entry barrier, which restricts the force of the potential entry threat, limiting firm density (Gilbert, 1989).

6 **Learning effect**   From the market's performance, firms can potentially learn about (in)effective conduct, which induces learning behavior through the adjustment of short and long-run strategies. For instance, a popular topic in IO is learning by doing in production and sales activities (Fudenberg and Tirole, 1984), implying that through accumulated experience a firm can improve demand and/ or technology knowledge. Here, both innovation and imitation processes play a role (Jovanovic, 1982). Modeling learning has clearly gained prominence in game theory (Selten, 1991). The underlying learning mechanisms are not IO-specific, however, but adopted from economics at large (Chen and White, 1998).

7 **Mobility effect**   From early times (Marshall, 1920), IO has considered processes of entry and exit by distinguishing the short from the long run. In the short run, productive capacities are assumed fixed; in the long run, they are not. In the long run, a high-profit industry is likely to attract newcomers, whereas in a low-profit

market a selection of firms is forced to depart. In this context, entry and exit barrier concepts play an important intermediate role (Bain, 1956). Together, processes of entry and exit determine firm density, a key aspect of market structure (Klepper and Graddy, 1990). Although IO's exit literature is not inappreciable (van Witteloostuijn, 1998), the bulk of mobility theorizing has focused on the entry processes and the entrant-*versus*-incumbent game; for an influential exception see Ghemawat and Nalebuff (1985).

8 **Environment effect**   IO has considered an enormous number of additional factors, which vary depending upon the issue at hand. Broadly speaking, these "covariates" constitute the industry's environment at large. Governmental legislation, for example, such as antitrust law and antidumping rules, is a basic feature of many industries (van Wegberg et al., 1994). The stability of cartel-types of (implicit) collusion is also viewed as very much dependent upon business cycle downturns and upswings (Rotemberg and Saloner, 1986). And, in IO's innovation literature much theorizing is focused on the effectiveness of different patenting regimes (Reinganum, 1989).

Table 30.1 complements Figure 30.1's eight-effect framework by offering an overview of eight illustrative IO studies from the set referred to above. Here, the emphasis is on theoretical modeling exercises that offer a look behind the scenes of IO theory. That is, the eight studies nicely shed light upon a number of key concepts, variables, findings, contributions and methods (without, of course, any pretension of completeness).

IO's first historical stage was devoted primarily to the theoretical analysis of the market structure, window, conduct and market form effects. In the second stage, IO turned to the empirical work in an attempt to provide empirical evidence for these four effects, adding insights about reciprocal causalities through the mobility effect. Subsequently, the third stage returned to a theoretical program, producing – in addition to further exploration of the other effects – complementary knowledge about commitment, learning, and environment effects through a wide array of game-theoretic models covering different mixtures of the eight effects. Now, IO is at the edge of a fourth stage directed at bridging the theory–evidence gap. Sutton's (1991, 1998) recent work, which derives robust across-model predictions about industry features (e.g., nature and size of sunk investment) and market structure (e.g., market concentration), subsequently tested through in-depth case and large sample empirical work, offers a view into IO's future.

Apart from the observation that much more can be said about each effect [for further reading see Schmalensee and Willig's (1989) *Handbook*], I must emphasize that, individually, IO studies work on a subset of the eight effects. While any game-theoretic IO model is inevitably involved with issues of market structure and firm conduct, to my knowledge, no integrative theory that encompasses the full eight-effect model has been advanced. Indeed, the Fisher–Shapiro (1989) discourse in the *RAND Journal of Economics* (Fisher, 1989; Shapiro, 1989) raised the question of whether there is – or can be – an overarching IO theory at all, given the plethora of disconnected, specialized oligopoly models that dominate the field but produce few robust across-model predictions. Even so, Figure 30.1's scheme offers an effective organizing device that congeals the many dimensions of IO into an overarching perspective. The frame also helps to sort out how different modeling fragments are interrelated in the context of the overall IO view of

Table 30.1 Eight illustrative IO studies

References	Key concepts	Key variables	Key findings	Key contributions	Key methods
Novshek and Sonnenschein, 1987	Perfect competition	• Price-taking strategies • Constant returns to scale • Free entry	• Market structure is endogenized • Zero-profit price taking • Perfect competition as the limit case of Cournot rivalry	Replication of perfectly competitive (with price-taking behavior) welfare result in a Cournot game setting (with quantity-setting conduct)	Cournot game with free entry
Baumol et al., 1982	Perfect contestability	• Price-setting strategies • U-shaped cost function with flat bottom • Hit-and-run entry (threat)	• Market structure is endogenized • Zero-profit pricing setting • Robustness for firm density	Generalization of the well-known perfectly competitive (with large density and price-taking behavior) welfare result to a context with density irrelevance and price-setting conduct	Bertrand game with free entry
Kamien and Schwartz, 1982	Dynamic–static efficiency tradeoff	• R&D investment • Market structure • Profitability level	• Positive R&D – profit association • Ambivalent R&D – firm size linkage • Monopoly power tends not to stimulate R&D	In-depth study of both Schumpeterian hypotheses: R&D (innovation) is stimulated by monopoly power and large scale	Dynamic decision analysis (maximizing discounted profit)
Kreps and Scheinkman, 1983	Bertrand–Cournot Nash game	• First-stage productive capacity choice • Second-stage price-setting choice • Demand rationing rules	The sequential capacity (Cournot) – price (Bertrand) choice can produce Cournot outcomes (in capacities and prices).	A revealing example of a sequential game that nicely exploits both key building blocks – Bertrand (price-setting) and Cournot (quantity-setting) games – in an overarching structure	Sequential Cournot–Bertrand game

References	Key concepts	Key variables	Key findings	Key contributions	Key methods
Dixit, 1982	Credible commitment	• Commitment • Credibility • Reputation	The credibility of strategic moves is essential, being reflected in the ex post profitability of ex ante threats.	An illuminating overview of game theory's key insights into the important issues of commitment and credibility in a sequential game setting	Sequential game with first-stage commitment strategies and second-stage product market rivalry
Jovanovic, 1982	Efficiency-driven firm entry, growth and decline	• Firm entry, growth and exit with infinite density • Cost efficiency level • Concentration and profitability	Firms enter, grow and exit according to their efficiency, which produces market structure (concentration) and market performance (profitability) outcomes.	A selection model in which efficient firms grow and survive, whereas their inefficient counterparts decline and fail	Perfect foresight market-clearing equilibrium with price-taking and profit-maximizing firms that face cost randomness
Klepper and Graddy, 1990	Market structure evolution	• Entry decision of a finite number of potential entrants • Efficiency imitation (with constant returns to scale) • Incumbents' efficiency-driven growth	Market structure (concentration and density) is endogenized in a setting with entry, imitation and growth, revealing an S-shaped density evolution.	A profit-maximizing equilibrium model that produces well-known industry evolution regularities	Price-taking, profit-maximizing and market-clearing equilibrium with stochastic efficiency at entry
Rotemberg and Saloner, 1986	Cyclical cartel behavior	• Implicit cartel collusion • Price-setting behavior • Demand fluctuation	Price or quantity wars occur if demand is high, implying that collusion breaks down in booming industries.	A comparison of Bertrand and Cournot iterative games, revealing that collusion is particularly likely to collapse in a booming period in a Bertrand setting with constant marginal cost	Bertrand and Cournot supergames with switching demand regimes

market performance, as well as revealing blind spots and weak links in IO's current state of the art. For example, although appreciable, work on the learning effect is still in its infancy, and studies on the mobility effect (i.e., entry and exit) are unbalanced with far greater attention to entry *versus* exit processes.

IO's Modeling Strategy

Methodologically, modern IO's heavy emphasis on mathematical modeling in general and game theory in particular distinguishes it from OS, and makes it difficult to understand without a basic understanding of game theory. Game theory is an analytical device for model building in the context of strategically interacting parties attempting to reach competing objectives (Morgenstern and von Neumann, 1944). The basic apparatus of game theory can be described with reference to five key modeling questions (Rasmusen, 1990).

1   **Which parties are involved?**   In IO this relates to the issue of market structure. How many firms take part in competitive rivalry, and what are their features? The answer to the latter sub-question may introduce firm heterogeneity in terms of, for instance, efficiency (relating to R&D, for example), origin (e.g., incumbent *versus* entrant) and/or size (implying an assumption as to market concentration).

2   **What motivates the parties?**   The parties' decision-making rule is framed in terms of the neoclassical utility-maximization notion. Which utilities? In IO nearly all of the literature takes profit maximization as the firms' driving force. The nature, size and movement of market demand are generally brought in by assumption, but without an active role of the demand side in the strategic game.

3   **What strategies can be brought into action?**   The next question pertains to the parties' strategy set, or conduct profile, which represents the behavioral means to the utility-maximization ends. In the context of IO, two sub-questions emerge in particular: is short-run rivalry of a Bertrand (price-setting) or Cournot (quantity-setting) nature, and what investment opportunities (if any) may be exploited (e.g., advertising, capacity buildup and/or R&D)?

4   **What is the information and time structure?**   This question has to do with the rules of the game: which party decides when about what, and on the basis of which knowledge? Game theory offers a wide array of specific devices. For example, firms may face different information regimes: is the complete history of the rivals' past decisions (e.g., investment behavior) known [(in)complete information]?; are the firms' features (e.g., efficiency) common knowledge [(im)perfect information]?; and is the movement of environmental variables (e.g., demand size) fully predictable [(un)certain information]? A game model can also be dynaminized assuming a multistage or supergame structure in which the order of the firms' decision making is fixed. A supergame involves the (finite or infinite) repetition of a similar game (e.g., a series of n Cournot games), whereas a multistage game is associated with a sequence of different games (e.g., a first-stage R&D-investment and a second-stage price-setting game).

5   **What is the equilibrium concept?**   To determine (likely) outcomes of the game, an equilibrium concept is needed. The dominant of game theory's equilibrium

concepts was developed by Nobel Prize winner John Nash. A "Nash equilibrium" (Nash, 1951) emerges if none of the game's parties faces an incentive to unilaterally deviate from the prevailing set of strategies. That is, in a duopoly setting, firm i's strategy is the best (i.e., profit-maximizing) reply to firm j's strategy, and *vice versa*. A well-known dynamic extension of the one-shot Nash equilibrium concept is "subgame perfectness" (being defined as a consistent series of Nash equilibria). For instance, in a finite game with common knowledge of the finite horizon, equilibrium is derived through backward inductive reasoning: if end game n is associated with Nash equilibrium z, then game n-1's Nash equilibrium y is to be determined given z, from which game n-2's . . . , and so on.

The calculus underlying by far the majority of IO's game modeling exercises is standard (though in many cases rather tedious) algebra (Fudenberg and Tirole, 1991). Much of the arithmetic follows from deriving players' first- and second-order conditions that pinpoint the existence of utility-maximizing decision alternatives that settle participants' strategies in a stable equilibrium. The equilibrium concept is particularly crucial. Much leading-edge game-theoretic work involves the development of equilibrium concepts that help to find a way out of the multiple equilibrium dilemma, e.g., Radner's (1980) ε-equilibrium notion. Without a strict definition of the equilibrium notion, many modeling exercises end up with numerous equilibria. This begs the question, of course: if there are many equilibria, then which equilibrium should be selected as the likely outcome of the game?

For sure, game theory is only a modeling tool. The creative application of the game-theoretic apparatus in a real-world context requires a sharp eye for translating the noisy practice of everyday life into the essential features that offer the building blocks for a game model. Then, tuning those building blocks, in ongoing interaction with the real world, might produce sharpened thinking and open up strategic opportunities that would otherwise have gone unnoticed. One course to sharpened thinking exploits the key game-theoretic concepts in an intuitive way by systematically answering game-theoretic questions and applying game-theoretic logic. This non-mathematical technique is nicely illustrated by Dixit and Nalebuff's (1992) *Thinking Strategically* or Brandenburger and Nalebuff's (1996) bestseller *Co-Opetition*. A second approach takes the analysis further by rigorously applying game theory's mathematical apparatus. Of course, this requires a basic knowledge of a number of game theory's mathematical tools.

For most OS-related applications, five pieces of mathematical game theory are likely to be particularly relevant:

1 Decision-making calculus through utility maximization
2 Normal-form games and payoff matrices
3 Supergames and the Folk Theorem
4 Sequential games and the extensive-form tree
5 Nash equilibrium and subgame perfectness concepts.

Obviously, there is much more mathematical game theory. However, for the purpose of applying mathematical game theory to real-world business issues insight into a limited number of key tools generally suffices. Accessible introductions are offered by Myerson's

(1991) *Game Theory* and Rasmusen's (1990) *An Introduction into Game Theory.*

A Dominant Contemporary Debate

A feature that characterizes much OS is limited use of mathematical modeling in general and game theory in particular, which clearly is an impediment to fruitful IO-OS cross-fertilization. One objection in OS against game theory (and mathematical modeling more generally, for that matter), and thus against modern IO, is the claim that game-theoretic models are unrealistic abstractions. Put differently, game theory is viewed as a *l'art pour l'art* corner of the social sciences that is, at best, only vaguely related to what happens in the real world. Fundamentally, this is a critique that is born of misunderstanding. Abstraction is inevitably bound up with any theoretical exercise – whether in OS or IO. Game theory, however, forces the modeler to be precise about the series of assumptions that is, by necessity, imposed upon the model. In other words, game theory's alleged downside is, in actual fact, a key strength. Without mathematical precision, the logic of the theory may be flawed as a result of implicit assumptions, redundant reasoning or faulty conclusions (Péli et al., 1994). That said, observing application of game theory's apparatus in IO's day-to-day practice, the OS critique is entirely correct in pointing out IO's nonhuman representation of the firm.

OS researchers also complain, more generally, of economic imperialism. The neoclassical utility-maximization paradigm is a powerful theory-producing device. The conceptual flexibility of the utility-maximization notion in combination with the analytical strength of the mathematical calculus apparatus offers a very productive toolkit for theory development (van Witteloostuijn, 1988). Moreover, with a shared method comes effective communication and cooperation within the economics' community. This theoretical and methodological homogeneity and the community's single-mindedness imply that today's work clearly relates to yesterday's achievement, which in turn paves the path to tomorrow's contribution, providing the field with a stimulating sense of progressive knowledge accumulation. The power of economics' and IO's dominant mathematical utility-maximization "paradigm" cannot be underestimated – especially given the apparent downsides of OS's heterogeneity (Pfeffer, 1993). Yet, in OS these advantages have resulted in economics being cast as the imperialist pupil in the class of the social sciences.

Regrettably, however, the way in which the modeling flexibility of the neoclassical apparatus has been exploited in IO is rather disappointing (van Witteloostuijn, Bunte and van Lier, 1999). By far the majority of IO starts from a strawman representation of the firm as an information-effective (discounted) expected profit-maximizing production function, and so assumes OS into irrelevance. These starting assumptions have three important implications.

1   The assumption that the firm is an effective **information machine** is firmly embedded in the rationality concept. That is, a firm is assumed to exploit all available and relevant information so as to reduce uncertainty by estimating the values of the unknown parameters in the decision model at hand (van Witteloostuijn, 1990). Of course, during the equilibrating process, learning behavior occurs (Selten, 1991). In equilibrium, however, all firms have settled into an

information-effective *status quo*. While the (in)availability issue leaves room for the game theory of incomplete, imperfect and uncertain information to play around with a wide variety of different information regimes (Fudenberg and Tirole, 1991), in practice this assumption is not relaxed, and firms, **by assumption**, absorb all relevant information **available**.

2   The notion of (expected and discounted) **profit maximization** as the firm's key driver is omnipresent in the IO domain. Virtually all IO modeling starts from the profit-maximization assumption without any discussion of its validity. With Friedman's (1953) famous "as-if" argument, the debate about the (non)sense of the profit-maximization assumption has all but ended. Nevertheless, the leading IO theorist Tirole (1988, p. 34–5) points out that "a widespread feeling that in practice . . . managers have other objectives (e.g., **maximizing the firm's size and growth** and the perquisites of the managerial position). . . . For instance, the shareholders' incomplete information . . . may allow the managers to inflate the need for personnel" (emphasis added).

3   An important auxiliary starting point of IO modeling is reflected by the *ceteris paribus* device of **firm symmetry**. That is, all firms behave alike if confronted with the same circumstances and if equipped with the same "objective" features (Boone et al., 1999). Here, IO is "dehumanized" by taking no notice of idiosyncrasies. However, firms are lead and managed by people. Who the CEO is and who the members of her top management team are clearly make a difference (Boone et al., 1996; Boone et al., 1998; Finkelstein and Hambrick, 1996).

To enhance IO's relevance to OS, these three assumptions must be relaxed and IO theory has to be humanized. IO has already produced several examples that demonstrate the feasibility and value of exploring such a relaxation. Of course, this is not to say that traditional IO is irrelevant to OS. To the contrary: Porter's (1980) *Competitive Strategy*, Brandenburger and Nalebuff's (1996) *Co-Opetition* and Shapiro and Varian's (1999) *Information Rules* are examples of translations of traditional IO highly relevant to OS.

A Central Question

Clearly, IO has much to say on OS-related issues, and *vice versa*. For example, Murnighan (1994) and Camerer and Knez (1996) provide revealing examples of the application of game theory to issues of organizational behavior, while Bates (1990) and Ichniowsky et al. (1997) are interesting cases of IO-related empirical work that focuses on the role of the people in explaining firm performance. Fruitful applications and translations of IO have also emerged in the OS literature. In addition to Porter's influential translation, IO has proven to be a source of inspiration in empirical OS work in such areas as multimarket rivalry (Barnett, 1993; Baum and Korn, 1996) and organizational ecology (Baum and Mezias, 1992; Boone and van Witteloostuijn, 1995; Amburgey and Rao, 1996; Baum and Haveman, 1997). Notwithstanding the current IO–OS overlap, because cross-fertilization is still the exception rather than the rule, much potential for further exchange remains to be exploited; see also the chapters in this volume by Silverman on organizational economics and Zajac and Westphal on intraorganizational economics.

Theoretically, much progress can be made by introducing OS-inspired assumptions to

IO's modeling strategy. From both sides of the IO–OS border, however, this is a controversial proposal – to say the least. After all, many IO scholars still believe that OS's contributions are too "soft" to be of use, while many of their OS counterparts distrust IO's mathematical *l'art pour l'art* tradition. I am convinced, however, that both groups are clearly off the mark. The two-sided condemnation, grounded in strawman characterizations and basic misunderstandings, is highly counterproductive indeed. Luckily, there are moderates at both sides of the border. The IO economist Mueller (1992, p. 166), for example, pleas for "[IO] techniques [to] be combined with a richer set of behavioral assumptions about the individuals whose actions are being explained, where such assumptions are appropriate. Modeling corporate managers' decisions regarding investment, mergers and the growth of the firm is an important example where alternative behavioral assumptions will have high payoffs." From the other side, OS researchers Zajac and Bazerman (1991, p. 52–3) argue that "strategic management research may benefit from taking an integrated behavioral / economic perspective toward specific topics from the industrial organization economics literature." I believe a humanized theory of the firm and market is a prime candidate for such a modeling strategy.

In the empirical arena, additional insight can be gained by testing hypotheses derived from a more humanized IO theory. From IO's perspective, this requires opening up the black box of the firm (Boone et al., 1998; Boone et al., 1999) and a shift from data-poor theorizing to theory-rich testing (Sutton, 1991, 1997). Here, a wide array of sources can – and must – be exploited, varying from archival documents and survey instruments to laboratory experiments and business interviews. This time-consuming strategy of primary data collection is, to say the least, not very popular in IO circles. Rather, empirical IO's emphasis is on the econometric analyses of secondary-source data. Although this reflects a legitimate and fruitful research agenda, bridging IO's theory-evidence gap (particularly in an OS-relevant context) will require IO researchers to dirty their hands in primary data collection.

Figure 30.2 summarizes the IO–OS cross-fertilization circle implied in the foregoing discussion. Within the circle, the strengths of both perspectives are combined. That is, IO's theoretical power is combined with OS's empirical richness. IO modeling feeds back into OS testing by deriving analytic hypotheses; OS testing feeds into IO modeling by providing evidence-based assumptions.

Two key barriers stand in the way of such an IO–OS cross-fertilization program. On the one hand, mathematical modeling without abstraction is a dead end (as is non-mathematical theorizing without abstraction!). Mathematical modeling, as with any other activity of the human brain, is inextricably bound up with abstraction. Inevitably, this is associated with a piecewise model building strategy. This implies that the OS audience must develop a tolerance for and understanding of applying the mathematical toolkit. On the other hand, sophisticated mathematical models tend to be filled with unobservables. IO can learn much from OS's rich tradition in the empirical arena and experience in 'transforming' unobservables into observables.

Theoretically, my emphasis on game theory should not be interpreted as a plea for exclusiveness – to the contrary. Although the game theory apparatus is particularly well-suited to analyze issues involving strategic interactions among parties with competing objectives, other modeling techniques bring in complementary strengths that should of course be taken on board. By way of illustration, two additional modeling techniques that have already entered the OS domain, are worthy of mention. First-order logic has recently

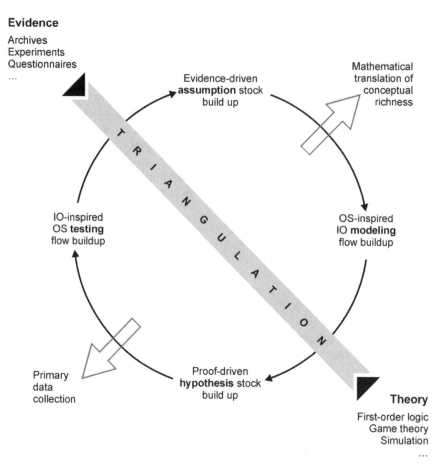

Figure 30.2   The IO–OS cross-fertilization circle

been applied to theory fragments in organizational ecology (Péli, et al., 1994). This device is a powerful tool for the analysis of the (il)logical structure of natural language theory. Second, computational techniques have a long history in OS, an early influential example being Cohen et al.'s (1972) garbage can model of organizational decision making. If a mathematical model is not analytically tractable, simulation techniques offer rich opportunities to explore the model's behavior in a wide range of different specifications; see, for examples, Dooley's simulation research methods chapter in this volume.

New and Emerging Directions for Future Research

For one reason or another, the flexible exploitation of the utility-maximization apparatus came to flourish outside the IO domain. The crowned king of this imperialist strategy is Nobel Prize winner Gary Becker, who applied the neoclassical utility-maximization devices to such controversial issues as drug addiction, child birth and partner choice

(Stigler and Becker, 1977). Particularly in the area of household behavior, which pertains to such issues as consumer demand and labor supply, Becker's flexible application of the utility-maximization toolkit is widespread. Just how far Becker's modeling strategy can be stretched, is clear from Margolis' (1982) Freudian utility-maximization model of human decision making in which the utility-maximizing ego and the utility-maximizing id fight for attention in the human brain. But as said, Becker's modeling strategy has, as yet, not gained a strong foothold in IO. However, although rare, IO is not without examples of pieces of a humanized theory of the firm and market that deviate from the standard assumption of the firm as an information-effective (discounted) expected profit-maximizing production function.

Below, I mark the contours of such humanized IO modeling by a nontechnical discussion of three examples. Technical summaries of the three examples' are provided in Figures 30.3, 30.4, and 30.5.

THE PROFIT-MAXIMIZATION PARADOX

The first example introduces a nonprofit-maximizing motive in IO's Cournot duopoly model, which introduces a market structure effect (duopoly structure) and window effect (Cournot's quantity setting). The notion of nonprofit-maximizing behavior in IO is rooted in the managerial economics of the 1950s and 1960s (Baumol, 1953). Management prestige, firm growth, managerial power and sales volume are just four examples of other objectives that may direct attention and behavior away from pure profit maximization. This heterodox IO assumption is a well-established "fact" in OS ever since, at least, the birth of the behavioral theory of the organization (Cyert and March, 1963). In the 1980s and 1990s, several IO economists took up the "managerial" challenge by exploring the consequences of sales-driven behavior in a game-theoretic oligopoly setting (Vickers, 1985; Fershtman and Judd, 1987; Sklivas, 1987; Basu, 1995; van Witteloostuijn, 1998). In a Cournot oligopoly model, the owner of a firm must (or, in Basu's case, may) sign a contract with a manager in which the latter's compensation is a function of realized profit and sales. In equilibrium, this principal-agent interaction is likely to induce nonprofit-maximizing managerial contracting, as – in the face of a (potentially) sales-motivated rival – sales-committed behavior facilitates profitability by increasing market share (or, for that matter, preventing a market share fall).

Van Witteloostuijn's (1998) model illustrates the wide-ranging consequences of this humanizing IO exercise by showing that a number of counterintuitive outcomes may result when a sales-motivated firm faces a profit-maximizing rival. Particularly, a sales-motivated firm may outperform a profit-maximizing rival. First, the sales-motivated firm is likely to develop into a Stackelberg-type of market leader (commitment effect), implying a larger market share and a higher profit level in comparison with the profit-maximizing follower, even if the former is associated with a cost inefficiency (conduct effect). Thus a preference for size may compensate for an efficiency disadvantage in the competitive Cournot duopoly game for market share (market form effect). Second, an inefficient and sales-motivated firm may develop into a monopolist by expelling the efficient and profit-maximizing rival from the market altogether, as the former's cut-throat expansion strategy drives the latter's profit below her zero-profit exit level (mobility effect). Third, van Witteloostuijn and Boone (1999) complement van Witteloostuijn's

In a Cournot oligopoly model, the owner of a firm must sign a contract with a manager in which the latter's compensation (C) is a function of realized profit (π) and sales (q).

$$C = A + ((1 - \alpha) . \pi + \alpha . q)) \tag{1.1}$$

where A is the manager's base salary, and α denotes the weight parameter that indicates the relative importance of sales (and thus, inversely, profit). The model is a straightforward Cournot duopoly game with product homogeneity, non-binding productive capacities and a combined profit-sales utility function. With product homogeneity, the demand side is simply represented by the linear downward-sloping curve

$$p = z - q_i - q_j \tag{1.2}$$

where z denotes a demand size parameter, and q_x ($x = i,j$ and $i \neq j$) is the quantity that firm x brings to the market. From Equation (1.1) firm i's (and similarly firm j's) decision goal, G, is

$$G_i = (z - q_i - q_j - v_i) . q_i + \alpha_i . q_i \tag{1.3}$$

for firm i (and *vice versa* for firm j). With α_i and/or α_j above zero, a deviation from orthodox profit maximization arises. Then, allowing for cost heterogeneity (that is, v_i may be different from v_j), the Cournot-Nash equilibrium fixes firm i's (and *vice versa* for firm j) output level at

$$q_i = \frac{(z - \alpha_j + 2\alpha_i - 2v_i + v_j)}{3} \tag{1.4}$$

Equilibrium quantity (1.4) is associated with firm i's (and *vice versa* for firm j) profit

$$\pi_i = \frac{(z - \alpha_i - \alpha_j - 2v_i + v_j) . (z + 2\alpha_i - \alpha_j - 2v_i + v_j)}{9} \tag{1.5}$$

Nonprofit-maximizing behavior may clearly pay off in terms of market share. After all, firm i is larger than rival j if

$$\alpha_i > \alpha_j + (v_i - v_j) \tag{1.6}$$

This reveals that a larger preference for size may compensate for an efficiency disadvantage (i.e., $v_i > v_j$) in the competitive game for market size. Moreover, an inefficient and sales-motivated firm i ($v_i > v_j$ and $\alpha_i > 0$) may even develop into a monopolist by expelling the efficient and profit-maximizing rival j ($\alpha_j = 0$) from the market as the former's cut-throat expansion strategy drives the latter's profit below her zero-profit exit level. Playing around with business cycle regimes (through varying values of z) does not produce a qualitative change in the outcomes.

Figure 30.3 Sales-motivated behavior

The model is a two-stage quality-price duopoly game. In stages 1 and 2, both duopolists simultaneously decide on quality and price, respectively. The utility U derived from consuming product variety a $\in$ {i,j} is

$$U_a = Q_a - p_a - (\lambda \cdot d_a) \tag{2.1}$$

where Q_a denotes variety a's quality, p is product a's price and $(\lambda \cdot d_a)$ represents the utility loss experienced if a is *not* the preferred variety b. Preference for variety is represented by a line running from 0 to 1, along which demand is uniformly distributed. Firms i and j are located at 0 and 1, respectively. A consumer buys a single product only, choosing the variety with the higher surplus (if positive). Firm i's demand is

$$D_i = \frac{1}{2\lambda} \cdot (Q_i - Q_j + p_j - p_i + \lambda) \tag{2.2}$$

Sunk cost investment (S) is incurred up-front so as to increse product quality, where the magnitude of S depends upon the aimed quality rise ΔQ. This is, for firm i,

$$S_i = \beta_i \cdot (\Delta Q_i)^2 \tag{2.3}$$

where β is random parameter (reflecting the investment's effectiveness). Assuming production efficiency homogeneity ($v_i = v_j = v$), firm i's total variable cost V is

$$V_i = v \cdot q_i \tag{2.4}$$

where v is average unit production cost and q the quantity produced. If the investment parameter $\beta_i = \beta_j = \beta$ is common knowledge, then first-stage profit π of firm i is

$$\pi_i = \frac{1}{18\lambda} \cdot (\Delta Q_i - \Delta Q_j + 3\lambda)^2 - (\beta \cdot \Delta Q_i)^2 \tag{2.5}$$

After substitution, the Nash-solution for firm i is

$$\Delta Q_i = \frac{1}{6\beta} \tag{2.6}$$

Rather than assuming $\beta_i = \beta_j = \beta$ to be common knowledge, both firms' estimates of β may be subject to heterogeneity and uncertainty. Heterogeneity may come in by, e.g., distinguishing rational (RE) and backward-looking (BE) expectational devices, where the backward-looking mechanism may pertain to three (BE3) previous observations. Assume that firm i expects (F) that firm j's estimate is equal to her own guess: $F_i[F_j[\beta_j]] = F_i[\beta_i]$. In the beginning of the game, both firms are at par, facing an identical cost and quality position. Moreover, throughout the game, both firms are equally investment-efficient: that is, the distribution of the random quality investment parameter β is the same for firms i and j. Because both firms employ a consistent estimator, firm i's expected value equals firm j's. Suppose that firm j applies a superior estimator (RE), whereas firm i sticks to an inferior expectation mechanism (BE3). Then, firm j's expected variance is lower than firm i's. Firm i's expectation of her own and the rival's quality increase is

$$F_i[\Delta Q_i] = \frac{1}{6F_i[\beta_i]} = \frac{1}{6F_j[\beta_j]} = F_j[\Delta Q_j] \tag{2.7}$$

However, since firm j's estimator is more accurate than firm i's, the former's expected variance (σ^2) is below the latter's: $M[(\sigma_j)^2] < M[(\sigma_i)^2]$, where M − contrary to F − denotes an expectation that is derived from the model, but which is unknown to both firms. The expected quality investment difference is

$$M\left[\frac{1}{6F_j[\beta_j]}\right] < M\left[\frac{1}{6F_i[\beta_i]}\right] \tag{2.8}$$

That is, the information-defective firm i is expected, on average, to outinvest her information-effective rival j. If both expectation formation devices are coupled in a 5000-run experiment, the result is that the information-defective firm i tends to outperform her information-effective rival j in terms of net profit.

Figure 30.4 Information-defective investment

In a Cournot duopoly setting with product homogeneity, non-binding productive capacities and a linearly downward-sloping demand curve (inversely, this is price $p = 1 - q_i - q_j$, where q_i and q_j are firm i's and rival j's sales volumes, respectively), a firm i maximizes utility, U,

$$U_i = ((1 - q_i - q_j) \cdot q_i) - (v_i \cdot q_i) + R_i \tag{3.1}$$

where q denotes sales volume, v represents average unit production cost and R is the firm's status in terms of relative size. That is,

$$R_i = \eta_i \cdot \frac{q_i}{q_i + q_j} \tag{3.2}$$

where η is a weight parameter. So, the utility from status increases with η and own sales, and decreases with the rival's quantity. The status motive is market-share driven. That is, a status-motivated firm seeks to outcompete the rival by increasing market share. After substituting equation (3.2) into utility function (3.1), the Cournot-Nash equilibrium can be calculated (Figure 30.3). From equations (3.1) and (3.2), firm i's first-order condition is

$$1 - 2q_i - 2q_j - v_i + \frac{\eta_i q_j}{(q_i + q_j)^2} = 0 \tag{3.3}$$

implying that

$$q_i(q_j = 0) = \frac{1 - v_i}{2} \tag{3.4}$$

which depends critically on the value of v_i. The slope of firm i's reaction curve is

$$\frac{dq_i}{dq_j} = \left(1 - \frac{\eta_i(q_i - q_j)}{(q_i + q_j)^3}\right) / \left(-2 - \frac{2\eta_i q_i}{(q_i + q_j)^3}\right) \tag{3.5}$$

which varies with the value of parameter η_i. Playing around with different sets of parameter values for average unit cost v and the status weight parameter η produces a wide array of different equilibrium regimes, including cyclical patterns of sales volumes. In the current context, the interesting case is associated with chaotic patterns of both firms' sales volumes. For example, with $v_i = 0.8$ and $\eta_i = 12$ for firm i in combination with $v_j = 0.9$ and $\eta_j = 0.6$ for firm j, Li-Yorke chaos emerges.

Figure 30.5 Status-driven rivalry

(1998) analysis by pointing out the profit-maximization paradox: a profit-maximizing owner may well have to impose nonprofit-maximizing behavioral incentives upon the firm's management. In effect, given knowledge about the rival's objectives, a firm can even calculate the "optimal" – that is, the profit-maximizing – level of sales-motivated behavior (learning effect).

THE COMPETITIVE ADVANTAGE OF FOOLISHNESS

The second example focuses on the consequences of expectational heterogeneity in a quality-price duopoly game, which relates to a market structure (duopoly structure) and window (quality-price game) effect. In the OS domain it is widely accepted that the management's perception of the environment "matters." Hambrick and Fukutomi (1991), for example, report that CEO tenure is negatively associated with strategic flexibility. Particularly, high firm tenure comes with reduced information search behavior. This argument is easily transferred to the issue of managerial expectation formation. For instance, Sutcliffe (1994) and Waller et al. (1995) present evidence that firms differ with respect to their expectation formation as a result of the top management team's heterogeneity regarding functional background and firm tenure. Expectation formation heterogeneity, in turn, is part of the explanation of firm performance differences in terms of profitability (Miller and Cardinal, 1994) and survival (Kelly and Amburgey, 1991). Managerial misperception may induce a blind spot that affects a firm's competitive strategies and thus the market's competitive outcomes (Zajac and Bazerman, 1991).

Van Witteloostuijn, Bunte and van Lier (1999) demonstrate that an information-defective firm may well outcompete an information-effective rival. In the model, both firms decide on R&D investment in product quality (commitment effect). The R&D process is associated with uncertainty. Here, expectational heterogeneity may be introduced. A firm may either exploit all information available, which reflects IO's rational expectations' case, or process a limited amount of information, which corresponds to OS's bounded rationality assumption (learning effect). In terms of relative firm performance (conduct effect), overinvestment has a negative and a positive effect for the information-defective firm (and only a negative effect for the information-effective rival). The overdose of sunk investment is a direct cost that reduces the information-defective firm's gross profitability. Overinvestment also produces a quality lead that, in turn, enhances the information-defective firm's gross profit through increased gross margin and market share. The net impact of these effects on relative profitability is not *a priori* clear. The information-effective rival's profit may decrease somewhat more than the information-defective firm's if the latter's relative overinvestment is not too large, because the latter's relative overinvestment is detrimental to the former's gross profit. For the information-defective firm's overinvestment to be sufficiently modest its relative information defection must be rather small and/or investment uncertainty must be rather low. Simulation experiments may help unraveling the effect of different types of expectational heterogeneity on firm performance (van Witteloostuijn and Maks, 1988). Van Witteloostuijn, Bunte and van Lier's (1999) simulation experiments reveal that the information-defective firm tends to outperform her information-effective rival in terms of net profit if the information gap is not too wide (market form effect).

THE BENEFIT OF STATUS-DRIVEN STRATEGIES

The third example introduces status-driven behavior in, again, a straightforward Cournot duopoly setup, which brings in a market structure (duopoly structure) and window (Cournot's quantity setting) effect. In the economics' domain the notion of status-oriented objectives has been explored in the context of consumer behavior, a well-known buying motive being to 'keep up with the Jones's' (Rauscher, 1992). However, a similar argument may be applied to firms: Philips wants to keep up with Sony and Volkswagen with Ford (and *vice versa*). Through the popular practice of benchmarking many firms thus mirror their own objectives to those of their key competitors. At least three forces foster such behavior. First, the management consultancy industry is a prominent promoter of best-practice exercises, implying that firms seek to learn from their best-performing rivals by mimicking their external and internal processes. This imitative behavior is a key driver of DiMaggio and Powell's (1983) 'mimetic isomorphism.' Second, a top manager's prestige is critically dependent upon the relative performance of the firm. Here, profit and size are crucial yardsticks. For example, an important – perhaps even dominant – stimulus of merger waves is top managers' egos (Mueller, 1992). Third, in the real-world practice of strategic management, market share objectives, which by their very definition refer to relative performance, are commonplace. Particularly at the level of competitive (SBU) strategies, market share figures prominently on the management's objectives list (Johnson and Scholes, 1999).

Van Witteloostuijn, van Lier and Boone (1999) introduce status-oriented objectives in a Cournot duopoly model by assuming that a firm may seek market share growth, next to a straightforward profit objective. The Cournot duopoly setting, again, introduces the market structure (duopoly) and window (Cournot's quantity setting) effect. Their model produces two interesting results. First, along the lines of van Witteloostuijn's (1998) sales objective model, a status-motivated firm may outperform her profit-maximizing rival in terms of profitability (conduct effect) and survival (mobility effect), even if faced by an efficiency disadvantage. Second, if both firms attribute a positive weight to status, different dynamic processes of output downturns and upswings may result from the firms' tit-for-tat type of strategic interaction (market form effect). In fact, for a specific interval of parameter values chaos emerges. That is, the pattern over time of both firms' sales volumes becomes erratic. So, although driven by non-stochastic decision making, the sales volumes' pattern resembles a random walk without the repetition of whatever recognizable (e.g., cyclical) sales volume sequence. Currently, metaphors of chaos and complexity are extremely popular in OS (Thiétart and Forgues, 1995). However, van Witteloostuijn, van Lier and Boone (1999) offer a revealing example of **mathematical** chaos in an OS-relevant setting of competitive rivalry; see also the chapters on complexity and computation in this volume.

EXPLORING THE IO–OS INTERFACE

These three modeling exercises illustrate how Figure 30.1's scheme plays out in practice if IO's assumption base is reoriented toward a humanized model of firm behavior. Clearly, humanized IO modeling, introducing alternative objective or perception assumptions on the basis of widespread OS evidence, produces competitive outcomes that would otherwise have gone unnoticed. For example, nonprofit-maximizing firms may well outperform their profit-maximizing rivals, even if faced by an efficiency disadvantage. Table 30.2 summarizes the key features of the three exemplary modeling exercises. Note that in each case, given the models' emphasis on introducing an OS-inspired assumption base, the focus is on *firm* rather than *market* performance (particularly implying a reinterpretation of the conduct effect).

The overall finding, that the market form effect produces asymmetries (in profitability and size), is not surprising as the introduction of utility heterogeneity is simply imposed in the three modeling exercises. What is counterintuitive from an IO perspective, though, is that in all three cases the inefficient firm may outcompete the efficient rival if the latter is associated with nonprofit-maximizing objectives or 'nonrational' expectations. This clearly is a result that originates from introducing an OS-inspired assumption in an otherwise standard IO setting. The next step, then, is to systematically test the new IO-OS hypotheses following OS's rich empirical tradition (Figure 30.2).

Connections Across Levels and Perspectives

Clearly, given my plea for integrating IO and OS, the connections across levels and perspectives are manifold indeed. From an IO perspective, OS at large offers numerous insights into likely candidates for assumptions that may enrich OS-inspired IO modeling; see Figure 30.2's IO–OS cross-fertilization circle. For example, OS research into cognition and interpretation – see, for example, Lant (this volume) – reveals many clues as how to humanize IO's abstraction of the over-rational firm such that new insights can be derived from "behavioral" game-theoretic modeling exercises; see Figures 30.3 to 30.5. From an OS perspective, IO's state of the art reflects an impressive stock of insights that can inform further OS work; see Figure 30.1's eight-effect framework. For example, OS's ecological research – see Baum and Amburgey (this volume) – can be enriched by introducing insights from IO theory (Boone and van Witteloostuijn, 1995; van Witteloostuijn, Boone and Carroll, 1999; van Witteloostuijn, 2000). There are many challenging opportunities for IO–OS cross-fertilization, both theoretically and empirically.

Of course, this chapter is anything but a lone ranger in emphasizing the integrative potential of cross-bordering OS and economics. The other economics chapters in this volume nicely communicate the very same belief. Zajac and Westphal's (this volume) overview of intraorganizational economics explicitly discusses a number of different routes toward cross-fertilization of OS and economics. In their context, the behavioral enrichment of economics' agency theory is particularly promising. Clearly, this relates to this chapter's introduction of insights from agency theory in an oligopoly model (Figure 30.3), which points to a challenging across-level integration of economics' agency and IO theories on the one hand and a wide variety of OS insights on the other hand. Silverman's (this volume) discussion of organizational economics explicitly relates to the clear connection between economics' transaction cost theory (TCE) and OS's resource-based view of the firm (RBV). From there, the step toward exploring many subtle IO–TCE–RBV linkages is within reach (Maijoor and van Witteloostuijn, 1996). These opportunities are immediately clear from the family resemblance between the theories'

Table 30.2 Three examples of humanized IO's theory

Illustrative literature	Eight-effect model	Theoretical mirror image	Humanized feature	Exemplary outcome
Van Witteloostuijn, 1998	Market structure effect Commitment effect Window effect Conduct effect Market form effect Mobility effect Environment effect	⇒ Duopoly structure ⇒ Stackelberg leadership ⇒ Cournot quantity game ⇒ Profitable inefficiency ⇒ Cournot asymmetric duopoly ⇒ Firm exit ⇒ Business cycle	A firm may reveal retrenchment inertia through a sales motive.	A sales-motivated and inefficient firm may outperform a profit-maximizing and efficient rival.
Van Witteloostuijn, Bunte and van Lier, 1999	Market structure effect Commitment effect Window effect Conduct effect Learning effect Market form effect	⇒ Duopoly structure ⇒ Stackelberg leadership ⇒ Quality-price game ⇒ Profitable information-defection ⇒ Expectational adaptation ⇒ Quality-price asymmetric duopoly	A firm may exploit an information-defective R&D expectation.	An information-defective firm may outperform an information-effective rival.
Van Witteloostuijn, van Lier and Boone, 1999	Market structure effect Commitment effect Window effect Conduct effect Market form effect Mobility effect	⇒ Duopoly structure ⇒ Stackelberg leadership ⇒ Cournot quantity game ⇒ Profitable inefficiency ⇒ Cournot duopoly tit-for-tat chaos ⇒ Firm exit	A firm may be driven by a status objective.	With status-driven behavior cyclical and chaotic quantity patterns may emerge.

seemingly different key concepts (e.g., IO's credible commitment, TCE's asset specificity and RBV's rent appropriability notions).

What distinguishes this chapter from fellow travelers in the economics–OS border area, though, is the emphasis on an important methodological issue. That is, my key argument is that OS can benefit from the IO tradition methodologically, too, particularly in the theory arena. This additional argument complements Silverman's and Zajac and Westphal's plea for further economics–OS integration. Hopefully, the arguments and examples above have convincingly communicated the message that mathematical modeling in general and game theory in particular are powerful theory-producing methodologies that can be molded into the OS mode easily by exploring a model's assumptional base. This potential is also clear from Dooley's chapter on simulation research methods. However, the current chapter includes a plea to apply the mathematical (game theory) methodology in OS at large. Perhaps the second edition of *The Blackwell Companion to Organizations* will include a research methods chapter about mathematical modeling techniques (and their fruitful application in OS)?

Conclusion

Interorganizational economics, particularly industrial organization (IO), has much to offer to those interested in competition and strategy. For one, IO's state of the art, as summarized in the eight-effect framework, offers an impressive overview of the many insights that this century-old branch of economics has produced. This stock of knowledge can be a source of inspiration for much OS research. Additionally, this chapter argues that particularly by combining IO's modeling apparatus with OS's empirical richness further progress can be obtained in our search for a deepened understanding of the many complexities of industry-level competitive processes and interfirm strategic maneuvering. In this context, the introduction of OS-inspired assumptions in an otherwise orthodox IO-based game setting is a promising producer of counterintuitive hypotheses that can subsequently be tested empirically, closing the IO–OS cross-fertilization circle. This research strategy offers great opportunities for theory integration and evidence accumulation across the IO–OS border.

Notes

1 Although interorganizational economics is dominated by IO, two prominent examples of non-IO interorganizational economics are evolutionary economics (Nelson and Winter, 1982) and transaction cost economics (Williamson, 1985). In this volume, the chapters by Silverman, and Zajac and Westphal are particularly relevant.

References

Amburgey, T. L., and Rao, H. (1996): "Organizational ecology: Past, present, and future directions," *Academy Management Journal*, 39, 1265–86.

Bain, J. S. (1956): *Barriers to New Competition*. Cambridge, MA: Harvard University Press.

Barnett, W. P. (1993): "Strategic deterrence among multipoint competitors," *Industrial and Corporate Change*, 2, 249–78.

Basu, K. (1995): "Stackelberg equilibrium in oligopoly: An explanation based on managerial incentives," *Economic Letters*, 49, 459–64.

Bates, T. (1990): "Entrepreneurial human capital inputs and small business longevity," *Review of Economics and Statistics*, 72, 551–59.

Baum, J. A. C., and Haveman, H. (1997): "Love thy neighbor? Differentiation and agglomeration in the Manhattan hotel industry, 1898–1990," *Administrative Science Quarterly*, 42, 304–38.

Baum, J. A. C., and Korn, H. J. (1996): "Competitive dynamics of interfirm rivalry," *Academy of Management Journal*, 39, 255–91.

Baum, J. A. C., and Mezias, S. J. (1992): "Localized competition and organizational failure in the Manhattan hotel industry, 1898–1990," *Administrative Science Quarterly*, 37, 580–604.

Baumol, W. J. (1953): *Business Behaviour, Value and Growth*. New York: McMillan.

Baumol, W. J. (1982): "Contestable markets: An uprising in the theory of industry structure," *American Economic Review*, 72, 1–15.

Baumol, W. J., Panzar, J. C., and Willig, R. D. (1982): *Contestable Markets and the Theory of Industry Structure*. New York: Harcourt, Brace Jovanovich.

Boone, C. A. J. J., and Witteloostuijn, A. van (1995): "Industrial organization and organization ecology: The potentials for cross-fertilization," *Organization Studies*, 16, 265–98.

Boone, C. A. J. J., De Brabander, B., and Witteloostuijn, A. van (1996): "CEO locus of control and small firm performance: An integrative framework and empirical test," *Journal of Management Studies*, 33, 667–99.

Boone, C. A. J. J., De Brabander, B., and Witteloostuijn, A. van (1999): "The impact of personality on behavior in five prisoner's dilemma games," *Journal of Economic Psychology*, 20, 343–77.

Boone, C. A. J. J., Olffen, W. van, and Witteloostuijn, A. van (1998): "Psychological top management team make-up and economic firm performance: An experimental study," *Journal of Economic Psychology*, 19, 43–73.

Brandenburger, A. M., and Nalebuff, B. (1996): *Co-Opetition*. New York: Currency Doubleday.

Camerer, C., and Knez, M. (1996): "Coordination, organizational boundaries and fads in business practice," *Industrial and Corporate Change*, 5, 89–112.

Chen, X., and White, H. (1998): "Nonparametric adaptive learning with feedback," *Journal of Economic Theory*, 82, 190–222.

Cohen, M. D., March, J. G., and Olsen, J. P. (1972): "A garbage can model of organizational choice," *Administrative Science Quarterly*, 17, 1–25.

Cyert, R. M., and March, J. G. (1963): *A Behavioral Theory of the Firm*. Englewood Cliffs, NJ: Prentice-Hall.

DiMaggio, P., and Powell, W. W. (1983): "The iron cage revisited: Institutional isomorphism and collective rationality in organizational fields," *American Sociological Review*, 48, 147–60.

Dixit, A. (1982): "Imperfect competition and public policy: Recent developments in oligopoly theory," *American Economic Review*, 72, 12–17.

Dixit, A., and Nalebuff, B. (1992): *Thinking Strategically: The Competitive Edge in Business, Politics, and Everyday Life*. New York: W. W. Norton.

Eaton, B. C., and Lipsey, R. G. (1989): "Product differentiation," in R. Schmalensee and R. D. Willig (eds), *Handbook of Industrial Organization*, Amsterdam: North-Holland, 723–70.

Fershtman, C., and Judd, K. L. (1987): "Equilibrium incentives in oligopoly," *American Economic Review*, 77, 927–40.

Finkelstein, S., and Hambrick, D. C. (1996): *Strategic Leadership: Top Executives and their Effect on Organizations*. Minneapolis: West Publishing.

Fisher, F. M. (1989): "Games economists play: A noncooperative view," *RAND Journal of Economics*, 20, 113–24.

Friedman, M. (1953): *Essays in Positive Economics*. Chicago: Chicago University Press.

Fudenberg, D., and Tirole, J. (1984): "The fat-cat effect, the puppy-dog ploy, and the lean and hungry look," *American Economic Review (Papers and Proceedings)*, 74, 361–66.

Fudenberg, D., and Tirole, J. (1991): *Game Theory*. Cambridge, MA: MIT Press.

Ghemawat, P. (1991): *Commitment: The Dynamic of Strategy*. New York: Free Press.

Ghemawat, P., and Nalebuff, B. (1985): "Exit," *RAND Journal of Economics*, 16, 184–94.

Gilbert, R. J. (1989): "Mobility barriers and the value of incumbency," in R. Schmalensee and R. D. Willig (eds), *Handbook of Industrial Organization*, Amsterdam: North-Holland, 475–536.

Hambrick, D. C., and Fukutomi, G. D. S. (1991): "The seasons of a CEO's tenure," *Academy of Management Review*, 16, 719–42.

Ichniowsky, C., Shaw, K., and Prennushi, G. (1997): "The effect of human resource management practices on productivity: A study of steel finishing lines," *American Economic Review*, 87, 291–313.

Johnson, G., and Scholes, K. (1999): *Exploring Corporate Strategy: Text and Cases*. Englewood Cliffs, NJ: Prentice-Hall.

Jovanovic, B. (1982): "Selection and the evolution of industry," *Econometrica*, 50, 649–70.

Kamien, M. I., and Schwartz, N. L. (1982): *Market Structure and Innovation*. Cambridge: Cambridge University Press.

Kelly, D., and Amburgey, T. L. (1991): "Organizational inertia and momentum: A dynamic model of strategic change," *Academy of Management Journal*, 34, 591–612.

Klepper, S., and Graddy, K. (1990): "The evolution of new industries and the determinants of market structure," *RAND Journal of Economics*, 21, 27–44.

Kreps, D. M., and Scheinkman, J. A. (1983): "Quantity precommitment and Bertrand competition yield Cournot outcomes," *Bell Journal of Economics*, 14, 326–37.

Maijoor, S. J., and Witteloostuijn, A. van (1996): "An empirical test of the resource-based theory: Strategic regulation in the Dutch audit industry," *Strategic Management Journal*, 17, 549–70.

Margolis, H. (1982): *Selfishness, Altruism, and Rationality*. Cambridge: Cambridge University Press,

Marshall, A. (1920): *Principles of Economics*. London: MacMillan.

Mason, E. S. (1939): "Price and production policies of large-scale enterprise," *American Economic Review*, 29, 61–74.

Miller, C. C., and Cardinal, L. B. (1994): "Strategic planning and firm performance: A synthesis of more than two decades of research," *Academy of Management Journal*, 37, 1649–55.

Morgenstern, O., and Neumann, J. von (1944): *Theory of Games and Economic Behavior*. Princeton, NJ: Princeton University Press.

Mueller, D. C. (1992): "The corporation and the economist," *International Journal of Industrial Organization*, 10, 147–70.

Murnighan, J. K. (1994): "Game theory and organizational behavior," *Research in Organizational Behavior*, 16, 83–123.

Myerson, R. B: Game Theory (1991): *Analysis of Conflict*. Cambridge, MA: Harvard University Press.

Nash, J. F. (1951): "Non-cooperative games," *Annals of Mathematics*, 54, 286–95.

Nelson, R.R., and Winter, S. G. (1982): *An Evolutionary Theory of Economic Change*. Cambridge, MA: Harvard University Press.

Novshek, W., and Sonnenschein, H. (1987): "General equilibrium with free entry: A synthetic approach to the theory of perfect competition," *Journal of Economic Literature*, 25, 1281–306.

Péli, G., Bruggeman, J., Masuch, M., and Ó Nualláin, B. (1994): "A logical approach to formalizing organizational ecology," *American Sociological Review*, 59, 571–93.

Pfeffer, J. (1993): "Barriers to the advance of organizational science: Paradigm development as a dependent variable," *Academy of Management Review*, 18, 599–620.

Porter, M. E. (1980): *Competitive Strategy: Techniques for Analyzing Industries and Competitors*. New York: The Free Press.

Radner, R. (1980): "Collusive behavior in noncooperative epsilon-equilibria of oligopolies with long but finite lives," *Journal of Economic Theory*, 22, 136–54.

Rasmusen, E. (1990): *Games and Information: An Introduction into Game Theory*. Oxford: Basil Blackwell.

Rauscher, M. (1992): "Keeping up with the Joneses: Chaotic patterns in a status game," *Economic Letters*, 40, 287–90.

Reinganum, J. F. (1989): "The timing of innovation: research, development, and diffusion," in R. Schmalensee and R. D. Willig (eds), *Handbook of Industrial Organization*, Amsterdam: North-Holland, 849–908.

Rotemberg, J. J., and Saloner, G. (1986): "A supergame-theoretic model of business cycles and price wars during booms," *American Economic Review*, 76, 390–407.

Scherer, F. M. (1980): *Industrial Market Structure and Economic Performance*. Chicago: Rand McNally.

Scherer, F. M., and Ross, D. (1990): *Industrial Market Structure and Economic Performance*. Boston, MA: Houghton Mifflin.

Schmalensee, R. (1989): "Inter-industry studies of structure and performance," in R. Schmalensee and R. D. Willig (eds) *Handbook of Industrial Organization*, Amsterdam: North-Holland, 951–1010.

Schmalensee, R., and Willig, R. D. (eds) (1989): *Handbook of Industrial Organization*. Amsterdam: North-Holland.

Schumpeter, J. A. ([1943] 1976): *Capitalism, Socialism and Democracy*. London: George Allen and Unwin.

Selten, R. (1991): "Evolution, learning, and economic behavior," *Games and Economic Behavior*, 3, 3–24.

Shapiro, C. (1989): "The theory of business strategy," *RAND Journal of Economics*, 20, 125–37.

Shapiro, C., and Varian, H. R. (1999): *Information Rules: A Strategic Guide to the Network Economy*. Cambridge, MA: Harvard Business School Press.

Sklivas, S. D. (1987): "The strategic choice of managerial incentives," *RAND Journal of Economics*, 18, 452–58.

Smith, A. ([1776] 1974): *The Wealth of Nations*. Hammondsworth: Penguin.

Stigler, G. J. (1968): The Organization of Industry, Homewood, IL: Irwin.

Stigler, G. J., and Becker, G. S. (1977): "De gustibus non est disputandum," *American Economic Review*, 67, 76–90.

Stiglitz, J. E. (1989): "Imperfect information in the product market," in R. Schmalensee, and R. D. Willig (eds), *Handbook of Industrial Organization*, Amsterdam: North-Holland, 771–848.

Sutcliffe, K. M. (1994): "What executives notice: Accurate perceptions in top management teams," *Academy of Management Journal*, 37, 1360–78.

Sutton, J. (1991): *Sunk Costs and Market Structure: Price Competition, Advertising and the Evolution of Concentration*. Cambridge, MA: MIT Press.

Sutton, J. (1997): "Gibrat's legacy," *Journal of Economic Literature*, 35, 40–59.

Sutton, J. (1998): *Technology and Market Structure: Theory and History*. Cambridge, MA: MIT Press.

Thiétart, R. A., and Forgues, B. (1995): "Chaos theory and organization," *Organization Science*, 6, 19–31.

Tirole, J. (1988): *The Theory of Industrial Organization*. Cambridge, MA: MIT Press.

Vickers, J. (1985): "Delegation and the theory of the firm," *Economic Journal*, 95, 138–47.

Waller, M. J., Huber, G. P., and Glick, W. H. (1995): "Functional background as a determinant of executives' selective perception," *Academy of Management Journal*, 38, 943–47.

Walras, L. (1954): *Elements of Pure Economics*. Homewood, IL: Irwin. Originally published (1874) as *Eléments d'Economie Politique Pure*. Lausanne: Corbaz.

Wegberg, M. J. A. M. van, Witteloostuijn, A. van, and Roscam Abbing, M. (1994): "Multimarket and multiproject collusion: Why European integration may reduce intra-Community competition," *De Economist*, 142, 253–85.

Williamson, O. E. (1985): *The Economic Institutions of Capitalism*. New York: Free Press.

Witteloostuijn, A. van (1988): "Maximising and satisficing: Opposite or equivalent concepts?" *Journal of Economic Psychology*, 9, 289–313.

Witteloostuijn, A. van (1990): "Learning in economic theory: A taxonomy with an application to expectations formation," *Journal of Economic Psychology*, 11, 183–207.

Witteloostuijn, A. van (1992): 'Theories of competition and market performance: Multimarket competition and the source of potential entry," *De Economist,* 140, 109–39.

Witteloostuijn, A. van (1998): "Bridging behavioral and economic theories of decline: Organizational inertia, strategic competition, and chronic failure," *Management Science,* 44, 501–19.

Witteloostuijn, A. van (2000): "Editorial: Organization ecology has a bright future," *Organization Studies,* 21, v–xiv.

Witteloostuijn, A. van, and Boone, C. A. J. J. (1999): "A game theory of organizational ecology: A model of managerial inertia and market selection," Research Memorandum, Warwick: Warwick Business School.

Witteloostuijn, A. van, and Maks, J. A. H. (1988): "Workable competition and the barrier market," *European Journal of Political Economy,* 4, 117–35.

Witteloostuijn, A. van, Boone, C. A. J. J., and Carroll, G. R. (1999): "A resource-based theory of market structure," Research Memorandum, Warwick: Warwick Business School.

Witteloostuijn, A. van, Bunte, F., and Lier, A. van (1999): "Competing as or against a fool: And the added value of orthodox unorthodoxy in industrial organization," Research Memorandum, Warwick: Warwick Business School.

Witteloostuijn, A. van, Lier, A. van, and Boone, C. A. J. J. (1999): "Labor force flexibility, long-term tenure, and firm performance in declining industries: The competitive advantage of high-commitment HRM," Research Memorandum, Groningen: University of Groningen.

Zajac, E. J., and Bazerman, M. H. (1991): "Blind spots in industry and competitor analysis: Implications of interfirm (mis)perceptions for strategic decisions," *Academy of Management Review,* 16, 37–56.

Part IV

Organizational Epistemology and Research Methods

31 Updating Organizational Epistemology   715
      Jane Azevedo

32 Contemporary Debates in Organizational Epistemology   733
      Mihnea C. Moldoveanu and Joel A. C. Baum

33 Model-Centered Organization Science Epistemology   752
      Bill McKelvey

34 Survey Research Methods   781
      David Knoke, Peter V. Marsden and Arne L. Kalleberg

35 Archival Research Methods   805
      Marc J. Ventresca and John W. Mohr

36 Simulation Research Methods   829
      Kevin Dooley

37 Grounded Theory Research Methods   849
      Deborah Dougherty

38 Field Research Methods   867
      Andrew H. Van de Ven and Marshall Scott Poole

Chapter Thirty-one

Updating Organizational Epistemology

JANE AZEVEDO

The study of organizations is characterized by a diversity of theory and method. This diversity is both its strength and its weakness. The strength results from bringing a range of disciplines and theoretical perspectives to bear on the problems associated with organizations – problems of design, function, management, operation, habitability and so on. It is the thematic nature of the subject that provides such cohesiveness as exists. The weakness stems from apparently irreconcilable conflicts between disciplines, PARA-DIGMS[1] and perspectives that fragment the area, leading to a general lack of consistency and coherence. This makes the application of organization science effectively useless except selectively, to bolster preexisting ideas. The study of organizations is best conceived as ideology rather than science.

But diversity need not lead to fragmentation. What is required to maintain the strengths that result from the diversity of organization science while avoiding the problems associated with fragmentation is a powerful epistemology capable of unifying diverse, even seemingly contradictory, approaches. In this chapter, I argue that an *evolutionary naturalist realist* epistemology best satisfies this requirement.

The study of organizations is not alone in being tarred with the brush of ideology. The social sciences in general face a similar set of problems. Both sociology and psychology, for example, abound with crisis talk (Fiske and Shweder, 1986). And then there is economics. The problems of organization science are perhaps compounded, based as they are in these disciplines, which are themselves often seen as incompatible.

For example, much mainstream organization theory stems from the sociology of Weber on bureaucracy and rationalization and that of Durkheim on the division of labor (Thompson and McHugh, 1995). While Weber and Durkheim were both critical of many features of modern organizations and society, the critical aspects of their work have generally been ignored by mainstream management theorists (Thompson and McHugh, 1995, p. 367). Critical alternatives to mainstream theory tend to be Marxist in flavor, or to take from Weber his conception of a social science rather than his criticisms of bureaucracy. Both Marxist and Durkheimian sociology tend to be hostile to the Weberian tradition, the former taking a REALIST approach to social entities while Weber's agency view of social science allowed social entities no existence independently of their place in the meaning systems of individual actors. The recent POSTMODERNIST and POSTSTRUCTURALIST moves in sociology challenge Weber's notion of rationality, as well as the realism associated with Marx and Durkheim. Sociology, then, comprises various competing perspectives. It operates with a variety of conflicting assumptions about the nature of the social world. It is multi-paradigmatic, where paradigms define what counts as research and set standards of validity and good explanation. Its multi-paradigmatic nature means that there is no consensual way of arbitrating conflicting truth claims. It is such lack of consensus that lies behind Kuhn's argument that to be multi-paradigmatic is to be PRE-SCIENTIFIC (Kuhn, 1970).

Mainstream organization theory has, as well as a sociological component, a social psychological component (Thompson and McHugh, 1995, p. 383). Psychology, too, is traditionally diverse; the major split being between behaviorism and cognitive psychology (Fiol, this volume). As in sociology, critical social psychologies have developed as a response to gaps and problems in mainstream theory, and in opposition to it. The stretching of economics, with its subideologies (such as game theory, agency theory, mathematical theory, and experimental economics), inside organizations adds still another element of discipline diversity.

But, with the rise of postmodernist epistemologies that applaud eclecticism and refuse to distinguish any claim to knowledge as privileged, even the so-called "hard" natural sciences such as physics are regarded simply as a claim to knowledge no better (and often worse) than any other.

So what is wrong with the fragmentation of knowledge? Simply, without consistency and coherence, claims to knowledge cannot be applied. They become, as is often argued by postmodernism, just so many language games. Inconsistent beliefs are of no practical use. If you hold the contradictory beliefs that

(a) getting in the way of moving cars is dangerous, and
(b) that getting in the way of moving cars is not dangerous

these beliefs lead you to opposite strategies for crossing roads. Together, they give no guidance to your actions.

While less extreme, a lack of coherence is almost as bad. Say you know through experience that you can't walk on Sydney Harbor. It is only because of a coherence between that belief and other beliefs, say, about the nature of water, the nature of the human body, and the nature of bodies of water, that you are able to generalize that belief so that you know without trying that you can't walk on the Macquarie River. If it weren't for the coherence of your beliefs, you'd spend an awful lot of time getting wet trying to walk on water.

As Thompson and McHugh (1995, pp. 362–3) argue, "Any account of contemporary organization must be at least *capable* of illuminating all levels, from the broader institutional constraints, through the sectional conflicts and down to real flesh and blood individuals." No single perspective or discipline can accomplish this task. This means that solutions to the problems of fragmentation in organization science are best found at the metatheoretical and epistemological levels.

Epistemological Traditions in Sociology

Within sociology, these issues have traditionally been addressed by discussing whether sociology is or is not a science. The more general issue is whether the social sciences are, or can be, scientific. This issue is worth exploring. It raises the pragmatic questions of the utility of funding social scientific research and the seriousness with which its findings are taken. By implication, and indeed in practice (McKelvey, this volume), the issue has serious consequences for the well being of organization *science*.

The fundamental parameters of the issue are simple. To determine whether the social sciences are, or can be, scientific, one must first know what it is to be scientific and what it is to be sociological, and then compare the two. On the assumption that if anything is scientific, the natural sciences are, the issue is usually resolved into a comparison of sociology in particular, or the social sciences in general, with the natural sciences, to ascertain whether there are any fundamental differences between them.

There are two possible solutions to this issue. The naturalist position is that, while there may be, and indeed are, differences between the social and the natural sciences, these differences are not fundamental. The social sciences, provided they adhere to the methods of the natural sciences (whatever they might be), can indeed be scientific. The humanist position, on the other hand, is that the differences between the social and the natural sciences are so fundamental as to require a quite different set of methodological principles. If the natural sciences are taken as paradigmatic for science, the social sciences must be considered non-scientific.

The archetypal naturalist epistemologies of the twentieth century are often referred to under the generic term "POSITIVISM," or in epistemological circles as "the RECEIVED VIEW." Positivism is a scientifically oriented form of empiricism first developed by the nineteenth century French philosopher Auguste Comte. The idea behind positivism was sound enough. The natural sciences were rightly seen as producing highly informative, reliable and useful knowledge about the natural world. With the social chaos that followed industrialization, intellectuals saw the need for an equally powerful way of knowing and understanding the social world, to ameliorate the appalling human conditions with the attendant unstable politics that threatened social order. An obvious way to develop the required social sciences was to model the natural sciences and base the social sciences on that model.

To the early positivists, natural scientific knowledge was seen as so powerful because it produced certain knowledge of the world. The foundations of that certainty were held to be sense experience and logic. Sensory experience was seen as incorrigible and the logic of the scientific method truth-preserving. Beliefs about the world could be regarded as knowledge only if they could be put to the test of experience. The incorrigibility of observation combined with the logic of the scientific method to produce certain knowledge. Thus, the appropriate objects of scientific knowledge were phenomena and the general relations between phenomena.

The positivists regarded all phenomena as subject to invariable laws of nature (see LAW-LIKE). The task of science was to discover these laws, and scientific explanation consisted in showing the links between particular phenomena and these general laws of nature. It was most definitely *not* the task of science to establish the underlying nature of phenomena, nor to search for causal GENERATIVE MECHANISMS. According to Comte, the search for these forms of knowledge belonged to the earlier "METAPHYSICAL" or pre-scientific stage in the development of knowledge. In the scientific or positivist stage, according to Comte,

> ... the human mind, recognizing the impossibility of attaining to absolute concepts, gives up the search for the origin and destiny of the universe and the inner causes of phenomena, and confines itself to the discovery, through reason and observation combined, of the actual laws that govern the succession and similarity of phenomena. The explanation of facts, now reduced to its real terms, consists in the establishment of a link between various particular phenomena and a few general facts, which diminish in numbers with the progress of science (Comte, in Andreski, 1974, p. 20).

For the positivists, then, scientific knowledge was characterized by several features. The objects of scientific knowledge were phenomena; such knowledge took the form of general laws that must be testable by experience; and explanation consisted in showing the logical links between specific phenomena and these laws. These tenets formed a general methodology for the acquisition of scientific knowledge. Such knowledge was certain and value-free, and only knowledge acquired via these general methodological principles had any claim to the term. It is these methodological principles that underlie the positivists' claim of the "UNITY OF SCIENCE" at an epistemological level. (Some positivists and later empiricists, although definitely not Comte, extend the idea of the unity of science to include the notion that each branch of science is reducible to the next most general branch, and ultimately to physics. This is an ONTOLOGICAL thesis rather than an epistemological one, though consistency demands a relationship between the two.) The social sciences, then, were subject to the same broad methodological principles as the natural sciences. In so far as they did not, or could not, comply, they were not producing knowledge at all.

Positivism in its various guises has been influential in all of the social sciences from their very beginnings. But it did not reign unchallenged. Max Weber, for example, held that the objects of study of the social sciences differed so fundamentally from those of the natural sciences that they required their own methodology. While the positivist method might serve to study human behavior, the object of sociological study was not behavior but social action (Weber, 1978, p. 4). Weber distinguishes "behavior" from "action" in terms of the subjective meaning that attaches to the latter. "Behavior" can be seen in purely physiological terms and can be explained causally from a physiological point of view. "Actions," on the other hand, are meaningful. But meaning, the feature that distinguishes behavior from action, is not OBSERVABLE. Simply to distinguish the subject matter of sociology requires interpretive understanding. Social action, the object of sociological knowledge, cannot be distinguished from behavior by observation alone.

Sociological explanation, then, according to Weber, differed from natural scientific explanation in that the latter explained an observable subject matter by subsumption under the laws of nature, whereas the former explained a non-observable subject matter by interpretive understanding. Interpretation involves understanding the meaning of a particular action, or placing it in a wider contextual setting. Moreover, Weber argued, the values of the social scientist unavoidably intrude on the study. Thus sociology requires the development of a fundamentally different methodology, the nature of which leads to criteria of objectivity quite different from those of a positivist natural science (Azevedo, 1997).

While there are various humanist positions, the methodological issues of causality, meaning and values that interested Weber are those upon which humanists tend to base their case for a fundamental distinction between the natural and the social sciences (Runciman, 1978, p. 65).

But the debate between humanism and naturalism arose against the backdrop of positivism. With positivism's fall from grace, complete by the late 1970s, most if not all of the arguments for a fundamental distinction between the natural and the social sciences disappeared. The problems of organization science, then, cannot be explained away as simply a function of their social scientific nature. Whether attaching the label "scientific" to the study of organizations will help resolve its problems is going to depend very much on whether scientific methodology can provide perspective-neutral mechanisms for arbitrating contradictory truth claims and for either choosing between, or somehow unifying, conflicting assumptions about the nature of the world.

The positivist models of science guaranteed such mechanisms. But internal difficulties with the positivist philosophies of science, in addition to studies in the history and sociology of science, have shown that none of the positivist models of science is an adequate description of the scientific process. Not only are the positivist models inadequate as descriptions of the scientific process, they are inadequate as normative models. Feyerabend has argued convincingly that had any of the positivist models actually been followed by scientists, science could not have progressed, though it obviously has (Feyerabend, 1978). Moreover, historical and sociological studies have pointed to the inevitable existence of many factors apart from value-free facts and logic in the scientific process, raising serious doubts about the ability of science to provide any such perspective-neutral mechanisms.

Positivism's fall from grace came with the realizations that

(a) observation was theory-laden, and
(b) there was more to the rational acceptance of theories than logic (either inductive or deductive).

Epistemic values such as simplicity, internal consistency and the potential to lead to further research, among others, may all be involved. But if theory choice involves values, and observation is theory-laden, the distinction between fact and value can no longer be seen as clear-cut. Observation and formal logic, then, cannot be seen as the foundation of a certain and objective science.

A common epistemological response to this loss of certainty is RELATIVISM. Postmodernism and poststructuralism are its most common contemporary forms. Relativism takes as its starting points the theory-ladenness of observation, and, following Kuhn and Feyerabend, the paradigm and/or cultural specificity of methodology. As a consequence, relativism regards science as FALLIBLE. For the relativist, once the incorrigibility of observation is denied and the inadequacy of formal logics to account for scientific methodology is recognized, there are no grounds for objectivity. Contemporary relativists do not usually take this to entail a retreat to SOLIPSISM, but rather to cultural frames of reference. Different cultures have been found to have different sets of values, and different ways of categorizing the world. Within each culture, it is held, common values and theories as to the nature of the world may ensure objective knowledge, but there can be no way of judging between the theories of different cultures. The point at issue, then, is the relativist claim that even if there is no fundamental difference between the social sciences and the natural sciences, the natural sciences themselves are not able to provide the perspective-neutral criteria necessary to solve the problems of organization science. Indeed, there is no way to distinguish science from any other knowledge production and maintenance system such as religion.

Evolutionary Naturalist Realism (ENR)

But relativism has not been alone in the field since the downfall of positivism. Realism, historically one of the major opponents of empiricism, offers promise of a different notion of objectivity, and has gained currency among contemporary philosophers of science. Realism is the thesis that there is a real world existing independently of our attempts to know it; that we as humans can have knowledge of that world; and that the validity of our knowledge claims is, at least in part, determined by the way the world is. Our knowledge of the world is not obtained simply from incorrigible perceptions and a content-free logic, as the positivists would have it; neither are its sources purely cognitive, as the relativists would have it. Rather, such knowledge has both cognitive and empirical content.

As modern versions of realism were developed against the background of the recent debate with positivism and realists were tackling the empiricists on their own ground, realism is now a well-developed epistemology (Hooker, 1987, 1995; Hahlweg and Hooker, 1989). But in contrast to positivism, it is a non-FOUNDATIONALIST epistemology. In the positivist schema, science discovered true theories because it followed the prescriptive and a prioristically derived method of combining objective facts with logic. To the naturalist realist, science is fallible. It does not so much discover true theories as provide reliable knowledge of the world. While a naturalist realist epistemology aims to be prescriptive, this is because it attempts to model the natural sciences well enough to abstract from them the best of their methods. It is based on a thorough study of scientific practice, and as such it too is fallible, bearing the same relation to scientific theories as the latter do to the world they are attempting to explain (Hooker, 1987, p. 88).

The notion that the naturalist realist epistemology is informed by science means that any methodology that it develops is going to be based not only on the study of science but on the results of scientific study. In other words, naturalist realism takes science seriously. So any epistemology and methodology is going to be informed by the best view that science can offer of what humans are and how they can know.

But from the definition of realism given above, it is clear that realism has an important ontological component, too, and one that is appealed to in justifying its notions of objectivity, for the realist claim is that the world itself is a perspective-neutral arbiter between competing truth-claims and theories. As realist ontology is important epistemically, I shall briefly discuss the ontological aspects of naturalist realism here.

The basic ontological position of realism is that a world exists independently of our knowledge of it, and that the nature of that world is such that we can have knowledge of it. Beyond that, the nature of the world is a matter for empirical investigation. Realism, then, is not committed a priori to any account of the specific nature of the world such as reductionism.

Nevertheless, realism is monistic in the sense that it holds that the nature of the world is such that it is, in principle, open to empirical investigation. So it is committed to an ontological unity of nature thesis in that it does not recognize ontologies that are in principle closed to empirical investigation. This unity of knowledge thesis can be seen as a special case of the naturalist unity of nature thesis. The naturalist thesis maintains that everything in the world is of such a nature that it can in principle interact with everything else. While causal isolations are possible, they are contingent, and the naturalist imposes no ontological distinctions for semantic or epistemic reasons. The realist thesis maintains that everything knowable in the world can interact with humans, because humans know the world via their interactions with it.

The notion of cause plays a vital role in naturalist realist accounts of science. The realist view of science holds that scientific theories aim to discover the real nature of the world, appearances notwithstanding. The realist is interested in discovering the generative/causal mechanisms underlying phenomena. Causal interactions between humans and the world form the basis of naturalist realist notions of validity.

This brief sketch of the naturalist realist ontological thesis, along with a fully fleshed out naturalist realist metaphilosophy of science such as that developed by Hooker (1987, 1995), makes sense of the realist response to the failure of positivism to provide criteria for the validity of theories. In response to the theory-ladenness of facts and the failure of logic to guarantee certainty, the realist, like the relativist, adopts a fallibilist approach to science. But in contrast to the relativist, the realist denies that it is rational to accept only what one is logically forced to. The process of acquiring knowledge involves taking risks – going beyond the evidence (Popper, 1979). Nonetheless, the realist wishes to maintain appropriate objective criteria for deciding whether a theory is good or bad. The realist, then, has to develop a quite different notion of rationality from the logic of the positivists, and a quite different notion of objectivity from the incorrigibility of observation. In other words, the realist has to develop a new methodology for science.

Once one realizes that science provides no "God's eye" view of reality (elaborated in Hendrickx, 1999) but is rather a fallible human activity, the search is on for an adequate epistemology and methodology of science that takes the biological nature of humans seriously. Much recent work by psychologists, anthropologists, philosophers, and historians of science has been directed at providing plausible naturalist models of sciencing as a human activity. These models have mainly been restricted to a discussion of human perceptual and/or cognitive mechanisms. As such, they make no contribution to the question of how scientific theories are selected, or whether, and if so how, they can be known to be valid. Such positions can do no more than argue that human perceptual and cognitive mechanisms are generally reliable within the range of the environmental interactions that selected them. The cross-cultural variation of belief systems, the persistence of false beliefs, and the fact that in some circumstances, false beliefs may be functional for survival and reproduction, all show that the nature of human perceptual and cognitive systems, while accounting for the fallibility of science, is insufficient to account for the reliability of science. Any account of the reliability of science must move beyond the nature of human perceptual and cognitive mechanisms to examine the ways in which beliefs are selected and justified; see Moldoveanu and Baum (this volume) for an application of such an approach to organizational epistemology.

CAMPBELLIAN NATURALIST EVOLUTIONARY REALISM

How beliefs are selected and justified has been addressed by Donald Campbell. Campbell provides a general model for inductive gains that takes full account of the social nature of scientific knowledge. One of the main features of his argument is that there is an analogy between biological evolution and scientific progress. Both evolve via a process of blind variation and selective retention. Science, seen as a problem-solving activity, is continuous with the problem-solving activity of all organisms. Some of the broad range of Campbell's thinking is apparent in the various contributions in the Baum and McKelvey (1999) anthology, and in McKelvey's (1999) review of Campbellian realism.

In an evolutionary sense, the main problems faced by organisms are survival and reproduction. But survival, even for simple organisms such as the paramecium, involves modeling the environment. The paramecium, for example, exhibits blind variation of locomotor activity until a nourishing or non-noxious setting is found. This solution is then retained as cessation of movement. In a world of only benign or neutral states, such organisms can operate without external sense organs. Wherever it is, the organism is trying to ingest the environment, and when starvation approaches, blind locomotor activity takes place until more food is found. But even at this simple level of organization, an internal organ is required to monitor the organism's nutritional states. This organ monitors nutritional levels and substitutes for the whole organism's death, indicating it's time for a move. Obviously, more complex perceptual/cognitive systems are needed if toxic environments are to be recognized and avoided. So there are evolutionary pressures for the development of such systems. But even with simple creatures like the paramecium, it is only indirectly, through selecting the selectors, that life-and-death relevance selects its response to the environment (Campbell, 1974, pp. 422–3).

Vicarious locomotor devices such as vision constitute an epistemological advance over such systems, but are less direct. With vision, an organism can scan ahead and move accordingly rather than just randomly running into trouble. Although enhancing the chances of an organism's survival, such devices, because less direct, are in an absolute sense more prone to error. This is because the penalty for error is decreased – it is less likely to result in the death of the organism – which is precisely why it constitutes an advantage in the first place. The exploration of a vicarious environment (as opposed to vicarious exploration of real environment) that occurs in sophisticated cognitive modeling and particularly in science is still less direct, more advantageous yet more prone to error (Rubinstein et al., 1984).

The problem, then, is to explain how (while their exploration of the world is so indirect) scientific beliefs increasingly improve their fit with the world. It cannot be just because humans have the perceptual and cognitive mechanisms that they do. Certainly, natural selection has validated the general operation of the visual system for middle-sized physical objects. But this does not of itself justify a visual-perceptual foundationalism, because the mechanisms that produce compelling experiential objectivity in the conscious mind are the same whether the perceptions are valid or illusory (Campbell and Paller, 1989, p. 236).

Campbell approaches the problem by considering the ways in which humans select and revise their perceptions. Illusory perceptions *can* be revised. Given a Muller–Lyer type illusion and a ruler, we can convince ourselves that our eyes are deceiving us. But when this happens, the perceptual belief is revised, not just by one other perception, but by trusting the great bulk of our other perceptions plus some constancy conditions (for example that the ruler is always the same length) that are only approximately true (Campbell and Paller, 1989, p. 234). Humans have a COHERENCE strategy of belief revision rather than one based on perceptual correspondence. Moreover, anthropological and sociological evidence to the effect that perceptual and cognitive frameworks are socially learned and vary from culture to culture indicates that the reliability of the human perceptual system comes not so much from the perceptual mechanisms of the individual as from the social cross-validation of beliefs.

Nonetheless, this does not lead to a cultural solipsism, as some sociologists of knowledge, postmodernist social theorists, and so on, have argued. Campbell argues convincingly that reality plays a part in editing beliefs, particularly in the sort of environment in which the organism's perceptual mechanisms evolved. Thus for humans there is general cross-cultural agreement over middle-sized objects and boundary acts. This can be shown by the way language "will cut nature at her joints" (Campbell, 1973, p. 1050). Not all languages, for example, will have words for pieces of trees (for example stems and leaves), but none that do will have a word for a twig plus the first centimeter or so of a leaf, or for a twig plus half a pine cone.

The point can be further illustrated by considering in detail the different ways that different cultures divide up the natural world. While species are the largest natural kind recognized by biology, the Linnaean system of classifying organisms is an hierarchical system that groups species further into genera and family groupings. Studies in folk taxonomy have shown that all known folk systems of classification are likewise hierarchical, assigning species into more general groups (Berlin, 1973). The principles that form the basis of folk classifications, particularly at a level equivalent to the Linnaean species, i.e. at the level of the folk genera, seem to be based primarily on the recognition of gross morphological similarities and differences. It is rare, at this level, for classification to be based on the functional attributes of the organism for the people concerned (Berlin et al., 1966; Bulmer and Tyler, 1968).

The groups represented both by scientific genera and families and by the higher levels of folk classification illustrate the different cognitive frameworks of different cultural groups. The frameworks reflect the significance of the items in the various groups to the culture concerned and have no objective reality. But the correspondence between different folk generic taxa and Linnaean species shows that at this level, nature edits classification and language.

Language, then, is not purely conventional. Moreover, language learning depends on shared perceptual reifications, which thus become "socially 'foundational' in achieving linguistic transfer of valid beliefs from person to person" (Campbell and Paller, 1989, p. 240). Language cannot be taught completely by telephone. Shared reference through language presupposes that reality has edited ostensibly transmitted vocabulary.

Valid beliefs, therefore, are achieved as a result of social processes rather than despite them. As with positivism, the basis of objectivity lies in inter-subjective, and even cross-cultural, agreement, at the level of middle-distance objects and boundary acts. Campbell, then, supports a fallible social perceptual foundationalism. But "foundationalism" in Campbell's sense differs from the a priori foundationalism of the positivists. Campbell's foundationalism is not of the FIRST PHILOSOPHY type. Rather, it is descriptive of the processes by which beliefs are tested for validity.

Reliable as perception may be at this level, it remains a puzzle how scientific beliefs, the social products of an elaborate social system, increasingly improve their fit with reality. For science extends far beyond middle-distance objects. Invisible theoretical entities lie outside the validity range of human perceptual mechanisms. And as anthropologists and sociologists are well aware, there are many social institutions whose business includes the production and maintenance of beliefs that palpably do not fit with reality. The question becomes, at this juncture, what is it that distinguishes the selection of scientific beliefs from those of other social belief-producing institutions.

All knowledge is physically embodied, and by the same token, all knowledge is subject to constraints and biases due to the nature of the system that embodies it. For example, a mosaic representation of some part of the countryside is necessarily incomplete, inaccurate, and distorted, as a result of the characteristics of the medium, for example, the size, shape and color of the pebbles available, the change from three dimensions to two dimensions, and the change of scale. So the validity of knowledge is constrained by the characteristics of the medium or vehicle of that knowledge (Campbell, 1979, pp. 183–4). It is also constrained by the structure of the vehicle. If the mosaic were attempted with colored drops of water rather than colored pebbles, the transferred information could not be retained. As Campbell (1979, p. 184) points out, ". . . if the vehicle is completely flexible, it lacks the rigidity to hold together the picture it carries." The carrier of scientific knowledge is the scientific community, so it is in the nature of the scientific community, and, in a broader sense, the institution of science itself, that the answer to the great reliability of scientific knowledge will be found.

Science, according to Campbell, differs from other social belief production and maintenance systems in two respects. The first is that its methods provide a narrow window through which "Nature" can speak. It shares this feature with several other social systems. The second is that science's social norms (in particular such norms as valuing truth seeking over tradition and making contribution to truth the only criteria of status in science), function to channel consensus in science in a way that maximizes the opportunity for physical reality to influence scientific knowledge (Campbell and Paller, 1989, p. 248). It is this that distinguishes science from all other social institutions. Together, these two features can account for the success of science in producing increasingly valid knowledge of reality.

THE MAPPING MODEL OF KNOWLEDGE

The adoption of such an evolutionary epistemology has profound implications for the methodology of science. Scientific knowledge cannot be known to be true in any absolute sense. Rather, from an evolutionary perspective, scientific knowledge is seen as a reliable guide to action and decision-making. The validity of scientific theory depends not on objective observation and truth-preserving logic, but on the extent to which it is a reliable guide to action.

The validity of scientific theories, it turns out, is determined in the same way as is the validity of maps. It is because maps and theories share the function of being guides to action and decision-making that the ultimate tests of both are practical. As the process of making and using maps is easily understood, the use of a mapping model of knowledge provides a powerful heuristic for determining the validity of scientific theories; see

Hahlweg (1989) and Azevedo (1997) for a full development of this model.

Both maps and theories are constructed with interests in mind. Basically, our judgement of how good a map is relates to how well it helps us carry out the task we have in mind. These interests affect both the form and the content of the map. A detailed topographical map, no matter how good in other respects, is not the best sort of map for navigating city streets. Maps are selective representations of the world, and their content and form are selected according to their relevance to the problems they are intended to solve. And because the usefulness of a map can only be assessed by how well it helps to solve the problems of the user, its validity is interest-related as well. Metrical accuracy is not necessarily an advantage. Indeed, it may at times be a disadvantage. A topological map such as a sketch map showing how to reach my place from the nearest highway, e.g., is valuable precisely because it is not metrically accurate. Rather, it ignores everything but clearly visible landmarks and turnings. It is not even strictly accurate *vis à vis* direction. But it is far more efficient and reliable than even a street directory.

It should be obvious, too, that the interests of the user very much affect the methods used to construct maps. Precise surveying methods are essential for detailed topographic maps, while the ability to abstract from the landscape what a stranger behind the wheel will see is rather more important to the construction of a sketch map. The point here is that there can be no prescription for scientific method. From an ENR perspective, methods turn out to be anything that works, and are constantly subject to improvement.

The point I wish to make here is that for maps and theories, what counts is how well they model the features of interest while ignoring those that are irrelevant; see McKelvey (this volume) for further implications of the use of models in theory. While values and interests obviously enter into the construction of maps and theories and are part of the assessment of their validation, the way the world is enters very much into how valid they are as well.

But the objectivity of mapping cannot lie in the use of any simple truth-preserving mechanism relating a map to its domain. Rather, it lies in a public judgement of how good the map is. Given a commonality of interest and purpose and an equal competence in map reading, a particular map should be as good (or bad) for one person as for another. Any competent map reader should be able, in theory, to check the validity of a map, bearing in mind the purposes for which it was made, by predicting from the map that certain features and the relationships between them are a certain way and then checking this with the domain itself. The same applies to scientific theories.

Maps may be tested via prediction. But there are further features of maps themselves that can also be used to assess their validity. Maps are multiply connected. A map cannot be significantly altered at one point without affecting neighboring relations. This means that a surveyor can, and does, collect redundant data (the equivalent in the social sciences is, not uncoincidentally, referred to as triangulation). The coordinates of a particular feature may be determined with reference to a variety of other features, which means that its position can be double-checked by means of the relations it holds to features other than those used originally to determine it. A good map, then, must be internally consistent and coherent, and the "fit" of any particular feature of the map with the territory may be checked with reference to its place in the map as a whole.

Moreover, maps of the same territory are deeply compatible. This is obviously so among maps that differ only in scale. But it is also the case among maps that abstract different features of the territory, such as road maps and railway maps, and also with topologic maps which abstract only the most general relationships. We can combine maps of different features of the same territory, for example a railway map and a road map, into a more general map that includes both features. A mapping relationship exists between any two maps of the same territory. Thus, whether a particular map is compatible with other maps of the same territory will be a further guide to validity. Maps should ideally be externally coherent, and at least externally consistent, to be valid.

Maps, then, are valid in so far as they enable us to act successfully in pursuit of our interests. Explanation is no less a feature here than prediction and coherence, for maps enable us to explain general connections among the data. For example, a topographic map (combined with background theories of the nature of water) will enable us to explain the positions of the water courses by reference to the contours. Some of these watercourses may be marked with a dotted line indicating they are not permanently flowing. This feature may itself be explicable in terms of the terrain as represented on the topographical map, combined with information from a general rainfall map of the territory in question.

Validity, then, can be assessed in a number of ways; empirically, and by internal and external consistency and coherency checks because maps are multiply connected and maps of the same territory are deeply compatible. But because maps are abstractions constructed with an interest in mind, there are limitations on the valid use to which even an excellent map can be put. Consider, for example, a street directory of a city. It would not be valid to assume that because all of the streets along both sides of a blank strip were indicated as dead ends, the strip marked a railway line. One might be able to guess that there was some blockage there, but it could as easily be a storm-water gully as a railway line. Indeed there might not be any blockage at all. Planners might have left the area free for a proposed motorway. It would be invalid to move beyond the scope of the map to arrive at such a conclusion. Of course, the presence of the strip might well prompt further investigation, but the map itself would not provide an explanation of the strip.

This limitation on the valid use of a map is directly related to the interest that guided its construction, the sorts of problem it was intended to solve for the user. This is what is used to select the data that is mapped. That maps of the same territory are deeply compatible means that any single map may indicate the existence of other areas to be mapped, and requires that the other maps be consistent with it. The more general the map, the wider its scope. Nonetheless, every map, no matter how wide its scope, has a limited range of valid applicability. No single map can encompass every feature of the reality in question. In all these of these respects, *scientific theories are like maps* (Azevedo, 1997). There can be no single (totalizing) theory under which all scientific knowledge can, even in theory, be subsumed.

This brief sketch of an ENR epistemology and methodology should be sufficient to show just how unlike positivism this form of realism is. It takes full account of the socially constructed, interest-related features of scientific knowledge. Moreover, it shows that it is precisely because of, rather than despite, the interest-related nature of knowledge that it can be assessed. The sketch should also show that despite its socially constructed and interest-related nature, scientific knowledge is not merely conventional. Rather, the way the world is plays a vital part in any assessment of validity. Reality is not completely malleable, and any map that assumes it is and is constructed accordingly will be just plain wrong. While it might be in the interests of railway makers to chart the minimum distance between Sydney and Canberra for a high speed railway line, a map that minimizes that distance at the expense of mapping the very difficult terrain involved would be worse than useless.

EVOLUTIONARY NATURALIST REALISM AND COMPLEXITY

While the mapping model of knowledge provides a good heuristic for the acquisition and assessment of scientific knowledge, it is what evolutionary epistemology implies about complex systems that is perhaps most valuable to the study of organizations, for the domain of such studies is without doubt complex (e.g., Carley, this volume).

An evolutionary view of the world is more compatible with a *process* metaphysics than an *object* based metaphysics (Hahlweg, 1983, 1989). This turns out to be an advantage for those interested in the study of complex systems, because a process metaphysics allows the coexistence of many relatively autonomous layers of reality. Under a process metaphysics, objects are just relatively stable or enduring patterns in a complex process. Objects such as rocks seem stable to us with our lifespans, but are highly unstable from the point of view of the much longer geological time spans. A tomato plant, ephemeral from our point of view, seems stable to the generations of insects that are born, reproduce, and die on it.

There is much to be learnt about the study of complex systems by looking at how organisms obtain knowledge of their environment. As Hahlweg (1983, p. 38) points out: "The world is too rich to be captured in its entirety by any one creature. Everything is in constant flux, thus stability cannot be anything absolute but is always relative to the dimension of time and to the sensory equipment of the organism." For the organism, the evolutionary problem is how to sort out, in this rich and changing world, those changes that are important to the survival of the organism from those that are not. This problem is reflected in the organism's perceptual and cognitive mechanisms.

Take our perceptual mechanisms. The structure of the human perceptual organs limits our perceptual input. Just as a result of this, we are selective in what we can see. We have a simplified view of the world. But simplified as it is, the input we receive from the world is highly ambiguous. In a constantly changing world, we have to learn how to distinguish those changes that occur independently of our act of perceiving from those that are related to that act. For example, if we are looking from the window of a moving train, we have to learn that the countryside is not rushing past us. We are rushing past it. And *if we are to perceive change at all, we must create a stable background or framework with which to compare it.*

The most important framework for humans is the spatiotemporal framework. The space–time framework and object independence are learned early in childhood. The various senses are coordinated at this time, and things that appear invariant across the senses are called objects. It requires at least two different senses to establish the robustness of an object. Sense perceptions that are not invariant across several sensory modalities can be regarded as noise resulting from the act of perception. The principle is: *Stability is established by the coordination of various sensory frames of reference.*

For humans, vision is the most powerful mode of perception. A big evolutionary advantage for humans was stereoscopic vision. The two eyes have slightly different projections, which, when coordinated by the brain, give the impression of depth. Additional information is achieved by coordinating different frames of reference.

The same principle applies to science (Hahlweg, 1989). With a complex and many-layered reality, the first major problem the scientist faces is that of ensuring that the changes at different levels of reality do not affect the kind of change being investigated. This is the problem of distinguishing "genuine" changes from noise, or creating a stable background against which change can be distinguished.

Now noise is as real as any other phenomenon. It is distinguishable from "genuine" phenomena only by the intentions of the observer to investigate a particular aspect of reality. Noise is eliminated as much as possible in the physical sciences by the use of rigidly controlled experiments. One of the consequences of this approach is that reality can be investigated only one level at a time. In the historical natural sciences, for example in biology and geology, and also in the social sciences, the elimination of noise may be somewhat more problematic. Controlled experiments are not always possible, and when they are, they may not always be useful, or ethical.

Nonetheless, even the historical sciences have some equivalent to rigidly controlled experimentation, in that they use the same principles of comparison and control that underlie experimental design. These principles are, however, applied in other ways. Sociology, for example, makes use of historical and cross-cultural comparisons. The result is that the historical sciences, too, at least aim to investigate one level of reality at a time, although they are unlikely to achieve the precision of the experimental sciences.

The other major problem scientists face is that of distinguishing change internal to the experimental apparatus from those external changes being studied. Just as the development of multiple perceptual frameworks allows us to distinguish those phenomena that are dependent on our acts of perception from those that are independent, the development of multiple conceptual frameworks may enable us to distinguish those features of our experience that are robust from those that are due to our involvement as perceivers.

If we consistently work within one conceptual framework, even a powerful and fruitful one like reductionism, this will likely lead to error:

> Consisting of a set of mutually reinforcing theories and practices, [a powerful conceptual framework] defines what is possible and easily leads to dogmatism. Being caught within its explanatory power, we are in danger of forgetting that our framework *is* a construction, that the world is far too rich to be captured by any one framework alone (Hahlweg, 1983, p. 57).

So, although it is only by the creation of a stable conceptual framework that external changes can be perceived and regularities in the changing world can manifest themselves, Hahlweg (1983, p. 60) argues that "as long as we remain within that framework we might not be capable of detecting error, and all our methodologies may mislead us." Multiple conceptual frameworks are as essential for establishing genuine invariance as are multiple perceptual frameworks.

Advantage from Multiple Perspectives

The complexity that bedevils organization science is of precisely the same nature as that faced by natural scientists. Organization researchers, too, are investigating a multi-layered and changing reality. They too have to create stable backgrounds against which to investigate change. They too have the problem of distinguishing the robust features of the world they are investigating from the noise from other layers of reality and from those features that are a result of the process of investigation. They are additionally constrained by the sheer number of factors that may be operating even at a single level of analysis, and by the fact that controlled experiments are either impossible, unethical, or irrelevant. But if Hahlweg is right about the way that knowledge of a complex and changing world is possible, then not only is the scientific study of organizations possible, but its multi-perspective nature starts to make sense.

The same thing applies to all of the social sciences. For example, the adoption of a particular perspective in sociology functions in much the same way as experimental controls in the physical sciences. As we have seen, each perspective has its own assumptions about the nature of the social world. While these assumptions do not simplify the reality to be studied, as experimental controls do, they can have a similar effect by suggesting other – conceptual – methods of control to the researcher. And of course, researchers eventually try to translate assumptions into actual control measures.

Let me illustrate. The structure of society has an effect on individuals, and at the same time, the behavior of individuals affects the structure of society. Both are constantly in a state of flux. Under these conditions, how can we have knowledge of the relationships between individuals and society? We are dealing here with two distinct levels of reality. But we can investigate only one level at a time. By assuming that the social structure is stable, we can investigate what individual characteristics or behaviors are affected by position in the social structure. But individual behavior is itself affected by many other factors besides the social structure. These factors can never be eliminated as we might eliminate factors in an experimental situation, but they can be controlled to a great extent in other ways – for example, by selecting for study those individuals who are as alike as possible regarding those other factors. This procedure allows the assumption that the remaining differences between the individuals are the result of the social structure.

Of course social structure does change, and indeed it changes as a result of individual behavior. But for the purposes of investigating the effects of social structure on different individuals, it can (and indeed must) be considered relatively stable. The greater numbers of variables involved in sociology, and the problems of achieving control, mean that one would expect the results of sociology to be less accurate than those of the physical sciences. Nonetheless, knowledge of the social world is possible. The use of various assumptions in sociology can be seen as a way of creating stability in a complex and changing world. Consequently, multiple perspectives are needed to establish the existence of genuine invariants and robust concepts in sociology. Robust concepts are those that are essentially invariant across theories, and are important to the unification of knowledge.

The use of multiple perspectives in sociology, then, need not be seen as a problem. It is better seen an essential part of doing sociology. The epistemic problems of sociology arise not from the existence of the different perspectives but from the way they are often viewed – i.e., as the only proper way to achieve knowledge of the social world. The structuralist perspectives, for example, point to social phenomena that cannot appear at all if the action perspectives alone are used, and vice versa. And the dichotomy between holism and individualism, reflected in the debate between the structuralists and the action theorists, disappears under a complex metaphysics that allows the existence of many relatively autonomous layers of reality, each with its own specific methods of investigation.

The assumptions that underlie the various sociological perspectives, then, are better seen not as rooted in different ontological specifications but as *methodological devices that facilitate the identification of stabilities in a complex and changing world*, for it is only against a stable background that genuine invariant relations can be established. But what counts as genuine change and what counts as noise depend on the intentions of the scientist. There are many ways of viewing the world.

The fact that there are many ways of studying reality is, given human perceptual and cognitive mechanisms, a good thing. In a complex world, different perspectives make accessible different sorts of information. In addition, it is through the coordination of multiple perspectives that robust features of reality can be distinguished from those features that are merely a function of the theoretical framework used. Scientific methodology is essentially pluralist.

To be multi-perspective does not mean to be multi-paradigmatic, as the relativists advocate. To be multi-paradigmatic, an area of study has to be sectarian, with little or no communication between perspectives. Communication across perspectives is a precondition for establishing the robustness of objects and processes, itself a precondition for establishing the validity of theories. Under the mapping model of knowledge sketched here, it is not that individual theories are considered true or false. Rather, their validity is a function not only of how well they model the aspect of the world in question but of how connected they are, in terms of consistency and coherence, with the greater body of scientific knowledge. These connections can be established in a number of ways not unproblematical (Azevedo, 1997) but communication across perspectives and a willingness to work toward establishing coherence is a precondition.

Thus the institutional structure of an area of study becomes very important to the worth, in epistemic terms, of the knowledge it generates. The institution has to be organized in such a way as not only to allow, but also to encourage multiple perspectives, as well as supporting the sort of work necessary to achieve disciplinary coherence (see Baum and Rowley, this volume). The rhetoric of postmodernism, with its praise of multidisciplinarity, goes part of the way. But multidisciplinarity these days is more often a code for rigid adherence to a postmodern perspective. Under the ENR epistemology I have sketched here, postmodernism and its relatives are best seen as perspectives like any other, valuable in that they provide another way of looking at the world, rather than as epistemologies in their own right.

It is in its thematic focus on organizations, then, that I see the major strength of organization science. It already has an institutional structure that encourages work from a number of different perspectives. What it lacks is the structure, and perhaps the will, to support theorists engaged in the work of establishing cross-disciplinary and cross-perspective coherence. It is through this work that, in the long run, good theory can be distinguished from bad, valuable work from that of little or no value. With the greater reliability that will result, the usefulness of organization science to all with an interest in the workings of organizations should increase. Organization science will seem less a series of fashions that provide managers with the latest jargon and more the important area of study, valuable to all humans, that it should be.

Notes

1   Further discussion of CAPITALIZED terms can be found in the 'Glossary of Epistemology Terms' (see pages 889–98, this volume).

References

Andreski, S. (1974): *The Essential Comte*, (trans. M. Clarke). London: Croom Helm.

Azevedo, J. (1997): *Mapping Reality: An Evolutionary Realist Methodology for the Natural and Social Sciences*. Albany, NY: State University of New York Press.

Baum, J. A. C., and McKelvey, B., (eds) (1999): *Variations in Organization Science: In Honor of Donald T. Campbell*. Thousand Oaks, CA: Sage.

Berlin, B. (1973): "Folk systematics in relation to biological classification and nomenclature," *Annual Review of Ecology and Systematics*, 4, 259–71.

Berlin, B., Breedlove, C., and Raven P. H. (1966): *Principles of Tzeltal Plant Classification: An Introduction to the Botanical Ethnography of a Mayan-Speaking People of Highland Chiapas*. New York: Academic Press.

Bulmer, R. N. H., and Tyler, M. J. (1968): "Karam classification of frogs," *Journal of the Polynesian Society*, 77, 333–85.

Campbell, D. T. (1973): "Ostensive instances and entitativity in language learning," in W. Gray and N. D. Rizzo (eds), *Unity Through Diversity: A Festschrift for Ludwig von Bertalanffy (Part 2)*, New York: Gordon and Breach, 1043–57.

Campbell, D. T. (1974): "Evolutionary epistemology," in P. A. Schilpp (ed.), *The Philosophy of Karl Popper* (vol. 14, I. & II), *The Library of Living Philosophers*, La Salle, IL: Open Court, 413–63. [Reprinted in G. Radnitzky and W. W. Bartley, III, (eds) (1987): *Evolutionary Epistemology, Rationality, and the Sociology of Knowledge*, La Salle, IL: Open Court, 47–89.]

Campbell, D. T. (1979): "A tribal model of the social system vehicle carrying scientific knowledge," *Knowledge*, 2, 181–201.

Campbell, D. T., and Paller, B. T. (1989): "Extending evolutionary epistemology to 'justifying' scientific beliefs (A sociological rapprochement with a fallibilist perceptual foundationalism?)," in K. Hahlweg and C. A. Hooker (eds), *Issues in Evolutionary Epistemology*, State University of New York Press, Albany, 231–57.

Feyerabend, P. K. (1978): *Against Method: Outline of an Anarchistic Theory of Knowledge*. London: Verso.

Fiske, D. W., and Shweder, R. A. (eds) (1986): *Metatheory in Social Science: Pluralisms and Subjectivities*. Chicago, IL: University of Chicago Press.

Hahlweg, K. (1983): "The evolution of science: A systems approach," unpublished PhD dissertation, The University of Western Ontario, Canada.

Hahlweg, K. (1989): "A systems view of evolution and evolutionary epistemology," in K. Hahlweg and C. A. Hooker (eds), *Issues in Evolutionary Epistemology*, Albany, NY: State University of New York Press, 45–78.

Hahlweg, K., and Hooker, C. A., (eds) (1989): *Issues in Evolutionary Epistemology*. Albany, NY: State University of New York Press.

Hendrickx, M. (1999): "What can management researchers learn from Donald Campbell, the philosopher?" in J. A. C. Baum and B. McKelvey (eds), *Variations in Organization Science: In Honor of Donald T. Campbell*, Thousand Oaks, CA: Sage, 339–82.

Hooker, C. A. (1987): *A Realistic Theory of Science*. Albany, NY: State University of New York Press.

Hooker, C. A. (1995): *Reason, Regulation, and Realism: Toward a Regulatory Systems Theory of Reason and Evolutionary Epistemology*. Albany, NY: State University of New York Press.

Kuhn, T. S. (1970): *The Structure of Scientific Revolutions*, 2nd edn. Chicago, IL: University of Chicago Press.

McKelvey, B. (1999): "Toward a Campbellian realist organization science," in J. A. C. Baum and B. McKelvey (eds), *Variations in Organization Science: In Honor of Donald T. Campbell*, Thousand Oaks, CA: Sage, 383–411.

Popper, K. R. (1979): *Objective Knowledge: An Evolutionary Approach*, 2nd edn. Oxford, UK: Clarendon.

Rubinstein, R. A., Laughlin, C. D., and McManus, J. (1984): *Science as Cognitive Process: Towards an Empirical Philosophy of Science*. Philadelphia, PA: University of Pennsylvania Press.

Runciman W. G. (1978): "Introduction to part 2," in W. G. Runciman (ed.), *Max Weber: Selections in Translation*, (trans. E. Matthews), New York: Cambridge University Press, 65–8.

Thompson, P. and McHugh, D. (1995): *Work Organizations: A Critical Introduction*, 2nd edn. Houndmills, Basingstoke, Hampshire, UK: Macmillan.

Weber, M. (1978): *Economy and Society: An Outline of Interpretive Sociology*, G. Roth and C. Wittich (eds), Berkeley, CA: University of California Press.

Chapter Thirty-two

Contemporary Debates in Organizational Epistemology

MIHNEA C. MOLDOVEANU AND JOEL A. C. BAUM

Epistemological Misattributions and "Paradigm Wars" in Organization Science

Person A makes a statement to person B about the relationship between firm level profits and industry-level concentration, citing some empirical evidence for the proposition. Person B knows that person A believes that statements do not *describe* reality, but rather *construct* it. By contrast, person B believes that statements describe reality, rather than construct it. She construes person A's statement not as a claim to truth, but rather as an attempt to shape person B's perceptions about what the "truth" is. Therefore, B cannot take A's proposition as a valid claim within B's own reference system. Moreover, B believes that A believes that B will interpret A's sentence differently from the way in which A intends the statement. Therefore, B will wonder how A intends his statement to be construed: if as a descriptive claim, then A has violated his own epistemological commitment, and is incoherent; if as an attempt to shape reality for B, then A has contradicted his own belief about the way in which B construes propositions, and therefore A is again incoherent. In B's view, A's assertion involves some internal contradiction. B concludes that A is an incoherent thinker.

This is a simplified model of arguments that have unfolded during the past ten years in organization science around differences in PARADIGMS[1] and the ways in which these differences should be resolved (Pfeffer, 1995; van Maanen, 1995a; McKelvey, 1997; Wicks and Freeman, 1998; Fabian, 2000). Researchers with a commitment to a SCIENTIFIC REALIST epistemological stance (sometimes misrepresented as a POSITIVIST stance) caricature researchers with a commitment to a CONSTRUCTIONIST stance (sometimes represented as a RELATIVIST stance or inaccurately as a post-positivist stance) by attributing to the latter epistemological commitments they do not hold, and vice-versa. Moreover, researchers from both cadres seem to base their defenses of their own epistemological commitments on further attributions about the others' attributions about their own epistemological commitments. Thus, realists believe that constructionists believe realists are positivists (incorrectly, as we shall show), while constructionists believe that realists believe that constructionists are nihilists, epistemological anarchists, or at best, relativists. These mutual attributions and meta-attributions (attributions about attributions) often lead to confusion between the epistemological issues that are being debated and the substantive changes that researchers from each cadre are proposing for the organization of "organization science."

We attempt to unpack this spiral of epistemological attributions, misattributions and meta-attributions that has characterized the so-called "paradigm wars" in organization science, and offer an analytic model that captures the dynamics of the ongoing debate. Unraveling the chain of epistemological misattributions in the field can help promote deeper and more meaningful exchanges between researchers representing different sides of the current debate. The model we advance is interactive in nature. Not only each cadre's own beliefs, but their beliefs about others' beliefs, and about others' beliefs about their own beliefs are drivers of the model. Scrutinizing the cross-paradigmatic dialogue with our interactive model of epistemological attributions exposes the logical structure of the arguments and counter-arguments that are being advanced, and offers prescriptions for the future of such debate in organization science.

We show that the often-false attribution of a particular epistemological stance – to oneself and to scholars working in different areas of organization science – creates much of the "fear and loathing" (van Maanen, 1995b) that characterize the "paradigm wars" in organization science. Our analysis suggests that the current state of misattribution is most likely to lead to an amplification of the mutual suspicion that besets researchers in different areas of the field. Moreover, the psychological literature suggests that because of the ways in which people believe their beliefs (sometimes dogmatically, sometimes reactively to the source of the beliefs, often unresponsively to counter-arguments), it may be very difficult to change the entrenched epistemological commitments of researchers in the field. If our characterization is correct, then one way to bring reasoned dialogue back to cross-paradigmatic debates is to introduce all participants to the authentic epistemological underpinnings of their respective positions, and to stimulate a responsive dialogue that includes debate about epistemological foundations.

Epistemological Stance and Epistemological Attribution

"Paradigm wars," like ideological battles, may be based on epistemological misattributions that, in turn, are failures of interactive reasoning. "How can you" – asks the "realist" of the "relativist" – claim that "truth" is a cultural construction whose meaning changes with time, place and purpose of the speaker, while even as you speak about the futility of arguing about "truth" you are making a claim to truth-likeness? (Implication: "you are incoherent.") "How can you" – echoes the "relativist" – defend the reliability of the empirico-deductive method on absolute grounds while at the same time making the obviously pragmatist argument that "objectivist" methods for studying social phenomena are more easily teachable to graduate students and more likely to gain majority representation in top journals? (Implication: "you are either naïve or disingenuous.") Below we examine in more detail the interactive EPISTEMOLOGY of cross-paradigmatic dialogue in organization science to account for the "rift" that has emerged in the field. Figure 32.1 charts the steps of our analysis and the flow of interactive reasoning that we uncover.

REALISTS THINK THEY ARE POSITIVISTS (BUT THEY ARE NOT)

One of the main epistemological traditions represented in organization theory attempts to emulate the methodological devices of the natural sciences. These principles stress the inter-subjective reliability of the methods for collecting and interpreting data (Pfeffer,

Realists think they
are positivists
a false self-attribution fuelling
rumours that realists are dogmatic

Constructionists think
they are realists
and therefore able to divine what
realists 'really' are

Realists think
constructionists are relativists
setting themselves up to call
constructionists 'incoherent'

Constructionists think
realists are pragmatists
and therefore hypocritical in their
insistence on a single 'normative'
methodology for the field

Realists think
constructionists think
realists are dogmatists
which they cannot understand,
either because they do not think
they are positivists, or because
they do not understand positivism
to be invalid as an epistemology

Constructionists think
realists think
constructionists are nihilists
and therefore fearful of the realist
'backlash' against qualitative
research and case studies as
examples of the breakdown in
the field

Figure 32.1 Epistemological misattribution in the "paradigm wars": Summary

1993), logical precision in the specification of theory and methods, making the resulting body of knowledge more easily codifiable and transferable to students and research assistants (Hartman, 1988; Aldrich, 1992; Pfeffer, 1993, 1995). They also stress the objective nature of data or of observations and focus on ways of reducing – wherever possible – the effects of researcher bias and interpretation in the process of building knowledge. Proponents of this particular point of view are known as – and have sometimes declared themselves to be – "positivist" in their epistemological stance. Following their cue, their critics have set themselves up in the "anti-positivist" or "post-positivist" camp (see "CONTRA SCIENCE"), which positivists have classified in the same group with "POSTMODERNISTS," who in turn have classified said positivists as "imperialists" and "dogmatists." Of course, this is just the sort of confusion we are trying to sort out.

To untangle the knot of attributions, it is useful to start with an understanding of POSITIVISM. Positivism was a philosophical position most powerfully represented by the physicist Mach ([1883] 1902), the logician Carnap (1951), and the philosopher Ayer (1959). Positivists attempted to draw a line of demarcation between sense and nonsense in language on the basis of the verifiability of a (sensible) sentence by a direct sensory experience. Only OBSERVATION LANGUAGE sentences that were directly verifiable by a sensory experience were "sensible" – according to the positivists, who thus aimed to tie "sense" to "sensibility."

Positivism has deep implications for how we should carry out organizational research. Linguistic products such as poetry, narrative of dream states and emotional states, and metaphysical theorizing and speculations about emotions and cognitive states are excluded by positivists as meaningless. Gone from organization theory should be terms such as "firms," "strategies," "capabilities" and "resources" in the generalized sense. They are meaningless. Gone, also, should be concepts such as "risk," "utility," uncertainty" and "ambiguity," as well as "causal laws" and "cause-and-effect relationships" for they too are meaningless. Thus, economics, the self-proclaimed "positive" science – using Friedman's (1953) peculiar interpretation of "positive" as a form of instrumentalism – is definitely *not* a positiv*ist* science.

The recent identification (and self-identification) of some organization theorists with positivism is particularly difficult to disentangle since the latter are also critics of the proliferation of multiple paradigms (Hartman, 1988; Pfeffer, 1993), much as the positivists attempted to "shut down" alternative forms of discourse by use of the verification principle as a gatekeeper to the realm of sense. LOGICAL POSITIVISM, as formulated by Carnap (1951) and defended by members of the Vienna Circle, can be understood as an attempt to do away with METAPHYSICAL discourse (and any other kind of discourse not amenable to verification), and to establish positivistic "scientific discourse" as the standard of linguistic "sense." A sentence that could not be "verified" was neither "false" nor "imprecisely formulated" – it was "meaningless." Proponents of unverifiable sentences could therefore be regarded as "incoherent." Such labeling, we will see, is a customary rhetorical device in cross-paradigmatic dialogue (as it is in the cross-partisan dialogue described above) and serves to heighten the mutual suspicion and distrust among the "opposing" sides.

Positivism had a short life and a violent death. The original verification principle proposed by Ayer (1936) was shown to be invalid by Isaiah Berlin (Hacking, 1984):

"This logical problem is bright green"

was, in Berlin's construction, a perfectly verifiable (albeit meaningless) sentence, which could be "verified" by the two sentences

"I dislike green"

and

"I dislike this problem"

in conjunction with Ayer's first formulation of the verification principle. Ayer's (1959) subsequent reformulation of the verification principle was refuted with another counter-example by the logician Alonzo Church (Hacking, 1984). No alternative reformulation of the verification principle has since appeared, leaving positivism in a logically indefensible position; see Hacking (1984) for a historical account. To say of someone that she is a positivist is, then, to accuse her of being logically incoherent. To declare oneself a positivist is, similarly, to admit to holding a logically incoherent position.

Since it is not likely that "positivist" organization scientists lack a commitment to logic (or subscribe to a view of themselves as incoherent) the question arises, "what are they *really*, epistemologically speaking?" One possibility is that they are metaphysical realists and methodological empiricists. As methodological empiricists, they demarcate between science and metaphysics on the basis of a criterion that posits scientific theories must have as their logical consequents a set of hypotheses that are intersubjectively observable. As metaphysical realists, they may believe that one, some, or all of the following propositions are true (Putnam, 1990):

1 The world consists of a fixed number of objects that are independent of the mind, acts or identities of any observer.
2 There is exactly one true description of the world, and that description is also a complete description of the world.
3 Truth involves a correspondence between words and objects or events.

Each of these propositions has been convincingly challenged in the ongoing epistemological "debate" surrounding the logical basis of realism. Propositions 1 and 2 were challenged by Putnam's (1990) argument that the "truth" of a sentence must always be "truth-in-a-language" rather than the language-independent truth originally sought by metaphysical realists (Popper, 1972), and proposition 3 by the difficulties owned up to by Wittgenstein (1953) – see Barnes et al. (1996) for an overview – of assigning a definitive correspondence between word and object.

To summarize, organization science "positivists" are not positivist. They cannot be. As McKelvey (1997) points out, organizational scholars who hold "objectivist" epistemological stances regularly misattribute to themselves an incoherent philosophy of knowledge. Since most of these practitioners are realists of one sort of another, we will refer to them henceforth as "realists," and continue our exploration of the interactive interactive epistemology of cross-paradigmatic misattributions by working our way up the hierarchy of interactive beliefs that now characterizes the field.

CONSTRUCTIONISTS THINK THEY ARE REALISTS

Another prominent school of thought in organization science is that of constructionists, who believe in an interpretative, creative and idiosyncratic element in human behavior that is irreducible to the set of causal laws that form the preferred set of explananda of natural scientists (Hempel, 1965). Constructionists defend multiparadigmaticity in organization science (van Maanen, 1995a, b, Burrell, 1996) both implicitly and explicitly, and this meta-theoretical position is well-harmonized with their view of knowledge as being "created" by individual minds, rather than logically built up from theory and observation of an independent reality. If knowledge – including knowledge about the logical bases of knowledge – is constructed rather than discovered, then there cannot be any favored "epistemological stance." Paradigm differences often boil down to differences in conceptions of what knowledge is, and so there is no "pan-paradigmatic" way to bridge across them. Any attempted resolution must address the *epistemological differences* between the researchers involved, not just their substantive differences about a particular research topic.

This view echoes Kuhn's (1962) view that different paradigms within a science create their own criteria for validity of a theory and model, and amplifies it. Now even *epistemological* positions and theories arise to justify particular theoretical commitments, which are in turn justified by data whose validity is guaranteed by the already sworn-to epistemologies. Constructionists thus believe in a "hermeneutic circle" (Mannheim, 1931) that is proper to each sub-network of mutually intelligible researchers in organization science.

It turns out, however, that constructionists' theory-in-use is often a sort of realism. Offended by the suggestion of their realist counterparts that organization science as a whole suffers from its multiparadigmatic intellectual geography, some constructionists aim to uncover the "real causes" of realists' concern for epistemological unity. They impute to the realists imperialist motives (van Maanen, 1995b), at times baldly stating that "knowledge *is* power" (Foucault, 1972). If "is" in this sentence is interpreted as

there exists x, and x = knowledge, and there exists y, and y = power and the world is such that, at all times, $x = y$,

then the sentence is either self-undermining (because it represents a piece of knowledge that *ex hypothesis* is an attempt to establish power) or makes a realist epistemological claim (referring to an object "out there" called knowledge, and an object out there called power, and equating the two objects).

Constructionists' claim to being "realists" seems to be amplified when van Maanen (1995b) asks Pfeffer (1995) for data that we can "trust" to support his claim that Weick's (1979, 1995) work is exceptionally difficult to build upon. (This claim seems to receive at least some indirect support from Usai and Turati's (2000) finding that Weick's work represents an "island" in the co-citation pattern observed in *Administrative Science Quarterly* in the 1980s and 1990s, as Weick is often cited but rarely co-cited with any other major researchers in organization theory.) What would convincing data for the constructionists look like? Relative frequency of "Weickian" research submitted? Relative frequency with which such research is accepted for publication? Is it likely that van

Maanen and Pfeffer can agree on a selection of journals that they deem relevant for this "critical test" of a contentious assertion? Is it likely that they would agree on a sample size appropriate for the test? Occasionally, constructionists speak the "language" of realists and may even "feel" more real than the realists – whom they often consider to be either devious or self-deceived ("disingenuous or naïve" (van Maanen, 1995b)). Naïve relative to *what?*

REALISTS THINK CONSTRUCTIONISTS ARE RELATIVISTS

Advocates of the deductive-empirical method as a standard of inquiry in organization science (Camerer, 1985; Montgomery et al., 1989) claim that proliferation of multiple theoretical paradigms is causally linked to the proliferation of unsound methodological and theoretical practices. The project of advancing organization science suffers as a result of the proliferation of multiple standards of reference of what constitutes a "publishable" scholarly contribution (Pfeffer, 1995). This is because theoretical plural-ism – the "realists" argue – leads to epistemological relativism of the field as a whole, to the detriment of the overall quality of the research contributions (Camerer, 1985). "Many standards means no standard" (of validity) – the argument goes; and it is only in the presence of a universally accepted standard of validity – which sets "rules of the competitive game" for academic scholarship – that academic research (and knowledge) can improve over time. To buy into this argument, one must subscribe to the economic metaphor for the organization of scientific inquiry. And, moreover, to the belief that rule-based competition must lead to "superior" research relative to a system of "com-petitive anarchy" in which different standards of success are competing against each other along with different pieces of scholarship that are geared to particular standards of success.

How is *paradigmatic pluralism* linked to epistemological relativism, at least according to the "realist" view? The logic is easy to follow (Montgomery et al., 1989). Ontology and epistemology, as McKelvey (1997) has observed, are somewhat connected. If we posit independent variables based on emotions, cognitions, group minds and interactive belief hierarchies, then we cannot very well be positivist in our epistemological stance. If we look for path-dependence and the effects of initial conditions on phenomena that we assume *ab initio* will be multiply determined and in turn have multiple effects, then we cannot very well apply the standard linear models of statistical inference, and we will have to carefully scrutinize our assumptions about "reference classes" and the constitution of our "sample space." This coupling between the "thing-hood" of the objects of study in organization science and the kinds of methods used to inquire into the nature and dynamics of the objects of study has been elegantly elaborated by McKelvey and Aldrich (1982) who argue that there are "many more" kinds of different sample populations – and reference classes for phenomena, objects and events – in organization science than there are in the natural sciences on which our current methods of inquiry are modeled.

If we also allow that social events are a by product of the interaction between ob-server and observed, and use this insight to construct theories of organizational phe-nomena, then we again cannot coherently subscribe to the "objectivist" approach to discovery that we have inherited from the natural sciences. Ontology influences epistemology here as well: the epistemology of "trust" (involving a "trusted" and a "trustor," each of whose behavior will change as a function of their beliefs about the trustworthiness of the other, of the other's beliefs about the first person's trustworthiness, and so forth) will be quite different from the epistemology of electrons (whose behavior does not change – to our knowledge – as a function of the theories about electron behavior published in *Physical Review A*).

Ontological commitments and epistemological stances thus go hand-in-hand. Proliferation of paradigms based on different kinds of variables and underlying mechanisms (i.e. ontological pluralism) leads to multiple conceptual frameworks and kinds of independent variables for explaining organizational phenomena, as well as a parallel proliferation of different methods of inquiry into the phenomena of interest (i.e., epistemological pluralism). Since publication in top journals is supposed to represent the endowment by the field as a whole of the published article with the status of "objective knowledge," epistemological fragmentation of a field is equivalent to epistemological relativism of the *agency* invested by that field to pick out excellent contributions: There is no single standard of excellence according to which any particular submission can be judged to be "superior" or "inferior" to others, which is the hallmark of value relativism. Hence, "realists" argue, constructionists are *really* relativist.

Constructionists think realists are pragmatists

Advocates of approaches based on interpretation and the construction of knowledge retort that the standards of excellence proposed by realists for unifying the field are nothing but ploys aimed at achieving greater popularity and political power. Ever since Nietzsche's (1884) indictment of truth-seekers as power-mongers and Foucault's (1972) identification of knowledge with power, practitioners of a field who seek a "reconstructed" logic of scientific discovery that validates current practices are seen as attempting to re-establish hegemony over the field.

Philosophically informed researchers and philosophers who study historical practice (Feyerabend, 1975) cite significant negative results in the philosophy of science that seem to negate the existence of a language-independent (or theory-independent) epistemological standard of excellence. Among these are Hume's and Popper's refutation of inductive logic (Popper, 1959), Berlin and Church's refutation of Ayer's verification principle (Hacking, 1984), Quine's (1961) rejection of the distinction between analytic and synthetic truths (vitiating the claim that claims to methodological rigor can be settled by *a priori* argumentation by rendering the distinction between *a priori* and *posteriori* knowledge far less sharp than we had thought it to be in the 200 years following Kant), Miller's (1994) proof that Popper's language-independent measure of truthlikeness for a theory is invalid, Popper's own proof of the incoherence of the project of representing degrees of belief by probability measures (Gemes, 1997), and the stubborn persistence of the "skeptic's problem" ("am I justified in believing that 'here is a hand'?") in analytic philosophy despite recent efforts at resolving it (Pryor, 1996).

It is easy enough, argue constructionists, to see why hegemony is an important goal for realists: It leads the "powerful" in the field to a greater share of resources in the form of grants, access to tenure-track appointments and graduate students, and consulting opportunities based on academic standing within the academic institution. It is also seemingly clear to constructionists why "canonical epistemological practices" are required for hegemony to be achieved: Without a standard of excellence there cannot be criteria for promotion within a hierarchy, without hierarchical organization, one cannot have a viable and lasting "institution," without which one cannot achieve the intended position in the field. Moreover, without consensus, there can be no standard of excellence, and without a normatively grounded epistemological platform, there can be no consensus. Hegemony depends on normality. Normality depends on the incontrovertible establishment of "normativity," which in turn depends on the incontrovertibility of the norms used to justify a particular way of thinking and writing. This is the reconstructed logic of the realists – according to the constructionists (Foucault, 1972, Burrell, 1996).

It is also what interpretive organization scientists react to most strongly in their counterparts' epistemological writings. Van Maanen (1995b) resonates to words in Pfeffer's (1995) article such as "domination of a field," "efficient in training graduate students," "taken over (applying to major journals)," "ability to readily reproduce," "technology for analysis," and so forth. It does not help this particular step of the mutual attribution process that Pfeffer himself argues for his epistemological position using the incentives of greater impact and power of practitioners of the field, rather than providing an argument for the foundations of a realist approach to organizational phenomena. Of what import could it possibly be to seek a *normative* basis for the epistemology of organization science that certain "well-organized" subfields of economics and political science have achieved – by virtue of their internal organization – hegemony over their disciplines in a short period of time?

Van Maanen, however, does not register the fact that Pfeffer's own arguments are aimed at consolidating a paradigmatic base of organization science that is conceptually broader and deeper than the conceptual base of rational choice theory, which he believes is "taking over" fields such as economics and political science, and may end up taking over organization theory as well. It is an apparently Churchillian strategy, aiming to cover the "truth in a bodyguard of lies": Rational choice theory, Pfeffer seems to argue, can provide the basis for paradigmatic consensus, but it is an inferior theory. "Letting all flowers bloom" in organization science will only allow rational choice theory to take over the field, as it has done in economics and political science. The call is therefore for a rally around a worthier rival paradigm, which must be supported by paradigmatic consensus.

Pfeffer's concern, then, is not an offensive one, but rather a defensive one for the field. He just happens to believe that the best defense is a good offense. But this belief is well supported by the historical study of PARADIGM SHIFTS in other fields (such as physics) wherein paradigms are not simply "given up," but rather replaced by other paradigms that polarize the imagination of practitioners. Pfeffer's concern about the proliferation rational choice theory arises from a concern about the evolution of economic discourse and thinking in business schools and policy-making bodies in spite of the overwhelming empirical refutation of the micro-analytic assumptions of economic science (Dawes, 1998; Thaler, 2000). Pfeffer is arguing for the replacement of a greater evil (conformity to a set of conventions that are empirically vacuous as a pre-requisite for publication) with a lesser evil (agreement on a set of epistemological norms that will help proliferate alternatives to rational choice theory).

Realists Think Constructionists Think Realists Are Dogmatists

Realists, however, do not fully respond to the charge of pragmatism (or imperialism) from the constructionists, because they have their own view of what constructionists *really* think is the problem with the empirico-deductivist approach. McKelvey (1997), for instance, in a contribution that spans many different fields of natural and social science and branches of philosophy, avers that the naturalistic epistemology often practiced by organization scientists is "eighteenth century" in its outlook. The "straitjacket of normal science" (Daft and Lewin, 1990) is "a Newtonian straitjacket" (McKelvey, 1997) positing linear laws and models and looking for nomological relationships among a restricted set of variables obtained after decomposition of complex social systems along the lines of conceptual maps drawn on a priori grounds by people who have never fully internalized the impact of quantum mechanics and statistical mechanics for *epistemology*. Organization scientists are still being indoctrinated with pre-Einsteinian epistemological practices.

McKelvey (1997) pleads "guilty" on behalf of realists to the charge of dogmatism (which realists believe they have to respond to, but constructionists never really raised explicitly). He interprets van Maanen's denunciation of Pfeffer's paradigm-centric view of organization science as "philosophically indefensible" as a reference to the demise of positivism in the philosophy of science. Because holding on to a belief after it has been shown to be incoherent is a sign of dogmatism, McKelvey infers from the cross-paradigmatic debate that constructionists believe that realists are dogmatists, and proceeds to show that they are not.

McKelvey proposes that constructionists' epistemological concerns can all be understood as ontological concerns. The idiosyncrasies of social phenomena are what make them so intractable to analysis by natural science methods. He suggests that idiosyncrasies are causally linked to the inherent complexity of social phenomena, and that applying the conceptual apparatus of complexity theory and concentrating on "rates" and "proportions" rather than discrete point events as dependent phenomena in organization science is the right approach for maintaining epistemological unity while freeing up ontological innovation.

McKelvey's proposal is bold, illuminating, and worth pursuing – but it will not, unfortunately, persuade many constructionists who might have tuned in because their main arguments are with the *epistemological* part of the realism, not only with the ontological part of it. Epistemological uniformity does not – as discussed earlier – allow unrestricted ontological innovation. Rather, the epistemology and ontology of a field coevolve (in a way that may be usefully studied by the kinds of methods that McKelvey proposes), so that imposing restrictions in one domain will often have an impact in the other. This particular kind of coevolution may be an interesting subject for an empirical study, but the results will be closely influenced by the epistemological devices that are considered legitimate in carrying out such a study: What is the research paradigm that allows us to study cross-paradigmatic dialogue and interchange?

CONSTRUCTIONISTS THINK REALISTS THINK CONSTRUCTIONISTS ARE NIHILISTS

Constructionists, in turn, feel obliged to protect themselves in their writing against the charge of nihilism – or of the denunciation of *any* value criterion for the adjudication of merit in academic research. They attempt to show that the basic constructionist view of ideas and propositions as end-states of "language-games" (Astley and Zammuto, 1992; Mauws and Philips, 1995) can provide a useful hermeneutic device for the understanding of the relationship between academics and practitioners, and also among academics.

Epistemological relativism, however, is, like positivism, not a coherent stance. 'Everything is relative' is a statement that courts paradox, because it relativizes itself. 'Everything *except this statement* is relative' is also a dubious statement because there is no foundation on which the statement itself lies. Although not incoherent per se, the statement is question-begging. Constructivism cannot therefore rely on relativism as a justification, without falling into nihilism, or to a renouncement of the commitment to logical coherence, which, itself, would be performatively incoherent because its proponents are *participating* in a dialogue that pre-supposes a commitment to a minimal logic.

The constructionists' cause is badly damaged, however, by the form and substance of writings of scholars such as Burrell (1996) who represent organization science as a "pandemonium" in which neither logical structure nor meaning can last or supply any sort of order and coherence. It is, indeed, easy to interpret the work of Burrell as a piece of nihilism which attempts to explode the semblance of cohesion and single-valuedness of the "utility function" of the field as a whole. According to Burrell, the aspirations of traditional researchers to produce a consensus on the kind of works that are valued as contributions to the field are illusory.

Researchers in the constructionist tradition try to move away from the claim that "knowledge" of a phenomenon is unattainable and refocus the debate on a redefinition of "knowledge." According to one formulation of this view, academics are involved in "language games" (Wittgenstein, 1953) in which they try to draw other participants – such as managers, consultants and the press. Academic jargon from various disciplines are both the outcomes of language games played by academics in those disciplines, and also form the basis for language games played between academics and practitioners. There are, of course, many kinds of language games, with some more successful than others. The success of certain language games can be traced to the logical structure of the "code" that they use. Parsimony of the resulting code, reliability of the code in use, and efficiency of the code in referring to particular events in the world are all desirable characteristics of scientific jargon (Moldoveanu, 2001). Economic discourse relying on the axioms of rational choice theory satisfies these requirements quite well, which may explain Pfeffer's fear that rational choice theory is a likely "conqueror" of organization studies.

Constructionists have thus hastened to put forth a view of knowledge as the outcome of functionally oriented behavior as a defense against the charge of "nihilism" that the radical critique of epistemology and ontology often invites. In doing so, they have ended up with a view of knowledge that resembles Campbell's (1974) realist epistemology with a twist: Epistemological commitments – not only the beliefs that epistemological commitments justify – are also units of selection in the evolutionary theory of knowledge.

SYNOPSIS: EPISTEMOLOGICAL MISATTRIBUTION AS AN EXPLANATION FOR THE
PARADIGM WARS

Much of the "fear and loathing" characterizing the paradigm wars in organization
science rests on misunderstandings that stem from epistemological misattributions. Realists are not positivists and constructionists are not relativists. Constructionists are not
nihilists (but think realists think they are) and realists are not dogmatists (but think
constructionists think they are). Defensive rhetorical maneuvers are often responsive
not to prima facie arguments, but to assumptions that researchers believe are embedded
in each other's arguments, which is the hallmark of parallel monologues. Parallel monologues breed fear and distrust in cross-paradigmatic coordination, as the grounds for
argument and rebuttal lie "hidden" from the discussants. Neither constructivism nor
realism is free of its own logical problems, and proponents of both positions can benefit
from authentic dialogue. Constructivism must guard against falling into solipsism (Popper, 1959) (and realists can help with arguments that highlight the role of the outer
world in the creation of knowledge), and realists must deal with the absence of any
language-independent measure of truthlikeness of a theory (Miller, 1994) (and
constructionists can help with arguments that highlight the objectivity of truth-in-a-
language). Realists and constructionists, it seems, are much farther apart rhetorically
than they are epistemologically.

Deliberative Style, Reflexivity and Entrenchment

We have thus far unraveled the interactive belief systems that seem to have become
entrenched among organization scientists engaged in paradigm wars (Figure 32.1).
Now we turn to the question of how researchers can *maintain* their beliefs and theories
– including theories about each other – in the face of refuting counter-arguments. To
answer this question, we must consider not only the *interactive* processes of mutual
(mis)attribution but the *reflexive* or *meta-cognitive* processes of deliberation about one's
own beliefs. We need to consider not only *what* beliefs researchers hold but also *how
researchers believe their beliefs* in order to document the persistence of paradigmatic affiliation in the face of vigorous dispute.

We may, for instance, hold a belief for a particular reason, and select as valid the
beliefs for which we have the greatest justification. If we did, we could then be called
justificationists (Lakatos, 1974; Albert, 1985). Alternatively, we may hold a belief not
because it is justified, but because it has not yet been falsified, despite the best efforts of
a person or a group of people to falsify it (Popper, 1959; Lakatos, 1974). Reconstructed
"logics of scientific discovery" (Popper, 1959) posit falsificationism – or critical rationalism (Albert, 1985) – as the cornerstone of the "scientific method." Criticisms of lay
people's cognitive habits (positing that they are poor "intuitive scientists") attempt to
show that they are not falsificationist believers of their beliefs, because they look for
confirming evidence when trying to adjudicate the validity of a proposition, rather than
for disconfirming evidence for it (Nisbett and Ross, 1980). Lay people, the argument
goes, fall short in their reasoning processes of the rigor of scientific reasoning because
they are not falsificationists.

Albert (1985) distinguishes among several different forms of justificationism. A person may justify a proposition by

1   recourse to absolute certainty (holding it to be true regardlessly of any evidence to the contrary, just as a dogmatist would)
2   infinite regress (searching for reasons for reasons for . . . for holding the belief), or
3   logical circularity (holding one belief because it follows by a syllogism from another belief which itself follows by logical syllogism from the first belief).

Albert (1985) regards all three forms of justificationism as pathological, and proposes that critical rationalism is the only tenable form of deliberation about the validity of beliefs. Critical rationalism is a general form of falsificationism that abandons the conflation of truth with certainty that has been a hallmark of Western reasoning since Aristotle (Popper, 1959). Instead, it holds that beliefs are not to be held for a reason, but rather as temporary claims to truthlikeness for which we must develop *counter-arguments* and *disconfirming* evidence.

Lakatos (1974) distinguishes four forms of falsificationism. Dogmatic falsificationism anchors the rejection of a belief in a refuting observation statement that is held to be true and not criticizable any further. Methodological falsificationism holds all beliefs – including observation statements – to be criticizable. Naïve methodological falsificationism advocates that some theories should be abandoned after they have been falsified by observation statements that have withstood falsification attempts. Lastly, sophisticated methodological falsificationism holds that theories should only be abandoned in favor of other theories that have fared better in the falsificationist game of "science."

Self-attributions about deliberative style can lead to entrenchment of one's own beliefs and epistemological commitments in the following way. Researchers who think of themselves as falsificationists, are likely to derive their confidence in their theories and beliefs (including their epistemological commitments) from the normative power of falsificationism as a logic of scientific discovery. "Reliable" or "VERISIMILAR" beliefs are beliefs that have been arrived at by the process of rigorous testing aimed at falsification that constitutes the scientific method. Paradoxically, the stronger the self-attribution "I am a FALLIBILIST," the more entrenched will become one's own beliefs (because they have been arrived at by the "right" method). The stronger one's self-attribution of fallibilism, the more like a justificationist (or like a dogmatist) one will behave.

If our reasoning is correct, then we should find that a) academics behave by and large like justificationists, while b) claiming to be falsificationists. That, indeed, is what has been found. Although academics often believe that they are conducting their inquiries in the falsificationist style contemplated by Popper's logic of scientific discovery (Popper, 1959), several studies have shown that academics are prey to justificationist biases. Early studies (Wason, 1966) showing justificationist tendencies in lay people have been replicated successfully (using slightly more complicated versions of similar problems) among academics, including natural and social scientists (Kahneman et al., 1982) even as academic psychologists excoriate lay people for being poor "intuitive scientists" (Gilovich, 1993). More recent studies of acceptance and rejection patterns by editors and reviewers of academic journals in the field of psychology (Greenwald et al., 1996) also show the distinctively "justificationist" pattern of the selective rejection of papers that contradict the reviewers' own theoretical commitments. Thus academics should tend to place a higher level of trust in their own beliefs and their theories than they would have had they fully internalized the actual practices in their fields.

The implication of these studies' findings is that researchers' own self-attributions about deliberative style will generally *increase* the level of their own epistemological commitments. The more open minded we think we are, the more closed minded we have become. What we should expect to see in cross-paradigmatic dialogue, then, is the *entrenchment* of individual epistemological commitments, not *in spite* of the alleged open-mindedness of researchers, but *because* of their self-attributed open-mindedness. In contrast, what we should expect to see in a "reflexive" stage of science, whose researchers have come to learn about their own failures *vis-à-vis* their *own* standards (for example, the failure of some "justificationist" psychologists *vis-à-vis* their own "falsificationist" standard) is a broadening of the dialogue and a disentrenchment of established epistemological commitments.

Autonomy, Responsiveness and Genuine Dialogue

Mutual epistemological misattribution and the self-attribution of a "normative" deliberative style seem to be at the root of the "fear and loathing" that has emerged within organization science. Epistemological commitments and unspoken assumptions underlie most of the substantive claims that researchers make in their published oeuvre. These epistemological commitments are rarely openly discussed in the literature, but they surface in "position pieces" that spell out the unifying axioms of a particular field. Misattributions about the epistemological commitments of other researchers underlie most of the misunderstandings and conflicts that are embodied in the "paradigm wars." Researchers that are committed to a particular paradigm often criticize the epistemological commitments of researchers from other paradigms on the basis of misattributed epistemological commitments and misattributed beliefs about their own epistemological commitments.

Interactive reasoning loops do not necessarily converge. As the "paradigm wars" literature unfolds, misattributions about epistemological commitments branch out and generate misattributions about beliefs about epistemological commitments, misattributions about beliefs about beliefs about epistemological commitments, and so forth. The net result of this unfolding interactive reasoning spiral is the genesis of parallel monologues, in which none of the various positions advanced are responding to the arguments that the other sides are raising, but rather taking alternative points to view to task for misattributed epistemological views. "Loathing" between proponents of different paradigms stems from the mutual imputation of incoherent epistemological positions. "Fear" between proponents of different paradigms stems from the mutual attribution of beliefs about one's own epistemological positions, whereby each side perceives the other side as making an attempt to "take over" the field by showing that no epistemological commitment (other than its own) is internally coherent.

One possible solution to both problems may be to ground the participation in the dialogue carried out in research publications, classrooms and editorial boardrooms in the ideals of autonomy and responsiveness, which Kant proposed as the cornerstones of reason. A commitment to responsiveness requires that constructionists, for instance, respond directly to the arguments advanced by realists for their epistemological commitment, instead of advancing an argument from an entirely different set of precepts and axioms that simply "talk past" the realists' arguments. Responsiveness to an argument requires that the claims of that argument (including the evidence statements on which the argument is based) be specifically addressed in the reply. They may be confirmed or refuted; but if they are left unanswered, then parallel monologues will once again emerge. A commitment to responsiveness requires both constructionist and realist researchers to abandon the self-justificationist practice of citing only the works in the philosophy and epistemology of science that substantiate their position, and that they specifically engage the counter-arguments that have been advanced to these positions.

Autonomy appears to be a pre-requisite for true responsiveness: In order to respond to epistemological arguments from the realist tradition, constructionist researchers will need to understand these arguments and make their own judgments about validity. Deference to the "higher authority" of philosophers and sociologists of science appears to be a factor in the propagation of parallel monologues in the field, because such appeals to authority imply that the authority itself is undiscussable. In absence of autonomy, it is not us that have our ideas, but rather our ideas that have us (Lynch, 1996). Yet, it is precisely the discussability of the authority that is required by a commitment to autonomy of the participant in the dialogue; and it is precisely this discussability of the authority that is required by the commitment to responsiveness. Thus, while we echo the proposal of Fabian (2000) that the difficult conversation on foundational issues in organization research should continue, we caution against researchers "taking sides" too quickly and too dogmatically: dis-solving epistemological questions is as much of a contribution to the field as is re-solving epistemological questions. We should not forget that some of the key insights in epistemology have come from the dis-solution of age-old distinctions, such as analytic-synthetic distinction (Quine, 1961) and the questioning of the fact-value dichotomy (Nietzsche, 1884).

Two Proposals for Transformation

Our analysis points to two concrete recommendations that might result in dialogue between researchers on epistemological issues adhering more closely to the principles of autonomy and responsiveness, thus sharpening and deepening their exchanges.

UPDATING EPISTEMOLOGICAL COMMITMENTS OF RESEARCHERS

Teaching future researchers about epistemological issues and possible epistemological commitments as part of "research methods" courses would produce researchers who are informed about epistemological commitments and more autonomous in making their own epistemological choices. Autonomy in deliberation involves being aware not only of the particular epistemological commitment that one is defending, but also of the arguments and counter-arguments against that position. Such awareness enables the researcher to make his or her own judgment about the validity of an argument, instead of deferring to the "higher authority" of philosophers of science and analytic philosophers, whose writings are often cited, but, we suspect, rarely read critically.

Of course, being able to teach epistemology to future researchers requires us to become aware of our own epistemological commitments, and to commit to updating them in light of advances in the field. Epistemology evolves, however, along with other beliefs, models and theories. Arguments and counter-arguments are consistently proposed and refuted. Positivism, as we have pointed out, has been argued into a logically indefensible position, as has pure relativism. Inductive logic has been a suspect way to ground theory ever since David Hume's initial objections to it, but the dialogue between inductivists and falsificationists continues in the epistemology literature (Gemes, 1997), with arguments brought forth by each side against the other. The Popperian argument that knowledge "evolves" towards greater degrees of truthlikeness has been seriously challenged by Miller's (1994) demonstration that Popper's measure of truthlikeness is invalid. Subsequent research aimed at proposing a new criterion of truthlikeness (Kuipers, 1987) has fallen short of providing a language-independent (i.e. theory-independent) measure of truthlikeness, confirming Kuhn's (1962) views on the connection between ontology and epistemology. Constructionists, in contrast, find it difficult not to lapse into full-fledged solipsism (von Glasersfeld, 1984), renouncing the very project of communicating about the world in which they are engaged. Open questions abound in epistemology, vastly outnumbering answers. A commitment to updating one's epistemological commitments translates into a commitment to becoming familiar with these questions and problems and to making contributions to the field not only analytically and empirically, but also ontologically and epistemologically. Azevedo's (this volume) welcome update on recent developments in the philosophy of science, with a particular emphasis on their relevance to organization science, provides a great opportunity to begin that process.

As an example of an inquiry that heeds epistemological concerns, McKelvey (1997) makes an illuminating and thorough attempt to rid organization science of some misconceptions about its own epistemological commitments, by revealing the underlying logic of "positivist" and "relativist" approaches, and by proposing a new approach to the study of organizations, starting from a commitment to realism – an endeavor he pursues further in this volume. That analysis – and the one he presents in this volume – can be usefully complemented by a critical consideration of the arguments on which realism is based, and incorporation of the link between epistemological commitments and research practices that would be one hallmark of a "reflexive" organization science.

TEACHING AND PRACTICING INTERACTIVE REASONING

Interactive reasoning, we have argued, provides a tool for the understanding of misunderstandings. Many exchanges that characterize the paradigm wars rest on implicit assumptions about one's own and others' epistemological commitments, as well as assumptions about others' assumptions, and so forth. Quite often it is the implicit assumptions that play the critical role in a dialogue (or paradigm war) because they fuel the apparent disagreement without themselves being part of the discussion. Quite often as well it is the implicit interactive attributions that create distrust and hostility between people on different sides of the paradigm wars, because these assumptions "frame" the other side's argument in the most disadvantageous way possible for the speaker.

Interactive reasoning is a skill that can be taught. It is a common tool of analysis in game theory since Aumann's (1976) use of Lewis' (1969) study of conventions and common knowledge, in which researchers have used it to uncover the logical foundations of Nash equilibria in games (Aumann and Brandenburger, 1995). It is, however, not a skill that one can take for granted. We often seem to fail to engage in interactive reasoning even when it is in our best interest to do so (Zajac and Bazerman, 1991). And, when we do engage in it, we seem to stop at fairly shallow levels of reasoning: "I think you think . . ." rather than "I think you think I think . . ." (Nickerson, 1999). We are just now beginning to understand the cognitive processes underlying interactive reasoning, and there is a clear opportunity to put these insights to work in the classroom where new researchers who may become tomorrow's paradigm warriors are being trained, so that war may turn to dialogue.

Conclusion

In this paper we proposed an explanatory model for "paradigm wars" in organization science. We documented the processes of mutual epistemological misattribution that characterize dialogue about the epistemological foundations of the field, and have shown that interactive reasoning can help uncover some of the implicit assumptions about the epistemological commitments of self and other than often turn dialogues into conflicts. We then described mechanisms through which researchers can become entrenched in particular epistemological commitments and worldviews, and showed that, in epistemology, as in moral philosophy, "the moment we think we have become better, we have just taken a step towards becoming worse" (Plesu, 1981, p. 3). Our analysis provides an account of *what* the phenomenon of epistemological misattribution is, *why* it came about, and *how* it became entrenched in our field.

Epistemological misattributions are often interactive in nature. Opposing sides of paradigm wars "psychoanalyze" each other's writing and criticize each other for implicit assumptions as much as for explicit arguments. Many explicit arguments are left unanswered, often because they do not accord with the writer's own conception of the opposing researcher's epistemological commitment. Epistemological commitments are entrenched – and are likely to remain entrenched – because of strong cognitive proclivities to discount counter-arguments, and because of meta-cognitive strategies for defending one's beliefs by attributing a "normatively correct" epistemological style to oneself. The implications of these findings is that the field, on its current path, can head towards decreased dialogue and intellectual "trade" between realist and constructionist researchers, and perhaps a long series of parallel monologues on epistemological issues that will serve the cause of neither side.

Powerful remedies for the rift in the field exist and are at hand. They rest on ancient requirements for autonomy and responsiveness to the environment that, in Kant's view, were the foundations of reason. And, they entail no more from us than a commitment to teaching and learning about epistemological problems, and a willingness to think interactively – like a detective – when engaging in potentially contradictory exchanges in order to increase the clarity and connectedness of the dialogue as a whole. We don't think this is too much to ask.

Notes

1 Further discussion of CAPITALIZED terms can be found in the "Glossary of Epistemology Terms" (see pages 889–98, this volume).

References

Albert, H. (1985): *Treatise on Critical Reason*. Princeton NJ: Princeton University Press.

Aldrich, H. E. (1992): "'Incommensurable paradigms?' Vital signs from three perspectives," in R. Meed and M. Hughes (eds), *Rethinking Organizations: New Directions in Organization Theory and Analysis*, London UK: Sage, 17–45.

Astley, W. G., and Zammuto, R. F. (1992): "Organization science, managers and language games," *Organization Science*, 3, 443–60.

Aumann, R. (1976): "Agreeing to disagree," *Annals of Statistics*, 4, 1236–39.

Aumann, R., and Brandenburger, A. (1995): "Epistemic conditions for Nash equilibrium," *Econometrica*, 63, 1161–80.

Ayer, A. J. (1936): *Language, Truth and Logic*. London: Dover.

Ayer, A. J. (1959): *Logical Positivism*. New York: Free Press.

Barnes, B., Bloor, D., and Henry, J. (1996): *Scientific Knowledge: A Sociological Analysis*. Chicago IL: University of Chicago Press.

Burrell, G. (1996): *Pandemonium*. London UK: Heinemann.

Camerer, C. (1985): "Redirecting research in business policy and strategy," *Strategic Management Journal*, 6, 1–15.

Carnap, R. (1951): *Logical Foundations of Probability*. Chicago IL: University of Chicago Press.

Campbell, D. T. (1974): "Evolutionary epistemology," in P. A. Schilpp (ed.), *The Philosophy of Karl Popper*, LaSalle: Open Court, 413–63.

Daft, R. L., and Lewin, A. (1990): "Can organization studies begin to break out of the normal science straitjacket?" *Organization Science*, 1, 1–9.

Dawes, R. (1998): "Behavioral decision theory," in S. Fiske, D. Gilbert, and G. Lindzey (eds), *Handbook of Social Psychology*, New York: Oxford University Press, 582–614.

Fabian, F. H. (2000): "Keeping the tension: Pressures to keep the controversy in the management discipline," *Academy of Management Review*, 25, 350–71.

Feyerabend, P. (1975): *Against Method*. London UK: Verso.

Foucault, M. (1972): *Power/Knowledge: Selected Essays and Interviews*. New York: Harper Collins.

Friedman, M. (1953): *The Methodology of Positive Economics*. Cambridge MA: MIT Press.

Gemes, K. (1997): "Inductive skepticism and the probability calculus I: Popper and Jeffreys on induction and the probability of law-like universal generalizations," *Philosophy of Science*, 64, 113–30.

Gilovich, T. (1993): *How We Know What Isn't So*. New York: Free Press.

Greenwald, A. G., Leippe, M. R., Pratkannis, A. R., and Baumgardner, M. (1996): "Under what conditions does theory obstruct research progress?" *Psychological Review*, 93, 216–29.

Hacking, I. (1984): *Why Does Language Matter to Philosophy?* New York: Cambridge University Press.

Hartman, E. (1988): *Conceptual Foundations of Organization Theory*. Cambridge: Ballinger.

Hempel, C. (1965): *Aspects of Scientific Explanation*. New York: Free Press.

Kahneman, D. P., Slovic, P., and Tversky, A. (1982): *Judgment under Uncertainty: Heuristics and Biases*. New York: Cambridge University Press.

Kuhn, T. (1962): *The Structure of Scientific Revolutions*. Chicago IL: University of Chicago Press.

Kuipers, T. (1987): *What is "Closer-to-the-Truth"?* Poznan Studies in History and Philosophy, Dordrecht: Kluwer.

Lakatos, I. (1974): "Falsification and the methodology of scientific research programmes," in I. Lakatos and A. Musgrave (eds), *Criticism and the Growth of Knowledge*, New York: Cambridge

University Press, 91–196.

Lewis, D. (1969): *A Study of Convention.* Cambridge: Harvard University Press.

Lynch, A. (1996): *Thought Contagion.* New York: Free Press.

Mach, E. (1883): *The Science of Mechanics: A Critical and Historical Account of Its Development,* (trans. 1902). Chicago IL: Open Court.

Mannheim, K. (1931): *Ideology and Utopia.* New York: Basic Books.

Mauws, M., and Philips, N. (1995): "Understanding language games," *Organization Science,* 6, 323–34.

McKelvey, B. (1997): "Quasi-natural organization science," *Organization Science,* 8, 352–80.

McKelvey, B., and Aldrich, H. E. (1982): "Populations, natural selection and applied organization science, *Administrative Science Quarterly,* 28, 101–28.

Miller, D. (1994): *Critical Rationalism.* Chicago IL: Open Court.

Moldoveanu, M. C. (2001): "Language, games and language games," *Journal of Socio-Economics,* forthcoming.

Montgomery, C. A., Wernerfelt, B., and Balakrishnan, S. (1989): "Strategy content and the research process: A critique with commentary," *Strategic Management Journal,* 10, 189–97.

Nickerson, R. (1999): "How we know – and often misjudge – what others know: Imputing one's knowledge to others," *Psychological Bulletin,* 125, 737–59.

Nietzsche, F. (1884): *Beyond Good and Evil,* (reprint 1996). New York: Dover.

Nisbett, R. E., and Ross, L. (1980): *Human Inference: Strategies and Shortcomings of Social Judgment.* Englewood Cliffs NJ: Prentice-Hall.

Pfeffer, J. (1993): "Barriers to the advance of organization science: Paradigm development as a dependent variable," *Academy of Management Review,* 18, 599–620.

Pfeffer, J. (1995): "Mortality, reproducibility and the persistence of styles of theory," *Organization Science,* 6, 681–86.

Plesu, A. (1981): *Minima Moralia.* Bucharest: Humanitas.

Popper, K. R. (1959): *The Logic of Scientific Discovery.* London: Routledge.

Popper, K. R. (1972): *Objective Knowledge.* London: Routledge.

Pryor, J. (1996): "How to be a reasonable dogmatist," unpublished doctoral dissertation, Princeton University.

Putnam, H. (1990): *Realism with a Human Face.* Cambridge MA: Harvard University Press.

Quine, W. V. O. (1961): "Two dogmas of empiricism", in W. V. O. Quine, *From a Logical Point of View,* Cambridge MA: Harvard University Press, 20–46.

Thaler, R. H. (2000): "From homo economicus to homo sapiens," *Journal of Economic Perspectives,* 14, 133–41.

Usai, A., and Turati, C. (2000): "Social network analysis applied to co-citation network data: An empirical view over the 'paradigm war' within the organizations studies debate," *Proceedings of the 20th International Sunbelt Social Network Conference, Vancouver, British Columbia,* 61.

Van Maanen, J. (1995a): "Style as theory," *Organization Science,* 6, 132–43.

Van Maanen, J. (1995b): "Fear and loathing in organization studies," *Organization Science,* 6, 687–92.

Von Glasersfeld, E. (1984): "An introduction to radical constructivism," in P. Watzlawick (ed.), *The Invented Reality,* New York: Norton, 84–101.

Wason, P. C. (1966): "Reasoning," in B. M. Foss (ed.), *New Horizons in Psychology,* Harmondsworth, UK: Penguin, 135–51.

Weick, K. E. (1979): *The Social Psychology of Organizing.* New York: Addison Wesley.

Weick, K. E. (1995): *Sensemaking in Organizations.* Newbury Park, CA: Sage.

Wicks, A. C., and Freeman, R. E. (1998): "Organization studies and the new pragmatism: Positivism, anti-positivism and the search for ethics," *Organization Science,* 9, 123–40.

Wittgenstein, L. (1953): *Philosophical Investigations.* Oxford UK: Basil Blackwell.

Zajac, E. and Bazerman, M. (1991): "Blind spots in industry and competitor analysis: Implications of interfirm (mis)perceptions for strategic decisions," *Academy of Management Review,* 16, 37–56.

Chapter Thirty-three

Model-Centered Organization Science Epistemology

BILL McKELVEY

WHAT *IS* THEORY? REALLY!

Reichenbach (1938) distinguishes between "JUSTIFICATION LOGIC" and "DISCOVERY LOGIC."[1] Weick (1989) sees theorizing as "disciplined imagination." Weick appropriately captures the essence of theory discovery/creation as "imagination." Indeed, after centuries of scientific development, no one has identified any systematic "logic" to the discovery of correct theory. But "justification" seems more appropriate than his "disciplined." Discipline might get the player to the piano practicing eight hours a day but the idea is to play the right notes. Justification logic is not about discipline and hard work. It is about developing more truthful theories.

Both the 1989 *AMR* and 1995 *ASQ* theory forums start with a problem that journal editors have trying to persuade authors to improve the quality of their theory. The gravity of the problem is indicated by the title of the *ASQ* forum: "What Theory Is Not." When asked for better theory, authors are not being cajoled to move from good theory to great theory. Instead, they appear quite off the track on what theory *is*, preferring instead to supply raw ingredients such as more references, data, variables, diagrams, or hypotheses (Sutton and Staw, 1995) instead of effective theory. But saying, for example, that a cake is *not* eggs, *not* flour, *not* sugar, *not* butter, *not* chocolate . . . does not say what it *is*. The kind of theory Sutton and Staw want to see is not just the result of more discipline and more imagination. But if it is not longer lists of references and variables, and if it is not guaranteed simply from more discipline and imagination – well, What *Is* Theory? Really!

Background

GOOD THEORY IS TRUTHFUL EXPLANATION

But how to decide what is "truthful" and what constitutes an explanation? This is what philosophy of science and justification logic do. The underlying problem is that justification logic has fallen into disarray in the latter half of the twentieth century. The dominant bases of current methodological legitimacy in ORGANIZATION "SCIENCE," as indicated by the *AMR* and *ASQ* theory forums (Van de Ven, 1989; Sutton and Staw, 1995) and the *Handbook* (Clegg et al., 1996), loosely reflect the RECEIVED VIEW and HISTORICAL RELATIVISM – both of which have been abandoned by philosophers (Suppe, 1977). The Received View is Putnam's (1962) label combining LOGICAL POSITIVISM (Ayer, 1959) and LOGICAL EMPIRICISM (Nagel, 1961; Kaplan, 1964). Historical relativism marks the recognition by Kuhn (1962) and Feyerabend (1975), among others, that the text of published scientific reports is the result of interpretation by individual scientists, social construction of meanings by scientific communities, PARADIGMS, PARADIGM SHIFTS, and INCOMMENSURABILITY. In their place we have seen the growth of POSTMODERNISM, a line of discourse that rejects science and rationality as not only wrong but for having caused science-driven atrocities like the holocaust (Burrell, 1996) and political excesses like the "Pasteurization of France" (Latour, 1984), not to mention anti-science in general (Holton, 1993; Gross et al., 1996; Norris, 1997; Gross and Levitt, 1998; Koertge, 1998; Sokal and Bricmont 1998;). For more on the dark side of postmodernism, see Weiss (2000). If (classical) POSITIVISM is dead, if the Received View is dead; if CLASSICAL EMPIRICISM is dead, if RELATIVISM is dead, and if modern science caused the holocaust, where does this leave justification logic? It is no wonder that journals focus on what theory is not and authors don't know what it is!

Vague justification logic is inevitable in multiparadigm disciplines, suggesting that multiparadigmaticism is at the core of the problem. The paradigm master himself, Kuhn (1962), says multiparadigm disciplines are prescientific – a view echoed by Azevedo (1997) and McKelvey (2001). Pfeffer (1993) presents data showing that multiparadigm disciplines are given low status by the broader scientific community, with a variety of negative consequences. Donaldson (1995) counts fifteen paradigms already and Prahalad and Hamel (1994) call for even more, as do Clegg et al. (1996). The natural sciences are held in high esteem because they are OBJECTIVIST – their use of external reality serves as the ultimate criterion variable for winnowing out inferior theories and paradigms (Campbell, 1995). Relativist PROGRAMS, on the other hand, in principle tolerate as many paradigms as there are socially constructed perspectives and interpretations. Hughes (1992, p. 297) says, "The naivety of reasoned certainties and reified objectivity, upon which organization theory built its positivist monuments to modernism, is unceremoniously jettisoned . . . [and] these articles of faith are unlikely to form the axioms of any rethinking or new theoretical directions. . . ." If he is correct organization "science" is destined to proliferate even more paradigms and sink to even lower status. The cost of the paradigm war is vague justification logic and loss of legitimacy from philosophers, and as Pfeffer (1993, 1995) details, from other scientists, and the external user community as well.

Multiparadigmaticism need not persist and philosophers are not dead. In the last 30 years they have developed a new, postpositivist, SELECTIONIST, FALLIBILIST, *scientific realist*

EPISTEMOLOGY that avoids the extremes of the Received View and the anti-science of relativism. Elsewhere (McKelvey, 1999c), I briefly present some of these trends under the label CAMPBELLIAN REALISM, along with arguments Suppe (1977) lodges against the Received View and relativism (particularly against paradigm shifts and incommensurability). Campbell develops an objectivist epistemology that also includes the interpretive and social constructionist dynamics of relativism. Included are key elements of *scientific* REALISM (Bhaskar, 1975, 1998; Hooker, 1987; Aronson et al., 1994) and EVOLUTIONARY EPISTEMOLOGY (Callebaut and Pinxten, 1987; Hahlweg and Hooker, 1989) that support Campbellian realism. Azevedo (1997) develops both at some length.

STOCHASTIC MICROSTATES

Clegg and Hardy (1996: p. 2) contrast thirty years of organization "science" into "NORMAL SCIENCE" and "CONTRA SCIENCE." Normal science includes "formal research design; quantitative data facilitate[d] validation, reliability, and replicability; [and] a steady accumulation and building of empirically generated knowledge derive[d] from a limited number of theoretical assumptions." Contra science (Marsden and Townley, 1996, p. 660) includes postpositivisms such as social constructionism, interpretism, phenomenology, radical humanism, radical structuralism, critical theory, and postmodernism, all focusing on "local, fragmented specificities" (Clegg and Hardy, 1996, p. 3), that is, *stochastic* IDIOSYNCRATIC MICROSTATES (McKelvey, 1997).

The dilemma is how to simultaneously accept the existence of idiosyncratic organizational events while at the same time pursuing the essential elements of justification logic defined by the new generation of normal science realists. Justification logic is based on prediction, generalization, and falsification. These require *non*idiosyncratic events (Hempel, 1965; Hunt, 1991). The dilemma is significant since idiosyncrasy will not disappear and realism is the only scientific method available that protects organization "science" from false theories, whether by distinguished authorities or charlatans. *The one singular advantage of realist method is its empirically based, self-correcting approach to the discovery of truth* (Holton, 1993).

REAL SCIENCE FROM CONTRA SCIENCE

I focus on whether one can apply the justification logic of normal science realist epistemology to organization theories purporting to explain or understand the nonlinear organizational ONTOLOGY recognized by contra science proponents. One might conclude that there must be some truth in each position, given the considerable discourse and level of feeling and commitment held by both sides. Suppose each side is *half* correct. The fight between normal and contra science is that the latter studies organizations as ontological entities that cannot be fruitfully studied via normal science epistemology because they are comprised of behaviors unique to each individual or subunit. Therefore they abandon normal science, calling for a new epistemology. Normal scientists see contra science epistemology as fraught with subjective bias and with no commitment toward protecting against even grossly untrue local statements let alone more generalizable ones. Wishing to follow the epistemology of "good" science, they adopt an ontology calling for levels of homogeneity among employees, behaviors, or events that do not exist – a clearly false ontology according to contra science adherents. Boiled down, we have four choices:

1 Normal Science Ontology with Normal Science Epistemology
2 Normal Science Ontology with Contra Science Epistemology
3 Contra Science Ontology with Normal Science Epistemology
4 Contra Science Ontology with Contra Science Epistemology

The paradigm war (Pfeffer, 1993, 1995; Perrow, 1994; Van Maanen, 1995a, b) pits choice 1 against choice 4. There are no present criteria for choosing one over the other, other than for each side to restate more loudly the "truth" of its position. It is equally clear that no one is advocating choice 2. The *only* untried alternative left is choice 3. Truthful explanation, thus, becomes *evolutionary realist truth* about a *contra science ontology*.

Though ignored by contra scientists, choice 3 is not new to normal science. It dates back to Boltzmann's statistical mechanics treatment (circa 1870) of Brownian Motion (circa 1830). Scientists have identified three methods of pursuing normal science epistemology, given idiosyncratic microstates (McKelvey, 1997):

1 *Assume them away* – as is characteristic of most Newtonian science, and more specifically, of economists' rational actor assumption.
2 *Translate them into probabilistic event arrivals* – either statistically (Hempel's (1965) deductive statistical model), or by mechanical artifice – what the container does for Boyle's Law by translating the random kinetic motion of gas molecules into directed pressure streams of probabilistic (molecule) arrivals at some measuring station (Cohen and Stewart, 1994).
3 *Analyze emergent structure* – complexity scientists studying how structure emerges in complex adaptive systems.

from the coevolution of heterogeneous agents (Holland, 1995; Mainzer, 1997).

REALISM

Though Suppe (1977) wrote the epitaph on positivism and relativism, a POSITIVIST LEGACY remains. Space precludes detailing it here, but essential elements are listed in McKelvey (1999c). From this legacy a *model-centered evolutionary realist epistemology* has emerged. Elsewhere (McKelvey, 1999c), I argue that model-centered *realism* accounts to the legacy of positivism and evolutionary realism accounts to the dynamics of science highlighted by relativism, all under the label *Campbellian Realism*. Campbell's view may be summarized into a tripartite framework that replaces the historical relativism of Kuhn et al. for the purpose of framing a dynamic realist epistemology. First, much of the literature from Lorenz (1941) forward has focused on the selectionist evolution of the human brain, our cognitive capabilities, and our visual senses (Campbell, 1974, 1988), concluding that these capabilities do indeed give us accurate information about the world we live in (reviewed by Azevedo, 1997).

Second, Campbell (1991, 1995) draws on the hermeneuticists' COHERENCE THEORY in a selectionist fashion to argue that over time members of a scientific community (as a tribe) attach increased scientific validity to an entity as the meanings given to that entity increasingly cohere across members. This process is based on hermeneuticists' use of coherence theory to attach meaning to terms (Hendrickx, 1999). This is a version of the social constructionist process of knowledge validation that defines Bhaskar's use of TRANSCENDENTAL IDEALISM and the sociology of knowledge components in his scientific realist account. The coherentist approach selectively winnows out the worst of the theories and thus approaches a more probable truth.

Third, Campbell (1988, 1991) and Bhaskar (1975) combine scientific realism with semantic relativism (Nola, 1988), thereby producing an ontologically strong relativist dynamic epistemology. In this view the coherence process within a scientific community continually develops in the context of selectionist testing for ontological validity. The socially constructed coherence enhanced theories of a scientific community are tested against real-world phenomena (the criterion variable against which semantic variances are eventually narrowed and resolved), with a winnowing out of the less ontologically correct theoretical entities. This process, consistent with the strong version of scientific realism proposed by de Regt (1994), does not guarantee error free "Truth" (Laudan 1981) but it does move science in the direction of increased VERISIMILITUDE. For a counter view see Stich (1990), who argues for PRAGMATISM over selectionist explanation.

Campbellian realism is crucial because elements of positivism and relativism remain in organization "science;" see chapters in Clegg et al. (1996). Campbell's epistemology folds into a single epistemology:

1 dealing with METAPHYSICAL TERMS
2 objectivist empirical investigation
3 recognition of socially constructed meanings of terms, and
4 a dynamic process by which a multiparadigm discipline might reduce to fewer but more significant theories.

Campbell defines a *critical, hypothetical, corrigible, scientific realist selectionist evolutionary* epistemology as follows: (McKelvey, 1999c, p. 403)

1 A scientific realist postpositivist epistemology that maintains the goal of objectivity in science without excluding metaphysical terms and entities.
2 A selectionist evolutionary epistemology governing the winnowing out of less probable theories, terms, and beliefs in the search for increased verisimilitude may do so without the danger of systematically replacing metaphysical terms with OPERATIONAL TERMS.
3 A postrelativist epistemology that incorporates the dynamics of science without abandoning the goal of objectivity.
4 An objectivist selectionist evolutionary epistemology that includes as part of its path toward increased verisimilitude the inclusion of, but also the winnowing out of the more fallible, individual interpretations and social constructions of the meanings of theory terms comprising theories purporting to explain an objective external reality.

The epistemological directions of Campbellian realism have strong foundations in the scientific realist and evolutionary epistemology communities (Azevedo, 1997). While philosophers never seem to agree exactly on anything, nevertheless, broad consensus does exist that these statements reflect what is best about current philosophy. As the debate about organization "science" epistemology goes forward, the points listed in Table 33.1 should be seriously considered as central elements of the field. These points combine key epistemological tenets developed by Campbell (1987), de Regt (1994), and Aronson et al. (1994) – discussed in McKelvey (1999c).

To date evolutionary realism has amassed a considerable body of literature, as reviewed by Hooker (1987, 1995) and Azevedo (1997, this volume). Along with Campbell (1987), and Lawson's (1997) realist treatment of economics, Azevedo (this volume) stands as principal proponent of realist *social* science. Key elements of her "MAPPING MODEL of knowledge" are listed here:

1   Realism holds "that there is a real world existing independently of our attempts to know it."
2   "The realist adopts a fallibilist approach to science" and truth.

Table 33.1 Suggested tenets for a Campbellian Realist organization science

Organization science:

1 Is an objectivist science that includes terms in all three REALMS.
2 Recognizes that though the semantic meanings of all terms are subject to interpretation and social construction by individuals and the scientific community, this semantic relativism does not thwart the eventual goal of an objective, though fallible, search for increased verisimilitude.
3 Includes a selectionist evolutionary process of knowledge development that systematically winnows out the more fallible theories, terms, and entities over time.
4 Does not, as a result of its selectionist process, systematically favor either operational or metaphysical terms.
5 Accepts the principle that the true/false dichotomy is replaced by verisimilitude and degrees or probabilities of truthlikeness.[a]
6 Includes theories that are eventually the result of fallible incremental inductions eliminating those having less probable verisimilitude.[a]
7 Because knowledge concerning Realm 1 and 2 terms and entities is at best probable, tentative belief in the probable existence and verisimilitude of Realm 3 terms is no less truthlike than the fallible truth associated with theories comprising Reams 1 and 2 terms and entities.[a]
8 Defines theories to consist of LAW-LIKE statements having predictive elements capable of being tested for analytical adequacy.[b]
9 Insists that theories be based on (preferably formalized) models representing that portion of phenomena within the scope of the theory and subject to tests for ontological adequacy.[b]
10 Defines verisimilitude in terms of the content of its models.[b]
11 Is based on a convergent realism in which there is a functional relationship such that increased verisimilitude serves to reduce the error in measures and predictions and vice versa.[b]
12 Holds that the relation between (1) theory and prediction; and (2) organizations and how they behave, remains independent of whether terms and entities are in Realms 1, 2, or 3.[b]

Notes:
[a] From de Regt (1994)
[b] From Aronson, Harré and Way (1994)

3   The rise of postmodernism is based on the "inadequacies of positivism."

4   "Postmodernists show a profound ignorance of contemporary realism and a reluctance to engage in serious debate."

5   "[H]umans are products of biological evolution ... [that] have evolved perceptual and cognitive mechanisms. ... Natural selection would not have left us with grossly misleading perceptual and cognitive mechanisms."

6   "Valid beliefs, therefore, are achieved as a result of social processes rather than despite them."

7   Being "scientific is tied up with the nature of the structure and the norms of the institution of science ... that distinguish science from other belief production and maintenance institutions" such as religion.

8   The "validity of theories is both relative to the interests that guide theory creation and a function of the reality that they represent."

9   [T]heories, like maps, are valid insofar as they are reliable guides to action and decision making."

10   "Causal analysis is the basis of validity."

11   "Explanations in terms of composition, structure, and function are as much a part of science as are causal explanations.

12   "[M]entalist explanations [based on meanings, motives, and reasons] turn out to be interpretative functional analyses ... [and] have a loose, but nonetheless specified, relationship with the [causal] transition theories they explain ... leaving the way open for a naturalist [realist] approach to the social sciences."

13   "[K]nowing a complex reality actually demands the use of multiple perspectives."

14   "The reality of some entity, property, or process is held to be established when it appears invariant across at least two ... independent theories." (pp. 255–69)

Though it might seem that the Campbellian Realist approach is more model-centered than hers, nothing is more central in Azevedo's analysis than the mapping model – making hers just as model-centered as mine. And both of us emphasize ISOLATED IDEALIZED STRUCTURES. Her analysis greatly elaborates the initial social constructionist applications of realism to social science by Bhaskar (1975) and Campbell (1991, 1995) and accounts for idiosyncratic microstates as well.

The New "Model-Centered" Epistemology

In my development of Campbellian Realism (McKelvey 1999c) I show, that model-centeredness is a key element of scientific realism, but I do not develop the argument. In this section, I flesh out the development of a model-centered science by defining the semantic conception and close with a scale of scientific excellence based on model-centering. As Cartwright puts it: "*The route from theory to reality is from theory to model, and then from model to phenomenological law*" (1983, p. 4; my italics). The centrality of models as autonomous mediators between theory and phenomena reaches fullest expression in Morrison (2000), Morrison and Morgan (2000), Morgan and Morrison (2000) as they extend the semantic conception.

MODEL-CENTERED SCIENCE

Models may be ICONIC or FORMAL. Much of organization "science" occurs in business schools often dominated by economists trained in the context of theoretical (mathematical) economics. Because of the axiomatic roots of theoretical economics, I discuss the AXIOMATIC CONCEPTION in epistemology and economists' dependence on it. Then I turn to the semantic conception, its rejection of the axiomatic definition of science, and its replacement program.

THE AXIOMATIC SYNTACTIC TRADITION

Axioms are defined as self-evident truths comprised of primitive syntactical terms. Thus, in Newton's second law, $F = ma$, most any person can appreciate the reality of force – how hard something hits something else, mass – how heavy something is, and acceleration – whether an object is changing its current state of motion. And the three terms, force, mass, and acceleration cannot be decomposed into smaller physical entities defined by physicists – they are primitive terms this sense (Mirowski, 1989, p. 223). A formal syntactic language system starts with primitives – basic terms, definitions, and formation rules (e.g., specifying the correct structure of an equation) and syntax – in $F = ma$ the syntax includes F, m, a, = and × (implicit in the adjoining of ma). An axiomatic formal language system includes definitions of what is an axiom, the syntax, and transformation rules whereby other syntactical statements are deduced from the axioms. Finally, a formal language system also includes a set of rules governing the connection of the syntax to real phenomena by such things as measures, indicators, operational definitions, and CORRESPONDENCE RULES all of which contribute to syntactic meaning.

The science of analytical mechanics (Lanczos, 1970) is the classic example of theories being governed by an axiomatic syntactic formalized language. It began with Newton's three laws of motion and his law of gravitational attraction (Thompson, 1989, pp. 32–3):

1 Every entity remains at rest or in uniform motion unless acted upon by an external unbalanced force;
2 Force equals mass times acceleration ($F = ma$);
3 For every action there is an equal and opposite reaction;
4 The gravitational force of attraction between two bodies equals the gravitational constant ($G = 6.66 \times 10^{-s}$ dyne cm.^{2}/gm.^{2}) times the product of their masses ($m_1 m_2$) divided by the square of the distance between them (d^2), that is, $F = G (m_1 m_2 / d^2)$.

During the 22 decades between Newton's *Principia* (circa 1687) and initial acceptance of quantum and relativity theory, physicists and eventually philosophers discovered that the syntax of these basic axioms and derived equations led to explanations of Kepler's laws of planetary motion, Galileo's law of free fall, heat/energy (thermodynamic) laws, electromagnetic force (Maxwell's equations), and thence into economics (Mirowski, 1989). Based on the work of Pareto, Cournot, Walras, and Bertrand, economics was already translating physicists' thermodynamics into a mathematicized economics by 1900. By the time logical positivism was established by the Vienna Circle circa 1907 (Ayer, 1959; Hanfling, 1981), science and philosophy of science believed that a common axiomatic syntax underlay much of known science – it connected theories as far removed from each other as motion, heat, electromagnetism, and economics to a common set of primitives. Over the course of the twentieth century, as other sciences became more formalized, positivists took the view that any "true" science ultimately reduced to this axiomatic syntax (Nagel, 1961; Hempel, 1965) – the origin of the "Unity of Science" movement (Neurath and Cohen, 1973; Hanfling, 1981).

Now, the axiomatic requirement increasingly strikes many scientists as more straightjacket than paragon of good science. After quantum/relativity theories, even in physics Newtonian mechanics came to be seen as a study of an isolated idealized simplified physical world of point masses, pure vacuums, ideal gases, frictionless surfaces, linear one-way causal flows, and deterministic reductionism (Suppe, 1989, pp. 65–8; Gell-Mann, 1994). But biology continued to be thought – by some – as amenable to axiomatic syntax even into the 1970s (Williams, 1970, 1973; Ruse, 1973). In fact, most formal theories in modern biology are not the result of axiomatic syntactic thinking. Biological phenomena do not reduce to axioms. For example, the Hardy-Weinberg "law," the key axiom in the axiomatic treatments of Williams and Ruse is

$$p = \frac{AA + \frac{1}{2}Aa}{N}$$

where p is the gene frequency, A and a are two alleles or states of a gene, and N is the number of individuals. It is taken as prerequisite to other deterministic and stochastic derivations. But instead of being a fundamental axiom of evolutionary theory, it is now held that this "law," like all the rest of biological phenomena is a *result* of evolution, not a causal axiom (Beatty, 1981, pp. 404–5).

The so-called axioms of economics also suffer from the same logical flaw as the Hardy-Weinberg law. Economic transactions appear to be represented by what Mirowski refers to as the "heat axioms." Thus, Mirowski shows that a utility gradient in Lagrangian form,

$$\mathbf{P} = \text{grad } U = \left[\frac{\partial U}{\partial x} \frac{\partial U}{\partial y} \frac{\partial U}{\partial z}\right] = \{P_x, P_y, P_z\}$$

is of the same form as the basic expression of a force field gradient,

$$\mathbf{F} = \text{grad } U = \left[\frac{\partial U}{\partial x} \frac{\partial U}{\partial y} \frac{\partial U}{\partial z}\right] = \{X, Y, Z\}$$

As Mirowski (1989, pp. 30–3) shows, this expression derives from the axiom $F = ma$. Suppose that, analogous to the potential or kinetic energy of planetary motion defined by the root axiom $F = ma$, an individual's movement through commodity space (analogous to a rock moving through physical space) is $U = ip$, (where i is an individual, p is the change in preference). The problem is that Newton's axiom is part of the causal explanation of planetary motion, but the economists' axiom could be taken as the *result* of the evolution of a free market capitalist economy, not as its root cause. Parallel to a

Newtonian equivalent of an isolated physical system where axioms based on point masses and pure vacuums, etc., are effective, the axiom, $U = ip$, works quite well in an isolated idealized capitalist economy – but as we have discovered recently – not in Russia. This "axiom" is not a self-evident expression that follows an axiomatic syntax common to all "real" sciences. It is the result of how economists think an economy *ought* to behave, not how economic systems *actually* behave universally. Economists are notorious for letting *ought* dominate over *is* (Redman, 1991) – economic theory still is defined by axiomatic syntax (Blaug, 1980; Hausman, 1992).

Sporadic axiomatic attempts in linguistics (Chomsky, 1965), various behavioral and social sciences, and even in organization "science" (Hage, 1965) have all failed. So much so that following the Kuhnian revolution the social sciences took historical relativism as license to invent various "alternative" relativist postpositivisms (Hunt, 1991), of which there are now many – ethnomethodology, historicism, humanism, naturalism, phenomenology, semioticism, literary explicationism, interpretism, critical theory, and postmodernism.

In logical positivism, formal syntax is "interpreted" or given SEMANTIC MEANING via correspondence rules (C-rules). For positivists, THEORETICAL LANGUAGE, V_T, expressed in the syntax of axiomaticized FORMAL MODELS becomes isomorphic to OBSERVATION LANGUAGE, V_O, as follows (Suppe, 1977, p. 16):

> The terms in *VT* are given an explicit definition in terms of V_O by correspondence rules C – that is, for every term '*F*' in V_T, there must be given a definition for it of the following form: for any *x*, $Fx \equiv Ox$.

Thus, given appropriate C-rules, scientists are to assume V_T in an "identity" relation with *VO*.

In the axiomatic conception of science one assumes that formalized mathematical statements of fundamental laws reduce back to a basic set of axioms and that the correspondence rule procedure is what attaches discipline-specific semantic interpretations to the common underlying axiomatic syntax. The advantage of this view is that there seems to be a common platform to science and a rigor of analysis results. This conception eventually died for three reasons (Suppe, 1977):

1 Axiomatic formalization and correspondence rules, as key elements of logical positivism, proved untenable and were abandoned.
2 Newer twentieth-century sciences did not appear to have any common axiomatic roots and were not easily amenable to the closed-system approach of Newtonian mechanics.
3 Parallel to the demise of the Received View, the semantic conception of theories developed as an alternative approach for attaching meaning to syntax.

ESSENTIAL ELEMENTS OF THE SEMANTIC CONCEPTION

Parallel to the fall of the Received View and its axiomatic conception, and starting with Beth's (1961) seminal work dating back to the World War II, we see the emergence of the semantic conception of theories, Suppes (1961), van Fraassen (1970), Suppe (1977, 1989), and Giere (1979, 1988). Cartwright's (1983) "simulacrum account" followed, as did the work of Beatty (1987), Lloyd (1988), and Thompson (1989) in biology; Read (1990) in anthropology. I present four key aspects:

1   From axioms to phase-spaces
2   Isolated idealized structures
3   Model-centered science and bifurcated adequacy tests
4   Theories as families of models

From axioms to phase-spaces   Following Suppe, I will use *phase-space* instead of Lloyd and Thompson's state-space or Suppes' set-theory. A phase-space is defined as a space enveloping the full range of each dimension used to describe an entity. Thus, one might have a regression model in which variables such as size (employees), gross sales, capitalization, production capacity, age, and performance define each firm in an industry and each variable might range from near zero to whatever number defines the upper limit on each dimension. These dimensions form the axes of an *n*-dimensional Cartesian phase-space. Phase-spaces are defined by their dimensions and by all possible configurations across time as well. They may be defined with or without identifying underlying axioms – the formalized statements of the theory are not defined by how well they trace back to the axioms but rather by how well they define phase-spaces across various state transitions. *In the semantic conception, the quality of a science is measured by how well it explains the dynamics of phase-spaces – not by reduction back to axioms.* Suppe (1977, p. 228) recognizes that in social science a theory may be "qualitative" with nonmeasurable parameters, whereas Giere (1979) says theory *is* the model (which for him is stated in set-theoretic terms – a logical formalism). Nothing precludes "improvements" such as symbolic/syntactic representation, set-theoretic logic, first predicate (mathematical) logic, mathematical proofs, or foundational axioms.

Isolated idealized structures   Semantic conception epistemologists observe that scientific theories never represent or explain the full complexity of some phenomenon. A theory may *claim* to provide a generalized description of the target phenomena, say, the behavior of a firm, but no theory ever includes so many variables and statements that it effectively accomplishes this. A theory

1   "does not attempt to describe all aspects of the phenomena in its intended scope; rather it abstracts certain parameters from the phenomena and attempts to describe the phenomena in terms of just these abstracted parameters" (Suppe, 1977, p. 223)
2   assumes that the phenomena behave according to the selected parameters included in the theory; and
3   is typically specified in terms of its several parameters with the full knowledge that no empirical study or experiment could successfully and completely control all the complexities that might affect the designated parameters.

Suppe (1977, pp. 223–4) says theories invariably explain *isolated idealized systems* (his terms). And most importantly, "if the theory is adequate it will provide an accurate characterization of what the phenomenon *would have been* had it been an isolated system. ..." Using her mapping metaphor, Azevedo (1997) explains that no map ever attempts to depict the full complexity of the target area – it might focus only on rivers, roads, geographic contours, arable land, or minerals, and so forth – seeking instead to satisfy the specific interests of the map maker and its potential users. Similarly for a theory. A theory usually predicts the progression of the idealized phase-space over time, predicting shifts from one abstraction to another under the assumed idealized conditions.

Classic examples given are the use of point masses, ideal gasses, pure elements and vacuums, frictionless slopes, and assumed uniform behavior of atoms, molecules, genes, and rational actors. Laboratory experiments are always carried out in the context of closed systems whereby many of the complexities of real-world phenomena are ignored – manipulating one variable, controlling some variables, assuming others are randomized, and ignoring the rest. They are isolated from the complexity of the real world and the systems represented are idealized. Idealization also could be in terms of the limited number of dimensions, the assumed absence of effects of the many variables not included, or the mathematical formalization syntax, the unmentioned AUXILIARY HYPOTHESES relating to theories of experiment, data, and measurement.

Model-centered science and bifurcated adequacy tests   Models comprise the core of the semantic conception. Figure 33.1a portrays the *axiomatic conception*:

1   Theory is developed from its axiomatic base.
2   Semantic interpretation is added to make it meaningful in, say, physics, thermo-dynamics, or economics.
3   Theory is used to make and test predictions about the phenomena; and
4   Theory is defined as empirically and ontologically adequate if it both reduces to the axioms and is INSTRUMENTALLY RELIABLE in predicting empirical results.

Figure 33.1b depicts the *organization "science" approach*:

1   Theory is induced after an investigator has gained an appreciation of some aspect of organizational behavior.
2   An ICONIC MODEL is often added to give a pictorial view of the interrelation of the variables, show hypothesized path coefficients, or possibly a regression model is formulated.
3   The model develops in parallel with the theory as the latter is tested for empirical adequacy by seeing whether effects predicted by the theory can be discovered in the real world.

Figure 33.1c illustrates the *semantic conception*:

1   Theory, model, and phenomena are viewed as independent entities.
2   Science is bifurcated into two not unrelated activities, ANALYTICAL and ONTOLOGICAL ADEQUACY.

Following Read (1990), my view of models as centered between theory and phenomena sets them up as autonomous agents, consistent with Morrison (2000), Cartwright (2000), and others in Morgan and Morrison (2000) – though I see model autonomy as coming more directly from the semantic conception than do Morrison or Cartwright.

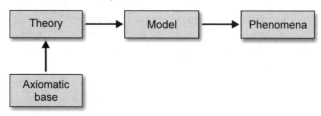

a Axiomatic conception

b Organization science conception

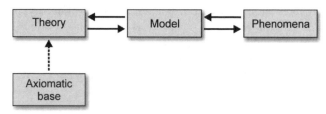

c Semantic conception

Figure 33.1 Conceptions of the axiom–theory–model–phenomena relationship

Read gives the most thorough analysis I have seen between analytical and ontological adequacy tests – which is frequently confused and misinterpreted. Read, a mathematician, also implicitly offers a litany of reasons why agent-based models will eventually dominate math models in model-centered social sciences.

Analytical adequacy focuses on the theory–model link. It is important to emphasize that in the semantic conception "theory" is always expressed via a model. "Theory" does not attempt to use its "If A, then B" epistemology to explain "real-world" behavior. It only explains "model" behavior. It does its testing in the isolated idealized world of the model. "Theory" is not considered a failure because it does not become elaborated and fully tested against all the complex effects characterizing the real-world phenomena. A mathematical or computational model is used to structure up aspects of interest *within* the full complexity of the real-world phenomena and defined as *"within the scope"* of the theory, and as Azevedo (1997) notes, according to the theoretician's interests. Then the model is used to test the "If A, then B" propositions of the theory to consider how a firm – as modeled – might behave under various possibly occurring conditions. Thus, a model would not attempt to portray all aspects of, say, laptop computer firms – only those within the scope of the theory being developed. And, if the theory did not predict *all* aspects of these firms' behaviors under the various relevant real-world conditions it would not be considered a failure.

Ontological adequacy focuses on the model–phenomena link. Developing a model's ontological adequacy runs parallel with improving the theory–model relationship. How well does the model *represent* real-world phenomena? How well does an idealized wind-tunnel model of an airplane wing represent the behavior of a full sized wing in a storm? How well does a drug shown to work on "idealized" lab rats work on people of different ages, weights, and physiologies? How well might a computational model from biology, such as Kauffman's (1993) *NK* model that Levinthal (1997), Baum (1999), McKelvey (1999a, b), and Rivkin (2000) apply to firms, actually represent coevolutionary competition in, for example, the laptop computer industry? In this case it involves identifying various coevolutionary structures, that is, behaviors, that exist in industry and building these effects into the model as dimensions of the phase-space. If each dimension in the model – called MODEL-SUBSTRUCTURES – adequately represents an equivalent behavioral effect in the real world, the model is deemed ontologically adequate (McKelvey, 2000).

Theories as families of models   A difficulty encountered with the axiomatic conception is the belief that *only one* theory–model conception should build from the underlying axioms. In this sense, only one model can "truly" represent reality in a rigorous science. Given this, a discipline such as evolutionary biology fails as a science. Instead of a single axiomatically rooted theory, as proposed by Williams (1970) and defended by Rosenberg (1985), evolutionary theory is a *family of theories* including theories explaining the processes of variation, natural selection, heredity, and a taxonomic theory of species (Thompson, 1989, ch. 1).

Even in physics, the theory of light is still represented by two models: wave and particle. More broadly, in other mature sciences there are competing theories/models about the age of the universe, the surface of the planet Venus, whether dinosaurs were cold or warm blooded, the cause of deep earthquakes, the effect of ozone depletion in the upper atmosphere, and so on.

Since the semantic conception does not require axiomatic reduction, it tolerates multiple theories and models. Thus, "truth" is not defined in terms of reduction to a single axiom-based model. Set-theoretical, mathematical, and computational models are considered equal contenders to more formally represent real-world phenomena. In physics both wave and particle models are accepted because they both produce highly reliable predictions. That they represent different theoretical explanations is not a failure. Each is an isolated idealized system representing different aspects of real-world phenomena. In evolutionary theory there is no single "theory" of evolution. In fact, there are even lesser families of theories (multiple models) *within* the main families. Organization "science" also consists of various families of theories, each having families of competing models within it. Most chapters in this volume, in fact, present families of theories pertaining to the subject of the chapter. Axiomatic reduction does not appear in sight for any of these theories. Under the semantic conception, organization "science" may progress toward improved analytical and ontological adequacy with families of models and without an axiomatic base.

AN EXAMPLE

Consider a recent paper by Contractor et al. (2000) using structuration theory (Giddens 1984) to predict self-organizing networks. It is not axiomatic nor does it offer more than a minimalist iconic model. Most importantly, it does not attempt to make a *direct* predictive leap from structuration-based hypotheses to real-world phenomena, noting that there are a "multitude of factors that are highly interconnected, often via complex, non-linear dynamic relationships" (Contractor et al., 2000, p. 4). Instead, the substructure elements are computationally combined into a model "outcome" and this outcome is predicted to line up with real-world phenomena. The model-substructures are easily identified (shown in Table 33.2) and each has research support.

There are three key steps embodied in the semantic conception:

1   A (preferably) *formalized model* is developed – either mathematical or computational;
2   *Analytical adequacy* is tested – theory and model coevolve until such time as the model (in an isolated idealized setting such as a lab or computer) correctly produces effects predicted by the theory, given the model-substructures and various other conditions or controls structured into the model;
3   *Ontological adequacy* is tested – substructures are tested against real-world phenomena, and if possible, the composite model outcome is also tested against predicted real-world behavior.

The Contractor et al. research implements Step 1 (Table 33.2), and begins Steps 2 and 3.

Step 2   The *analytical adequacy* test – using the model to test out the several causal propositions generated by the theory. This involves several elements in the coevolution of the *theory–model link*. Contractor et al. start with structuration theory's recursive interactions among actors and contextual structure. Structuration and negotiated order are linked to network dynamics and evolution (Barley, 1990; Stokman and Doreian, 1997). Monge and Contractor (in press) identify ten GENERATIVE MECHANISMS posited to cause emergent network dynamics. Contractor et al. end with ten model-substructures – each a causal proposition – rooted in structuration theory and hypothesized to affect network emergence. Each rests on considerable research. These reduce to ten equations (Table 33.2): seven exogenous factors, each represented as a matrix of actor interactions; and three endogenous factors with more complicated formalizations. For example, in the equation $\Delta C_{wij} = W_{ij}$ the value of ΔC_{wij}, "the change in communication resulting from interdependencies in the workflow" represented as the matrix W_{ij}, "is a workflow matrix and the cell entry W_{ij} indexes the level of interdependence between individuals i and j" (p. 21).

Contractor et al. begin the lengthy process of theory–model coevolutionary resolution, but:

1   Debate remains over which elements of structuration theory are worth formalizing;
2   Not all generative mechanisms thought to cause network emergence are represented; additional theorizing could mean additions and/or deletions;

Table 33.2 Model substructures defined[a]

Exogenous mechanisms

$\Delta C_{S_{ij}} = S_{ij}$ — Cell S_{ij} is coded 1 if i is the superior of j (or vice versa) – because supervisors initiate more communication with subordinates than the reverse.

$\Delta C_{HL_{ij}} = HL_{ij}$ — Cell HL_{ij} is weighted more if i and j are higher level managers – because coordination oriented communication is directly related to level in the hierarchy.

$\Delta C_{P_{ij}} = P_{ij}$ — Cell P_{ij} is weighted to indicate the proximity of i to j.

$\Delta C_{E_{ij}} = E_{ij}$ — Cell E_{ij} is coded 1 if i and j email each other.

$\Delta C_{W_{ij}} = W_{ij}$ — Cell W_{ij} is indexed to reflect workflow interdependency between i and j.

$\Delta C_{F_{ij}} = F_{ij}$ — Cell F_{ij} is coded 1 if i reports that j is a friend (or vice versa).

$\Delta C_{A_{ij}} = A_{ij}$ — Cell A_{ij} is indexed to show the number of common activity foci between i and j.

Endogenous mechanisms

$\Delta C_{tr_{ij_t}} = \sum_{k=1}^{N} C_{ik_{t-1}} C_{kj_{t-1}}$ — Cell C_{ij} is indexed upward if i and j both communicate with k, reflecting Heider's (1958) balance theory.

$\Delta C_{co_{ij_t}} = \left(g_{d_{t-1}} - g_{d_{mean_{t-1}}} \right)$ — Cell C_{ij} is indexed to show the level of network density of i and j's group relative to the mean of all group network densities – because groups with higher levels of cohesion have higher levels of communication among members, reflecting Homans (1950).

$$\Delta C_{HO_{ij_t}} = -\left(\sum_{k=1}^{N} \frac{C_{jk_{t-1}} C_{ki_{t-1}}}{(C_{max_{t-1}})^2} + \sum_{k=1}^{N} \frac{C_{ki_{t-1}}}{C_{SE_{jk_{t-1}}} - C_{SE_{min_{t-1}}} + 1} \right)$$

Cell C_{ij} is weighted downward to the extent that structural equivalence reduced the need for i and j to communicate directly with each other, following Burt's (1992) structural hole theory.

[a] From Contractor et al. (2000).

3 Formalization of model-substructures could take a variety of expressions; and
4 "*Blanche*" is only one of many computational modeling approaches that could be used.

In short, it will take a research program iteratively coevolving these four developmental process elements over some period of time before theory, the derived set of formalized causal statements, and modeling technology approach optimization – recognizing that evolutionary epistemologists hold that this seldom, if ever, fully materializes.

Step 3 The *ontological adequacy* test – comparisons of model-substructures with functionally parallel real-world subprocesses. Empiricists are not held to the draconian objective of testing model-to-real-world isomorphism for all substructures at the same time – that is, matching the composite outcome of the model against equivalent real-world phenomena. Experience in classical physics shows that if each of the substructures is shown to be representative, then the whole will also refer. This means that model–phenomena tests may be conducted at the substructure or composite outcome levels.

The increased probability of nonlinear substructure effects (individually or in combination) in social science, demonstrates the increased importance of model-centered science. Given nonlinear substructure interactions, it is more likely that the model's *composite* outcome will fair better in the ontological test. Contractor et al. actually do both kinds of tests. In a quasi-experiment, they collect data pertinent to each of the model-substructures and to the composite outcome of the model. Their sample consists of 55 employees measured at 13 points over two years. They do not test whether a specific model substructure predicts an equivalent subcomponent of the emergent network. For example, they do not test the relation between the model's workflow interdependence matrix and the equivalent real-world matrix. They could claim, however, that each causal substructure has already been well tested in previous research. They find that the model's composite outcome predicts the empirically observed emergent network. Four of the ten substructures also significantly predict the observed emergent network.

Testing the *model–phenomena link* also involves several coevolutionary developments:

1 Decompose the model into key constituent substructures, which may need further ontological testing.
2 Identify equivalent generic functions in real-world phenomena, perhaps across a variety of quasi-experimental settings, presumably improving over time as well.
3 Define the function of each substructure in generic real-world operational terms; here, too, improvement over time is expected.
4 Test to see if (a) the model substructures are isomorphic with the real-world functions; and (b) if the model's composite outcome represents real-world phenomena – both expected to develop interactively over time.

Needless to say, several empirical tests would be required before all aspects of the model are fully tested. In the Contractor et al. study, six of the substructure expressions do not separately predict the real-world outcome. This could be because of the nonlinear interactions or because the substructures do not validly represent real-world phenomena in this instance. The ontological adequacy of the model is not fully resolved. More generally, sensitivity analyses would test the presence or absence of specific substructures against changes in level of ontological adequacy. Furthermore, since theory and model coevolve toward analytical adequacy, it follows that tests for ontological adequacy would have to be updated as the theory–model link coevolves.

A GUTTMAN SCALE OF EFFECTIVE SCIENCE

So far I have identified four nonrelativist postpositivisms that remain credible within the present-day philosophy of science community: the *Legacy* of positivism, *Scientific Realism*, the *Semantic Conception*, and *Selectionist Evolutionary Epistemology*. As a simple means of

1 summarizing the most important elements of these four literatures; and
2 showing how well organization "science" measures up in terms of the institu-

tional legitimacy standards inherent in *these* postpositivisms, I distil seven criteria essential to the pursuit of effective science (Figure 33.2).

The list appears as a GUTTMAN SCALE. It goes from easiest to most difficult. To be institutionally legitimate and effective, current epistemology holds that theories in organization "science" must be accountable to these criteria. Existing strong sciences such as physics, chemistry, and biology meet all of them. Many, if not most, organization "science" theory applications to firms do not meet any but the first. I submit that this is why organization "science" has so little institutional legitimacy from scientific, philosophical, and user communities.

1   AVOIDANCE OF METAPHYSICAL TERMS

This criterion *could* have been the most difficult for organization "science" to meet and is seen as a significant issue (Godfrey and Hill, 1995). If we were to hold to the "avoid metaphysical entities at all costs" standard of the positivists, organization "science" would fail even this minimal standard since even the basic entity, the firm, is hard to put one's hands on – that is, gain direct knowing about. Scientific realists, and especially Aronson et al. (1994), remove this problem by virtue of their "PRINCIPLE OF EPISTEMIC INVARIANCE." They argue that the "metaphysicalness" of terms is independent of scientific progress toward truth. The search and truth-testing process of science is defined as fallibilist with "probabilistic" results. Given this, it is less important to know for sure whether the fallibility lies

1   with fully *metaphysical* terms (e.g., "corporate strategy"), eventually DETECTABLE TERMS (e.g., "idiosyncratic resources"), or as measurement error with regard to OBSERVATION TERMS (e.g., "# of company cars"), or

2   the probability that the explanation or model differs from real-world phenomena (discussed in McKelvey 1999c).

Whatever the reason, empirical findings are only true with some probability and selective elimination of any error improves the probability. Since metaphysicalness has been taken off the table as a standard by the scientific realists, it is one standard organization "science" meets, if only by default.

2   NOMIC NECESSITY

NOMIC NECESSITY holds that one kind of protection against attempting to explain a possible accidental regularity occurs when rational logic can point to a strong relation between an underlying structure – force – that, if present, produces the result – if force *A*, then regularity *B*. Consider the "discovery" that "legitimization affects rates of [organizational] founding and mortality ..." (Hannan and Carroll, 1992, p. 33). Is this an accidental regularity? The posited causal proposition is "If legitimacy, then growth." But, there is no widely agreed upon underlying causal structure, mechanism, or process that explains the observed regularity (Zucker, 1989). Thus, if legitimacy is removed, do (most) growing firms disappear? Since there are many firms with no legitimacy that

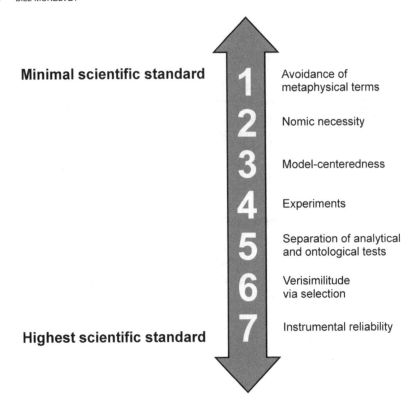

Minimal scientific standard

1 — Avoidance of metaphysical terms

2 — Nomic necessity

3 — Model-centeredness

4 — Experiments

5 — Separation of analytical and ontological tests

6 — Verisimilitude via selection

7 — Instrumental reliability

Highest scientific standard

Figure 33.2   Guttman scale

have grown rapidly because of a good product, the proposition seems false (Baum and Oliver, 1992; Hybels et al., 1994).

A different aspect of the theory of population dynamics, however, is clearly not an accidental regularity. In a niche having defined resources, a population of firms will grow almost exponentially when the population is small relative to the resources available, and growth will approach zero as the population reaches the carrying capacity of the niche (Hannan and Freeman, 1989). This proposition explains changes in population growth by identifying an underlying causal mechanism – the difference between resources used and resources available – formalized as the Lotka–Volterra logistic growth model:

$$dN \,/\, dt = rN(K - N/K)$$

In this case, the law came to organization "science" before the discovery of the hypothesized organizational regularities since it was imported from theoretical ecology (Levins, 1968) by Hannan and Freeman (1977), hence the prospect of an accidental regularity is reduced. The model expresses the underlying causal mechanism and it is presumed that if the variables are measured and their relationship over time is as the model predicts then the underlying mechanism is *mostly likely* present – truth always being a probability and fallible.

3 BIFURCATED MODEL-CENTERED SCIENCE

My use of "model-centeredness" has two meanings:

1 Are theories mathematically or computationally formalized?
2 Are models the center of bifurcated scientific activities – the theory–model link and the model–phenomena link?

Carley's (1995) review of the use of formal models in organization "science" shows around 100 instances (see also her chapter in this volume). More now appear in the journal she co-edits, *Computational and Mathematical Organization Theory*, as well as in books such as Masuch and Warglien (1992), Carley and Prietula (1994), Burton and Obel (1995), and Prietula, Carley, and Gasser (1998). Yet a review of journals such as *ASQ, AMR, AMJ, OS*, and *SMJ*, not to mention Academy of Management presentations, indicates that organization "science" is a long way from routinely formalizing the meaning of a theoretical explanation, as is common in physics, economics, and in the journal, *Management Science*. And almost no data-based empirical studies in *ASQ*, etc. have the mission of empirically testing the real-world fit of a formalized model – they invariably try to test unformalized hypotheses directly on the full complexity of the real world.

4 EXPERIMENTS

Witchcraft, shamanism, astrology, and the like, are notorious for attaching *post hoc* explanations to apparent regularities that are frequently accidental – "disaster struck in '38 after the planets were lined up thus and so." Though nomic necessity is a necessary condition, using experiments to test the propositions reflecting the law (LAW-LIKE relation) in question is critically important. Meeting nomic necessity by specifying underlying causal mechanisms is only half the problem, as has been discovered with the "legitimacy explanation" in population ecology. The *post hoc* use of "legitimacy" is an example of sticking an explanation to an accidental regularity absent the correct underlying causal mechanism. Cartwright (1983) goes so far as to say that even in physics all theories are attached to causal findings – like stamps to an envelope. The only recourse is to set up an experiment, take away cause A and see if regularity B also disappears – add A back in and see if B also reappears. Unlike marketing research and micro OB, both of which use experiments frequently, organization "science" seldom does. Organization theory and strategy are fields particularly vulnerable to pinning theories to accidental regularities. Given that lab studies of firms are borderline impossible, naturally occurring quasi-experiments and computational experiments offer constructive substitutes.

5 SEPARATION OF ANALYTICAL AND ONTOLOGICAL TESTS.

This standard augments the nomic necessity, model-centeredness, and analytical results criteria by separating theory-testing from model-testing. In mature sciences theorizing and experimenting are usually done by different scientists. This assumes that most people are unlikely state-of-the-art on both. Thus, if we are to have an effective science applied to firms, we should eventually see two separate activities:

1   Theoreticians working on the theory–model link, using mathematical or computational model development, with analytical tests carried out via the theory–model link
2   Empiricists linking model-substructures to real-world structures

It is possible that some researchers would be able to compare model analytic results with real-world quasi-experimental results, as do Contractor et al. (2000). Without evidence that both of these activities are being pursued independently, as per Figure 33.1c, organization "science" will remain amateurish, immature, illegitimate, and unrecognized. The prevailing organization "science" focus on only a direct theory–phenomena link is a mistaken view of how science progresses.

6   VERISIMILITUDE VIA SELECTION

I ranked this standard here because the selection process happens only over time. For selection to produce any movement toward less fallible truth there need to have been numerous trials of theories of varying quality, accompanied by tests of both analytical and ontological adequacy – as defined by Steps 2 and 3 in the Contractor et al. (2000) example. So, not only do all of the previous standards have to have been met, they have to have been met across an extensive mosaic of trial-and-error learning adhering to separate analytical and ontological adequacy tests. Population ecology meets this standard quite well. As the Baum (1996) review indicates, there is a 20-year history of theory–model and model–phenomena studies with a steady inclination over the years to refine the adequacy of both links by the systematic removal of the more fallible theories and/or model ideas and the introduction and further testing of new ideas. The lack of contrived experiments has already been noted – though quasi-experiments are possible when population regulation dynamics are shown to readjust after a technological or deregulation discontinuity (Tushman and Anderson 1986, Baum et al., 1995).

7   INSTRUMENTAL RELIABILITY

A glass will fall to earth every time I let go. This is 100 percent reliability. Four hundred years ago Kepler, using Tyco Brahe's primitive (pretelescope) instruments, created astronomical tables that improved the reliability of predicting the locations of planets to within $\pm 1'$ compared to the up to $5°$ of error in the Ptolemaic/Copernican tables. Classical physics achieves success because its theories have high INSTRUMENTAL RELIABILITY, meaning that they have high analytical adequacy – every time a proposition is tested in a properly constructed test situation the theories predict correctly and reliably. It also has high ontological adequacy because its formal models contain structures or phase-space dimensions that very accurately represent real-world phenomena "within the scope" of various theories used by engineers and scientists for many of their studies. Idealizations of models in classical physics have high isomorphism with the physical systems about which scientists and engineers are able to collect data. But, as Gell-Mann (1994) observes, laws in modern physics are no longer exact but probabilistic. *The more accurate physicists' measures, the more probabilistic their laws!*

It seems unlikely that organization "science" will ever be able to make individual event predictions (McKelvey, 1997). Even if organization "science" moves out from under its archaic view of research – that theories are tested by looking directly to real-world phenomena – it still will suffer in instrumental reliability compared to the natural sciences. The "*isolated idealized systems*" of natural science are more easily isolated and idealized, with lower loss of reliability, than those studied by social scientists. Natural scientists' lab experiments more reliably test nomic-based propositions and their lab experiments also have much higher ontological representative accuracy. In other words, their "closed systems" are less different from their "open systems" than is true for socio-economic systems. Consequently natural science theories produce higher instrumental reliability.

The instrumental reliability standard is truly a tough one for organization "science". The good news is that the semantic conception makes this standard easier to achieve. Our chances improve if we split analytical adequacy from ontological adequacy. By having some research focus only on the predictive aspects of a theory–model link, the chances improve of finding models that test propositions with higher analytical instrumental reliability – the complexities of uncontrolled real-world phenomena are absent. By having other research activities focus only on comparing *model-structures* and *processes* across the model–phenomena link, ontological instrumental reliability will also improve. In these activities, reliability hinges on the isomorphism of the structures causing both model and real-world behavior, not on whether predictions occur with high probability. Thus, in the semantic conception instrumental reliability now rests on the joint probability of two elements:

1 *predictive analytic reliability*
2 *model-structure reliability*, each of which is higher by itself.

Of course, instrumental reliability is no guarantee of improved verisimilitude in transcendental realism. The semantic conception protects against this with the bifurcation above. Instrumental reliability does not guarantee "predictive analytical reliability" tests of theoretical relationships about transcendental causes based on nomic necessity. If this part fails the truth-test fails. However, this does not negate the "success" and legitimacy of a science resulting from reliable instrumental operational-level event predictions even though the theory may be false. Ideally, analytic adequacy eventually catches up and replaces false theories in this circumstance.

If a science is not based on nomic necessity and centered around (preferably) formalized computational or mathematical models it has little chance of moving up the Guttman scale – it is not even on the same playing field. Such is the message of late twentieth-century (postpositivist) philosophy of normal science. This message tells us very clearly that in order for organization "science" to avoid or recover from scientific discredit, and institutional illegitimacy it must become model-centered. The nonlinearity of much of our phenomena makes model-centeredness even more essential, as Contractor et al. (2000) observe.

Conclusion

Organization "science" has lost its legitimacy with two external institutions, philosophy of science and user community. Philosophical legitimacy is missing for three reasons:

1 Bench scientists have never followed the Received View, whether logical positivism or logical empiricism (Suppe, 1977).

2 Whatever partial legitimacy organization "science" might have gained from the Received View or historical relativism (Kuhn, 1962; Feyerabend, 1975) disappeared when these two epistemological programs were abandoned by philosophers in the 1970s (Suppe, 1977).

3 Organization "science" seems largely ignorant of the normal science postpositivisms emerging after the abandonment, with an active subgroup bent on setting up postmodernism and other relativist postpositivist epistemologies (Reed and Hughes, 1992; Hassard and Parker, 1993; Burrell, 1996).

Pfeffer (1993) more than anyone worries about the lack of legitimacy among external user communities – managers and consultants largely ignore the Academy of Management and our research findings do not make front page news.

Instead of the postmodernists' anti-science path, my proposal emphasizes the four *other* postpositivisms in current philosophy of science: The *Legacy* tenets remaining from the Received View; *Scientific Realism* and *Selectionist Evolutionary Epistemology* as interpreted for organization "science" via *Campbellian Realism* (McKelvey, 1999c); and the *Semantic Conception*. In essence, scientific activities bifurcate, focusing on

1 the coevolutionary development of the *theory–model* link and truth-testing for *analytical adequacy* – the ability of the model to test the predictive nuances of the theory, given various conditions; and

2 the coevolutionary development of the *model–phenomena* link and truth-testing for *ontological adequacy* – the ability of the model to represent real-world phenomena defined as within the scope of the theory.

I conclude with a Guttman scale of scientific effectiveness criteria. It is clear that organization "science" barely registers on this scale and that much work remains to be accomplished before its research hits the top of the scale. Population ecology does best by this scale. Perhaps this explains why it has grown so quickly in organization "science" while remaining a minor subfield in biology.

Empirical tests in organization "science" typically are defined in terms of a direct "theory–phenomena" corroboration, with the result that:

1 We do not have the bifurcated separation of theory–model analytical and model–phenomena ontological tests;

2 The strong analytical type of theory confirmation is seldom achieved because the attempt is to predict real-world behavior rather than model behavior;

3 Model-structures are considered invalid because their inherent idealizations usually fail isomorphically to represent real-world complexity – instrumental reliability is very low; and

4 Our models are not formalized – though this may be optional.

While the semantic conception in no way represents a shift away from formalized models, Suppe (1977, p. 228) does admit the possibility of qualitative models. Though formal models exist in organization "science" (Carley, 1995), they are marginally used at best – most theory articles do not end with a formal model, whether computational or mathematical, and most empirical studies do not begin their model–phenomena test with a formalized model.

Organization "science" could move to a stronger epistemological footing if it followed the semantic conception. Bifurcating activity into theory–model predictions and model–phenomena comparisons would enhance both analytical and ontological adequacy – it would actually make the task of producing a more effective science easier. If model-structures representing a complex real world can be developed, then:

1 theoreticians can work on developing formalized mathematical or computational models, both activities of which require technical skills outside the range of many organization scientists;
2 the organization "science" equivalent of laboratory scientists can work on enhancing model–phenomena adequacy by making and testing predictions to test analytical statements;
3 empiricists can make comparison tests between model and phenomena "within the scope" of the theory and work on generating findings comparing model-structures with functionally equivalent real-world structures.

Campbellian realism combined with the model-centered semantic conception makes effective science a more realistic organization "science" objective for several reasons:

1 A fallibilist realist epistemology lowers the standard of truth-seeking from unequivocal Truth with a capital T, to a more approachable human scale definition of verisimilitude, that is, more truthlike theories remain after the more fallible ideas have been selectively winnowed away.
2 A model-centered epistemology that separates the theory–model link from the model–phenomena link makes each activity more manageable, sets up differentiated standards for truth-testing, and allows scholars to become more specialized in one or another side of science, if they wish.
3 The new normal science postpositivisms are actually closer to the logic-in-use in organization "science" than reconstructions following narrowly from the Received View, though the standards imposed by the Guttman scale are still far from being achieved.
4 An organization "science" that is more legitimate in terms of the current normal science postpositivisms should produce results that in fact will also increase legitimacy in terms of criteria held dear by user constituencies.

The best way to fend off the anti-science attack by the postmodernists is to develop an organization "science" that works better because it better meets the institutional legitimacy requirements of both academic and external user communities. I consider how organization studies might best become a more legitimate science in McKelvey (forthcoming).

Acknowledgments

I wish to thank Andy Van de Ven for commenting on an earlier version, Jane Azevedo for helpful comments along the way, and Joel Baum and Margie Morrison for commenting on the penultimate one. All remaining errors and oversights are my responsibility.

Notes

1 Further discussion of CAPITALIZED terms can be found in the "Glossary of Epistemology Terms" (see pages 889–98, this volume).

References

Aronson, J. L., Harré, R., and Way, E. C. (1994): *Realism Rescued*. London: Duckworth.

Ayer, A. J., (ed.) (1959): *Logical Positivism*. Glencoe, IL: Free Press.

Azevedo, J. (1997): *Mapping Reality: An Evolutionary Realist Methodology for the Natural and Social Sciences*. Albany, NY: State University of New York Press.

Barley, S. R. (1990): "The alignment of technology and structure through roles and networks," *Administrative Science Quarterly*, 35, 61–103.

Baum, J. A. C. (1996): "Organizational ecology," in S. R. Clegg, C. Hardy and W. R. Nord (eds), *Handbook of Organization Studies*, Thousand Oaks, CA: Sage, 77–114.

Baum, J. A. C. (1999): "Whole-part coevolutionary competition in organizations," in J. A. C. Baum and B. McKelvey (eds), *Variations in Organization Science: In Honor of Donald T. Campbell*, Thousand Oaks, CA: Sage, 113–35.

Baum, J. A. C., and Oliver, C. (1992): "Institutional embeddedness and the dynamics of organizational populations," *American Sociological Review*, 57, 540–59.

Baum, J. A. C., Korn, H. J., and Kotha, S. (1995): "Dominant designs and population dynamics in telecommunications services, 1969–1992," *Social Science Research*, 24, 97–135.

Beatty, J. (1981): "What's wrong with the received view of evolutionary theory?" in P. D. Asquith and R. N. Giere (eds), *PSA 1980, Vol. 2*, East Lansing, MI: Philosophy of Science Association, 397–426.

Beatty, J. (1987): "On behalf of the semantic view," *Biology and Philosophy*, 2, 17–23.

Beth, E. (1961): "Semantics of physical theories," in H. Freudenthal (ed.), *The Concept and the Role of the Model in Mathematics and Natural and Social Sciences*, Dordrecht, The Netherlands: Reidel, 48–51.

Bhaskar, R. (1975): *A Realist Theory of Science*. London: Leeds Books. 2nd edn. (1997) London, Verso.

Bhaskar, R. (1998): *The Possibility of Naturalism*, 3rd edn. London: Routledge.

Blaug, M. (1980): *The Methodology of Economics*. New York: Cambridge University Press.

Burrell, G. (1996): "Normal science, paradigms, metaphors, discourses and genealogies of analysis," in S. R. Clegg, C. Hardy and W. R. Nord (eds), *Handbook of Organization Studies*, Thousand Oaks, CA: Sage, 642–58.

Burt, R. S. (1992): *Structural Holes: The Social Structure of Competition*. Cambridge, MA: Harvard University Press.

Burton, R. M., and Obel, B., (eds) (1995): *Design Models for Hierarchical Organizations: Computation, Information, and Decentralization*. Boston, MA: Kluwer.

Callebaut, W., and Pinxten, R. (eds) (1987): *Evolutionary Epistemology: A Multiparadigm Program*. Dordrecht, The Netherlands: Reidel.

Campbell, D. T. (1987): "Evolutionary epistemology," in G. Radnitzky and W. W. Bartley, III (eds), (1987), *Evolutionary Epistemology, Rationality, and the Sociology of Knowledge*, La Salle, IL: Open

Court, 47–89. Originally published in P. A. Schilpp (ed.), *The Philosophy of Karl Popper* (Vol. 14, I. & II), *The Library of Living Philosophers*, La Salle, IL: Open Court, 413–63.

Campbell, D. T. (1988): "Descriptive epistemology: Psychological, sociological, and evolutionary," in E. S. Overman (ed.) *Methodology and Epistemology for Social Science: Selected Papers, D. T. Campbell*, Chicago, IL: University of Chicago Press, 435–86.

Campbell, D. T. (1991): "Coherentist empiricism, hermeneutics, and the commensurability of paradigms," *International Journal of Educational Research*, 15, 587–97.

Campbell, D. T. (1995): "The postpositivist, non-foundational, hermeneutic epistemology exemplified in the works of Donald W. Fiske," in P. E. Shrout and S. T. Fiske (eds), *Advances in Personality Research, Methods and Theory: A Festschrift Honoring Donald W. Fiske*, Hillsdale, NJ: Erlbaum, 13–27.

Carley, K. M. (1995): "Computational and mathematical organization theory: Perspective and directions," *Computational and Mathematical Organization Theory*, 1, 39–56.

Carley, K. M., and Prietula, M. J., (eds) (1994): *Computational Organization Theory*. Hillsdale, NJ: Erlbaum.

Cartwright, N. (1983): *How the Laws of Physics Lie*. New York: Oxford University Press.

Cartwright, N. (2000): "Models and the limits of theory: Quantum Hamiltonians and the BCS models of superconductivity," in M. S. Morgan and M. Morrison (eds), *Models as Mediators: Perspectives on Natural and Social Science*, Cambridge, UK: Cambridge University Press, 241–81.

Chomsky, N. (1965): *Aspects of the Theory of Syntax*. Cambridge, MA: MIT Press.

Clegg, S. R., and Hardy, C. (1996): "Organizations, organization, and organizing," in Clegg et al. (1996, pp.1–28).

Clegg, S. R., Hardy, C., and Nord, W. R., (eds), (1996): *Handbook of Organization Studies*. Thousand Oaks, CA: Sage.

Cohen, J., and Stewart, I. (1994): *The Collapse of Chaos: Discovering Simplicity in a Complex World*. New York: Viking/Penguin.

Contractor, N. S., Whitbred, R., Fonti, F., Hyatt, A., O'Keefe, B., and Jones, P. (2000): "Structuration theory and self-organizing networks," paper presented at Organization Science Winter Conference, Keystone, CO.

de Regt, C. D. G. (1994): *Representing the World by Scientific Theories: The Case for Scientific Realism*. Tilburg, The Netherlands: Tilburg University Press.

Donaldson, L. (1995): *American Anti-Management Theories of Organization*. Cambridge UK: Cambridge University Press.

Feyerabend, P. K. (1975): *Against Method*. Thetford, UK: Lowe and Brydone.

Gell-Mann, M. (1994): *The Quark and the Jaguar*. New York: Freeman.

Giddens, A. (1984): *The Constitution of Society: Outline of the Theory of Structuration*. Berkeley, CA: University of California Press.

Giere, R. N. (1979): *Understanding Scientific Reasoning*. New York: Holt, Reinhart and Winston.

Giere, R. N. (1988): *Explaining Science: A Cognitive Approach*. Chicago, IL: University of Chicago Press.

Godfrey, P. C., and Hill, C. W. L. (1995): "The problem of unobservables in strategic management research," *Strategic Management Journal*, 16, 519–33.

Gross, P. R., and Levitt, N. (1998): *Higher Superstition: The Academic Left and its Quarrels with Science*, 2nd edn. Baltimore, MD: Johns Hopkins University Press.

Gross, P. R., Levitt, N., and Lewis, M. W. (eds) (1996): *The Flight from Science and Reason*. Baltimore, MD: Johns Hopkins University Press.

Hage, J. (1965): "An axiomatic theory of organizations," *Administrative Science Quarterly*, 10, 289–320.

Hahlweg, K., and Hooker, C. A. (eds) (1989): *Issues in Evolutionary Epistemology*. New York: State University of New York Press.

Hanfling, O. (1981): *Logical Positivism*. Oxford, UK: Blackwell.

Hannan, M. T., and Carroll, G. R. (1992): *Dynamics of Organizational Populations*. New York: Oxford University Press.

Hannan, M. T., and Freeman, J. (1977): "The population ecology of organizations," *American Journal of Sociology*, 83, 929–84.

Hannan, M. T., and Freeman, J. (1989): *Organizational Ecology*. Cambridge, MA: Harvard University Press.

Hassard, J., and Parker, M. (eds) (1993): *Postmodernism and Organizations*. Thousand Oaks, CA: Sage.

Hausman, D. M. (1992): *Essays on Philosophy and Economic Methodology*. New York: Cambridge University Press.

Heider, F. (1958): *The Psychology of Interpersonal Relations*. New York: Wiley.

Hempel, C. G. (1965): *Aspects of Scientific Explanation*. New York: Free Press.

Hendrickx, M. (1999): "What can management researchers learn from Donald Campbell, the philosopher?" in J. A. C. Baum and B. McKelvey (eds), *Variations in Organization Science: In Honor of Donald T. Campbell*, Thousand Oaks, CA: Sage, 339–82.

Holland, J. H. (1995): *Hidden Order*. Reading, MA: Addison-Wesley.

Holton, G. (1993): *Science and Anti-Science*. Cambridge, MA: Harvard University Press.

Homans, G. C. (1950): *The Human Group*. New York: Harcourt, Brace.

Hooker, C. A. (1987): *A Realistic Theory of Science*. Albany, NY: State University of New York Press.

Hooker, C. A. (1995): *Reason, Regulation, and Realism: Toward a Regulatory Systems Theory of Reason and Evolutionary Epistemology*. Albany, NY: State University of New York Press.

Hughes, M. (1992): "Decluding organization," in M. Reed and M. Hughes (eds), *Rethinking Organizations: New Directions in Organization Theory and Analysis*, Newbury Park, CA: Sage, 295–300.

Hunt, S. D. (1991): *Modern Marketing Theory: Critical Issues in the Philosophy of Marketing Science*. Cincinnati, OH: South-Western.

Hybels, R. C., Ryan, A. R., and Barley, S. R. (1994): "Alliances, legitimation, and founding rates in the U. S. biotechnology field, 1971–1989," paper presented at the Academy of Management Meetings, Dallas, Texas, August.

Kaplan, A. (1964): *The Conduct of Inquiry*. New York: Chandler.

Kauffman, S. A. (1993): *The Origins of Order: Self-Organization and Selection in Evolution*. New York: Oxford University Press.

Koertge, N. (1998): *A House Built on Sand: Exposing Postmodernist Myths about Science*. New York: Oxford University Press.

Kuhn, T. S. (1962): *The Structure of Scientific Revolutions*. Chicago, IL: University of Chicago Press.

Lanczos, C. (1970): *The Variational Principles of Mechanics*, 4th edn. Toronto: University of Toronto Press.

Latour, B. (1984): *Les Microbes: Guerre et Paix Suivi de Irréductions*. Paris: Editions A. M. Métailié. Translation by A. Sheridan and J. Law (1988): *The Pasteurization of France*. Cambridge, MA: Harvard University Press.

Laudan, L. (1981): "A confutation of convergent realism," *Philosophy of Science*, 48, 19–48.

Lawson, T. (1997): *Economics and Reality*. New York: Routledge.

Levins, R. (1968): *Evolution in Changing Environments: Some Theoretical Explorations*. Princeton, NJ: Princeton University Press.

Levinthal, D. A. (1997): "Adaptation on rugged landscapes," *Management Science*, 43, 934–50.

Lloyd, E. A. (1988): *The Structure and Confirmation of Evolutionary Theory*. Princeton, NJ: Princeton University Press.

Lorenz, K. (1941): "Kants Lehre vom apriorischen im Lichte gegenwärtiger Biologie," *Blätter für Deutsche Philosophie*, 15, 94–125. Reprinted in L. von Bertalanffy and A. Rapoport (eds), (1962): *General Systems, vol. VII*, Ann Arbor, MI: Society for General Systems Research, 23–35.

Mainzer, K. (1997): *Thinking in Complexity: The Complex Dynamics of Matter, Mind, and Mankind*, 3rd edn. New York: Springer-Verlag.

Marsden, R., and Townley, B. (1996): "The Owl of Minerva: Reflections on theory in practice," in S. R. Clegg, C. Hardy and W. R. Nord (eds), *Handbook of Organization Studies*, Thousand Oaks, CA: Sage, 659–75.

Masuch, M., and Warglien, M. (eds) (1992): *Artificial Intelligence in Organization and Management Theory: Models of Distributed Activity*. Amsterdam, The Netherlands: North Holland.

McKelvey, B. (1997): "Quasi-natural organization science," *Organization Science*, 8, 351–80.

McKelvey, B. (1999a): "Avoiding complexity catastrophe in coevolutionary pockets: Strategies for rugged landscapes," *Organization Science*, 10, 294–321.

McKelvey, B. (1999b): "Self-organization, complexity catastrophes, and microstate models at the edge of chaos," in J. A. C. Baum and B. McKelvey (eds), *Variations in Organization Science: In Honor of Donald T. Campbell*, Thousand Oaks, CA: Sage, 279–307.

McKelvey, B. (1999c): "Toward a Campbellian realist organization science," in J. A. C. Baum and B. McKelvey (eds), *Variations in Organization Science: In Honor of Donald T. Campbell*, Thousand Oaks, CA: Sage, 383–411.

McKelvey, B. (2000): "Model-centered strategy science: More experiments, less history," in R. Sanchez and A. Heene (eds), *Research in Competence-Based Management*, Stamford, CT: JAI Press, 217–53.

McKelvey, B. (forthcoming): "From fields to science," in R. Westwood and S. R. Clegg (eds), *Point/Counterpoint: Central Debates in Organization Theory*, Oxford, UK: Blackwell, forthcoming.

Mirowski, P. (1989): *More Heat than Light*. Cambridge, UK: Cambridge University Press.

Monge, P., and Contractor, N. S. (forthcoming): "Emergence of communication networks," in F. M. Jablin and L. L. Putnam (eds), *Handbook of Organizational Communication*, Thousand Oaks, CA: Sage, in press.

Morgan, M. S., and Morrison, M. (eds) (2000): *Models as Mediators: Perspectives on Natural and Social Science*. Cambridge, UK: Cambridge University Press.

Morrison, M. (2000): "Models as autonomous agents," in M. S. Morgan and M. Morrison (eds), *Models as Mediators: Perspectives on Natural and Social Science*, Cambridge, UK: Cambridge University Press, 38–65.

Morrison, M. and Morgan, M. S. (2000): "Models as mediating instruments," in M. S. Morgan and M. Morrison (eds), *Models as Mediators: Perspectives on Natural and Social Science*, Cambridge, UK: Cambridge University Press, 10–37.

Nagel, E. (1961): *The Structure of Science*. New York: Harcourt, Brace.

Neurath, O., and Cohen, R. S. (eds) (1973): *Empiricism and Sociology*. Dordrecht, The Netherlands: Reidel.

Nola, R. (1988): *Relativism and Realism in Science*. Dordrecht, The Netherlands: Kluwer.

Norris, C. (1997): *Against Relativism: Philosophy of Science, Deconstruction and Critical Theory*. Oxford, UK: Blackwell.

Perrow, C. (1994): "Pfeffer slips," *Academy of Management Review*, 19, 191–94.

Pfeffer, J. (1993): "Barriers to the advancement of organizational science: Paradigm development as a dependent variable," *Academy of Management Review*, 18, 599–620.

Pfeffer, J. (1995): "Mortality, reproducibility, and the persistence of styles of theory," *Organization Science*, 6, 681–86.

Prahalad, C. K., and Hamel, G. (1994): "Strategy as a field of study: Why search for a new paradigm?" *Strategic Management Journal*, 15, 5–16.

Prietula, M. J., Carley, K. M., and Gasser, L. (eds) (1998): *Simulating Organizations: Computational Models of Institutions and Groups*. Boston, MA: MIT Press.

Putnam, H. (1962): "What theories are not," in E. Nagel, P. Suppes and A. Tarski (eds), *Logic, Methodology, and Philosophy of Science: Proceedings of the 1960 International Congress*, Stanford, CA: Stanford University Press, 240–51.

Redman, D. A. (1991): *Economics and the Philosophy of Science*. New York: Oxford University Press.

Read, D. W. (1990): "The utility of mathematical constructs in building archaeology theory," in

A. Voorrips (ed.), *Mathematics and Information Science in Archaeology: A Flexible Framework*, Bonn: Holos, 29–60.

Reed, M., and Hughes, M., (eds) (1992): *Rethinking Organization: New Directions in Organization Theory and Analysis*. London: Sage.

Reichenbach, H. (1938): *Experience and Prediction*. Chicago, IL: University of Chicago Press.

Rivkin, J. W. (2000): "Imitation of complex strategies," *Management Science*, 46, 824–44.

Rosenberg, A. (1985): *The Structure of Biological Science*. Cambridge, UK: Cambridge University Press.

Ruse, M. (1973): *The Philosophy of Biology*. London: Hutchinson.

Sokal, A., and Bricmont, J. (1998): *Fashionable Nonsense: Postmodern Intellectuals' Abuse of Science*. New York: Picador.

Stich, S. (1990): *Fragmentation of Reason*. Cambridge, MA: MIT Press.

Stokman, F. N., and Doreian, P. (1997): "Evolution of social networks: Processes and principles," P. Doreian and F. N. Stokman (eds), *Evolution of Social Networks*, New York: Gordon and Breach, 233–50.

Suppe, F. (1977): *The Structure of Scientific Theories*, 2nd edn. Chicago: University of Chicago Press.

Suppe, F. (ed.) (1989): *The Semantic Conception of Theories & Scientific Realism*. Urbana-Champaign, IL: University of Illinois Press.

Suppes, P. (1961): "A comparison of the meaning and use of models in mathematics and the empirical sciences," in H. Freudenthal (ed.), *The Concept and the Role of the Model in Mathematics and Natural and Social Sciences*, Dordrecht, The Netherlands: Reidel, 163–77.

Sutton, R. I., and Staw, B. M. (1995): "What theory is *not*," *Administrative Science Quarterly*, 40, 371–84.

Thompson, P. (1989): *The Structure of Biological Theories*. Albany, NY: State University of New York Press.

Tushman, M. L., and Anderson, P. (1986): "Technological discontinuities and organizational environments," *Administrative Science Quarterly*, 31, 439–65.

Van de Ven, A. (1989): "Nothing is quite so practical as a good theory," *Academy of Management Review*, 14, 486–89.

van Fraassen, B. C. (1970): "On the extension of Beth's semantics of physical theories," *Philosophy of Science*, 37, 325–39.

Van Maanen, J. (1995a): "Style as theory," *Organization Science*, 6, 133–43.

Van Maanen, J. (1995b): "Fear and loathing in organization studies," *Organization Science*, 6, 687–692.

Weick, K. E.: "Theory construction as disciplined imagination," *Academy of Management Review*, 14 (1989), 516–531.

Weiss, R. (2000): "Taking science out of organization science: How would postmodernism reconstruct the analysis of organizations?" *Organization Science*, 11, 709–31.

Williams, M. B. (1970): "Deducing the consequences of evolution: A mathematical model," *Journal of Theoretical Biology*, 29, 343–85.

Williams, M. B. (1973): "The Logical Status of Natural Selection and Other Evolutionary Controversies," in M. Bunge (ed.), *The Methodological Unity of Science*, Dordrecht, The Netherlands: Reidel, 84–102.

Zucker, L. G. (1989): "Combining institutional theory and population ecology: No legitimacy, no history," *American Sociological Review*, 54, 542–5.

Chapter Thirty-four

Survey Research Methods

DAVID KNOKE, PETER V. MARSDEN, AND
ARNE L. KALLEBERG

An organizational survey assembles data on the characteristics or attributes of a large number of organizational entities by administering interviews or questionnaires to organizational informants or participants.[1] Data collected may pertain to entities ranging from teams or departments to entire establishments, multi-establishment firms, or interorganizational linkages and networks. Often these organizational data are linked with individual-level survey data on organizational members. Well-designed, successfully executed surveys describe, and permit inferences about, distributions of organizational characteristics and their bivariate and multivariate relationships.

Organizational surveys have become common, both in the academic world and in applied research conducted by government agencies such as the US Bureau of the Census or Department of Labor. Both narrowly and broadly defined populations have been sampled and a diverse range of substantive issues has been investigated. In this chapter, we first illustrate the variety of designs and applications using several prominent examples of organizational surveys. Next, we examine the sequence of decisions that organizational surveys confront regarding study design, sampling frames and methods, identifying key informants, questionnaire construction, gaining access to organizations, data collection and dataset management. We conclude with a brief discussion of the strengths and drawbacks of surveys as an approach to organizational research.

Examples of Organizational Surveys

The most basic organizational survey design assembles data on organizational entities of a single type – for example, establishments or firms – at one point in time. In the very simplest case, data are obtained from a single informant for each organization, who reports on all the aspects of his or her unit that are of interest to a research project. This minimal design can be made more elaborate in several ways. Multiple, rather than single organizational informants may be queried. Multilevel data may be collected on several types of entities nested within one another, as in a study of departments within establishments within firms. Data on organizations may be linked to individual-level information for one or more employees, members, or other participants. Finally, information about organizational properties may be collected at multiple points in time.

Table 34.1 provides examples of organizational surveys. The first three surveys listed use one-time, cross-sectional designs in studying job training, programmable automation, and employment practices, respectively. The National Association Study (NAS) and the Indianapolis-Tokyo Work Commitment Project exemplify two-level designs in which surveys of association members and employees accompany organization-level surveys. The National Organizations Study (NOS) and the National Congregations Study (NCS) are organizational studies of employers and religious organizations, each linked to a representative sample survey of individuals. Longitudinal organizational surveys in Table 34.1 include the National Employer Surveys, the National Establishment Surveys (NES), and the Workplace Industrial Relations Surveys (WIRS). The final entry in Table 34.1, the National Policy Domains Study (NPDS), is a network survey of two theoretical populations of "core organizations" involved in policy fields.

The examples in Table 34.1 are by no means exhaustive, but they do illustrate a broad range of applications and designs. Among many other studies including organizational surveys are the Metropolitan Employer-Worker Survey (Bridges and Villemez, 1994), the Employment Opportunity Pilot Project (Barron and Bishop, 1985), the Multi-City Study of Urban Inequality (Holzer, 1996), and the Swedish Establishment Survey (le Grand et al., 1994). Callus et al. (1991) describe an Australian counterpart to the WIRS surveys, while Knoke et al. (1996) use the Laumann and Knoke (1987) policy domain methodology to compare organizational networks surrounding labor policy across the USA, Germany, and Japan. Bills (1992) gives an overview of employer surveys used in studies of labor market phenomena prior to 1990. National statistical agencies conduct numerous organizational surveys to obtain official statistics and maintain national accounts (Cox and Chinnappa, 1995).

Implementing an Organizational Survey

This section follows the implementation guide in Table 34.2, which highlights a series of key decision points and selection criteria that researchers must consider when designing and conducting an organizational survey project. Fundamental problems include the development of suitable sampling frames, difficulties in gaining access and cooperation from authorities, the selection of informants and organizational measures, and data collection and distribution.

STUDY DESIGN AND TARGET POPULATION

Several important parameters of organizational surveys are set at the outset of a project based on the research questions to be investigated and/or the resources available. These include unit(s) of analysis to be covered, the number of time points at which units are to be surveyed, and definition of the target population to which survey findings are to be generalized.

UNIT(S) OF ANALYSIS

Freeman (1978) recounts complexities in determining the appropriate units of analysis in organizational research, pointing to the permeability of unit boundaries, the nesting of some units within others, and to longitudinal considerations. He suggests that the selection of a unit of analysis should be guided by the level of analysis at which important dependent variables are conceptualized.

In practice, five common units of analysis – the individual participant or employee, the subunit or department, the establishment, the multi-establishment firm, and the interorganizational network – are used in organizational surveys. When organizational surveys gather data on individual participants, these are usually accompanied by information on supra-individual units, since theories suggest that organizational context shapes individual phenomena. Departments or work units are groups of participants involved in a coordinated set of activities. Many of the surveys in Table 34.1 examine establishments, that is, the organizational participants and activities located at a single site. Establishments are often, in turn, parts of larger organizational complexes that operate at two or more sites, such as firms or school districts.[2] For example, General Electric operates many manufacturing plants across the USA; an establishment-level sampling frame would include these GE establishments as well as its corporate headquarters as distinct eligible units, while GE would be only one element within a firm-level sampling frame. Interorganizational networks, such as the policy domains of the NPDS, consist of a set of establishments or firms and the relationships among them.

Many research projects involve phenomena at multiple levels of analysis, and organizational surveys commonly use hierarchical or multi-level designs that gather information about several types of units. The NOS, for example, was primarily a survey of work establishments. Limited data also were gathered, however, about the larger firm (if any) of which an establishment was part. Within establishments, some information was assembled about up to three occupations; the NOS data were also linked to individual responses to the General Social Survey (GSS). The Indianapolis-Tokyo Project and the NAS also had hierarchical designs in which data were collected on numerous participants within plants and voluntary associations, respectively.

CROSS-SECTION OR LONGITUDINAL DESIGN

Organizational surveys are usually conducted at a single point in time. Trend studies of independent samples at different time points make possible the measurement of net change, while panel studies of the same units at two or more time points enable analysts to study within-organization change. The WIRS studies contain elements of both of these longitudinal designs.

Designing longitudinal studies requires decisions about the time intervals at which remeasurement should take place; to a degree such judgments depend on anticipated rates of change in the phenomena under study. Panel studies also require that researchers make judgments regarding continuity and change in unit boundaries over time, as establishments (for example) change ownership, location, or name, merge with or acquire others, and so on. Successful panel studies require that researchers retain tracking information on how to contact a sampled establishment or firm. A common complication not encountered in panel studies of individuals is substantial turnover in organizational informants between waves of a panel study.

Table 34.1 Examples of organizational surveys

Study	Design	Target population	Sampling method	Major topics	References
Survey of employer-provided training	Cross-sectional	Private-sector workplaces	Size/industry stratified random sample, list frame	Formal job training	Frazis et al., 1995
Survey of machine tool use in manufacturing	Cross-sectional	Plants in 21 metalworking industries	Size-stratified random sample, list frame	Diffusion of programmable automation	Kelley and Brooks, 1988
Three-state study	Cross-sectional	Organizations with 50+ employees in 13 industries	Simple random sample, list frame	Employment practices	Dobbin et al. 1993
National Association Study (NAS)	Cross-sectional Linked survey of members	"Collective-action" voluntary associations	Size-stratified random sample, list frame	Governance, services, political activities	Knoke, 1990
Indianapolis-Tokyo Work Commitment Project	Cross-sectional Linked survey of employees	Manufacturing plants in 7 industries	Size-stratified random sample, list frame	Commitment, satisfaction, participatory structures, employee services	Lincoln and Kalleberg, 1990
National Organizations Study (NOS)	Cross-sectional Linked to survey data on one employee	Work establishments in USA	Hypernetwork sample linked to 1991 General Social Survey	Organizational structures, human resource practices	Kalleberg et al. 1996
National Congregations Study (NCS)	Cross-sectional Linked to survey data on one congregant	Religious organizations	Hypernetwork sample linked to 1998 General Social Survey	Congregational composition, structure, activities, programming	Chaves et al. 1999
National Employer Surveys	Two distinct panel surveys	Private-sector workplaces, 20+ employees	Size- and sector-stratified random sample	Educational preparedness; workplace ties to schools	Cappelli et al. 1998

National Establishment Surveys (NES)	Panel survey, new organizations added in second wave	Private-sector establishments, 50+ employees	Size-stratified random sample, list frame	Innovative workplace practices, family policies	Osterman, 1994, 1995, 1999
Workplace Industrial Relations Surveys (WIRS)	Trend survey with panel components in some years	Workplaces with 25+ employees (10+ in 1998)	Size-stratified random sample, list frame	Industrial relations and human resource practices	Marginson, 1998
National Policy Domain Study (NPDS)	Network study	"Core organizations" in health and energy fields	All active organizations identified via several archival sources	Organizational networks, participation in legislative events	Laumann and Knoke, 1987

Table 34.2   Implementation guide for organizational surveys

Implementation step	Key decision	Key decision criteria
Set major design parameters	Cross-section, panel or trend study? Sample or census? Single or multiple levels?	Research questions Research budget
Define units of analysis	Persons, work teams/subunits, establishments, and/or firms?	Level(s) at which phenomena of interest occur
Define target population	Restrict by size, industry, geographic area?	Research questions Research budget
Select sampling frame	List, area, or implicit?	Is a high-quality list available?
Sampling design	Simple random sample or stratified sample? Draw a multiplicity sample?	Minimize sampling variance given available resources Is a list frame available? Is an individual-level survey to be conducted?
Identify informants	How many per organization? What organizational positions to approach?	Who is best informed and least biased? How much between-informant agreement on items of interest?
Instrument construction	What measures and questions to include? How much time required to complete?	Research questions Availability of prior measures Pretest findings and experience
Mode of administration	Mail, telephone, in-person, or electronic?	Research budget Type(s) of data sought
Gaining access	Obtain advance permission or make direct approaches?	Does study design require within-organization survey of participants? Research budget
Maximizing response rate	Number and mode of contacts, follow-up attempts?	Research budget
Weighting	Use weights to present findings?	Take perspective of individual participants or organizations?
Data preparation and archiving	Protect informant confidentiality? Enrich survey data with contextual and archival materials	What data sources to merge in? Where to archive data base? Identifying information to mask

DEFINITION OF TARGET POPULATION

The target population designates that set of organizational units to which a study's findings are to be generalized. Some studies define this quite broadly. The NOS, for example, took the population of all US work establishments as its target. This excludes organizations such as clubs or associations (unless these have paid staff) but is otherwise rather comprehensive. The target population is often restricted, however, usually on the basis of industry, size, or geographic area.

Limitations on the target population are introduced for several reasons. A study may be confined to organizations that operate within a particular industry – such as hospitals, religious congregations, or law firms – because these types of organizations are of intrinsic substantive concern. Sometimes a single-industry focus is required because key concepts cannot be measured in comparable ways across industrial settings. There also may be analytic criteria for industry restrictions; Kelley's (1990) study of the impact of programmable automation on work organization, for instance, obtained some control over variability in "technology" by limiting the study to establishments in metalworking industries.

Size limitations usually exclude those organizations that fall beneath a particular threshold, as in the NES or the WIRS surveys. Such exclusions may be based on a belief that phenomena of interest are unlikely to be observed in small organizations having simple structures. Because of the substantial skew in the distribution of organization size, however (Table 34.3), such limitations serve to exclude a large fraction of otherwise eligible organizations.

Restricting the target population to organizations that operate in a particular geographic area is very common; indeed, even the most expansive population definitions include only those organizations located in a particular nation-state. Further limitations may ease the data collection process by confining it to a particular region or metropolitan area, as in the Bridges and Villemez (1994) or Lincoln and Kalleberg (1990) studies. Such restrictions also permit analysts to draw on contextual knowledge about that area – such as labor market conditions – when interpreting findings. A design may also contrast organizations operating in areas known to have distinct institutional arrangements, as in the three-state study of Dobbin et al. (1993).

CENSUS OR SAMPLE?

A final parameter for the design of an organizational survey is whether data will be sought on all organizations in the target population – an organizational census or "dense sample" – or whether a sample is to be drawn. Target populations may be defined sufficiently narrowly that it is possible to obtain data on all units, as in the studies of employment security agencies reported by Blau (1972). Surveys that focus on the largest corporations, such as the Fortune 500 or 1000 (Lawler et al., 1992), also attempt to collect data on all elements in the target population. Likewise, network studies seeking to depict the structure of an organizational field or policy domain require data on all units within the population or "system." More typically, however, researchers administer surveys to a representative sample of organizations.

Table 34.3 Private-sector employment by organization size, 1994

Firm employment size (Number of employees)	Firm (%)	Establishment (%)	Employment (%)
0–4	60.8	49.4	5.5
5–9	18.3	15.1	6.5
10–19	10.7	9.4	7.8
20–99	8.6	9.7	18.3
100–499	1.4	4.4	14.6
500 or more	0.3	12.1	47.3
Total	100.1[a]	100.1[a]	100.0
(Number of observations)	(5276,964)	(6509,065)	(96,721,594)

[a] Totals to more than 100.0% due to rounding
Source: Standard Statistical Establishment List (SSEL) maintained by the US Bureau of the Census. This source covers business establishments other than those operated by government or in private households. For more information on the SSEL and its uses, see http://www.census.gov/econ/www/mu0600.html.

SELECTING A SAMPLING FRAME

The target population is a theoretical construction. By contrast, the sampling frame provides an operational enumeration of the organizations eligible for inclusion in a study. Generalizing the findings of a study to the target population is legitimate only to the degree that the sampling frame corresponds to the population. A sampling frame may also provide information needed to stratify a sample (on, e.g., size or industry) and/ or on how to establish contact with those organizations selected. A business register (Colledge, 1995) is a database maintained over time to provide sampling frames for a program of surveys conducted by a statistical agency.

"List" and "area" frames are typical in organizational surveys (Colledge, 1995). A list frame consists of a list of organizations, often accompanied by supplementary data. An area frame includes a set of geographic areas; organizational units are enumerated within a subset of these to establish a sampling frame. The two types of frames may be used together in a particular study.

Some list frames used in organizational research are maintained commercially. For example, Dun and Bradstreet makes data on US businesses available in the form of its Market Identifier File (DMI). This data base contains financial and other information on organizations in virtually all industry sectors besides public administration. Osterman's (1994, 1999) NES surveys used the DMI as a sampling frame. Other sources that offer sampling frames for studies of diverse organizations include records maintained for tax purposes (ES202), telephone directories, and membership lists kept by Chambers of Commerce (Kalleberg et al., 1990).

List frames for studies of organizations within particular industries often can be found in published directories. Gale Research Company, for example, regularly publishes an *Encyclopedia of Associations*, a worldwide directory of 140,000 organizations including trade and professional associations, sports and hobby groups, and religious organizations. Knoke (1990) used this *Encyclopedia* together with two similar compendia listing other membership organizations as a sampling frame for the NAS. Studies of law firms can use sources such as the *Martindale-Hubbell Law Directory* as a sampling frame. Other list frames for industry studies can be obtained from peak organizations such as the Association of American Colleges and Universities, the American Hospital Association, or the National Association of Manufacturers.

Area frames are considerably less common in organizational research, since much effort and expense is entailed in developing lists of organizations within geographic areas. Aldrich, Zimmer and McEvoy (1989) relied on an area frame in a study of Asian businesses in English cities. They purposively selected wards within cities, compiling a complete business census for each ward, from which businesses were subsequently sampled.

Substantial expense can be associated with obtaining and maintaining a sampling frame. Colledge (1995) suggests that this can account for as much as a fifth of the survey program budget for a national statistical agency. That substantial costs are entailed in direct enumeration for area frames is self-evident; often this approach will be viable only when a frame is to be used for drawing several samples. The direct costs of obtaining list frames from commercial or published sources are usually more modest.

Nonetheless, researchers confront a number of practical problems in working with such frames. Among the most serious of these is undercoverage, when eligible units are omitted from a sampling frame. This may occur because of lags between the founding of an organization and its inclusion in a list frame. Aldrich, Kalleberg, Marsden and Cassell (1989) compared an area frame to several list frames, demonstrating that the latter tended to omit newer establishments. Undercoverage may also result because criteria for entry into the list frame differ from those used to define the target population; lists such as Chamber of Commerce directories or rosters kept by peak associations include only those organizations that have chosen to be members.

Coverage problems can also arise in the use of area frames. The enumeration required is especially challenging when organizations do not have a visible on-street presence. Kalleberg et al. (1990) found, for example, that direct enumeration within a geographic area often failed to locate construction-industry businesses that were found in list frames they examined. Organizations such as voluntary associations that often lack visible markers such as signs or facilities may also not be identified when an area frame is compiled.

List frames may also include "ineligible" organizational units. Listings may be defunct, or may not meet the criteria that define the target population. Inclusion of ineligibles is not a special problem if they are readily recognizable in the frame. Ineligibility increases study costs if it is discovered only in the course of fieldwork, as is often so with units that have disbanded. Duplication of listings can also pose problems if it is not immediately evident, since this may affect the likelihood that a given unit is selected as part of a sample. Duplication would occur, for example, in a frame based on telephone listings when organizations have varying numbers of telephone lines.

Further problems with sampling frames arise if there is a disjunction between the units listed in the frame and those defined by a study. A frame might contain a listing for a firm, for instance, while the study's units of analysis are establishments. Lists containing supplementary data on size or industry are useful because they facilitate stratification of a sample, but there are often inaccuracies in such data. These may lead to erroneous inclusion or exclusion of a unit, or to its placement in an incorrect stratum. Location and contact information too may be inaccurate. This may happen because the location or representative of an organization has changed, but it also occurs when records list the name and address of the person whose report places an establishment on a list – which might be a headquarters office or an independent accountant – rather than someone at the establishment itself.

For all of these reasons, lists that may serve as organizational sampling frames should be examined carefully. One such study compared four list frames and a direct enumeration approach (area frame) for a North Carolina county. Kalleberg et al. (1990: p. 658) summarized its findings as follows:

> Direct enumeration is an effective approach for locating young organizations but is expensive to implement and likely to miss establishments in construction. Unemployment Insurance [UI] records and DMI [Dun's Market Identifier] files are practical: they are machine-readable and contain substantial auxiliary information about each unit. Neither is available on a timely basis, however, and they therefore tend to include somewhat older establishments. The coverage of the Chamber of Commerce Directory is poor, and it contains a strong bias towards older businesses. White Pages of the telephone book give the broadest coverage and the least overall bias but are cumbersome to work with because they are not machine readable and contain numerous duplicate and ineligible entries.

The sampling method known as hypernetwork or multiplicity sampling (McPherson, 1982) establishes a sampling frame for organizational units implicitly, relying on known relationships between organizational units and sampling frames for individuals or households. We discuss this approach in more detail in the following section.

Sampling methods

A 1982 review of research methods used in over 700 organizational studies (Drabek et al., 1982) revealed that only about 13 percent were based on simple or stratified random sampling designs which readily permitted generalization to a large population. A substantial fraction of other studies used dense samples including all available units within a specified class or population.[3] The broad majority of the studies reviewed involved convenience samples or case studies. We have not reviewed more recent studies as systematically as did Drabek et al., but it is evident from the examples in Table 34.1 that there has been increased attention to representativeness in organizational research designs since their review (see also Carroll and Hannan, 2000, p. 87).

Once a sampling frame is constructed, organizational surveys usually make use of relatively straightforward simple or stratified random sampling designs. Lincoln and Kalleberg (1990), for example, randomly sampled plants within three size-industry strata. Osterman (1994) also used a size-stratified sample. Dobbin et al. (1993) drew simple random samples of organizations meeting their selection criteria in each of the three states they studied.

Sampling from list frames often seeks to minimize sampling variance given cost (Sigman and Monsour, 1995). This suggests sampling of organizations with probability proportional to size (PPS), since most organizational populations include units that differ widely in size (Cox and Chinnappa, 1995), and because the variance of most organizational characteristics tends to rise with size. The size distribution of units typically exhibits a marked positive skew, as illustrated in Table 34.3 for employment in private-sector US work units in 1994. More than six out of ten firms, and nearly five of ten establishments, have fewer than five employees; less than one percent of firms, and only 12 percent of establishments, have 500 or more workers. Such skewness in the size distribution means that a simple random sample would include predominantly smaller organizational units. This would yield very imprecise estimates of the characteristics of the larger organizations.

HYPERNETWORK OR MULTIPLICITY SAMPLING

A major alternative approach both provides an implicit sampling frame for organizations and draws a PPS sample from it. Variously known as hypernetwork (McPherson, 1982), multiplicity (Parcel et al., 1991), and network sampling (Johnson, 1995), this approach relies on a well-defined affiliation relationship between individuals and organizations. Respondents sampled from an individual- or household-level sampling frame are linked to organizational units – such as workplaces, voluntary associations, or religious congregations – and asked for information that permits researchers to locate those organizations. Organization-level data collection occurs via separate contacts with organizational informants. This approach was used in the NOS (Spaeth and O'Rourke, 1994), in the NCS (Chaves et al., 1999) and in employee-employer studies in Chicago (Bridges and Villemez, 1994) and Columbus, Ohio (Parcel et al., 1991).

Hypernetwork sampling leads to a PPS sample at the organizational level; the likelihood that an organizational unit falls into the sample increases with its number of individual members. As McPherson (1982: p. 230) puts it, "[t]he key insight . . . is that the larger the organization, the more likely one or more of its members will be picked in a sample of individuals." Studies using this sampling design must obtain measures of organizational size in order to estimate the organizational size distribution and to weight the estimated distributions of other measured organizational characteristics by size.

Hypernetwork sampling is an attractive approach to sampling organizations because it avoids the costs of developing a separate sampling frame for organizations, relying instead on existing sampling frames for individuals. Cost savings are particularly notable if a study design requires individual-level respondents, since obtaining the representative organization-level sample is then nearly cost-free. This sampling method is especially advantageous for units of analysis such as departments or work units, which rarely are listed for more than one organization. Finally, the PPS feature of hypernetwork samples is often desirable, as discussed earlier.

The individual-level respondents targeted by a hypernetwork design must constitute a representative sample of the population of interest, whether that is composed of church members, volunteers, or business employees. When the individual-level sample has a complex design that requires weighting to be representative of the underlying population, adjustments are also necessary for the associated organizational sample. The membership relation between individual-level respondents and organizational units must be clearly defined to yield precise weights for estimating distributions at the organizational level. Special problems of nonresponse arise in the two-stage data collection procedures required by hypernetwork sampling (Johnson, 1995). Both individual respondents and organizational informants may fail to participate in a survey, and individuals do not always provide information that permits researchers to locate the organizations with which they are affiliated. Spaeth and O'Rourke (1994) reflect on the use of hypernetwork sampling in the NOS, and offer practical suggestions about conducting research projects using this sampling design.

IDENTIFYING INFORMANTS

Careful attention to sampling frames and random sampling plans is essential to ensure that an organizational survey is representative of an underlying population. In general, however, the same principles do not apply when choosing informants to be asked for organizational data from among eligible organizational participants. Researchers assume that participants differ systematically in their knowledge of the organization, and place a premium on locating those who are best informed, since they are apt to provide the most reliable organization-level reports.[4]

Huber and Power (1985) suggest that ideal informants will possess the needed information, be motivated to respond, and lack significant perceptual biases or cognitive limitations. Seidler (1974) observes that vested interests of participants may systematically affect their reports, particularly on perceptual items, and points to situational differences – such as organizational size – that affect the capacity of respondents to provide accurate reports.

If study resources permit only a single interview or questionnaire per organization, the response should be sought from the most knowledgeable informant available. Who this person is will depend on the substantive focus of a survey. Different participants would be approached, for example, by surveys that focus on financial, personnel, strategic, production, or marketing issues. Usually, positional criteria are used to identify appropriate informants: human resources managers are approached about hiring, compensation, and fringe benefit policies, financial officers about money matters, production supervisors about workgroup organization, and so on. In smaller organizations that do not have an extensive functional division of labor, the head of the organization may be responsible for all significant personnel, financial and strategic decisions. There researchers seek contact with "the person in charge here" or "the person responsible for hiring" rather than with someone having a specific job title.

Systematic studies of the relative capacity of different informants to report on organizational properties are rare. In a study of perceptions of conflict within Catholic dioceses, Seidler (1974) asked outside experts to rate the bias expected of incumbents holding different positions within the Church, and used those ratings in selecting a balanced set of informants within dioceses. Studying marketing channels, John and Reve (1982) found that wholesalers made somewhat more reliable reports for structural measures than did retailers, and very low convergent validity for reports on sentiments like domain consensus. Kumar, Stern and Anderson (1993) examined perceptions of dealer performance from the standpoint of a supplier organization, and found sales managers to be somewhat better informants than were fleet managers. McPherson and Rotolo (1995) studied the capacity of officials and ordinary members to report on characteristics of face-to-face voluntary groups, finding that officials provide reports of slightly higher quality. Edwards and Marginson (1988) found limited perceptual differences between establishment-level and higher-level managers who answered the WIRS surveys.

Multiple informants may be useful in organizational surveys, in two distinct ways. First, variations in knowledge across participants may require surveys to contact more than one informant in order to obtain an informed answer to each survey question. The NOS, for example, used two or more informants for about a sixth of the organizations it sampled (Spaeth and O'Rourke, 1994); these tended to be larger establishments that were part of multi-site firms. Alternatively, multiple informants may answer all items on a survey. The multiple responses are then combined to yield organization-level measures. Typically this involves averaging the replies of different informants, but measures of inter-informant variation are used occasionally. Kumar et al. (1993) suggest a consensus procedure for combining reports from multiple informants.

Seidler (1974) suggests a minimum of five respondents per organization as a guideline. Aday (1991), however, concludes that one informant is usually adequate to describe structurally undifferentiated organizations. The number of informants needed to obtain an aggregate-level measure with adequate reliability may depend on the extent of within-organization variation on the characteristic in question. Knoke et al. (1991) show that this differs widely across kinds of items often administered in organizational surveys. Agreement among informants is high on such features as organizational age and size – there a response from single informant will often be sufficient. Perceptions of organizational culture (Zammuto and Krakower, 1991) or descriptions of the division of labor, on the other hand, have much lower inter-informant reliability; measuring such properties requires correspondingly more informants.

List sampling frames will occasionally provide information that identifies appropriate informants, though its accuracy should not be taken for granted. Otherwise, finding the targeted informant(s) may require telephone calls or visits to the organization's central reception area or website to obtain the phone extension or office number of a specific department. A short series of referrals usually suffices to identify a participant who is a suitable informant about the survey issues. It can be important to make such inquiries even when a survey is to be conducted via mail questionnaire, since addressing questionnaires to named individuals promotes better response rates (Paxson et al., 1995).

INSTRUMENT CONSTRUCTION

The survey questionnaire or interview schedule usually consists of a sequence of sections focusing on the various topics of interest. Unique or innovative questions that measure the phenomena of central concern to a study must often be created *de novo*. In many instances, however, items may be drawn from questionnaires used in previous studies; these will frequently suggest useful strategies for formulating questions even when not used verbatim. One inventory of such questions appears in the periodically updated *Handbook of Organizational Measurement* (Price 1997; Price and Mueller 1986). The current *Handbook* classifies numerous measures and scales under 28 headings such as commitment, environment, formalization, innovation, power, size, and technology. After describing a measure's origins and previous usage, the volume presents a formal definition, item wordings, methods for combining multiple items into composite measures, and available evidence on validity and reliability. Van de Ven and Ferry (1980) provide an additional compendium of this kind.

Because researchers often adapt existing measures or create original items suitable to a specific organizational population and set of substantive topics, draft instruments must be pretested. Sometime pretesting occurs in focus groups that elicit discussion of survey concepts and proposed indicators (Dippo et al., 1995), but eventually pretests should be conducted under conditions that resemble those anticipated in the actual field period. A number of eligible organizations should be drawn from the target population, and suitably trained interviewers should administer the interview or questionnaire to appropriately selected informants. Valuable feedback can be obtained by debriefing pre-test interviewers about the process of gaining access and conducting the interview, as well as informant difficulties in following instructions or comprehending questions. Debriefing of pretest respondents can help to identify items that are regarded as vague, awkward, or sensitive.[5] Behavior coding and cognitive techniques such as think-aloud protocols can identify problems in the formulation of questions (Presser and Blair, 1994; Dippo et al., 1995). Effective questionnaires are often subjected to two or more pretests; these may experiment with alternative forms for sensitive questions, for example.

Importantly, pretest data allow researchers to estimate the time required to complete an interview or questionnaire, essential information for ensuring that data collection costs remain within budget. A very difficult stage in the development of most questionnaires comes when investigators must remove items to keep the length of an instrument within tolerable bounds.

Prior to fieldwork, completed questionnaires and other research plans must be reviewed by a human subjects committee or institutional review board. This helps to insure that the research will not create significant risks for participants. Among other things, researchers must indicate how informed consent will be obtained from prospective participants in the study.

DATA COLLECTION

Procedures for conducting field operations differ little between organizational and household surveys. Both have the objective of conducting data collection in a way that maximizes data quality within the constraints of available resources. In this section, we outline issues regarding data collection mode, techniques for gaining access to informants, training of interviewers, and controlling rates of nonresponse.

MODE

Survey data have usually been collected via three major modalities. In decreasing order of costs, these are in-person interviews, telephone interviews, and self-administered mail-back questionnaires. Relatively recent innovations in computer-assisted data collection include computer-assisted telephone interviewing (CATI) and computer-assisted personal interviewing (CAPI) (Saris, 1991). These modes can enhance data quality by preventing technical mistakes in administration, such as the omission of items due to errors in following filtering instructions. They also offer methodological opportunities, such as randomization of the order in which survey items composing attitude scales are presented (thus avoiding order effects), or the immediate verbatim transcription of responses to open-ended items, while the respondent is available for further probing. Significant capital costs are associated with computer-assisted interviewing, and such methods require higher skill levels on the part of both questionnaire designers and field interviewers.

Christianson and Tortora (1995) report on a survey of 21 statistical agencies in 16 countries, which revealed that mail was the major mode in use. Cost savings are one important reason for the preponderance of mail. Another is that these surveys often require informants to report data residing in an accounting system. Retrieving such data is not readily accomplished within the limited time period available for an in-person or telephone survey.

Organizational surveys conducted by social science researchers have used all three of these survey modes. For example, Lincoln and Kalleberg (1990) interviewed plant managers in person; the NOS, NES, NAS and NCS were conducted exclusively or primarily via telephone; Dobbin et al. (1993) and Frazis et al. (1995) relied on mail questionnaires.

Developments in information technology make electronic data interchange (Ambler et al., 1995) attractive as a survey mode. This is particularly so to the extent that requests for economic or financial data are compatible with formats in which organizations store such information. Such approaches have the potential to lower data collection and data processing costs, and reduce recording errors. Some, but not all, of these advantages apply to surveys requesting that informants supply structural or perceptual data, which may not be recorded by organizations in any form.

Christianson and Tortora's (1995) study revealed that nearly half the surveys conducted by statistical agencies used more than one mode; mail remained the predominant approach, even in combination with others. Multiple modes may be used because different items are amenable to different approaches to data collection: perceptual data may be more readily gathered by in-person or telephone interview, while information regarding budgets or sales may be more easily reported via mail. Alternatively, multiple modes may be used because some informants will reply to a mail questionnaire but are unable or unwilling to schedule an interview (Spaeth and O'Rourke, 1994).

GAINING ACCESS

When a study's field period begins, gaining access to the targeted organizational informants and obtaining their cooperation become a top priority. As Tomaskovic-Devey et al. (1994) point out, informants in organizational surveys must have the authority to respond, as well as the capacity and motive required of all survey respondents. It can be useful to seek advance approval from an upper-level participant, via a letter, telephone call, or in-person visit that outlines the purpose of the study, the investigator's credentials, and the importance of the project to academic researchers and participating organizations alike. A by-product of this contact could be that the official who grants permission also directs the researcher toward qualified informants. Advance approval is essential if a study design requires that the organization supply a list of, e.g., employees or clients to be surveyed. Obtaining such access can be a delicate matter that requires approval of other groups, such as a board of directors or a union; see, for example, Knoke (1988, p. 316) or Lincoln and Kalleberg (1990: pp. 40–1).

Not all organizational surveys use advance recruitment procedures; instead survey interviewers often contact informants directly after identifying them. Considerable persistence is required of interviewers at this stage. Barriers to reaching informants include secretaries and voicemail systems. Informants often indicate that their schedules do not permit them to set aside the sometimes-substantial block of time needed to complete an interview. They may state that their organization has a policy against participating in surveys or that they must obtain permission from authority figures before answering. Survey staff must be prepared to explain patiently why scientific sampling does not permit the interviewer to replace the prospective informant's organization with another similar one. Survey directors must budget for multiple contacts with prospective informants. Fieldwork for the NOS, for example, required a median of two contacts just to reach respondents; on average, five contacts were needed in order to complete an interview (Spaeth and O'Rourke, 1994).

INTERVIEWER TRAINING

Together with complexities of gaining access, the fact that the subject matter of organizational surveys differs from that in typical household surveys often requires special and extensive training. Spaeth and O'Rourke (1994) indicate that NOS telephone interviewers were trained for three days, with special attention to techniques for converting reluctant respondents. Dippo et al. (1995) describe training procedures and performance standards used by the Bureau of Labor Statistics for interviewers administering its establishment surveys.

MINIMIZING UNIT AND ITEM NONRESPONSE

Surveys based on appropriate sampling frames and careful sampling procedures produce representative samples only when a sufficient fraction of eligible units approached do, in fact, cooperate. Achieving a high response rate can be challenging, since there appears to be a trend toward increased reluctance to participate in surveys (Steeh, 1981; Bradburn, 1992). It is nonetheless possible to achieve adequate response rates in organizational surveys if a sufficient fraction of study resources is devoted to doing so. Field staff must be persistent in making numerous callbacks, patiently reschedule broken appointments, and be prepared to substitute a mailed version for an interview – if the alternative is no reply at all. Directors may wish to pay bonuses to interviewers able to convert respondents who initially decline to participate.

In their review of organizational surveys conducted by statistical agencies, Christianson and Tortora (1995) found an interquartile range of 6-22 percent for *non*response rates; these high completion rates reflect the fact that participation in some of the surveys covered is legally obligatory. Response rates differed by survey mode; surveys using mail tended to have lower response rates. Paxson et al. (1995) report completion rates ranging from 57 percent to 96 percent, with an average of 84 percent, for a set of 20 business mail surveys conducted by the Census Bureau. Substantially lower completion rates (average, 51 percent; range, 28–95 percent) were achieved for a set of 26 business surveys conducted by a survey research center. Response rates for some of the surveys discussed above include 64.5 percent for the NOS (Spaeth and O'Rourke, 1994), 65.5 percent for the 1992 NES (Osterman, 1994), 80 percent for the NCS (Chaves et al., 1999), and 93 percent for the NAS (Knoke, 1990).[6]

The total design method (TDM; Dillman, 2000) uses combinations of mail and telephone contacts to maximize rates of response to mail surveys. Paxson et al.

(1995: p. 304) review the application of this technique to organizational surveys, stating that

> The details include (1) a carefully timed sequence of four first-class mailings, the last of which is certified, (2) personalized correspondence, and (3) an attractive booklet question-naire designed to increase the perceived salience of the questions and ease of responding.

Paxson et al. note that financial incentives can further increase response rates, even when all TDM specifications are followed. Their review of response rates to organizational surveys conducted by a survey research center indicates that higher rates were achieved when more of these steps were taken. Contacting a named individual (rather than addressing surveys to, e.g., "Owner/Manager") seemed to be particularly effective. Paxson et al. observe that getting past organizational gatekeepers is a special barrier to be surmounted in achieving adequate cooperation rates for organizational surveys.

Tomaskovic-Devey et al. (1994) examined factors that differentiated responding and non-responding organizations in a survey of North Carolina businesses. Cooperation was more common in headquarters units than in subsidiary ones. The authors reason that subsidiary personnel lack authority to respond. Smaller, regulated, and publicly traded businesses participated more often; Tomaskovic-Devey and colleagues attribute this to differences in informant capacity and motive. A telephone follow-up of nonrespondents revealed that time burden, claims that headquarters were responsible for answering surveys, company prohibitions against participation, and reluctance to provide confidential information were among the most common reasons given for non-participation.

Some respondents may reply to part or most of a questionnaire, but refuse to provide responses to certain items. It is of course desirable that such item nonresponse also be minimal. Tomaskovic-Devey et al. (1995) apply their ability–motive–authority framework to item nonresponse. Finding that refusals to respond are particularly high for financial information, they recommend posing such questions only when the information is central to a survey's objectives. Relatively high rates of item nonresponse were also encountered for open-ended items in the Tomaskovic-Devey et al. employer survey. They suggest that seeking information from headquarters and/or obtaining advance approval of headquarters officials may reduce levels of item nonresponse.

Weighting

As noted above, there are good reasons that PPS samples should be drawn for organizational surveys. After data are collected using such a sampling design, researchers must decide whether to apply weights when presenting findings. Unweighted PPS data describe the organizational contexts encountered by a typical participant, member or employee; thus they depict the size of the religious congregation attended by an average worshiper, the formalization of the workplace as seen by an average employee, or the sex composition of a voluntary association from the viewpoint of a typical member. Weighting PPS data inversely to unit size will instead describe the distribution of organizational units, counting large and small organizational units equally.

Because organizational size distributions tend to have a pronounced positive skew, adjustments in distributions as a consequence of weighting can be dramatic. This is illustrated for private-sector employment by the last two columns of Table 34.3 above. Unweighted PPS data would yield the "employment percent" distribution in the last column, while weighting PPS observations inversely to establishment size would produce a distribution like that in the "establishment percent" column. Most *workers* are employed by moderate-to-large establishments, but *establishments* are on average quite small.

Because many organizational variables are closely associated with unit size, using a weighted rather than an unweighted PPS sample can make a large difference in substantive conclusions. For example, raw NOS data from the PPS sample indicate that 70 percent of establishments responding provided formal training within the past two years. When weighted such that each establishment is counted equally (irrespective of its number of employees), the estimated percentage providing training drops to 22 percent. Both interpretations of the data are valid: only a minority of all establishments offers formal job training programs, but a large majority of the labor force works in places offering such programs.

Whether to use weights depends on the purpose of a given analysis. When depicting the experiences of typical participants, PPS-weighted distributions are preferable. If, however, the goal is to describe distributions of organizational features, such as the percentage of CEOs with financial backgrounds or the mean level of foreign investment, then observations should be given equal weight, regardless of unit size. (These remarks about the use of weights refer to descriptive statistics such as percentages, measures of central tendency, or measures of variation. See Winship and Radbill (1994) for a discussion of the use of weights in regression analyses.)

CONSTRUCTION AND ARCHIVING OF DATA SETS

Once data collection is complete, information assembled must be coded, cleaned, and entered into machine-readable form. Automated modes such as CATI, CAPI, or electronic data interchange facilitate this process. Other data in the sampling frame or information from published and archival sources may be merged with the survey data. This could include such publicly available information as stock price, or financial data from annual company reports and SEC filings. Additional secondary data may be obtained from government sources, such as Census reports on the primary industries and geographic areas in which the sampled organizations operate. The NOS database, for example, includes data on both industrial and geographic contexts of the sampled establishments.

At this point, data from different stages of multi-level organizational surveys (of, e.g., members within organizations, as in the NAS) must be linked. Different components of such surveys must use suitable case-identification codes to ensure proper between-level matches. If the survey project involves a panel design, care must be taken to preserve information sufficient to re-locate participating organizations and informants at subsequent time points.

The primary products of data preparation are one or more machine-readable data sets, a manual describing data collection procedures, and a codebook listing all questions and response codes – usually accompanied by copies of all research instruments.

Investigators should prepare and disseminate feedback promised to organizations in return for their participation in the project. This ranges from brief written reports to presentations of seminars.

Ordinarily the researchers who construct and assemble survey data have exclusive access to the database for a period of time after its completion, in order to examine the data and develop findings pertaining to their research questions. At the end of this period, many investigators make data available to the wider organization studies community for secondary analyses. The US National Science Foundation requires that all funded projects archive their data, for example, through the Interuniversity Consortium for Political and Social Research (ICPSR).[7] The British WIRS datasets are distributed by Essex Survey Research Center Data Archive; a recent bibliographic report tallied 196 publications and papers using these data (Millward, Woodland, Bryson and Forth 1998).[8]

Protecting the confidentiality and anonymity promised to the organizations and informants in public-domain datasets is especially difficult because a few key variables such as size, industry, and geographic location may suffice to identify a specific firm. For this reason US government agencies do not release their organizational survey data to the public; see, for example, Spletzer (1997). One security precaution that permits public archiving while protecting participant identities is to remove all geographic identifiers below the regional level. Secondary analysts wishing to conduct research involving such sensitive data (for example, measures of local labor market conditions) can obtain access by posting a bond and signing a protocol, approved by their human subjects committee, which describes the steps taken to prevent persons outside the project from gaining access to the data.

Conclusion

Much early knowledge about organizations and organizational behavior was acquired via case study methods. These provide richly detailed portraits of participants and activities within particular organizations, and remain valuable in illuminating new phenomena. Archival materials yield data on organizations and organizational populations over long periods of time. Though they sometimes lack ideal measures of important concepts, archival materials provide unobtrusive data that have led to important insights about processes of organizational change.

The survey research methods covered by this chapter are especially valuable for organizational studies when representativeness and generalization are central study objectives. Survey methods are often essential tools for answering research questions about the prevalence of organizational structures or practices such as team organization, internal promotion ladders, formal training or performance-contingent compensation. Since organizations do not maintain records about such structures and practices in a standardized form amenable to archival inquiry, surveys are the only practical method of assembling representative information about them. Used in tandem with targeted case studies, survey methods permit assessment of the generality of the findings uncovered by more in-depth methodologies. Case studies, for example, pinpoint emergent, innovative phenomena; surveys using representative samples can reveal how ordinary or atypical such phenomena are.

Sample survey methods do have drawbacks. They are not well-suited to capturing subtle socially constructed processes that take place within organizations, such as the interpretive frames that emerge from workers' collective interactions. Data on sensitive topics such as malfeasance or discriminatory employment practices are not readily assembled via surveys. Any lack of subtlety in surveys is, however, more than offset by their comprehensive scan and highly transparent research methods (Marginson, 1998). Survey designs make it possible to venture generalizations – within calculable bounds of error – about characteristics of an organizational population. As Millward, Marginson, and Callus (1998, p. 135) put it:

> National surveys of employing units ... have provided comprehensive mapping of the structures, practices, and policies of industrial relations at workplace and enterprise levels; have progressively enabled key changes in practice and important continuities to be identified; and have enabled researchers to confirm or challenge conventional industrial relations wisdom.

Though much of our discussion here has been oriented to the common case of cross-sectional surveys of organizations and their participants, survey designs have much to contribute to understanding organizational change. By using identical indicators in surveying repeated cross-sectional samples or panels of organizations at several time points, changes in organizational structure and behavior can be systematically tracked. Examples of phenomena that have been examined in this manner are high-performance workplace practices (Osterman 1999) and industrial relations practices (Marginson, 1998).

We expect that future organizational surveys will give increased attention to dynamic questions about trends in organizational practices and organizational change. Likewise, we anticipate more multi-level surveys that address questions about the interaction between distinct hierarchical levels of complex organizations, or about inter-organizational relationships. We hope to see the strengths of surveys combined with complementary approaches, especially case studies, in multi-method research designs. These and other design variations, together with innovations in modes and methods of data collection, will sustain the vitality of survey data for research on organizations and organizational behavior.

Notes

1 We thus expressly distinguish our usage of "organizational survey" from one that refers to surveys of members within single organizations (e.g. Kraut, 1996). The respondents to organizational surveys are individuals, but they are surveyed only as spokespeople or informants for their organizations (Cox and Chinnappa, 1995).

2 One can, of course, anticipate that establishments within a complex will be similar to one another since they are subject to common controls and policies; hence it is often important to obtain firm-level contextual data in studies taking establishments as the unit of analysis.

3 Carroll and Hannan (2000) advocate such sampling plans on the grounds that they yield greater information about conditions that are key to understanding population dynamics. With this sort of study design, the potential generalizability of findings is explored by repeating a study across several distinct populations.

4 This applies in the collection of *organizational* data. When a survey examines the contextual influences of organizational properties on individual attainments or attitudes, as in Knoke's

(1990) NAS or Lincoln and Kalleberg's (1990) Indianapolis-Tokyo study, it is best that the individual-level respondents be representative of organizational members, employees, etc. Similarly, when a subjective organizational property – such as climate or cultural orientation – is defined in terms of sentiments about values or purposes that prevail among participants, it is also important that participants be representatively sampled.

5 For example, many government-relations informants approached in the NPDS (Laumann and Knoke [1987]) felt uncomfortable answering an item asking that they identify other organizations to which they gave and received "confidential advice" on energy or health policy matters, on the grounds that they "never give out confidential information." Rewording the question using a different criterion for information exchange might have reduced the number of refusals and the loss of important information.

6 Calculation of a response rate depends both on the number of completed interviews or questionnaires and on the number of actual attempts made with eligible units. Some sample units approached prove to be ineligible (because, e.g., they have dissolved or do not meet geographical or size criteria for inclusion), while others cannot be located (if, e.g., the individual-level respondent in a hypernetwork sampling design does not provide sufficient identifying information). Such cases ordinarily are not counted as attempts, and therefore do not reduce the response rate.

7 The NOS, for instance, is available through ICPSR; see http://www/icpsr.umich.edu. Marsden et al. (2000) review both original and secondary analyses based on this survey.

8 See http://www.esrc.ac.uk for WIRS data and research reports.

References

Aday, D. P. Jr. (1991): "Organizational research, structural data and the informant method: Problems of reliability," in G. Miller (ed.), *Studies in Organizational Sociology: Essays in Honor of Charles K. Warriner*, Greenwich, CT: JAI Press, 107–22.

Aldrich, H., Kalleberg, A., Marsden, P., and Cassell, J. (1989): "In pursuit of evidence: Sampling procedures for locating new businesses," *Journal of Business Venturing*, 4, 367–86.

Aldrich, H., Zimmer, C., and McEvoy, D. (1989): "Continuities in the study of ecological succession: Asian businesses in three English cities," *Social Forces*, 67, 920–44.

Ambler, C. E., Hyman, S. M., and Mesenbourg, T. L. (1995): "Electronic Data Interchange," in B. G. Cox, D. A. Binder, B. N. Chinnappa, A. Christianson, M. J. Colledge and P. S. Kott (eds), *Business Survey Methods*, New York: John Wiley & Sons, 339–52.

Barron, J. M., and Bishop, J. (1985): "Extensive search, intensive search, and hiring costs: New evidence on employer hiring activity," *Economic Inquiry* 23, 363–82.

Bills, D. B. (1992): "A survey of employer surveys: What we know about labor markets from talking with bosses," *Research in Social Stratification and Mobility*, 11, 3–31.

Blau, P. M. (1972): "Interdependence and hierarchy in organizations," *Social Science Research*, 1, 1–24.

Bradburn, N. M. (1992): "A response to the nonresponse problem," *Public Opinion Quarterly*, 56, 391–97.

Bridges, W. P. and Villemez, W. J. (1994): *The Employment Relationship: Causes and Consequences of Modern Personnel Administration*. New York: Plenum.

Callus, R., Morehead, A., Cully, M., and Buchanan, J. (1991): *Industrial Relations at Work*. Canberra, Australia: AGPS.

Cappelli, P., Shapiro, D., and Shumanis, N. (1998): "Employer participation in school-to-work programs," *Annals of the American Academy of Political and Social Science*, 559, 109–24.

Carroll, G. R., and Hannan, M. T. (2000): *The Demography of Corporations and Industries*. Princeton, NJ: Princeton University Press.

Chaves, M., Konieczny, M. E., Beyerlein, K., and Barman, E. (1999): "The National Congregations

Study: Background, methods, and selected results," *Journal for the Scientific Study of Religion*, 38, 458–76.

Christianson, A., and Tortora, R. D. (1995): "Issues in surveying businesses: An international survey," in B. G. Cox, D. A. Binder, B. N. Chinnappa, A. Christianson, M. J. Colledge and P. S. Kott (eds), *Business Survey Methods*, New York: John Wiley & Sons, 237–56.

Colledge, M. J. (1995): "Frames and business registers: An overview." in B. G. Cox, D. A. Binder, B. N. Chinnappa, A. Christianson, M. J. Colledge and P. S. Kott (eds), *Business Survey Methods*, New York: John Wiley & Sons, 21–47.

Cox, B. G., and Chinnappa, B. N. (1995): "Unique Features of Business Surveys." in B. G. Cox, D. A. Binder, B. N. Chinnappa, A. Christianson, M. J. Colledge and P. S. Kott (eds), *Business Survey Methods*, New York: John Wiley & Sons, 1–17.

Dillman, D. A. (2000): *Mail and Internet Surveys: The Tailored Design Method*. New York: Wiley.

Dippo, C. S., Chun, Y. I., and Sander, J. (1995): "New and tested strategies for designing the data collection process," in B. G. Cox, D. A. Binder, B. N. Chinnappa, A. Christianson, M. J. Colledge and P. S. Kott (eds), *Business Survey Methods*, New York: John Wiley & Sons, 283–301.

Dobbin, F., Sutton, J. R., Meyer, J. W., and Scott, W. R. (1993): "Equal opportunity law and the construction of internal labor markets," *American Journal of Sociology*, 99, 396–427.

Drabek, T. E., Braito, R., Cook, C. C., Powell, J. R., and Rogers, D. (1982): "Selecting samples of organizations: Central issues and emerging trends," *Pacific Sociological Review*, 25, 377–400.

Edwards, P. K., and Marginson, P. (1988): "Differences in perception between establishment and higher level managers," in P. Marginson, P. K. Edwards, R. Martin, J. Purcell and K. Sisson (eds), *Beyond the Workplace: Managing Industrial Relations in the Multi-Establishment Enterprise*, New York: Basil Blackwell, 227–57.

Frazis, H. J., Herz, D. E., and Horrigan, M. W. (1995): "Employer-provided training: Results from a new survey," *Monthly Labor Review*, 118(5), 3–17.

Freeman, J. H. (1978): "The unit of analysis in organizational research," in M. W. Meyer and Associates (eds), *Environments and Organizations*, San Francisco: Jossey-Bass, 335–51.

Holzer, H. J. (1996): *What Employers Want: Job Prospects for Less-Educated Workers*. New York: Russell Sage Foundation.

Huber, G. P., and Power, D. J. (1985): "Retrospective reports of strategic-level managers: Guidelines for increasing their accuracy," *Strategic Management Journal*, 6, 171–80.

John, G., and Reve, T. (1982): "The reliability and validity of key informant data from dyadic relationships in marketing channels," *Journal of Marketing Research*, 19, 517–24.

Johnson, A. E. (1995): "Business surveys as a network sample," in B. G. Cox, D. A. Binder, B. N. Chinnappa, A. Christianson, M. J. Colledge and P. S. Kott (eds), *Business Survey Methods*, New York: John Wiley & Sons, 219–33.

Kalleberg, A. L., Marsden, P. V., Aldrich, H. E. and Cassell, J. W. (1990): "Comparing organizational sampling frames," *Administrative Science Quarterly*, 35, 658–88.

Kalleberg, A. L., Knoke, D., Marsden, P. V., and Spaeth, J. L. (1996): *Organizations in America: Analyzing Their Structures and Human Resource Practices*. Newbury Park, CA: Sage.

Kelley, M. R. (1990): "New process technology, job design, and work organization: A contingency model," *American Sociological Review*, 55, 191–208.

Kelley, M. R., and Brooks, H. (1988): *The State of Computerized Automation in U.S. Manufacturing*. Cambridge, MA: Center for Business and Government, Harvard University.

Knoke, D. (1988): "Incentives in collective action organizations," *American Sociological Review*, 53, 311–29.

Knoke, D. (1990): *Organizing for Collective Action: The Political Economies of Associations*. New York: Aldine de Gruyter.

Knoke, D., Pappi, F. U., Broadbent, J., and Tsujinaka, Y. (1996): *Comparing Policy Networks: Labor Politics in the U.S., Germany, and Japan*. New York: Cambridge University Press.

Knoke, D., Reynolds, P. D., Marsden, P. V., Miller, B., and Kaufman, N. (1991): "The reliability of organizational measures from multiple-informant reports," manuscript, Department of Sociology, University of Minnesota, Twin Cities.

Kraut, A. I. (1996): *Organizational Surveys: Tools for Assessment and Change*. San Francisco: Jossey-Bass.

Kumar, N., Stern, L. W. and Anderson, J. C. (1993): "Conducting interorganizational research using key informants," *Academy of Management Journal*, 36, 1614–32.

Laumann, E. O., and Knoke, D. (1987): *The Organizational State: A Perspective on the Social Organization of National Energy and Health Policy Domains*. Madison, WI: University of Wisconsin Press.

Lawler, E. E., III, Mohrman, S., and Ledford, G. (1992): *Employee Involvement and Total Quality Management: Practices and Results in Fortune 1000 Companies*. San Francisco: Jossey-Bass.

le Grand, C., Szulkin, R., and Tåhlin, M. (1994): "Organizational structures and job rewards in Sweden," *Acta Sociologica*, 37, 231–51.

Lincoln, J. R., and Kalleberg, A. L. (1990): *Culture, Control, and Commitment: A Study of Work Organization and Work Attitudes in the United States and Japan*. New York: Cambridge University Press.

Marginson, P. (1998): "The survey tradition in British industrial relations research: An assessment of the contribution of large-scale workplace and enterprise surveys," *British Journal of Industrial Relations*, 36, 361–88.

McPherson, J. M. (1982): "Hypernetwork sampling: Duality and differentiation among voluntary organizations," *Social Networks*, 3, 225–49.

McPherson, J. M., and Rotolo, T. (1995): "Measuring the composition of voluntary groups: A multitrait-multimethod analysis," *Social Forces*, 73, 1097–115.

Marsden, P. V., Kalleberg A. L., and Knoke, D. (2000): "Surveying organizational structures and human resource practices: The National Organizations Study," in R. T. Golembiewski (ed.), *Handbook of Organizational Behavior*, 2nd edn, New York: Marcel Dekker, Inc., 175–201.

Millward, N., Marginson, P., and Callus, R. (1998): "Employer-based surveys: Mapping, monitoring and theory development in large-scale national surveys," in K. Whitfield and G. Strauss (eds), *Researching the World of Work*, Ithaca, NY: Cornell University Press, 135–56.

Millward, N., Woodland, S., Bryson, A., and Forth, J. (1998): *The British Workplace Industrial Relations Survey Series: A Bibliography of Research Based on the WIRS*. London: Policy Studies Institute.

Osterman, P. (1994): "How common is workplace transformation and who adopts it?" *Industrial and Labor Relations Review*, 47, 173–88.

Osterman, P. (1995) "Work/family programs and the employment relationship," *Administrative Science Quarterly*, 40, 681–700.

Osterman, P. (1999): *Securing Prosperity. The American Labor Market: How It Has Changed and What To Do About It*. Princeton, NJ: Princeton University Press.

Parcel, T. L., Kaufman, R. L., and Jolly, L. (1991): "Going up the ladder: Multiplicity sampling to create linked macro-to-micro-organizational samples," in P. V. Marsden (ed.), *Sociological Methodology 1991*, Oxford, UK: Blackwell Publishers, 43–79.

Paxson, M. C., Dillman D. A., and Tarnai, J. (1995): "Improving response to business mail surveys." in B. G. Cox, D. A. Binder, B. N. Chinnappa, A. Christianson, M. J. Colledge, and P. S. Kott, *Business Survey Methods*, New York: John Wiley & Sons, 303–16.

Presser, S., and J. Blair, (1994): "Survey pretesting: Do different methods produce different results?" in P.V. Marsden (ed.), *Sociological Methodology 1994*, Oxford, UK: Basil Blackwell, 73–104.

Price, J. L. (1997): "Handbook of organizational measurement," *International Journal of Manpower*, 18(4/5/6), 303–558.

Price, J. L., and Mueller, C. W. (1986): *Handbook of Organizational Measurement*. Marshfield, MA: Pitman.

Saris, W. E. (1991): *Computer-Assisted Interviewing*. Newbury Park, CA: Sage.

Seidler, J. (1974): "On using informants: A technique for collecting quantitative data and controlling measurement error in organization analysis," *American Sociological Review*, 39, 816–31.

Sigman, R. S., and Monsour, N. J. (1995): "Selecting samples from list frames of businesses," in B. G. Cox, D. A. Binder, B. N. Chinnappa, A. Christianson, M. J. Colledge, and P. S. Kott, (eds), *Business Survey Methods*, New York: John Wiley & Sons, 133–52.

Spaeth, J. L., and. O'Rourke, D. P. (1994): "Designing and implementing the National Organizations Survey," *American Behavioral Scientist*, 37, 872–90.

Spletzer, J. R. (1997): *Longitudinal Establishment Microdata at the Bureau of Labor Statistics: Development, Uses, and Access*. Washington, DC: Bureau of Labor Statistics.

Steeh, C. (1981): "Trends in nonresponse rates, 1952–1979," *Public Opinion Quarterly*, 45, 40–57.

Tomaskovic-Devey, D., Leiter, J., and Thompson, S. (1994): "Organizational survey nonresponse," *Administrative Science Quarterly*, 39, 439–57.

Tomaskovic-Devey, D., Leiter, J., and Thompson, S. (1995): "Item nonresponse in organizational surveys," in P. V. Marsden (ed.), *Sociological Methodology 1995*, Oxford, UK: Basil Blackwell, 77–110.

Van de Ven, A. H., and Ferry, D. L. (1980): *Measuring and Assessing Organizations*. New York: Wiley. (Out of print; online version made available by one of the authors at http://www.umn.edu/~avandeve.)

Winship, C., and Radbill, L. (1994): "Sampling weights and regression analysis," *Sociological Methods and Research*, 23, 230–57.

Zammuto, R. F., and Krakower, J. Y. (1991): "Quantitative and qualitative studies of organizational culture," *Research in Organizational Behavior*, 5, 83–114.

Chapter Thirty-five

Archival Research Methods

MARC J. VENTRESCA AND JOHN W. MOHR

Archival research methods include a broad range of activities applied to facilitate the investigation of documents and textual materials produced by and about organizations. In its most classic sense, archival methods are those that involve the study of historical documents; that is, documents created at some point in the relatively distant past, providing us access that we might not otherwise have to the organizations, individuals, and events of that earlier time. However, archival methods are also employed by scholars engaged in non-historical investigations of documents and texts produced by and about contemporary organizations, often as tools to supplement other research strategies (field methods, survey methods, etc.) Thus, archival methods can also be applied to the analysis of digital texts including electronic databases, emails, and web pages.

As such, the methods we discuss in this chapter cover a very broad sweep of organizational analysis and include a wide range of other more specific methodological practices – from fundamental historiographic skills and strategies for archival investigations to formal analytic techniques such as content analysis and multidimensional scaling. The theoretical topics and substantive areas of investigation to which these methods are applied are broader still – perhaps as broad as the domain of organization science itself. In sum, archival methods can be thought of as a loosely coupled constellation of analytic endeavors that seek to gain insights through a systematic interrogation of the documents, texts, and other material artifacts that are produced by and about organizations.

Contributions of Archival Methods to Organization Science

In his discussion of the characteristics of modern bureaucracy, Weber noted that "(t)he management of the modern office is based upon written documents (the 'files'), which are preserved in their original or draft form, and upon a staff of subaltern officials and scribes of all sorts" (Weber, 1968, p. 957). Yates (1989) highlights this dimension of organizational life in her study of the rise of the large-scale modern organization. Yates demonstrates how the evolution of official document genres – such as the office memo – provided necessary infrastructure for the emergence of modern forms of control-at-a-distance and administration.

The linkage of text and power is not new. As Giddens (1987) reminds us, written texts have long been associated with forms of administrative power; writing systems were originally invented in response to the need to count, survey, prescribe and control the activity of others across both time and space (Goody, 1986; Latour, 1987; Ventresca, 1995). But it is in the modern bureaucratic organization that the production and use of files comes into its most full and powerful expression. Indeed the production of written documents may well be the most distinctive quality of modern organizational life. Few official actions of any sort are conceived, enabled, or enacted without having been written down both in advance, in retrospect, and invariably several more times in between. As the telltale email messages from the Iran-Contra hearings, or more recently, the emergence of incriminating archival records in tobacco arbitration cases demonstrate, even questionable or illegal organizational activities have a tendency to be textually recorded by those who inhabit modern organizations.

Organizations are fundamentally systems of "talk" – more or less formalized, more or less direct, more or less freighted with power. Organizational texts thus represent forms of social discourse – literally, ways of communicating, producing, and enacting organizational life (Riles, 2000; Smith, 1984). As Smith (1984) has argued, written texts play an especially significant role in organizations because they codify in a potent fashion, that which has been said and thought. Once it is written down, organizational talk takes on new dimensions of veracity, credibility, and efficacy – an authoritatively instrumental life of its own – often traveling well beyond the intent or expectations of the author.

This makes organizational files – the embodiments of sedimented, accumulated talk – an especially appealing data source. These texts enable researchers to view the ebb and flow of organizational life, the interpretations, the assumptions, the actions taken and deferred from a range of differing points of view as events unfold across organizational space and time. Archival materials provide unobtrusive measures of process for the study of contemporary organizations (Covaleski and Dirsmith, 1988; see papers in Jermier and Barley, 1998) and invaluable means of access in historical investigations (for the obvious reason that archival materials are among the few resources we have available for learning about past events). The examination of archival materials is thus important because they are ubiquitous, consequential and strategically useful.

It is especially through the shifting character of historical research, shaped in fundamental ways by alternative approaches to archival materials, that these methods have had their most profound impact on organization science. The investigation of organizational practices as they occurred in a different time allows scholars to gain perspective on how shifting social and historical conditions affect the character of organizational life (Kieser, 1989). Archival work provides a basis for defining key questions, establishes a base of evidence, and supports debate about familiar forms and mechanisms (Kieser, 1994; Zald, 1993). Particular practices, ideologies, or social arrangements can be better understood by exploring their origins, what Piore and Sabel (1984) describe as the key historical "branching points" or path dependencies. More than this, historical study allows for the analysis of organizational change in increments of time that captures significant institutional processes – what Braudel (1980) refers to as the *long durée*.

But the use of archival materials is never innocent or transparent. The conditions of their production and of their persistence mean that materials often offer partial or contradictory evidence for an interpretation. Recognition of the inherently political and residual features of archival material is thus a central methodological concern, the basis for significant decisions about design and analysis (Guillen, 1994; Casadesus-Masanell and Spulber, 2000). The skillfulness of scholars' abilities to master this ambiguity is a distinguishing feature of exemplary research in this tradition; see for example Baron et al. (1986) and the methodological commentaries by Jennings et al. (1992). Moreover the complexity of the task leaves open an especially wide space for intellectual disagreement. Thus Fligstein's (1990) archival work leads to a reconsideration of Chandler's (1962) classic arguments regarding the sources of the modern multi-divisional form. And so too do the alternative accounts in Freeland's (2000, 2001) detailed archival study of GM, Yates' (1989) analysis of the rise of communication and control infrastructures within the firm, Roy's (1997) analysis of the contested origins of the modern corporation in the U.S., and Djelic's (1998) comparative study of the rules and resources shaping the spread of the multidivisional form in France, Italy, and Germany. In short, as researchers turn to archives and put them to different uses they make possible alternative kinds of insights about the nature and character of organizational events, structures, and processes.

Modes of Archival Research

Three very different approaches to archival study can be distinguished in organizational research. The first is the historiographic approach. We include in this approach the traditions of historically-oriented work that found their way into the canon of organizational research through the early 1980s. Up until this time the use of archival materials in organization science was still relatively rare (Daft, 1980; Scott, 1965; Stablein, 1996).

Two streams of historiographic research were notable. One was the work of scholars who employed historical materials to study the emergence of distinctive institutional arrangements, politics, and change (Lounsbury and Ventresca, 2002). Selznick (1949) investigated the history of the TVA, Zald and Denton (1963) studied the transformation of the YMCA and Clark (1970) followed the histories of individual colleges to identify organizational sagas, contested values, and the interplay of broader social structure and organization. The second stream includes the work of business historians who used archival materials to examine the origins of modern business practices and business forms (Chandler, 1962; 1977; Galambas, 1770; John, 1997; McKenna, 2001). A more radical contingent of labor historians and organization theorists used archival materials to explore the origins and character of class conflicts and control in the work place (Braverman, 1976; Clawson, 1980; Perrow, 1991).

The distinctive character of the historiographic tradition was its attention to the rich details of organizational life, rendering what were essentially ethnographic studies of organizations conducted through the medium of archival materials. These studies identified particular individuals, chronicled their lives and careers, interpreted mindsets and ideologies, and revealed conflicts, contests and power relationships. Explanations were sought for the creation of particular institutional configurations, modes of operation, and management styles. A wide range of archival materials was typically employed, including organizational documents, internal office memos, public announcements, and personal narratives. Most often the materials were read and notes taken, but little formal measurement or quantitative analysis conducted. These efforts were influential and widely discussed, although they represented a relatively small proportion of the research work being conducted in organization science then and since (Kieser, 1994).

In the mid-1970s, however, a new tradition of archival research based on ecological analysis established a foothold. The methodological shift was dramatic. In place of the more traditional engagement with historical materials, ecological research ushered in an era of archival studies in which small amounts of information gleaned from the life histories of large numbers of organizations were marshaled to tell a story about the dynamics of organizational environments and organizational populations (Baum and Amburgey, this volume; Rao, this volume). Inspired by Stinchcombe's (1965) suggestion that we turn away from the study of particular organizations toward an analysis of historically embedded classes of organizations, or "organizational forms," this shift in focus opened a novel approach to archival research.

Hannan and Freeman (1977; 1984) were the first to link this conceptualization to a viable methodology. Their focus was on the development of formal models in the tradition of demography and a substantive argument about ecological variation and change mechanisms in organizational populations. The ecological approach diverged dramatically from prevailing research designs, requiring samples of historically complete organizational populations, rather than conventional representative random (or convenience) samples of diverse organizations.

A resurgent cultural institutionalism in organizational analysis also took form during this period, a second stream within this larger archival tradition. Although Meyer's early work (Meyer, 1977; Meyer and Rowan, 1977) focused on theoretical foundations of collective orders and cultural analysis, the collaboration with Hannan and colleagues (Meyer and Hannan, 1979) on studies of education and national development connected the new institutional stream to the ecological strategy in archival analysis. The institutionalist studies of this period collected and analyzed small amounts of information on a large number of organizations sampled over time in contrast to the earlier historiographic approach. The arguments focused on how authority and expertise drove field-level structuration and organizational change, tested over the years on a wide variety of organizational populations – schools (Meyer et al., 1987), juvenile justice institutions (Sutton, 1988), firms (Edelman, 1990; Mezias, 1990; Suchman, 1994; Sutton and Dobbin, 1996), and nation states (Thomas et al., 1987; McNeely, 1995; Ventresca, 1995; Palmer and Biggart, this volume; Strang and Sine, this volume).

In contrast to the historiographic tradition, the ecological approach is far more formal in its orientation. The empirical strategy is not based on nuanced readings of the actions, understandings, or careers of individual persons, groups, or organizations. Rather, the measurement of the degree of similarity and difference of specified structural characteristics among a large number of organizations provides evidence and insight. Measures of variation are used to support broader interpretative schemas about the logic of macro-organizational processes. As the institutional and ecological research streams gained professional momentum, the use of archival materials overall became widely accepted in organization science and reliance on archival methods grew. A count of articles published in the *Administrative Science Quarterly* between 1970 and 1998 confirms this point. Figure 35.1 shows the proportion of articles published in *ASQ* in this period that em-

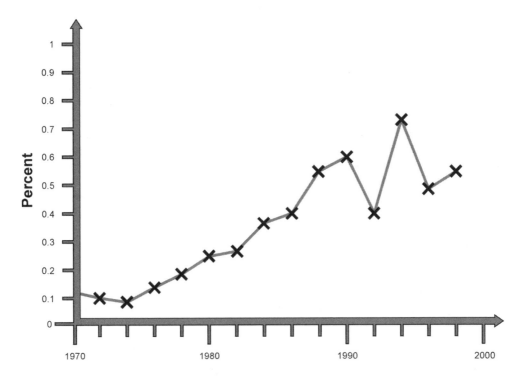

Figure 35.1 Articles employing archival methods published in the *Administrative Science Quarterly*, 1970–98 (proportion)*
Note: * Articles were coded at two-year intervals starting in 1970.

ployed some form of archival methods. The graph shows a clear and sustained increase in the use of these methods from the mid-1970s to the present period.

Much of this growth can be attributed to publications by scholars who identified directly with the institutional and ecological theoretical traditions. Carroll and Hannan's (2000, p. 86–8) review of the research design features of articles published in the *ASQ* supports this interpretation. Their analysis showed a marked increase in the use of representative samples (up from 3 in 1960s to 17 in 1990s) and in homogeneous population-specific samples (up from 2 to 18 over the same period). The most dramatic change, however, was in the lengthening of the observation periods. Although the number of empirical studies covering relatively short time spans (≤ 5 years) increased from 5 to 14, the number of studies with timeframes spanning more than 25 years increased from 1 to 25.

While those details rather dramatically demonstrate the increased prevalence of the ecological approach to archival materials, other kinds of archival studies were also on the rise during this period. Indeed, in our analysis of articles published in the *ASQ* we found a substantial increase over time in the number of archival articles that relied exclusively on *qualitative* methodologies (including more than a third of all the archival articles published after 1992; see Locke and Golden-Biddle, 1997). In some cases, researchers returned to traditional historiographic methods as a way to supplement or respond to questions raised by the ecological tradition. Langton (1984), for example, used an in-depth analysis of a specific, historical case – the Wedgwood pottery company – to answer questions about ecological change. Others went to the archives to more closely investigate the kinds of change processes that had been demonstrated with quantitative methods by the new institutionalists. Westney (1987), for example, investigated the coupled processes of imitation and innovation that resulted from efforts of Meiji reformers to incorporate "modern" organizational patterns from the West. DiMaggio (1991) used traditional historiographic methods to explore struggles among organization forms in the field of art museums. Kogut and Zander (2000) used corporate and other archives and a comparative design to identify how broader social structure organized firm strategies and development.

But something else is also afoot in the contemporary legacies of this archival work. A new archival approach in organization science has been emerging over the last decade. Like the ecological strategy before it, this "new archivalism" is steeped in the ethos and methods of formal social science. However, its practitioners dissent variously (at times, vigorously) from the methodological conventions of ecological research. Indeed, the new archivalists tend to share key sensibilities in the historiographic approach, sharing its concerns for exploring the nuanced, meaning-laden, action-oriented foundations of organizational processes. We turn now to a more detailed discussion of this emergent archival tradition.

Exemplars of the New Archival Tradition

New archivalists, like their predecessors, are a heterogeneous lot. They come from different theoretical traditions and pursue different empirical agendas. But they nonetheless partake of a common vocabulary of research strategies and goals that together define a new set of principles for archival work. These include:

1 reliance on formal analytic methodologies
2 focus on the measurement of social organization and its constituent elements rather than on organizations themselves
3 emphasis on the study of relations rather than objects or attributes
4 concern with measuring the shared forms of meaning that underlie social organizational processes and finally
5 interest to understand the configurational logics that tie these various elements together into organized activity.

Take the first of these principles. A defining feature of the new archival project is the premise that archival materials can and should be treated as data to be analyzed. The new archivalists, like the ecologists before them, are aggressively social scientific. They enter the archives in search of datasets, they rely on formal methods to reveal features of social life that would otherwise be difficult if not impossible to perceive and they put their analytic findings up front, at the core of their interpretative endeavor. In this respect, the new archivalists are heirs of the ecological turn in archival analysis.

However, they quickly part company with the ecological research strategy in a number of fundamental ways. Perhaps the most significant is the turn away from an organization-centered approach to the study of social organization. Whereas organizational ecologists talk a great deal about broader social phenomena such as legitimacy, these elements of social organization are generally not measured directly. Rather organizations (and their features or behaviors) are measured and used to infer the existence, the effect, and the transformation of broader social organizational processes. Many studies in the institutional analysis of organization reported through the early 1990s continue this research strategy (Schneiberg and Clemens, 2001). Isomorphism and structuration are highlighted in the theory (and in the discussion sections of published research articles) but it is the attributes of organizations that are measured and compared to one another in the analyses.

In contrast, work in the new archivalists traditions consistently theorizes and measures social organizational processes directly. In this work, organizations become a feature of the landscape, not the entirety of it (Mohr, forthcoming; Scott, 2001; Stinchcombe, 1965). Consider, for example, the research by Baum and Oliver's (1991, 1992) on childcare centers in Toronto. These papers exemplify an early shift away from the standard ecology tradition. They employ archival materials in the ecological spirit but incorporate relational data coded from public agency registries as evidence of legitimating logics. Baum and Oliver use these data to measure institutional linkages in order to test arguments about the nature and consequence of public authorization on the survival and founding of organizations. The papers represent early efforts to augment the indirect measurement of legitimacy and competition with direct, varied measures that test empirical variations in linkages of social structures of authority and resources on organizational form dynamics.

The Baum and Oliver papers also point to a third distinguishing characteristic of this new archival tradition, the shift away from analytic projects that emphasize organizations as independent objects towards the measurement of relations among objects and the inherent connectivity of social organization. The ecological tradition begins from a demographic perspective in which every organization population is treated as a discrete and distinct observation within a larger population. Organizations are thus treated as a scatter of data points arrayed across time. The new archivalists have been reluctant to accept this approach, preferring instead to attend to the ways in which elements of broader social organization are related to one another in distinctive, patterned ways (Dacin et al., 1999).

This is most clear in papers such as McLean and Padgett's (1997) network analysis of economic markets in fifteenth century Florence. Inspired by contemporary debates in institutional economics, McLean and Padgett explore whether market transactions in this early capitalist exchange arena were strictly arm's length transactions or embedded within relatively enduring social relationships. With evidence preserved in the Florentine municipal tax archives, they set about the painstaking task of piecing together a coherent map of the economic transactions which linked (nearly) all of the active companies in the core of the Florentine economy in the year 1427. They coded detailed information on more than a quarter of all the transactions (sales and purchases) that occurred during that year (including information on some 60 percent of the total value of debts and credits). With these data, they model the exchange networks between firms in order to determine the guiding firm strategy and behavior – choosing exchange partners according to considerations of price alone, as neoclassical arguments would contend – or whether the firms worked through ties of social familiarity.

Of course, McLean and Padgett were not the first to analyze these types of social relations – their work is moored in a long tradition of archival research on organizational networks, a tradition that provides one analytic foundation for the new archivalists (Burt and Lin, 1977; Aldrich and Whetten, 1981; Schwartz and Mizruchi, 1988). But unlike traditional network analysts, the new archivalists are generally reluctant to limit themselves to the formal analysis of social networks. Rather they are interested in the full range of relational systems that operate to produce forms of social organization, including the forms of knowing, styles of understanding, and sets of shared beliefs that constitute organizational activity (Mohr, 2000).

This concern links the new archivists to yet another stream of archival work in organization science which has focused on the application of content analysis to annual reports and other corporate documents. Some of this work follows in a tradition pioneered by Salancik and Meindl (1984) who used a content analysis of annual reports to identify and test claims about attributions of responsibility for losses, reduced earnings, or other turbulence in shareholder expectations. Recent developments in content analysis techniques and software (Pollock, 1998) make more varied uses of these data possible. For example, a stream of papers by Porac, Wade, Pollock and colleagues extend traditional content analysis to investigate industry-level models of rivalry and meaning (Porac et al., 1995), broader field-level frames provide justifications for CEO compensation (Porac et al., 2000), and support dominant managerial logics in high growth firms (Porac et al., 2000).

This use of formal methods to analyze shared systems of meaning is a fourth focus, one of the most intriguing and vibrant sectors of the new archival tradition. Increasingly scholars are finding innovative ways to use formal methods to extract the same kinds of interpretative readings of archival texts that had once been the sole purview of the historiographic tradition. For example, Shenhav (1994, 1995, 1999) uses a content analysis of professional engineering and union publications at the turn of the century to understand the engineering origins of modern management concepts and practices. Barley and Kunda (1992) code data from the academic literature on research strategies to provide evidence of alternating periods of "design and devotion" in management ideologies. Studies by Abrahamson (Abrahamson, 1991; 1997) analyze journal articles over a 20-year period to explore variations in the diffusion of conceptual innovations such as quality circles and TQM. Guillén (1994) uses content coding to help explain the diffusion of management ideologies in Great Britain, Germany, Spain, and the USA. And Orlikowski and Yates (1994) analyze an archive of over 1,300 email messages from a virtual community of computer language experts to identify a repertoire of communicative genres – standardized ways of communicating that facilitate shared understanding – in distributed organizational initiatives.

Part of what is so exciting about this work is that the formalization of such data makes vivid underlying social structures of meaning that shape how organizational activity gets accomplished. Orlikowski and Yates' study of the emergence of repertoires of communicative genres illustrates this in the context of how stylized conventions enable communication. But it is also important to see how organizational activities are themselves bundled in standardized packets of what Charles Tilly (1978) has called repertoires of action. Clemens (1993; 1997; 1999) does exactly this, borrowing from Tilly and social movement theory to explain the institutional changes that foster the emergence of alternative repertoires of organizational action. She shows how late nineteenth century US women's activism, blocked from expression by the existing system of political parties, drew upon alternative organizational models (founded on women's social movement organization) to contest and ultimately supplant the existing institutional structures of politics, paving the way for the development of modern interest group politics.

Pentland and Reuter (1994) report a kindred accomplishment at the level of the firm. They use archival materials taken from a software manufacturer's call-tracking database to understand the basic repertoires of action that are deployed to manage calls for software service and assistance. Individual "calls" may comprise many actual phone conversations and other actions, which they code as a sequence of activities or moves. They analyze a random sample of 335 calls from an archival software database to identify the set of action sequence or "moves," that constitute what they refer to as the "grammar for [the firm's] software support process" (1994, p. 490); that is, they explain through a systematic analysis of empirical data precisely how and in what manner organizational activity happens.[1]

Each of these concerns represents a part of the puzzle that the new archivalism explores. That puzzle concerns the assembly of the basic building blocks of organizational life, the ways in which sets of practical activities and shared systems of understanding combine to make up a recognized arena of institutional life (Meyer and Rowan, 1978). It is the combinatorial logic itself, of how sets of practices fit together with particular ways of understanding, which reflects a final set of concerns that are constitutive of the new archival project. Friedland and Alford (1991) clearly articulate this agenda in their conception of institutional logics, which they defined as "a set of material practices and symbolic constructions" which provide the governing principles for a given field of organizational activity (1991, p. 248); see also Heimer (1998; 2001).

Several papers in the new archival tradition have sought to give empirical substance to this notion of component assembly. Mohr and Duquenne (1997) do this in the context of nineteenth century social welfare organizations. Their goal is to trace how particular organizational practices (e.g., social investigations, giving advice, food or money, providing job training, employment, temporary shelter or long-term asylum) were matched to and defined by different conceptual categories of the poor (the distressed, destitute, fallen, deserving, homeless, indigent, misfortunate, needy, poor, strangers, and worthy). By mapping out precisely how different categories of the poor were treated in New York City over a forty-year period, Mohr and Duquenne are able to offer concrete interpretations of how and why alternative professional ideologies emerged. And, central to the preoccupations of the new archivalism, they are able to measure the degree of institutionalization and structuration within the organizational field by assessing the levels of structural congruence between meanings and practices.

A recent article by DiMaggio and Mullen (2000) provides a second example. The paper focuses on the events of National Music Week in 1924. Using data on types of celebrations that occurred in 419 different cities and towns spread across the United States, DiMaggio and Mullen raise the question of how the kinds of civic rituals that occurred in these localities reflected (and constituted) alternative institutional logics. They focus on three analytical dimensions – the types of actors involved (churches, schools, recreational associations, professional groups, etc.), the types of actions taken (lectures, slide shows, recitals, parades, etc.), and the objects of action (or types of audiences) that were targeted (children, members of particular church or ethnic communities, the general public, etc.). What they discover is that there were clear differences in the logics according to which different communities organized their ritual activities. Some rituals were constructed in such a way as to ratify the existing social order while others were organized so as to draw citizens into a broader civic mass public or alternative corporate identities.

In this discussion we have used examples from recent books and articles to highlight the basic principles of what we propose as a significant, emergent new archivalist tradition in organization science. We turn now to a more focused discussion of the kinds of practical decisions and research strategies that are involved in conducting archival research on organizations.

Doing Archival Research on Organizations

Researchers who use archival materials to study organizations have tended to use three broad strategies that we have labeled historiographic, ecological, and new archivalist. These divisions reflect basic differences in research design, the selection of archival materials, and data analysis. We review these issues here.

TYPES OF ARCHIVAL RESEARCH DESIGNS

Four distinctions in how archival research is designed strike us as fundamental. The first two concern how researchers approach archival materials. The other two pertain to how researchers interpret their data. Table 35.1 shows how these distinctions map onto the three major modalities of archival analysis.

Table 35.1 Major analytic distinctions and the three modes of archival analysis

	Levels of analysis	Input method	Causality theory	Measurement theory
Historiographic	Few	Read	Both	Both
Ecological	Many	Measure	Descending	Objects
New archivalist	Both	Both	Ascending	Relations

FEW VS. MANY

This refers to basic differences in the level of analysis that conditions the type of materials that one chooses to pursue. The ideal-typical distinction is between studies that make intensive use of archival materials from a single or a few organizations, in contrast to studies that make use of small amounts of information taken from a large number of organizations. Historiographic research is typically restricted to the careful and detailed scrutiny of the archival materials of one or a few organizations. Ecological projects use information from many organizations, while the new archivalists make use of both types of research designs.

READ VS. MEASURE

A second basic distinction has to do with how the data are collected – the input method. In historiographic investigations, the researcher reads through large amounts of archival information (often from unstandardized sources) in a disciplined fashion as a way to gain insights, make discoveries and generate informed judgments about the character of historical events and processes. This method relies upon intensive note-taking and a carefully managed pattern of strategic reading. In contrast, archival materials can be used to enable more conventional social scientific measurement by "coding" them as data. This latter approach depends upon a careful assessment of the relevant variables that are implicitly embedded within the material and a systematic method of recording the constituent information in order to apply formal quantitative methodologies. Insights here stem from attention to systematic variations, patterns, or configurations within formally measured data fields.

DESCENDING VS. ASCENDING

Other differences occur in how the data are put into the service of a particular analytic agenda, a distinction that says something about the implicit theory of causality that a scholar brings to the materials. One important distinction in this regard is whether the researcher uses a more macro-historical interpretative framework to motivate the data gathering process or whether she seeks to identify local constellations of practices and interpretations that can be used to build up a larger narrative interpretation. Foucault (1980) describes this as the difference between a "descending model of analysis" in which more macro patterns of social life are expected to explain more micro processes, and an "ascending model of analysis" in which local practices and logics of action are presumed to develop in their own fashion after which they are incorporated at higher levels of social organization. The latter is the approach most valued by the new archivalists who are concerned with identifying and specifying the nuts and bolts of institutional life, the modes of understanding, the grammars of action, the relational networks that tie elements of organizational life together. It differs in this sense from the tendency to embrace a grand explanatory narrative which is then applied to generate interpretations of archival material. In this sense, both Chandler (1962) and, in their own way, the organizational ecologists are more likely to embrace a descending explanatory model.

OBJECTS VS. RELATIONS

A final analytic distinction concerns whether the archival data are employed chiefly as a means of learning about individual social objects or used in the service of understanding the relations among objects. This is a distinction that speaks to the implicit theory of measurement that is brought to bear upon the data. In an object-oriented approach to the data, the distinguishing characteristics of people, organizations, and other social entities are seen as central to developing an adequate explanation. The primary analytic issue concerns which features, traits, or characteristics of the objects in question can and should be used to explain the observed behavior or stance. Analysis focuses on connecting attributes to outcomes. In contrast, a relational approach tends to look at the relations that connect individuals, organizations or elements of a discourse system together into some more systemic whole. In this model it is the features of the relations, rather than the characteristics of the objects, that are expected to yield explanatory value. It is the social network tradition which has most vigorously advocated an approach to social scientific measurement that privileges relations over objects (Emirbayer, 1997). However, it is also a basic tenet of semiotic theory and structural linguistics more generally that meanings are constituted through systems of difference and it is through the application of relational methods that formal methods can be most fruitfully brought to bear on interpretative problems (Mohr, 1998a; 2000). The new archivalists have been especially interested in paying attention to how organizational activities, meanings, and logics of action are linked together as relational systems.

TYPES OF ARCHIVAL MATERIALS AND ANALYSIS

There are two more specific methodological questions that arise when designing a study using archival materials:

1   What types of materials will be selected for analysis?
2   How will those materials be analyzed?

It is difficult to give an answer to either question in general terms. We have already noted the great diversity of methodological approaches that are associated with archival research. An even greater diversity exists in the types of archival materials that might be employed in organizational research. Indeed, one could say that there are as many kinds of archival materials as there are types of organizational talk that produce archives. A quick (and incomplete) inventory of general categories of organizational talk would include, for example, how organizations talk about: who they are, what they do, what happened, what they want, what's ahead, who other organizations are and what they do, and on and on.[2] Burton's (1995, 2001) study of high technology firms illustrates this wide variety of firm- and field-level data from "talk" by, about, and among emerging companies – some talk generated from the routines of administrative data production, some from retrospective interviews, and still other data compiled from corporate directories, media accounts, and other non-standard sources. Other studies make use of talk generated by reflexively instrumental forms of rhetoric (Hirsch, 1986; Kunda, 1992), or in response to extraordinary demands (Vaughan, 1996).

In some well-structured genres of organizational science, established conventions for choosing archival materials *do* exist. In organizational ecology, for example, these conventions have been carefully developed and empirically tested. Carroll and Hannan (2000, ch. 8) provide a comprehensive review of archival sources commonly used in ecology and corporate demography research. These include industry directories, encyclopedic compilations, governmental registries, census government, proprietary databases, survey data, and lists of prominent firms. Carroll and Hannan discuss tradeoffs made in the choice of archival materials that affect sampling. They describe four typical errors in observation plans: *organizational coverage*, which refers to the inclusiveness of the sample of organizations within the definition of a population or industry; *temporal coverage*, which concerns the extent to which the observation period cover the critical times in a population's history; *precision in timing*, which refers to the specificity and completeness of data on organizational changes and their timing; and *accuracy of information*, which refers to the quality and completeness of detailed data available for individual organizations such as ownership, strategy, technology, and size.

However, the same degree of clarity or convention does not yet exist in the new archival research traditions. Indeed, one of the distinguishing features of the new archivalism's exemplars has been the creativity and convention-shattering abandon with which new sources and types of materials have been brought into empirical use.

Consider, for example, Jones' (2001) study of the early US film industry. She relies on an extraordinary dataset containing entries for every American film that was produced during these years, including information on the individuals and firms that produced and distributed the film, release dates, film length, genre and story synopsis. Her measures also include time series data on the career histories of key individuals, their relationships with others (e.g. litigation, partnerships, kinship, etc.), personal attributes (ethnicity, religion, gender), and then similar data on firms including: foundings, production function, (and changes in function, e.g., from distribution into production), name changes, mergers and acquisitions, key personnel changes, legal actions, and exits. Also included are the histories of strategic networks (information on their founding, memberships, and types of relationships within the network), and, finally, key industry events such as law suits, court decisions, and broader political and economic circumstances. Jones takes in the broad sweep of social organization, treating organizational forms, entrepreneurial careers, institutional rules, and cultural models as complexly interwoven, co-evolving and equally worthy of empirical analysis.

Or, look at Guerra-Pearson's (2000) investigation of nineteenth century custodial institutions based on her detailed tracking of the usage and design of the buildings which they occupied. Her dataset consists of several thousand observations, one for each building "event" for each of some sixty organizations. Whenever a new building was built, added to, remodeled, redesigned, sold, rented, purchased or simply put to a different use, that information is recorded. What makes Guerra-Pearson's database especially distinctive, however, is that the entries are not simply numbers or a small sample of predefined codes, but literally thousands of pages of rich, verbatim primary archival texts. Her database is accessed through a content analysis program that returns complex sweeps of information about the architectural details of buildings, the rationale behind various decisions, the varied allocation and amounts of money spent, the architect's comments, the practices that were embodied within the organization, classifications of inmates, and on and on. Moreover she uses these data to show how architecture was, quite literally, the material embodiment of the ideas which both defined and fundamentally shaped the organizational character and competitive success of these institutions.

Finally, consider Ventresca et al. (2001) study of e-business models using data coded from the features of electronic shopping carts (ESCs) on the websites of online retailers of books, records, and equities. This project, at the intersection of institutional theories of organizations, entrepreneurship research, and technology studies in the actor network tradition, explores ESCs (order processing systems) as empirical "boundary objects" that align and focus the activities of entrepreneurs, technologists, web designers, and venture capitalists. For the comparative study, they code over 60 websites for US and European firms, extending principles of "net-nography" (Kozinets, 1998) developed by ethnographers in marketing. Their coding protocol records several layers of data embedded in the webpages including:

1   technical foundations (e.g., language)
2   analogy to design and use of physical shopping carts
3   structure of the order process
4   options incorporating choice for the consumer, and
5   features that enable personalization (e.g., use of "cookies").

Our point is that it is difficult, if not impossible, to lay out specific prescriptions or strategies for the use of textual sources that will hold for all types of archival work given the enormous variety of archival materials and the ingenuity of design that characterizes archival work today. Indeed, it is difficult to say very much at all about the actual decision points and practicalities of archival research without specifying the research goals in question. Because these vary widely by theory and analytic perspective we restrict ourselves here to those research desiderata that we have already identified with the new archivalist tradition and offer general observations on the relationship between research goals, archival materials and methods of analysis.

MATCHING GOALS, MATERIALS, AND METHODS

Above we propose four kinds of research goals as being central to the new archivalist project:

1   Concern with the structural embeddedness of organizations and their components
2   Focus on the shared systems of understanding and meanings that facilitate organizational action
3   Interest in identifying and specifying the formal grammars and repertoires of action that are deployed by organizations
4   Understanding and mapping the institutional logics that set all of these processes in motion

Researchers have pursued each of these goals through the use of distinctive types of archival materials and methods of analysis. We will briefly review the options we discuss and the conventions in addressing them. Table 35.2 summarizes each of these in turn.

STUDYING STRUCTURAL EMBEDDEDNESS

The *research goal* is to understand how individuals, organizational units, and firms are embedded within relational networks that facilitate the flow of communications, interactions, material transactions, ideas, social sentiments (and so on) through the social order. Patterns of similarity of compositional attributes can also be modeled to identify the structural positions of objects within a field. A network approach treats the relational structure as foundational. Relations and their logics effectively constitute the objects that are connected by them.

Archival materials are used to identify *relational ties* that link elements of a given structure together. Many different kinds of relations can be extracted from archival data. Evaluations made about others can be taken from textual narratives such as annual

Table 35.2 Research goals, data sources, and methods for archival research on organizations

Objects of investigation	Data source	Analytic methodologies
Structural embeddedness	Relational ties (Corporate interlocks, exchange agreements, market transactions, reference groups, etc.)	Network analysis Blockmodels
Meaning systems	Professional discourse (journal articles, trade publications) Procedural talk (emails) Organizational identity statements (directories, IPOs, annual reports)	Content analysis Semantic grammars Semiotics Multidimensional scaling
Grammars and repertoires of action	Event sequences Organizational practices (procedural records)	Sequence analysis Boolean algebra Fuzzy sets
Institutional logics	Classification statements (directories, industry reports, organizational narratives)	Galois lattice Correspondence analysis Hierarchical classification model

reports (Porac et al., 2000). Transactions that link firms or sub-units together can be taken from archives of accounting materials such as tax records (McLean and Padgett, 1997). Linkages between larger aggregates (such as product markets) can be derived from published government data (Burt, 1992). Interactions between firms can be deduced from interlocking directorate patterns (Mintz and Schwartz, 1985) or from evidence of co-membership of firm managers in clubs or associations (Galaskiewicz, 1985). Burt and Lin (1977) describe useful strategies for creating network data taken from a variety of archival sources (organizational archives, journal articles, minutes of meetings, court records, newspaper accounts, etc.).

There is a long and well-developed tradition of *formal methodologies* that have been built up over the years for analyzing these kind of data (Wasserman and Faust, 1994). Often a key distinction is made between methods that rely on calculations of network cohesiveness (Aldrich and Whetten, 1981) and those that rely on measures of structural equivalence (DiMaggio, 1986). Burt (1978; 1980) reviews this distinction.

STUDYING MEANING STRUCTURES

The *research goal* is to assess relevant features of shared understandings, professional ideologies, cognitive frames or sets of collective meanings that condition how organizational actors interpret and respond to the world around them, to measure essential properties of these ideational systems and to use them to explain the strategies and actions of individuals and organizations.

A wide range of *archival materials* have been used to study meaning systems. The study of managerial ideologies and belief systems has often relied on analysis of repositories of professional discourse in professional journals, trade publications, and academic literatures (Shenhav, 1995, 1999; Barley and Kunda, 1992; Abrahamson, 1997,

Guillén, 1994). Archival data from organizations has also been used. For example, some studies make use of procedural documents, information gleaned from the normal flow of work in organizations (Orlikowski and Yates, 1994). Others have focused on analytic accounts that organizations are often called upon to produce – organizational directories, initial public stock offerings, annual reports, governmental accounting demands, and routine compilations by advocacy organizations and other agencies (Proffitt and Ventresca, 2002).

Another long tradition of *formal methodologies* is relevant. Content analysis (which dates back to propaganda analysis techniques developed in World War II) are useful here. Two recent developments in content analysis are especially important. One is the shift in data gathering techniques, away from basic word counts toward more context-specific treatments such as the coding of semantic grammars (Franzosi, 1989, 1990). The other development has had to do with how meanings are analyzed. Early work by Osgood and colleagues relied on semantic differential analysis (Osgood et al., 1971). Recent developments have drawn on structural linguistics, semiotic theory, and network analysis (Mohr, 1998a). Multidimensional scaling analysis is a common analytic tool. For a review of theoretical issues and software packages, see Dohan and Sanchez-Jankowski, 1998. For more general discussions of methodological strategies see Jepperson and Swidler (1994), Franzosi and Mohr (1997), Wade et al. (1997), Ruef (1999) and Mohr (2000).

STUDYING GRAMMARS OF ACTION

The *research goal* is to understand how things are done by analyzing the raw elements of organizational activity, the sequences of actions that go together, and the underlying grammars or combinatorial principles that account for these configurations. While organizational scholars have long been interested in understanding technologies as specific ways of accomplishing tasks, recent work shifts the focus more toward a relational understanding of activities organized through time.

The *archival materials* that are likely to be most appropriate for this kind of research either involve detailed sequences of events (Van de Ven and Garud, 1993, 1994; Garud and Lant, 1997) or the daily communications that flow within and between organizations as a natural part of organizational life. Again, Pentland and Reuter's (1994) work on assistance calls is an example.

A relatively new strand of *formal methodologies* have emerged in the social sciences over the last decade and a half that lend themselves particularly well to the analytic problems defined by this research goal. Boolean algebra is a means of linking qualitative data to a more formal metric of analysis by identifying irreducible and non-redundant combinations of features which are associated with specified outcomes (Ragin, 1987). Recently Ragin (2000) has extended his method by the inclusion of fuzzy-set theory. Sequence analysis is another qualitatively oriented formal methodology which can be used. These methods find reduced form patterns in the sequencing of events through time (Abbott and Forrest, 1986; Abell, 1987; Abbott and Hrycak, 1990).

STUDYING INSTITUTIONAL LOGICS

The *research goal* is to understand how ways of knowing and ways of acting are combined together into a broader package or logic of action. The study of institutional logics brings together the analysis of meaning structures and the study of grammars of action (Heimer, 1999; 2001; Jackall, 1988; Padgett and Ansell, 1992). A central presumption is that the two orders – practical and symbolic – are mutually constitutive.

The best *archival materials* contain classificatory statements that invoke fundamental distinctions between classes or categories of things. These kinds of classifications are especially powerful because they usually link understandings together with actions. They also tend to be fairly stable and to be organized around institutional assumptions (Mohr, 1998b; Mohr and Guerra-Pearson, forthcoming). DiMaggio and Mullen (2000) extract classificatory distinctions from summary reports of community ritual activities. Mohr and Duquenne (1997) draw upon categories listed in an organizational directory.

The most useful *formal methodologies* are those intended for the analysis of two-mode data. The goal is to highlight the relevant relations that link a set of meanings into an organized structure by seeing how they are differentially embedded within a set of activities. Correspondence analysis is probably the most well known of these methods (Weller and Romney 1990). Galois lattices (Duquenne, 1986) and hierarchical classification models are also appropriate (de Boeck and Rosenberg, 1988). Mohr (1998a) provides an overview of these methods. Breiger (2000) demonstrates the practical utilities of each method in a comparative manner.

Conclusion

This chapter answers two key questions about archival methods – what archival materials are and how to analyze them. We have identified three traditions here – the historiographic, the ecological, and an emergent project we have referred to as the new archivalists – and demonstrated how they vary in terms of four basic criteria: their level of analysis (few/many), their input method (read/measure), their implicit approach to causality (descending/ascending) and their conception of measurement (objects/relations).

We have spent most of our energy detailing the character of the new archivalism strategies and goals that we see as leading the field of organizational science in useful and important directions. It is these approaches in particular that we believe begin to take up a difficult challenge posed to the organizations research community by Zald (1993). In that gentle polemic, Zald proposes that organizational researchers have not yet effectively bridged the gap between the demands of the more interpretative and humanistic dimensions of organizational life and the ambitions of their enterprise as a formal social science. Drawing on his appreciation of what the humanists have to teach us, Zald suggests that organization scholars should seek to render behavior in specific time and societal contexts, attend to the coherence and the transformation of symbols and sign systems, and focus on the ways in which organizations embody substantive meanings in presentational forms such as rhetoric and narrative. To do all this and yet preserve the canons of organizational science is a tall order and one that requires innovations of both theory and method.

As we show in this chapter, the use of archival methods presents an especially rich opportunity for advancing Zald's precepts in practical research. The use of archival methods and materials has frequently been the occasion through which core questions of organization theory, strategy, and practice have been confronted and reframed. Archives contain the residues of organizational life, stretched out across time and space, available for all to come and see. As we have shown with examples highlighted in this chapter, archival studies afford scholars the opportunity to do things differently, to tell new tales, to make their own path. Such is the exuberance of insight evident in contemporary archival work.

Acknowledgments

The order of authors is reverse alphabetical; both are full contributors. We thank Lisa Amoroso, Lis Clemens, Barry Cohen, Marie-Laure Djelic, Tyler Colman, Bob Freeland, Roger Friedland, Amin Ghaziani, Mike Lounsbury, John W. Meyer, Candace Jones, Peter Levin, Trex Proffitt, Marc Schneiberg, Sarah Soule, and participants in the Workshop on Organizations, Institutions, and Change at Northwestern University for early comments on this chapter, for direction to relevant exemplary sources, and for sharing their wisdom about archival methods in organization research. We thank Craig Rawlings for superb research assistance on the project. We owe a special debt to the editorial wisdom and collegial spirit of Joel Baum. We also acknowledge with appreciation research support from the Department of Sociology, and the Institute for Social and Behavioral Research at UCSB and from the Kellogg School of Management, Northwestern University.

Notes

1 Van de Ven and colleagues (Van de Ven and Garud, 1993; 1994) developed an "event analysis" research strategy to describe key infrastructural processes in industry, organization, and technological change. This work draws from the unstandardized data sources characteristic of the historical approaches, but reaches toward more formal analysis and thus can be seen as an important antecedent to this project.
2 Clemens and Hughes (2001) provide an alternative framework intended for social movement researchers but also useful for organizational analysts: organizational archives, government documents, newspapers, and biographical dictionaries.

References

Abbott, A., and Forrest J. (1986): "Optimal matching methods for historical sequences," *Journal of Interdisciplinary History*, 26, 471–94.
Abbott, A., and Hrycak, A. (1990): "Measuring resemblance in sequence data: An optimal matching analysis of musicians' careers," *American Journal of Sociology*, 96, 144–85.
Abell, P. (1987): *The Syntax of Social Life: The Theory and Method of Comparative Narratives*. Oxford: Clarendon.
Abrahamson, E. (1991): "Management fads and fashion: The diffusion and rejection of innovations," *Academy of Management Review*, 16, 586–612.
Abrahamson, E. (1997): "The emergence and prevalence of employee–management rhetorics: The effect of long waves, labor unions and turnover, 1875–1992," *Academy of Management Journal*, 40(3), June, 491–533.
Aldrich, H. E., and Whetten, D. A. (1981): "Organization-sets, action-sets, and networks: Making the most of simplicity," in P. C. Nystrom and W. H. Starbuck (eds), *Handbook of Organizational Design*, Oxford: Oxford University Press, 385–408.
Barley, S., and Kunda, G. (1992): "Design and devotion: Surges of rational and normative ideologies of control in managerial discourse," *Administrative Science Quarterly*, 37(3), September, 363–99.
Baron, J. N., Dobbin, F. R., and Jennings, P. D. (1986): "War and peace: The evolution of modern

personnel administration in U.S. industry," *American Journal of Sociology*, 92, 250–83.

Baum, J. A. C., and Oliver, C. (1991): "Institutional linkages and organizational mortality," *Administrative Science Quarterly*, 36, 187–218.

Baum, J. A. C., and Oliver, C. (1992): "Institutional embeddedness and the dynamics of organizational populations," *American Sociological Review*, 57, 540–59.

Braudel, F. (1980): *On History*. Chicago: University of Chicago Press.

Braverman, H. (1976): *Labor and Monopoly Capital*. New York: Monthly Review Press.

Breiger, R. L. (2000): "A tool kit for practice theory," *Poetics*, 27(2–3), 91–116.

Burt, R. S. (1978): "Cohesion versus structural equivalence as a basis for network subgroups," *Sociological Methods and Research*, 7, 189–212.

Burt, R. S. (1980): "Models of network structure," *Annual Review of Sociology*, 6, 79–141.

Burt, R. S. (1992): *Structural Holes: The Social Structure of Competition*. Cambridge, MA: Harvard University Press.

Burt, R. S., and Lin, N. (1977): "Network time series from archival records," in D. Heise (ed.), *Sociological Methodology*, San Francisco: Jossey-Bass, 224–54.

Burton, M. D. (1995): "The evolution of employment systems in new firms," unpublished dissertation, Stanford University.

Burton, M. D. (2001): "The company they keep: Founders' models for organizing new firms," in C. B. Schoonhoven and E. Romanelli (eds), *The Entrepreneurship Dynamic: Origins of Entrepreneurship and the Evolution of Industries*, Stanford, CA: Stanford University Press, 13–39.

Carroll, G. R., and Hannan, M. T. (2000): *The Demography of Corporations and Industries*. Princeton, NJ: Princeton University Press.

Casadesus-Masanell, R., and Spulber, D. F. (2000): "The fable of fisher body," *Journal of Law and Economics*, 63(1), April, 67–104.

Chandler, A. D., Jr. (1962): *Strategy and Structure: Chapters in the History of the American Industrial Enterprise*. Garden City, NJ: Doubleday.

Chandler, A. D., Jr. (1977): *The Visible Hand: The Managerial Revolution in American Business*. Cambridge, MA: Belknap Press.

Clark, B. (1970): *The Distinctive College: Antioch, Reed and Swarthmore*. Chicago: Aldine.

Clawson, D. (1980): *Bureaucracy and the Labor Process: The Transformation of U.S. Industry, 1860–1920*. New York: Monthly Review Press.

Clemens, E. S. (1993): "Organizational repertoires and institutional change: Women's groups and the transformation of U.S. politics, 1890–1920," *American Journal of Sociology*, 98(4), January, 755–98.

Clemens, E. S. (1997): *The People's Lobby: Organizational Innovation and the Rise of Interest Group Politics in the United States, 1890–1925*. Chicago: University of Chicago Press.

Clemens, E. S. (1999): "Securing political returns to social capital: Women's associations in the United States, 1880s–1920s," *Journal of Interdisciplinary History*, 29(4), Spring, 613–38.

Clemens, E. S., and Hughes, M. D. (2001): "Recovering past protest: Historical research on social movements," in S. Staggenborg and B. Klandermans (eds), *Methods in Social Movement Research*, Minneapolis: University of Minnesota Press.

Covaleski, M. A., and Dirsmith, M. W. (1988): "An institutional perspective on the rise, social transformation, and fall of a university budget category," *Administrative Science Quarterly*, 33(4), 562–87.

Dacin, M. T., Ventresca, M. J., and Beal, B. (1999): "The embeddedness of organizations: Dialogue and directions," *Journal of Management*, 25(3), 317–56.

Daft, R. L. (1980): "The evolution of organizational analysis in ASQ: 1959–1979," *Administrative Science Quarterly*, 25(4), 623–36.

de Boeck, P., and Rosenberg, S. (1988):"Hierarchical classes: Model and data analysis," *Psychometrika*, 53, 361–81.

DiMaggio, P. J. (1986):"Structural analysis of organizational fields," in B. Staw and L. L. Cummings (eds), *Research in Organizational Behavior*, Greenwich, CT: JAI Press, 335–70.

DiMaggio, P. J. (1991): "Constructing an organizational field as a professional project: U.S. art museums, 1920–1940," in W. W. Powell and P. J. DiMaggio (eds), *The New Institutionalism in Organizational Analysis*, Chicago: University of Chicago Press, 267–92.

DiMaggio, P. J., and Mullen, A. L. (2000): "Enacting community in progressive America: Civic rituals in national music week, 1924," *Poetics*, 27(2–3), 135–62.

Djelic, M. L. (1998): *Exporting the American Model: The Post-War Transformation of American Business*. New York: Oxford University Press.

Dohan, D., and Sanchez-Jankowski, M.S. (1998): "Using computers to analyze ethnographic field data: Theoretical and practical considerations," *Annual Review of Sociology*, 24, 477–98.

Duquenne, V.: (1986): "What can lattices do for experimental designs?" *Mathematical Social Sciences*, 11, 243–81.

Edelman, L. (1990): "Legal environments and organizational governance: The expansion of due process in the American workplace," *American Journal of Sociology*, 95, 1401–40.

Emirbayer, M. (1997): "Manifesto for a relational sociology," *American Journal of Sociology*, 103, 281–317.

Fligstein, N. (1990): *The Transformation of Corporate Control*. Cambridge, MA: Harvard University Press.

Foucault, M. (1980): "Lecture Two: 14 January 1976," in C. Gordon (ed.), *Power/Knowledge*, New York: Pantheon Books, 92–108.

Franzosi, R. (1989): "From words to numbers: A generalized and linguistics-based coding procedure for collecting textual data," *Sociological Methodology*, 19, 263–98.

Franzosi, R. (1990): "Computer-assisted coding of textual data: An application to semantic grammars," *Sociological Methods and Research*, 19(2), 225–57.

Franzosi, R., and Mohr, J. W. (1997):"New directions in formalization and historical analysis," *Theory and Society*, 26(2-3), 133–60.

Freeland, R. F. (2000): "Creating holdup through vertical integration: Fisher body revisited," *Journal of Law and Economics*, 63(1), April, 33–66.

Freeland, R. F. (2001): *The Struggle for Control of the Modern Corporation: Organizational Change at General Motors, 1924–1970*. New York: Cambridge University Press.

Friedland, R., and Alford, R. (1991): "Bringing society back in: Symbols, practices, and institutional contradictions," in W. W. Powell and P. J. DiMaggio (eds), *The New Institutionalism in Organizational Analysis*, Chicago: University of Chicago Press, 232–63.

Galambos, L. (1970): "The emerging organizational synthesis in American history," *Business History Review*, 44, Autumn, 279–90.

Galaskiewicz, J. (1985): *Social Organization of an Urban Grants Economy*. New York: Academic Press.

Garud, R., and Lant, T. (1997): "Navigating Silicon Valley: Kaleidoscopic experiences," working paper, Stern School of Business, New York University.

Giddens, A. (1987): *The Nation-State and Violence: Volume Two of a Contemporary Critique of Historical Materialism*. Berkeley: University of California Press.

Goody, J. (1986): *The Logic of Writing and the Organization of Society*. Cambridge: Cambridge University Press.

Guerra-Pearson, F. (2000): "'The chief ornaments of the Christian metropolis': Charitable, moral, and benevolent institution building in New York City, 1736–1920," unpublished dissertation, University of California, Santa Barbara.

Guillén, M. F. (1994): *Models of Management: Work, Authority, and Organization in Comparative Perspective*. Chicago, IL: University of Chicago Press.

Hannan, M. T., and Freeman, J. (1977): "The population ecology of organizations," *American Journal of Sociology*, 82, 929–64.

Hannan, M. T., and Freeman, J. (1984): "Structural inertia and organizational change," *American Sociological Review*, 49, 149–64.

Heimer, C. A. (1999): "Competing institutions: Law, medicine, and family in neonatal intensive care," *Law and Society Review*, 33(1), 17–66.

Heimer, C. A. (2001): "Cases and biographies: An essay on the routinization and the nature of comparison," *Annual Review of Sociology*, 27, 46–76.

Hirsch, P. M. (1986): "From ambushes to golden parachutes: Corporate takeovers as an instance of cultural framing and institutional integration," *American Journal of Sociology*, 102(6), 1702–23.

Jackall, R. (1988): *Moral Mazes: The World of Corporate Managers*. New York: Oxford University Press.

Jennings, P. D., Dobbin, F. R., and Baron, J. N. (1992): "Making war and peace," in P. J. Frost and R. E. Stablein (eds), *Doing Exemplary Research*, Newbury Park, CA: Sage, 182–92.

Jepperson, R. L., and Swidler, A. (1994): "What properties of culture should we measure?" *Poetics*, 22, 359–71.

Jermier, J. M., and Barley, S. R. (eds) (1998): "Critical perspectives on organizational control," *Administrative Science Quarterly*, 43(2), June, Special issue.

John, R. R. (1997): "Elaborations, revisions, dissent: Alfred D. Chandler, Jr.'s 'The Visible Hand' after twenty years," *Business History Review*, 71, Summer, 151–200.

Jones, C. (2001): "Coevolution of entrepreneurial careers, institutional rules, and competitive dynamics in American film, 1893–1930," *Organization Studies*, 22, in press.

Kieser, A. (1989): "Organizational, institutional, and societal evolution: Medieval craft guilds and the genesis of formal organizations," *Administrative Science Quarterly*, 34(4), December, 540–64.

Kieser, A. (1994): "Why organization theory needs historical analyses – And how this should be performed," *Organization Science*, 5, 608–20.

Kogut, B. and Zander, U., (2000) "Did socialism fail to innovate? A natural experiment of the two Zeiss companies," *American Sociological Review*, 65(2), 169–90.

Kozinets, R. V. (1998): "On netnography: Initial reflections on consumer research investigations of cyberculture," in J. Alba and W. Hutchinson (eds), *Advances in Consumer Research*, Provo, UT: Association for Consumer Research, 366–71.

Kunda, G. (1992): *Engineering Culture: Control and Commitment in a High-Tech Corporation*. Philadelphia: Temple University Press.

Langton, J. (1984): "The ecological theory of bureaucracy: The case of Josiah Wedgewood and the British pottery industry," *Administrative Science Quarterly*, 29, 330–54.

Latour, B. (1987): *Science in Action: How to Follow Scientists and Engineers Through Society*. Cambridge, MA: Harvard University Press.

Locke, K., and Golden-Biddle, K. (1997): "Constructing opportunities for contribution: Structuring intertextual coherence and "problematizing," *Academy of Management Journal*, 40(5), 1023–62.

Lounsbury, M., and Ventresca, M. J. (2002): "Social structure and organizations, revisited," in *Research in the Sociology of Organization*, London: JAI Press, Elsevier.

McKenna, C. D. (2001): "Two strikes and you're out: Why forty million dollars and a team of consultants from McKinsey could not save the *New York Herald Tribune*," *The Historian*, 63(2), winter, 287–308.

McLean, P. D., and Padgett, J. F. (1997): "Was Florence a perfectly competitive market? Transactional evidence from the Renaissance," *Theory and Society*, 26, 209–44.

McNeely, C. L. (1995): *Constructing the Nation-State: International Organization and Prescriptive Action*. Westport, CT: Greenwood Press.

Meyer, J. W. (1977): "The effects of education as an institution," *American Journal of Sociology*, 83, 53–77.

Meyer, J. W., and Hannan, M. T. (1979): *National Development and the World System: Educational and Political Change, 1950–1970*. Chicago: University of Chicago Press.

Meyer, J. W., and Rowan, B. (1977): "Institutionalized organizations: Formal structure as myth and ceremony," *American Journal of Sociology*, 83, 340–63.

Meyer, J. W., Scott, W. R., and Strang, D. (1987): "Centralization, fragmentation, and school district complexity," *Administrative Science Quarterly*, 32(2), 186–201.

Meyer, J. W., and Rowan, B. (1978): "The structure of educational organizations," in M. W. Meyer (ed.), *Environments and Organizations*, San Francisco, CA: Jossey-Bass, 78–109.

Mezias, S. J. (1990): "An institutional model of organizational practice: Financial reporting at the *Fortune* 200," *Administrative Science Quarterly*, 35, 431–57.

Mintz, B., and Schwartz, M. (1985): *The Power Structure of American Business*. Chicago: University of Chicago Press.

Mohr, J. W. (1998a): "Measuring meaning structures," *Annual Review of Sociology*, 24, 345–70.

Mohr, J. W. (1998b): "The classificatory logics of state welfare systems: Towards a formal analysis," in C. McNeely (ed.), *Public Rights, Public Rules: Constituting Citizens in the World Polity and National Policy*, New York: Garland Publishing, 207–38.

Mohr, J. W. (2000): "Structures, institutions, and cultural analysis," *Poetics*, 27(2–3), 57–68.

Mohr, J. W. (forthcoming): "Implicit terrains: Meaning, measurement, and spatial metaphors in organizational theory," in M. J. Ventresca and J. Porac (eds), *Constructing Industries and Markets*, London: Elsevier Science.

Mohr, J. W. and Duquenne, V. (1997): "The duality of culture and practice: Poverty relief in New York City, 1888–1917," *Theory and Society*, 26(2–3), 305–56.

Mohr, J. W., and Guerra-Pearson, F. (forthcoming): "The differentiation of institutional space: Organizational forms in the New York social welfare sector, 1888–1917," in W. W. Powell and D. Jones (eds), *How Institutions Change*, Chicago: University of Chicago Press.

Orlikowski, W. J., and Yates, J. (1994): "Genre repertoires: The structuring of communicative practices in organizations," *Administrative Science Quarterly*, 39(4), December, 541–74.

Osgood, C. E., Suci, G. J., and Tannenbaum, P. H. (1971): *The Measurement of Meaning*. Urbana, IL: The University of Illinois Press.

Pentland, B. T., and Reuter, H. H. (1994): "Organizational routines as grammars of action," *Administrative Science Quarterly*, 39(3), September, 484–510.

Perrow, C. (1991): "A society of organizations," *Theory and Society*, 20, 725–62.

Piore, M. J., and Sabel, C. F. (1984): *The Second Industrial Divide: Possibilities for Prosperity*. New York: Basic Books.

Pollock, T. G. (1998): "Risk, reputation, and interdependence in the market for initial public offerings: Embedded networks and the construction of organization value," unpublished doctoral dissertation, University of Illinois.

Porac, J. F., Mishina, Y., and Pollock, T. G. (2000): "Entrepreneurial narratives and the dominant logics of high growth firms," in A. Huff and M. Jenkins (eds), *Mapping Strategy*, Thousand Oaks, CA: Sage.

Porac, J. F., Thomas, H., Wilson, F., Paton, D., and Kanfer, A. (1995): "Rivalry and the industry model of Scottish knitwear producers," *Administrative Science Quarterly*, 40(2), June, 203–29.

Proffitt, W. T., and Ventresca, M. J. (2002): "Rationalized conflict, field logics, and mobilization: Evidence from U.S. shareholder activism, 1949–1997," *Review of Social Movements, Conflict, and Change*, 22, forthcoming.

Ragin, C. (1987): *The Comparative Method: Moving Beyond Qualitative and Quantitative Strategies*. Berkeley: University of California Press.

Ragin, C. (2000): *Fuzzy-Set Social Science*. Chicago: University of Chicago Press.

Riles, A. (2001): "Introduction," in A. Riles (ed.), *Documents: Artifacts of Modern Knowledge*, Durham, NC: Duke University Press.

Roy, W. G. (1997): *Socializing Capital: The Rise of the Large Industrial Corporation in America*. Princeton: Princeton University Press.

Ruef, M. (1999): "Social ontology and the dynamics of organizational forms: Creating market actors in the healthcare field, 1966–1994," *Social Forces*, 77(4), June, 1403–32.

Salancik, G. R., and Meindl, J. R. (1984): "Corporate attributions as strategic illusions of management control," *Administrative Science Quarterly*, 29, 238–54.

Schneiberg, M., and Clemens, E. S. (2001): "The typical tools for the job: Research strategies in institutional analysis," in W. W. Powell and D. Jones (eds), *How Institutions Change*, Chicago: University of Chicago Press.

Schwartz, M., and Mizruchi, M. (eds) (1988): *The Structural Analysis of Business*. New York: Cambridge University Press.

Scott, W. R. (1965): "Field methods in the study of organizations," in J. G. March (ed.), *Handbook of Organizations*, Chicago, IL: Rand-McNally.

Scott, W. R. (2001): *Institutions and Organizations*, 2nd edn. Thousand Oaks, CA: Sage.

Selznick, P. (1949): *TVA and the Grass Roots*. Berkeley: University of California Press.

Shenhav, Y. (1994): "Manufacturing uncertainty and uncertainty in manufacturing: Managerial discourse and the rhetoric of organization theory," *Science in Context*, 7, 275–305.

Shenhav, Y. (1995): "From chaos to systems: The engineering foundations of organization theory, 1879–1932," *Administrative Science Quarterly*, 40(4), December, 557–85.

Shenhav, Y. (1999): *Manufacturing Rationality: The Engineering Foundations of the Managerial Revolution*. Oxford: Oxford University Press.

Smith, D. E. (1984): "Textually mediated social organization," *International Social Science Journal*, 99, 59–75.

Stablein, R. (1996): "Data in organization studies," in S. R. Clegg, C. Hardy, and W. R. Nord (eds), *Handbook of Organizations Studies*, Thousand Oaks, CA: Sage, 509–25.

Stinchcombe, A. L. (1965): "Social structure and social organization," in J. G. March (ed.), *Handbook of Organizations*, Chicago, IL: Rand-McNally, 142–93.

Suchman, M. (1994): "Localism and globalism in institutional analysis: The emergence of contractual norms in venture finance," in W. R. Scott and S. Christensen (eds), *The Institutional Construction of Organizations: International and Longitudinal Studies*, Thousand Oaks, CA: Sage.

Sutton, J. R. (1988): *Stubborn Children: Controlling Delinquency in the United States, 1640–1981*. Berkeley: University of California Press.

Sutton, J. R., and Dobbin, F. (1996):"The two faces of governance: Responses to legal uncertainty in U.S firms, 1955–1985," *American Sociological Review*, 61, 794–811.

Thomas, G. M., Meyer, J. W., Ramirez, F. O., and Boli, J. (1987): *Institutional Structure: Constituting State, Society, and the Individual*. Beverly Hills, CA: Sage.

Tilly, C. (1978): "Repertoires of contention in America and Britain, 1750–1830." in M. Zald and J. McCarthy (eds), *The Dynamics of Social Movements*, Cambridge: Cambridge University Press, 126–55.

Van de Ven, A. H., and Garud, R. (1993): "Innovation and industry development: The case of cochlear implants," in R. Burgelman and R. Rosenbloom (eds), *Research on Technological Innovation, Management, and Policy*, 5, Greenwich, CT: JAI Press.

Van de Ven, A. H., and Garud, R. (1994): "The co-evolution of technological and institutional innovations," in J. A. C. Baum and J. Singh (eds), *Evolutionary Dynamics of Organizations*, New York: Oxford University Press.

Vaughan, D. (1996): *The Challenger Launch Decision: Risky Technology, Culture, and Deviance at NASA*. Chicago: University of Chicago Press.

Ventresca, M. J. (1995): "When states count: Institutional and political dynamics in the modern census, 1800–1990," unpublished doctoral dissertation, Stanford University.

Ventresca, M. J., Ghaziani, A., Kaghan, W., and Sakson, J. (2001): "Electronic shopping carts as boundary objects: Cultural-institutional perspectives on 'New Economy' artifacts," Working paper, Kellog School of Management, Northwestern University.

Wade, J., Porac, J., and Pollock, T. G. (1997): "'Worth' words and the justification of executive pay," *Journal of Organization Behavior*, 18, 641–64.

Wasserman, S., and Faust, K. (1994): *Social Network Analysis: Methods and Applications*. Cambridge: Cambridge University Press.

Weber, M. (1968): *Economy and Society: An Outline of Interpretive Sociology*, 3 vols, G. Roth and C. Wittich (eds), Berkeley, CA: University of California Press, trans.

Weller, S. C., and Romney, A. K. (1990): *Metric Scaling: Correspondence Analysis*. Newbury Park, CA: Sage Publications.

Westney, D. E. (1987): *Imitation and Innovation: The Transfer of Western Organizational Patterns to Meiji, Japan*. Cambridge, MA: Harvard University Press.

Yates, J. (1989): *Control through Communication: The Rise of System in American Management*. Baltimore, MD: The Johns Hopkins University Press.

Zald, M. N. (1993): "Organization studies as a scientific and humanistic enterprise: Towards a reconceptualization of the foundations of the field," *Organization Science*, 4(4), November, 513–28.

Zald, M. N., and Denton, P. (1963): "From evangelism to general service: The transformation of the YMCA," *Administrative Science Quarterly*, 8, 214–34.

Chapter Thirty-six

Simulation Research Methods

KEVIN DOOLEY

Simulation Research Methods

Computer simulation is growing in popularity as a methodological approach for organizational researchers. Other research methods must make various assumptions about the exact cause and effect nature of the system under study; for example, in survey research, one must define the form and content of cause and effect a priori in order to learn from the data observed. Simulation allows for researchers to assume the inherent complexity of organizational systems as a given. If other methods answer the questions "What happened, and how, and why?" simulation helps answer the question "What if?" Simulation enables studies of more complex systems because it creates observations by "moving forward" into the future, whereas other research methods attempt to look backwards across history to determine what happened, and how. Because the nature of living systems is to either increase in entropy (disorder) or complexity (order), looking backwards is inherently more difficult than moving forwards.

There are three main schools of simulation practice:

- Discrete event simulation, which involves modeling the organizational system as a set of entities evolving over time according to the availability of resources and the triggering of events.
- System dynamics, which involves identifying the key "state" variables that define the behavior of the system, and then relating those variables to one another through coupled, differential equations.
- Agent-based simulation, which involves agents that attempt to maximize their fitness (utility) functions by interacting with other agents and resources; agent behavior is determined by embedded schema which are both interpretive and action-oriented in nature.

Simulation researchers typically remain in one camp and are not facile and do not work in all three domains. This will likely change in the future, however, as complex organizational systems really require elements of all three approaches in order to be their complexity to be appropriately captured.

The Purpose of Simulation

Axelrod (1997) outlines seven different purposes of simulation in the social sciences: prediction, performance, training, entertainment, education, proof, and theory discovery. Numerous examples can be found of each of these uses.

PREDICTION

Simulation takes a model, composed of a structure and rules that govern that structure and produces output (observed behavior). By comparing different output obtained via different structures and governing rules, researchers can infer what might happen in the real situation if such interventions were to occur. The validity of such predictions depends on the validity of the model. The vast majority of models used in the operations research and operations management field, for example, fall into this category. Predictions are made concerning how certain changes in (e.g.) inventory control, quality, productivity, material handling, etc. will impact operations (positively). If predictions turn out as expected, then there is more impetus to try such changes in the real system.

Examples include numerous simulation studies done concerning the scheduling of production in flow lines, assembly shops, and job shops (Law and Kelton, 1982). A model of the production or service facility, usually of a discrete event nature, is developed whereby the system is defined by events (e.g. a customer order arrives, a machine starts work, a machine finishes work), entities (the jobs that go through the system, and resources (e.g. machines, people, transports). The prediction in question might concern, for example, whether scheduling of jobs at the bottleneck workstation according to "earliest due date" led to better delivery performance than scheduling jobs according to a "first come first served" rule. This hypothesis would be tested over a number of different configurations to determine how robust the answer was; for example, the scheduling by due date might make a significant difference if the number of jobs in the system is large (utilization is high), but might make no difference if the system is not very busy.

Simulation for prediction is a substitute for experimentation and intervention on the actual system. It is undertaken when such experimentation is too dangerous, costly, untimely, or inconvenient. This is often the case with the "human system", and with the larger-scale elements of the organization (e.g. its information systems, its supply chain, its strategy), because of scaleability problems. Changes can be made at a task level of the organization in such a manner that the change can be scaled down appropriately and attempted on a very small component of the organization, with little (relative) cost. This often cannot be done with larger organizational systems, including human systems.

For example, human resource policy cannot be altered for one small group of individuals, and observations made about the appropriateness of such intervention. Even if it were feasible to practically do so, the results would be biased by the fact that there was a differential treatment; such an effect could not be separated from the experimental effect. Additionally, there may be network and contagion effects that could impact the results from an organization-wide implementation that would not be observed in a small experiment. Thus simulation for prediction is common in organizations because large-scale change in organizations is difficult, and one wants to be relatively sure of a change's potential before investing greatly in the change effort.

THEORY DISCOVERY

Simulation can uncover phenomena that in turn focus theoretical attention. One concept that has gotten much attention in organization circles is the so-called "edge of chaos" (Brown and Eisenhardt, 1998). Theories concerning the "edge of chaos", and what it might have to do with running real organizations came about first because simulation made discovery of the phenomena possible, and second because people then reframed the structure of their simulations to reflect the conditions under which the "edge of chaos" emerged, using simulation in its predictive mode.

The edge of chaos was discovered in a particular class of agent-based simulations known as cellular automata (CA) (Waldrop, 1992). A CA model has entities (agents) that have certain states (e.g. on, off), connections between entities (typically local), and behavioral rules. A CA simulation evolves the state of system entities over time; for each entity, it uses the corresponding behavioral rules and the states of other entities to which it is connected to determine its future state. One such set of simulations could be described by a single parameter, "lambda" value. Researchers found that when lambda was near zero, the CA's tended to generate patterns that were simple; when lambda was near one, the CA's tended to generate patterns that were extremely complex. With an initial "random" starting condition, and a complex (lengthy) periodic cycle, these patterns appeared to the human eye as random, or as they were (perhaps inappropriately) coined, "chaotic." As lambda was brought into the middle region of the parameter space, geometry emerged that was termed "complex" – they had a pattern that was visible yet not immediately repetitive.

The conclusion was that "interesting things" happened at that region between boring repetition and high dimensional behavior – the so-called edge of chaos. From this, it was concluded that all life takes place at the edge of chaos. This interpretation in general has some logical appeal. If a system is too repetitive in its response to external stimuli, then it is possible to get "stuck" in an unhealthy spot without any hope of adaptation and continued survival. If the system is too variable in its response to stimuli, then it cannot predict anything to do with the effects of its future behavior, which leaves it helpless to develop internal models that are predictive in any effective manner. It is that region of system response that is neither too dead nor too haphazard that represents a healthy, adaptive state. Taken beyond the conceptual though, the "edge of chaos" concept is hard to prove in real living systems, and is yet to be universally accepted as an axiom of life. Nevertheless, it has inspired numerous organizational theorists to posit theories concerning organizations at the edge of chaos. For example, Brown and Eisenhardt (1998) talk extensively about how effective organizations balance the predictable and the unpredictable at the edge of chaos.

Performance

With an appropriately calibrated and validated model, simulation can be used to perform real tasks for an organization, such as diagnosis or decision-making. In the organizational realm, simulation as a decision-aid is more likely to occur. In organizational decision making, uncertainty and randomness are often a natural context of the system. While decisions require taking uncertainty into account, this is not easily done with analytical formulations. Hence, simulation is used to mimic this uncertainty in the form of a Monte Carlo simulation. A Monte Carlo simulation is similar to discrete event simulation in approach, but does not emphasize the variable of "time."

An example is the use of simulation models in project portfolio management (Cooper, 1993). Given a set of potential projects to engage in, but limited resources, an organization must decide what projects to invest its resources in. The portfolio of projects undertaken should maximize some benefit, such as return on investment; however such numbers can be difficult to predict using formulae, given that they depend on the confluence of many variables that are random in nature. For example, market penetration (for a new product), competitive actions, and development time, each of which could be described by a statistical distribution, may determine investment return. A Monte Carlo simulation would consist of hundreds or thousands of trials, each trial sampling from the distribution of the element specified, and then aggregate the composite answer; thus return would be characterized not by a single number, but by a distribution of possible outcomes.

Training

A simulation environment makes it quick, easy, and safe for users to make decisions that mimic the decisions they (will) make in reality. "Flight simulators" – both the real and the so-called – fall into this realm. Two organizations where such simulation is used extensively are military organizations and nuclear plants. In both cases reaction to a given set of conditions must be rapid and yet calculated, almost to the point of automaticity. Because these "crisis" situations are too difficult, expensive, and dangerous to set up in a physical context, computer simulation can be used, perhaps coupled with virtual reality. Such training can fulfill many different learning purposes:

- What type of environmental data is available for scanning? What are the important variables to pay attention to? What are the cause and effect mechanisms in place?
- How should decisions be appropriately framed?
- What is the timing and pacing required for decision-making?
- How will other people around me react?
- How can we effectively deal with the stress associated with such situations?

EDUCATION

As opposed to using simulation for training purposes, simulation can also provide users more general education about how complex systems work. Users can gain a deeper conceptual, and perhaps metaphorical and symbolic understanding of mechanisms such as feedback, noise, reciprocity, self-organization, nonlinearity, etc. "Fractals" provide an example. Fractals are naturally occurring shapes with no clearly defined boundaries: clouds, trees, mountains, leafs, etc. While fractals have always existed, their operationalization was not possible until the advent of the computer, which allowed scientists to show how simple rules, iterated back into themselves, could produce such complex patterns.

At first glance the concept of fractals may appear as irrelevant to the world of organizations. Yet, people interested in organizations (especially organizational development researchers and practitioners) who observed these fractal shapes being constructed became inspired by the images they saw. They thought: organizations have complex boundaries; organizations have self-similar structure across multiple scales. Perhaps if these complex shapes were developed from a set of iterated, simple rules, perhaps organizations are constituted by simple rules iterated repeatedly (Eoyang and Dooley, 1996)? Such simulations inspired organizational scholars and practitioners to learn more about complexity theory and dynamical systems in general, thus a simulation's educational benefits may have secondary value in that they may inspire further inquiry and learning.

ENTERTAINMENT

While the simulation "SimCity" is used for training city planners, it is also simply "played" by millions of users interested in seeing if they can build a metropolis. Educational benefits can accrue however from such entertainment uses (Rushkoff, 1996).

PROOF

Simulation can be used to prove existence of a possible solution to a problem. This is not in common usage in the social science realm.

Approaches to Simulation

There are three different approaches to simulation in the organizational sciences:

- *Discrete event* simulation models are best used when the organizational system under study can be adequately characterized by variables and corresponding states, and events occur that change the value of these variable states in some rule-oriented but stochastic manner. Discrete event simulation is not appropriate when state variables interact with one another and change on a continuous basis, and when entities and their internal mechanisms are a more important element of the simulation than events, *per se*.

- *System dynamics* (or continuous) simulation models are best fit for situations where the variables in question are numerous, and can be related to one another in terms of how their rates of change interact with one another. System dynamic models tend to treat systems rather mechanistically, so it would not be the appropriate paradigm for modeling systems where individuals within the system were highly differentiated, or when behavior is best defined by people (and other entities) rather than the state variables themselves. System dynamics, as contrasted to the other two modeling approaches, is a "top-down" modeling approach, and thus requires fairly extensive knowledge about how the state variables of the system interact with one another.

- *Agent-based* simulation models are best fit for situations when the organizational system is best modeled as a collection of agents who interpret the world around themselves and interact with one another via schema. Agent-based models usually emphasize change in agents' schema via learning and adaptation, and also highlight the phenomena of emergent, self-organizing patterns in complex organizational systems. Agent-based models are considered "bottom-up" models in that one describes individual agents and their patterns of connectivity and interaction, without necessarily knowing what might emerge as patterns of behavior in the larger, aggregate system.

Table 36.1 summarizes the basic characteristics of these methods.

Table 36.1 Characteristics of three different simulation approaches

Simulation approach	Conditions for use	Main characteristics
Discrete event	System described by variables and events that trigger change in those variables	Events that trigger other events sequentially and probabilistically
System dynamics	System described by variables that cause change in each other over time	Key system variables and their interactions with one another are explicitly (mathematically) defined as differential equations
Agent-based	System described by agents that react to one another and the environment	Agents with schema that interact with one another and learn

DISCRETE EVENT SIMULATION

Discrete event simulation is a term used to describe organizational simulations that are discrete, dynamic, and stochastic (Law and Kelton, 1982). If a system can be adequately defined by some collection of variables that at any given moment characterize the "state" of the system, then a discrete system is one in which the state variables only change a finite number of times, at specific instances in time. If one were to plot the quantitative values associated with the state of the system, it would be piecewise continuous, making discrete jumps at particular times and then remaining constant for other periods of time. A model of a system is considered stochastic if its behavior is determined by one or more random variables. Models are dynamic to the extent that time is an over-arching component of the model and its corresponding behavior.

A discrete event simulation is characterized by the following elements (Law and Kelton, 1982):

- *Entities*: Objects that comprise the system
- *System state*: the state variables that describe a system at a given moment, often associated with specific entities
- *Simulation clock*: denoting the passage of simulated time
- *Event list*: a list specifying the events to occur in the future, and the time at which they will occur
- *Statistical counters*: for collecting data during the simulation run, to record history, and be analyzed later
- *Initialization routine*: some means by which to prepare the model for an experimental run
- *Timing routine*: a subroutine that manages the event list
- *Event routine*: a subroutine for each different type of event, that specifies the actions (creation of other events, change in state variables) that are associated with triggering of the event
- *Report generator*: reports the aggregate results as obtained from the statistical counters
- *Main program*: a program that coordinates activity between all of the various other elements of the simulation system

Many of these elements are common across all types of simulations. They are often embedded in a user-friendly (often graphically-driven) software package.

March's (1991) influential study of organizational learning as exploitation and exploration is an example of a discrete event simulation. Entities are considered individual people within the organization, and the state variables that define the system are an "external reality" (an m-dimensional vector made up of +1 and −1 values), an "organizational code" (a similar vector with different values), and n "individual codes." The system does not use a variable time clock, as is common in discrete event models, but rather a fixed clock (e.g. events are timed at regular intervals). As time moves forward, the external reality state vector remains constant, while parts of any individual's code evolve toward the state code according to some probability p_1 (learning from the organizational code), and parts of the organizational code evolve toward individuals with codes that are closer to the external reality than it itself is, with some probability p_2 (learning by the organizational code). March reports results from an experimental design that fixes the dimension of the reality vector, the number of individuals, and the number of replications (to obtain results), and then varies the probabilities to determine the effect of different learning rates.

From this simulation come the following observations, which can then be appropriated into theoretical propositions:

- Higher rates of learning lead to achieving equilibrium in the system's states earlier.
- Rapid individual learning may not lead to rapid organizational learning.
- Having some small percent of individual "slow learners" may increase organizational learning rates, but having too many slow learners can decrease organizational learning rates.
- Moderate amounts of turnover, in some circumstances, can accelerate organizational learning.

One characteristic strength of March's simulation work is that explanations for the simulation results are always strongly coupled with – in a sense triangulated by – strong theoretical arguments.

SYSTEM DYNAMICS

System dynamics modeling grew out of the socio-technical systems movement in the 1950s, coupled with cybernetics and the desire to use systems theory (including the mathematics of Weiner's control theory) on problems in the social domain. It is best characterized by Jay Forrester's work in the 1960s; it had a "re-birth" of interest in the organizational world, following the popularity of Senge's (1990) book "The Fifth Discipline" (which used the models of, but not the computational elements of, system dynamics).

Forrester (1961, p. 13) defines system dynamics (actually, industrial dynamics) as "the study of the information-feedback characteristics of industrial activity to show how organizational structure, amplification (in policies), and time delays (in decisions and actions) interact to influence the success of enterprises. It treats the interaction between the flows of information, money, orders, materials, personnel, and capital equipment in a company, an industry, or a national economy . . . It is a quantitative and experimental approach for relating organizational structure and corporate policy to industrial growth and stability."

As in discrete event simulation, one has to define the variables that capture the state of the system. These variables need not be entities or physical items; nor must there be consistency in the *type* of variable that is chosen. For example, in simulating an information systems development team, one might define state variables such as group stress, the amount of workload present, morale of the team members, and external pressures and incentives for performance. In system dynamics, the next step is to characterize the relationship between the state variables, in terms of a functional equation relating one to the other. Using language from its historical roots, these state variables are often referred to as *sinks*, and the relationships between sinks are called *flows*.

There is one twist however to how these functional relationships, or flows are defined. Rather than being stated in the form of the state variables' natural metrics, they are stated in terms of the first derivative of the state variable. Thus flows define how rates of change in one variable impact rates of change in another. This gives the simulation a dynamical quality that would not otherwise be obtained. This also means that system dynamic models tend to be the only type to conform to McKelvey's (1997) plea for modeling rates rather than states.

Computationally what this means is that a system dynamics model is essentially a set of coupled, differential equations. More often than not, the differential equation is linear and thus system behavior, while it may be complex, is confined to periodic trajectories. One can use nonlinear flows and stochastic elements or events can be incorporated to enhance the complexity of the model.

An exemplar of system dynamics modeling is Sterman et al.'s (1997) work on paradoxes of organizational improvement. They used a system dynamics model to simulate the internal and external dynamics of the company *Analog Devices*, over a several year period, as the industry was going through trying times and the company itself was implementing a total quality management program. The model is quite complex – it is not uncommon to see system dynamic models with hundreds of variables – and contains variables such as the rate at which breakthrough new products were being innovated, market share, the effectiveness of process improvement, workforce commitment and morale, cash flow, pricing, labor variances, and R&D spending.

Sterman et al. first present a base case representing what actually happened to Analog Devices during the time frame in question. Analog Device's TQM program led to successful waste reduction in manufacturing, leading to excess capacity. Because new products were not available to take up this slack, the company laid off workers, eventually deteriorating the trust and support for the TQM effort.

Besides the intriguing subject matter, what makes this study stand out as an exemplar is the rigor attended to in validating the simulation's behavior to that of the real system. Unfortunately such care is rarely taken in simulation studies in organizational science. Sophisticated statistical methods for determining goodness of fit (between the simulated and real) were used and results clearly demonstrate high validity for the base case. This makes the subsequent experiments all the more believable.

From the base case, they explore several alternative lines of action, including maintaining a no-layoff policy, maintaining morale while downsizing, and maintaining operating margins. Key organizational performance variables are compared between the base and experimental case to determine the impact of such interventions.

AGENT-BASED SIMULATION

Agent-based modeling is an outgrowth of artificial intelligence models in computer science. Whereas discrete event and system dynamic models focus on variables and events, agent-based simulation models focus on organizational participants (companies, teams, employees, etc.) and their larger collective behavior. Agents are considered "sentient beings" inside the computer, and are embodied with schemas that are both interpretive and behavioral in their nature. Since their advent, agent-based modeling has coupled with the discipline of complexity science (Anderson, 1999). As complexity science gains more acceptance as *the* normative description of living systems, agent-based simulation has the potential to become the dominant simulation-modeling paradigm for organizational researchers. Holland (1995) discusses the basic components of agent-based models:

- *Internal models*: schemas that are implemented computationally using behavioral rules. Adaptation is implemented via either genetic algorithms or schemes that change degree of belief parameters associated with behavioral rules.
- *Building blocks*: schema can combine with other schema into higher order behavioral models; a building block is the simplest form of a schema.
- *Tagging*: the explicit labeling of an agent in order to assign a class of attributes to the agent (i.e., through object-oriented methodology).
- *Aggregation*: agents can combine into meta-agents and behave as individuals and/or collectives.
- *Nonlinearity*: computationally, nonlinearity is implemented via rules that embed nonlinearity in agent behavior. Nonlinearity is a common but not required feature of agent-based models.
- *Flows*: computationally, flows represent the simultaneous change of attributes of agents.
- *Diversity*: implemented via the heterogeneity of internal models, tags and associated hierarchical aggregations, flows and agent attributes, and fitness functions.
- *Fitness function*: the utility function that determines how healthy each individual agent is. Fitness functions inform behavior because as certain rules become associated with certain outcomes that help or hurt the fitness value, these rules can be made to be evoked more or less often in the future (i.e. learning).

Cellular automata (CA) models are perhaps the simplest form of agent-based simulation, and thus serve as a useful demonstration of this approach. To simplify, consider a one-dimensional CA, where a "cell" represents an agent, and each agent possesses a "state". In the simplest arrangement, the state is considered binary, and can be represented visually by two numbers (0,1) or colors (white, black) (Walker and Dooley, 1999). The CA is finite in size, e.g. it has a fixed number of cells (agents). Each cell evolves its state in a discrete manner, such that the state of cell "j" at time t, state(j, t) is determined by the state of cell "j" at time $t - 1$, state($j, t - 1$), and the state of some neighboring cells at time $t - 1$, for example, state($j - 1, t - 1$) and state($j + 1, t - 1$). The cells are lined up in a specific and fixed spatial order. In order to visualize change in the states over time, the combined state vector is plotted down the screen, thus becoming a two dimensional object. Each column of the graphical object represents the evolution of a cell over time, and each row represents the combined states of all cells at a particular time.

Consider a 5-cell CA; assume that the cells at the left and right end "wrap-around" and consider their neighbor at the other end to be connected to them. We denote the states by (0,1), and start-off with a random initial configuration: {0, 1, 0, 1, 1}. Now consider the following set of rules:

- If the sum of yourself and left and right neighbors is less than two, change to a 1.
- If the sum of yourself and left and right neighbors is two or greater, change to a 0.

Given the initial condition above, several iterations of the CA are shown in Figure 36.1.

By examining the types of patterns that exist over time (Is there a periodic pattern?

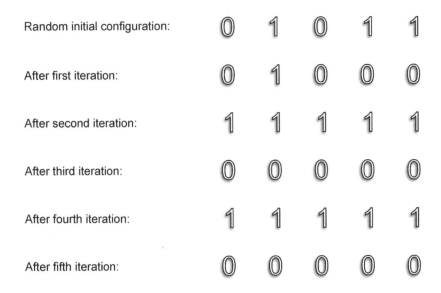

Figure 36.1 Cellular automata example

If so, is it simple or complex? Is there sensitivity to small changes in the initial condition?) one can use CA models, and agent-based models in general, for the set of purposes outlined earlier. Studying the behavior of an agent-based simulation can be difficult though, because they demonstrate self-organization and emergence. (These two behaviors also can exist in discrete event simulation, but are rarely talked about in that domain.)

Behavior in a simulation is induced not by a single entity but rather by the simultaneous and parallel actions of many entities within the system itself. Thus, we refer to the simulation as self-organizing as it undergoes "a process … whereby new emergent structures, patterns, and properties arise without being externally imposed on the system. Not controlled by a central, hierarchical command-and-control center, self-organization is usually distributed throughout the system" (Goldstein, 1998). Self-organization leads to emergent behavior. Emergence is "the arising of new, unexpected structures, patterns, properties, or processes in a self-organizing system. These emergent phenomena can be understood as existing on a higher-level than the lower level components from which (emergence took place). Emergent phenomena seem to have a life of their own with their own rules, laws and possibilities unlike the lower level components" (Goldstein, 1998).

Self-organization and emergence are important organizational phenomena that are just beginning to be recognized and understood (Anderson, 1999). For example, the evolution of Napster.com, a free music-sharing Internet site whose presence eventually challenged the fundamental assumptions of the music industry, can best be understood as an emergent event shaped by the actions of semi-autonomous actors coupled together in a complex web of interaction.

Consider, for example, a simulation of bird flocking. At first glance, one may be tempted to believe that the complex order observed in the flocking pattern is the result of either a predetermined plan, or the result of unilateral control employed by the lead bird. In fact, flocking patterns emerge as part of the system's self-organizing behavior (this has been proven to be true in reality). Individual birds behave according to simple rules that are enacted based on local information. Any individual bird determines their speed and direction by flying towards the center of the flock, mimicking the velocity of birds around them and staying a safe distance away from neighboring birds. We also observe this same type of self-organizing behavior in complex organizational systems, where simple behavior based on local information can, in the aggregate, lead to complex global behavior.

Many agent-based simulation models go beyond the simplifying assumptions of CA models, by incorporating fitness functions (measures of how well, or "healthy" an agent is; its utility function), learning and adaptation (typically incorporated by genetic algorithm-type formulations), systemic and institutional constraints (represented by non-local connections), global influences, and agent idiosyncrasies (implemented by differentiating fitness function, connectivity, learning rates, and/or behavioral rules). One such model is Axtell's (1999) very detailed computational model of the emergence of firms.

In Axtell's model, an agent is an individual who self-organizes into a firm as it so benefits their own fitness function. First, each agent is assigned an "income-leisure" parameter that determines the amount of time it would prefer to spend working (making income) versus at leisure (any amount of time not allocated to work effort). These assignments are made randomly so agent heterogeneity is maintained. The agent's fitness is a multiplicative function of the amount of effort they are expending, the return on that effort at the firm level, and the amount of leisure time available. At random intervals of time an agent will consider their current position and either

(a)   maintain their current effort level
(b)   increase or decrease their current effort level
(c)   start a new firm (by themselves), or
(d)   migrate to one of two friend's firms.

The amount of return that a firm gets from the aggregated efforts of its members depends on the number of members, their individual efforts, and any synergistic effects that may be included (e.g. increasing returns). Returns to the individual are equally divided among all members of the firm.

Despite the number of different parameters and starting conditions that can be varied, and the fact that the simulation itself is based on some rather simplistic assumptions about human nature, the corresponding results support the convergent and predictive validity of the model:

- As firms become large, an individual agent's contribution becomes miniscule compared to the whole, which produces "free riders."
- As free-riding becomes more commonplace, firm productivity decreases and those who most want "work" leave for other firms, bringing the large firm into decline.
- While "equilibrium" conditions theoretically exist that would lead to a static situation, there is sufficient dynamic instability such that these equilibrium conditions never arise.

- The history of any firm is emergent and path dependent.
- At the aggregate level, firm size, growth and death rates mimic existing empirical evidence.

Axtell's model demonstrates the potential power of computational models to mimic actual behavior in complex organizational and market systems.

There are at least two important methodological issues that must be considered when developing agent-based simulation models (Dooley and Corman, 2002). First, it is difficult to evaluate the impact of structural and behavioral changes to such models, because emergent macro-patterns that depend on shifting micro-patterns tend to invalidate the assumption base of most modern statistical methods. One of the challenges in simulation research is to invent means by which emergence and self-organization in simulations can be visualized, operationalized and measured, and statistically modeled. The fractal nature of self-organization and emergence, both over time and space, make it difficult to use existing statistical methods that make restrictive assumptions about equilibrium, constancy of structure, and independence. This is an arena where advances in the modeling of these phenomena in the physical domain will come first, and be exported into the social science domain.

The second problem is related to the trade-off between model parsimony and model validity. Viewed as a simple trade-off, the analyst simply has to decide which perspective to favor and live with the consequences. There is a side effect – Bonini's paradox (1963) – induced by model complexity, however that tends to give favor to more parsimony and less model complexity for validity. The paradox states that as a model of a complex system becomes more complete, it becomes less understandable. Since understandability is major consideration in any simulation study, having too much complexity can be deadly for a simulation study.

The Implementation of Simulation Modeling

It is rare for a simulation study to be flawed because simulation was an inappropriate selection for a research method; or flawed because someone chose to do a simulation using one approach (e.g. discrete event) when another approach (e.g. system dynamics) would have been more appropriate. Simulation studies often falter, however, when it comes to implementation. This is especially true in disciplines where simulation has not been a common component of research training, as is the case in the areas of organizational structure, strategy, and behavior.

Implementing a simulation model involves the following steps and challenges (see Table 36.2 for summary):

CONCEPTUAL DESIGN

The user must determine what is to be modeled, what questions are to be asked via such a model, who will be using the model, and what their requirements are. An elegant conceptual design will also simultaneously consider the medium in which the computational model is to be developed. In determining the conceptual design, preference is

Table 36.2 Issues and challenges in organizational simulation

Implementation step	Key decisions	Key decision criteria	Common problems	Follow-up resources
Conceptual design	Boundaries of system, key variables, agent/entity attributes	Driven by theoretical propositions or research questions	Lack of linkage between model and theory(ies) of interest	Exemplars: March, 1991; Sterman et al., 1997
Code development	How to effectively manage the software development project	Effective project management practice	No explicit requirements Poor change control Little reuse of code Untested code Lengthy development times	McConnell, 1997
Validation	Match between simulation results and real system	Extent to which validity is important	Validity completely ignored	Axelrod, 1997; exemplar: Sterman et al., 1997
Experimental design	How to manipulate variables across experimental conditions	Effective experimental design practice	No (formal) experimental design used	Box et al., 1978
Implementation	Initial configuration, transient versus steady-state behavior	Statistical theory	Simulation runs not long enough, or not enough runs	Law and Kelton, 1982
Analysis	Determination of significant effects	Statistical theory	Transient and steady-state behavior intermixed Independence assumptions violated Dynamics not examined	Law and Kelton, 1982; Dooley and Van de Ven, 1999
Interpretation	Link simulation results back to theory	Logical arguments	Over-interpretation of results	Exemplar: Sterman et al., 1997

often given to models that are more parsimonious, that is, all things being equal, one should choose a simpler model over a complex model, unless the increase in complexity is well-justified.

A number of different design errors could occur during this stage:

- Behavior may be insufficiently specified, especially at the "boundaries" of the system.
- The researcher may include too many rules, thus making the model more difficult to test and validate, with little added value; or may exclude some important elements of the system (this is rare).
- Researchers may make erroneous assumptions about the sequencing of activities. For example, since many of the behaviors in an agent-based simulation occur simultaneously, but the computer is sequential, appropriate decisions must be made about sequencing and interval times.

In many papers there is a lack of cohesion between the theoretical propositions put forth and the model that is eventually developed. A simulation model is indeed the codification of a set of theoretical propositions, and in that sense is no different than the operationalization given to a set of survey items representing a construct. Researchers must pay careful attention to the alignment of their propositions, and the corresponding assumptions and boundaries of their theories, and the operationalization of those propositions, assumptions, and boundaries in the form of a simulation model.

In many ways the domain of the simulation model is much more limiting and constrained than the domain of theoretical propositions and assumptions. There are some things that simulation simply cannot do effectively; some concepts are not well addressed by computer modeling. In such instances it may be more effective to work backwards, that is, use the developed simulation model to suggest how specific theoretical propositions should be framed and stated.

Another problem often associated with the conceptual design of a simulation model is its relationship to reality – again a problem of aligning the research questions to the model. This is not to say that the model should attempt to mimic reality – that would be self-defeating. Rather, the modeler should make choices about the simulation that make it more realistic, thus enhancing its potential validity and generalizability. For example, a simulation model of behavior in a cross-functional team can use a model that differentiates the agents in an essentially "blind" and uninformed manner; alternatively, one can specify what functions would realistically be working together, and then differentiate them in a specific manner that relates to what we know about such differences from other studies and theories.

CODE DEVELOPMENT

The computational model is implemented in software code and tested. Today, simulation languages exist that enable the user to write statements that then refer back to lower-level computer languages such as Fortran or BASIC. These second generation languages reduce the amount of code that needs to be developed by an order of magnitude, or more. Even more sophisticated software packages enable a user to construct a simulation model completely using click, drag, and drop objects on a computer screen. In general, the more user-friendly the modeling environment, the more complexity is hid from the user and therefore difficult to access, if indeed such complexity is needed. Most research projects require the flexibility of the more general languages.

One problem present in many simulation studies is a lack of discipline concerning the development of what often turns out to be a complex and very large software project. There is a lack of appreciation for the software development process; indeed researchers typically believe that all is required to "get going" is to learn the intricacies of the particular simulation language. For small models this might suffice, but for large models an ad hoc development process is more likely than not to lead to significant errors (which may or may not ever be discovered), thus leading to loss of productivity and/or validity.

Researchers involved in the development of large simulation models should follow basic software development practices (McConnell, 1997):

- Maintain a documented set of requirements.
- Implement a change control process, whereby changes to requirements and/or code are documented, dated, and explained; and a corresponding document (or version) control process.
- Develop the architecture independently of the features of the model, to the extent possible.
- Reuse code (that has been validated for its quality) whenever possible. Write code for future potential reuse.
- Develop code in a modular fashion, to the extent possible, so that it can be easily reused, tested, and integrated.
- Use a variety of testing methods, including code walk-throughs, scenario testing, and user testing.
- Develop a project plan for coding and testing.
- Use trained personnel only.

VALIDATION

A simulation might be technically without error – but it may have no truth, or validity associated with it. Model validity concerns how close the computed behavior is to the "real" answer. In some cases there is no real answer and validity can only be determined "at face," by an expert – do the results make sense? Sometimes though there may be actual quantitative behavior that can be compared to. There are three ways in which the computational model can match quantitative system history – exactly, distributionally, or pattern-wise. Since most simulations involve random variables, one rarely seeks an exact fit. A distributional fit means that a variable of interest demonstrates the same mean and covariance structure as seen in reality. A pattern-wise fit means variables are generally related to one another in a valid manner, but their actual numerical values have no relationship to real behavior. Validity checks are too often found missing from computational studies of social systems.

EXPERIMENTAL DESIGN

The user must design a set of experiments, indicating particular initial and run-time parameter values that will be used to determine answers to questions posed. This is another area where there is often a mismatch between the goals of the research embodied in the research questions and theoretical propositions, and the operationalization of that in an experimental design. There is considerable room for improvement of rigor and use of state-of-the-art methods in organizational studies. At the present time I am hard-pressed to find even a single example of high quality, let alone exemplary experimental design in the organizational studies area. The dominant mode of experimentation in such studies is "one-variable-at-a-time," which is known to be a woefully inadequate methodology (Box et al., 1978), incapable of determining interactions between variables, and dismally inefficient.

Researchers should be drawing from the family of experimental designs known as full and fractional factorials, and other similar experimental design models (Box et al., 1978). These experimental designs enable the researcher to examine the effects of specified variables in a cost effective manner. They also generate data that is "optimized" for ease of analysis and interpretation (e.g. estimated statistical effects of variables are independent). Additionally, researchers should differentiate experimental variables into control factors and nuisance factors, and use Taguchi's methods – or variations thereof; see Dooley and Mahmoodi (1992) for example – to determine robustness of their results. Good experimental design not only makes the discovery process more efficient, but it makes analysis easier ("cleaner"), and gives one the potential to begin to see quasi-nonlinearities (in terms of variable interactions).

IMPLEMENTATION

The user must execute the experimental design, which will likely include replicates; a replicate is a multiple-run of a single experimental condition, but using a different stream of random numbers. There are various ways of managing random number streams associated with the stochastic elements of the model that make it more or less easy to make comparisons (Law and Kelton, 1982). Another issue that must be addressed is the transient behavior of the simulation. When a simulation model begins to run, it is initialized to some starting condition (often randomly). There is a period of time when observed the observed behavior is overwhelmingly due to the particular initial configuration – this data should be ignored, unless one is specifically interested in transient behavior. It is assumed that after some time, the simulation behavior will reach a "steady state," whereby further observation is unlikely to yield new information. First, researchers should be aware that there are sophisticated methods that can be used to determine when transient conditions have curtailed. Second, the notion of "steady-state" was developed in a world of equilibrium-based systems, and therefore may have not as much relevance (or more specifically, a different type of relevance) for complex, nonlinear models such as found in agent-based models.

ANALYSIS

Replicates are averaged over an experimental condition for subsequent analysis, and the standard error of replicates can be used to determine confidence intervals for other subsequent work. The user analyzes the output data according to the model being hypothesized.

Again, practice in the organizational research area lags behind other disciplines with respect to analysis of simulation results. Often, no statistical analysis is done at all – a graph of the time-oriented behavior for the different experimental cases is shown. This is adequate for system dynamic models that are completely deterministic (and thus there is not uncertainty associated with the outcomes), but it is not adequate for simulations with stochastic components. Under such circumstances, several "problems" might exist that should be addressed by appropriate and powerful statistical techniques:

- There may be correlation between the averages of different replicates, thus necessitating the need to take into account the covariance structure when doing hypothesis testing.
- There is almost certainly correlation between the different variables of interest within a single replicate. This correlation structure should be analyzed and understood. Coupling this issue to the previous statement, researchers may need to use techniques such as MANCOVA in order to appropriately analyze their results.
- Transients (temporal behavior that is solely due to the initial configuration of the simulation) should be identified and removed.
- There is almost certainly autocorrelation within many of the variables temporal behavior. This does not cause a problem with calculation of the mean, as the mean is unbiased by such dynamical behavior. Variance estimates, however, are likely to be inflated and thus make comparisons more difficult. The autocorrelation structure of the corresponding time series should be taken into account when making a variance estimate.
- To go further, this autocorrelation structure should be analyzed as an outcome of the simulation itself. Knowledge of internal dynamics may well inform the researcher of generative mechanisms that would otherwise be blind to them (Dooley and Van de Ven, 1999).

INTERPRETATION

Observations from analysis are noted, and results are discussed in order to sense-make. A common mistake is over-interpretation of the results, as the researcher attempts to link the simulation results back to the theory(ies) of interest.

Conclusions

Simulation is a powerful research method that enables researchers to look at an artificial world move forward into the future, giving the user the unprecedented opportunity to intervene and attempt to make improvements to performance. As such it is a laboratory, safe from the risks of the real environment, for testing out hypotheses and making predictions.

For organizational researchers, simulation can be used as a theory testing mechanism, although it is perhaps more frequently and successfully used in this domain as a theory building mechanism. Whereas other research methods discussed in this book help researchers answer questions such as "What happened? Why? How?", simulation is best used to answer the question "What if?"

Three different approaches to simulation modeling have emerged over time. Discrete event simulation is historically the most common, and assumes the organizational system can well be described as a "machine" where inputs (entities) arrive and are transformed (by events) into outputs (entities). Uncertainty associated with "real life" is implemented in the form of random variables. Discrete event simulation is good for studying the more mechanical, predictable, and orderly elements of the organization.

System dynamics models also treat the organizational system as somewhat mechanical, and perhaps even deterministic. To the extent that one can describe an organization by its constituent states and their interrelationships in terms of rates, system dynamics offers a rich modeling paradigm. Corporations oft use system dynamic models for strategic planning purposes, but rarely do such efforts reach the light of day of the public. Researchers would be best to use system dynamic models for specific purposes and instantiations; its usefulness on "generic" problems is marginal. Therefore, if one was going to study "organizational learning" using system dynamics, one would be much more likely to obtain useful results if the developed model came from observation of a real organization. System dynamic models that are created abstractly rarely inform.

Agent-based models treat the organizational member as all-important, and expect that organizational behavior will somehow emerge from the coupled interactions of organizational members. These models borne from artificial intelligence have merged with complexity science to offer a more complete and theoretically sound landscape within which to develop interesting and informative models. Agent-based models are probably best suited to answer the typical questions that organizational researchers have; they also probably have a steeper learning curve, as the field is still relatively young.

I have made editorial comments in this chapter noting the disparity between the state-of-the-art in simulation research, as exhibited in other disciplines such as operations management, industrial engineering, and computer science, and current practice in the organizational research area. In particular, organizational researchers must pay much closer attention to the following issues:

- Alignment of theory and model
- Testing of code, and disciplined project management of the simulation (software) development process
- Validation of model and results
- Rigorous experimental design
- Appropriate and rigorous statistical analyses.

I hope this overview increases the frequency and rigor of simulation research in the organizational sciences.

Acknowledgments

This work in part has been sponsored by the *Laboratory for Organization, Communication, and Knowledge Studies* (LOCKS), at Arizona State University.

References

Anderson, P. (1999): "Complexity theory and organization science", *Organization Science*, 10, 216–32.

Axelrod, R. (1997): "Advancing the art of simulation in the social sciences," Santa Fe Institute paper no. 97-05-048.

Axtell, R. (1999): "The emergence of firms in a population of agents," Santa Fe Institute paper no. 99-03-019.

Bonini, C. P. (1963): *Simulation of Information and Decision Systems in the Firm*. Englewood Cliffs, NJ: Prentice-Hall.

Box, G., Hunter, J., and Hunter, W. (1978): *Statistics for Experimenters*. New York: Wiley and Sons.

Brown, S., and Eisenhardt, K. (1998): *Competing on the Edge*. Cambridge, MA: Harvard Business School Press.

Cooper, R. G. (1993): *Winning at New Products*. Reading, MA: Addison Wesley.

Dooley, K., and Corman, S. (2002): "Agent-based, genetic, and emergent computational models of complex systems," *Encyclopedia of Life Support Systems* (EOLSS), L. D. Kiel (ed.), Oxford, UK: UNESCO/EOLSS Publishers.

Dooley, K., and Mahmoodi, F. (1992): "Identification of robust scheduling heuristics: Application of Taguchi methods in simulation studies," *Computers and Industrial Engineering*, 22, 359–68.

Dooley, K., and Van de Ven, A. (1999): "Explaining complex organization dynamics," *Organization Science*, 10, 358–72.

Eoyang, G., and Dooley, K. (1996): "Boardrooms of the future: The fractal nature of organizations," in C. A. Pickover (ed.), *Fractals Horizons: The Future Use of Fractals*, New York: St. Martin's Press, 195–203.

Forrester, J. (1961): *Industrial Dynamics*. Cambridge, MA: Productivity Press.

Goldstein, J. (1998): "Glossary," in B. Zimmerman, C. Lindberg and P. Plsek (eds), *Edgeware*, Irving, TX: VHA, 270.

Holland, J. H. (1995): *Hidden Order*. Reading, MA: Addison-Wesley.

Law, A., and Kelton, D. (1982): *Simulation Modeling and Analysis*. New York: McGraw-Hill.

March, J. (1991): "Exploration and exploitation in organizational learning," *Organization Science*, 2(1), 71–87.

McConnell, S. (1997): *Software Project Survival Guide*. Redmond, WA: Microsoft Press.

McKelvey, B. (1997): "Quasi-natural organization science", *Organization Science*, 8, 351–80.

Rushkoff, D. (1996): *Playing the Future*. New York: Harper-Collins.

Senge, P. (1990): *The Fifth Discipline*. New York: Doubleday.

Sterman, J., Repenning, N., and Kofman, F. (1997): "Unanticipated side effects of successful quality programs: Exploring a paradox of organizational improvement," *Management Science*, 43, 503–21.

Waldrop, M. (1992): *Complexity*. Carmichael, CA: Touchstone Books.

Walker C., and Dooley, K. (1999): "The stability of self-organized rule following work teams," *Computational and Mathematical Organization Theory*, 5, 5–30.

Chapter Thirty-seven

Grounded Theory Research Methods

DEBORAH DOUGHERTY

Grounded Theory Building Research: Some Principles and Practices

The purpose of qualitative research is to delineate some of the essential qualities of complex social phenomena. Many concepts in organizational theory, such as learning, replicating routines, power, authority, dynamic capabilities, or chaos, involve intricate webs of causes, effects, processes, and dynamics. Qualitative analysis characterizes these intricate webs so we can appreciate what a phenomenon is really like in practice, how it works, and how it is affected by other patterns in the organization. Qualitative research is based on the principle that social life is inherently complex, which means that organizational issues are inextricably bound up in ongoing social action among people in the situation (Geertz, 1973; Giddens, 1979; Strauss, 1987; Azevedo, this volume). People are continually making sense of and enacting organizational life by interacting with each other and by invoking taken-for-granted practices and understandings. Organizational issues are sticky, or connected with, part of, and influential on the context. The goal of qualitative research is to capture the essence of these sticky inter-relations for a particular research purpose.

This chapter summarizes my approach to the qualitative analysis of complex organizational phenomena, which is grounded theory building. Grounded theory building (GTB) *builds theory;* it does not test or verify theory. GTB theories capture the inherent complexity of social life by conceptualizing organizational issues *in terms of* their interactions with the context of practice. The goal of grounded theory is to tease out, identify, name, and explicate themes that capture the underlying dynamics and patterns in the blooming, buzzing confusion that is organizational life. GTB reaches into the "infinite profusion" (Weber, see Giddens, 1971) of social action in organizations to sift out the gist of a particular phenomenon. GTB is a way to understand why and how structures, conditions, or actions might arise, to ferret out generative mechanisms (Van de Ven and Polley, this volume), to explore conditions under which their effects might change or stay the same, and to qualify their temporary and emergent aspects.

The inconsistencies in some organizational theories and the limited variance that many theories explain indicate that these theories need to be re-fashioned, indeed re-grounded, to capture a richer, more realistic understanding of ongoing organizational action. Grounded theory building is a way to systematically capture richer, more realistic understandings. The method therefore contributes significantly to the quality and to the reach of organization studies.

The goal of this chapter is to articulate, in a pragmatic fashion, both the promises and the challenges of GTB for the field of organization studies. A hands-on emphasis is useful two reasons. Epistemological discourse provides important information about the underlying logics of this kind of study, and the knowledge it develops and why (see Azevedo, this companion). Methods literature reviews highlight core differences between, boundaries around, and possible connections among various approaches. But a pragmatic discussion, like grounded theory building in general, provides additional insight by illustrating the approach's contribution to organization studies within the actual flow of everyday research practice. Moreover, my basic argument is that grounded theory building brings important (and I think essential) capabilities to the field, but to realize its potential the community of researchers as a whole needs to address the challenges GTB faces. These challenges are not particular to this method, but reflect growing pains for organization studies overall as the field attempts to mature. Rather than exhort organization researchers to "do something," this hands-on emphasis allows me to suggest several particular practices through which we as a community can address certain challenges of both GTB and organization research more generally.

Four Principles for GTB

Even a practical description of a research approach begins with a general conceptual framework for two reasons. First, putting our conceits aside for a moment, many organization theorists know very little about qualitative methods. Few receive the same extensive training in qualitative methods as they do in quantitative ones, and so may unthinkingly apply inappropriate or irrelevant research principles to the development or peer review of a grounded theory study. While general values for good research may apply to all methods, grounded theory's particular techniques for choosing a topic, gathering and organizing data, carrying out the analysis, and drawing systematic inferences differ fundamentally from the familiar techniques of theory testing research in which most people have been trained. A research effort based on mixed up principles may result in less than sensible or useful results. Second and more pragmatically, any research is a complex enterprise, and researchers become stuck and confused. The principles map this particular terrain, helping to identify problems and alternate possibilities.

Table 37.1 outlines four principles that guide grounded theory building research so it captures the inherent complexity of social life in an effective, useful manner. The table also notes the research task(s) that each principle in particular illuminates, and two rules of thumb that connect each principle to research practice.

Table 37.1 Principles that guide GTB research

Principles	Research tasks addressed	Rules of thumb for applying principle to research practice
GTB should capture the inherent complexity of social life.	Kinds of research questions asked How questions are examined	Rule 1: Explore unique characteristics of a phenomenon. Rule 2: Look for social action that underlies manifest structures.
The researcher must interact deeply with the data.	Kinds of data to be gathered, and how analysis proceeds	Rule 3: Data must reflect, convey social action, meaning. Rule 4: Subjectivity cannot be eliminated
Grounded theory intertwines research tasks: Each is done in terms of others.	How the analysis unfolds	Rule 5: Ground problem statement in the phenomenon. Rule 6: The analysis process determines what data to get, how much data.
GTB stands on its own merits.	All of the above, plus how to write up research	Rule 7: GTB should not be confused with exploratory or pre-testing studies. Rule 8: "Validity" and "reliability" depend on coherence, consistency, plausibility, usefulness, and potential for further elaboration.

PRINCIPLE 1: GTB SHOULD CAPTURE THE INHERENT COMPLEXITY OF SOCIAL LIFE

The first principle re-iterates the overarching perspective for qualitative research: grounded theory building should capture the inherent complexity of social life. This principle frames the research questions and how they are approached, since the subject of this method is always the actual, ongoing organizational phenomena themselves, not theory or constructs about them. GTB *centers on* the blooming, buzzing confusion of social life, going beneath or beyond such constructs as "density dependence," "job satisfaction," "race," or "functional structure," for example, to see what people actually do and think, how they enact such structures, how the many processes in the situation might interact dynamically, and how, why, or under what conditions these enactments might "slip." The object is to create new theory or to elaborate upon existing ones by discovering and articulating core themes and patterns among them that explain the particular organizational phenomenon being studied. Grounded theory is more a "process" than "variance" approach (Mohr, 1982; Langley, 1999; Pentland, 1999), and emphasizes the views of the people in the situation, which is referred to as "verstehen"; see Van Maanen (1979) for a primer on the social self (Strauss, 1987). While some suggest that qualitative research occurs in natural settings (Lee et al., 1999), it is more than that: qualitative research is about what actually goes on as people in the situation understand it.

RULE 1: EXPLORE UNIQUE CHARACTERISTICS OF A PHENOMENON

Exploring unique aspects of the phenomenon helps to capture the inherent complexity of social life because it pushes the researcher to get deeply into the actual situation and try to understand all the nuances, interplay, and connections. Exploring unique characteristics is less about looking at outliers and more about delving into a phenomenon deeply enough to understand how all the issues interact. For example, in his analysis of the Mann Gulch Disaster (a major forest fire in which 13 smoke jumpers died), Weick (1993) delved deeply into unique events, thoughts, and actions of these men in that situation. From that, he produced a general theory of how organizations unravel, what the social conditions of such unraveling are, and how organizations can be made more resilient. In part because he explored the unique characteristics of this event, Weick's theory about the relationships of role structure and meaning takes a variety of possible contingencies into account, and enables us to think about the unraveling of structure when these and other contingencies might vary. Capturing unique events in general terms reflects deepness.

RULE 2: LOOK FOR SOCIAL ACTION THAT UNDERLIES MANIFEST STRUCTURES

Second, look for the social action that underlies apparent order and generates unique, complex variations. "Social action" refers to the patterns of thinking and acting that are collectively meaningful to people in the situation, and includes the interactions through which people generate and enact shared interpretive schemes, those schemes themselves, and the frameworks of roles, rules, procedures, routines, and so on that embody meanings (Weber, 1947; Hinings et al., 1991; Barley, 1996). In other words, how is the situation meaningful to those in it, what is the structure of these meanings, and why do these particular meanings hold sway? I emphasize interpretive schemes, but one might study other kinds of social action such as grammars (Pentland and Reuter, 1994) or the variety of ideas that constitute feminist approaches (Calas and Smircich, 1996). My point: get past a construct and its presumptions of order, and explore the actual social order in practice. GTB does not assume that a certain structural element or condition will operate in the theoretically proscribed manner, since people can understand that element or enact it in surprisingly diverse ways. The complexity of social life tells us that many organizational issues have an emergent quality, since any instance of a general phenomenon may be a unique, contingent actualization of it (Sahlins, 1985). Suchman and Trigg (1993) emphasize "situated action," which means that people do not plan actions and then follow through without reflection, but rather are guided by partial plans that are locally contingent.

For example, one might theorize that the more an organization relies on specialized labor, the more knowledge it can absorb. A theory testing study would measure specialization and knowledge absorption, and then correlate the two. Grounded theory building seeks to understand how, why, and under what conditions does specialization lead to knowing more, and to develop a theoretical understanding about the underlying processes and actions. GTB goes past the construct "specialization of labor" to ask how do people understand their own specialization and its relationships to work and responsibility? Do they see their work in terms of the work of the group, or do they insist that their work be translated into the principles of their own specialization before they tackle it (Leonard-Barton, 1995)? What properties of the organizational context affect these understandings? (See also Bailyn and Lynch (1983) who explore how and why engineers are and are not satisfied with their careers over time; these dynamics would also inform an exploration of organizational knowledge.)

One promise of GTB research is that it addresses different research questions. Theory testing research asks whether or not a construct operates, or how much is the effect, while GTB asks how, when, and why. It may be important to know whether or how much something affects something else, but it also may be important to know what that something really is in practice, and how, when, and why its effects occur. This promise also challenges the community of organization researchers to recognize and appreciate the role of these different kinds of questions. How GTB data are gathered and analyzed helps to explicate these different questions.

PRINCIPLE 2: THE RESEARCHER MUST INTERACT DEEPLY WITH THE DATA

The second principle of grounded theory building is that the researcher interacts deeply with the data, carrying out a detailed, microscopic investigation. Some practices for how to engage in a deep interaction with the data are illustrated in the next section, so here I summarize two rules of thumb that guide the development of data for grounded theory building.

RULE 3: DATA MUST CONVEY SOCIAL ACTION

Interacting deeply with the data means that one examines the data closely, looking at minute changes and exploring "what is going on here." The data must enable such close interaction, and usually come from observations, interviews, letters, stories, photographs, archival details, and other text-like material that convey social action. However, a study might incorporate a variety of data types and sources, mingling in abstracted measures perhaps with richer archival accounts and interviews. Provided the researcher can articulate clear, reasonable connections between data and the underlying complex of social action being studied, what constitutes data is open.

I use open interviews to capture people's stories of everyday practice in new product development, because these reflect people's interpretive schemes about customers, technology, and product work (my subjects). To understand connections between behaving and thinking, it would be appropriate to observe behavior as in ethnography, or perhaps to participate in the social action as in participant observation or action research; see Denzin and Lincoln (1998) for one of many overviews of the numerous methods in qualitative research. Hirsch (1986) explored the transformation of corporate governance as takeovers became prominent during the 1980s, by examining the language used in newspaper stories to frame and explain this heretofore unacceptable behavior. Goffman (1979) used photographs in advertisements to delve into how we as a society think men and women behave, reflecting back some important insights about the complex social action of gender. Dougherty and Kunda (1990) used photos of customers in annual reports to explore how the notion of market orientation varied across firms in an industry over time. Each example also details why the data source is appropriate for the purpose.

This rule of thumb means that the data must capture the subject – the actual organizational phenomenon. Consider the study of the processes of knowledge transfer by Szulzanski (1996), or absorptive capacity by Cohen and Levinthal (1990). Rather than gather data that directly reflect these processes and their emergent relations with the social context, these studies used outcome indicators to see if the theorized process was there. Neither study examined the processes directly to see how they actually work, what people understand and do, what else beyond what was measured was going on, and what affected these patterns of social action in what way. These studies contribute by "verifying" that these complex processes of knowing and knowledge transfer are important, and by sorting out some contextual factors. They cannot deepen our understanding of these processes except by ungrounded inference. By the same token, GTB cannot verify that a process exists across diverse settings, nor properly estimate relative importance for some outcome. Both kinds of research do different things in different ways.

RULE 4: SUBJECTIVITY CANNOT BE ELIMINATED

GTB researchers worry about biases from subjectivity, but subjectivity is inherent so eliminating it is not an option. The analysis process is subjective since the researcher must interpret her data in a situated fashion to discern the unique issues or emergent characteristics of the meanings. One reason that grounded theory builders work so closely with their data is to reduce the negative effects of subjectivity, by continually "pushing" possible inferences. Van de Ven and Poole (this volume) summarize many of the subjectivity challenges of field research, and how to work with them.

GTB studies different questions with different kinds of data than theory testing research, challenging organization researchers to develop different standards for research practice. Some concerns about subjectivity arise from the failure to recognize the different research question. Recently, a manager was worried that since I would talk to only some of the people at his plant I might get a biased view of the situation. He thought I would use the data to determine if they (and he) were doing the right things in the right way. Grounded theory building cannot make such determinations. Instead, I was seeking to understand how the issue (in this case, a strategic redirection) was grounded in this particular situation, to explore what people were doing that seems to be working and not, and why and how these processes were unfolding. Standards for judging how well subjectivity is handled are based on whether or not the researcher adequately addressed *these* questions of what, how, and why. However, there are no precisely articulated, recipe-like standards for GTB, which relies instead on the structuring of the research process.

PRINCIPLE 3: GROUNDED THEORY INTERTWINES RESEARCH TASKS: EACH DONE *IN TERMS OF* OTHERS

The third principle frames the overall GTB research process to heighten the researcher's heedfulness about bias and about doing good work in general. As Strauss (1987) argues, the theories and inferences that emerge from this research approach must be plausible, useful, and allow for their own further elaboration. Intertwining the particular research tasks helps to assure plausibility, usefulness, and potential for further elaboration.

Put simply, research comprises four basic tasks: planning the study, gathering the data, analyzing the data, and writing it up. Grounded theory building relies on the parallel development of these tasks, as each proceeds in terms of each other task. Consider an analogy with product innovation, often based on the parallel development of market, design, manufacturing, and other activities which proceed in parallel and which play off of each other (Clark and Fujimoto, 1991; Yang and Dougherty, 1993). In innovation, unfamiliar problems arise constantly and are often most quickly and effectively addressed for the product by working each out in terms of the possibilities and constraints in all the functions. The intertwining of functions limits options, focuses attention on critical performance issues, and otherwise helps to structure the problem.

The same kind of parallel processing structures grounded theory building for the same reasons, and provides checks on the inferences being developed. Planning the study, gathering and analyzing the data, and writing the work up all occur together over time, and each is informed by the other. The problem being studied is unstructured (since the objective is to articulate it), so structure comes from the process of study. As Bailyn (1977) puts it, research is based on a constant interplay between the conceptual and empirical planes. A researcher gathers data to explore a question, but discovers new possibilities in that data and so hypothesizes about this other effect, gathers more data, and thinks through alternate conceptual issues. Similarly, Strauss (1987) argues that grounded theory building combines deduction, induction, and hypothesis testing. The ongoing iterations among the research tasks and processes of deduction, induction, and hypothesis testing help hone insights so that they plausibly represent some aspect of social life, are useful in that they articulate dynamics that were heretofore hidden from view, and can be elaborated further because the deliberate searching through alternate events allows one to articulate possible effects fairly precisely.

RULE 5: GROUND THE PROBLEM STATEMENT IN THE PHENOMENON

The research question or problem should be stated in terms of the phenomenon being studied, since a simple, real question helps one stay grounded empirically. The complexity of social life means that any problem will encompass multiple issues – it will explode out. If the researcher starts with a construct that abstracts issues from the context, the high level of abstraction broadens the scope, so the researcher may be trying to make sense of far too much from far too narrow a purview. For example, examining whether formal versus informal structure inhibits innovation could drop a researcher into a black hole, since the answer to such a question will be "yes and no." We already know that innovation, like any complex work, requires some formal or articulated mapping of roles, relationships, priorities, and responsibilities; see Nord and Tucker (1987) and Jelinek and Schoonhoven (1990) for good examples of GTB. To state this question in terms of the phenomenon in real life as informed by other studies, one asks: What kinds of activities are formalized, how, and why, in successful versus unsuccessful projects? How does formality occur, and how do the various manifestations of formality help to order or disorder the collective work?

One should also frame the question with a thorough literature review of the phenomenon, not a literature review of abstracted constructs about the phenomenon. Glaser and Strauss (1967) warn against becoming so immersed in theory that we miss the real insights in the data. While true, we must be aware that a vast literature already exists for how things actually work, even if a certain construct has received little attention. A good literature summary moves a study past re-invention of the wheel, leverages real wisdom, and connects the work to existing theory so other researchers can make sense of the findings. Pragmatically, the inherent complexity of social life means that the researcher needs some focus and a way to keep generating focus. A good frame helps to make sense of what is seen and maps the way to other studies for more help as the analysis unfolds. The various studies cited in this chapter provide many examples of the use of literature, and illustrate how literature summaries can help justify and specify the question, shape the analysis, help with coding and data display, and draw useful conclusions.

RULE 6: THE ANALYSIS PROCESS DETERMINES THE AMOUNT AND KIND OF DATA NECESSARY

The data are developed as the analysis proceeds. The researcher delves into "what is going on here" in the data, articulates preliminary themes, and creates generative questions about them. He or she then explores these possibilities by examining other events, incidences, or activities in which this theme is likely to occur, proceeding via "theoretical sampling" until the theme or category is "saturated." Theoretical sampling, according to Strauss (1987), is directed by the evolving theory: one samples incidents, events, and actions to compare and contrast them, seeing whether and how the emerging themes actually capture and help understand the social action as it occurs in alternate events and incidences. When additional analyses do not provide any new insights, the theme is "saturated," and the researcher moves on to other themes.

The subtitle for this rule of thumb should be: contrast, contrast, contrast! The data must contain opportunities for multiple comparisons and contrasts among events, incidences, and activities *in order to* trace the potential theoretical theme thoroughly. A good set of data always captures alternate situations or variations of some kind, so that the researcher can see how (and if) emerging insights and their implications actually play out.

Unfortunately, there are no hard and fast standards for how much data one needs for grounded theory building. The answer depends on the researcher's judgment of whether or not the emerging theory plausibly and usefully captures the underlying complexity of the particular piece of social action being examined. Does the theory make good sense of this phenomenon, address the focal question well, and clearly articulate central dynamics – what they are, how they work and evolve, how they interact with other themes? Can the researcher provide a plausible justification for the data: why they fit the problem and are an adequate basis for theory? Were the themes discovered really run to the ground, so to speak? That is, did the researcher go beyond induction to iterate among deduction, induction, and hypothesis generating?

Obviously one cannot study everything about a phenomenon, since any study brackets out a slice of organizational life. But the researcher should both develop a thorough enough understanding of this slice to propose specific, observable, and insightful implications for how it interacts with other aspects of organizing, and present these results coherently. If the best one can do at the end of a study is to make a broad, general call for "more research," then one definitely has not done enough analysis. And the research probably does not have enough data. How GTB presents the analysis and the resulting data of course differs from theory testing work, since the logic of analysis differs. The challenge to the field of organization studies is to develop ways to capture and present the results from this different logic of analysis.

PRINCIPLE 4: GROUNDED THEORY BUILDING STANDS ON ITS OWN MERITS

These principles indicate that grounded theory building is (or should be) very systematic, very carefully executed, and very comprehensively analyzed. Grounded theory building provides unique insights into organizational life and therefore stands (or falls) on its own merits. It is not a prelude to nor subset of quantitative research, and must not be confused with the latter, since it intent is different. Two rules of thumb help to frame the overall research enterprise.

RULE 7: GTB SHOULD NOT BE CONFUSED WITH PRE-TESTING

This rule of thumb drives home the idea that grounded theory building differs fundamentally from the more familiar quantitative work and needs to be judged on its own merits. Quantitative researchers may pre-test an instrument to verify that how they measure a variable makes sense to people, but the variable itself remains given. The purpose of this prelude is quite distinct from grounded theory building. Research designed to verify an instrument does not ask grounded theory building questions, like: Do the variables actually fit the situation? Are they useful in some way to the people involved? How well do they capture the underlying social action? For example, a quantitative researcher in a pre-test might ask if the measures of "union commitment" make sense to people, and measure "commitment" reliably (using quantified techniques for so measuring). A qualitative researcher might ask what "union commitment" really means to people and how it informs, or not, their choices at work and at home. The two are not the same.

RULE 8: "VALIDITY" AND "RELIABILITY" DEPEND ON COHERENCE AND CONSISTENCY, PLAUSIBILITY, USEFULNESS, AND POTENTIAL FOR FURTHER ELABORATIONS

Finally, validity and reliability for GTB on depend on epistemological judgments for how the study is developed, not on the application of particular techniques such as proper sampling, or measures of consistency for indices. Azevedo (this companion) explains that theories are like maps of a particular terrain, and thus "are valid in so far as they enable us to act successfully in pursuit of our interests." She adds that while different maps abstract different features of the territory, to be valid and reliable they should be coherent and consistent with other maps. Or the emerging theory is, as Strauss (1987) puts it, plausible, useful, and allows for its further elaboration. Because of the infinite profusion of social life, no one can explain everything about a social phenomenon, and there may be other explanations or narratives for other purposes; see Van de Ven and

Poole (this volume) for discussion of this idea. The goal is to capture the dynamics and interactions in the situations studied well enough to explain 'what is going on here,' and to generalize from this situation by hypothesizing in clear, specific effects and interactions for other situations.

Unfortunately, there are no widely agreed upon standards for how to judge any of these characteristics of good qualitative research. Moreover, there are many conflicting or incommensurate standards to choose from (Czarniawska-Joerges, 1992; Glaser, 1992). I doubt that agreement upon a single set of standards is useful for qualitative study, or even possible. To be sure, validity and reliability for any good research that addresses the complexities of organizing are judgment calls. My point is that judgment is all grounded theory building has. People in a multi-disciplinary domain like organization studies find it hard to make such complex judgments. It is easier and more comfortable to reject an article because it has respondent bias than because it is not plausible. To help overcome the challenge of judging the merits of a grounded theory building study, the researcher must articulate the study's grounds for validity and reliability sharply, fully, and clearly. The researcher must make a clear, cogent case for why this approach to this question is useful and important, how the analysis was carefully and heedfully done, and how and why the theory being built contributes to our ongoing understanding of organizational life. However, for their part readers, especially editors and reviewers, must learn to hear and understand these arguments, and to appreciate the study on its own merits based on the principles of grounded theory building.

Practices for Analyzing Data for GTB

GTB is also enormously gratifying and very doable, despite the lack of standards, and this section details some practices for it. While all research tasks are important, guides already exist for the overall research approach and how to gather data – e.g., ethnography, case study, clinical analysis, interviews, content analysis, archival studies; see Denzin and Lincoln (1998), and for how to write up the results, Van Maanen (1988) or Golden-Biddle and Locke (1997). Relatively less is written on what to do with the data once you have it, so I develop some practical tips for this aspect of GTB. Van de Ven and Poole (this volume) provide practical tips for mapping out processes and their generative mechanisms from the enormous amount of data from field studies. These GTB practices for data analysis both complement their broad mapping techniques and provide a way to discern underlying mechanisms.

Strauss (1987) outlines three facets of data analysis that I use (and no doubt twist). The facets proceed simultaneously, but the first facet is emphasized more in the beginning of a study, and the last facet more near the end. The goal is to discover and name categories (or as I call them, themes) that capture the pattern of social action that the study is seeking to understand.

1   *Open coding* – finding, labeling the themes or categories in the data. This facet of analysis runs throughout, but in the early stages the researcher tries to generate as many themes as possible, to assure that the data are thoroughly analyzed, and to assure that the analysis is open to what is really going on. Open coding includes what Strauss calls dimensionalizing, or making distinctions within the

theme on such issues as conditions, consequences, interactions, tactics and strategies. One engages in open coding any time a new insight arises, or any time the theme remains less than crisply labeled or articulated.

2   *Axial coding* – intense analysis around one category at a time across the data. The analysis revolves around the axis of one theme at a time, as the researcher checks to see whether and how much a particular theme permeates the data. Axial coding generates cumulative knowledge about the relationships between that theme and others.

3   *Selective coding* – coding systematically and concertedly for the few core themes that best capture, hold together, and/or link up with other themes. As theory building, the object is to arrive at a nice, simple understanding that also accounts for, or is in terms of, the complexity of social life. Selective coding searches for the main concern or problem for people in the setting, what sums up the substance of what is going on in the data. Other themes are subservient to this one: if one "pulls" the core theme out, most of the other important themes will be pulled along with it.

This illustration emphasizes the first facet, open coding, but some selective and axial coding processes are summarized at the end. The study concerns the organizational capabilities that enable sustained product innovation, and this example focuses on one capability: market-technology linking. My basic question: what is the nature of the capability that enables people in organizations to gather the right knowledge about markets and technologies at the right time and put it all together in the right way for multiple products? I cannot review the extensive literature on this question here, but bear in mind that the analysis always is framed by these insights (Dougherty, 1996; Dougherty et al., 2000).

The following example of data represents less than 1 of 8 pages of one interview, from 1 of 125 interviews (or, 0.1 percent of the whole data set). In this excerpt, a marketing manager compares his unit's former, non-effective approach to product development with their current practices:

(Director of market analysis and planning for a small business unit in large textiles manufacturer, comprised of over 50 business units): I came to the business 7 years ago. It had a traditional organization with a director of development and a bunch of engineers, and a marketing manager and salesmen. They would go find customers and get a quote on a product, and bring it back and drop it in a box, and the engineers would pick them up and do them. The salesman would go back to the customer and show it and say is this OK. We were doing hundreds of these costings, and very few would get to the sample stage, and of those very few succeeded. Our hit rate was very low. Bob [unit mgr] recognized that we needed a new organization, so we turned the organization upside down ... The salesmen were horrified if anyone visited with their customers. They would say this is my customer and I have him fat, dumb, and happy. Everything the engineers worked on was screened through the sales people. They never heard the voice of the customer. We had marketing, and engineering teams were doing maintenance work to keep the customer happy.

Then with the new organization we had the new ventures team to do new markets and innovation, and pull in people from across the organization. To see if they will work on this, we would say this is a wonderful opportunity ... You need the right people. We have a variety of people, some people with more leadership than others. I was on the new venture team for years. You need a good basic understanding of some portion of manufacturing – you can't understand all of it. We are really a team – strong in yarn, weaving, chemical engineering. We draw on resources inside the team, really do this in the early stages. For example the luggage project. We did a screen and it looked like a very good idea. We got a list of all luggage and backpacking manufacturers and divided it up and we were all making phone calls. We looked inside to see what resources we had. Team members leave the security of the team and select people cross functionally. We selected a yarn plant and got them involved. We sit down with a plant manager and ask who can I work with. The same thing at the weaving, dyeing and finishing plants. We help them understand the needs and wants, do the QFDs, have manufacturing on the team to help with the QFD, and ask them if they have time to go with me to the customer plant. The development engineers take the process engineers to several customers.

The goal of open coding is to surface a variety of possible themes in the data. To do so, look closely at the data and stick to what is there. Do not make second-hand attributions about psychology or industry effects, or based on imaginary answers to better questions, or anything else that is not in the data. Ask questions like: What is actually happening in the data? What study are these data pertinent to? What are the basic problems faced by the people? What is the main story here (from Strauss, 1987)? Initial analyses are always sentence by sentence, and I typically spend 2 or more hours with assistants analyzing just a few pages of one interview.

The following is verbatim from one page of coding notes on the excerpt above that illustrate our very first "cut" at surfacing and exploring possible themes. Following the notes I go back and "dimensionalize" a few of them to illustrate the coding process:

1   "They would go find a customer and get a quote on a product," physicality of product
2   "drop it in a box," objectified customer needs, turned them into a thing
3   "costings" very narrow criteria, slim view
4   "were doing maintenance work," disconnected from customers, were doing dumb work; a very sequential process.

Compare to the second paragraph:

5   "this is a wonderful opportunity," contrasts significantly with "costings"
6   One student said: I am struck by this being a story of separation plus integration.
7   Unless they focus on customers it is an amorphous world, need a focus to make sense; it is difficult to have cohesion without customer focus.
8   In first para, everything is an abstraction, now a switch in language; before was boxed, bounded; switched to things scattered around and are drawing in, like crystallization.
9   "They never heard the voice of the customer." He invokes front end, and then says, "You need a good basic understanding of manufacturing." This is a starting point and then they anchor in the customer. They can see both ends, and have a grip on the back end and the front end of the process, versus a sequential process in the first para. They "had a basic understanding of manufacturing . . ." – it is an opening, front and back, integration is always possible; it is a dual

thing, they are integrated. They begin to know what questions to ask, like can we do it, solve technical problems. They are asking the right questions, what is feasible. Manufacturing is transformation, not a commodity; they input transformation.

10 "strong in yarn ..." reflects deep interdependencies, organic integration like Durkheim said; it is a moral thing (we read Durkehiem's *Division of Labour in Society* and we were able to draw in common understandings from theory).

11 Technology is created from the skills as applied to the customer, customer satisfaction and technology are deeply enmeshed in each other. These technologies are skill sets, not hardware. (Student drawing on her chemical engineering expertise): These are processes which are flexible, provide an infinite pool of resources, lots of potential; they are not like a refinery or a distillation column, but are in terms of potential. Versus fixed, tangible in first para

12 "You need the right people ..." "We draw on resources." So, maybe humanizing? He never talks about functions, is that it?

13 Resources: good language; people seen as resources; the team connects together the separate skills

Hang on to the research question (the capability for market-technology linking), since any good data will have many insights on lots of issues, and one can bog down easily. This initial cut is entirely provisional, but by thinking through possible themes, one quickly surfaces a variety of ideas that might have bearing on market and technology knowledge.

The first item is about how people linked their product with customers. It struck us that people framed the product and the technology as a physical entity. Strauss's dimensionalizing regime helps to get past the manifest structures to the underlying social action. Consider the conditions of physicality, or why people treated the product as a physical entity. Looking back at the data, we see that the person describes "the traditional organization," or fixed managerial roles that segment bunches of engineers and marketing people. The separation of these functions perhaps reduced technology knowledge to an abstraction? Consequences of the physical nature: they would "go find customers" as if customers are also physical entities that can be matched up to the technology. Physicality makes the linking process physical? In addition, the technology seems given, fixed, closed off like Latour's (1987) "black boxing." As part of the iterative nature of analysis (principle 3), the researchers draw on comparisons including other studies to help surface possible themes. Latour suggests that once a technology has been black boxed, knowledge of how it was developed and why and how to change it are cut off. This insight opens up another seam in the data: how knowledge of technology becomes limited, stilted.

The other three coding items from the first paragraph of the excerpt elaborate upon the objectified nature market and technology knowledge. Both kinds of knowledge are stripped of their nuances and emergent possibilities. Dimensionalizing the idea about narrowness or "slimness" of the criteria suggests the following: conditions – perhaps the sequential nature of the work required an articulated bridge between departments; consequences – since knowledge is stripped away, people cannot judge what should be linked to what. Consider item 4 along with item 1, on the relationship with customers. We inferred that the engineers were disconnected from customers. "Doing maintenance work" suggests that they were not thinking about new approaches to solving customer problems, but rather tweaking existing solutions and products. They were "doing costings," or meeting an abstracted idea of a price quote, not really developing new products.

Comparing coding items 1 through 4 with items 5 through 13 from the second paragraph describing their more effective product development practices demonstrates the power of contrast. Item 5 indicated that labeling the product as a "wonderful opportunity" differed significantly from labeling it as a "quote." Dimensionalizing articulates potential aspects of a possible theme. Conditions: now product developers work in a team to attract other participants rather than process a quote. The work shifts from processing to attracting others. The term "opportunity" presents the work as an important activity perhaps, no longer "maintenance work." The technology becomes an activity, not a fixed, physical thing. Product development itself becomes a full-blown flow of events, not just a "quote" on a piece of paper. Consequences: the more innovative view involves people, while the costing is just an outcome of engineering work. Consider item 11, where we see technology and customer satisfaction "go hand in hand:" analytically perhaps they are mutually constitutive (i.e., one creates the other over time), while in the former approach the link between technology and the market was like sticking things together.

Just these few coding ideas on this tiny fraction of the data indicate very different views of "the market," of working with customers, and of the meaning of the product and the technology. I usually continue with open coding for a number of weeks or months (with bi-weekly coding sessions), looking at different interviews in this company, in other innovative companies, and in less innovative companies. After each session I write up an analytical memo to summarize our thinking along with the original coding notes. This process generates many possible themes, hones others, and transforms yet others.

A combination of axial coding and just plain iterating back and forth between the empirical and theoretical planes led us to identify possible core themes – those few that capture much of what is going on, and which become the theory. One possible core theme is "work is defined as relationship with customer," which emerges when we compare the second paragraph with the first, since working with customers is central to effective innovative work but not to ineffective work. This relationship is embedded directly in their day-to-day work, and seems to ground their efforts, framing the work so that numerous nuances and possibilities can be considered. Also in this brief paragraph and our preliminary analysis are several ideas that suggest tensions between market and technology. Item 6 in our notes is about a ". . . a story of separation plus integration," suggesting that both go together in juxtaposition. Item 8 suggests "crystallization" as a metaphor. The dynamics of linking market and technology knowledge are clearly different: sequential and disconnected in the non-effective approach, but transforming and creative in the effective one. We eventually realized that the "linking" relationship was one of sensemaking (Weick, 1995), or iterating between intersubjective sense from working with customers and technology on the one hand and generically subjective sense captured in rules for business and opportunity on the other. This core theme captures a number of ideas from the open coding, connects with literature concerning tacit versus articulated knowledge, and redefines the relationship as juxtaposing, not just balancing or translating. Other core themes include how knowledge itself was framed at different levels of innovative action. Each of these core theme possibilities is subjected to axial and selective coding, to see if they hold across the data and through the situation, respectively, and to fully ground them in these data.

The process can be aided with various computerized techniques (the researcher must always interact deeply with the data since a computer cannot, but the computer can help store ideas, flag possibilities, and surface patterns). The data analysis process is onerous, exacting, time consuming, but robust and systematic if done right. Also if done right, one can readily produce some frequency counts, and even generic indicators of core themes. For a particular example, Dougherty and Heller (1994) used content analysis to enumerate problems and solutions with new product development across 134 interviews to help analyze the illegitimacy of innovation (their core theme). The frequency counts helped to display the idea that innovation was illegitimate, and allowed the researchers to examine different relationships in the data that might not be obvious otherwise. Other studies cited here used a variety of techniques for counting, displaying, and categorizing the data.

Conclusion

I have focused on how to deliver the unique promises of GTB by presenting some principles and practices for defining questions, developing and analyzing data, and formulating grounded theory. Each and every one of one the rules of thumb here can be extensively critiqued along a variety of epistemological or ontological dimensions, and such philosophical wrestling is important. Staying in the practical realm, however, this essay also highlights some challenges in the practice of GTB that prevent its promises from being exploited fully. I suggest that the same challenges may prevent organization research in general from addressing the complexities of organizational action fully. Grounded theory researchers must of course do good work and present their work fully, cogently, and coherently, but the onus cannot be only on a subset of researchers if the whole field is to benefit. The rest of the organization research community must also work hard to judge these studies appropriately, and to leverage their findings usefully. I briefly outline three areas of practice through which the field as a whole can advance both grounded theory building and research more generally.

One area of practice that needs to be developed concerns framing research questions, and more generally articulating the purpose of the study. GTB does not ask whether or not, but rather examines how, when, and why. GTB therefore fits into the literature a bit "sideways," since theory testing work tends to emphasize theories by themselves, while GTB studies reflect how a number of theories and constructs might affect a phenomenon being studied. This uncomfortable fit prompts GTB researchers to be a bit vague about the purpose and point of the study. We must do a better job of clarifying the particular contribution of our research and of explaining crisply why that is important. However, the field needs to maintain a rich view of our subject (organizations), and keep the phenomena in our research framing. A dialogue about how to ask questions, how to connect issues, and how to approach real organizational problems would be a good start. As well, every study, regardless of approach, should be expected to articulate its contributions and limits for understanding actual practice (which may have little to do with the often rather vague "implications for managers" sections). Research that tests alternate theories against each other rather than against a null hypothesis would strengthen our understanding of phenomena. Theory journals that contrast grounded theory building with deductive theory building, rather than exclude GTB because it is empirical, would advance the practice of theorizing significantly.

The second practice the field needs to develop more fully concerns data presentation and display. One of the major advantages of GTB is its sheer depth and breadth of analysis as an idea is literally run to the ground. However, demonstrating this depth and breadth is a real challenge, and any three grounded theory builders use three wildly distinct approaches. I have no particular solutions, except that some so-called "standards" do not fit all data or all purposes. One approach at the problem is to ask how can the more familiar data display approaches better convey the complexities of organizational life, and then try to build from there into the qualitative realm. Another approach is to ask consumers of research what they need to know in order to feel that the results are plausible, useful? These questions push us to articulate and debate openly what we need from all studies in order to make the complex judgments we actually make about them.

The third practice we need to work on is writing up studies. The linear, step-by-step presentation of the entire study – theory, data, results, or data, results, theory – seriously misrepresents how GTB actually occurs (principle 3, intertwined). However, presenting the study as it actually unfolded, in a complex spiraling over time among theory, data, questions, answers, and write-ups, can be very confusing. Some GTB writers put theory at the end as if it were inducted, even though they surely used some theory to frame the study. While other GTB writers properly go back and forth (Weick is a master), most of us cannot pull this off very well. The onus for making a case for a study is on the researcher. However, thoughtful dialogue and debate about how to present the whole study among writers and readers of all approaches would help to clarify expectations, sort out plausible options, and place responsibility more properly on the field as a whole.

Grounded theory building makes unique and important contributions to organizational analysis by providing a way to generate theories that really reflect how the subject of interest works in practice. Like any research, grounded theory building is systematic, is framed and ordered, draws on complex skills learned through experience, and is deeply informed by a social science discipline (for me, sociology, for others communication, social psychology, political science). One perhaps can achieve similar theoretical insight through abstracted and imaginative induction or deduction. But GTB provides a more systematic, and to me a more sensible, approach to building good organization theory.

References

Bailyn, L. (1977): "Research as a cognitive process: Implications for data analysis," *Quality and Quantity*, 11, 97–117.

Bailyn, L., and Lynch, J. (1983): "Engineering as a life-long career: Its meaning, its satisfactions, its difficulties," *Journal of Occupational Behaviour*, 4, 263–83.

Barley, S. (1996): "Technicians in the workplace: Ethnographic evidence for bringing work into organization studies," *Administrative Science Quarterly*, 41, 404–41.

Calas, M., and Smircich, L. (1996): "From 'the women's' point of view: Feminist approaches to organization studies," in S. Clegg, C. Hardy, and W. Nord (eds), *Handbook of Organization Studies*, London: Sage, 218–58.

Clark, K., and Fujimoto, T. (1991): *Product Development Performance*. Boston: Harvard Business School Press.

Cohen, M., and Levinthal, D. (1990): "Absorptive capacity: A new perspective on learning and innovation," *Administrative Science Quarterly*, 35, 128–52.

Czarniawska-Joerges, B. (1992): *Exploring Complex Organizations*. Newbury Park: Sage.

Denzin, N., and Lincoln, Y., (eds) (1998): *Collecting and Interpreting Qualitative Materials*. Thousand Oaks, CA.: Sage.

Dougherty, D. (1996): "Organizing for innovation," in S. Clegg, C. Hardy, and W. Nord (eds), *Handbook of Organization Studies*, London: Sage, 424–39.

Dougherty, D., and Heller, T. (1994): "The illegitimacy of successful product innovation in established firms," *Organization Science*, 5, 200–18.

Dougherty, D., and Kunda, G. (1990): "Photograph analysis: A method to capture organizational belief systems," in P. Gagliardi (ed.), *Symbols and Artifacts: Views of the Corporate Landscape*, Berlin: Walter de Gruyter, 185–206.

Dougherty, D., Borrelli, L., Munir, K., and O'Sullivan, A. (2000): "Systems of organizational sensemaking for sustained product innovation," *Journal of Engineering and Technology Management*, 17, 321–55.

Geertz, C. (1973): *The Interpretation of Cultures*. New York: Basic Books.

Giddens, A. (1971): *Capitalism and Modern Social Theory: An Analysis of the Writings of Marx, Durkheim, and Max Weber*. Cambridge: Cambridge University Press.

Giddens, A. (1979): *Central Problems in Social Theory*. Berkeley: University of California Press.

Glaser, B. (1992): *Basics of Grounded Theory Analysis*. Mill Valley, CA: Sociology Press.

Glaser, B., and Strauss, A. (1967): *The Discovery of Grounded Theory*. Chicago: Aldine.

Goffman, E. (1979): *Gender Advertisements*. New York: Harper Colophon Books.

Golden-Biddle, K., and Locke, K. (1997): *Composing Qualitative Research*. Thousand Oaks, CA: Sage.

Hinings, C. R., Brown, J., and Greenwood, R. (1991): "Change in an autonomous professional organization," *Journal of Management Studies*, 28(4), 375–93.

Hirsch, P. (1986): "From ambushes to golden parachutes: Corporate takeovers as an instance of cultural framing and institutional integration," *American Sociological Review*, 91, 800–37.

Jelinek, M., and Schoonhoven, C. B. (1990): *The Innovation Marathon: Lessons From High Technology Firms*. Oxford: Basil Blackwell.

Langley, A. (1999): "Strategies for theorizing from process data," *Academy of Management Review*, 24, 4, 691–710.

Latour, B. (1987): *Science in Action*. Cambridge, MA, Harvard University Press.

Lee, T., Mitchell, T., and Sablynski, C. (1999): "Qualitative research in organizational and vocational psychology, 1979–1999," *Journal of Vocational Behavior*, 55, 161–87.

Leonard-Barton, D. (1995): *Wellsprings of Knowledge*. Boston: Harvard Business School Press.

Mohr, L. (1982): *Explaining Organization Behavior*. San Francisco: Jossey-Bass.

Nord, W., and Tucker, S. (1987): *Implementing Routine and Radical Innovations*. Lexington, MA: Lexington Books.

Pentland, B. (1999): "Building process theory with narrative: From description to explanation," *Academy of Management Review*, 24, 4, 711–24.

Pentland, B., and Reuter, H. (1994): "Organizational routines and grammars of action," *Administrative Science Quarterly*, 39, 484–510.

Sahlins, M. (1985): *Islands of History*. Chicago, University of Chicago Press.

Suchman, L., and Trigg, R. (1993): "Artificial intelligence as craftwork," in S Cahiklin and J. Lave (eds), *Understanding Practice*, New York: Cambridge University Press, 144–78.

Strauss, A. (1987): *Qualitative Analysis for Social Scientists*. New York: Cambridge University Press.

Szulanski, G. (1996): "Exploring internal stickiness: Impediments to the transfer of best practice within the firm," *Strategic Management Journal*, 17, 27–43.

Van Maanen, J. (1979): "On the understanding of interpersonal relations," in W. Bennis, J. Van

Maanen, E. Schein, and F. Steele (eds), *Essays in Interpersonal Dynamics*, Homewood, IL: Dorsey Press.

Van Maanen, J. (1988): *Tales of the Field: On Writing Ethnography*. Chicago: University of Chicago Press.

Weber, M. (1947): *The Theory of Social and Economic Organization*, A. H. Henderson and T. Parsons (eds), with introduction by T. Parsons, New York: Free Press.

Weick, K. (1993): "The collapse of sensemaking in organizations: The Mann Gulch Disaster," *Administrative Science Quarterly*, 38(4), 628–52.

Weick, K. (1995): *Sensemaking in Organizations*. Thousand Oaks, CA: Sage.

Yang, E., and Dougherty, D. (1993): "Product innovation: More than just making a new product," *Creativity and Innovation Management*, 2, 137–55.

Chapter Thirty-eight

Field Research Methods

ANDREW H. VAN DE VEN AND MARSHALL SCOTT POOLE

Studying Processes of Organizational Change

There is a growing interest in understanding how and why events unfold over time as individuals, groups, and organizations change. Process studies of organizational change typically employ many methods of field research. Field research includes a wide variety of methods for studying organizational life in its natural setting with first-hand observations from the viewpoint of a particular individual or group. An extensive literature is available to guide an investigator in conducting field research. This chapter applies some of this knowledge to gain insights on less known methods for studying processes of organizational change in their natural field settings.

Process studies pose a number of challenges that traditionally have received little methodological attention. These challenges include designing field studies so they can address process questions, collecting process data about what happened and who did what when – that is, events, activities, and choices over time – and analyzing these data into coherent and useful process theories. In recent years more attention has been given to methods for conducting field research on process questions (Poole et al., 2000). This chapter takes up the challenges and summarizes some new methods for designing and conducting field research on processes of organizational change.

What Field Research Is and Isn't

In organization science, *field research* involves the study of ongoing organizational life in its naturally occurring settings with first-hand observations from a particular subject's frame of reference (Van Maanen, 1988). A variety of other labels are often used to describe field research methods, including qualitative research, case study, participant observation, ethnography and clinical research. It is useful to clarify distinctions among these related approaches to field research.

Some call field studies "qualitative" (as opposed to "quantitative") research because observations are often presented in a narrative style using descriptive everyday language of the people and organizations observed. We think that the term "qualitative" is misleading, as it implies that field research does not include quantitative data. The sheer volume of qualitative data typically collected in a field study – thousands of pages of field notes of events that were observed over several years – vastly exceeds our human information processing capabilities. Systematic analysis of such a mass of data necessitates a simplifying strategy of coding and assigning numbers to observations. Typically, field research also includes gathering quantitative data on the frequency and distribution of certain behaviors and events using surveys, archival records, or in-depth interviews. As Singleton et al. (1993, p. 321) point out, "What brings these methods together, aside from the desire to describe the social world as subjects see it, is that they always take place *in the field* – in a natural social setting familiar to the subject."

Others have referred to field research as "participant observation" (Whyte, 1984), suggesting that the researcher adopts the partisan perspective of a participant engaged in events unfolding in the natural setting (Schein, 1987). This label is also somewhat misleading. Not only is observation of naturally occurring events common to many forms of scientific inquiry (Johnson, 1975, p. 21), the view that scientific observations can be impartial or detached has been severely discredited (Popper, 1972). Most social scientists now concede that no research is value free; a researcher should therefore disclose his/her values and perspective (Van Maanen, 1996; Calas and Smircich, 1999).

Every act of observing something represents countless choices not to observe other things and perspectives. Any organizational topic or issue can be examined from the viewpoints of many different individuals or stakeholders, some of which are accessible to the researcher, others not. It is difficult, if not impossible, for a researcher to assume an impartial and detached perspective or to obtain a balanced representation of all stakeholders involved in any complex organizational change process. It is better to be explicit about which stakeholder's interests and viewpoints are favored (and accessible) than to be silent or naïve about whose interests are served and ignored in any study. Following this recommendation, field researchers often aim to see organizational life from the perspective of a specific participant or stakeholder in the process. This requires more than a backstage view of reality; indeed, field researchers may actively participate in the lives of the people and situations that they are studying (Singleton et al., 1993).

"Ethnography" and "clinical research" are two other terms frequently used to reflect the basic and applied research ends (respectively) of fieldwork. *Ethnography*, a term derived from cultural anthropology, typically refers to fieldwork conducted by a single investigator who "lives with and lives like" those who are studied for a lengthy period of time (usually a year or more)" to describe their culture (Van Maanen, 1995, p. 5). In contrast, Schein (1987, p. 32) discusses the *clinical researcher*, who is typically hired as a consultant and uses a model of action science to solve a client's problems. The clinical researcher assumes that the only way to understand an organization is to change it through deliberate intervention and diagnosis of the responses to the intervention. The ethnographer in contrast starts with the assumption that the organization is there to be understood and left intact.

Although ethnographers and clinicians have different basic or applied goals, they employ similar field research methods. Schein (1987, p. 57) notes they both have common commitments to scientific rigor in the collection and analysis of data, to learn to observe, to develop relationships with clients and subjects, to listen attentively, to elicit information in conversations and interviews, and to use structured devices for gathering and analyzing data. Moreover, both ethnographers and clinicians seek to understand what is occurring in a given place and time. "What is going on here?" and "From who's perspective?" are the most elementary field research questions, yet the most difficult to answer adequately (Van Maanen et al., 1982, p. 16). Field research begins with close-up detailed observation. The specific and local are sought as a primary database within which patterns may or may not be found. An investigator may enter the field with some general questions, preconceived concepts, and expectations, but is open to revising them based on observations. In the course of field research, clinical and ethnographic roles can become highly intertwined. The field researcher "must be able to function in both the clinical and ethnographic roles, and furthermore, must be highly aware of when he or she is in which role so that neither relationship is fundamentally compromised" (Schein, 1987, p. 29).

In summary, the main objective of field research is to describe organizational life as it unfolds in its natural settings with intimate first-hand observations from a particular subject's frame of reference. An abundant literature discusses how to gain entrée, compose the research team, ask questions, listen, observe meetings and events, take field notes, and transform the field data into a sociological narrative. In particular, we recommend Van Maanen et al. (1982), Whyte (1984), Weick (1985), Schein (1987), Singleton et al. (1993), Denzin and Lincoln, (1994), Van Maanen (1995), and Calas and Smircich (1999). In addition a new journal, *Field Methods*, devoted to "methods for the collection or analysis of data about human thought or human behavior in the natural world" (Bernard, 1999, p. ii) is now available.

Designing Longitudinal Field Studies of Organizational Change Processes

Field studies of organizational change processes pose a number of challenges that have received little methodological attention. These challenges, summarized in Table 38.1, include: formulating the research plan, gathering and tabulating field process data, and transforming observational data into forms useful for analysis. While we discuss these topics in sequential order, they are highly interdependent; designing a particular field study entails many interdependent decisions and tradeoffs.

FORMULATING THE RESEARCH PLAN

THE SUBJECT OF ORGANIZATIONAL CHANGE

Consider the bewildering array of change processes ongoing in organizational life and theories that might be used to explain them. For example, Figure 38.1 shows a typology developed by Van de Ven and Poole (1995) of four alternative process theories for explaining organizational change. To stay in business, most organizations follow routines to reproduce a wide variety of recurring changes, such as adapting to economic cycles, periodic revisions in products and services, and ongoing instances of personnel turnover and executive succession. These commonplace changes within organizations are typically programmed by pre-established rules or institutional routines. They can be

Table 38.1   Key steps, decisions, and suggestions for process research in field studies

Implementation step	Key decision(s)	Suggestions
Formulating the field research plan		
1 The subject	What is organizational change?	A difference in an entity over time
2 The research question	Variance or process research?	Process research is geared to studying how questions.
3 Frame of reference	Who's viewpoint is featured?	Observe change process from a specific participant's viewpoint.
4 Mode of inquiry	Deductive, inductive or retroductive?	Iterate between deduction and retroduction.
5 Conceptual model	Examine one or more models?	Compare alternative models.
6 Observational method	Real-time or historical observations?	Observe before outcomes are known.
7 Source of change	Age, cohort or transient sources?	Develop parallel, synchronic and diachronic research design.
8 Sample diversity	Homogeneous or heterogeneous?	Compare the broadest range possible.
9 Sample size	Number of events and cases?	Focus on number of temporal intervals and granularity of events.
Analyzing Field Process Data		
1 Developing process concepts	What concepts or issues will you look at?	Begin with sensitizing concepts and revise with field observations.
2 Defining incidents and events	What activities or incidents are indicators or what events?	Incidents are observations, events are unobserved constructs.
3 Specifying an incident	What is the qualitative datum?	Develop decision rules to bracket or code observations.
4 Measuring an incident	What is a valid incident?	Ask informants to verify incidents.
5 Identifying events	What strategies are available to tabulate and organize field data?	Apply a mix of qualitative and quantitative data analysis methods.
6 Developing process theory	How to move from surface observations to a process theory?	Identify five characteristics of narrative theory.

analyzed and explained using a life cycle theory of change. At the industry or population level, evolutionary theory is useful for explaining many changes brought on by market competition as the probabilistic workings of variation, selection, and retention processes.

Occasionally, organizations also experience unprecedented changes for which no established routines or procedures exist. They include organizational creation, innovation, turnaround, reengineering, cultural transformation, merger, divestiture, and many other issues the organization may not have experienced. These kinds of novel changes can be

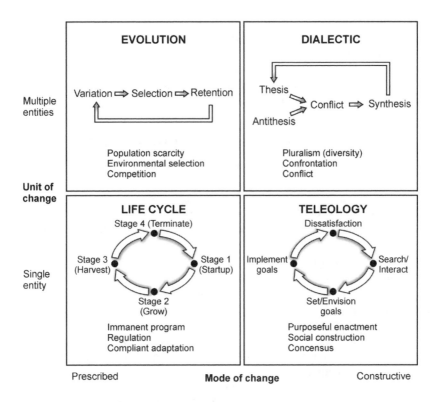

Figure 38.1 Process theories of organizational development and change
Note: Arrows on lines represent likely sequences among events, not causation between events

explained with a planned (or teleological) theory if they are triggered by a frame-breaking goal of powerful people in control of the organization. Alternatively, a dialectical theory might better explain the novel change process when conflicts and confrontations between opposing groups occur to produce a synthesis out of the ashes of the conflict engagements. The processes through which these novel changes unfold are far more complex and unpredictable than routine changes because the former require developing and implementing new change routines, while the latter entail implementing tried-and-tested routines. Novel changes entail the creation of originals, whereas routine changes involve the reproduction of copies. Novel changes represent organizational innovations, whereas routine changes are viewed as business as usual.

Three basic concepts are essential in studying these kinds of organizational changes:

1   a noticeable difference
2   at different temporal moments
3   between states of an organizational unit that is being observed.

Organizational change is defined as a difference in form, quality, or state over time in an organizational entity (Van de Ven and Poole, 1995). The entity may be an individual's job, a work group, an organizational subunit, strategy, or product, the overall organization, or a community or population of organizations. Change in any of these entities can be determined by observing the entity at two or more points in time on a set of dimensions, and then calculating the differences over time in these dimensions. If there is a noticeable difference we can say that the organizational entity has changed. Much of the voluminous literature on organizational change focuses on the nature of this difference, what produced it, and what are its consequences.

RESEARCH QUESTIONS ABOUT ORGANIZATION CHANGE

Studies of organizational change tend to focus on two kinds of questions (Van de Ven and Huber, 1990):

- What are the antecedents or consequences of the change?
- How does a change process emerge, develop, grow or terminate over time?

Although the vast majority of research to date has focused on the "What" question, we focus on and encourage much greater research attention to the "How" question. Process studies are fundamental to gaining an appreciation of dynamic organizational life, and to developing and testing theories of "how" organizational adaptation, change, innovation, and redesign occur.

The "What" question usually entails a "variance theory" (Mohr, 1982) explanation of the input factors (independent variables) that statistically explain variations in some outcome criteria (dependent variables). The "How" question requires a "process theory" explanation of the temporal order and sequence in which a discrete set of events occurred based on a story or historical narrative (Abbott, 1988). In terms of causality, the "What" question requires evidence of co-variation, temporal precedence, and absence of spurious associations between the independent and dependent variables (Blalock, 1972). The "How" question explains an observe sequence of events in terms of some underlying generative mechanisms that have the power to cause events to happen in the real world and the particular circumstances or contingencies when these mechanisms operate (Tsouskas, 1989).

A variance researcher is inclined to decompose organizational processes into a series of input-output analyses by viewing each event as a change in a variable (e.g., the number of product innovations), and then examining if changes in this variable are explained by some other independent variable (e.g., R&D investment). From a variance theory perspective, events represent changes in variables, and these changes are the building blocks of process in an input-process-output model. But since our process question is not whether, but *how*, a change occurred, we first need a story that narrates the sequence of events that unfolded as the product innovation emerged. Once the sequence or pattern of events in a developmental process is found, then one can turn to questions about what the causes or consequences are of the event sequence.

Having distinguished the two questions, it is important to appreciate their complementary relationship. To answer the "What" question, one typically assumes or hypothesizes an answer to the "How" question. Whether implicit or explicit, the logic underlying an answer to a variance theory is a process story about how a sequence of events unfold to cause an independent (input) variable to exert its influence on a dependent (outcome) variable. For example, to say that R&D investment causes organizational innovativeness is to make important assumptions about the order and sequence in which R&D investment and innovation events unfold in an organization. Thus, one way to significantly improve the robustness of answers to the first (variance theory) question is to explicitly examine the process that is assumed to explain why an independent variable causes a dependent variable.

By the same token, answers to "How" questions tend to be meaningless without an answer to the corresponding variance theory questions. As Pettigrew (1990) argues, theoretically sound and practically useful research on change should explore the contexts, content, and process of change through time. Just as change is only perceptible relative to a state of constancy, an appreciation of a temporal sequence of events requires understanding the starting (input) conditions and ending (outcome) results.

FRAME OF REFERENCE TO VIEW THE RESEARCH QUESTION

Field researchers often aim to see organizational life from the perspective of a specific participant or stakeholder in the process. This requires a degree of access and familiarity with key stakeholders that few researchers have been able to develop. Gaining access has been problematic for many researchers because they seldom place themselves into the frame of reference of the stakeholders who sponsor the study or wish to use its results. Typically, managers are key stakeholders of field studies in their organizations. Without observing a change process from the manager's perspective, it becomes difficult for a researcher to understand the dynamics confronting managers who are directing the change effort, and thereby generate new knowledge that advances the theory and practice of managing change. If organizational participants do not understand the relevance of a study, there is also little to motivate their providing access and information to an investigator. At issue here is *not* that researchers become consultants. The issue is one of negotiating and addressing important research questions that capture the attention and motivation of scholars and practitioners alike.

For example, in launching the Minnesota Innovation Research Program (MIRP) (Van de Ven et al., 1989), we found that a useful way to begin formulating a longitudinal field study is to conduct periodic meetings with small groups of managers from various organizations engaged in comparable change efforts or new ventures. In these meetings we discussed the meanings and implications of the research question (e.g., "How and why do innovations develop over time?") and explored ways of studying the question so that it might advance theory and practice from a manager's viewpoint. These meetings produced many useful ideas that guided our research, and many participants also agreed to provide access to conduct the research.

DEDUCTION, INDUCTION, AND RETRODUCTION

Reflecting their styles of inquiry and clarity of the subject matter, researchers can adopt a continuum of strategies that are grounded in theory or data. While *deduction,* a theory-driven approach, is familiar to most readers, *retroduction,* and its relationship to the more popular term, *induction,* may not be. Induction refers to the inference we draw from direct observation of a phenomenon that results in assigning a probability of the likelihood of an occurrence in the future. Retroduction, refers to the inference in which we posit a theory or substantive hypothesis to explain previously observed patterns (Peirce, 1955). Such theory or hypothesis is supposed to go beyond the specific case. Retroduction more accurately describes the research process than induction; and so we use the term retroduction as the opposite of induction.

Taking a deductive approach, the basic steps in designing research might consist of adopting one or more process theories of change (Figure 38.1), developing an operational template for the theory, and then using it to determine how closely an observed process matches the theory. Proceeding by retroduction, the steps might include observing processes of stability and change over time in a few organizational entities, sorting data into meaningful categories, developing propositions explaining the observations, and corroborating them with a different sample or on the same sample at a different time. One could also start somewhere in between, with a partial theory and flesh it out through retroduction and induction.

As discussed in the Dougherty chapter, there is a tight iterative cycle between deduction, retroduction, and verification in grounded theory building studies. Strauss (1987) emphasized that all scientific theories require that they be conceived, then elaborated, then checked.

> "Few working scientists would make the mistake of believing these stood in a simple sequential relationship. . . . Many people mistakenly refer to grounded theory as "inductive theory" . . . All three aspects of inquiry (induction, deduction, and verification) are absolutely essential" (Strauss, 1987, pp.11–12).

In the course of a field research study, most researchers move back and forth between deduction and retroduction. Deduction will raise questions or adventitious observations that lead to retroductive theory building. Retroduction will generate theories that stimulate deductive research.

EXAMINING A SINGLE MODEL OR COMPARING SEVERAL MODELS

Most researchers conduct their field studies with one model or theory in mind. Working with a single model or perspective of change has the advantage of sharpening and focusing data collection and analysis. A single perspective or model is also easier to operationalize and fit to field data. Stinchcombe (1972) argued, in contrast, that having two or more models enables the researcher to make stronger inferences by positing a series of critical tests of assumptions that differentiate the models. Another advantage of comparing alternative models is that null results on one model are less likely to leave the researcher in a cul-de-sac of knowing only what is not the case.

Organizational change processes can be exceedingly complex, and far beyond the explanatory capabilities of any single process theory found in the literature. Typically there are several different perspectives which capture different aspects of the same process and which are equally valuable in understanding it (Pettigrew, 1990). Moreover, when researchers and practitioners have only a single perspective or theory, they tend to twist and rationalize facts to fit their model (Mitroff and Emshoff, 1979). Consequently, we believe it is generally better to develop and juxtapose alternative theories, and then to determine which theory better explains the data or how they can be combined.

This comparative method also facilitates taking a retroductive strategy. It reduces complexity because it is very difficult to analyze a large array of field data without conceptual guidance. This approach emphasizes that testing a process theory should be based the relative explanatory power of alternative theories that are available or that can be developed to explain the phenomena. This comparative approach is consistent with the principle that knowledge advances by successive approximations and comparisons of competing alternative theories (Lakatos, 1978)

OBSERVING PROCESSES IN REAL TIME OR RELYING ON RETROSPECTIVE ACCOUNTS

Because change is defined as an observed difference in an organizational entity over time, the study of organizational change processes necessarily entails collecting longitudinal data. These data can be obtained either by observing the sequence of change events as they occur in real time, or by relying on archival data to obtain a retrospective account of the change process. Most studies of organizational change are retrospective, conducted after outcomes are already known before data collection begins. Retrospective studies provide the advantage of knowing the "big picture," how things developed and the outcomes that ensued. This *post hoc* knowledge is helpful for interpreting events that unfolded, and for constructing a narrative of the process. However, prior knowledge of the outcome of an organizational change also may bias a study. This is especially true if the final assessment valorizes the outcome as a success or failure, effective or ineffective. There is a tendency to filter out events that do not fit or that render the story less coherent, censoring in particular minority views.

A promising approach is to initiate historical study before the outcomes of an organizational change effort becomes apparent. It is even better to observe the change process in real time as it unfolds in the field setting. This approach maximizes the probability of discovering short-lived factors and changes that exert important influence. As Pettigrew (1985) notes, "the more we look at present-day events, the easier it is to identify change; the longer we stay with an emergent process and the further back we go to disentangle its origins, the more likely we are to identify continuities." At one point or another, most field studies of organizational change involve many forms of longitudinal data collection: archival, retrospective, and real time observations.

COMPONENT SOURCES OF CHANGE

In the study of human development, Schaie (1965) discussed three common sources of temporal change:

1 *Age*: The age or temporal duration of the individual at the time of measurement. This variable represents that part of development and change that is produced by unfolding biological or institutional processes.
2 *Cohort*: The set of characteristics of all individuals who are born at the same time and go through similar developmental processes, such as classes in school. This variable represents the common historical conditions that shape the development of a given cohort.
3 *Transient*: All the temporary or immediate and non-cumulative factors that influence outcomes or the dependent variables at the time of measurement.

Organizational change studies should be designed to disentangle these three sources of change. What appears to be a developmental change due to some immanent mechanism could also be due to a cohort effect or to a unique effect at the time of measurement. Taking into account age, cohort and time of measurement as well as organization type and context will result in more effective research designs.

Barley's (1990) exemplar study design, shown in Figure 38.2, permits systematic study of these different sources of change. In his field study of the adoption of a technology (CT scanners), Barley drew comparisons between two parallel hospitals with synchronic (one point in time) observations of different radiology technologies, and with diachronic (repeated over time) observations of CT scanning behavior by radiology department staffs. Reflecting on his study, Barley (1990, p. 227) explains how conclusions become problematic when research questions and comparative design are not matched correctly:

> ... synchronic data may seem to suggest that similar outcomes are rooted in similar processes. However, similar outcomes may arise from different processes and different outcomes may arise from similar dynamics ... Only diachronic data can disentangle such possibilities. By itself, a parallel study of a class of events, objects, or activities may also lead

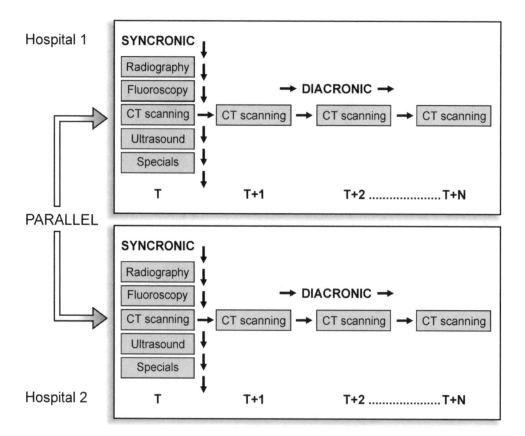

Figure 38.2 Barley's parallel, synchronic, and diachronic research design
Source: Barley (1990)

to wrongful conclusions. Suppose, for instance, that one were to investigate the effects of new technologies by studying CT scanning in a number of hospitals. Even if one found that all CT scanners occasion similar phenomena, one could not be sure whether the findings would apply to all computationally based imaging devices or only to CT scanners. A synchronic analysis of several technologies conducted in tandem could resolve this issue. In other words, the synchronic, the diachronic, and the parallel represent three distinct axes of comparison that, when used in combination, allow researchers to examine explicitly the spatial and temporal boundaries of their claims.

SAMPLE DIVERSITY: HOMOGENEOUS OR HETEROGENEOUS CASES

There is no one best sampling scheme for process research. A homogeneous sample has the advantage of keeping to a minimum the multitude of alternative explanations for developmental processes. This is especially advantageous in the case of lengthy sequences of events, because they are particularly vulnerable to accidental or adventitious occurrences that shift the course of development. Comparing cases that are similar in as many respects as possible facilitates identifying whether change processes are due to such transient events or to more basic developmental models, but does not control for cohort effects. A homogeneous sample also facilitates the development and investigation of very precise, focused questions or hypotheses. Hence homogeneous sampling is useful when a well-specified theory of change or development is available. A broad, heterogeneous sample, however, may provide a better opportunity to detect whether sources of change are due to temporal development, cohort, or transient factors.

The comparative method is perhaps the most general and basic strategy for generating and evaluating valid scientific knowledge. This strategy involves the selection of comparison groups that differ in the scope of the population and conceptual categories of central interest to the research. Kaplan (1964, p. 52) pointed out that scientific knowledge is greatly enhanced when we divide the subject matter into concepts and cases that "carve at the joints" over the widest possible ranges, types, conditions, and consequences. In this way researchers can develop and evaluate the limits of their propositions. Given the tradeoffs between homogeneous and heterogeneous samples, Pettigrew (1990, pp. 275–7) suggests four guidelines for selecting cases to study:

1   "Go for extreme situations, critical incidents and social dramas." By choosing unusual cases, cases that are critically important or highly visible cases, researchers select cases in which the process is "transparently observable." However, such cases may have nongeneralizable features precisely because they are unusual.
2   "Go for polar types." Choose cases that seem very different in terms of the processes under study. For example, compare successful and unsuccessful program startups. Or, choose cases which differ from patterns in earlier cases. By successive sampling of polar types, it will eventually be possible to cover the range of possible cases.
3   "Go for high experience levels of the phenomena under study." Choose cases that have a long track record of experience with a process. This strategy may not be feasible for some cases: new program startups, for example, may best be illuminated by inexperienced agencies, since they will make the mistakes and experience the learning that highlights key requirements for successful startups.
4   "Go for more informed choice of sites and increase the probabilities of negotiating

access." Cases must often be selected on the basis of who will cooperate, rather than on grounds of optimal sampling. As Campbell and Stanley (1963) noted, this introduces a sampling bias that must be considered in drawing conclusions from the study.

SAMPLE SIZE: NUMBER OF EVENTS AND/OR CASES

The central sample size consideration in longitudinal field research is the number of temporal intervals or events on which data are obtained from beginning to end on each case. The number of temporal intervals or events observed depends on what constitutes the "natural" flow of experience in the organizational change cases being studied. Organizational change processes vary in *temporal duration* and *granularity*. In terms of temporal duration, some organizational change processes, such as group decision making, may occur in committee meetings lasting no more than a few hours. Other change processes, such as the development of technological and administrative innovations, may span several years.

Granularity refers to the preciseness or discreteness of events that are recorded throughout the temporal duration of a case being studied. The granularity of events varies greatly, ranging from events of such large scope that only 5 to 20 might be observed over the period of study to events of such small scope that several thousand occur. Event granularity typically increases with the micro-analytic detail of the change process being investigated.

Events that require a great amount of time and effort to observe and code are likely to be observed in shorter sequences than those less costly to observe. Because there are inherent tradeoffs between the temporal duration and granularity of events that can be sampled, most studies of fine-grained events tend to focus on change processes of relatively short temporal duration, while studies of lengthy change processes tend to adopt course-grained events.

GATHERING AND TABULATING PROCESS DATA

Consider the challenge confronting researchers who conduct longitudinal field studies of organizational change processes. During a typical one to five-year study, a researcher might collect quantitative and qualitative data including:

- survey questionnaires completed by all participants every six months
- interviews with key managers and participants every six months
- direct observations of regularly scheduled meetings
- a diary recording frequent informal discussions with participants
- in-house memos and reports, and stories in trade journals or newspapers about the organization undergoing change.

Whatever data collection methods are used to observe change processes in the field or from archival records, over time data mount astronomically and overload the information processing capacity of even the most insightful mind. Drawing careful inferences require methods that go beyond subjective "eyeballing" of raw data to identify patterns.

But it is difficult to reconstruct field methods, because they are rarely reported in detail in published field studies. One cannot ordinarily follow how the researchers arrived at their conclusions from hundreds of pages of field observations, even though the reports may be sprinkled with vivid – yet idiosyncratic – quotes from organizational participants.

PROCESS CONCEPTS

Whether a researcher adopts a deductive, inductive, or retroductive approach the collection of field data requires a set of categories or concepts. These concepts provide selective focus for observing the change process; one cannot study everything, and different categories can produce very different findings. When a particular process model(s) is proposed or known beforehand, category development proceeds deductively by operationalizing theoretical constructs into empirical indicators of those constructs. When a more inductive or retroductive approach is taken, these initial categories are best viewed as "sensitizing constructs" for conducting exploratory research. The categories become clear as they are grounded in field observations. Eventually, these grounded concepts can be codified in a final category system (Dougherty, this volume).

In our Minnesota Innovation Research Program (MIRP), for example, we began with five "sensitizing categories" to study innovation development: ideas, people, transactions, context, and outcomes (Van de Ven et al., 1989). As is typical in longitudinal studies, our assumptions and definitions of these concepts changed substantially and became progressively clear with field observations over time. Table 38.2 compares our starting assumptions of these concepts drawn from the literature at the time, with how we came to view them as a result of two years of field studies (Van de Ven, 1999). The latter disclosed a different reality from the rather orderly and naive conceptions of the former. As this example illustrates, the development of research constructs involves an iterative process of conceptualization, observation, and reformulation.

INCIDENTS AND EVENTS

It is useful to distinguish between *incidents* and *events* when building or testing a process theory (Abbott, 1984). Incidents are empirical observations. Events are meaningful bracketings of the stream of incidents. They are constructions based on more or less systematic interpetations of what is relevant to the process. The stream of incidents, a first-order construction, is translated into a sequence of events, a second-order construction. This implies that some incidents may be embedded in different conceptual domains and utilized as constituents of different events.

Events may differ in temporal and spatial scope, and as a result, incidents may indicate more than one, overlapping event. For example, a meeting with "firm Q" can indicate the event "meeting with a partner," but it may also indicate a longer event, "negotiation with firm Q regarding partnership." Events may be embedded within other different types of events of larger scope. Both levels may be important for understanding the change process, because interleaving narratives clarify it better than either narrative could on its own.

Another complication is the possibility that the incident-event relationship may change over time (Abbott, 1984). The significance of events may change as the process unfolds. The same change is possible in incident-event relations. For example, the first time a

Table 38.2 Evolution of innovation concepts during MIRP

	Starting definitions from literature	*But we see this in field studies*
Ideas	One invention to be operationalized	Reinvention, proliferation, reimplementation, discarding and termination of many ideas
People	An entrepreneur with a fixed set of full time people over time	Many entrepreneurs, distracted, fluidly engaging and disengaging in a variety of roles over time
Transactions	Fixed network of people/firms working out the details of an innovative idea	Explanding and contracting network of partisan stakeholders converging and diverging on innovation ideas
Context	Environment provides opportunities and constraints on innovation process	Innovation process constrained and created by multiple enacted environments
Outcomes	Final result orientation: a stable order comes into being	Final results may be indeterminate; multiple in-process assessments and spinoffs Integration of new order with the old
Process	Simple cumulative sequence of stages and phases of development	From simple to multiple progressions of divergent, parallel, and convergent paths; some are related and cumulative, others not

Source: Van de Ven et al. (1989, p. 11)

potential partner is encountered may signal an expansion of an organizational program, whereas the sixth encounter with a potential partner may signal desperation for ideas or resources. Thus, while events are constructs indicated by incidents, the indication relationship is more complicated for qualitative data than it is for quantitative scores. The assumption of uniformity across respondents and responses in psychometrics and scale theory may not hold for data used to define events. What quantitative analysis would classify as error may be quite important nuances for qualitative data.

DEFINING AN INCIDENT: A QUALITATIVE DATUM

In survey research, a *quantitative datum* is commonly regarded to be

1 a numerical response to a question scaled along a distribution
2 about an object (the unit of analysis)
3 at the time of measurement, which is
4 entered as a variable (along with other variables on the object) into a record (or case) of a quantitative data file, and
5 is subsequently recoded and classified as an indicator of a theoretical construct.

In comparison, we define a *qualitative datum* as

1   a bracketed string of words capturing the basic elements of information
2   about a discrete incident or occurrence (the unit of analysis)
3   that happened on a specific date, which is
4   entered as a unique record (or case) in a qualitative data file, and
5   is subsequently coded and classified as an indicator of a theoretical event.

The basic element of information in a qualitative datum is a bracketed string of words about a discrete incident. Raw words, sentences or stories collected from the field or from archives cannot be entered into a series until they are bracketed into a datum(s). Obviously, explicit decision rules that reflect the substantive purposes of the research are needed to bracket raw words.

In our MIRP studies, the decision rule used to bracket words into a qualitative datum was the definition of an incident that occurred in the development of an innovation. An incident occurred whenever changes were observed to occur in any one of our five core concepts: innovation ideas, people, transactions, context, and outcomes. When an incident was identified, the bracketed string of words required to describe it included: date of occurrence, the actor(s) or object(s) involved, the action or behavior that occurred, the consequence (if any) of the action, and the source of the information. As with any set of decision rules, discussions among researchers were necessary to define innovation incidents in an operationally consistent manner.

Decision rules may vary in the level of specificity and the temporal duration of incidents they construct. Some rules specify fine-grained definitions of incidents that interpret each action as a separate incident; others adopt coarse-grained definitions that require longer episodes for incidents. The proper granularity of incidents depends on the rates of development of various kinds of innovations, and the differing research questions associated with these rates.

RELIABILITY AND VALIDITY OF INCIDENT CONSTRUCTION

It is important to establish the reliability of classifying raw data into incidents. An equally important, though often neglected issue is the validity of this bracketing procedure (Folger et al., 1984; Poole et al., 1987). Researchers often assume that the meaning of incidents is clear and that establishing reliability is equivalent to showing clear meaning of codings. However, attaining reliability among coders simply indicates that the meaning of incidents is clear to the particular group of researchers who designed the coding system, not necessarily to participants or key stakeholders. It is necessary to test empirically whether researchers' classifications coincide with practitioners' perceptions of events. If the evidence indicates inconsistency, then no claims about the meaning of events to the participants are valid. Researchers can still sustain claims about the meaning of the incident from their theoretical position, but no claims about the "social reality" of the event are appropriate.

Two basic procedures can enhance the reliability and validity of incident coding. First, coding of incidents from raw data sources can be performed by two or more researchers. Consensus among coders increases the consistency of interpretations of the decision rules used to identify incidents. Second, incident codings can be reviewed by key organizational informants. It is useful to ask informants if any incidents are missing or incorrectly described.

QUALITATIVE STRATEGIES FOR IDENTIFYING EVENTS FROM INCIDENTS

The next step is to identify theoretically meaningful events from the incident data. Since the temporal sequence of events is a central organizing device for process data, this next step typically consists of identifying the order and sequence of events from observed incident data. Several approaches are available for tacking back and forth between incident data and event sequence categories.

Inductive approaches go first to the data – the incidents – and sift through the various instances, deriving categories from the ground up, using the constant comparative method for identifying concepts from data (Dougherty, this volume). Langley (1999) discusses two additional strategies for making sense of process data:

- *Visual mapping*   As the saying goes, "a picture is worth a thousand words." A diagram of how incidents unfolded by event categories or actors over time is a useful method for organizing incident data. Visual graphical representations permit the compact presentation of large quantities of information, and are particularly useful for analyzing process data because they allow the simultaneous display of a large number of dimensions, and show precedence, parallel processes, and the passage of time. Miles and Huberman (1994) provide many different formats with examples of how these graphical displays might be constructed. Meyer (1991) provides a creative application of visually mapping major changes unfolding at different levels of a health care system.
- *Temporal bracketing*   Various categories of events identified through visual mapping can be arrayed over time by phases, stages, or distinct periods of activities. In their study of technology adoption in small manufacturing firms, for example, Langley and Truax (1994) decomposed decision, activity and context events into three periods: rivalry between projects and management turnover (1987), financial and technical difficulties and union strike (1988), and major project investment stimulated by customers (1989). They observed continuity in the activities within each period and discontinuities between the periods. Importantly, these periods are not "phases" in the sense of a predictable sequential process but simply a way of structuring the description of events (Langley, 1999).

Deductive approaches make use of theory to specify the expected order and sequence of event categories.

- *Template matching*   In this strategy, operational templates of one or more process theories, such as those illustrated in Figure 38.1, are used to determine how closely an observed event sequence matches each theory. Pentland (1999:719) poses an important challenge to template matching by asking: "How can we tell which motor is running?" Many specific theories of organizational change are combinations of two or more of basic "motors" (e.g., life cycle plus teleology in Figure 38.1). The problem is that these deep structures [process theories] are never directly observed. All we have in empirical research is the "surface structure" captured in our observations. This is the problem of construct validation; given some data, what is the underlying construct?

A number of steps can be taken to enhance the reliability and validity of coding incidents into indicators of event constructs or events into higher-order constructs. Operational definitions and coding conventions can be drafted for the coded constructs, and periodic meetings can be conducted with researchers and other colleagues to evaluate the construct validity of these definitions. Van de Ven and Ferry (1980) found that a useful way to conduct such meetings is to begin with an overall presentation of the conceptual model being studied, then specific definitions of each construct in the model are presented along with the measurement indicators to be used. Participants can then be asked to "suggest better indicators for measuring this construct as defined previously." Comments from these review sessions are especially helpful in sharpening correspondence between definitions of constructs and event indicators, and to clarify ambiguities in decision rules for coding event indicators.

- *Synthetic strategy*   Another deductive approach to analyzing process data is to transform sequence data into summary statistics such as: the total number of events in various categories in the entire sequence or in segments of it; or the total number of phases in the process. This "synthetic strategy," as Langley terms it, can then be used to test developmental models with variance analysis. While this transformation is one of the most common in developmental research (Eisenhardt, 1989), caution must be taken to preserve the temporal sequence in observed change processes. Too often the categories that researchers use collapse the data over time, and thereby remove the temporal information that is central to any process story.

Poole et al. (2000) point out that in practice, inductive and deductive strategies are frequently combined in a *retroductive* approach. A literature search is undertaken to derive a scheme for categorizing and coding events, and categories are adjusted in view of what is workable and informative after trying them out on the data. Another common approach is to generate a set of categories based on theory and then refine and adjust them as they are applied to data.

QUANTITATIVE STRATEGIES FOR CODING EVENT SEQUENCE DATA

The foregoing qualitative approaches to ordering and making sense of event process data are useful for identifying and displaying general patterns in event sequence data. However, they only take us so far. Longitudinal field data on organizational change incidents typically far exceed our limited capacity to analyze qualitative data. Further information reduction strategies are often needed to analyze process patterns in the data.

A limitation of many quantitative coding systems is that they reduce rich qualitative data to a single dimension of meaning. One way to organize multidimensional data to analyze change processes is to array them on multiple tracks corresponding to conceptually meaningful categories. The procedure of coding incidents along several event tracks was used in Poole's (1983) studies of decision development in small groups, which coded acts with a three-track coding system that took into account the impact of each incident (a group member's statement) on group work process and group relationships, and also indexed incidents on which of several topics it referred to. By coding each incident on several conceptually relevant dimensions simultaneously, Poole was able to derive a richer description of group processes than previous studies had achieved.

Abbott (1990) describes methods for analyzing sequence, order, and causal relationships in coded event data. They involve different forms of transforming a chronological listing of coded incidents into dichotomous indicators of event constructs. Such transformations of qualitative codes into quantitative dichotomous variables permits applying various statistical methods to examine time-dependent patterns of relations among the event constructs. *Sequence analysis*, a family of methods concerned with the problem of determining the temporal order among events, is particularly useful for such analyses (Abbott, 1984). Analogous to analysis of variance that determines differences or correlations between spatial orders (variables), sequence analysis examines similarities and differences between temporal orders (discrete events).

Poole et al. (2000) review a variety of statistical methods that can be used to identify substantively interpretable time-dependent patterns (or lack thereof) and relationships in event sequence data. These techniques include:

1   stochastic modeling techniques (e.g., Markov and logit analysis) to examine probabilistic relationships between the occurrence of events
2   granger causality and vector autoregression to identify possible causal relationships between dichotomously coded events
3   phasic analysis of temporal patterns in event sequence data
4   linear time-series regression analysis on incidents aggregated into fixed temporal intervals to examine causal relationships among coded event time series
5   a variety of diagnostic procedures for examining non-linear dynamic patterns in event time series.

Other statistical methods are also being explored to examine the temporal duration and sequence among coded events. For example, "renewal theory" can be used to examine whether the duration between two consecutive events in a change process are distributed according to some known probabilistic distribution, such as the exponential or more general Weibull distribution. In addition, Tuma and Hannan (1984) show how "hazard rates" can be computed to determine the likelihood of occurrence of certain coded events based on a set of predictor variables.

FROM EVENT SEQUENCE TO STORY NARRATIVE

The fundamental scientific goal in conducting field studies of organizational change is to develop a *process theory of change*. A process theory needs to go beyond a surface description to penetrate the logic behind observed temporal progressions. This explanation should identify the generative mechanisms that cause observed events to happen in the real world, and the particular circumstances or contingencies when these causal mechanisms operate (Harré and Madden, 1975; Tsoukas, 1989).

Thus, as we move from surface observations toward a process theory, we move from description to explanation (Simon, 1992). Explanation requires a *story*, and stories can be understood as process theories (Pentland, 1999). In narrative theory the story is an abstract conceptual model; it identifies the generative mechanisms at work. At a minimum this story must describe a progression or sequence of events. In narrative theory, however, the 'story' includes a great deal more than just event sequence. In particular, a process theory should include the following features in the story (Pentland, 1999, 712–13):

1 *Sequence in time* Narrative should include a clear beginning, middle, and end. Chronology is a central organizing device. The events or actions referred to in a narrative are understood to happen in a sequence.

2 *Focal actor or actors* Narratives are always about someone or something. There is a protagonist and, frequently, an antagonist as well. The characters may not be developed or even identified by name, but, along with sequence, they provide a thread that ties the events in a narrative together.

3 *Identifiable narrative voice* A narrative is something that someone tells (Bal, 1985), so there should always be an identifiable voice doing the narrating. That voice reflects a specific point of view (Rimmon-Kenan, 1983).

4 *"Canonical" or evaluative frame of reference* Narratives carry meaning and cultural value because they encode, implicitly or explicitly, standards against which actions of the characters can be judged. But even without any explicit moral, narratives embody a sense of what is right and wrong, appropriate or inappropriate, and so on.

5 *Other indicators of content or context* Narrative texts typically contain more than just the bare events. In particular, they contain a variety of textual devices that are used to indicate time, place, attributes of the characters, attributes of the context, and so on. These indicators do not advance the plot, but they provide information that may be essential to the interpretation of the events (e.g., knowing that the scene is a wedding changes the significance of the utterance "I do").

We admit that these five steps in theory building are "easier said than done." Developing a process theory that embodies these features requires considerable ingenuity and creativity in applying the repertoire of methods described in this chapter. Becoming a skillful field process researcher requires repeated use and practice of these methods.

Conclusion

Research design invariably requires the exercise of what Aristotle termed "practical wisdom." There is no definitive best design for a given project, and any design requires giving up some data so as to focus on others. We outlined a number of methods for moving from field data on observed incidents to a process theory that does not betray the richness, dynamism, or complexity of the story. Each strategy reduces some aspect of raw data complexity by focusing on some anchor point for guiding the analysis. Langley discusses the strengths and weaknesses of alternative methods based on Thorngate's (1976) and Weick's (1979) tradeoffs between the *accuracy, generality,* and *simplicity* of any theory.

Some strategies tend to stick closely to the original data, whereas others permit greater abstraction. Close data fitting reflects what Weick (1979) calls "accuracy." However, accuracy may act against generality – another desirable quality related to the potential range of situations to which the theory may be applicable. Finally, simplicity concerns the number of elements and/or relationships in a theory. It affects the theory's aesthetic qualities. Simple theories with good explanatory power may actually be preferred to complex ones that explain a little more; as Daft (1983) suggests, good research is more like a poem than a novel (Langley, 1999, pp. 694–5).

Fortunately, the methods discussed in this chapter are not mutually exclusive. They complement each other. Each method can provide useful information for deciding how and what other methods to use in the next step in the analysis. In this sense, the methods serve as building blocks for developing process theories. Our experiences have been to use all the strategies for analyzing various aspects and questions in the course of designing and analyzing field data on processes of organizational change. In practice our objective is to combine the information that quantitative and qualitative approaches provide for understanding organizational change processes. By themselves quantitative data provide a skeletal configuration of structural regularities, often devoid of life, flesh, and soul. Qualitative data, by themselves, are like an amoeba, rich with life but absent apparent structure. Only by combining quantitative and qualitative data in a balanced way do we come to understand the richness of life in its varied regularities.

We conclude on a personal note. Studying real-time processes of organizational changes through fieldwork has become a normal part of our everyday work lives. A normal working week includes about a day of field work in conducting site visits, interviews, observing meetings and events, and talking to people related to the organizational changes that are unfolding in real time. While frustrating at times, some of our greatest insights have come from field research, and they strongly influenced a growing appreciation of dynamic organizational change processes. These experiences lead us to believe that letting go of initial conceptions and remaining open to new ideas and directions from field observations are fundamental dispositions of field researchers. We recommend undertaking field research, for it provides a rich laboratory for personal learning and development. We encourage you to place field studies of organizational change processes high on your research agenda. An understanding of how organizations change lies at the very core of our field.

References

Abbott, A. (1984): "Event sequence and event duration: Colligation and measurement," *Historical Methods*, 17, 192–204.

Abbott, A. (1988): "Transcending general linear reality," *Sociological Theory*, 6, 169–86.

Abbott, A. (1990): "A primer on sequence methods," *Organization Science*, 1(4), 375–92.

Bal, M. (1985): *Narratology: Introduction to the Theory of Narrative.* Toronto: University of Toronto Press.

Barley, S. R. (1990) "Images of imaging: Notes on doing longitudinal fieldwork," *Organization Science*, 1(3), August, 220–47.

Bernard, H. R. (1999): "Editor's note," *Field Methods*, 11(1), August, 3–4, AltaMira Press.

Blalock, Jr., H. M. (1972): *Social Statistics*, New York: McGraw-Hill.

Calas, M. B., and Smircich, L. (1999): "Past postmodernism? Reflections and tentative directions," *Academy of Management Review*, 24(4), 649–71.

Campbell D. T., and Stanley J. C. (1963): *Experimental and Quasi-Experimental Designs for Research.* Chicago, IL: Rand McNally and Company.

Daft, R. L. (1983): "Learning the craft of organizational research," *Academy of Management Review*, 89, 539–46.

Denzin, N. K., and Lincoln, Y. S (eds) (1994): *Handbook of Qualitative Research.* Thousand Oaks, CA: Sage.

Eisenhardt, K. M. (1989.): "Building theories from case study research," *Academy of Management Review*, 14(4), 532–50.

Folger, J. P., Hewes, D. E., and Poole, M. S. (1984): "Coding social interaction," in B. Dervin and M. Voight (eds) *Progress in Communication Sciences, vol 5*, Norwood, NJ: Ablex, 115–61.

Harré, R., and Madden, E. A. (1975): *Causal Powers.* Totowa, NJ: Littlefield Adams.

Johnson, J. M. (1975): *Doing Field Research.* New York: Free Press.

Kaplan, A. (1964): *The Conduct of Inquiry: Methodology for Behavioral Science.* New York: Chandler.

Lakatos, I. (1978): *The Methodology of Scientific Research Programmes, Philosophical Papers, vol 1.* Cambridge, UK: Cambridge Univ. Press.

Langley, A. (1999): "Strategies for theorizing from process data," *Academy of Management Review*, 24(4), 691–710.

Langley, A., and Truax, J. (1994): "A process study of a new technology adoption in smaller manufacturing firms," *Journal of Management Studies*, 31, 619–52.

Meyer, A. D. (1991): "Visual data in organizational research," *Organization Science*, 2, 218–36.

Miles, M. B., and Huberman, A. M. (1994): *Qualitative Data Analysis: A Sourcebook of New Methods.* Beverly Hills, CA: Sage.

Mitroff, I., and Emshoff, J. (1979): "On strategic assumption making: A dialectical approach to policy and planning," *Academy of Management Review*, 4(1), 1–12.

Mohr, L. B. (1982): *Explaining Organizational Behavior.* San Francisco: Jossey-Bass.

Pentland, B. T. (1999): "Building process theory with narrative: From description to explanation," *Academy of Management Review*, 24(4), 711–24.

Peirce, C. S. (1955): *Philosophical Writings of Peirce*, J. Buchler (ed.), New York: Dover.

Pettigrew, A. M. (1985): *The Awakening Giant: Continuity And Change in ICI.* Oxford: Basil Blackwell.

Pettigrew, A. M. (1990): "Longitudinal field research on change: Theory and practice," *Organization Science*, 1(3), August, 267–92.

Poole, M. S., (1983): "Decision development in small groups, III: A multiple sequence model of group decision development," *Communication Monographs*, 50, 321–41.

Poole, M. S., Folger, J. P., Hewes, D. E. (1987): "Analyzing interpersonal interaction," in M. E. Roloff and G. R. Miller (eds), *Interpersonal Processes*, Beverly Hills: Sage, 220–56.

Poole, M. S., Van de Ven, A. H., Dooley, K., and Holmes, M. (2000): *Organizational Change and Innovation Processes: Theory and Methods for Research.* New York: Oxford Univ. Press.

Popper, K. (1972): *Objective Knowledge.* New York: Oxford Univ. Press

Rimmon-Kenan, S. (1983): *Narrative Fiction: Contemporary Poetics.* London: Routledge.

Schaie, K. W. (1965): "A general model for the study of developmental problems," *Psychological Bulletin*, 64, 92–107.

Schein, E. G. (1987): *The Clinical Perspective in Fieldwork*, (*Sage University Papers Series on Qualitative Research Methods, vol. 5*). Thousand Oaks, CA: Sage.

Simon, H. A. (1992): "What is an 'explanation' of behavior?" *Psychological Science*, 3, 150–61.

Singleton, Jr., R. A., Straits, B. C., and Straits, M. M. (1993): *Approaches to Social Research*, 2nd edn. New York: Oxford Univ. Press.

Stinchcombe, A. (1972): *Constructing Social Theories.* New York: Harcourt, Brace and World.

Strauss, A. L. (1987): *Qualitative Analysis for Social Scientists.* New York: Cambridge Univ. Press.

Thorngate, W. (1976): "Possible limits on a science of social behavior," in J. H. Streckland, F. E. Aboud, and K. J. Gergen (eds), *Social Psychology in Transition*, New York: Plenum: 121–39.

Tsoukas, H., (1989): "The validity of idiographic research explanations," *Academy of Management*

Review, 14, 551–61.

Tuma, N. B., and Hannan, M. T. (1984): *Social Dynamics: Models and Methods*. San Diego, CA: Academic Press.

Van de Ven, A. H., and Ferry, D. L. (1980): *Measuring and Assessing Organizations*. New York: Wiley.

Van de Ven, A. H., and Huber, G. P. (eds), (1990): "Longitudinal field research methods for studying processes of organizational change," *Organization Science*, 1(3) August, Special Issue.

Van de Ven, A. H. and Poole, M. S., (1995.): "Explaining development and change in organizations, *Academy of Management Review*, 20, 510–40.

Van de Ven, A. H., Angle, H. L., and Poole, M. S. (eds) (1989): *Research on the Management of Innovation*. New York: Ballinger/Harper and Row.

Van Maanen, J. (1988): *Tales of the Field: On Writing Ethnography*. Chicago: University of Chicago Press.

Van Maanen, J. (1995): *Representation in Ethnography*. Thousand Oaks, CA: Sage.

Van Maanen, J., Dabbs, Jr., J. M., and Faulkner, R. R. (1982): *Varieties of Qualitative Research, (Sage Series on Studying Organizations: Innovations in Methodology, Vol. 5)*. Beverly Hills, CA: Sage.

Weick, K. E., (1979): *The Social Psychology of Organizing*. Reading, MA: Addison-Wesley.

Weick, K. E. (1985): "Systematic observational methods," in G. Lindzay and E. Aronson (eds), *The Handbook of Social Psychology*, vol. 1, 3rd edn, New York: Random House, 567–634.

Whyte, W. F. (1984): *Learning from the Field: A Guide from Experience*. Beverly Hills, CA: Sage.

Appendix

Glossary of Epistemology Terms

BILL McKELVEY

Unless otherwise specified the definitions are based on discussions in Hunt (1991) and Audi (1995).

ANALYTICAL ADEQUACY indicates the ability of a model to accurately match or represent the real-world phenomena within the scope of the theory upon which the model is based.

AUXILIARY HYPOTHESES are unstated relationships presumed to be true in any specific empirical test. For example, suppose an investigation explicitly states the hypothesis that poor performance leads to diversification and includes several control variables. The many economic, psychological, social, and strategic governing relationships presumed true, other effects presumed randomized, and theories of experiment, method, and data not explicitly stated, all exist as unstated auxiliary hypotheses.

AXIOMATIC CONCEPTION presumes that all laws in a science can be mathematically deduced from basic axioms stated in mathematical syntax. In physics, Newton's three laws of motion (including $F = ma$) and law of gravity considered the root axioms. Once it was discovered that laws of motion, heat/energy, and electromagnetism all could be reduced to axioms of common mathematical SYNTACTICAL form, POSITIVISTS concluded that fields of study not built on this aspect were not science. As Mirowski (1989) argues, economists base the legitimacy of their field on the axiomatic conception.

CAMPBELLIAN REALISM is a concept of REALISM begun by Donald Campbell and elaborated by McKelvey (1999) holding that social science can be objective even when using METAPHYSICAL TERMS; move toward improved truth via the evolutionary selection out of poorer theories; describe a changing science using RELATIVIST assumptions; without excluding individual interpretation nor SOCIAL CONSTRUCTION.

CLASSICAL EMPIRICISM holds that knowledge of the real world rests only upon direct human observation and experience and is build up from atomized facts. See POSITIVISM.

COHERENCE THEORY is an element of hermeneutics focusing on how scholars come to agreement, given initially varying interpretations of language, a key feature being the "principle of charity" wherein scholars initially presume that the views of each participating scholar have merit.

CONSTRUCTIONISTS believe in an interpretative, creative and idiosyncratic element in human behavior that is irreducible to a set of causal laws. They hold that knowledge is not inevitable, but instead a social product, historically situated in social interactions that led to the knowledge being established (Hacking, 1999). Although constructionists do not deny the objective nature of scientific knowledge, they do emphasize that historical and social factors are highly relevant to the stabilization of some beliefs as knowledge.

CONTRA SCIENCE is a label Clegg and Hardy (1996) use to refer to EPISTEMOLOGIES outside NORMAL SCIENCE, such as RELATIVISM, interpretism, functionalism, phenomenology, radical humanism, POSTMODERNISM, etc.

CORRESPONDENCE RULES are used by LOGICAL POSITIVISTS to define THEORETICAL TERMS, guarantee their cognitive significance, and to specify the procedure by which they are attached to OBSERVATION TERMS. Since theory terms are not allowed independent meaning, but could not be METAPHYSICAL either, the CORRESPONDENCE RULES were required to tie theory terms explicitly to real-world phenomena. For example, these rules would tie the number seen on a particular kind of scale with the abstract, general concept of mass.

DETECTABLE TERMS (REALM 2 terms) fall in between the REAL and METAPHYSICAL ends of a continuum. REAL TERMS are those that are, in principle, accessible by the human senses. METAPHYSICAL TERMS are not, given today's conception of science and the real world. Detectable terms, in principle, could become real. For example, Jupiter's moons were not real for Kepler since he did not have a telescope; were more real for Galileo since he saw through his telescope what he thought were moons; and are very real if, eventually, one was in a rocket that crashed on one of them.

DISCOVERY LOGIC is a misnomer. There is no "logic" to discovery. "Many, if not most, major scientific discoveries are flashes of perceptual insight" (Hunt, 1991, p. 24). A classic is Kekulé's reputed "discovery" of the structural formula for the benzene ring because of seeing imaginary snakes in the flames in his fireplace when one seemed to form a ring by biting its tail.

EPISTEMOLOGY is the study of kinds of knowledge, how we come to know, by what right we can believe some statement to be true, which is to say, by what rules of justification logic have we come to a particular belief about the real world.

EVOLUTIONARY EPISTEMOLOGY, a key element of Campbellian realism, holds that the dynamics of science are best interpreted as an evolutionary Darwinian selectionist process in which a less fallible version of truth results as the more fallible individual interpretations of facts and expositions of theory and social constructions of facts by scientific communities of real-world (causal) processes, are winnowed out over time. This is not to say there is any guarantee of convergence on a nonprobabilistic, absolutist Truth (Laudan, 1981), only that inferior ideas are winnowed out over time.

FALLIBILIST (realist) epistemology lowers the standard of truth-seeking from unequivocal, absolutist Truth, to a more approachable human-scale definition of verisimilitude, that is, more truthlike theories remain after the more fallible ideas have been selectively winnowed away.

FIRST PHILOSOPHY is the metaphysical analysis of "being" or entitativity. If an entity is to be taken as "real" it must either be an individual thing, or an event, or a property, or a relation or distance to other things and events. First philosophy developed criteria for defining these characteristics. At issue is whether the things, et al. are "material" (real) or in the minds of observers and, thus unreal or "idealistic." The debate continues between normal science realists and postmodernist anti-realists.

FORMAL MODEL is one stated in a formal language such as set-theory, mathematics, symbolic logic, or computer programming language.

FOUNDATIONALISM   In this view there are two kinds of beliefs or statements: Foundational beliefs (or statements) are not inferentially justified by reference to other beliefs. They stand on their own as true – hence "foundational." The second kind of beliefs become true because they are inferentially justified by reference to foundational statements. This is the *radical* form of foundationalism. The *modest* view recognizes both kinds of statements, but does not hold that foundational statements are guaranteed with certainty to be true (Audi 1995, p. 277).

GENERATIVE MECHANISMS are the (usually) unobservable processes, that realists believe are nonetheless real, at higher or lower levels of analysis that cause behavior at a given level of analysis and, thus, are the bases of scientific explanation.

GUTTMAN SCALE is one in which each higher level of the scale includes all of the information, attributes, or elements measured at lower levels of the scale – it is cumulative.

HISTORICAL RELATIVISM, built upon the founding works of Kuhn (1962) and Feyerabend (1975), holds that an objective view of phenomena and cause cannot exist because individual scientists interpret means of terms "relative to a *Weltanschauung* [world view] or conceptual perspective upon which the meanings of terms are dependent" (Suppe, 1977, p. 120). Depending upon the *Weltanschauung* of which they are members, scientists have idiosyncratic interpretations of what they see, what they read, and how they apply the rules of JUSTIFICATION LOGIC, leading to an "anything goes" standard of what qualifies as truth. This is particularly true over time as scientific communities shift from one dominant PARADIGM or *Weltanschauung* to another. This leads to INCOMMENSURABILITY.

ICONIC MODEL is a pictorial, graphic, physical, or mechanical representation – could be boxes-and-arrows, an airplane wind tunnel model, a working mechanical device, and so on.

IDIOSYNCRATIC MICROSTATES, called agents in agent-based modeling, are below the lower bound of normal puzzle solving in a science. Traditionally they were assumed uniform, and therefore ignored for the sake of instrumental convenience, but now they are often assumed stochastically idiosyncratic (McKelvey, 1997) with the question becoming, How does order emerge from such agents?

INCOMMENSURABILITY is a term dating back to Kuhn's 1962 book. Given that PARADIGMS SHIFT, Kuhn held that there would be sufficiently dramatic enough changes in

1   problems to be solved
2   meanings of theoretical terms and concepts, and
3   standards and methods of JUSTIFICATION LOGIC that it would be impossible for

adherents of the previous PARADIGM to assess the truth value of the new paradigm.

INSTRUMENTAL RELIABILITY pertains to the level of accuracy and consistency that event *a* at time *t* predicts event *b* occurring at time $t + n$.

ISOLATED IDEALIZED STRUCTURES are simplified views of complex real-world phenomena such as pure elements and vacuums, ideal gases, frictionless surfaces, perfectly round masses (planets), 'standard conditions', unmutated genes, and rational actors – what the semantic conception view holds that theories attempt to explain. This is to say that no theory is actually about real-world phenomena in its full complexity.

JUSTIFICATION LOGIC refers to the rules and criteria a scientific community imposes on its members in an attempt to assure that they have an objective, replicable, and useful (operational) means of assessing the truth value of their hypotheses, laws, and theories.

LAW-LIKE STATEMENTS are statements have a high probability of truth (in scientific realist terms) and but are not yet proven to be universally true (in positivist terms). Thus, the law of gravity is accepted as universally true, whereas the population ecology statement, that organizational failures happen because environmental carrying capacity has been reached, is highly corroborated, and reasonably lawlike, but not yet accepted as a universal law.

LOGICAL EMPIRICISM is exemplified in the work of Nagel (1961), Kaplan (1964), and Hempel (1965). It attempted to recover from the misguided excesses of logical positivism. It gave up the notion of VERIFIABILITY and, thus, "positivism" in favor of Carnap's "gradually increasing confirmation" and "testability" and Reichenbach's introduction of probability. It emphasized laws, theories, and explanation. It continued the positivist's aversion to metaphysical terms including causality, maintained the distinction between theory and observation terms and because of this retained CORRESPONDENCE RULES, and equated explanation and prediction. Hempel's (1965) deductive-nomological and deductive statistical models of explanation represent it best. "Causality" is a term assiduously avoided throughout the Hempel and Kaplan books!

LOGICAL POSITIVISM began with the so-called Vienna Circle in 1907 as a response against German idealism. It emphasized the analysis of scientific language and especially the use of formal logic such as mathematics – hence the "logical." The use of "positivism" in the label emphasized its: abhorrence of METAPHYSICAL TERMS, including causality; its reliance on facts directly accessible to the human senses; reliance on instrumentalism (one variable predicts another) instead of searching for underlying, seemingly unreal (metaphysical) causal GENERATIVE MECHANISMS; strict separation of theory terms from observation terms and as a result of this; use of correspondence rules to allow tight connection between empirical facts and theories. All for the purpose of assuring VERIFICATION of Truth – a statement is either totally and verifiably true or it is false.

MAPPING MODEL is Azevedo's (1997) way of connecting theory to the semantic conception's 'isolated idealized structures'. A "map" in her usage is a simplified (isolated idealized) rendition of a complex reality designed with the specific interests of the map maker in mind – location of forests and minerals, identification of rivers and mountains, delineation of roads, etc. It is useful simply because it does not attempt to describe all of a complex reality. Semantic conceptionists view theory similarly.

METAPHYSICAL TERMS and concepts (REALM 3) are those LOGICAL POSITIVISTS believe have no likelihood of being directly observable or potentially DETECTABLE by methods currently imaginable by a scientific community. To Ernst Mach, atoms were metaphysical. To other scientists, seeing tracks in a cloud chamber, atoms are accepted as "detected." The reader can decide whether psychological needs, norms, transaction costs, strategies, or transcendental causes are real, detectable, or metaphysical.

MODEL-SUBSTRUCTURES are identified by semantic conceptionists as components of a model that represent a usually causal element of complex real-world phenomena thought within the scope of the theory the model depicts.

NOMIC NECESSITY holds that the occurrence of any phenomenon cannot be due to chance but instead is due to some other phenomenon. The requirement of nomic necessity is to protect against attempting to build a theory or explanation on an accidental regularity – the occurrence of an event by chance. Any theoretical statement must have one or more elements that meet the nomic necessity requirement. This requirement is an element of the legacy of logical positivism that still has philosophical legitimacy.

NORMAL SCIENCE is the stage of science (including normal puzzle solving) that occurs between paradigm shifts in Kuhn's framework. For others "normal science" usually refers to what natural and life scientists do as they conduct their investigations – whether or not paradigm shifts are underway. Relativists and postmodernists use the term to refer to people doing (modernist) science that more or less looks like what is seemingly (really falsely) described by logical positivism and logical empiricism.

OBSERVATION LANGUAGE refers to OBSERVATION TERMS or concepts designed to explicitly measure observable phenomena. For POSITIVISTS this means facts directly accessible to the human senses – and for LOGICAL POSITIVISTS no theoretical term can be an observation term (a distinction impossible for them to maintain).

OBSERVATION TERMS refer to observable facts directly accessible by the human senses. LOGICAL POSITIVISTS held that they were strictly separate from theoretical terms. CORRESPONDENCE RULES were devised to connect the two. Eventually it was found impossible to keep them separate – one of the many critiques against the RECEIVED VIEW. An OBSERVATION TERM may have one or more competing OPERATIONAL TERMS.

ONTOLOGICAL ADEQUACY in the semantic and realist conceptions refers to the ability of a model to represent the real-world phenomena (entities and properties) within the scope of the theory. Ontological adequacy may be tested substructure by substructure when the phenomena covered by the model (and theory) cannot reasonably be separated out as an ISOLATED IDEALIZED behavior, that is, reasonably disconnected from extraneous effects not included in the model.

ONTOLOGY is the study of beingness – whether anything actually exists as an entity in the real world having properties of some kind. Scientific realists take an ontologically strong view that entities and relationships do exist in the world "out there" and serve as criteria against which models are to be tested for representation (Aronson et al., 1994).

OPERATIONAL TERMS are not the same as observation terms (making up observation language) in logical positivism. An operational term is the actual measure – a "number" coming from a mercury barometer vs. one from an aneroid barometer. An observation term accessible to the human senses could be measured any one of several competing operational terms.

ORGANIZATION "SCIENCE" A reading of Kuhn (1970, ch. 2) makes it quite clear that organization science is "prescience" and not "science," as does Azevedo (this volume). I elaborate on this at some length in McKelvey (forthcoming). I could have used organization studies, as did Clegg et al. (1996) in the title of their Handbook of Organization Studies, but then I would be confusing their postmodernist anti-science predilections with my pro-science recognition of organization "science"'s' prescience state. Consequently I simply remind the reader of its questionable status by using "organization 'science'."

PARADIGM SHIFTS, in Kuhn's (1962) framework, separate one program of normal puzzle solving from a subsequent one. Based mainly on a reading of physics, Kuhn argued that stable periods of normal puzzle solving were punctuated by revolutions – called paradigm shifts. His view of scientific change as a series of revolutions was a dramatic departure from the prevailing view of LOGICAL EMPIRICISTS – that change was a slow, smooth, cumulative, and incremental process as new facts forced revisions in theories. During a prolonged period of normal puzzle solving, anomalies accumulate to the point where they topple an existing paradigm. After the shift INCOMMENSURABILITY results.

PARADIGMS became one of the most discussed elements of epistemological discourse after Kuhn's (1962) book appeared. A paradigm is "a set of scientific and metaphysical beliefs that make up a theoretical framework within which scientific theories can be tested, evaluated, and if necessary, revised" (Audi, 1995). They define: legitimate problems to be studied, exemplar methods, concrete problem solutions underlying JUSTIFICATION LOGIC, and the nature of scientific training programs. These all create inertia preventing change. Masterman (1970) shows that Kuhn uses paradigm in twenty-one different ways. As a result of this and other complaints, Kuhn (1970, Postscript) introduces "disciplinary matrix" to avoid the definitional confusion. Disciplinary matrix represents the totality of beliefs connected to "paradigm." He substitutes "exemplar" where a paradigm plays the role of setting up standards and defining training programs.

POSITIVISM (classical positivism) dates back to August Comte and Ernst Mach's views that any theory not based on observable fact is meaningless. An organizational version of classical positivism is Pfeffer's (1982) call for a focus on observable organizational demographics – which Lawrence (1997) shows was unsuccessful in that subsequent organizational demographers kept using metaphysical terms anyway!

POSITIVIST LEGACY Suppe (1977) identifies ten elements remaining from the RECEIVED VIEW that continue to have value in subsequent epistemology – reference to empirical reality, logical rigor, AUXILIARY HYPOTHESES, FORMAL MODELS, and semantic interpretation. Hunt (1991) adds six additional elements emphasizing NOMIC NECESSITY and experiments. These are listed in McKelvey (1999). These elements are carried forward – all too often rather implicitly – in the recent scientific realist literature.

POSTMODERNISM is a many faceted statement against the Enlightenment. More specifically it is against reason, rationality, and instrumental rationality – the idea that the main purpose of knowledge is for social control and to direct innovation and change (Hassard, 1993). Postmodernists focus "on the constructed nature of people and reality, emphasizing language as a system of distinctions which are central to the construction process, arguing against grand narratives and large-scale theoretical systems such as Marxism or functionalism, emphasizing the power/ knowledge connection and the role of claims of expertise in systems of domination, emphasizing the fluid and hyperreal nature of the contemporary world and role of mass media and information technologies, and stressing narrative/fiction/ rhetoric as central to the research process (Alvesson and Deetz 1996, pp. 192–3). At its core, postmodernism rests on relativism.

POSTSTRUCTURALISM   Structuralists have their origin in Saussure's "scientific" model of language as a closed system of elements and rules. They place equal emphasis on the "*signifier*" ("the sound image made by the word 'apple'") and the "*signified*" (the apple), with the linguistic "*sign*" or relationship between the two a matter of social convention. Poststructuralists, starting with Derrida, made the signifier dominant with little determinable relation to extra-linguistic referents. "Structuralism sees truth as being 'behind' or 'within' a text, poststructuralism stresses the interaction of reader and text" Poststructuralism is "quite radically anti-scientific" (Sarup, 1993, pp. 2–3)

PRAGMATISM holds that true beliefs are those that lead to desirable actions and results. The development of knowledge is guided by interests and values – it is an instrumental tool for organizing experience. Truth cannot be determined solely by epistemological criteria.

PRE-SCIENTIFIC   Kuhn (1970) emphasizes the "class of schools" (paradigms) as the dominant indicator the pre-scientific status of a field. Other signs are low consensus on problems, more speculative theories, high journal rejection rates, books the preferred medium, gathering of "random" readily available facts as low hanging fruit, less separation of field from society (Hoyningen-Huene, 1993, p. 190; Pfeffer, 1993).

PRINCIPLE OF EPISTEMIC INVARIANCE holds that "When it comes to gathering evidence for our beliefs, *the epistemological situation remains the same for observables and unobservables alike*, no matter whether we are dealing with observables, possible observables or unobservables [REALMS 1, 2, and 3]" (Aronson et al., 1994, p. 194; their italics). This epitomizes the scientific realists' blurring of the consequences of real vs. metaphysical concepts and terms. Their argument is that since the truth of a statement or theory is more or less probable – (as opposed to VERIFIABLY True or False as absolutes), and since there are various probabilities associated with any research method, the relative realness or metaphysicalness of terms is just another probability to be included amongst the others as a statement or theory becomes more truthlike and/or LAW-LIKE.

PROGRAM is a label applied to a body of work that extends beyond a few articles and represents a significant, extended, and coherent intellectual or epistemological development. Hooker's several books on naturalist EVOLUTIONARY EPISTEMOLOGY are an example, as is Bhaskar's book on TRANSCENDENTAL REALISM. Campbell's accumulation of papers about his "*critical, hypothetical, corrigible, scientific realist selectionist evolutionary* epistemology" also fits.

REAL TERMS See REALM 1 entities.

REALISM (scientific or metaphysical realism) holds that there are

1 real entities in the world "out there"
2 that exist independently of our perception, experience, or knowledge of them, and
3 that they have properties and relationships that are independent of the concepts or language we use to describe them (Audi, 1995, p. 488).

Scientific realists blur the distinction between METAPHYSICAL and REAL terms, holding that underlying GENERATIVE MECHANISMS or causes not directly accessible to the human senses are nevertheless real, and not to be relegated to the scientific dustbin.

REALMS *Realm 1* entities are currently observable (number of employees in a firm); *Realm 2* entities are currently unobservable but potentially detectable (process event networks in a firm); and *Realm 3* entities are metaphysical and beyond any possibility of observation by any conception of current science (psychological need, environmental uncertainty, underlying cause) (Harré, 1989). Pols (1992) terms Realm 1 observations "*direct knowing*" and Realm 3 observations "*indirect knowing.*"

RECEIVED VIEW refers to LOGICAL POSITIVISM and its evolved successor, LOGICAL EMPIRICISM.

RELATIVISM Cognitive (here epistemological) relativism holds that the world has no intrinsic characteristics – there are just different ways of interpreting it. Rorty is quoted as saying, "objective truth is no more and no less than the best idea we currently have about how to explain what is going on" (Audi, 1995, p. 690). Relativism "denies the existence of any standard or criterion higher than the individual by which claims to truth and knowledge can be adjudicated" (Siegel quoted in Hunt, 1991, p. 218). For many, relativism especially characterizes the work of Kuhn (1962) and Feyerabend (1975) to the effect that "anything goes" – since each scientist has an idiosyncratic interpretation of facts and linguistic terms, there can be no such thing as a universally objective justification logic. See HISTORICAL RELATIVISM.

SELECTIONIST is an adjective used to describe any approach that more or less follows Darwinian natural selection theory – over time, in the context of external criterion variables, less favorable entities are winnowed out.

SEMANTIC MEANING is attached to formal theoretical terms via CORRESPONDENCE RULES. Thus, the syntax, $x = yz$, could appear as the more familiar $F = ma$ with meanings from the study of motion attached via correspondence rules. Or different rules could attached different meanings to the $x = yz$ syntax in thermodynamics, electromagnetism, economics, etc.

SOLIPSISM (broadly) holds that behavior is a function of desires, hopes, and fears that are psychological states occurring inside the mind or brain and, thus, are the only causes of observable human behavior. Each individual is said to be isolated from all other persons or external things as a result of egocentrism and unique: experiences, semantic interpretations, and psychological states. This leads to ontological solipsism, which holds that there is no reality external to our minds, and that we are epistemologically isolated from the real world as well.

THEORETICAL LANGUAGE consists of theoretical terms. These are allowed by logical positivists as useful abbreviations of more complicated and varied OBSERVATIONAL and

OPERATIONAL descriptions. Thus, there is the theory term, mass; descriptions of mass or weight meaningful to human senses such as planet, ball, big truck; and various operational weight measures with numbers. The danger was that theory terms could become disassociated from observation terms, thereby becoming meaningless metaphysical terms. But if they are they same as operational terms they are unnecessary. This is known as the theoretician's dilemma (Hempel, 1965, p. 186). CORRESPONDENCE RULES were to avoid this.

TRANSCENDENTAL IDEALISM (from Kant) holds that it is possible for a scientific community to move toward an intersubjectively valid and even objectively based imagining of properties such as sound and color as existing relative to our sensibilities while at the same not accepting that they exist as real entities. Transcendental idealism accepts that social construction exists in scientific communities. Bhaskar (1975) appropriately places transcendental idealism between classical realism (science can only be based on atomistic facts having observed regularity) and transcendental realism which holds that there are intransitive entities and relations among them existing independently of human perception.

UNITY OF SCIENCE   A view, held mainly by logical empiricists, that all sciences could eventually be reduced to a universal observation language, and that all theories could eventually be reduced to one basic theory (in physics). This view gained headway when it was discovered that analytical mechanics, thermodynamics, electrodynamics, and economics could be reduced to the root axiom, $F = ma$. This led to the AXIOMATIC CONCEPTION of science.

VERIFICATION PRINCIPLE holds that all scientific statements are to be logically or empirically shown to be True or False, otherwise they are meaningless. Statements are subdivided into elements, each of which is then logically (formally) analyzed as to Truth or Falseness or connected to a fact. Elements are recombined into a truth-table to ascertain the Truth of the more complex statement. Absent this, statements are meaningless.

VERISIMILITUDE is the same as truthlikeness. Because philosophers moved away from an absolutist view of theoretical statements as either True or False (that is, the logical positivists' verification of theories), toward Carnap's testability and evolutionary epistemology, Popper (1979) developed the idea of verisimilitude. As poorer theories are winnowed out in selectionist fashion, theories with improved verisimilitude remain.

References

Alvesson, M., and Deetz, S. (1996): "Critical theory and postmodernism approaches to organizational studies," in S. R. Clegg, C. Hardy and W. R. Nord (eds), *Handbook of Organization Studies*, Thousand Oaks, CA: Sage, 191–217.

Aronson, J. L., Harré, R., and Way, E. C. (1994): *Realism Rescued*. London: Duckworth.

Audi, R. (1995): *The Cambridge Dictionary of Philosophy*. Cambridge, UK: Cambridge University Press,

Azevedo, J. (1997): *Mapping Reality: An Evolutionary Realist Methodology for the Natural and Social Sciences*. Albany, NY: State University of New York Press.

Bhaskar, R. (1998): *The Possibility of Naturalism*, 3rd edn. London: Routledge.

Clegg, S. R., and Hardy, C. (1996): "Organizations, organization, and organizing," in Clegg et al., 1–28.

Clegg, S. R., Hardy, C., and Nord, W. R., (eds), (1996): *Handbook of Organization Studies*. Thousand Oaks, CA: Sage.

Feyerabend, P. K. (1975): *Against Method*. Thetford, UK: Lowe and Brydone.

Hacking, I. (1999): *The Social Construction of What?* Cambridge, MA: Harvard University Press.

Harré, R. (1989): "Realism, reference and theory," in A. P. Griffiths (ed.), *Key Themes in Philosophy*, Cambridge, UK: Cambridge University Press, 53–68.

Hassard, J. (1993): "Postmodernism and organizational analysis," in J. Hassard and M. Parker (eds), *Postmodernism and Organizations*, Thousand Oaks, CA: Sage, 1–23.

Hempel, C. G. (1965): *Aspects of Scientific Explanation*. New York: Free Press.

Hoyningen-Huene, P. (1993): *Reconstructing Scientific Revolutions*, (trans. A. T. Levine). Chicago, IL: University of Chicago Press.

Hunt, S. D. (1991): *Modern Marketing Theory: Critical Issues in the Philosophy of Marketing Science*. Cincinnati, OH: South-Western.

Kaplan, A. (1964): *The Conduct of Inquiry*. New York: Chandler.

Kuhn, T. S. (1962): *The Structure of Scientific Revolutions*. Chicago, IL: University of Chicago Press.

Kuhn, T. S. (1970): *The Structure of Scientific Revolutions*, 2nd edn. Chicago, IL: University of Chicago Press.

Laudan, L. (1981): "A confutation of convergent realism," *Philosophy of Science*, 48, 19–48.

Lawrence, B. L. (1997): "The black box of organizational demography," *Organization Science*, 8, 1–22.

Masterman, M. (1970): "The nature of a paradigm," in I. Lakatos and A. Musgrave (eds), *Criticism and the Growth of Knowledge*, Cambridge, UK: Cambridge University Press, 59–90.

McKelvey, B. (1997): "Quasi-natural organization science," *Organization Science*, 8, 351–80.

McKelvey, B. (1999): "Toward a Campbellian realist organization science," in J. A. C. Baum and B. McKelvey (eds), *Variations in Organization Science: In Honor of Donald T. Campbell*, Thousand Oaks, CA: Sage, 383–411.

McKelvey, B. (forthcoming): "From fields to science," in R. Westwood and S. R. Clegg (eds), *Point/Counterpoint: Central Debates in Organization Theory*, Oxford, UK: Blackwell.

Mirowski, P. (1989): *More Heat than Light*. Cambridge, UK: Cambridge University Press.

Nagel, E. (1961): *The Structure of Science*. New York: Harcourt, Brace.

Pfeffer, J. (1982): *Organizations and Organization Theory*. Marshfield, MA: Pitman.

Pfeffer, J. (1993): "Barriers to the advancement of organizational science: Paradigm development as a dependent variable," *Academy of Management Review*, 18, 599–620.

Pols, E. (1992): *Radical Realism: Direct Knowing in Science and Philosophy*. Ithaca, NY: Cornell University Press.

Popper, K. R. (1979): *Objective Knowledge: An Evolutionary Approach*, revised edn. Oxford, UK: Oxford University Press.

Sarup, M. (1993): *An Introductory Guide to Post-Structuralism and Postmodernism*, 2nd edn. Athens, GA: University of Georgia Press.

Suppe, F. (1977): *The Structure of Scientific Theories*, 2nd edn. Chicago: University of Chicago Press.

Subject Index

abandonment 510
  and transformation of organizational
    practices 509
absolute certainty 745
absorption 602
absorptive capacity 87, 296, 427, 645, 649,
  651
access 282, 290
accidents, normal 213
accumulation of competence 424
accuracy 885
  action 718
  communication acts 353
  decision accuracy 184
action(s)
  grammars of 820
  individual 417
  learning 643
  observable 718
  organized 353
  situation action theory 356
  social 718
activation factors 112
activity-based normative boundaries, relational
  8
actor-task-tool networks 436
adaptation 328, 445, 676
  adaptationism 108
  adaptive sensemaking perspective 357
  complex adaptive systems 453
  evolutionary theories of 442
  individual 52

learning as an example of 336
Markovian conception of organizational
  adaptation 629
of aspiration levels 429
of goals 419
production and adaptation of rules and
  routines 418, 420
program adaptation 416
reactive adaptation 53
adequacy
  analytical adequacy 763, 764, 766, 889
  model-centered science and bifurcated
    adequacy tests 763
  ontological adequacy 763, 765, 766, 767,
    893
administrative man, Simon's 4
adolescence, liability of 307
adulteration, institutional 509
advanced manufacturing technology see AMT
advantage
  first mover 673
  from multiple perspectives 729
  sustainable 677
advocacy organizations 562
age
  and size dependence 306, 307
  liability of aging 308
agent(s)/agency
  agency theory 19, 234, 250
  agent schemata 462
  agent-based simulation models 829, 834,
    837

agent(s)/agency (*cont'd*)
  change agent 503
  IT-as-agent computational theories 218
  normative agency 234, 235
  ORGAHEAD multi-agent model 215, 217
  positive agency 234, 235
  power, experience and agency costs 249
agglomeration 564
  agglomeration economies 635
aggregation
  aggregates and ensembles 318
  theoretical 236, 241
AGIL – adaptation, goal attainment,
    integration, latency 6
algorithmic complexity 218
alignment, incentives 236, 242, 247
alliance(s) 471, 477
  alliancing 625
  centrality in alliance networks 623
  horizontal alliances 601
  learning 87
  prior 284
  scope 474
  strategic 622, 631, 632, 635, 649
  success 293
  vertical 601
ally-or-make-or-buy decision 476, 478
ambidextrous organization 386, 396, 398
ambidextrous senior management teams 401
ambiguity 355, 736
  in the causes of success 305
  learning under 417, 419
  mission ambiguity 80
  of CEO performance 246
AMT (advanced manufacturing technology)
    160, 165
analysis/es 846
  ascending/descending models of 815
  causal analysis 758
  cross-industry 293
  intelligent analysis tools 227
  levels of 61, 360
  of economic transactions 527
  of industry rhetoric 585
  of top-down institutional reform 507
  sequence 884
  social network 115
  units of 783
analysts, ecological 808
analytic-synthetic distinction 747
analytical adequacy 763, 764, 766, 889

analytical and ontological tests, separation of
    771
anarchists, epistemological 734
anti-positivist 736
anti-trust 266, 335, 377, 503, 688
appeal, upward 147
apprenticeship 106
appropriability 469, 471, 474
architecture(s)
  architectural innovation 84, 393, 394,
    396
  connectionist architectures 124
  mixed 125
  of complexity 115
  standard interfaces and system architecture
    174
  symbolic architectures 121
archiving
  archival research 805, 807, 810
  data sets, collection and archiving 798
  on-line data archives 226
area frame 788
artifacts, language and apprenticeship 106
artificial intelligence 221, 223
"as-if" argument 696
ascending model of analysis 815
aspiration
  aspiration levels 416, 419, 425, 429
  dispersed learning and aspirations 433
assertiveness 146
assets
  asset-specificity 468, 471, 473, 476, 478,
    707
  depletion of 420
assignment network 225
Association of South East Asian Nations
    (ASEAN) 275
asymmetry, information 247, 248
asynchronous updating 679
attainment discrepancy models 421
attention 185, 420
  human 91
  organizational 366
attribution
  epistemological 734
  fundamental attribution error 59, 145
audience learning 417, 419
authority 141
  authority relations 542
  obedience to 150
autocorrelation, network 68

automatic and controlled cognitive processes 129

autonomy 59, 747
   autonomous processes 79, 105
   responsiveness and genuine dialogue 746
   structural autonomy model 603
auxiliary hypothesis 763, 889
avoidance
   of metaphysical terms 769
   of interfirm ties 525
axial coding 859
axioms 759, 760, 762, 763, 765, 889
   conceptions of the axiom-theory-model-
      phenomena relationship 764

bank(s)
   bank power 610
   centrality in corporate interlock networks
      610
Barley's parallel, synchronic, and diachronic
     research science 876
Barnard's inducement-contribution theory of
     organizational participation 367
barriers
   entry and exit 690
   to imitation 672
behavior 425, 718
   behavioral game-theoretic modeling 705
   behavioral sources of power 142, 146
   behavioral theories 16
   behavioral theory of the firm 4, 699
   behaviorism 119
   chaotic 209
   cyclical cartel 692
   emergent 215
   innovation 622, 632
   interfirm political 610
   market 686
   mindless 130
   sales-motivated 700
   simple schemata, complex behavior 450,
      452
   types of learning behaviors 681
belief 348
   belief consensus 594
   belief structures 348
   boundary 585, 588
   evolution 595
   individual 417
   industry belief systems 580, 583, 585, 593
   market stories and the enactment of the

belief hierarchy 584
   taken-for-granted 37, 48, 591
   verisimilar 745
Bénard processes 213
Berlin and Church's refutation of Ayer's
     verification principle 740
Bertrand–Cournot Nash game 691
Bertrand–Cournot oligopoly distinction 689
best-practices 298, 672, 699
   transfer of 189
betweenness measure of centrality 144, 289
bias 854, 878
bifurcated-model-centered science 771
birth
   birth rates of organizations 264
   form at 264
blackboxing 861
blind variation 722
   Campbell's (blind) variation-selection-
     retention (VSR) model 7, 14, 25, 77, 101,
     588, 722
blockmodels 459
   three-dimensional blockmodeling 521
bluffing 148
board(s)
   control of 365
   independence of 236
   interlocks 244, 635, 654
   social exchange and board monitoring 244
   social influence and board independence 244
   strategic side-effects of board monitoring
     245
Bonini's paradox 841
boundaries
   boundary beliefs 585, 588
   locus of organizational boundaries 407
   market 591
   mutable 224
   of competition 583, 584
   relational activity-based normative
     boundaries 8
   transmission of technical knowledge across
     firm boundaries 634
bounded rationality 366, 467, 468, 480
bracketing, temporal 882
brainstorming 185, 191
bridging tie 289, 290
broken learning cycles 419
broken ties studies 607
brokerage 66
   social capital as 60

Brown's political phenomenology of
organizations 376
building intraorganizational institutions 44
bureaucracy 4, 100, 366, 599, 715
    bureaucratic proliferation 420
    patrimonial 366
    Weber's analysis of bureaucratic domination
    363
    Weber's "iron law of bureaucratic
    proliferation" 424
business register 788
buying
    buyer community 583
    make-or-buy decisions 470, 471, 486

Campbell
    (blind) variation-selection-retention model 7,
    101
    Campbellian realism 754, 755, 756, 758,
    889
    fish-scale model of omniscience 21
    naturalist evolutionary realism 722
    rule 91
canonical versus non-canonical practice 423
capabilities 477, 478, 736
    capabilities gap 476
    capabilities network 225
    capabilities replication 102
    dynamic learning 283
    firm 283
    relational 297
capital
    availability of 264
    capital network 225
    social capital 60, 66, 237, 366, 380, 616,
    634
capitalism 499, 513
    capitalists 506, 599
    finance capitalists 606
Carnegie School 4, 364, 579, 593
cartels 264
    cyclical cartel behavior 692
Cartwright's simulacrum account 761
catastrophe(s)
    complexity 443, 678, 681
    catastrophe theory 442
    error catastrophe 443
categorization 44, 53, 347
cause
    and effect relationships 736
    causal analysis 758

causal laws 736, 738
causal primacy 568
causality theory 814
    downward causation 92
    notions of 721
    reciprocal causalities through the mobility
    effect 690
    upward causation 92
cellular automata 665, 668, 675, 677, 679,
    831, 838
census or sample? 787
centrality 59, 60, 61, 294, 372, 606, 616
    betweenness measure of 144, 289
    closeness 144, 289
    degree 288
    joint 284
    network 288, 612, 623
    of banks 610
CEO(s)
    ambiguity of CEO performance 246
    compensation 237
    dismissal of 236
    succession 241, 404
    turnover 407
certainty, absolute 745
chaebol 504
change
    change agent 503
    change histories 309
    changing basis of competition 314
    component sources of 875
    consequences of 306
    discontinuous 402
    economic change 79
    endogenous evolutionary change 331, 338
    eras of incremental change 405
    formation, change and collapse of
    communities 548
    hazardousness of 310
    in institutional environments 266
    in antitrust law 377
    in power over time 152
    institutional 260, 266, 269, 507
    interorganizational origins and change 559
    legal changes 562
    legitimating change 508
    macro change model 404
    managing 873
    Marxist accounts of revolutionary change
    506
    measuring changes in performance 182

membership changes within organizations 188

organizational 309, 422, 867, 869, 871, 872

process theory of 884

punctuated 365

stability versus 90

strategic 79, 354

technological 386, 621

chaos 209, 213, 442, 665, 704

edge of 17, 228, 320, 443, 447, 449, 459, 462, 682, 831

charisma 145, 146, 407

as personal source of power 142

choice theory, rational 19, 741, 743

circularity, logical 745

circulation theory of power 365

city manager form of government 263

class struggle, Marx's model of 513

classical empiricism 753, 889

classical sociological theories of Marx and Weber 599

classification system 78

clinical researcher 868

closed system approaches within organizational theory 599

closeness centrality 144, 289

clustering, geographic 633

co-location in geographic space 114

coalitions

coalition formation 147, 433

political 365

coding

axial 859

codifiability 103

codification traps 426, 432

open 858

selective 859

coercive isomorphism 610, 614

coercive pressures 259, 262

coevolution 338, 569

evolution and 341

public policy and industry coevolution 567

cognition 658

and interpretation 15, 27

automatic and controlled cognitive processes 129

cognition affect 128

cognitive (vs. normative) elements of institutions 12

cognitive and sociopolitical legitimacy 313

cognitive manipulation 44

cognitive maps 122, 680

cognitive measures of taken for grantedness 511

cognitive mechanisms 727

cognitive micro-processes of market-making 580

cognitive nature of routines 109

cognitive overload 89

cognitive strategic groups 588

cognitive structures 128, 259

cognitive taxonomy of organizational forms 583

cognitivism 119

collective cognition 356, 360, 593

distributed and shared 130

distributed cognition and transactive systems of knowledge 594

human perceptual and cognitive mechanisms 730

interorganizational 119, 579

locus/loci of 355, 358

organizational 122, 344, 355, 398

schema-based cognitive processing 121

situated cognition 356, 357

coherence

coherence strategy 723

coherence theory 755, 890

of communities 549

cohesion 66, 267, 613

and conflict in dominant political coalitions 379

cohesive tie 289, 290

elite 605

interorganizational model of cohesion 610

social capital as cohesion and network closure 60

cold cognitive structures 128

cold intraorganizational institutions 52

Coleman School 66

collaborative experience 657

collapse of communities, formation, change and 548

collectives

collective cognition 356, 360, 593

collective learning 354

collective mind 353

collective strategic concepts 584

types of 2

commensalism 541, 545, 546

commitment(s)
  commitment effect 689, 690, 699, 703, 706
  credible 692, 707
  epistemological 743, 746, 747
  social 371
common third parties 284
communication acts 353
community/ies
  buyer 583
  coherence of 549
  definition 542
  evolution 543
  formation, change and collapse 548
  of learners 423, 427
  organizational 541, 583
  organizations of 550
  producer 583
  structure 544
comparability, frame of 583, 588
comparative diffusion across nations and
    practices 500
comparative studies 565
compensation
  contingent 235
  for CEOs 237
competence
  accumulation of 424
  competency network 225
  competency trap 17, 420, 423, 426, 429,
    432
  search competencies 419
  transmission of manufacturing competences
    109
competition 264, 304, 318, 467, 526, 528,
    541, 622, 666, 707
  as lack of differentiation 631
  between routines 81
  boundaries of 583, 584
  changing basis of competition 314
  competitive advantage of foolishness 703
  competitive experience 643, 647
  competitive-innovation relationship 631
  competitive intensity 306, 314, 625, 626
  competitive interdependence 602
  competitive rivalry 693
  density and competitive processes 315
  ecology of technology-based competition 631
  exposure to competitors 423
  full competition 545
  game theory of competitive rivalry 686
  industry competitiveness experience 644

intensity of 677
intercommunity 544
interfirm interaction norms and
    competitiveness 567
learning and 652
localized 314
microeconomics of imperfect 687
monopolistic 689
partial 545
perfect 688, 689, 691
Schumpeterian 672
complementarity
  between routines 82
  fit as 198
completed institutions 513
complexity 103, 704
  algorithmic complexity 218
  and computation 17, 29
  architecture of 115
  as a metaphor 210, 213
  complex adaptive systems 453, 454
  complex organizations 4
  complex systems 210, 212
  complexity catastrophe 443, 678, 681
  computational theory building about
    complex systems 214
  ENR and 727
  in population dynamics 320
  integrative 190
  interorganizational 66
  intraorganizational 208
  of social life, inherent 851
  organizational complexity and computation
    442
  predatory 545
  simple schemata, complex behavior 450,
    452
  strategic 236
  theory 115, 209
component sources of change 875
comps 78, 101
computation
  complexity and 17, 29
  interorganizational complexity and 664
  intraorganizational complexity and 208
  organizational complexity and computation
    442
computational approach 345
computational organization theory 209, 210
computational stream of research 15
computational theory building about complex

systems 214
computer aided design (CAD) 163–4, 165
computer aided manufacturing (CAM) 165
computer integrated manufacturing (CIM) 165
concentration 316
conceptions
    conceptual scheme of variation, selection and
        retention 558
    multiple conceptual frameworks 728
    network conception of control 529
    of control 366, 530
    of institutions and institutional effects 498,
        510
    of learning 428
    of the axiom-theory-model-phenomena
        relationship 764
    semantic 761, 763, 768
conditioning, operant 147
conduct
    conduct effect 688, 699, 703, 704, 706
    firm conduct 687
    structure-conduct-performance (SCP) 18,
        475
conflict 140
    cohesion and conflict in dominant political
        coalitions 379
    of interest 530
    resolution of 376
    role of 110
conformity
    cycle of 433
    to institutional constraints 272
congenital experience 647
congenital learning 644
conglomerate firms, deinstitutionalization of
    529
conjoint exchange activities 531
connectionist architectures 124
consensus 355, 741, 757
    belief consensus 594
    content consensus 354
    in science 724
    lack of 360
    paradigmatic 741
constrained variation 333
constraint
    emergence and 222
    institutional 260
constructed reality 351
constructionist(s) 734, 739, 740, 742, 743,
    744, 748, 890

constructionist stance 733
    theory in use 738
consumer leagues 333
    watchdog groups 512, 562
contagion
    contagion studies 64
    institutional 433
    of legitimacy 498
content
    content consensus 354
    relational 60
contestability, perfect 691
contestation 365, 378
contingency 66
    contingency theories 16, 213, 621
    contingent compensation 235
    historical contingency 558
    role of, in interorganizational evolutionary
        process 569
    strategic contingencies 15, 153
    structural contingencies 364, 365, 368
continuous incremental improvement 396
contra science 736, 754, 890
    real science from 754
contracting 471
    contract design 251
    contractual hazards 471, 476, 478
    nexus of contracts 461, 508, 509
control 262
    conceptions of 267, 269, 366, 377, 500,
        529, 530
    controlled cognitive processes 129
    managerial 52
    of board 365
    of capital 609
    over uncertainty 374
    spin control 148
convergence 365
    and reorientation 422
    theoretical convergence and methodological
        variety theory 341
co-optation 261, 600, 607, 612
coordination
    coordination costs 476
    embedded 167
    motivation and coordination of managers
        486
    under uncertainty 476
core competence 509
core markets 535
core organizational features 309

core technology 542
core values, exploration of culture and, in sustaining ambidextrous designs 407
corporations
  corporate conceptions of control 500
  corporate diversification, direction of 479
  corporate elite 15
  corporate governance 242, 252
  corporate greenmail 241
  corporate innovation, direction of 632
  corporate venturing, internal 79
  interlocks between 606
correspondence rules 759, 890
corroboration, empirical 677
costs
  of monitoring top management 240
  transaction 18, 252, 442, 467, 468, 471, 476, 478, 483, 484, 705
coupling
  degree of 228
  loose 78, 167, 261, 269, 444, 446, 462, 676
creation
  meaning 352
  path 455
creativity 191
  creating knowledge 181, 190
  creative destruction 390
credible commitment 692, 707
crisis reaction 39
critical hypothetical corrigible scientific realist selectionist evolutionary epistemology 756
critical rationalism 744, 745
critical theory 761
cross-industry analyses 293
cross-national differences in management and governance 557
cross-paradigmatic dialogue, epistemology of 735
cross-section or longitudinal design 783
cultivation of luck 406
culture 38, 498, 658
  Carley's construct model of culture formation 220
  cultural and political sources of variability in legitimacy 510
  cultural evolution assumption 98, 106
  cultural-frame perspectives 333
  cultural solipsism 723
  exploration of culture and core values in sustaining ambidextrous designs 407

Harrison and Caroll's model of culture formation 220
  single factor model of organizational culture 220
customization, mass 166
cycle
  cyclical cartel behavior 692
  learning 417, 419
  of conformity 433
  technology cycles 388, 390, 406

Darwinian assumption 98, 101
Darwinian selection 328
data
  data collection 794
  data sets, collection and archiving 798
  on-line data archives 226
  qualitative datum 881
  quantitative datum 880
death
  mortality rates 564
  of routines 88
  organizational 668
decisions
  decision accuracy 184
  decision making 398
  make-or-buy decisions 470, 471, 486
decline, institutional 510
decomposability, near 167
decoupling 379
  institutional 238
deductive empirical method 739
  empirico-deductivist approach 742
degenerating theories 23
degree
  degree centrality 288
  of coupling 228
  of interconnectedness (K) 447
deinstitutionalization 497, 510, 529
  sources of 507
delay, density 314, 673
deliberative style, reflexivity and entrenchment 744
demand models 59
demise of a dominant corporate form 500
demography 365
  demographic processes 305, 307
  demographic similarity and incentive alignment 243
  of organizational founding 317
  organizational 370

dense samples 790
density 372
  and competitive processes 315
  and institutional processes 313
  and legitimacy 270, 314
  as a form of experience 423
  density delay 314, 673
  density dependence model 314, 337, 673
  density dependent explanations for founding
    and failure 312, 313
  density dependent selection 262
  dense versus sparse social networks 196,
    198
  ecological models of density dependence
    509
  firm density 690
  relational 315, 318
  rule 424
dependence 306, 313, 317, 366
  age and size 306, 307
  firm heterogeneity and path dependence 481
  interorganizational power and 570, 599
  intraorganizational power and 138
  location 314
  mass dependence 314
  organizational power and 363
  power-dependence framework 368
  power and 11, 15, 27, 138, 365
  resource dependency 153, 272, 282, 364,
    365, 368, 369, 371, 381, 467, 481, 528,
    599, 600, 603, 605, 606, 612, 616, 621,
    677
  Weberian perspectives on power and
    dependence 373
deparadoxification 134
depletion of assets 420
  model of rule change 424
deregulation 676
descending model of analysis 815
description, *ex post* 339
design
  contract 251
  cross-section or longitudinal 783
  dominant 250, 386, 390, 391, 395, 570,
    622, 672
  evolution as 113
  experimental 845
  longitudinal 783
  organization 681
  search design 681
  study design and target population 782

total design method (TDM) 796
destruction, creative 390
detail 222
detectable terms 769, 890
determinism 305
development
  development process, improving the
    effectiveness of 163
  key success factors in new product
    development 159
  of new technology 158
diffusion
  comparative, across nations and practices
    500
  diffusion studies 502
  intraorganizational 107
  of innovations 107, 622
  of technology in intraorganizational
    ecologies 109
dimensionalizing 858, 861
director experience and information asymmetry
    248
director interlocks 606, 609, 612
disaggregation 171
discontinuities
  discontinuous change 402
  discontinuous innovation 393, 396
  innovation streams and discontinuous
    organization change 402
  technological 391
discovery
  discovery logic 752, 890
  theory discovery 831
discrete event simulation 829, 834
discretion 374
dismissal of CEOs 236
dispersed learning and aspirations 433
displacement, goal 85
disruptive technologies 395
dissemination of organizational knowledge
    423, 427
dissolution
  hazards of 528
  risks of 525
distance, technology 292
distributed cognition
  and transactive systems of knowledge 594
  distributed and shared cognition 130
distributed expertise 184
districts, industrial 557
divergent thinking 190

diversification 476, 477, 478, 485
  corporate diversification, direction of 479
  effect of, on firm performance 479
  firm 630
  growth through 335
diversity 304
  managing 190
  of experience 200, 434
  sample 877
division of labor 715
dogmatism 742
  dogmatic falsificationism 745
  dogmatists 736, 742
dominance 145
  demise of a dominant corporate form 500
  dominant designs 250, 386, 388, 390, 391,
    395, 570, 622, 672
  Weber's analysis of bureaucratic domination
    363
double interacts 101
downward causation 92
drift, goal 261, 265, 269
duration, temporal 878
dyads 523, 524
  studies of 62
dynamic learning capability 283
dynamic-static efficiency tradeoff 691
dynamics, rule 421

EEO law, impact of, on employment practices
  504
ecology/ies 13, 29, 442
  ecological processes 305, 311
  ecological models of density dependence 509
  ecological theory 13
  integration of institutional and population
    ecology theory 270
  interorganizational 541, 546
  intraorganizational 75, 109
  of a technical system 546
  of formal jobs 109
  of organizational rules 99, 109
  of technology-based competition 631
  organizational 304, 621, 677
  population 270, 622
  rule 424, 427
  social ecology of jobs 420
  structural 366
  technology structure as an ecology of
    organizational positions 622
economic transactions, effects of social

  structure on 527
economics 18, 28
  axioms of 760
  economic change 79
  economic imperialism 695
  economic leverage 611
  economic perspective 11
  evolutionary 18
  information 247
  interorganizational 686
  intraorganizational 233
  organizational economics 467, 485
  spatial 677
economy
  Internet 277
  political 15, 601
edge of chaos *see* chaos
effect(s)
  cause and effect relationships 736
  commitment 689, 690, 699, 703, 706
  conduct effect 688, 699, 703, 704, 706
  dysfunctional 48
  environmental 690, 706
  exhaustion 653
  forms and effects of intraorganizational
    institutions 38
  frog-pond 153
  institutions and institutional 12, 498, 510
  learning 689, 690, 699, 703, 706
  market structure 688, 706
  Matthew 644, 648
  mobility 689, 699, 703, 706
  of diversification on firm performance 479
  of economic performance on organizational
    power 377, 378
  of equal rights law 503
  of group norms 39
  of multiple networks 295
  of social structure on economic transactions
    527
  of turnover on knowledge retention 191
  Red Queen 338, 570, 652
  relative 340
  window 687, 706
effectiveness, organizational 365
efficiency 19
  dynamic-static efficiency tradeoff 691
  efficiency-driven firm entry, growth and
    decline 692
  static versus dynamic efficiency dilemma 688
egocentric network 63, 281, 282, 287, 536

role of social psychological processes 293
either-or thinking 134
elites 506, 508, 560, 614
  corporate 15
  elite cohesion 605
  managerial 372
  social 513
  social ties among 607
  social ties to 604
embeddedness 13, 482, 527, 520
  embedded coordination 167
  institutional 314
  interorganizational 530
  relational 502, 510
  structural 818
emergence
  and constraint 222
  emergent behavior 215
  of complex adaptive systems 453
emotion 129, 226
  role of 53
empiricism 720, 753, 889
  deductive empirical method 739
  empirical corroboration 677
  empirico-deductivist approach 742
  logical 753, 892
  methodological empiricists 737
employee governance, model of 263
employment
  employment practices 784
  impact of EEO law on employment practices
    504
  private-sector employment by organization
    size 788
emulative models 222
enactment 10, 353
  and meaning creation 352
  enacted environment 365
  enactment perspective 351, 353, 355
  market stories and the enactment of the belief
    hierarchy 584
  of industry belief systems 585
  of organizational communities 583
endogenous dynamics 512
  endogenous dynamic of rationalization 513
endogenous evolutionary change 331, 338
endogenous experience 432
ENR *see* evolutionary naturalist realism
ensembles, aggregates and 318
entrenchment
  deliberative style, reflexivity and 744

versus contestation 378
entrepreneurship 92
  entrepreneurial activity 623
  institutional entrepreneurs 505
entropy 498
entry and exit barriers 690
environment
  enacted environment 365
  environmental effect 690, 706
  environmental responses 417
  environmental variability 78, 311
  environmental volatility 667
  fine-grained 311
  institutional 9, 250, 259, 266, 273
  organizational 8
  spatial and temporal environmental
    variation 312
  task 8
  technical 8, 260, 274
epistemic invariance, principle of 769, 895
epistemology 890
  epistemological anarchists 734
  epistemological attribution 734
  epistemological commitments 743, 746, 747
  epistemological misattributions 733, 744
  epistemological pluralism 740
  epistemological relativism 743
  epistemological stance 734
  epistemological traditions in sociology 717
  epistemological uniformity 742
  evolutionary 754, 890
  glossary of terms 889
  model-centered evolutionary realist 755
  model-centered organizational 752, 758
  nonfoundationalist 720
  objectivist epistemological stance 737
  of cross-paradigmatic dialogue 735
  of truth 740
  ontologically strong relativist dynamic
    epistemology 756
  organizational epistemology 19, 713, 715,
    733
  postpositive selectionist fallibilist scientific
    realist epistemology 753
  selectionist evolutionary epistemology 768
equal rights law, effect of 503
equifinial meaning 353
equilibria
  frozen 570
  Nash 694, 749
  punctuated 364, 369, 404

equilibria (*cont'd*)
  Radner's ε-equilibrium notion 694
equity perceptions 51
equivalence, structural 267, 631
eras
  of ferment 388, 395, 405, 622
  of incremental change 405
error catastrophe 443
esteem 59
estimation, reduced form 474
ethno methodology 761
ethnography 868
  ethnographic studies of organizations 807
  industry 586
  of conflict resolution 376
European Economic Community (EEC) 275
event(s)
  discrete event simulation 829, 834
  event history analysis 459
  incidents and 879
evolution 14, 29
  and co-evolution 341
  as design 113
  belief 595
  community 543
  cultural 98, 106
  endogenous evolutionary change 331, 338
  evolutionary economics 18
  evolutionary epistemology 754, 890
  evolutionary game theory 115
  evolutionary theories of adaptation 442
  evolutionary theory 462, 558
  evolutionary theory perspective 621
  evolutionary transformation 329, 330
  hierarchical 98, 103, 105, 109
  interorganizational 557, 569, 629
  intraorganizational 98
  law evolving 567
  learning as evolution of knowledge 430
  market evolution 567
  market structure evolution 692
  naturalist evolutionary realism 722
  of evolution 91
  organizational 327, 386, 398
  recombination and 455, 457
  selectionist evolutionary epistemology 768
  sociocultural 7, 77
  structural 340
  see also coevolution
evolutionary naturalist realism (ENR) 442,
    462, 558, 720

  and complexity 727
ex ante prediction 339
ex post description 339
exchange 15
  exchange hazards 469
  exchange power tactic 147
  role of 530
  social 244, 247, 365, 379, 599, 600, 607,
    616
exclusive market centers 535
executive succession 377
exhaustion effects 653
exit
  and entry barriers 690
  strategic business exit 77
expanded institutionalism 529
expansion of theories 273
expectancy, life 564
expectation
  expectation based learning 221
  rational expectation models 421
  status 433
experience
  collaborative 657
  competitive 643, 644, 647
  congenital 647
  diversity of 200, 434
  endogenous 432
  experiential learning 221, 642
  industry operating 643
  learning from one's own experience 200
  operating 643, 657
  power, experience and agency costs 249
  quality of 431
  related 653
  sensory 717
  similarity of 200
  types of 657
  unrelated 653
experimentation 426
  experimental design 845
  experiments 771
expertise 145, 184
  progressivist emphasis on predictability and
    expertise 508
explanation, truthful 753
explanatory fiction 131
explicationism, literary 761
exploitation 426, 448
  exploitive learning 643
  of knowledge 397

exploration 397, 426, 448
  and exploitation 82, 111, 285, 399, 422
  and exploitation, tension between 197
  explorative learning 435, 643
  of culture and core values in sustaining
    ambidextrous designs 407
exposure to competitors 423
expression, representation and 111
extinction, speciation and 330, 332

fact-value dichotomy 747
failure
  density dependent explanations for founding
    and failure 312, 313
  failure traps 426
  performance 507
  risks of organizational failure 643
fallibilist 745
fallibilist (realist) epistemology 719, 890
fallible social perceptual foundationalism 723
false beliefs, persistence of 721
falsificationism 744
  dogmatic falsificationism 745
  falsificationists 748
  methodological falsificationism 745
FDI *see* foreign direct investment
feedback, performance 421, 425
ferment, eras of 388, 395, 405, 622
fiction 131
field(s)
  field research methods 867
  longitudinal field studies 869
  organizational field 526, 259
finance capitalists 606
finance conception of control 267, 269, 377
financial hegemony 609, 612
financial institutions, role of 609
financial resources 286
fine-grained environments 311
fine-grained population substructures 317
firm(s) 736
  as an information machine 695
  as portfolio model 267, 331, 334, 508
  behavioral theory of the firm 4, 699
  effect of diversification on firm performance
    479
  efficiency-driven firm entry, growth and
    decline 692
  firm capability 283
  firm conduct 687
  firm density 690

firm disaggregation and the adoption of
    modular organizational forms 171
firm diversification 630
firm heterogeneity and path dependence 481
firm performance 282, 287, 294, 295, 705
firm risk 236
firm size, R&D investment, and industry
    structure 162
firm strategy 686
firm symmetry 696
  interfirm interaction norms and
    competitiveness 567
  interfirm mobility 636, 637
  interfirm political behavior 610
  interfirm power 605
  measuring firm performance 293
  micro-level interactions between firms 666
  virtual 509
first mover advantage 673
first order logic 697
first philosophy type 723, 891
fiscal sociology 528, 529
fish-scale model of omniscience 21
fit
  as complementarity 198
  as similarity 198
  of organizational components 195
  versus misfit tension 197
fitness
  inclusive 91
  fitness landscape 113, 336, 447, 459, 670
flexible manufacturing systems (FMS) 165
foolishness, competitive advantage of 703
forbearance 423
  forbearance law 470
foreclosure, vertical 485
foreign direct investment (FDI) 472, 485
foreign entry experience 657
form(s)
  and effects of intraorganizational institutions
    38
  at birth 264
  institutionalized 267
  market form effect 689, 699, 703, 704, 706
  network organizational 529
  organizational forms 171, 542, 583
formal jobs
  ecology of 109
  training 784
formal model 759, 761, 891
formal organizational policies 500

formal rules 432, 434
formation, change and collapse of communities 548
foundationalism 891
  fallible social perceptual 723
founding conditions 261
  density dependent explanations for founding and failure 312, 313
fractals 833
fragmentation of knowledge 716
frame(s)
  area frame 788
  cultural-frame perspectives 333
  list frame 788
  of comparability 583, 588
  political framing 148
  selecting a sample frame 788
framework
  members–tool–tasks 183, 659
  multiple conceptual 728
  spatiotemporal 727
  structure-conduct-performance (SCP) 18
French Conventions School 275
frog-pond effects 153
frozen equilibria 570
full competition 545
full mutualism 545
functional heterogeneity 190
functional perspectives 364, 616
functional reconstitution 607
fundamental attribution error 59, 145

game theory 693, 748
  Bertrand–Cournot Nash game 691
  evolutionary 115
  game-theoretic model building 687, 705
  language games 743
  of competitive rivalry 686
  Prisoner's Dilemma 679
  subgame perfection 694
garbage can model of organizational decision making 211, 215, 222, 461, 698
gatekeeper 194
  organizational 797
gender 67
  inequalities 371
  organizational sex composition 371
general systems theory 442
generalists 311, 318
generality 885
generalized reciprocity 365

generation and recognition problems 424
generative mechanisms 717, 766, 891
genotype 111
geographic space
  co-location in 114
  geographic clustering 633
glass ceiling 67
glossary of epistemological terms 889
goal
  goal adaptation 419
  goal displacement 85
  goal drift 261, 265, 269
  goal material, and methods 818
  goal setting theory 246
  instrumental 266
  stated 542
God's eye view of reality 721
golden parachutes 268, 502
governance
  corporate governance 242, 252
  governance inseparability 483
  governance structures 484, 561, 530
  model of employee governance 263
government, city manager form of 263
grammars of action 820
grantedness
  cognitive measures of taken for 511
  taken-for-granted beliefs/norms/recipes 37, 48, 591
granularity 878
greenmail, corporate 241
grounded theory building (GTB) 849, 850
  research methods 849
group(s)
  group norms 39, 276
  group sources of power 148
  voluntary 336
  watchdog 333, 512, 562
growth
  Lotka–Volterra logistic growth model 544, 770
  through diversification 335
Guttman scale 770, 891
  of effective science 768

hazard(s) 471
  contractual hazards 471, 476, 478
  exchange hazards 469
  hazard rate 884
  hazard rate model 365
  hazardousness of change 310

of dissolution 528
hedging, organizational 334
hedonism 499
hegemony 740
    financial 609, 612
herd theory 658
heterogeneity
    firm heterogeneity and path dependence 481
    functional 190
    homogeneity versus heterogeneity in senior
        team composition 407
    in founding 317
    resource 485
hierarchy/ies
    hierarchical evolution assumption 98, 103
    hierarchical evolution in populations of
        strategic initiatives 105, 109
    hierarchical teams 184
    hierarchically nested nature of
        organizational phenomena 7
    market stories and the enactment of the belief
        hierarchy 584
    of rules 419
    versus informal uses of power 150
history/ies
    event history analysis 459
    historical contingency 558
    historical origins of institutional structures
        262
    historical relativism 753, 891
    historicism 761
    historiographic research 807
    organizational 509
    rule 421
homogeneity versus heterogeneity in senior
    team composition 407
homophily 62, 68, 365
horizontal alliances 601
horizontal and vertical interorganizational
    relationships 612
hot-cold debate 129
    hot intraorganizational institutions 52
human attention 91
human perceptual and cognitive mechanisms
    730
humanism 719, 761
Hume and Popper's refutation of inductive logic
    740
hypernetwork or multiplicity sampling 790,
    791

iconic model 759, 763, 891
idealism, transcendental 756, 897
identity 41, 276
    identity management by organizational
        subgroups 39
    network 283
    organizational 50
idiosyncratic microstates 891
ignorance 355
illusory perception 722
imitation 666
    barriers to 672
    imitation learning 221
    organizational 340
    outcome 645
    trait 645
imperfect competition, microeconomics of 687
imperialism 742
    economic 695
    imperialists 736
implementation
    implementing organizational surveys 782
    rule 432
impression management 238, 243, 247
improvement
    continuous incremental 396
    learning as improving 428
in-degree 59
incentives 236, 252
    demographic similarity and incentive
        alignment 243
    incentives alignment 236, 247
    managerial incentives and risk aversion
        240
    symbolic management and incentive
        alignment 242
    to learn 652
    versus monitoring 251
incidents
    and events 879
    reliability and validity of incident
        construction 881
inclusive fitness 91
incommensurability 753, 891
incorporation, law of 260
incremental change
    eras of 405
    incrementalism versus punctuation 90
    incremental innovation 392, 396
incubation 185
independence of boards 236

individual(s)
  individual action 417
  individual adaptations 52
  individual beliefs 417
  individual network 63
  individual power 142, 152
induced process(es) 79, 105
inductive logic 748
industrial districts 557
industrial organization (IO) 686
  exploring the IO-OS interface 704–5
  IO studies 691
  IO-OS cross-fertilization circle 697, 698, 705
  IO's model of market performance 688
  IO's modeling strategy 693
industry belief systems 580, 583, 585, 593
industry competitiveness experience 644
industry ethnography 586
industry macro-cultures 584
industry operating experience 643
industry recipe(s) 584, 585
  as logics for market action 590
industry rhetoric, analysis of 585
industry structure, firm size, R&D investment,
  and 162
inequalities, gender 371
inertia 365, 627
  and interorganizational evolution 629
  organizational inertia 398, 622
  structural 90, 261, 306, 309, 339, 650
infinite regress 745
influence 354
  social 44, 244
informal networks 365
informal routines 434
informants, identifying 792
information
  asymmetry of 247
  director experience and information
    asymmetry 248
  firm as an information machine 695
  information-defective investment 701
  information economics 247
  information network 225
  information processing perspective 348, 355,
    476
  information processing systems 15
  knowledge and information resources 287
  neo-information processing paradigm 216,
    224
  sharing of unshared information 189

information technology (IT) 218
  impact of 168
  IT-as-agent computational theories 218
  IT focus 224
ingratiation 146
inheritance 14, 87
injunctive norms 48
innovation(s) 426
  challengers as institutional innovators 505
  diffusion of 107, 622
  direction of corporate 632
  discontinuous 393, 396
  incremental 392, 396
  innovation behaviors 622, 632
  innovation search 419
  innovation streams 387, 392, 393, 394
  innovation streams and discontinuous
    organization change 402
  innovation types 392, 394
  institutionalization of a deviant innovation
    501
  market based innovations 395
  patents as innovation indices 632
  service innovation 407
innovativeness 59
  innovative learning 642
inseparability, governance 483
insider versus outsider succession 376
instability, market 676
institution(s) 12, 27
  and institutional effects 498, 510
  cognitive (vs. normative) elements of
    institutions 12
  completed 513
  financial 609
  interorganizational 497
  intraorganizational 37, 41, 42, 52
  life cycle of 510
  organizational 259
  process 38, 42
  structure 38
  value 38, 52
institutional adulteration 509
institutional change 266, 269
  sociology of 497
  triggers of 507
institutional constraints 260
institutional contagion 433
institutional decline 510
institutional decoupling 238
institutional dimensions of organizations 3

institutional effects 12
   institutions and 498, 510
institutional embeddedness 314
institutional entrepreneurs 505
institutional environments 9, 250, 259, 273
   change in 266
institutional forms, sociology of 497
institutional innovators, challengers as 505
institutional isomorphism 500, 614
institutional locus, shift of 332
institutional logics 366, 820
institutional perspective 10, 366, 373, 380
institutional pillars 499
institutional practice 261
institutional processes, density and 313
institutional reform
   analysis of top-down 507
   reformers at the top 503
institutional resources 287
institutional rules 501
institutional structures, historical origins of
      262
institutional theory 269, 621, 680
   integration of institutional and population
      ecology theory 270
institutionalism
   expanded 529
   Selznick's old institutionalism 506
institutionalization 5, 89, 528, 366, 520
   and institutional decline 510
   as a determinant of power and politics in
      organizations 375
   institutionalized forms 267
   institutionalized group norms 276
   naturalistic accounts of 502
   normative approach to 375
   of a deviant innovation 501
   of power 377
   process of 263
instrument construction 793
instrumental goals 266
instrumental reliability 763, 772, 892
integration
   integrating approaches 151
   integrative complexity 190
   of institutional and population ecology
      theory 270
   of TCE and RBV 483
   strategic 407
   theoretical 237, 242
   vertical 473, 476, 483, 676, 667

intellective models 216, 222
intellectual property 621
intelligent analysis tools 227
intensity of competition 677
intent
   internalization 650
   substitution 650, 655
interaction
   double interacts 101
   interaction processes 76, 80
   interfirm interaction norms and
      competitiveness 567
   micro-level interactions between firms 666
   teaching and practicing interactive
      reasoning 748
   topology of 112, 114
intercommunity competition 544
interconnectedness (K), degree of 447
intercorporate partnering 632
interdependence 284, 602, 666
   reciprocal 664
   sequential 664
   symbiotic 602
   transaction 484
interdisciplinary research 247
interest(s)
   conflict of 530
   shareholder 245
interfirm interaction norms and
      competitiveness 567
interfirm mobility 636, 637
interfirm political behavior 610
interfirm power 605
interfirm ties, avoidance of 525
interlocks
   between corporations 606
   board 244, 635, 654
   director interlocks 606, 609, 612
   networks of interlocking markets 531, 532
   networks of interlocking organizations 531
intermarket structure 531
internal corporate venturing 79
internalization intent 650
Internet economy 277
interorganizational cognition and
      interpretation 579
interorganizational complexity and
      computation 664
interorganizational ecology 541, 546
interorganizational economics 686
interorganizational embeddedness 530

interorganizational evolution 557
  inertia and 629
  role of contingency in interorganizational
    evolutionary process 569
interorganizational institutions 497
interorganizational learning 187, 642
interorganizational level 7, 495
interorganizational mimicry 658
interorganizational model of cohesion 610
interorganizational networks (ION) 225, 520
  ION box 522
interorganizational origins and change 559
interorganizational power
  and dependence 570, 599
  sources of 607
interorganizational relationships
  and interorganizational learning 654
  horizontal and vertical 612
  types of 654
interorganizational technology 176, 621
interpretation 351, 846
  cognition and 15, 27
  interorganizational 579
  interpretism 761
  interpretive approach 15, 345
  interpretivist research 590
  intraorganizational 119
  managerial issue 347
  organizational cognition and 344
  perception and 345
  shared interpretive schemes 353
  strategic issue interpretation 348
interrelations, heedful 353
Interstate Commerce Act of 1887 266
interviewer training 796
intra-plant transfer of knowledge 109
intra-regional mobility 656
intraorganizational cognition and
    interpretation 119
intraorganizational complexity and
    computation 208
intraorganizational diffusion 107
intraorganizational ecology 75
  diffusion of technology in intraorganizational
    ecologies 109
intraorganizational economics 233
intraorganizational evolution 98
intraorganizational institutions 37
  forms and effects of 38
  hot 52
intraorganizational learning 181

intraorganizational level 7
intraorganizational networks 58
intraorganizational power and dependence 138
intraorganizational process institutions 42
intraorganizational selection 99
intraorganizational technology 158
intraorganizational value institutions 41
invariance, principle of epistemic 769, 895
investment
  information-defective 701
  irreversibility of 689
  R&D investment and industry structure 162
IO *see* industrial organization
ION *see* interorganizational networks
iron cage 263, 461
iron triangle 525
isolated idealized structures 762, 758, 892
isolationism as an impediment to
    interdisciplinary research 246
isomorphism 261, 264
  coercive 610, 614
  institutional 500, 614
  mimetic 87, 704
Israel 265
issue identification 348

jargon 743
jobs
  ecology of formal 109
  employment practices 784
  job deaths 81, 418
  social ecology of 420
joint centrality 284
joint RBV-TCE 478
justice 51
  procedural 294
justification logic 752, 892
justificationists 744

knowledge 475, 642, 738, 743
  and information resources 287
  creating 181, 190
  dissemination of organizational 423, 427
  distributed cognition and transactive systems
    of 594
  effect of turnover on knowledge retention
    191
  exploitation of 397
  Foucalt's identification of knowledge with
    power 740
  fragmentation of 716

intra-plant transfer of 109
knowing-doing gap 49
knowledge management systems 49, 87
knowledge network 225
knowledge repositories 201
knowledge sharing 283, 655
knowledge spillovers 644
knowledge structures 122
knowledge transfer 17, 185
  learning as evolution of 430
  mapping of 724, 757
  model of knowledge combination 430
  nature of 127
  organizational 415, 432, 427
  prior 649
  receivers of 649
  retaining 181, 191
  scientific 724
  senders of new knowledge 647
  status of knowledge creator 644
  stickiness of 427
  tacit 102
  transactive systems of 594
  transfer of 17, 181, 185, 193, 634

labor, division of 715
Lamarckian inheritance 87
Lamarckian selection 328
landscape(s)
  fitness 336, 447, 459, 670
  structured 680
language 723
  artifacts, language and apprenticeship 106
  language games 743
  language learning 723
  observation 736, 761, 893
  theoretical 761, 896
  truth-in-a-language 744
law(s)
  anti-trust 266, 335, 377, 503, 688
  causal 736, 738
  effect of equal rights law 503
  forbearance law 470
  Interstate Commerce Act of 1887 266
  law evolving 567
  law-like relation 771
  law-like statements 717, 757, 892
  Moore's Law 172
  of incorporation 260
  power law distribution 217
leadership 189, 460

charismatic leaders 146, 407
  role of team leaders 163
learners, communities of 423, 427
learning 16, 28, 221
  and competition 652
  as an example of adaptation 336
  as evolution of knowledge 430
  as improving 428
  as recording 429
  audience 417, 419
  by doing 406, 570, 689
  collective 354
  conceptions of 428
  congenital 644
  dispersed learning and aspirations 433
  dynamic learning capability 283
  expectation based 221
  experiential learning 221, 642
  exploitive learning 643
  explorative learning 435, 643
  from one's own experience 200
  from others 651
  imitation 221
  incentives to learn 652
  innovative 642
  interorganizational 187, 642, 654
  intraorganizational 181
  language 723
  learning actions 643
  learning alliances 87
  learning behaviors, types of 681
  learning curve(s) 17, 106, 429, 642, 651,
    654, 657
  learning cycle 417, 419
  learning effect 689, 690, 699, 703, 706
  learning races 297, 653, 655
  learning substitution 432
  learning theory perspective 621
  limits of 422, 426, 429
  nested 429
  organizational 335, 399, 415, 416, 419
  population-level 187, 319
  prior 433
  role-constrained 417, 419
  rule-based organizational 100
  search and 108
  self-learning 651
  social learning theory 680
  sources of 431
  structural 221
  superstitious 85, 417, 419, 429

learning (*cont'd*)
  transfer 17
  under ambiguity 417, 419
  vicarious 319, 644
  winner-take-all learning situations 653
legal changes 562
legalization of the workplace 263
legitimacy 272, 502, 509, 580
  cognitive and sociopolitical 313
  contagion of 498
  cultural and political sources of variability in
    legitimacy 510
  density and 270, 314
  impact of legitimacy on survival rates 271
  legitimate power 141
  legitimating change 508
  legitimation 666
  measures of 510
  quest for 616
  sociopolitical 313
  versus status 511
levels
  interorganizational 7, 495
  intraorganizational 7
  macro-level patterns 90
  macro-level population dynamics 666
  multilevel approach 7
  of analysis 61, 360
  of organization 7
leverage
  economic 611
liability/ies 307, 308
life cycle
  life cycle theories 89
  of institutions 510
life expectancy 564
limits of learning 422, 426, 429
links-in-time 84
list frame 788
literary explicationism 761
lobbying of state officials 601
local search 622
localized competition 314
location dependence 314
locus/loci
  and essence of organizational cognition 355
  of cognition 355, 358
  of organizational boundaries 407
  of power 614
  of technological variation 407
  shift of institutional locus 332

logic(s)
  discovery 752, 890
  first order logic 697
  inductive 748
  institutional 366, 820
  justification 752, 892
  logical circularity 745
  logical empiricism 753, 892
  logical positivism 736, 753, 892
  rules and 379
logistic and Lotka–Volterra equations 320
longitudinal design 783
longitudinal field studies 869
loose coupling 78, 167, 261, 269, 462
  and NK phenomena 444, 446
  loosely coupled organizations 676
Lotka–Volterra logistic growth model 544, 770
  logistic and Lotka–Volterra equations 320
luck, cultivation of 406
Lyapunov exponent 213

Machiavellianism 145
macro change model 404
macro-cultures, industry 584
macro-level patterns 90
macro-level population dynamics 666
mafia 525
maintenance and loss of power 152
make-or-buy decisions 470, 471, 486
Malthusian assumption 98, 99
management
  cross-national differences in management
    and governance 557
  identity 39
  impression 238, 243, 247
  knowledge management systems 49, 87
  monitoring 248
  scientific 4
  symbolic 53, 242
managerial cognition
  managerial and organizational cognition
    122
  role of 407
managerial control 52
managerial dimensions of organizations 3
managerial elites 372
managerial incentives and risk aversion 240
managerial issue interpretation 347
managerialist school 233
managing change 873
managing diversity 190

manipulation
  organizational 52
  proactive 53
Mann Gulch disaster 39, 43, 852
manufacturing competences, transmission of
    109
mapping(s)
  cognitive maps 122, 680
  model 892
  objectivity of 725
  of knowledge 724, 757
  visual mapping 882
market(s) 532
  boundary beliefs as market identities 588
  cognitive micro-processes of market-making
    580
  core 535, 586
  exclusive market centers 535
  industry recipes as logics for market action
    590
  intermarket structure 531
  market based innovations 395
  market behavior 686
  market boundaries 591
  market evolution 567
  market form effect 689, 699, 703, 704, 706
  market instability 676
  market network 225, 531, 532, 583
  market performance 687
  market stories and the enactment of the belief
    hierarchy 584
  market strategy 542
  multimarket contact 486
  peripheral 535
  regulated internal labor markets 506
  single market center 535
  sociology of 13
market status orders, reputational rankings as
    591
market structures 557, 559, 687, 693
  market structure effect 688, 706
  market structure evolution 692
  unified market structure 535
Markovian conception of organizational
    adaptation 629
Marx
  classical sociological theories of Marx and
    Weber 599
  Marx's model of class struggle 513
  Marxist accounts of revolutionary change
    506

mass customization and modularity 166
mass dependence 314
matching, template 882
Matthew effect 644, 648
meaning
  enactment and meaning creation 352
  equifinial 353
  meaning creation 355
  meaning structures 819
  semantic 761, 896
  socially shared 594
  systems of 15, 344
measures
  measurement problems 273
  measuring changes in performance 182
  measuring firm performance 293
  nondensity 314
  of legitimacy 510
  patent-based measures of resources 479
members–tool–tasks framework 183, 659
membership
  changes within organizations 188
  rotating 196
  stability versus fluidity in 196
memes 91
memory, transactive 187, 193, 195, 435,
    659
mental models 579
  overlapping 594
mentoring programs 58, 70
mergers, vertical 472
meta-network approach (PCANS) 224
meta-routines 83, 87, 104
metaphor approach 212
metaphysical discourse 736
metaphysical realists 737
metaphysical terms 718, 756, 893
  avoidance of 769
methodological empiricists 737
methodological falsificationism 745
methodological variety theory 341
methodology of science 724
metrics
  performance 585
  technical 592
micro- and macro-processes, linking 336
micro-level interactions between firms 666
microeconomics of imperfect competition 687
microstates
  idiosyncratic 891
  stochastic 754

mimicry
  interorganizational 658
  mimetic isomorphism 87, 704
  mimetic processes 64, 259, 262
  mimetic, normative and coercive pressures 262
mind, collective 353
mindlessness 40, 46, 52
  mindless behavior 130
mindsets 584
misattributions, epistemological 733, 744
misfit tension, fit versus 197
mission 80, 366
mobility
  interfirm 636, 637
  intra-regional 656
  mobility effect 689, 699, 703, 706
  mobilization of social groups 505
  reciprocal causalities through the mobility effect 690
models/modeling
  attainment discrepancy 421
  behavioral game-theoretic modeling 705
  bifurcated-model-centered science 771
  Campbell's (blind) variation-selection-retention (VSR) model 7, 14, 25, 77, 101, 588, 722
  conceptions of the axiom-theory-model-phenomena relationship 764
  demand models 59
  density dependence 314, 337, 673
  ecological models of density dependence 509
  emulative models 222
  firm as portfolio 267, 331, 334, 508
  fish-scale model of omniscience 21
  formal 759, 761, 891
  game-theoretic model building 687, 705
  hazard rate model 365
  iconic model 759, 763, 891
  intellective 216, 222
  interorganizational model of cohesion 610
  IO's model of market performance 688
  knowledge mapping 724, 757
  Lotka–Volterra logistic growth 544, 770
  macro change 404
  Marx's model of class struggle 513
  mental 579, 594
  model-centered evolutionary realist epistemology 755
  model-centered organizational epistemology 752, 758

model-centered science 759
model-centered science and bifurcated adequacy tests 763
model realism 675, 679
model structure reliability 773
model substructures 765, 893
multiform 314
nexus of contracts 509
NK 443, 444, 446, 665, 670, 675, 765
NKC 677
of employee governance 263
of knowledge combination 430
of organizational population dynamics 11
ORGAHEAD multi-agent 215, 217
organizational consultant expert system model 216
overlapping mental 594
p-star 69
parsimony 841
political cultural model of organizational change 269
rational expectation 421
reach 59
realism 682
resource partitioning 318
simulation 841
single factor model of organizational culture 220
structural autonomy 603
structural modeling approach 485
system dynamics (or continuous) simulation models 834
validity 841
valuation and portfolio balancing 163
variation-selection-retention (VSR) 7, 14, 25, 77, 101, 588, 722
modularity 622
  mass customization and 166
  modular organizations 166, 167, 171
  modular products and processes 170
momentum
  organizational 306, 309, 332
  repetitive 433
monitoring
  costs of monitoring top management 240
  incentives versus 251
  monitoring capacity 236
  monitoring management 248
  monitoring when the principal is a group 248
  performance 245, 247
  social exchange and board monitoring 244

strategic side-effects of board monitoring 245
Moebius strip organizations 509
monopoly 689
Moore's Law 172
moral sentiments 501
mortality rates 564
motivation
  and coordination of managers 486
  power motive 145
movement, personnel 196
MRQAP (multiple regression quadratic
    assignment procedure) 69
multi-agent model, ORGAHEAD 215, 217
multidisciplinarity 730
multidivisional form, rise of the 529
multiform models 314
multilevel approach 7
multimarket contact 486
multiparadigmaticism 753
multiple conceptual frameworks 728
multiple networks, effects of 295
multiple perceptual frameworks 728
multiple perspectives 12, 729
multiplex networks 340
museums 263
mutability of schemas 498
mutable boundaries 224
mutualism 318, 545
myopia 422, 426, 429

naive methodological falsificationism 745
Nash equilibrium 694, 749
natural system 2, 5, 12, 15
natural-open systems 15
naturalism 719, 761
  evolutionary naturalist realism (ENR) 442,
    462, 558, 720, 727
  naturalist evolutionary realism 722
  naturalistic accounts of institutionalization
    502
near decomposability 167
needs 142, 225
negotiations, repeated 47, 53
neoclassical utility-maximization notion 693
neo-information processing paradigm 216, 224
neo-institutional approach 12
nesting
  hierarchically nested nature of
    organizational phenomena 7
  nested learning 429
  nested processes 103

networks 13, 217, 225, 366, 431
  actor–task–tool 436
  and social capital 371
  and task fit 69
  assignment of 225
  centrality in alliance networks 623
  dense versus sparse social networks 196, 198
  egocentric 63, 281, 282, 287, 536
  individual 63
  informal 365
  information 225
  interorganizational 225, 520
  intraorganizational 58
  knowledge 225
  market 225, 583
  meta-network approach (PCANS) 224
  multiple networks, effects of 295
  multiplex 340
  needs 225
  network approach 223
  network autocorrelation 68
  network benefits and constraints 284
  network centrality 288, 612, 623
  network conception of control 529
  network configuration 283
  network constraints 286
  network identity 283
  network organizational form, rise of 529
  network organizations 167
  network perspective 10
  network resources 283, 286
  network structures 60
  network theory 616
  of interlocking markets 531, 532
  of interlocking organizations 531
  old boy 67
  organizational 281
  precedence 225
  requirements 225
  role of social psychological processes 293
  skills 225
  social capital as cohesion and network
    closure 60
  social network analysis 115
  sparse personal 616
  subnetworks 182
  substitution 225
  technological 626
  value 395
neutrality 545
newness 88, 307

Newtonian straitjacket 742
nexus of contracts 461, 508, 509
niche(s)
    niche width 306, 311
    organizational niche overlap 314
    status of 625
nihilists 734, 743, 744
NK models 443, 665, 670, 675, 765
    loose coupling and NK phenomena 444, 446
    NKC model 677
noise 728
nomic necessity 769, 771, 893
nominalist approach 8
non-substitutability 149
nondensity measures 314
nonfoundationalist epistemology 720
nonlinear dynamical systems 442
nonresponse, minimizing 796
normal accidents 213
normal science 754, 893
    straitjacket of 742
normative agency literature 234
normative approach to institutionalization 375
normative boundaries, relational activity-based
    8
normative influences 40
normative processes 259, 262
normative structures 259
normative theories 375
norms
    effects of group norms 39, 276
    injunctive 48
    interfirm interaction norms and
        competitiveness 567
    of reciprocity 244
    taken-for-granted 37, 48, 591
    temporal norms at work 39
North America Free Trade Act (NAFTA) 275
notoriety 433

obedience to authority 150
object oriented programming (OOP) 174
objectivity
    notion of 721
    objectivist epistemological stance 737
    objectivists 10, 744, 753
    of mapping 725
observable action 718
observation language 736, 761, 893
observation terms 769, 893
obsolescence 306, 365

risks of 308
old boy network 67
oligopoly 689
omniscience, fish-scale model of 21
on-line data archives 226
ontology 718, 739, 754, 893
    ontological adequacy 763, 765, 766, 767,
        893
    ontological pluralism 740
    ontologically strong relativist dynamic
        epistemology 756
    product ontologies 583, 584, 585, 586, 588,
        591
    separation of analytical and ontological tests
        771
open coding 858
open systems 2, 6, 621, 665
operant conditioning 147
operating experience 657
    industry 643
operational terms 756, 894
opportunism 467, 468, 476, 479
orderly systems 664
ORGAHEAD multi-agent model 215, 217
organization(s)
    advocacy 562
    ambidextrous 386, 396, 398
    as classes of traders 534
    as enactors of environments and creators of
        meaning 351
    as information processing systems 344, 345
    as interpretation systems 346
    as political coalitions 364
    basic elements of 182
    birth rates 264
    Brown's political phenomenology of 376
    computational organization theory 209, 210
    definitions of 2
    dimensions of 3
    dual nature of, as process and product 24
    ethnographic studies of 807
    industrial organization (IO) 686
    institutionalization as a determinant of
        power and politics in organizations 375
    interlocking 531
    levels of 7
    loosely coupled 676
    membership changes within 188
    modular 166, 167, 171
    Moebius strip 509
    network 167, 529

of communities 550
organization-level technology 175
oversocialized view of 268
private-sector employment by organization
    size 788
self-organization 455, 462, 839
spatial organization of high technology 633
standards and testing 333
tightly coupled 676
virtual 167, 170
organization design 681
organization science (OS) 686, 753, 763, 894
organization set 526
organization structure 484
organizational action 417
organizational adaptation, Markovian
    conception of 629
organizational attention 366
organizational boundaries, locus of 407
organizational change 309, 422, 867, 869,
    871, 872
organizational character 366
organizational cognition 398
  and interpretation 344
  locus and essence of 355
  managerial and 122
organizational community 541
  enactment of 583
organizational complexity and computation
    442
organizational components, fit of 195
organizational consultant expert system model
    216
organizational culture, single factor model of
    220
organizational decision making, garbage can
    model of 211, 215, 222, 461, 698
organizational demography 370
organizational dysfunctions 49
organizational ecology 304, 621, 677
organizational economics 467
  and sociology-based organization theory 485
organizational effectiveness 365
organizational environments 8
organizational epistemology 715, 733
  and research methods 19, 713
organizational evolution 327, 386, 398
organizational failure 305
  risks of 643
organizational features, core 309
organizational field 526, 259

organizational forms 542
  cognitive taxonomy of 583
  firm disaggregation and the adoption of
    modular organizational forms 171
organizational founding, demography of 317
organizational gatekeepers 797
organizational hedging 334
organizational histories 509
organizational identity 50
organizational imitation or transfer 340
organizational inertia 398, 622
organizational inheritance and transmission 14
organizational institutions 259
organizational knowledge 415
  dissemination of 423, 427
organizational learning 335, 399, 415
  origins of 416, 419
  rule-based 100
organizational level 7
organizational manipulation 52
organizational momentum 306, 309, 332
organizational networks 281
organizational niche overlap 314
organizational phenomena, hierarchically
    nested nature of 7
organizational policies, formal 500
organizational populations 542
  model of organizational population dynamics
    11
  variation across 510
organizational positions, technology structure
    as an ecology of 622
organizational power
  and dependence 363
  effect of economic performance on 377, 378
organizational practices, abandonment and
    transformation of 509
organizational reorientation and convergence
    421
organizational replicators 101
organizational reputation 582
organizational rules, ecology of 99, 109
organizational sex composition 371
organizational simulation 842
organizational slack 365
organizational subcultures 39
organizational surveys 781, 782
organizational survival 265, 272
organizational systems, status and power in
    627
organizational technology 386

organizational theory, closed system
approaches within 599
organizational transfer 340
organized action 353
orientation
social constructionist or phenomenological
orientation 12
see also reorientation
OS *see* organization science
outcome imitation 645
outsourcing 168
overlapping mental models 594
overload, cognitive 89
oversocialized view of organizations 268
own and others' experience 431

p-star models 69
paradigms 715
multiparadigmaticism 753
neo-information processing paradigm 216,
224
paradigm shifts 741, 753, 894
paradigm war(s) 20, 733, 734, 735, 746,
753, 755
paradigm wars, explanation for 744
paradigmatic consensus 741
paradigmatic pluralism 739
parsimony 841
partial competition 545
partial mutualism 545
partitioning, resource 312, 317, 318
partners
intercorporate partnering 632
partner profiles 71, 292, 294
prestige exchange 628
prominence of 285
status 292
patching 455, 462
patents 647, 648, 678
as innovation indices 632
patent-based measures of resources 479
patent-to-patent ties 626
patenting 625
path creation 455
path dependency 114, 327, 432, 455, 498,
563, 564, 806
firm heterogeneity and path dependence 481
patrimonial bureaucracy 366
perception(s) 10
and interpretation 345
human perceptual and cognitive

mechanisms 730
illusory 722
of equity 51
of power 140
of uncertainty 349
perceptual and cognitive mechanisms 727
perfect competition 688, 689, 691
perfect contestability 691
perfection, subgame 694
performance 293, 419, 477, 484, 832
ambiguity of CEO performance 246
effect of diversification on firm performance
479
effect of economic performance on
organizational power 377, 378
firm performance 282, 287, 294, 295, 705
market performance 687
measuring changes in 182
measuring firm performance 293
performance-alignment relationship 484
performance consequences of TCE and RBV
484
performance failure 507
performance feedback 421, 425
performance metrics 585
performance monitoring 245, 247
survival as a proxy for 293
peripheral features 309
peripheral markets 535
personal networks, sparse 616
personal sources of power 145
personal theories 16
personnel movement 196
personnel turnover 186
perspective(s) 10
cultural-frame 333
economic 11
enactment 351, 353, 355
functional 364, 616
information processing 348, 355, 476
institutional 10, 366, 373, 380
learning theory 621
multiple 12, 729
network 10
plurality of 20
social capital 380
structural 365, 370
symbolic management perspective on
organizations 376
upper echelon 372
value-expressive 51

Weberian perspectives on power and dependence 373
phenomenology 761
philosophy type, first 723, 891
phenotype 111
pluralism
   epistemological 740
   ontological 740
   paradigmatic 739
   plurality of perspectives 20
poison pill(s) 236, 241, 268, 502, 528, 604
policy arenas 557
politics
   cultural and political sources of variability in legitimacy 510
   institutionalization as a determinant of power and politics in organizations 375
   interfirm political behavior 610
   political coalitions 365
   political contestation 378
   political-cultural approaches 376
   political cultural model of organizational change 269
   political economy 15, 601
   political framing 148
   political theories 364
polythetic groupings 77
pooled interdependence 664
population(s) 99
   fine-grained population substructures 317
   organizational 542
   population dynamics 11, 312, 320, 666, 770
   population ecology 270, 622
   population-level learning 187, 319
   target 782, 787, 788
   variation across organizational populations 510
portfolio model
   firm as 267, 331, 334, 508
   valuation and portfolio balancing models 163
positive agency
   positive agency literature 234
   positive and normative agency theories, connecting 235
positivism 717, 719, 720, 743, 748, 753, 894
   anti-positivist 736
   inadequacies of 758
   legacy of 755, 768, 894

logical 736, 753, 892
positive stance 733
positivists 20, 734, 744
postpositive selectionist fallibilist scientific realist epistemology 753
postpositive stance 733, 736
postmodernism 716, 719, 730, 736, 753, 758, 761, 894
poststructuralism 716, 719, 895
power 237, 251, 738, 806
   and dependence 11, 15, 27, 138, 365
   bank power 610
   behavioral sources of 142, 146
   change in power over time 152
   circulation theory of 365
   effect of economic performance on organizational power 377, 378
   exchange power tactic 147
   Foucalt's identification of knowledge with power 740
   group sources of 148
   hierarchy versus informal uses of power 150
   individual 152
   institutionalization as a determinant of power and politics in organizations 375
   institutionalization of 377
   interfirm 605
   interorganizational 570, 599
   intraorganizational 138
   legitimate 141
   locus of 614
   maintenance and loss of 152
   needs and charisma as personal sources of 142
   Nietzsche's indictment of truth-seekers as power-mongers 740
   of contrast 862
   of institutions 275
   organizational 363, 377, 378
   perception of 140
   personal sources of 145
   potential 143
   potential, vs. power use 149
   power-dependence framework 368
   power law distribution 217
   power motive 145
   power relationships 365
   power use 143
   power, experience and agency costs 249
   referent 145

power (*cont'd*)
  social networks as structural sources of
    individual power 142
  status and power in organizational systems
    627
  structural sources of 141, 142
  theory of power and dependence 15
  transitivity of 150
  Weberian perspectives on power and
    dependence 373
pragmatism 740, 742, 756, 895
pre-scientific status 716, 895
pre-testing 857
precedence network 225
predatory competition 545
prediction 830
  ex ante prediction 339
  predictive analytical reliability 773
  progressivist emphasis on predictability and
    expertise 508
prestige dynamics 627
prestige exchange partners 628
pressures
  mimetic, normative and coercive 262
  to confirm 268
pretests 794
price mechanism 467
primitives 759
prior alliances 284
prior knowledge 649
prior learning 433
Prisoner's Dilemma game 679
private benefits 653
private knowledge sharing 655
private-sector employment by organization size
  788
proactive manipulation 53
probabilism 305
procedural justice 294
procedures, rules and 101
process(es)
  density and institutional 313
  dual nature of 'organization' as process and
    product 24
  ecological 305, 311
  induced 79, 105
  interaction 76, 80
  mimetic processes 64, 259, 262
  modular products and processes 170
  nested 103
  normative processes 259, 262

process institutions 38, 42
process theory of change 884
replication 76, 80, 86, 102
role of social psychological processes in
    egocentric organizational network
    formation 293
search process 680, 682
stage-gate 163
see also institutionalization
producer community 583
producer positions 625
product(s)
  dual nature of 'organization' as process and
    24
  key success factors in new product
    development 159
  modular products and processes 170
  product conceptualization 587
  product families 394
  product platforms and families 395
product ontology/ies 583, 584, 585, 588, 591
  as market cores 586
production
  and adaptation of rules and routines 418, 420
  production technologies 164
profession(s) 263, 503, 504, 561
  professionalization 266, 513
professional sovereignty 508
profit-maximization paradox 699
program(s) 419, 753, 895
  mentoring programs 58, 70
  object oriented programming (OOP) 174
  program adaptation 416
progressive theories 24
  progressivist emphasis on predictability and
    expertise 508
proletariat 506
proof 833
  social verification and social proof 48
property, intellectual 621
proprietary strategists 308
proximity 112, 171
  role of 172, 174
public benefits 653
public goods problems, solving 501
public policy and industry coevolution 567
punctuation
  incrementalism versus 90
  punctuated change 365
  punctuated equilibrium 364, 369, 404
pure relativism 748

purpose 366

qualitative datum 881
qualitative research 849
quality circles 504, 505, 582, 591, 595
quality function deployment 163
quality of experience 431
quantitative datum 880
Quine's rejection of the distinction between analytic and synthetic truth 740

R&D investment and industry structure 162
races
   learning 297, 653, 655
   Red Queen 338, 570, 652
radical inventions 633
Radner's ε-equilibrium notion 694
random systems 665
random variation 333
rankings, reputational 584, 585, 591
rates
   hazard rate 884
   mortality 564
   of change 306
rational choice theory 19, 741, 743
rational expectation models 421
rational-open systems 18
rational system 2, 3
rationalism, critical 744, 745
rationality 147, 695
   bounded 366, 467, 468, 480
rationalization 715
   endogenous dynamic of 513
RBV *see* resource based view
reach models 59
reaction
   crisis 39
   reactive adaptation 53
   reactive reorientations (turnarounds) 405
real science from contra science 754
real terms 896
realism 738, 755, 896
   Campbellian realism 754, 755, 756, 758, 889
   commitment to 748
   metaphysical realists 737
   model realism 675, 679
   naturalist evolutionary realism 722
   realism models 682
   realist approach 8, 715
   realists 734, 735, 738, 739, 740, 742, 743

scientific 23, 733, 754, 756, 768
   virtual realism in virtual realities 339
reality 726
   constructed 351
   God's eye view of 721
   ways of studying 730
realms 757, 896
reasoning, interactive 748
received view 717, 753, 761, 896
receivers of knowledge 649
receptivity 650
recipes
   industry 584, 585, 590
   taken-for-granted 37, 48, 591
reciprocity 617, 654
   norms of 244
   reciprocal causalities through the mobility effect 690
   reciprocal interdependence 664
   rule of 451
recognition problems, generation and 424
recombinant property 334
recombination 630
   and evolution 455, 457
reconstitution, functional 607
recording, learning as 429
Red Queen effect/races 338, 570, 652
reduced form estimation 474
reductionism 720, 728
redundancy 631
referent power 145
referrals 282, 290
refinement search 419
reflexivity, deliberative style and entrenchment 744
reform, institutional 503, 507
regress, infinite 745
regulated internal labor markets 506
regulative structures 259
reinforcement theory 147
related experience 653
relation(s)
   law-like 771
   structures and 59
   symbiotic 545
relational activity-based normative boundaries 8
relational capabilities 297
relational content 60
relational density 315, 318
relational embeddedness 502, 510

relationships 201
  authority relations 542
  between cognition and social interaction 360
  between firm age and performance 670
  between market share, market
    concentration, competitiveness and
    innovation 159
  between network configuration and firm
    success 292
  between organizations that learn from each
    other 650
  between power and efficiency 251
  cause and effect 736
  competitive-innovation relationship 631
  conceptions of the axiom-theory-model-
    phenomena relationship 764
  etiology of 62
  interorganizational 612, 621, 654
  performance-alignment 484
  power 365
  relative importance of 654
  social 654
  social exchange 247
relative effects 340
relative impact of task 221
relativism 719, 720, 896
  epistemological 743
  historical relativism 753, 891
  pure 748
  relativist stance 733
  relativists 20, 734, 739, 744
  semantic 756, 757
reliability 857
  and validity of incident construction 881
  instrumental 763, 772, 892
  model structure reliability 773
  of science 721
  predictive analytical reliability 773
renewal theory 884
reorientation
  convergence and 421, 422
  reactive reorientations 405
  strategic reorientation 184
repeated negotiations 53
  and interactions 47
repetitive momentum 433
replication processes 76, 80, 86, 102
replicators, organizational 101
repositories, knowledge 201
representation 221
  and expression 111

reproduction 86
reputation 592
  organizational 582
  reputational rankings 584, 585
  reputational rankings as market status
    orders 591
requirements network 225
research
  archival 805, 807, 810
  computational stream of 15
  field research methods 867
  historiographic 807
  interdisciplinary 247
  interpretivist 590
  organizational epistemology and research
    methods 19, 713
  qualitative 849
  simulation research methods 829
  survey research methods 781
  VSLI 632
resolution of conflict 376
resource(s) 736
  financial 286
  institutional 287
  network 283, 286
  patent-based measures of 479
resource based view (RBV) 18, 296, 468, 475,
  476, 477, 705
  integration of TCE and RBV 483
  joint RBV-TCE 478
  performance consequences of TCE and RBV
    484
resource dependency 153, 272, 282, 364,
  365, 369, 371, 381, 467, 481, 528,
  599, 600, 603, 605, 606, 612, 616, 621,
  677
  structural contingencies and 368
resource heterogeneity 485
resource partitioning 312, 317, 318
resource profile 478, 479
resource uncertainty 80
resource variation 80
responses, environmental 417
responsiveness and genuine dialogue 746
retaining knowledge 181, 191
retention 304, 543, 558, 564, 567, 570
  effect of turnover on knowledge retention
    191
  selective 722
  see also variation selection retention
retroduction 873, 883

rhetoric, analysis of industry 585
rights, effect of equal rights law 503
risk(s) 658, 736
    firm risk 236
    managerial incentives and risk aversion
        240
    of dissolution 525
    of obsolescence 308
    of organizational failure 643
    risk preferences 421
    risk taking 425, 426
rivalry
    competitive 693
    game theory of competitive rivalry 686
    status-driven rivalry 702
role(s)
    of conflict 110
    of emotion 53
    of financial institutions 609
    of managerial cognition 407
    of proximity 172, 174
    of social psychological processes 293
    of teams and team leaders 163
    of the state 528
    role-constrained learning 417, 419
    role structures 39
    structural 60
rotating membership 196
rotten apple theory 65
routines 78, 79, 101
    cognitive nature of 109
    competition between 81
    complementarity between 82
    informal 434
    meta-routines 83, 87, 104
    production and adaptation of rules and
        routines 418, 420
    Schumpeterian recombination of pre-existing
        routines 102
rule(s)
    and logics 379
    and procedures 101
    correspondence 759, 890
    ecology of organizational rules 99, 109
    formal 432, 434
    hierarchies of 419
    institutional 501
    of exchange 530
    of reciprocity 451
    of the game 505
    production and adaptation of rules and

    routines 418, 420
rule-based organizational learning 100
rule density 424
rule dynamics 421
rule ecologies 424, 427
rule histories 421
rule implementation 432

sales-motivated behavior 700
sampling methods 790, 816
    dense samples 790
    sample diversity 877
    sample size 878
    selecting a sample frame 788
scanning and search 345
schemata
    mutability of schemas 498
    schema-based cognitive processing 121
    simple schemata, complex behavior 450,
        452
Schumpeterian competition 672
Schumpeterian recombination of pre-existing
        routines 102
science
    consensus in 724
    contra 736, 754, 890
    Guttman scale of effective science 768
    methodology of 724
    model-centered 759, 763
    normal 742, 754, 893
    organization science (OS) 686, 753, 763,
        894
    real science from contra science 754
    reliability of 721
    unity of 718, 760, 897
scientific knowledge 724
scientific management 4
scientific realism 23, 754, 756, 768
    epistemological stance 733
SCP (structure-conduct-performance) *see*
    structures
search
    and learning 108
    innovation 419
    local 622
    refinement 419
    scanning and 345
    search competencies 419
    search design 681
    search process 680, 682
selecting a sample frame 788

selection 304, 389, 543, 558, 570, 765
density dependent 262
intraorganizational 99
Lamarckian 328
of ties 525
selection mechanism 84, 328
selectionism 108
selectionist approach 896
selectionist evolutionary epistemology 768
strong 329
verisimilitude via 772
weak 329
see also variation
selective coding 859
selective retention 722
self-learning 651
self-organization 455, 462, 839
selfish gene 91
Selznick's normative approach to
institutionalization 375
Selznick's old institutionalism 506
semantic conception 761, 763, 768
semantic meaning 761, 896
semantic relativism 756, 757
semi-structures 83
semioticism 761
semiotic theory 816
senders of new knowledge 647
senescence 306
liability of 308
senior teams 392
homogeneity versus heterogeneity in senior
team composition 407
sensemaking 39, 122, 133, 349, 352, 354,
502, 520, 584, 862
adaptive sensemaking perspective 357
sensory experience 717
sequence analysis 884
sequential interdependence 664
service innovation 407
sex composition, organizational 371
shared interpretive schemes 353
shareholder interests 245
sharing, knowledge 283, 655
similarity of experience 200
Simon's "administrative man" 4
simplicity 885
similarity
demographic similarity and incentive
alignment 243
fit as 198

simulacrum account, Cartwright's 761
simulation
agent-based simulation models 829, 834,
837
approaches to 833
discrete event 829, 834
organizational 842
purpose of 830
simulation modeling, implementation of 841
simulation research methods 829
system dynamics (or continuous) simulation
models 834
single factor model of organizational culture
220
single market center 535
situated cognition theory 356, 357
situation action theory 356
situativity theory 356
size
private-sector employment by organization
size 788
sample 878
size dependence 306, 307
size-localized competition 316
skeptic's problem 740
skills network 225
slack
organizational 365
slack search 419, 422, 425
smallness, liability of 307
smart talk 50
social action 718
social capital 66, 237, 366, 616, 634
as brokerage 60
as cohesion and network closure 60
social capital perspectives 380
social commitments 371
social construction of technology 390
social constructionist or phenomenological
orientation 12
social ecology of jobs 420
social elites 513
social exchange 365
and board monitoring 244
social exchange relationships 247
social exchange theory 244, 379, 599, 600,
607, 616
social groups, mobilization of 505
social influence 44
and board independence 244
social learning theory 680

social life, inherent complexity of 851
social network(s) 225, 252, 433, 502, 633
   as structural sources of individual power 142
   dense versus sparse social networks 196, 198
   social network analysis 115
social proof 53
social relationships 654
social structure(s)
   effects of, on economic transactions 527
social ties 188, 372, 560
   among elites 607
   to elites 604
social understandings 502
social values 266
social verification and social proof 48
socialism 513
socially shared meanings 594
sociocultural evolution 77
   variation-selection-retention model of 7
sociology
   classical sociological theories of Marx and
      Weber 599
   epistemological traditions in 717
   fiscal 528, 529
   of institutional change 497
   of institutional forms 497
   of markets 13
   of Weber 715
   organizational economics and sociology-
      based organization theory 485
   sociological concept of status 511
   sociological critiques 481
   Weber's sociology of domination 373
sociopolitical legitimacy 313
solipsism 719, 744, 748, 896
   cultural solipsism 723
solitude, death by 668
sources
   of deinstitutionalization 507
   of interorganizational power 607
   of learning 431
   structural sources of power 141, 142
sparse personal networks 616
sparse social networks, dense versus 196, 198
spatial and temporal environmental variation
   312
spatial economics 677
spatial organization of high technology 633
spatial structure 337, 563
spatiotemporal framework 727
specialists 311, 318

directory specialists 435
speciation and extinction 330, 332
spillovers 292, 624, 647, 651, 652, 655
spin control 148
stability
   versus change 90
   versus fluidity in membership 196
stage-gate processes 163
stance
   epistemological 734
   objectivist epistemological 737
   positive stance 733
   postpositive stance 733, 736
   relativist stance 733
standard interfaces and system architecture
   174
standards
   and testing organizations 333
   standards strategists 308
state 503, 561, 562
   impact on employment practices 504
   lobbying of state officials 601
   role as an institutional entrepreneur 504
   role of 528
stated goals 542
static versus dynamic efficiency dilemma 688
status 592, 606, 622, 648
   and power in organizational systems 627
   benefit of status-driven strategies 704
   legitimacy versus status 511
   of a niche 625
   of knowledge creator 644
   partner 292
   pre-scientific 716, 895
   sociological concept of 511
   status-driven rivalry 702
   status expectations 433
   status transfer 285
stickiness of knowledge 427
stochastic microstates 754
stock repurchase plans 249
stories
   market stories and the enactment of the belief
      hierarchy 584
   story-based nature of market sensemaking
      585
straitjacket of normal science 742
strategy/ies 101, 484, 707, 736
   cognitive strategic groups 588
   coherence 723
   collective strategic concepts 584

strategy/ies (*cont'd*)
  firm 686
  market 542
  proprietary strategists 308
  status-driven 704
  strategic alliances 622, 631, 632, 635, 649
  strategic business exit 77
  strategic change 79, 354
  strategic complexity 236
  strategic contingencies 15, 153
  strategic integration, methods of 407
  strategic issue interpretation 348
  strategic reorientation 184
  strategic side-effects of board monitoring 245
  synthetic 883
streams, innovation 387, 392, 393, 394, 402
strong selection 329
strong tie 290, 291
  versus weak ties 290
structural autonomy model 603
structural contingency/ies 364, 365
  and resource dependencies 368
structural ecology 366
structural embeddedness 818
structural equivalence 267
  as a measure of redundancy 631
structural evolution 340
structural holes 59, 194, 299, 460, 462, 623
  structural hole benefits 144
  structural hole theory 61, 63, 363, 371,
    380, 525, 616, 632, 767
structural inertia 261, 306, 650
  structural inertia theory 90, 309, 339
structural learning 221
structural modeling approach 485
structural perspectives 365, 370
structural roles 60
structural sources of power 141
  social networks as structural sources of
    individual power 142
structural theories 16
structure(s)
  and relations 59
  belief 348
  cognitive 259
  cold cognitive structures 128
  effects of social structure on economic
    transactions 527
  governance 484, 561, 530
  historical origins of institutional 262
  intermarket 531

  isolated idealized 762, 758, 892
  knowledge 122
  market 535, 557, 559, 687, 688, 692, 693,
    706
  meaning 819
  model structure reliability 773
  model substructures 765, 893
  network 60
  normative 259
  of communities 544
  of social ties 462
  organization 484
  regulative 259
  role 39
  role of, in adaptive processes 682
  semi-structures 83
  spatial 337, 563
  structure-conduct-performance (SCP) 475
  structure-conduct-performance (SCP)
    framework 18
  structure institutions 38
  structured landscapes 680
  team 186
  technology structure as an ecology of
    organizational positions 622
study design and target population 782
study of emergent behavior 215
subcultures, organizational 39
subgame perfection 694
subjectivity 854
  subjectivists 10
subnetworks 182
substitution
  learning substitution 432
  non-substitutability 149
  substitution intent 650, 655
  substitution network 225
succession
  executive 377
  insider versus outsider 376
  of CEOs 241, 403
suffocation, death by 668
superstitious learning 85, 417, 419, 429
surveys
  organizational 781, 782
  survey research methods 781
survival
  as a proxy for performance 293
  impact of legitimacy on survival rates 271
  organizational 265, 272
sustainable advantage 677

symbiosis 541, 546
  symbiotic interdependence 602
  symbiotic relations 545
symbolism 354
  symbolic architectures 121
  symbolic management 53
  symbolic management and incentive
    alignment 242
symmetry, firm 696
synchronous or asynchronous updating 679
synergy 664
system(s)
  chaotic 665
  classification 78
  complex 210, 212
  complex adaptive 453
  general systems theory 442
  information processing 15
  knowledge management 49, 87
  natural 2, 5, 12, 15
  natural-open 15
  nonlinear dynamical 442
  of meaning 15, 344
  open 2, 6, 621, 665
  orderly 664
  organizational 627
  random 665
  rational 2, 3
  rational-open 18
  transactive memory 187, 193, 195
  transactive systems of knowledge 594
system dynamics modeling 829, 836
  system dynamics (or continuous) simulation
    models 834
systems theory 677

tacit knowledge 102
taken-for-granted beliefs/norms/recipes 37, 48,
  591
  cognitive measures of taken for grantedness
    511
takeovers 263, 501, 502, 560
target population 787, 788
  study design and 782
task environments 8
taxonomy of organizational forms, cognitive
  583
TCE (transaction cost economics) *see*
  transaction costs
TDM *see* total design method
teaching

and practicing interactive reasoning 748
  teachability 103
teams
  hierarchical 184
  role of teams and team leaders 163
  team structure 186
technical environment 8, 260, 274
technical metrics 592
technical system, ecology of a 546
technical, managerial and institutional
  dimensions of organizations 3
technology 16, 28
  choosing new technology development
    projects 173
  core technology 542
  development of new technology 158
  diffusion of technology in intraorganizational
    ecologies 109
  disruptive technologies 395
  dominant designs, technology cycles and
    388, 390
  ecology of technology-based competition 631
  eras of ferment 388, 395, 405, 622
  interorganizational 176, 621
  intraorganizational 158
  locus of technological variation 407
  organizational 386
  organization-level 175
  production 164
  social construction of 390
  spatial organization of high technology 633
  technological change 386, 621
  technological discontinuities 391
  technological network 626
  technological spillovers 624
  technological trajectories 395
  technological uncertainty 676
  technology cycles 406
  technology distance 292
  technology structure as an ecology of
    organizational positions 622
template matching 882
temporal bracketing 882
temporal duration 878
temporal norms at work 39
theories
  as families of models 765
  behavioral theory of the firm 4
  catastrophe 442
  categorization 347
  causality 814

theories (*cont'd*)
  chaos 213, 442
  circulation theory of power 365
  coherence 755, 890
  complexity 115, 209
  computational organization theory 209, 210
  conceptions of the axiom-theory-model-
    phenomena relationship 764
  constructionist's theory in use 738
  contingency 16, 213, 621
  critical 761
  degenerating 23
  density dependence 314, 337, 673
  ecological 13
  evolutionary 442, 462, 558, 621
  expansion of 273
  game 115, 686, 687, 691, 693, 705, 748
  general systems 442
  goal setting 246
  herd 658
  institutional 269, 621, 680
  integration of institutional and population
    ecology theory 270
  IT-as-agent computational 218
  learning theory perspective 621
  life cycle 89
  network 616
  normative 375
  of fitness landscape 113
  of organization failure 305
  of power and dependence 15
  organizational 599
  personal 16
  political 364
  positive and normative agency theories 235
  process theory of change 884
  progressive 24
  rational choice 19, 741, 743
  reinforcement 147
  renewal 884
  resource dependence theory of organizational
    and interorganizational power 369
  rotten apple 65
  semiotic 816
  situated cognition 356, 357
  situation action 356
  situativity 356
  social exchange 244, 379, 599, 600, 607,
    616
  social learning 680
  structural 16

  structural hole 61, 63, 363, 371, 380, 525,
    616, 632, 767
  structural inertia 90, 309, 339
  systems 677
  theoretical aggregation 236, 241
  theoretical convergence and methodological
    variety 341
  theoretical integration 237, 242
  theoretical language 761, 896
  theory discovery 831
  Weberian 373
thinking
  divergent 190
  either-or 134
threats 347, 348, 579
three-dimensional blockmodeling 521
thrifts 508, 559, 567
ties
  avoidance of 525
  bridging 289
  broken ties studies 607
  cohesive 289
  cohesive versus bridging 290
  configuration of 71, 289, 294
  patent-to-patent 626
  selection of 525
  social ties 188, 372, 560, 604, 607
  strong vs. weak 290, 291
  weak 59, 60, 63, 194, 196, 290, 291, 460
tightly coupled organizations 676
time
  links-in-time 84
  timing 282, 290
tinkering 433
tipping points 228
topology/ies
  belief 595
  of interaction 112, 114
total design method (TDM) 796
total quality management (TQM) 287, 298,
  504
trader participation 532
traditions in sociology, epistemological 717
training 784, 832
  interviewer 796
  training tools 223
trainwrecks 448
trait imitation 645
trajectories, technological 395
transactions
  effects of social structure on economic

transactions 527
transaction interdependence 484
transaction costs 252
    integration of TCE and RBV 483
    joint RBV-TCE 478
    performance consequences of TCE and RBV
        484
    transaction cost economics (TCE) 467, 468,
        471, 476, 705
    transaction cost theory 18, 442
    Williamson's transaction costs perspective
        252
transactive memory 435
    concept of 659
    transactive memory systems 187, 193, 195
transactive systems of knowledge, distributed
        cognition and 594
transcendental idealism 756, 897
transfer
    of best practice 189
    of knowledge 17, 181, 185, 193
    organizational 340
    status transfer 285
    transfer learning 17
transformation
    evolutionary 329, 330
    proposals for 747
transitivity of power 150
transmission
    of manufacturing competences 109
    of technical knowledge across firm
        boundaries 634
    organizational 14
trap(s)
    codification 426, 432
    competency 17, 420, 423, 426, 429, 432
    failure traps 426
    levels of analysis 360
triads 524, 525
triangulation 725
triggering conditions 507
trust 226, 294, 297, 299, 480, 616, 650
    between firms 291
    in relationships 245, 654
truth 737, 765
    as a bodyguard of lies 741
    distinction between analytic and synthetic
        truth 740
    epistemology of 740
    Nietzsche's indictment of truth-seekers as
        power-mongers 740

true/false dichotomy 757
truth-in-a-language 744
truthful explanation 753
truthlikeness 744, 748, 757
turnarounds (reactive reorientations) 405
turnover 403, 407
    effect of, on knowledge retention 191
    personnel 186
typology 164

uncertainty 60, 149, 367, 468, 471, 473, 627,
        632, 658, 657, 703, 736
    control over 374
    coordination under 476
    coping with 143
    perceptions of 349
    resource 80
    technological 676
    uncertainty reduction 560
unified market structure 535
uniformity, epistemological 742
unions 506
unity of science 718, 760, 897
unlearning 408
unrelated experience 653
unshared information, sharing of 189
updating
    synchronous or asynchronous 679
    updating epistemological commitments of
        researchers 747
upper echelons perspective 379
upward appeal 147
upward causation 92
    and downward causation 321
upward influence styles as behavioral sources of
        power 142
utility 736
    neoclassical utility-maximization notion 693

validity 857
    of modeling 841
    reliability and validity of incident
        construction 881
value/valuation
    fact-value dichotomy 747
    intraorganizational value institutions 41
    of weak ties 60
    social values 266
    valuation and portfolio balancing models
        163
    value-expressive perspective 51

value/valuation (*cont'd*)
  value institutions 38, 52
  value networks 395
variability 406
  cultural and political sources of variability in
    legitimacy 510
  environmental 78, 311
variation 88, 304, 389, 543, 558, 563, 570,
    765
  across organizational populations 510
  Campbell's (blind) variation-selection-
    retention (VSR) model 7, 14, 25, 77, 101,
    588, 722
  constrained variation 333
  generating, by innovating niches 560
  locus of technological variation 407
  random 333
  resource 80
  spatial and temporal environmental
    variation 312
variety theory, methodological 341
VDT *see* virtual design team
verification
  social verification and social proof 48
  verification principle 897
verisimilitude 756, 757, 897
  verisimilar beliefs 745
  via selection 772
verstehen 5, 851
vertical alliances 601
vertical foreclosure 485
vertical integration 473, 476, 483, 667, 676
vertical interorganizational relationships,
    horizontal and 612
vertical mergers 472
vicarious learning 319, 644
Vienna Circle 736, 760
view, received 717, 753, 761, 896
virtual design team (VDT) 215, 217, 222
virtual firms 509

virtual organizations 167, 170
virtual realism in virtual realities 339
visual mapping 882
volatility, environmental 667
voluntarism 305
voluntary groups 336
VSLI research 632
VSR *see* variation selection retention

watchdog groups 333, 512, 562
weak selection 329
weak ties 59, 60, 63, 194, 196, 290, 291, 460
Weber
  classical sociological theories of Marx and
    Weber 599
  sociology of 715
  Weber's analysis of bureaucratic domination
    363
  Weber's iron cage 263
  Weber's "iron law of bureaucratic
    proliferation" 424
  Weber's sociology of domination 373
  Weberian perspectives on power and
    dependence 373
  Weberian theories 373
Williamson's transaction costs perspective
    252
window effect 687, 706
winner-take-all learning situations 653
Women's Christian Temperance Movement
    266
Woodward typology 164
work
  legalization of workplace 263
  temporal norms at 39
  work network 225
  workflow centrality 149
world-as-text 122

zaibatsu 504

Name Index

Abbott, A. 551, 872, 879, 884
　and Forrest, J. 820
　and Hrycak, A. 820
Abell, P. 820
Abernathy, W. J. 392, 622
　and Clark, K. 402
　and Utterback, J. M. 633
Abrahamson, E. 513, 591, 812, 819
　and Fairchild, G. 513, 582, 584, 591
　and Fombrun, C. J. 584
Acheson, J. A. 473, 482
Achrol, R. S. 167
Aday, D. P. Jr. 793
Adler, P. S. 89, 165, 374
　and Borys, B. 432
　and Clark, K. B. 181, 429
Aguilar, F. 345
Ahuja, G. 623, 630, 637
Aiken, M. and Hage, J. 282
Aitken, H. 388
Albert, H. 744, 745
Alchian, A. A.
　and Demsetz, H. 486
　and Woodward, S. 169
Aldrich, H. E. 76, 77, 78, 85, 91, 107, 304,
　　321, 328, 408, 526, 542, 543, 545,
　　549, 550, 557, 558, 568, 569, 570, 608,
　　736
　and Auster, E. R. 307, 634
　and Kalleberg, A., Marsden, P. and Cassell, J.
　　789
　and Mueller, S. 84

and Reese, P. R. and Dubini, P. 67
and Whetten, D. A. 812, 819
and Zimmer, C. and McEvoy, D. 789
Allen, M. P. 602
Allen, R. W., Madison, D. L., Porter, L. W.,
　　Renwick, P. A. and Mayes, B. T. 146
Allen, T. J. 193, 194
Allison, G. T. 233, 429
Almeida, P. and Kogut, B. 193, 196, 634, 647,
　　656
Alstyne, M. V. and Brynjolfsson, E. 218
Alvesson, M. and Deetz, S. 895
Ambler, C. E., Hyman, S. M. and Mesenbourg,
　　T. L. 795
Amburgey, T. L.
　and Dacin, T. and Kelly, D. 316
　and Kelly, D. and Barnett, W. P. 306, 309,
　　328, 330, 332, 335, 340, 433
　and Miner, A. S. 86, 310
　and Rao, H. 696
Amit, R. and Schoemaker, P. 480
Amram, M. and Kulatilaka, N. 173, 174
Anand, B. N. and Khanna, T. 282, 288, 293
Ancona, D. 405
　and Caldwell, D. F. 58
Anderson, C. J., Wasserman, S. and Crouch, B.
　　69
Anderson, E. and Schmittlein, D. 470
Anderson, J. R. 119, 125, 128, 129
Anderson, P. 443, 444, 450, 455, 665, 837,
　　839
　and Tushman, M. 82, 388, 391

Anderson, P. W., Arrow, K. J. and Pines, D. 320, 443

Andreski, S. 718

Appleyard, M. 655, 656

Argote, L. 182, 192, 193, 429, 642
  and Beckman, S. L. and Epple, D. 183, 185, 187, 192, 650, 657
  and Darr, E. 182, 195
  and Epple, D. 182, 429
  and Epple, D., Rao, R. D. and Murphy, K. 191
  and Gruenfeld, D. and Naquin, C. 181, 182
  and Ingram, P. 183, 195, 199, 201
  and Insko, C. A., Yovetich, N. and Romero, A. A. 192

Argyres, N. S. 168, 478, 483
  and Liebeskind, J. P. 482, 483

Argyris, C. and Schon, D. A. 85

Aronson, J. L., Harré, R. and Way, E. C. 754, 757, 769, 893, 895

Arrow, H., McGrath, J. E. and Berdahl, J. L. 182, 183

Arrow, K. 106

Arthur, W. B. 443

Asch, S. E. 638

Ashforth, B. E.
  and Fried, Y. 40, 43, 46, 52, 515
  and Mael, F. 197

Ashkenas, R., Ulrich, D., Jick, T. and Kerr, S. 166

Astley, W. G. 43, 543, 557
  and Fombrun, C. J. 551
  and Sachdeva, P. S. 141
  and Zammuto, R. F. 743

Attewell, P. 107

Audi, R. 889, 891, 894, 896

Aumann, R. 748
  and Brandenburger, A. 749

Axelrod, R. M. 434, 443, 451, 452, 458, 830, 842
  and Cohen, M. D. 101, 112, 113, 115, 209, 443, 450, 455, 665
  and Mitchell, W., Thomas, R., Bennett, D. S. and Bruderer, E. 451, 452, 458

Axtell, R. 840
  and Axelrod, R., Epstein, J. M. and Cohen, M. D. 220

Ayer, A. J. 736, 737, 753, 760

Azevedo, J. 718, 725, 726, 730, 753, 754, 755, 757, 762, 764, 892

Bachrach, P. and Baratz, M. S. 600

Bailyn, L. 855
  and Lynch, J. 853

Bain, J. S. 475, 687, 690

Bak, P. 209, 229, 448

Baker, W. E. 65, 70, 289, 291, 521, 524, 526, 529, 530, 532, 535, 560, 603, 611, 613
  and Faulkner, R. R. 147, 521, 524, 531
  and Faulkner, R. R. and Fisher, G. A. 524, 526, 528, 536, 605
  and Obstfeld, D. 524, 525

Bal, M. 885

Bala, V. and Goyal, S. 658

Balci, O. 220

Baldwin, C. Y. and Clark, K. 166, 171, 391, 392, 462

Banaszak-Holl, J. 316

Bandura, A. 680

Banerjee, A. V. 658

Bantel, K. A. and Jackson, S. E. 190

Barkema, H. G.
  and Bell, J. H. J. and Pennings, J. M. 657
  and Vermeulen, F. 434, 649

Barker, J. R. 374

Barley, S. R. 152, 270, 515, 766, 852, 876
  and Freeman, J. H. and Hybels, R. C. 341
  and Kunda, G. 584, 812, 819

Barnard, C. A. 468

Barnard, C. I. 367, 453

Barnes, B., Bloor, D. and Henry, J. 737

Barnett, W. P. 314, 543, 546, 547, 549, 570, 571, 623, 625, 696
  and Amburgey, T. L. 314
  and Carroll, G. R. 104, 321, 386, 405, 406, 543, 546, 547
  and Greve, H. R. and Park, D. Y. 85, 314, 423, 427, 429, 565
  and Hansen, M. T. 328, 331, 338, 341, 570, 652

Barney, J. B. 172, 296, 469, 475
  and Hansen, M. H. 294
  and Hesterly, W. 467, 481, 487

Baron, J. N.
  and Dobbin, F. R. and Jennings, P. D. 260, 503, 504, 515, 558, 567, 568, 605, 807
  and Kreps, D. M. 83

Barron, D. N. 314, 316, 674
  and West, E., Hannan, M. T. 308

Barron, J. M. and Bishop, J. 782

Bartlett, C. A. and Ghoshal, S. 87

Bartunek, J. 352, 353, 359

Bar-Yam, Y. 442

Basalla, G. 626
Basu, K. 699
Bates, T. 696
Baum, J. A. C. 308, 311, 314, 316, 319, 542, 545, 765, 721, 772
 and Berta, W. B. 183, 187, 194, 195
 and Calabrese, T. and Silverman, B. S. 283, 293, 408, 625, 628, 652, 653
 and Haveman, H. A. 314, 318, 531, 532, 565, 696
 and Ingram, P. 194, 195, 319, 647, 650, 651, 654, 657
 and Korn, H. J. 543, 550, 565, 696
 and Korn, H. J. and Kotha, S. 391, 772
 and Li, S. X. and Usher, J. M. 437
 and McKelvey, B. 209, 571, 722
 and Mezias, S. J. 314, 316, 318, 564, 652, 656, 668, 696
 and Oliver, C. 270, 286, 293, 294, 314, 315, 502, 547, 790, 811
 and Powell, W. W. 270, 315, 510
 and Rao, H. 543, 544, 549, 550
 and Silverman, B. S. 320, 678
 and Singh, J. V. 77, 101, 103, 104, 306, 310, 314, 315, 321, 323, 532, 543, 547, 549, 552, 553, 557, 571, 631
Baumol, W. J. 689, 699
Baumol, W. J., Panzar, J. C. and Willig, R. D. 688, 691
Beatty, J. 760, 762
 and Zajac, E. J. 235, 236, 240
Belliveau, M. A., O'Reilly, C. A. III. and Wade, J. B. 237, 243, 372
Benaroch, M. and Kauffman, R. 174
Bendix, R. 276
Benjamin, B. A. and Podolny, J. M. 511, 582, 592
Benner, M. and Tushman, M. 387, 405, 408
Bercovitz, J. E. L. 484
Berg, S. V., Duncan, J. and Friedman, P. 286, 293
Berger, P. L. and Luckmann, T. 44, 351, 373, 502, 511
Berle, A. and Means, G. C. 233, 234
Berlin, B. 723
 and Breedlove, C. and Raven, P. H. 723
Berliner, P. F. 444, 450
Bernard, H. R. 869
Bernheim, B. D. and Whinston, M. D. 486
Berry, D. C. and Broadbent, D. E. 181, 193
Beth, E. 761

Bhaskar, R. 754, 756, 758, 897
Biggart, N. W. 276
 and Guillén, M. 262, 276
Bijker, W. E., Hughes, T. and Pinch, T. J. 391, 586
Bikhchandani, S., Hirshleifer, D. and Welch, I. 569
Bills, D. B. 782
Black, B. S. 246
Black, D. 536
Blackmore, S. J. 87, 91, 92
Blair-Loy, M. 571
Blalock, Jr., H. M. 872
Blau, P. M. 63, 295, 371, 453, 600, 601, 787
Blaug, M. 761
Blundell, R., Griffith, R. and Van Reenen, J. 159, 163
Boeker, W. 236, 241, 372, 378, 401, 542
Boer, F. P. 174
Boerner, C. and Macher, J. 470
Bogner, W. C. and Barr, P. 357
Boisot, M. and Child, J. 443
Bonini, C. P. 345, 841
Boone, C. A. J. J.
 and De Brabander, B. and Witteloostuijn, A. van 696, 697
 and Olffen, W. van and Witteloostuijn, A. van 696, 697
 and Witteloostuijn, A. van 696, 705
Borja, J. and Castells, M. 172
Bougon, M. G. 359
Boulding, K. E. 346
Bowman, C. and Johnson, G. 589
Bowman, E. H. and Hurry, D. 174
Box, G., Hunter, J. and Hunter, W. 842, 845
Boyd, R. and Richerson, P. J. 87, 106
Boyer, K. K., Leong, G. K., Ward, P. T. and Krajewski, L. J. 165
Bradach, J. L. 396, 397, 445, 446, 456, 461
Bradburn, N. M. 796
Brandenburger, A. M. and Nalebuff, B. 694, 696
Brandyberry, A., Rai, A. and White, G. P. 160, 165
Brass, D. J. 59, 67, 138, 141, 142, 144, 145, 151, 153
 and Burkhardt, M. E. 138, 141, 143, 144, 145, 149, 150, 381
Braudel, F. 806
Braverman, H. 807
Breiger, R. L. 821

Bresnahan, T. 474
Brewer, M. B. 45, 197
Bridges, W. P. and Villemez, W. J. 782, 787, 791
Brinig, M. 473
Brint, S. and Karabel, J. 41, 497, 498, 506, 507
Brittain, J. W. and Wholey, D. H. 542, 545, 546, 547
Brown, J. S. and Duguid, P. 107, 356, 423, 427, 459
Brown, L. D. 508
Brown, R. H. 373, 376
Brown, S. L. and Eisenhardt, K. M. 83, 90, 163, 320, 387, 388, 396, 402, 404, 406, 442, 443, 444, 448, 449, 450, 454, 455, 456, 458, 459, 460, 682, 831
Bruderer, E. and Singh, J. V. 84, 110, 328, 331, 335, 339, 340, 342
Brynjolfsson, E. 168
  and Malone, T. W., Gurbaxani, V. and Kambil, A. 160, 169
Buckley, P. J. and Carter, M. J. 430, 431
Bulmer, R. N. H. and Tyler, M. J. 723
Burgelman, R. A. 76, 77, 79, 81, 85, 88, 99, 104, 105, 108, 109, 396, 398, 400, 407, 451, 452, 458, 571, 572, 629
  and Grove, A. 388, 402
Burkhardt, M. E. and Brass, D. J. 143, 144, 145, 152
Burns, L. and Wholey, D. 649, 651
Burns, T. and Stalker, G. M. 396, 447
Burrell, G. 738, 741, 743, 753, 774
Burt, R. S. 58, 59, 60, 61, 63, 64, 66, 67, 144, 145, 194, 281, 282, 289, 290, 297, 363, 366, 371, 380, 460, 462, 481, 521, 525, 527, 603, 608, 611, 612, 616, 622, 630, 631, 632, 634, 767, 818, 819
  and Knez, M. 297
  and Lin, N. 612, 819
Burton, M. D. 407, 816
Burton, R. M. and Obel, B. 210, 214, 216, 771
Butts, C. 219
Byrne, J. A. 170

Calas, M. B. and Smircich, L. 852, 868, 869
Callebaut, W. and Pinxten, R. 754
Callus, R., Morehead, A., Cully, M. and Buchanan, J. 782
Calori, R., Johnson, G. and Sarnin, P. 589
Camerer, C. 739
  and Knez, M. 696

Campbell, D. T. 76, 77, 85, 91, 101, 304, 321, 322, 459, 549, 552, 558, 722, 723, 724, 743, 753, 755, 756, 757, 758
  and Paller, B. T. 722, 723, 724
  and Stanley, J. C. 878
Campbell, J. L. and Pedersen, O. K. 498
Cannella, A. A. and Lubatkin, M. 241, 378
Cappelli, P., Shapiro, D. and Shumanis, N. 784
Carley, K. M. 183, 186, 192, 214, 218, 219, 220, 430, 447, 462, 771, 774
  and Gasser, L. 214
  and Hill, V. 214, 226
  and Lin, Z. 431
  and Newell, A. 214, 222
  and Prietula, M. J. 214, 771
  and Svoboda, D. M. 211, 214, 215, 217, 443, 681
Carnap, R. 736
Carpenter, M. and Westphal, J. D. 248
Carroll, G. R. 312, 542, 546, 547, 561
  and Delacroix, J. 312
  and Hannan, M. T. 265, 271, 313, 314, 387, 558, 790, 800, 809, 816
  and Harrison, J. 557, 569, 571, 666, 673
  and Swaminathan, A. 312, 551
  and Teo, A. 386, 405
  and Wade, J. B. 314, 668
Cartwright, N. 758, 761, 763, 771
Casadesus-Masanell, R. and Spulber, D. F. 807
Cavalli-Sforza, L. L. and Feldman, M. W. 106
Caves, R. M.
  and Porter, M. E. 475
  and Porter, M. E. and Spence, A. M. 479
Chandler, A. D. 445, 807, 815
Chang, S-J. 310
Chatman, J. and Barsad, S. 407
Chaves, M., Konieczny, M. E., Beyerlein, K. and Barman, E. 784, 791, 796
Chen, X. and White, H. 689
Cheng, Y-T. and Van de Ven, A. H. 320
Chesbrough, H. 407
  and Christensen, C. M. 171
  and Teece, D. 167
Chi, T. 483
Child, J. 345
Chomsky, N. 761
Christensen, C. M. 387, 392, 393, 394, 395, 397, 406, 407
  and Bower, J. L. 310, 386
  and Overdorf, M. 406
  and Suarez, F. and Utterback, J. 391, 392, 393

Christianson, A. and Tortora, R. D. 795, 796

Churbuck, D. and Young, J. S. 167

Cialdini, R. B. 46, 48, 147, 148
and Bator, R. J. and Guadagno, R. E. 40, 48, 52
and Kallgren, C. A. and Reno, R. R. 48

Ciborra, C. U. 455

Cilliers, P. 209

Clark, B. 514, 807

Clark, K. B. 391
and Fujimoto, T. 855
and Wheelwright, S. C. 163

Clawson, D. 807
and Neustadtl, A. and Scott, D. 610

Clegg, S. R.
and Hardy, C. 754, 890
and Hardy, C. and Nord, W. R. 753, 756, 894

Clemens, E. S. 812
and Cook, J. M. 498
and Hughes, M. T. 822

Coase, R. H. 442, 467, 468

Cohen, J. and Stewart, I. 755

Cohen, L. E., Broschak, J. P. and Haveman, H. A. 371

Cohen, M. D. 110, 434, 678
and Bacdayan, P. 89, 102, 109, 182, 183, 186, 192, 201, 434
and Burkhart, R., Dosi, G., Egidi, M., Marengo, L., Winter, S. and Warglien, M. 102, 111
and Levinthal, D. A. 854
and March, J. G. and Olsen, J. P. 211, 215, 216, 222, 698

Cohen, W. M.
and Levin, R. C. 162
and Levin, R. C. and Mowery, D. C. 631
and Levinthal, D. A. 87, 193, 296, 427, 430, 431, 432, 435, 476, 629, 630, 645, 651

Cole, R. E. 500, 505

Coleman, J. S. 58, 59, 60, 66, 290, 380
and Katz, E. and Menzel, H. 64

Colledge, M. J. 788, 789

Collins, J. and Porras, J. 401

Comfort, L. K. 431

Commons, J. R. 468

Conner, K. R. 476
and Prahalad, C. K. 480

Contractor, N. S., Whitbred, R., Fonti, F., Hyatt,
A., O'Keefe, B. and Jones, P. 766, 767, 772, 773

Cook, K. S. 602
and Emerson, R. M. 371

Cook, S. D. N. and Yanow, D. 418, 430

Cool, K. O., Dierickx, I. and Szulanski, G. 107, 108, 109, 177

Cooper, A. and Smith, C. 400

Cooper, R. G. 832
and Kleinschmidt, E. J. 159, 163, 164

Covaleski, M. A. and Dirsmith, M. W. 604, 806

Covington, C. R. 431

Cox, B. G. and Chinnappa, B. N. 782, 790, 800

Crane, D. 511

Craswell, R. 480

Crawford, V. 115

Crouch, B., Wasserman, S. and Contractor, N. 69

Crozier, M. 139, 145, 363, 366, 368, 373, 374

Cusumano, M.
and Mylonadis, Y. and Rosenbloom, R. 390, 391, 405
and Selby, R. 401
and Yoffee, D. 391, 404

Cyert, R. M. and March, J. G. 105, 192, 201, 233, 309, 332, 344, 345, 346, 363, 364, 365, 367, 372, 378, 379, 380, 416, 419, 425, 429, 629, 658, 699

Czarniawska-Joerges, B. 122, 125, 130, 132, 134, 594, 858

Dacin, M. T., Ventresca, M. J. and Beal, B. D. 525, 811

Daft, R. L. 807, 886
and Lewin, A. 742
and Weick, K. E. 346, 579

Dahl, R. A. 138, 140, 149, 600

Dalton, D. R. and Kesner, I. F. 241

Damanpour, F. 163

D'Andrade, R. G. 593

Daniels, K., De Chernatony, L. and Johnson, G. 589

Darr, E. D.
and Argote, L. and Epple, D. 194, 642, 646, 647, 650, 651, 654, 657
and Kurtzburg, T. 195, 198, 200, 647, 651, 652, 654

Darwin, C. 110, 113

D'Aveni, R. A. 570

David, P. 667, 674

Davidow, W. H. and Malone, M. S. 167, 170

Davis, G. F. 236, 241, 381, 528, 604, 615, 651, 654
   and Diekmann, K. A. and Tinsley, C. H. 328, 331, 334, 335, 339, 500, 505, 507, 508, 529, 560, 569
   and Greve, H. R. 58, 267, 298, 500, 502, 560
   and Mizruchi, M. S. 543, 609, 611, 615
   and Thompson, T. 381
   and Yoo, M. and Baker, W. E. 614, 617
Davis, J. A. 524, 525
Davis, L. E. and North, D. C. 483
Dawes, R. 741
Dawkins, R. 91
de Boeck, P. and Rosenberg, S. 821
De Chernatony, L., Daniels, K. and Johnson, G. 589
De Figueiredo, J. M. and Tiller, E. H. 483
de Regt, C. D. G. 756, 757
Dean, J. W. Jr., Yoon, S. J. and Susman, G. I. 165
Dearborn, D. C. and Simon, H. A. 347
Deephouse, D. L. 272
Delacroix, J.
   and Carroll, G. R. 312, 313
   and Rao, H. 315
   and Swaminathan, A. and Solt, M. E. 313
Delaney, K. J. 562, 567
Della Porta, D. and Vannucci, A. 524, 525
Demsetz, H. 467
Dennett, D. C. 91
Denzin, N. K. and Lincoln, Y. S. 853, 858, 869
Devadas, R. and Argote, L. 192
Dierickx, I. and Cool, K. 296, 475
Dill, W. R. 579, 601
Dillman, D. A. 796
DiMaggio, P. J. 263, 269, 497, 498, 513, 520, 521, 526, 528, 529, 549, 561, 631, 810, 819
   and Mullen, A. L. 813, 821
   and Powell, W. W. 41, 44, 52, 87, 259, 261, 315, 376, 497, 500, 513, 514, 515, 524, 526, 528, 543, 557, 558, 571, 590, 610, 704
Dippo, C. S., Chun, Y. I. and Sander, J. 794, 796
Dixit, A. 689, 692
   and Nalebuff, B. 694
Djelic, M. L. 807
Dobbin, F. R. 504, 561, 562, 567, 571
   and Dowd, T. J. 264, 266, 268, 274
   and Edelman, L., Meyer, J. W., Scott, W. R.

   and Swidler, A. 261, 263
   and Sutton, J. R., Meyer, J. W. and Scott, W. R. 263, 500, 503, 504, 784, 787, 790, 795
Dohan, D. and Sanchez-Jankowski, M. S. 820
Domhoff, G. W. 614
Donaldson, L. 480, 753
Donnellon, A., Gray, B. and Bougon, M. G. 352, 353, 359
Dooley, K. J. 320
   and Corman, S. 841
   and Mahmoodi, F. 845
   and Van de Ven, A. 447, 842, 846
Dore, R. 276
Dougherty, D. 859
   and Borrelli, L., Munir, K. and O'Sullivan, A. 859
   and Heller, T. 863
   and Kunda, G. 853
Douglas, M. 434, 593
Douthit, M. W. 63
Dow, S. C. and Earl, P. E. 213
Doz, Y. L. and Hamel, G. 287, 294, 297
Drabek, T. E., Braito, R., Cook, C. C., Powell, J. R. and Rogers, D. 790
Dunbar, K. 190
Duncan, R. B. 345, 388, 396, 397
   and Weiss, A. 430
Duquenne, V. 821
Durkheim, E. 670
Dutton, J. E. and Jackson, S. E. 579
Dutton, J. M. and Thomas, A. 182
Dyer, J. H. 474
   and Nobeoka, K. 283, 286, 287, 294, 648, 652
   and Singh, H. 288, 294, 476

Easton, G. and Jarrell, S. 509
Eaton, B. C. and Lipsey, R. G. 689
Eccles, R. and White, H. 524, 525
Edelman, L. B. 263, 434, 503, 562, 808
   and Suchman, M. C. 557
   and Uggen, C. and Erlanger, H. S. 504
Eden, C. and Spender, J. C. 122, 123, 125, 129, 130, 131, 132, 133, 134
Edmondson, A. O. 402, 404, 407, 408
   and Bohmer, R. M. J. and Pisano, G. P. 181
Edwards, J. R. 198
Edwards, P. K. and Marginson, P. 792
Edwards, R. 506
Egidi, M. and Narduzzo, A. 102

Ehrenberg, E. 406
Eisenhardt, K. M. 234, 402, 883
  and Bourgeois, L. J. 147, 372
  and Brown, S. L. 455
  and Galunic, D. C. 455, 461
  and Martin, J. A. 450
  and Santos, F. M. 460
  and Sull, D. 450, 451, 458
  and Tabrizi, B. N. 190, 396
Eldredge, N. and Gould, S. J. 90
Ellickson, R. C. 482
Elsbach, K. D. 39, 41, 45, 50, 51, 52
  and Kramer, R. M. 50, 52, 584
Emerson, R. M. 138, 139, 144, 147, 149, 368,
  371, 381, 600, 601, 610
Emirbayer, M. 816
Engeström, Y., Brown, K., Engeström, R. and
  Koistinen, K. 191
Eoyang, G. and Dooley, K. 833
Epple, D.
  and Argote, L. and Devadas, R. 106, 109,
  429
  and Argote, L. and Murphy, K. 201
Epstein, J. M. 442
  and Axtell, R. 210, 214, 222
Espeland, W. N. and Hirsch, P. M. 263, 267
Etzioni, A. 212
Evan, W. M. 295, 524, 526
Evans, W. N. and Kessides, I. N. 565
Eve, R. A., Horsfall, S. and Lee, M. E. 209, 665

Fabian, F. H. 733, 747
Faloutsos, M., Faloutsos, P. and Faloutsos, C.
  217
Fama, E. F. and Jensen, M. C. 234
Faulkner, R. R. 535
Feld, S. L. 62
Feldman, M. S. and March, J. G. 352
Fershtman, C. and Judd, K. L. 699
Festinger, L., Schachter, S. and Back, K. W.
  634
Feyerabend, P. K. 719, 740, 753, 774, 891,
  896
Fichman, M. and Levinthal, D. A. 307, 424
Fiegenbaum, A. and Thomas, H. 572
Finkelstein, S. 372
  and D'Aveni, R. A. 372
  and Hambrick, D. C. 392, 686, 696
Fiol, C. M. 123, 354, 355, 359
  and Huff, A. S. 130
  and Lyles, M. A. 434

Firebaugh, G. 153
Fisher, F. M. 690
Fiske, D. W. and Shweder, R. A. 715
Fiske, S. T. and Taylor, S. E. 121
Fleming, L. 630, 633
  and Sorenson, O. 678, 682
Fligstein, N. 37, 41, 262, 266, 267, 268, 269,
  366, 373, 376, 377, 380, 381, 500, 503,
  512, 529, 530, 551, 560, 604, 807
  and Brantley, P. 267
Folger, J. P., Hewes, D. E. and Poole, M. S. 881
Fombrun, C. J. 144, 584, 585, 592
  and Shanley, M. 582, 592
Fontana, W. and Ballati, S. 443
Forrester, J. 836
Foss, N. J. 480
Foster, R. 405
Foucault, M. 738, 740, 741, 815
Fox-Wolfgramm, S. J., Boal, K. B. and Hunt,
  J. G. 82
Frank, D. J. 557
Franzosi, R. 820
  and Mohr, J. W. 820
Frazis, H. J., Herz, D. E. and Horrigan, M. W.
  784, 795
Freeland, R. F. 807
Freeman, J. H. 783
  and Lomi, A. 312
Freeman, L. C. 59, 60, 144, 288, 289
French, J. R. P. and Raven, B. 141, 145
Friedel, R. 586
Friedland, R. and Alford, R. 509, 813
Friedman, M. 696, 736
Fruin, M. and Nishiguchi, T. 451
Fudenberg, D. and Tirole, J. 689, 694, 696
Fulmer, R. M., Gibbs, P. and Keys, J. B. 429

Galambos, L. 807
Galaskiewicz, J. 41, 604, 608, 819
  and Burt, R. S. 58, 267, 604
  and Wasserman, S. 528, 604, 654
  and Wasserman, S., Rauschenbach, B.,
    Bielefeld, W. and Mullaney, P. 603
Galbraith, C. S. 193
Galbraith, J. R. 345, 476
Galunic, D. C.
  and Eisenhardt, K. M. 81, 104, 406, 408,
    443, 455, 456, 457, 458
  and Rodan, S. 84, 88
Gambetta, D. 525
Gandz, J. and Murray, V. V. 138

Gargiulo, M. 150, 524, 525
 and Benassi, M. 69
Garud, R.
 and Ahlstrom, D. 407
 and Kotha, S. 166
 and Kumaraswamy, A. 166, 167, 171
 and Lant, T. K. 588, 820
 and Rappa, M. A. 572, 581, 586
 and Van de Ven, A. H. 85
Garvin, D. A. 429
Gatignon, H.
 and Anderson, E. 472
 and Tushman, M., Anderson, P. and Smith,
  W. 406
Gavetti, G. and Levinthal, D. A. 388, 401, 406,
  407, 675, 679, 680
Geertz, C. 849
Geletkanycz, M. A. and Hambrick, D. C. 654
Gell-Mann, M. 442, 443, 458, 460, 760, 772
Gemes, K. 740, 748
Gemser, G., Leenders, M. A. and Wijnberg,
  N. M. 286, 293
Gersick, C. J. G. 90
 and Hackman, J. R. 86
Ghemawat, P. 689
 and Nalebuff, B. 690
Ghosh, M. and John, G. 483
Ghoshal, S.
 and Bartlett, C. A. 166
 and Moran, P. 480
Gibbons, R. 252
Gibson, D. 214
Giddens, A, 453, 462, 766, 806, 849
Giere, R. N. 761, 762
Gilbert, R. J. 689
Gilfillan, S. 678
Gilovich, T. 745
Gilson, R. J. 638
Gimeno, J. 565
 and Woo, C. Y. 565
Ginsberg, A. and Baum, J. A. C. 310
Gioia, D., Thomas, J., Clark, S. and Chittipeddi,
  K. 352, 354, 355
Glaser, B. 858
 and Strauss, A. L. 856
Glassmier, A. 386
Glynn, M. A.
 and Abzug, R. 54
 and Lant, T. and Milliken, F. 356
Godfrey, P. C. and Hill, C. W. L. 769
Goffman, E. 853

Golden-Biddle, K. and Locke, K. 858
Goldstein, J. 839
Gomes-Casseres, B. 287
Gompers, P. A. and Lerner, J. 634
Goodman, P., Fichman, M., Lerch, J. and
  Snyder, P. 487
Goody, J. 806
Gordon, D. M. 442, 443
Gort, M. 476
Gould, S. J. 558
Gouldner, A. 363, 373
Granovetter, M. S. 58, 59, 60, 63, 249, 291,
  370, 453, 462, 481, 527, 528, 560, 634,
  664
Grant, R. M. 418, 436
Greeno, J. G. and Moore, J. L. 356, 357
Greenwald, A. G.
 and Leippe, M. R., Pratkanis, A. R. and
  Baumgardner, M. 745
 and Pratkanis, A. R., Leippe, M. R. and
  Baumgardner, M. H. 197
Greenwood, R. and Hinings, C. R. 85, 87, 405,
  498, 506, 507, 513
Greve, H. R. 194, 195, 306, 311, 422, 426,
  433, 437, 561, 564, 565, 567, 571, 651,
  655, 690
 and Taylor, A. 584
Griffin, A. and Hauser, J. R. 163
Griliches, Z. 162
Gross, P. R.
 and Levitt, N. 753
 and Levitt, N. and Lewis, M. W. 753
Grossman, S. J. and Hart, O. 486
Grove, A. 386
Gruenfeld, D. H. 190
 and Hollingshead, A. B. 190, 199
 and Mannix, E., Williams, K. and Neale, M.
  199
 and Martorana, P. V. and Fan, E. T. 181,
  183, 188, 190, 193, 196
Guerra-Pearson, F. 817
Guetzkow, H. and Simon, H. A. 193
Guillén, M. F. 506, 512, 557, 565, 567, 569,
  807, 812, 820
Gulati, R. 281, 282, 288, 289, 291, 292, 295,
  297, 310, 484, 521, 529
 and Nohria, N. and Zaheer, A. 282, 296
 and Dialdin, D. 296
 and Gargiulo, M. 282, 284, 297, 310, 452,
  453
 and Kumar, N. and Zajac, E. 297

and Lawrence, P. 288, 297
and Singh, H. 290, 297, 476, 529
and Wang, L. 288, 291
and Westphal, J. D. 239, 245, 252, 295
Gupta, A. K. and Govindarajan, V. 649, 650
Gusfield, J. R. 266

Hacking, I. 736, 737, 740, 890
Hage, J. 761
Hagedoorn, J. and Schakenraad, J. 473
Hahlweg, K. 725, 727, 728
and Hooker, C. A. 720, 754
Hall, P. A and Taylor, R. 498
Hall, R., Haas, J., Johnson, E. and Norman, J.
212
Halliday, T. C., Powell, M. J. and Granfors,
M. W. 328, 329, 330, 332, 335, 340
Hambrick, D. C. 372, 379, 401, 407
and Cho, T. S. and Chen, M. 190
and D'Aveni, R. 401
and Fukutomi, G. D. S. 703
and Mason, P. A. 372, 379
and Nadler, D. and Tushman, M. 405
Hamel, G. 645, 649, 655
and Prahalad, C. 387, 400, 401
Hamilton, G. G. and Biggart, N. W. 503
Hamilton, W. D. 91
Han, S. 605
Hanfling, O. 760
Hannan, M. T. 559, 570, 627, 670
and Carroll, G. R. 265, 271, 313, 315, 510,
571, 673, 769
and Carroll, G. R., Dundon, E. A. and Torres,
J. C. 262, 306, 313, 314, 315, 675
and Freeman, J. H. 90, 104, 108, 305, 307,
309, 311, 315, 369, 434, 442, 502, 542,
544, 557, 558, 622, 629, 665, 668, 770,
808
Hansen, M. T. 172, 174, 183, 188, 194, 196,
430, 431, 445
and Podolny, J. M. and Pfeffer, J. 69
Hardin, C. D. and Higgins, E. T. 48
Hardy, C. and Clegg, S. R. 140
Hargadon, A. and Sutton, R. I. 83, 191, 192
Harré, R. 896
and Madden, E. A. 884
Harrison, B. 564, 571
Harrison, J. R.
and Carroll, G. R. 210, 220
and March, J. G. 431
Hart, O.

and Moore, J. 486
and Tirole, J. 485
Hartman, E. 736
Haspeslagh, P. C. and Jemison, D. B. 87
Hassard, J. 895
and Parker, M. 774
Hatch, M. J. and Weick, K. E. 450
Haunschild, P. R. 267, 604, 654
and Beckman, C. M. 267, 658
and Miner, A. S. 274, 298, 528, 645, 648,
658
and Ni, B. 200
Hausman, D. M. 761
Haveman, H. A. 84, 510, 561, 649
and Rao, H. 271, 501, 508, 543, 548, 557,
559, 567, 568, 569, 570
Hawley, A. H. 541, 543, 545, 548, 563, 602
Hayek, F. 468
Hayes, R. H. and Abernathy, W. J. 250
Heath, C., Larrick, R. P. and Klayman, J. 429
Hedlund, G. and Nonaka, I. 430
Heide, J. B.
and John, G. 473
and Miner, A. S. 293
Heider, F. 767
Heimer, C. 821
Heise, G. and Miller, G. 193
Helper, S. 294
Hempel, C. G. 738, 754, 755, 760, 892, 897
Henderson, A. D. 306, 308
Henderson, R. M. 393, 396, 405
and Clark, K. B. 84, 88, 171, 386, 391, 392,
393, 394, 406, 455, 622, 629
and Cockburn, I. 477, 479, 644, 647, 652,
653, 654
Hendrickx, M. 721, 756
Henisz, W. J. 470
Hennart, J. F. 470
Herrigel, G. 566
Herriott, S. R., Levinthal, D. A. and March, J. G.
427
Hey, J. D. 432
Hickson, D. J., Hinings, C. R., Lee, C. A.,
Schneck, R. E. and Pennings, J. M. 138,
153, 363, 364, 365, 368, 374, 380
Higgins, M. C.
and Gulati, R. 292
and Kram, K. E. 63
Hinings, C. R.
and Brown, J. L. and Greenwood, R. 506,
852

Hinings, C. R. (*cont'd*)
  and Hickson, D. J., Pennings, J. M. and
    Schneck, R. E. 143, 149, 369
Hirsch, P. M. 263, 268, 497, 501, 502, 560,
  584, 816, 853
Hitt, L. M. 161, 169
Hodgkinson, G. P. 588
  and Johnson, G. 582, 588, 589
Hoffman, A. J. 557, 561, 562
Hofstader, D. R. 552
Holland, J. H. 110, 111, 209, 442, 837
  and Miller, J. H. 443
Hollander, S. 392
Hollenbeck, J. R., Ilgen, D. R., Sego, D. J.,
  Hedlund, J., Major, D. A. and Philips, J.
  183, 184, 192
Hollingshead, A. B. 193
Hollingsworth, J. R., Schmitter, P. C. and
  Streeck, W. 557, 565, 569
Holm, P. 561, 571
Holmstrom, B. and Roberts, J. 252
Holton, G. 753, 754
Holzer, H. J. 782
Homans, G. C. 767
Hooker, C. A. 720, 721, 754, 757
Hooks, G. 561
Horgan, J. 458
House, R. J. 141, 145, 146
  and Spangler, W. D. and Woycke, J. 141,
    142, 146, 407
Hoyningen-Huene, P. 895
Huber, G. P. 431
  and Power, D. J. 792
Huberman, B. and Glance, N. 679
Huff, A. S. 121, 122, 123, 125, 127, 131, 134,
  584
Hughes, M. 753
Hughes, T. 388, 390, 391, 626, 627
Hummon, N. P. 214
Hunt, C. S. and Aldrich, H. E. 408, 543, 548
Hunt, S. D. 754, 761, 889, 890, 894, 896
Hunter, F. 59
Hurry, D., Miller, A. T. and Bowman, E. H. 173
Hurst, D. 388, 401, 406
Hutchins, E. 214
  and Hazelhurst, B. 107
Hybels, R. C.
  and Ryan, A. R. 273, 510
  and Ryan, A. R. and Barley, S. R. 315, 770

Iansiti, M. and Clark, K. 396, 402, 404

Ibarra, H. 58, 67, 153, 370
Ichniowsky, C., Shaw, K. and Prennushi, G.
  696
Imai, K., Nonaka, I. and Takeuchi, H. 396
Ingram, P.
  and Baum, J. A. C. 284, 286, 287, 319, 643,
    644, 651, 654, 655, 657, 660
  and Clay, K. 483
  and Inman, C. 286, 564
  and Roberts, P. R. 650, 652, 654
  and Simons, T. 194, 260, 262, 265, 274,
    647, 650, 651, 653, 654, 657
Irwin, D. A. and Klenow, P. J. 642, 647, 652,
  654, 657
Iwai, K. 431

Jackall, R. 363, 366, 373, 374, 380, 821
Jackson, S. E. and Dutton, J. E. 347, 348
Jacobs, D. 602
Jacoby, S. 506
Jaffe, A., Trajtenberg, M. and Henderson, R.
  172, 624, 633
Jehn, K. A. 39, 43, 52
Jelinek, M. and Schoonhoven, C. B. 855
Jennings, P. D., Dobbin, F. R. and Baron, J. N.
  807
Jensen, M. C.
  and Meckling, W. H. 233, 234, 248, 486
  and Murphy, K. J. 234
Jensen, R. 431
Jepperson, R. L. 38, 498
  and Swidler, A. 820
Jermier, J. M.
  and Barley, S. R. 806
  and Slocum Jr., J. M., Fry, L. W. and Gaines, J.
    39, 41, 42, 45, 52
Jin, Y. and Levitt, R. 211, 214, 215, 216, 217,
  222
John, G. and Reve, T. 792
John, R. R. 807
Johne, F. A. and Snelson, P. A. 163
Johnson, A. E. 791
Johnson, G. 458
  and Scholes, K. 704
Johnson, J. M. 868
Johnstone, B. 566
Jones, C. 817
  and Hesterly, W. S. and Borgatti, S. P. 167,
    482
Joskow, P. L. 469, 470, 471, 473
Jovanovic, B. 689, 692

Kahneman, D. P., Slovic, P. and Tversky, A. 745

Kale, P. J.
and Dyer, J. and Singh, H. 297
and Singh, H. and Perlmutter, H. 294, 297

Kalleberg, A. L.,
and Knoke, D., Marsden, P. V. and Spaeth, J. L. 784
and Marsden, P. V., Aldrich, H. E. and Cassell, J. W. 788, 789, 790

Kamien, M. I. and Schwartz, N. L. 689, 691

Kanter, R. M. 67, 68, 363, 365, 370, 380
and Stein, B. and Jick, T. 405

Kaplan, A. 753, 877, 892

Kaplan, D. 218

Karnøe, P. and Garud, R. 675

Katz, M. L. and Shapiro, C. 627, 628

Katz, R. 198, 199

Kaufer, D. S. and Carley, K. M. 218

Kauffman, S. A. 114, 209, 222, 320, 442, 443, 447, 448, 453, 455, 456, 459, 544, 550, 570, 672, 682, 765
and Levin, S. 672

Kearns, D. and Nadler, D. 393, 405

Keenan, D. and O'Brian, M. 668

Keister, L. A. 286,

Kelley, M. R. 787
and Brooks, H. 784

Kelly, D. and Amburgey, T. L. 310, 703

Kelly, G. A. 124

Kets de Vries, M. 407

Khanna, T.
and Gulati, R. and Nohria, N. 653
and Palepu, K. 286, 287
and Rivkin, J. 286

Kiel, D. and Elliott, E. 229

Kieser, A. 806, 808
and Koch, U. 435

Kiesler, S. and Sproull, L. 346

Kilduff, M. and Krackhardt, D. 148, 150

Kim, D.-J. and Kogut, B. 630

Kim, J. Y. 653, 657

Kim, N. and Srivastava, R. K. 177

Kim, S. 563

Kipnis, D.
and Schmidt, S. M. 142, 146, 147
and Schmidt, S. M. and Wilkinson, I. 146, 149

Kirsch, D. 674

Klatzky, S. R. 212

Klein, B., Crawford, R. A. and Alchian, A. A. 468

Klein, K. J. and Kozlowski, S. W. J. 462

Klein, P. 487

Klepper, S. 395
and Graddy, K. 690, 692
and Sleeper, S. 406

Klimecki, R. G. and Lassleben, H. 430

Klimoski, R. and Mohammed, S. 131

Knoke, D. 784, 789, 795, 796, 800
and Burt, R. S. 144
and Pappi, F. U., Broadbent, J. and Tsujinaka, Y. 782
and Reynolds, P. D., Marsden, P. V., Miller, B. and Kaufman, N. 793

Koenig, T., Gogel, R. and Sonquist, J. 606

Koertge, N. 753

Kogut, B. 452, 476, 654
and Kulatilaka, N. 173
and Walker, G. and Kim, D. J. 624, 631
and Zander, U. 87, 172, 431, 482, 654, 810

Kono, C., Palmer, D., Friedland, R. and Zafonte, M. 563, 634, 635

Koput, K. and Powell, W. W. 451, 458

Korn, H. J. and Baum, J. A. C. 543

Kosnik, R. D. 236, 241

Kotha, S. 166
and Swamidass, P. 160, 165

Kozinets, R. V. 817

Kraatz, M. S. 651
and Zajac, E. J. 505

Krackhardt, D. 68, 69, 140, 144, 145
and Brass, D. J. 58
and Carley, K. M. 70, 214, 226
and Hanson, J. R. 65
and Porter, L. W. 58, 64

Kramer, R. M. 40, 45, 46, 197

Kraut, A. I. 800

Kreps, D. M. 434
and Scheinkman, J. A. 689, 691

Krugman, P. 563

Kuhn, T. S. 299, 507, 674, 716, 738, 748, 753, 774, 891, 894, 895, 896

Kuipers, T. 748

Kuklinski, J. H., Luskin, R. C. and Bolland, J. 124, 132

Kumar, N., Stern, L. W. and Anderson, J. C. 792, 793

Kunda, G. 816

Kuwada, K. 85, 91

Labianca, G., Brass, D. J. and Grey, B. 58
Lacey, R. 584
Lafontaine, F. 473
Lakatos, I. 744, 745, 875
Lanczos, C. 759
Landes, D. 388, 390
Lane, P. J. and Lubatkin, M. 430, 435, 460
Lang, J. R. and Lockhart, D. E. 603
Langfield-Smith, K. 131
Langley, A. 851, 882, 886
  and Truax, J. 882
Langlois, R. N. 166, 171
  and Foss, N. J. 475, 476, 481, 483
Langton, J. 810
Lant, T. K. 214, 356, 421, 425, 429
  and Mezias, S. J. 197, 422, 426, 429, 431
  and Milliken, F. J. and Batra, B. 183, 184,
    190, 421, 425, 429
  and Phelps, C. 356
  and Shapira, Z. 344, 359
Larsen, E. R. and Markides, C. 668
Larson, A. 523, 524
Larson, J. R.
  and Christensen, C. 131
  and Christensen, C., Abbott, A. S. and Franz,
    T. M. 183, 189, 195
Latour, B. 626, 753, 806, 861
Laudan, L. 756, 890
Laughlin, P. R. and Hollingshead, A. B. 199
Laumann, E. O.
  and Galaskiewicz, J. and Marsden, P. V. 281,
    525
  and Knoke, D. 524, 526, 608, 782, 785, 801
  and Marsden, P. V. 521
  and Pappi, F. U. 59, 608
Lave, C. A. and March, J. G. 417, 428, 429
Lave, J. and Wenger, E. 107
Law, A. and Kelton, D. 830, 834, 835, 842,
  845
Lawler, E. E. III, Mohrman, S. and Ledford, G.
  787
Lawrence, B. L. 894
Lawrence, P. R. and Lorsch, J. W. 447
Lawson, T. 757
Lazerson, M. 559, 564, 659
le Grand, C., Szulkin, R. and Tåhlin, M. 782
Leavitt, H. J. 183, 193
Leblebici, H., Salancik, G. R., Copay, A. and
  King, T. 501, 505, 513, 559
Lee, B. 165
Lee, T., Mitchell, T. and Sablynski, C. 851

Lei, D., Hitt, M. A. and Goldhar, J. D. 165, 167
Leifer, E. M. 583, 588
Lempel, A. and Ziv, J. 219
Leonard-Barton, D. 107, 387, 396, 400, 853
  and Deschamps, I. 107
Levin, P. and Espeland, W. N. 583
Levins, R. 770
Levinthal, D. A. 111, 114, 228, 387, 396, 443,
  446, 447, 462, 572, 666, 765
  and March, J. G. 319, 419, 425, 426, 429,
    431, 432
  and Warglien, M. 114, 455, 461
Levitt, B.
  and March, J. G. 100, 101, 181, 191, 197,
    200, 396, 415, 418, 420, 426, 427, 429,
    431, 432, 435
  and Nass, C. 605
Levy, D. 84
Lewin, A. Y.
  and Long, C. P. and Carroll, T. N. 569
  and Volberda, H. W. 442, 444, 448, 455,
    458
Lewis, D. 748
Lewis, K. 181
Lewis, M. 119
Liang, D. W., Moreland, R. and Argote, L. 181,
  183, 187, 193, 199, 201, 435
Lichtenstein, B. 665
Lie, J. 557
Lieberman, M. B. 429
Liebeskind, J. P., Oliver, A. L., Zucker, L. and
  Brewer, M. 649
Lin, N. 58, 66
Lincoln, J. R. 69
  and Kalleberg, A. L. 784, 787, 790, 795,
    801
Lindell, P., Melin, L., Gahmberg, H. J., Hellqvist,
  A. and Melander, A. 123, 125, 128, 130
Lindgren, K. and Nordahl, M. 219
Lippman, S. A. and Rumelt, R. P. 87, 475, 677
Lloyd, E. A. 762
Locke, E. 147
Locke, K. and Golden-Biddle, K. 809
Lomi, A. 314, 317, 561, 564
  and Larsen, E. R. 328, 331, 337, 338, 339,
    452, 453, 571, 569, 666, 668, 669, 670,
    677
  and Larsen, E. R. and Ginsberg, A. 431
Lord, R. G. and Maher, K. J. 119, 121, 124,
  125, 126, 127, 128, 129, 133
Lorenz, K. 755

Lorenzoni, G.
  and Lipparini, A. 454, 455, 456
  and Ornati, O. 559
Lorrain, F. and White, H. C. 631
Lörsch, A. 677
Lorsch, J. W. and MacIver, E. 245
Louis, M. R. and Sutton, R. I. 130, 401, 407
Lounamaa, P. H. and March, J. G. 429, 432
Lukes, S. 140, 600
Luo, Y. and Peng, M. W. 435
Lusht, K. M. and Farber, D. 172
Lyles, M. A. 288
  and Schwenk, C. R. 128, 131
Lynch, A. 747

McCaffrey, D. P. 268
McCall, M. W. 149
McClelland, D. C. 145
McConnell, J. J. and Nantell, T. J. 293
McConnell, S. 842, 844
McEvily, B. and Zaheer, A. 194, 196, 287, 290, 291
McGrath, J. E. 322
  and Argote, L. 182
McGrath, R. 396, 402
  and MacMillan, I. 396
McGrath, R. T. 173, 174
Mach, E. 736
Macintosh, R. and MacLean, D. 443, 460
Macken, C., Hagan, P. and Perelson, A. 672
McKelvey, B. 76, 77, 78, 99, 101, 104, 209, 212, 213, 304, 320, 321, 442, 443, 447, 448, 455, 542, 550, 551, 676, 677, 722, 733, 737, 739, 742, 748, 753, 754, 755, 756, 757, 758, 765, 769, 772, 774, 775, 837, 889, 891, 894
  and Aldrich, H. E. 78, 739
McKendrick, D. and Carroll, G. R. 674
McKenna, C. 504
McLean, P. D. and Padgett, J. F. 811, 819
McNeely, C. L. 808
McPherson, J. M. 315, 631, 790, 791
  and Rotolo, T. 328, 331, 336, 338, 792
  and Popielarz, P. A. and Drobnic, S. 572
Macy, J., Jr., Christie, L. and Luce, R. 193
Macy, M. W. 214, 222
Madison, D. L., Allen, R. W., Porter, L. W., Renwick, P. A. and Mayes, B. T. 141
Mael, F. and Ashforth, B. E. 45
Maguire, S. and McKelvey, B. 209, 450
Maher, M. and Palmer, D. 268

Mahoney, J. T. and Pandian, J. 475
Maier, N. F. 356
Maijoor, S. J. and Witteloostuijn, A. van 705
Mainzer, K. 209
Malone, T. W., Yates, J. and Benjamin, R. I. 169
Mandell, T. 58
Mann, C. C. 172
Mannheim, K. 593, 738
March, J. G. 29, 82, 90, 91, 111, 113, 197, 214, 355, 397, 399, 417, 421, 422, 425, 426, 431, 435, 568, 643, 653, 675, 835, 842
  and Olsen, J. P. 375, 416, 419, 431
  and Schulz, M. and Zhou, X. 201, 421, 424, 427, 429, 430, 431, 432, 433, 435
  and Shapira, Z. 425
  and Simon, H. A. 86, 106, 214, 344, 345, 364, 367, 368, 416, 419, 429, 579
  and Sproull, L. S. and Tamuz, M. 199, 429
Marginson, P. 785, 800
Margolis, H. 699
Marris, R. L. 233
Marsden, P. V. 63, 139
  and Kalleberg, A. L. and Knoke, D. 801
Marsden, R. and Townley, B. 754
Marshall, A. 172, 677, 687, 689
Martin, R. and Sunley, P. 563
Marx, K. 599
Mason, E. S. 687
Masten, S. E. 470, 471, 484
  and Crocker, K. J. 473
  and Meehan, J. W. and Snyder, E. A. 472, 474, 485
Masterman, M. 894
Masuch, M. and Warglien, M. 771
Mathews, K. M., White, M. C. and Long, R. G. 229
Mauws, M. and Philips, N. 743
May, R. 673
Mechanic, D. 144
Meindl, J. R., Stubbart, C. and Porac, J. F. 122, 125
Merton, R. C. 627
Merton, R. K. 511, 648
Messick, D. M. and Mackie, D. M. 197
Meyer, A. D. 346, 882
  and Brooks, G. and Goes, J. 405
  and Goes, J. B. 194
Meyer, J. W. 808
  and Boli, J. and Thomas, G. M. 489, 513
  and Hannan, M. T. 808

Meyer, J. W. (*cont'd*)
  and Jepperson, R. L. 513
  and Rowan, B. 87, 260, 261, 263, 269, 272,
    376, 483, 497, 500, 511, 513, 514, 665,
    680, 808, 813
  and Scott, W. R. 210, 213
  and Scott, W. R. and Strang, D. 504, 808
Meyer, M. W. 84, 91, 104
Meyerson, D. E. 40, 44, 47, 52
Meyerson, E. M. 58
Mezias, S. J. 37, 274, 429, 605, 808
  and Glynn, M. A. 430, 431, 432
  and Lant, T. K. 680
Miles, M. B. and Huberman, A. M. 882
Miles, R. E. and Snow, C. C. 167
Milgram, S. 141, 150
Milgrom, P. and Roberts, J. 234
Miller, C. C. and Cardinal, L. B. 703
Miller, D. 386, 400, 401, 405, 740, 744, 748
  and Friesen, P. H. 83, 90
Miller, R. 172
Milliken, F. J. 349, 350
  and Lant, T. K. 396, 401, 407
Millward, N.,
  and Marginson, P. and Callus, R. 800
  and Woodland, S., Bryson, A. and Forth, J.
    799
Miner, A. S. 76, 77, 80, 81, 82, 85, 88, 99,
    109, 418, 420
  and Amburgey, T. L. and Stearns, T. 318
  and Anderson, P. 319
  and Haunschild, P. R. 319, 408
  and Kim, J. Y., Holzinger, I. W. and
    Haunschild, P. R. 200, 657
  and Mezias, S. J. 85, 182, 428
Minkoff, D. C. 562
Mintz, B. and Schwartz, M. 289, 543, 609,
    611, 612, 819
Mintzberg, H. 145, 149, 234
  and McHugh, A. 448, 449, 450, 456, 459,
    461, 462
Mirowski, P. 759, 760, 889
Mitchell, W.
  and Shaver, J. M. and Yeung, B. 310
  and Singh, K. 293
Mitroff, I. and Emshoff, J. 874
Mizruchi, M. S. 281, 289, 381, 521, 528, 530,
    604, 607, 610, 613
  and Fein, L. C. 273, 614
  and Stearns, L. B. 58, 60, 64, 69, 603, 609
Moe, T. 473, 558

Moen, J. and Tallman, E. 548
Mohanram, P. and Nanda, A. 293
Mohr, J. W. 594, 811, 812, 816, 820, 821
  and Duquenne, V. 813, 821
  and Guerra-Pearson, F. 821
Mohr, L. B. 851, 872
Moldoveanu, M. C. 721, 743
Molm, L. D. 147
Monge, P. and Contractor, N. S. 766
Monteverde, K. and Teece, D. J. 470, 471, 473,
    674
Montgomery, C. A.
  and Hariharan, S. 476, 477
  and Wernerfelt, B. 477, 479
  and Wernerfelt, B. and Balakrishnan, S. 739
Moon, J. Y. and Sproull, L. 358
Moore, W. L. and Pfeffer, J. 152
Moorman, C. and Miner, A. S. 88, 89, 190,
    435, 450
Morel, B. and Ramanujam, R. 209, 448, 458
Moreland, R. L., Argote, L. and Krishnan, R.
    187, 193, 198
Moreno, J. L. 59
Morgan, M. S. and Morrison, M. 758, 763
Morgenstern, O. and Neumann, J. von 693
Morison, E. E. 89, 391
Morone, J. 386, 400
Morrill, C. 376, 551
Morrison, F. 320
Morrison, M. 758, 763
  and Morgan, M. S. 758
Moscovici, S. and Duveen, G. 593
Mowery, D. C.
  and Oxley, J. E. and Silverman, B. S. 454,
    455, 456, 476, 477, 479, 630, 632, 637,
    647, 654, 655
  and Rosenberg, N. 629
Mueller, D. C. 697, 704
Mullen, B., Johnson, C. and Salas, E. 191
Murnighan, J. K. 147, 696
  and Brass, D. J. 147
Myers, S. and Marquis, D. 392
Myerson, R. B. 694

Nadler, D. 405
  and Shaw, R. and Walton, E. 405
  and Tushman, M. 396, 402, 408
Nagel, E. 753, 760, 892
Nahapiet, J. and Ghoshal, S. 174, 430, 431
Narayanan, S., Bodner, D. A., Sreekanth, U.,
    Govindaraj, T., McGinnis, L. F. and

Mitchell, C. M. 174
Narduzzo, A., Rocco, E. and Warglien, M. 112
Nash, J. F. 694
Nelson, R. R. 386, 407, 408
  and Winter, S. G. 76, 77, 79, 84, 86, 87,
    101, 102, 103, 104, 105, 192, 418, 431,
    434, 475, 629, 653, 707
Nemeth, C. J. 190
  and Kwan, J. L. 190
  and Wachtler, J. 190
Nemetz, P. L. and Fry, L. W. 165
Neurath, O. and Cohen, R. S. 760
Neustadtl, A. and Clawson, D. 521
Nickerson, J. A. 483, 484
  and Hamilton, B. and Wada, T. 483
  and Silverman, B. S. 484, 485
Nickerson, R. 749
Nielsen, E. and Hannan, M. T. 542, 544, 547
Nietzsche, F. 740, 747
Nisbett, R. E. and Ross, L. 744
Noble, D. 391
Noda, T. and Bower, J. L. 310
Nohria, N. and Garcia-Pont, C. 287
Nola, R. 756
Nonaka, I. 181, 396, 401, 430
  and Takeuchi, H. 86, 593
Nord, W. and Tucker, S. 855
Norris, C. 753
North, D. C. 260, 483
Novshek, W. and Sonnenschein, H. 688, 691
Nowak, M. and May, R. 679

O'Reilly, C. A. 58
  and Chatman, J. 38
  and Snyder, R. and Booth, J. 401, 403
Ocasio, W. 273, 365, 372, 376, 377, 378,
    379, 380
  and Kim, H. 269, 273, 377, 378
Okhuysen, G. A. and Eisenhardt, K. M. 450,
    460
Oliver, C. 269, 481, 498, 507, 511, 529, 543
Ophir, R., Ingram, P. and Argote, L. 200
Orlikowski, W. J. and Yates, J. 812, 820
Ornstein, M. D. 606, 607
Orr, J. 107
Orrú, M., Biggart, N. W. and Hamilton, G. G.
    260, 557, 569
Orton, J. and Weick, K. 167
Osgood, C. E., Suci, G. J. and Tannenbaum,
    P. H. 820
Osterman, P. 785, 788, 790, 796, 800

Oxley, J. E. 469, 471, 473, 485

Padgett, J. F. 115, 214, 222, 443
  and Ansell, C. K. 528
Palay, T. 483
Palmer, D. A. 606
  and Barber, B. 267, 269
  and Barber, B. M. and Zhou, X. 560
  and Barber, B. M., Zhou, X. and Soysal, Y.
    560, 604
  and Friedland, R. and Singh, J. V. 603, 607
  and Jennings, D. P. and Zhou, X. 262, 267,
    605, 654
Parcel, T. L., Kaufman, R. L. and Jolly, L. 791
Park, S. H., Li, S. and Tse, D. K. 272
Parkhe, A. 293
Parsons, T. 511
Parthasarthy, R. and Sethi, S. P. 165
Pattison, P. E.
  and Wasserman, S. 69
  and Wasserman, S., Robins, G. and Kanfer,
    A. M. 69
Paulus, P. B. and Yang, H. 183, 185, 191
Paxson, M. C., Dillman, D. A. and Tarnai, J.
    793, 796
Pea, R. D. 357
Peirce, C. S. 874
Péli, G.
  and Bruggeman, J., Masuch, M. and
    Ó Nualláin, B. 695, 698
  and Nooteboom, B. 675
Pennings, J. M. 603, 608
Penrose, E. T. 467
Pentland, B. T. 851, 882, 885
  and Reuter, H. H. 434, 813, 820, 852
Perlitz, M., Peske, T. and Schrank, R. 174
Perreault, W. and Miles, R. 147
Perrow, C. 210, 213, 268, 269, 481, 487, 511,
    600, 755, 807
Pescosolido, B. A. and Rubin, B. A. 520, 529
Peteraf, M. A. 475, 480
Petroski, H. 581, 586, 587, 588
Pettigrew, A. M. 140, 372, 405, 873, 874,
    875, 877
Pfeffer, J. and Salancik, G. R. 282
Pfeffer, J. 40, 42, 46, 52, 138, 140, 141, 145,
    147, 148, 152, 154, 234, 247, 253, 352,
    363, 369, 376, 378, 401, 487, 602, 608,
    695, 733, 735, 736, 738, 739, 741, 753,
    755, 774, 894, 895
  and Moore, W. L. 148, 369

Pfeffer, J. (*cont'd*)
  and Nowak, P. 282, 602
  and Salancik, G. R. 269, 274, 363, 364, 365,
    369, 371, 376, 378, 380, 381, 481, 528,
    561, 602, 608, 612, 665, 667
  and Sutton, R. I. 46, 49, 50, 51, 402, 404
Philips, J. 183, 184, 192, 197
Phillips, D. J. 637
Phillips, M. E. 582, 584, 590, 591
Pianka, E. R. 550
Pimm, S. L. 544
Pinch, T. J. and Bijker, W. E. 391, 581, 583,
    587, 627
Pine II, B. J. 166
Pines, D., Cowan, G. and Meltzer, D. 209
Piore, M. J. and Sabel, C. F. 806
Pisano, G. P. 431, 471, 473
Plesu, A. 749
Podolny, J. M. 59, 69, 481, 511, 521, 560,
    567, 571, 627, 675
  and Baron, J. N. 58, 60, 64, 67, 144, 295
  and Philips, D. J. 482
  and Stuart, T. E. 408, 623, 626, 627, 644,
    647
  and Stuart, T. E. and Hannan, M. T. 295,
    623, 626, 631
Polanyi, K. 527, 528
Polanyi, M. 86
Pollock, T. G. 812
Polos, L., Hannan, M. T. and Carroll, G. R. 542
Pols, E. 896
Poole, M. S. 883
  and Folger, J. P. and Hewes, D. E. 881
  and Van de Ven, A. H., Dooley, K. and
    Holmes, M. 867, 883, 884
Popper, K. R. 678, 721, 737, 740, 744, 745,
    868, 897
Poppo, L. and Zenger, T. R. 478, 487
Porac, J. F.
  and Mishina, Y. and Pollock, T. G. 812, 819
  and Rosa, J. A. 579
  and Thomas, H. 583
  and Thomas, H. and Baden-Fuller, C. 582,
    584, 591
  and Thomas, H., Wilson, F., Paton, D. and
    Kanfer, A. 581, 588, 589, 591, 595, 812
  and Wade, J. B. and Pollock, T. G. 237, 243
Porter, M. E. 475, 563, 696
Powell, W. W. 498, 520, 529, 617
  and DiMaggio, P. J. 37
  and Koput, K. W. and Smith-Doerr, L. 201,

    408, 524, 529, 623, 632, 646, 651,
      657
  and Smith-Doerr, L. 520
Prahalad, C. K. and Hamel, G. 753
Prechel, H. 601
Presser, S. and Blair, J. 794
Price, J. L. 793
  and Mueller, C. W. 793
Prietula, M. J., Carley, K. M. and Gasser, L.
    771
Prigogine, I. and Stengers, I. 448
Probst, G. and Buchel, B. 429
Proffitt, W. T. and Ventresca, M. J. 821
Provan, K. G. and Sebastian, J. G. 560
Pryor, J. 740
Puccia, C. J. and Levins, R. 550
Putnam, H. 737, 753

Quine, W. V. O. 740, 747
Quinn, J. B. 407, 461
Quinn, R. and Cameron, K. 406

Radner, R. 694
Ragin, C. 820
Rajagopalan, N. and Spreitzer, G. 406
Ranger-Moore, J. 306, 308
  and Breckenridge, R. S. and Jones, D. L. 316,
    668
Rao, H. 314, 328, 330, 332, 334, 335, 339,
    340, 342, 512, 551, 561, 562, 571
  and Amburgey, T. L. 91
  and Morrill, C. and Zald, M. 551
  and Singh, J. V. 542, 558, 570
Rapping, L. 182
Rasmusen, E. 693, 695
Ratcliff, R. E. 606
Rauscher, M. 704
Read, D. W. 763–4
Reagans, R. E. 63
Redman, D. A. 761
Reed, M. and Hughes, M. 774
Reger, R. K. and Huff, A. S. 581, 588
Reichenbach, H. 752
Reinganum, J. F. 690
Rich, P. 542
Richardson, R. J. 603, 609
Riles, A. 806
Rimmon-Kenan, S. 885
Rindfleisch, A. and Heide, J. B. 481, 487
Ring, P. S. and Van de Ven, A. 293, 480
Riolo, R. L. 113

Ritti, R. R. and Silver, J. H. 502
Rivkin, J. W. 443, 447, 666, 672, 673, 680, 765
RoAne, S. 58
Roberts, E. and Berry, C. 396
Roberts, P. W. and Greenwood, R. 481
Rogers, E. M. 59, 87, 103, 107, 108, 558
Romanelli, E. 542
  and Schoonhoven, K. 408
  and Tushman, M. 388, 405
Romer, P. 172
Rosa, J. A., Porac, J. F., Runser-Spanjol, J. and Saxon, M. S. 583, 584, 587
Rosenberg, A. 765
Rosenbloom, D. and Christensen, C. M. 397, 405
Rosenbloom, R. S. 386, 405
  and Christensen, C. M. 629
Rosenkopf, L.
  and Nerkar, A. 408, 626, 629
  and Tushman, M. L. 389, 402, 408, 570
Rosenthal, E. A. 58
Ross, S. 233, 234
Rotemberg, J. J. and Saloner, G. 162, 690, 692
Rothwell, R. 193
Rowley, T., Behrens, D. and Krackhardt, D. 285, 291, 292, 293, 294, 445, 460, 648
Roy, D. F. 37, 42
Roy, W. G. 807
Rubin, E. L. 470
Rubinstein, R. A., Laughlin, C. D. and McManus, J. 722
Ruef, M. 572, 820
  and Scott, W. R. 271, 273, 510
Rulke, D. L.
  and Galaskiewicz, J. 194
  and Rau, D. 199, 435
  and Zaheer, S. and Anderson, M. H. 190, 435, 656
Rumelt, R. P. 296, 475, 476, 477, 480
Runciman, W. G. 719
Rura-Polley, T. 571
Ruse, M. 760
Rushkoff, D. 833

Sackman, S. A. 41, 45, 52
Sahlins, M. 852
Salancik, G. R.
  and Meindl, J. R. 812
  and Pfeffer, J. 138, 139, 141, 142, 148, 153, 369, 378

Sanchez, R. 166, 167, 171
  and Mahoney, J. 166, 167, 171
Sandelands, L. E. and Stablein, R. E. 345, 356, 430, 431
Sanderson, S. and Uzumeri, M. 391, 394, 395
Saris, W. E. 794
Sarup, M. 895
Sastry, A. 388, 404
  and Lee, F. 450, 458
Sastry, M. 104, 214
Saxenian, A. 446, 447, 456, 461, 543, 544, 546, 547, 557, 563, 567, 633, 656
Schaie, K. W. 875
Scharfstein, D. and Stein, J. 658
Schein, E. G. 86, 263, 868, 869
Scherer, F. M. 162, 687
  and Ross, D. 687
Schilling, M. A. 166, 167, 171, 174, 391, 392, 462
  and Hill, C. W. L. 163
  and Ployhart, R. E., Vidal, P. and Marangoni, A. 200
  and Steensma, K. 161, 167, 168
Schmalensee, R. 689
  and Willig, R. D. 690
Schneiberg, M. and Clemens, E. S. 273, 510, 811
Schriber, J. B. and Gutek, B. A. 39, 43
Schulz, M. 88, 99, 100, 109, 342, 418, 420, 423, 424, 426, 427, 429, 430, 431, 432, 433, 571
  and Beck, N. 424, 430, 433, 434
  and Jobe, L. A. 201, 429
Schumpeter, J. A. 162, 467, 529, 631, 678, 688
Schwartz, M. and Mizruchi, M. S. 812
Scott, R., Ruef, M., Mendel, P. J. and Caronna, C. A. 271, 273
Scott, W. R. 38, 41, 78, 87, 89, 259, 497, 498, 528, 543, 557, 664, 807, 811
  and Meyer, J. W. 212
  and Ruef, M., Mendel, P. J. and Caronna, C. A. 524, 548
Searle, J. R. 359
Seidler, J. 792, 793
Selten, R. 695
Selznick, P. 261, 264, 266, 366, 373, 375, 380, 497, 498, 502, 514, 526, 600, 612, 807
Senge, P. M. 85, 429, 836
Shan, W., Walker, G. and Kogut, B. 289, 293

Shane, S.
  and Sine, W. D. 511
  and Stuart, T. E. 635
Shapiro, C. 686, 690
  and Varian, H. R. 545, 696
Shapiro, D. L., Buttner, E. H. and Bruce, B. 51
Shaver, J. M. 485
Shaw, M. E. 193
Shelanski, H. A. and Klein, P. G. 487
Shenhav, Y. 504, 812, 819
Sherif, M. 45
  and Harvey, O. J., White, B. J., Hood, W. R.
    and Sherif, C. W. 45
Shrivastava, P. 432
Sigman, R. S. and Monsour, N. J. 790
Silverman, B. S. 396, 407, 478, 479, 483
  and Nickerson, J. A. and Freeman, J. H. 472,
    485
Simmel, G. 525
Simon, H. A. 115, 127, 130, 167, 222, 345,
    677, 884, 416, 436, 442, 458, 468, 470
Simonin, B. L. 460
  and Helleloid, D. 657
Sine, W. D. 499, 507, 510, 511
Singh, H. and Montgomery, C. A. 479
Singh, J. V. 270, 322
  and Tucker, D. J. and House, R. J. 270
Singleton, Jr., R. A., Straits, B. C. and Straits,
    M. M. 868, 869
Sirsi, A. K., Ward, J. and Reingen, P. 587
Sitkin, S. B. 85, 431
  and Bies, R. J. 434
Sklivas, S. D. 699
Smircich, L. and Stubbart, C. 352
Smith, A. 688
Smith, D. and Alexander, R. 406
Smith, D. E. 806
Smith, K., Olian, J., Sims, H. and Scully, J. 401,
    402, 403
Snow, C., Miles, R. and Coleman, H. J. 166
Sober, E. and Wilson, D. S. 544, 549
Sokal, A. and Bricmont, J. 753
Solow, D.
  and Burnetas, A., Roeder, T. and Greenspan,
    N. 681
  and Burnetas, A., Tsai, M. and Greenspan, N.
    672
Sørensen, J. B. 668
  and Stuart, T. E. 386, 387, 405, 624, 629,
    630
Sorenson, O. 667, 668, 676, 677

  and Audia, G. P. 564, 668, 675
  and Stuart, T. E. 175, 635
Spaeth, J. L. and. O'Rourke, D. P. 791, 792,
    793, 795, 796
Spender, J. C. 584, 590, 591
Spiller, P. T. 472
Spletzer, J. R. 799
Stablein, R. 807
Stacey, R. D. 461
Starbuck, W. H. 191, 346
  and Milliken, F. J. 579
Stark, D. 328, 330, 334, 335, 339, 340, 342,
    456, 457, 458, 461
Starr, P. 504, 512
Stasser, G.
  and Stewart, D. D. 194
  and Titus, W. 189
  and Vaughan, S. I. and Stewart, D. D. 195
Stata, R. 429
Staw, B. M. 131
Stearns, L. B.
  and Allan, K. D. 560, 562
  and Mizruchi, M. S. 445, 607
Steeh, C. 796
Stephan, W. G. and Stephan, C. W. 45
Sterman, J.
  and Repenning, N. and Kofman, F. 837, 842
  and Wittenberg, J. 674
Stevenson, W. B., Pearce, J. L. and Porter, L. W.
    147
Stewart, D. D. and Stasser, G. 195
Stich, S. 756
Stigler, G. J. 689
  and Becker, G. S. 699
Stiglitz, J. E. 689
Stinchcombe, A. L. 261, 264, 272, 307, 308,
    498, 506, 511, 523, 570, 664, 670, 808,
    874
Stokman, F. S. and Doreian, P. 766
Storper, M. and Salais, R. 276
Stovel, K., Savage, M. and Bearman, P. 571
Strang, D.
  and Bradburn, E. M. 503, 504, 508
  and Macy, M. W. 513, 569, 571
  and Soule, S. A. 502, 558, 622, 638
Strauss, A. L. 849, 851, 854, 855, 856, 857,
    858, 860, 874
  and Schatzman, R. B., Erlich, D. and Sabshin,
    M. 47
Stuart, T. E. 282, 288, 289, 292, 408, 626,
    628, 630, 631, 632

and Hoang, H. and Hybels, R. C. 285, 292, 482, 623, 627, 628, 635, 658
and Podolny, J. M. 226, 292, 293, 310, 626, 629, 630, 632
Suchman, L. and Trigg, R. 852
Suchman, M. C. 511, 524, 526, 527, 528, 546, 548, 570, 808
Sull, D. 386, 395, 405
and Tedlow, R. and Rosenbloom, R. 395
Sundstrom, E. and Altman, I. 53
Suppe, F. 753, 754, 755, 760, 761, 762, 774, 891, 894
Suppes, P. 761
Sutcliffe, K. M. 703
Sutton, J. R. 486, 687, 689, 690, 697, 808
and Dobbin, F. 434, 562, 808
and Dobbin, F., Meyer, J. W. and Scott, W. R. 263, 266, 562
Sutton, R. I. and Staw, B. M. 752, 753
Swaminathan, A. 306, 312, 561
and Wade, J. B. 551
Swedberg, R. 525, 557
Szulanski, G. 83, 87, 181, 183, 193, 194, 197, 201, 427, 430, 460, 854

Taylor, A. H. and Clement, M. 592
Taylor, D. G. and Coleman, J. S. 59
Teece, D. J. 388, 396, 402, 468, 469, 470, 476, 487
and Pisano, G. P. and Shuen, A. 84, 88, 475
Tegarden, L., Hatfield, D. and Echols, A. 391
Thaler, R. H. 741
Thelen, K. 459
Thiétart, R. A. and Forgues, B. 213, 442, 704
Thomas, G. M., Meyer, J. W., Ramirez, F. O. and Boli, J. 808
Thomas, J. B.
and Clark, S. M. and Gioia, D. A. 347, 350
and McDaniel, R. 347, 348
and Shankster, L. J. and Mathieu, J. E. 356
Thompson, J. D. 368, 371, 476, 612
and McEwen, W. J. 601
Thompson, K. R. and Luthans, F. 147
Thompson, L., Gentner, D. and Lowenstein, J. 195
Thompson, L. L.
and Fine, G. A. 593, 599
and Levine, J. M. and Messick, D. M. 38, 44
Thompson, P. 759, 762, 765
and McHugh, D. 715, 716
Thorndike, E. L. 658

Thorngate, W. 885
Thornton, P. H.
and Ocasio, W. 274, 363, 366, 377, 380, 381
and Ventresca, M. J. 586
Thye, S. R. 511
Tilly, C. 812
Tilton, J. E. 629
Tirole, J. 686, 687, 696
Tolbert, P. S.
and Sine, W. D. 505, 509, 510, 514
and Zucker, L. G. 37, 263, 269, 510, 511
Tolman, E. C. 124
Tomaskovic-Devey, D., Leiter, J. and Thompson, S. 795, 797
Tripsas, M. 386, 390, 445, 446, 456, 459, 461
and Gavetti, G. 386, 393, 395, 398, 400, 401, 405, 406, 407
Trow, D. B. 192
Tsoukas, H. 872, 884
Tuma, N. B. and Hannan, M. T. 459, 884
Turner, J. C. 249
Tushman, M. L.
and Anderson, P. 82, 90, 406, 448, 622, 626, 629, 772
and Murmann, J. P. 82, 391, 392, 393, 406
and Nelson, R. R. 386, 631
and O'Reilly, C. 386, 387, 388, 396, 397, 400, 406, 407
and Romanelli, E. 90, 104, 144, 364, 365, 369, 378, 405, 426
and Rosenkopf, L. 370, 391, 627
Tyler, T. R. 51
and Boeckmann, R. J., Smith, H. J. and Huo, Y. J. 51

Ulrich, K. and Eppinger, S. 391
Usai, A. and Turati, C. 738
Useem, M. 372, 381, 609, 611, 615
Usher, J. M. and Evans, M. G. 81, 88
Utterback, J. M. 387, 388, 402, 626
and Abernathy, W. 570
Uzzi, B. 291, 445, 446, 456, 460, 462, 481, 524, 526, 527, 530, 560, 650, 654
and Gillespie, J. J. 527, 530

Van de Ven, A. H. 753, 880
and Angle, H. and Poole, M. 391, 406, 873, 879, 880
and Ferry, D. L. 793, 883
and Garud, R. 391, 569, 820, 822

Van de Ven, A. H. (*cont'd*)
  and Huber, G. P. 872
  and Poole, M. S. 89, 134, 869, 871
van Fraassen, B. C. 761
Van Maanen, J. 733, 734, 738, 739, 741, 755,
  851, 858, 867, 868, 869
  and Dabbs, Jr., J. M. and Faulkner, R. R. 869
Van Valen, L. 338
Vaughan, D. 816
Venkatraman, N. 171
Ventresca, M. J. 806, 808
  and Ghaziani, A., Kaghan, W. and Sakson, J.
  817
  and Lacey, R. 586
Vera, A. H. and Simon, H. A. 359
Vickers, J. 699
Vincenti, W. G. 587
Virany, B., Tushman, M. L. and Romanelli, E.
  192, 369, 401, 404, 405
von Bertalanffy, L. 442
Von Glasersfeld, E. 748
Von Hippel, E. 626

Wade, J. B. 561, 625
  and Porac, J. and Pollock, T. G. 820
  and Swaminathan, A. and Saxon, M. S. 564
Waldrop, M. M. 448, 451, 831
Walker, C. and Dooley, K. 838
Walker, G. 281
  and Poppo, L. 487
  and Weber, D. 473
Waller, M. J., Huber, G. P. and Glick, W. H. 703
Walras, L. 687
Walsh, J. P. 121, 122, 124, 127, 129, 130,
  347, 356
  and Ungson, G. R. 191, 434
Warglien, M. 99, 104, 110, 571
Wason, P. C. 745
Wasserman, S.
  and Anderson, C. 69
  and Faust, K. 281, 289, 530, 532, 819
Watson, W. E., Kumar, K. and Michaelson, L. K.
  190
Weber, E. U., Hsee, C. K. and Sokolowski, J. 658
Weber, M. 100, 363, 373, 499, 525, 600, 718,
  805, 852
Wegberg, M. J. A. M., van, Witteloostuijn, A.
  van and Roscam Abbing, M. 690
Wegner, D. M. 193, 195, 435
Weick, K. E. 39, 43, 76, 77, 78, 88, 101, 105,
  122, 125, 129, 131, 133, 167, 346, 351,

396, 408, 418, 429, 430, 431, 444, 447,
  450, 462, 579, 584, 738, 752, 852, 862,
  869, 885, 886
  and Quinn, R. 405, 406
  and Roberts, K. H. 131, 193, 352, 353, 356,
  359, 430
Weinberger, E. 672
Weingast, B. R. and Marshall, W. J. 473
Weiss, G. 223
Weiss, R. 753
Weller, S. C. and Romney, A. K. 821
Wells, W. P. and Pelz, D. C. 192, 196
Wernerfelt, B. 296, 475, 480
  and Montgomery, C. A. 479
West, G. P., III and Meyer, G. D. 430
West, J. 407
Westney, D. E. 514, 590, 810
Westphal, J. D. 238, 244
  and Gulati, R. and Shortell, S. M. 287, 295,
  298, 514
  and Milton, L. 249
  and Seidel, M-D. 246
  and Zajac, E. J. 237, 238, 242, 243, 244,
  245, 249, 250, 270, 365, 372, 379, 380,
  381
Wheelock, D. C. 548
Whetten, D. A. and Godfrey, P. C. 50
White, H. C. 319, 531, 535, 583, 584, 588,
  589, 592, 594, 622, 637
  and Boorman, S. A. and Breiger, R. L. 459
  and Eccles, R. 588
White, M. C., Marin, D. B., Brazeal, D. V. and
  Friedman, W. H. 213
Whitt, J. A. 610
Wholey, D. R., Christianson, J. B. and Sanchez,
  S. M. 316, 546, 547
Whyte, W. F. 868, 869
Wicks, A. C. and Freeman, R. E. 733
Wilkinson, J. 276
Williams, K. Y. and O'Reilly, C. A. 190, 402,
  404, 407, 408
Williams, M. B. 760, 765
Williamson, O. E. 233, 252, 442, 467, 468,
  469, 470, 476, 480, 481, 483, 484, 485,
  487, 568, 707
Willis, P. 42
Wilson, E. O. 76
Wind, Y. and Mahajan, V. 163
Winship, C. and Radbill, L. 798
Winter, S. G. 87, 103, 429, 484
Witteloostuijn, A. van 688, 690, 695, 699,

703, 704, 705, 706
and Boone, C. A. J. J. 699
and Boone, C. A. J. J. and Carroll, G. R. 705
and Bunte, F. and Lier, A. van 695, 703, 706
and Lier, A. van and Boone, C. A. J. J. 704,
  706
and Maks, J. A. H. 703
Wittenbaum, G. M. 199
Wittgenstein, L. 737, 743
Woodward, J. 165, 621
Worren, N. 166
Wright, S. 447, 670

Yang, E. and Dougherty, D. 855
Yates, J. 805, 807
Yelle, L. E. 642
Young, P. 115

Zaheer, A., McEvily, B. and Perrone, V. 294
Zajac, E. J.

and Bazerman, M. H. 234, 697, 703, 749
and Fiss, P. 251
and Olsen, C. P. 253, 293
and Westphal, J. D. 236, 237, 240, 241,
  242, 246, 250, 269, 270, 401
Zald, M. N. 600, 601, 608, 612, 806, 821
and Denton, P. 807
Zammuto, R. F. and Krakower, J. Y. 793
Zander, U. and Kogut, B. 86, 87, 91, 103, 109,
  195, 429, 460, 462, 479
Zeigler, B. P. 174
Zeitlin, M. 605, 606
and Ewen, L. A. and Ratcliff, R. E. 521
Zenger, T. R. and Hesterly, W. S. 167, 168, 170
Zhou, X. 88, 99, 420, 424, 430, 433
Zirger, B. J. and Maidique, M. A. 159, 163, 164
Zucker, L. G. 37, 270, 315, 489, 509, 511,
  513, 769
and Darby, M. R. and Brewer, M. B. 635
Zuckerman, E. W. 524, 584, 592